W9-DIW-119

CURRENT
BIOGRAPHY
YEARBOOK
1971

CURRENT BIOGRAPHY YEARBOOK

1971

EDITOR

CHARLES MORITZ

ASSOCIATE EDITORS

EVELYN LOHR
HENRY SLOAN
KIERAN DUGAN
DONNA LAMBSON

NEW YORK

THE H. W. WILSON COMPANY

PREFACE

The aim of CURRENT BIOGRAPHY YEARBOOK 1971, like that of the preceding volumes in this series of annual dictionaries of contemporary biography, now in its fourth decade of publication, is to provide the reference librarian, the student, or any researcher with brief, objective, accurate, and well-documented biographical articles about living leaders in all fields of human accomplishment the world over.

CURRENT BIOGRAPHY YEARBOOK 1971 carries on the policy of including new and updated biographical sketches that supersede earlier, outdated articles. Sketches have been made as accurate and objective as possible through careful researching by CURRENT BIOGRAPHY writers in newspapers, magazines, authoritative reference books, and news releases of both government and private agencies. Immediately after they are published in the eleven monthly issues, articles are submitted to biographees to give them an opportunity to suggest corrections in time for CURRENT BIOGRAPHY YEARBOOK. To take account of major changes in the careers of biographees, sketches have also been revised before they are included in the yearbook. With the exception of occasional interviews, the questionnaire filled out by the biographee remains the main source of direct information.

In the back of the volume under *Organizations* can be found the names of men and women who head organizations. Persons who are not professional authors but who have written books are listed under *Nonfiction* or *Literature* in addition to their vocational fields. The annual bestowal of Nobel Prizes and other significant awards has added articles about their winners to the volume.

The pages immediately following contain: *Explanations; Key to Reference Abbreviations; Key to Pronunciation;* and *Key to Abbreviations.* The indexes at the end of the volume are *Biographical References; Periodicals and Newspapers Consulted; Classification by Profession;* and *Index, 1971.* The 1940-1950 index can be found in the 1950 yearbook; the 1951-1960 index, in the 1960 yearbook; and the 1961-1970 index, in the 1970 yearbook. A *Necrology* of persons whose biographies have appeared in previous volumes can be found at the back of the book.

For their assistance in preparing CURRENT BIOGRAPHY YEARBOOK 1971, I should again like to thank the associate editors.

Charles Moritz

Explanations

Authorities for biographees' full names, with some exceptions, are the bibliographical publications of The Wilson Company. When a biographee prefers a certain name form, that is indicated in the heading of the article: for example, Niemöller, (Friedrich Gustav Emil) Martin means that he is usually referred to as Martin Niemöller. When a professional name is used in the heading, as for example, Anne Bancroft, the real name (in this case Annemarie Italiano) appears in the article itself.

The heading of each article includes the pronunciation of the name if it is unusual, date of birth (if obtainable), and occupation. The article is supplemented by a list of references to sources of biographical information, in two alphabets: (1) newspapers and periodicals and (2) books. (See the section *Biographical References,* found in the rear of this volume.)

Key to Reference Abbreviations

References to newspapers and periodicals are listed in abbreviated form; for example, "Sat Eve Post 217:14 S 30 '44 por" means *Saturday Evening Post,* volume 217, page 14, September 30, 1944, with portrait. (For full names, see the section *Periodicals and Newspapers Consulted,* found in the rear of this volume.)

January—Ja	July—Jl	Journal—J
February—F	August—Ag	Magazine—Mag
March—Mr	September—S	Monthly—Mo
April—Ap	October—O	Weekly—W
May—My	November—N	Portrait—por
June—Je	December—D	Review—R

KEY TO PRONUNCIATION

ā	āle	ō	ōld	ü	Pronounced approximately as ē, with rounded lips: French u, as in *menu* (mē-nü); German ü, as in *grün*
â	câre	ô	ôrb		
a	add	o	odd		
ä	ärm	oi	oil		
		o͞o	o͞oze		
ē	ēve	o͝o	fo͝ot		
e	end	ou	out		

g go

ə the schwa, an unstressed vowel representing the sound that is spelled
a as in sofa
e as in fitted
i as in edible
o as in melon
u as in circus

th *then*
th thin

ī īce
i ill

к German ch as in *ich* (iк)

ū cūbe
û ûrn; French eu, as in *jeu* (zhû), German ö, oe, as in *schön* (shûn), Goethe (gû'te)

N Not pronounced, but indicates the nasal tone of the preceding vowel, as in the French *bon* (bôN).

u tub

zh azure

' = main accent

" = secondary accent

KEY TO ABBREVIATIONS

AAAA	Amateur Athletic Association of America
A.A.U.	Amateur Athletic Union
ABA	American Bar Association
ABC	American Broadcasting Company
A.C.L.U.	American Civil Liberties Union
ADA	Americans for Democratic Action
AEC	Atomic Energy Commission
AEF	American Expeditionary Force
AFL	American Federation of Labor
AFL-CIO	American Federation of Labor and Congress of Industrial Organizations
ALA	American Library Association
AMA	American Medical Association
A.P.	Associated Press
ASCAP	American Society of Composers, Authors and Publishers
ASNE	American Society of Newspaper Editors
B.A.	Bachelor of Arts
BBC	British Broadcasting Corporation
B.D.	Bachelor of Divinity
B.L.S.	Bachelor of Library Science
B.S.	Bachelor of Science
CAA	Civil Aeronautics Administration
CAB	Civil Aeronautics Board
C.B.	Companion of the Bath
C.B.E.	Commander of (the Order of) the British Empire
CBS	Columbia Broadcasting System
C.E.	Civil Engineer
CEA	Council of Economic Advisers
C.E.D.	Committee for Economic Development
CENTO	Central Treaty Organization
CIA	Central Intelligence Agency
CIO	Congress of Industrial Organizations
C.M.G.	Companion of (the Order of) St. Michael and St. George
Com.	Commodore
CORE	Congress of Racial Equality
D.A.R.	Daughters of the American Revolution
D.C.L.	Doctor of Civil Law
D.D.	Doctor of Divinity
D.Eng.	Doctor of Engineering
DEW	Distant Early Warning Line
D.F.C.	Distinguished Flying Cross
D.J.	Doctor of Jurisprudence
D.Lit.	Doctor of Literature
D.Mus.	Doctor of Music
DP	Displaced Person
D.Pol.Sc.	Doctor of Political Science
D.Sc.	Doctor of Science
D.S.C.	Distinguished Service Cross
D.S.M.	Distinguished Service Medal
D.S.O.	Distinguished Service Order
ECA	Economic Cooperation Administration
ECOSOC	Economic and Social Council
EDC	Economic Defense Community
ERP	European Recovery Program
ESA	Economic Stabilization Administration
FAO	Food and Agriculture Organization
FBI	Federal Bureau of Investigation
FCC	Federal Communications Commission
FEPC	Fair Employment Practice Committee
FHA	Federal Housing Administration
FOA	Foreign Operations Administration
FPC	Federal Power Commission
FSA	Federal Security Agency
FTC	Federal Trade Commission
GATT	General Agreement on Tariffs and Trade
G.B.E.	Knight or Dame, Grand Cross Order of the British Empire
G.C.B.	Knight Grand Cross of the Bath
G.O.P.	Grand Old Party
H.M.	His Majesty; Her Majesty
IBM	International Business Machine Corporation
ICBM	Intercontinental Ballistic Missile
ICC	Interstate Commerce Commission
I.C.F.T.U.	International Confederation of Free Trade Unions
IGY	International Geophysical Year
I.L.A.	International Longshoremen's Association
I.L.G.W.U.	International Ladies' Garment Workers' Union
I.L.O.	International Labor Organization
INS	International News Service
IRO	International Refugee Organization
J.D.	Doctor of Jurisprudence
K.B.E.	Knight of (the Order of) the British Empire
K.C.	King's Counsel
K.C.B.	Knight Commander of the Bath
L.H.D.	Doctor of Humanities
Litt.D.	Doctor of Letters
LL.B.	Bachelor of Laws
LL.D.	Doctor of Laws
M.A.	Master of Arts
M.B.A.	Master of Business Administration
MBS	Mutual Broadcasting System
M.C.E.	Master of Civil Engineering
M.D.	Doctor of Medicine
M.E.	Master of Engineering
METO	Middle East Treaty Organization
MGM	Metro-Goldwyn-Mayer
M.Lit.	Master of Literature
M.P.	Member of Parliament
M.P.P.D.A.	Motion Picture Producers and Distributors of America
MRP	Mouvement Républicain Populaire

MSA	Mutual Security Agency	SCAP	Supreme Command for the Allied Powers
M.Sc.	Master of Science		
Msgr.	Monsignor, Monseigneur	SEATO	Southeast Asia Treaty Organization
		SEC	Securities and Exchange Commission
NAACP	National Association for the Advancement of Colored People	SHAEF	Supreme Headquarters, Allied Expeditionary Force
NAB	National Association of Broadcasters	SHAPE	Supreme Headquarters, Allied Powers Europe
NAM	National Association of Manufacturers		
NASA	National Aeronautics and Space Administration	S.J.D.	Doctor of Juridical Science
		SLA	Special Libraries Association
NATO	North Atlantic Treaty Organization	S.T.B.	Bachelor of Sacred Theology
NBC	National Broadcasting Company	S.T.D.	Doctor of Sacred Theology
NEA	National Education Association		
NLRB	National Labor Relations Board	TVA	Tennessee Valley Authority
N.M.U.	National Maritime Union	T.W.U.A.	Textile Workers Union of America
NRA	National Recovery Administration		
NRPB	National Resources Planning Board	UAR	United Arab Republic
NYA	National Youth Administration	U.A.W.	United Automobile, Aircraft, and Agricultural Implement Workers of America
O.A.S.	Organization of American States		
O.B.E.	Officer of (the Order of) the British Empire	UMT	Universal Military Training
		U.M.W.A.	United Mine Workers of America
OCD	Office of Civilian Defense	U.N.	United Nations
OEEC	Organization for European Economic Cooperation	UNESCO	United Nations Educational, Scientific, and Cultural Organization
OPA	Office of Price Administration	UNICEF	United Nations Children's Fund
OPM	Office of Production Management	UNRRA	United Nations Relief and Rehabilitation Administration
OWI	Office of War Information		
P.E.N.	Poets, Playwrights, Editors, Essayists and Novelists (International Association)	U.P.I.	United Press and International News Service
		USO	United Service Organizations
Ph.B.	Bachelor of Philosophy	U.S.S.R.	Union of Soviet Socialist Republics
Ph.D.	Doctor of Philosophy	U.S.W.A.	United Steel Workers of America
PWA	Public Works Administration		
		VA	Veterans Administration
Q.C.	Queen's Counsel	V.F.W.	Veterans of Foreign Wars
RAF	Royal Air Force		
RCA	Radio Corporation of America	W.F.T.U.	World Federation of Trade Unions
REA	Rural Electrification Administration	WHO	World Health Organization
RFC	Reconstruction Finance Corporation	WMC	War Manpower Commission
RKO	Radio-Keith-Orpheum	WPA	Work Projects Administration
ROTC	Reserve Officers' Training Corps	WPB	War Production Board
SAC	Strategic Air Command	YMCA	Young Men's Christian Association
SALT	Strategic Arms Limitation Talks	YMHA	Young Men's Hebrew Association
S.J.	Society of Jesus	YWCA	Young Women's Christian Association

CURRENT BIOGRAPHY

YEARBOOK

1971

ABZUG, BELLA (SAVITSKY)

1920- United States Representative from New
York; lawyer
Address: b. House of Representatives, Congress
of the United States, Washington, D.C. 20515;
252 7th Ave., New York 10001; h. 37 Bank St.,
New York 10011

BELLA ABZUG

The Ninety-second Congress has a number of new
Representatives who are impatient with archaic
House rules and anxious to make the national legislative body more responsive to the needs of the
people, but none is more vocal than flamboyant,
fearless Bella Abzug, Congresswoman from the
Nineteenth Congressional District of New York.
Representative Abzug has eschewed the meek role
traditionally assumed by freshman legislators to
challenge the House seniority system, assume
leadership in the House antiwar movement, and
espouse aggressively such causes as women's rights,
abolition of the draft, and statehood for New York
City. Such impassioned crusading, while rare in
the House, has long been the style of the New
York civil rights lawyer, peace activist, and Reform Democrat. Mrs. Abzug reached the House of
Representatives in her first try for public office,
defeating seven-term Congressman Leonard Farbstein, a regular Democrat, in the 1970 primary
and Republican-Liberal candidate Barry Farber in
the November 1970 election. She is one of twelve
women in the House and the first Jewish woman
ever to be sent to Capitol Hill.

Bella Savitsky Abzug was born in the Bronx in
1920, the daughter of Emmanuel and Esther Savitsky. She has one sister. Her father, who emigrated
from Russia, was the proprietor of the Live and
Let Live Meat Market on Ninth Avenue in Manhattan until his death during her teen-age years.
Bella attended local Bronx schools and was graduated from Walton High School. At Hunter College in Manhattan she became president of the
student council and an active Zionist. After graduating in 1942 she enrolled at Columbia Law
School but soon dropped out to aid the war effort
by working in a shipbuilding factory.

Back at Columbia after World War II, Mrs.
Abzug became an editor of the *Columbia Law
Review*. In 1947 she was awarded the LL.B. degree and admitted to the bar. As a specialist in
labor law she represented, among other union
groups, fur workers, restaurant workers, auto work-

ers, and the first rank-and-file longshoremen strikers. A large proportion of her work outside of the
labor field over the years was done gratis or for
a minimal fee for civil rights and civil liberties liti-
gants. She served as a lawyer for the Civil Rights
Congress and the American Civil Liberties Union,
for example, and she was chief counsel in the two-
year appeal of Willie McGee, a young Mississippi
black man convicted of raping a white woman and
sentenced to death. The case drew worldwide attention, and some Southern newspaper editorials
attacked McGee's "white lady lawyer" in ominous
language of the kind calculated to whet the blood-
lust of vigilantes. In her appeal arguments Mrs.
Abzug concentrated on challenging the injustice
of excluding blacks from juries and of applying
the death sentence for rape virtually exclusively
to blacks. The arguments fell on deaf ears and
McGee was executed in Mississippi in 1951.

Mrs. Abzug defended several persons accused
of subversive activities by the late Senator Joseph
McCarthy, and she was defense lawyer for New
York State teachers accused of leftist activities by
the Rapp-Coudert state legislative committee. In
such civil liberties litigation she was among the
first lawyers to appeal to the First Amendment's
guarantee of the rights to free speech, press, and
association. During the 1950's she also counseled
tenants and minority groups and helped to draft
legislation that was incorporated into the Civil
Rights Act of 1954 and Voting Rights Act of 1965.

Regarding participation in the peace movement, Jimmy Breslin remarked in *New York* (October 5, 1970), "Some came early, others came late. Bella has been there forever." When the Soviet Union and the United States resumed nuclear testing in 1961 Bella Abzug helped to found Women Strike for Peace. As its national legislative representative throughout the 1960's she led lobbies and mass demonstrations to Washington on behalf of the nuclear test ban, disarmament, and an immediate end to the war in Vietnam.

In New York City Mrs. Abzug mobilized peace groups to back the campaigns of several peace candidates, most notably Paul O'Dwyer, who unsuccessfully ran for the United States Senate in 1968. On the national level, she helped to rally peace forces and insurgent Democrats into a united front in the "Dump Johnson" movement of 1967 and 1968; she was a founder of the Coalition for a Democratic Alternative, which supported the Presidential candidacy of Senator Eugene McCarthy; and in the summer of 1968 she helped form the Coalition for an Open Convention. After the Democratic defeat of November 1968 she was a founder of the New Democratic Coalition, in which she remains a member of both the New York state and national executive committees. In the New York City mayoral campaign of 1969 she organized and served as chairman of the Taxpayers' Campaign for Urban Priorities, which boosted Mayor John V. Lindsay's successful reelection campaign. She continues to serve as a member of the New York Mayor's advisory committee.

After announcing her candidacy for the Democratic nomination to Congress from the Nineteenth Congressional District on March 14, 1970, Bella Abzug was endorsed as the official candidate of the Reform Democrats. The Nineteenth C.D., predominantly Jewish but ethnically diverse, is a fish-hook-shaped district that encompasses the Lower East Side, Chinatown, Little Italy, Greenwich Village, and much of the Upper West Side. Its constituents are both rich and poor, living in luxury co-ops and in some of the worst slum housing in New York City. For fourteen years the district had been represented by Leonard Farbstein, a Democrat who sat quietly in the House, keeping his fences mended at home while maintaining a safe, moderately liberal voting record to please or pacify his constituents. The reform wing of the party had unsuccessfully tried to unseat him several times, and in 1970 the Farbstein forces were confident that they would prevail once more. But they underestimated the infectious enthusiasm and energy of the Abzug campaign. Running on the slogan, "This woman belongs in the House," Mrs. Abzug accused Farbstein of lack of initiative and promised to offer her constituents a strong voice in Washington, a voice that would work to secure better housing, cuts in the defense budget, equal rights for women, and an immediate end to the war in Indochina. In the June 23 primary Mrs. Abzug scored an upset, defeating Farbstein 17,341 votes to 14,642.

With the primary hurdle passed, Mrs. Abzug's campaign continued to gain momentum as it girded for the final electoral contest with Republican-Liberal contender Barry Farber, the host of a local radio talk show. Citywide, Mrs. Abzug had a wide range of supporters, including Mayor Lindsay, peace groups, and a legion of Broadway entertainers, who gave a benefit show in her honor. An early women's liberation supporter and a sponsor of the nationwide Women's Strike for Equality in August 1970, she drew cadres of young women to her campaign organization, and her Greenwich Village headquarters doubled as a day-care center so that mothers could go out to canvas.

Mrs. Abzug's campaign drew a degree of attention in the national media unusual for a local political candidate, even a New York candidate. The focus of the attention was the candidate herself, undoubtedly one of the most vividly colorful political personalities New York has ever produced. Out on the streets from dawn to dusk, Bella Abzug greeted voters with her knuckle-cracking handshake and addressed them in her raspy, Bronx-accented voice, punctuating her statements with swift jabs of her fist. She was loud, good-natured, plain-talking, and seemingly indestructible. Reporters vied in coming up with imaginative epithets for her, such as "Battling Bella," "Hurricane Bella," and "Mother Courage."

Because the Nineteenth Congressional District has more than four registered Democrats for every Republican, Mrs. Abzug was heavily favored to win. However, many regular Democrats, smarting from the Farbstein defeat, spitefully defected to her opponent, and some voters were put off by her aggressive manner and strong views on such controversial issues as women's lib. Farber attempted to convince Jewish voters that Mrs. Abzug was not sufficiently pro-Israel, a charge she hotly denied, and the battle grew increasingly acrimonious as election day neared. In the balloting on November 3, 1970, Bella Abzug won handily, with 47,128 votes to Farber's 38,438.

Representative Abzug lost no time in making her presence known on Capitol Hill. On her first day in Congress, January 21, 1971, she introduced a resolution on the floor of the House calling for the withdrawal of all troops from Indochina by July 4, 1971, and when House proceedings ended that afternoon she stood on the steps of the Capitol while fellow New York Congresswoman Shirley Chisholm administered a special peace oath to her. Looking on were some 600 members of Women Strike for Peace, a few Congressmen, and a Harlem youth group shouting, "Give 'em hella, Bella."

Beginning on her first day in Washington, Mrs. Abzug demanded appointment to the House Armed Services Committee—a choice assignment seldom awarded to a freshman Representative—on two grounds: she was a woman, and a woman had not served on the committee since Margaret Chase Smith left for the Senate in 1949; and she was an outspoken critic of the military, and the committee had no such critic to offset its "symbiotic relationship" with the Pentagon. Despite personal appeals to Wilbur Mills, who was in charge of committee assignments, to House Speaker Carl Albert, and to Armed Services chairman F. Edward Hebert,

Mrs. Abzug failed in her attempt and was assigned to the Government Operations and Public Works committees.

When, in March 1971, the House Democratic caucus failed by two votes to pass a resolution calling for the withdrawal of all American troops from Indochina by the end of 1971, Mrs. Abzug read into the *Congressional Record* the names of those Congressmen who had voted for the resolution and of those who had contributed to its defeat by their absence. When she brought the resolution before the caucus two months later the session was so poorly attended that no vote could be taken. According to some Capitol Hill observers, House doves had blocked a vote on the resolution because they believed that more could be accomplished by behind-the-scenes lobbying than by forcing the issue to a showdown through the resolution.

Describing compulsory military service as "slavery," Mrs. Abzug called for an end to the draft and abolition of the Selective Service System in testimony before the House Armed Services Committee in March 1971. A month later she was among a group of House doves who announced that they would hold unofficial public hearings on war crimes in Vietnam. Mrs. Abzug's peace activities again made headlines in May, when she and three other Representatives invited peace demonstrators to gather on the steps of the Capitol. Even as the Congressmen were speaking to their invited guests police moved in and broke up the gathering by arresting many of the young people. In a speech before the Federal Bar Association a few days later Representative Abzug questioned the constitutionality of the mass arrests made during the May demonstrations in Washington and called for a House Judiciary Committee investigation of them.

Early in the first session of the Ninety-second Congress, Representative Abzug testified before the House Judiciary Committee in favor of the proposed Equal Rights Amendment to the Constitution; announced at a public hearing in New York City that she planned to sponsor legislation for the federal financing of twenty-four-hour-a-day child care centers; called for a thorough Judiciary Committee probe of the Federal Bureau of Investigation and the competence of its director, J. Edgar Hoover; and launched a drive to obtain statehood for New York City.

Broad-shouldered, husky-looking Bella Abzug is often described by reporters as "chunky." She has brown eyes and short reddish-brown hair, and her large collection of wide-brimmed hats has become a trademark. Mrs. Abzug, who suspended her law practice when she went to Washington, spends much of her time fulfilling speaking engagements. Gifted with a dynamic delivery, she is much in demand on campus podiums and before Democratic, antiwar, and women's lib groups across the country.

She usually returns to New York City on weekends, to visit her district office in the Veterans Building on Seventh Avenue and spend some time with her husband, Martin, a stockbroker and the author of two published novels, in their duplex apartment in Greenwich Village. The Abzugs, who were married in June 1945, have two daughters, Isobel, a student at Boston University, and Eve Gail, a recent graduate of Hofstra University. "You try to adjust the family situation to the realities of your life," Representative Abzug told a reporter for *New Woman* (June 1971). "You don't put one ahead of the other. There is a balance, and you strive to keep that balance. The family grows with it. And the kids also know that the mother is a woman, wife, and lawyer. A total person. It makes them better people."

References

N Y Post p21 N 7 '70
Washington (D.C.) Post G p1+ Jl 5 '70 pors; C p1+ F 12 '71 por
Congressional Directory (1971)

AICHI, KIICHI (ä-ē-chē kē-ē-chē)

Oct. 10, 1907- Former Foreign Minister of Japan
Address: 3-17-1 Yushima, Bunkyo-ku, Tokyo, Japan

Although he is perhaps best known internationally as the man who conducted the negotiations with the United States for the scheduled return of Okinawa to Japan in 1972, former Japanese Foreign Minister Kiichi Aichi has consistently worked to broaden the scope of his country's leadership in international affairs. Aichi began his career as a civil servant with the Finance Ministry in 1931, and he occupied key sub-Cabinet and Cabinet posts in the crucial years of recovery that followed Japan's defeat in World War II. During his tenure as Foreign Minister, from December 1968 to July 1971, he steadily moved Japan away from the passive role in international politics that it has assumed since World War II toward an increased participation in the affairs of Asia and of the world at large. Since his removal from the Cabinet by Premier Eisaku Sato in a government reshuffle following elections in the early summer of 1971, Kiichi Aichi has served as the head of the Japanese delegation to the United Nations.

Kiichi Aichi, the son of Professor Keiichi Aichi and of Yoshi Aichi, was born in Tokyo on October 10, 1907. He grew up in the northern Japanese city of Sendai, where his father, a physicist, was a member of the science faculty of Tohoku University. In the early 1920's, Aichi, then, according to a profile in the New York *Times* (June 2, 1969), a "chubby, sports-loving" junior high school student, met visiting Professor Albert Einstein, who advised him to become a scholar. When he met Einstein again many years later in the United States, the eminent physicist approved of his choice of a career as a public servant and urged him to "work as a statesman to prevent wars." Aichi won his first "political" victory in 1927 when, as a high school student in Sendai, he led

KIICHI AICHI

a successful student strike against the appointment of an authoritarian headmaster. He graduated from the University of Tokyo in 1931, after studying political science under its law faculty.

Aichi began his public service career in April 1931 as a secretary with the Ministry of Finance, with which he remained intermittently for nineteen years. Sent to Europe by his government in November 1932, he served for more than two years in secretarial posts in Great Britain and France. In May 1933 he was appointed a secretary with Japan's plenipotentiary mission to the International Economic Conference at London. After his return to Japan in February 1935, Aichi continued to serve in a succession of civil service positions, including that of secretary with the North China liaison department of the China Affairs Board, to which he was appointed in 1939. By 1946 he had worked his way up to the post of director of the Finance Minister's secretariat, and in September 1947 he became director of the Finance Ministry's banking bureau.

In 1950 Aichi—who was then slated for the post of vice-minister, the highest civil service position in the Finance Ministry—decided to abandon his secure civil service career and enter the more precarious realm of politics. Disregarding the advice of friends, he resigned as director of the banking bureau to run as a Liberal party candidate for a seat in the Sangiin, or House of Councillors, the upper house of Japan's bicameral Diet. He won the seat in the June 1950 election by a comfortable majority of the vote.

Aichi's intimate involvement in economic affairs in the crucial post-World War II period convinced him that economic health was a prime prerequisite for the nation's political recovery, and in the years following the end of the American military occupation in April 1952, he devoted himself to restoring Japan's strength as a competitor in the world market. He returned to the Finance Ministry in November 1952, this time in the non-civil service post of parliamentary vice-minister, while continuing to fulfill his duties as a legislator. In

January 1954 he was appointed to his first Cabinet post, that of Minister of International Trade and Industry, by Premier Shigeru Yoshida. Concurrently he held the post of minister of state in charge of the Economic Planning Agency.

In January 1955 Aichi resigned as Minister of International Trade and Industry, and the following month he was the successful candidate of the Liberal Democratic party—formed not long before by a merger of Liberals and Democrats—for a seat in the Shugiin, or House of Representatives, the lower, more powerful house of the Japanese Diet. He was subsequently reelected three times to that seat. In July 1957, Liberal Democratic Premier Nobusuke Kishi appointed Aichi chief Cabinet secretary. When Kishi formed a new Cabinet in June 1958, Aichi was named Minister of Justice, a post he occupied until June 1959. Concurrently, beginning in October 1958, he served as minister of state in charge of the Local Autonomy Agency. His term as Justice Minister was marked by widespread political and industrial unrest that, he warned the Cabinet in November 1958, could easily be used by Communists to ignite a serious national rebellion.

Kishi's successor, Hayato Ikeda, appointed Aichi in July 1964 to serve as Minister for Education and, concurrently, as minister of state in charge of the Science and Technology Agency. When Ikeda resigned as Premier in November 1964 for reasons of ill health, Aichi continued to head the Education Ministry under his successor, Eisaku Sato, until 1966. From August to December 1966 Aichi served as Sato's chief Cabinet secretary, with the rank of minister of state.

When Foreign Minister Takeo Miki resigned in November 1968 to challenge Sato for the leadership of the Liberal Democratic party and the Premiership, Aichi was appointed to succeed him in Sato's new Cabinet. Aichi was described at the time by a correspondent for the New York *Times* (December 1, 1968) as "strongly pro-American" and as a man "with close personal ties to Premier Sato and a reputation as a brilliant politician and diplomat." At a news conference following his appointment, Aichi defined as his most important tasks the "solid maintenance" of the Japan-United States Mutual Security Treaty, which was due for renewal in 1970, and the return to Japan of Okinawa and the other islands of the Ryukyu chain, which had been under United States control since the end of World War II.

When Aichi left for Washington, D.C. on May 30, 1969 to open Okinawa negotiations, some 5,000 riot police guarded the Tokyo airport against leftist demonstrators demanding an end to the security treaty and the removal of all United States bases from Okinawa. The Okinawa issue was an immensely popular one, both in Japan and on the island itself, and the survival of the Sato government was said to hinge upon its settlement. Faced by opposition from American military spokesmen who argued that unrestricted use of the Okinawa base by the United States was essential for Far Eastern security, Aichi failed to obtain any definite agreement on the return of the islands in his meetings in early June with President Richard Nixon and other government officials. In the discussions, Aichi stressed the importance of Japan's internal political stability, which might be jeopardized if a satisfactory agreement regarding Okinawa was not reached. On a second visit to Washington, in September 1969, Aichi conferred with Secretary of State William P. Rogers and, although there remained "differences of views with regard to some key issues," the discussions paved the way for an agreement between Sato and Nixon during the Premier's visit to the United States in November.

In their joint communique, dated November 21, 1969, the President and the Premier announced that Okinawa and the other islands would be returned to Japan in 1972. United States bases on Okinawa would become subject to the terms of the security treaty applying to bases in Japan itself; nuclear weapons would be forbidden; and consultation with the Japanese government would be required before the launching of any combat mission. As part of the agreement, United States forces in Japan would be permitted greater flexibility to carry out security commitments in Asia. The two statesmen affirmed the intention of both governments to extend the security treaty beyond June 23, 1970 and to enter discussions on economic matters. A formal treaty for the return of Okinawa and the other Ryukyu Islands was signed on June 17, 1971, after its specific terms had been agreed upon earlier that month by Aichi and Rogers.

In the elections of December 1969 the voters of Japan, apparently showing their satisfaction with the Okinawa agreement, returned the Liberal Democratic party to power with an increased majority. Aichi was one of five ministers to return to the Cabinet, reorganized by Sato on January 14, 1970 to balance increasingly disparate elements within the party. In February 1970, Japan—the only nation to have experienced attack by nuclear weapons—became the ninety-fifth country to sign the nuclear nonproliferation treaty. "Our country has been supporting the spirit of the treaty, and thought it proper to sign the treaty before it becomes effective in order to state Japan's stand more clearly and effectively," Aichi declared in announcing the government's decision. He added, however, that ratification must be considered "prudently," with full regard to the national interest.

On the economic level, some friction had developed between Japan and the United States in the late 1960's as a result of the flooding of the American textile market with Japanese imports. During Aichi's visit to the United States in June 1969, Commerce Secretary Maurice H. Stans suggested to him that Japan impose voluntary quotas on its textile exports to lessen American pressure for protectionist legislation. In March 1970, Aichi asserted that Japan might have to accept some voluntary restraints in its textile exports to the United States. Continued textile negotiations between the two nations broke down in the summer of 1970, despite efforts by Aichi and others to bring about a compromise. Some hope for the improvement of Japanese-American economic relations was revived in June 1971, when the Japanese government announced an eight-point program for the liberalization of trade.

Although he believes that the United States presence is the "mainstay of security in the Far East," Aichi favors friendly relations with all countries, including the Communist powers. His efforts to reach a territorial settlement with the Soviet Union have, however, met with little success. When he visited Moscow in September 1969 to press demands for return of the Southern Kurile Islands—known as Japan's Northern Territories—which had been under Soviet occupation since the end of World War II, he was told by Premier Aleksei N. Kosygin that balance-of-power considerations demanded their continued control by the Soviet Union. While Japan recognizes the government of the Republic of China on Taiwan, Aichi has also encouraged better relations with the Peking government, in view of the fact that Communist China has become Japan's largest trading partner.

Aichi believes that Japan should take the diplomatic initiative in promoting peace in Asia and elsewhere in the world. "We need peace . . . perhaps more than any other nation," he told a reporter for the *Guardian* (July 15, 1970). "As an island nation . . . densely populated and extremely poor in natural resources, Japan is in a highly vulnerable position. Even conflicts far from our shores can have the most adverse effects on our economic stability." As head of the Japanese delegation at the June 1969 meeting of the nine-nation Asian and Pacific Council (ASPAC)—established in 1966 for regional cooperation—Aichi was the leading spokesman of the group favoring conciliation rather than confrontation between Communist and non-Communist nations in Asia. In response to United States proposals that ASPAC should develop into a post-Vietnam regional military association, he declared at the meeting that "a clear and positive agreement now exists among the member countries that ASPAC is not intended to be a military alliance." In May 1970 Aichi took part in the Asian Conference on Cambodia that met in Djakarta to help resolve the Southeast Asian conflict. Kiichi Aichi helped organize the eight-nation Ministerial Conference on the Economic Development of Southeast Asia, which convened in May 1971 at Kuala Lumpur, Malaysia.

Economic and technical aid is, in Aichi's view, Japan's natural instrument of diplomacy. "I intend to strengthen our cooperation for the peace and prosperity of the Asian-Pacific area and eventually the entire world," he declared in a report to the national Diet in February 1970, in which he outlined plans for increased economic aid to Asian countries and other underdeveloped regions. Despite misgivings of Finance Ministry officials, who argued that domestic needs had priority, Aichi induced the Japanese government to adopt a target of 1 percent of the gross national product as the amount to be spent for foreign aid by 1975.

Japan came close to that target in 1970, when its foreign aid expenditures amounted to $1.824 billion, or .93 percent of the gross national product.

Aichi does not, however, believe in granting long-term or interest-free loans, such as are offered by other leading foreign aid donors. "We have a proverb: 'Nothing is so expensive as that which is offered free,'" he told David K. Wills of the *Christian Science Monitor* (September 11, 1970). "The recipient doesn't know what the obligations might be. If Japan gave such aid, people would certainly criticize us." In the past, Japanese foreign aid had often been the target of critics who charged that it was given only in response to United States pressure and that it was largely geared to the development of private commercial interests and to the promotion of Japanese exports. More recently, observers have noted, there has been considerable improvement in both the quantity and quality of Japanese aid.

In view of Japan's phenomenal economic recovery since World War II and what appears to be a gradual disengagement of the United States from active participation in Asian affairs, Aichi foresees a greatly expanded role for his country in the years to come. "I, for one, am an optimist," he wrote in *Foreign Affairs* (October 1969), "and one of my favorite sayings is: 'Listen to the call of the twenty-first century.' It is my hope that with hard and sometimes painful work, my people by that time will have transcended the discontinuities of their past, and will be vital participants in the affairs of both the Asian and the world communities."

Kiichi Aichi and Tomiko Uda were married on May 28, 1936. Their only daughter, Ayako, lives in New York with her two children and her husband, the former Kazuo Nakata (who adopted his wife's family name), an employee of the Nihon Kokan steel company. A short, stocky, soft-spoken man, Aichi was described by Takashi Oka in the New York *Times* (June 2, 1969) as having the "wide-eyed, innocent look characteristic of a young master brought up without a care in the world." He is fond of literature, especially the works of the Nobel Prize-winning novelist Yasunari Kawabata and of the younger writer Yukio Mishima. Some years ago, when Mishima was working under him in the Finance Ministry, Aichi was among the first to recognize his literary talents and advised him to become a professional writer. Aichi's athletic skills range from rugby and golf to judo and Japanese fencing. The home of Aichi and his wife is a traditional Japanese house, owned by them, near Tokyo University.

References

Christian Sci Mon p1+ S 11 '70 por
N Y Times p23 D 1 '68; p3 Je 1 '69; p12 Je 2 '69 por
Asia Who's Who (1960)
International Who's Who, 1970-71
Japan Biographical Encyclopedia and Who's Who, 1964-65
Who's Who in the World, 1971-72

ALLENDE (GOSSENS), SALVADOR (ä-yen'dä)

July 26, 1908- President of Chile
Address: El Palacio de la Moneda, Santiago, Chile

A prevailing myth of the cold war has been the cherished belief that a Marxist government could never come to power through free, democratic elections. It was shattered on November 3, 1970, when Dr. Salvador Allende, a Marxist Socialist heading a coalition dominated by Communists, succeeded Christian Democrat Eduardo Frei for a six-year term as president of Chile. Allende began his political activities as a medical student and helped to found the Chilean Socialist party in 1933. A veteran legislator, and a former Minister of Health and president of the Chilean Senate, he won a narrow plurality over two opponents in his fourth bid for the presidency, on September 4, 1970. Since his inauguration, Allende has implemented his "anti-imperialist" and "anti-oligarchic" program without forfeiting cordial relations with the United States or justifying the fears of those who are concerned that he might turn Chile into a totalitarian state.

A member of a freethinking, upper middle-class family, Salvador Allende Gossens was born in Valparaiso on July 26, 1908 to Salvador Allende Castro, a lawyer, and Laura Gossens. One of his grandfathers, a physician, organized the medical services of the Chilean army during the War of the Pacific. His other grandfather, a Serene Grand Master of the Masonic Order in Chile, served as a Senator of the anti-clerical Radical party and founded the country's first secular school. His sister, Laura Allende de Pascal, is a member of the national Chamber of Deputies and serves on the Socialist party's central committee. Educated in the liceos of Tacna, Valdivia, and Valparaiso, Allende completed his secondary schooling at sixteen. He then volunteered for military service with the Coraceros Cavalry Regiment at Viña del Mar, later earning an officer's rank in the army reserve.

At the School of Medicine of the University of Chile, Allende excelled in his studies. He was president of the student medical center and later became vice-chairman of the student federation and a delegate to the university council. His encounters with poverty and his reading of Marx and Lenin convinced him that revolutionary measures were needed to solve Chile's social and economic problems. Allende's radical student activities—including his participation in an occupation of the University of Chile—caused him to be imprisoned twice and led to his expulsion from the university. He was later permitted to return and complete his studies and obtained his medical degree in 1932.

Because of his reputation as a student activist, Allende had difficulty in finding employment in the medical profession. In the course of his career he worked as an assistant coroner, a dental school assistant, a physician in a mental hospital, and an official reporter at medical conventions. He has practised medicine in provincial towns and among public welfare patients in Valparaiso.

In 1933 Allende, along with other prominent leftists, founded the Socialist party of Chile as an alternative for Marxists who objected to the Communist party's rigid adherence to Soviet policies. Over the years, Allende has occupied administrative posts within the party, and he has twice served as its secretary general. Elected in 1937 to the Chamber of Deputies, the lower house of the Chilean Congress, as a Socialist from Valparaiso, Allende soon attained a nationwide reputation as a champion of the underprivileged. During his long career as a legislator he initiated over 100 bills, most of them dealing with public health, social welfare, and women's rights.

In 1938 Allende managed the successful presidential campaign of Pedro Aguirre Cerda, who in the following year appointed him Minister of Health in his Popular Front coalition government of liberals and leftists. In the aftermath of the disastrous earthquake of January 1939, Allende personally directed relief efforts. As Minister of Health, he was also responsible for reforms in the government's social insurance program and in the industrial safety laws. In his book *La realidad médico-social chilena* (The Medical-Social Reality in Chile), which was published by the Ministry of Health in 1939 and was awarded a Van Buren prize, Allende found capitalism to blame for much of the prevailing poverty and sickness, and presented an elaborate program for reforms in public health, housing, nutrition, and social security. He remained with the Ministry of Health until 1942.

Allende was elected in 1945 to his first eight-year term in the Senate, or upper house, representing the south of Chile. In his three subsequent Senate terms he represented first the northern district of Tarapacá and Antofagasta, then the district of Valparaiso and Anconcagua, and finally the southern district of Magallanes. He was vice-president of the Senate for about five years. As its president, from 1965 to 1969, Allende was its highest-ranking and most powerful member.

Making his first bid for the presidency of Chile, in 1951 Allende struck up an electoral alliance with the then outlawed Chilean Communist party. In the prevailing cold war climate the Socialist party shunned the Communists and for the 1952 presidential election backed the candidacy of the former military dictator General Carlos Ibañez. Because of his pact with the Communists and his refusal to support Ibañez, Allende was temporarily expelled from the Socialist party. He told Norman Gall, as quoted in the New York *Times Magazine* (November 1, 1970): "The working class in Chile is represented basically by Communists and Socialists. . . . I was motivated by . . . the creation of an authentic instrument for the liberation of the working class and the liberation of Chile." In the election of September 4, 1952 Ibañez won the presidency, and Allende, backed by the Communists, came in last in a four-man race, with 51,948 votes—less than 6 percent of the total.

Again backed by the Communists, who had recently recovered their legality, in 1958 Allende waged a vigorous campaign for the presidency, in which he called for an evolution toward state so-

SALVADOR ALLENDE

cialism. The presidential election of September 4, 1958 was won by Jorge Alessandri, the candidate of a Conservative-Liberal coalition, who received 387,297 votes, but Allende, with 352,915 votes, came in as a close second in the five-way race.

The presidential election of 1964 developed into a contest between Allende and the moderately leftist Senator Eduardo Frei, a Christian Democrat, following the collapse of the Democratic Front, a coalition of moderate and rightist forces. As candidate of the Popular Action Front (FRAP), a six-party leftist coalition including the Socialists and Communists, Allende promised to "establish a government that will recover Chile for the Chileans." The two candidates, who were boyhood friends, avoided personal recriminations during the campaign. In the election of September 4, 1964 Frei received 1,418,101 votes—about 56 percent of the total—while Allende, with 982,122 votes, had about 39 percent.

Allende's nomination in August 1969 as the Socialist candidate for the 1970 presidential election met with opposition from party militants who took a dim view of his credentials as a revolutionary. In January 1970 Allende became the candidate of Unidad Popular (Popular Unity), a new coalition of Socialists, Communists, middle-class Radicals, dissident Christian Democrats, and others. Although Frei's liberal reforms during his six years as president had brought him considerable popularity, he was not permitted under the constitution to serve for two consecutive terms. The Christian Democrats therefore nominated Radomiro Tomic, a former ambassador to the United States, who held views to the left of the incumbent president's. Representing the nation's conservatives was the aging ex-president Jorge Alessandri, who entered the three-way presidential contest as an independent candidate of the right.

In his campaign speeches, on television, and at election rallies, Allende unemotionally outlined his plans for ending inflation and unemployment; for nationalization of "monopolies"; for an extensive agrarian reform program; for revisions in the judicial system and the replacement of the bicameral Congress by a "people's assembly"; and for the establishment of "dignified diplomatic and commercial relations with all countries." Although he played down revolutionary Marxism and emphasized "Chilean socialism," Chile's powerful, 60,000-member Communist party played a major role in the campaign and was said to manipulate most of the 8,500 "action committees" organized in Allende's behalf. A Communist bogeyman was conjured up by Allende's right-wing opponents, who evoked horrendous images of Soviet tanks patrolling the streets of Santiago.

In the election of September 4, 1970 Allende, with 1,075,616 votes, or 36.3 percent of the total, had only a slight plurality over Alessandri, who received 1,036,278 votes, or 34.9 percent, while Tomic came in third with 824,849 votes. Since Allende failed to obtain a majority, the final choice was to be made by a joint vote of the fifty Senators and 150 members of the Chamber of Deputies. Although Congress traditionally confirmed the front-running candidate, at this time Allende's right-wing opponents tried to block his confirmation. Unidad Popular controlled eighty of the 200 votes in Congress, and to obtain a majority Allende also required support from some of the seventy-five Christian Democrats. In the aftermath of the election an estimated 15,000 Chileans, mostly upper-class, left the country, and heavy withdrawals from Chilean banks almost caused a financial crisis.

In the weeks that followed, Allende reassured his countrymen that his government would be "a nationalist, popular, democratic, and revolutionary government that will move toward socialism" in a manner "that fits Chilean reality." Marxism was, in his view, as he told a correspondent for *Time* (September 21, 1970), "not a prescription for making a government" but a "scientific method for interpreting history and the economic and social facts of the world." According to Allende, 98 percent of Chileans would have "nothing to fear" from his government but he warned that his supporters would "answer reactionary violence with revolutionary violence."

On October 9, 1970 Allende reached an agreement with the Christian Democrats, who promised to support him after he agreed to the adoption of ten constitutional amendments designed to safeguard freedom of political parties, labor unions, civic associations, and the communications media, and an educational system free from political interference. He was confirmed in the presidency at a joint session of the two houses of Congress on October 24, two days after the commander in chief of the Chilean army, General René Schneider, was fatally wounded, apparently by right-wing extremists who wanted to provoke a coup. In the runoff Allende won 153 votes, while Alessandri, who had officially conceded the election a few days earlier, received thirty-five.

At his inauguration on November 3, 1970, attended by dignitaries from over sixty countries, including the United States, Cuba, and Communist China, Allende pledged to "maintain the integrity and independence" of Chile. His first official act was the swearing in of his fifteen-member Cabinet, in which three key economic ministries—those of Finance, Labor, and Public Works—were tendered to Communist party members.

Cautiously and steadily, Allende proceeded toward his goal of creating a "republic of the working class." He soon took steps under existing laws to take over certain firms on the grounds of "mismanagement"—including Chile's largest textile manufacturer. In the months that followed, the coal, steel, and nitrate industries and a Ford Motor Company assembly plant were also nationalized. Allende's primary goal, however, was the complete nationalization of Chile's partly foreign-owned copper mines, in which the Frei government had already acquired a controlling interest. To facilitate the acquisition of the mining properties from the three United States corporations—Anaconda, Kennecott, and Cerro—that owned them, Allende introduced a constitutional amendment in December 1970, giving the government the right to the nation's mineral wealth, with considerable leeway in determining compensation. The amendment was unanimously passed by both houses of Congress in May 1971 and signed by Allende in July.

Because Christian Democrats opposed his plans to establish a state monopoly of banking by outright nationalization, Allende worked to achieve it by purchasing private bank stock with government bonds. By mid-1971 the government had acquired some 60 percent of the nation's private banks, and it had reached agreement with two major foreign banks—the Bank of America and the Bank of London—to buy out their Chilean operations. Implementing the land reform program begun under Frei, by early spring 1971 the Allende government had taken over some 350 latifundios, or large estates, totaling about 2,593,000 acres, to be converted into farm cooperatives. A rash of illegal land seizures, many by landless peasants or impoverished Indians spurred on by radical students, posed a problem for the Allende government, which in the spring of 1971 began to remove the illegal occupants.

Ten days after taking office Allende resumed diplomatic ties with Cuba, broken off in 1964, and in January 1971 Chile became the first country in South America to establish diplomatic relations with Communist China. Allende has also begun to cement diplomatic and economic ties with the Communist countries of Eastern Europe. In the ideological conflict between China and the Soviet Union Allende considers himself neutral and has expressed the desire for good relations with both powers.

Relations between the Allende government and the United States were at first strained. On Allende's election President Richard Nixon failed to send the customary congratulations, although he later sent a brief verbal message through Assistant Secretary of State Charles Meyer, who attended the inauguration. Eventually recognizing the Marxist government of Allende as an accomplished fact, the Nixon administration later mellowed in its attitude. In early 1971 Nixon conceded that the Chilean government had the right to conduct its internal affairs as it saw fit and declared that the United States was ready for good relations with Chile if the latter reciprocated. To have what he calls "the very best" relations with the United States, Allende has affirmed that Chile will continue to work within the framework of the inter-American system and that it will never permit military bases on its soil that might be used against the United States. To encourage investments and to restore the free flow of credit, Allende has sent economic representatives to the United States.

Some observers have maintained that Allende has begun to move in the direction of militant Marxism, citing in particular his policy, instituted in early 1971, of permitting wage increases ranging from 35 to 47 percent while imposing a strict freeze on prices. The Allende government has been accused of trying to strangle freedom of the press by applying economic pressure on opposition newspapers; instituting a neighborhood surveillance program on the Soviet pattern; importing Cuban security agents; and making Chile a haven for Latin American revolutionists. On the other hand, Allende appears to realize that the extreme left represents a major threat to his government. Although at first indulgent toward such student-based extreme leftist movements as the Movement of the Revolutionary Left (MIR) and the People's Revolutionary Vanguard, the assassination of the Christian Democratic leader Edmundo Pérez Zujovic in June 1971, allegedly at the instigation of the latter movement, made him determined to eliminate all illegally armed organizations.

Allende has continued to meet with opposition from the Christian Democrats, who have blocked a number of his proposals, such as his plan for neighborhood courts. He has indicated that in order to obtain passage of some of his key constitutional reform measures he might bypass Congress and invoke his constitutional privilege to call a plebescite. In the municipal elections of April 1971 Allende found his position considerably strengthened when his Unidad Popular received 49.7 percent of the vote and the Socialists replaced the Communists as the strongest party in the coalition. He suffered a setback in June, however, when the Unidad Popular candidate was defeated in a Congressional by-election in Valparaiso.

Allende has served as a director of Casas Prefabricadas, S.A. and other business firms. He is a past president of the Chilean Medical Association and of the Pan-American Medical Confederation, a former chairman of the College of Physicians, and a former editor of *Boletín médico de Chile* and *Medicina social*. In the 1960's he helped to found the Organization of Latin American Solidarity, a Havana-based pro-Castro group, and he directed its Chilean branch.

In 1939 Salvador Allende married Hortensia Bussi of Valparaiso, a teacher. They have three daughters—Carmen Paz, a nursery school teacher; Beatriz, who studied medicine; and Isabel, a sociologist—and two grandchildren. The Allendes' town house in the exclusive Providencia section of Santiago is decorated with the President's collection of Oriental art objects, pre-Columbian ceram-

ics, impressionist paintings, and photographs of his visits to Cuba, North Vietnam, and Communist China. Allende, who is five feet seven inches tall and stocky, has gray hair and a small, neatly trimmed mustache, wears thick glasses, and dresses fastidiously. An active Mason and a connoisseur of music and feminine beauty, he relaxes by playing checkers, watching detective movies, walking his collie dogs, or going for a spin in his ten-foot sailboat, which he keeps moored near his weekend beachfront house. He does little reading and is not considered a scholar, but he is known as a skilled political maneuverer and a dynamic speaker. Among the books in his study is an autographed copy of the late Che Guevara's *Guerrilla Warfare* with the inscription: "To my friend Salvador Allende, who is trying to do the same thing by different means."

References

Christian Sci Mon p1+ Ap 26 '71 pors
N Y Times p9 S 7 '70 por
N Y Times Mag p26+ N 1 '70 pors
Visión 38:14+ N 20 '70 pors
Diccionario Biográfico de Chile, 1965-67
Who's Who in Latin America Pt 4 (1947)

ARAFAT, YASIR

1929- Palestinian commando leader
Address: b. c/o Palestine Liberation Organization Information Service, 801 2d Ave., New York 10009

To millions of Arabs throughout the world Yasir Arafat, the foremost leader of the Palestinian commandos, represents a kind of latter-day Saladin, dedicated to liberating Palestine from the Israelis as the medieval Sultan drove the Crusaders from the Holy Land. A Palestinian by birth, Arafat fought in the Egyptian army as a demolitions expert and became an early organizer of the Arab movement to gain control of the territory now incorporated in the state of Israel. His specialty became the training of cells of guerrilla troops that could be sent behind Israeli lines, and by the late 1950's he was associated with Al Fatah, a militantly nationalistic Palestinian organization. At first the members of Al Fatah and similar commando groups were regarded as outlaws, operating clandestinely and often imprisoned by the Arab countries from whose borders they launched their attacks on Israel. But after the humiliating defeat inflicted on the Arab states by Israel in June 1967, many Palestinians and other Arabs began to look toward the commandos for leadership. Since 1969 Yasir Arafat has been the chief spokesman and leader of the Palestinian commandos, not only as leader of the largest group, Al Fatah, but as head of the Palestinian Liberation Organization, an alliance of Palestinian refugee groups that has been accorded the status of a government-in-exile within the Arab League.

According to various estimates, from 1,500,000 to 2,500,000 Arab Palestinians are now living in

YASIR ARAFAT

the Arab states surrounding Israel, refugees or the children of refugees who left their homeland after the creation of Israel in 1948. Most of the Palestinian commandos, or *fedayeen* (Arabic for "those who sacrifice themselves for the homeland") are recruited from the squalid camps that still shelter many of those refugees. Although their methods vary from small Israeli border harassments to spectacular international airline hijackings, the fedayeen are united in their goal to bring about the downfall of the Israeli state through armed struggle.

Reportedly the descendant of Palestinian nobility, Yasir Arafat was born in Jerusalem in 1929. He has a sister and two brothers, Jamal and Fathi, who is now a physician in Kuwait. The Arafat family had at one time owned valuable property in Cairo, but they were deprived of it through a legal tangle that Arafat's father spent much of his life trying to unravel in the Egyptian courts without success. According to one account, the Arafats left Jerusalem long before 1948 for Cairo, where the father opened a small store. Other reports say that the family were refugees in Gaza after Israel's establishment. In any case, it appears that young Yasir aided the Arabs during the fighting of 1948-49 as a gun runner.

In Cairo after the war, Arafat attended Fuad I (now Cairo) University, where he majored in civil engineering and was elected chairman of the Palestinian Student Federation. Around the same time he began studying guerrilla tactics, and became a trainer and leader of Palestinian and Egyptian commandos who harassed the British at the Suez Canal in 1951 and 1952. Following his graduation from college Arafat attended the Egyptian military academy and received training in the use of explosives. Commissioned a lieutenant in the Egyptian army, he served as a demolitions expert in 1956, fighting the French and British at Port Said and Abu Kabir.

Returning to civilian life, Arafat worked briefly in Egypt as an engineer and then moved to Kuwait, where he set up a contracting firm. In 1958 he became an engineer with the Kuwaiti public works department. Meanwhile his activities with the

Palestine movement continued, as he edited an ultranationalistic magazine called *Our Palestine* and trained Palestinian commandos for assignments behind Israel's borders. Assuming the pseudonym Abu Amar, he became part of a clandestine organization of militant Palestinians called Al Fatah.

Varying accounts place the birth of Al Fatah in the early or middle 1950's, although it did not begin to carry out commando raids until as late as 1962 or 1964. Al Fatah is an acronym for the organization's full name, Harakat al Tahrir al-Falastin (Movement for the Liberation of Palestine). The initials H.T.F. form the Arabic word for death, and the initials reversed—F.T.H.—spell *fath,* the Arabic word for conquest. Although Al Fatah was only one of many similar groups forming around the same time, it was distinctive for its militancy and fierce independence, pledging fealty to no Arab government but accepting aid from all. Many of its strategists and fund raisers were rich Arab businessmen, but the only man whose face was revealed to the public was Abu Amar, or Arafat, who left his job in Kuwait in 1965 to become head of Al Assifa (the Storm), the military arm of Al Fatah.

In 1965 the predominant fedayeen organization was not Al Fatah, however, but the Cairo-based Palestine Liberation Organization, an alliance of Palestinian groups formed during a conference of the Arab League in 1964. Although the PLO enjoyed the status of a government-in-exile within the league, its powers were severely limited and its leadership was firmly controlled by Egyptian President Gamal Nasser. Already largely moribund by 1967, the PLO was humbled along with Egypt, Jordan, and Syria in June of that year when its army was one of the first fighting forces to be defeated by the Israelis. After June, Arabs began to look with new favor on the outlawed guerrilla groups untainted by defeat in the Six-Day War. Much of their support went to Al Fatah, the largest and best-organized fedayeen group, and the only one to have a leader who dared to reveal his identity and allow his photograph to be circulated. Despite his protests against becoming the focus of a personality cult, Arafat quickly emerged as a kind of Arab folk hero. Money, volunteers, and supplies started to pour in to Al Fatah, and the fedayeen began to obtain widespread grassroots support from the people. Politically, Arafat steered Al Fatah on a steady course, maintaining that the organization's sole political stance was its belief that the Palestine question could be solved only through armed struggle. Beyond that he professed no interest in political ideologies of the left and the right. By February 1969 Al Fatah had gained control of the Palestinian Liberation Organization and Arafat was named its executive chairman.

The fedayeen have never entertained any illusions that by acting alone they would be able to inflict a military defeat on Israel. Rather their strategy has been to foment trouble between Israel and the Arab states so that no political settlement could be concluded between them. To that end Al Fatah and similar groups "pinprick" Israel with small-scale acts of death and destruction such as the mortaring of *kibbutzim*, the ambushing of Israeli patrols, and the mining of roads, vehicles, and bridges. Most of their targets are military and economic, but marketplaces, movie houses, and school buses have also been blown up. Only about 20 percent of the commandos sent behind Israeli lines return safely, and Arab border towns that harbor commandos are subjected to swift retaliatory attacks by Israeli soldiers. Yet, despite the high rate of mortality among fedayeen and their supporters, Arafat has insisted that they are willing to continue their struggle for generations if necessary.

By 1970 there were ten main commando organizations, based mainly in Jordan and Lebanon. About half of the 20,000 men in Jordan and one-third of the 4,000 in Lebanon were reportedly members of Al Fatah. The second largest organization was Al Saiqah, sponsored by the ruling political party of Syria, and the other groups included the Peking-oriented Popular Front for the Liberation of Palestine (PFLP) and several of its splinter groups. More extreme than the other commando groups, the PFLP has been responsible for a number of international airline skyjackings. In 1970 PFLP fedayeen held sixty foreigners hostage in Amman, Jordan hotels for three days, and they dynamited three aircraft, including a TWA Boeing 707, on an airstrip outside Amman. Arafat has been able to exercise little control over the PFLP, even though he managed to bring them into a new Central Committee of commando groups that he headed in June 1970. (The PFLP had refused to join the Palestine Liberation Organization.)

The build-up of fedayeen strength has seriously threatened the internal stability of both Lebanon and Jordan. Reluctant to suffer Israeli air attacks in reprisal for commando raids from her borders, Lebanon tried to curb commando activities in 1969. There were clashes between fedayeen and government troops in April and October, and in November an uneasy truce was agreed to by Arafat and Lebanese officials. When fighting broke out in February and June 1970 in Jordan, King Hussein took a conciliatory attitude toward the guerrillas' demands. However, after the King agreed to back Egypt in a ceasefire and negotiations with Israel that August, the fedayeen attempted to take control of Jordanian cities, forcing King Hussein to a showdown. After ten days of bloody fighting Jordanian troops defeated the commandos, and a truce was signed by Arafat and Hussein on September 27, 1970.

Since the Jordanian civil war many observers have felt that the commando movement has been foundering. Plagued by rivalry and dissension among groups, crippled by military losses, and largely out of favor with the Arab masses, the fedayeen have had little strength left for bellicose activities. The continuation of the Arab-Israeli ceasefire and the apparent receptivity of the Arab states to a negotiated settlement with Israel have also weakened their cause. Arafat, however, shows no signs of losing his control of the movement and has been engaged in efforts to reorganize and revitalize his forces.

Yasir Arafat is a bachelor who once told a Western correspondent that he had "married a woman called Palestine." Short and paunchy, he scarcely cuts the figure of a daring guerrilla leader, but he does dress the part, usually sporting a three-day beard, Arab headdress, and khaki army fatigues. He is seldom without his Soviet-made *kalashnikov* submachine gun, the weapon that has almost become the trademark of the commando movement. To C. L. Sulzberger of the New York *Times* (October 30, 1970) the fedayeen leader resembled "a cliché Hollywood villain" with "heavy, sensuous features, pale skin and glittering eyes, often shaded by dark glasses." Arafat's main strength lies in his political shrewdness and gift for oratory, but he has earned the grudging respect of Israeli intelligence agents by slipping into and out of Israel without detection. Several attempts have been made on his life. Although many Palestinians have vowed to "drive the Jews into the sea," Arafat has steadily maintained that he is working for a Palestinian state that will provide equal rights for Moslems, Christians, and Jews.

References

N Y Times p2 S 26 '70 por
Time 92:29+ D 13 '68 por
Washington (D.C.) Post D p1+ Mr 29 '70 pors

ARROYO, MARTINA (är-rō'yō)

1936(?)- Singer
Address: b. c/o Maurice Feldman, 745 5th Ave., New York 10022; c/o Metropolitan Opera Company, Lincoln Center for the Performing Arts, Lincoln Center Plaza, New York 10023

Metropolitan Opera audiences in New York first heard the lyrical and dramatic soprano Martina Arroyo as the offstage voice in *Don Carlos* in 1959 and first saw her a season or so later as an anonymous Rhinemaiden in a *Ring* production. Then an eleventh-hour substitution in *Aïda* in 1965 brought her sudden stardom at the Met. By that time the lustrous, velvety voice of the young Harlem-bred singer had been acclaimed in the concert halls and opera houses of the music capitals of Europe. She has since then ensured her place in the front ranks of American operatic artists through concert tours in Israel and South America as well as the United States and Europe, through recordings with many prominent orchestras, and through her creation of some dozen leading roles at the Met, including Elvira in *Ernani*, which opened the 1970-71 season. Like Leontyne Price, Grace Bumbry, and several other black singers, she has helped to break down racial barriers in the operatic world.

Born about 1936 in New York City, Martina Arroyo is the second child of Demetrio Arroyo, who had moved to the United States mainland from Puerto Rico at the age of eleven, and of Lucille (Washington) Arroyo, originally of Charleston, South Carolina. Her father, who had studied engineering at the University of Florida,

MARTINA ARROYO

was a mechanical engineer at the Brooklyn Navy
Yard. Her brother, sixteen years older than she, is
pastor of a church in New York. Growing up in
Harlem, on West 111th Street near St. Nicholas
Avenue, Miss Arroyo attended P.S. 170 and Junior
High School 101, where she attained high grades
and especially enjoyed taking part in school plays
and carnivals. Although she received little formal
musical training as a child, she was taught to play
the piano by her mother and often sang in the
choir of the Baptist Temple as well as in school
vocal groups. She also took ballet lessons for years.

To give their children "a better life than they
had," Demetrio and Lucille Arroyo made a determined effort to teach their daughter about the
world beyond the ghetto, and even when Martina
was very young they provided a rich cultural life
by taking her downtown to attend plays, films,
concerts, and other kinds of performances. On
graduating from junior high, Martina Arroyo was
admitted to the special high school for gifted
children operated by Hunter College. She soon
developed an interest in opera when hanging
around during sessions of the Hunter College
Opera Workshop, directed by Joseph Turnau. One
day she asked for an opportunity to sing and
favorably impressed Turnau by her rendition of
the "Jewel Song" from Gounod's *Faust*, even
though her French was incomprehensible because
she had learned it from a recording of that aria.
He introduced Miss Arroyo to Thea Dispeaker,
who later became her manager, and to Madame
Marinka Gurewich, who since then has been her
only voice teacher.

From Hunter High School Miss Arroyo went
on to attend Hunter College. Through the inter-
cession of her guidance counselor and of Turnau,
the college administration gave her special permission to enroll in the opera workshop, a privilege
not normally granted to undergraduates. In her
growing devotion to opera, she often waited on
long lines to buy a standing-room place at the
Metropolitan Opera, especially when her favorite
diva, Renata Tebaldi, was performing. Because

there were only limited opportunities for Negroes
in opera, Miss Arroyo, while working diligently
at her musical studies, prepared also for an alternate career as a schoolteacher. She majored in
Romance languages and comparative literature
and obtained her B.A. degree in three years instead of the usual four.

Following her graduation from Hunter around
1954, Miss Arroyo taught for a year at Draper
High School in the Bronx while taking graduate
courses at New York University and continuing
her musical studies at the workshop and with
Madame Gurewich. Although she enjoyed teaching, and has asserted that she would gladly return to that profession "the day the sheen rubs
off her voice," she found her schedule too demanding and gave up teaching to take a job as
a caseworker with the New York City Welfare
Department at the East End Welfare Center. Despite a heavy caseload of over 100 people, the
job apparently allowed her more free time than
teaching. "You take nothing home with you except
your own shock," she told Sally Hammond of the
New York *Post* (January 27, 1968). Discussing
her two years of social work in another interview,
for the *New Yorker* (April 8, 1967), she recalled,
"It was a terribly important experience for me—
my life had been centered on music for so long,
and suddenly there I was, deeply involved in other
people's problems."

In March 1958 Miss Arroyo entered the Metropolitan Opera's Auditions of the Air. Although
she chose somewhat recklessly to sing the challenging "O Patria Mia" aria from Verdi's *Aïda*,
she was selected as one of the four national winners and received a guest contract with the Met,
as well as a $1,000 prize. Miss Arroyo's first impor-
tant professional singing engagement was scheduled for the planned American première of Ilde-
brando Pizzetti's opera *Murder in the Cathedral*
at the Empire State Music Festival in Ellenville,
New York in August 1958. The event ended in
nerve-wracking disaster when the performance
was canceled at the last minute, after the tent in
which it was to have been held was destroyed by
a storm. She sang her role, therefore, at Carnegie
Hall, where the opera later had its première. In
another early performance, on September 9, 1958,
she appeared in the outdoor Salute to Summer
concert at the Wollman Memorial in Central Park,
New York City.

Realizing that she might best advance her career in Europe, as have many other talented American singers, Miss Arroyo became a frequent
visitor to England and the Continent. She made her
first trip in 1959 as a member of an American
House Tour sponsored by the United States Information Service. Since 1960 she has spent as
many as six or eight months each year touring
abroad. The pace of the concert circuit is so hec-
tic that once she sang in forty-five different cities
within a single forty-eight-day period. In 1963
Miss Arroyo became a permanent member of the
Zurich Opera Company. She has often appeared
also at the Vienna State Opera, the Deutsche
Oper Berlin, Covent Garden in London, the Tel

Aviv Opera, La Scala in Milan, the Teatro Colón in Buenos Aires, and many other famous opera houses. She was chosen the United States delegate to the First International Conference of Negro Artists, held in Dakar, West Africa in April 1966.

Meanwhile, on December 14, 1959, Miss Arroyo had made her debut at the Metropolitan Opera in New York as the offstage Celestial Voice in Verdi's *Don Carlos*. Except for a few minor roles during the 1960-61 season in the production of Wagner's *Ring* cycle, Miss Arroyo did not perform again at the Met until 1965. She made, however, many nonoperatic appearances in America over the next few years, and those performances, combined with her work in Europe, enabled her to develop professional poise and a solid critical reputation.

During 1960, for instance, Miss Arroyo performed the Bach B Minor Mass as a soloist with the Dessoff Choirs at Carnegie Hall on May 10; sang in an Evening by the River concert at the East River Amphitheater in New York City on July 5; and had a recital at the National Gallery in Washington, D.C. on December 5. In her first solo recital in New York, at Town Hall on February 17, 1961, Miss Arroyo sang several lieder of Brahms and Richard Strauss as well as songs by Stradella, Mozart, Pianna, and other composers. Praising her "interpretative insight and real musicianship," John Gruen commented in the New York *Herald Tribune* (February 18, 1961) especially on the "contrasting hues" of her voice in handling the lieder, which she made "miniature works of art, blending all the right ingredients in all the right places and doing so without, in fact, possessing a voice of great size."

On April 4, 1963 Miss Arroyo made her debut with the New York Philharmonic, singing the lead role in the world première of Samuel Barber's *Andromache's Farewell*. Evaluating her performance in the *Herald Tribune* the next day Paul Henry Lang was pleased with her "fine and substantial voice under excellent control," although he expressed some reservations about her enunciation. Harriett Johnson asserted in the New York *Post* that Miss Arroyo had never before sung with "such maturity, understanding, or transcendence." Since that time Miss Arroyo has often appeared with the Philharmonic, garnering critical tributes, in particular, for her solo performances in Beethoven's Ninth Symphony on May 14, 1964 and in Verdi's Requiem on January 13, 1966 and for her rendition of the role of Marguerite in Berlioz' *Damnation of Faust* on July 21, 1965.

Among the many other orchestras in the United States with which she has sung are the Little Orchestra Society in New York, the Pittsburgh Symphony, and the Philadelphia Orchestra. Following Miss Arroyo's performance of Dvořák's Requiem with the Musica Aeterna Orchestra and Chorus in New York City on February 26, 1964, Harriett Johnson warmly praised her "pure, limpid soprano . . . soaring to high places with ease and spiritual rapture."

The long-awaited opportunity arrived for Martina Arroyo on February 4, 1965, when, with only two days' advance notice, she was asked by Rudolph Bing, general manager of the Metropolitan Opera Association, to replace Birgit Nilsson in the title role of the company's February 6 production of *Aïda*. She had learned the role of the Ethiopian princess at the Hunter Opera Workshop and had sung it in European productions. Although she had never rehearsed with the Met cast, Miss Arroyo accepted the challenge, and as a result of her stirring performance, which received a standing ovation from the audience, she was given a "star" contract with the Metropolitan Opera Company.

Miss Arroyo has appeared at the Met in every subsequent season, performing the leading roles in ten or more operas, including *Il Trovatore, Don Carlos, Un Ballo in Maschera,* and *Madama Butterfly*. On January 22, 1968 she made opera history by singing the part of Elsa, for which she wore a reddish-brown wig, in Wagner's *Lohengrin,* a role traditionally reserved for blond women of Germanic coloring and appearance.

The Met's 1970-71 season opened on September 14 with Martina Arroyo starring as Elvira in a new production of Verdi's *Ernani*. In her vocally exacting role she provided, a critic for *Time* (September 28, 1970) observed, "the kind of feathery high notes, creamy middle range and sheer power that have made her one of the Met's most reliable prima donnas." Other roles that Miss Arroyo was scheduled to sing, for performances and broadcasts, at the Met during 1970-71 were Aïda, Amelia in *Un Ballo in Maschera,* and Leonore in *Il Trovatore*. She was also booked with the Royal Opera at Covent Garden in London, for her third season, and had a later engagement at the Teatro Colón. In another scheduled appearance she was to sing in the centennial performance of *Aïda* in Verona in 1971, and she was reported to be preparing both a new Aïda for a 1972 production at La Scala and the title role in Bellini's *Norma* for a future presentation at the Met.

Miss Arroyo has sung leading roles in the complete recordings of Mozart's *Don Giovanni* (Deutsche Grammophon), Verdi's *La Forza del Destino* (Angel), and Meyerbeer's *Les Huguenots* (London). Among her orchestral and oratorio recordings are Verdi's Requiem (Columbia), Handel's *Samson* (Deutsche Grammophon), Beethoven's *Missa Solemnis* and Ninth Symphony (both Columbia), Rossini's *Stabat Mater* (Columbia), and Stockhausen's *Momente* (Nonesuch). She sang at the world première performance of the last-named work in 1966.

Some critics feel that Miss Arroyo requires more experience and polish before she reaches her peak. Harold C. Schonberg, for instance, commenting on her performance in *Ernani*, wrote in the New York *Times* (September 15, 1970) that "as yet she is not a perfect technician," but that she "continues to grow in artistry and vocal authority." Her voice is remarkable for its richness and range and is so versatile that critics have difficulty classifying it in conventional musical terms, but they delight in its "effulgence," "warmth," "beautiful color," and "heroic ease."

While in Perugia, on a tour of Italy in 1959, Martina Arroyo met Emilio Poggioni, a violinist with the Società Cameristica Italiana of Florence. They were married in New York City in 1961. Because they both maintain such busy professional schedules and are often on separate tours, Miss Arroyo and her husband are able to be together for only a few months each year. They have an apartment in Zurich and a house in Perugia, her husband's native town, as well as an apartment in Manhattan near Lincoln Center, which Miss Arroyo shares with her widowed mother. She and her husband own some land in St. Croix, the Virgin Islands, where they plan someday to build a home.

Characterizing Martina Arroyo as "Junoesque," Fern Marja Eckman went on to describe her in the New York *Post* (September 12, 1970) as five feet seven and a half inches tall, "billowy, rollicking, mocha-skinned . . . about as fragile as a cyclone." Offstage she radiates the same personal charm that captivates her audiences, and interviewers find her candid and unpretentious, with a lively sense of fun. In joking self-derision she says her favorite role is "Madame Butterball." She enjoys preparing, and eating, high-caloried and spicy Italian foods. Her pastimes include reading detective stories and listening to jazz.

References

After Dark 12:26+ S '70 pors
Christian Sci Mon p6 Ja 27 '66 por
Guardian p8 F 16 '70 por
Hi Fi 18:MA-5 Je '68
N Y Post p21 Ja 27 '68 por; p13 S 12 '70 por
N Y Sunday News mag p4+ N 8 '70 pors
N Y Times II p21 Ap 28 '68 por
New Yorker 43:33+ Ap 8 '67
Time 96:37 S 28 '70 por

AUDEN, W(YSTAN) H(UGH) (od'n)

Feb. 21, 1907- Anglo-American writer
Address: b. c/o Random House, 201 E. 50th St., New York 10022; h. 77 St. Mark's Place, New York 10003

When W. H. Auden left England for the United States in 1939, he forfeited his chances to be crowned poet laureate of his native land, but not his right to the higher distinction he now enjoys of being acclaimed, by his admirers and many literary scholars, the successor to William Butler Yeats and T. S. Eliot as "the greatest living poet of the English language." Auden is an essayist, playwright, librettist, teacher, editor, and translator, but he is chiefly a poet of dazzling technical virtuosity, as dexterous in his use of the rhythms of the blues, music hall, or haiku as in his experiments with the traditional meters of English poetry.

In some twenty books of poetry Auden has interpreted the times by confronting the moral, aesthetic, and theological problems that make up the modern predicament. Although primarily, perhaps, a satirist and an antiromanticist, he has written much beautiful and moving lyrical verse. His idealism offsets his urbanity, just as his buffoonery and mock pomposity offset his formidable erudition. Most of his poetry has been published in England by Faber and Faber and in the United States by Random House.

Wystan Hugh Auden was born in York, England on February 21, 1907, the youngest of three sons in a well-to-do professional British family of Icelandic descent. His father, Dr. George Augustus Auden, was a professor of public health at Birmingham University and the school medical officer for the city of Birmingham; his mother, Constance Rosalie (Bicknell) Auden, had been a nurse. Both parents loved books. His two grandfathers were ministers of the Anglican church, as were four of his uncles, and Auden has mused in recent press interviews that if he had not become a poet he might now be an Anglican bishop.

The Midlands' industrial landscape of Auden's boyhood, with its slag heaps and often-abandoned mills, became "the ideal scenery" of much of his poetry. Machinery, mining, and metallurgy fascinated him. "When I was a child, I/Loved a pumping-engine,/Thought it every bit as/Beautiful as you," he recalled in his poem "Heavy Date." At one time he longed to be a mining engineer. Then one March afternoon when he was fifteen, a friend asked him whether he wrote poetry. As he related in "Letter to Lord Byron": "I never had, and said so, but I knew/That very moment what I wished to do."

When he turned to writing poetry, Auden enjoyed the advantage of having been a choirboy taught to enunciate words distinctly. "Long before I took a conscious interest in poetry," he remarked in his "autobiographical" commonplace book, *A Certain World* (Viking, 1970), "I had acquired a sensitivity to language which I could not have acquired in any other way." He was educated in boarding schools, at St. Edmund's School in Grayshott, Surrey and Gresham's School in Holt, Norfolk.

Science still strongly appealed to Auden when he entered Christ Church College, Oxford in 1925, but then and there he discovered that he wanted to spend all his time reading. His literary interests and influences extended from Thomas Hardy, who had been an early inspiration, to Anglo-Saxon and Middle English poetry and eventually encompassed the entire range of English literature, as well as much of the literature of the world. In college he helped to edit two volumes of *Oxford Poetry* (1926 and 1927) and also wrote poetry of his own. In 1928 one of his friends, the poet Stephen Spender, printed thirty copies of twenty-six of Auden's poems on his handpress at Oxford.

In his early poetry Auden was chiefly concerned with personal relationships, love, hatred, family conflicts, alienation, and psychosomatic illness. Similar themes, reflecting his interest in modern psychology, occur in his verse play about family feuds, *Paid on Both Sides*, which he wrote during a visit to Berlin in 1928. T. S. Eliot, who eventually became Auden's editor at Faber and Faber, praised *Paid on Both Sides* as a "brilliant piece of work." The first volume of Auden's poetry published by Faber was *Poems* in 1930.

Auden's early attitude was one of detachment. As a young writer, he told Spender, he believed that "the subject of a poem is a peg to hang the poetry on." His style showed some indebtedness to the experimental techniques of Eliot, Wilfred Owen, and Gerard Manley Hopkins. From the first his craftsmanship was assured, giving promise of his becoming "one of the most challengingly adroit versifiers there has ever been," as John Fuller called him in *A Reader's Guide to W. H. Auden* (1970).

From 1930 to 1935 Auden made his living as a schoolmaster, teaching first at Larchfield Academy in Helensburg, Scotland and then at Downs School in Colwall, near Malvern, England. As a writer, meanwhile, he turned to large issues of public concern in *The Orators; An English Study* (1932), a difficult and controversial work employing a variety of literary forms in prose and poetry, to delineate, often satirically, a sick culture. His social consciousness linked him with a group of young poets, including Spender and Cecil Day Lewis, who became known as the Auden Circle or, because of their technological imagery, the Pylon Poets.

Discussing Auden's work of the 1930's, Spender wrote in his autobiography, *World Within World* (1951), "Auden was a highly intellectual poet, an arranger of his world into intellectual patterns, illustrated with the brilliant imagery of his experience and observation. His special achievement was that he seized on the crude material of the unconscious mind which had been made bare by psychoanalysts, and transformed it into a powerful poetic imagery." The originality and audacity of his perceptions revitalized English poetry, as did his readiness to deal vigorously in poetry with the spiritual bankruptcy and economic crises of the times, the horror of fascism, and the forebodings of war. Particularly in some of the poems of *Look, Stranger!* (1936, American title *On This Island*) he captured the insecurity of the decade.

With Rupert Doone and Robert Medley, Auden founded the Group Theatre in 1932. Soon afterward he wrote his first play for production, *The Dance of Death* (1933), inspired as a playwright by what he considered "the most living drama of today": England's indigenous Christmas pantomime, music hall, and country house charade. There are Brechtian touches, also, in the three plays on which Auden collaborated with Christopher Isherwood: *The Dog Beneath the Skin* (1935), *The Ascent of F6* (1936), and *On the Frontier* (1938). During the mid-1930's, in a further diversification of his talent, Auden was also engaged in writing for motion pictures, collaborating as a member of the General Post Office film unit on the scripts of *Night Mail, Coal-Face*, and other documentary films.

In another collaboration, with the poet Louis MacNeice, Auden wrote *Letters from Iceland* (1937), a travel book of prose and poetry based on their visit to Iceland, to which Auden was attracted by his love of Icelandic saga. He traveled

W. H. AUDEN

to Spain in 1937, during the civil war, apparently in the desire to become personally involved in the battle against fascism, and he expressed his faith in the Republican cause in "Spain 1937," a poem he later disowned. Since the late 1920's his views had been decidedly left wing, in his repudiation of the traditional values of his own upper-bourgeois class, including the Anglican creed. But although drawn to Marxist ideology, he opposed all forms of totalitarianism and apparently never joined the Communist or any other party.

A trip to China in 1938, at the time of the Sino-Japanese War, produced the prose record *Journey to a War* (1939), which Auden wrote with Isherwood, his traveling companion. His next departure from England, in 1939, again with Isherwood, led to his taking up permanent residence in the United States and becoming an American citizen in 1946. His move to New York, where he continued his search for the Just City, coincided with what some scholars regard as a new phase of his work, beginning with his collection of lyrics and topical poems, *Another Time* (1940).

The outbreak of World War II had made Auden acutely aware of the ineffectiveness of his efforts in poetry against fascism. Convinced now that a work of art does not influence political events, he gave less attention to politics than to the moral and spiritual problems of mankind, using poetry to make life more enjoyable in a troubled century. At about the same time he transferred his allegiance from Freud and Marx to Sören Kierkegaard and Reinhold Niebuhr. The idea of choice and free will became a central theme in his poetry. His *New Year Letter* (1941; American title *The Double Man*) and his Christmas oratorio, *For the Time Being* (1944), which present the spiritual predicament of modern man, make apparent the changes in Auden's thinking that led to his recommitment to Christianity and his rejoining the Anglo-Catholic church. In *The Sea and the Mirror* (1944), a companion piece to *For the Time Being*, he discussed his aesthetic views, as they relate to his spiritual quest, in a semidramatized commentary in poetry and prose on Shakespeare's *The Tempest*.

The Age of Anxiety: A Baroque Eclogue (1947), the fourth of Auden's long poems of the 1940's, is set in New York City, first in a bar and then in a West Side apartment, on All-Souls' Night during World War II. Its four characters, three men and a woman, speaking in alliterative verse, represent, in terms of Jungian psychology, the separate faculties of man's fragmented personality: Thinking, Feeling, Intuition, and Sensation. One admirer of the poem, Marianne Moore, described it in the New York Times Book Review (July 27, 1947) as "a morality play showing us the route to hope and health; a deep and fearless piece of work, matched by a mechanics of consummate virtuosity." The Age of Anxiety won the Pulitzer Prize in poetry for 1948, gave a name to an era, and, along with other poems of Auden, inspired Leonard Bernstein's The Age of Anxiety (Symphony No. 2).

In 1948 Auden began to spend his summers on the Mediterranean island of Ischia. The date marks the appearance of yet another of the several periods discernible in his work. His poetry made increased symbolic use of landscape and became more relaxed and ruminative, somewhat Horatian, in tone, often abounding in charm and good humor. He gave free play to his wry wit and his fondness for rare and obsolete words. His inventiveness and dexterity remained undiminished, as did his sensitivity to issues and events of the time. Most of his poetry—short poems and sequences dealing with a common theme—was collected in Nones (1952), The Shield of Achilles (1955), Homage to Clio (1960), About the House (1966), and City without Walls (1969). He also compiled Collected Shorter Poems, 1927-1957 (1966) and Collected Longer Poems (1968), revising at will and omitting poems he considered "dishonest, or bad-mannered, or boring."

After moving to the United States, Auden devoted considerable time to writing libretti for opera, beginning with Benjamin Britten's Paul Bunyan (1941). His major libretti, written in collaboration with Chester Kallman, are those for Igor Stravinsky's The Rake's Progress (1951), Hans Werner Henze's Elegy for Young Lovers (1961), and Henze's The Bassarids (1966). Monroe K. Spears credits Auden and Kallman with having "rehabilitated the art of the libretto."

That special art is one of the many subjects, along with detective stories and Shakespeare, that Auden commented on in The Dyer's Hand (1963), his collection of literary and other essays. He discussed the difficulties of libretto writing at greater length in Secondary Worlds (1969), his four lectures inaugurating the T. S. Eliot Memorial Lectures at the University of Kent in Canterbury, England in 1967. Another, and earlier, book of Auden's masterly literary analyses, The Enchaféd Flood; or The Romantic Iconography of the Sea (1950), was also made up of lectures, those delivered at the University of Virginia in 1949.

It was by lecturing and teaching that Auden earned the greater part of his living in the United States. Among the colleges and universities at which he taught were the University of Michigan (1941-42), Swarthmore College (1942-45), and

Smith College (1953). "I think Auden has left his mark on the work of the young American poets as much as a teacher as through the influence of his own poetry," Spender wrote in World Within World. ". . . Genuinely didactic by nature, he was one of the outstanding teachers of his time." His most distinguished academic appointment was to Oxford, where he lectured as professor of poetry from 1956 to 1961.

Auden's contribution to literature in the form of editing, translating, and book reviewing would seem to constitute a lifetime career in itself. His translations range from such opera libretti as The Magic Flute, with Chester Kallman, to the Russian Andrei Voznesenski's Antiworlds (1966) and to the Icelandic The Elder Edda (1970), with P. B. Taylor. Among the scores of books he has edited, many of them with introductions, are Oxford Book of Light Verse (1938), The Portable Greek Reader (1948), and the five-volume anthology Poets of the English Language (1957, with Norman Holmes Pearson). One of his recent book reviews, of Oliver Sachs's Migraine, for the New York Review of Books (June 3, 1971), reaffirms the diversity of his concerns and his continuing interest in psychosomatic illness.

While still living in England, Auden received one of his country's highest literary awards, the King's Gold Medal for Poetry (1937). The tributes paid to him in the United States have been no less prestigious. In addition to the Pulitzer and other prizes, he was awarded the Merit Medal of the American Academy of Arts and Letters (1945), the Bollingen Prize in Poetry (1954), the National Book Award (1956), the National Medal for Literature (1967), and the Gold Medal for Poetry of the National Institute of Arts and Letters (1968). He also has several international awards. In 1967 he was made a fellow of Christ College, Oxford.

In the mid-1930's Auden married Thomas Mann's daughter, the writer Erika Mann, then a political refugee from Nazi Germany, in order to provide her with a British passport. They remained remotely associated until Erika Mann's death in 1969. For more than a decade Auden has been spending his summers in Kirchstetten, Austria, where he shares with Chester Kallman the farmhouse described in About the House. In the fall he customarily returns to his apartment in New York's East Village. Auden, who stands five feet eleven inches tall and has hazel eyes, was described by Raymond A. Sokolov in Newsweek (January 29, 1968) as "an aging man with a face like a drought-furrowed wadi." Sokolov also observed, "The real W. H. Auden hides behind many masks." In A Certain World Auden protested that a writer's "private life is, or should be, of no concern to anybody except himself, his family, and his friends."

From time to time Auden has been accused of slickness, superficiality, and frivolity. But in A Certain World he declared, "A poet must never make a statement simply because it sounds poetically exciting; he must also believe it to be true," conveying "a view of reality common to all, seen from a unique perspective." In his acceptance speech for the National Medal for Literature he said that an artist must not attempt anything else than "to make an object, be it an epic or a two-line epigram, which will remain permanently on hand in the world." Devoted to crossword puzzles, the works of J. R. R. Tolkien, and the *Oxford English Dictionary*, Auden has a profound respect for words. He deplores what he regards as the present-day debasement of language. "Whatever else it may or may not be," he once asserted, "I want every poem I write to be a hymn in praise of the English language."

References

Atlan 220:84+ Jl '67
Esquire 73:137+ Ja '70 por
Life 68:52+ Ja 30 '70 pors
London Observer p25 Je 28 '70 por
London Times Lit Sup p404 Je 7 '63
N Y Daily News p46 Ja 13 '71 por
N Y Rev of Books 10:3 F 15 '68 por
Newsweek 71:77+ Ja 29 '68 por

Auden, W. H. A Certain World (1970)
Contemporary Poets of the English Language (1970)
Fuller, John. A Reader's Guide to W. H. Auden (1970)
Hoggart, Richard. W. H. Auden (1957)
International Who's Who, 1971-72
Twentieth Century Authors (1942; First Supplement, 1955)
Two Hundred Contemporary Authors (1969)
Who's Who, 1971-72
Who's Who in America, 1970-71

BADILLO, HERMAN (bä-dē'yō)

Aug. 21, 1929- United States Representative from New York; lawyer; accountant
Address: b. Longworth House Office Bldg., Washington, D.C. 20515; h. 405 W. 259th St., Bronx, N.Y. 10471

The nation's most prominent Puerto Rican politician is Herman Badillo, freshman New York City Representative in the Ninety-second Congress. Since 1965, when he was elected Bronx borough president, Badillo has been the highest office-holder of Puerto Rican extraction in the United States, and in 1969 he made an impressive showing in the Democratic primary for mayor of New York City. Born in Puerto Rico, orphaned early, and raised largely in New York's East Harlem *barrio*, Badillo entered the maze of New York City politics in 1960 as a Reform Democrat, and he served as Mayor Robert F. Wagner's Commissioner of Relocation from 1962 to 1965. Elected to the United States House of Representatives in 1970 as an antiwar candidate, Badillo brings to his office a conviction that the nation must give priority to solving the problems of poverty and urban blight.

Herman Badillo was born in Caguas, Puerto Rico on August 21, 1929, the only child of Francisco and Carmen (Rivera) Badillo. He can trace his lineage back to the earliest Protestant settlers

HERMAN BADILLO

on the island, and it is said that his ancestors brought the first Protestant Bible to Puerto Rico. (According to varying sources his ancestry is Spanish, Italian, or both.) The Badillo family traditionally sent its sons into the ministry or law, but Francisco Badillo became an English teacher. A studious intellectual whose hero was Abraham Lincoln, Herman's father was compiling a Spanish-English dictionary when he died in 1930 at the age of twenty-five. Both he and his wife had ministered to the poor during the Depression, which had a worse impact in Puerto Rico than it did in the United States. The island was swept with recurrent epidemics of tuberculosis, and both husband and wife succumbed to the disease, within four years of each other.

Left an orphan at the age of five, Badillo went to live with relatives and at eleven was sent to the United States to stay with an aunt. Shunted among relatives, he lived first in New York, then Chicago, California, and finally New York again. In New York City he completed his secondary education at Haaren High School and enrolled at City College to study accounting, meanwhile supporting himself as a dishwasher, cook, and pinboy in a bowling alley. In 1951 he received the B.B.A. degree *magna cum laude* and went to work as an accountant in the firm of Ferro, Berdon and Company, Certified Public Accountants. While working full time he attended Brooklyn Law School at night, and in 1954 he obtained the LL.B. degree *cum laude*, graduating as valedictorian of his class. In 1955 Badillo was admitted to the New York Bar, and a year later he earned his accreditation as a C.P.A. From 1955 to 1962 he practised law in New York City as a partner in the firm of Permut and Badillo.

Badillo first plunged into New York politics in 1960, as chairman of the East Harlem Kennedy for President committee. The next year he tried to unify Puerto Rican and black voters in East Harlem by founding the John F. Kennedy Democratic club, which allied itself with the Reform wing of the party. (Despite the overwhelming majority of Puerto Rican residents, East Harlem was still politically controlled by Italians.) Badillo's club supported Mayor Robert F. Wagner's successful bid for reelection as an "anti-boss" candidate in the Democratic primary of 1961. At the same time Badillo challenged the regular Democratic party organization's candidate, Alfred E. Santangelo, for the post of district leader of the Sixteenth Assembly District. Badillo lost by seventy-five votes and demanded a recount, but before the courts had handed down a decision, Mayor Wagner appointed him deputy real estate commissioner. Eleven months later, in November 1962, Wagner named him commissioner of the newly created department of relocation, the highest appointive office ever held by a Puerto Rican in New York.

Not long after his defeat in his try for the district leadership Badillo moved to the Bronx, where the Puerto Rican population was growing rapidly, and where it was possible to broaden his base of support among the Puerto Rican community. As relocation commissioner, however, he did not always endear himself to Puerto Rican community groups, and he was often called the man in charge of "minority removal." He especially clashed with Puerto Rican leaders over his enthusiastic support of the West Side urban renewal project.

Nonetheless, by 1965 Badillo felt strong enough to challenge the entrenched regular Democratic party organization of the Bronx, headed by Charles A. Buckley, for his party's nomination for Bronx borough president. He resigned from the relocation department to conduct his campaign. In the September primary Badillo defeated the handpicked Buckley candidate, Ivan Warner, by a slim margin, providing the Reform Democrats with their first major victory over the regular organization.

Election controversies have plagued Badillo throughout his political career. In a press conference after his primary election victory Badillo charged the Buckley organization with "the most intensive effort to harass, intimidate, and prevent eligible voters from exercising their rights that this city has seen since the heyday of Tammany Hall." He warned that if similar tactics were used in the November election he would protest directly to President Lyndon B. Johnson. Under a provision of the 1965 Voting Rights Act, enacted late in the summer, many new Puerto Rican voters would be eligible to vote in the November election, and they were expected to cast their votes for Badillo. Up until that time voters had been required to pass a literacy test in English, but the act gave the franchise to persons able to prove they completed the sixth grade in any school "under the American flag." When the election took place on November 2, 1965, Badillo was declared the winner, polling 2,086 votes more than the incumbent Republican candidate, Joseph F. Periconi. Two weeks later, however, a three-judge Federal Court in Washington invalidated the sixth-grade provision of the Voting Rights Act, and Periconi called for a new election, claim-

ing that the ruling voided 4,023 of his opponent's votes. The question was settled in December, when a New York court upheld Badillo's victory.

As borough president, Badillo devoted little time to ceremonial functions and appearances. "I think it's a waste of time," he explained to Fred Ferretti in an interview for *New York* magazine (February 10, 1969). "I went to a few right after I took office, but it was always the same 400 people honoring one of their number. The same thirty-five organizations. It was like an interlocking directorate." On the other hand, he made every attempt to meet with concerned members of his constituency on a neighborhood level. He initiated public capital budget hearings in the fourteen neighborhoods, or community planning districts, of the Bronx, where he went to listen to people's requests. Although his advisers warned him that his constituents' demands would be unrealistic, Badillo told Timothy Lee of the New York *Post* (June 5, 1969), "This proved not so. From a request for a library in the Italian section of Throgs Neck to emergency boiler repairs in the Puerto Rican South Bronx, the requests were reasonable and . . . necessary." On the basis of information obtained at those hearings, Badillo then prepared his own municipal budgets in minute detail, unlike the usual borough president, who customarily submits only requests for capital construction projects and leaves the rest of the budget-making to City Hall. Badillo told Fred Ferretti of *New York* magazine that in his three years as borough president he obtained some $1 billion of improvements and new construction for the Bronx.

While serving the Bronx, Badillo expanded his influence into other political spheres. At the 1967 New York State Constitutional Convention he served as chairman of the health, housing and social service committee. A vigorous opponent of the war in Vietnam, Badillo supported the Presidential bid of Senator Robert F. Kennedy, and, after Kennedy's assassination, that of Senator Eugene J. McCarthy. At the 1968 Democratic National Convention in Chicago, where he was a delegate and a member of the credentials committee, Badillo made a speech urging the seating of the insurgent Georgia delegation led by Julian Bond.

Fortified with those liberal credentials, Badillo declared himself "the only liberal candidate" on the Democratic ticket when he announced his intention to run for mayor of New York on April 3, 1969. The six other candidates in the running he dismissed as either "conservatives" or "party machine men." In the primary campaign Badillo sought liberal votes with endorsements by Eugene McCarthy, unsuccessful New York Senate candidate Paul O'Dwyer, and Senator Jacob K. Javits, counting on his major support from blacks, Puerto Ricans, and the Jewish middle class who vote for Reform Democrats. Aware that his strength lay with the same voters who endorsed Lindsay, Badillo nevertheless took an aggressive stance against the mayor even in the primary. While praising Lindsay's "liberal principles," Badillo accused him of being a poor administrator who discriminated in favor of Manhattan and was unable to prevent tensions and divisiveness, particularly racial, from growing in New York City.

By the time the primary election was held on June 17, 1969 there were five Democratic candidates, including Badillo's former political patron, Robert Wagner, whom he dismissed as a "man of the past." When the votes were counted Badillo placed third, behind Mario Procaccino and Wagner, in what was generally considered to be an excellent showing by a politician making his first entry into citywide politics. Soon after the primary, Badillo joined with Paul O'Dwyer and others in forming the New Democratic Coalition, a coalition largely of Liberals and Reform Democrats, and he became its vice-chairman. The NDC and Badillo supported Lindsay's successful race as a Liberal-Independent against the Republican-Conservative candidate John A. Marchi and the Democrat Procaccino.

Early in 1970 Badillo was succeeded by Robert Abrams as Bronx borough president, and he became a partner in the distinguished Wall Street law firm of Stroock and Stroock and Lavan. A few months later he declared himself a candidate for the Democratic nomination for Congressman from the newly created Twenty-first Congressional District. Although the triborough district, consisting of sections of Manhattan, the Bronx, and Queens, superficially seemed tailor-made for a Puerto Rican candidate, the district was actually only about 30 percent Puerto Rican, and 30 percent black, 30 percent Irish and Italian, and 10 percent Jewish. In the June primary Badillo found himself in a difficult race against a large number of candidates who could splinter the vote of the relatively small district, among them two Puerto Rican candidates. His primary victory in June was challenged by the runner-up, and he became the official Democratic nominee barely a month before the election. In a clearly polarized contest with George B. Smaragdas, the Conservative candidate, Badillo won the November election by a wide margin.

When Badillo took office in the Ninety-second Congress in January 1971 he became the first Puerto Rican ever to hold a voting membership in that body, and he vowed to represent the people of Puerto Rico as well as of his New York district. (The island of Puerto Rico sends its resident commissioner to the House of Representatives, but he does not vote.) When the freshman Congressman was appointed to the Agriculture Committee a furor broke out, with a New York Times editorial (February 1, 1971) calling the appointment "an insulting waste of [Badillo's] talents and his experience." When Badillo challenged the assignment in the House's Democratic caucus, he succeeded in getting the assignment changed to the Education and Labor Committee, which also handles most antipoverty legislation. In his first major speech on the House floor, in March, Badillo called for the federal government to lend $20 billion to America's cities until a federal revenue-sharing program is enacted.

Herman Badillo has with reason called himself a "one-man integration ticket." A Baptist, he has a Jewish wife, the former Mrs. Irma (Deutsch) Leibling, whom he married on May 18, 1961. Mrs. Badillo has two adult sons by a previous marriage, and her husband has a teenage son, David Alan, by his former wife, Norma (Lit) Badillo, whom he married in 1949 and divorced in 1960. Badillo is six feet one inch tall, weighs 160 pounds, and has curly brown hair and brown eyes. He has often expressed resentment at being called a "tall Puerto Rican," maintaining that poor diet and extreme poverty prevent most of his people from growing taller. He has told interviewers that he grew six inches the first summer he was in the United States, having had not "more than three gallons of milk or four dozen eggs" during the previous six years. Badillo is considered a reserved man who is difficult to know, and the journalist Murray Kempton has compared his face to the intelligent but guarded portraits painted by the cinquecento artist Bronzino. During the mayoral campaign an aide told Fred Ferretti of *New York* magazine, "[Badillo] thinks he doesn't need anybody. It's not arrogance. It's rather . . . a belief in his destiny."

References

N Y Post p47 S 1 '65 por; p53 Je 5 '69 por
N Y Times p51 N 4 '65 por
New York 2:26+ F 10 '69 por
Who's Who in America, 1970-71
Who's Who in American Politics, 1969-70

BAKER, JANET

Aug. 21, 1933- British singer
Address: b. c/o Hurok Concerts, Inc., 730 5th Ave., New York 10019; h. "Bamford Cottage," South Hill Ave., Harrow, Middlesex, England

Excelling equally in lieder, oratorio, and opera, the British mezzo-soprano Janet Baker remains uncompartmentalized, one of the most flexible and versatile singers on the international scene. She is an artist of much warmth, intelligence, and control, of flawless technique, who has been called a "thinker-singer" because of the searching interpretation she gives to whatever music she performs, whether a Mahler song, Bach's B Minor Mass, or an operatic role. In the United States, where she made her Town Hall debut in 1966, she is best known as a concert and recital singer, but in England she has been singing with the English Opera Group and other opera companies since the early 1960's, distinguishing herself particularly in the roles of Berlioz' and Purcell's Dido and Britten's Lucretia.

Janet Abbott Baker was born to Robert Abbott and May (Pollard) Baker on August 21, 1933 in York, England, the site of a famous cathedral. "I got used to hearing the best English church music," she has recalled, commenting on the ambiance of her girlhood, "and found, as a child, that the long phrases of the plainsong soaked in." Her enthu-

JANET BAKER

siasm for the performing arts was encouraged both
by her music-loving father and by her mother, a
theatre buff who took Janet to the York repertory
theatre every week. In childhood she began to
acquire the stage sense that is one of her major
assets as an opera singer. The family was not well-
off, and for some years, when her parents could
not afford a piano and music lessons, she had to
rely on BBC programs to enlarge her musical experience. Even at an early age she had what she
calls "an instinctive thing": a standard, an ability
to distinguish between the good and the bad in
music.

In choirs at school and church Janet Baker sang
high soprano until her voice began to change at
about the age of fifteen. Letting her voice "settle"
for a couple of years, at the advice of a teacher,
she found when she began singing again that her
voice was markedly lower. At seventeen she left
school, the College for Girls in York, to work as
a clerk in a bank in Leeds and earn money for
singing lessons. While attending a local production of Haydn's Lord Nelson Mass, the bank manager heard her in a small part, in which she was
substituting for an indisposed singer, and arranged
for her to be transferred to the bank's headquarters in London, where she would have better opportunities for musical study.

Stowed in a back room of the London bank,
Miss Baker could practise singing for hours while
working on a coin-sorting machine. During her
free time she took singing lessons in Hampstead
with Helene Isepp, mother of the pianist and
harpsichordist Martin Isepp, who now often accompanies Miss Baker. To Mrs. Isepp, who trained
her to sing lieder, she owes her apparently effort-
less technique. "Her theory was that if it isn't
easy, it's wrong," Miss Baker has explained in
press interviews. "Singing is a natural function.
You clear away the debris to let what's there come
through." Another teacher, Meriel St. Clair, later
coached her in repertoire. As an established performer, she also learned much from the conductors with whom she worked, including Sir John

Barbirolli, Otto Klemperer, and George Szell. "The
great conductors are the best sort of coaches a
singer can get, because there is an exchange of
ideas among musicians," she told Robert Jacobson, who interviewed her for an article in Lincoln
Center programs (1971).

As part of her apprenticeship Janet Baker gave
recitals under the sponsorship of the Arts Council
in small towns in England and Wales. In 1956
she won the Daily Mail Kathleen Ferrier Prize,
which brought her welcome publicity and enabled
her to study at the Mozarteum in Salzburg. She
also boosted her career by joining the Glyndebourne Festival chorus in 1956 and by attending
a master class with Lotte Lehmann at Wigmore
Hall. Scattered praises of her singing began to appear in British opera and recording magazines.
The distinguished critic Desmond Shawe-Taylor,
reviewing a 1957 Oxford University Opera Club
presentation of Smetana's The Secret, singled out
Miss Baker's performance for special commendation and forecast a notable career for her.

By 1959 Janet Baker had assumed operatic
roles as diverse as those of the Sorceress in Purcell's Dido and Aeneas in a production conducted
by Colin Davis, Eduige in a Sadler's Wells presentation of Handel's Rodelinda with Joan Suther-
land, and Pippo in Rossini's La Gazza Ladra. During 1960 she gave a recital at the Edinburgh
International Festival and sang Sosostrice's aria
from Michael Tippett's A Midsummer Marriage at
the Promenade Concerts in London's Albert Hall.
Her remarkable musicianship was acknowledged
in the awards of the Queen's Prize from the Royal
College of Music in 1959 and an Arts Council
grant in 1960 for further study.

Joining Benjamin Britten's English Opera Group
in the early 1960's, Miss Baker toured the British
Isles with that company and traveled to Sweden,
France, and the Soviet Union. The roles that she
added to her repertoire included Lucretia in Britten's The Rape of Lucretia, and Polly Peachum
in Britten's The Beggar's Opera. In her continuing
association with the English Opera Group she
sings opera in England for several months a year
and then is left free for extensive concert work.
Britten has created some of his operatic roles especially for her voice and style of singing, including a part in the recent Owen Wingrave, composed for BBC television.

Meanwhile, with other groups, including the
Handel Opera Society, Janet Baker performed in
Jeptha and Orlando furioso, among other operas
of Handel. She particularly enjoys singing Handel
because it is close to the oratorio style that suits
her well. During the early 1960's, in addition to
opera she sang Bach's St. John Passion, Mahler's
Second Symphony (under Otto Klemperer), Mozart's C Minor Mass, Beethoven's Ninth Symphony,
Brahms's Alto Rhapsody, and Verdi's Requiem,
appearing in some of the great music capitals of
Europe.

The impressive reputation that Janet Baker had
acquired in England and on the Continent and
through recordings, especially as a concert artist,
preceded her to the United States, where she

made her debut in 1966. On the West Coast in the spring of that year she sang in Mahler's *Das Lied von der Erde* with the San Francisco Symphony Orchestra under Josef Krips. In the fall she was heard first on the East Coast at Hunter College in Manhattan with the Melos Ensemble of London in a program that included music by Handel and Spohr. At Carnegie Hall later in November 1966 she sang Smeton in the American Opera Society's concert version of Donizetti's *Anna Bolena* with Marilyn Horne and Elena Suliotis and also performed in the Handel Society's production of *Xerxes*.

Miss Baker "wrapped a Town Hall audience tightly around her little finger" in her first recital there, on December 2, 1966, as Howard Klein reported in the New York *Times* two days later. He went on to say, "She can do just about anything vocally and dramatically in a variety of contexts, and she does it all with a communicative radiance and personal warmth that borders on magic." So enthusiastic was her reception by New Yorkers that her manager Sol Hurok booked her for a Carnegie Hall concert in January 1967.

One of the operatic roles for which Janet Baker has been warmly acclaimed is Purcell's Dido. At the request of Anthony Lewis she sang that role in the English Chamber Orchestra's recording of *Dido and Aeneas* in 1965. She also portrayed Dido in productions of the opera in Aldeburgh, Liège, and in the Drottningholm Theatre near Stockholm and in thirteen performances at the Glyndebourne Festival in the summer of 1966. With the Scottish Opera in Edinburgh in the spring of 1969 she sang and acted the part of another Dido, the one Berlioz created in his *Les Troyens*. Desmond Shawe-Taylor commented at that time in the London *Sunday Times*, "Not even her finest achievements . . . had prepared us for the dramatic fire and intensity of her Dido."

The following autumn Miss Baker had the opportunity to repeat her portrait of Berlioz' Dido, this time at England's most distinguished opera house, Covent Garden in London, where she had made the first of her rare appearances in 1967 as Hermia in Britten's *A Midsummer Night's Dream*. When Josephine Veasey, who had been assigned the Dido role, suddenly fell ill, Janet Baker received an urgent summons to Covent Garden to replace her. While the rest of the cast sang in French, she sang her part in English, as she had learned it with the Scottish Opera. Accomplishing that difficult task with cool proficiency, she drew rave notices. She later recorded the Act V arias from *Les Troyens* for Angel Records.

Other operatic roles in Miss Baker's repertoire are Dorabella in *Così fan tutte* and Sextus in *La Clemenza di Tito*. Operas in which she was scheduled to perform in 1971 included *Calisto, Damnation de Faust*, and *Incoronazione di Poppea*. As the tempo of her career has accelerated in recent years, she has traveled around the world concertizing, and has performed in Japan with Barbirolli and the New Philharmonia Orchestra of London to celebrate Expo '70. During a six-week tour of the United States in early 1971 she appeared in solo concerts, in a joint recital with Dietrich Fischer-Dieskau accompanied by Daniel Barenboim, and with the New York Philharmonic. Commenting on Miss Bakers performance in the program of vocal duets with Dietrich Fischer-Dieskau at Carnegie Hall, Harold C. Schonberg of the *Times* (January 28, 1971) found her to be a "sensitive musician," but not a "heart-on-sleeve artist."

Much of the program in which Miss Baker collaborated with Fischer-Dieskau and Barenboim had been previously presented in London. Recorded at that time, it is one of some thirty discs, most of them on the Angel label, testifying to the breadth of her musical interests. They include Berlioz' *Les Nuits d'été*, Bach's *Magnificat*, Ravel's *Shéhérazade*, Elgar's *The Dream of Gerontius*, Vaughan Williams' *Hodie, A Christmas Cantata*, and many songs. Refusing to be "put in a box," she constantly varies roles, types of music, styles, and possibly even ranges (she has more than once been referred to as a contralto, and one critic regards her as a soprano rather than a mezzosoprano). The pianist Gerald Moore, who has accompanied some of the world's most celebrated singers, once associated, as quoted in *Time* (September 21, 1970), "My idea of a great singer is one who can do everything: baroque, modern, Italian, German, opera, oratorio. Janet can do all that with absolute ease and conviction. She and baritone Dietrich Fischer-Dieskau are the two greatest singers in the world today."

Miss Baker's voice is not remarkable for its volume or weight, as she is well aware, having refused to assay Wagnerian roles. "Still, it is a voice that puts Miss Baker among the elite of the century," Alan M. Kriegsman wrote in the Washington *Post* (February 17, 1969). "It can swell to thrilling intensity, or it can pour forth with unutterably lithe fluidity, maintaining its loveliness of texture even in the most ephemeral pianissimos. Equally amazing is Miss Baker's control over this remarkable instrument. Trills emerge like ripples of liquid silver, and treacherous coloratura passages are negotiated with flawless accuracy and speed."

Because her technique has become second nature to her, Miss Baker is able to concentrate fully on using her voice as an instrument of interpretation. Her concern with communication and verbal meaning distinguishes her approach to singing. Her enunciation is impeccable, and she has the rare ability to impart significance through beautiful phrasing, to draw out a pianissimo while imbuing it with shades of meaning—what Irving Kolodin of the *Saturday Review* has called an "ability to color sound." Critic after critic has commented on the subtlety and acuity of the interpretation conveyed in her phrases.

In acting as well as singing Miss Baker has a refreshing, pristine quality, a style unencumbered by intrusions of technique, and a naturalness in stage manner. She has said that for her the process is the same in performing both lieder and opera. "I do Dido exactly as I do in a great Schubert song," she told Jacobson. Lionel Markson observed in *Records and Recording* (December 1969) that besides being an "intellectual singer with a voice of exceptional beauty," she has a wealth of "elemental passion" and "histrionic power." In *Time* (September 21, 1970) she was commended for her singular skill in projecting both the "purity and passion" of the complex title character of the *Rape of Lucretia*. Reviewing her performance in that work in *Opera* (November 1966), Stanley Sadie wrote, "Others sing the great outbursts with more vehemence but none with greater intensity or understanding."

Since 1957 Janet Baker has been married to James Keith Shelley, formerly an executive of a national driving school. He gave up his own business interests to manage his wife's career and to travel with her on her many trips abroad. When the Shelleys are at home, they live in a cottage at the foot of Harrow Hill, not far from London. The singer's recreations are taking walks, playing tennis, and reading—mostly books of history and philosophy. Among the tributes paid to her is an honorary D. Mus. degree awarded by the University of Birmingham in 1968. She was named a commander of the Order of the British Empire in 1970.

After meeting Miss Baker between flights at Kennedy International Airport a few years ago, the music critic Howard Klein described her in the New York *Times* (December 18, 1966): "Her hair is auburn, her eyes blue, her figure rounded but trim and her face a relaxed bit of sunlight, the upturned nose and easy smile bright signs of welcome." Her speech retains traces of a Yorkshire accent. Interviewers are impressed by Miss Baker's candor, earnestness, and level-headed attitude toward her career. She refuses to think of herself as a kind of legend in the making: "There's always somebody as good as you are or better. . . . I try not to bother myself about it." Generous in her admiration of Marilyn Horne and other first-rank singers, she is not at all imitative. "I believe I'm employed to deliver my own thing. I'm Janet Baker and no one else," she asserted on one occasion. Fame and wealth are rewards that she neither shuns nor pursues. "In singing a song, one must be willing to stand aside all the time and not use the song as a vehicle for the personality, which is a dangerous temptation. It *is* a vehicle, but it must be for the right reason. The fundamental idea I have about my own singing," she explained to Klein, "is that it is a God-given gift to me and that the only way that it can work is if I give it back unstintingly."

References

Esquire 70:58+ N '68
Guardian p7 Mr 4 '67 por
N Y Times II p19+ D 18 '66 por; p42 Ja 28 '71
Opera N 34:28+ Mr 7 '70 por
Time 96:68+ S 21 '70 por

Concise Biographic Dictionary of Singers (1969)
International Who's Who, 1971-72
Who's Who, 1970-71

BARBER, ANTHONY (PERRINOTT LYSBERG)

July 4, 1920- British government official
Address: b. House of Commons, London, S.W. 1, England; h. 11 Downing St., London, S.W. 1, England; "Red House," Wentbridge, Pontefract, Yorkshire, England

The restoration of Great Britain's ailing economy to a state of health is the main concern of Anthony Barber, who succeeded the late Iain Macleod as Chancellor of the Exchequer in the Conservative government of Prime Minister Edward Heath on July 25, 1970. A lawyer specializing in financial matters, Barber entered Parliament in 1951 and served his political apprenticeship as parliamentary private secretary to Prime Minister Harold Macmillan and as a junior official in the treasury. He was Minister of Health in 1963-64, and he rose steadily through the ranks of the Conservative party as a protégé of party leader Heath and as a leading parliamentary spokesman for the Opposition. Appointed Conservative partly chairman in 1967, Barber helped to engineer the party's surprising victory at the polls in June 1970, which has been attributed to widespread public dissatisfaction with economic conditions under the Labour government of Harold Wilson. During the first month of the Heath government, Barber headed negotiations for Great Britain's entry into the Common Market. Since taking office as Chancellor of the Exchequer, he has introduced far-reaching and controversial measures reducing taxes and sharply curtailing public expenditures.

A native of England's industrial north, Anthony Perrinott Lysberg Barber was born in Hessle, near Hull, Yorkshire on July 4, 1920, the youngest of the three sons of John and Katy (Lysberg) Barber. His brothers are Kenneth Barber, who is secretary of the Midland Bank; and Noel Barber, an author and journalist. His father was personal assistant to Lord Leverhulme, the founder of the Unilever soap and margarine empire, and later became managing director of Radiance of Doncaster, a small candy manufacturing firm. Barber's mother was born in Denmark, and he had a French grandmother. He grew up in Doncaster, Yorkshire and attended Retford Grammar School in Retford, Nottinghamshire.

In 1939 Barber joined a Doncaster unit of the British Territorial Army and received a commission. Called to active duty with the outbreak of World War II, he was sent to France with an artillery unit and fought at Dunkirk. In 1940 he was assigned to the Royal Air Force and served as a Spitfire pilot on photo-reconnaissance missions. While he was returning from a mission to Gibraltar in 1942 his plane ran out of fuel, and he was forced to bail out over the English Channel. Captured by the Germans, he was sent to the prison camp Stalag Luft III in Poland. There he directed the escapes of a number of prisoners, an activity that earned him favorable mention in British war dispatches. He once managed to escape through a tunnel, but the Germans soon recaptured him and placed him in solitary confinement.

During his three years as a prisoner of war, Barber studied law by correspondence under the auspices of the International Red Cross and earned a British law degree with first class honors. He has attributed his scholastic excellence to "lack of other temptations." At the end of the war he was a prisoner of the Russians, who occupied the area of Poland where the prison camp was located. On his return to England after the war he attended Oriel College, Oxford University, on a state grant and took an M.A. honors degree in Modern Greats (philosophy, politics, and economics). Having won an Inner Temple Scholarship, he was made a barrister-at-law in 1948, and he soon acquired a reputation as a successful lawyer, specializing in tax law.

Barber has said that his entry into politics was motivated by his desires to alleviate the poverty he had witnessed in prewar northern England and to help prevent tyranny like that of Nazism from ever threatening the country again. A member of the Conservative party, he successfully contested the Doncaster constituency in the House of Commons in the general election of 1950. Taking his seat in Parliament in the fall of 1951, he delivered his maiden speech on his first day, having been selected for the honor of seconding the address in reply to the King's speech.

From 1952 to 1955, Barber served as parliamentary private secretary to the undersecretary of state for air. In June 1955 he was named to the unpaid position of assistant government whip, and in 1957-58 he served as a full-time government whip and as lord commissioner of the treasury. Barber was appointed in March 1958 as parliamentary private secretary to Prime Minister Harold Macmillan. In that position he accompanied the Prime Minister on a trip to Moscow in the spring of 1959 and on visits to other capitals. He maintains that he learned more about politics from Macmillan than from anyone else.

Appointed economic secretary to the treasury in October 1959, Barber served in that post until July 1962. In February of 1962 he took on the added responsibility of helping to coordinate the government's domestic information services. From July 1962 until October 1963 he was financial secretary to the treasury. During his four years in sub-Cabinet posts at the treasury Barber worked closely with three Chancellors of the Exchequer on budgets and financial legislation. His coworkers of that period remember him as something of a liberal, who seemed to find the conventional conservatism of Chancellor of the Exchequer Selwyn Lloyd uncongenial, and who apparently felt more at home after Reginald Maudling took over the Cabinet post in 1962.

In October 1963 Barber was appointed to his first Cabinet post, that of Minister of Health, by Prime Minister Sir Alec Douglas-Home, and was made a Privy Councillor at the same time. In the general election of October 1964, which brought the Labour party to power, Barber lost his Doncaster constituency by a narrow margin. He was returned to the House of Commons in February 1965, however, after defeating three opponents in

ANTHONY BARBER

a by-election in the northwestern constituency of Altrincham and Sale.

One of the most effective speakers for the opposition, Barber was named by Conservative party leader Edward Heath as the principal spokesman on trade, industry, and power in the shadow Cabinet. In the summer of 1966 Barber launched an elaborate and skillful attack on a plan by Prime Minister Harold Wilson's Labour government to renationalize the steel industry. He characterized the nationalization scheme as "lunacy" and "wicked," pointing out that it would require large-scale borrowing at a time of economic crisis, and he maintained that it was based on political expediency rather than sound economic principles. Although the measure passed in the House of Commons by a vote of 328 to 247, Barber's effort earned him a special citation from the Conservative leadership and contributed to his rise through the party's ranks.

To create a more effective opposition, Heath appointed Barber on February 22, 1967 to the party post of liaison officer on home affairs between the Conservative central office, the shadow Cabinet, and Conservative back-benchers. As such, he attended twice-weekly meetings of a liaison committee and worked with the party's eighteen policy groups and with its specialized committees in an effort to establish a common ground for action among Conservatives within and outside of Parliament. In March 1967 he added the position of president of the Young Conservatives to his other responsibilities.

On September 11, 1967, after several months of rumors of an impending shakeup of the Conservative party, Heath appointed Barber as party chairman, to succeed Edward du Cann, who had resigned, reportedly because of business and family commitments. The chairman heads the party's central office, supervises organizational work, evaluates parliamentary candidates, organizes election campaigns, and plays a key role in formulating policy. Accepting the post, Barber called on party workers to be prepared for an early general election. He charged the Labour government with ineptitude and maintained that it was responsible for "an incredible situation, with industrial stagnation, mounting unemployment, rising prices, and a continuing balance-of-payment problem." Barber's prestige suffered something of a setback in the fall of 1969, when his challenge of Labour's overseas trade figures was proved wrong in a House of Commons debate.

In preparation for the general election scheduled for June 18, 1970 Barber concentrated the party's resources into seventy marginal constituencies and organized a vigorous "grass-roots get-out-the-vote" campaign. He was given much of the credit for the Conservatives' unexpected victory, which brought the party a thirty-seat majority in the House of Commons and placed Edward Heath into the Prime Ministership. In the new Cabinet, which was chosen on June 20, 1970 and sworn in two days later, Barber was named Chancellor of the Duchy of Lancaster and was placed in charge of forthcoming negotiations for Great Britain's entry into the European Economic Community (EEC) or Common Market, a position that made him the second-ranking official in the Foreign Office.

Accompanied by Sir Alec Douglas-Home, the British Foreign Minister, Barber went to Luxembourg on June 30, 1970 for preliminary talks with representatives of the six Common Market nations —France, the Netherlands, Luxembourg, Belgium, West Germany, and Italy. (On two previous occasions, in 1963 and 1967, British application for membership in the EEC was vetoed by France.) Representatives of three other applicant nations— Norway, Denmark, and the Republic of Ireland— were also present. In addressing the meeting, Barber outlined the British negotiating position and pointed out that the Common Market needed Britain as much as Britain needed the Common Market. Although he recognized the need for Britain to accept the EEC's financial regulations, he called attention to the cost that the country would have to bear under the market's agricultural financing system, and he stressed the need for finding a fair solution that would not place an excessive burden on the British consumer. He also noted that the problem of Britain's special economic ties with non-European members of the Commonwealth of Nations would have to be resolved.

At the first formal business session of the British negotiations for EEC membership, held at Brussels on July 21, 1970, Barber pledged his government's acceptance of Common Market regulations. He asked, however, that some of Britain's special needs be taken into consideration, proposing a one-year grace period that would enable Britain to adapt its laws to EEC policy. At his suggestion, the Common Market's executive commission agreed to undertake special studies of problems posed by Britain's application, until the next formal meeting, scheduled for October.

On July 21, 1970 Chancellor of the Exchequer Iain Macleod died of a heart attack. Four days later, Prime Minister Heath appointed Anthony Barber to the post. With almost total freedom to levy taxes and to impose economic regulations, the Chancellor occupies the most powerful office in the British government next to that of the Prime Minister. Heath's appointment of a close professional associate like Barber was seen by political observers as an indication that the Prime Minister intended to keep a tight rein on the economy. Despite Barber's qualifications, the appointment was not universally acclaimed. An editorial in the *Guardian* (July 25, 1970), for example, while acknowledging that Barber was "intelligent, energetic, and courageous," noted that he was "not known for any broad economic philosophy" and questioned whether he had "the weight or intellectual tenacity" needed for the office. Barber was succeeded in the negotiations with the EEC by Geoffrey Rippon, and he relinquished the party chairmanship to Peter Thomas. "Everything we want to achieve as a nation is dependent on getting our economy and our taxation onto a sound footing," Barber said on accepting the office of Chancellor.

In the months that followed, Barber worked closely with Heath in formulating the Conservative government's "quiet revolution," aimed at combating mounting inflation and the deteriorating balance of payments. At a conference of the International Monetary Fund at Copenhagen in September 1970 he pointed out the dangers of a flexible exchange rate, indicating that his government was firmly committed to the existing dollar-sterling rate of exchange. Addressing the Conservative party conference at Blackpool in the following month, Barber denounced as "blackmail" the exorbitant wage demands and strike threats of some trade unions.

On October 27, 1970 Barber presented an extensive economy program to the House of Commons, under which certain cutbacks in welfare were made, the free-milk program for schools was eliminated, and charges for medicines and dental care under the National Health Service were increased. Fewer funds were made available for railroad and highway construction and for housing subsidies, and limits were placed on military expenditures. Museums and galleries were instructed to introduce admission charges for the public. A system of agricultural import levies was introduced, apparently in anticipation of Britain's entry into the Common Market. Corporation income taxes were reduced by 2.5 percent, and personal income tax rates were also decreased. For the very poor, an income supplement plan was introduced. Certain government agencies, such as the Prices and Incomes Board and the Industrial Reorganization Corporation were abolished. According to Barber, the reduction of government spending would result in net savings of some $792,000,000 for the coming fiscal year and of an estimated $2.6 billion by 1974-75. In answer to Labour party spokesmen who denounced the plan as a boon for the well-to-do and a burden for the poor, Barber declared that by reducing governmental activity the program would give the individual "greater incentive to increase his earnings and greater freedom in how he spends or saves his income."

In recent years, Barber seems to have turned away from his earlier liberalism to a more right-wing position. In Parliament he voted against the abolition of capital punishment and other liberal measures, and he has consistently defended United States military involvement in Southeast Asia. Although he is opposed to apartheid, he became the first senior Conservative to commit his party abroad to the lifting of the ban on the sale of arms to South Africa when he visited that country in March 1970. Firmly committed to private enterprise, he has said, as quoted in the New York *Times* (July 1, 1970): "Socialism will never bring out the best in man because its very nature is calculated to erode personal responsibility. Choice is the essence of liberty, and there is no more effective way of improving the quality of life."

Aside from government and politics, Barber had for some years been active in the management of his father-in-law's glass manufacturing company, which was merged into Redfearn National Glass Ltd. He became chairman of the latter firm in 1967. In addition, he joined the board of directors of British Ropes, a Yorkshire concern, in November 1964, and he became a director of the Chartered Bank in 1966. Barber relinquished his business interests when he joined the Cabinet in June 1970.

Anthony Barber was married on September 5, 1950 to Jean Patricia Asquith, a former secretary of the Oxford University Conservative Association and an unsuccessful candidate for Parliament in the 1950 election. They have two daughters, Louise and Josephine. Described in the New York *Times* (July 1, 1970) as "the archetype civil servant and Conservative party official," Barber is slight in build and balding, and he dresses fastidiously. Fair-haired and brown-eyed, he stands at five feet ten inches and weighs 154 pounds. Although he is generally soft-spoken and tends to avoid unpleasant confrontations, he also has a reputation as an aggressive debater and as a man of restless energy who cannot brook inefficiency. Barber has a flair for interior decoration and for collecting antiques. His favorite recreations are riding and swimming; he likes to listen to pop music and to watch old movies on television, and he limits his reading mainly to political literature. He belongs to the Church of England but does not attend church regularly. His club is the Carlton. Barber holds Great Britain's Territorial Decoration.

References

Christian Sci Mon p5 Jl 29 '70 por
London Observer p1+ Jl 26 '70 pors
N Y Times p2 S 12 '67 por; p10 Jl 1 '70 por
International Who's Who, 1970-71
Who's Who, 1971-72
Who's Who in America, 1970-71

BARING, GEORGE ROWLAND STANLEY *See* Cromer, 3d Earl of

BARRY, RICK

Mar. 28, 1944- Professional basketball player
Address: b. New York Nets, 1 Old Country Rd., Carle Place, N.Y. 11514; h. 8 Hilton Place, Hempstead, N.Y. 11550

Rick Barry, the shooting, passing superstar of the New York Nets of the American Basketball Association, is the only player to have won scoring titles in both of professional basketball's major leagues. Playing with the San Francisco Warriors in 1966-67, his second season as a pro, he scored the highest average of points per game in the National Basketball Association, then the only league, and two years later, playing with the Oakland Oaks, he was highest scorer in the new ABA. When the Oakland franchise was transferred to Washington, D.C., in 1969, Barry was unhappy, and a year later, when it was moved to Virginia, he rebelled in such a way as to force the owner of the franchise to trade him to New York. The Net forward's brilliant career has been chronically interrupted by injuries and clouded by complex contract litigation. Legally committed to returning to the Warriors after the 1971-72 season, he has expressed the hope that Net president Roy Boe can negotiate an out-of-court settlement with the San Francisco club.

Richard Francis Barry 3d was born on March 28, 1944 in Elizabeth, New Jersey to Richard Francis Barry 2d, a travel and conference supervisor for the Bell Telephone Company, and the former Alpha Monique Stephanovich. Barry was raised in Roselle Park, New Jersey. His father, who once played semi-pro basketball, transmitted his love of the sport to his two sons. Regarding his brother, Dennis, four years his senior, Rick has recalled, in an interview with Arnold Hano of *Sport* (February, 1967): "Everything he did I wanted to do. When I was five years old I used to tag after him. . . . I played basketball with him and his friends. I guess I could keep up with him because I was much taller than kids my age."

When he was in the fifth grade Barry became the youngest member of the basketball team at Saints Peter and Paul parochial school, coached by his father. "My father was a strict fundamentalist and a strict disciplinarian. He was a perfectionist. He drilled the fundamentals into me. . . . [But] the game was never forced on me. Always, I would get interested first. I'd say, 'Show me,' and my father would show me. Take the way I shoot fouls. He taught me to shoot them underhand. . . . I shoot five percent more fouls because I shoot underhanded."

As outstanding scorer at Roselle Park High School, Barry made the New Jersey All-State team, and in his senior year in high school he was already six feet four and a half inches tall. When he graduated, at least twenty-five colleges were offering him scholarships and he had an alternate appointment to the United States Naval Academy. He chose to go to the University of Miami, whose basketball coach, Bruce Hale, he knew and liked. (Hale, alerted to Barry's prowess by a friend who

RICK BARRY

was a New Jersey high school coach, had gone to the trouble of traveling north to meet the young player and his family.)

At the University of Miami, Barry majored in marketing, belonged to Omicron Delta Kappa honor society, and in his spare time sold life insurance. On the basketball court, he matured rapidly under Bruce Hale's tutelage. "Coach Hale put my game together," he recalled in the interview with Arnold Hano. "He helped me get rid of my temper. I used to stew or pout on the court. I would get mad easily if something happened that I didn't like, if I did something wrong, or if I thought the official had called one wrong against me. I wouldn't run back on defense. I'd stop playing. Coach Hale explained that . . . I couldn't be a kid all my life." With Barry on its roster, the University of Miami basketball team gained national prominence for the first time. In his junior year he was the fifth best scorer in the country, with an average of 32.2 points per game, and the eleventh best rebounder, with 16.6 points. In his senior year he averaged 37.4 points per game and was a unanimous All-America selection.

In June 1965, when he took his B.B.A. degree, Barry married Coach Hale's daughter Pamela, who was then a professional swimmer. There was some doubt about his immediate prospects for a berth in professional basketball, because, at 205 pounds, he was light for his height by pro standards. But the skeptics were confounded when the San Francisco Warriors, then one of the weakest teams in the National Basketball Association, selected him in the first round of professional basketball's 1965 "draft" of college graduates and signed him to a three-year contract.

In his first season with the Warriors, Barry scored 2,059 points, for an average of 25.7 per game, and he was voted the league's Rookie of the Year. (Only three other rookies in NBA history had scored more than 2,000 points.) Alex Hannum, who was then coaching the Warriors, later attributed Barry's success to "guts," "speed," and "quickness." "He has absolute courage under

that basket. No one pushes him around, and that's a necessity for success. . . . He moves real well for a big man on the fast break and he has great hands. If he's going after a loose ball with somebody you can generally bet that Rick will get it." Bill Sharman replaced Hannum as San Francisco coach after the 1965-66 season.

In the 1966-67 season Barry won the NBA individual scoring championship with a total of 2,775 points, for an average of 35.6 per game, and he led the Warriors to the finals of the NBA championship playoffs, where they lost to Philadelphia. In the fifteen playoff games he averaged 34.7 points a game, and in the All-Star game that season he scored thirty-eight points and was voted the Most Valuable Player. His impressive season and post-season scoring was done despite the heavy guard that opposition teams had learned to put on him. "They don't stop you . . . ," he commented to Frank Deford of *Sports Illustrated* (February 13, 1967). "They play you close and they make you work for every shot. But it all comes down to whether you can put them in or not. In the final analysis it is not them stopping you but you missing it."

For eighteen years, beginning in 1949, the National Basketball Association was the only major league in professional basketball. In 1967 a new league was formed, the American Basketball Association, with an Eastern Division of six teams and a Western Division of five teams. One of the franchises in the Western Division went to the Oakland Oaks, who hired Barry's father-in-law as its general manager and sought to lure Barry himself across San Francisco Bay. Barry was happy with the Warriors but the offer made by the Oaks was more than he could resist: a salary of $75,000 a year, 15 percent ownership of the club, and a 5 percent share in gate receipts over $600,000.

Although his contract with the Warriors still had a year to run, Barry signed a five-year contract with the Oaks. Sidelined for a year by a court ruling won by the Warriors, he did not play with the Oaks until 1968-69. That season he scored the highest average in the ABA, 34 points per game, but a knee injury restricted his playing to thirty-five games, and while the Oaks were winning the championship playoffs, he was in the hospital, having cartilage removed. According to his wife, the injury turned Barry into a "hypochondriac." "The knee was a traumatic experience," Mrs. Barry told an Associated Press interviewer two years later (Washington *Post*, January 17, 1971). "He was never injured in college and it hit Rick worse than it would others. It was his first time in the hospital, his first operation. After the operation, he was lying in bed saying, 'I can't feel the leg. I'll never walk again' . . . . He kept thinking about injuries after he hurt his knee. He would only jump a few inches off the floor, except . . . [when] he would forget himself."

In 1969 Earl Foreman, a wealthy Washington, D.C. lawyer, bought the ABA's Oakland franchise and moved the Oaks to Washington, changing their name to the Capitols. Reluctant to leave the San Francisco Bay area, Barry went back to the

San Francisco Warriors and signed a five-year, million-dollar contract with them. But court orders forced him to adhere to his prior contract with the Oaks-Caps, and he played fifty-two games with the Caps in 1969-70, scoring an average of 27.7 points per game. (In the playoffs his average was 40.1.) Hospitalization and recuperation following re-injury of his left knee kept him out of thirty games. His career totals up to the end of the 1969-70 season were 7,466 points scored in 245 games, 2,256 rebounds, and 769 assists. He succeeded in making 48 percent of the 2-point field goals he attempted, 26 percent of the 3-pointers, and 88 percent of the free throws.

The Washington Caps moved to Virginia to become the Virginia Squires in 1970. In an interview published in Sports Illustrated (August 24, 1970), Barry made some remarks about the Old Dominion calculated to insure that he would be persona non grata there. The ploy worked. Explaining that "Barry's continued presence on the Squires would be an affront to the sports fans of the state of Virginia," Foreman traded him to the New York Nets. In return, the Squires received an estimated $200,000 and the Nets' first round choice in the 1971 college draft. At a press conference called to announce the trade, Barry apologized for his derogatory remarks about Virginia: "I really have nothing against Southern accents, but I'm used to the metropolitan area type of living. I used that article [the Sports Illustrated interview] as a wedge."

Midway through the 1970-71 season, the Nets were in third place in the ABA's six-team Eastern Division. Barry, who was averaging approximately 25 points per game, had played only about half the Nets' schedule, because of chronic knee problems." The injuries have really depressed him . . . ," his wife observed in the Associated Press interview published in the Washington Post. "Every time he starts to get back into form he gets injured again. He hasn't played well all year and I know it's bothering him." Barry's low estimate of his performance was valid only in relation to his own high standard. The league judged him worthy of membership on the Eastern All-Star team, and in the East-West game, in Greensboro, South Carolina on January 23, 1971, he scored the tying and the winning points.

As Joe Donnelly noted in Newsday (January 25, 1971), the biographical paragraph about Barry in the All-Star program broke surprisingly from bland, complimentary tradition. It ended: "Bitter about not being able to return to that team (San Francisco) . . . somewhat spoiled . . . complains to referees a lot." Barry was abashed for a moment when he saw the paragraph but took it in good-natured stride. "People like to ride Barry," Donnelly observed. "Some of the time the person getting on him is Rick Barry. That, and his shooting, are his saving graces." Publicly, Net coach Lou Carnesecca half-humorously chides Barry for playing to the crowd, but privately, according to Donnelly, he makes such statements about him as: "I hope he never loses that sophomoric urge to win."

Rick Barry lives in Hempstead, New York with his wife and two sons, Richard F. 4th, known as Scooter, born in 1966, and Jon Alan, born in 1969. The Net forward is six feet seven and a half inches tall, weighs 220 pounds, and has brown hair and eyes. His favorite recreations are golf, power boating, snowmobiling, tennis, horseback riding, and sports car driving, and his religious affiliation is with the Roman Catholic Church. He does not, at least publicly, identify himself with any political party, but otherwise he is, by his own description, "the type of person who speaks up on most everything, especially if it concerns me." In addition to his major injuries—the knee problems and a broken foot—Barry regularly suffers more minor injuries than the average basketball player. "He's accident prone, I guess," his wife said in the AP interview, adding that he has a tendency to magnify minor ailments. "Rick feels a twinge of pain and he dies. As soon as he gets hurt he thinks the worst. . . . He panics. Maybe he just has a low tolerance for pain." But Mrs. Barry was quick to point out that, in the long run, her husband's will to work and win always proves stronger than his worry about injuries. "He's like a spirited race horse. He kicks and bites, but he'll put out for you. He has his quirks, but he puts out for you." Barry adds to his sizeable basketball income by doing commercial endorsements, and he invests his money wisely, if the number of business consultants in his entourage is any indication. Prentice-Hall is planning to publish an autobiographical book by Barry.

References

Life 62:54+ Ja 6 '67
Nat Observer p42 N 8 '68 por
Sat Eve Post 240:80+ Mr 11 '67 por
Sport 43:67+ F '67 por
Sports Illus 26:32+ F 13 '67 por; 27:22+ Ag 14 '67 por
Washington (D.C.) Post mag p7+ Ap 12 '70 por; D p2 Ja 17 '71

BAZELON, DAVID L(IONEL)

Sept. 3, 1909- Judge
Address: b. United States Courthouse, Washington, D.C. 20037; h. 2700 Virginia Ave., N.W., Washington, D.C. 20037

Since his appointment in 1949 to the United States Court of Appeals for the District of Columbia Circuit, David L. Bazelon, now chief judge of the court, has written a series of landmark decisions whose revolutionary effect on the judiciary has reached far beyond his own courtroom. Judge Bazelon first stirred up international controversy in 1954 with his formulation of the Durham Rule, redefining the test of criminal insanity. Throughout his career he has consistently defended the rights of the individual against the impersonal machinery of law enforcement and the judiciary, stressing the need for rehabilitation as opposed to retribution and consideration of the social and

DAVID L. BAZELON

psychological situation of the defendant in each criminal case. His philosophic involvement with questions of law and punishment and his support for an informed use of the behavioral sciences, especially psychiatry, in the courtroom have brought him both honor and criticism in abundance from the press and from members of his own and related professions.

David Lionel Bazelon was born on September 3, 1909 in Superior, Wisconsin, the last of nine children (three girls and six boys) of Israel and Lena (Krasnovsky) Bazelon. His father, the proprietor of a general store, died two years later, leaving his wife and children virtually penniless. The family moved to Chicago, where David Bazelon attended the city's public schools and graduated from Senn High School in 1926. He financed his college education with jobs as a store clerk and movie usher. Bazelon enrolled at the University of Illinois in 1928, but remained for only one year. He then entered Northwestern University, where he studied in the schools of liberal arts and law and eventually obtained his B.S.L. degree in 1931.

The following year, on being admitted to the bar in Illinois, Bazelon opened a private law practice. In 1935 he entered the United States Attorney's Office in Chicago as an assistant United States attorney for the northern district of Illinois, where he was assigned to federal tax matters. He resigned that post after five years to join the private law firm of Gottlieb and Schwartz, of which he became a senior partner. During the late 1930's he was politically active in the Independent Voters League, which sponsored Paul H. Douglas, who later became a Senator from Illinois, for a seat on the city council of Chicago.

President Harry S. Truman appointed Bazelon to the position of Assistant Attorney General of the United States on April 29, 1946. Leaving his lucrative law practice, he moved to Washington, where during his first year he was in charge of the lands division of the Justice Department. In 1947 he became head of the department's office of alien property, which had taken over the functions of the alien property litigation unit. Bazelon was tagged a "New Dealing Lawyer" in a short article in *Time* (March 8, 1948) concerning his action against the North American Rayon Corporation, whose dealings in the "gray" market and German ownership had attracted the notice of the office of alien property.

In October 1949 Bazelon's name was included in a list of nineteen nominations sent by President Truman to the Senate for judgeships in the United States Courts of Appeals, following the creation by Congress of twenty-seven new judgeships. Within two days the Senate Judiciary Committee had postponed consideration of all the nominations, on the grounds that there was insufficient time to act before Congress adjourned. It was not, therefore, until February 8, 1950 that Bazelon's nomination to the bench for the United States Court of Appeals for the District of Columbia Circuit was confirmed by the Senate. He was the youngest man ever named to a federal appellate bench. His appointment attracted only the usual notice and no objection, with the exception of Harold L. Ickes' comment in the *New Republic* that the President had been "imposed upon" by Bazelon's supporters, including Supreme Court Justice Tom C. Clark. In 1962 Bazelon became by seniority the chief judge of the court, a position that is considered prestigious, though the added duties are largely administrative.

From the beginning of his career on the bench Bazelon has been concerned with the insanity defense in criminal cases. The prevalent test of criminal responsibility continues to be the McNaghten Rules, which ask whether the defendant is able to distinguish between "right" and "wrong." Those who cannot make the distinction are considered undeserving of blame for the criminal acts they have committed. In the federal courts and those of a quarter of the states, those rules are supplemented by the so-called "irresistible impulse test," which would relieve the defendant of legal responsibility if the behavior could not be controlled because of a mental disorder. Judge Bazelon, in a decision in a 1954 case, *Durham v. United States*, established a broader rule to be applied in the District of Columbia court in cases where the issue was the mental condition of the defendant. It states that an "accused is not criminally responsible if his unlawful act was the product of mental disease or mental defect."

Since the formulation of the Durham Rule, its significance has been debated in law reviews and medical journals. It has been considered by other courts, and although adopted only by the Virgin Islands in 1957, it has stimulated interest in challenging the limitations of the old rules. Much criticism has centered on the philosophical issue of free will as opposed to social and mental determinations. Other criticisms have dealt with the wording of the Bazelon doctrine, contending that the term "mental disease" cannot be closely defined; with the possibility of an exaggerated influence of psychiatry in criminal trials; and with the risk of permitting juries to acquit those defendants who have relatively minor mental disturbances.

Supporters of the rule see it not so much as a device to increase the number of insanity acquittals, but rather as a device to expand the information about human behavior which is available to a jury. Bazelon has defended his rule not only in court opinions, but also in lectures and magazine articles. In "Imperative to Punish," which he wrote for the *Atlantic Monthly* (July 1960), Bazelon asserted, "If we were not so set on punishing the offender for the sake of punishment, if we did not justify this practice by reference to its deterrent effect, we could understand that rehabilitation lies at the spiritual heart of any vital moral system."

In the classroom too Bazelon has worked to establish and clarify relationships between mental illness and mental defects and the law. He was lecturer in law and psychiatry at the University of Pennsylvania from 1957 to 1959; Sloan Visiting Professor at the Menninger Clinic in Topeka, Kansas in 1960-61; and Regent's Lecturer at the University of California at Los Angeles in 1964. Since 1964 he has been lecturer in psychiatry at the Johns Hopkins University School of Medicine, and since 1966 he has been clinical professor of psychiatry in its social and legal aspects at George Washington University.

In speeches before professional groups Bazelon has often prodded psychiatrists to take a greater interest in the mentally disturbed criminal defendant and to explain their court testimony more adequately to members of the jury unfamiliar with psychiatric terms. Over the years he has urged that juvenile courts appoint psychiatrists for youthful offenders. Another of his concerns has been with the lack of information and understanding about mental retardation and with the treatment of mentally retarded persons by the law. In a 1964 dissent he argued that narcotics addiction was a form of illness that required treatment and of itself should not be cause for imprisonment.

An exchange of letters between Bazelon and Attorney General Nicholas deB. Katzenbach, made public in August 1965, revealed their differing views on a proposal of changes in criminal procedure being considered by the American Law Institute. The proposal would permit a suspect to retain legal counsel during police interrogation, but would not require the police to provide counsel for persons who could not afford it. Bazelon argued that such a code would discriminate against the poor. Katzenbach's reply was that the purpose of a criminal investigation was to discover the guilty and not to insure equal treatment. Bazelon was supported some months later by professor of criminal law at Michigan University, Yale Kamisar, who believed that the judge had lost his case in the mass media but won it in the courts and law schools.

Continuing to issue majority decisions that have provoked controversy for their reversals of precedents, in 1965 Bazelon's court held that the federal government could not dismiss an employee on unspecified charges of homosexuality. A 1969 decision held that homosexuality justifies dismissal only if conduct affects job performance, not simply if it is judged to be immoral. The court was divided in a 1967 ruling that prison sentences for related "common law crimes" could not run consecutively. In 1970 Bazelon led the court in ruling in favor of a suit filed by conservation groups to pressure the Department of Agriculture into banning the insecticide DDT. In the first court case, in 1970, testing the new federal law giving eighteen-year-olds the right to vote in all elections, he was one of three judges on a special United States district court to uphold the constitutionality of the law.

One of Bazelon's chief concerns has been the youthful offender, and his court has often been required to fill what he has called the gap between the legal promises of the juvenile statutes and the reality of inadequate facilities. In a speech to psychiatrists in 1969 he asked whether American society has given up on ghetto youth, who represent the majority of youthful offenders. Observing that the young ghetto offender "may be twice cursed," he explained, "The very conditions which made him a mental or emotional cripple, . . . that make us feel we owe him special care, may make us feel such care is futile." He has long believed that the answer for both juvenile and adult criminals is psychiatric treatment in mental hospitals and in community health clinics as an "alternative to prison commitment." His views have brought attacks from law enforcement officials as well as lawyers and judges and members of Congress. To help alleviate the conditions he sees as contributing to crime in Washington, he served from 1964 to 1966 as chairman of the advisory committee of the model school division of the District of Columbia Public Schools, known as the Cardozo Project. During his first year and a half he criticized the lethargy and intellectual timidity of some educators associated with the project, but in June 1966 he released a letter praising proposals for the coming year as being innovative and responsive to suggestions offered in his committee's report.

Judge Bazelon has worked with many groups involved in matters of law and mental health and related problems. He served in 1961-62 as chairman of the task force on law of the President's Panel on Mental Retardation. In present affiliations he is a member of the board of the Salk Institute for Biological Studies, the Washington School of Psychiatry, the Center for the Study of Violence of Brandeis University, and the Joint Commission on Mental Health of Children, Inc. He is on advisory committees for the Boston University Center for Law and Life Sciences (chairman), Center for Law and Psychiatry of the Psychiatric Institute Foundation, the Harvard University Program on Technology and Society, and the National Association of State Mental Health Program Directors, and others. He is also a member of the working conference on an action program for psychiatry in mental retardation of the American Psychiatric Association. In September and October 1967 he was a member of the United States Mission on Mental Health to the

U.S.S.R. More than a score of articles by him on law, civil liberties, and psychiatry have appeared in medical and law journals and in popular periodicals.

Among Bazelon's several lectureship awards were the American Psychiatric Association's Isaac Ray Award Lectures at the University of Chicago in 1961 and the David K. Niles Memorial Lecture at the Hebrew University of Jerusalem in 1966. The certificate of commendation of the Isaac Ray Award declared that "he has removed massive barriers between the psychiatric and legal professions and opened pathways wherein together they may search for better ways of reconciling human values with social safety." In 1962 he was elected an honorary fellow of the American Psychiatric Association and in 1969 a fellow of the American Academy of Arts and Sciences. He holds honorary LL.D. degrees from Colby College and from Boston University Law School.

David L. Bazelon and Miriam M. Kellner were married on June 7, 1936. They have two grown sons, James A. and Richard L. Bazelon. The family is Jewish. Politically, Bazelon is a Democrat. A reporter for the New York *Times* described the white-haired judge as "speaking in measured tones and peering over tortoise shell half-glasses" while making a speech. "Despite the fame of his works," Thomas W. Lippman wrote of him in the Washington *Post* (August 5, 1969), "the man himself remains an enigma. . . . People who have associated with him professionally for years have no idea of what he does on his day off." He belongs to the Cosmos Club in Washington and has a summer home in Massachusetts, although it is said that he seldom relaxes. Bazelon, who regards his critics dispassionately, once remarked, "Any court decision that even smacks of novelty can be counted upon to spawn a rash of commentary."

References

Washington (D.C.) Post C p1 + Ag 5 '69
Directory of American Judges (1955)
International Who's Who, 1970-71
Who's Who in America, 1970-71
Who's Who in World Jewry (1965)

BÉJART, MAURICE (bā-zhär')

Jan. 1, 1927- Ballet director-choreographer
Address: Ballet du XXe Siècle, Opéra National, Théâtre de la Monnaie, 4 Rue Léopold, Brussels, Belgium

The most lionized, avant-garde ballet master in Europe is Maurice Béjart, the controversial director-choreographer of the Ballet of the Twentieth Century (Ballet du XXe Siècle), Belgium's national dance company. The classically trained Béjart founded the Brussels troupe in 1959, after six years of experience with his own company in Paris, where he was a pioneer in electronic and intermedia compositions. Béjart is known for his flamboyant theatricality and his treatment of dance

as total spectacle, as visual music rather than as moving sculpture; his penchant for massive patterns; his intermingling, or fusion, of diverse musical styles, themes, and movements, such as Oriental with Occidental, and classical with modern and natural; and his daring revamping of traditional materials.

Much of Béjart's revamping, or contemporizing, has reflected an *engagé*, New Leftish political position and a desire to evoke healthy animality or eroticism, as in his *Boléro* (Ravel), in which forty men, in turn, and one ballerina thrust pelvises. But in his basic philosophy he is mystical, viewing ballet theatre as neo-religious ritual. "Those who approach dance as an intellectual exercise," critic Greer Johnson of *Cue* magazine has observed, "are likely to be left unpersuaded by Mr. Béjart." Those most persuaded by him, apparently, are the precise audiences he is avowedly trying to attract, the young and the unsophisticated "masses" untouched by conventional balletomania. Béjart, a prolific choreographer, relishes nothing more than mounting his more grandiose works, such as the *Ninth Symphony* (Beethoven) before such audiences in sports stadiums and other large amphitheatres. "Ballet is popular art of the twentieth century," he has asserted. "But for the large public, ballet must change as much as music and painting have."

Maurice Béjart was born Maurice Jean Berger in Marseilles, France on January 1, 1927 to Gaston and Germaine (Capeillères) Berger. He has two brothers, Alain and Philippe, and a sister, Claudette (Berger) Verges. Béjart was exposed to Oriental philosophy from earliest childhood by his late father, an extraordinary man as described by Béjart in an interview with Elenore Lester for the New York *Times* (January 24, 1971): "My father was too poor to go to school when he was young, but he taught himself while he supported the family working as a fertilizer salesman. He studied the conventional school subjects but also taught himself Chinese and became a Vedanta disciple. At the age of thirty-five he took his baccalaureate examinations with eighteen-year-olds. He became a teacher and rose to become general chief of universities."

As a child, Béjart was attracted to theatre generally. He became interested in ballet specifically when his parents enrolled him, at the age of fourteen, in the ballet school of the Marseilles Opéra for therapeutic reasons, because he was physically frail. When he graduated from the Lycée de Marseilles in 1945 his parents wanted him to matriculate at a university, but instead he went to Paris, studied ballet under Leo Staats, Lubov Egorova, and Madame Rousanne (Rousanne Sarkissian), and served a two-year apprenticeship in Roland Petit's dance company. Then, in London, he studied under Vera Volkova and danced with Mona Inglesby's International Ballet, which was trying to attract new, young audiences. In 1952 he was a guest artist with the Royal Swedish Ballet, dancing, among other roles, Jason in Birgit Cullberg's *Medea*. He began trying his hand at choreography while with the Royal Swedish Ballet.

In 1953, following his compulsory tour of service in the French army, Béjart, with writer-critic Jean Laurent, organized Les Ballets de l'Étoile, named for the Théâtre de l'Étoile, the company's first home. Later, when the troupe moved from the Théâtre de l'Étoile to perform at other Paris theatres and on tours of Europe, its name was changed to Le Ballet-Théâtre de Paris. Early in the history of the company he choreographed for it *L'Inconnu* (Scarlatti), *La Belle au Boa* (Rossini), *Voyage au coeur d'un enfant* (Pierre Henry), and *Haut-Voltage* (Marius Constant, Pierre Henry), based on Jean-Paul Sartre's play *Huis Clos*. Later Béjart created *Le Teck* (Gerry Mulligan), *Orphée* (Henry), and *Sonate à trois* (Bartók).

By the time that Béjart formed his Paris company, Pierre Schaeffer had been experimenting for several years with his *musique concrète* (taped music produced by the combining and electro-acoustical manipulation of sundry sounds, not necessarily instrumental). Béjart became interested in it because of the obviously vast new range it opened in musical concordances for bodily movements and emotions.

According to critic-historian Arnold L. Haskell, Béjart's *Symphonie pour un homme seul*, with music by Schaeffer and Pierre Henry, was the first *musique concrète* ballet ever created. After witnessing its première at the Théâtre de l'Étoile in July 1955, with Béjart in the leading role, Haskell reported in his *Ballet Annual 1957*: "In this work the daily loneliness of contemporary man is represented not, as hitherto, by violincellos, but by footsteps, voices, and other familiar noises distorted and confused as in a nightmare. . . . On a bare stage swept by shafts of pale light, he [Béjart] wanders among shadows which resemble automatons and moves to the rhythm set by the shrieks and whispers of *musique concrète*. Woman, played with savage intensity by Michele Seigneuret, symbolizes a morbid, egotistical love which is powerless to rescue man from his anguish. Classical and modern dance vocabularies intermingle. A perfect cohesion is achieved between gesture, rhythm, and sound. This is the masterpiece of the new genre, a work of brutal, hallucinatory power." Two years later Haskell wrote of another Béjart creation, *Promethée*: "It is amazing, the feeling of size and importance that he [Béjart], and his artistic collaborator, Bernard Daydé, were able to give to a ballet for a handful of dancers. The familiar legend was told with strong dramatic effect and with a feeling of antiquity but without any archaistic tricks."

Commissioned by Maurice Huisman, director of the Théâtre Royal de la Monnaie, home of the Brussels Opéra, Béjart choreographed his own version of *Le Sacre du printemps* to Stravinsky's music, a version without classical steps and with groupings daring in their novelty, such as fifty dancers writhing as one mass. With an expanded company, Béjart staged the première of the powerful work at the Théâtre Royal de la Monnaie in December 1959. The performance was an extra-

MAURICE BÉJART

ordinary triumph with public and critics, and after it the Béjartists remained in Brussels as the Ballet of the Twentieth Century, with Béjart as its director.

When the Brussels troupe performed Béjart's *Le Sacre du printemps* at the Festival of Nations in Paris in 1960, Béjart won the festival's Grand Prix in choreography, critics raved about his unusual "gymnic forms," "staggering motions," and "perfection of overall groupings," and one predicted that the work would "leave its mark upon the history of ballet." In collaboration with the painter Salvador Dali, who conceived the idea, Béjart choreographed the dance spectacle *Gala* for presentation in Venice in the summer of 1961. Dali angrily disassociated himself from the production before its presentation, objecting to such scenes as one involving destruction of national flags and another, a stage full of bloody cattle carcasses.

In staging operas for the Brussels Opéra, Béjart from the first used heavy, surrealistic visual embellishment, or the reverse. For the Bacchanale in Wagner's *Tannhäuser*, in 1961, he prescribed costumes simulating nudity (along with explicitly sexual movements). His production of Offenbach's *Tales of Hoffman*, in 1962, had an ostrich doing a Charleston-like dance, an enormous eye hanging from the ceiling, and a disembodied, pulsating lung in a rib cage that opened and closed. Descendants of Viktor Leon and Leo Stein, the librettists, sued Béjart when he added to the operetta *The Merry Widow* such scenes as the heroine dancing on a corpse-laden battlefield and hobnobbing with beggars. In Béjart's version of Berlioz's *The Damnation of Faust* (1963), Marguerite did a striptease.

Béjart conceived of his *Ninth Symphony* (Beethoven) as a religious-like rite, with the audience participating in a spirit of brotherhood. The large-scale work, employing fifty dancers and a full orchestra and chorus, with soloists, premièred in the Royal Circus (Cirque Royal) in Brussels in 1964. Two years later the same site was chosen for the initial presentation of Béjart's *Romeo and Juliet* (Berlioz), in which the Shakespearean text was twisted to accommodate antiwar and antityranny sentiments. Later, when *Romeo and Juliet* was performed in Lisbon, Portugal, Béjart appended some topical political comments in a spontaneous speech to the audience and Portuguese authorities expelled him immediately.

Béjart's liturgical concept was developed most explicitly in *Messe pour le temps présent,* first performed at the papal palace in Avignon, France as part of the Avignon Festival of the Arts in 1967. That long work is eclectic in its sparse music (some jazz, rock, and raga and much wooden percussion—usually done by Béjart offstage, with blocks —and chanting) and its philosophy (which includes elements of Eastern mysticism), and it is open-ended, with the audience participating differently on different occasions. (Some performances end with the members of the cast, and members of the audience who wish to join them, sitting in silent meditation.) Like other Béjart works of monumental scale, *Messe pour le temps présent* uses virtually no costumes or scenery, which, Béjart believes, "were once a valuable part of ballet—but that is now over."

In 1968 Béjart, who has since retired as a dancer, was still performing principal parts in some of his productions, including *La Nuit obscure,* based on St. John of the Cross's *Dark Night of the Soul.* "Like many of Béjart's works," a writer noted in *Dance* (October 1968), "this one is conceived as a highly theatrical fusion of speech, gesture, and movement." The Béjartians received thunderous applause from the tens of thousands of arena spectators who witnessed their contribution to the inaugural festivities at the Olympic Games in Mexico City in 1968. At the 1969 Avignon Festival of the Arts politically agitated young people reportedly showed greater affinity for the Béjart troupe, along with the Living Theatre, than for any of the other participants.

Greer Johnson visited the Théâtre Royal de la Monnaie in September and reminisced about his "too-brief stay" four months later (*Cue,* January 23, 1971): "People who are not 'prepared' for Béjart's work tend to react to it with immediate, almost visceral enthusiasm. Adequately briefed on controversial critical opinion about the Ballet of the Twentieth Century, I was myself quite unprepared for what so electrifyingly happened the moment the curtain went up." In Johnson's opinion, Béjart succeeded, "more often than not," in his calculated breaches of tradition and accepted taste, such as his mixing of Wagner's *Tristan und Isolde* with the *Wesendonck Lieder* and his bending of some of Richard Strauss's songs "into passionate convolutions." "Perhaps the musical mélange is, by the book, tasteless, but it works, it fascinates, and it creates some new unity on its own."

Walter Terry, who went to Brussels to write a two-installment article on Béjart and his company for the *Saturday Review* (December 19 and 26, 1970), described Béjart's newest work, *Firebird* (Stravinsky): "This *Firebird* is truly a remarkable creation. Its principal figure is not a ballerina but a male dancer; it is not staged as a Russian ballet but, rather, as an abstract work. . . . Here . . . is a Firebird who breathes life into man's consciousness, who flashes brilliantly across the spectrum, but who must die. But as he dies, he is replaced by the phoenix . . . and there is hope for tomorrow."

Terry watched Béjart rehearse his recently recruited star, Suzanne Farrell, the protegée of George Balanchine who had defected from the New York City Ballet. "One could see Béjart adapt the previously composed choreography to Farrell's high leg extensions and spinal flexibilities; but, more, as he guided her and her cavalier, one saw the presence of shrewdly calculated choreographic patterns (his discipline) combined with his desire to release the animal in the human (his drive). Perhaps this is the secret of the man—discipline and drive."

In the decade following its formation, the Ballet of the Twentieth Century toured Japan, Canada, most of Europe, and much of Latin America, gathering legions of ardent supporters, and a few detractors, as it went. The company made its United States debut in a two-week engagement at the Brooklyn (New York) Academy of Music beginning on January 25, 1971. The program on opening night in Brooklyn comprised *Erotica* (Tadeusz Baird), a pas de deux, and *Bhakti,* based on a Hindu theme and set to Indian music, and the world première of *Choreographic Offering* (J. S. Bach), a tour de force devised by the dancers of the company themselves. The offerings on the following days included *Bach Sonata, Nomos Alpha,* and *Le Sacre du printemps.*

The reception accorded the Béjart troupe by New York newspaper critics was disappointing. The opening night review by Clive Barnes in the New York *Times* and another *Times* review by Anna Kisselgoff two days later seemed as much concerned with debunking Béjart's reputation as an innovator as with the company's performances. Miss Kisselgoff argued that Béjart's experimentalism was old-fashioned in terms of the American ballet of the past thirty years. "If you had never seen Balanchine . . . Cunningham . . . Graham . . . Sokolow . . . Robbins . . . , Béjart's supposedly 'with it' ballets might have seemed hip." She also accused Béjart of pandering to the tastes of a youthful audience. "Béjart is out to *épater les petits bourgeois.* There is a hint of demagogic appeal here that has no place in art." Hubert Saal of *Newsweek* (February 8, 1971) judged his choreographic vocabulary "anemic" and his ideas "obscure" but thought that he succeeded in his unconventional way in *Bhakti* and, above all, in *Messe pour le temps présent,* in which he worked through "the ordinary, the simplistic, and the mystic" to evoke, finally, "an irresistible, shattering apocalyptic vision of mankind."

The roster of the Ballet of the Twentieth Century now numbers more than sixty dancers, from all parts of the world. Among the company's powerful male principal dancers are Antonio Cano, Paolo Bortoluzzi, and Jorge Donn. The leading ballerinas include Miss Farrell, Menia Martinez,

Maina Gielgud, Duska Sifnius, and Tania Bari. The company's school, called the Mudra (a Hindu word meaning gesture), has eight teachers. Early in 1971 Béjart was planning to write a *pas de deux* for two men—Paolo Bortoluzzi of his own company and Rudolf Nureyev—and a ballet inspired by Antonin Artaud's "very pure and very decadent" novel *Héliogable*.

Maurice Béjart is five feet four inches tall, weighs 143 pounds, and has dark chestnut hair, heavy brows, a pointed beard, and piercing, luminous eyes that have been variously described as "hypnotic" and "disconcertingly wide-open." Elenore Lester, interviewing him for the New York *Times* (January 24, 1971), saw in his profile "a Satanic cast" and in his "white-toothed" smile a "determined" affability, and she described him as "a man of driven and driving energies." According to Miss Lester, he speaks English "well but somewhat hesitantly." Walter Terry noted that at rehearsals Béjart illustrates his instructions "with physical facility and enormous intensity." The intense Béjart confesses to one passionate recreation, motion pictures. "I love Von Stroheim, Godard, Fellini. . . . I'm not put here to relax, but to create. When I come out of the movies I am ready to work. I can see things with clear eyes. I am full of energy." The director-choreographer has written a novel, *Mathilde, ou le temps perdu* (R. Julliard, 1963).

References

Cue 40:12+ Ja 23 '71 por
Dance 42:34+ O '68 pors; 45:42+ Ja '71 pors
Guardian p7 My 24 '65 por
N Y Times II p1 Ja 24 '71 por
Chujoy, A., and Manchester, P. W., eds. Dance Encyclopedia (1967)
Who's Who in France, 1965-66

BENCH, JOHNNY

Dec. 7, 1947- Baseball player
Address: b. Cincinnati Reds, 100 Riverfront Stadium, Cincinnati, Ohio 45201

Catching is the most crucial and complex job in baseball—and also the most thankless. While the pitcher gets the glory, the inconspicuous man calling the game from behind the plate generally goes unsung. One of the rare exceptions to that rule is Johnny Bench, catcher and field leader of the Cincinnati Reds in the Western Division of the National League. Bench is the first receiver in league history to have been named Rookie of the Year (1968) and the first in fifteen years to have been chosen Most Valuable Player (1970). Sportswriters have tagged him "the most valuable property in baseball" and predicted that he will be the first player to arrive at a $200,000 salary; Cincinnati pitcher Wayne Granger sees him as "more valuable to this team than anyone was to any other team in the history of baseball"; and astute

JOHNNY BENCH

old pro Ted Williams has judged him "a Hall of Famer for sure."

Behind the plate Bench is agile in both mind and body, calling pitches in combinations calculated to exploit the specific weaknesses of each individual batter, picking runners off base with sudden, precise bullet thrusts, and signaling to fielders the anticipated direction of a ball before it is hit. What makes him stand out, however, is his extraordinary—especially for a catcher—power at bat. As he entered the 1971 season his slugging totals, compiled over less than four complete years, were 101 doubles, eight triples, eighty-seven home runs, and 326 runs batted in, and his batting average was .281. In occasional respites from his catching chores, the big Cincinnati right-hander plays first base, third base, and the outfield.

Johnny Lee Bench was born on December 7, 1947 in Oklahoma City, Oklahoma and, with his sister and two older brothers, was raised in the nearby small town of Binger, Oklahoma. Bench is one-eighth Choctaw Indian, through the paternal line of descent. His parents are Mr. and Mrs. Ted Bench, who now live near Cincinnati, in a home purchased for them by Johnny. The father, a semi-professional catcher before he became the driver of a heating-oil delivery truck in Oklahoma, early instilled major league ambitions in Johnny, and he was his first mentor, as William Barry Furlong noted in the New York *Times Magazine* (August 30, 1970): "He taught him to grab the ball across the seams to get the greatest possible velocity; with any other grip, Johnny might throw a curve ball to second base, one that would tail away from the fielders. His father also taught Johnny to throw to specific targets—the belt buckle, the knee, or the corner of the base. Instead of teaching Johnny to throw the distance from home to second base—127 feet and a few inches—he taught him to throw double that distance, training Johnny to fire the ball as much as 250 feet with micrometrical accuracy—from a crouch."

While concentrating on catching, Bench also played first base, third base, and outfield with a local American Legion team and with the Binger High School team, with which he also pitched. His high school batting average was a phenomenal .675, his pitching record was 29-1, and several of his victories on the mound were no-hitters. Outside of baseball, he won national honors as a guard on the high school basketball team, and scholastically, he was valedictorian of the Binger High class of 1965.

The Cincinnati Reds chose Bench in the second round of the 1965 free-agent draft and sent him to their Tampa farm team in the Florida State League, where he batted .248. In 1966 with the Peninsula (Florida) club in the Class A League he batted .294 and hit twenty-two home runs. In mid-season he was promoted to Buffalo in the Triple A International League, but he broke his right thumb in his first game there and that injury, together with injuries sustained later in an automobile accident (precipitated by a near collision with a drunken driver) kept him out of the lineup for the rest of the season.

Bench started the 1967 season with Buffalo and finished it in the majors. In ninety-eight games with Buffalo he batted .259, hit twenty-three home runs, drove in sixty-eight runs, and earned the minor-league Player of the Year citation. In twenty-six games with the Cincinnati Reds at the end of the season he had a batting average of .163. Because he was at bat only eighty-six times, five short of the decisive ninety-one, his freshman status with Cincinnati was carried over into 1968.

In a baseball team's batting order the first three places are traditionally filled by men who consistently get on base. In the fourth, or "cleanup," position comes the team's leading slugger, who is expected to drive in the men on base. In 1968 Bench began the season batting seventh, but as his dependable power became manifest he advanced in the lineup, ultimately to fourth place. During the season he drove in eighty-two runs, hit fifteen home runs, and compiled a .275 batting average. When he won the Rookie of the Year distinction, Al Stump of Sport (January 1967) observed that he did so not only on the strength of his offensive record and defensive proficiency but also on that of "all the intangibles you look for in a potential superstar." Stump reported: "To a man, the old pros said they had seldom if ever seen a youngster as poised, tough, self-reliant and full of leadership as Bench."

Bench's batting averages, home runs, and runs batted in were, respectively, .296, twenty-six, and ninety in 1969 and .296, forty-five, and 148 in 1970. His 1970 home-run and RBI figures led the league, and the RBI tally was the highest of any since 1938 except Tommy Davis' 151 in 1962. The 1970 performance won him, in addition to Most Valuable Player, the Mercer, the Sporting News, and, for the third consecutive year, the Golden Glove awards. Under Manager Sparky Anderson, who had succeeded Dave Bristol, the Reds won the National League pennant in 1970 but lost the World Series to Baltimore. In the 1971 season both Bench and the Reds slumped. By mid-summer Bench was out of contention for National League slugging honors, and at the end of the season the Reds were tied for fourth and fifth place in standing with the Houston Astros among the six clubs in the league's Western Division. As for himself, however, Bench was not unduly perturbed, because his catching during the season had been up to his usual high standard. In the 1971 All-Star game, which the National League lost, Bench hit a two-run homer and a single.

Bench's teammates have dubbed him "the little general" because of his commanding presence as a field leader and game strategist. Even as a rookie he acted old, addressing pitchers many years his senior as "kid," coaxing their best from them, calming or agitating them as needed. In his New York Times Magazine article William Barry Furlong called Bench "the archetype of the cerebral catcher," meaning that his sharp intelligence and memory are always at work, noting and filing away the batting patterns of his opponents and computerizing the combinations of pitches to use against them. Catching one-handed (formerly a heresy in baseball), he can handle any pitch with seeming ease. (At one time he had difficulty with low pitches, but that fault has been overcome.) Because of his fast reflexes and quick wrists and his powerful, accurate arm few base-runners dare to attempt to steal on him, and less than half of those who do succeed.

Large-framed, tough-sinewed Johnny Bench is six feet one inch tall and weighs about 195 pounds. His hands are so huge that in the right one, his throwing hand, he can hold as many as seven baseballs. His round face, with its tranquil, seemingly unblinking eyes, has a Buddha-like composure that reflects what one observer has called his "preternatural calm." Although he admits to "a fear of failure" in living up to "the expectations not only of yourself but of others," his self-control and self-confidence are such that apparently no amount of pressure can shake Bench's cool poise. When accused of "cocky" self-complacency and conceit by some critics, he has explained that a catcher-field leader cannot afford a humble pose and, furthermore, that he believes in flaunting the truth as he sees it. "There are too many false things in the world and I don't want to be part of them. . . . If you have an object in life you shouldn't be afraid to stand up and say it. I want to be the greatest catcher ever to play the game."

Bench's salary, $40,000 in 1970, was raised to nearly $90,000 in 1971. A believer in hard work and "purposeful" living, he is careful in investing his money, as is his business partner, teammate Pete Rose. He owns a bowling alley in Cincinnati, and bowling is one of his own favorite recreations. Among the others are bridge, golf, and listening to and singing country music. In the winter of 1970-71 he began singing professionally in nightclubs, and during the same period he toured Vietnam with the Bob Hope troupe. In 1970 he had a cameo role in a drama in the television adventure series Mission Impossible, and in the summer of 1971 he began hosting MVP—

Johnny Bench, a half-hour weekly syndicated television show in which he interviews sports figures and others. "Bench comes through the piercing eye of the TV camera as boyishly enthusiastic, charming, and vigorous," Maury Allen reported in *Coronet* (May 1971). "He is not Joe Namath, not long-haired and anti-establishment, not smart-alecky, not flip; just wholesome, clean, and apple-pie America." But Bench has been compared to Namath in the way that he is, according to some observers, always "on-stage," grooming his public image as a superstar not only on the field but in life, through conspicuous consumption of stylish clothes and beautiful women. In *Life* (June 5, 1970) Bill Bruns quoted a teammate: "He won't take a girl out unless she's good looking. He likes to show them off," and then Bench himself: "My girls aren't going to embarrass me. I can afford to be choosy." The Reds catcher lives in the Forum, a "swinging singles" apartment building in Cincinnati.

References

Christian Sci Mon p6 Jl 19 '71 por
N Y Times Mag p8+ Ag 30 '70 pors
Sport 48:50+ D '69 por
Sports Illus 30:26+ Mr 31 '69 pors; 34:
69+ Je 7 '71 por
Who's Who in Baseball, 1971

BENTLEY, HELEN DELICH

Nov. 28, 1923- United States government official; newspaperwoman
Address: b. Federal Maritime Commission, 1405 I St., N.W., Washington, D.C. 20573; h. 408 Chapelwood Lane, Lutherville, Md. 21093

In an appointment of unquestioned merit President Richard Nixon chose as a member and the chairman of the Federal Maritime Commission a redoubtable veteran newspaperwoman, Helen Delich Bentley, whom he credited with having "established a record of professional excellence unsurpassed by any maritime expert in the country." As maritime editor of the Baltimore *Sun* since 1952 and producer of documentary television programs from 1950 to 1965, Mrs. Bentley had acquired a vast store of knowledge about shipping throughout the United States and the world. On a leave of absence from the Baltimore *Sun,* she took her oath of office as chairman of the five-member regulatory agency on October 27, 1969. Mrs. Bentley has long been an impassioned advocate of a more powerful American merchant marine, whose strength is currently being threatened by labor disputes, cut-throat competition from other nations, changing patterns in overseas trade, and a host of other challenges.

Helen Delich Bentley was born on November 28, 1923 in the copper-mining town of Ruth in Nevada's mountainous White Pine County, some 8,000 feet above sea level, and was reared in the nearby town of Ely. Her parents, Yugoslavian im-

HELEN DELICH BENTLEY

migrants, Michael Ivanesevich and Mary (Kovich) Delich, had six other children, two girls and four boys, of whom two are no longer living. When Helen was eight, her father, who worked in a copper mine, died of an occupational disease, silicosis. Her mother, now Mrs. Mary Grubich, lives in Carson City, Nevada.

Faced with economic hardship after her husband's death, Mrs. Delich took in boarders to help provide for her children. Helen went to work in a local dress shop at the age of twelve and continued to work all through high school and college. Her naturalized parents had imbued her with a sense of gratitude for having been born in the United States, and she took full advantage of the opportunities provided by the American educational system. At White Pine High School in Ely, she compiled a record, 5,452 merits, for extracurricular activities that still stands. Prominent in every organization in the school, she was president of her senior class and of the Quill and Scroll Society, business manager of the yearbook, and a member of the debating team and dramatics club. While in high school she also began her career in journalism, as a part-time reporter on the Ely *Record* in 1939. Charles Russell, editor of the *Record* and later Governor of Nevada, encouraged her to become a newspaperwoman and a Republican. She graduated as valedictorian of her class in 1941.

In the fall of that year Helen Delich entered the University of Nevada with two scholarships—a first prize from the Elks National Scholarship Foundation, awarded to her as the nation's outstanding girl high school graduate of 1941, and a Serb National Federation scholarship. She wanted to become a lawyer, but because the long preparation seemed beyond her means, she chose to major in her next favorite subject, journalism. During her 1942 summer vacation she managed the campaign in two Nevada counties of James G. Scrugham, a successful candidate for the United States Senate. She transferred to the University of Missouri in the fall of 1942, supporting herself as a drugstore clerk.

When Scrugham took his seat in the Senate in January 1943, Miss Delich went to Washington, D.C. to work in his office as a secretary. She also attended evening classes at a local university. In October 1943 she returned to the University of Missouri, where besides working on the university paper, the *Columbian Missouri,* she was employed as a waitress in the dining hall, as an assistant to a professor of photography, and as a stringer for United Press. She was awarded the Bachelor of Journalism degree in September 1944, having completed her college education in three years instead of four by receiving extra credits for high grades.

For seven months after graduation Helen Delich continued her association with the U.P. as a reporter and bureau manager in Fort Wayne, Indiana. Then while working briefly as telegraph editor on the Lewiston (Idaho) *Tribune,* she applied by letter to several Eastern newspapers. One of them, the Baltimore *Sun,* hired her as a reporter in June 1945. With the eruption of labor strife across the country at the end of World War II, she began to concentrate primarily on labor matters in her reporting for the *Sun.* In San Francisco in 1947 she became the first newspaperwoman to cover an American Federation of Labor convention. One day in 1948 the city editor offered her a change of assignment: "Go down and take a look at the port; we've had nobody there since before the war."

Through on-the-spot observation of waterfront events, investigation of both sides of a story, and conversation with dockhands, industrial leaders, and government officials, Helen Delich educated herself in the problems of the nation's shipping. In her hard-hitting, factual maritime coverage she not only shared with her *Sun* readers the love of the sea and ships that she believes is inherent in everyone, but conveyed through an educational effort her concern for the declining United States merchant fleet. Miss Delich, who changed her byline to Helen Delich Bentley after her marriage in 1959, was promoted to the position of maritime editor of the *Sun* in 1952. Traveling throughout the world for her paper, she wrote national and international labor and transportation stories in addition to reporting on maritime developments. Her "Around the Waterfront" column was syndicated in fifteen newspapers.

One piece in her column, about union featherbedding on ships, brought a suit, still pending, against her and the Baltimore *Sun* by a union of marine radio officers, asking $26,000,000 in damages for alleged defamation. Having cultivated innumerable friendly waterfront news sources, she has been credited with scoops of national and international importance, such as breaking the story of the exchange of ransom goods for Cuban Bay of Pigs prisoners in 1962. Her articles and exposés have helped bring about the passage of a considerable amount of maritime legislation.

Beginning in 1950 Mrs. Bentley wrote and produced her own television show called *The Port that Built a City and State.* The thirty-minute program was seen every Sunday afternoon on Balti-

more's WMAR-TV from 1950 to 1965 and on Washington, D.C.'s WTTG-TV from 1955 to 1959. The show was so well received that in 1959 she was asked to produce a similar series on the ports of the Delaware Valley for WFIL-TV in Philadelphia. The programs alerted viewers to the importance of shipping and foreign trade in their everyday lives. Characteristically involved in many activities at the same time, Mrs. Bentley also engaged in public relations counseling for the American Association of Port Authorities; edited *Seaport Histories of the Ports of the Americas, History and Development,* published by that association in 1961; and did free-lance writing and film producing.

Mrs. Bentley's rise to national prominence as a journalistic expert on the maritime industry, a province completely dominated by men, was due in part to her capacity for hard work. In one not atypical day, she covered the shakedown cruise of the SS *Gulfbeaver,* hailed a tugboat to take her ashore, and drove to Washington, where she covered an important shippers' meeting and a Congressional hearing. All three stories were filed that night. She is said to possess, and to use when her patience is tried, a vocabulary as salty as the sea and as pungent as stack gas. While reporting a story by radio from the icebreaking tanker SS *Manhattan* during its historic voyage in September 1969 through the Northwest Passage to the North Slope Alaskan oilfields, she used a four-letter Anglo-Saxon expletive that led to the barring of her and her fellow journalists from the ship's radio room for the rest of the voyage.

The incident was played up in the press because of the celebrity that had come her way the preceding month when, on August 9, President Nixon nominated her chairman of the Federal Maritime Commission, to fill out the unexpired term of John Harllee, a retired United States Navy rear admiral who had resigned the chairmanship. Although not the first woman to head a federal regulatory agency (a Lyndon B. Johnson appointee, Mrs. Virginia Mae Brown, chairman for a one-year term in 1969 of the Interstate Commerce Commission, holds that honor), Helen Bentley is the first chairman of a regulatory agency to be appointed by President Nixon. She had not been particularly active in politics before her appointment, but she had supported Spiro T. Agnew's election as Governor of Maryland in 1966 and had served as staff adviser on shipping matters during Nixon's 1968 Presidential campaign.

During the Senate hearing on her nomination Mrs. Bentley was questioned closely on the possibility of compromise arising from her public relations work for port agencies and shipping lines. Senators from Great Lakes states asked about her partiality to the port of Baltimore. She denied any conflicts of interest and stated that she had always considered the St. Lawrence Seaway and the Great Lakes ports America's "fourth coast," along with the Atlantic, Pacific, and Gulf of Mexico. Impressed with her knowledge of the shipping industry, the Senate confirmed her appointment on October 3, 1969, and Vice-President

Agnew administered the oath of office on October 27. She was reappointed, for a full five-year term, on May 5, 1970. Mrs. Bentley's $40,000 annual salary makes her the highest-ranking woman in the Nixon Administration.

Mrs. Bentley took the helm of an agency created in 1916 as the United States Maritime Commission. That agency was reorganized and renamed the Federal Maritime Board in the 1940's and again restructured in 1961 and given its present name, the Federal Maritime Commission. The commission was established to regulate rates charged by United States steamship lines to carry cargo and passengers. Regulation was found necessary to eliminate rate wars and cut-throat competition between American shippers that threatened to drive the smaller lines off the high seas and leave one or two giant lines with a stranglehold on America's foreign commerce.

Among the commission's present additional responsibilities is making sure that cruise ship operators deliver what their advertisements promise and that they carry adequate liability, fire, and collision insurance. Since the regulation of the maritime industry is fragmented among several federal agencies, the United States Coast Guard is responsible for setting safety standards for cruise ships and for inspecting them to ensure compliance. The commission licenses freight forwarders and checks on all United States merchant vessels of 300 tons or larger to see that they carry insurance adequate to compensate victims of their accidental or intentional oil spills. The assignment of that job to the Maritime Commission rather than to the Environmental Protection Agency was taken by many as a sign of President Nixon's confidence in Mrs. Bentley.

Although her commission is responsible for only a part of federal maritime policy, Mrs. Bentley has not hesitated to speak out on the state of United States shipping in general. She recently told a convention of the 129,000-member International Longshoremen's Association that they were in danger of pricing the United States out of world markets. Many technological inventions designed to reduce shipping and cargo handling costs have been developed in the United States, but only foreign countries were reaping the profits from them because of American labor disputes and outmoded work rules.

"In two or three years the [United States merchant] fleet will be so old and decayed that we'll be in real trouble," she has asserted, as quoted in the Chicago *Daily News* (August 21, 1969). "The shipowners are not going to be able to continue operating these tubs once the Vietnam War dies down. Military leases are supporting them now, but if nothing is done, we'll be totally in the hands of foreign shipping powers." She laments that the United States has slipped from first to sixth or seventh place among maritime nations.

Neither has Helen Bentley hesitated to speak out on broader national issues. She is one of the Nixon Administration's most-sought-after speakers and has acquired a reputation as a fiery defender of the United States Constitution and its guaran-tees of liberty, lambasting those "who incite the young and malcontents to riot" while hiding behind the Constitution. On one occasion her enthusiasm for helping her party led to criticism in the Washington press: in September 1970 she was accused of impropriety in soliciting campaign contributions from shipping magnates for C. Stanley Blair, Republican candidate for Governor of Maryland and former assistant to Agnew.

While not a militant feminist, Mrs. Bentley, having herself undergone prejudice, does try to help other women rise to the more intellectually satisfying jobs they are capable of performing. She hired a woman admiralty lawyer as a trial attorney for the Maritime Commission and appointed a woman, Mirian Evelyn Wolff of San Francisco, to the $30,000 a year post of managing director of the commission, its highest staff position.

In January 1970 the University of Maryland awarded Mrs. Bentley an honorary LL.D. degree. Her honors include an award from the Steamship Trade Association in Baltimore in 1954 for distinguished labor reporting and an award for meritorious service to the nation's maritime industry by the AFL-CIO Maritime Port Council of the Maritime Trades Department of the Port of Greater New York. In 1957 and again in 1958 the American Merchant Marine Institute gave Mrs. Bentley and *The Port that Built a City and State* its Atlas Award for advancing the cause of a strong merchant fleet. She has twice received the American Merchant Marine Writers award from the Propeller Club of the United States and has twice been named "Woman of the Year" by the Women's Advertising Club of Baltimore. Mrs. Bentley belongs to several professional organizations, the Maryland Historical Society, the Star-Spangled Banner Association, and the Zonta Club. Her church is the Greek Orthodox.

Mrs. Bentley is five feet three inches tall, weighs 130 pounds, and has brown eyes and blond, formerly brown, hair. According to one of countless anecdotes told about her, she once punched the jaw of a dockworker at a longshoremen's convention because he likened her nose to a ski jump. She had her nose reshaped in 1956, possibly to enhance her appearance for her television show, which also gave her the opportunity to exploit her fondness for stylish hats. Dancing and cooking are among her recreations. She shares another hobby, collecting antiques, with her husband, William Roy Bentley, whom she married on June 7, 1959. Bentley gave up his job as a schoolteacher in Baltimore to devote full time to operating an antique shop that he and his wife opened in 1968. Antiques abound in their home in the suburban Fox Chapel area of Baltimore, where they also enjoy the company of six poodles.

References

N Y Post p21 Ag 16 '69 por
N Y Times p1+ Ag 10 '69 por; p36 Ja 6 '70 por
St. Louis Post Dispatch p41 O 30 '68 por
Washington (D.C.) Post B p1+ Ag 12 '69
Who's Who of American Women, 1972-73

BERIO, LUCIANO (bä′ryō)

Oct. 24, 1925- Italian composer; teacher
Address: b. Juilliard School of Music, Lincoln
Center for the Performing Arts, Lincoln Center
Plaza, New York 10023; h. 53 Potter Place,
Weehawken, N.J. 07087

The career of the Italian composer Luciano Berio
is dedicated to the challenge of creating a musical
idiom suited to the tastes, needs, thought patterns,
and techniques of modern society. A controversial, inventive, and outspoken critic of the musical establishment, Berio has innovated a highly evocative form of expression that, because of
its effective synthesis of diverse musical, aural,
electronic, and dramaturgical elements, has been
described as "total theater," while his experiments
with the musical use of sound in its widest range
and fullest dimensions have opened an exciting
new area of musical experience. Although his
works have often received adverse criticism and
sometimes have provoked members of the audience to leave the concert hall prematurely, Berio
is widely admired as one of the most talented and
original of present-day composers. Since 1965 he
has been teaching composition at the Juilliard
School of Music in New York.

Descended from a family with a long musical
tradition, Luciano Berio, the second child of
Filippo Ernesto and Ada (dal Fiume) Berio, was
born on October 24, 1925 in Oneglia, Imperia
province, Italy. Both his father and grandfather
were church organists and composers, as were several of his ancestors. Among them the most notable was Steffano Berio, who in 1782 composed
an oratorio. Berio's older sister, Miriana, is a professor of Latin and Italian literature at the University of Milan.

From the age of six Berio took organ and piano
lessons, first with his grandfather and then with
his father. While still a child he often assisted
them both in the performance of their musical
duties at church. He attended the elementary
school, grammar school, and Licèo Classico in
Oneglia. On graduating from the latter in 1943,
the year of the Allied invasion of Italy during
World War II, he was drafted into the Italian
Army. He deserted soon afterward and spent the
early months of 1945 fighting along with the Italian partisans against the German forces occupying
northern Italy.

When the war ended, Berio enrolled in the
faculty of law of the University of Milan. During
his first months in Milan a new musical world
was opened to him: the works of Stravinsky,
Webern, Bartók, and other modern composers
whose music had been outlawed during the Fascist
domination of Italy. Years later he explained in
an autobiographical article in the *Christian Science Monitor* (July 15, 1968) how the angry realization that he had been "until that moment deprived . . . of knowledge of the most essential
musical achievements of [his] own culture" left
him with an undying hatred of all forms of thought
control.

In 1946 Berio dropped out of the university
and enrolled instead in the Conservatorio Giuseppe
Verdi in Milan, where during the next few years
he studied composition with Ghedini and Paribeni,
choral and orchestral conducting with Giulini,
and piano. He supported himself by coaching
opera seminars and conducting operas in small
towns in the Milan vicinity, where he remained
after he had graduated with honors in 1951. While
working as a coach and conductor in opera houses
throughout Italy as well as the Milan region, he
composed several innovative but essentially traditional works, such as *Due Pezzi* for violin and
piano (1951), five *Variazioni* for piano (1952),
and *Chamber Music* for voice, clarinet, cello, and
harp (1952)—a setting for poems by James Joyce.

During his first visit to the United States, in
1952, Berio, who had never before heard electronic music, attended an electronic concert at the
Museum of Modern Art in New York City. He
was profoundly influenced by that experience,
which made him suddenly aware of the artistic
potential of the new electronic medium. The recipient of a Koussevitzky Foundation Fellowship,
Berio spent the summer of 1952 at the Berkshire
Music Center at Tanglewood in Lenox, Massachusetts, where he took a course in composition with
Luigi Dallapiccola, who introduced him to twelve-
tone music, or serialism. Berio later rejected
twelve-tone composition as "formalistic and escapist . . . ignoring what sound really is," but in the
next few years, while still visiting the United
States, he used serial technique in several orchestral and chamber works, although in a free, flexible
manner.

Back again in Milan, in 1954 Berio joined the
staff of RAI, the Italian State Radio system. Shortly afterward he founded both the Studio di Fono-
logia Musicale in Milan, a radio laboratory for
electronic music, and the progressive music journal
Incontri Musicali, of which he is still proprietor
and director. With *Perspectives*, in 1956, he composed his first significant electronic work. In
Thema (Omaggio a Joyce) (1958), as much a vocal
as an electronic piece, he combined his developing grasp of electronic techniques with his fascination for the aural resources of the writings of
James Joyce by setting to music the first forty
lines of *Ulysses*, achieving, as Alfred Frankenstein
described it in *High Fidelity* (February 1968) a
"rich, elaborate and dramatic polyphony of pure
sound."

Berio's one-act opera-ballet *Allez-hop*, his first
attempt to liberate modern opera from the constraints of operatic tradition, was premièred at
the La Fenice Opera Festival in Venice in October
1959. It employed serial technique in a fluent,
fast-paced manner, had a biting ideological theme,
and was provided with an elaborate mimed
choreography by producer Jacques Lecoq. Another
1959 composition, *Differences*, a work for five instruments and stereophonic tape, reflects Berio's
interest in the musical aspects of sound and his
growing realization that even noises have musical
potential. A live chamber ensemble is made to
play against a recording of its own performance

in which the individual sounds are separated and distorted.

Exploration and exploitation of sounds and combinations of sounds not traditionally musical also characterize Berio's later compositions. In 1960 he returned to the Berkshire Music Center as a teacher and guest composer-in-residence. On August 1 his *Circles for Voice, Harp, and Percussion*, a setting of some poems by e. e. cummings selected for their aural value rather than their meaning, had its world première as part of the Fromm Foundation Concert at Tanglewood. That unorthodox piece, which utilized the human voice and a wide variety of sound-producing instruments, including noisemakers, was praised by Jay S. Harrison in the New York *Herald Tribune* (August 3, 1900) as "an edifice of exotic sound—not all of it musical, to be sure, but all of it vigorous and fresh and alive."

In *Visage*, a related experiment completed by Berio in 1961, a single voice—supplemented and supported by diverse electronic sounds—repeatedly articulates a single word, *parole*, which in Italian means "words," exploring all its possible nuances, emotional qualities, and tonal variations in an effort to attain a depth of feeling beyond that attainable through conventional musical expression.

Passagio, which Berio has termed a *"messa en scena,"* or a "staged mass," had its world première performance at La Scala in Milan in 1963 and its American première at the Juilliard School on January 9, 1967. An expressionistic monodrama with completely atonal music, *Passagio* dramatizes the passage through life of an Everywoman character identified only as "Her," who appears alone on stage, to be abused and tormented by a chorus in the pit and a chorus dispersed through the audience. Her voice victoriously drives her persecutors, perhaps the forces of conformism, from the theatre at the conclusion of the performance. Although some critics dismissed *Passagio* as "amateurish" and "sophomoric," Alan Rich, in the New York *World Journal Tribune* (January 10, 1967), found it a "powerful, surging, maddening work . . . violent and totally compelling . . . almost the essence of theatrical communication divorced from concrete representation."

In 1968 Berio's *Epifanie* for orchestra, *Chemins II* for viola and nine instruments, and the opera-ballet *Laborinthus II* were all performed to enthusiastic audiences. The greatest triumph of his career to date took place on October 10, 1968, when he conducted the New York Philharmonic Orchestra and the Swingle Singers in the première of his *Sinfonia* at Philharmonic Hall in Lincoln Center, New York City. The Philharmonic had commissioned the work for its 125th anniversary season. Utilizing a multilingual sung and spoken text drawn from a great variety of sources, including Claude Lévi-Strauss, Joyce, Beckett, and student grafitti, as well as substantial musical quotation from the works of Mahler, Debussy, Stravinsky, and others, *Sinfonia* is a brilliant collage, described in *Time* (October 18, 1968) as "a new kind of dramaturgy encompassing music, drama,

LUCIANO BERIO

word sounds, and, eventually, lighting and stage effects." Harold C. Schoenberg of the New York *Times* (October 11, 1968) praised its synthesis of "serialism, Dada, electronic and a touch of aleatory."

To the original four sections, or movements, of *Sinfonia*, one of which paid homage to Martin Luther King, Berio added a fifth section in 1969, improving the symmetry of his composition. The expanded version was performed by the Philharmonic in October 1970 under the direction of Leonard Bernstein. Several music critics have commented on Berio's rewarding use of the *objet trouvé*, or "found object," in *Sinfonia*, weaving into his work more or less familiar fragments from writers and other musicians, in somewhat the same way that certain modern sculptors and other artists incorporate existing objects into their constructions.

Berio's *This Means, That . . . ,* performed at Carnegie Hall on February 17, 1970, was less enthusiastically received than *Sinfonia*. A musical "project" that, as Berio explained in a *Newsday* interview (February 18, 1970), "doesn't really exist as a piece of music, [but] may have the metaphorical structure of a dream," *This Means, That . . .* is a confusing and apparently confused conglomeration of effects that may have been intended as "camp." There was almost no applause from an audience composed mainly of music professionals, and most critics found the work disappointing. The reception of that particular presentation need not have discouraged Berio, who regards the piece as "a commentary on a ritual whose content can be modified each time it is performed."

On August 12, 1970 the Santa Fe (New Mexico) Opera company gave the world première of Berio's *Opera*, an event eagerly awaited by the musical world. *Opera* is a somewhat fragmentary nonlinear collage with an outspoken ideological theme related to the technological arrogance of modern bourgeois man as exemplified in the tragic sinking of the SS *Titanic* in 1912. The title word is the plural form of "opus." Not an opera in the usual sense, *Opera* is so named because it includes elements of many of Berio's previous works, as well as extensive quotations from the classical operatic repertory.

Opera was admirably staged and performed, in the opinion of some critics who thought it effective as theatre, especially in the sections done by members of Joseph Chaikin's Open Theater Company from New York. Nonetheless, the view was widely held that the work was a musical failure and critical reactions, as John Rockwell pointed out in *Opera News* (October 10, 1970), were "torn between the heavily guarded and the overtly hostile."

Among the recordings of Berio's work are *Circles* (Mainstream), *Sequenza for Solo Flute* (Mainstream), *Visage* (Columbia), and *Epifanie* (RCA). His *Sinfonia* (Columbia) won the 1969 National Academy of Recording Arts and Sciences Grammy Award for the best classical choral performance. In 1970 Philips released an eclectic record that included *Differences, Sequenza III, Sequenza VII, Due Pezzi*, and *Chamber Music*. Walter Trampler performed in a recording of a viola series by Berio released in 1971 by RCA.

Since the early 1960's Berio has spent most of his time in the United States, making frequent trips to Europe to teach and conduct. He taught at Mills College in Oakland, California in 1962 and 1963. He later joined the music faculty of Harvard University and for a time taught classes at both Harvard and the Juilliard School, commuting to New York from his home in Cambridge, Massachusetts. In 1967 he left Harvard to become a full-time professor of composition at Juilliard. He has also taught summer school in Darmstadt, Germany and elsewhere.

The extraordinary solo voice heard in several recordings and many concert performances of Berio's music is that of the American soprano Cathy Berberian, whom Berio married in November 1950. Some of his compositions use her particular virtuosity as an instrument in experimenting with sound. After their divorce in 1965 she continued to be an invaluable interpreter of his work. While on the faculty of Mills College, Berio met Susan Oyama, a Japanese-American student whom he married on May 25, 1967. They have two children, Marina and Stefano. Berio also has a daughter, Cristina, by his marriage to Cathy Berberian.

In an article for the New York *Times* (January 8, 1967) Joan Peyser described Luciano Berio as "short, hurried, overbearing, articulate . . . thoroughly Mediterranean, both in his volatile behavior and charming manner." He has brown hair and brown eyes and bears some physical resemblance to the English actor Peter Sellers. He often dresses in khaki work clothes and enjoys boating and fishing in his free time. Politically, he is a radical, unreservedly opposed to the United States involvement in Vietnam. During a concert of his work at the Whitney Museum in New York in the spring of 1970, he turned briefly from conducting to tell the audience his views on the Vietnam war and the radical student movement.

References

BMI p11 My '70 por
Christian Sci Mon p8+ Jl 15 '68 por
N Y Times II p15 Ja 8 '67 por; II p15 F 15 '70 por
Newsday A p9 F 25 '70 por
Time 92:56 O 18 '68 por

Ewen, David. Composers Since 1900 (1969)
International Who's Who, 1970-71
Who's Who in America, 1970-71

BERKELEY, BUSBY

Nov. 29, 1895- Dance director
Address: b. c/o Directors Guild of America, 7950 Sunset Blvd., Hollywood, Calif. 90046; h. Palm Desert, Calif. 92260

Scores of pretty girls dancing in kaleidoscopic patterns or posed in elaborate geometric formations are the hallmarks of the work of Busby Berkeley, Hollywood's king of the big production number during the golden age of film musicals in the 1930's. Until recently Berkeley's giddy film extravaganzas, numbering some seventy-five made between 1930 and the early 1950's, were regarded merely as "camp" curiosities for insomniacs watching late night television. But by the late 1960's recognition of Berkeley's innovations in cinematography and an upsurge of nostalgia for the 1930's caused new audiences to escape into the wonderland of such Berkeley classics as *Forty-second Street, Footlight Parade,* and the *Gold Diggers* series. Before going to Hollywood in 1930, Busby Berkeley had staged dances for twenty-one Broadway musicals, and in 1971 he emerged from retirement to make a triumphant return to Broadway as production supervisor of the hit revival *No, No, Nanette,* starring Berkeley's favorite leading lady, Ruby Keeler.

Busby Berkeley was born William Berkeley Enos on November 29, 1895 in Los Angeles, California. His father, Wilson Enos, was a theatrical director and his mother, Gertrude (Berkeley) Enos, was an actress. At the time of the boy's birth Enos was director of Frawley's stock company in Los Angeles, but the family moved to New York when William was about three months old. (Berkeley's first name eventually evolved from the name of the Frawley company's leading lady, Amy Busby.) Although Berkeley made his stage debut at the age of five, his early career was far removed from the theatre. In 1914 he graduated from the Mohegan Lake Military Academy, about fifty miles from New York City, and for the next three years he worked at a shoe factory in Athol, Massachusetts. On the day the United States declared war in April 1917, Berkeley enlisted in the Army. As a second lieutenant he served briefly with the 312th Field Artillery, 79th Division and as General John J. Pershing's entertainment officer in Chaumont, France. During his war service Berkeley had his first experience with "choreography," putting his battalion through intricate maneuvers on the parade ground.

By late 1917 Berkeley was out of the Army and in New York City, where he was soon lured into the theatre by a family friend's offer of a part in the touring company of *The Man Who Came Back.* After cross-country appearances with that play he appeared in the hit musical *Irene,* which opened in New York on November 18, 1919. By 1921 he had taken up directing, and he staged stock productions—often a new one each week—in such cities as Rochester, New York, Baltimore, Maryland, and Springfield, Massachusetts. Despite his never having had a dancing lesson, he was asked to direct a musical in Boston, and with that production his career was launched in earnest.

Berkeley's first assignment on Broadway was to stage the dances for a short-lived musical production called *Holka Polka* in October 1925, and two years later he directed the dancers in Rodgers and Hart's hit musical comedy *A Connecticut Yankee.* Over the next few years Berkeley was affiliated with a number of productions including *Present Arms* (1928), as dance director and in the part of Douglas Atwell; *Good Boy* (1928), as dance director; *Street Singer* (1929), as director and producer; and *The International Review* (1930), as dance director.

In 1930 Samuel Goldwyn brought Berkeley to Hollywood as a dance director, where his first job was to stage the production numbers for *Whoopee* (United Artists, 1930), an Eddie Cantor movie. Before even starting, Berkeley roamed from set to set, watching to see how cameras were used. "I soon realized that in the theater your eyes can go any place you want," he told William Murray in an interview for the New York *Times Magazine* (February 2, 1969), "but in pictures the only way I could entertain an audience was through the single eye of the camera. But with that single eye I could go anywhere I wanted to." Berkeley was the first to reach that conclusion, for until then, Hollywood musical numbers had been shot as if the camera were a front-row spectator in the theatre. In *Whoopee* Berkeley changed all that by introducing close-ups of the chorus girls and "top shot" views of the dancers made from the rafters. He also abolished the traditional four cameras for one, whose every angle he could dictate.

Berkeley's other films for Goldwyn included *Palmy Days* (UA, 1931), *The Kid from Spain* (UA, 1933), and *Roman Scandals* (UA, 1933), in which he presented a line of chorines clad only in long blond wigs. But Berkeley's production numbers for Goldwyn were only warm-ups for those that he started devising when he began his seven-year association with Warner Brothers in 1932. It was for his Warners creations that the term "busby berkeley" came into the language (defined in the *American Thesaurus of Slang* as a "very elaborate musical number"). His first film at that studio, *Forty-second Street* (1933), starred Dick Powell and Ruby Keeler and set the pattern for most of his subsequent extravaganzas. Its flimsy backstage story line served only as a backdrop for the production numbers, which included Miss Keeler tapdancing on top of a taxi and an overhead view of chorus girls arranged to form the

BUSBY BERKELEY

petals of a flower. The movie reportedly saved Warners from bankruptcy, and in recent interviews Berkeley has boasted that, although his cinematic conceptions could cost up to $10,000 a minute to produce, "no one ever lost a dime on any of my pictures."

For *Gold Diggers of 1933* Berkeley created a number that used sixty girls carrying illuminated violins. As the girls waltzed about on the darkened set the camera followed them, and because of strategically placed mirrors it appeared that hundreds of violins were floating in the dark. With such elaborate production devices, the choreography could be reduced to a minimum. Indeed, Berkeley told an interviewer from *Cahiers du Cinema* in 1966, "A great part of my work has not been the work of a choreographer strictly speaking, because, for me . . . it is the camera that must dance."

Berkeley staged his first aqua ballet for a song called "By a Waterfall" in *Footlight Parade* (1933). At the outset he arranged his beautiful girls in rows astride a pyramided fountain that was reflected in a pool and photographed spectacularly from the ceiling to create lush patterns of legs and thighs. Later the girls cascaded down the sides of the fountain into the pool and swam in unison around a large tank outfitted with mirrors. Another number in *Footlight Parade* involved a chorus of hundreds of sailors who assume formations of the American flag, the eagle, and a portrait of President Franklin D. Roosevelt. (The studio also filmed English and French versions substituting the appropriate flags and heads of state.)

Although every film he worked on bears his inimitable stamp, Berkeley was not given responsibility for overall direction until *Gold Diggers of 1935,* which was released by First National. That film contains one sequence in which a stage is filled with girls playing white baby grand pianos, and another that Berkeley calls his favorite number. The latter, entitled "Lullaby of Broadway," opens with a tiny pinpoint of light on a dark screen. As the dot enlarges the audience sees that it is the face of the "Broadway playgirl" who is singing her song, "Lullaby of Broadway." Gradually the volume of the song increases as the camera draws closer and closer until the girl's face fills the whole screen. By the end of the sequence the heroine has plunged to her death from a skyscraper and voices are singing "Good night, Baby," while the camera pans the dead girl's apartment, empty except for a kitten waiting to be fed. The scene was nominated for an Academy Award, and earned Berkeley a special recognition plaque from the Dance Directors section of the Academy.

The production problems were so complicated in *Gold Diggers of 1935* that Berkeley built a special monorail to transport his camera about the rafters without the more cumbersome camera boom. As his cinematic ideas became more grandiose, his methods of operation became more streamlined, a natural outgrowth of his practice of using only one camera. A careful planner, he would pre-edit his ideas, plot every camera angle, and shoot scenes exactly as they were finally to appear—without ever having to retake a scene, he claims. In this way, Berkeley had complete creative control. "Nobody but me ever knew what the number would look like on the screen until it was in the can," he told William Murray for his New York *Times Magazine* article.

Other Warner Brothers motion pictures that Berkeley directed or staged the production numbers for include *Dames* (1934), *I Live for Love* (1935), *Hollywood Hotel* (1937), *Singing Marine* (1937), *Garden of the Moon* (1938), and *Gold Diggers in Paris* (1938). In addition he directed two dramatic films for Warners, *Men Are Such Fools* (1938) and *They Made Me a Criminal* (1939). While under contract to Warner Brothers, Berkeley made musicals that were released by First National, including *Gold Diggers of 1937* (1936), *Stage Struck,* and *Wonder Bar,* for which he had created an octagonal hall of mirrors that made 100 girls look like 1,600.

By the time Berkeley moved to the studios of MGM in 1939, his most innovative work was completed, but he continued to provide excellent dance numbers for such musicals as *Broadway Serenade* (1939), *Lady Be Good* (1941), *Ziegfeld Girl* (1941), and *Girl Crazy* (1943). Perhaps the last pure Berkeley confection was *The Gang's All Here,* which he directed for Twentieth Century-Fox in 1943. It contained one number in which chorus girls holding five-foot papier maché bananas dance around Carmen Miranda and another in which the dancers are photographed from so high above that they appear to be tiny, disembodied heads flitting about the screen. For MGM Berkeley directed the Mickey Rooney-Judy Garland vehicles *Babes in Arms* (1939), *Strike Up the Band* (1940), and *Babes on Broadway* (1941), and he introduced Gene Kelly to filmgoers in *For Me and My Gal.* A few years later Berkeley directed the successful Kelly vehicle *Take Me Out to the Ball Game* (1949), which received the *Photoplay* magazine Blue Ribbon Award for 1949.

During the early 1950's Berkeley directed the production numbers for such musicals as *Two Tickets to Broadway* (RKO, 1951), *Call Me Mister* (Fox, 1951), and *Rose Marie* (MGM, 1954). For *Small Town Girl* (MGM, 1953) he cut holes in the sound stage floor so that Ann Miller could tap dance around the seemingly disembodied hands and instruments of an orchestra hidden beneath. But Berkeley found the most spectacular outlet for his talents in staging the water ballets for Esther Williams in *Million Dollar Mermaid* (MGM, 1952) and *Easy to Love* (MGM, 1953). In the latter Miss Williams led a troupe of a hundred water skiers through their breakneck paces and dived from a trapeze suspended seventy-five feet above the water by a helicopter. By the 1950's, however, the public had tired of clichéd backstage plots and gigantic production numbers, and after 1954 Hollywood had no call for Berkeley's resources except once, in 1962, when he directed the circus acts in MGM's unabashedly old-fashioned "family show" spectacular about circus life entitled *Jumbo*.

By the mid-1960's, however, interest had developed in early film making and especially the Hollywood of the 1930's. Originally designed to entertain, Berkeley's films became historical documents as well. A retrospective of his work was given in 1965 at festivals in San Francisco and the Gallery of Modern Art in New York and later in Europe. Suddenly Berkeley emerged from obscurity and was granting interviews, appearing at festivals, and lecturing. With Berkeley's films cropping up in art houses around New York, critic Vincent Canby contended in an article in the New York *Times* (April 12, 1970) that they were much more than just camp. While conceding that Berkeley's movies contain flaws, such as an overbearing symmetry in his production numbers, Canby asserted that the dance director "liberated movie musicals from a sense of oppressive realism, from the restraints of theatrical logic. There is an immensely satisfying feeling of freedom in his production numbers in the way he places his camera at impossible angles and multiplies sets into a kind of drunken infinity."

In all his personal appearances Berkeley called for a return to the entertainment values of his heyday, predicting that they would still be good box office. "In my musicals people forgot the Depression; they forgot their troubles. My God, why can't we do the same today?" he told a press conference at a Grand Bahamas film festival in 1969. It appeared that Berkeley's claims had been vindicated when on January 19, 1971 *No, No, Nanette* opened on Broadway and became a smash hit. Originally presented in 1925 without Berkeley's participation, the musical was produced for the contemporary stage under his general supervision, and with the presence of a large tap-dancing chorus and Ruby Keeler, grand staircases and grand pianos, and a big Atlantic City number in which the girls balance on beach balls, the audience is taken back to the days when Berkeley reigned supreme.

A large man with gray hair, blue eyes, and a fairly trim figure, Busby ("Buzz") Berkeley displays an energy that belies his age. He has told interviewers that he still has many ideas he would like to produce, such as an abstract dance for 100 copper cuspidors and 200 black hands that he would stage as the dream of a Negro cleaning woman. On January 23, 1958 Berkeley was married for the sixth time, to Etta Dunn, who has had no professional experience in show business. He has no children. For the past ten years the Berkeleys have lived modestly in a small, pink stucco house in the residential community of Palm Desert, near Palm Springs, California. Until his recent flurry of activity, they lived very quietly, with Etta feeding all the neighborhood stray cats, and Berkeley reading, playing a little golf, and working on his autobiography, which he calls "Girls, Glamour and Glory."

References

Dance Mag 42:34+ F '68 pors
N Y Times Mag p26+ Mr 2 '69 pors
Newsweek 76:63 Ag 3 '70 por
Variety 263:1+ Ag 11 '71
Washington (D.C.) Post B p3+ Ap 7 '70;
    B p4 Jl '71
Biographical Encyclopaedia & Who's Who
    of the American Theatre (1966)
Gruen, John. Close-Up (1968)
Who's Who in America, 1970-71

BLATCHFORD, JOSEPH H(OFFER)

June 7, 1934- United States government official
Address: b. Action, 806 Connecticut Ave., N.W., Washington, D.C. 20525; h. 3036 P St., N.W., Washington, D.C. 20007

When he took office as the third director of the Peace Corps in May 1969, Joseph H. Blatchford pledged to make that agency "more relevant to '69" in promoting goodwill and self-help in developing nations. During his two years as head of the Peace Corps he worked to transform what he has called "the most flexible and innovative arm of the United States government" into an organization capable of operating efficiently within an international context that has markedly changed since the agency was launched under the directorship of R. Sargent Shriver in 1961. Since July 1, 1971 Blatchford has been director of Action, a new federal agency that merges the Peace Corps, VISTA, and other volunteer service programs. For eight years before joining the Nixon administration in 1969, Blatchford had administered his own version of the Peace Corps, ACCION, a still flourishing privately financed, multinational organization dedicated to combating social problems and their causes in Latin American slum communities.

Joseph Hoffer Blatchford was born in Milwaukee, Wisconsin on June 7, 1934, the oldest in a family of three children. His twin sisters, Barbara Winslow and Beatrice Hannigan, are both actresses living on the East Coast. When he was ten years old, the family moved to Los Angeles, where his father, George N. Blatchford, became comptroller of the United Artists motion picture studios. "We

JOSEPH H. BLATCHFORD

were just this far from the tracks," Blatchford once remarked, as quoted in the Washington *Post* magazine (October 11, 1970), suggesting that he never quite belonged to glamorous, opulent Hollywood.

Educated in local public schools, Blatchford graduated from Beverly Hills High School in 1952. At the University of California at Los Angeles he majored in political science and served as president of the Phi Kappa Psi fraternity. As he had in high school, he excelled in tennis, becoming the captain of the varsity tennis team in his senior year. During his undergraduate years the UCLA team won three consecutive national collegiate tennis championships. In the summer of 1956, following his graduation from college, he competed in the Wimbledon championships and then toured Europe, occasionally playing in tennis tournaments to pay his expenses.

While a student at UCLA, Blatchford had taken part in the ROTC program. Commissioned a second lieutenant in the United States Army, he was sent on his return from Europe in 1956 to Fort Knox, Kentucky, where he served six months of active duty as a tank commander in the armor school. In the spring of 1957 he went to Washington, D.C. to work as a researcher on a subcommittee of the House of Representatives Committee on Education and Labor. The following September he enrolled in the Law School of the University of California at Berkeley, where he was elected president of his class.

News of the hostile reception that Richard Nixon, then Vice-President, had to endure in Peru and Venezuela during a tour of South America in May 1958, greatly disturbed Blatchford, who felt that increased effort should be made to reverse the deterioration in United States relations with Latin America. Taking a year off from law school, he solicited donations from well-wishers, including various corporations like IBM International, to finance a goodwill tour of South America organized around the universal languages of music and sports. From March through June 1959 he and several other students visited about thirty Latin

American countries, giving tennis exhibitions and jazz concerts, mainly at universities.

Many times during his Latin American tour Blatchford was troubled by the squalor of city slums and the miserable living conditions in the shantytowns that had sprung up with the sudden influx of peasants to the city as unskilled laborers during a period of urban expansion. He returned to the Berkeley law school to work for his degree, but was also determined to try to alleviate the unemployment, overcrowding, and other potentially explosive social problems that he had seen. In formulating a workable plan, he was influenced, he has recalled, as quoted in *Newsday* (April 18, 1969), "by a William James essay on 'The Moral Equivalent of War,' where he argued that if young people didn't march off to war they would have to exert their manliness by fighting poverty, disease and illiteracy." He was also guided in part by conversations with Eugene Burdick, the co-author of *The Ugly American,* an indictment of American diplomatic and economic missions in Southeast Asia.

In the fall of 1959, eighteen months before President John F. Kennedy created the Peace Corps, Blatchford conceived of ACCION (Americans for Community Cooperation in Other Nations; *acción* is the Spanish word for *action*) as a means of sending trained community organizers to the barrios to set up local self-help groups, an attempt to spread democratic ideals at neglected levels, guided by "the principle of self-help as the key to self-government." Blatchford began canvassing private corporations and individuals in the United States and Venezuela for financial support and rounding up volunteers. ACCION field work started in Venezuela in the fall of 1961 on a budget of $160,000, which supported some 2,000 projects in civic development, job training, construction, and education. At first the workers were volunteers from the United States and a few other countries, but they were gradually replaced by trained, salaried nationals.

During its first eight years ACCION, under Blatchford's guidance, carried out over 45,000 projects in Venezuela, Peru, Brazil, and Argentina with more than 1,000 field workers and staff members from nine countries. It attracted contributions in cash and services totaling $9,000,000 from some 3,000 companies. In 1965 Blatchford founded and became executive director of ACCION International, with headquarters in New York City, which supports programs already underway and develops new projects by providing seed money and trained personnel to initiate eventually self-sustaining community action institutions. The president of the board of ACCION International is Donald M. Kendall, president of PepsiCo, Inc.

Taking a leave of absence from his ACCION post, Blatchford campaigned in 1968 on the Republican ticket for the seat in the House of Representatives from the Seventeenth California Congressional District. In that heavily Democratic district, one of several covering the county of Los Angeles, he lost to his opponent, Glenn M. Anderson, a former Democratic lieutenant governor of the state. It was the 1968 election that won the Presidency for Richard Nixon, and during the transition from the Democratic to Republican administrations Blatchford was summoned to Washington to work briefly on Latin American policy.

Among the important appointive positions affected by the Republicans' gaining control of the federal government was that of director of the Peace Corps. Although that agency is nonpolitical in spirit, President Nixon decided to replace Jack Hood Vaughn, who had served as Peace Corps director under a Democratic administration. Appointed to succeed Vaughn, Joseph H. Blatchford was confirmed by the Senate on May 1, 1969 and was sworn into office four days later at a ceremony in the rose garden of the White House. The relationship of the United States to the rest of the world was at that time considerably different from what it had been when President Kennedy proposed the Peace Corps in 1961 as a bold experiment in volunteer service abroad. Anti-American sentiment had generally increased, partly because of the United States' involvement in the Vietnam conflict, which had also alienated many young people, from whose ranks the first Peace Corps volunteers had been drawn by idealism. Certain host countries had become less eager to receive corpsmen, sometimes resenting what they considered an intrusion into domestic matters and sometimes rejecting good intentions as a substitute for technical skills among the volunteers.

In reevaluating the purposes and programs of the Peace Corps, Blatchford called in the individual directors of the agency's projects in sixty countries for discussion and then embarked on a tour of several of the countries whose Peace Corps programs were considered typical to talk to staff, officials, and volunteers. The result was Joseph Blatchford's "New Directions," a list of proposals that amounted to a basic reinterpretation of the agency's function and identity. The Peace Corps' unspoken purpose previously had been the creation of the intangible bonds of personal understanding; Blatchford proposed to engage the Peace Corps in projects with concrete, practical results.

High on Blatchford's list of priorities was an effort to attract a wider spectrum of volunteers, specifically craftsmen from unions, experienced farmers, and vocational education specialists. To encourage skilled volunteers, Blatchford asked unions and employers to protect seniority and fringe benefits for those who left their jobs for overseas service and to assist in making mortgage and loan payments. In addition, he lifted the organization's strictures against families with dependents and allocated more liberal living allowances. Among his proposals also was a plan to recruit retirees, job corps graduates, and a greater number of blacks and Hispano-Americans. The "professionalization" of the Peace Corps was intended to help answer the host countries' increasingly specific requests. Bolivia, for instance, needed electricians, plumbers, and construction workers; Kenya asked for hydrologists. Blatchford also planned to expand that area of Peace Corps service that had met with the most tangible success, such as improvements in quantity and quality of agricultural products.

Another significant proposal of Blatchford's New Directions provided for "internationalization" of the Peace Corps. The host countries were called upon to play an increasingly larger role in directing and administering the projects and in selecting volunteers. "Binationalism" was expected eventually to lead to a "reverse" Peace Corps, which would bring skilled foreigners to the United States to work on American domestic problems.

Blatchford has also called attention to a "need for the closer integration of personnel with other government agencies involved in overseas development." The success or failure of his programs is likely to depend largely on Congress, some of whose members are concerned, among other things, over Peace Corps volunteers who have publicly criticized United States foreign policy, charging that the Peace Corps is an extension of American "imperialism" and supports oppressive governments. Critics, furthermore, of Blatchford's proposal to professionalize the Peace Corps have voiced skepticism over the ability of middle-aged volunteers to adapt to different cultures. Even Blatchford's detractors, however, concede that he is an aggressive and proficient administrator.

Addressing the students and faculty at the University of Nebraska in January 1971, President Nixon disclosed a plan to ask Congress to combine the Peace Corps, Volunteers in Service to America (VISTA), and other federal programs into a single agency that would give young volunteers expanded opportunity for service. The consolidation of government efforts in helping the underprivileged at home and abroad would advance what he called the forging of "an alliance of generations." Following Congressional approval of the merger, Nixon inaugurated the new agency on July 1, 1971 with Blatchford as its director.

While serving as executive director of ACCION, Blatchford also worked for a time with the Misereor Foundation in Germany; was chairman of the 1965 Anglo-American Conference on Volunteer Service Overseas, held in England; and took part in the 1964 UNESCO Conference in Buenos Aires. He has been an adviser to the New York-based Interracial Council for Business Opportunity, which offers aid to black businessmen, and has lectured in North and South America and in Europe on Latin American affairs and on urban problems.

In December 1967 Joseph H. Blatchford married Winifred Marich of San Pedro, California, an ACCION veteran. Blatchford, who stands just under six feet tall, is a trim, smooth-featured man, with blue eyes and wavy hair. Tennis remains his favorite sport, and he also finds recreation in listening to jazz and Brazilian folk music and riding his small motorcycle through the Virginia countryside. In childhood he attended Christian Science Sunday school, but he is no longer a practising Christian Scientist. He believes, however, in "the perfectibility of man," and although the terms used in the press to describe his complexity— "idealist and pragmatist," "optimist and realist"—

imply conflict, the quality of his leadership is certain and dynamic.

References

N Y Post mag p2 My 17 '69 por
N Y Times p27 My 6 '69 por; p12 Ja 5 '71 por
Newsday B p2 Ap 18 '69
Newsweek 72:56 Je 2 '69 por
Washington (D.C.) Post mag p10+ O 11 '70 por
International Who's Who, 1970-71

BOK, DEREK C(URTIS)

Mar. 22, 1930- University president; educator; lawyer
Address: b. Harvard University, Office of the President, Massachusetts Hall, Cambridge, Mass. 02138

The twenty-fifth president of Harvard University is Derek C. Bok, formerly dean of the Harvard Law School. Bok's appointment was announced in January 1971 after an exhaustive eleven-month search for a successor to Nathan M. Pusey, who retired from Harvard to become president of the Mellon Foundation. Relatively unknown nationally, Bok was chosen to head the nation's oldest and most prestigious university largely because of the way in which he successfully mediated differences between students and faculty at the law school during the period of campus strife in the late 1960's. An expert on collective bargaining, Bok taught antitrust and labor law at Harvard Law School for ten years before becoming dean in 1968. When he took office as president of Harvard on July 1, 1971 he became one of the youngest presidents in the university's long history and the first not to have been a Harvard undergraduate since the seventeenth century.

The scion of a wealthy and distinguished Philadelphia Main Line family, Derek Curtis Bok was born in Bryn Mawr, Pennsylvania on March 22, 1930 to Curtis and Margaret (Plummer) Bok. Bok's father, who died in 1962, was an associate justice of the Supreme Court of Pennsylvania and a novelist. His grandfather, Edward William Bok, an immigrant from the Netherlands, was the first editor of the *Ladies' Home Journal* and the author of *The Americanization of Edward Bok*, which won the Pulitzer Prize for biography in 1921. One of Bok's great-grandfathers was Cyrus H. K. Curtis, the founder of the Curtis Publishing Company.

When Bok was a small child, his parents were divorced and he moved to Beverly Hills, California with his mother, who later married William Kiskadian. After graduating from Emerson Junior High School in Beverly Hills, Bok went on to the Harvard School, an Episcopal Church-affiliated institution in North Hollywood not connected in any way with Harvard University. Upon completion of his secondary education he entered Stanford University, where he majored in political science

DEREK C. BOK

and was a member of the basketball team, the student council, and Phi Kappa Sigma fraternity. He graduated Phi Beta Kappa in 1951 with a B.A. degree.

Determined to accomplish something on his own rather than go into the Curtis family's publishing business, Bok considered joining the United States Foreign Service but finally chose law as a field that would offer a wide range of opportunities. In the fall of 1951 he enrolled at Harvard Law School. As a law student he edited the *Harvard Law Review*, and during a summer vacation he traveled in India. In 1954 he received the LL.B. degree *magna cum laude*.

In 1954-55 Bok studied economics on a Fulbright scholarship at the Institute of Political Science of the University of Paris, where he wrote a report entitled *The First Three Years of the Schumann Plan*, published in 1955 by the International Finance School of Princeton University. After returning to the United States he entered the United States Army, and while stationed in Washington, D.C. as a first lieutenant in the office of the Judge Advocate General he studied economics at George Washington University. In 1958 he was discharged from the Army and awarded an M.A. degree in economics.

Having decided on a career in university teaching, Bok joined the faculty of Harvard Law School at the behest of Professor Kingman Brewster Jr., one of his former teachers there and now president of Yale University. He began as an assistant professor in 1958 and was promoted to professor in 1961. Beginning in 1965, he also taught in Harvard's John F. Kennedy School of Government. He was a popular and accessible teacher, one whose seminars were always oversubscribed and who made a point of attracting to his classes students from the bottom third of the class, because he felt that the challenge they presented forced him to be a better teacher. At the time he was appointed law school dean he was serving as a member of the faculty-student committee and the curriculum committee.

When Bok succeeded Dean Erwin N. Griswold on July 1, 1968 he was confronted with a student body seething with unrest and dissatisfaction regarding participation in decision-making processes and the ordering of teaching priorities, among other issues. Early in his tenure he faced a major test, when a sit-in was conducted by first-year students demanding that they be graded on a pass/fail basis, an innovation strongly opposed by much of the faculty. The new dean ordered coffee and doughnuts sent to the demonstrators and joined them for a "rap session" that lasted several hours. The student protesters then dispersed, and later a compromise was reached whereby a pass/fail system was instituted on an optional basis.

Besides the new grading procedure, Dean Bok was credited with a number of other innovations at the law school, including a stepped-up recruitment program for black and women students; the widening of a curriculum stressing corporate law to include more poverty, criminal, and environmental law courses; and the establishment of joint degree programs with the Harvard Business School and the John F. Kennedy School of Government. He also encouraged the students to hold mass meetings to discuss their grievances and problems, asked faculty committees to open their hearings to students, and initiated the founding of a law school newspaper as a means of closing the communications gap between students and faculty.

While Dean Bok was thus responding to student-faculty problems at the law school, Nathan M. Pusey was faring less well in the Harvard presidency. Pusey, already regarded as too aloof in some campus circles, turned a great many students and faculty against his administration by his handling of the student protests of April 1969. When about fifty student radicals occupied the main administration building the Harvard president lost little time in calling in the police to clear the building, reportedly over the strenuous objections of Bok and some of the other deans. The "Harvard bust," in which 197 persons were arrested and forty-five were injured, was followed by a week-long strike and months of bitter division within the university.

Early in 1970 Pusey announced his decision to retire and the Harvard Corporation launched an unprecedented selection process to find his successor. It sent letters to over 200,000 Harvard and Radcliffe alumni, faculty members, students, and employees, inviting them to submit names in nomination and to comment generally on the kind of person who ought to fill the presidential office. Some 1,100 names were submitted, and a special committee screened out nominations until, in December 1970, there was a final list of twenty-three. On January 11, 1971 the university's Board of Overseers announced that it had formally elected Bok to assume the presidency upon Pusey's retirement six months later.

In a statement issued after Bok's election President Pusey declared, "I could not be happier for myself or the University. . . . [Dean Bok] has shown himself admirably equipped to cope with the intensified demands posed for administrative officers in these difficult times. . . . He knows the institution and its people. He is sympathetic to student needs, intelligent, energetic, imaginative, good-humored, conscientious, resilient, and—not least—willing." Aside from isolated critics who considered him *too* sensitive to student moods, all segments of the Harvard community, from liberal to conservative, hailed the selection of Bok, the proven peacemaker, as an ideal choice in a time of campus tension. Bok himself said that he was approaching his new post with the following attitude: "It is really terribly important that you be as open as you can be about what you're doing, be very careful about what you promise and break your back to fulfill the commitments you make—and in that way very very slowly build up trust."

Bok is frequently compared to Yale University's President Kingman Brewster Jr., who has also been successful in dealing with campus crises. While acknowledging a possible resemblance to his former mentor and long-time friend, Bok has asserted that Brewster's peacemaking abilities have been overpublicized and that he will eventually be remembered for other accomplishments at Yale. "In the last analysis the business of a university is the quality of its education and its research," he told William Woodward of the New York *Post* (January 16, 1971), "and although those can be temporarily deflected by a particular crisis, they depend on different matters that are largely independent of student crises from one year to the next." As president, Bok has plans to revamp the university's administration and is giving serious thought to the feasibility of a three-year undergraduate program. But the matter that will demand a major portion of his attention in the coming years is money, for Harvard, like most of the nation's educational institutions, is facing a growing deficit and can look forward to a protracted period of belt-tightening.

With Archibald Cox, Bok edited the fifth, sixth, and seventh editions of *Cases and Materials on Labor Law* (Foundation Press, 1962, 1965, 1969), which is regarded as the basic textbook on labor law. With John T. Dunlop, the Harvard economist, he wrote a study of the history and problems of the American labor movement entitled *Labor in the American Community* (Simon and Schuster, 1970), and he has contributed widely to law journals. He was a member of President Lyndon B. Johnson's Committee on Labor Management and a consultant to the Department of Labor and the Equal Employment Opportunities Commission, and he has served as arbiter of many labor disputes, including the Florida East Coast railway strike. While dean of Harvard Law School Bok taught a course in legal education, and he served on a committee that conducted a survey of legal education in Colombia.

While he was studying in Paris, Derek C. Bok met Sissela Ann Myrdal, a psychology student at the Sorbonne, and they were married on May 7, 1955 in France by former French Premier Pierre Mendes-France. Mrs. Bok, who is the daughter of the Swedish social scientist Gunnar Myrdal, received a Ph.D. degree in philosophy from Har-

vard in 1970 and has taught at Tufts University and Harvard. With their three children, Hilary Margaret, Victoria, and Thomas Jeremy, the Boks lived for many years in Belmont, a suburb of Boston. At the time he was named Harvard president Bok told reporters that he planned to move his family from Belmont to Cambridge but not into the official presidential residence on Quincy Street in Cambridge.

President Bok is a handsome six-footer with a deep voice and dark hair that is graying at the temples. As law school dean he did not hesitate to speak out on political issues, denouncing the United States invasion of Cambodia and President Nixon's nomination of G. Harrold Carswell to the Supreme Court, and he has said that he intends to follow the same policy in his new position. Bok is a Democrat. In his spare time he enjoys gardening, tennis, skiing, and taking his children to sports events. He is a trustee of the Cyrus H. K. Curtis estate.

References

N Y Post p22 Ja 16 '71 por
N Y Times p1+ Ja 12 '71 por
Newsweek 77:70+ Ja 18 '71 pors
Time 97:60+ Ja 25 '71 por
Directory of American Scholars (1969)
Who's Who in America, 1970-71

BORCH, FRED J.

Apr. 28, 1910- Corporation executive
Address: b. General Electric Co., 570 Lexington Ave., New York 10022

Chairman of the board and chief executive officer of the General Electric Company, Fred J. Borch directs the far-flung enterprises of the fourth-largest corporation in the United States. Since the firm was founded by Thomas A. Edison and associates in 1892, G.E. has mushroomed from a manufacturer of light bulbs and small home appliances to an industrial empire with 400,000 employees and plants throughout the world. Since he succeeded Ralph J. Cordiner as chief executive in December 1963, G.E.'s sales volume has almost doubled, amounting to $9.14 billion in 1970. Despite considerable risks Borch has maneuvered the company into such new areas of technology as nuclear reactors and jet engines. He denies that G.E. is too big to operate efficiently, insisting that, like the Pentagon, it has "*got* to be run." As outlined in *Nation's Business* (February 1971), his formula is to organize it "into segments" and to take "the very best people you've got and give them clear-cut assignments."

Fred J. Borch, the son of Frederik and Antonette (Mikkelsen) Borch, was born on April 28, 1910 in Brooklyn, New York, where his father was an electrical engineer with the Brooklyn Edison Company. As a child he also lived in Newark and Elizabeth, New Jersey, and in Ohio. In 1918 the family moved to Cleveland, when the father took a job with the Northern Ohio Traction and

Light Company in Akron. He later became associated with the Cleveland Electric Illuminating Company, where he supervised the electrical engineering department until he retired. Fred Borch obtained most of his schooling in the Cleveland area, and during his school years he worked two summers as an office boy with the Cleveland *News*. In 1927 he entered Western Reserve University (now Case Western Reserve University) as an economics major. To help meet expenses, he took a summer job as a timekeeper on a construction project for an electric power line. He obtained his B.A. degree in economics in 1931.

Borch had intended, after his graduation, to do graduate work at the Harvard School of Business, but since his funds amounted to about $500 less than what he would have needed for tuition and expenses, he decided to look for a job. He had received an offer from IBM through the business school dean at Western Reserve, but taking the advice of the alumni president of his fraternity, he applied at General Electric and was hired. Several months passed, however, before he was placed in the auditing department of G.E.'s lamp division in Cleveland's Nela Park, at a salary of $115 a month. According to Allan T. Demaree, writing in *Fortune* (October 1970), "the lamp division virtually carried G.E. through the Depression, and it became so independent that it was known throughout the company as the Irish Free State." After eighteen months, as business conditions worsened, Borch agreed to accept an across-the-board pay cut that reduced his salary to $78 a month, although, as a traveling auditor, he also had an expense account. In 1940, at the age of thirty, Borch was named general manager of the lamp division's customer service section, the youngest man ever to serve in that post. Borch was promoted to manager of the sales operation department in 1947 and joined the administrative staff of the lamp division in 1952.

Late in 1952 Borch was sent to New York City to handle a special assignment for the General Electric Management Consultation Services, a customary procedure for screening employees proposed for advancement. He returned to Cleveland in 1953 and was assigned to reorganize the lamp division into six separate departments in compliance with a general companywide directive to decentralize operations. Under the chairmanship of Ralph J. Cordiner the company pursued the policy that each department be made small enough to be supervised by one man. After completing that assignment Borch moved up to the top levels of G.E. management. In 1954 he became vice-president in charge of marketing services, working closely with Cordiner. Borch became vice-president and group executive for consumer goods in September 1959, with responsibility for supervising a highly profitable department that manufactured a line of products ranging from alarm clocks to industrial air conditioners. His election as executive vice-president in July 1962 indicated that he would eventually succeed Cordiner, since the post was, according to *Time* (October 18, 1963), intended to "accommodate an heir apparent." As executive vice-president Borch was elected to the board of directors and assumed responsibility for the company's operating components on a worldwide basis.

Borch was elected on October 7, 1963 to succeed Cordiner—who had announced his retirement—as chief executive officer of G.E. He was also named president, a title previously held by Gerald L. Phillippe, who was at that time elected to succeed Cordiner as chairman of the G.E. board of directors. Borch took office on December 21, 1963, becoming the fifth chief executive officer in the company's history. As the world's largest and most diversified producer of electrical equipment, the General Electric Company had at the time some 211 plants producing over 200,000 products. Its sales in 1963 amounted to about $4.9 billion, assets were $2.8 billion, and net income was over $270,000,000, or $3 a common share. The company ranked fourth in the American industrial structure, surpassed only by General Motors, Standard Oil of New Jersey, and the Ford Motor Company. Although G.E. was in sound financial condition in 1963, Borch anticipated several problems. Company morale was low, and G.E.'s public image and reputation had been threatened as a result of a price-fixing conspiracy that received much publicity in 1960. Some 1,800 damage suits had been filed against G.E. by utility firms, charging violation of the antitrust laws. Borch was also concerned with overexpansion in the electrical equipment industry and competition from domestic and foreign firms. He took the reins firmly resolved to let people know that G.E. was "on the move again." As Allan T. Demaree noted in *Fortune* (October 1970), Borch was determined "to launch bold, aggressive ventures, taking considerable risks."

When Borch took over the presidency of G.E. he reportedly formulated a confidential set of plans outlining the company's goals for a period extending to 1975. His chief aim was to increase production and efficiency at G.E. in order to achieve higher sales volume, greater profits, and better earnings per share for his stockholders. As the company's chief strategist he supervised the allocation of funds for research and development, moving G.E. into far-reaching enterprises that would yield future growth possibilities. Aware that G.E. could not remain an electrical manufacturing company exclusively, he developed plans for balanced corporate growth through a program of diversified production. Borch depended on G.E.'s decentralized structure to absorb the costs of expanding into such new areas as the production of computers, commercial jet engines, nuclear reactors, and aerospace equipment and still permit the company to reach a sales goal of $10 billion within the decade.

In 1964 Borch announced that G.E. had settled most of the claims in the price-fixing conspiracy out of court. Although the payments had some adverse effect on 1964 earnings, sales exceeded $5 billion and earnings before price adjustments for the anti-trust actions rose 10 percent to $312 million or $3.44 a share. "Our consumer products business continues to break records as it has each year since 1960," Borch declared in December 1964. The trend continued through 1965 with profit margins at a high of 11 percent. Aerospace and defense sales took an upward swing in 1965 and the demand for heavy electric utility equipment reached an all-time high, although computers and nuclear reactors still remained liabilities on G.E.'s earnings record. In April 1965 Borch announced that G.E. would start to manufacture an improved model of a television color picture tube that would allow for simpler installation and reduced service charges. The company anticipated customer demand for color television, which Borch called "the most rapidly growing segment of the consumer goods market."

Despite a costly strike in 1966 and a downward trend in the economy, G.E. sales soared to $7.2 billion. They reached $7.8 billion in 1967 and rose by 8 percent to $8.4 billion in 1968. The earnings ratio, which had been 6.2 percent in 1959, declined, however, amounting to 4.7 percent for the years 1966 through 1968. Borch attributed the imbalance to the excessive costs of establishing new businesses, but he saw those ventures as "challenges that, with our resources and technologies, we simply could not walk away from." To increase the earnings of G.E.'s heavy equipment industry, in 1967 Borch introduced a $600,000,000 program to modernize the manufacturing of transformers, nuclear power reactors, and turbine generators.

Concerned with improving administrative efficiency, in 1968 Borch called for a reorganization of G.E.'s corporate structure. While remaining chief executive officer, Borch was elected in December 1968 to the board chairmanship, vacated by Phillippe's death in October, and the title of president was abolished. Borch created a corporate executive office with three vice-chairmen to assist him in making high level decisions and he established scores of new departments to facilitate tighter control and more constructive long-range planning. For the first time, staff groups were permitted to function at all levels with responsibility for streamlining the bureaucratic maze. Borch has been criticized for adhering to two standard G.E. policies—moving men up through the ranks instead of recruiting outside talent and rotating executives between divisions before they had the opportunity to know the product. He was convinced, however, that the new organizational policies allowed G.E. to know "where we will be five years hence and how to get there and fill the gap in between," as he told an interviewer for *Business Week* (October 17, 1970).

In Borch's view, the decade of the 1960's was demanding but promising, and he was optimistic that earnings would grow and the new technologies would enter a more profitable and productive period in the 1970's. General Electric's financial structure was, however, seriously threatened by a fourteen-week strike that began in October 1969, resulting in company losses of $42,600,000 for the first quarter of 1970. Borch was concerned with the adverse effect the strike had on earnings, which appeared to be on the rise before labor walked out. Once the settlement had been signed, G.E. production resumed quickly, and Borch credited the "constructive spirit with which employees returned to work," according to the *Wall Street Journal* (April 10, 1970).

Early in 1970 Borch and his corporate staff made an appraisal of the assets and liabilities incurred by the new divisions that G.E. had been developing. The computer business demanded a heavy cash outlay, and after fourteen years of research and development, G.E. had succeeded in capturing only 4 percent of the world sales market. Borch knew that much more money and effort would have to be expended before G.E. could compete successfully with IBM and other giants in the field. "When you make these major investments, they have . . . elements of a gamble in them," Borch told an interviewer for *Forbes* (May 15, 1971). "We've learned that if the investment is not viable, you should be in a position to make a good deal for your shareholders. You should hedge your bets." Hoping to expand G.E.'s interests in the computer line, Borch wanted to buy out Honeywell, Inc., a leading producer of computers. But when federal authorities, fearing possible violation of antitrust laws, vetoed such an arrangement, Borch decided to take G.E. out of the computer business. By July 1970 the two companies had reached an agreement whereby G.E. transferred all of its computer interests to a new subsidiary of Honeywell while temporarily retaining some of the equity.

As a major supplier to utility companies, G.E. went into the business of producing nuclear power plants in the 1950's. The original contracts were written on a "turnkey" basis, requiring G.E. to construct a complete plant at a fixed price. Substantial losses were incurred because G.E. did not foresee the runaway inflationary trend in construction costs. In 1966 Borch called a halt to turnkey bidding, and earnings in the nuclear energy division began to improve. Development of commercial jet engines took a promising turn when G.E. obtained contracts for Douglas and Boeing aircraft, but a recession in the domestic airlines industry and the cancellation of a government-financed supersonic transport project in 1971 has posed some problems for the company in that area. Concerned with foreign competition in the production of aircraft equipment, Borch wrote to President Richard Nixon in May 1971, urging that requests for federal financial backing made by the Lockheed Aircraft Corporation be rejected unless that company agreed to use American-made engines for its Tristar jet airbus instead of the British-made Rolls-Royce engine it had planned to use on the project.

Chosen Businessman of the Year for 1970 by the *Saturday Review* (January 23, 1971), Borch received twice as many votes as any other candidate for that honor in American business, finance, or government. In 1964 he was given the Ohio Governor's Award in recognition of his distinguished professional achievements. That same year, Clarkson College of Technology in Potsdam, New York conferred an honorary doctorate in engineering on him. Borch is a former vice-chairman of the Committee for Economic Development and a past president of the prestigious Business Council, whose membership includes over 100 presidents and board chairmen of leading United States corporations. He has served on the Industry Advisory Council of the United States Department of Defense, the Public Advisory Committee on United States Trade Policy, the Economic Development Council and Mayor's Management Advisory Council of New York City, and the board of trustees of Case Western Reserve University. Other organizations in which Borch has played an active role include the Council on Foreign Relations, the Center for Inter-American Relations, the Sales Executives Club, and ACTION Inc.

Borch is said to have an uncanny talent for choosing "the right man for the job, for sizing up people and then getting the best out of them." Charles Sievert once wrote of Borch in the New York *World-Telegram and Sun* (December 22, 1964) that he "virtually carries a mental picture of everything G.E. does and owns" and that he "can spout figures without turning to a reference book, and explain the why of operations and changes without hesitation." Although Allan T. Demaree depicted Borch in *Fortune* as "a decisive, no-nonsense executive" with "a cocksure personality that at times borders on the arrogant," his associates call him by his first name and, according to the profile in *Saturday Review,* consider him the sort of person "who makes you feel as comfortable as an old shoe." Borch pictures himself as an "impatient" man who tries to keep "the ball rolling" at G.E. He admits that he loves the pressures of his job but believes that it is necessary for an executive to retain a sense of humor.

By his first marriage, to the former Martha A. Kananem, Fred J. Borch has two children, Richard F. Borch and Mrs Kay B. Otterstrom. Martha Borch died in 1969, and Borch was remarried in August 1970, to Mrs. Lucia Lowles. Borch makes his home in Darien, Connecticut, and although he is rarely away from the office more than ten days at a time he likes to take long weekends in Florida with his wife. A sandy-haired six-footer, Borch is described in the *Saturday Review* as "a slender man with abundant energy and crackling eyes." He enjoys fishing with members of his family, and he is an avid golfer. His clubs are the Wee Burn Country Club in Darien, the Augusta (Georgia) National Golf Club, the Lyford Cay in Nassau in the Bahamas, the Blind Brook in Port Chester, New York, and the Links and University clubs in New York City.

References

Forbes 103:53 F 15 '69 por; 107:59 My 15 '71 por
Fortune 82:88+ O '70 por
N Y Times p68 O 8 '63 por; p36 O 12 '63 por
Nations Bsns 59:31+ F '71 por
Who's Who in America, 1970-71
World Who's Who in Finance and Industry, 1970-71

BORLAUG, NORMAN E(RNEST)

Mar. 25, 1914- Plant pathologist and geneticist; international consultant
Address: b. Rockefeller Foundation, Londres 40, Mexico City 6, Mexico; h. Sierra Gorda 69, Lomas de Chapultepec, Mexico City, Mexico

The first agricultural scientist to receive the Nobel Peace Prize is the American plant pathologist Dr. Norman E. Borlaug, who was honored with the award in October 1970 for his leadership in the "Green Revolution" that has helped to dispel the specter of famine from underdeveloped countries. Now head of the wheat research and production project of the International Maize and Wheat Improvement Center in Mexico, Dr. Borlaug and his associates have engineered new varieties of high-yield cereal that, in the words of the Nobel Committee, gave "the developing nations the possibility of breaking out of hunger and poverty." "The apostle of wheat" is the fifteenth American to win the Nobel Peace Prize and the first to win it since 1964, when it was bestowed on the late Martin Luther King Jr. Because of Dr. Borlaug and his coworkers the world has been granted another three decades of grace in which to attack its most urgent problem—the population explosion.

The son of Norwegian immigrants, Norman Ernest Borlaug was born on March 25, 1914 to Henry O. and Clara (Vaala) Borlaug, who owned a 56-acre farm near Cresco, Iowa. The area around Cresco is still spoken of as Iowa's "little Norway," and Borlaug grew up surrounded by neighbors who lauded the virtues of hard work and proper living. He graduated from the local high school in Cresco, where he captained the football team, in 1932. He might have been content to become a farmer himself if his grandfather had not constantly urged him to go on to college. The urging won out; Borlaug enrolled at the University of Minnesota, and, doing odd jobs, worked his way through to a B.S. degree in forestry, which he received in 1937. At the University of Minnesota, as in high school, his extracurricular activities included wrestling and football.

The year before he took his B.S. degree Borlaug worked as a field assistant with the United States Forest Service, and as a graduate student of plant pathology he divided his time between studying and earning a living at forestry-related jobs. In 1937 he served in the Idaho National Forest, and in 1939 he was a junior forester in Massachusetts. He returned to the campus of the University of Minnesota in 1940 as a research assistant, and the following year, when he was promoted to instructor, he received his doctor of philosophy degree in plant pathology.

When Borlaug emerged from graduate school, American organic chemists were synthesizing thousands of new chemicals aimed at controlling insect pests and plant diseases and at killing weeds without damaging crops and ornamental plants. It was not surprising that in 1941 E. I. du Pont de Nemours and Company recruited Dr. Borlaug as a promising plant pathologist from the University of Minnesota to study the effects of the new chemicals on plants and plant diseases. He remained with du Pont in Delaware as a plant pathologist for three years

In 1944 the Rockefeller Foundation, at the request of the Mexican Ministry of Agriculture, appointed George Harrar, a plant pathologist, to assemble a small team of American agricultural scientists, including himself, to "export the United States agricultural revolution to Mexico." The men whom Harrar chose to accompany him were Edward Wellhouse, a corn breeder, William Colwell, an agronomist, and Borlaug. Each of the men was convinced that the application of scientific methods in agriculture could benefit poor countries even more than it had benefited the affluent United States.

When, late in 1944, that team of young enthusiasts gathered in the hills outside Mexico City, they knew that many obstacles lay ahead. Corn, which is still the principal bread grain in Mexico, was cultivated there by the Indians for centuries before the first Spaniards arrived. With them the European conquerers brought wheat, and at the time they began its cultivation, in the early 1520's, they probably expected it to become eventually the staple grain. But four centuries later wheat culture in Mexico was still in a primitive state. Although some mechanization had taken place in Sonora, the northwestern coastal state, everywhere else the cultivation of wheat resembled that of the early Spaniards. Land was prepared for planting with the Egyptian wooden plough, pulled by mules or oxen. Harvesting was done with hand sickles, oxen trod out the grain just as they had done in Biblical times, and the grain was winnowed by being thrown into the air for the wind to blow the chaff away.

As Borlaug later recalled for members of the third international Wheat Genetics Symposium, held in Canberra, Australia in 1968: "When the

NORMAN E. BORLAUG

program was established there were only a very few qualified agricultural scientists in Mexico. A wheat-breeding program was nonexistent. Only one qualified scientist was available for wheat breeding, but because of other responsibilities he spent only about ten percent of his effort in wheat research. No soil fertility or agronomic research of any type was being done. Nothing was being done on research to control losses from diseases, insects, and weeds."

As one of his primary goals, Borlaug aimed at a drastic improvement of the tall, thin-stemmed varieties of Mexican wheat that had evolved over the centuries to compete with weeds for sunlight. As soon as those varieties were given enough fertilizer and water to increase the yield, they became top-heavy and fell over, or "lodged," to use the jargon of the field. New varieties with shorter and stronger stems were needed.

At about that time the Japanese had developed a sturdy, short-stemmed wheat variety, called the Norin dwarf, that could carry a heavy head and still stand sturdily erect. Soon afterward, the agronomist Dr. Orville A. Vogel, of Washington State University, succeeded in crossing the Japanese dwarf with breeding varieties having other superior characteristics to produce a new dwarf called Gaines. In the favorable growing conditions of the Pacific Northwest, and under the best cultivation practices, Gaines wheat produced enormous yields.

Borlaug obtained Gaines seeds from Vogel and began making crosses of Gaines with the Mexican varieties. He could have followed the common practice of growing one experimental crop each year, but since he was a man in a hurry, he grew two alternate crops each year at different sites. The summer site was in upper Sonora, just south of the United States border, and the winter site was some 800 miles south, near Mexico City. The elevation at Sonora was not far above sea level and the latitude some 30°, and near Mexico City, the elevation was over 7,000 feet and the latitude about 20°, with a corresponding difference in length of days. By exposing his progressive new crosses to repeated alternations of such differences in climate and photoperiod, Borlaug bred into them a revolutionary new adaptability to a wide range of conditions. They have been successful all the way from the Equator to Turkey, near the fortieth parallel.

Borlaug's development of high-yield, highly adaptable dwarf wheats has won him international acclaim, but he sees his achievement as just one element in the many-pronged attack needed to solve the food and population problems of the underdeveloped countries. He has been called on for technical advice to West Pakistan, to India, and more recently to Turkey, Afganistan, Tunisia, and Morocco. Where his advice has been followed, cereal production has risen as much as 50 percent within two years. Government officials in some countries have not always been happy about the programs that Borlaug recommends. Bluntly pointing out that the new grain varieties—by themselves—cannot solve any country's food problem, he hammers home a list of conditions that a host country must meet before technical assistance can have a significant effect.

A host country, insists Borlaug, must have political stability, and its top-level officials must commit themselves to an aggressive program of action. The government must adopt fiscal policies that will stimulate agricultural production rather than stifle it and must guarantee that fertilizers, pesticides, weed killers, and modern machinery will be available so that new seed varieties can achieve their full potential. The program must be organized around the wheat crop, by a government willing to streamline administrative procedures and cut through red tape. Above all, the government must support a program of training young native scientists who can be counted on to develop and maintain a stable research program. Such continuing research is critical, for the best-yielding wheat varieties become increasingly susceptible to rust, and varieties with greater resistance to disease must continually be developed.

Borlaug's deep-rooted impatience with red tape has led him to fight throughout his career against administrative routines that stand in the way of getting the job done. Unintermittedly devoted to his dusty and sweaty chores, he still spends most of each day in the fields with young scientists from many countries (the so-called "Borlaug apostles"), pointing out to them that they should listen closely to what the plants themselves are saying. They tell more, he insists, than textbooks. Characteristically, Borlaug was working in an experimental plot fifty miles outside Mexico City on October 21, 1970, when his excited wife drove out to tell him that word had reached Mexico from Norway that he had won the Nobel Peace Prize. He pushed his sports hat back on his head and grinned. "That's just fine," he said, "but I still have a day's work to do here. After that we'll celebrate."

The Nobel Peace Prize of $78,400, which Borlaug received at Oslo University in Norway on December 10, 1970, climaxed a long series of awards and honors. Among them were a citation and award from the government and farmers of Tlaxcala, Mexico, in 1955; a diploma of honor from the wheat farmers of Queretaro, Mexico, in 1956; the outstanding achievement award of the University of Minnesota, in 1959; the national award of the Agricultural Editors' Association, in 1967; the International Agronomy Award of the American Society of Agronomy, in 1968; and the Distinguished Service Medal of Pakistan, in 1968. The University of Punjab, India awarded him an honorary doctorate in 1969. The citizens of Ciudad Obregón, Mexico's wheat capital, have named a street in Borlaug's honor. He is a member of many professional societies and of the National Academy of Sciences.

Although Borlaug has been too busy with field work to write many scientific papers, he has been called on to deliver keynote addresses at international symposia. Outstanding among them was the public lecture with which he opened the third international Wheat Genetics Symposium in Canberra in August 1968, an address titled "Wheat Breeding and its Impact on World Food Supply."

Bronzed, trim, and vigorous from his work in the fields, Norman Borlaug still weighs the 155 pounds that he did as a champion wrestler at the University of Minnesota. Shortly after he completed his undergraduate work in forestry there he married Margaret G. Gibson, on September 24, 1937. For many years now the couple have made their home in Mexico City. They have two children, a daughter, Norma Jean (Mrs. Richard H. Rhoda), and a son, William Gibson Borlaug.

When Borlaug visited Cresco after winning the Nobel Prize, the townspeople honored him with Borlaug Day festivities, on December 19, 1970. Returning the tribute, he said, as quoted in the *Farm Quarterly* (January-February 1971), "Whatever I have become, these people are a part of it. They taught me to give the best that is within me."

Borlaug takes a cautious view of the ultimate benefit of his work to human society, believing that population growth transcends all other problems. He thinks that all of his own work, and that of his fellow scientists, has won only a temporary truce in man's war against hunger and deprivation. Still, he is no pessimist. "Since man is potentially a rational being," he has said, as quoted in *National Observer* (March 1, 1971), "I am confident that within the next two decades he will recognize the self-destructive course he steers along the road of irresponsible population growth, and will adjust the growth rate to levels which will permit a decent standard of living for all mankind."

References

N Y Times p1 O 22 '70 por
Nat Observer p7 O 26 '70
Read Digest 98:104+ Mr '71 por
Science 170:518 O 30 '70 por

American Men of Science 11th ed (1965)
International Who's Who, 1970-71
Who's Who in America, 1970-71

BOUMEDIENNE, HOUARI (boō'mā-dē·en oō'är-ē)

Aug. 23, 1932(?)- President and Premier of
the Algerian Democratic People's Republic; army
officer
Address: Cabinet Building, Algiers, Algeria

A dedicated socialist as well as a devout Moslem,
Colonel Houari Boumedienne, President of the ruling Revolutionary Council of the Algerian Democratic People's Republic, remains, after more than
five years in power, one of the most enigmatic and
elusive personalities among the world's heads of
state. Even his name adds to the enigma; Houari
Boumedienne is a *nom de guerre* he assumed early
in the Algerian revolution against France, in which
he played a key role. Despite the air of mystery
about his personal life, however, there is no question that Boumedienne has succeeded remarkably
in providing political stability and economic progress for Algeria's 13,500,000 people since he seized
power from Ahmed Ben Bella in June 1965, and
he commands much respect in the councils of the
Arab states. Boumedienne is also Algeria's Premier
and Minister of Defense.

Houari Boumedienne's life and his name are in-
separably linked with the Algerian revolution. Facts
about his earlier years are hazy and often contradictory, and Boumedienne has made little attempt
to clear up his background. Even his age is in
dispute; his date of birth has been placed variously
between 1925 and 1932. Much of what is known
of his childhood and student days may be traced
to an interview of his father by a group of journalists in the fall of 1965, an account of which was
published by Peter Braestrup and David Ottaway
in the New York *Times Magazine* (February 13,
1966). According to that account, Boumedienne,
one of seven children, was born on August 23,
1932, in Clauzel, a hamlet near Guelma, in the
impoverished eastern part of Algeria. His name was
originally Mohammed Ben Brahim Boukharouba.
The elder Boukharouba was a wheat-growing small-
holder and a devout Moslem, who never learned
French. Boumedienne was remembered by his
father as a "shy, silent boy" who preferred reading
to sports, and even to eating.

When Boumedienne was six he entered a French
elementary school at Guelma, enrolling at the same
time in a local Koranic school for religious training and Arabic grammar. He may have had his
first taste of the conflict between Algerian nationalists and French authorities at Guelma, in 1945,
when he witnessed French police breaking up a
Moslem street demonstration. At fourteen Boumedienne began the part of his education that
set him apart from most of his young compatriots.
Since Algeria was considered part of metropolitan
France, Algerians were at the time generally educated according to the French curriculum. Boumedienne, on the other hand, studied for six years
at the Kettani Médersa in Constantine, one of the
few secondary schools in Algeria that followed the
traditional Arabic-Islamic curriculum.

In 1952 Boumedienne went to Cairo to complete his education at the prestigious Islamic uni-

HOUARI BOUMEDIENNE

versity, al-Azhar. According to his father's account,
he had been called up for service in the French
Army, and when his father's pleas for a deferment
were rejected, he and four friends fled east across
the Tunisian border and went from there to Cairo.
Boumedienne is said to have become a full-fledged
revolutionary while studying in Cairo, which in
1952 was in the midst of the revolution of young
army officers that overthrew King Farouk. In Cairo
he became associated with a small group of Algerian nationalists including Ahmed Ben Bella—
who were destined to be among the "historic chiefs"
of the Algerian revolution. Some sources indicate
that Boumedienne was for a time a student at the
Zitouna faculty of the University of Tunis, that he
worked briefly at a factory in France, and that he
was employed as a teacher at Guelma before joining the Algerian revolutionary organization, known
as the National Liberation Front (FLN).

By the time the FLN first rebelled openly against
French rule in Algeria in November 1954, Boumedienne had apparently become a key member of
the group. French press reports that he was trained
in Moscow or Peking seem unsubstantiated and
have been dismissed by his close associates. He is
believed to have obtained his first military training about 1954 at a training camp at Hilwân,
Egypt. Later he was apparently at an Egyptian-
supported guerrilla training camp at Nador, Spanish Morocco.

Boumedienne and eight others secretly crossed
the border from Morocco into Algeria in early
1955 to begin guerrilla activities. His area of operations was Oran, where the presence of a large
French population and the apathy of the Arabs
had discouraged nationalist activity. It was then
that he chose his *nom de guerre* from the name
of a mountain range near Oran. By 1957 Boumedienne had become commander of the Fifth Wil-
laya—comprising the military district of Oran—one
of six willayas into which the FLN had divided
Algeria. In June of 1958 he moved back across
the frontier to the sanctuary of Morocco and became commander of forces of the National Liberation Army (ALN)—the military arm of the FLN—

on both sides of the border. A provisional government of the Republic of Algeria, with headquarters in Cairo, was established by the FLN in September 1958 under the premiership of Ferhat Abbas. Boumedienne reportedly became a member of the National Council of the Algerian Revolution—the national parliament of the provisional government—while continuing to command the frontier forces.

On March 15, 1960 Boumedienne—who had by that time become a colonel, the highest rank in the ALN—was made chief of the ALN general staff, with headquarters at Ghardimaou, Tunisia. He thus became de facto head of the Algerian Army, then a frontier force of some 20,000 or 30,000 men. Since the ALN was by that time no longer strong enough to challenge the increasingly effective French border defenses between Algeria and Tunisia, Boumedienne did not personally take part in any further military operations inside Algeria. Instead, he devoted his effort in the period that preceded Algerian independence to shaping the ALN into a disciplined fighting force, indoctrinating it with a sense of mission. Ideologically, he emphasized Algerian tradition and Arab culture, rather than Marxist or Maoist theory. Surviving several attempts to depose him, he won the loyalty of his subordinates and thereby created the power base from which he took over as President of Algeria a few years later.

The Algerian revolution ended on March 28, 1962 when, after five months of secret negotiations with the FLN at Evian-Les-Bains, the French government agreed to Algerian independence. On July 1, 1962 a referendum was held throughout Algeria, in which 91 percent of the voters chose independence; two days later the independence of Algeria was officially proclaimed by French President Charles de Gaulle. By that time most of Algeria's European population had departed.

A provisional government, established pending elections, was headed by Benyoussef Ben Khedda and included other "centralist" politicians who had predominated in the government-in-exile in Tunisia. Boumedienne had little regard for the centralists, who, he felt, had lived too ostentatiously in exile and had conceded too much to the French at Evian. The centralists, in turn, distrusted Boumedienne, and on July 25, 1962 Ben Khedda, fearing a coup, dismissed him, along with the two other members of the army general staff. Boumedienne retained the loyalty of the army, however, and threw his support to Ahmed Ben Bella, the popular hero of the revolution, recently released from imprisonment in France. On July 11, 1962 Boumedienne and Ben Bella entered Algeria from Morocco and established a rival headquarters at Tlemcen. Consolidating their power, the Ben Bella forces isolated the centralists. In the national elections on September 20, 1962 a handpicked slate of Ben Bella supporters was elected to the National Assembly by some 90 percent of the voters, and Ben Bella was chosen Premier. Boumedienne was appointed Minister of Defense in the Cabinet, approved on September 29, 1962, and

he also became First Vice-Premier on May 17, 1963.

During his thirty-three months in power, Ben Bella gained a reputation abroad as one of the major leaders of the Afro-Asian bloc, but at home was unable to alleviate the political and economic chaos in the wake of the devastation of eight years of war and the departure of most European professionals and skilled workers. The personalized style and socialist experimentation of Ben Bella's regime caused dissatisfaction among several of the "historic chiefs" of the revolution, notably in the poor and traditionally independent Kabylia district. At first Boumedienne supported Ben Bella against attempts at insurrection. In the summer of 1963 he quelled an uprising in Kabylia, led by Colonel Mohand Ou El Hadj and by Ait Ahmad; a year later he suppressed a revolt led by the southern area commander, Colonel Mohammed Chaabani, who was eventually captured and executed.

Meanwhile, Boumedienne concentrated on beefing up the Algerian army—which had made a poor showing in a border war with Morocco in the winter of 1963-64. He visited Moscow in late 1963 to negotiate for Soviet military equipment and instructors. With a minimum of publicity he took steps to make the army practically a state within a state. Military salaries were raised, and cooperatives were organized to run such enterprises as army printing plants, a chicken farm, and a furniture factory. A bi-weekly magazine, *El Djeich* (The Army), was published under military auspices. In the summer of 1964 foreign observers noted that Boumedienne's 50,000-man National People's Army seemed the "sole organized force" in Algeria.

When Ben Bella was elected President in September 1963 for a five-year term under a new constitution, Boumedienne became Vice-President, while continuing to serve as Defense Minister and army commander. Relations between the two men were, however, becoming increasingly strained as Ben Bella concentrated more and more power in his own hands. In April 1963 Ben Bella had ousted Mohammed Khider as FLN general secretary and personally assumed the post. To tighten his own control over the army and undercut Boumedienne's authority, Ben Bella in March 1964 appointed Colonel Tahar Zbiri as chief of the army general staff. Boumedienne reached an agreement with Zbiri, however, and continued to run the army himself. In July 1964 Ben Bella ordered the fifteen regional administrators to report directly to him, rather than to the Minister of the Interior, Ahmed Medeghri, a close associate of Boumedienne, and shortly thereafter Medeghri resigned from the Cabinet in protest.

By the spring of 1965 a showdown between Ben Bella and Boumedienne seemed inevitable. In May, Ben Bella tried to force the resignation of Foreign Minister Abdelaziz Bouteflika, one of Boumedienne's chief allies in the Cabinet. The scheduling of an Afro-Asian conference to be held in Algiers on June 29, 1965 was seen by some observers as a move by Ben Bella to enhance his power and prestige and facilitate his planned removal of Buomedienne as head of the army. Informed by Colonel Zbiri of Ben Bella's plot to oust him, Boumedienne, assured of the army's loyalty, led a bloodless coup on June 19, 1965 with a force of about 1,000 troops. Ben Bella was placed under arrest, along with five of his aides. The Afro-Asian conference was at first postponed, then cancelled.

On July 5, 1965 Boumedienne formally assumed the title of President of the twenty-six-man Revolutionary Council in which political authority was vested, and in a radio address affirmed the country's desire for friendly relations with all nations. He declared that the army coup aimed at restoring "legitimate state institutions . . . permitting the free expression of the people's will and elaborating a constitution in accordance with the revolutionary principles" of the independence struggle. The United States recognized the Boumedienne regime the next day. A new twenty-member Cabinet, formed on July 10, was largely composed of men noted for their technical knowledge and included several holdovers from the Ben Bella regime including Bouteflika as Foreign Minister, and Medeghri as Minister of the Interior.

Originally, little was known about Boumedienne's political orientation. Some observers regarded him as a "Maoist" or "Castroite," while others believed him to be a right-wing militarist. Soon, however, he emerged as a pragmatic socialist, influenced more by Algerian nationalism and by the precepts of Islam than by Marxist ideology. "Our socialism is without philosophy," he said shortly after he came to power. "The underprivileged classes have to benefit from our revolution. That is our only criterion."

To relieve Algeria's economic woes, Boumedienne adopted a pragmatic policy of blending socialism with state capitalism, and to obtain an impartial picture of Algeria's needs, he asked both the Soviet state planning agency and the World Bank to make economic development surveys of the country. He nationalized mines and insurance companies in 1966 and domestic petroleum distribution companies in 1967; but he returned some previously nationalized enterprises, such as small businesses and farms, to their original owners. Although his regime expropriated some foreign holdings, Boumedienne also tried to encourage foreign investments. Aided by his cadre of capable young technocrats, Boumedienne has embarked on a large-scale program of industrialization, especially in the production of petroleum, which remains the cornerstone of Algeria's economy. In June 1970 he announced an ambitious four-year plan for the country's economic development. Although such problems as massive unemployment remain unsolved, foreign observers have commented favorably on the economic achievements of Boumedienne's regime.

Boumedienne has brought some stability to Algeria, which remains a one-party state under the FLN. At first he faced a challenge from the Marxist-oriented Algerian labor movement, but he brought it under control in 1966. His erstwhile ally, Colonel Zbiri, staged an unsuccessful coup

against him in December 1967 and was forced to flee into exile. In April 1968 Boumedienne survived an assassination attempt by unknown assailants. Since then his authority has not been seriously challenged.

In foreign policy Boumedienne has tried to reconcile socialist ideology with Algeria's national interest and independence. Although Algeria has received considerable aid from the Soviet Union and other Communist countries, it has remained outside the Soviet orbit. Despite occasional friction between Algeria and France, cooperation between the two nations, especially in the economic sphere, has remained a major facet of Boumedienne's foreign policy. Within the context of Middle Eastern politics, Boumedienne's has been one of the most militant anti-Zionists and a strong supporter of the Palestinian guerrilla movement. During the six-day Israeli-Arab war of June 1967 he criticized the Soviet Union for not giving greater aid to the Arab states, and he broke off relations with the United States because of its aid to Israel. On an informal level, however, Algeria's relations with the United States have recently improved. Boumedienne has also met with some success in settling Algeria's border disputes with Morocco and Tunisia.

Of medium height, gaunt, soft-spoken, and ascetic-looking, Colonel Houari Boumedienne has green eyes and sandy red hair. He was once nicknamed "the Swede." In the New York *Times Magazine* article he was described as appearing "more like a starving Irish poet than a guerrilla veteran." A chain-smoker who reportedly switched from cigarettes to Havana cigars a few years ago, he drinks large quantities of black coffee, and he is a skillful chess player. Some sources suggest that Boumedienne was once married and is now divorced, but those close to him deny that. "His only wife," said one associate, "has been the army."

References

N Y Times p5 Je 23 '65 por
N Y Times Mag p36+ F 13 '66 pors
Newsweek 76:33 Jl 20 '70 por
International Who's Who, 1970-71
Middle East and North Africa, 1969-70
Ottaway, David and Marina. Algeria; The Politics of a Socialist Revolution (1970)

BOUTON, JIM (bou'tən)

Mar. 8, 1939- Television sportscaster
Address: b. WABC-TV, 77 W. 66th St., New York 10023

Nonconformist television sportscaster Jim Bouton, a Holden Caulfield among the "jocks," was a topranking major-league baseball pitcher for three years, until his arm went sore in 1965. Gamely, Bouton "hung in there" for five years, toward the end as a journeyman relief hurler using an ingenious, elusive knuckleball to compensate for his loss of brute speed. Just before bowing out he issued a swan song that shocked the baseball establish-

JIM BOUTON

ment but delighted the reading public: the best-
selling book *Ball Four; My Life and Hard Times
Throwing the Knuckleball in the Big Leagues*
(World, 1970), a candid, iconoclastic insider's
diary of the 1969 season, written with the editorial help of Leonard Schecter. Baseball's angry
reaction to *Ball Four* was among the matters chronicled in a sequel, *I'm Glad You Didn't Take It
Personally* (Morrow, 1971), also written in collaboration with Schecter. With his blond cowlick
and impish grin—and the same irreverent sense of
humor that went into his books—Bouton now appears nightly as a sports reporter and commentator on WABC-TV in New York City.

The oldest of three sons, James Alan Bouton
was born in Newark, New Jersey on March 8,
1939 to George H. Bouton, of French Huguenot
descent, and Trudy (Vischer) Bouton, of Dutch
and German descent. George H. Bouton was a
salesman of Flex-Seal pressure cookers (invented
by Trudy Bouton's father), and later he became an
executive with the Flex-Seal Company. Jim Bouton
grew up in Rochelle Park and Ridgewood, New
Jersey and, after his father's job took him to Chicago, in Chicago Heights, Illinois. Physically a
late starter, he was short for his age in childhood
and did not immediately display a superiority in
athletics, but by dint of effort he developed prowess as a baseball player in elementary school in
Rochelle Park and at Bloom Township High
School in Chicago Heights.

In one of the chapters of *I'm Glad You Didn't
Take It Personally* Bouton traces his development
as a cheerfully mischievous maverick to not-so-
happy feelings of inferiority and alienation that he
experienced in childhood, despite "a lot of love"
in his family. Aside from studies, he put fierce
effort into almost everything he did, from pocket-
money chores to sports, but invariably he finished
looking like "the bad guy." (His brother Bob was
"the good guy.") "Also I had the world's worst
case of acne. And braces on my teeth. I was an
absolute squirrel, and I often wondered why I
should be alive. The feelings I had of not being

one of the guys, not being able to make the team
[in his first year at Bloom Township High], not
dating cheerleaders, being the kind of kid that the
athletes pointed at and snickered about, made me
forever aware of the outsider, the underdog. It's
the kind of thing you remember every time you
join in with the big boys, putting down the little
guy. It has made me shut up more than once."

In 1957 Bouton entered Western Michigan
University, where he vacillated between business
and liberal arts before finally settling on a business finance major. "The only thing I was sure of
was that I didn't want to be a salesman. I saw
myself as more an entrepreneur, but I didn't know
of what," he has written. On the basis of his pitching for the university's freshman baseball team he
was granted a scholarship at the beginning of his
sophomore year, but a proffered contract with the
American League's New York Yankees was more
attractive and he signed with the Yankees on
Thanksgiving Day in 1958. "As soon as I signed,
I seemed to get a lot more confidence in myself,"
Bouton has recalled. "Along about this time my
acne went away and the braces came off my teeth
and my name was in the local paper and I felt
like, well, the ugly duckling that was starting to
turn into a swan."

Bouton completed the first semester of the 1958-
59 academic year at Western Michigan before reporting for training with the Yankees, and he returned to the university winters during his three
years in the Yankee farm system. (Later he
studied at Fairleigh Dickinson University, without
taking a degree.) In his first season in the minor
leagues, with Auburn, New York and Kearney,
Nebraska, he won three games; in his second, with
Greensboro, North Carolina, he won fourteen; and
in his third, with Amarillo, Texas, he won thirteen. His earned-run average with Amarillo was
a healthy 2.97.

In 1962 Bouton moved up to the mother club
in New York as a relief pitcher, and he became
a starter with the Yankees the following year. His
annual won-lost records during his first three full
seasons with the New York club were 7-7, 21-7,
and 18-13. In the 1964 World Series he won two
games for the Yankees. In 1965, when his arm
gave out, he won only four games out of nineteen.
The following season his earned-run average of
2.7 was the best on the club but his won-lost record was only 3-8. Early in the 1967 season, when
his record was 1-0, the Yankees shipped him back
to the minors, to Syracuse, New York. He returned
to New York City the following year, but manager
Ralph Houk, who was antipathetic to his free-
wheeling ways, gave him little chance to perform
and sold him to Seattle of the Pacific Coast League
in June 1968, when his record for the year stood
at 2-1.

A week after the Yankees sold Bouton, George
Vecsey of the New York *Times* (June 23, 1968)
eulogized the departing hurler as "much more than
a typical pitcher" and predicted that the "sense
of dialogue" and "feeling of involvement" he had
brought to the team "will not be replaced easily."
"The Yankees were traditionally close-mouthed

heroes with little inclination to share even the time of day [with sportswriters] when Bouton . . . arrived with his eyes open, his brain switched on, and his mouth working on all twelve cylinders." Bouton was free and easy with reporters, "willing to share his observations" and "not afraid to reveal the group dynamics of the Yankee clubhouse." In his relationships with his teammates, he "felt secure enough to question . . . political and religious beliefs" and "he took a missionary's responsibility toward his roommates."

Vecsey further observed: "In the last year, Jim developed a terminal madness/sanity, grasping each day as if it were his last, certainly aware that his major league career could end at any moment. As the ballplayers say, Bouton did it all: he ordered a la carte from gourmet menus in Mexico City, he supported the exclusion of South Africa from the Olympics, he appeared at McCarthy [the Presidential peace candidate] rallies during Yankee road trips, he sought out hippies in Haight-Ashbury on a trip to Oakland, he investigated extrasensory perception, and he and his wife applied to adopt a Korean-American child."

The Seattle Pilots became a major league club when the American League expanded in 1969. That year Bouton revived a delivery he had tried in adolescence: the knuckleball, a pitch depending on surprise rather than speed for its effectiveness. Thrown from the fingertips with a locked wrist, the knuckleball floats toward the batter "dead," with little or no rotation, and as it reaches the plate it suddenly veers in a direction—up, down, or to either side—that even the pitcher cannot predict. Many pitchers past their peak resort to the arm-saving "flutter" pitch, but good knuckleballers are rare because the delivery is not only baffling to batters—and, unfortunately, to most catchers—but difficult for pitchers to control. Few of them attain sufficient mastery of it to keep the ball consistently in the strike zone.

In 1969 Bouton made fifty-seven appearances, mostly in relief roles, with the Pilots, won two games, and lost one. At one point during the season the Pilots farmed him out briefly to the Vancouver Mounties, and before the season's end they sold him to the Houston Astros in the National League. With Houston that year he lost two games and won none, and in 1970 he lost six and won two. His earned-run average with Houston was 5.42. On July 31, 1970 the Astros sent him "down" to their farm club in Oklahoma City, where he pitched two games and lost both. Ten days later he announced that he was retiring from professional baseball because he was having "so much trouble with this pitch" (the knuckleball) that a major-league comeback was unlikely and he did not want to subject his family to long-term minor-league life.

Meanwhile *Ball Four* had made its explosive appearance. Bouton had talked the book into a tape recorder day by day during the 1969 season, setting down without malice but with uninhibited frankness, a running account of nitty-gritty professional baseball life as it is actually lived, with all its follies and foibles. The latter included voyeurism and other sexual escapades, locker-room horseplay, salary machinations, bitter feuds, bullpen banter, and the widespread use of "greenies" (amphetamines) by ballplayers.

When typed out, Bouton's monologues totaled 450,000 words filling 1,500 manuscript pages. After Leonard Schecter, a veteran sportswriter, edited the manuscript down to 520 pages, *Look* magazine published excerpts in two installments early in June 1970 and World Publishing Company issued the complete *Ball Four* later in the same month. It quickly became the most popular and most commercially successful sports book in the history of publishing. It was on the New York *Times* best-seller list for seventeen weeks; sold 200,000 copies in hardcover; and in paperback sold at a rate unprecedented in the sports field. In 1970 alone Bouton estimated his share of profit from the book in tens of thousands of dollars.

Literary reviewers (as opposed to sportswriters) generally found the book "hilarious" and refreshing, a revelation of the humanity usually hidden by baseball's falsely heroic public-relations facade. Wilfrid Sheed, writing in *Life* (August 2, 1970), called it "not only the best and funniest account I know of that strange gypsy caravan known as a ball team and its trackless wanderings through the endless season, but a serious moral investigation of a profession, a distant cousin of *From Here to Eternity*."

But men who made their living in baseball tended to view *Ball Four* as indiscreet, perfidious, tales-out-of-school muckraking. Angry reactions came from many of them, from superstars whom Bouton had reduced to human scale to Baseball Commissioner Bowie Kuhn, who gave Bouton an official scolding. ("You've done the game a grave disservice. Saying players kissed on the Seattle team bus—incredible! Or that some of our greatest stars were drunk on the field. What can you be thinking of?")

In September 1970 Bouton joined the staff of WABC-TV in New York City as sports correspondent for that station's daily 11:00 P.M. news program. His starting salary was $40,000, about twice what he had been making in baseball. Bouton has said that he tries to report and comment on athletic news with "humor," "perspective," and "the realization that sports are not the most important thing in the world." He categorizes himself as a member of the "chipmunk" school of sportscasters, which gets across "the story and the enjoyment of the game without a lot of mush about how wonderful things are."

Bouton acknowledges that he is not a polished television performer, but his irrepressible comic sense of life, expressed with a combination of nonchalance and enthusiasm, fits in well with the WABC-TV news team's spirit, which is characterized by relaxed badinage. A favorite butt of Bouton's sly wit is the station's senior newscaster, Howard Cosell, a veteran observer of the athletic scene who looks as tough as he sounds. With friendly sarcasm, Bouton may dismiss Cosell as "just another pretty face," or, with hyperbole, describe him as "out walking his pet rat." His life at WABC-TV is among the areas of experience chronicled in Bouton's second book, *I'm Glad You Didn't Take It Personally*. Among the other subjects covered are his feud with World Publishing Company over the handling of *Ball Four*.

Jim Bouton and Barbara Heister were married in 1962. They have three children: Michael, Laurie, and the Korean-American boy they adopted, whose name has been given in conflicting sources as David and Kyong Jo. The Boutons live in Wyckoff, New Jersey. Bouton used to paint and sculpt, but his chief recreation now is baseball, which he plays with the Ridgewood-Paramus Barons in the semipro Metropolitan League in New Jersey. A liberal in politics, Bouton has campaigned for such candidates as Allard K. Lowenstein, the former United States Representative from New York and leader of the successful "Dump Johnson" movement in the Democratic party. He has contributed his name and energy to such causes as the peace movement, the American Committee on Africa, the campaign against cystic fibrosis, and Zero Population Growth. In the cause of population control he has undergone a vasectomy, or sterilization operation.

References

Christian Sci Mon p7 O 16 '64 por
N Y Times V p3 Je 23 '68 por; II p19 O 4 '70 por
Newsday W p3+ My 22 '71 pors
Sport 50:22+ Jl '70 por

Bouton, Jim. Ball Four (1970); I'm Glad You Didn't Take It Personally (1971)

BREL, JACQUES

Apr. 8, 1929- Composer; lyricist; singer
Address: c/o Ivan Black, 900 W. 190th St., New York 10040

In the mid-1960's Belgium-born Jacques Brel was the leading chansonnier, or "troubadour pop" artist, in France, enthralling cabaret audiences and discophiles with "Les Biches," "Les Vieux," and other dark ballads of his own composition. At that time Marlene Dietrich called him "the greatest singer in the world," while others resorted to epithets like "lyric genius." If Miss Dietrich's hyperbolic assertion no longer applies, now that Brel has quit the concert circuit, "lyric genius" is certainly still appropriate, as the intense, sensitive Brel concentrates on the writing of his soul-searching songs, which number in the hundreds. Musically, the compositions are rooted in old Flemish and French forms, but they have a contemporary sound. In theme they range the gamut of simple, universal, bittersweet human experience—bewildered first love, painful lost love, rueful old age, horrific death. In tone they build from tenderness to explosion, and they encompass a variety of moods, including cynical irony but never excluding warm compassion for suffering humanity. But there is never a hint of cloying romanticism. As Leroy F. Aarons observed

in the Washington *Post* (February 11, 1967), "A listener to one of Brel's albums is impressed with the raucous, Brechtian intensity of his delivery, far different than the sweetness of an Aznavour or the sensuality of a Montand."

American audiences know Brel chiefly through the revue *Jacques Brel Is Alive and Well and Living in Paris*, containing twenty-five of his songs (translated and adapted by Eric Blau and Mort Shuman), which is now in its fourth year Off Broadway. "Youth dies. Life hurts. Love warms. Understanding heals," a reviewer for *Time* (May 18, 1970) wrote. "The wounds and balms of the human condition are so commonplace that men eventually experience them without noticing. It is only when art magnifies truth that audiences become aware of it. One of the most powerful magnifiers currently in use is . . . *Jacques Brel Is Alive and Well and Living in Paris*."

The son of a cardboard carton manufacturer, Jacques Brel was born in Brussels, Belgium on April 8, 1929. He taught himself to play the guitar when he was fifteen. As a student at Roman Catholic schools he was an incorrigible mischief-maker, and before finishing secondary school he was expelled. He worked in his father's factory for four years, and during that time he began to compose songs. After doing his year of obligatory military service, he went to Paris and began singing his songs in small Left Bank *caves*, accompanying himself on the guitar.

Brel's first regular engagement as a professional performer was at the Theâtre des Trois Baudets in the Pigalle section of Paris in 1953. That was followed by gigs in the Écluse, the Patachou, and other cabarets, and in 1954 he won second billing at the Olympia, the top music hall in Paris. A correspondent for *Variety* (July 14, 1954) who witnessed his performance at the Olympia described him as a "young, gaunt-looking Belgian . . . [who] sings of emotions and desires that are thwarted by misunderstandings and pettiness." In the ensuing years his popularity grew steadily, not only in France but in other European countries, especially after he began recording his songs. When he returned to the Olympia with star billing in November 1959, the *Variety* critic noted his "big voice, projection, and electric personality."

During one of his frequent sojourns in Paris, Eric Blau, an aspiring American poet and confirmed Francophile who was then earning a living by ghostwriting sports autobiographies, heard a Brel LP. "I was knocked out when I heard his work," Blau later said, as quoted in the *Time* article. "I had never known any songwriter to address himself to the human condition." Elsewhere ly informed." "Brel did two things: He took the "a guy writing pop songs who was really poetically informed." "Brel did two things: He took the song form seriously and he knew that, although the lyric is not poetry, the songs as such could be art."

Back in New York, Blau was asked by impresario Art D'Lugoff if he would try his hand at a revue for the Village Gate, the cabaret that D'Lugoff had recently opened in the spacious basement of the old Greenwich Hotel on Bleecker Street in Greenwich Village. In collaboration with composer Doris Schwerin, Blau created *O, Oysters!*, which included two songs by Jacques Brel, "Carousel" and "Ne Me Quitte Pas," with the lyrics translated by Blau. Elly Stone (who later married Blau) sang both Brel songs in the show, which was presented at the Village Gate during the 1960-61 Off-Broadway season.

Like *O, Oysters!*, as a whole Brel's songs had only a lukewarm reception, which Blau analyzed in retrospect for Kaspars Dzeguze of the Toronto *Globe and Mail* (October 1, 1970): "The songs ran against the American grain then. They just wouldn't go." Elly Stone told Dzeguze that the later acceptance and success of Brel's work in the United States "has a lot to do with what the kids are up to and what they're saying. Bob Dylan's coming on the scene changed American tastes considerably. People started listening to the lyrics and that made it easier for Brel."

An early Brel watcher among American critics was Robert Alden of the New York *Times*. Reporting from Paris in January 1963, when Brel had just finished a benefit performance at the Salle Pleyel and was preparing for a month's engagement at the Olympia, Alden wrote: "Mr. Brel is youthful, lean, energetic, and attractive. He could easily be taken as a teen-age idol. But Mr. Brel . . . has many dimensions that lift him above the crooner category. He too, like Mr. [Léo] Ferré and Mr. [Georges] Brassens, is a poet who sets his poetry to music. In his performance, Mr. Brel . . . builds climax upon climax, scarcely pausing even to accept applause. The effect upon the music hall audiences is electric." When Brel made his American debut at Carnegie Hall in December 1965, Alden reported (December 6, 1965): "It was clear on Saturday night that Mr. Brel . . . had stepped ahead of even the gifted Mr. Ferré and the gifted Mr. Brassens. . . . It was even possible for a member of the audience who did not understand a word of French to understand emotionally and to be swept along by what Mr. Brel had to say. . . . Using his large hands, supple body, expressive arms, a strong voice, and even mischievously humorous legs, . . . he becomes the bitter sailor drinking in the port of Amsterdam, the old person who is waiting for death, the timid suitor, even the bull dying under a hot Spanish sun so that an Englishman can pretend for a moment that he is Wellington."

Brel returned to Europe immediately after the Carnegie Hall performance, leaving behind a concert LP (Reprise 6187) in which a critic for the New York *Herald Tribune* (January 23, 1966) found "the drama and personal intensity that marked the style of Edith Piaf." After Brel performed in Albert Hall, London, the critic for the *Observer* (November 20, 1966) wrote: "Brel, like others in the French intellectual pop section, is anti-clerical, anti-militarist, and anti-bourgeois. He attacks humbug, small-mindedness, and bigotry, but what puts him in a class of his own are his vigor, honesty, and sympathy even for his victims. He doesn't pose as a poet with right entirely on

JACQUES BREL

his side. His range of sympathies is wide-sixteen-stone drunks, old people, a thick-headed German corporal struggling to make friends in Occupied France. . . . Most of Brel's songs [some with sixteen and seventeen bar lines] are hard to hum. He makes sense of them musically with a razor-sharp flair for timing and a voice that can bellow and manage tenderness. A Brel recital isn't a smooth ride. He shoots images and rhythms and melodies at you without any pause for patter."

In a press conference in New York during a second brief American tour, in February 1967, Brel inadvertently revealed what is probably the basis of his rapport with audiences: "There are people as unhappy and bored as I sometimes am. . . . They feel a little better that somebody knows and tells them that he knows." His interpreter in the press conference was Mort Shuman, an American pop song writer who, like Eric Blau, had become an aficionado of Brel's work in Paris years before. "The first thing that impressed me," Shuman has recalled, "was the virility in his voice. The only time I'd heard this virility was in black singers. Here was a man who combined raw force with the most meaningful lyrics I had heard in songs, a deep understanding of the human condition. I began to translate the songs. This was what I wanted to bring back to America. No more 'yummy-yummy-yummy, I've got love in my tummy.' "

At the time of the New York press conference, Shuman was in the process of collaborating with Blau—to whom he had been introduced by a mutual friend, former recording executive Nat Shapiro—on the translation of twenty-five of Brel's songs for theatrical presentation. The product of that collaboration was *Jacques Brel Is Alive and Well and Living in Paris*, which opened at the Village Gate on January 22, 1968. The members of the original cast were Shuman himself, singing "Mathilde," "Jackie," "Amsterdam," "Funeral Tango," and "Next"; Elly Stone, rendering "I Loved," "My Death," "Sons of," "Old Folks," "Marieke," "You're Not Alone," and "Carousel";

Shawn Elliott, singing "Alone," "Bachelor's Dance," "The Statue," "The Bulls," and "Fannette"; and Alice Whitfield, singing "Timid Frieda." The other songs—"Marathon," "Madeleine," "Girls and Dogs," "Desperate Ones," "Brussels," "The Middle Class," and "We Only Have Love"—were duets or company songs. Marilyn Stasio of *Cue* (February 3, 1968), who especially liked the "honestly felt" interpretations of "Carousel" and "Amsterdam," described the American adaptation of Brel as "intelligent," "compassionate," and "(intensely!) dedicated."

In retrospect, the writer of the 1970 *Time* article gave a large measure of the credit for the show's enduring success to the initial contribution of Elly Stone, "a phosphorescent waif . . . who breathed life and passion into Brel's hard-edged depictions of soul *v.* circumstance." "Audiences that witness . . . [her] tours de force know what it must have been like in the '30's, when the young Lotte Lenya sang the works of Brecht and Weill and cabaret fused with art. The resemblance to Brecht and Weill does not end with Elly. The elusive melodies seem, at first, to be mere cloaks for Brel's verse. But they bear constant repetition. . . . As for his lyrics, the terse, iron-clad couplets recognize revelations beyond politics and fashion; they know that every man is an expatriate from youth." In addition to the revue's present New York cast there are now three touring companies, including an international troupe headed by Elly Stone and Mort Shuman that has done the show on French television and at the Olympia in Paris. An original cast recording has been released on the Columbia label.

While in New York during his second American tour, Jacques Brel saw *Man of La Mancha*, the hit musical by Mitch Leigh, Joe Darion, and Dale Wasserman based loosely on the life and works of Cervantes. Immediately enamored of the show, he subsequently made arrangements for a French version, translated by and starring himself. The Gallic production opened in Brussels in November 1968 and moved to the Théâtre des Champs Elysées in Paris for a brief engagement the following month. French audiences, traditionally inhospitable to musicals of American origin, responded enthusiastically to the production.

In the motion picture *Mont-Dragon* (Films Jacques Leitienne, 1971), Brel plays the straight dramatic leading role of Georges, a career army man who seeks vengeance on the family of the colonel who is responsible for his dishonorable discharge, and he intends to appear in a cameo role, singing "Ne Me Quitte Pas," in a projected film version of *Jacques Brel Is Alive and Well and Living in Paris*. But otherwise he is concentrating on writing music to the exclusion of performing. (He gave up concert tours in 1967, and he has not performed on stage since 1968.) On stage, he has explained, "one has too much power," the one-sided power of the monologist, and that power, he feels, tends to make an artisan (as he thinks of himself—"when you die you become an artist") complacent and "immobile." In writing, he has the insecure, open-ended sense of being in "dia-logue" with people, not the public ("a false notion"). "Besides, the writing, the idea, is the most important thing. Faulkner never sang."

Jacques Brel is short (five feet seven inches) and slight. A writer for the *Observer* (November 20, 1966), citing his "large mouth and big teeth," called him "boyishly ugly," but Leroy F. Aarons in his Washington *Post* article conveyed a different impression: "He is Gallicly handsome . . . with a high-cheekboned, wide-nostriled virility not unmindful of Belmondo." Aarons rounded out his description: "He is very much the individualist who gives the impression during an interview that the fame, riches and other trappings of success are unimportant to him. . . . Brel is . . . a pleasant, animated sort, given to chain-smoking Gauloise Disque Bleu and lapsing regularly into a favorite, if obscene, gesture with his arms." Like other interviewers, Aarons found in Brel's conversation the introspective quality that characterizes his songs.

Brel, once married but now divorced, lives a life relatively untethered to property, except for a private airplane in which he hops about Europe. He has said that his chief interests outside of writing songs are "making love and flying my plane." He also likes to sail. According to the *Time* article, "He professes a love for Americans, . . . but he will not [again] pay a visit to the United States until the war in Vietnam is over." But Brel has said, "Vietnam is not the issue. War is only the manifestation of power. Power is the real problem."

References

London Observer p23 N 20 '66
N Y Times p28 F 10 '67 por
Time 95:64+ My 18 '70 por
Washington (D.C.) Post C p9 F 11 '67
Blau, Eric. Jacques Brel Is Alive and Well and Living in Paris (1971)
Who's Who in France, 1965-66

BRESSON, ROBERT (brə-sôɴ')

Sept. 25, 1907- French motion picture director; scriptwriter
Address: h. 49 quai de Bourbon, Paris 4ᵉ. France

Among that select group of motion picture directors whose reputations are international and solidly grounded in the continuing respect accorded their work by discerning critics and filmgoers alike, Robert Bresson of France has, for almost thirty years, maintained front-rank status as a "director's director." The achievement is the more remarkable in view of the fact that in his entire career he has only nine feature-length films to his credit, including the multiple-award-winning *Le Journal d'un curé de campagne* (1950) and *Un Condamné à mort s'est échappé* (1956). Bresson's austere cinematography weds a subdued soundtrack to carefully selected images that resemble the compositions of a painter, uninfluenced by popular tastes, artistic trends, or commercial rewards. He has made only one film in color, his recent *Une Femme douce* (1969).

Robert Bresson was born on September 25, 1907 at Bromont-Lamothe, Puy-de-Dôme, France to Léon and Marie-Elisabeth (Clausels) Bresson. Of solid, bourgeois background, he attended the Lycée Lakanal à Sceaux, where he studied classics and philosophy, and took a bachelor of arts diploma. On completing his formal education, he attempted a career as a painter, but his efforts evidently met with indifferent success. He turned to scenario writing, collaborating on the screenplays of *C'était un musicien* (1933), directed by Frédéric Zelnick; *Les Jumeaux de Brighton* (1936), directed by Claude Heymann; and *Courrier sud* (1937), directed by Pierre Billon. The first film that Bresson himself directed was *Les Affaires publiques* (1934), a medium-length comedy produced by Arc Films. In 1939, about the time of the outbreak of World War II, he worked as an assistant to René Clair on the unfinished "Air pur." He then spent a year in a German prisoner-of-war camp.

The atmosphere of the French movie industry of the 1930's, in which Bresson learned his craft, differed greatly from Hollywood's. Production budgets were comparatively small and emphasis was on quality and experimentation rather than on spectacle and mass appeal. From the first, the French approached movies as a serious art form and the realistic treatment of social themes was encouraged by grants from the French Ministry of Culture. Long before the American public as a whole became aware of "new wave" films, thoughtful movie critics and the patrons of small off-beat movie houses in major American cities acknowledged that the French had moved out in front in their realistic depiction of the human condition on the screen. By World War II the work of French actors such as Jean Gabin, Harry Baur, Raimu, Michel Simon, Fernandel, and Louis Jouvet, as well as cameraman Claude Renoir and directors Marcel Carné, René Clair, and Jean Renoir, was being accorded critical, if not commercial, success in avant-garde movie houses in America.

With the German occupation, the export of French films ceased, and it was not until the late 1940's that Robert Bresson became known in America through the belated transatlantic release of *Les Anges du péché* (1943, *The Angels of Sin*) and *Les Dames du Bois de Boulogne* (1945, *The Women of the Bois de Boulogne*). In his discussion of *Les Anges du péché*, Raymond Durgnat observed in *The Films of Robert Bresson* (1970) that Bresson was among those directors who "ceaselessly transpose and refine a vision almost mature in their first feature."

The "vision" of Robert Bresson has been a matter of controversy and differing interpretation on both sides of the Atlantic by film critics and fans, but all agree that its basic elements are a profound distaste for theatrical performances and traditional dramatization, a subordination of purely human values and themes to spiritual ones, and a ruthless pruning of all details, both auditory

ROBERT BRESSON

and visual, that do not contribute directly to the dominant mood of the film. The last factor has become the hallmark of Bresson's film style.

In his first two feature-length films Bresson used professional actors and engaged experts to write the dialogue, Jean Giraudoux for *Les Anges du péché* and Jean Cocteau for *Les Dames du Bois de Boulogne*. Dissatisfied with those films because of the performances of the professional actors, he has insisted upon casting nonprofessionals in all of his succeeding motion pictures— *Le Journal d'un curé de campagne* (1950, *Diary of a Country Priest*); *Un Condamné à mort s'est échappé* (1956, *A Man Escaped*); *Pickpocket* (1959); *Le Procès de Jeanne d'Arc* (1061, *The Trial of Joan of Arc*); *Au Hasard, Balthazar* (1966, *Balthazar*); *Mouchette* (1967); and *Une Femme douce* (1969, *A Gentle Woman*). For those films Bresson also wrote the dialogue. He has always been his own scriptwriter, adapting two novels of Georges Bernanos for the screenplays of *Le Journal d'un curé de campagne* and *Mouchette* and a story by Dostoievsky for the screenplay of *Une Femme douce*. Two of his films seem almost documentary: *Un Condamné à mort s'est échappé* is based on a firsthand account of an actual escape by André Devigny, and *Le Procès de Jeanne d'Arc* follows rigorously the minutes of Joan's trial and the historical account of the rehabilitation process.

Directing nonprofessional actors requires abundant patience and a special skill. In filming *Un Condamné à mort s'est échappé*, Bresson reportedly asked François Leterrier, who portrayed the Resistance fighter escaping from a Gestapo prison, to repeat one line of dialogue some 300 times in order to get the exact intonation. The line was "Va te coucher" (Go to sleep). Before making *Le Journal d'un curé de campagne*, he talked with Claude Laydu every Sunday for a year before he was satisfied that Laydu comprehended what was wanted of him in the title role. It was only after seeing the finished film that Laydu, who had never acted in a film before, realized that he had been portraying a saint.

Bresson's rigid attitude toward the paramount importance of the director's role in the creation of film and his insistence that actors key their performances to his conception of their role has made him a hero to directors and an arch villain to actors. His film technique derives in part from his study of painting. A motion picture, he has pointed out, must express itself through the relationship of images in a sequence. "There must, at a certain moment, be a transformation," he has explained, as quoted by Roy Armes in *French Cinema Since 1946* (1970); "if not, there is no art." He therefore chooses flat, inexpressive, functional images, which are transformed more readily than striking images in association with other images. "Painting taught me to make not beautiful images but necessary ones," he has remarked. He also has found that "the images must share some unity of tone if the flow and transformation is to be maintained." For that reason Bresson directs all the performers in his film to act and speak in a certain uniform manner. The camera itself reveals the personality of the characters: "Plastically, one must sculpt the idea into a face by means of light and shade." His images are accompanied by natural sounds, such as the creaking of wheels or crackling of flames, and an occasional background score of the music of Mozart, Lully, Schubert, or Monteverdi.

In an interview for the Manchester *Guardian* (November 5, 1962) Bresson maintained that performances of experienced, professional actors, however expert, destroy the rhythm, or essence, of a motion picture. He argued that the instincts and training of an actor militate against docility, prevent his submission to the director's vision of the whole. If Bresson has scant sympathy for the rebellious impulses of professional actors, the same cannot be said for the social types portrayed in his films. Many of his characters may be considered rebels, both those who operate within the accepted social structure and those outside of it. That was as evident in his first feature film, *Les Anges du péché* (where the chief protagonists were an unruly nun, at odds with her order, and a young woman whom she befriends and who eventually murders her lover), as in his recent *Une Femme douce* (where an emotionally bankrupt antique dealer drives a young girl student he has married to suicide with his jealousy and inability to love). In between are a gallery of off-beat heros and heroines: an obsessively revengeful woman in *Les Dames du Bois de Boulogne*; a tormented priest struggling for the soul of an intransigent countess in *Le Journal d'un curé de campagne*; an imprisoned lieutenant of the French Resistance; a Parisian pickpocket; a medieval saint; a carnival donkey in *Au Hasard, Balthazar*; and a biker's girl who commits suicide in *Mouchette*. All of them are explicit, if fragmentary, versions of Robert Bresson's "vision" of the human condition: whatever spiritual values life grudgingly reveals are found in travail and only he who simultaneously accepts and struggles against his fate is capable of winning through to spiritual peace and freedom.

Bresson's fundamentally transcendental perspective on life has led to his being accused by some European film critics of Jansenism, a peculiarly French variant of an ancient heresy, condemned by the Roman Catholic Church for teaching that the nature of matter is essentially evil—that the world and the flesh are the devil's domain and the sooner man relinquishes them the better are his chances for eternal salvation. To accusations of religious nonconformism Bresson is indifferent, but he seeks identification as a Christian intellectual. In an interview in *Télérama*, the French critical review devoted to the appreciation of movies as an art form, Bresson said of his then forthcoming movie *Un Condamné à mort s'est échappé*, "I would like to show this miracle: an invisible hand over the prison, directing what happens and causing such and such a thing to succeed for one and not for another. . . . The film is a mystery. . . . The Spirit breathes where It will." Lest there be any mistake about the religious approach he took to the protagonist's role in the film Bresson chose as the subtitle *Le Vent souffle où il veut* (The Wind Bloweth Where It Listeth).

The films of Robert Bresson lose something in their transatlantic voyage to avant-garde movie houses in America, largely because of the exhibitor's tendency to trim and edit scenes to suit the American taste, for reasons that have little or nothing to do with either their artistic merit or relation to the film as a whole. In a letter to Bosley Crowther, the movie critic, reprinted in the New York *Times* on May 2, 1954, Bresson complained, "I have the terrible surprise to hear that my picture, *Diary of a Country Priest*, has been entirely mutilated by the distributor, who took on himself to cut out a considerable number of scenes in order to shorten the picture by a whole half hour! . . . What I am sure of is that it is impossible (I have tried myself) to cut even one scene of the film without making it absolutely ununderstandable. I had built it with utmost care and precautions. And every little detail is indispensable. Besides, a picture is also made of proportions, rhythms. . . ." In his own review of the film for the New York *Times* (April 6, 1954) Crowther had found it difficult to understand "the motivations and maneuverings of the characters." But when commenting on Bresson's letter, he was not convinced that restoring the cuts would make the theme less bewildering.

Despite the alleged mutilation of his films for American audiences, Bresson's reputation as a director and an artist has suffered little. American critics, while not uniformly enthusiastic over his tendency ruthlessly to exclude details extraneous to the central theme and his unwavering insistence upon authentic settings, are virtually unanimous in paying tribute to his stature as an artist. In the same review in which he saw some weaknesses in *Diary of a Country Priest*, Crowther voiced the general critical appreciation of Bresson in the United States: "His cinema technique is brilliant. Reflective of the work of Carl Dreyer, the old Danish master of the close-up and the hard, analytical camera style, it is a compound of searching realism and a tempo of movement that approaches poetry."

Two of Bresson's films won him the Grand Prize of the French Cinema, *Les Anges du péché* in 1943 and *Le Journal d'un curé de campagne* in 1951. For the latter picture he was also awarded the Louis Delluc Prize in 1950 and the Grand Prize of the Venice Film Festival in 1951. *Un Condamné à mort s'est échappé* received the Best Director Award at the Cannes Film Festival in 1957 and was named the best picture of the year by the French Film Academy. Another award for best picture of the year went, in 1960, to *Pickpocket,* which was also chosen by international film critics of *Sight and Sound* magazine as one of the all-time best films in motion picture history. Bresson's other honors include the Special Award of the Jury at the Cannes Film Festival in 1962 for *Le Procès de Jeanne d'Arc* and the Grand Prize of the Festival of Panama in 1968 for *Mouchette.*

Robert Bresson is honorary president of the Society of French Film Directors and a Chevalier in the French Legion of Honor. When discussing his cinematographic views, the slim, whitehaired director expresses himself readily, in English as well as French—"entirely without affectation," as one interviewer remarked—but he seems reticent about his private life. He has been married since December 1926 to Leida (Van der Zee) Bresson. His recreations are collecting modern paintings and first editions. He seldom goes to the movies and dislikes the few films he does see.

References

Armes, Roy. French Cinema Since 1946 vol 1 (1970)
Cameron, Ian, ed. The Films of Robert Bresson (1970)
Dictionnaire de Biographie Française (1964-)
International Who's Who, 1970-71
Who's Who, 1970-71
Who's Who in France, 1965-66

BROCK, WILLIAM EMERSON, 3D

Nov. 23, 1930- United States Senator from Tennessee
Address: b. Senate Office Bldg., Washington, D.C. 20510; h. Dogwood Dr., Lookout Mountain, Tenn. 37350; 10837 Stanmore Dr., Potomac, Md. 20854

Outstanding among the limited gains made by the Republicans in the national election of November 1970 was the victory in Tennessee of Representative William Emerson Brock 3d against the veteran liberal Democrat Albert Gore, seeking reelection to the United States Senate. Brock, who is heir to the Brock Candy Company in Chattanooga, represented the Third Congressional Tennessee District for three terms, from 1963 to 1971, in the House of Representatives, where his voting record

WILLIAM EMERSON BROCK 3D

generally followed party lines and his outlook seemed customarily, though not uniformly, conservative. His election to the Ninety-second Congress, convening in January 1971, gave the Republicans, for the first time in memory, both of Tennessee's seats in the Senate, the other being occupied by Senator Howard H. Baker Jr. of Knoxville.

The oldest of the three sons of William Emerson Brock Jr. and his wife, the former Myra Kruesi, William Emerson Brock 3d was born on November 23, 1930 in Chattanooga, Tennessee. His brothers are Frank and Paul K. Brock. Early in the century his grandfather, William Emerson Brock, had moved to Chattanooga, where he started a candy-making business. At the time of his grandson's birth he was serving a brief term, from 1929 to 1931, in the United States Senate, as a Democrat. William 3d attended Lookout Mountain Grade School and the McCallie School, a preparatory school in Chattanooga, before enrolling in his father's alma mater, Washington and Lee University. Majoring in business administration, he obtained the Bachelor of Science degree in commerce in 1953. His fraternity is Sigma Alpha Epsilon.

In the same year Brock joined the United States Navy as an ensign. From 1954 to 1956 he saw duty with the Seventh Fleet in the Far East, and by the time he returned to civilian life he had advanced to the rank of lieutenant (j.g.). Since 1961 he has served in the rank of lieutenant as a member of the Naval Reserve. For his active service he was decorated with the Korean Battle and United Nations Service ribbons.

On his release from the Navy in 1956, Bill Brock entered the family business in Chattanooga, the Brock Candy Company, of which his father had become chairman of the board. Starting as an assistant in the production control department, he was then occupied successively as manager of production control, as direct sales representative in southern Florida, and as member and eventually head of the market research department. In 1961 he was made a director of the company and vice-president in charge of marketing. He served in the latter position only until taking his seat in Congress in January 1963. He has, however, retained his directorship in the Brock company, which by 1970 enjoyed annual sales of between $10,000,000 and $15,000,000 and employed about 460 workers.

Early dedicated to the advancement of civic standards, Brock became especially concerned with improvements in local education. "He was appalled by a survey that showed widespread functional illiteracy below the levels of the Chattanooga society in which he lived," as reported in *Time* (November 16, 1970). "He and his friends organized their own training program, and Brock started coming down from his plush home atop Lookout Mountain to teach reading and writing to impoverished blacks." From 1960 to 1962 he was a member of the steering committee of the Chattanooga Area Literacy Movement and in 1960-61 served as its treasurer. He was in addition a member of the steering committee of the Citizens Committee for Better Schools and in 1961-62 a director and chairman of the education committee of the Tennessee Junior Chamber of Commerce. As part of an effort to facilitate integration of Chattanooga public facilities, he initiated a program that enrolled some fifty black pupils in schools. Other civic betterment organizations in which Brock has been active include the local Law Enforcement Committee, the Good Government League, the Industrial Committee of 100, the Golden Gateway Citizens Committee (for urban renewal), and the 365 Club of the Handicapped.

Politically, meanwhile, Brock, who had rejected the Democratic affiliation of his father and grandfather, was becoming prominent in local Republican circles. During the 1960 Presidential campaign he supported the Republican candidate, Richard Nixon, against the Democratic candidate, John F. Kennedy. In 1961 he was elected a national committeeman for the Tennessee Young Republicans National Federation and chairman of the National Young Republican Teen Committee. Brock also served as chairman of the Republican central committee for Hamilton County, which includes Chattanooga and its suburbs, becoming chairman of the finance committee in 1962.

By his victory over his Democratic opponent, Wilkes T. Thrasher, in the November 1962 election, Brock became the first Republican in more than forty years to serve as Representative for the Third Congressional Tennessee District, which includes Hamilton and several more rural counties in the southeast corner of the state. When he took his seat in the Eighty-eighth Congress in January 1963, he was assigned at his own request to the Banking and Currency Committee, the only standing committee of the House on which he was to serve. He was also named to the Republican Congressional Committee, the campaign committee for G.O.P. candidates seeking election to the House.

Representative Brock lost little time in asserting his Republicanism. Early in the 1963 session when the White House, instead of the Civil Service Commission, undertook to coordinate the assignment of students to summer civil service jobs, Brock commented that he supposed "many sons and daughters of Kennedy supporters will find their way to summer jobs in the nation's capital at the taxpayer's expense" (quoted in the *Congressional Quarterly Almanac,* 1963). In the spring of 1963 Brock joined eight out of the thirteen Republicans on the Banking and Currency Committee in opposing through a minority report the Democratic administration's urban mass transportation bill. The minority report pointed out that under the bill more than 6,000 communities would be eligible for aid, but that the federal government is not responsible for local transportation problems. One of his noteworthy votes in the Eighty-eighth Congress was that against the Civil Rights Act of 1964. "We exceeded our constitutional authority," he explained.

Reelected in November 1964 by 71,005 votes to 59,027, Brock continued to hold an increased majority in the 1966 and 1968 elections. In the Eighty-ninth Congress, 1965 and 1966, he added to his responsibilities those of membership in his party's Planning and Research Committee and during the same Congress was appointed assistant, or regional, minority whip. His record on roll call votes shows a clear, though not rigid, adherence to conservatism. In 1965 he opposed both the Appalachian regional development bill and the Republican-sponsored alternative, although in 1969 he supported authorization of development funds, and in 1966 he voted against the $1.75 billion appropriations bill for the war on poverty and the $10.5 billion appropriations bill for the Department of Labor and the Department of Health, Education and Welfare. He also voted against funds for the antipoverty program in 1967 and against an appropriation of more than $4 billion for NASA, but among the measures he approved in 1967 were those providing funds for the House Un-American Activities Committee and $115,700,000 for the Peace Corps. The $1.8 billion appropriations bill for military construction won his support in 1968, but not the proposed $5.5 billion for agriculture.

As a delegate to the 1968 Republican National Convention, Brock staunchly supported the candidacy of former Vice-President Nixon for the Presidential nomination. In August, following the convention, Nixon named Brock among the prominent Republicans who would speak for him on major issues. One of Nixon's concerns after he took office as President in January 1969 was the storm of student unrest sweeping the American campuses. During the spring of that year Brock organized a group of twenty-two Republican Representatives into six teams to make unpublicized tours of colleges and universities and speak with as many students as possible to learn the causes of their discontent. Brock was among the team leaders who reported directly to the President.

Their report, which advised against repressive measures and cited student complaints against materialistic and dehumanized university administration among other dissatisfactions, resulted in the appointment by Nixon of the Scranton Commission on Campus Unrest.

Among the measures on which Brock voted affirmatively during the first session of the Ninety-first Congress were a $480,000,000 United States contribution to the International Development Corporation, a $4.5 billion appropriation for public works and the Atomic Energy Commission, funds for housing and urban development, and the voting rights bill. In November 1969 he spoke out against the Blackburn amendment to the banking regulation bill, which would have restricted the activity of cooperatives and which if passed, Brock predicted, would have a "chaotic effect" on business.

In key voting of the 1970 session Representative Brock opposed overriding President Nixon's veto of the Department of Health, Education and Welfare appropriations bill. He approved a 15 percent increase in retirement benefits for railroad workers and a pay increase for civil service employees, and voted against the appropriation bill for foreign aid in fiscal 1971 eventually passed by the House. During the Ninety-first Congress Brock served on the Joint Committee on Defense Production and Joint Economic Committee, as well as on his regular standing House committee.

"Today," Representative Brock informed his supporters on April 3, 1970, first in Chattanooga and then in the other major cities of the state, "I am announcing my candidacy for the United States Senate." His declaration followed by about six months the decision of another potential Republican candidate, Representative Dan Kuykendall of Memphis, not to run against the incumbent liberal Democrat, Senator Albert Gore, who would be seeking a fourth term in 1970. Neither Brock nor Gore went unchallenged in the August primaries: Brock had to fight a strong bid for nomination by the folk singer Tex Ritter, and Gore narrowly won over Hudley Crockett, a segregationist and former television newscaster.

Enjoying the favor of President Nixon and the benefits of the Republican National Committee's campaign fund, Brock accelerated his efforts to unseat Gore. Brock was "one of the first candidates to receive the on-the-scene endorsement of Vice-President Spiro Agnew," as reported in the Boston *Globe* (October 4, 1970) by R. M. Weintraub, who also observed that in the ensuing bitter contest Brock's "political rhetoric" was a "carbon copy of the Vice-President's." The two Republicans made much of Gore's votes in the Senate against confirming the Southern judges Clement Haynsworth and G. Harrold Carswell for the Supreme Court. Defending the sending of American troops into Cambodia and Nixon's other policies in Southeast Asia, Brock excoriated the veteran Democrat for his consistent opposition to the Vietnam war. Gore contrasted his support of federally financed hospitals, dams, and schools

with Brock's negative vote on many appropriation bills. He also emphasized a contrast in backgrounds: "When I grew up, I had dirt on my hands, not chocolate." The fairly close outcome of the November election was 559,556 votes for Brock to 513,212 for Gore. With the election of Brock and that of another Republican, Winfield Dunn, as governor of the state, G.O.P. politicians claimed a clear-cut victory in Tennessee for the Nixon administration's so-called "Southern strategy."

Soon after the opening of the Ninety-second Congress, Brock was named to the Senate Banking, Housing and Urban Affairs Committee and the Government Operations Committee. On a roll call vote of early 1971 he joined other Southerners and conservative Republicans in defeating an attempt in February to curb filibusters in the Senate. The following month in support of the stand of the Nixon administration he voted with the minority for an amendment to provide $134,000,-000 to continue federal funding for the supersonic transport plane project. In late October 1971 he voted with the majority of Senators to defeat legislation authorizing foreign aid.

While in the House of Representatives, Brock worked closely with business and industrial groups in his district to increase economic opportunities and attract new investments to eastern Tennessee. He had been active in the Better Business Bureau and in both the Chattanooga Chamber of Commerce and the Tennessee Junior Chamber of Commerce, serving the latter as vice-president in 1960-61. The Jaycees named him "Outstanding Young Man in Tennessee" of the year 1964. He belongs to the American Legion and the Chowder and Marching Society.

William Emerson Brock 3d and Laura Handly ("Muffet") were married on January 1, 1957 and are the parents of three boys, William Emerson 4th, Oscar Handly, and John Kruesi, and one girl, Laura Hutcheson Brock. The brown-eyed, brown-haired Senator is six feet tall and weighs 170 pounds. "Nothing in Brock's personal life and tastes," according to *Time* (November 16, 1970), "dims the image of regularity that he carries in public. . . . His clothes and hair reflect no effort at compromise with today's youthful fashions. He likes semiclassical music and Winston Churchill, and privately and publicly projects total sincerity." His outdoor diversions are sailing and water-skiing and roaming the woods. He attends the Lookout Mountain Presbyterian Church, where he used to teach Sunday school.

References

Cong Q 28:2606 O 23 '70 por
N Y Times IV p3 N 1 '70; p1+ N 4 '70 por
New Yorker 47:34+ Jl 10 '71
Time 96:18 N 14 '70 por
U S News 69:45+ N 16 '70 por
Congressional Directory (1970)
Who's Who in America, 1970-71
Who's Who in American Politics, 1969-70

BROTHERS, JOYCE

1927(?)- Psychologist; television and radio personality
Address: b. National Broadcasting Company, 30 Rockefeller Plaza, New York 10020; h. 305 E. 86th St., New York 10028

Dr. Joyce Brothers has been "psychologist extraordinaire" to the radio and television public since 1958, when she first conducted her own show for the National Broadcasting Company. Well qualified for her post, Dr. Brothers holds advanced degrees, is a certified psychologist in the State of New York, and has lectured at Columbia University and Hunter College. Thousands of letters reach her each week from the dejected, the lonely, and the troubled who comprise her loyal audiences. If she sometimes sounds like "a smooth blend of Dorothy Dix and Sigmund Freud," the articulate Dr. Brothers makes up for it by offering her mass therapy with suavity, gentleness, and sincerity. Professional clinicians may criticize Dr. Brothers' tendency to reduce complex questions to simplistic solutions, but she has given new courage to many despairing listeners.

Dr. Joyce Brothers was born Joyce Diane Bauer, one of the two daughters of Morris K. and Estelle (Rapoport) Bauer, possibly around 1927. Joyce and her sister Elaine, who is now an attorney married to a pediatrician, grew up in Far Rockaway, Queens, then a suburb of New York City. Both lawyers, the Bauers instilled in their daughters a high regard for hard work and academic achievement. Even as a child in the local public schools, Joyce set high goals for herself, and she demonstrated great powers of concentration when she was trying to learn something. "There could be an explosion in the house and she wouldn't hear it," her father recalled many years later in Coronet (November 1968). She was an honor student at Far Rockaway High School, where her intelligence, charm, and poise made her popular with her contemporaries.

While attending Cornell University as an undergraduate, Joyce Brothers became absorbed in psychology and decided to major in that field. She took a B.S. degree with honors from Cornell in 1947 and then enrolled at Columbia University for advanced work in behavior and personality. From 1948 to 1953 she was an assistant in psychology at Columbia and an instructor at Hunter College in New York City. She obtained the M.A. degree from Columbia University in 1949. A few weeks later she married a medical student, Dr. Milton Brothers, and she managed after her marriage to continue with her teaching and research. During 1949-50 she was a research fellow on a United Nations leadership project. Joyce Brothers received the Ph.D. degree from Columbia in 1953. Her dissertation concerned an experimental investigation of anxiety avoidance and escape behavior as measured by action potential in muscle.

Although many women with advanced degrees do not elect to become housewives, Joyce Brothers thought it important to remain at home to raise her new-born daughter. She left her teaching posts at Columbia and Hunter, which swiftly reduced the couple's income to Dr. Milton Brothers' fifty dollar-a-month salary as a medical resident. To get them out of their financial straits, Joyce Brothers tried for an appearance on a popular television quiz show called The $64,000 Question. During the mid-1950's there was considerable brouhaha about quiz shows that featured extravagant giveaways of many thousands of dollars. Choosing contestants who could qualify for unusual categories, the producers quickly recognized the entertainment potential of an attractive female psychologist who was an expert on boxing, "just to please her husband." Joyce Brothers enriched her knowledge of the ring by memorizing twenty volumes of a boxing encyclopedia. "I studied from six in the morning to 12:00 at night," Dr. Brothers recalled for Coronet (November 1968). "I had good motivation because we were hungry."

Appearing on the show for the first time in the late autumn of 1955, Dr. Brothers was an immediate success. As she reached each new plateau in the game, she built up her winnings from week to week, until she won the $64,000 question in December. She knew such extraneous bits of information as the full name of the Marquis of Queensberry and the number of rounds fought in the 1923 Dempsey-Firpo contest. When she analyzed her own reactions to the show, Dr. Brothers remembered that the day after the telecast she felt relaxed and "triumphant," but then the pressure began to build like that inside a balloon, until it "reached a state of excruciating tension." She has compared entering the quiz booth with going into battle. Dr. Joyce Brothers was the second person and the only woman ever to win the top prize of $64,000.

When audiences wearied of the $64,000 Question, it was replaced by the $64,000 Challenge, which pitted the contestant against experts in his field. In September and October 1957 Dr. Joyce Brothers gamely appeared on the show against seven ex-fighters in a battle that seemingly put her at a great disadvantage but turned out to be what the New Yorker (September 13, 1958) called "one of the high points in the annals of boxing." To the dismay of the experts, all of them living immortals of the ring, she answered every level of questioning correctly. Her moment of triumph came when she upset a challenge by champion Tommy Loughran by maintaining that Archie Moore knocked out Bobo Olson in the third round of their light-heavyweight title bout. Joyce Brothers' total earnings from the two shows amounted to $134,000, a figure that made her one of the biggest winners in the television quiz business.

When, in 1959, hearings were held that exposed corruption in the quiz shows, the public learned that contestants had been coached and often provided with answers in advance. Dr. Brothers not only came through the hearings unscathed but was cleared of any duplicity when testimony revealed that she had actually caused an upheaval on the *$64,000 Challenge* show by winning when the producers had intended her to lose. "They were going to knock me out with impossible questions, but they didn't," Dr. Brothers recalled for a *Newsday* (June 22, 1970) reporter. "I'd memorized everything it is possible to know on the subject."

Unlike the other quiz show contestants, Joyce Brothers remained on television. In 1956 she was cohost of *Sports Showcase,* commenting on sports events and interviewing prominent sports figures. She often appeared on television "talk shows," where her mercurial intelligence, charm, and dignity reinforced her favorable image. In September 1958 the National Broadcasting Company offered Dr. Brothers an opportunity to try out an afternoon show given over to counseling and advice on love, marriage, sex, and child-rearing. To the surprise of the producers, who had planned the show partly as a publicity stunt, Joyce Brothers was an immediate success, apparently because she filled a void in television programming. Although she had originally signed to a four-week contract to appear on a local station in the New York metropolitan area, Dr. Brothers was telecast nationally when she began to receive more than one thousand letters a week from her listeners. Within a year, Dr. Brothers added a late-night program to her schedule, expanding her discussions to canvass topics previously tabooed on the air, such as frigidity and impotence, sexual satisfaction and menopause. Although Harriet Van Horne demurred that her shows were "too intimate for public airing," Marya Mannes wrote in the *Reporter* (February 15, 1962) that Dr. Brothers had a flair for making private areas public without being embarrassing or offensive.

A sizeable and dedicated audience has been listening to Dr. Brothers' opinions for more than a decade. "Whatever feelings the sophisticates might have about Dr. Brothers," wrote a reporter for *Coronet* (November 1968), "large sections of the public take her very seriously." Much of her success stems from her genuinely sympathetic manner and her ability to dispense sound advice in simple language unencumbered by professional jargon. The original format of *The Dr. Joyce Brothers Show* was revamped several times and reintroduced as *Consult Dr. Brothers* and *Ask Dr. Brothers.* She is also heard on radio stations of the ABC and NBC networks and in taped short talks that go out on *Emphasis* and *Monitor* news spots. Dr. Brothers is also featured on station WMCA in New York City, answering personal questions from on-the-air telephone callers. Taped in advance, the television programs are thoroughly prepared, and Dr. Brothers often devotes fourteen to sixteen hours of background work to every half hour of discussion. The live radio shows, on the other hand, are spontaneous, realistic, and sometimes invested with drama. Dr. Brothers once intervened directly to arrange a meeting between army officials and a young soldier who had gone AWOL. She has also had two tense incidents on the air with disturbed individuals who threatened suicide. In 1965 she saved a man's life, and early

JOYCE BROTHERS

in 1971 she prevented an hysterical woman from taking an overdose of sleeping pills while comforting her over the phone. Dr. Brothers talked calmly to the woman for three hours, ninety minutes of it on the air, while the police traced the telephone number in a rescue operation. After the woman was taken to the hospital and the ordeal was over, Dr. Brothers admitted she "shook" from fright.

Consulting psychologists hold mixed opinions about Dr. Brothers' shows. Most of them are concerned that she gives advice without knowing the intimate details of a caller's life and that her listeners will accept her "psychological uplift" rather than deal directly with a trained therapist. Those who are familiar with her work believe it is excellent group therapy, offering an individual a chance to look at a personal problem with some detachment and know that it is shared by others and not at all unique. "I think she is sound and tactful," a psychiatrist reported to a writer for *Coronet* (November 1968). "There's a lot of sour grapes in the profession." Dr. Brothers insists that she is merely a link between the viewer and professional literature. "I attempt to give people information which will be of some service to them in everyday living . . . ," Dr. Brothers told an interviewer for *Newsweek* (September 29, 1958). "I do not and will not talk about problems of mental illness. I am not trying to do therapy on the air. If I think there is even a possibility that people need therapy, I suggest they seek professional help."

Although she prescribes tranquility for others, Dr. Brothers herself leads a fast-paced existence. In addition to fulfilling her television and radio commitments, she writes a syndicated column that appears in some 350 daily newspapers throughout the nation. She furnishes a monthly column for *Good Housekeeping* and is a special feature writer for the Hearst newspapers and United Press International. In 1957 Dr. Brothers collaborated with E. P. F. Egan to write *Ten Days to a Successful Memory* (Prentice-Hall), a resource manual for remembering people's faces and names. She serves as business consultant for Magee Carpet Company, Greyhound Bus Lines, and Sperry and Hutchinson Company, advising them on feminine tastes. Dr. Brothers is also an executive director of the Reading Development Center, a nationally franchised chain teaching rapid reading techniques. She is associated with the Lighthouse for the Blind, the Federation of Jewish Philanthropies and the fund-raising committee for the Olympics. Dr. Brothers received a merit award from Bar-Ilan University in Israel and she has been cited by the Federation of Jewish Women's Organizations (1964) and the Professional Women's Clubs (1968). Awards have also been conferred upon her by the Mennen Baby Foundation (1959), the Newhouse Newspapers (1959), and the American Academy of Achievement.

Despite her fragile, porcelain doll-like proportions of five feet of height and one hundred pounds of weight, Dr. Joyce Brothers works like a towering dynamo. She rejects the view that she is a "compulsive achiever" and attributes her ability to get things done to efficient organizing of time so that not a moment is wasted. In private life she is Mrs. Milton Brothers, the wife of a Park Avenue internist whom she married on July 4, 1949, and the mother of a daughter, Lisa, who now attends Princeton University. In ranking her multiple roles, she considers herself first a woman, then a mother, a wife and a psychologist. Despite her $100,000 yearly salary, she lives unostentatiously and dresses demurely in skirts, blouses, and shirtwaist dresses. She and her husband live in an unpretentious East Side apartment, attending to their separate careers and limiting their social life to family and a few close friends. She has been described as "terribly shy," and much more secure before an audience of thousands than at private parties. "She's very quiet and polite; I've never heard her raise her voice," a friend told a writer for Coronet (November, 1968). "She's a very humorous fun gal. Anybody with this kind of quick mind is very entertaining to be with."

References

Coronet 6:118 N '68 por
N Y Times p71 Ja 5 '71 por
Newsday p15 Je 22 '70 por
Who's Who in America, 1970-71
Who's Who of American Women, 1970-71

BROWN, GEORGE H(AY)

Feb. 4, 1910- United States government official; economist
Address: b. United States Bureau of the Census, Washington, D.C. 20233; h. 1103 N. Watergate East, Washington, D.C. 20037

As the United States government expands its services, statistics on population and the economy take on increasing significance. The prime responsibility for collecting and interpreting such statistical data is shouldered by George H. Brown, who became director of the United States Bureau of the Census on September 9, 1969, in time to direct the 1970 census on population and housing. An authority on marketing, he taught that subject for seventeen years at the University of Chicago. He joined the staff of the Ford Motor Company in 1954 and served as its director of market research from 1960 until his appointment as Census Bureau director by President Richard Nixon.

The United States Constitution prescribes that a population census be taken at the beginning of each decade. The main purposes of the decennial census are to allow for the allocation of the 435 seats in the House of Representatives according to population and to provide data needed by the government in developing economic and social programs. In addition, the Bureau of the Census—established as a permanent agency in 1902 and now a unit of the Department of Commerce—conducts periodic surveys and provides up-to-date information on agriculture, industry, international trade, and other aspects of the economy. It collects data for other federal agencies in such areas as public health, housing, and employment; and it cooperates with state and local authorities, private business, and foreign governments. Its many publications include the monthly Current Population Survey and the annual Statistical Abstract of the United States.

George Hay Brown was born on February 4, 1910 in Denver, Colorado, the son of Dr. Orville G. Brown, a physician with the United States Army, and Clara Amsden (Topping) Brown. He has two sisters, Dr. Emily C. Brown and Elizabeth B. McGuire. Brown grew up in Michigan and attended Western High School in Detroit, where his extracurricular activities included tennis and golf. After graduating from high school in 1925, at fifteen, he enrolled as a premedical student at Oberlin College in Ohio, which conferred a B.A. degree on him in 1929. Having in the meantime decided on a career in marketing, he then entered Harvard University to study marketing and statistics. In 1931 he obtained his M.B.A. degree.

Brown began his career in marketing in 1931 as a divisional sales manager with the Mallinckrodt Chemical Works in St. Louis, where he remained until 1936. In 1937 he joined the faculty of the University of Chicago as an instructor of marketing and began graduate studies in economics and international trade. In 1943 he took time out to serve as a consultant to the War Production Board. In 1945 he obtained his Ph.D. degree in economics at the university, and two years later he was promoted to the rank of professor. Brown also served the university as director of development for the biological, physical, and social science divisions of the School of Social Service and the School of Business from 1948 to 1950; and as director of the Business Problems Bureau from 1950 to 1954. Concurrently he was a marketing consultant to Armour & Company, the Chicago Tribune, General Mills, Inc., the Toni division of Gillette, Inc., Motorola, and other business organizations.

While at the University of Chicago, Brown undertook several projects in marketing research —a relatively new field. Much of his work focused on measuring consumer preference to determine the degree of acceptance of a product by quantitatively evaluating relative preferences for a group of items and then inferring acceptance from a random sample of the population. Reporting in 1940 on a study of the relationship between advertising and sales in department stores, he concluded that advertising was not necessarily a direct cause of increased sales volume. As sample research became more common, the problem arose of what kind of samples to use. In 1947 Brown urged that because of the high cost of obtaining truly random samples, marketing research should consider increasing the use of stratified sampling. Noting that at times "we take our research too seriously," he suggested that in some instances simple low-cost research into consumer attitudes might be enough.

In an article in the *Journal of Marketing* (July 1951) Brown noted that the teaching of marketing —originally centering on the training of marketing executives—was broadened in the 1940's to include studies of economic theory and institutions, and he suggested that scholars in the field of economics could, in turn, benefit considerably from the study of marketing techniques. In 1952 he reported on a four-year study that substantiated the prevalence of brand loyalty among consumers, particularly in non-food items. As part of his studies in international trade, Brown wrote the monograph *The International Economic Position of New Zealand* (University of Chicago Press, 1946), covering the years 1920 to 1938, with emphasis on New Zealand's adjustment to the decline in the value of exports during the Depression. He also edited *Readings on Marketing* (Holt, 1955).

Brown left the University of Chicago in 1954 to join the Ford Motor Company at Dearborn, Michigan as consumer research manager for its Ford Division. Soon he became marketing research manager, and in 1960 he was appointed director of marketing research. Under Brown's direction the Ford company pioneered research on such subjects as the sales effectiveness of advertising, price elasticity, dealer location, and market segmentation. In 1959 he conducted a study that examined the decision-making process involved when an American family buys an automobile. He reviewed all marketing research studies in Ford's worldwide operations and helped to interpret their findings to the company's management when Ford was expanding its facilities in Western Europe.

President Nixon nominated Brown in July 1969 to succeed A. Ross Eckler as director of the Bureau of the Census. Brown was confirmed by the Senate on August 8 and sworn into office by Secretary of Commerce Maurice H. Stans on September 9, 1969. Resigning his position at Ford, Brown came to Washington just in time to prepare the bureau for the mammoth job of conducting

GEORGE H. BROWN

the nineteenth decennial population and housing census, scheduled to begin April 1, 1970. The 1970 census—the largest undertaking of its kind in the world—involved the hiring of some 180,000 workers and the printing of about 150,000 pages of information and 235,000 maps. Its cost has been estimated at $200,000,000.

Census figures have taken on added importance in recent years because of the increase in state and federal aid to local areas. About $16 billion in federal aid is currently granted to local communities. An administration bill pending before Congress would provide for the distribution of all federal funds on the basis of population figures. Local officials, as well as the Census Bureau, make periodic checks on population changes, but although records are kept of births and deaths, there is no accurate way of determining how many people move into or out of areas each year, and the reliability of such indirect indicators as changes in school enrollment, car registrations, and building permits has been increasingly questioned. Furthermore, the Census Bureau had announced in 1967 that the 1960 census had undercounted the population by about 5,700,000, and that a large percentage of those missed were black inner-city residents. Outlining the procedures for 1970, Brown reported that extensive improvements had been made to eliminate the errors of 1960 and noted special efforts to enlist the cooperation of minority groups. Census Bureau officials have pointed out that in 1970 the bureau had for the first time a complete register of the addresses of all dwelling units in the country but that a new problem was posed by the great increase of nomadic young people who have left home and shift from one part of the country to another.

Early in September 1970 the Census Bureau issued the first of a number of reports scheduled to be released over a two-year period. Although the report indicated that the rate of population growth had tapered off as had been previously estimated, an anticipated slowdown in population shifts did not appear to have taken place. Black families were leaving the rural South at as high a rate as before, the central cities were still losing large numbers to the suburbs, metropolitan areas were growing rapidly, and the westward movement continued at the same pace. Of the twenty-five largest cities, twelve declined in population. On the other hand, for the first time the suburbs included more people than the cities. While the overall growth of the central cities since 1960 amounted to about 1 percent, the suburbs grew by 28 percent during that period. Another notable feature of the census was the indication that about one out of every eight Americans now lived either in Florida or in California, whereas twenty years earlier the ratio had been one out of eleven. The census figures also indicated that during the 1960's, for the first time, more people moved into the South than left it, and that its population was becoming metropolitan at twice the rate of the North. The median income of Southern families increased by 48 percent within a decade, and corresponding improvements occurred in educational levels and state expenditures. Brown has attributed the development of the "new South" to the decreasing importance of agriculture in that region and to the exodus of poor black families. In 1950, 68 percent of American Negroes lived in the South, but by 1970 only 52 percent of the country's black population lived there.

On the basis of early census reports, spokesmen for several hundred cities claimed that the census count was low, particularly in ghetto areas. The high stakes involved made some complaints inevitable. For example, in one Michigan suburb where the census showed 12,000 fewer people than had been estimated, the community stood to lose a quarter of a million dollars. At hearings of the House Subcommittee on Census and Statistics, which began on September 15, 1970, Mayor John V. Lindsay of New York City, the first of several big-city mayors to testify, maintained that one-sixth of the New Yorkers who were spot-checked had not been counted. Brown countered that reviews of the first 185 complaints indicated that the census had only missed .07 percent of the population. He expressed skepticism toward most of the complaints and suggested that the increase in such indicators of population as automobile registration was the result of the increased affluence of Americans and did not necessarily mean an increase in population. He urged that a census be conducted every five years to reduce the inevitable errors that occur between censuses.

On November 30, 1970, Brown and Commerce Secretary Stans formally presented the final census figures to President Nixon, revealing that the population of the United States had increased from 179,323,175 in 1960 to 204,765,770 as of April 1970. The proportionate growth of 13.4 percent was smaller than that of any previous decade except the 1930's, a phenomenon that Brown attributed in part to a decline in fertility rate. The figures on regional population shifts, which more or less confirmed earlier estimates, indicated that eleven Congressional seats would change in January 1973, with California gaining five Representa-

tives, Florida three, and Texas, Colorado, and Arizona one each. New York and Pennsylvania, on the other hand, are each scheduled to lose two seats, while Ohio, Alabama, Tennessee, Iowa, Wisconsin, West Virginia, and North Dakota are slated to lose one seat each. Although municipal officials and minority group spokesmen renewed charges of undercounting after the release of the final figures, Stans affirmed that the 1970 census was the most accurate ever undertaken, and that the amount of verifiable error was no more than about .05 percent.

Brown delivers about twenty-five speeches a year on topics related to the census. In a major speech entitled "1985," which he presented in New York City on October 7, 1970, he asserted that the population growth rate would continue to taper off for the foreseeable future. He predicted that in fifteen years there would be an affluent majority; that the average annual family income would rise during that period from $8,600 to $15,000, as measured in constant purchasing power; and that nearly half of the population would be suburban by 1985. He warned, however, that such problems as crime, pollution, drug abuse, and congestion of urban ghettos were likely to continue to plague the nation unless Americans made a determined effort to use their newly found affluence to combat those conditions.

A member of the American Marketing Association since 1937, Brown served as its president in 1951-52. In 1970 he became a fellow of the American Statistical Association, which he had originally joined in 1938. He was made an affiliate by invitation of the consumer division of the American Psychological Association in 1967, and he was on the board of trustees of the Marketing Science Institute from 1962 to 1969. Brown was an executive committee member of the Commerce Department's National Marketing Advisory Committee from 1965 to 1969 and a member of the research committee of the Better Business Bureau Research and Education Foundation from 1967 to 1969. In 1968-69 he was a director of the Advertising Research Foundation, and in the latter year he was treasurer of its executive committee. From 1961 to 1969 he was a trustee of the Foundation for Research on Human Behavior. He was elected to Beta Gamma Sigma, the national honorary business fraternity, in 1945, and he is also a member of Delta Sigma Pi. Other organizations with which he has been affiliated include the American Economic Association and the Econometric Society.

George H. Brown was married on June 11, 1932 to Catherine Smith, who died in May 1962. His daughter, Ann Catherine, lives in New York City. A former resident of Bloomfield Hills, Michigan, Brown now has an apartment in the nation's capital. He is five feet ten inches tall, weighs 165 pounds, and has brown hair and blue eyes. According to the New York *Times* (July 31, 1970) he remained "accommodating and unargumentative" while under hostile questioning by Congressmen. Brown considers working with numbers and statistics a labor of love. His favorite recreations are golf, swimming, travel, visiting art galleries, and listening to opera. He is a Republican and a member of the United Presbyterian Church.

References

Newsday p36 N 28 '70
Who's Who in America, 1970-71
Who's Who in American Politics, 1969-70

BUCKLEY, JAMES L(ANE)

Mar. 9, 1923- United States Senator from New York
Address: b. 452 Old Senate Office Bldg., Washington, D.C. 20510; h. "The Elms," Sharon, Conn. 06069

JAMES L. BUCKLEY

As the architect of a new pragmatic conservatism, James L. Buckley seeks to combine traditional conservative philosophy with a commonsense regard for the realities of contemporary politics. His election as United States Senator from New York State—the stronghold of liberal Republicanism—on the Conservative party ticket was one of the ironies of the 1970 national election. Campaigning on a platform that stressed traditional middle-class values, Buckley defeated his liberal Republican and Democratic opponents with a plurality of 38.7 percent of the vote and became the first candidate to win a Senate seat on a third-party ticket since Robert M. La Follette Jr. was elected as a Progressive in Wisconsin in 1940. Previously, Buckley had been serving since 1953 as vice-president and director of the Catawba Corporation, a consultant firm in oil speculation established by his father. In the Senate, Buckley has, with some notable exceptions, generally supported the policies of President Richard Nixon, and he has taken a special interest in problems concerning conservation of the natural environment.

James Lane Buckley was born in New York City on March 9, 1923, the fourth of the ten children of William Frank Buckley Sr. and Aloise (Steiner) Buckley. James Buckley's grandfather, John Buckley, the Canadian-born son of an Irish immigrant, established the family's maverick tradition as a Roman Catholic sheep rancher in the Baptist cattle country of Texas, where he became sheriff of Duval County. William F. Buckley Sr., who began his career as a lawyer in Texas, later moved to Mexico as a speculator in oil but was expelled by the revolutionary government there in the early 1920's, allegedly for aiding counterrevolutionary forces, and had to abandon over $1,000,000 worth of properties. Moving to New York, he made the family fortune some years later through oil concessions in Venezuela. At his death in 1958 he left $17,000,000 to each of his children. The Senator's mother, who came from a prominent New Orleans family, now presides over a clan of more than fifty children and grandchildren. His older brother, John, is president and manager of the Catawba Corporation; his younger brother William F. Buckley Jr. is the noted conservative philosopher, polemicist, author, and tele-

vision personality and the founder and editor of the magazine *National Review;* a third brother, F. Reid Buckley, is a writer, living in Spain. His sisters are Priscilla Buckley, the managing editor of *National Review;* Jane (Mrs. William Smith 2d); Patricia, who is married to L. Brent Bozell, the editor of the conservative Roman Catholic magazine *Triumph;* and Carol (Mrs. Ray Learsy). Two sisters, Aloise (Mrs. Benjamin W. Heath) and Maureen (Mrs. Gerald O'Reilly), are no longer living.

The Buckley children grew up on the family estate in Sharon, Connecticut. According to *Newsweek* (November 16, 1970), they were raised to be "pure American and delightfully, deliberately, incorrigibly creatures of the eighteenth century. . . . They were educated as little *philosophes,* sheltered on great estates, escorted on grand tours," and nourished on Roman Catholicism and the doctrine of individual responsibility. One member of the family was quoted in the same article as saying about Buckley *père:* "There was nothing complicated about Father's theory of child rearing. He brought up his sons and daughters with the quite simple objective that they become absolutely perfect." From early childhood, Jim Buckley's interests centered around nature and wildlife. He has said that as a boy he considered becoming an ornithologist and that he might have pursued the study of ecology if it had been an established subject when he was growing up. Once, while he was a student at the Millbrook School in upstate New York, he persuaded his father to allow his favorite biology teacher to spend a summer at Sharon and instruct all the members of the family in the natural sciences.

After graduating from the Millbrook School, Jim Buckley entered Yale University, where he majored in English literature and was tapped for the exclusive society, Skull and Bones. He wrote a column on world affairs for the *Yale Daily News,* took a conservative stance in campus politics, and was a member of Yale's debating forum, the Political Union. He also gained campus fame as the owner of a pet boa constrictor named Martha, until the university authorities "expelled" her. Having attained an officer's rank in the naval ROTC, Buckley enlisted in the United States Navy after his graduation from Yale with a B.A. degree in 1943. He went on active duty in the Pacific in 1944, and as a deck officer on an LST he took part in invasions of Leyte, Lingayen, and Okinawa, spending almost two years at sea. Shipmates recall that he was something of a "Boy Scout," using his time ashore to explore marine life rather than the local night life. After his discharge, in 1946, as a lieutenant, junior grade, he entered Yale Law School, where he obtained his LL.B. degree in 1949. During the next four years he practised law as an associate with the New Haven firm of Wiggin & Dana.

In 1953 James Buckley joined the Catawba Corporation—owned in equal shares by the surviving Buckley children—as vice-president and right-hand man to his brother John. The firm holds stock in several small oil companies in various parts of the world. Those companies buy land on speculation and, aided by Catawba geologists and lawyers, contract the drilling to larger companies. Jim Buckley's major assignment was to travel to the speculation sites and to negotiate agreements with government agencies and private companies. His travels, which occupied about one-fourth of his time and averaged some 60,000 miles a year, took him to Canada, Latin America, Asia, Africa, and Australia. During his years with Catawba, Buckley had occasion to pursue his ecological interests by joining two expeditions to the Arctic organized by Professor John J. Teal Jr. of the University of Alaska. Their purpose was to capture musk oxen and repatriate them in Alaska and Norway, to enable natives to develop a fur industry. A friend has observed that the undertaking perfectly combined Buckley's interests in conservation and free enterprise, in that "he cared about preserving the animals and he thought the Eskimos should be supporting themselves."

When in 1965 William F. Buckley Jr. decided to run for mayor of New York City as the candidate of the New York State Conservative party, which he had helped found in 1962, he enlisted his brother Jim to serve as his campaign manager. Disturbed by the liberal orientation of the New York State Republican party under the leadership of Governor Nelson A. Rockefeller and Senator Jacob K. Javits, the Buckleys were not deeply concerned with victory in the mayoralty contest but saw the race as an opportunity to publicize the conservative viewpoint and, in the long run, to influence Republican party policy. Pitted against Republican John V. Lindsay and Democrat Abraham D. Beame, Bill Buckley waged a witty and incisive campaign, concentrating his fire on Lindsay's liberal record as a Congressman. Although Lindsay won the election, Buckley was well satisfied when he received 339,137 votes, or 19 percent of the total.

In 1968 the Conservative party leadership persuaded James Buckley to make his first bid for public office and run for the United States Senate.

Less extroverted than his brother Bill, he was at first reluctant to step into the limelight, but he finally accepted the nomination as a further means of publicizing the conservative viewpoint. In his campaign, Buckley characterized his opponents—incumbent Republican Senator Javits and Democrat Paul O'Dwyer, a strong peace and civil rights advocate—as speaking "with one voice," and he termed himself "a better Republican than Javits." He hammered away at big government and federal spending, called for stronger law enforcement and, criticizing the Paris peace talks, which had recently begun, he urged a return to a full offensive position in Vietnam. Although Javits won reelection in November, Buckley received over 1,100,000 votes, or 17.3 percent of the total. On a statewide basis, the Conservatives outpolled the Liberal party, and in some areas they challenged the Democrats for second place.

Returning to the United States in March 1970 after several months abroad on a business trip, Buckley was dismayed to find the country engulfed in popular unrest and felt morally obligated to enter politics. "We had the Chicago Seven trial, all the student unrest, and the Panther trials, and when I returned . . . the whole weight of what was going on sort of crowded in on me," he recalled, as quoted in *Newsweek* (November 16, 1970). At the urging of F. Clifton White, who had organized Senator Barry Goldwater's bid for the Republican Presidential nomination in 1964, he embarked on the first serious attempt by a Conservative candidate to win a United States Senate seat. The incumbent junior Senator from New York, Charles Goodell, had been appointed in 1968 by Governor Rockefeller to fill out the unexpired term of the late Robert F. Kennedy. Originally a moderately conservative Republican, Goodell emerged as a strong liberal and a leader of the opposition to President Nixon's Vietnam policy, and fell into disfavor with the administration. As a result, Buckley, whose views corresponded more closely with the President's, was able to obtain a tacit agreement from the White House that he might try to obtain funds from Republican contributors, and he soon managed to raise $1,700,-000. Meanwhile, White assembled an effective organization from among Conservative party ranks, and by Labor Day 1970 Buckley was established as a credible candidate, capable of winning. His original plan, to launch an all-out attack on Goodell, was revised after it appeared that most of the liberal votes would go to the Democratic candidate, Congressman Richard Ottinger. Vice-President Spiro T. Agnew's attacks on Goodell, in September, greatly enhanced Buckley's chances for victory by furthering the split among the liberals, many of whom threw their support to Goodell in sympathy, while at the same time clearly establishing Buckley as the choice of the Republican establishment.

Avoiding extreme right-wing rhetoric, Buckley proclaimed himself "the voice of the new politics" and appealed to "Middle America" with his emphasis on such traditional middle-class values as patriotism, social stability, and individual initiative and his catchy campaign slogan—"Isn't it time *we* had a Senator?" He focused on the issues of crime, campus unrest, drug abuse, and pollution of the environment. Although he endorsed most of Nixon's policies, he criticized the President's welfare reform program, which, he maintained, required too prodigal an expenditure of federal funds. While referring to his two opponents as "white flag candidates," who favored "surrender" in Southeast Asia, he did not treat the Indochina war—which under Nixon's Vietnamization policy appeared to be winding down—as a major issue.

Buckley's candidacy was endorsed by the State Police Conference, the Uniformed Firefighters Association of Greater New York, and a number of Republican clubs throughout the state. Mayor John V. Lindsay's two opponents in the 1969 election—Democrat Mario Procaccino and Republican State Senator John J. Marchi—both supported Buckley. Also in Buckley's camp were several thousand young people, many of them university students, who campaigned enthusiastically on his behalf. Although Governor Rockefeller remained in Goodell's camp, his support for the Senator was lukewarm, and he concentrated mainly on his own reelection campaign.

In the election of November 3, 1970 Buckley received 2,288,190 votes, or 38.7 percent of the total, while Ottinger received 2,171,232 and Goodell came in third with 1,434,472. Election analyses indicated that Buckley had won by cutting across traditional party and class lines. While he made the best showing in upstate and suburban Republican regions, he also received strong support in urban areas, where his lack of appeal to black, Latin American, and Jewish voters was offset by the support he received from blue-collar workers, many of them Roman Catholic and of ethnic European background, who had traditionally voted Democratic. Political observers attributed Buckley's victory to his personality and to a general popular frustration. An editorial in the New York *Times* (November 5, 1970), calling Buckley "a man of intelligence and capacity," asserted that the vote for him was a protest vote against crime in the streets, mounting budgets, taxes, and welfare costs, and the deterioration of schools and municipal services.

After the election, Buckley reaffirmed his adherence to the "Nixon team" and outlined some of his proposals for legislation, including a plan under which industries would obtain tax incentives for combating pollution. He also proposed a self-help program for slum residents, asserting that "a man can call himself conservative and still care about people in the ghetto." He also advocated an all-volunteer military force and limitation of future combat duty in Vietnam to volunteers. In dealing with campus disorders, he has suggested legislation to permit students to file damage suits against those who close down universities.

Taking his place in the Senate at the opening of the Ninety-second Congress in January 1971, Buckley was at first uncertain as how to classify himself. Although he basically believed in the two-party system, he did not want to disavow the Conservative label. He therefore compromised by calling himself a Conservative-Republican. After rejecting a move by Senator Javits that his Republican credentials be examined, the GOP Senators decided on January 21, 1971 by a vote of thirty-six to three to accept him as a member of the Republican Conference. A few days later Buckley was named to the Republican Senatorial Campaign Committee, a group that had been organized to promote the election of GOP Senate candidates in 1972. Hoping to be placed on one of the committees where he could pursue what he called his number one goal, the protection of the environment, he was pleased to be named to the Public Works Committee. Buckley was also assigned to the Committee on Astronautical and Space Sciences and the Committee on the District of Columbia.

Taking what he calls a common sense approach to current problems, Buckley is less doctrinaire than some of his conservative colleagues. He considers his conservatism as a "frame of reference," rather than a "set of principles." During his first year in the Senate he generally backed the Nixon administration, with several carefully chosen and notable exceptions. He endorsed the general aim of the President's revenue-sharing plan, which would reduce restrictions on federal aid to the states, but he drew up an alternative tax-sharing plan under which each state would request that the federal government collect and give it a percentage of the taxes its residents had paid. The scheme would reserve a larger share for the big industrial states than Nixon's plan, and it would make the local governments responsible for requesting the funds they spent. In line with his fight against drug traffic Buckley introduced a bill that would cut off economic aid to any country that failed to take necessary steps to end the importation of narcotics to the United States.

Buckley has supported the Nixon administration in voting for the lowering of the voting age to eighteen and in opposing the McGovern-Hatfield amendment calling for the withdrawal of United States troops from Vietnam by the end of 1971. He was one of only three Senators to support the President in voting against the extension of the Appalachian Regional Development Commission. Although he entertained misgivings about the proposed government-financed supersonic transport plane, which, environmentalists claim, might harm the environment, he voted for the appropriation, arguing that those claims can be proven or disproven only by in-flight tests. He added that he had the President's assurance that the plane would not be put into operation if it were found to cause pollution. Angered by the courtroom tactics of attorney William Kunstler in his defense of black militants and members of the New Left, Buckley asked Congress in June 1971 to authorize the Justice Department to initiate disciplinary proceedings against lawyers guilty of "conduct prejudicial to the administration of justice" or other offenses.

On several occasions, Buckley has tried to influence the administration to take what he considers a more conservative position. In June 1971 he and Senator William Brock of Tennessee began to deliver a series of pro-defense speeches to counteract antimilitary sentiment which, he claimed, was causing the United States defense establishment to deteriorate. When Nixon requested legislation guaranteeing $250,000,000 in loans to the Lockheed Aircraft Corporation, which claimed to be on the verge of bankruptcy, Buckley voted against it, claiming that it would entail government intervention and erode free competition. In July 1971 spokesmen for the New York State Conservative party, including William F. Buckley Jr., expressed alarm over Nixon's overtures to Communist China and declared that they were suspending support of the administration. Although James Buckley, who shared the misgivings of his party colleagues, did not go along with their declaration, he warned the President that the defection of the conservatives might have "serious implications" for the 1972 elections.

James L. Buckley's wife is the former Ann Frances Cooley of Rye, New York, whose brother had been his roommate at Yale. They renewed their acquaintance while she was in Washington, D.C., working for the Central Intelligence Agency, and were married in May 1953. The Buckleys, who have five sons and one daughter, make their home near the family estate in Sharon, Connecticut, and they also maintain a residence in New York City. The Senator and his wife both enjoy sports and the theatre. Jim Buckley, who speaks French and Spanish fluently, wears his graying hair in a brushed-back crew cut and often sports a bow tie. L. Clayton Dubois describes him in the New York *Times Magazine* (August 15, 1971) as "youthful, handsome . . . , with the kind of natural warmth and good humor that Richard Nixon could only dream of." According to *Newsweek* (November 16, 1970), Buckley's speeches are "so cool and affable that even [his] enemies could never work up much venom against him."

References

Life 69:34+ D 18 '70 pors
N Y Post p55 S 18 '68 por; mag p22 N 7 '70 por
N Y Times p31 N 5 '70 por
N Y Times Mag p10+ Ag 9 '70 pors; p8+ Ag 15 '71 pors
Newsweek 76:37+ N 16 '70 pors
Americana Annual, 1971
Congressional Directory (1971)

BURROUGHS, WILLIAM S(EWARD)

Feb. 5, 1914- Author
Address: b. c/o Grove Press, 80 University Place, New York 10003

William S. Burroughs, an underground progenitor of the "beat generation," has since surfaced as a significant figure in American letters, recognized for his radical innovations in the novel form, especially his departure from linear language and narrative.

Burroughs, scion of the affluent family of adding-machine fame, was a heroin addict for some fourteen years, and out of that long period of living death he emerged with two benefits. One was a familiarity with a subculture he might otherwise never have known, what he has described as the "whole carny world" of "old-time pickpockets and sneak thieves and short-change artists." The other was a cosmic vision in which addiction to "junk" is but an analogue of a universal spiritual bondage in which the general run of men are unwittingly trapped, comparable to that in which a bodily cell is captured by and made to serve the malignant purposes of an invading virus. Burroughs isolated the "virus" that degrades humanity in his first major novel, *Naked Lunch* (1959), a surreal reconstruction, at once horrific and hilarious, of his experiences as a drug addict, and he suggested a remedy—essentially a deconditioning—in some of his later works, notably the science-fiction collage *Nova Express* (1964), in which forces hostile to the human image and spontaneous individual life become interplanetary. Norman Mailer, reviewing *Naked Lunch* in 1962, called Burroughs "the only American novelist living today who may conceivably be possessed by genius."

William Seward Burroughs is the grandson and namesake of the inventor of the adding machine, or, as Burroughs puts it more accurately, "the gimmick that made it [the adding machine] work." He was born on February 5, 1914 at 4664 Pershing Avenue in what was then the most elite section of St. Louis, Missouri, to Perry Mortimer Burroughs and Laura [Lee] Burroughs, a Southern aristocrat. Nina Suttor, after interviewing Burroughs for the *Guardian* (July 5, 1969), related his misogynism to childhood influences: "He himself admits that he has probably been prejudiced by his upbringing in what he calls a malignant matriarchial society." The British literary critic Tony Tanner has observed that "the dull respectability of his [childhood] milieu seems to have engendered a predilection for the outlaw, the deviant."

Burroughs was educated at the John Burroughs School and the Taylor School, both in St. Louis, at a prep school in Los Alamos, New Mexico, and at Harvard University, where he took a B.A. degree in English, in 1936, and did some graduate work in ethnology and archeology. From Harvard University he went to New York, where he worked as a bartender, private detective, exterminator, factory hand, newspaper reporter, and advertising copy writer. During World War II he was a glider pilot trainee with the United States Army for three months, until September 1942, when he was discharged for physical reasons.

In 1944 Burroughs became addicted to heroin. At first, he recounted in an interview with Conrad Knickerbocker for the *Paris Review* (Fall, 1965), it had an hallucinatory effect, "a sense of moving at high speed through space," but as soon as addiction was established there was nothing but a narrowing of consciousness. "The hallucinogens [such as mescaline and LSD] produce visionary states, sort of, but morphine and its derivatives decrease awareness of inner processes, thoughts, and feelings.

They are painkillers, pure and simple. They are absolutely contra-indicated for creative work, and I include in the lot alcohol, morphine, barbiturates, tranquilizers—the whole spectrum of sedative drugs."

After the war, to escape the legal difficulties inseparable from addiction in the United States, Burroughs moved to Mexico. There, at the age of thirty-five, he began writing *Junkie,* a straight narrative account of his experiences as an addict. (His only previous attempt at writing, outside of scholastic assignments, had been a short story done in 1938 in collaboration with a friend, Kells Elvins.) Under the pseudonym William Lee, *Junkie* was published by A. A. Wyn in 1953, and Ace Books later brought out a paperback edition, in 1964. Burroughs himself has assessed *Junkie* as "not much of a book," explaining that it was written when he was still an addict and that he "knew very little about writing at that time."

After accidentally shooting his wife to death while handling a revolver, Burroughs left Mexico and traveled in Colombia, Peru, and Ecuador, "just looking around." In the Amazon region of Peru he sought out, successfully, the mescaline-like drug *yage,* which was administered to him by a native medicine man. Concerning the *yage* episode he corresponded with Allen Ginsberg, and the correspondence was later published as *The Yage Letters* (City Lights, 1963). His experiences in South America generally, after lying fallow for years, were surrealized in the novel *The Soft Machine* (Olympia, 1961; Grove, 1966).

Following his travels in South America, Burroughs lived for about six years in Tangier, Morocco. There, in 1957, he decided to cure himself of narcotics addiction, partly because he realized that he was doing nothing day after day but "staring at the toe of my foot" and feared he was "dying" and partly because his interest in writing had taken precedence over that in drugs. Having heard of British physician John Yerby Dent's success with apomorphine (a nonaddicting chemical obtained by boiling morphine in hydrochloric acid), he went to London and submitted himself to Dr. Dent's treatment. According to his own account, after two brief relapses he lost all desire for heroin.

"What the apomorphine did was regulate my metabolism . . . ," Burroughs explained to Conrad Knickerbocker in the *Paris Review* interview. "I'd already taken the cure . . . [but] there was a physiological residue. Apomorphine eliminated that. . . . I don't have to use any will power. Dr. Dent always said there is no such thing as will power. You've got to reach a state of mind in which you don't want it [heroin] or need it." He told Nina Suttor of the *Guardian* that, in his opinion, efforts to introduce the apomorphine treatment into the United States have been unavailing because "all the hysteria and laws" put "the police in charge of a problem that shouldn't concern them any more than tuberculosis" and the police and narcotics agents have "vested interests in addiction."

William Burroughs Jr., then fourteen years old, lived with his father briefly in Tangier, in "a houseful of 'fags,' " as one of Burroughs Sr.'s housemates

WILLIAM S. BURROUGHS

described the ménage. In an article in *Esquire* (September 1971) the son recalled: "There was . . . an orgone box in the upstairs hall in which my father would sit for hours at a time smoking kif and then rush out and attack his typewriter without warning."

What William Burroughs Sr. was pounding out on the typewriter was *Naked Lunch* (Olympia, 1959; Grove, 1962), which created a sensation in the literary underground and then, after three years, burst controversially into the world of established letters. Mary McCarthy, Norman Mailer, and Jack Kerouac, among others, hailed it as a landmark in twentieth-century American literature, while writers such as Dame Edith Sitwell denounced it as psychopathological filth.

The meaning of the title of *Naked Lunch* is explained by Burroughs in his introduction: "a frozen moment when everyone sees what is on the end of every fork." The kaleidoscopic work is a nightmare carnival of fragmented grotesqueries, many of them obscene homosexual fantasies, such as orgastic hangings. Among its funny but sinister cartoon-like characters are the Shoe Store Kid, a drug pusher who seeks out his prey with hands of "rotten ectoplasm"; Dr. Benway, head of a Reconditioning Center devoted to "Automatic Obedience Processing" by all available chemical and surgical means, who fights off rats with one hand while performing with the other the parodic ego-altering operations by which he programs his patients; and Dr. Schafer, or the Lobotomy Kid, another mind-raping physician, who effects "the Complete All-American De-anxietized Man," one "all-purpose blob" of viscous jelly with a huge black centipede at its center. The blackest, most revolting episodes in *Naked Lunch* are those in which lower forms of life parasitize and subsume higher ones. A man is consumed by his own anus; a city becomes the inside of a sick intestinal system; and "larval entities" dot the entropic landscape, "waiting for a Live One" as "the Planet drifts to insect doom."

In his chapter on Burroughs in *City of Words* (1971), critic Tony Tanner wrote of *Naked Lunch*: "The feeding metaphor is an appropriate one, since

Burroughs is really writing about the different ways human identity is devoured in the modern world, how the self is dissolved or pre-empted by nameless forces radically antipathetic to the human image. Just what the origin of this malign enemy is Burroughs cannot immediately say. But he can produce a whole range of images to make us perceive its agencies and its modes of operation." The most conspicuous of the agencies is what Burroughs calls the Senders, the masters of the mass media taken to their logical conclusion, which in Burroughs' view is not the transmission of significant information but virus-like infiltration and control. "The Sender . . . is the human virus. . . . The broken image of man moves in minute by minute and cell by cell. . . . Poverty, hatred, war, police-criminals, bureaucracy, insanity, all symptoms of the human virus."

"In *Naked Lunch* and *The Soft Machine* I have diagnosed an illness," Burroughs stated in a BBC radio interview quoted in *Les Langues Modernes* (January-February 1965), "and in *The Ticket That Exploded* [Olympia, 1962] and *Nova Express* [Grove, 1964; Cape, 1966] is suggested a remedy." By "the soft machine" is meant the biologic device that punches into or stamps onto "fleshly identity" (the ticket to a spurious "garden of delights") the virus code that makes one the slave of an alien symbol system. In *The Ticket That Exploded* the programming device is seen as a prerecording, and one of the ways suggested for escaping its thrall is to counter-record—to tape the actual ugliness that surrounds one—and then destroy the playback. In *Nova Express* what appears to be reality is actually a motion picture, foisted on the planet's population by the "nova mob," which intends to blow up the planet. Underground rebels, together with the nova police, whom the rebels have summoned for help, get into the darkroom where the film is processed and are thus in a position to destroy footage and prevent events from happening, but the police by their habitual attitude cause the venture to fail.

Since 1960 Burroughs has been using collage techniques, "cutting up" and "folding into" his own writing quotations from other authors, newspapers, and so on in order to break set patterns, create new associations, and emulate the peripheral impressions experienced constantly by consciousness in actual life. His friend Brion Gyson, a poet and painter, who suggested the technique to him, collaborated with him on the small book *The Experimentor* (Auerhahn Press, 1960). Burroughs' other works include *Minutes to Go* (Two Cities, 1960); *Dead Fingers Talk* (Calder, 1963), which consists of excerpts from *Naked Lunch*, *The Soft Machine*, and *The Ticket That Exploded*, along with passages added to connect the excerpts; and a film script about the late American gangster Dutch Schultz. In recent years he has reportedly been working on science fiction for children and planning a Western novel. His favorites among other writers include C. S. Lewis, James Joyce, Joseph Conrad, Jean Genet, Franz Kafka, Graham Greene, Richard Hughes, and Raymond Chandler.

In keeping with his collage technique, Burroughs' daily journal has three columns, one for what he is doing, another for what he is thinking, and the third for what he is reading; he carries gigantic files of notes, clippings, and photographs wherever he travels; and scissors, paste pot, camera, tape recorders, and scrapbooks are essential tools of his craft. He constantly does what he calls "exercises in . . . time travel, in taking coordinates . . . to expand consciousness, to teach me to think in association blocks rather than words," and he puts great significance on the often apt juxtaposition of random observations and events that results. He characterized himself to Bill Butler of the *Guardian* (November 27, 1965) as "a public agent" who doesn't know for whom he works, who gets his "instructions from street signs, newspapers, and pieces of conversation" snapped "out of the air." Elsewhere he has called himself "a recording instrument."

William S. Burroughs has been married twice. His first wife was a German-Jewish refugee who was still living in New York City in the 1960's. Joan Vollmer, whom he married in January 1945 and who died in the revolver accident in Mexico, was the mother of his son. Physically, Burroughs is tall, trim, and bony, in manner he is calm and gentle, and in dress and personal habits he is immaculately neat and decorous, in contrast with the public image of him as an anarchic outlaw generated by his books. Conrad Knickerbocker described his voice as "sonorous, its tone reasonable and patient" and his accent as "mid-Atlantic." "He speaks elliptically, in short, clear bursts," and while "he did not smile during the interview and laughed only once, . . . he gives the impression of being capable of much dry laughter under other circumstances." At last report, Burroughs was still a chain smoker.

After leaving Tangier, Bill Burroughs, as his friends call him, lived for several years in Paris. According to his son, he has a "respectable working vocabulary" in French but his accent is "abominable." After years of absence, Burroughs visited the United States in 1965, and he returned in 1968 to cover the Democratic Convention in Chicago for *Esquire* magazine. He now lives in London, where he writes in solitude. In order to work, he has said, he needs to be alone for "ten to twelve hours at a stretch."

Burroughs is apolitical because he sees no escape from the "forces operating through human consciousness [to] control events" except in inner freedom. While he does not consider such hallucinogens as LSD inimical to creative work he regards them as "dangerous." As his novels manifest, he has studied Scientology but is apparently not an unqualified believer in it. He characterizes his work as "picaresque" and "satirical" and he has acknowledged as correct Mary McCarthy's judgment that it has a deep moral purpose. In the *Guardian* interview with Nina Suttor he said that he was warning of "unimaginable disasters" toward which our system is heading, and he told Conrad Knickerbocker in the *Paris Review* interview: "I do definitely mean what I say to be taken literally, yes, to make people aware of the true criminality of our times, to wise up the marks. All of my work is directed against those who are bent, through stupidity or design, on blowing up the planet or rendering it uninhabitable. . . . I'm concerned with the precise manipulation of word and image to create . . . an alteration in the reader's consciousness."

References

N Y Post mag p4 Mr 10 '63 por
Contemporary Authors vol 9-10 (1964)
Odier, Daniel. The Job; An Interview with William Burroughs (1970)
Writers at Work; The Paris Review Interviews, 3d series (1967)

CÂMARA, HELDER PESSOA

Feb. 7, 1909- Roman Catholic prelate
Address: Avenida Rui Barbosa, Recife, Estado de Pernambuco, Brazil

ARCHBISHOP HELDER PESSOA CÂMARA

In Latin America, where a privileged minority, however good its intentions, willy-nilly maintains its wealth at the expense of an oppressed majority, the Roman Catholic Church has traditionally been identified with the elite rather than the masses. Young priests in increasing numbers have been calling for an about-face on the part of their church, but relatively few members of the hierarchy have dared, or cared, to do so. The loudest of the progressive episcopal voices has been that of Dom Helder Câmara, Archbishop of Recife and Olinda in the poverty-stricken northeast corner of Brazil, a country where other voices of dissent have been effectively stifled by the military regime that took power by coup in 1964. "Dom Helder is all that remains of peaceful political opposition within Brazil," Joseph A. Page, a veteran observer of the Brazilian scene wrote in the New York *Times Magazine* (May 23, 1971). "His is the only voice to denounce the widening gulf between the rich and the poor in Northeast Brazil and the rest of the country, to fault the government for its cultivation of this status quo, to advocate radical social and economic reform as a more effective, humane, and Christian solution to Brazil's problems, and to urge that these basic changes be achieved through nonviolent means."

One of thirteen children (only four of whom lived to adulthood), Helder Pessoa Câmara was born on February 7, 1909 in the port city of Fortaleza, the capital of Ceará state in northeastern Brazil. According to Joseph A. Page in his New York *Times Magazine* article, Câmara's mother was a devout Catholic and his father was a Mason who was skeptical of organized religion. Page quoted the Archbishop: "My father taught me to see that it is possible to be good without being religious." In his youth Câmara contracted tuberculosis, from which he has never completely recovered.

In 1923 Câmara entered the seminary, where his most memorable experience was the visit of one Father Cicero, a controversial, fiercely ascetic old priest opposed by the ecclesiastical establishment but venerated by the peasants of northeastern Brazil as a saint and miracle-worker. "He was very intelligent and knew well the psychology of the poor," Dom Helder has reminisced. "He was upset because the Catholic newspapers were attacking him and gave him no chance to reply. But he said that in the heart of a Christian there is no room for hate and that we must work to demonstrate it is impossible to have hatred in the heart of a priest. I have always remembered this."

After his ordination, in 1931, Camara was stationed in his native city for five years. At that time he was an active partisan of the Integralists, or "Green Shirts," the Brazilian fascist party, because he was then "under the impression that the world was going to divide itself into two parts labeled 'communist' and 'anticommunist.'" The humiliation he feels in looking back at that period in his life is, in his view, a blessing in disguise, because it "makes it easier for me to understand the weaknesses of others."

In 1936 Câmara was transferred to Rio de Janeiro, where he underwent a transformation that he later described in an article for the *Christian Century* (December 10, 1969): "I began little by little to recognize the fallaciousness of the communism-anticommunism dichotomy, to see that such things as 'capitalism' and 'socialism' do not exist in the singular. All around me . . . I see millions of people who are ill and underfed, who live in miserable shacks and have no opportunity to improve their lot. They suffer the consequences of an extremism—a massive, hysterical anticommunism. . . . Any new idea or any suggestion aimed at improving the condition of the poor is instantly and efficiently labeled 'communism'. . . . To me the evidence indicates that the most threatening clash of our time is not that between East and West but rather that between the developed and underdeveloped countries."

In 1952 Dom Helder was consecrated a bishop and named auxiliary bishop of Rio de Janeiro, and two years later he was elevated to auxiliary archbishop. Soon after joining the episcopacy he founded the Brazilian National Conference of Bishops, with the permission of Vatican Secretary of State Giovanni Battista Montini, now Pope Paul VI, who has remained his friend and protector ever since. Dom Helder presided over the conference for eleven years, and during that time he also helped to found the Council of Bishops of Latin America.

In Rio de Janeiro, Dom Helder spent much of his time visiting the *favelas,* the shanty-town slums built on the slopes of the city, eating in working-class restaurants, and frequenting other places where prelates were rarely seen. Among other projects, he organized the São Sebastião Crusade which, with capital borrowed by him from concerned wealthy citizens, built a block of cooperative apartments for 250 *favela* families. His work for the poor and his lively sermons on television at that time made him a popular figure, lionized by the press. President Juscelino Kubitscek offered him the mayoralty of Rio de Janeiro and Jânio Quadros asked him to be his running-mate in a presidential election, but Dom Helder rejected both offers.

During the first session of Vatican Council II, in 1962, Dom Helder prepared a sermon criticizing the council for not dealing with urgent social issues, but Archbishop Pericle Felici, secretary general of the council and a member of the Curia, censored the sermon and ordered destroyed the translations that had been prepared for distribution to reporters. On the eve of the opening of the second session, in 1963, Dom Helder issued an open letter to his "brothers in the episcopate" in which he urged them to abdicate honorifics, luxuries, and privileges that create distance between them and working-class Catholics and obstruct reunion with "our separated brethren." He suggested, for example, that they renounce the following: such titles as "excellency" and "eminence"; silver-buckled shoes, rings with precious stones, gold and silver pectoral crosses, and other "expensive" or "ridiculous" items of decoration or attire; and symbols of wealth that "scandalize and revolt," such as limousines. He also proposed that they encourage church architects henceforth to design simple instead of "grandiose" structures. "Let us end once and for all the impression of a bishop-prince, residing in a palace, . . . more feared than loved, . . . served rather than serving."

Running on separate tickets in October 1960, Jânio Quadros and João Goulart were elected, respectively, president and vice-president of Brazil. When Quadros resigned in August 1961, the legislature was reluctant to confirm Goulart's succession to the presidency, because of his leftist sympathies. It compromised by severely limiting presidential powers before permitting his inauguration, in September 1961. Full presidential powers were restored in January 1963, but as soon as Goulart began to use them to effect radical economic reforms, such as nationalization of oil refineries and redistribution of land, the military overthrew him, on March 31 and April 1, 1964.

That same spring Pope Paul VI named Câmara archbishop of Olinda and Recife, an archdiocese encompassing the drought-ridden state of Pernambuco, where Brazil's root problems are most severe. Writing of the country as a whole in the *Wall Street Journal* (January 23, 1970), Bowen North-

rup described those problems as follows: "One bishop points out that 3 percent [other estimates range up to 12 percent] of the people in Brazil own 62 percent of the land. . . . Great numbers of peasants in the interior live in semi-feudal bondage to landowners. Millions of Brazilians live entirely outside the money economy, and the per capita income isn't more than $350 a year. The educational system caters to the elite. Literacy is about 50 percent."

Humberto Castello Branco, the first president set up by the military regime, was relatively sympathetic to Dom Helder and did his best to keep the army from obstructing his archdiocesan social and economic programs. The latter included a literacy program, a peasant-worker self-help program based in local councils, and Action, Justice, and Peace, a crusade that enlisted middle-class liberal Catholics in bringing moral pressure to bear on factory owners paying less than subsistence wages. But in 1968 the regime became more repressive. Castello Branco was replaced by Artur da Costa Silva; the Fifth Institutional Act was passed, virtually abolishing civil liberties; and a wave of political arrests effectively silenced overt reform movements. In October 1968 right-wing terrorists machine-gunned Dom Helder's episcopal residence, and during the months following student leaders and other prominent progressives in Recife were subjected to similar acts of terrorism. One student leader was wounded, and in May 1969 a close associate of Dom Helder's, Rev. Antonio Henrique Pereira da Silva, chaplain to the students at the University of Recife, was found murdered.

There were also reports that political prisoners, including Catholic priests and lay leaders, were being tortured. In December 1969, two months after he took office, General Emilio G. Medici, the present president of Brazil, ordered an end to any and all use of torture, but early in 1970 sixty-one leading European Roman Catholic clergymen submitted to the Vatican "Black Book: Terror and Torture in Brazil," a report documenting the torture of thousands of prisoners. At about the same time Dom Helder himself reported to Pope Paul on the same subject, and on May 26, 1970 he gave a speech denouncing political torture in Brazil before an overflow crowd, including members of the French hierarchy, in the Palais des Sports in Paris.

After Dom Helder returned home he was the target of a vituperative campaign in the government-toadying Brazilian press, which accused him of being a slandering, treacherous "Red Bishop," and the government's repression of political dissent was stepped up. Among other priests, Rev. Antonio de Magalhaes Monteiro was arrested for subversion and, allegedly, tortured. Even usually silent segments of the hierarchy protested to the government, and the latter, backing away from the church-state confrontation, took steps to restrain the more zealous of its extreme right-wing army officers and police.

Dom Helder's influence within Brazil has been limited by the government's barring of his voice and message from newspapers, television, and radio (except for a Sunday sermon weekly over local Radio Olinda). Aside from that ban, the government has not touched him, for several reasons. First, he is popular with the people of his archdiocese. Second, he has the friendship and confidence of Pope Paul. (Despite that relationship, conservative elements in the Vatican and in the Brazilian hierarchy have been able to effect a Papal restraint on his public statements, and close observers saw the same forces at work when Pope Paul surprised prognosticators by passing over Dom Helder in naming two Brazilians to the College of Cardinals in March 1969. The Cardinals named by the Pope were Alfredo Scherer and Eugenio Sales, both conservatives, as are all three of the previously named living Brazilian Cardinals.)

According to Bowen Northrup's report in the *Wall Street Journal*, 500 to 1,000 of Brazil's 13,000 priests are progressives, and a Vatican spokesman was quoted in *Time* (February 9, 1970) as saying that some of them were further to the revolutionary left than Soviet Communists. The writer of the *Time* article commented: "Some bishops are heeding the growing number of rebel priests who insist that Catholicism can transform society —and save its own soul—only by embracing revolution, even a Marxist variety." A Vatican survey cited in the article found that among Brazil's 245 bishops, only fifteen supported the military regime, but, on the other hand, Bowen Northrup knew of only six bishops who might be classified as "liberal." However, the number has been increasing, if for no reason other than the fact that the church's ties to the oligarchy are weakening the strength of both its constituency and its leadership. Nominally, Brazil has the largest Roman Catholic population in the world—90 percent of the 90,000,000 inhabitants—but only 10 to 15 percent actually practise their faith and that percentage is steadily diminishing. Seminary enrollment is dropping and the rate of defections from the priesthood is higher than in any other country in the world. Protestant denominations of the fundamentalist and revivalist variety have been growing, and there is a resurgence of pre-Christian Afro-Brazilian and spiritualist cults, including voodoo and animism.

For three centuries, Dom Helder points out, the church has "accepted the ethic of slavery" and "acquiesced in the social order—really the social disorder—that keeps millions of human creatures living in subhuman conditions." If the church does not now "join the battle for development and social justice," people will later say that it "deserted them in their hour of need" and "if that happens, the church will suffer the consequences."

By the standards of Latin America's militant radicals, Dom Helder is a moderate. True, he respects the memory of revolutionary heroes like Camilo Torres and Che Guevara "as much . . . as that of Martin Luther King" and he considers their guerrilla tactics to be "secondary violence." The "primary violence" is in the conditions that make armed rebellion necessary. But he does not consider violence to be an option open to him personally. He wants an end to "internal colonialism,"

and he believes that the social and economic reforms necessary to that end, such as land redistribution, peasant education, and free trade unions, could be achieved peacefully within the present political structure—if that structure could be freed of "external colonialism" (represented chiefly by the United States' Pentagon and by foreign business interests). As a model for effective dialogue between social and economic reformers and a military regime he points to Peru, where nationalization of certain industries and other socialistic measures are liberating peasants and workers from colonialistic oppression. The kind of socialization he envisions is inspired by encyclicals of the popes rather than by Marxist examples. "I have a pattern of development in my heart for Latin America," he has said. "It is not capitalistic but it is not any of the present socialistic systems."

Ecclesiastically he is no radical either. Although generally open to changes that will make the church more relevant to the problems of humanity today, especially in underdeveloped countries, he is cautious in approaching issues that might be divisive. He has been careful not to contradict Pope Paul on the issue of birth control, for example, and regarding a married clergy he has said: "I would like to see the celibacy rule relaxed, but it is not the number one problem of the church at the moment."

Two books of essays and addresses by Dom Helder have been translated into English: *Revolution Through Peace* (Harper, 1971) and *The Church and Colonialism* (Dimension Books, 1969). Reviewing the latter in the *Christian Century* (November 5, 1969), Richard Shaull described the author as one of those "few men who, out of their anguish in the midst of great human suffering and injustice, are becoming the Christian conscience of the modern world." In 1970 Dom Helder was nominated for the Nobel Peace Prize and was awarded the Martin Luther King Prize. He feels that his cause in Brazil has much in common with the nonviolent civil rights struggle initiated by the late Dr. King in the United States. In March 1970 he and Ralph Abernathy, King's successor as head of the Southern Christian Leadership Conference, issued a joint declaration of their solidarity.

Helder Pessoa Câmara is a frail, diminutive man, five feet four inches tall and weighing 120 pounds, with glowing eyes, delicate hands, an energetic manner, and an animated pulpit style. Practising what he preaches to his episcopal colleagues, Dom Helder prefers to be called "Padre," like an ordinary priest, and he leads a simple life, free of ostentation. Using his episcopal palace only as an office, he lives in a Spartanly furnished room a short distance away. He lives alone, without housekeeper or secretary, answering his own phone, which has often disturbed his sleep with threats on his life or crank calls. Joseph A. Page in his New York *Times Magazine* article ascribed to the Archbishop "the charm of a precocious child," and a reporter for the *Guardian* (April 9, 1969) described him thus: "There are many Catholic prelates of the avant-garde . . . who preach fundamental change in their church and in society but who, individually, hold themselves in; the caste mark of the seminary and the breeding grounds of obedience. Câmara is not among them. The elfin face is constantly acrease with wide-eyed mirth. He lays his hand on your arm to make a point and jabs you in the ribs to put it good and strong. 'My vocation,' he says with a great and fierce grimace, 'my vocation is to argue, argue, argue for moral pressure upon the lords.' And he rolls up his sleeve to show how vigorously the argument must go." But Joseph A. Page, who saw Dom Helder more recently, found him showing "unmistakable signs of weariness," among which were "his blue-gray eyes sunken in their sockets." Page quoted a former Brazilian dock union official's assessment of the Archbishop: "Perhaps a little bit of a demagogue, but nevertheless a fabulous man."

References

Le Monde Weekly Selection in English p4 S 30 '70
N Y Herald Tribune p2 S 8 '63 por
N Y Times p6 O 28 '70 por
N Y Times Mag p26+ My 23 '71 por
International Who's Who, 1970-71

CARINGTON, PETER ALEXANDER RUPERT, 6th BARON CARRINGTON *See* **CARRINGTON, 6th BARON**

CARRINGTON, 6th BARON

June 6, 1919- British Secretary of State for Defence
Address: b. Ministry of Defence, Main Bldg., Whitehall, London, S.W. 1, England; h. 32A Ovington Sq., London, S.W. 3, England; "The Manor House," Bledlow, near Aylesbury, Buckinghamshire, England

As Secretary of State for Defence of Great Britain, Lord Carrington faces the difficult assignment of curtailing excessive defense expenditures in a limited economy at the same time that he tries to maintain his nation's status as a world power. For more than twenty-five years, Peter Alexander Rupert Carington, the sixth Baron Carrington, has played an increasingly important role in the Conservative party, serving as first lord of the admiralty, ambassador to Australia, and party leader and opposition leader in the House of Lords. By attempting to broaden England's international responsibilities, he has gained the support of Prime Minister Edward Heath and the Conservative party. He has worked tirelessly for political and military cooperation with the European community of nations and has advanced the view that Great Britain must guarantee the protection of former dependencies. Although the once mighty British Empire has been fragmented, Lord Carrington believes that England's continuing pres-

ence in the world arena assures international peace and prevents threatening powers from creating new spheres of influence.

Peter Alexander Rupert Carington was born on the family estate in Buckinghamshire on June 6, 1919, the only son of the fifth Baron Carrington (the title is spelled with two R's) and the Honorable Sibyl Marion, a noblewoman and the daughter of the second Viscount Colville. Carington's ancestors were drapers or textile merchants and the family is descended from the mercantile class that was the bulwark of the expanding British economy in recent centuries. As his ancestors prospered, they became provincial bankers and elected members of Parliament. King George III named the first Baron Carrington in Ireland in 1796, and the title was created in Great Britain the following year. For several generations the family has maintained a manor house and land holdings in Bledlow, near Aylesbury in Buckinghamshire, where each baron has taken part in the local government councils in the tradition of British nobility. Lord Carrington's great-uncle, the Marquess of Lincolnshire, was appointed by Queen Victoria to serve as governor of New South Wales in Australia from 1885-1890.

Lord Carrington was raised on the family estate near Aylesbury and educated at Eton, the fashionable preparatory school for boys. He grew up during the tenebrous and uncertain period between the two World Wars, when Europe was undergoing social and political turmoil. On the death of his father in 1938, Peter Carington succeeded to the title of sixth Baron with its accompanying privileges, including a seat in the House of Lords. When he was nineteen he began officers' training at the Royal Military College at Sandhurst, England's West Point. Commissioned in the Grenadier Guards, during World War II he advanced to the rank of major. Serving in many military campaigns, in 1944 Lord Carrington was recognized for conspicuous heroism for single-handedly holding the bridge at Nijmegen in the Netherlands against the Germans and preventing them from cutting off a British unit on the opposite side of the river.

When Lord Carrington left military service in 1946, he returned to his estate full of ideas for improving its agricultural yield and raising his farm revenues. Not content to be merely a gentleman farmer, he introduced mechanized equipment and cross-breeding techniques for Hereford cattle. Lord Carrington became a member of the Buckinghamshire County Council and deputy chairman of the agricultural executive committee of the county. When, in 1946, he took his hereditary seat in the House of Lords, he naturally made agricultural affairs his special interest; and when Sir Winston Churchill's Conservative government was returned to power in 1951, he was appointed joint parliamentary secretary to the Ministry of Agriculture and Fisheries. Just thirty-two years old, Lord Carrington was one of the youngest men in the Churchill government, which faced the formidable task of stabilizing the balance of payments by making England agriculturally self-sufficient. Lord Carrington provided constructive leadership in his post. He headed the British delegation to the 1951 international conference of the Food and Agricultural Organization, served as a member of the working party on agricultural education established in 1952 by the Ministry of Agriculture and Fisheries, and chaired the Hill farming and advisory committee for England, Wales and Northern Ireland.

Shortly after Lord Carrington was appointed parliamentary secretary to the Ministry of Defence in October 1954, he became embroiled in a heated controversy over naval preparedness. Critical of Britain's inadequate and antiquated fleet, the nation's leading naval authorities called for new construction to replace the battleships, cruisers, and carriers they deemed unseaworthy. As the government spokesman, Lord Carrington justified the change of emphasis in the defense program away from traditional shipbuilding to the development of guided weapons. In the fall of 1956 Lord Carrington was sent to Australia as British High Commissioner, a post similar to that of ambassador to the Commonwealth nations. During his three-year tenure in Australia he earned a reputation as a skillful administrator and a popular and "unstuffy" representative of the mother country.

While on his way back from Australia to Great Britain in October 1959, Lord Carrington was created a Privy Councillor and offered the post of First Lord of the Admiralty. Many great leaders, including Sir Winston Churchill, had served in that high-ranking post, which was considered a stepping stone to even more distinguished appointments. When Prime Minister Harold Macmillan selected the forty-year-old Carington, he intended to revitalize some of the hidebound ministries by staffing them with younger men with a new approach. As titular head of the British Navy, Carington made his first objective the boosting of morale and the implanting of a spirit of confident optimism. He was given extensive powers to make policy decisions affecting the future development of the navy, which he insisted could not "afford to be second-rate." Committed to maintaining England's position as a great naval power, Carington endorsed a program for a more modern, though necessarily smaller, navy. He advocated using new ships "with their life in front of them," instead of maintaining a larger force with cumbersome and outdated vessels. "We believe that the value of sea power is as great and, if anything, greater than it was," Carington said.

In his official post as First Lord of the Admiralty, Lord Carrington made an inspection tour of Australia, New Zealand, and Singapore. During his term in office the first British nuclear submarine, the *Dreadnaught,* was launched and the keel of a second sub was laid. The navy gained cruisers, conventional submarines, frigates (to act as escort ships) and guided missile destroyers designed to fight aircraft as well as surface targets. Carington approved plans to arm helicopters with antisubmarine torpedoes and to construct an unusual landing-craft assault ship that would advance the development of amphibious warfare.

LORD CARRINGTON

The influential British newspaper the *Guardian* (February 17, 1961) criticized Lord Carrington for giving priority to surface shipping at a time when both the Soviet Union and the United States were concentrating on submarine power, but Carington insisted that he had based his decision on a close analysis of the military thrust and potential of the British Navy. He believed that British naval power depended on the expansion of amphibious task forces to transport commando units to trouble spots and sustain them while on shore.

In 1963 Lord Carrington became Conservative party leader in the House of Lords, having served as the assistant deputy leader during the previous year, and he simultaneously held an appointment as one of the two ministers without portfolio in the Conservative Cabinet of Prime Minister Alec Douglas-Home. Although he was not responsible for the operations of a particular ministry, Lord Carrington handled diverse assignments connected with the Foreign Office. He represented Great Britain at international conferences and acted as liaison official between the government and the House of Lords on issues related to the Commonwealth nations.

At a meeting of the Western European Unity in December 1963 Lord Carrington advocated continued economic ties between Great Britain and the Common Market countries and indicated his government's interest in taking part in future negotiations involving European political union. When the issue of arms exports to South Africa set off impassioned political debate in the House of Lords, Carington refused to consider the shipment of "arms or equipment for arms manufacture which would enable the policy of apartheid to be enforced," despite losses to British industry. The Minister also handled Anglo-American talks concerning the integrity of the Malaysian Federation, and in January 1964 he announced that England would guarantee the independence of Malaysia and prevent Indonesia from taking further aggressive action against it.

In 1964 the general elections brought the Labour government of Harold Wilson into power, thrusting the Conservatives into the ranks of the loyal opposition. While the Labourites held office, Lord Carrington was opposition leader in the House of Lords and an adviser in the consultative committee or "Shadow Cabinet" formed by Edward Heath, Conservative party leader in the House of Commons. That inner circle formulated Conservative policy and decided how party members should vote on Labourite legislation. Having made one of his major campaign promises the evaluation and reform of the House of Lords, Wilson established an interparty committee to develop a new set of criteria to alter the composition and powers of the peerage, including an attempt to abolish hereditary rights in favor of an elected body and to curb the Lords' constitutional, though rarely used, power to interfere with the passage of legislation. Faced with those threats to reduce the House of Lords to political impotence, Lord Carrington and his Conservative majority decided to use their decisive veto power to oppose a Labour bill giving the United Nations the right to implement harsher sanctions against Rhodesia. He believed that the delaying tactic could probably be used only once until the elected members of the House of Commons restricted the privilege.

In a tense atmosphere the House of Lords voted 193-184 to reject the Labour government's order, indicating their fear that Great Britain was gradually relinquishing her traditional rights in Rhodesia. Denouncing the Lords' defiance as a "squalid political maneuver," Wilson accused the Conservatives of working only for their party. But Lord Carrington insisted that the peers had "done nothing unconstitutional, nor put the country in default of its international obligations."

Despite his combative leadership in the Rhodesian affair, Lord Carrington has a reputation as a moderate Tory who can steer a middle-of-the-road course and restrain some of the more vehement members of his party. His statesmanship made him Edward Heath's trusted friend and adviser, and when the Conservatives won a majority in the June 1970 elections, Prime Minister Heath appointed Lord Carrington Secretary of State for Defence.

Soon after taking office he proposed to deliver more defense for less money, since Britain's budget was $6.1 billion or 5½ percent of the gross national product as compared with America's 8 percent. Although he soon advanced a plan for stronger ties with the European community of nations and for a British-French nuclear agreement, Lord Carrington wanted to direct British policy away from the Labour government's emphasis on Europe alone and focus more on England's global commitments. According to the defence minister, it was "illogical and unrealistic" to restrict Great Britain's defenses to the Continent while the Soviet Union remained a world threat. In light of what they saw as that danger, the Conservatives reversed former Labour policy by advocating a military assistance pact with New Zealand, Australia, Singapore and Malaysia, under which joint defense effort Great Britain guaranteed those countries "modest" aid in manpower and naval and air supplies. When they met in London in April 1971 the members of the pact agreed to accept Lord Carrington's flexible proposals that permitted the nations to consult each other as equal partners without becoming entangled by political and military treaties.

When Rolls-Royce, Ltd., declared itself bankrupt early in February 1971, the British government took over ownership and Lord Carrington was put in charge of negotiations. The firm defaulted before it could complete the Rolls-Royce RB-211 engine for the Lockheed TriStar airbus, and Lockheed interests feared that Rolls-Royce had given false assurances and had failed to act equitably. In a London radio interview on February 28, 1971 Lord Carrington hinted plainly that a large American cash outlay would be necessary to continue production. Economists on both sides of the Atlantic feared that the crisis could bring disastrous consequences for both Great Britain and the United States, since the economies are so tightly entwined. The Lockheed Company, the largest defense contractor in America, seemed headed for bankruptcy, while British employment figures were slated to decline by 20,000 to 40,000. As a compromise, Lord Carrington proposed in the spring of 1971 that his government assume research and development costs while the United States pay an additional $230,000,000 for the engines, but as of late summer no agreement between the two nations had been reached.

Since 1942 Lord Carrington has been married to the former Iona McClean, the youngest daughter of Sir Francis McClean, a pioneer in British aviation. They have one son and two daughters. His colleagues in the House of Lords have said that Lord Carrington's Latin family motto, *Tenax in Fide* (Persevering and Faithful) might serve as an apt capsule description of his own character. For all his briskness of manner, Lord Carrington is a modest man, who would rather talk about Australia or farming problems, his favorite conversational gambits, than his own achievements. He lists no recreations in *Who's Who, 1970-71*. Every year Lord Carrington visits Australia as chairman of the Australian and New Zealand Bank, and he is a director of both the Hambros and Barclays banks, the British Metal Corporation, and Schweppes, Ltd. The defence minister is a Knight Commander of the Order of St. Michael and a Fellow of Eton College. His London clubs are the Turf, the Beefsteak, and Pratt's.

References

    Guardian p10 O 16 '59 por
    London Observer p2 Je 21 '70
    N Y Times p2 Je 21 '68 por; p27 Je 21 '70
    Newsweek 75:33 Je 29 '70 por
    Burke's Peerage, Baronetage & Knightage,
      1963
    International Who's Who, 1970-71
    International Year Book and Statesmen's
      Who's Who, 1970
    Who's Who, 1970-71
    Who's Who in Finance and Industry, 1972-
      73

CARTER, JAMES EARL, JR. *See* Carter, Jimmy

CARTER, JIMMY

Oct. 1, 1924- Governor of Georgia
Address: b. Governor's Mansion, Atlanta, Ga.
30303; h. Plains, Ga. 31780

Hailed as the harbinger of a new political and social era in the South, Jimmy Carter became the seventy-sixth Governor of Georgia on January 12, 1971, when he succeeded Lester G. Maddox for a four-year term. A farmer, businessman, and former member of the Georgia State Senate, Carter is one of a new generation of progressive governors of Southern states who have rejected the doctrine of white supremacy that had traditionally dominated the South and are committed to social and economic progress. Making his second bid for the governorship, Carter defeated former Governor Carl Sanders in the 1970 Democratic primary after a campaign in which he sometimes reverted to an old-style populist appeal, and he then went on to win an easy victory over his Republican opponent, Hal Suit, in the November election. Carter gained wide publicity when in his inaugural address he proclaimed an end to racial discrimination, a statement that marked a radical departure from the traditional oratory of Southern politicians.

An eighth-generation Georgian, whose ancestors —including cotton farmers, merchants, and Civil War soldiers—have lived in the southwestern region of the state for about 150 years, James Earl Carter Jr. was born in the small town of Plains, in Sumter County, on October 1, 1924, the son of James Earl Carter Sr. and the former Lillian Gordy. He has a brother, William A. Carter 3d, and two sisters, Gloria C. Spann and Ruth C. Stapleton. His father, the manager of a grocery store and owner of the town's icehouse and dry-cleaning establishment, later acquired land outside of Plains and set up a business selling farm supplies and buying peanuts from local farmers for resale to processors. At the time of his death in 1953 he had been a representative in Georgia's state legislature. Carter's mother, who had long been active in social causes in her home state, joined the Peace Corps in 1967 and served for two years in India on birth-control information projects.

Growing up in a rural atmosphere, Jimmy Carter attended Plains High School, where he played basketball. After graduating in 1941 he studied at Georgia Southwestern College in nearby Americus for a year. He then spent one year at the Georgia Institute of Technology in Atlanta, where he studied mathematics to qualify for admission to the United States Naval Academy at Annapolis, to which he had won an appointment. Carter entered the academy in 1943, and after completing an accelerated wartime program he graduated in 1946 with distinction and obtained a commission. During his seven years in the United States Navy he served two years on battleships and five years on submarines and attained the rank of lieutenant

JIMMY CARTER

commander. In 1951 he began to work with Admiral Hyman G. Rickover on the nuclear submarine program under the auspices of the Atomic Energy Commission. He took postgraduate night courses in nuclear physics at Union College in Schenectady, New York and became a senior officer in the precommissioning crew of the *Seawolf*—one of the first submarines to operate on atomic power.

His father's death in 1953 prompted Carter to resign from the Navy and return to Georgia to manage the family interests, including Carter Warehouses—which grossed an estimated $800,000 a year by early 1971—and some 2,500 acres of farmland in Sumter and Webster counties. He has been considerably successful as a peanut farmer. Carter's civic activities in his home town have been many and varied. From 1955 to 1962 he was chairman of the Sumter County board of education, and he also served as chairman of the county hospital authority. In 1963 he became president of the Plains Development Corporation and the Sumter Redevelopment Corporation, and in 1964 he helped organize and became the first chairman of the West Central Georgia Planning and Development Commission. He was president of the Georgia Planning Association and of the Georgia Crop Improvement Association in 1968-69. Carter has also been a state chairman of the March of Dimes and a district governor of Lions International.

Jimmy Carter made his first bid for elective office in 1962, when he became a candidate for the Georgia State Senate. Although the original election returns seemed to indicate that his opponent had won by a narrow margin, Carter suspected foul play at the ballot box and filed suit to challenge the result. According to *Time* (May 31, 1971), "Carter had been beaten by voters who were dead, jailed, or never at the polls on Election Day. The election was reversed in his favor." He was elected to a second term two years later. During his four years in the State Senate he maintained a moderately liberal voting record, and he was designated by a poll as one of its most effective members. Taking a special interest in education, Carter served on the educational matters committee and on its higher education subcommittee, which is responsible for operation of the state's university system, and he sponsored several education bills. He also served on the highways, agriculture, and appropriations committees.

During the civil rights demonstrations in Americus in the summer of 1965 the Plains Baptist Church, of which Carter was a deacon, was faced with a vote on whether to exclude Negroes from the congregation. Carter's impassioned speech against exclusion caused some members of his church to try to organize a boycott of his business, but it also won him considerable publicity as a liberal on the issue of race relations. Although still relatively unknown, Carter decided to become a candidate in the Democratic gubernatorial primary of September 1966 and came in an impressive third in the six-man race. After restaurant owner Lester G. Maddox, a rabid segregationist, won the Democratic nomination in a runoff contest with former Governor Ellis Arnall, some liberals organized a write-in campaign to provide an alternative in the November elections to Maddox and his opponent, Representative Howard H. Callaway, a Goldwater Republican. Although Carter enjoyed considerable support, the liberals chose Arnall as the write-in candidate. (Because of the write-in votes for Arnall, neither Maddox nor Callaway received a majority in the November election. The choice of a governor was therefore left up to the State General Assembly, which elected Maddox on January 10, 1967.)

After his defeat in the 1966 primary race, Carter returned to his business and civic activities. At the same time he made serious—but unannounced —preparations for the 1970 gubernatorial campaign. In the four years between elections Carter made some 1,800 speeches throughout the state, building an effective political organization and gaining wide publicity, especially at the important grassroots level.

For the 1970 primary campaign Carter adopted a populist, down-to-earth approach, promoting himself as a "simple country boy" in contrast to the aloof and sophisticated manner of his principal opponent, Carl E. Sanders, a liberal, who had served as Governor of Georgia from 1963 to 1967. To win votes away from Sanders—whom he sometimes called "Cufflinks Carl"—Carter tried to appeal to popular sentiments in the conservative rural areas and among urban blue-collar workers by criticizing the practice of busing public school pupils to attain a racial balance, defending private schools, and inviting Alabama's segregationist Governor George C. Wallace to visit Georgia. While avoiding the sulphurous rhetoric that has often characterized Southern political campaigns, he attacked the "Establishment power brokers" and "big-money boys" and implied—without concrete evidence—that Sanders had used the governorship to line his own pockets, that he practised favoritism, and that he had allowed the state Democratic party organization to deteriorate. Carter's campaign tactics were viewed as opportunism by some observers and as evidence of his shrewdness by others.

Endorsed by the state's political and business leaders and backed by most of the larger newspapers, Sanders began the campaign as the definite favorite and did little to meet Carter's challenge. But Carter apparently benefited from the prevailing "anti-Establishment" and "anti-politician" sentiments among the voters, and his popularity grew steadily. In the primary election of September 8, 1970 Carter obtained a plurality among the nine Democratic gubernatorial candidates, with 48.6 percent of the vote, while Sanders, his nearest opponent, polled 37.7 percent. In third place, with 8.8 percent of the vote, was the attorney C. B. King, the state's first black candidate for governor since Reconstruction. In the two-week runoff campaign between Carter and Sanders, the latter bowed to pressure to reveal his net financial resources, which, he claimed, amounted to about $700,000. Carter had previously issued his financial statement, indicating net assets of some $400,-000. In the runoff election of September 23 Carter won with nearly 60 percent of the votes cast.

Carter's Republican opponent in the general election of November 3, 1970 was Hal Suit, a television newscaster and a friend of Georgia's Democratic Senator Richard B. Russell. To broaden his base for the November election, Carter solicited support not only from the state's established white political bosses but also from the black leaders of the Southern Christian Leadership Conference. In the primary runoff contest Carter had received less than 10 percent of the state's Negro vote, but in the general election it appeared that the black voters remained overwhelmingly with the Democratic party. Although President Richard Nixon campaigned for Suit, Carter's victory in November was decisive. He won 620,419 votes, or 59.3 percent, against 424,983 votes received by Suit.

In view of his conservative campaign, superimposed upon a long-standing reputation as a moderate liberal, Carter emerged from the election as something of an enigma. His inaugural address, on January 12, 1971, did much to dispel doubts as to his orientation, at least on the race issue. "I say to you quite frankly that the time for racial discrimination is over," he declared. "No poor, rural, weak, or black person should ever have to bear the additional burden of being deprived of the opportunity of an education, a job, or simple justice."

Press commentary after Carter's inauguration gave due credit to his iconoclasm in taking a stand against racial discrimination, but there was also a tendency to view the Governor's statements in the context of a changing South, rather than as a manifestation of individual idealism. Tom Wicker commented in the New York Times (January 14, 1971) that after decades of resistance to desegregation the South was left with an "exhausted compliance with the law of the land. Hence it became politically safe for a moderate like Mr. Carter to speak out." Carter later told Wicker, as quoted in the Times (April 25, 1971), that he viewed himself as a product of a "particular time and mood in the South," rather than as a creator of a movement. State Senator Leroy Johnson, a leader of the black community of Atlanta, has said: "Carter represents all the people of Georgia, and he is being effective in delivering. I think he is going to be the most effective Governor this state ever had."

The priorities of the Carter administration include reforms in education, a conservative but productive fiscal policy, and coordinated planning. Carter has managed to maintain a reasonably good relationship with the state legislature, a traditional problem of governors. He was able to secure adoption of a series of environmental protection bills and to obtain authorization for a number of governmental reforms. While trying to meet the needs of Georgia's large rural population, Carter is also aware of the necessity for realistic urban planning. Among the measures initiated in the early months of his administration was a bill, adopted in March 1971, giving the city of Atlanta authorization for the construction of a rapid transit system.

Although Carter has on occasion tried to placate right-wing sentiments among his constituents by such actions as his proclamation, on April 5, 1971, of "American Fighting Man's Day" in protest against the court martial conviction of Lieutenant William L. Calley for war crimes in Vietnam, he has also appealed to young and liberal voters. Shortly before the inauguration he named Ellis C. MacDougal, a professional criminologist, as director of the state's prison system, with a mandate for reform and rehabilitation. On February 1, 1971 Carter named the Atlanta lawyer David H. Gambrell to fill the seat vacated by the recent death of United States Senator Richard B. Russell. Gambrell, a liberal, had been serving as chairman of the state Democratic party organization.

Carter has given little publicity to his religious work, centering around the Baptist Church, nor has he tried to derive political capital from it. In recent years he has spent several months in Baptist laymen's evangelistic campaigns in various states, and he once did religious and social work in a slum area of San Juan, Puerto Rico. In the summer of 1970, at the height of the gubernatorial primary campaign, he unostentatiously spent a week working at a Baptist mission in an Atlanta slum. He is a member of the Southern Baptist Convention's brotherhood commission. Before moving to the state capital, Carter was a deacon and Sunday school teacher at the Plains Baptist Church.

On July 7, 1946 Jimmy Carter married Rosalynn Smith, a childhood neighbor. They have four children, John William, James Earl 3d, Jeffrey, and Amy. The soft-spoken and articulate Governor, who resembles the late John F. Kennedy, is five feet ten inches tall, weighs 160 pounds, and has hazel eyes and sandy hair. His favorite sport is auto racing, and he is said to have a predilection for serious poetry. Carter's political philosophy, which he calls "enlightened conservatism," stresses self-reliance, personal responsibility, and individual participation in government.

References

Life 70:31+ Ja 29 '71 pors
Time 98:14+ My 31 '71 pors
Who's Who in American Politics, 1969-70

CHALK, O(SCAR) ROY

June 7, 1907- Transportation and communications executive
Address: b. Transportation Corp. of America, 714 5th Ave., New York 10019; h. 1010 5th Ave., New York 10028

Although he is a product of the twentieth century, the self-made tycoon O. Roy Chalk represents an atavistic throwback to the breed of nineteenth-century American entrepeneurs. The son of a Russian immigrant shopkeeper, Chalk has either owned or controlled vast blocs of choice real estate, an airline, a railroad, television and radio stations, an advertising firm, newspapers, and the largest private single-city transit system in the United States. So harried has he sometimes been in annexing his holdings that he has not always had enough time to investigate all the ramifications of his enterprises before undertaking them. According to Chalk, ignorance—if not always bliss, as Thomas Gray insisted—can confer other benefits. "A lack of knowledge is a great advantage," he has said. "With ignorance, you proceed with confidence where you would otherwise proceed with trepidation."

Oscar Roy Chalk was born on June 7, 1907 in London, England to Bennett and Sophie (Stern) Chalk. He has a sister, Blanche. His parents, who had emigrated from Russia, moved the family from England to the United States when Chalk was three and settled in the Bronx in New York City. A shopkeeper, Bennett Chalk doubled as a cantor at Sabbath services at a synagogue near their home.

The family soon moved to 111th Street on Manhattan's Upper West Side, where Chalk attended Public School 165 and the High School of Commerce. After school he used to play stickball with other boys on his block. Among them were Lou Gehrig, who went on to become a star on the New York Yankees, and George and Ira Gershwin. Chalk learned to be self-sufficient at an early age. "I always had to make the decisions," he recalls. "My parents were interested, but they were busy with other things."

After graduation from high school, Chalk entered night classes at New York University, where he worked towards a law degree. During the day he worked at odd jobs, including that of door-to-door salesman. He received his law degree in June 1931, and the following year was admitted to the New York State Bar. Chalk opened a law office in midtown Manhattan, specializing in real estate transactions and landlord-tenant disputes. With the financial help of his father-in-law, Herman Cole, a prominent New York real estate man, Chalk bought a sixteen-story apartment house at 1010 Fifth Avenue for 1,000,000 dollars. The transaction proved successful and soon Chalk owned choice properties in Manhattan and the Bronx. In 1942 he entered the construction business by founding the O. Roy Chalk Realty and Construction Company.

During World War II Chalk worked as a civilian lawyer with the armed forces and served as consultant to the aeronautics training divisions of the Navy and Army Air Corps. He also founded a

O. ROY CHALK

lucrative company, Metal Associates, Inc., which made electronic training devices for the Army and Navy air forces. When the war ended, Chalk bought two beaten up DC-3's for $60,000 and converted the planes for civilian operation. Aware of the large influx of Puerto Ricans into New York City, he started operating a nonscheduled airline called Trans Caribbean Airways between New York and San Juan.

Despite competition from two scheduled airlines, he soon had a flourishing business by cutting his fares lower than his competitors and by offering such inducements as free box lunches and in-flight entertainment. Chalk made a profit of between $3,000 and $4,000 every time one of his planes made a round trip. His competitors, Pan American and Eastern, with higher overhead, higher fares, and far more empty seats, ended up with less.

When the Korean War broke out in June 1950, Chalk foresaw another golden opportunity for his airline. Finding itself short of planes for carrying cargo and troops, the Army's Military Air Transport Service (MATS) turned to the nonscheduled air-lines' association, the Air Coach Transport Association (ACTA), which parceled out business on an equitable basis. To get more of the contracts for Trans Caribbean, Chalk formed an association of his own, including other independent operators as well as himself. Called the Independent Military Air Transport Association (IMATA), the group, especially Trans Caribbean, got a far larger share of the pie than if it had remained in the Air Coach Transport Association. Chalk readily admits that one of the reasons for Trans Caribbean's success was his ability to cultivate the goodwill of politicians. "Let's face it," he once said, "airlines operate by the grace of the government. To get along in this business you have to get along with the government." When, in 1957, Trans Caribbean Airways was certified by the Civil Aeronautics Board to fly scheduled routes between Aruba, San Juan, and New York, it became the first nonscheduled airline to receive certification in two decades.

Equally interested in the possibilities of ground transportation, in 1956 Chalk offered to buy the decrepit Washington, D.C. Transit System from financier Louis Wolfson, only to discover that another firm had already been given a conditional sales contract. Undeterred, Chalk began making the rounds of his influential friends, informing them that he had ready cash with which he planned to pump new life into the moribund system. Chalk bought the firm, with its $26,000-000 in assets, for $13,500,000, of which he put up $540,000 himself, got a loan from the Chase Manhattan Bank for $9,000,000, and financed the rest with a fifteen-year, $4,000,000 mortgage to Wolfson. Having friends in the nation's capital had helped Chalk, who was quoted in *Forbes* magazine (June 1, 1965) as saying: "If you run a business company, you must be on close terms with the city mayor and the city council. In Washington, the mayor is the President of the United States and the council is the Congress."

Chalk rejuvenated the feeble transit company by introducing new air-conditioned buses, adding express routes, and expanding service into the suburbs. He had the buses painted with such color combinations as coral, white, and green, eliminated most of the streetcar lines, and even branched into the tour business with pretty girl guides. Net income shot up 97 percent, partly because he succeeded in getting the fare raised from twenty to twenty-five cents and in obtaining exemptions on fuel taxes and a subsidy for carrying school children at reduced fares. Within two years Chalk paid off his loan to Chase Manhattan, four years ahead of time, and the following year, twelve years before it fell due, Chalk paid off his $4,000,000 mortgage to Wolfson.

Looking for new investments, Roy Chalk offered to buy the city-owned New York City bus and subway system, then running $2.1 billion in the red, for $615,000,000. The deal fell through when New York politicians learned that Chalk proposed to raise the fare, then fifteen cents, to twenty-five cents, and possibly even higher to put the system on a profit-making basis. Undiscouraged, Chalk found consolation by adding to his empire other losing propositions that he transformed into profit-making properties.

By 1965 Chalk's vast holdings represented assets worth more than $112,000,000. Largely through acquisition by Trans Caribbean Airways, his holdings in 1965 included the D.C. Transit System, the Capital Transit Company, and the Washington, Virginia & Maryland Coach Company, Inc., which put Chalk in control of the largest private single-city transit system in the nation; International Railways of Central America, a 795-mile freight line in Guatemala and El Salvador; Transportation-Communications of America, Inc.; Radio San Juan (WRSJ); and prime pieces of real estate in New York City, Falls Church, Virginia, and Washington, D.C. (In 1965 it was estimated that the Fifth Avenue apartment house that Chalk bought in the 1940's for $1,000,-000 was worth $5,000,000.)

In 1962 Chalk entered newspaper publishing by acquiring the Spanish-language daily *El Diario de Nueva York* for about $1,000,000—a bargain at that price because its owners were eager to retire.

The daily, which won the hearts of the members of New York City's huge Puerto Rican population because it spoke directly to their problems and interests, cleared about $200,000 a year after taxes. Soon Chalk set out to take over its rival, *La Prensa,* a smaller Hispanic-American newspaper owned by the Pope family, by using the strategy of dropping *El Diario's* newsstand price from seven cents to a nickel and publishing some types of classified advertising free. Within six months *La Prensa's* publishers sold out to Chalk, and he merged the two newspapers.

The newspaper's crusading editorial policy became a powerful voice in city and national politics. Although Chalk had been a staunch supporter of Dwight D. Eisenhower at the time he bought Washington's transit system, he wrote signed editorials endorsing Democratic candidates and lambasting the Republicans. He instituted a unique and enormously popular human relations department at the newspaper that undertook to solve the many daily problems of Puerto Rican migrants in New York. The triumph of *El Diario-La Prensa* helped to solace Chalk for the failure of another of his publishing enterprises, the weekly Washington, D.C. *Examiner,* which before it finally folded, was given away free to passengers on his transit system.

In the latter part of the 1960's Chalk's fortunes began to wane. Along with the rest of the American airline industry, Trans Caribbean Airways started to run up a large deficit, although it had won new routes to other major Caribbean vacation areas. Plagued with high labor and equipment costs without comparable fare increases or subsidies, the Washington transit system began to run in the red, and there were suggestions in Congress that the government take it over. As quoted in the Washington *Post* (February 23, 1971), Chalk's reply to murmurs of discontent in official quarters was: "Unless the government is willing to support the bus system, it should not continue to completely control the services, fix the fares, establish the routes, determine the frequencies, or in any other way prevent the company from exercising good business judgement under the great American free enterprise plan. Uncontrolled regulation without contributing financial support is worse than tyranny."

Embarking on an extensive retrenchment program, Chalk began to sell off some of his more unprofitable enterprises. When he sold Trans Caribbean Airways to American Airlines in 1970 for $18,000,000 in stock, it was with the agreement that Chalk would receive $4,300,000 in American Airlines stock, plus a seven-year $40,000 annual consulting fee. And by the summer of 1971 the outlook had brightened for the D.C. Transit System, which reported that it had slashed its losses by 82 percent in the first half of the year compared to the same period the year before, thanks to a hike in fares. Obviously, although O. Roy Chalk was temporarily down, he was far from out.

When Chalk merged Trans Caribbean Airways with American Airlines, a prearranged stock spin-off left him in control of a group of former airline subsidiaries known as Diversified Media, Inc., which on December 31, 1970 cheerfully reported assets of $7,800,000. The holdings of Diversified Media, Inc., include 80 percent control of *El Diario,* which with its more than 80,000 daily circulation was the largest foreign-language newspaper in the country; full ownership of Transit Card Advertising, Inc., a profitable advertising agency; three television stations in Puerto Rico; a number of radio stations; and select holdings of real estate.

On December 24, 1931 Oscar Roy Chalk married Claire Cole. They have one daughter, Barbara (Mrs. Henry M. Hupshman). The Chalks live in a twelve-room apartment in a building that the entrepreneur owns at 1010 Fifth Avenue, from which they occasionally retreat to their thirty-acre Walnut Hill estate in Falls Church, Virginia or to their yacht, *Blue Horizon.* Wherever they happen to be holding forth, they are much given to lavish entertaining of political, social, and show business celebrities, who are free to admire the sunken bathtubs, the Rolls Royce with the initials on the license plates, the tack room in the Virginia stable with its wall-to-wall carpeting, and the walls hung with Renoirs, Vlamincks, Rouaults, and Dufys.

O. Roy Chalk (he bridles at "Oscar" and prefers to be called "Roy") stands five feet six inches tall and is of medium build. He has receding gray hair that he combs straight back and a scrupulously neat moustache. A flashy but fastidious dresser, he likes to splurge on vests with lapels and pleated shirts. He not only received an honorary LL.D. from Seoul (Korea) University but was named an honorary citizen of that nation in 1957. He was named vice-chairman and director of the American-Korean Foundation in 1954. Chalk is national chairman of the American Jewish Committee, vice-chairman of the United Negro College Fund, and a member of the board of trustees of Virgin Islands College and Finch College, the New York State Board of Regents, the president's council of Georgetown University, and the council of the Catholic University of Puerto Rico. He is chairman of the finance committee of the United States Committee for the United Nations and a fellow of the Institute of Aeronautics and Sciences. His honors include the award of achievement of the Advertising Club of Washington and the merit award of the United States Navy Bureau of Aeronautics.

References

    Coronet 4:146+ Ag '66 por
    Forbes 95:45+ Je 1 '65
    N Y Herald Tribune p19 D 8 '62
    Newsweek 59:92+ Je 4 '62 por; 70:84 Jl
      17 '67 por
    Status 2:102 Ja-F '66 por
    Time 95:20+ My 4 '70 por
    Washington (D.C.) Post L p2 O 28 '62 por;
      E p2 D 12 '65 por; A p1+ Ja 24 '71 por;
      H p1 Jl 11 '71 por
    Who's Who in America, 1970-71

CHILES, LAWTON (MAINOR, JR.)

Apr. 3, 1930- United States Senator from Florida
Address: b. 421 Old Senate Office Bldg., Washington, D.C. 20510; h. 940 Lake Hollingsworth Drive, Lakeland, Fla. 33801

Among the new personalities who appeared on Capitol Hill when the Ninety-second Congress opened in 1971 is Florida's junior Senator, Lawton Chiles, whose low-key, grass-roots campaign symbolized a reaction against glossy campaigning based on lavish budgets and wide media exposure. A member of the Florida state legislature since 1958, Chiles was determined in 1970 to contest the seat of retiring United States Senator Spessard L. Holland. Lacking adequate funds and organizational support, Chiles walked more than 1,000 miles, from one end of Florida to the other, and came into direct contact with thousands of people. After defeating former Governor Farris Bryant in the Democratic primary he went on to win the November 1970 election against the Republican candidate, William C. Cramer, who had the solid support of the Nixon administration. Chiles's actions during his early months in the Senate—where he is a member of the powerful Democratic Steering Committee—reflect, among other things, his interests in environmental problems, drug control, Latin American affairs, and an end to the Vietnam war.

Lawton Mainor Chiles Jr. was born on April 3, 1930 in Lakeland, Florida, the son of Lawton Chiles Sr. He and his sister Jeanette grew up in Lakeland, and as a student at Lakeland High School he played football and was a member of the Key Club and of Boys' State. He has credited the latter experience with giving him his initial interest in lawmaking and government. After graduating from high school in 1948 Chiles entered the University of Florida in Gainesville, where he majored in business administration and obtained his B.S. degree in 1952. He interrupted his education during 1953-54 to serve with the United States Army artillery in Korea. After his discharge with the rank of first lieutenant, he resumed his education at the University of Florida school of law, which conferred an LL.B. degree on him in 1955. At the university Chiles belonged to Alpha Tau Omega and the legal fraternity Phi Delta Phi. He was elected to the Florida Blue Key leadership honorary society and the University of Florida Hall of Fame.

After his admission to the bar Chiles established a law practice in Lakeland, where he became active in the local Democratic party organization. In 1958 he decided to run for a seat in the state House of Representatives and was elected to the first of four consecutive two-year terms after conducting what he has termed a "shoestring, shoe-leather campaign." He won election to the state Senate in 1966 and was reelected two years later. The legislative district that Chiles represented comprises Polk County, including the city of Lakeland, and is located at about the geographical center of the state, in the heart of Florida's rich citrus-growing region.

During the 1950's and the early 1960's the Florida state government was dominated by what Robert G. Sherrill, writing in *Harper's Magazine* (November 1965), called the "pork chop state of mind." Although Florida, with the ninth-largest state population and a 37.1 percent rate of population growth in the 1960's, experienced considerable urban expansion in recent years, its state legislature continued to be controlled by conservative rural officials popularly known as "pork choppers." Legislation was designed primarily to protect property interests. Although the state generously allocated funds for measures benefiting large citrus growers and other vested interests, it kept welfare payments among the lowest in the country, and it generally maintained both taxes and expenditures at minimum levels. Until 1963 Florida had what was probably the most inequitably apportioned legislature in the United States. Those inequities were partly remedied when, in accordance with a United States Supreme Court decision, the Florida legislature was reapportioned, in 1963 and again in 1967.

During his twelve years in the legislature Chiles remained aloof from the "pork chop" clique and pursued what he has termed a "progressive conservative" approach. Although he had grown up in the largest urban center in his county he was conditioned by the influence of the surrounding rural areas, which are basically conservative, and has referred to himself as a "third generation cracker." A reporter for the *National Observer* (November 9, 1970) noted, however, that although Chiles likes to think of himself "as a country boy," he is also a successful lawyer in Lakeland, and his family owns several restaurants and real estate tracts in Polk county. Chiles also typifies what a writer for *Time* (May 31, 1971) calls the "historic and fundamental Southern notion of populism; defending the little man, attacking the Establishment." As a member of the Florida House of Representatives, Chiles served on the code of ethics, education, urban affairs, game and fresh water fish, citrus industry, and apportionment committees. In the state Senate he was chairman of the ways and means committee, the legislative staff internship sponsoring committee, and the appropriations subcommittee, and he also served on the education, rules and calendar, and governmental organization committees.

In 1960 Chiles became chairman of a joint legislative study committee to examine pollution problems in Florida. He held hearings in various parts of the state and was discouraged to find much apathy about such problems as chemical pollution. The committee's inquiries resulted in legislation, passed in 1961, that established the Florida Pollution Control Commission, the first agency of its kind in the state. On his own, Chiles sponsored a number of pollution control laws, and as a member of the Florida Constitution Revision Commission he fought to ensure that the Pollution Control Commission remained an independent agency directly responsible to the Governor.

As a champion of conservation, Chiles worked for the adoption by the Florida legislature of measures dealing with such subjects as the protection of alligators and the expansion of recreational areas and state parks. He was also interested in quality education for teachers, vocational training, and improved school facilities. In 1961 he gained national attention as the sponsor of a bill that would allow self-employed professionals to set themselves up as corporations, thereby gaining substantial tax advantages. During his last session Chiles sponsored legislation to provide the public with guaranteed access to Florida beaches. The controversial measure was defeated by two votes.

Late in 1969 Chiles decided to run for the seat held by the retiring United States Senator Spessard L. Holland, a veteran Florida Democrat. His campaign staff soon realized that a traditional campaign would not be feasible, since a poll indicated that Chiles's name was recognized by only 5 percent of the people interviewed, and there was not enough money in the till for an effective campaign on the mass media. Recalling his first "shoeleather" campaign of 1958, Chiles hit on the idea of a walk along the entire length of Florida as a means of gaining exposure and talking directly with its inhabitants. Setting out in the late spring of 1970, he covered 1,003 miles in ninety-two days, with a stop along the way in Tallahassee, where he attended a session of the state legislature. Often joined by members of his family and by other state senators, he chatted with at least 40,000 persons along the way and earned the nickname "Walkin' Lawton."

In an article in *Look* (January 12, 1971) Frank Trippett reported that political professionals at first thought that Chiles was making a big mistake in dispensing with the media, but his unconventional method of campaigning became more and more effective. Walking along highways, stopping at towns, and speaking to small groups, he gained more public exposure than he had counted on. He also gained insights into people's problems in talking with them about their aspirations and frustrations. He modified his own thinking on issues, changing from a hawk to a dove on the Vietnam conflict.

In the primary race for the Democratic Senate nomination, on September 8, 1970, Chiles, with 26 percent of the vote, came in second among six candidates, thus becoming eligible for a runoff contest against the front-runner, former Governor Farris Bryant, who had received 33 percent. Supported by Senator Holland's organization and considered the favorite, Bryant campaigned on his record as Florida's governor from 1961 to 1965, while Chiles, backed by a majority of the state senators, spoke about the failure of federal money to benefit the state. In the runoff election, on September 29, 1970, Chiles won a stunning upset with 65.8 percent of the vote.

Chiles's opponent for the November election, Congressman William C. Cramer, had won the Republican primary by defeating Judge G. Harrold Carswell, President Richard Nixon's unsuccessful nominee for the United States Supreme Court. A

LAWTON CHILES

well-known conservative Republican, Cramer served eight terms in Congress and helped to build up the GOP organization in Florida. Although Florida, like all other states in the deep South, is predominantly Democratic in terms of voter registration, the Republican party has had a phenomenal growth in recent years. In 1966 Claude R. Kirk Jr. became Florida's first Republican governor in ninety-four years, and in the first election after the 1967 reapportionment, the Republicans gained enough strength to achieve what has been called the South's first two-party state legislature.

Reportedly Nixon's handpicked choice for the Senate candidacy, Cramer was backed by the national Republican organization with funds and speakers. The President spent two full days in Florida, campaigning for Cramer. During the campaign, rigged out in a plastic helmet to identify with the "hard hats," Cramer derided his opponent as "Liberal Lawton" and accused him of being soft on crime and campus disorders. Chiles kept his own campaign low key and on a grass-roots level by walking through a town in each county, talking with its people about bread-and-butter issues. When Cramer held a fund-raising affair at $1,000 a ticket, Chiles responded with a $1-a-box chicken supper in a Miami park. In the election of November 3, 1970 he won with 902,438 votes, or 53.9 percent of the total, while Cramer received 772,817 votes.

On January 23, 1971, the day after he was sworn into the Senate, Chiles was selected by the majority leader, Senator Mike Mansfield, to serve on the seventeen-member Democratic Steering Committee, which controls all Senate committee assignments. Committed to select a Southerner to replace the late Senator Richard B. Russell of Georgia, Mansfield bypassed all the other Southern Senators with greater seniority, and appointed Chiles to the committee to give it a "more liberal orientation." In the Senate, Chiles was assigned to the Committee on Agriculture and Forestry and its subcommittees on environment, soil conservation and forestry and on agricultural research and general legislation, and he was named chairman of the subcommittee on agricultural exports. He also serves on the Committee on Government and its subcommittee on national security and international affairs and on the Joint Committee on Congressional Operations.

During his first six months in office Chiles sponsored or cosponsored several environmental bills, including the National Coastal and Estuarine Zone Management Act to assist states in developing plans for coastal areas and a bill to require the Secretary of the Army to undertake public works for the control of water pollution. Other proposed legislation for which he was in whole or in part responsible included a plan for recruiting and retraining unemployed Aerospace personnel and returning servicemen for employment in the Model Cities Program; a bill to provide incentives for industrial growth in rural areas; an amendment to the Social Security Act to allow recipients to earn up to $3,000 a year without penalty; and several bills to control the importation and abuse of narcotics. In voting on key issues in 1971, Chiles supported a move to end government sponsorship of the supersonic transport plane and voted for the McGovern-Hatfield amendment, requiring an end to United States military involvement in Indochina by the end of 1971. After the defeat of the latter, Chiles introduced a compromise amendment—also defeated—that would have set the withdrawal deadline at July 1, 1972.

Chiles's long-standing interest in Latin America was heightened by his encounters with Cuban refugees in Dade County during his campaign walk. He wants the United States to make a greater effort to pursue programs that will earn it the goodwill of Latin Americans. As chairman of the subcommittee on agricultural exports Chiles visited Mexico in February 1971, and in May he again went to Mexico, to attend an interparliamentary conference. To prepare himself to become an authority on Latin America he has been taking daily lessons in conversational Spanish.

A trustee of the University of Florida Law Center, Chiles has been a legislative counselor to Boys' State and was chairman of the Lakeland March of Dimes in 1964, of the United Fund of Greater Lakeland in 1967, and of the Polk County Cancer Crusade in 1968. He is a member of the Kiwanis Club and the YMCA Century Club. Among the many awards and honors he has received over the years are the Distinguished Service Award of the Florida Association for Retarded Children; the Wildlife Conservation Award of the National Wildlife Federation; the Agricultural Commendation Award of the Florida Agriculture Council; the Victory Crusade Award of the American Cancer Society; and the United Fund Award of Special Merit. In 1959 he was named Jaycee's Outstanding Young Man.

Lawton Chiles and Rhea May Grafton of Coral Gables were married on January 27, 1951. They have two sons, Lawton Mainor 3d and Edward C., and two daughters, Tandy M. and Rhea Gay. Projecting what has been described as "boyish amiability" or "good-natured earnestness," Chiles is six feet one inch tall, weighs 175 pounds, and

has brown hair and blue eyes. He enjoys hunting, fishing, and football and keeps fit by walking and jogging. He belongs to the Presbyterian Church. One of his associates once commented that Chiles is not the "crash-program type," but that he sets his goals and then gives himself tactical room to adjust and remain flexible. "You try not to compromise your principles," Chiles told a reporter for the *National Observer* (February 1, 1971), "but government is the art of the possible."

References

Cong Q 28:2605 O 23 '70 por
Look 35:46+ Ja 12 '71
Congressional Directory (1971)
Who's Who in American Politics, 1969-70
Who's Who in the South and Southwest, 1971-72

CLARKE, RON

Feb. 21, 1937- Australian runner
Address: b. c/o Victoria Amateur Athletic Association, 12 McKillop St., Melbourne, Australia

If the sheer weight of statistics were the criterion, Ron Clarke of Australia would have to be judged the best distance runner of all time. In the 1960's Clarke set nineteen world records, and in 1970, when his retirement was announced—and received with a grain of salt by some observers—he still held five of them, for two, three, and six miles and 5,000 and 10,000 meters. Despite the brilliance of his career, Clarke has never won an Olympic or a Commonwealth medal. "Ron Clarke remains an enigma," Australian fellow runner John Landy wrote in 1966. "He is a performer of fantastic feats of endurance who can be beaten by a relative unknown in a club event, and seemingly be unmoved by either eventuality. . . . He runs for the sake of the race itself and not specifically for winning. He accepts races as he accepts life—as it comes, wishing to be judged, if at all, on the whole of his career rather than on the [disappointing] 10,000 meters at Tokyo or his superb three miles at White City, London in 1965."

Clarke's ancestors emigrated from Ireland to Australia in the nineteenth century, and for several generations the men of the family worked in the gold mines of Ballarat, Victoria. Ron Clarke was born in Queen Victoria Hospital in Melbourne on February 21, 1937, and he was raised in the Essendon section of Melbourne. His father, a famous Australian Rules football (rugby) player, was a sailmaker by trade, but when his health forced him to seek outdoor employment he became greenkeeper for the Essendon Football Club. Jack Clarke, Ron's older brother, now an architect, was a star centreman for the Essendon team. Ron, tall for his age but overweight, was also a good football and cricket player but never quite as agile in those sports as his brother. His early development as a runner was, as he describes it, "haphazard." "Running meant nothing more than a means of locomotion. . . . It was usually simpler to run or cycle to wherever we wanted to go than to walk a fair way to catch a tram."

"Dad not only aroused in us an enthusiasm for sport, but helped also to mould our attitudes," Clarke recalled in his autobiography, *The Unforgiving Minute* (Pelham Books, 1966). "He used to tell us not to feel upset when our team was beaten; that the only sensible response to defeat was to learn from it and be determined to try harder the next time. At the dinner table he encouraged discussion and rational argument, and we learned not to accept anything at face value, but rather to assess all theories, extracting from them what we thought was good and rejecting the bad." On the playing field, the elder Clarke did not drive or dominate his sons. "After showing us the rudiments and playing with us, he sat back and let us develop in our own way." He also constantly reminded them that sport was a recreational avocation, "that the serious part of life was in preparing oneself for a sound trade or profession."

Clarke's mother remembers him as a "mischievous" child whom she enrolled in the Essendon State School when he was barely four so that he would be kept busy and out of trouble. At the primary school he eventually played on the football and cricket teams, and his physique and athletic skill improved year by year, especially after he entered Essendon High School, where he captained both teams. During his high school years he also played with the Youden Kensington Cricket Club and with the junior squad of the Essendon Football Club. Track at that time interested him less than the other sports, especially football, partly because he was, by his own description, "atrocious" at jumping and hurling. In running, however, he won the school district cross-country title twice and the mile and the 880-yard championships once each.

After receiving his Leaving Certificate at Essendon High, Clarke qualified for matriculation in the advanced commercial course offered at highly rated Melbourne High School, on the other side of the city. Encouraged by the track coach and track captain at Melbourne High, he became serious about running, although still not so interested in it as in football.

In 1954 Clarke completed his studies at Melbourne High and took a job in a chartered accountant's office. That summer he set his first Victorian junior record, 4:31.1 for the mile, and the following season he set Australian junior records for 3,000 meters, 1,500 meters, and two miles. His chief aspiration, however, still was to win admission to the senior roster of the Allendon Football Club. He renounced that ambition in favor of running when he broke his hand playing with the Allendon juniors early in 1955.

At the time that he quit the Allendon team, Clarke weighed 175 pounds, about fifteen more than the ideal track weight for a runner his height (then five feet eleven inches). In the spring of 1955 he placed himself under the guidance of track coach Franz Stampfl, under whose regimen he reduced his weight and did interval training,

RON CLARKE

which he later rejected as unrealistic. "The effort is not continuous, as it has to be in a race. By running fast lap times and then allowing himself time to recover, an athlete is deceiving himself as to his fitness."

By the end of the 1955-56 season, his last as a junior, Clarke had set twelve Australian junior records. He competed and failed in the Olympic trials in 1956, but he participated in the Olympiad as the runner who carried the torch into Melbourne Olympic Stadium to initiate the Games. Running as a senior, he set an Australian record of 5:20.6 for 2,000 meters in October 1956, but soon afterward he dropped out of racing, because a chronic sinus infection was bothering him and, besides, he wanted to concentrate on his long-drawn-out accountancy certification examinations and his work with Lamson Paragon Ltd. in the Richmond district of Melbourne.

Clarke trained sporadically until he married in 1959. After the marriage he and his wife moved to Dromana on the Mornington Peninsula, forty miles from Melbourne, because he had been advised that the seaside climate would help clear his sinuses. Traveling two or three hours a day between work and home left him little time for training, and he did none, until late in 1960. By then, he and his wife had again moved, to Heathmont, which is much closer to Melbourne, his sinus infection had cleared up, and he had passed his final accounting examination. Encouraged by a friend, veteran runner Les Perry, Clarke resumed his training, working out evenings with runners Trevor Vincent and Tony Cook.

Returning to competition in the 1960-61 season, Clarke regained his form gradually. In 1962 he broke the Australian records for the ten-mile and the one-hour races, and the following year he set four additional national marks. In the summer of 1963 he broke the European records for three meters and 10,000 meters, and the following December he set his first world marks, in the six-mile and 10,000-meter categories. A year later he broke the world records for three miles and for 5,000 meters.

In the 1964 Olympics in Tokyo, Clarke finished ninth in the 5,000-meter event. Referring to the occasion later, he called it "the one performance of which I am ashamed," explaining: "At the crucial moment in the race I quit. Frustrated and rattled, I allowed myself to be too unbalanced by the way the race was run." In the 10,000-meter at Tokyo he finished third. His previously set 10,000-meter record remained unsurpassed, however, until he himself bettered it in 1965, pushing his mark first to 28:14.0 and finally to 27:39.4. In 1965 he also improved on his three-mile record twice, with a final mark of 12:52.4; recovered world leadership in the six-mile category with a time of 26:47.0; and set new world records for 20,000 meters (59: 22.8), the one-hour run (twelve miles, 1,006 yards), ten miles (47:12.0), and 5,000 meters (successive marks of 13:34.8, 13:33.6, and 13: 25.8). Kipchoge Keino of Kenya later did the 5,000 meters 1.6 seconds faster, but in 1966 Clarke took the 5,000-meter title back from Keino with a clocking of 13:16.6. In the same year he set a new world indoor record for two miles, with 8:28.8, and bettered his three-mile record, with 12:50.4.

In 1967 in Stockholm, Clarke set a new world record for two miles with 8:19.8. The clocking was almost three seconds faster than the mark previously set by Michel Jazy. More significantly, as a revelation of the progressively higher speeds attained by runners over the generations, it was 46.8 seconds better than the record set by Alf Shrubb in 1904. In 1968 Clarke brought his two-mile time down even lower, to 18:19.6. In the 1968 Olympic Games in Mexico City, Clarke, unaccustomed to the high altitude with its thin air, finished fifth in the 5,000-meter race. In the 10,000-meter event he did well until three laps from the finish, when he began to collapse from lack of oxygen. He staggered to the finish line, in sixth place, and fell unconscious there. Oxygen was administered to him for ten minutes before he revived.

Clarke won almost all his races in 1968-69 and 1969-70. On July 12, 1970 he announced that he was retiring from track. "The 1972 Olympics in Munich are out of the question for me," he said, according to an Associated Press dispatch. "I just couldn't reach the top again." His recollection of the 1968 Mexico City Olympics was "very bitter," he confessed. "I was at my prime then. . . . I think I can beat any runner in the world at this distance. But I can't beat the thin air. Now I'll be able to spend more time with my wife, Helen, and the children." But a couple of weeks later, when a reporter reminded him of his retirement announcement, Clarke said: "Did I really say that? Oh, I'm enjoying it more now. I think I'll be back."

When in training, Clarke runs three times a day, before each meal. Before dinner he jogs between twelve and fifteen miles, and on weekends he extends the distance to twenty miles or so. He also lifts weights, and his physical recreations, squash, tennis, and swimming, help to keep him in shape in and out of training. In running, he has an unorthodox arm motion that is, as he once said, essentially "clumsy and inefficient" but "sometimes

erroneously taken as a model by aspiring young runners."

Ron and Helen Clarke and their three children still live in the foothills of the Dandenong Mountains, about nineteen miles from Melbourne. Clarke is six feet tall and weighs about 168 pounds. In his autobiography he wrote of his work as a "cost accountant" for the British Tobacco Company in Melbourne, but in the AP dispatch reporting his announcement of retirement he is described as a "travel agent." In addition to his autobiography, Clarke has written, with Norman Harris, *The Lonely Breed* (Pelham, 1967), containing the stories of twenty-one all-time great distance runners.

References

Christian Sci Mon p11 Jl 23 '69 por
Guardian p12 Ag 28 '68
Sports Illus 24:18+ F 21 '66 por; 31:38 Jl 28 '69
Clarke, Ron. The Unforgiving Minute (1966)

COLOMBO, EMILIO

Apr. 11, 1920- Premier of Italy
Address: b. Palazzo Chigi, Rome, Italy; h. Via Aurelia 239, Rome, Italy

The chief architect of Italy's postwar economic boom has been Emilio Colombo, who became the Premier of Italy's thirty-second post-fascist government on August 6, 1970. A quiet, behind-the-scenes economic expert and skilled negotiator, Colombo was little known to the public at the time he took office, even though he had been a member of almost every Italian Cabinet since World War II and had most recently served as Treasury Minister for seven years. When Colombo, a Christian Democrat, managed to end a month-long government crisis by patching together a center-left coalition Cabinet, most observers felt that he would do little better than his predecessor, Mariano Rumor. (Rumor's last center-left government fell on July 6 after some 100 days.) Yet, as of late 1971 Colombo had not only held together the dissident factions of his coalition administration but had succeeded in stabilizing the lira and putting in motion a number of badly needed social and economic reforms.

Born to a lower-middle-class family on April 11, 1920 in the provincial capital city of Potenza, eighty miles southeast of Naples, Emilio Colombo is the son of Angelo and Rosa (Tordela) Colombo. Colombo entered politics early as an officer in the local Catholic Action youth group, and after obtaining a law degree from the University of Rome he was elected vice-president of Italy's national Catholic Action organization. In 1946 he was elected a member of Italy's interim constituent assembly, and in 1948 he was sent to the Chamber of Deputies of the newly created Italian Parliament by his constituency of Potenza. He has been returned to the legislature in every subsequent election.

Colombo obtained his first subcabinet post in 1948, as undersecretary of Agriculture, and his rise in the Italian government from then on was steady. In 1953 he became undersecretary of Public Works, and starting in 1955 he served for three years as Minister of Agriculture. During those years Colombo helped to formulate many of Italy's basic postwar reforms, such as land redistribution, nationalization of the electrical power industry, and developmental programs for the impoverished south, including the Twelve-Year Plan and the rebuilding of the "Sassi" district in Matera, 130 miles southeast of Naples.

Since 1958 Colombo has played a vital part in the economic life of Italy, serving successively as Minister of Foreign Trade (1958-59), Minister of Industry and Commerce (from 1959 to 1963, except for a few months in 1960), and as Minister of the Treasury (from 1963 until his appointment as Premier). Colombo's boldest stroke in helping the Italian economy came in the early 1960's, when the nation's postwar economic growth was seriously threatened by inflation. Despite the unpopularity of such measures, the Treasury Minister insisted on increased sales taxes and other austerity measures that proved highly effective.

Since 1963 Italy has been governed by a center-left coalition of Christian Democrats, Republicans, and socialists. A chief objective of the coalition's strategy has been the exclusion from power of the Communist party, which, with 28 percent of the vote, is the nation's second largest party and western Europe's strongest Communist organization. (The Christian Democrats control 38 percent of the national vote.) The coalition worked fairly smoothly until 1969, when the United Socialist party divided over the issue of Communist participation in government. The leftist Socialists favored a degree of cooperation with the Communists, while the more conservative Social Democrats adamantly opposed any such action. The socialist dissension was largely responsible for the downfall of three governments, all headed by Mariano Rumor, who resigned as Premier on July 6, 1970.

After Rumor's resignation President Giuseppe Saragat called on Christian Democrat Giulio Andreotti to form a new center-left government, but he was unable to do so. On July 25, 1970 Colombo was named Premier-designate, and by August 6, 1970 he had formed a government with a Cabinet almost identical to his successor's by effecting a compromise over the Communist issue that was acceptable at least for the time being to both the Socialists and the Social Democrats. His solution was to allow the Socialists to ally themselves with Communists in regional administrations where a center-left coalition was numerically impossible provided they continued to oppose Communist participation at the national level.

When Colombo took office Italy was in the midst of an economic crisis largely resulting from the widespread labor strikes of the "hot autumn" of 1969. Labor costs were up, productivity was down, and capital was fleeing the country at a prodigious rate. To check inflation and promote

EMILIO COLOMBO

social reforms, Colombo issued an emergency fiscal decree on August 27, 1970 aimed at raising an estimated $1 billion a year in taxes on gasoline and many other luxury or semiluxury items. Under the Italian constitution the decree would expire after sixty days if it were not enacted into law by Parliament within that time. Although the emergency measures could theoretically be extended indefinitely if the Premier kept reissuing slightly different versions of the decree every sixty days, in fact the political climate demanded that Parliament be consulted. Faced with adamant leftist opposition to the austerity measures in the Chamber of Deputies, Colombo was forced to reissue the decree shortly before it was due to expire in October, and when the measures came to the test in Parliament in November his government had its first crisis. After much parliamentary maneuvering, Colombo succeeded in breaking a filibuster in the Chamber of Deputies on November 28 by demanding and receiving a vote of confidence for his government based on the government's version of the fiscal bill. To win the vote, Colombo committed his Roman Catholic church-backed Christian Democratic party to voting for final passage of Italy's first divorce bill, which was backed by the secular parties in his coalition government. The historic divorce bill was passed in the Chamber of Deputies two days later.

By early 1971 Colombo had succeeded in unifying Parliament to pass urgently needed health, education, and public housing reforms. Colombo has also taken steps to free his country from the stifling and outmoded bureaucracy that controls almost all aspects of governmental services. In June 1970 Parliament had divided Italy into twenty regions, each of which was to elect its own local parliament. By January 1971 Premier Colombo had worked out a timetable for gradually expanded self-government in the regions, transferring such responsibilities as local police, welfare, and health services from Rome to the regional governments. Reforming Italy's antiquated tax laws has been another of the Premier's aims, and in October 1971 he succeeded in pushing an income tax reform bill through the Chamber of Deputies.

Colombo has pledged that the major focus of his administration will be on developing Italy's under-privileged south and that up to 80 percent of all public investments will be siphoned to that region of the country. The south's problems have been exacerbated by a steady population drain to the north, where immigrants crowd into the industrialized cities. To stop that displacement of society, Colombo has determined to "transfer capital where there is labor, and not the other way around." In an interview with J. W. Anderson of the Washington *Post* (February 21, 1971), he outlined his government's strategy for the south. In the beginning capital will be put into irrigation systems to increase agricultural productivity. Then money will be poured into the development of such facilities as better schools and roads, so that finally the south will be ready to benefit from the establishment of modern industry and services.

Reggio di Calabria, a small city on the tip of Italy's boot, has become the best-known symbol of southern Italy's poverty and backwardness. Shortly before Colombo took office it was announced that Reggio was being passed over in favor of a smaller rival city, Catanzaro, to serve as the capital of the newly created region of Calabria. Although the location of the capital has little practical import beyond bringing a few government jobs to the town, the issue brought out all the frustrations engendered by generations of neglect by Rome, and, partly at the instigation of neo-fascists, violence and rioting have broken out intermittently in Reggio di Calabria since July 1970. To pacify the city's inhabitants, Colombo has promised them a steel mill, but observers have pointed out that one highly automated industrial plant will do little to assuage the town's deep-rooted problems.

Internationally Colombo has staunchly supported the European Common Market and Italy's interests within it. He is credited with having drafted much of the Treaty of Rome, which mandated the creation of the European Economic Community in 1958, and he subsequently served as chairman of the Common Market's Ministerial Council. The Italian politician has steadfastly endorsed Great Britain's inclusion in the Market and plans for a supranational Europe.

Premier Colombo's government recognized Communist China on November 6, 1970, becoming the seventh NATO country to do so, and within three months the two nations were to have established formal diplomatic relations. Just before making his first diplomatic visit to the United States in February 1971, Colombo told New York *Times* correspondent Paul Hofmann (February 15, 1971) that he hoped Italy's recognition of China would help to bring Peking out of its isolation from the world community. At the same time he emphasized that the Western nations must maintain "solidarity" in their relations with the Communist world. "We deeply believe in a peaceful international community whose members are all able to respect one another," he told Hofmann. "To respect one another they must know one another."

An unemotional, reserved bachelor who wears dark, sharply creased suits and drab ties, Emilio Colombo has been likened in appearance and manner to a British civil servant or even to a "proper, prosperous undertaker." His piety and political skill have earned him the nickname of the "lay cardinal," and one leading Italian newspaperman wrote when he became Premier, "Politics for Colombo is not a profession, it is a form of priesthood." Colombo has few interests outside of his work, but he does collect French vintage wines, sing in a choral group on occasion, and attend a few movies and plays. He has served as president of the Italian National Committee for Nuclear Research (1961) and as a member of the central committee of the Christian Democratic party (1952-53).

References

N Y Times p10 Ag 10 '70 por
Chi è? (1961)
International Who's Who, 1970-71
Panorama Biografico degli Italiani d'Oggi (1956)
Who's Who in Italy, 1957-58

CONIGLIARO, TONY

Jan. 7, 1945- Retired baseball player
Address: b. c/o California Angels, Anaheim Stadium, 200 S. State College St., Anaheim, Calif. 92806

One of the most dramatic comebacks in recent sports history was made by Tony Conigliaro in 1969. Conigliaro, a slugging outfielder who led the American Baseball League in home runs in 1965, his second year with the Boston Red Sox, was severely "beaned" in August 1967. The vision in his left eye was so seriously impaired by the injury that physicians did not give him much chance of ever playing again, but his retina seemed to heal, as if miraculously, and he returned to the Boston lineup in 1969. Conigliaro related the story of his arduous recovery in an autobiography, *Seeing It Through* (Macmillan, 1970), written with the late Jack Zanger. Unfortunately, however, the story of Conigliaro's comeback had an unhappy ending. Traded to the California Angels in October 1970, the outfielder played the first half of the 1971 season before announcing, on July 10, 1971, that he was retiring from baseball because he lacked complete vision in his left eye.

Anthony Richard Conigliaro was born in Revere, Massachusetts on January 7, 1945 to Salvatore and Theresa Conigliaro. His father at that time was a factory worker who also tried, not very successfully, a variety of small business enterprises, including a doughnut shop, a backyard chicken farm, and a small music-stand manufacturing shop. During Conigliaro's childhood the family moved from Revere to East Boston, within commuting distance of Lynn, where the father is now a plant manager at the Triangle Tool and Die Company. The ex-

California Angel outfielder has two brothers, Billy, right fielder with the Boston Red Sox, and Richard. Salvatore Conigliaro introduced his sons to baseball as soon as they were able to handle the ball, at the age of four or five. Tony remains very close to his parents, who now live in Swampscott, Massachusetts, and in his autobiography he said of them: "I more than love them; without them I am nothing. Having them behind me has been the most important thing in my life."

In the autobiography Conigliaro also recalled that he always hated school and that his bleakest years as a reluctant scholar were those in the lower half of elementary school, when he felt "apart" from his fellow students as well as his teachers. "I wasn't as quick as other kids. . . . It took me longer than anyone else to learn how to read and write. A lot of kids made fun of me, so I stayed by myself mostly. As a result I'd skip school quite a bit, in spite of my father's warning [of punishment], and I accepted the beatings." In compensation for his dismal scholastic status, Conigliaro sometimes acted, in his words, the mischievous "smart aleck."

Conigliaro's relations with his peers improved when he began playing Little League baseball, at the age of eight. As a Little Leaguer and, later, a Pony Leaguer, he pitched and played shortstop. His success, and especially his better than .400 batting average, encouraged him to set his sights on a professional career, and he practised with that goal in mind. He also excelled at other sports, especially hockey (until his father made him abandon it, for fear that an injury on the ice would hurt his baseball prospects), basketball, and football. He was quarterback on the football team at St. Mary's High School in Lynn, where he commuted daily with his father by automobile.

On the baseball team at St. Mary's, Conigliaro alternated between the pitcher's mound and short stop, as he had in the Little and Pony leagues. In his junior and senior years he won about sixteen games as a pitcher, and his batting average was an extraordinary .600-plus. During the summer following his graduation from high school he played for an American Legion team and continued to bat over .600.

The Boston Red Sox, who had been scouting Conigliaro for a year or so, signed him to a $20,000-bonus in September 1962. To warm him up for spring training, they sent him to Bradenton, Florida, in the Winter Instructional League, where he realized that he was outmatched physically. (He was then at his full height—six feet three inches—but weighed only 170 pounds, and he lacked strength in his arms and legs.) "I went on a weight-lifting campaign . . . ," he recalled in his autobiography, "and I put myself on a training program. I . . . worked and worked and worked. I knew what I had to do to improve myself and I did it."

Although he performed fairly well in the training sessions at Ocala, Florida in the spring of 1963, it was obvious that Conigliaro needed more confidence, and the Red Sox assigned him to Wellsville, New York, in the New York-Pennsyl-

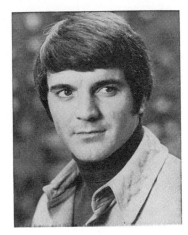

TONY CONIGLIARO

vania League, a medium-paced A league. In eighty-three games as an outfielder with Wellsville during the 1963 season, he batted .363, hit forty-two doubles, four triples, and twenty-four homers, and batted in eighty-four runs. He was named Most Valuable Player and Rookie of the Year in the New York-Pennsylvania League.

Conigliaro was called up to Boston as a center fielder in 1964. (Later he also played in left and right fields.) In his first game with the Red Sox he tapped Whitey Ford of the New York Yankees for his first major-league hit, a single. Injuries later hampered his play and kept him on the bench for long periods, but he finished the season with a .290 batting average, twenty-four home runs, and fifty-two runs batted in. The following season his tallies in the same categories were .269, thirty-two, and eighty-two. Meanwhile, Boston sportswriters were creating sensational copy about him, inflating his reputation as a "playboy," and Conigliaro entered into a running feud with them. "I'm no angel," he said later. "But I am all business when it comes to baseball." In addition, there was friction between him and Boston manager Billy Herman. During the 1965 season he was fined a total of $1,500 in penalties for misconduct.

In 1966 Conigliaro tried, with some success, to reform his deportment, and he was voted Boston's Most Valuable Player that year, when his average at the plate was .265 and he hit twenty-eight home runs and batted in ninety-three runs. The following year Dick Williams succeeded Billy Herman as manager and led the Red Sox from ninth place to the pennant. Conigliaro did not get along with Williams any better than he had with Herman, but he contributed significantly to Boston's success with a batting average of .287, twenty home runs, and sixty-seven runs batted in.

Conigliaro's contribution to Boston's successful pennant race came to a halt on August 18, 1967. In his autobiography he told what happened on that day: "We were playing a night game with the California Angels. . . . I came to bat in the fourth inning. . . . Jack Hamilton was pitching for the Angels. . . . When the ball was about four feet from my head I knew it was going to get me. And I knew it was going to hurt because Hamilton was such a hard thrower. I was frightened. I threw my hands up in front of my face and saw the ball follow me back and hit me square on the left side of the head. . . . Just before everything went dark I saw the ball bounce straight down on home plate. It was the last thing I saw for several days."

After hospitalization and recuperation, Conigliaro reported for spring training with the Red Sox in 1968, but the vision in his damaged left eye had deteriorated to 20/300 and physicians warned that exercise of the eye might result in a detached retina. "I love being on a baseball field," Conigliaro once said. "It is my life." The prospect of being cut off from his "life" was crushing to him, and to distract himself he turned to music. The possessor of a pleasant voice, he had already recorded some songs—the best known of which was "Playing the Field"—for RCA-Victor, and now he formed a rock group called Tony C. and the All Night Workers, consisting of a lead vocalist (Conigliaro), two guitar players, a drummer, an organist, a trumpet player, and a trombonist. The group played a few dates at O'Dee's, a small nightclub in the Cambridge section of Boston.

In June 1968 physicians were surprised to find that Conigliaro's vision had improved to 20/100, and he began working out with the intention of returning to baseball. While he was playing in the Winter Instructional League in Sarasota, Florida at the end of 1968, nearly normal vision suddenly returned to his left eye. A physician at Retina Associates examined the eye and told him: "I can't explain it, but that large hole you had in [the retina of] your eye is gone, except for a small piece of scar tissue." Conigliaro commented in his autobiography: "All of this they [the opthalmologists] regarded as remarkable and never could have predicted. . . . To me it all said one word: Miracle."

Returning to the Red Sox in 1969, Conigliaro batted .255, hit twenty home runs, and drove in eighty-two runs. The following season he retained his form at the plate and, in fact, was one of the most feared sluggers in the American League, with thirty-six home runs and 116 runs batted in. But he and Dick Williams were still at odds, and on October 11, 1970 Conigliaro was traded to the California Angels along with catcher Jerry Moses and pitcher Ray Jarvis for pitcher Ken Tatum, outfielder Jarvis Tatum, and minor-league infielder Douglas Griffin.

Tony Conigliaro has brown hair and brown eyes and he now weighs 202 pounds. His favorite recreations are travel, fishing, golf, tennis, and karate. He owns an employment agency, Tony C.'s Girls, Inc., and he is planning to do testimonials for commercial products in television ads. A Roman Catholic, he saw a religious significance in his comeback: "I must be a special kind of guy. God has always been good to my family, but this time I think he went out of his way." Regarding his bachelorhood, he wrote in his autobiography: "I made up my mind not to get married until I got my complete fling out of life. . . . I'm experimenting. . . . I'm very moody, I like quiet. Any girl who married me . . . would have to be completely mine. . . . When I get married . . . I hope to have a tight family held together by prayer, love, and respect."

References

Look 29:102+ My 4 '65 pors
N Y Post p92 Mr 13 '70 por
Sport 47:28+ Jl '69 por
Sports Illus 21:49+ Ag 3 '64 por
Conigliaro, Tony. Seeing It Through (1970)

CROMER, 3D EARL OF

July 28, 1918- United Kingdom Ambassador to the United States; banker
Address: b. British Embassy, 3100 Massachusetts Ave., N.W., Washington, D.C. 20008; h. "Frenchstreet Farm," Westerham, Kent, England

As Great Britain prepared to draw economically closer to Europe through eventual membership in the Common Market, George Rowland Stanley Baring, the third Earl of Cromer, arrived in Washington, D.C. in early February 1971 to serve as British Ambassador to the United States at a difficult time of shifting international alliances. In a career about equally divided between private banking and public service, Lord Cromer has acquired a solid background in both world monetary affairs and diplomacy. He is a former governor of the Bank of England and former chairman and managing director of the family merchant bank, Baring Brothers & Company Ltd. On an earlier mission in Washington he held the key post of economic minister at the British Embassy from 1958 to 1961.

The heir of Rowland Thomas Baring, the second Earl of Cromer, George Rowland Stanley Baring was born on July 28, 1918 in Hitchin, Hertfordshire, England. King George V stood sponsor at his christening. His mother is the former Lady Ruby Elliott, and he has two older sisters, Lady Rosemary Ethel (Mrs. John D. Hills) and Lady Violet Mary (Mrs. Sidney B. Vernon). The Baring family is one of England's most aristocratic, steeped in a tradition of public and royal service going back more than 200 years. Lord Cromer's great-granduncle, Alexander Baring, was sent to Washington on a diplomatic mission in 1842, to help negotiate the United States-Canada border. His grandfather, Evelyn Baring, the first Earl of Cromer, was British agent and consul general in Egypt from 1884 to 1907. His maternal grandfather, the fourth Earl of Minto, was Governor General of Canada and Viceroy of India. In government service and royal service throughout his life, Lord Cromer's father for some years held the position of Lord Chamberlain at the court of King George V, in which one of his duties was licensing plays.

Baring spent his childhood and school holidays at his parents' house in the West country, near

Exmoor on the Bristol Channel, where he enjoyed swimming, riding, shooting, and playing golf. He early acquired a lifelong interest in photography and cinematography. When he was about thirteen he became a page of honor to King George V, whom he attended until 1935. At the coronation of King George VI in 1937, when he was a page of honor to Queen Mary, he handed the Princesses Elizabeth and Margaret their coronets.

At the age of eight George Baring had been sent to a school near Broadstairs in Kent to prepare for Eton College. He completed his studies at Eton with credit rating in seven subjects and then spent eight months at Grenoble University in France learning French. In 1937 he entered Trinity College, Cambridge University, to read law. "I was not enthralled with my studies," he has recalled, "and wanted to start earning some money." Leaving college after a year, he began working at Baring Brothers & Company Ltd. as a junior clerk at an annual salary of £100. That merchant bank, one of the most respected in England and the oldest in the City of London, was founded by his great-great-grandfather, Sir Francis Baring, in 1765. During the summer of 1938 George Baring spent his vacation serving as the private secretary to the Marquis of Willingdon, whom he accompanied on an official goodwill tour of Argentina, Uruguay, and Brazil.

Just before the outbreak of World War II, Baring joined the Supplementary Reserve of Officers of the Grenadier Guards. He was called to active military service in September 1939, when Britain declared war on Germany. The army released him briefly from duty in early 1940 so that he could again serve the Marquis of Willingdon as private secretary, this time on a trip to New Zealand, a journey made by flying-boat. After his return to England he was eventually appointed to the Guards Armoured Division, with which he saw action in Normandy. His division was among the first Allied troops to reach Brussels. Baring was mentioned in dispatches, was awarded the decoration of Member of the British Empire at the end of the war, and was demobilized in April 1946 in the rank of lieutenant colonel.

In 1947 Baring Brothers & Company sent George Baring to New York to study American banking practices. For about a year he worked in the offices of four well-known financial organizations: J.P. Morgan & Company, Inc.; Kidder, Peabody & Company; Morgan Stanley & Company; and the Chemical Bank and Trust Company. When he returned to London in 1948 he became managing director of Baring Brothers. In later years he held directorships in the Royal Insurance Company Ltd., Liverpool London and Globe Insurance Company Ltd., Daily Mail and General Trust Ltd., Lewis's Investment Trust Ltd., Anglo-Newfoundland Development Company Ltd., and Harris & Partners Ltd., Toronto.

The title of the Earl of Cromer passed to George Baring on the death of his father in 1953. As quoted in the Washington *Post* (November 9, 1970), the British writer Anthony Sampson has observed that Lord Cromer's title, combined with

LORD CROMER

his ability and charm, "made a large mark" when he served at the British Embassy in Washington, D.C. as economic minister from 1958 to 1961. His position entailed the multiple functions of head of the United Kingdom treasury and supply delegation and executive director for his country of the International Monetary Fund, of the International Bank for Reconstruction and Development, of the International Finance Corporation, and, after September 1960, of the International Development Association, with the establishment of which he was closely connected.

While carrying out his mission in Washington, Lord Cromer was on leave of absence from Baring Brothers & Company. He formally severed his relationship with the merchant bank when he succeeded Cameron F. Cobbold as governor of the Bank of England in 1961. The appointment by Prime Minister Harold Macmillan of Lord Cromer to head Great Britain's national central bank had caused some surprise in government and financial circles because of the relative youth of the Earl and because, unlike many of his predecessors, he had never served on the bank's court of directors. Lord Cromer left Washington in January 1961 to work as a part-time director of the Bank of England until assuming the governorship for a five-year term on July 1, 1961. He became the bank's 113th governor and, at the age of forty-two, its youngest in more than two centuries. While head of the Bank of England, he was also a director of the Bank of International Settlement in Basel, Switzerland and a governor of the World Bank.

The Bank of England was founded as a privately owned commercial bank in 1694, during the reign of William and Mary, and was nationalized in 1946. With headquarters in the financial district of the City of London, it has been nicknamed "The Old Lady of Threadneedle Street." The bank issues currency, manages the national debt, sets basic interest rates, administers foreign exchange transactions, serves as a depository for government funds, and on occasion acts to stabilize prices for gold and the pound sterling. The governor of the Bank of England is considered the most important financial figure in the country after the Chancellor of the Exchequer.

In November 1964, when world confidence in the British pound was low, Lord Cromer saved it from a sudden, forced devaluation by persuading, within a single afternoon, the top bankers in ten countries to give the Bank of England $3 billion in credit. "The reserves were just going to run out," he later explained in an interview with Terry Coleman of the *Guardian* (November 13, 1970). "My job was to deal with the situation. I literally got on the telephone to all the other leading central banks, having worked out on an envelope before how much we needed, to ask if they would give us credit. . . . [The pound] was saved at that moment. There would have been a worldwide collapse."

During the last year of Lord Cromer's term as head of the Bank of England, and shortly before the crisis of the pound sterling, Macmillan's Conservative government was voted out and replaced by the Labour government of Harold Wilson. Lord Cromer, who had earlier criticized the Conservatives for heavy spending, soon found himself at odds with the new Prime Minister over economic policies. The Labour government, dedicated to a high rate of public spending, would, according to Lord Cromer, bring about the downfall of the pound unless it mended its ways. He favored a severe reduction in government expenditures and a boost in productivity to restore balance.

At a meeting of the Institute of Bankers in Scotland in mid-February 1965 Lord Cromer warned that the international rescue of the pound the preceding November "no more guarantees our future than Dunkirk presaged swift victory in 1940." In his open criticism of Labour's expansionist policy he broke with the traditional practice of the governor of the Bank of England usually to offer only private advice to the government. One London financial editor described his speech as "the stiffest ever made by the governor of the Bank." Coming at a time when the Labourites were shaping policies for the new fiscal year, Lord Cromer's charges of government extravagance precipitated calls for his dismissal from several left-wing members of Parliament. He remained in office, however, until the end of his term, resigning as governor of the Bank of England on June 30, 1966, when he was succeeded by Leslie Kenneth O'Brien.

Lord Cromer resumed work at Baring Brothers & Company in 1966 as senior partner. Soon afterward he also became a director of Union Carbide Corporation, chairman of IBM (UK) Ltd., and honorary chairman of Harris & Partners Ltd., Toronto. At the request of the president of the Board of Trade he undertook an investigation of the subject of financing major overseas capital projects, and for Lloyds of London he made a study of the working of the insurance market. He was also associated with the business and industrial advisory council to the Organization for Economic Cooperation and Development, serving as chairman of a subcommittee concerned with freedom of movement of capital.

Continuing to denounce what he regarded as Labour's breaking of the rules of sound finance, Lord Cromer may very well have influenced a considerable number of voters in favor of the Conservatives during the June 1970 election campaign, of which the most hotly debated issue was the state of the British economy. In that election the victorious Conservatives ended almost six years of rule by the Labour party. The following November Prime Minister Edward Heath, the Conservative party leader, named Lord Cromer to succeed Labourite John Freeman as British Ambassador to the United States. On February 8, 1971 Lord Cromer, who had resigned his positions with Baring Brothers & Company, presented his credentials to President Richard Nixon in Washington. The British Embassy is the largest diplomatic establishment in the capital, with a total personnel of 670.

The selection of Lord Cromer as Ambassador to the United States indicates the importance that Heath attaches to having an expert in international finance deal with the many changes in Anglo-American relations expected to result from Britain's closer economic alliance with the Continent. "I see the important part of my job in the area of commerce and trade and in the dollar-sterling relationship during the coming Common Market monetary developments," the Ambassador said in a press interview soon after his appointment. "It will be important to explain to the Americans why Britain must move closer to Europe."

About the time of his arrival in Washington, in early February 1971, Lord Cromer was appointed a knight commander of the Order of St. Michael and St. George. He was made a member of the Queen's Privy Council in 1966. Among his honors is a LL.D. degree from New York University conferred in November 1966, when he delivered the fifth annual Arthur K. Salomon Lecture, on the world's capital markets, at the university's Graduate School of Business Administration. He has written several articles on British economy, including "Sterling and the Common Market," which was published during 1967 in *The World Today*. His clubs are Brooks's and Beefsteak in London, Brook in New York City, and the Metropolitan in Washington. He is a member of the Church of England.

On January 10, 1942 George Rowland Stanley Baring married Esmé Harmsworth, whose father, Arthur Harmsworth, Viscount Rothermere, owns the London *Daily Mail* and is reportedly one of the wealthiest men in England. Lord and Lady Cromer have three children: their older son, Evelyn, Viscount Errington, is a journalist; their younger son, Vivian, attends agricultural college; and their daughter, Lady Lana, is married to Anthony Grey, a stockbroker.

The Earl and Countess of Cromer have a house in London and a Provence-style villa in the south of France near Cannes. In 1948 they bought from Winston Churchill a farm in Kent on which Lady Cromer won modest renown as a breeder of pedigreed Jersey cattle. For some years she held the position of Lady of the Bedchamber (lady in waiting) to Queen Elizabeth II. Lord Cromer, known to his friends as Rowley, has been described in the Washington *Post* as a "burly" man who laughs and talks easily, but chooses his words cautiously. He is six feet tall, weighs 170 pounds, and has blue eyes and graying dark-brown hair. He smokes cigarettes, using a long holder. Among his interests and hobbies are yachting, swimming, electronics, and wood and metal working.

References

Guardian p11 N 13 '70 por
N Y Post p21 F 27 '71
N Y Times p21 Jl 1 '61 por; p53+ N 23
   '66 por; p2 N 9 '70 por
Newsweek 76:55+ N 23 '70 por
Time 85:90 F 26 '65 por
Washington (D.C.) Post A p41+ D 27 '70
   por; p29 F 19 '71
International Who's Who, 1970-71
International Year Book and Statesmen's
   Who's Who, 1970
Who's Who, 1970-71
Who's Who in America, 1970-71

DASSIN, JULES (das'in jōōlz)

Dec. 12, 1911- Film and theatre director; producer; writer; actor
Address: b. c/o Alain Bernheim, 16 Avenue Hoche, Paris 8°, France

The expatriated American film maker Jules Dassin is perhaps best known for having given the world Greece's enchanting actress, Melina Mercouri, now his wife. *Never on Sunday*, his ebullient ode to Greece, made Miss Mercouri an international star in 1960, and she has since been featured in most of his films. A director with an acute sense of atmosphere, mood, and the big dramatic—or melodramatic—moment, Dassin has produced such absorbing crime thrillers as *Rififi* (1956), *Topkapi* (1964), and *The Naked City* (1948), which was made in the United States before he left in 1953. To many, however, his finest film is *He Who Must Die* (1958), a stark retelling of Christ's Passion that was filmed in a Greek village. The Hollywood blacklist of the McCarthy era forced Dassin to seek employment in Europe, where he has remained. In recent years he has returned to the United States to stage the Broadway musical *Illya Darling* (1967) and to film the racial drama *Uptight!* (1969).

Jules Dassin was born in Middletown, Connecticut on December 12, 1911, one of eight children of Samuel Dassin, a barber, and his wife Berthe (Vogel) Dassin. Both parents were Jewish emigrants from Russia. The Dassins moved to Harlem, in New York City, when Jules was a child, and the boy later graduated from Morris High School in the Bronx. For a short time in 1936 he studied drama in Europe, but he soon returned to New York, where he became involved in various leftist theatrical ventures. As a member of the Artef

JULES DASSIN

Players Collective, he acted in a production of *The Good Soldier Schweik* (1937) and in *Clinton Street* (1939), a melodrama about life on the Lower East Side. For the WPA Federal Theatre Project in 1937 Dassin played the lead in *Revolt of the Beavers*, a Marxist musical for children that treated the struggle of the working classes in terms of an allegory about beavers.

Dassin has acknowledged that he joined the Communist party around that time, in the late 1930's, but he reportedly left it in 1939. By 1940 he was writing for Kate Smith's radio show and had created a radio adaptation of Gogol's *The Overcoat*. That year he made his debut as a director with *Medicine Show*, a Broadway production of a script originally prepared for the Federal Theatre Project. The play utilized the Living Newspaper technique, and John Mason Brown of the New York *Times* (April 13, 1940) called it "a plea for socialized medicine" that was "directed with uncommon felicity."

In 1941 Dassin left New York for Hollywood with an RKO contract as an apprentice director. After eight months in which he did nothing but "sit and observe" the veteran directors Garson Kanin and Alfred Hitchcock, Dassin left RKO for MGM. His first assignment was to make a short film based on a story by Edgar Allan Poe. The result, *The Tell-Tale Heart* (1941), was described by Gordon Gow of *Films and Filming* (February 1970) as "a small masterpiece of accelerating tension," and it won a number of awards.

After several indifferent feature films for MGM—*Nazi Agent* (1942), *The Affairs of Martha* (1942), *Reunion in France* (1942), and *Young Ideas* (1943)—Dassin scored a modest hit with *The Canterville Ghost* (MGM, 1944), a genial comedy based on the Oscar Wilde story. His next effort was *A Letter for Evie* (MGM, 1946), a sentimental comedy about a correspondence between a soldier and a girl who have never met. His final film for MGM was *Two Smart People* (1946), starring Lucille Ball and John Hodiak as government bond thieves.

After his exit from MGM, Dassin directed a series of naturalistic, gritty melodramas that established his early reputation. Teamed up with the producer Mark Hellinger he made *Brute Force* (Universal-International, 1947), a violent thriller about an attempted prison escape that starred Burt Lancaster as the convict leader and Hume Cronyn as a sadistic guard who beat his prisoners to the strains of Wagner. Again with Hellinger he filmed *The Naked City* (Universal-International, 1948), an absorbing yarn about the detection and capture of a murderer by the New York City homicide squad that critics honored for its tough but loving view of the people, sights, and sounds of Manhattan. Like *The Naked City, Thieves' Highway* (Twentieth Century-Fox, 1949) was shot on location, this time in California, in the fruit orchards, on the highways, and in the teeming San Francisco produce markets that made up the environment of the film's truckdriver hero. In London Dassin filmed the less successful *Night and the City* (Twentieth Century-Fox, 1950), a murky, turgid depiction of the London underworld.

In between his Hollywood film melodramas, Dassin tried his hand at music and comedy on Broadway. His first effort was *Joy to the World,* a comedy lampooning Hollywood commercialism that he staged early in 1948. When that venture closed about four months later, Dassin began direction of *Magdalena,* an ambitious production brought to New York from the Los Angeles Civic Opera Association. Despite lavish and expensive staging, fine performances, and a superior musical score by the distinguished Brazilian composer Heitor Villa-Lobos, the musical play received mixed reviews when it opened on September 20, 1948, and it closed after only eighty-eight performances, reportedly at a disastrous loss to its backers. Dassin's next Broadway assignment did not come until late 1952, when he staged the revue *Two's Company,* a change of pace for its star Bette Davis in her first song and dance role.

By the time he began work on *Two's Company* his career had already been jeopardized by the House Un-American Activities Committee investigations of Communist infiltration in Hollywood. In 1951 Edward Dmytryk in committee testimony named Dassin as a member of the Hollywood "Communist faction," and he was later named by Frank Tuttle. In the fall of 1952 Dassin was subpoenaed by the committee to testify, but he was able to obtain a postponement because of his work on the Bette Davis revue. In an interview with Thomas M. Pryor of the New York *Times* (March 17, 1959) Dassin recalled that after obtaining a subsequent postponement, he was informed by the committee early in 1953 that his testimony had been "postponed indefinitely." Nonetheless, he found himself unemployable in the United States and left for France with his wife and children in 1953. Even in that more permissive climate he was unable to find work, because European producers feared that American exhibitors would blacklist his films. Chronically in debt, Dassin managed to support himself and his family by writing plays and poems.

After several years of struggle, Dassin found a French producer willing to back him on the making of a low-budget film based on a novel by Auguste le Breton, the French Mickey Spillane. A spellbinding thriller about a jewelry robbery in Paris, *Rififi* created a sensation in Europe and in the United States, where it was released by the United Motion Picture Organization in 1956. Besides directing the film, Dassin was coauthor of the screen play and, under the pseudonym Perlo Vita, played one of the jewel thieves, a rascally little safecracker with a weakness for women. Alton Cook of the New York *World-Telegram and Sun* (June 5, 1956) wrote of Dassin, "As a director, he has composed his scenes with an unfailing eye for human tension. He catches the emotions of men under stress, especially in his frequent close-ups of the eyes." The most admired—and imitated—section of the film was a tense, wordless, thirty-five-minute sequence in which the robbery was executed. *Rififi* won several international film awards for Dassin, and it encouraged producers to consider his work despite his unofficial blacklisting.

At the 1956 Cannes Festival Dassin met Melina Mercouri, and the couple soon became inseparable, although Dassin was still married and so was the Greek actress. With the help of Miss Mercouri's father, a member of the Greek parliament, Dassin went to Greece to make his next film, *Celui Qui Doit Mourir (He Who Must Die,* Kassler, 1958), on the island of Crete. Dassin adapted the screenplay with Ben Barzman from Nikos Kazantzakis' powerful novel *The Greek Passion,* a twentieth-century retelling of Christ's suffering and death. The theme is the inevitability of Christ's crucifixion, and the modern counterpart to Jesus is a shepherd who plays the Son of God in a Passion Play presented by the members of a Greek village under the Turkish occupation. Although it did not achieve the commercial success of *Rififi, He Who Must Die* was equally praised and feted. It proved that Dassin's art could reach depths unfathomed by his crime thrillers. Richard L. Coe of the Washington *Post and Times Herald* (April 23, 1959) expressed the consensus of critical opinion when he called the film "a screen classic—beautiful in concept, exciting in execution, absorbing to think about."

Although Melina Mercouri portrayed the village Mary Magdalene in *He Who Must Die,* she did not attain international stardom as Dassin's leading lady until the release of *Never on Sunday* in 1960. After conceiving and writing the screen play, Dassin produced that film on a low budget for United Artists and directed it on location in Greece. He has claimed that he cast himself opposite Miss Mercouri, in the role of a priggish American tourist who tries to reform the happy Greek prostitute, because he did not have the money to hire a leading man. A few critics complained of the film's dependence on the clichéd "whore-with-heart-of-gold" theme, but most of them warmed to *Never on Sunday*'s gayety, spontaneity, and Greek charm. Bosley Crowther of the New York *Times* (October 12, 1960) wrote of the starring team: "Both . . . are superb—she in a flashy, forceful fashion and he in a Chaplinesque vein." The film packed houses on both sides of the Atlantic; its theme song became a hit tune; and it reportedly caused a boom in tourism to Greece. Dassin received an Academy Award nomination for his direction.

The success of *Never on Sunday* prompted the American release of Dassin's French-Italian produced *La Loi* under the title *Where the Hot Winds Blow* (MGM, Embassy, 1960). Written and directed by Dassin, it was shot on location in Southern Italy with an international cast including Melina Mercouri, Gina Lollobrigida, Yves Montand, and Marcello Mastroianni. Despite some admiring reviews, the film received little promotion and failed to make a stir in the United States. Nor was the reception enthusiastic for *Phaedra* (Lopert, 1962), an ambitious but essentially unbelievable modern version of the ancient Greek Phaedra legend that was coauthored, produced, and directed by Dassin. Again set in Greece, this time on the island of Hydra, *Phaedra* starred Melina Mercouri as a Greek shipping magnate's wife destroyed by love for her half-English stepson (Anthony Perkins).

Dassin reinstated himself at the box office with *Topkapi* (United Artists, 1964), a jewel-robbery thriller, based on an Eric Ambler novel, that combined the suspense of *Rififi* with a witty script and the abundant charms of Melina Mercouri. Produced and directed by Dassin, and filmed in extravagant, kaleidoscopic color in Istanbul, *Topkapi* dealt with an eccentric gang of amateur jewel thieves, including Robert Morley, Peter Ustinov, and Miss Mercouri, out to steal the world's choicest emeralds from the Topkapi Palace in Istanbul, Turkey.

The critics panned Dassin's next film, *10:30 P.M. Summer* (Lopert, 1966), finding it pretentious and grotesquely moody. Based on a Marguerite Duras novel that was adapted for the screen by the author and Dassin, the film starred Melina Mercouri as an alcoholic wife losing her husband to a younger woman. Slightly more successful was the director's next picture, *Uptight!* (Paramount, 1968), a remake of John Ford's 1935 classic *The Informer* that shifted the setting from Sinn Fein Ireland to today's black American ghetto. Although most critics found the transplantation unsatisfactory, many were impressed with the film as the first attempt underwritten by a major studio to express with honesty the feelings of black militants and moderates. *Uptight!* starred black actors and used a nearly all-black cast, but in *Promise at Dawn* (Avco-Embassy, 1971) Dassin again featured Melina Mercouri, as the undaunted mother who dominates Romain Gary's autobiographical novel on which the film is based.

Since his European exile Dassin has twice returned to the United States to stage Broadway plays. The first was *Isle of Children*, a lugubrious drama about a dying fourteen-year-old girl that, despite a masterly performance by Patty Duke, closed after only eleven performances in March 1962. Five years later he returned triumphantly

with Melina Mercouri to mount *Illya Darling*, his musical comedy adaptation of *Never on Sunday.* Although most critics felt that the story lost much of its freshness when saddled by the cumbersome conventions of the Broadway musical stage, it remained a splendid vehicle for Miss Mercouri, who won a Tony Award as the best musical actress of the year. After a nine-month run the play closed on January 13, 1968.

Slight and white-haired, Jules Dassin has the face "of a Medici cardinal," according to John Skow of the *Saturday Evening Post* (January 25, 1969). He has three children—Joseph, Richelle, and Julie—by his first wife, Beatrice Launer, whom he married in 1933 and divorced in 1962. He was married to Melina Mercouri on May 18, 1966. The films that Dassin made with Miss Mercouri in Greece helped to establish a thriving Greek film industry, but since the military takeover in 1967 the couple has not worked there. Of the Communist scare that curtailed his career in his native country Dassin has said, "I do not believe that the American movie public ever created a blacklist. The blacklist was always a fraud, an extraordinary fraud." Collaborating with Irwin Shaw, Dassin filmed a documentary on the June 1967 Arab-Israeli war entitled *Survival 1967.*

References

Films and Filming p?? + F '70; p66 + Mr '70
N Y Herald Tribune IV p12 Ap 9 '61 por
PM p23 Mr 9 '48
International Who's Who, 1970-71
Who's Who in America, 1970-71
Who's Who in France, 1965-66

DIEBENKORN, RICHARD (CLIFFORD, JR.)

Apr. 22, 1922- Artist
Address: b. Department of Art, University of California at Los Angeles, Los Angeles, Calif. 90024; c/o Marlborough-Gerson Gallery, 41 E. 57th St., New York 10022; h. 334 Amalfi Dr., Santa Monica, Calif. 90403

Independent of aesthetic vogues in his still-evolving career, the West Coast artist Richard Diebenkorn has been guided by his devotion to painting as a "physical thing, an involvement with a tangible feeling of sensation." But with action painting, or abstract expressionism, as it is more commonly called, he gradually combined elements of other styles, and to the avant-garde he brought many influences of the past, among them fauvism, neo-impressionism, and American realism. His inspiration, and often his subject, has been his natural environment, California.

Richard Clifford Diebenkorn Jr. was born in Portland, Oregon on April 22, 1922, the son of Richard Clifford and Dorothy (Stevens) Diebenkorn. After he had completed his high school education, he attended the University of California at Berkeley. He served from 1943 to 1945 in the United States Marines and then resumed his art

RICHARD DIEBENKORN

training at the California School of Fine Arts in San Francisco as a recipient of the Albert Bender Grant-in-Aid in 1946, and other California art schools, finally obtaining his B.A. degree from Stanford University in 1949.

Meanwhile, in 1947 Diebenkorn had begun a three-year teaching stint at the California School of Fine Arts, where he had studied under Mark Rothko and Clyfford Still, two of America's foremost abstract expressionists, who continued to exert a decisive influence on his early work. The postwar abstract expressionist movement, which marked the emergence of the United States as the world leader in modern art, began on the East Coast under the pioneering guidance of Rothko, Jackson Pollock, and Franz Kline, among other painters. Rothko, along with Still, then became a central figure in the California group of abstract expressionists belonging to the San Francisco bay area movement that flourished under the encouragement of the San Francisco Museum of Art.

Stimulated by the work of Still and Rothko, Diebenkorn skimmed over the representational phase that is a customary part of the training of young artists. He began painting in an abstract manner almost immediately, and in 1948 his work won him a one-man show at San Francisco's California Palace of the Legion of Honor. Critically well received, the show contributed much to his early recognition as one of the West Coast's top abstract painters.

While continuing to paint in the abstract expressionist manner over the next few years, Diebenkorn gradually moved away from executing purely abstract canvases like those of Pollock or Rothko. His work was closely linked to the California terrain in a landscape element often suggested or clearly visible. Especially preoccupied with space in painting, he communicated a feeling of space through large geometric areas of color that gave the impression, sometimes, of patterns of fields, mountains, or hills. His colors were strong and bright; the paint was laid on thickly and with a free, noticeable brush stroke, characteristic of the action painters.

The appearance of the landscape motif in the horizontal-vertical structures of Diebenkorn's pictures has been attributed to his leaving California and his colleagues of the abstract expressionist persuasion around 1950. According to an article in *Life* (November 4, 1957), "When he moved away from the group and went to live in New Mexico, he began to create a less abstract art based on recollections of the California landscape he had left behind." Diebenkorn was awarded his M.A. degree at the University of New Mexico in 1952. Then after a year of teaching at the University of Illinois, he returned to California, settled in Berkeley, and in early 1955 became assistant professor of drawing and painting at the College of Arts and Crafts in Oakland, a post he held for about five years.

Californians saw Diebenkorn's work in a one-man show at the San Francisco Museum of Art in 1954 and in several group shows in other cities. Outside his own state he became better known through his inclusion in the Guggenheim Museum's "Younger American Painters" show in New York in 1954, in the Walker Art Center's "Vanguard '55" show in Minneapolis in 1955, and in group shows at the Carnegie Institute in Pittsburgh in 1955 and the Whitney Museum of American Art in New York in 1955. He was also represented in a group exhibition at the Poindexter Gallery in New York in late 1955, when he received special mention in the New York *Times* review of the show, having impressed the critic by his ability to suggest vast spaces even when working in a small format.

Soon afterward, in March of 1956, Diebenkorn had the first of his periodical one-man shows at the Poindexter. Calling him a "rising star" of the abstract expressionist movement, the reviewer for the New York *Times* (March 4, 1956) went on to say, "His compositions are vast and stratified irregularly, bedecked with lumps of pigment and run through with snake-like lines. In short, they resemble aerial photographs of a big varied landscape with shore-line, mountains, cliffs and fields, the contours, perhaps, of California."

Although barely recognizable, the horizons and deserts of Diebenkorn's pictures foreshadowed a decision he had reached some months before his New York exhibition, to abandon abstract expressionism. By that time nonobjectivism had become dominant in American painting, but no longer answered Diebenkorn's own aesthetic problems. "I was encumbered with style and too concerned with style," he once explained, as quoted in *Time* (March 17, 1958). "There were a good many things I wanted to say—to talk about—that a more strict style prevented. My painting was too inbred. Representation was a challenge I hadn't had before."

When Diebenkorn introduced human figures into his pictures, however, he retained much of the abstract expressionist technique of applying paint. His own individual style remained largely the same: the bright color was only occasionally muted, and his interest in space and geometric form still prevailed. His one or two personages became the focal point of his vertical-horizontal structures, as in *Girl on Terrace* (1956), *Girl with Cups* (1957), *Man and Woman in a Large Room* (1957), *Man and Woman Seated* (1958), and *Woman in Profile* (1958). "It is here [at the figure] that the directional lines converge, that color becomes most intense and the pattern more varied," Peter Selz observed in *New Images of Man* (1959). "Thus the spaciousness of the surrounding areas is greatly enhanced by the familiar measure of the human figure." Others have commented on the tension arising from the contrast between the interior or exterior open space and the introspective figure.

In the treatment of his personages, therefore, Diebenkorn may be said to have been formal rather than primarily humanistic. And yet, according to an art critic for *Time* (March 17, 1958), change of mood constituted the chief difference between his objective and nonobjective work: "His abstractions recalled sunlit, freshly green California hills . . . ; his representations introduce man as a somber, lonely figure, and hark back to an early admiration for such realist painters as Edward Hopper." Diebenkorn's new pictures, however, integrated his abstract expressionism perhaps not so much with American realism as with the French modernists Manet, Vuillard, and Bonnard.

With two other West Coast artists, David Park and Elmer Bischoff, who joined him in breaking away from abstractionism, Diebenkorn exhibited his figurative paintings at the Oakland Museum of Art in 1957. That show, like Diebenkorn's one-man show at the Poindexter Gallery early the following year, generated much excitement as a fresh and unexpected aesthetic departure. The New Realists, as the three Californians came to be called, were not interested in organizing a movement for or against any artistic credo. As John Canaday later wrote in the New York *Times* (May 26, 1968), "Diebenkorn and his colleagues issued no manifesto, indulged in no professional diatribes, and neither sought nor shied away from publicity. They merely painted, and their survival outside the system of competitive exploitation remains one strong indication of their merits as artists."

Some of the paintings seen in Diebenkorn's 1958 show in New York were selected for inclusion in an exhibition, "Seventeen American Painters," held at the United States Pavilion at the Brussels World's Fair. From there the show moved to London as the inaugural exhibition of the new gallery of the United States Information Service. Of the seventeen painters represented, Diebenkorn was reported to have been among the two or three most generally admired by the British. After having his work exhibited widely and regularly throughout his own country, he returned to London in 1964 for a one-man show at the Tate Gallery. During that year he also visited the Soviet Union on a cultural exchange program arranged by the State Department. The Russians greeted him warmly, but criticized the lack of social message in his work, which he showed them in about a hundred slides.

A more important event for Diebenkorn of the year 1964 was the opening at the Washington (D.C.) Gallery of Modern Art of a major retrospective of his work. The show moved the following year to New York's Jewish Museum and then to the Pavilion Gallery in Newport Beach, California. Besides being enthusiastically reviewed in local papers, it came to national attention in *Newsweek* (November 30, 1964), whose delighted critic felt that the retrospective demonstrated that Diebenkorn "belongs in the big leagues." Referring to the abstract and representational phases of the artist's work, he observed, "Instead of a split personality, what Diebenkorn exhibits is stunning evidence of integration." He went on to say, "Retrospectives usually have an air of finality. But this one is the sum total of a man at half time. Armed with honesty, bedeviled by conscience, in search of risk and difficulty, Diebenkorn has still half a lifetime to pull out the big plays, to put on the big show."

The conclusion of the *Newsweek* review of the retrospective proved to be prophetic in an unexpected direction: the disappearance in 1967 of the figure from Diebenkorn's canvases. The result of the change was an abstract style moored, as always, to reality and showing the effect of the discipline acquired through the years of representational work. His careful structuring of color in the manner of Matisse, a constant in all phases of his work, became more pronounced and more personalized. Some of the paintings, notably the "Ocean Park" series, inspired by the surroundings of his new home at Ocean Park, Santa Monica, were shown at the Poindexter in May 1968 and at the Los Angeles County Museum in August 1969.

"Diebenkorn is a draftsman of remarkable gifts," is the opinion of the New York *Times* critic Hilton Kramer, who has written highly approving reviews of several of Diebenkorn's exhibitions of drawings in New York. In early 1971 he praised the tonal delicacy of drawings related to the "Ocean Park" series of paintings, but in general he preferred the drawings of Diebenkorn's representational period. "His drawings of the figure, in particular," he wrote in the New York *Times* (March 20, 1971), "were often so breathtaking in their virtuosity that at times they looked even better than the paintings."

Drawing is the subject of a book by Diebenkorn that was published in 1965. He taught at the San Francisco Art Institute from 1960 to 1966 and has since then been teaching as professor of art at the University of California at Los Angeles. In 1963-64 he was artist in residence at Stanford University. Among his awards are the Samuel Rosenberg Fellowship, the Tamarind Fellowship, and the Emanuel Walter Purchase Prize. His paintings are in the permanent collections of the Phillips Memorial Gallery in Washington, D.C., the Albright Gallery in Buffalo, the Toronto Museum, the San Francisco Museum of Art, and other major galleries and museums.

Richard Diebenkorn is a tall, dark-haired man of sturdy build. He married Phyllis Gilman on

June 16, 1943, and they have two children, Gretchen Gilman and Christopher James. From 1966 to 1969 he was a member of the National Council on the Arts. He became a member of the American Academy of Arts and Letters in 1962 and is also a member of the National Foundation on Arts and the Humanities.

References

> N Y Times II p37 My 26 '68
> Newsweek 64:97 N 30 '64 por
> Time 71:64 Mr 17 '58; 94:50+ Ag 1 '69 por
> International Who's Who, 1971-72
> Nordness, Lee, ed. Art USA Now vol 2 (1962)
> Selz, Peter. New Images of Man (1959)
> Who's Who in America, 1970-71
> Who's Who in American Art, 1970

DOMS, KEITH (dämz)

Apr. 24, 1920- Librarian; organization official
Address: b. The Free Library of Philadelphia, Logan Sq., Philadelphia, Pa. 19103; h. 3101 Coulter St., Philadelphia, Pa. 19129

When Emerson Greenaway retired as director of the Free Library of Philadelphia in 1969, the library's board of trustees looked for "the best librarian in America" to replace him. After considering twenty-five other candidates, they chose Keith Doms, then the librarian of the Carnegie Library of Pittsburgh, an authority on library physical-plant planning and a man known for his concern with the expansion of services, especially for the disadvantaged, and his ability to raise funds to implement that concern. In addition to heading Pennsylvania's greatest public library, Doms is serving as president of the American Library Association for 1971-72. Although the ALA declined sharply in membership between 1969 and 1971, from 39,115 to 32,774, after a sharp increase in its annual dues, it is still the largest national organization of librarians in the world. The association's executive offices are in Chicago.

Keith Doms was born in Endeavor, Wisconsin on April 24, 1920 to Reinhard Edward Doms, a banker, now retired, and Lillian Linda (Gohlke) Doms, and he grew up in Wisconsin and Minnesota. When he was a student at Omro (Wisconsin) High School his favorite extracurricular activity was boating on the Fox River. In 1938 he graduated from high school and matriculated at the University of Wisconsin in Madison, where he majored in modern languages, minored in social science, and worked part time at various jobs, including janitor, waiter, newspaper reporter, and truck driver.

In 1942 Doms took senior honors at Wisconsin, received his B.A. degree, and entered the United States Army, where his specialty was cryptology. Under army sponsorship he studied for nine months in 1943-44 at the School of Far Eastern Studies at Harvard University. About the factors that helped influence him in his choice of a career, Doms has said: "I have always placed high value on self-education and self-development. I saw early that public libraries had exceptional opportunities in these areas. Coupled with my own enjoyment of reading and my interest in education and people, I saw that librarianship offered an excellent opportunity for both professional and personal satisfaction."

After his discharge from the army, in 1946, Doms enrolled in the Graduate Library School of the University of Wisconsin, where he was elected president of his class. He took his B.L.S. degree with highest honors in 1947, after the acceptance of his dissertation on federal legislation for libraries. Doms was city librarian in Concord, New Hampshire from 1947 to 1951 and city librarian in Midland, Michigan from 1951 to 1956, when he went to the Carnegie Library of Pittsburgh (Pennsylvania) as assistant director.

Doms became associate director of the Carnegie Library in 1963 and its director in 1964. As director he built three new branch buildings and initiated plans for two more, established a mobile library for disadvantaged neighborhoods, a poetry forum, an annual poetry prize, and, in cooperation with Pennsylvania State University, a program facilitating business and industry's access to technical and scientific literature. He also established a regional film library, completed plans for a regional reference center, expanded the Carnegie Library's services for the blind, found a sponsor for the training of two black students a year for library service in the ghetto, and persuaded the city government to take over the funding of a library program for juvenile delinquents that the federal government was going to abandon. During his tenure in Pittsburgh, in 1964, Doms conducted a seminar on public library development in Karachi, Pakistan at the request of the United States Department of State.

In September 1969 Doms succeeded Emerson Greenaway as director of the Free Library of Philadelphia. At last count the library had more than 6,500,000 books and other items, about 5,000,000 of which were available to the general public, 600,000 card-holding patrons, and forty-three branches employing 600 people, under the direction of Alan Thomas. There is a large regional library, twenty-two miles away from the central library, and there are also a mercantile library, a library for the blind and physically handicapped, a regional film center, three bookmobiles, and six stationary trailer units.

At a seminar for library trustees at Columbia University on June 25, 1970, Doms spoke of some of the basic problems and issues confronting library administrators in their daily work. The first problem he discussed was that of money in relation to library service and structure in an age of rapid social change and compelling political and economic problems. Although "the competition for funds will be critical for the balance of the seventies," he said, there will be funds for libraries, along with other national priorities, but "they will not be doled out to librarians on the basis of the notion that libraries are a 'good thing,'" so that "the library administrator must give increasing attention to justification of his budget requests." With the flight of the relatively affluent to the suburbs, the question of who should support central city libraries, with reference and research facilities open to the greater metropolitan community, is now a crucial one. In that connection Doms pointed to the suggestion of Emerson Greenaway that "the central libraries of major metropolitan cities be operated as part of a federal system of reference-research libraries" and that "all other public libraries be organized into a state system."

Regarding the library as a community information center, Doms contended in his Columbia address that "there is room for experimentation in this area" and he gave as an example the alliance of the Free Library of Philadelphia with the local Model Cities Agency. "The Model Cities Agency planned a Community Information Center which would be a sophisticated system to deliver referral services and information to residents of the neighborhood via telephone and computer. While the Model Cities Agency will take the lead in computerizing referral services data, the Free Library in its supportive role will identify and encode appropriate information for storage in the data bank. The next step will be installation of computer terminals in all of our branches in the Model Cities Neighborhood. I believe that this program has great potential and can be extremely valuable to large numbers of citizens who might never relate their information needs to the public library."

Doms next discussed community participation or control. Libraries, he pointed out, have long been accustomed to consulting, or at least trying to sound the consensus of, their middle-class clients. "Now that new community voices are being heard, we must be responsive to these new voices as well. . . . To hear and work affirmatively with upward-bound citizens is central to the survival of cities, public libraries, and democratic traditions." His final points of discussion in the talk at Columbia were the problem of dealing with unionized manpower, interlibrary cooperation, and the freedom to read.

Freedom to read became a practical issue for Doms four months later, when two patrons of the Free Library objected to the inclusion of Jerry Rubin's radical political tract *Do It!* in the library's collections. Doms issued the following statement on October 9, 1970: "The Free Library of Philadelphia has always considered it a primary obligation to provide books for its public which are representative of all current significant political and social outlooks, no matter how controversial. . . . Once the library begins to censor the unpopular and disrespectful from its collections, it will have renounced its basic obligation to serve and strengthen a free society. Finally I want to point out that the book selection policy of the Free Library of Philadelphia embodies the American Library Association's Freedom to Read statement and the Library Bill of Rights." The American Book Association also endorses the statement.

KEITH DOMS

In an interview with Sandy Padwe of the Philadelphia *Inquirer* (December 7, 1970), Doms observed that decentralization is necessary in contemporary urban library service because "we have to meet the needs of specific communities." He went on: "But the whole fiscal dilemma of the American city affects what a library can do. This has been a frustrating problem for the whole staff. They should be spending their time thinking of creative programming, but we have to spend as much time holding the line and thinking of belt-tightening measures." He was alluding to a city budget crisis that threatened the jobs of approximately 100 library employees, without whom the central library would probably have to cut its hours from seventy to forty-five a week and the branches would have to curtail many services. Questioning the prevailing scale of priorities, in which education ranks far behind police, fire, and health services, he told Padwe that with "the society changing so rapidly," libraries should take on not lesser but "greater importance." "If we want to remain viable as humans, we have to make education and informing ourselves a lifelong experience."

Doms has held office in the American Library Association, at least on the state and administration division levels, ever since he began his library career in New Hampshire, and he has often made state and local surveys of library buildings and furnishings for or through the ALA. From 1963 to 1967 he was on the executive board of the association. Elected to the ALA's highest office in June 1970, he was inaugurated in the presidency on June 25, 1971, during the association's ninetieth annual conference, in Dallas, Texas.

The Philadelphia librarian is a member of the Pennsylvania Governor's Council on Library Development, the Pennsylvania Advisory Council on Library Service for the Blind and Physically Handicapped, the Pennsylvania Advisory Council on International Cooperation, and the Joint Committee on Coordination of Public Research Agencies of Philadelphia. He is president of the Pennsylvania Home Teaching Society and a director of the World Affairs Council of Philadelphia, the Freedom to Read Foundation, the Historical Society of Western Pennsylvania, Pennsylvania Union Catalogue, and station WQED-WQEX in Pittsburgh, and he is on the board of visitors of the Graduate School of Library and Information Sciences at the University of Pittsburgh. Articles on library planning and related subjects by Doms have appeared in the *Pennsylvania Library Association Bulletin*, the *Wilson Library Bulletin*, and *Local Public Library Administration* (International City Managers Association, 1964), among other publications.

Keith Doms and Margaret Ann Taylor were married on April 1, 1944. They have two sons, Peter Edward and David Laurance. Doms is five feet nine inches tall, weighs 165 pounds, and has hazel eyes and brown, brush-cut hair. He lists his political affiliation as Democrat and his religious as Protestant. His favorite recreations are reading, fresh water fishing, and camping, and he collects political memorabilia and antiques. His clubs are the Philobiblon, the Franklin Inn, and the Science and Art Club of Germantown, and he is a member of the Philadelphia Art Alliance and the Museum Council of Philadelphia. Honors bestowed on him include the Pennsylvania Library Association's Award of Merit and the Distinguished Citizens Award of the Alpha Epsilon chapter of Delta Sigma Theta. In 1963-64 Doms was president of Beta Phi Mu, the national honorary fraternity for librarians.

References

Philadelphia Inquirer mag p24 N 23 '69
    pors; D 7 '70 por
Biographical Directory of Librarians in the
    United States and Canada (1970)
Who's Who in America, 1970-71

DOWELL, ANTHONY

Feb. 16, 1943- British ballet dancer
Address: b. Royal Opera House, Covent Garden, London, W.C. 2, England

A principal of the Royal Ballet since 1966, Anthony Dowell is generally recognized as the outstanding male dancer of that company and as one of the finest dancers of his generation. Endowed with an impeccable line, aristocratic bearing, and an elegantly pure technique, he is often compared to the great Danish *danseur noble*, Erik Bruhn. Although Dowell has been acclaimed for such dance portrayals as the Messenger of Death in MacMillan's *Song of the Earth* and the Boy with Matted Hair in Tudor's *Shadowplay*, he is best known for his *pas de deux* with Antoinette Sibley, and their partnership has become almost as heralded as that of Margot Fonteyn and Rudolf Nureyev, the Royal Ballet's much publicized guest artists. As well as representing the cool, lucid British style of dance at its best, Dowell and Sibley achieve a breathtaking fusion of movement

and spirit, whether dancing together in classics like *Swan Lake, Sleeping Beauty,* and *The Nutcracker,* or in such modern works as MacMillan's *Romeo and Juliet* and Ashton's *The Dream.*

Anthony James Dowell was born in London on February 16, 1943 to Arthur Henry and Catherine Ethel Dowell. His dancing career began early, and almost by chance. Dowell's mother, who had studied dancing but had never performed professionally, envisioned a career in dance for his older sister, and the girl was enrolled at the Hampshire School, a private elementary school in London that included dancing in its curriculum. At the age of five Anthony was sent along to the same school and put into the dancing class, where he began studying ballet, tap, and musical comedy routines. Dowell remembers his dance teacher there, the late June Hampshire, as "marvelous," and he was soon captivated by the magic of the stage, which he experienced while performing in the annual student recitals Mrs. Hampshire produced at a London theatre.

Mrs. Hampshire recognized Dowell's flair for dancing and recommended that he audition for the Royal Ballet School, the official school of the Royal Ballet. (Dowell's sister evidently flourished under Mrs. Hampshire's tutelage also, for she went on to dance in West End musicals.) The boy was accepted at the Royal Ballet, after performing only a simple routine of warm-up exercises, and at the age of ten he enrolled at the Royal Ballet's junior school at White Lodge. Dowell was disappointed to discover at White Lodge that the emphasis was on academic studies, which he loathed, and that he was allowed to dance for only an hour a day. Nor were there any recital performances. Nevertheless, he endured the regimen, kept up the required high grades, and found artistic solace in painting and drawing and making paper sculptures.

Once enrolled at the senior school of the Royal Ballet, at Baron's Court, Dowell found himself much happier. There dance was the principal activity, and the students attended regular classes in ballet technique, character dancing, and *pas de deux*, in which men and women dance together in supported movement. Even more important, senior students were used as extras in big ballet productions at Covent Garden. To his consternation, Dowell was one of the last boys in his class to be invited to perform, but he finally made his debut as a Hunter in *Swan Lake.*

Not long afterward, in 1960, Dowell was admitted to the Covent Garden Opera Ballet. For a year he divided his time between occasional performances and classes, until in July 1961 he was invited to join the corps of the Royal Ballet, just as that company was preparing for a tour of the Soviet Union. The following season Erik Bruhn chose Dowell for a solo in Bournonville's *Napoli Divertissement,* which he was staging for the Annual Benevolent Fund Gala. Dowell came down with the measles and missed the gala, but his solo received favorable notice when that ballet entered the repertory later in the year. Also in 1962 he danced the Country Boy in Andrée Howard's *La*

Fête étrange and the Boy in Kenneth MacMillan's *The Invitation*. By November 1962 the British magazine *Dance and Dancers* could cite him as an important newcomer in the ballet world.

On his first tour of the United States in 1963 with the Royal Ballet, he scored a personal success with *Napoli*, and in 1964 he created his first part, that of Oberon in *The Dream*, Frederick Ashton's one-act ballet based on *A Midsummer Night's Dream*. After its London première on April 2, 1964 Dowell was praised for his noble bearing and elegant technique. The occasion also marked the first appearance together of Dowell and Antoinette Sibley, one of the company's younger principal ballerinas whose training closely paralleled his. Recalling their early partnership in *The Dream*, Olga Maynard of *Dance Magazine* (April 1970) wrote, "We . . . saw at once that Dowell and Sibley were ideally suited to each other; in physical proportions, in temperaments, and in classical style."

In 1965 Dowell created the role of Benvolio in Kenneth MacMillan's *Romeo and Juliet*, and he later danced Romeo to Sibley's Juliet. (In the color film of the ballet, however, he appears as Benvolio.) When the Royal Ballet visited the United States in 1965 Dowell and Sibley danced together in both *Romeo and Juliet* and *The Dream*, and were featured in a *pas de deux* from the latter on the *Ed Sullivan Show* (CBS-TV).

By 1966, when he was promoted to the rank of principal dancer, Dowell's versatility was in evidence in such ballets as MacMillan's *Song of the Earth*, to music of Mahler; Ashton's *Monotones 1 and 2*, both *pas de trois* requiring superb classic line; Cranko's abstract *Brandenburg Nos. 2 and 4*, to music of Bach; and Bronislava Nijinska's dramatic and expressionistic ballet, *Les Noces*.

Early in 1967 Dowell created the role of the Boy with Matted Hair in *Shadowplay*, the first ballet ever choreographed for the Royal Ballet by the expatriate British choreographer Antony Tudor. Based on the coming of age of Kipling's jungle boy Mowgli, it is a ballet of considerable psychological subtlety and a superb showcase for Dowell's sensitivity of movement and interpretation. The dancer was widely acclaimed when the work was premièred in London on January 25, 1967, and those accolades were repeated in the spring when the Royal Ballet visited the United States.

That United States tour, Dowell's third, established him as a major artist. After his performance as the Messenger of Death in the American première of *Song of the Earth*, Walter Terry wrote in the New York *World Journal Tribune* (April 26, 1967), "He played it with taut strength, and he danced it with a movement power and with a muscle beauty which sang out with the radiance of the songs themselves. Indeed, an unforgettable dance portrayal by one of the Royal Ballet's most striking young stars." Having recently added Prince Siegfried and Count Albrecht to his repertoire in London, Dowell was given the opportunity to perform those choice classical roles in New

ANTHONY DOWELL

York. For Clive Barnes his *Swan Lake* with Antoinette Sibley was a "historic performance." Of Dowell as Siegfried in that performance Barnes wrote (New York *Times*, May 8, 1967), "Young Mr. Dowell shared his ballerina's triumph. In the last two years, he has improved immeasurably, and he now has the manner and distinction of a true premier danseur. His youthful interpretation of a Prince thrown into a sea of adolescent despair was both sensible and appropriate, and his partnership with Miss Sibley had the kind of incandescence that every great ballet partnership requires." Of his performance in *Giselle*, however, Barnes was more critical, finding that, as Albrecht, Dowell "looks rather too boyishly immature to be a convincing seducer. He seemed more like a kid brother with problems than a lover." Yet, in the same review (New York *Times*, May 15, 1967) Barnes wrote, "[Dowell's] partnership [with Merle Park] was exemplary, and his dancing in the second act was both noble and exquisite."

Since 1967 Dowell has added the major male roles in *The Nutcracker*, *Cinderella*, and *The Sleeping Beauty* to his credits, as well as the leads in several one-act ballets, most notably revivals of Ashton's *Daphnis and Chloe* and *Symphonic Variations* and the part of Troyte in Ashton's masterpiece *Enigma Variations*, premièred in October 1968. Of his Daphnis, Barnes wrote in the New York *Times* (April 30, 1970), "Mr. Dowell is a beautifully ardent dancer—his nerve-ends are in his technique, his very smile, tight and yet gracious, is part of his characterization."

In London and in the United States, where they have toured most recently in 1969 and 1970, Anthony Dowell and Antoinette Sibley are an increasingly magnetic box-office draw. Their partnership is fast becoming legendary—the distinguished dance critic P. W. Manchester has called it "all but unique"—and the dancers themselves seem to regard it as almost magical. In an interview with Olga Maynard for *Dance Magazine* (April 1970) Dowell tried to explain its essence: "From the beginning of our partnership nothing ever jarred. . . . Antoinette's body always feels right to me; in balance, everything. Dancing together is somehow never awkward, or wrong. There is the way we make contact, in various moods—just the way of looking at each other, as well as moving, behaving—that seems natural to us."

Anthony Dowell has wavy brown hair and hazel eyes that often appear blue onstage. He is said to be unusually conscientious and hardworking. Because of the large roster of principal dancers with the Royal Ballet and the paucity of their London performances (seven every two weeks), he has reportedly felt that he does not get enough chance to perform. In 1970 he and Miss Sibley signed contracts with the Royal Ballet that allow them freedom to perform elsewhere when they are not busy at Covent Garden or on company tours. (Up until that time Dowell had never danced outside the Royal Ballet, except for a few performances of *La Fille Mal Gardée* in Johannesburg and of *Song of the Earth* in Stuttgart). Although they still appear occasionally with other partners, Dowell and Sibley think of themselves as a team on a long-range basis. When asked by Miss Maynard in the *Dance Magazine* interview what they wanted to perform in the future, Dowell replied, "Everything, and especially things that are created for us. . . . The classics are the greatest ballets because they are the hardest—you are pitted against the legends and that is an awesome challenge. But it is exciting to go into new things, things that are created specifically for you, and dancers need that excitement to survive."

References

Dance Mag 41:54 Je '67 pors; 44:50+ Ap '70 pors
N Y Times p52 My 8 '67; p55 My 15 '67
N Y World Journal Tribune III p34 Ap 26 '67
Chujoy, Anatole, and Manchester, P. W., eds. Dance Encyclopedia (1967)
Who's Who (1970-71)

DRINAN, ROBERT F(REDERICK)

Nov. 15, 1920- United States Representative from Massachusetts; Roman Catholic priest; lawyer; educator
Address: b. 509 Cannon Bldg., Washington, D.C. 20515; h. 140 Commonwealth Ave., Newton, Mass. 02167

The first Roman Catholic priest ever to serve as a voting member of the United States Congress is the Rev. Robert F. Drinan, S.J., who scored an upset victory in the midterm Congressional elections of 1970 over Philip J. Philbin, longtime Democratic Representative from Massachusetts. (The only other Roman Catholic priest to sit in Congress was the Rev. Gabriel Richard, a nonvoting delegate to the House from the territory of Michigan in 1823.) Chosen by a caucus of independent Democratic antiwar groups to oppose Philbin, an influential Congressional "hawk,"

Drinan waged a successful campaign against the incumbent in the September 1970 primary and in the November election, in which Philbin was a write-in candidate. The Jesuit priest's victory was widely hailed as a triumph of the New Politics, which combines efficient campaign organization with an ideological appeal to issues.

Before entering politics, Father Drinan had long been an activist in civil rights and antiwar causes as well as an articulate and moderate Roman Catholic spokesman on such issues as birth control, abortion, and public aid to parochial schools. A lawyer, Drinan has been dean of the Boston College Law School since 1956 and is now on leave from that post. From 1969 to 1970 he served as provost and vice-president of Boston College.

Robert Frederick Drinan was born on November 15, 1920 in Boston, Massachusetts to the late James John and Ann Mary (Flanagan) Drinan. He has one brother, Francis W., a Newton, Massachusetts physician, and one sister, Catherine (Mrs. Otfried) Brauns-Packenius, who lives with her husband in Frankfurt, Germany. Growing up in the Hyde Park section of Boston, Robert Drinan learned to play the clarinet and was a clarinetist with the Boston Civic Symphony.

As a day student at Boston College, Drinan was on the debating team. After earning his B.A. degree in 1942, he entered the Society of Jesus and then studied at Weston College in Weston, Massachusetts, where one of his classmates was Daniel Berrigan, the Jesuit radical peace activist. In 1947 Drinan received an M.A. degree from Boston College. From the Georgetown University Law Center the young scholastic received the LL.B. degree in 1949 and the LL.M. in 1950. After being ordained into the priesthood at Weston in June 1953 Drinan went to Rome, where he completed the requirements for the Licentiate in Sacred Theology at Gregorian University in 1954. Then, for a year, he studied in Florence, Italy.

Father Drinan was admitted to practice before the Washington, D.C. bar in 1950, the United States Supreme Court in 1955, and the Massachusetts state bar in 1956. In 1955 he joined the faculty of the Boston College Law School as associate dean and professor of family law and church-state relations. Promoted to dean a year later, Drinan continued as dean and professor at the law school until going on leave in 1969 to run for Congress. Under Drinan's leadership the law school began to publish the *Boston College Law Review* and rose from being what a federal jurist once called "a moribund institution" to one of the nation's top twelve or fifteen law schools in terms of the calibre of its student body.

Over the years Father Drinan brought his legal expertise to bear on a number of social issues. In his book *Religion, the Courts and Public Policy* (McGraw-Hill, 1963) he argued persuasively for aid to parochial schools and made a critical analysis of the Supreme Court's decision on prayer in public schools. As chairman of the family law section of the American Bar Association (1966-67) Father Drinan advocated separate counsel for children in divorce proceedings and a mandatory reconciliation system for couples seeking divorce. He also helped to draft a marriage code that would require a mandatory waiting period between the time a couple takes out a marriage license and their wedding.

On the controversial issues of birth control and abortion Drinan has taken moderate stands. Speaking before the Catholic Association for International Peace in October 1967 he pointed out that although natural law forbids artificial birth control it also imposes the duty on both individuals and states to limit procreation to the number of individuals that can be adequately cared for. For that reason Roman Catholics can in good conscience support tax-financed family planning clinics as long as provisions are made for methods acceptable to them. Two years later the priest was one of a group of Massachusetts clergymen who asked Governor Francis W. Sargent to pardon William Baird, the birth-control advocate, who had been jailed for giving birth control supplies to a Boston University coed in violation of the state's archaic statutes.

At an international conference on abortion held in Washington in September 1967 Father Drinan opposed a provision in the American Law Institute's model penal code that allowed abortion when there is a substantial risk of the child's being born defective. He deplored the power that such legislation would give a state to permit the selective destruction of life, and he suggested that a similar law recently adopted in North Carolina might have been intended to cut down the number of Negro births. Although he denounced abortion, he suggested that the abolition of all laws prohibiting abortion during the first six months of pregnancy might be a preferable alternative to laws allowing selective abortion.

As chairman of the advisory committee for Massachusetts to the United States Commission on Civil Rights (1962-70), Drinan conducted open hearings during the spring of 1966 in Boston's black ghettoes. The committee's report, documenting the need for urgent reforms and predicting violence in the streets, was not released by the federal government for over a year, until after their prediction had been fulfilled in the June 1967 rioting in Boston's Roxbury district. Late in 1969 Drinan took a key role in a widely publicized dispute between black militant students and the Volpe Construction Company over its discriminative hiring practices on a construction project at Tufts University.

Long a critic of American involvement in Indochina, Father Drinan traveled to South Vietnam in June 1969 as part of an ecumenically sponsored study team on its political and religious freedom. According to a series of articles that he wrote for the Boston *Globe,* the team discovered that, contrary to State Department reports, the number of political prisoners in South Vietnam was increasing rapidly. According to Father Drinan's figures, 60 percent of that country's 35,000 prisoners were called "political prisoners," "Communists," or "Vietcong sympathizers," and many of those prisoners were actually non-Communists held for op-

REV. ROBERT F. DRINAN

posing President Nguyen Van Thieu. Furthermore, Drinan and his colleagues found significant evidence that many political prisoners were subjected to torture. The following year he published a book entitled *Vietnam and Armageddon: Peace, War and the Christian Conscience* (Sheed and Ward), in which he urged the Roman Catholic church to condemn war as "morally objectionable."

In February 1970 a caucus of independent Democrats, including supporters of former Senator Eugene J. McCarthy and the late Senator Robert F. Kennedy, endorsed Drinan to run for Congress from the Third Congressional District in Massachusetts. His opponent in the September primary, Philip J. Philbin, had been a Congressman since 1942 and was vice-chairman of the House Armed Services Committee. Philbin was fairly liberal on domestic issues but had incurred the wrath of antiwar groups by his hawkish policy on Vietnam. His support had come from the working-class mill towns and rural areas of his district, until the 1967 reapportionment took some of those areas away from him and replaced them with the affluent but antiwar Boston suburbs. In 1968 Philbin barely won the primary, and he was obviously vulnerable in 1970.

In other parts of the United States many antiwar candidates emphasized domestic issues, but Father Drinan based his campaign squarely on the war in Southeast Asia. For many voters, however, the main issue of his candidacy was the propriety of a priest running for Congress. Although a number of Protestant clergymen have held political office in the United States, Roman Catholic clerics have traditionally remained aloof from the political arena. A poll taken by the Boston *Globe* in April 1970 found that 30 percent of the voters in Drinan's district felt that it was improper for a priest to run for office, with the figure running higher for Catholics polled. (The Third Congressional District is about 75 percent Roman Catholic.) Many of the faithful believed that a priest abandoned his proper place in the rectory when he sought office, but Drinan viewed politics as a natural extension of the active role he had taken in public affairs as a priest.

Drinan's campaign was one of some sixteen conducted by American clergymen, Protestant and Catholic, in the 1970 elections. In response to the new involvement of priests in politics the 1970 meeting of American Catholic bishops passed a resolution urging bishops to "discourage" their priests from seeking public office. Drinan's superior, however, the late Richard Cardinal Cushing, kept silent on his candidacy, as did the Superior General of the Society of Jesus, Father Pedro Arrupe.

Father Drinan's well-financed campaign was conducted by a highly efficient organization that drew on the services of hundreds of young people. Under the direction of campaign manager John Marttila, a former Republican at one time employed by the Republican National Committee, volunteers canvassed 70 percent of the district's 80,000 registered Democrats—some 41,000 households. Each person was questioned about the war and other issues, and their answers were fed into a computer programed to identify potential voters for Drinan. Those identified were then bombarded with mailings, personal visits, and telephone calls on election day. Drinan also waged an effective television campaign, and he was aided by endorsements from such noted liberals as New York Mayor John Lindsay and former Attorney General Ramsey Clark.

When the September primary votes were counted, Drinan had won handily by 28,612 votes to Philbin's 22,132. Refusing to accept defeat, the incumbent Congressman waged a write-in campaign for the November election. Both Philbin and the Republican nominee, John McGlennon, made a vigorous bid for conservative votes. According to Scott Pecker of the *Christian Science Monitor* (November 2, 1970) Philbin attacked Drinan as a disseminator of "unrest, hatred, violence, and radical ideas" and McGlennon hit hard at the priest's past statements and writings advocating unilateral disarmament and disobedience to unjust laws. Their tactics failed to impress the voters, however, and on election day Father Drinan won by 3,000 votes.

In January 1971 Drinan was sworn into the Ninety-second Congress. Appointed to the House Judiciary Committee, he was also named as a member of the Internal Security Committee two days after he had introduced a bill in the House that would in effect abolish that committee and transfer its functions to the Judiciary. A longtime foe of the Internal Security Committee, formerly called the House Un-American Affairs Committee, Father Drinan is now the sole civil libertarian in its membership.

Besides the books previously mentioned, Father Drinan has written *Democracy, Dissent, and Disorder* (Seabury, 1969), in which he studied the violence that has shaken the United States in recent years and the "law and order" reaction provoked by it. He edited *The Human Right To Be Educated* (Corpus Books, 1968) and contributed to several volumes, including *The Wall of Separa-*

tion Between Church and State (Univ. of Chicago Press, 1964), *Religion and the Public Order* (Univ. of Chicago Press, 1966), and *Abortion and the Law* (Western Reserve Univ. Press, 1967). Father Drinan has written articles for the *Harvard Law Review*, the *Georgetown Law Review*, *Commonweal*, and other legal and religious journals. Since 1958 he has been a corresponding editor of *America*, a national Catholic weekly magazine, and since 1967 he has been editor in chief of the *Family Law Quarterly*. He has lectured on church-state relations at Andover Newton Theological School in Newton Centre, Massachusetts, and he was a visiting professor at the University of Texas Law School in 1966-67.

Long active in local, state, and national bar associations, Father Drinan served as vice-president of the Massachusetts Bar Association from 1961 to 1964. He is a Fellow of the American Bar Foundation and a member of the American Law Institute, the National Conference of Lawyers and Social Workers and the executive committee of the National Citizens Committee for Broadcasting. In 1966 he was elected to the American Academy of Arts and Sciences.

At the time he took office as a Congressman the Rev. Robert F. Drinan told reporters that he intended to continue wearing clerical attire in Congress because, as he put it, "It's the only clothes I have." In Washington he makes his home in the Jesuit community at Georgetown University and spends most of his $42,500 a year salary on services for his Massachusetts district. Often described as a cheerful extrovert with a dry wit and a quick mind, Father Drinan nonetheless admits to having a hot temper. The Jesuit priest is six feet tall, weighs 180 pounds, and has brown hair and blue eyes.

References

Boston Sunday Globe p9+ O 29 '67
Sign Jl '70
American Catholic Who's Who, 1970-71
Dictionary of International Biography (1968)
Directory of American Scholars (1969)
Who's Who in America, 1970-71

DUFFEY, JOSEPH D(ANIEL)

July 1, 1932- Urban specialist; political leader; clergyman
Address: h. 175 Ridgefield St., Hartford, Conn., 06112

For both major American political parties the election of November 1970 served as the arena for attempts to forge new coalitions of voters. While the Republicans waged an aggressive campaign directed at a broad middle-to-conservative spectrum, the Democrats tried to capitalize on the nation's economic problems and draw together workers, minority groups, and liberals. One of the most closely watched nationally of the Democratic campaigns was that of the Reverend Joseph D. Duffey of Connecticut in his unsuccessful bid for the Senate seat held by Democratic Thomas J. Dodd. A minister of the United Church of Christ, Duffey is also a specialist in urban affairs who served from 1966 to 1970 as director of the Hartford Seminary Center for Urban Ethics. Since 1969 he has been national chairman of Americans for Democratic Action. Challenging the Democratic party organization in Connecticut, headed by John Bailey, former Democratic National Chairman, in the spring of 1970, he forced the first Democratic primary in the state's history and won the Senatorial nomination. In the three-way fall election against the incumbent Senator Dodd, running as an independent, and the Republican nominee, Lowell P. Weicker Jr., Duffey ran second to Weicker, but gained the reputation of a skilled politician and a liberal with a broad nonideological appeal.

Of Irish extraction, Joseph Daniel Duffey was born to Joseph Ivan and Ruth (Wilson) Duffey on July 1, 1932 in Huntington, West Virginia. His father had been an occasional professional prizefighter and coal miner in Logan, West Virginia before undergoing, at the age of twenty-three, a mining accident in which his leg was crushed by a mule car and had to be amputated. At that time there were no workmen's compensation laws. He moved with his wife, a telegraph operator, to nearby Huntington, where he worked as a barber and raised a family of five children. Joseph Duffey was the oldest; he has a brother, Robert Duffey, who also now lives in Connecticut, and three sisters, Mrs. Helen Phillips, Mrs. Ida Plymale, and Mrs. Patricia Keesee.

His father's modest career in politics, as a councilman and state legislator, brought Joe Duffey his first encounter with campaigning. He has recalled that in his boyhood politicians sometimes courted voters by giving away two-shot bottles of whiskey wrapped in a sample ballot indicating what candidates should be chosen. As he became aware of the contrast between the rich and the poor and of the exploitation of the poor, he developed an anger toward poverty and for a time in high school his ambition was to be a labor lawyer. Among the early influences on his attitudes was the Baptist church, which he and his family attended. Duffey has since remarked that, perhaps surprisingly, the Baptist church in some Southern cities is "one of the more liberal centers."

Although his father hoped that he would go to West Point, when Duffey graduated from Huntington High School in 1950, he enrolled in Marshall University near his home. Becoming involved in Baptist church youth work, he began thinking about a career in the ministry. He took a job as an apprentice carpenter on the railroads and then worked for about a year and a half in a steel mill. At college he majored in history and belonged to the debating team, taking part in state and national contests. He was a member of Omicron Delta Kappa, a national leadership fraternity, and Pi Delta Kappa, a forensic fraternity.

By the time he obtained the B.A. degree from Marshall, in 1954, Duffey had made up his mind

REV. JOSEPH D. DUFFEY

to enter the ministry. He attended Andover Newton Theological School in Massachusetts, where he took the Bachelor of Divinity degree in 1957. Ordained a minister of the Congregational church, now the United Church of Christ, he spent three years, from 1957 to 1960, as pastor of the First Congregational Church in Danvers, Massachusetts. He then moved into teaching and research as an assistant professor of urban studies at Hartford Seminary in Connecticut. Continuing with his own education he took courses at the Divinity School of Yale University, which awarded him the Master of Sacred Theology degree in 1963. In further graduate work, carried out in part under a Rockefeller Foundation doctoral grant in 1965-66, he completed a dissertation entitled "Lewis Mumford's Philosophy of Technology and Culture" to earn his Ph.D. in social ethics, conferred by Hartford Seminary in 1969. Meanwhile, in 1966, he had been appointed director of the seminary's Center for Urban Ethics, a position that he held until the center closed in June 1970.

Through such influences as the social ethics writings of the theologian Reinhold Niebuhr and the example of John F. Kennedy, Duffey was gradually stirred to political activism. In his early direct involvement in the civil rights cause, he took part in a protest during 1963 on behalf of an attempt to desegregate a construction union in Brooklyn's Bedford-Stuyvesant district and was briefly jailed. He became involved in Hartford politics at the precinct level and in 1967 broadened his involvement by working in the Negotiation Now movement to end the war in Vietnam.

In the spring of 1968 Senator Eugene McCarthy launched a campaign for the Democratic Presidential nomination, with Duffey, who was drawn to McCarthy's strong stand against the war, as cochairman of the campaign in Connecticut. That post provided him his first experience in challenging the state party machine run by the powerful John Bailey, described in *U.S. News & World Report* (August 31, 1970) as one of the country's two "remaining old-time political bosses," along with Mayor Richard J. Daley of Chicago. Enlisted by Allard Lowenstein in his effort to coalesce sentiment against the leadership of Democratic President Lyndon B. Johnson in early 1968, Duffey came to be regarded, according to James A. Wechsler of the New York *Post* (June 18, 1969), as "one of the most effective spokesmen of the political rebellion of 1968." The Duffey-McCarthy forces included nine of Connecticut's forty-four delegates to the Democratic National Convention in Chicago, where the McCarthy supporters were soundly defeated by those of Vice-President Hubert H. Humphrey. A delegate to that convention, which became notorious for its bitter controversy, Duffey told William Rudy of the New York *Post* (October 11, 1970), "I came back numbed and shocked as anyone else. But I supported Hubert Humphrey. I said at the time there was too much at stake." In December 1968, following the Democratic defeat in the national election, Duffey helped found and became chairman of the Caucus of Connecticut Democrats, a coalition of former supporters of Senators McCarthy and Robert F. Kennedy, who had been assassinated during his own campaign for the Presidential nomination.

Duffey also gained in political prominence in his state as chairman of the Connecticut branch of Americans for Democratic Action, which he had joined in 1964. A liberal organization of some 65,000 members, with headquarters in Washington, D.C., ADA publishes a newsletter, *ADA World,* to inform and influence public opinion on important policy and legislative issues. At its twenty-second annual convention in June 1969, ADA delegates elected Duffey national chairman, to succeed the well-known Harvard University economist John Kenneth Galbraith. Wechsler observed in the New York *Post* that the election of the thirty-seven-year-old clergyman meant a "dramatic transformation in the age level of ADA leadership and conceivably the beginning of a new chapter in the history of American liberalism." That possibility was strengthened by Duffey's insistence on rational politics rather than doctrinaire sloganeering and by his desire to make ADA a means of communication between generations. In his acceptance speech he said that his major concerns would be to defeat President Richard Nixon and to end the Vietnam war so that Americans could begin to tackle their domestic problems. Duffey also proposed to shift the organization's activities from the "legislative halls of Congress to local wards and precincts" and to begin putting ADA resources into elections at local levels. He was reelected ADA national chairman in 1970. Also during that year Duffey became a member of the Democratic National Policy Council.

On November 10, 1969 Duffey announced that he was a candidate for the Democratic nomination for the United States Senate. The incumbent Connecticut Senator Thomas J. Dodd had fallen out of favor with the party organization after the Senate censured him in 1967 for misuse of campaign funds, although he retained many loyal supporters throughout the state. John Bailey, party chief since 1946, reportedly felt that the Democrats should offer an Irish Catholic candidate because of the predominance of Catholics in the state, and he backed Alphonsus J. Donahue. A 1955 Connecticut law provides that any candidate who gets 20 percent of the votes at the state party convention can run against the convention's choice in a party primary. With 960 delegates at the convention, a candidate would need 192 votes to force a popular election.

To challenge the convention's expected choice, in November 1969 Duffey and his campaign manager, Mrs. Anne Wexler, who has been called an "organizational genius," began organizing groups in 120 towns and cities across the state and researching election laws and statistics. In small towns delegates were selected by town caucuses; traditionally, a dozen people might attend, but the Duffey forces often brought out as many as 100, a practice that Mrs. Wexler maintained netted Duffey 101 delegates.

At the Democratic convention in May, Donahue won the party designation, but both Duffey and State Senator Edward Marcus polled more than 20 percent of the votes, receiving 231 and 221 respectively, thus forcing a primary. Meanwhile, Dodd had decided to run in November as an independent. In the primary campaign Donahue ran as a unity candidate who could win in November and Marcus ran on a law and order platform. Supplementing Duffey's moderate tone and broadly appealing style in the primary race was his attempt to deal with a wide range of issues relevant to liberals, blacks, and blue-collar workers. "My concern is with building a campaign of diverse people—people everyone has told us can't stand together—the kids, the mechanics, the bartenders, and the housewives," he explained, as quoted in the New York *Times* (August 23, 1970).

Much of Duffey's attention focused on economic problems, a salient issue because residents of Connecticut, with the second largest number of defense-related industries in the country, were concerned over the rise in national unemployment. Duffey had long advocated the late Walter Reuther's conversion plan, which would require defense industries to set aside 25 percent of their profits for conversion to nonmilitary production. He often discussed such bread and butter matters as better housing, unemployment benefits for strikers, collective bargaining rights for teachers, higher tariffs to protect domestic workers, and a tough occupational safety bill, and he proposed the creation of new public service jobs to deal with social problems and rising unemployment.

When Duffey talked about the Vietnam war it was usually to stress its economic costs. While avoiding moral rhetoric, he remained committed to a dovish, but not a radical, position. He urged that the United States government set forth a clear timetable for withdrawal of troops and send a top negotiator to the peace talks in Paris to work out a settlement. In addition, he argued that Congress should take a larger role in shaping foreign policy. Duffey also came out strongly for such liberal proposals as national health insurance, control of pollution, tax reform, and Congressional creation of a national railroad authority to improve commuter service. His candidacy was endorsed by Senator Abraham A. Ribicoff; Richard Lee, former mayor of New Haven; former Governor Chester Bowles; and other Connecticut political leaders. Ribicoff's support was especially vital.

Duffey won the primary election on August 19, 1970 in an upset victory by a 12,000-vote margin. The returns showed that he had run well in the antiwar suburbs, several industrial areas, and black sections in the cities; he had carried both Hartford and New Haven, the state's two largest cities. "Pound for pound, Duffey's campaign may be the best organized in America," James M. Perry commented in the *National Observer* (October 19, 1970) in weighing Duffey's chances for success in his ensuing race against Republican Lowell P. Weicker Jr. and independent Senator Dodd. Duffey had earlier been endorsed by many local unions, especially the Machinists and the United Auto Workers. Then in September 1970 he won the backing of the state AFL-CIO. Analyzing, however, a preelection poll taken in blue-collar neighborhoods of Connecticut, the columnists Rowland Evans and Robert Novak reported in the Washington *Post* (October 7, 1970) that Weicker had been effective in picturing Duffey as a radical and that many workers felt he did not hit hard enough on the issue of law and order, which seemed more important to them than economic questions.

On November 3, 1970 the Republicans nearly swept the state. Duffey ran second to Weicker, losing by a vote of about 360,000 to Weicker's 443,000; and Dodd trailed with some 261,000 votes. After controlling the state house for sixteen years, the Democrats lost the governorship to the conservative Republican Thomas J. Meskill, and Republicans gained four of the five state offices on the ballot. It was not apparent whether Dodd drew votes from Weicker or from Duffey, but observers generally blamed the division within the Democratic party for the Republican victory. Duffey emerged, however, as a symbol of Democratic coalition politics and as an influential liberal politician. In January 1971 Evans and Novak reported in the Washington *Post* that Senator Edmund Muskie was seeking Duffey's endorsement to gain credence with the liberal wing of the Democratic party in his drive for the Presidential nomination in 1972.

While a student at Marshall University, on August 24, 1952 Joseph D. Duffey married Patricia Fortney of Morgantown, West Virginia. They have two sons, Michael Robert and David King, and a foster son, Alex. Several years ago the family moved away from the Hartford Seminary area and nearer to the inner city to try to help stabilize a changing urban neighborhood. "Boyish-looking" is a term often used to describe Duffey, who has hazel eyes and brown hair, stands five feet ten inches tall, and weighs 180 pounds. He is said to be self-assured and unaffected, with a quiet, "easy-going, nice-guy manner." His recreation is cruising with his family in his twenty-five-foot sloop.

References

Hartford Courant My 15 '70 por
N Y Post p57 Je 18 '69; p37 Jl 9 '70; p31 O 1 '70 por
N Y Times p73 Ap 5 '70; p27 Ag 20 '70
Who's Who in American Politics, 1969-70

EASTWOOD, CLINT

May 31, 1931(?)- Actor
Address: b. c/o William Morris Agency, Inc., 151 El Camino, Beverly Hills, Calif. 90212

After several years of playing an innocuous cowpuncher on the American television serial *Rawhide*, Clint Eastwood gained European stardom in 1964 as The Man With No Name in *A Fistful of Dollars*, a bloody, Italian-produced "spaghetti" western filmed in Spain. As the flinty-eyed antihero of that film, a hired killer without fear or moral scruple, Eastwood created a campy embodiment of male escapist fantasy somewhat in the tradition of James Bond. So popular was the role that he repeated it in two more Spanish-Italian westerns, *For a Few Dollars More* and *The Good, the Bad, and the Ugly*. When the three films—sometimes known as the "paella trilogy"—reached the United States a few years later, they became camp institutions, and Eastwood became a star at home as well as abroad. He has gone on to star in several violent, action-packed westerns, war stories, and adventure melodramas that usually score low with film critics but high with audiences. In 1971 he was named the second biggest box-office draw in the United States, following Paul Newman, and the most popular international film actor.

Impassive on screen as a rule, Eastwood can hardly be said to act at all, but he projects a magnetic presence that dominates every frame in which he appears. Although women often find him irresistible, men make up the bulk of his audience. His films are especially popular in the black ghettoes of northern cities. "The character Eastwood plays is invariably a man in total control, able to handle anything," wrote Judy Fayard for a cover story on the actor in *Life* (July 23, 1971). "He is his own law, and his own morality—independent, unfettered, invulnerable, unfathomable and unbelievable. He is a nondimensional symbol of man as pure superiority. He is a heavy dude. He is superstud."

The older child of Clinton and Ruth Eastwood, Clinton Eastwood Jr. was born in San Francisco, California around 1931. His birthday is May 31, but sources vary on the exact year of his birth. During the Depression Eastwood's father had difficulty in getting and keeping jobs, and the family lived successively in a number of small northern California towns, wherever the father could find work. Clint and his sister Jeanne were always being switched from school to school as the family moved, until Clinton Sr. became an executive for the Container Corporation of America in Oak-

CLINT EASTWOOD

land. By then Clint was a teenager, and at Oakland Technical High School he had the chance to become a basketball star.

"I can't remember how many schools I went to," Eastwood told Wayne Warga in a syndicated interview carried by the Washington *Post* (July 6, 1969). "I do know that we moved so much that I made very few friends. Moving has become sort of my life style. Basically, I'm a drifter, a bum. As it turns out I'm lucky because I'm going to end up financially well-off for a drifter." After graduating from Oakland Technical High, Eastwood took to the road, working in Oregon as a lumberjack. When he was drafted in 1951 his proficiency at swimming got him an assignment as a swimming instructor at Fort Ord in California. Two years later he arrived in Los Angeles to study at Los Angeles City College on the G.I. bill. Undecided about a career, he studied business administration until a friend who worked as a cameraman at Universal Studios persuaded him to take a screen test, which landed him a contract with the studio.

"They made a lot of cheapies in those days, a lot of B-pictures," Eastwood explained to Ann Guerin of *Show* (February 1970), "and I'd always play the young lieutenant or the lab technician who came in and said, 'He went that way' or 'This happened' or 'Doctor, here are the X-rays' and he'd say, 'Get lost, kid,' I'd go out and that would be the end of it." After eighteen months, Universal let him go. Some lean years followed during which he played a few more lab technicians, drew unemployment, and worked as a lifeguard and as a swimming-pool digger. In 1958 he had a minor role in *Ambush at Cimarron Pass* (Twentieth Century-Fox), which he has described as "a cheap little western that . . . was even worse than the title."

Eastwood has told interviewers that he was about to give up acting and return to college, when he obtained his role in *Rawhide* by a fluke. Drinking coffee with a friend one day in the cafeteria at CBS's television studios, he was spotted by *Rawhide*'s producer, who was having trouble

casting the part of Rowdy Yates, the second lead in the new series. The CBS executive thought Eastwood looked properly young, handsome, and well built and, after a screen test, offered him the part.

Rawhide had its première in the spring of 1959, and for the next seven years Eastwood played the assistant trail boss on a seemingly endless trail drive to Sedalia, Missouri. "One thing a series affords somebody is great security," the actor told Ann Guerin. "In a series you're going to work every week and if you try something one week and it doesn't work, you're going to be employed the next week so it doesn't make any difference. So you can . . . try anything you want and file all the things that work for you in your brain and discard what doesn't work—it's a great training ground." For the first few seasons the show ranked high in the Nielsen ratings, but by 1961-62 it had slumped to thirteenth place. The following year it fell to twenty-second place and then for three seasons languished in the forty-fourth position. In 1965 CBS tried to refurbish the serial by making several changes, including firing its star, Eric Fleming, and elevating Eastwood to the position of trail boss. Nothing worked, however, and the show was dropped.

By the time *Rawhide* finally reached the end of the trail, Eastwood's fortune was assured, however. On his 1964 summer vacation from filming the series, he had gone to Spain to appear in a low-budget "spaghetti western" directed by Sergio Leone, an Italian moviemaker whose credits included the screenplay for *The Last Days of Pompeii*. Although Eastwood has admitted that part of his motivation for agreeing to work with Leone was the chance of a free trip to Europe, he was also intrigued with the script the Italian had sent to him. For some time the Italian movie industry had been churning out shoddy westerns that were gory versions of the old Hollywood good-guys-versus-bad-guys formula. By adapting a story from a Japanese film about a fourteenth century samurai (*Yojimbo,* directed by Akira Kurosawa), Leone was aiming to bypass that formula, however. He envisioned a film that would retain the obsessive violence of the Italian genre, while presenting a new kind of hero, an antihero who scorned law and morality in his lust for money and who could not be clearly distinguished from the bad guys.

Under Leone's direction Eastwood created the scruffy protagonist of *A Fistful of Dollars,* an ill-shaven, cheroot-smoking gunman, rootless, lawless, and fearless. The plot of the film was simple and violent. The Man With No Name arrives in a small town where he encounters two rival gangs. He manages to hire himself out as a gunman to both gangs and to turn them against each other. By the end of the film the town is strewn with bodies, Eastwood himself has sustained a beating that would have killed a lesser man, and he is ready to leave town with both gangs' money. *Fistful* was made for $200,000, of which $15,000 went to Eastwood. The movie immediately broke box-office records all over Europe, grossing about

$4,000,000 in Italy alone, and a sequel was hastily assembled. Eastwood was reportedly paid $50,000 for *For a Few Dollars More*, which was even more popular than the original, and $250,000 plus a percentage for *The Good, the Bad, and the Ugly.* Meanwhile, in 1965, he was featured in one segment of *The Witches*, an Italian omnibus film starring Silvana Mangano that was produced by Dino De Laurentiis and released in the United States by United Artists in 1969.

Release of *A Fistful of Dollars* in the United States was delayed because of legal problems arising from its indebtedness to *Yojimbo,* but it finally made its debut in February 1967 as a United Artists release. The reviewers found little to admire. Writing in the New York *World Journal Tribune* (February 2, 1967), Judith Crist described the film as "an ersatz western" dedicated to proving that "men and women . . . can be gouged, burned, beaten, stomped and shredded to death." Bosley Crowther (New York *Times,* February 2, 1967) at least hailed the character created by Eastwood as "a morbid, amusing, campy fraud." Bad reviews did not deter filmgoers from attending *Fistful,* however, and United Artists quickly released *For a Few Dollars More* later in 1967 and *The Good, the Bad, and the Ugly* early in 1968.

Meanwhile, Eastwood starred as the gun-toting hero in several American-made action melodramas. The first was a western about frontier justice entitled *Hang 'Em High* (United Artists, 1968). In *Coogan's Bluff* (Universal, 1968), an "Eastern western," Eastwood played an Arizona lawman searching for a criminal in contemporary New York City. He then costarred with Richard Burton in *Where Eagles Dare* (MGM, 1969), a World War II story.

Eastwood changed his pace completely to play the romantic lead in *Paint Your Wagon* (1969), Paramount's costly fiasco that was based on Lerner and Loewe's Broadway musical comedy about the California Gold Rush. Eastwood had cut a few records early in his career and was able to carry the singing part of his role, crooning as Vincent Canby of the New York *Times* commented, "in an early Frankie Avalon mode." But most critics found Eastwood incongruous within the setting of a conventional Hollywood musical, and Ann Guerin of *Show* observed that he managed to give the impression that "if only someone would hand him a gun, he could whip . . . the whole soggy film into shape."

Since making *Paint Your Wagon*, Eastwood has not deviated from the slightly seedy he-man roles he handles convincingly. In *Two Mules for Sister Sara* (Universal, 1970) he portrayed an American mercenary soldier in old Mexico who is reluctantly pressed into being gallant to a prostitute (Shirley MacLaine) disguised as a nun. He was one of a band of larcenous American soldiers who steal $17,000,000 worth of gold bullion from the Nazis in *Kelly's Heroes* (MGM, 1970). In *The Beguiled* (Universal, 1971), a gothic tale set during the Civil War, Eastwood played a wounded Union soldier seeking refuge in a Southern 'girls'

school, where he is eventually murdered by the sex-starved students.

By 1971 Eastwood's films had grossed an estimated $200,000,000, and he was able to command a fee of about $1,000,000 plus a percentage of the gross for each film he contracted to make. Reportedly, his films in the future will be produced by his own company, Malpaso Productions, which has already produced *Hang 'Em High* and *The Beguiled.* Eastwood has directed sequences in several of his starring films and undertook complete direction, as well as the starring role, in *Play "Misty" For Me* (Universal), which was released to mixed reviews late in 1971.

Clint Eastwood's self-image as a "drifter" does not preclude his having a stable family life. Since December 19, 1953 he has been married to the former Maggie Johnson, and they have one child, Kyle Clinton, who was born in 1968. The Eastwoods make their home in a large but unostentatious house overlooking the ocean in Carmel, California. A health enthusiast, Eastwood exercises regularly and strenuously, eats organic foods, and limits his drinking to an occasional few beers. He recently acquired a chain of health food stores. Eastwood has never smoked cigarettes. The actor has a sensitive and youthfully handsome face framed by thick, unruly dark blond hair. He is six feet four inches tall and weighs 198 pounds. Invariably described as unpretentious, Eastwood prefers the company of old friends to Hollywood society and likes to drive around in his old Chevy pickup truck. (He also owns a Ferrari and several motorcycles.) Although he does not consider himself an activist, the actor is interested in conservation and he refuses to hunt. Once he even refused to kill a rattlesnake for a scene in one of his films. Politically he is a conservative.

References

Life 71:45+ Jl 23 '71 pors
N Y Post p29 O 25 '69 por
N Y Sunday News mag p4 D 3 '61 por; II p9 Ap 4 '71 por
N Y Times II p11 Ja 22 '67 por; II p9 Ag 10 '69 por
Nat Observer p30 F 6 '67 por
Who's Who in America, 1970-71

ERDMAN, JEAN

Feb. 20, 1917(?)- Dancer; choreographer; teacher
Address: b. Jean Erdman Theatre of Dance, 110 W. 14th St., New York 10011; h. 136 Waverly Place, New York 10014

For over three decades Jean Erdman has enriched modern dance with her intellectual breadth, wit, and passion for experimentation. After five years with the Martha Graham Dance Company, Miss Erdman struck out on her own in 1943 and since then has performed in the United States and abroad, alone or with her own groups. Perhaps the most striking feature of her work is the way she has

JEAN ERDMAN

explored the relationship between music and dance, making dance into a spatial counterpoint of the music rather than an accompaniment to it or a visual elucidation. Although she has worked with traditional music, she has achieved her greatest success with contemporary compositions, and her musical collaborators have included John Cage, Louis Horst, Lou Harrison, Ezra Laderman, Milton Babbitt, and Luciano Berio.

But music is by no means Miss Erdman's only concern, and she has always been fascinated by the possibilities of relating dance to literature, the visual arts, or the dramatic theatre. She has choreographed or directed several plays and has written, staged, and starred in *The Coach With the Six Insides*, a "total theatre" presentation of music, dance, mime, and dialogue based on James Joyce's *Finnegans Wake*. The play captured the Obie and Vernon Rice awards when it opened Off Broadway in 1962 and has since had a second Off-Broadway run and performances abroad. Since 1948 Jean Erdman has had a dance school in New York City, and she has headed the dance departments at Bard College, Teachers College of Columbia University, and New York University.

Jean Erdman was born in Honolulu, Hawaii on February 20, in or around 1917. (She does not give her exact age to interviewers.) Her mother, the former Marion Dillingham, was a singer whose parents had emigrated from New England to Hawaii in the 1820's. Her father, John Pinney Erdman, was a nondenominational Protestant minister who settled in Hawaii as a missionary after completing his doctor of divinity degree. Both parents encouraged their daughter's artistic bent, and dancing became her mode of expression, probably because, as she told Jane Mary Farley of the Milwaukee *Journal* (February 18, 1957), in Hawaii "people dance almost as naturally and easily as they walk. . . . After supper on the beach there would be waves coming in. Someone would have a ukelele and one by one people got up and did the hula."

Besides her early exposure to the native dancing of Hawaii, Miss Erdman had what she has called the "sublime luck" to be introduced to the dance

technique of Isadora Duncan by a gym teacher at the Punahou School in Honolulu. Her parents sent her to the mainland to complete her secondary education, and she was graduated from Miss Hall's School in Pittsfield, Massachusetts in 1934. She then entered Sarah Lawrence College in Bronxville, New York, where she studied contemporary dance and the theatre. By the time she graduated in 1938 she had decided to become a professional dancer, but before launching her career she went on a round-the-world tour with her parents and sister that enabled her to see the dance in such places as Bali, Java, Cambodia, India, and Spain. Ethnic dances, especially those of the Orient, have remained an important source of inspiration for her, as she recalled to Jane Mary Farley: "This trip came at a crucial point in my dance life. . . . I'll never forget it. I discovered things that really served me artistically later."

Returning to the United States late in 1938, Miss Erdman joined the Martha Graham Dance Company and made her professional debut in New York City at Carnegie Hall. Among her solo roles over the next five years with the Graham group were the Ideal Spectator in *Every Soul is a Circus* and the dancing-speaking parts in *Punch and the Judy* and in *Letter to the World*, Miss Graham's dance legend about the life of the New England poet Emily Dickinson. After seeing a performance of the latter work, John Martin wrote in the New York *Times* (April 8, 1941), "Jean Erdman gives . . . [Martha Graham] admirable assistance in the role of an alter ego. It is she who speaks the actual Dickinson verses and she brings to them a beautiful variety and a radiantly youthful feeling for their quality."

During the summers Miss Erdman studied dancing and composition at the Bennington College modern dance school, and in 1942 she made her debut as a choreographer at the Bennington Summer Festival with a performance of her solo composition *The Transformations of Medusa* (music by Louis Horst). She has since pointed to the evolution of that work to show how a choreographer should never depend on personal style but rather create for each new dance a unique style of movement intrinsic to its subject. Miss Erdman began to develop *The Transformations of Medusa* while imitating the angular, highly stylized positions of figures on ancient Greek bas-reliefs. In so doing she realized, as she later told Isabel Ferguson of the *Christian Science Monitor* (March 15, 1962), that the postures contained "a whole state of being or attitude toward life, a one-pointedness . . . , an enthusiasm for some special thing." Creating around that feeling, she was able to complete her composition, and she later decided to name her dance character Medusa, after the beautiful priestess of Greek mythology who was turned into a Gorgon.

To pursue her dance ideas more fully, Jean Erdman decided to leave the Martha Graham Company in 1943. She founded the Jean Erdman Dance Group soon afterward and over the next few years presented annual concerts in New York City of her solo and group works. At the same time she taught and performed with the New Dance Group, an avant-garde group of New York-based young dancers and choreographers. Still convinced that ethnic dance forms can make a vital contribution to modern dance, Miss Erdman returned to Hawaii in the summer of 1945 to refresh her understanding of Far Eastern and Polynesian dancing and to study the ancient Hawaiian ceremonial dance under Mary Kawena Pukui and Japanese dance at the Hisamatsu School. When she returned to New York she enrolled at the American School of Ballet and at José Hernandez' Spanish dance school and continued her study of Hawaiian dance with Huapala.

Among Jean Erdman's important works of the 1940's were *Daughters of the Lonesome Isle* (1945) and *Ophelia* (1946), both with music commissioned from John Cage, and *The Perilous Chapel* (music by Lou Harrison), a group work that was named one of the three best new compositions of 1949 by *Dance Magazine*. Of *The Perilous Chapel* dance critic Doris Hering wrote, "When the dance was over one realized that by means of purely physical and visual elements, Miss Erdman had succeeded in giving a moving picture of the experience of an artist through phases of isolation and realization."

From 1950 to 1954 Miss Erdman took her dance group on annual tours, and in 1954-55 she made a solo tour through the Orient, becoming the first American dancer to perform in the East since World War II. Everywhere she found audiences responsive to modern dance, particularly in India, and a report she submitted to the United States government on her return helped to initiate America's cultural exchange program with India and other countries in the Orient.

Back in the United States Joan Erdman made solo tours around the country for the next five years, presenting many of her best known pieces, including *Changingwoman* (to music of Henry Cowell, 1951), a work in which she dances through a kaleidoscopic range of emotions, punctuating the sections of the work with strange, throaty cries; *Fearful Symmetry* (Ezra Laderman, 1957), based on William Blake's poem "The Tiger"; *Four Portraits from Duke Ellington's Shakespeare Album* (to music by Ellington, 1958), her comic portrayals of some of the Bard's heroines; and *Now and Zen—Remembering* (to music by Laderman, 1959), a gentle satire on modern dance.

The collaboration between Miss Erdman and Ezra Laderman, a dance enthusiast as well as a composer, began when Laderman approached her with his *Duet for Flute and Dancer* (1956). Throughout that composition he had envisioned a dancer participating as a kind of percussion instrument. His score notations indicated types or moods of movement rather than specific directions, and he asked Miss Erdman to amplify them into a choreographic composition. Pleased with that venture, the next year the two collaborated in a similar fashion on *Harlequinade*, a group number that Miss Erdman first danced with Donald McKayle.

In 1960 Miss Erdman reorganized her dance company and named it the Jean Erdman Theatre of Dance. With it she has toured the United States and given several concerts in New York. Among them was the first New York dance concert on an arena stage, at the Circle-in-the-Square in 1960, when she gave the première of her *Twenty Poems of E.E. Cummings* for eight dancers and an actor, and a Brooklyn Academy of Music concert in 1970, when she presented *The Castle*, an unusual collaboration with the jazz clarinetist-saxophonist Jimmy Giuffre that consisted of structured group sections and improvised duets between Miss Erdman and Giuffre.

Jean Erdman's most significant work during the 1960's was *The Coach With the Six Insides*, which won both the Vernon Rice and Obie awards for best Off Broadway play of the 1962-63 season. Miss Erdman's involvement in drama had actually begun many years before. In 1947 she choreographed a production of Jean-Paul Sartre's *The Flies* for the Vassar Experimental Theatre and three years later she choreographed the Broadway production of Jean Giraudoux's *The Enchanted*. In 1954 she collaborated with William Saroyan and composer Alan Hovhaness on a ballet-play called *Otherman—Or the Beginning of a New Nation*, which was produced under her direction at Bard College.

Finnegans Wake had long fascinated Miss Erdman. Her husband, Joseph Campbell, the well-known authority on myth, had collaborated with Henry M. Robinson on *A Skeleton Key to Finnegans Wake*, a guide for the uninitiated through Joyce's labyrinth of puns and esoterica. Commissioning a score from Teiji Ito, who had composed the music for *Twenty Poems*, Miss Erdman set out to write a play with music that would capture the mood of *Finnegans Wake*, which takes place in the dreaming mind of a Dublin tavern keeper.

The Coach With the Six Insides premièred at the Village South Theatre on November 26, 1962. Joseph Morgenstern of the New York *Herald Tribune* wrote the next day: "Miss Erdman . . . has done an audacious thing and done it very well. Taking a sampling of characters, phantasms, distortions, mutations and text that occur in *Finnegans Wake*, she has staged in dance, pantomime and witty vignettes. . . . It is odd and difficult, but excellent entertainment for anyone who wants to give his mind a stretch." After a four-month run Off Broadway Miss Erdman took the play on tour, first to Europe, where it was ecstatically received in Paris, Dublin, and at the Festival of Two Worlds in Spoleto, Italy, and then to Tokyo for a two-month run. Over the next few years she appeared with it on three North American tours, winding up with an engagement at the Seventy-fourth Street Theatre in New York City in 1967.

Since staging *The Coach With the Six Insides* Miss Erdman has become involved in a number of other theatrical ventures, either as director or choreographer. In 1964 she staged the Helen Hayes Repertory Theatre production of *Hamlet*, and in 1966 she choreographed movement for the Lincoln Center Repertory Company production of *Yerma*. For television she codirected an Atlanta (Georgia) Municipal Theatre production of Jean Cocteau's *The Marriage on the Eiffel Tower* in 1967, and in 1968 she was the director of Tom Anderson's *The Municipal Water System Is Not Trustworthy*, which played Off Broadway at the Sullivan Street Theatre.

Miss Erdman's recent dance compositions have shown her to be a vanguard experimenter with modern music and with multimedia. Recently at the Minneapolis Institute of Arts she improvised dances in spatial relation to sculptural forms before an audience of architects and sculptors. For a multi-media concert at Manhattan's Whitney Museum in 1969 she prepared a group dance entitled *Ensembles* that was accompanied by a composition in lights by Anthony Martin and music by Milton Babbitt played on the Mark II synthesizer. In collaboration with Luciano Berio she created *Voracious* in 1969, and she has choreographed several dances to electronic scores by Michael Czajowski, including *Safari* (1969) and *Vulnerable as an Island Is Paradise* (1969).

Since 1948 Jean Erdman has maintained her own dance school in New York City. Because she considers the constant restudying of the fundamentals of movement as central to her dance philosophy, she has been unusually active in teaching throughout her career and has instructed at many educational institutions. Among the colleges and universities with which she has been affiliated are Teachers College of Columbia University, where she directed the modern dance department from 1949 to 1951; the University of Colorado, where she was artist in residence and head of the dance department during the summers from 1949 to 1955; and Bard College, where from 1954 to 1957 she was chairman of the dance department, an associate professor, and director of dance productions. She has been a guest faculty member at many other schools, including Sarah Lawrence College, the University of British Columbia, the University of Hawaii, and the University of California at Los Angeles. She now heads the dance theatre program that she created at New York University School of the Arts at Washington Square in 1966.

Jean Erdman met Joseph Campbell when she was a student in one of his literature classes at Sarah Lawrence College, and they were married on May 5, 1938. Campbell still teaches at Sarah Lawrence as a professor of literature and comparative mythology. Since their marriage the Campbells have made their home in a two-room apartment on Waverly Place, near New York University in Manhattan. Jean Erdman is five feet six inches tall and weighs 120 pounds. She has long brown hair and brown eyes. Over the years she has contributed several articles to dance journals, including a long piece on the Japanese theatre for *Impulse: the Annual of Contemporary Dance* in 1955. Miss Erdman has served three times on the dance panel for Fulbright grants and is a reader and special consultant for the United States Office of Education.

References

Christian Sci Mon p9 Mr 15 '62 por
N Y Herald Tribune p16 N 29 '65
N Y Post p31 My 29 '67 por
N Y Times p44 N 27 '62
Variety 258:64 My 13 '70
Chujoy, Anatole, and Manchester, P. W., eds. Dance Encyclopedia (1967)

ERIKSON, ERIK H(OMBURGER)

June 15, 1902- Psychoanalyst; author; educator
Address: b. c/o W. W. Norton Co., 55 5th Ave., New York 10003

Erik H. Erikson, the nondogmatic, emancipated Freudian who introduced the term "identity crisis" into the language, is the most influential living psychoanalyst in America today. Trained under the Freuds in Vienna, Erikson has been in the United States for four decades, teaching and researching at Harvard University and other institutions, doing clinical work with children, and writing the widely used textbook *Childhood and Society* (1950) and the prize-winning psychohistorical biography *Gandhi's Truth* (1969), among other works. He retired from the Harvard faculty in 1970 with the title of professor emeritus.

Erikson has significantly broadened Freudian theory and technique to illuminate the successive stages of individual psychosexual development within the unfolding history of a given society. Going beyond Freud's notion that the personality is decisively bent, once and forever, in the earliest years of life, Erikson asserts that the whole of an individual life is lived in crucial stages, that an emotional crisis occurs at each stage, and that the dynamics of the society in which one lives contribute to or detract from the successful resolution of each crisis. Thus he has made psychoanalysis a viable, descriptive tool for the "normal" as well as the "sick" personality and opened new relationships between psychoanalysis and social science.

Erik Homburger Erikson was born of Danish parents in Frankfurt, Germany on June 15, 1902. His religious background was mixed. On his mother's side, one of his ancestors was chief rabbi of Stockholm; on his father's, there was a Protestant church historian and pastor. Erikson's parents separated before his birth, and when he was three years old his mother married Dr. Theodor Homburger, a Jewish pediatrician, in Karlsruhe. When he was growing up he was known as Erik Homburger, and for many years mother and stepfather led him to believe that he was Homburger's son. "This loving deceit," as he later called it, was undoubtedly a prime influence in the development of his interest in problems of identity.

Erikson's experiences at school and synagogue compounded his personal identity confusion. Although born a Dane, he thought of himself as a German, but anti-Semitic German classmates rejected him, and at synagogue he was called "the goy" because of his Nordic features. At the Humanistische Gymnasium, the classical high school, in Karlsruhe, he was a disinterested, mediocre student, but one who showed artistic talent. After graduation, trying to find himself in art, he led a bohemian, itinerant life, wandering through the Black Forest, the Alps, and Italy, working, drawing pictures, reading, and taking notes as he went, and he studied painting in Karlsruhe and Munich. He has described that period of his youth as one of "morbid sensitivity," on the "borderline" between psychosis and neurosis.

At the invitation of his friend Peter Blos, the child analyst, Erickson moved to Vienna in 1927, and there he became a teacher in an experimental school set up by Blos for the children of Sigmund and Anna Freud's patients and friends. Chosen by the Freuds for analytic training, he was analyzed by Anna Freud and he specialized in child analysis at the Vienna Psychoanalytic Institute. At the same time he earned certification as a Montessori teacher.

In 1933 Erikson completed his psychoanalytic training and became a full member of the Vienna Psychoanalytic Institute. Shortly afterward, because of the rise of Hitler in Germany, he migrated, via Denmark, to the United States. Settling in Boston, he established a private practice as that city's first child analyst and served as staff member or consultant at Massachusetts General Hospital, the Judge Baker Guidance Center (for treatment of emotionally disturbed juvenile delinquents from poor families), and the Harvard Psychological Clinic. In his work with university students at Harvard he experimented with play situations that revealed the traumatic content of normal psyches.

A powerful influence was exerted on Erikson by the Cambridge intellectual community, anthropologists Margaret Mead, Ruth Benedict, and Gregory Bateson and psychologists Henry Murray and Kurt Lewin. He began working for a Ph.D. degree in psychology at Harvard but cut short his studies to accept a full-time research position at the Yale University Institute of Human Relations in 1936. While doing research at the Institute, he taught at the Yale Medical School, first as an instructor and later as a professor. In 1938 he and a faculty colleague, anthropologist Scudder Mekeel, studied the early childhood training methods of the Sioux Indians on a reservation in South Dakota. His "Observations on Sioux Education," published in the *Journal of Psychology* (January 1939), marked the beginning of his lifelong effort to demonstrate how the universal events of childhood are affected and molded by a particular society.

In 1939 Erikson moved to San Francisco, where he resumed private practice and did training analysis for the San Francisco Psychoanalytic Institute. At the same time, he participated in a long-term study of normal children at the University of California's Institute of Child Welfare at Berkeley. The Berkeley project was an attempt to fit all available information about the first ten years of each child's life into a summary and predictive prognosis, and his contribution was to disclose internal psychodynamics through experimental play situations, as he had done at Harvard. "Problems of Infancy and Early Childhood," published in the *Cyclopaedia of Medicine, Surgery and Specialties* (Davis, 1940), was characterized by Erikson as "a restatement of the theory of infantile sexuality." It was his first formal attempt to relate the Freudian stages of psychosexual development to emergent social capacities and needs within particular milieus.

ERIK H. ERIKSON

During World War II Erikson did government-sponsored research into Nazi propaganda, the psychology of submarine crews, and information obtained from prisoners-of-war. "Hitler's Imagery and German Youth," published in *Psychiatry*, (Volume 5, 1942) indicates, for the first time, Erikson's interest in innovative historical figures. Not a clinical study of Hitler, it is an attempt to show how Hitler's childhood experiences paralleled those of other Germans, and how Hitler skillfully used allusions to those experiences, in *Mein Kampf* and other writings and speeches, to strike sympathetic psychic chords in his countrymen.

In 1943 Erikson and anthropologist Alfred Kroeber studied the Yurok, a tribe of salmon-fishing Indians in northern California. A distrustful, thrifty, cautious people, the Yurok would probably have been characterized as "anal neurotic" by most psychoanalysts. Erikson, however, was not interested in pinning psychological labels on the Yurok or in establishing pathology in terms of Western middle-class values. In his monograph *Observations on the Yurok: Childhood and World Image* (University of California Publications in American Archaeology and Ethnology, 1943), he related the restrictive childhood training of the Yurok to the realistic requirements of their arduous way of life.

After World War II, Erikson treated emotionally disturbed veterans in the rehabilitation center of Mount Zion Hospital in San Francisco. In his work with the bewildered, anxious men he was struck by the fact that most of them were not really mentally ill but were normal men undergoing normal crises that postwar society in the United States was exacerbating. It reinforced Erikson's conviction that psychoanalysis must be made into a tool for understanding "the vicissitudes of normal life." It also made him aware that psychoanalysis can be used as a political weapon, as a tool to force conformity, because many of the patients took on the symptoms of mental illness in compliance with what they thought was expected of them by psychiatrists, analysts, and therapists.

"Ego Development and Historical Change" published in Volume 2 of *Psychoanalytic Study of the Child* (International Universities Press, 1946) was Erikson's first theoretical exploration of the concept of group identity and of the social and historical forces that make for the ego's strengths and weaknesses. The essay, which contains an analysis of the identity roles open to most Negro Americans, is noteworthy for its assertion that factors such as racism and joblessness affect the mind not superficially but on the deepest layers of the unconscious.

Beginning in 1946, Erikson spent one day a week in a friend's beach house writing *Childhood and Society* (Norton, 1950), a book that has continued to sell steadily over the years, in many languages. In it, Erikson asserts that the stages of psychosexual development posited by Freud are paralleled by psychosocial stages, in each of which the ego must re-establish itself and reorient itself socially, and that the stages cover virtually the entire life cycle. He identifies eight stages: infancy, or the oral sensory stage, in which the emotional conflict is between basic trust and mistrust; muscular-anal, in which autonomy conflicts with shame and doubt; the locomotor-genital, where the conflict is between initiative and guilt; latency, in which the positive component is industry and the negative is inferiority; adolescence, where the identity crisis, or role confusion, normally occurs; young adulthood, in which intimacy vies with isolation; adulthood, in which the crisis poles are generativity and stagnation; and maturity, when ego integrity is threatened by despair.

In June 1950 Erickson left the University of California rather than sign a loyalty oath. (Not a Communist, he objected to the oath on principle.) From 1950 to 1960 he was a senior staff member of the Austin Riggs Center, a treatment center for severely disturbed young people from well-to-do families, in Stockbridge, Massachusetts. During the same decade he commuted biweekly to Pittsburgh to work with disturbed children from working-class and poor families at the University of Pittsburgh School of Medicine's Western Psychiatric Institute and at the Arsenal Health Center, where he collaborated with Dr. Benjamin Spock.

Erikson's contributions to professional journals in the 1950's were predominantly on the subject of identity, by which he means, roughly, a basic confidence in one's inner continuity in the midst of change. A sense of identity, emerging at the end of adolescence, "denotes certain comprehensive gains which the individual must have derived from all of his preadult experiences in order to be ready for the tasks of adulthood." The crisis that precedes its emergence is a normal stage in human development, but in some cases, especially those of creative individuals, it may be acute, prolonged, and accompanied by intense neurotic suffering. Among the essays were papers exploring the

identity crises in the lives of Freud and George Bernard Shaw.

Erikson's first full-length psychohistorical study, *Young Man Luther* (Norton, 1958), is an extension of his efforts to trace the difficult process whereby certain men of great gifts discover themselves and their role in relation to their times. Focusing on Martin Luther's famous fit in the monastery choir, Erikson traced the events in Luther's childhood that led to this "identity crisis" and showed how Luther, in transcending those events, not only freed himself from the authority of a severe father but also emancipated himself— and his followers—from the authority of a rigid medieval church. *Young Man Luther* was widely acclaimed by both social scientists and theologians, including Reinhold Niebuhr, who called it "a very profound study."

In 1960 Erikson, while remaining consultant to the Austin Riggs Center, returned to Harvard as professor of human development and lecturer in psychiatry. Until his retirement in 1970 he taught a popular undergraduate course, The Human Life Cycle, and conducted a graduate seminar, History and Life-History, in which the identity crises in the lives of a variety of historically innovative figures were explored. He was also a fellow at Harvard's Center for Advanced Study in the Behavioral Sciences, and he taught some classes in the Center for International Studies at the Massachusetts Institute of Technology.

In essays published in learned journals during the 1960's Erikson ranged widely in exploring the implications and applications of his ideas. The subjects included the status of women in American society, the attitudes and motivations of young people, racism, ethics, and current political and social events. Many of the essays were collected in *Insight and Responsibility* (Norton, 1964) and *Identity: Youth and Crisis* (Norton, 1968). Erikson was editor of *Youth: Change and Challenge* (Basic Books, 1963).

Erikson spent long periods in India, beginning in 1962, preparatory to writing *Gandhi's Truth: On the Origins of Militant Nonviolence* (Norton, 1969). Using as his focus the point in middle life when Gandhi first used the tactic of fasting— leadership of a textile workers strike in Ahmedabad in 1918—Erikson traced the personal history of Gandhi and the social and political history of India to show how the two came together at the historical moment when the man was ready to lead a movement of nonviolent civil disobedience and the country was ready to follow such revolutionary leadership. At the conclusion of the book Erikson looked into the possibility of human nature now being open to "Gandhi's Truth" as a way of averting world annihilation. He dedicated *Gandhi's Truth* to Martin Luther King Jr., and when the work won the National Park Award, he donated the $1,000 stipend to "men and women who are working and suffering for causes that Gandhi would have considered his own." A reviewer of the book in the *Times of India* (December 19, 1969) wrote: "Few are likely to improve on Erik Erikson's immensely rewarding and clinically competent study of the Mahatma and his methods. . . . What this modest scholar . . . has done is to reveal to us, his countrymen, many of whom have seen him in flesh and blood, the full extent of Gandhiji's greatness."

The spirit of Gandhi was evident in the essay "Reflections on the Dissent of Contemporary Youth" (*Daedalus,* Winter 1970), in which Erikson looked hopefully to the possibility of "quite different images of both youth and young adulthood" than those now prevailing. "New models of fraternal behavior may come to replace those images of comradeship and courage that have been tied in the past to military service and probably have contributed to a glorification of a kind of warfare doomed to become obsolete in our time." Such models, Erikson went on, "would make it possible for adults to contribute true knowledge and genuine experience without assuming an authoritative stance beyond their actual competence and genuine inner authority." He pointed out that we must be wary not only of youthful but also of elderly irrationality. Young activists react scornfully to their elders' "display of that brittle dignity which is supposed to protect occupational identity and status" because "to them a career that is not worth sacrificing for professed ideals is not worth having." In the summer 1970 issue of *Daedalus* Erikson's essay "Autobiographic Notes on the Identity Crisis" was published.

Erik H. Erikson and Canadian-born Joan Mowat Serson were married in Vienna in 1930. They have three grown children: Kai, a sociologist, Jon, a photographer, and Sue, a social anthropologist. The Eriksons spend their summers in a cottage at Cotuit, Massachussets, on Nantucket Sound, and live the rest of the year in Stockbridge, Massachusetts, where he holds seminars in his home. Mrs. Erikson, who edits all her husband's manuscripts, is the author of *The Universal Bead* (1969), a book on Indian weaving, among other works. Erikson is a member of the National Academy of Education, a life member of the American Psychoanalytic Association, and a fellow of the American Academy of Arts and Sciences.

Erikson is a white-haired, moustached man who, according to Robert Coles, is "reassuring" in manner and speaks in a "straightforward" way, using "good and plain English" with a German accent. David Elkind, writing in the New York *Times Magazine* (April 5, 1970), observed that "in his approach to his work Erikson appears neither drawn nor driven, but rather to be following an inner schedule as natural as the life cycle itself." Since leaving the Harvard faculty Erikson has begun to review his early observations in the light of contemporary change, and he has continued his field work, among, for example, the Sioux, black farmers in Mississippi, and ghetto children. Erikson generally dislikes honorary degrees—although he has accepted some—and similar distinctions, but is happy to be associated by name (and occasionally as a consultant) with the Erikson Institute for Early Childhood Education at Loyola University in Chicago, which trains teachers for work with children in slums and rural areas. John Leonard wrote of Erikson in the New York *Times* (November 24, 1970): "I can't help thinking how little it seems to matter which words our saints employ, what manner they lay hands upon our wounds, how they describe themselves and comfort us, so long as they are saints."

References

New Yorker 46:51+ N 7 '70 por; 46:59+ N 14 '70 por
Time 96:51+ N 30 '70 por
Coles, Robert. Erik H. Erikson: The Growth of His Work (1970)
Who's Who in America, 1970-71

EVANS, WALKER

Nov. 3, 1903- Photographer
Address: b. School of Art and Architecture, Yale University, New Haven, Conn. 06520; h. Old Lyme, Conn. 06371

In junkyards, shuttered windows, gas stations, people on the street, and countless other familiar sights, the American photographer Walker Evans recognized "sorts of perfection," which through his camera became images of broad relevance that collectively symbolize the American experience. His pictures, mainly in black and white, have an unmistakable style of detachment, understatement, and precise delineation, with no gimmickry and little, if any, of the excitement of photojournalism. But for all their insistence on factual exactness, Evans' own perception of his subjects endows them with both mystery and poetry. Besides influencing the photography of a younger generation and other visual arts, he has affected the way Americans look at the twentieth century, especially the 1930's. "It is difficult to know with certainty whether Evans recorded the America of his youth, or invented it," John Szarkowski wrote in his introduction to *Walker Evans* (Museum of Modern Art, 1971). "Beyond doubt, the accepted myth of our recent past is in some measure the creation of this photographer, whose work has persuaded us of the validity of a new set of clues and symbols bearing on the question of who we are." Evans now teaches a course in photography at Yale University and previously, from 1945 to 1965, held the position of associate editor of *Fortune.*

Walker Evans was born in St. Louis, Missouri on November 3, 1903 to Walker and Jessie (Crane) Evans. The family moved to Toledo, Ohio not long after his birth and from there to Kenilworth, Illinois, an exclusive suburb of Chicago, which they could well afford because of the father's success in advertising as a copywriter for Lord & Thomas in the midwestern metropolis. From early boyhood Walker enjoyed painting pictures, and in Kenilworth he

WALKER EVANS

learned to play golf. When his parents separated, he went with his mother to New York City, but afterward spent most of his time in expensive private schools. He attended first the Loomis School in Windsor, Connecticut and then Phillips Academy in Andover, Massachusetts, from which he graduated in 1922.

Attracted to literature at Andover, Evans aspired to become a writer. At the end of what seemed to him an unrewarding freshman year at Williams College, however, he dropped out of school, rejoined his mother in Manhattan, and worked nights as an attendant in the map room of the New York Public Library. A small allowance from his father enabled him to live in Paris for the year 1926. He audited classes at the Sorbonne, read the works of Flaubert and Baudelaire, and frequented the bookstore of Sylvia Beach, where he caught a glimpse of James Joyce but lacked the self-assurance to brave an introduction to that celebrated author. Nor did he meet any of the American expatriates, like Ernest Hemingway, who later achieved fame as writers. Visually, however, his visit to Paris was invaluable. "The School of Paris painting was so incandescent then, a revolutionary eye education," he told Jerry Tallmer, who interviewed him for an article in the New York Post (March 5, 1971). "In recollection I was really in Paris to absorb intellectual stimulus. The best training in the world."

In another interview, for the New Yorker (December 24, 1966), Evans observed, "I wanted so much to write that I couldn't write a word." In 1928, about a year after he had left Paris, he turned to photography, discovering that even technically he felt immediately at home with a camera. If a reverential attitude toward literature had blocked his ambition to be a writer, he was not at all frustrated in his new pursuit by any similar regard for the art of photography as he saw it practised in the late 1920's. He "disdained aesthetically," he has said, the work of the two most highly acclaimed photographers of the time, Edward Steichen and Alfred Stieglitz. In angry rebellion against what he considered commercialism and pretentious artiness, Evans set out on a ground-breaking venture

to achieve "the elevated expression, the literate, authoritative, and transcendent statement which a photograph allows," as he described his intention to Landt Dennis of the Christian Science Monitor (March 12, 1971).

During the penurious, bohemian years of his apprenticeship in photography Evans held several temporary jobs, including that of stock clerk in the Wall Street firm of Henry L. Doherty. One of his fellow workers there, briefly, was his friend Hart Crane, the poet. Three of Evans' photographs, his first published work, appeared as illustrations in the first edition of Crane's The Bridge (Black Sun Press, Paris, 1930). In the late 1920's Evans had begun his documentation of American architecture, and to advance that interest in the spring of 1931 he joined another friend, Lincoln Kirstein, in photographing Victorian houses in and around Boston.

The year before, Kirstein had published in his magazine, Hound & Horn, several photographs by Evans that the critic James Thrall Soby admired, as he later wrote in the Saturday Review (February 18, 1956), for "their uncanny precision and directness combined with their acute sense of mood." The personal standards that Evans followed in developing his style were "both exacting and original," John Szarkowski has pointed out. "He thought of photography as a way of preserving segments out of time itself, without regard for the conventional structures of picture-building. Nothing was to be imposed on experience; the truth was to be discovered, not constructed." Scorning technical tricks, Evans relied on an unerring intuition in determining the precise light, angle, and distance required for his camera to capture the unadorned and significant character of his subject. As a lucid record of fact his work shows an affinity with the earlier photographic concepts of Mathew Brady and Eugène Atget.

Evans had his first exhibition at the Julien Levy Gallery in New York in 1932. The following year thirty-one of his photographs appeared in The Crime of Cuba (Lippincott), illustrating Carleton Beals's story of the suffering of Cubans under the tyrannical regime of Machado y Morales. For another commission, in 1934 he photographed the sculpture in the Museum of Modern Art's exhibition "African Negro Art." Many of his photographs were later printed in the Bollingen Foundation's African Folktales & Sculpture (1952).

Over a period of about a year and a half, from late 1935 to 1937, Evans was "a roving social historian" with the photographic unit of the Resettlement Administration, which was renamed the Farm Security Administration soon after he joined it. He is credited with having had considerable influence on that unit in its pioneering documentation of rural poverty during the Depression. His months of service with the FSA, when for the first time he enjoyed a steady income, were the most prolific of his career. He produced hundreds of photographs of quality in what Szarkowski has called "an astonishing creative hot streak."

Nearly half of the pictures in American Photographs, the monograph accompanying a major exhibition of Evans' work at the Museum of Modern Art in 1938, were taken when he was engaged on the Farm Security Administration project. In more than forty other pictures—of storefronts, doorways, torn posters, streets, churches, interiors, and portraits—he called attention to what he found most meaningful in the American environment. Elegiac in tone, with many touches of paradox and some of humor, his pictures seem to warn of the perishability and evanescence of earthly things.

Evans' *American Photographs*, which was reissued in 1962, has become a classic of the documentary approach in photography. As the years passed Kirstein's appraisal of Evans' work in his introductory essay no longer seemed extravagant: "Compare this vision of a continent as it is, not as it might be or as it was, with any other coherent vision that we have had since the war. What poet has said as much? What painter has shown as much? Only newspapers, the writers of popular music, the technicians of advertising and radio have in their blind energy accidentally, fortuitously, evoked for future historians such a powerful monument to our moment. And Evans' work has, in addition, intention, logic, continuity, climax, sense and perfection."

Taking a leave of absence from the FSA, in 1936 Evans joined the writer James Agee on an assignment from *Fortune* magazine to investigate conditions among sharecroppers in the South. For several months they lived with an impoverished Alabama sharecropper, observing his family and neighbors. Their report, in Evans' thirty-one pictures and Agee's embittered prose, was published not by *Fortune*, but by Houghton Mifflin in *Let Us Now Praise Famous Men: Three Tenant Families* (1941). The naked realism of Evans' uncaptioned, eloquent photographs impressed many reviewers. The book was described in *Time* (October 13, 1941) as "the most distinguished failure of the season." After it was reissued in 1960 with sixty-two photographs and a foreword by Evans, and later published as a paperback, the photographs that he made in his collaboration with Agee became perhaps Evans' most widely known work. Although Evans' compassion speaks out of every photograph, he was not concerned with the reform of social ills, but with describing experience—the effect of the Depression on the nation, which he regards as even more cataclysmic than its wars.

Evans' characteristic photographs are reticent, contemplative studies of motionless subjects viewed from human-eye level. In 1938, however, he began a number of experiments in which he sacrificed photographic controls, such as choice of angle, to take advantage of the element of chance. Using a Contax camera concealed in his topcoat, in 1938 and 1941 he secretly photographed a series of passengers on the New York City subway. Forty-one of his portraits, remarkable for what they revealed of the mental states of his fellow riders, were exhibited at the Museum of Modern Art in 1966. Concurrently with that show, eighty-nine photographs of subway riders were published in *Many Are Called* (Houghton Mifflin). In the mid-1940's Evans made a somewhat similar series of portraits of people on Chicago streets. Later reversing the fixed position of the camera and the moving subject, he made photographs from a train window of the passing industrial landscape.

When the United States entered World War II, Evans tried without success to enter a Naval unit of photographers organized by Steichen. In 1943 he took a job as contributing editor of *Time*, where Agee was then employed. "Two years and I was just drained dry," Evans recalled in his interview with Tallmer for the New York *Post*. "Hard work, and also intellectually degrading and insulting. You had to figure out how not to die, and that was useful too; it toughened you."

The experience in writing that Evans had gained at *Time* helped him to assert his independence when he transferred to *Fortune* in 1945 as associate editor. Over the next twenty years he conceived and executed his own ideas for photo-essays, took the pictures, and wrote the captions and text. His camera explorations of Chicago and of the American landscape seen from a moving train were among his picture essays for *Fortune*. The subjects of his other articles included workers in Detroit, the Wall Street district, New England resort hotels, railroad stations, Early American river mills, locomotives, antique Rolls-Royce cars, primitive churches, and American masonry. His touching pictures on unemployment in the March 1961 issue of *Fortune* recall his photographs of the Depression years.

Some of Evans' photographs, at times accompanied by a text, were also published in the *Cambridge Review*, *Architectural Forum*, and *Life*. The concessions, if any, that he may have made to popular taste have not impaired the integrity of his art. "In the best of the *Fortune* portfolios Evans has worked with the same impetus and conviction as before," Soby acknowledged in the *Saturday Review* (September 22, 1962); "the edge of his commentary still cuts clean and deep; his poetry (and the word is not too strong) has not lost its melancholy, piercing ability to make unadorned reality suggest evocative metaphor."

The metaphorical quality of Evans' work distinguishes, for example, the twelve photographs of *Message from the Interior* (Eakins Press, 1966). Most of the pictures, made between 1931 and 1962, are unpeopled scenes of the inside of buildings, and like Evans' photographs of the exteriors of buildings, they tell much about their occupants and about America. "Mr. Evans affects to see only what his camera, or any camera, can see, but in fact his pictures are full of ghostly presences," a reviewer commented in the *New Yorker* (January 7, 1967). "Even if the pictures have been taken in a blazing sun, they convey the sense of an ominous twilight to come."

Since 1965 Evans has held the title of Professor of Graphic Design at Yale University, where he teaches a seminar-type, wide-ranging graduate course in what he calls "seeing." He has continued his work as a photographer, and several pictures of recent years were among the 200 selected for his retrospective exhibition at the Museum of Modern Art in 1971. In some of the critical commentary on his widely reviewed show it was suggested that his prevailing images of billboards, signs, and advertising artifacts led the way to Pop Art. Szarkowski, however, finds the differences between Evans' photographs and Pop painting more important than similarities: "The descriptive and elusive complexity, the richer ambiguity, the reticence of Evans' pictures result not in parody but in mystery."

Photographs by Evans are included in the permanent collections of the Metropolitan Museum of Art, the Museum of Modern Art, and the Art Institute of Chicago. He is a fellow of the American Academy of Arts and Sciences and was the recipient of a Guggenheim fellowship in 1941, a Carnegie Corporation award in 1962, and an honorary Litt.D. degree from Williams College in 1968. His club is the Century Association in New York City.

On October 29, 1960 Walker Evans married Isabelle Boeschenstein. He is a small, slender man with hazel eyes, gray hair, and—according to press interviewers—a reserved and courtly manner and a "spunky" outlook. Even in his bohemian days he maintained a dapper appearance. Walter McQuade, an editor of *Fortune*, recently described him in *Life* (March 5, 1971): "He has an entrancing, self-indulgent wit, a finely polished peskiness, a zone defense of personality traits that makes him even more impenetrable than his pictures."

References

Christian Sci Mon p13 Mr 12 '71 por
Life 70:12 Mr 5 '71
N Y Post p53 Mr 5 '71
New Yorker 42:26+ D 24 '66
Sat R 39:28+ F 18 '56; 45:57+ S 22 '62
Time 50:73 D 15 '47
Walker Evans (1971)
Who's Who in America, 1970-71

FAIRCHILD, JOHN B(URR)

Mar. 6, 1927- Publisher
Address: b. Fairchild Publications, Inc., 7 E. 12th St., New York 10003

As the owner and guiding light of *Women's Wear Daily,* the American fashion industry's gossipy and irreverent trade journal, John B. Fairchild wields what one well-known couture designer has called "the power of the devil." When Fairchild took over the then sedate *WWD* in 1960 it had a reputation for reliability; under his aegis it soon became the most influential publication on American fashion, providing breezy, if opinionated, reportage on everything from "in" restaurants and films to the latest migrations of the jet-set. Throughout the 1960's society matrons and prominent fashion designers smarted from snubs or snidery directed at them from the columns of *WWD*, but nothing caused an uproar to match the newspaper's all-out campaign in 1970 to lower women's skirts. Although Fairchild and *Women's Wear* only partly succeeded in making 1970 the year of the midi, they proved for the first time that fashion editors as well as designers and retailers could dictate fashion to substantial numbers of women.

Women's Wear Daily is the best known of the eight trade journals published by Fairchild Publications, which was founded by John's grandfather, Edmund Fairchild. John served in the family business as head of the Paris bureau of *Women's Wear Daily* for six years before his appointment as publisher of *WWD* in 1960. In 1966 he succeeded his father, Louis W. Fairchild, as president of Fairchild Publications, and in 1970, upon the retirement of his uncle, Edgar W. B. Fairchild, he became board chairman of the family enterprise.

John Burr Fairchild was born on March 6, 1927 to Louis and Margaret (Day) Fairchild in Newark, New Jersey. At first he had little interest in joining the family business, and after he graduated from the Kent School in Kent, Connecticut in 1946 he entered Princeton University with vague ideas of becoming a doctor or a scientist. His lack of aptitude for math soon discouraged him from pursuing those careers, and at the end of his freshman year he dropped out of school. After a stint in the Army as a speechwriter at the Pentagon, however, he returned to Princeton and studied humanities, working for *WWD* during the summers and earning his B.A. degree in 1949.

Fairchild worked for the Detroit department store J. L. Hudson Company in its research department for a time before joining Fairchild Publications full time in 1951 as a reporter for *Women's Wear Daily*. His beat was the New York City retail scene; his approach was aggressive. "From the moment he started," John's father has recalled, "he stirred things up." Transferred to Paris as head of the Paris bureau of *WWD* in 1954, John Fairchild soon became known as Un-Fairchild or "Blouson Noir" (Black Jacket or the Tough One). While his predecessors had often been ignored, Fairchild earned fame—or notoriety —by panning top designers' collections, printing sketches before release dates, and reporting often unverified gossip on Parisian high society. In 1960 he managed to get a couturier's assistant to show him a sketch of Yves St. Laurent's new silhouette for Dior several weeks before its release date and then had the audacity to describe it as "a toothpaste tube on top of a brioche."

When Fairchild returned to New York in October 1960 to take over as publisher of *WWD*, he made his presence felt immediately. Factual and useful trade stories continued in the journal, but they were replaced on page one by photographs of society women, sketches, notes on fashion trends, and gossip. On the inside pages Fairchild introduced reviews of plays, books, films, and restaurants, and the paper's market news column, "Eye," became a gossip column that was soon supplemented by "Eye Too."

It soon became obvious that Fairchild was determined not merely to chronicle the fashion industry but to shape it. Until his arrival on the scene the most influential fashion journalists had been the fashion editors of certain daily newspapers and mass circulation magazines. (Monthly fashion magazine editors had great prestige but little actual leverage.) Although the circulation of *WWD* was much lower than that of mass-circulation journals, Fairchild pressed his advantage through daily coverage. Five days a week he presented his readers with his attitudes and opinions on fashion and with photographs and sketches of admired European women and the work of top European designers. He praised those American designers who, he believed, had flair and originality, but scorned those who had been pirating fashion ideas from Europe.

Among the designers championed by *Women's Wear Daily* are Yves St. Laurent, Oscar de la Renta, Geoffrey Beene, and Adolfo. According to many observers, other prestigious designers have been virtually ignored because of Fairchild's spitefulness. They point, for example, to Norman Norell, who used to be a court favorite but has not appeared in *WWD* since he reportedly had a falling out with Fairchild. Other designers who are supposedly blacklisted include Mainbocher, Pauline Trigère, and Mollie Parnis, who several years ago reportedly fell out of favor because she refused to release advance sketches of clothing for Lady Bird Johnson to *WWD* reporters.

In a similar apparently arbitrary way *WWD* began building up certain society women with photographs and tidbits of news on the pages of "Eye" and "Eye Too." Women to receive the royal treatment included Gloria Guinness, Isabel Eberstadt, Amanda Burden, and Baby Jane Holzer. Other prominent women came in for ridicule, especially the wives of politicians, for whom *WWD* writers invented such catty titles as Her Goodiness for Mrs. Nixon and Her Efficiency for Mrs. Johnson. (Britain's Princess Margaret became known as Her Drear). For *WWD* the buying habits and fashion preferences of celebrities became top news. On his arrival in New York in 1960 Fairchild created a Presidential campaign issue when he broke the news that Jacqueline Kennedy and her mother-in-law, Rose Kennedy, had spent $30,000 on a Paris shopping spree. Later *WWD* scored scoops with Princess Margaret's wedding dress, Lady Bird Johnson's inaugural wardrobe, "Happy" Rockefeller's trousseau, and Jackie Kennedy's leopard coat. Their advance sketch of Luci Johnson's wedding dress so infuriated the White House that *WWD* reporters were banned from the wedding.

Although Fairchild and the editors of *Women's Wear Daily* innocently denied that they set out to blitz the fashion world with the midi, or "longuette," as Fairchild decided to call it, nobody seemed to believe them. In 1970 women did not find their photographs in *WWD* unless they were long-skirted, and designers received coverage in proportion to their devotion to the longer look, ranging from just below the knee to ankle length. With millions of American women outspokenly committed to the mini length, manufacturers and retailers were caught in a mini-midi dilemma of major financial consequences. Some gambled that women would remain loyal to their legs, others that they would soon seek the new fashions. Still others hedged with pants suits. By the end of the year some manufacturers had been forced out of business in the confusion, while many stores were left with racks of spurned midis. By 1971 a hodgepodge of short pants, long pants, knickers, and skirts of every length could be observed on the

JOHN B. FAIRCHILD

streets of New York and elsewhere, but Fairchild continued to forecast the eventual victory of the longuette.

The *WWD* midi campaign intensified the fear and hatred felt for Fairchild on Seventh Avenue, but it did nothing to impair the journal's status as obligatory reading for anyone in the women's wear business. Since 1960 its circulation has risen from 48,000 to 85,000. A substantial number of *WWD*'s newer readers are the rich, fashionable "Ladies," as the trade paper calls them with a capital "L," who find their activities chronicled therein. Once asked by reporters if she reads *WWD*, Jacqueline Kennedy Onassis sighed and replied, "I try not to."

With less fanfare, John Fairchild enlivened the other journals that comprise the Fairchild family business. In addition to *WWD* he also was put in charge of the *Daily News Record*, the trade paper of the men's clothing industry, in 1960, and in 1964 he was named editor in chief of all Fairchild publications, including *Electronic News, Footwear News, Home Furnishings Daily, Metalworking News, Supermarket News,* and *Men's Wear* magazine. When he was named vice-president of Fairchild Publications in 1965, he relinquished his post as publisher of *WWD* to James Brady, but his influence prevailed unabated at the paper's editorial offices, and in 1971 he resumed the title of publisher after Brady's departure to join Hearst publications. After becoming president of Fairchild Publications in 1966, he negotiated a merger of his company with the Capital Cities Broadcasting Company. When Fairchild Publications became a subsidiary of the larger company in 1968, John Fairchild was named one of its directors and its executive vice-president. Since December 1, 1970 he has been chairman of the board of Fairchild Publications. Besides its trade journals, the Fairchild enterprise maintains a book division and a *Women's Wear Daily* syndicated news service. In the future John Fairchild has plans for launching a weekly magazine to be called *W*, which would be an expanded form of *WWD* without the trade stories.

John B. Fairchild has often been compared to a mischievous English schoolboy. Brown-haired, blue-eyed, and bedimpled, he has a cherubic face and a manner that Willa Petschek of the *Guardian* (November 6, 1970) has described as "nervy, brash, and disarming." On June 8, 1950 he married Jill Lipsky, the Vassar-educated daughter of a Russian father and an English mother. With their four children—John Longin, James Burr, Jill, and Stephen—the Fairchilds live in a large East Side Manhattan apartment. They also maintain a farmhouse in Connecticut and a beach house in Bermuda. The publisher enjoys going to films or spending time with his family, but he shuns the company of the beautiful people his newspaper lionizes. "Those people are a joke, wasteful and unimportant," he told an interviewer for a cover story in *Time* (September 14, 1970). "To be living like that in this day and age is unforgivable." Several years ago he wrote what the *Time* story called a "terrible novel" about the beautiful people entitled *The Moonflower Couple* (Doubleday, 1967). Much better received was Fairchild's vivid account of Parisian and New York couture, *The Fashionable Savages* (Doubleday, 1965), which has gone through several printings. Writing about the latter book in her column in the *Herald Tribune* (August 30, 1965), Eugenia Sheppard commented: "I hate most books about fashion. They don't see the forest for the trees. John Fairchild, though, not only sees the forest, but the forest exactly as it is. . . . Paris is the exotic forest. New York's Seventh Avenue is a forest primeval." Among his clubs are the University of New York, the Travellers of Paris, and the Royal Bermuda Yacht. Fairchild is an Episcopalian.

References

    Guardian p9 N 6 '70 por
    N Y Herald Tribune Mag p20+ F 2 '64
       por
    Time 96:76+ S 14 '70 pors
    Ephron, Nora. Wallflower at the Orgy
       (1970)

FELD, ELIOT

July 5, 1942- Dancer; choreographer
Address: b. c/o The American Dance Foundation, Inc., 2291 Broadway, New York 10024

To Eliot Feld, who has been involved in dance since early childhood, ballet represents a kinetic response to the pure feeling engendered by music. He has lived up to that creed in the dozen ballets he has created since 1967, when his *Harbinger* was premièred by the American Ballet Theatre. Although rooted in classical forms, his movement vocabulary is original and free of balletic excesses. While abstract, his works are thematic, and their characters range over a wide spectrum of emotional progressions.

After a stint as a dancer on the Broadway musical stage, Feld began dancing with the American Ballet Theatre in 1963 and was later appointed a resident choreographer. In 1969 he struck out on his own to found the American Ballet Company, of which he became a principal dancer and the manager and chief choreographer. Although Feld's company achieved considerable artistic success, money problems forced it to disband in mid-1971. Since that time Feld has been staging his works for ballet companies and has been commissioned to create two new works for the American Ballet Theatre.

Eliot Feld was born in Brooklyn, New York on July 5, 1942, to Benjamin Noah Feld and Alice (Posner) Feld. His parents still live and work in Brooklyn, where his father practises law and his mother is a travel agent. He has a younger sister, Erica. In childhood Feld underwent rigorous religious training in a Hebrew school that he attended beginning at six in the morning; later in the day he reported to public school. His formal training in dance began at about the age of six, when he began rhythm classes with Ronne Aul. Later he entered the school of American Ballet, and in 1954 he donned royal raiment for his first major stage appearance as the child prince in George Balanchine's New York City Ballet production of *The Nutcracker*.

At twelve Feld enrolled at the High School of Performing Arts in New York City, where he took classes in modern dance and studied ballet with Bella Malinka and Nina Popova. Meanwhile, he was a precocious performer with the modern dance groups of Pearl Lang and Donald McKayle. Late in 1954 Sophie Maslow hired him for her dances for the Phoenix Theatre musical *Sandhog*, and he turned up in a performance of Ravel's one-act opera *L'Enfant et les Sortilèges*, with the Little Orchestra Society. By the time that Feld graduated from the High School of Performing Arts in 1958 he had joined the cast of *West Side Story*, first as a member of the Sharks and later in the role of Baby John, which he also played on tour and in the film version.

Back home in New York, Feld entered what he described to Jack Anderson in an interview for *Dance Magazine* (July 1967) as a "morbid" period. "I stopped going to class," he recalled. "I got out of shape. I didn't work. I just sat in my apartment until my money ran out and I ran crying home to my parents. That sort of life lasted until I was twenty. It was a real bad time." He rallied out of his funk permanently when he joined the company of *I Can Get It for You Wholesale*, which opened on Broadway in March 1962. Resuming his ballet classes, he studied under Richard Thomas, about whom Feld said to Jack Anderson: "He's been just wonderful to me. He really helped me along at a tough time. When I saw how out of shape I was, I'd cry and curse and rant and throw fits. But Richard Thomas always managed to calm me down."

Urged by Thomas, Feld auditioned for American Ballet Theatre, which finally accepted him in 1963. After several years in the corps he took solo roles in such repertory works as *Les Noces, Wind in the Mountains* and *Dark Elegies*. His most memorable interpretations were the First

Sailor in *Fancy Free,* Billy in *Billy the Kid* and Hermes in *Helen of Troy.* His performance of Hilarion in *Giselle* raised some eyebrows because of his interpretation and style, but, aware of his inadequacies in the role, Feld looked for someone to help him eliminate them.

The impetus for the first ballet that Feld choreographed—*Harbinger*—was the music to which it was set—Prokofiev's Concerto No. 5 in G for Piano —which had so interested him that he learned to read the orchestral score. Soon he was improvising steps to the second movement, gradually developing the swift pas de deux. The first two minutes of finished choreography required some 300 hours of work. When Jerome Robbins saw a fragment of *Harbinger* he encouraged Feld to continue, and when he had seen more, he persuaded the directors of the American Ballet Theatre to make it an official project.

After *Harbinger* had its première at the New York State Theatre on May 11, 1967, Clive Barnes's column in the next morning's New York *Times* was headlined: "Ballet Theater Introduces Eliot Feld—and a New Phase in Choreography." "Choreographers are seldom born—they explode," Barnes wrote. "One exploded last night. His name is Eliot Feld. . . . Here is the most important indigenous talent in classic ballet since Jerome Robbins." Barnes praised Feld's "sense of the inevitability of steps . . . flow of genuine invention . . . feel of a construction in space." Feld has explained that in *Harbinger* he is talking about himself and the people he knows: "It's like showing some of the personal games we play."

Before the year was out, Feld had a chance to prove that the success of *Harbinger* had been no mere fluke, when his second pure dance work, *At Midnight,* was given its world première by the American Ballet Theatre at City Center on December 1. Set to Mahler's brooding *Five Rückert Songs* and danced in settings by Leonard Baskin, *At Midnight* had to do with the anguish of loneliness and the search for love, as contrasted to the felicity of belonging. By demonstrating the depth of Feld's choreographic gifts and the dimensions of his vision, *At Midnight* confirmed the promise of his earlier work.

That season Eliot Feld was also winning praise as a dancer in the American Ballet Theatre's repertory. In *Saturday Review* (December 23, 1967) Walter Terry touched on the relationship between Feld's dancing and his choreographic gifts: "His dancing . . . is rooted, as it should be, in a powerful exposition of male bravado, yet the sensitive being is inescapable in one who could create a new masterful ballet, *At Midnight,* because he could admit with reluctance but with honesty, that at the witching hour, 'I don't sleep, I cry.'"

Early in 1968, soon after touring with the American Ballet Theatre, Feld resigned from the company over conflicts that were apparently impossible to resolve in spite of the concessions made to him as resident choreographer. That spring he told Clive Barnes of his determination to form his own company because he believed that he needed total administrative control to accomplish his aims

ELIOT FELD

in dance. Shortly thereafter, at Barnes's suggestion, Feld was commissioned to create a work for the Royal Winnipeg Ballet. His lyrical *Meadowlark* premièred in Winnipeg, Manitoba on October 5, 1968, and although it toed a lighter line than *Harbinger* or *At Midnight,* it once more affirmed Feld's creative authenticity. When Beryl Grey, director of London's Festival Ballet, invited Feld to restage the work for her company, the second production received mixed notices from the London critics who traveled to Bristol to view it at the Hippodrome. In his dispatch to the New York *Times* (December 13, 1968), John Percival suggested that Feld had fallen victim to his own reputation in that "people went expecting to be astonished and were disappointed that they were only pleased."

In the fall of 1968 Feld persuaded Harvey Lichtenstein, with whom he had once danced in Pearl Lang's company, and now director of the Brooklyn Academy of Music, to launch his own company and provide it with a permanent base of operations. Tentatively named the American Ballet Players, the new resident company began auditions around the end of 1968, under Feld and Richard Thomas, then ballet master. Its first small roster included Christine Sarry, John Sowinski, Elizabeth Lee, and David Anderson, Feld's former colleagues at the American Ballet Theatre. David Coll was recruited from the San Francisco Ballet, and Olga Janke, just turned sixteen, came from the Pennsylvania Ballet.

Insisting on the luxury of live music, Feld demanded a full orchestra and a music director, in the person of Christopher Keene. Money trickled in from the state and federal governments, private endowments, and individuals, and the nonprofit American Dance Foundation, Inc., became the board of trustees and sponsoring organization for Feld's American Ballet Company. Invited by Gian-Carlo Menotti to the Umbrian hill town of Spoleto, Italy, the American Ballet Company gave its first public performance on June 27, 1969, at the opening of the Festival of Two Worlds. Its program, consisting of Feld's *Harbinger, At Mid-*

night, and *Cortège Burlesque* and Herbert Ross's *Caprichos,* earned eight curtain calls, and Feld's *Intermezzo,* introduced the following night, was called by Clive Barnes "one of the best ballets of the year."

A few days before the company made its scheduled American debut at the Brooklyn Academy of Music on October 21, 1969, Feld fractured a bone in his foot, precipitating a crisis that was weathered when Bruce Marks, Edward Verso, and Richard Rutherford agreed to pinch-hit for him. Although shadowed by the near-disaster that cost them the presence of Feld, the company won unanimous acclaim. Before the second week was out, Feld was dancing again, with the aid of pain-killing drugs.

That first season of the American Ballet Company brought the premières of three new works by Feld. Many aficionados consider *Cortège Burlesque* (to music of Chabrier) to be Feld's contribution to high camp, parodying as it does the genre of bravura ballet. *Pagan Spring* (Bartók), which to some critics seemed unfinished, has not been performed in succeeding engagements. When *Intermezzo,* set to Brahms piano pieces, was performed on the second night, its lyric purity confirmed Clive Barnes's earlier raptures. Critics and audiences alike have noted its similarity to *Liebeslieder Walzer* and *Dances at a Gathering,* but as Anna Kisselgoff pointed out in the New York *Times* (October 24, 1969) "it is the originality of the movement that gives the work its great distinction."

Feld's flurry of creativity continued throughout 1970. In two seasons at the Brooklyn Academy of Music he choreographed four new ballets, convincing dance enthusiasts that he intended to stay around. His poetic *Early Songs* (Richard Strauss) was acclaimed by Hubert Saal of *Newsweek* (April 13, 1970) as "the best work so far by the brilliant young American choreographer." *Cortège Parisien* (Chabrier) is a saucy divertissement, while *The Consort,* with a score arranged by Christopher Keene from Renaissance music, is structured around court dances whose sedate patterns and intricate cadences evolve into a peasant bacchanal. A kind of kinetic précis of a life, Feld's *A Poem Forgotten* was called by Walter Terry in the *Saturday Review* (November 21, 1970) "an engrossing work that has the curious power of making the onlooker search his own kinetic memories of how it all began, how patterns were formed, how a bundle of senses became an 'I'."

For his spring of 1971 season at the Brooklyn Academy of Music, Feld created three new ballets. Set to Brahms piano pieces, *Romance* presents an ensemble of four couples whose vague yearnings and discontent blend with an economy of movement to achieve what is possibly Feld's most sophisticated work to date. *Theater,* to music of Richard Strauss, is an opulent piece in which a tragic Pierrot searches vainly for identity among the tawdry trappings of a commedia dell'arte world. Debussy's *Sacred and Profane Dances* inspired *The Gods Amused,* a pas de trois for Daniel Levins, Elizabeth Lee, and Christine Sarry.

Despite their variety in theme and content, Feld's ballets flow from a wellspring that is unmistakably his own. He explained to Herbert Kupferberg in an interview for the *National Observer* (November 3, 1969): "My company is different from others because it is based on me. . . . My basic belief is that movement is an expression of feeling, and that in ballet a dancer or a choreographer must make his feelings clear to the audience so that it can share them. To me theatre must be felt, must affect the emotions, not the mind. Ballet is not an intellectual art." Feld will continue to dance as long as he can, because dancing enriches his choreography. "If you're going to invent movement, you've got to be sensitive to movement, and that means you've got to move," he told a writer for *Dance Magazine* (July 1971).

Eliot Feld is five feet nine inches tall, weighs about 145 pounds, and has dark brown hair and hazel eyes. Apart from dance his interests include music, literature, and painting. He particularly admires Leonard Baskin, some of whose work he owns. His dream, according to *Dance Magazine* (July 1971), is "to play the Met for two eight-week seasons a year."

References

Dance and Dancers 20:38+ Ja '69 pors
Dance Mag 41:44+ Jl '67 pors
N Y Times p14 S 6 '70 por; II p29 N 15 '70

FITZSIMMONS, FRANK E(DWARD)

Apr. 7, 1908- Labor union official
Address: b. International Brotherhood of Teamsters, Chauffeurs, Warehousemen, and Helpers, 25 Louisiana Ave., N.W., Washington, D.C. 20001

The biggest and richest trade union in the world today is the International Brotherhood of Teamsters, Chauffeurs, Warehousemen, and Helpers of America—generally known as the International Brotherhood of Teamsters (IBT) or simply Teamsters—with 2,100,000 members in 870 locals in the United States and Canada. At its core the membership is composed of truck drivers and others involved in freight hauling, from airline workers to garagemen, but it extends beyond cartage into such distant areas as the Western Union Company and the broadcasting industry. The newly elected president of this labor giant is former vice-president Frank E. Fitzsimmons, loyal lieutenant and crony of longtime president James R. Hoffa since the 1930's, when they were organizers together in Detroit. The feisty Hoffa entrusted the reins of power to the quiet Fitzsimmons in 1967, when he began serving an aggregated federal prison sentence of thirteen years for malfeasance in office and in the courts.

Gainsaying those skeptics within the union who mistook his low-keyed, self-effacing style, so different from Hoffa's, for weakness, Fitzsimmons has proved himself to be a cool, efficient administrator and a shrewd, stalwart negotiator, level-headed and calm under pressure. The frustrated opposition to Hoffa within Teamster ranks apparently sprang not from any significant belief in the government's charges against him but rather from resentment of his autocratic exercise of authority, and by decentralizing administrative procedures, Fitzsimmons has brought relative peace and contentment to the IBT's chain of command. The respectability he has regained for the Teamsters in external relations is reflected in the Alliance for Labor Action, a loose, socially-oriented partnership of the IBT and the United Auto Workers, and in the apparently imminent rapprochement of the IBT and the AFL-CIO, the labor federation from which the Teamsters were ousted in 1957. After the rejection of Hoffa's second bid for parole, in March 1971, the Teamsters elected Fitzsimmons to the office of president at their convention in the summer of 1971.

The fourth of five children of Frank and Ida May (Stahley) Fitzsimmons, Frank Edward Fitzsimmons was born on April 7, 1908 in Jeannette, Pennsylvania, where his father was employed by the Pittsburgh Brewing Company. When he was fifteen the family moved to Detroit, and there the father went into partnership with a relative in a garage business. Two years later the elder Fitzsimmons suffered a stroke from which he never recovered and Frank dropped out of school to help support the family.

Fitzsimmons' first job was an eight-month stint as time clerk with the Ternstadt Company, manufacturers of automobile hardware. At eighteen, by lying about his age, he became a bus driver with the Detroit Motor Company, and when he was in his early twenties he worked briefly away from Detroit, as a driver and instructor with the Brooklyn-Manhattan Transportation Company in New York City. After his return to the Motor City he drove trucks for, successively, the National Transit Corporation and the 3-C Highway Company.

While with National Transit, in 1934, Fitzsimmons joined Teamster Local 299, in Detroit. Jimmy Hoffa, then the newly elected president of Local 299, was so impressed with Fitzsimmons' militant union activism that he selected him to be the local's business agent in 1937. Fitzsimmons was elected vice-president of 299 in 1940 and appointed secretary-treasurer of the IBT's Michigan Conference three years later. At that time the general president of the Teamsters was Daniel Tobin, in office since 1907. Under Tobin, the union's central administration served chiefly as a coordinating point for largely autonomous regional and area units. That structure began to change centripetally, in 1952, when Dan Tobin retired and Dave Beck was elected to succeed him. At the same time Jimmy Hoffa was elected an international vice-president of the union.

Beck's administration was clouded by allegations of corruption that culminated in the conviction of Beck for embezzlement, larceny, and income tax evasion and the eviction of the Teamsters from the AFL-CIO. Hoffa, elected to replace

FRANK E. FITZSIMMONS

Beck in October 1957, took office in January 1958. His presidential power was exercised under the surveillance of three federally-approved monitors for three years, until 1961. In the latter year Fitzsimmons joined the Teamsters' executive board, as an international vice-president.

Bending the Teamster constitution, Hoffa encouraged local union leaders to bypass intermediary councils and officials and "call Hoffa" directly for strike authorizations, financial aid, and help in solving problems. The resulting centralization of power irked not only area council members and regional vice-presidents but also many local officials because, as one of the latter pointed out, it meant that "someone from Washington [was] on the phone every other day messing in their local affairs." But the centralization also made possible the first national contract in the trucking industry, signed in January 1964. Hoffa was generally able to force locals to accept the complex contract, although there were pockets of resistance in New England, New York City, Chicago, and San Francisco.

In 1964 federal courts sentenced Jimmy Hoffa to eight years in prison for jury tampering and five years for conspiracy and fraud in connection with use of a union pension fund, but the union leader remained free for three years pending appeal. At the Teamster convention (an event held every five years) in Miami Beach, Florida in 1966, the delegates reelected Hoffa to the presidency. At Hoffa's request they also created the office of general vice-president, for the purpose of filling any vacancy in the presidency, and elected Fitzsimmons to the new, $45,000-a-year post.

When Hoffa began his incarceration in Lewisburg (Pennsylvania) Federal Penitentiary, in March 1967, Fitzsimmons replaced him in the master freight contract negotiations then in progress and led the Teamsters to a settlement at least as good as, if not better than, any contract Hoffa might have won. The agreement, signed by Trucking Employers Inc. (representing 1,500 companies) on April 12, 1967 and ratified by the Teamster membership a week later, guaranteed the workers an increase of seventy-six cents an hour over a three-year period. Fifty-five cents of the increase was to be in wages and the rest in fringe benefits.

Once the arduous contract bargaining was out of the way, Fitzsimmons and the Teamster executive board addressed themselves to the task of returning the exercise of authority and the flow of grievances and money to the chain of command envisioned in the union constitution, beginning with local leadership and moving up through the area joint councils (fifty in number) and regional vice-presidents (twelve) to the general international leadership. With constitutional channels reestablished, Fitzsimmons was able to spend more time on the union's national business, such as lobbying Congress, and on matters transcending self-serving "bread-and-butter" unionism, such as those issues of concern to the Alliance for Labor Action.

The ALA was formed by Fitzsimmons and the late Walter Reuther, president of the United Auto Workers, in 1969. They dedicated the loose federation of Teamsters and the UAW to broad goals not only in the field of labor but also in the wider community: assisting isolated community unions by various means, including an emergency defense fund; helping the unorganized, such as migrant farm workers, to unionize themselves; strengthening collective bargaining procedures; and setting up programs designed to contribute to the solution of problems relating to racism, employment, and income, health and medicine, agriculture, the aged, housing and urban affairs, politics and legislation, the schism between blue collar workers on the one hand and liberals, intellectuals, and alienated young people on the other, and the quality of national life. "We are formalizing," Fitzsimmons later explained, "our basic commitment to the total welfare of the community." Also in 1969, Fitzsimmons and the IBT executive board founded the Teamster Labor Institute, a school for educating local IBT leaders and prospective representatives in labor-management and community relations. The institute is housed in a leased building adjacent to the Everglades Hotel in Miami, Florida.

In bargaining with Trucking Employers Inc. between January and April 1970, Fitzsimmons won a settlement giving the Teamsters a wage increase of $1.10 an hour over a thirty-nine-month contract term. But dissident truck drivers in Chicago held out for more and local employers gave them what they demanded: a $1.65-an-hour increase over thirty-six months. Fitzsimmons and Trucking Employers Inc., renegotiated the national contract to bring it into line with the Chicago settlement and the agreement finally reached, in July 1970, was for $1.85 an hour over thirty-nine months. The contract brings the basic Teamster wage to approximately six dollars an hour.

Frank E. and Mary Patricia Fitzsimmons were married in 1952, after the death of Fitzsimmons' first wife. They have two children, Gary and Carol Ann. The Fitzsimmonses, formerly residents of Dearborn, Michigan, now live in Bethesda, Maryland, within commuting distance of the luxurious marble building that is the Washington headquarters of the Teamsters. (The "main and principal" office of the union, according to the IBT letterhead, is at 2801 Trumbull Avenue in Detroit.) At last report, the presidential office that Fitzsimmons uses was almost exactly as Hoffa had left it, with pictures of the jailed ex-president's grandchildren on the wall, for example, and his nameplate on the desk.

Fitzsimmons, known as "Fitz" to friends and associates, is a bespectacled, stout man, five feet ten inches tall and weighing 192 pounds, with a full head of graying black hair surmounting a round face. In personality he is diametrically different from that of the aggressive Hoffa—amiable, cautious, deliberate, soft-spoken, and reserved, but his subdued manner can be deceptive. Underneath it, according to those who know him, is a sense of humor, an "ability to make decisions," an impatience with "nonsense," and a toughness that becomes evident when he is angry. Although Hoffa relished giving histrionic performances before standing-room audiences of staff and hangers-on at executive board meetings, Fitzsimmons restricts the meetings to those whose attendance is required, and he conducts them tightly and expeditiously. And while Hoffa, in the words of one union official, used to "say good night to his wife and mix with the boys, Fitz would rather go to the beach with his wife and kids." And another Teamster officer has said: "If you were going to look for a nice grandfather for your kids—kindly, congenial, very warm—you'd pick a guy like Fitz." Outside of family life, Fitzsimmons' favorite recreations are playing golf and poker and watching baseball.

References

American Labor 3:20+ O '70 pors
N Y Times IV p2 Ap 16 '67; p67 Ag 27 '67 por
Wall St J p1+ Ap 18 '68
Who's Who in America, 1970-71

FLEISHER, LEON

July 23, 1928- Pianist; conductor
Address: b. c/o Columbia Artists Management Inc., 165 W. 57th St., New York 10019; h. 1723 Park Ave., Baltimore, Md. 21217

Surviving the ordeal of a childhood as a piano prodigy, Leon Fleisher benefited from ten years of study with Artur Schnabel to become one of the most highly regarded pianists of his generation. In the mid-1960's, however, while at the peak of his career, he was stricken by a mysterious disability that paralyzed his right hand and limited his playing to the specialized repertoire of one-handed piano music. Still determined to expand his horizons in the musical world, he successfully launched a new and promising career as a conductor with the "Mostly Mozart Festival" at New York's Philharmonic Hall in August 1970.

Leon Fleisher was born in San Francisco on July 23, 1928 to Isidor and Bertha (Mittelman) Fleisher. His parents had emigrated to the United States from Russia. Fleisher began to study the piano at an early age, and because his musical studies took up much of his time, he was privately educated. Being a child prodigy was "a painful experience" for him, because it deprived him of normal boyhood activities. "My mother had cultural ambitions for my older brother and me," Fleisher told Gerald Nachman of the New York *Post* (August 4, 1964), "but he got out of it somehow—baseball and so forth. When I was five I sat down at the piano because it was already there, and when I was seven my parents decided to exploit me." Recalling that his mother wanted him to become either President of the United States or the world's greatest pianist, he added: "I thought it would be easier to become a pianist."

In 1935 Leon Fleisher gave his first public recital in San Francisco. When he was nine, the great pianist Artur Schnabel was persuaded to listen to him and was much impressed. Breaking his own rule against teaching child prodigies, Schnabel agreed to take the boy as a pupil and tutored him for ten years, from 1938 to 1948, at first at Tremezzo, on the shores of Lake Como, Italy and, after the outbreak of World War II, at his Central Park West apartment in New York City. Lessons usually lasted two to three hours. While one of the students played, the others would listen so that all could benefit from the master's comments. In an interview with John Briggs in the New York *Times* (November 29, 1964) Fleisher said: "It was wonderful. He was giving us sixty years of knowledge about a piece. There was so much to learn, so much to remember. We used to reel out of our lessons." Writing in the New York *Herald Tribune* (November 20, 1964), Fleisher remembered Schnabel as "one of the first musicians to assume the responsibility of an 'honest' approach to music, with fidelity to the composer of prime importance." After a decade, Schnabel apparently decided that he had taught Fleisher all he could, and he ended the lessons, saying simply: "Enough!"

Meanwhile, in 1943 Fleisher made his concert debut with the San Francisco Orchestra under Pierre Monteux. He first performed in New York City on November 4, 1944 as a soloist with the New York Philharmonic, again under the baton of Monteux, who called the sixteen-year-old Fleisher "the pianistic find of the century." A New York *Times* critic about that time described him as "one of the most remarkably gifted of the younger generation of American keyboard artists." Despite his continued success, Fleisher decided at twenty to interrupt his career and "bum around" Paris for two years. "I just got sick of looking at big black pianos," he said in the New York *Post* interview, "and I also wanted to get out of the house."

Fleisher gained international stature as an artist in 1952, when he became the first American to win a major European music competition. As one of seventy-one competitors representing twenty-eight countries, he took first prize at Brussels in the Concours International Reine Elisabeth de Belgique, which is considered by some to be the most rigorous competition of its kind. An eminent panel of judges,

LEON FLEISHER

including Artur Rubinstein, Rudolf Firkusny, and Olin Downes, named Fleisher "the best young pianist in the world." His performance evoked so much applause that eventually the audience had to be silenced by the ringing of a bell.

After his triumph in Brussels, Fleisher embarked on a series of concert appearances throughout Europe. Over the next few years he became one of the most widely traveled pianists, dividing his time between Europe, the United States, Canada, and Latin America. His popularity was so great in Buenos Aires that an Asociación Leon Fleisher was founded there, and under its auspices a symphony orchestra, a concert series, and an instrumental competition were established. Fleisher was among the first American artists chosen to represent the United States at the Brussels World's Fair in 1958.

Fleisher's career as a pianist prospered in the years between 1952 and the mid-1960's, and his mastery of the classic and romantic repertoire was acclaimed by fellow musicians, audiences, and critics. Among the critics were Ross Parmenter of the New York *Times* (March 2, 1962), who praised his "purity of style" and "beguilingly clear . . . sound"; and Howard Klein in the New York *Times* (November 18, 1963), who found his playing "technically brilliant and musically penetrating." Writing in the New York *Herald Tribune* (January 8, 1965), William Bender called him "a virtuoso with the refined instincts of a chamber musician, . . . whose brilliant technique and scholarship blend in a state of assured perfection. In the field of the Viennese classicists—Beethoven, Mozart, and Schubert—he is virtually unsurpassed." Fleisher's repertoire also included such modern works as Leon Kirchner's Second Piano Concerto, which he commissioned through the Ford Foundation and first performed in November 1963 with the Seattle Symphony Orchestra.

During his apogee as a pianist, Fleisher made recordings for Epic Records and Columbia Masterworks, often with the Cleveland Symphony under the direction of George Szell. Probably the most important were his performances of all five of Beethoven's piano concertos, released by Epic in 1961. Fleisher was one of the youngest pianists ever to undertake that project, which had generally been reserved for veteran performers. Commenting on the Beethoven set in the New York *Times* (September 3, 1961), Raymond Ericson noted that "a vitality, a kind of joy in making music suffuses the recordings, even when the music is at its most profound. This, coupled with the intellectual penetration that marks the work of Mr. Szell and Mr. Fleisher, gives the set a special aura."

By late 1964 some critics began to observe flaws in Fleisher's playing. Winthrop Sargeant, commenting in the *New Yorker* (November 7, 1964) on his Carnegie Hall performance of Mozart's Concerto in D (K. 451), remarked; "At times his right hand did not seem to know what his left was doing; there were many fumbles in matter of detail, a very prominent one in the middle of the cadenza of the last movement." In fact, Fleisher had begun to suffer the paralysis of his right hand that threatened to bring his career to an end. He remembers that his affliction began with symptoms usually attributed to writer's cramp —a tingling sensation, followed by a cramping of the fingers. In 1965, following a concert with Szell and the Cleveland Orchestra, he found himself incapable of playing. "I was pretty desperate," he told an interviewer for *Newsweek* (August 31, 1970). "The means by which I made music were gone, and music was the very core of my existence. And it wasn't easy for those around me. When I wasn't wandering in a valley of depression I treated them like the ogre of the Andes."

Determined not to give up playing the piano completely, Fleisher began to specialize in the limited repertoire of music written for the left hand alone. That repertoire consists largely of piano concertos commissioned by the pianist Paul Wittgenstein, who lost his right arm in World War I, from such composers as Ravel, Prokofiev, Richard Strauss, and Benjamin Britten. "I have a public following gracious enough to listen to me play with five fingers instead of ten," Fleisher told the *Newsweek* interviewer. But despite the success of his one-handed recitals he was not content to restrict himself to such a limited amount of musical activity.

Fleisher had long considered the possibility of a career as a conductor. When he was eleven, he asked Pierre Monteux to let him try to conduct the orchestra, but he was dissuaded by the maestro, who told him: "Once you get the stick in your hand you'll never want to let it go." In 1968 Fleisher became music director of the newly established Theatre Chamber Players of Washington, D.C., a group that includes such noted musicians as pianist André Watts, cellist Leslie Parnas, and violinist Berl Senofsky. Fleisher has planned the group's programs to include a wide range of music, classical as well as modern, and he has personally conducted a number of its programs. Apart from those intimate Washington concerts Fleisher had virtually no preparation for his professional debut as a conductor with the New York Chamber Orchestra at Philharmonic Hall in

the Lincoln Center's "Mostly Mozart Festival" on August 24, 1970. A few days earlier, Fleisher told Donal Henahan of the New York *Times* (August 18, 1970): "I'm not really a conductor yet. I have to study. . . . Naturally, I'm very nervous about my Philharmonic Hall concerts. I'm old to be starting. A whole new bunch of reflexes must be developed."

Conducting without a baton, Fleisher was seated on a tall rehearsal stool because he felt that he could communicate better with his players if he could "be among them, rather than above." Despite his qualms, his New York debut as a conductor proved successful. Reviewing his performance in the New York *Times* (August 26, 1970), Harold C. Schonberg wrote: "Whether or not he has a great deal to learn, he has the instincts of a conductor: . . . fluid rhythm, plenty of authority, a good though somewhat tight beat, and his own ideas about the music. Some conductors have worked for years on less." Miles Kastendieck observed in the *Christian Science Monitor* (September 9, 1970) that Fleisher "demonstrated his awareness of chamber music ensemble, showed how musically intelligent he is, and suggested a self-effacing approach by conducting while seated on the podium. There was quality if not distinction in his direction, leaving a desire for more profile to performances of Schubert's Symphony No. 5 and Mozart's 'Haffner' Symphony."

Since 1959, Fleisher has also been professor of piano at the Peabody Conservatory of Music in Baltimore. He follows the example of his mentor, Artur Schnabel, by teaching his students all he knows, rather than limiting his instruction to what they are ready to assimilate. "Teaching has taught me a great deal," he says. "When you clarify something for a student you also clarify it for yourself." Fleisher is a member of the American Association of University Professors. He was elected a director of the Walter W. Naumburg Foundation in 1965, and he has also served on the boards of directors of the Center Stage in Baltimore and of the Baltimore City Ballet Company. In 1970 he added the position of conductor of the Annapolis (Maryland) Symphony, an amateur orchestra, to his other responsibilities. Aware that an artist cannot remain isolated from the outside world, Fleisher has consistently refused to perform before segregated audiences in the South.

After five years of tests and treatments, medical authorities have still not determined the cause or found a cure for Fleisher's baffling paralysis. Psychotherapy, physiotherapy, shock treatment, and traction have all failed to alleviate the condition, which by 1970 had become so aggravated that he could sign his name with his right hand only with great difficulty. One treatment that he has been considering is what he calls "a kind of Pavlov conditioning in reverse—deconditioning the reflexes so they can be conditioned again."

Leon Fleisher was first married in 1951 to Dorothy Druzinsky. Three children—Deborah, Richard, and Leah—were born to that marriage. Divorced in March 1962, Fleisher was married a second time, on April 1, 1962, to Risselle Rosenthal, a former dancer. With their two children—Paula Beth and Julian—they live in Baltimore, in a three-storied Victorian house that is roomy enough to accommodate their many antiques. Six feet two inches tall, the bespectacled, dark-haired virtuoso currently wears a beard and mustache. Among his pastimes are poker, bridge, and ping-pong. His sense of humor has sustained him during his crisis. He once half jokingly announced plans to write an autobiography, to be titled: "Eighty-eight Keys and No Lock, or, I Was a Kindergarten Dropout."

References

Mus Courier 157:9 Je '58 por
N Y Post p23 Ag 4 '64 por
N Y Times p28 Ag 18 '70 pors
Newsweek 76:64+ Ag 31 '70 por
Time 96:47 S 7 '70 por
Who's Who in America, 1970-71

FLETCHER, ARTHUR A(LLEN)

Dec. 22, 1924- United States government official
Address: b. United States Department of Labor, 14th St. and Constitution Ave., N.W., Washington, D.C. 20210; h. 5101 W. Running Brook Rd., Columbia, Md. 21043

As the highest-ranking black official in the Nixon administration, Arthur A. Fletcher, the Assistant Secretary for Wage and Labor Standards in the United States Department of Labor, is largely responsible for implementing the President's program to improve employment conditions for minorities. A former football star and teacher, and a dedicated Republican, Fletcher came to the attention of Richard Nixon as a result of a successful community self-help program that he organized in East Pasco, Washington in 1966. Since taking office as Assistant Secretary of Labor in May 1969, Fletcher has concentrated on opening job opportunities, especially in the skilled construction trades, for blacks and other minorities through such means as his Philadelphia Plan. In his view, mandatory requirements must be established to overcome resistance by contractors and trade unions to equality of opportunity in employment. "In implementing these requirements," Fletcher wrote in *Ebony* (August 1970), "we must apply the same techniques used in attaining the national goal of putting a man on the moon."

Arthur Allen Fletcher, the son of Andrew A. and Edna (Miller) Fletcher, was born in a black ghetto in Phoenix, Arizona on December 22, 1924. His father (or, according to one source, his stepfather) was a career soldier in an all-black cavalry regiment in the United States Army. The family lived in a succession of ghettoes, including the Watts district of Los Angeles, where Arthur Fletcher was a youth gang leader at thirteen. By the time he reached the eighth grade he had attended seventeen different schools. His mother, who had college degrees in education and nursing

ARTHUR A. FLETCHER

but was unable to find professional employment, worked as a live-in maid, and as a result, Arthur was brought up by various families, including Indians and Mexican-Americans. At one time, during his boyhood, he wanted to study for the ministry.

In high school in Kansas, Arthur Fletcher distinguished himself as a halfback and defensive end on the school football team, and in 1942 he became the first Negro to be chosen for an all-state team in Kansas. Racial antagonism was common at the time, and Fletcher recalls that he and a Negro teammate used to charge themselves up for games against white teams by reading about lynchings of blacks.

At eighteen Fletcher was married, and at nineteen he entered the United States Army. Wounded after a year of combat duty in Europe, he was discharged in 1945. Offered football scholarships by Northwestern, Iowa, and Indiana universities, Fletcher enrolled at Indiana in 1946 but, unable to find suitable housing in Bloomington, decided to accept a scholarship offer from Washburn University in Topeka, Kansas. As a member of the Washburn team he earned Little All-American honors as the sixth leading rusher among small college teams in the United States. While majoring in political science, Fletcher gained some practical experience in government by working part time for one of the state agencies and for legislative committees. He obtained his B.A. degree from Washburn University in 1950.

Deciding on a career in professional football, Fletcher joined the Los Angeles Rams in 1950. Since their quota allowed only five Negroes on the team, he was sold after a short time to the Baltimore Colts. He was their first black player. In 1951 he served with the Hamilton (Ontario) Tiger Cats of the Canadian Football League but found the salary of $5,100 a year not enough to support his family, which by that time included five children. Returning to Kansas, where he tried unsuccessfully to find a job as a high school football coach, he held menial jobs during the next few years, often working sixteen hours a day. In 1953 he took a factory job with the Goodyear

Tire and Rubber Company in Topeka, after his application to join its management trainee program was turned down. During 1953-54 he did postgraduate work in economics and education at Kansas State University.

Meanwhile, Fletcher had entered Republican politics. In 1954 Lieutenant Governor Fred Hall of Kansas, a liberal Republican, asked him to manage his gubernatorial campaign in the black community. Fletcher reportedly delivered some 17,000 votes for Hall and was credited with ensuring his victory at the polls. While waiting for a job in Hall's administration, Fletcher had begun to teach in a rural elementary school and, overwhelmed by the inadequacies of black education, helped raise funds for the pending *Brown vs. School Board of Topeka* desegregation suit, which eventually was successfully fought up to the United States Supreme Court.

As assistant public relations director of the Kansas Highway Commission from 1954 to 1957, Fletcher obtained an inside view of the ways and means by which government contracts are awarded and urged black businessmen to compete for some of the lucrative state contracts. He also served as a legislative liaison officer and as chairman of a commission on racial problems. From 1954 to 1956 he was vice-chairman of the Kansas State Republican Central Committee.

Hall was defeated for reelection in the primaries in 1956, and the next administration abolished Fletcher's job. Meanwhile he had opened a used-car business in Topeka, but according to one source, city officials, resenting his role in the desegregated school suit, forced him out of business. In 1957 he was appointed assistant football coach at Washburn University, becoming its first black staff member, and the first Negro in the United States to coach at a predominantly white institution. In late 1958 he followed Hall to California to work as management control coordinator with the Aerojet Corporation. Later he worked with an Oakland tire company and tried the restaurant business, but with little success. Tragedy struck the family in 1960, when his wife, Mary, broke under the strain of prejudice and economic insecurity and committed suicide after being refused rental of a house in a white section of Berkeley.

Through his involvement in local politics Fletcher managed to get back on his feet. As a paid staff member of the Nixon-Lodge campaign organization, he was charged with the task of "Republicanizing" the heavily Negro and almost totally Democratic Seventeenth Assembly District in the East Bay Area. Although the local Republican candidate for Congress was defeated in the 1960 election by a large margin, Fletcher created a functioning Republican organization in the district with about 200 volunteers. Between 1960 and 1965 Fletcher taught at the Burbank Junior High School in Berkeley, and as a special project director with the Berkeley board of education he helped to desegregate that city's school system. In 1962 he ran for the state Assembly, and although he lost by a two-to-one margin, he put up

a good fight against the Democratic incumbent. From 1962 to 1965 he served on the Alameda County Republican Central Committee, and from 1962 to 1964 he was chairman of an advisory commission on civil rights of the California Republican Assembly. During 1964-65 he did additional postgraduate work at San Francisco State College.

Invited by YMCA officials, in 1965 Fletcher went to the state of Washington to accept a $12,000-a-year position as director of a federally-funded manpower development project training hard-core unemployed in East Pasco, a small, isolated Negro ghetto community on the outskirts of the city of Pasco, in the southeastern part of the state. Its residents were largely semi-literate migrants from the rural South. Although Fletcher succeeded in training 380 men, differences with local welfare officials caused the program to founder. Meanwhile, on his own initiative, Fletcher organized the East Pasco Self-Help Cooperative Association to help the local residents cope with government plans for urban renewal. The association used local capital to buy land, build a service station, establish a credit union, and construct a $650,000 shopping center. All of the jobs and businesses were used to train people in skills that would enable them to work outside of the ghetto. In 1967 Fletcher, as a candidate for the Pasco city council, carried every precinct in town. He served as a councilman in 1968-69. From 1967 to 1969 he also worked as an employee relations specialist at the Hanford Atomic Energy Facility at Richland, Washington.

Fletcher's work in East Pasco brought him to the attention of the national Republican party organization in 1968. He was invited to address the party's platform committee, and his self-help scheme provided the basis for the "black capitalism" program endorsed by the Republican National Convention in Miami that summer. In the Washington state primaries in September he defeated two white opponents for the Republican nomination for lieutenant governor, becoming the first black nominee for statewide office in a state in which only 2 percent of the population was Negro. In the November election, Fletcher polled a surprising 49 percent, losing to his Democratic opponent, John A. Cherberg, by only a few thousand votes. During the first few months of 1969 Fletcher worked for the newly elected Republican Governor, Daniel J. Evans, as a special assistant to coordinate relations between the state government and local communities and served on his urban affairs advisory council.

On March 14, 1969 Fletcher was appointed by President Richard Nixon as Assistant Secretary for Wage and Labor Standards in the Department of Labor. He was confirmed by the Senate on May 1 and sworn into office on May 5, 1969. In his $38,750-a-year post, Fletcher administers a budget of $50,000,000 and establishes policy for some 3,400 employees in ten regional offices. As head of the Wage and Labor Standards Administration he is also responsible for the Office of Federal Contract Compliance, the Bureau of Labor Standards, the Women's Bureau, the Wage and Hour and Public Contract Divisions, the Bureau of Employee's Compensation, and the Office Wage Determinations.

Convinced that without economic security, all the social gains that blacks have made are meaningless, Fletcher has concentrated his efforts on using federal power to push for equal employment opportunities. His major vehicle for that task is the Office of Federal Contracts Compliance (OFCC), which was set up by the Johnson administration in the Labor Department in 1965 and has the power to cancel or suspend government contracts of firms that practise discrimination. This was a powerful weapon, since over half of the 86,000,000-member labor force in the country is employed by some 260,000 government contractors. When Fletcher took office, the OFCC had an inadequate staff and no clearcut guidelines with which to operate. In fact, Fletcher had to struggle during his first year in office to retain the OFCC in his department. He reorganized it, boosted its staff from twenty-eight to 118, and issued a directive that progress in equal employment was to be measured by actual numbers of minority group members on the job, and not by projected plans. Finally, he set up a compliance review system that called for a monthly report on firms receiving government contracts. He appointed John Wilks, a San Francisco public relations executive, as director of the OFCC.

In the late summer of 1969 Fletcher turned his attention to the burgeoning construction industry, noting that blacks held only about 2 percent of the 800,000 highest paying construction jobs and only 7.2 percent of all 2,900,000 jobs in the building trades. His main targets were such highly paid crafts as plumbing and pipefitting, in which the unions were accused of limiting apprenticeship openings, often to the exclusion of racial minorities. The problem of minority employment in the building trades took on a special significance in view of predictions that in the 1970's some 1,000,000 new construction workers would be needed, and that in twenty-five urban areas where blacks are heavily concentrated, two-thirds of the bill would be paid by public funds. The problem of union resistance to job integration was dramatized in September 1969, when Fletcher held hearings in Chicago on the conflict of that summer between local black groups and union workers in the building trades industry. Some 500 white construction workers packed the meetings, held them up for two days, and forced Fletcher to barricade himself in his hotel suite.

A program of mandatory goals for the employment of racial minorities on federal construction projects, devised by Fletcher and OFCC director Wilks during the summer of 1969, was put into effect that September by Secretary of Labor George P. Shultz. Known as the Philadelphia Plan, it ordered that on federally assisted construction projects in the Philadelphia area, valued at more than $500,000, minority group workers were to constitute 4 percent of the labor force in 1969 and 26 percent by 1973. Labor leaders, including AFL-CIO president George Meany, immediately denounced the plan. They were supported by Comptroller General Elmer B. Staats, who maintained that the plan's goals were, in effect, "quotas," which had been banned by the Civil Rights Act of 1964. On the other hand, black civil rights spokesmen criticized the plan for not going far enough, noting that it did not mandate penalties against violators, and that its effectiveness depended wholly on the way it was administered. In June 1970, after it appeared that the plan had failed to achieve its desired results, Fletcher initiated suits against several contractors.

Fletcher has pursued his economic policy on several fronts. In February 1970 the Labor Department issued "Order No. Four," establishing more stringent rules for minority hiring, which, according to Fletcher, shifted the emphasis from relying on voluntary compliance to enforcement procedures. In the five months that followed, twenty-seven "show cause" orders were issued to firms, requiring them to show why they should not be debarred from bidding for defense contracts. Fletcher delayed a $1 billion contract with Newport News Shipbuilding and Drydock Company for fifteen weeks, until he received assurance that blacks in the 27,000-man work force faced equal chances for promotion. During 1970 he also experimented with voluntary hiring programs, called "home town plans," but indicated that if they failed, compulsory programs like the Philadelphia Plan would be put into effect. A task force to devise local voluntary hiring plans in nineteen cities was set up by the OFCC in the summer of 1970.

In view of the somewhat negative image that the Nixon administration projects among large segments of the black community, Fletcher's position has been the subject of considerable controversy. Rejecting his solutions, some militant spokesmen have argued for the totally independent development of the black community, including the formation of black unions and construction firms. Others, like the NAACP official Clarence Mitchell and the black Congressman Augustus F. Hawkins of California, have charged the White House with trying to drive a wedge between black and white workers through its attacks on unions. Fletcher has defended the President's record on civil rights and has disputed charges by Herbert Hill and other NAACP spokesmen that the administration was racially biased, indicating that he would not remain in his post if that were true. He has said that he has constant access to the White House, and that he is allowed considerable freedom from restraint in the performance of his job. "I don't try to defend everything the administration does," he said, as quoted in Ebony (April 1971), adding, however, that he felt that the Republicans could do more for black Americans than was done by "a decade of Democrats."

Arthur A. Fletcher was married a second time, on May 5, 1965, to Bernyce Ayesha Hasson. He has six children—Phyllis, Sylvia, Arthur J., Paul, Phillip, and Joan—and four grandchildren. The

Fletchers live in the planned community of Columbia, Maryland, to the north of the nation's capital. The Assistant Labor Secretary, who is six feet four inches tall and weighs 240 pounds, is described by friends, cited by Rex Adkins in the San Francisco *Sunday Examiner and Chronicle* (March 23, 1969) as "immensely popular, humorous, . . . creative, understanding, [and] a dynamo of energy." A devout Methodist, he reads the Bible every morning; his favorite passages are from the Sermon on the Mount. He is a member of the NAACP and the American Legion. Fletcher was awarded the George Washington Honor Medal by the Freedoms Foundation of Valley Forge in 1969, and he received an honorary doctorate from Malcolm X College in Chicago and the Russwurm Award from the black National Newspaper Publishers Association in 1970. President Nixon appointed him a member of the United States delegation to the twenty-sixth session of the United Nations General Assembly in 1971.

References

Ebony 26:95+ Ap '71 pors
N Y Post p29 S 28 '71 por
Who's Who in America, 1970-71
Who's Who in American Politics, 1969-70

FORD, EILEEN (OTTE)

Mar. 25, 1922- Business executive
Address: b. Ford Model Agency, 344 E. 59th St., New York 10022; h. 160 E. 78th St., New York 10021

Largely because of Eileen Ford's flair for finding the world's most beautiful models—stars like Suzy Parker and Jean Shrimpton as well as less-known but equally successful models—the Ford Model Agency has become the world's most famous and thriving model agency, with an annual billing of over $5,000,000. After a brief modeling career of her own, Eileen Ford founded the Ford agency with her husband, Jerry Ford, in 1946. As president of the agency, Ford has handled its administrative and financial side, introducing efficient business practices that have become standard in the business; as vice-president, Mrs. Ford has exercised her talent for recruiting and training models and getting them work with top photographers and advertising agencies. The Ford Model Agency's main offices, which include a smaller men's division headed by Jerry Ford, are located in New York City. There is a branch office in Paris.

The only daughter of Loretta (Laine) Otte and the late Nathaniel Otte, Eileen Otte Ford was born on March 25, 1922 in New York City. With her three brothers and her parents, both of whom worked as credit raters, she grew up in Great Neck, an affluent suburb of New York. In an interview with Mary Brannum, author of *When I Was Sixteen* (1967), Mrs. Ford recalled her early life as carefree and uncomplicated: "At sixteen . . . I was very content and very confident. I had everything it took to make me . . . happy.

My parents thought I was fine. I had reasonable marks, nice clothes and a car, a home where I could give a party every week, plenty of boyfriends. There was none of this problem of wondering 'Who am I?' which we hear about so endlessly now. None of my friends had identity problems, either. . . . We all had perfectly marvelous lives."

Eileen Otte attended public schools in Great Neck and graduated from Great Neck High School in 1939. Although, according to her interview with Miss Brannum, she had little interest in attending college, she enrolled at Barnard College in New York City at the prodding of her mother, a former model who wanted her daughter to become a lawyer. While in college Eileen did some modeling for the now-defunct Conover Model Agency, which specialized in girls with a wholesome, coed look. After her graduation in 1943, with a bachelor's degree in psychology, she had vague ideas of pursuing a law career, but she continued to model for a short time and then worked at a series of jobs that made her familiar with fashion and advertising. The first was as a secretary and stylist for the photographer Elliot Clark, followed by positions as a stylist for the William Becker Studio, as a copywriter for the Arnold Constable department store, and as a fashion reporter for the Tobé Reports.

In 1944 Eileen Otte met Jerry Ford, a midwestern college student and varsity football player who had come East to finish his studies. They were married on November 20, 1944. By 1946 the Fords were expecting a child, and, since they needed extra money, Eileen began handling bookings for two friends of hers who were models. Soon the Fords opened the Ford Model Agency, which within a year was managing the careers of twenty-two models.

When the Fords started their enterprise, the modeling business was conducted in a haphazard manner that did little to protect the interests of either the agency or the model. Agencies would obtain bookings, but the models were usually responsible for setting their own fees and collecting them. Since the models were often unable to collect their fees, the agencies often went without their commissions. "It was a way of doing business that was partly responsible for the demise of John Robert Powers, Bob Taft, and Harry Conover, agencies that once led the field," Jerry Ford told Bernadette Carey of the New York *Times* (December 21, 1966). Setting out to put modeling on a sound business basis, Ford worked out a system under which the models are paid by the agency each week and the agency collects from the photographers and advertising agencies later. That procedure soon became standard throughout the business, along with Ford's 20 percent commission, half from the model and half from the client. The Fords were also largely responsible for standardizing modeling fees. The regular rate for "print" work—photographs for magazine advertising—is now about $60 an hour, and for television advertising the model is paid a certain amount each time her commercial is telecast. Because a great deal of money depends on getting orders exactly right, the Ford agency keeps a taped record of every telephoned order or cancellation that comes into the office.

While her husband handles the business end of the Ford Model Agency, Eileen Ford recruits the talent, managing to enlist the services of a sizable percentage of the world's great models, including Suzy Parker, Jean Shrimpton, Capucine, and Wilhelmina. Jane Fonda, Elsa Martinelli, Ali MacGraw, and Candice Bergen were all Ford girls before going into films, and the agency's recent stars have included Penelope Tree, Samantha Jones, Sunny Griffin, Babette, Lauren Hutton, and Gunilla Knutson, the Swedish blonde who seductively urges the males in TV audiences to "take it all off" with Noxzema Medicated Shave Cream. Although not all those models are known to the public by name, each one can command soaring fees that make it possible for her to earn $100,000 a year, which means $20,000 for the Ford agency. Only a few of the nearly 200 girls registered are big stars, however.

Eileen Ford has built her reputation on her ability to spot the stars of tomorrow and to see to it that they come to the Ford Model Agency instead of to its competitors. Every girl who aspires to a modeling career must have a photogenic face, healthy hair, and long willowy proportions, but once in a while a girl comes along with something beyond that. Asked to define star quality, Mrs. Ford told James Mills of *Life* (November 13, 1970), "There's a cockiness to them, and a . . . *way* about them. . . . They're just *going* to be good and you can just tell it. It's a way they have of moving, and it's a way of talking to you. I see girls that I know—I absolutely *know*—will be star models within just a matter of weeks, and they always are."

She is constantly on the lookout for such girls, both in the United States and in Europe, which she visits several times a year. (Over half the models in the Ford agency are American; the rest come from Europe, especially from Sweden.) Although the ideal age to begin a modeling career is probably eighteen, Mrs. Ford does not hesitate to recruit especially promising girls of seventeen or even sixteen. Girls under eighteen, however, are usually housed in the Ford home, where they are treated like one of the family's daughters. There the young models are expected to help out with the chores and conduct themselves with due propriety. Occasionally, unruly girls have been shipped back home. Mrs. Ford has wryly commented, "I'm not what you'd call permissive."

Mrs. Ford is scarcely less protective toward the girls who do not live in her home. Ford girls are prescribed diets, assigned to dermatologists and hairdressers, and offered advice on emotional problems and life in New York. Yet there is a steel edge to Eileen Ford's motherliness, and she tolerates no deviation from her standards of discipline and professionalism. In an interview with Marian Christy of the White Plains (N.Y.) *Reporter Dispatch* (April 6, 1971) she repeated the ultimatum that she delivered to one of her best

EILEEN FORD

models, after she had arrived at the office looking tired and drawn from staying up nights with her boyfriend: "Look, dear, you're a mess. If you want to model, fine. If you want to fool around, that's fine, too. But you can't do both. So make up your mind, and that's it."

A neophyte model goes through a training period at the agency, working with photographers to acquire modeling techniques and to assemble a portfolio. Then she is systematically introduced to photographers and advertising agencies. Ford models make most of their money posing for magazine advertisements, although the agency has been conducting a campaign to get more television work, which accounted for only 10 percent of its billings in 1968. Really successful models may be chosen to pose for the pages of *Vogue* and the other slick fashion magazines, but those jobs bring more prestige than money. Less glamorous but far more lucrative are the mail order catalogs, which account for the largest single source of income at the agency. An experienced model can expect a career of about ten years, during which she should earn at least $25,000 a year.

Eileen Ford and her husband, Gerard William Ford, live with their son, Bill, and their daughters, Jamie, Katie, and Lacey, in a town house on the Upper East Side of Manhattan. The Fords also have a summer house at Quogue, Long Island, where they frequently play host to Ford models. A confident, brisk woman, who demands the same discipline from herself that she does from her models, Mrs. Ford keeps her figure at a trim size eight with yoga exercises and dieting. She is five feet five inches tall, weighs 115 pounds, and has gray eyes and brown hair. For relaxation she enjoys gardening and cooking and plans to write a cookbook someday. Mrs. Ford writes a newspaper column entitled "Eileen Ford's Model Beauty" that is syndicated by the Daily News and the Chicago Tribune. She is also the author of *Eileen Ford's Book of Model Beauty* (Trident Press, 1968) and *Eileen Ford's Secrets of the Model's World* (Trident, 1970). In France she has published a book entitled *21 Leçons de Beauté*. She is a member of the President's People to People Committee and a trustee of the Village of Quogue.

References

Life 69:63+ N 13 '70 pors
N Y Herald Tribune p18 O 26 '61 por
N Y Post p41 Ag 10 '68 por
Brannum, Mary. When I Was Sixteen (1967)

FORMAN, MILOS (mē'losh)

Feb. 18, 1932- Czech film director
Address: Chelsea Hotel, 222 W. 23d St., New York 10011; Mjr. Schramma 31, Prague 6, Czechoslovakia

With *Black Peter, The Loves of a Blonde,* and *The Fireman's Ball,* Czech film director Milos Forman helped to create the internationally celebrated new wave of film making in Czechoslovakia during the mid-1960's. In those gentle comedies of contemporary life, Forman probed everyday situations to reveal eternal truths. Fascinated by the problems of youth and the generation gap, the Czech director chose teen-age runaways and their parents as the subjects for *Taking Off* (1971), his first film made in the United States. Although he regards Czechoslovakia as his permanent home, Forman has lived mostly in the United States since 1968.

The youngest son of Rudolf Forman, a schoolteacher, and his wife, Anna (Svabova) Forman, Milos Forman was born in Caslav, a small city forty-five miles east of Prague, on February 18, 1932. He and his brother, Pavel, a painter, are the only surviving members of his immediate family. Both parents died in Nazi concentration camps, and another brother, Blahoslav, died in an accident in 1961. After his parents, one of whom was Jewish, were seized by the Germans in 1940, Forman and his brothers were cared for by a succession of relatives and family friends. Although the boys and those who harbored them were in considerable danger, the motion picture director has recalled that because he was too young to understand, he looked upon the war merely as an adventure. Nor did he grasp the horror of the circumstances of his parents' deaths. (His mother died at Auschwitz in 1943, his father at Buchenwald a year later.) It was not until he was sixteen years old that an old newsreel of a Nazi death camp drove home the full impact of his parents' fate.

Meanwhile, he was growing up and attending schools in Nachod, Caslav, Kutna Hora, Podebrady, and, finally, Prague. In part, at least, his sharp eye for familial relations dates from those gypsy-like years. "Because I wasn't emotionally involved," he told James Conaway of the New York *Times Magazine* (July 11, 1971), "I became very objective. Most children aren't consciously aware of what is going on around them, but I was always following the action, trying to fit myself into the group."

After graduating from secondary school in 1950 Forman tried unsuccessfully for admission to the drama division of the Prague Academy of Music and Dramatic Art. He then flirted briefly with the idea of studying law, but abandoned that notion when he learned of openings at the academy's Film Faculty. On the advice of a friend he applied for the screenwriting section instead of the director's branch, which was overcrowded, and his application was accepted.

The Prague Film Faculty offers one of the world's finest and most comprehensive courses on film. During his four years at the school Forman studied—besides scriptwriting—directing, camera technique, film history and criticism, and production. He had the opportunity to see hundreds of film classics, and the works of Charlie Chaplin, Buster Keaton, and Marcel Carné considerably influenced his ideas on film making. By the time he graduated from the Film Faculty, in 1954, Forman had collaborated on one feature-length film and a dozen shorts as part of his required course work.

While holding down his first job, as director of film presentations for Czechoslovak Television, Forman assisted in writing the screenplay of *Leave It To Me* (1955), was the assistant director of Alfred Radok's *Old Man Motor-Car* (1956), and was coauthor and assistant director of *Puppies* (1957). In 1958 he staged part of Radok's *Magic Lantern,* a mixed media spectacle of film, slides, and live performance, at the Brussels World's Fair, and continued to work on *Magic Lantern* presentations under Radok's direction for four years.

In 1962 Forman went to work for Barrandov, the foremost studio in Czechoslovakia's nationalized film industry, as a production assistant. He soon persuaded the studio to let him make his own films by showing them a forty-five minute documentary-like short he had made on his own about teen-age girls trying out for a musical show. Barrandov was impressed enough to transfer the film, called *The Audition,* from 16mm to 35mm for distribution to theatres and authorized Forman to create a companion piece. That short, about two young boys playing in brass bands, was completed in 1963. (Both short subjects were released in the United States five years later by Brandon Films under the title *Competition.*)

Late in 1963 Forman completed his first feature-length film, entitled *Black Peter* (released in Europe under the title *Peter and Pavla*). Like *Competition,* its subject was youth, this time in the person of Peter, a not too bright lad attempting to adjust to the problems of adult life. In the humorous and sympathetic treatment of the relationship between the boy and his father, Forman revealed a preoccupation with the generation gap that was to become a hallmark of much of his later work. *Black Peter* won the Czechoslovak Film Critics' Award in 1963 and the grand prize of the Locarno, Switzerland International Film Festival in 1964.

The favorable reception accorded *Black Peter* assured Forman of a chance to make more films, and in 1964 he completed *The Loves of a Blonde.*

The heroine of that film is a romantic small-town factory girl who is seduced by a youthful dance-band musician from Prague. Taking up his casual invitation, she follows him to his home in the city, only to discover that he lives with his excessively protective parents. As with his other films, Forman recruited the professional and amateur actors for *Loves of a Blonde* from among his friends and acquaintances, and he encouraged improvisation as the shooting proceeded by keeping his actors from seeing the entire script. (All of Forman's Czech films were written by him in collaboration with Ivan Passer and Jaroslav Papousek.)

The Loves of a Blonde created even more of an international stir than *Black Peter*, winning the jury prize of the 1965 Venice Film Festival and the 1966 best foreign film award of the French Film Academy. Yet both films were nearly relegated to the late-night television circuit in the United States. It was only after the commercial, as well as artistic success of Jan Kadar's *Shop on Main Street* there in 1965 that Czech films began to be seriously considered for commercial distribution.

Before its commercial release late in 1965, *Black Peter* was entered in the September New York Film Festival, but the critics greeted it with little enthusiasm. Reviewing it for the New York *Herald Tribune* (September 12, 1965), John Molleson conceded that the film "does capture with considerable wit and sensitivity the growing awareness of a bashful boy of seventeen." Still, Molleson concluded, "Peter . . . and his parents do seem unusually backward for this day and age." Six years later, however, the critics were having second thoughts. Roger Greenspun in the New York *Times* (July 23, 1971) reminisced that he "didn't much like" *Black Peter* when he first saw it in 1965. "But I liked it a lot when I saw it again the other day, which may prove . . . that certain works of art, and especially certain movies, only get to look as good and as individual as they really are after their time has past." In its 1971 rerelease by Altura Films, *Black Peter* won nearly unanimous praise from American critics.

The Loves of a Blonde (Prominent Films, 1966), however, proved to be an immediate success in the United States. After its triumphs on the festival circuit in Europe it was chosen to open the 1966 New York Film Festival, and Judith Crist wrote in the New York *World Journal Tribune* the next morning (September 13): "Once again we are left to marvel at the peculiar ability of Czech film makers to find universal truths in the simplest situations, to discern both the humor and the heartbreak in the human comedy and to translate them to film with a sharp but compassionate eye." *Loves of a Blonde* went on to receive an Academy Award nomination as the best foreign film of the year.

The Fireman's Ball (Cinema V, 1968) is perhaps the most richly meaningful film that Forman has made to date, and it was the only one that encountered political attacks in Czechoslovakia. When it was first screened privately in Prague in 1967 high officials were so scandalized by the film

MILOS FORMAN

that the Italian producer Carlo Ponti, who had financed the film with Barrandov, withdrew his backing in order not to offend the Novotny regime with which he was negotiating a cultural treaty. The film was rescued from oblivion and Forman from possible imprisonment when the French film makers Claude Berri and François Truffaut raised the money to make up for Ponti's decampment. *The Fireman's Ball* has to do with a retirement party held for a fire-chief. On one level the film affords a tragicomic view of the foibles and frailties of a group of small-town firemen, but the film can also be interpreted as a satire on bureaucracy and the fumblings of committee rule. Forman has at times advocated both views. When the film was released in Czechoslovakia 40,000 firemen walked out on strike until Forman mollified them with the assurance that *The Fireman's Ball* was a political allegory. Later, when it was released in Europe, Forman added a short preamble in which he certified that the film is merely about firemen.

By the time *The Fireman's Ball* had its American première at the New York Film Festival in September 1968, the liberal Dubcek regime in Czechoslovakia had been ousted by the Soviets, leading some viewers to find a new and tragic significance in Forman's satire. "With the Russian occupation," wrote a *Time* reviewer (December 6, 1968), "the farce is suddenly open to newer and darker interpretations—of men too weak and ill-equipped to fight, while liberty and hard-won independence are stolen or reduced to ashes." Three years later writers were still finding tragic import in *The Fireman's Ball*. "In *The Fireman's Ball* there is a scene in which an old man's home burns," wrote James Conaway in his *Times Magazine* article. "The man, wearing only a nightshirt, is seated on a chair outside in the snow, close enough to the blaze to keep warm, but with his back to it so he won't see his house burn down. Taken at face value, the scene represents Forman at his best: poignant, sad-funny, totally realized. Taken as a metaphor for contemporary society, it is devastating."

From time to time Forman had contemplated making a screen version of Kafka's novel *Amerika* or creating a film that would feature Jimmy Durante as a rich American hunter stalking a bear through the forests of Slovakia. But not until 1968 did the director have a serious offer from an American studio to produce one of his pictures, when Paramount agreed to back his projected film about youthful American runaways. When Paramount asked for a revision of Forman's script, the Czech director settled down in New York City for a year to study American youth culture at first hand. The resulting script, on which Forman had three collaborators, including two Americans, may or may not have been to Paramount's liking, but by that time the company was in financial difficulties and the Forman project was dropped. Eventually it was picked up by Universal, and the film was finally shot on location in the East Village and Queens, using many nonprofessionals recruited from the hippie hangouts of Manhattan.

By the time *Taking Off* was eventually released in March 1971 its story focused less on the dropped-out flower children than on their parents, and the stars of the film were Buck Henry and Lynn Carlin as a bewildered suburban couple in search of their runaway daughter. Most reviewers, like the one for *Variety* (March 17, 1971), found the film to be "a very compassionate, very amusing contemporary comedy," but some were bothered by Forman's lack of familiarity with American culture. But Richard Schickel wrote in *Life* (April 2, 1971), "Perhaps only a humane, gentle, and intelligent foreigner can at this time restore to us some perspective about our national life, suggest that our problems stem not from the System, the Establishment or other abstractions convenient for self-indictment, but from the fact that we are only human, entangled in absurdities not entirely of our own making." As a United States entry at the 1971 Cannes Film Festival *Taking Off* was awarded the jury prize.

In the summer of 1971 Milos Forman was still in the United States, where he was scheduled to begin filming a second American picture, entitled "Bulletproof," in August. Although some journalists have assumed that the Czech director has expatriated himself, Forman contends that he is only visiting the United States to make films. "Confronted with questions about politics, or comparisons between this country and his own, Forman hunches his shoulders and assumes a mien as inscrutable as a Bohemian dumpling," reported James Conaway in his New York *Times Magazine* article. Forman's wife and children still live in Prague. Since 1964 he has been married to Vera Kresadlova, a singer, and they have twin sons, Petr and Matej. Formerly he was married to Jana Brejchova, a popular Czech film actress. In appearance Conaway suggested that Forman resembles "a fanciful cross between an aging James Dean and the Good Soldier Schweik." He is nearly six feet tall and has brown eyes and brown hair. A trencherman, he whittles his weight down to about 185 pounds by skiing and playing basketball. When in New York, Forman usually stays at the Chelsea Hotel, the hostelry so favored by artists, writers, composers, anad other creative persons.

References

Life 62:77+ Ja 20 '67 pors
N Y Times II p13 O 23 '66 por
N Y Times Mag p8+ Jl 11 '71 pors
Britannica Book of the Year, 1969
Cowie, Peter, ed. International Film Guide (1969); Screen Series: Eastern Europe (1970)
International Who's Who, 1970-71
Who's Who in America, 1970-71
Who's Who in the World, 1971-72

FOSTER, JOHN S(TUART), JR.

Sept. 18, 1922- United States government official; physicist
Address: b. United States Department of Defense, The Pentagon, Washington, D.C. 20301; h. 6382 Lakeview Drive, Falls Church, Va. 22041

One of the key nonpolitical members of the Nixon administration is Dr. John Stuart Foster Jr., director of research and engineering in the United States Department of Defense. Appointed by President Lyndon B. Johnson in 1965, he was kept in office by President Richard Nixon. A former director of the University of California's Lawrence Radiation Laboratory at Livermore, Foster has contributed significantly to the application of nuclear energy to peaceful as well as military uses. Concerned that the United States might lag behind the Soviet Union in the nuclear armaments race, Foster insists that the quality as well as the quantity of American defense research and development must be maintained at the highest level, but some critics feel that he has overstated the extent of the Soviet threat. "It is absolutely essential that the free world be technologically superior to the Soviet Union," he has said, as quoted in *Fortune* (May 1971). "There is no room here for parity."

John Stuart Foster Jr., the son of the noted Canadian nuclear physicist Dr. John Stuart Foster and of Flora (Curtis) Foster, was born on September 18, 1922 in New Haven, Connecticut, while his father was teaching at Yale University. He has a brother, Curtis, who became an executive with the Zenith Radio Corporation. The senior Foster, who died in 1964, was a professor of physics at McGill University in Montreal for many years and received the United States Medal of Freedom for his World War II research on radar scanners and cyclotrons at the Massachusetts Institute of Technology.

Growing up in Canada, John S. Foster Jr. was exposed to an academic environment from childhood, and he decided early in life that he would follow his father's footsteps and become a physicist. He interrupted his studies during World War II and joined the staff of the radio research laboratory at Harvard University in 1942 to work on defense projects involving radar and electronic interference devices. Two years later he went overseas as a civilian consultant to the United States Air Force, training service crews in the Mediterranean Theatre of Operations in the handling of radar countermeasure equipment. At the end of the war Foster returned to Canada and enrolled at McGill University to complete his undergraduate education. During the summers of 1946 and 1947 he worked with the National Research Council at Chalk River, Ontario, the site of an atomic power plant. Foster graduated from McGill with honors, with a B.S. degree in physics, in 1948.

Continuing his studies in physics at the University of California at Berkeley, Foster was one of the original group of young men who worked at the university's radiation laboratory under the direction of Dr. Ernest O. Lawrence, winner of the 1939 Nobel Prize in Physics and inventor of the cyclotron. He did his graduate work in plasma physics and wrote his dissertation on ion properties. After receiving his Ph.D. degree in 1952, Foster was appointed a division leader in experimental physics at the radiation laboratory in Livermore, California. The research center was established by the Atomic Energy Commission for Dr. Lawrence and his staff to develop advanced technology in nuclear weaponry. While Foster directed a research project in high vacuum techniques, he invented a large-scale ion pump that was later used in the Van de Graaf accelerator and in a high-intensity linear accelerator, as well as in some of the early experiments for Project Sherwood, which involved the study of controlled thermonuclear reactions.

Like many of his colleagues during his years at Livermore, Foster worked closely with the military, advising them on strategy and keeping them informed of the latest developments in weaponry at the laboratory. From 1953 to 1958 Foster concentrated on the design of small nuclear armaments, adapting weapons used in strategic warfare for tactical purposes, such as in air-to-air and air-to-surface combat operations. He also perfected the command-control system for maintaining directional signals over nuclear missiles and warheads. Concerned with national security, Foster does not feel that his work on weapons represents any departure from morality. "Force—nuclear, or any other—is not in itself immoral," he has said, as quoted in *Fortune* (April 1962). "Morality involves how it is used."

As associate director of the Livermore radiation laboratories from 1958 to 1961, Foster directed projects that contributed to a major breakthrough in the study of hydrodynamics. He pioneered in the development of thermonuclear explosives with reduced fission yields and devised the computational and experimental tools that made possible "clean" thermonuclear explosives, producing a minimum of radioactive fallout. Those nuclear explosive devices were lighter in weight and had a greater yield in relation to the amount of fissionable material used. Because of their increased

JOHN S. FOSTER JR.

flexibility and efficiency, the explosives were used in Project Plowshare, which applied the vast potential of nuclear energy to peaceful purposes. Foster was enthusiastic about the unlimited possibilities of nuclear energy in large-scale excavations for canals and for exploration of natural gas deposits, petroleum, and other mineral resources. "It's exciting to think of changing the face of the world in our lifetime," says Foster, who provided dynamic and influential leadership for the program.

Foster was promoted to director of the Lawrence Radiation Laboratory at Livermore in 1961, succeeding Dr. Harold Brown, who took a post with the Department of Defense. Taking charge of some 5,300 employees—including more than 350 with Ph.D. degrees—and a budget of $100,-000,000, Foster assumed the post about the time the Soviet Union unilaterally ended the moratorium on nuclear testing, posing what some observers considered a great security threat to the United States. The quality and strength of Soviet technology was reported to be steadily increasing, and the Soviet Union was known to allocate a high percentage of its capital budget to defense-related projects. Many scientists feared that the United States would not be able to maintain a nuclear balance and would lose its position of leadership. According to *Science* (October 1, 1965), "Foster did his best to keep the radiation laboratory in a state of readiness, and he is generally credited with having held it together during that period." An outspoken advocate of a vigorous research and development program in the United States, Foster was one of the few scientists in the country to testify in 1963 against Senate ratification of the nuclear test ban treaty.

On September 11, 1965 President Lyndon B. Johnson appointed Foster to succeed Dr. Harold Brown as director of research and engineering in the Department of Defense, the third-ranking civilian job in the Pentagon. Although he was regarded as a "hawk" in the scientific community and his views differed from those held by many Pentagon officials, including the Secretary of Defense, Robert S. McNamara, the Senate Armed

Services Committee confirmed his appointment with record speed. One commentator suggested in *U.S. News and World Report* (September 27, 1965) that "if the Defense Department were to adopt his views, the whole United States weapons pattern could be in for extensive revision." Foster's main responsibility is to apportion a research budget of several billion dollars and to advise the Secretary of Defense in matters relating to the research, development, testing, and evaluation of new weapons systems and defense materiel.

Although Foster's opinions on weapons development are controversial and he has often been criticized by colleagues and by the Federation of American Scientists for allegedly playing on fears and encouraging false concern about Soviet arms buildup, he has been an influential policy-maker in the Johnson and Nixon administrations. According to *Fortune* (May 1971), "no man has more to say about what military contracting will be like than John Foster Jr." He defended the antiballistic missile system in Senate testimony and disputed charges by other qualified scientific witnesses that the ABM was a technical failure. Foster encouraged President Nixon to take a hard line in pressing for passage of the ABM program as a strategic deterrent to enemy attack. He also supported the development of an almost foolproof over-the-horizon warning system that would allow American missiles almost thirty minutes to get off the ground before enemy missiles could attack. In 1967 there was some public concern over potential escalation of strategic warfare when Foster admitted that the United States was planning an X-ray missile defense system to destroy incoming warheads at high altitudes.

Late in 1967 Foster announced that the United States had made "a major breakthrough in missile technology" by creating a single missile capable of multi-city bombardment. The new weapon, known as the multiple independently targeted re-entry vehicle (MIRV) and nicknamed the "space bus," could carry a load of thermonuclear warheads to several enemy cities, altering its course in a zig-zag line rather than moving on a single direct trajectory. According to the New York *Times* (December 14, 1967), Foster's statements were apparently intended to offset criticism of the Johnson administration for not dealing effectively with a Soviet missile buildup and the deployment of the Russian fractional orbital bombing system. Both the United States and the Soviet Union admitted testing MIRV weapons, and the issue of placing a ban on MIRV flight tests figured heavily in the strategic arms limitation talks (SALT) which began in November 1969. Scientists of both nations emphasized that MIRV production was difficult to detect once it got beyond the testing stage and it appeared unlikely that either nation would permit on-site inspection of individual missiles. Foster opposed a moratorium on the development of MIRV because he believed the United States would be unable to monitor secret Soviet development of those high-accuracy warheads. He told a Senate subcommittee in June 1970 that the deployment of multiple missile warheads was not irreversible and could be stopped if a joint accord were reached by the two powers. An analyst for *Time* (June 7, 1971) surmised that if Foster could convince the administration that the threat of Soviet superiority in the missile race was real, "the spirit if not the substance of the SALT negotiations" could be destroyed.

Described in *Fortune* (May 1971) as "a man with a mission, devoted single-mindedly to containing the formidable threat" of Soviet military might and scientific progress, Foster has tried by means of press reports and speeches to arouse the American public from its apathy on defense spending and space research. His concept of "asymmetry" calls for the proper combination of weapons to maintain United States superiority at all times and to keep the Soviet Union guessing and spending because of an ever-changing American arsenal. Foster has encountered resistance in the academic community where, because of anti-war attitudes and antagonism to the military-industrial complex, there has been a decline in the number of scientists willing to work on government-supported military research programs.

Foster believes that "the universities must play their role in examining and understanding possible future threats" to national security. He has committed the Defense Department to the support of projects that "are relevant to long-range defense probelms" and to the promotion of graduate education "adequate to the defense needs of the country." Alarmed at the prospect that American scientific apathy towards military projects may give the Soviet Union an advantage that the United States might never regain, Foster has warned that Soviet achievements by the mid-1970's could reduce the United States to the status of a second-rate power. He has recommended that Congress increase the arms budget to expand air-to-air missile production and permit the development of strategic bombers and new adaptable fighter planes.

President Dwight D. Eisenhower presented Foster with the Ernest O. Lawrence Memorial Award in 1960, citing him for "unique contributions, demanding unusual imagination and technical skill, to the development of atomic weapons." In 1969 Foster received the Distinguished Public Service Medal of the Department of Defense and was elected to the National Academy of Engineering. The James Forrestal Memorial Award was conferred on him in 1970. Foster is a member of Theta Delta Chi fraternity and Sigma Xi honor society. Before his appointment to the Defense Department post he served on the Army Scientific Advisory Panel, the Air Force Scientific Advisory Board, the advisory board of the United States Naval Ordinance Testing Station, and the Ballistic Missile Defense Advisory Committee. From 1959 to 1965 he was also a panel consultant to the President's Scientific Advisory Committee, and he has served as a consultant to the Boeing Company and to Thompson Ramo Wooldridge, Inc.

Dr. John S. Foster Jr. and his wife, the former Barbara Anne Wickes of Montreal, whom he married on May 23, 1946, have four children: Susan

(Mrs. Patrick Duffy), Bruce, Scott, and John. Tall and wiry, with a shock of light-brown hair, Foster has been described as "ruggedly handsome" and is said to look more like a matinée idol than a scientist. He is highly respected, even by his critics, for his imaginative ideas and his dedication and commitment to his work. His persuasive personality has also been an asset in Washington, especially when he has requested Congressional appropriations for research and development. Among his favorite quotations is one attributed to the late Dr. Albert Einstein: "The concern for man and his destiny must always be the chief interest of all technical effort. Never forget it among your diagrams and equations."

References

Washington (D.C.) Post A p1 S 14 '65 por
American Men of Science 11th ed (1966)
McGraw-Hill Modern Men of Science, 1966
Who's Who in America, 1970-71
World Who's Who in Science (1968)

FRAZIER, JOE

Jan. 17, 1944- Prizefighter
Address: b. c/o Cloverlay Inc., 1306 Philadelphia National Bank Bldg., Broad and Chestnut Sts., Philadelphia, Pa. 19107

The most publicized event in pugilistic history was the multimillion-dollar contest between the world's ranking gladiators, Joe Frazier and Muhammad Ali, held in Madison Square Garden, New York City, in March 1971. In that prizefight the undefeated Philadelphia mauler outpointed the previously unbeaten Ali, also known as Cassius Clay, to become the world's undisputed heavyweight boxing champion. The championship had been moot since 1967, when the colorful Ali, champ since 1964, was stripped of his title for violating the federal Selective Service Act. The W.B.A. conferred the crown on Frazier in February 1970, but millions of fight fans sympathetic to Ali regarded the coronation as usurpation and refused to recognize the new champion until he actually entered the ring with the voluble, bombastic Black Muslim and "whupped" him in what was ballyhooed as "the fight of the century."

Frazier, Olympic boxing champion in 1964, has been a professional since 1965, with an unbroken record of twenty-eight pro victories, twenty-three of them by knockouts—the highest knockout percentage in the history of modern boxing. He himself has been knocked down—never out—only three times —by Mike Bruce once and Oscar Bonavena twice —and, like Ali, he was unscathed up to the time that the two fighters pulped each other's faces in "the fight." Unlike Ali—a high-headed, elusive boxing stylist with a long flashing left jab—Frazier is a stubby, steady, two-fisted slugger, a crouching infighter who whirs relentlessly forward—and only forward—into his opponent like a pummeling machine. With head down and bobbing, thick

JOE FRAZIER

legs implacable, and short arms arcing in a merciless rhythm, he savages his enemy's torso with both fists until the arms come down to break the blows and the head is left open for the *coup de grâce.* "If you kill the body," his favorite slogan goes, "the head dies." Observers sometimes attribute to Frazier a "killer instinct," but he explains his attitude in the ring strictly in terms of survival, "If there's an obstacle there, I'm going to destroy it."

Joseph Frazier—who acquired the nickname Billy in childhood—is the second youngest of thirteen children of Dolly Frazier and the late Rubin Frazier. He was born at 9:30 P.M. (EST) in Beaufort, South Carolina, where the family owns a small hog and vegetable farm. His father had lost his left arm in an accident, and Frazier "became his left arm," as he told Martin Kane of *Sports Illustrated* (November 16, 1970): "He'd hold a bolt with his right hand and I'd screw it. By the time I was seven I could drive a tractor, and when I was eight I was driving an automobile. He taught me everything I know about life."

The Fraziers were devout Baptists, and Joe—who now heads his own rock-blues group—learned to sing in church. "I never sang in the choir," he has recalled, "but I would often lead a song from the audience. You know, someone would start singing and then everyone would join in." Regarding racial relations in Beaufort, he has said: "I just don't understand why some people . . . make it tough for other people. They say they read the Bible. . . . When I was down there, and I'm champion, y'know, I can't even get a check cashed uptown. They don't feel a boy like me should have that kind of money."

"I had my share of street fights as a kid," Frazier told Peter Wood in an interview for the New York *Times* (November 15, 1970), "and nobody ever beat me and I just figured nobody could whip me. It's like I still feel." According to Frazier, his mother taught him "respectfulness," and she would not let him play football for fear that he might seriously injure himself. In childhood he liked to watch boxing matches on TV.

When he was fourteen and in the tenth grade Frazier beat up a white man for calling him "nigger." Following his mother's advice, he dropped out of school and left home. Traveling north, he settled in Philadelphia, where he found a job cutting meat in a slaughterhouse. At that time he tended to obesity, and to lose weight he began working out in a Philadelphia Police Athletic League gym, where Yancy (Yank) Durham, still his manager, saw his potential as a boxer and took him under his wing.

Frazier lost but two of his thirty-seven fights as an amateur, both to Buster Mathis. One of the losses was in the Olympic tryouts of 1964, but Frazier went to the Olympics in Japan anyway, after Mathis injured a hand. In Tokyo he himself broke his left hand but fought through the finals despite the injury and won the gold medal for the United States. While his hand was healing, the Rev. William H. Gray Jr., pastor of the Bright Hope Baptist Church in Philadelphia, gave him a part-time job as parish janitor, and later, when Frazier decided to turn pro, the minister put him and Durham in touch with F. Bruce Baldwin, Horn & Hardart executive and boxing aficionado. To provide financial backing for Frazier, Baldwin formed Cloverlay Inc. and sold eighty shares in the corporation at $250 each. Within two years the total value of Cloverlay shares was close to half a million dollars, and it has gone on rising over the years.

Durham let Frazier develop slowly, matching him with relatively easy opponents until he was ready for tougher competition. Frazier's first really difficult test was his twelfth fight, against Oscar Bonavena in Madison Square Garden on September 21, 1966. A slow starter and fast finisher, Frazier came close to losing in the second round, when Bonavena floored him twice, but he plodded on to a split decision. In March 1967 he knocked out Doug Jones in the sixth round of a bout in Philadelphia, and four months later in Madison Square Garden he injured George Chuvalo's right eye so badly that the referee stopped the fight in the fourth round.

In June 1967, when Muhammad Ali, a Black Muslim (now temporarily suspended but still true-believing) and draft resister on religious grounds, was convicted of evading military conscription, the New York State Athletic Commission and the World Boxing Association took away his title and his prizefighting license. To determine Ali's successor as champion, the W.B.A. held a tournament, which was won by Jimmy Ellis. Frazier refused to participate in W.B.A. competition at that stage and instead fought Buster Mathis under the aegis of the New York State Athletic Commission, in March 1968. He knocked Mathis out in the eleventh round, thus becoming the heavyweight champion of—or recognized in—New York, Massachusetts, Illinois, and Maine.

In 1968 and 1969 Frazier successfully defended his title against Manuel Ramos, Oscar Bonavena, Dave Zyglewicz, and Jerry Quarry, and he was named Fighter of the Year (1969) by the Boxing Writers Association. On February 16, 1970 he went after the ambiguous W.B.A. crown in a fight with Jimmy Ellis and, after knocking Ellis down twice, won by a technical knockout in the fifth round. Nine months later he knocked out light heavyweight champion Bob Foster in the second round in Detroit.

In October 1970 a federal court ruled that the revocation of Muhammad Ali's boxing license was "arbitrary and unreasonable." Ali returned to the ring, defeating Quarry in Atlanta in October and Bonavena in New York two months later. Finally, Fight of the Century Inc., headed by publicity agent Jerry Perenchio and millionaire sportsman Jack Kent Cooke, arranged a match between Ali and Frazier, for March 8, 1971 in Madison Square Garden. Perenchio had no problem in selling the event as a show business spectacular to a public that had long been lusting for the showdown match. The popular thirst for gladiator blood was whetted by the verbal war the two boxers waged for weeks beforehand. Ali, glib, versifying, and boastful, insulted Frazier with a stream of epithets, including "Uncle Tom," and Frazier, in his more somber, pedestrian way, made it a rule always to call Ali by his "slave" name, Clay. Gambling odds on the event were 7-5 in Frazier's favor in the United States and 11-8 in Ali's favor in England.

During the week preceding the fight Frazier was warned anonymously, by phone and letter, to "lose or else," and an unprecedentedly large force of police and private security agents was on hand to protect both fighters and maintain order on the night of the contest. Celebrities vied for ringside seats, priced at $150 each but sold by scalpers for three or four times that amount. Altogether, 20,445 people paid $1,352,951 for seats in Madison Square Garden, a million and a half closed circuit television watchers in the United States and Canada paid about $17,000,000 in admissions, and television stations in foreign countries willing and able to pay for the rights brought the fight, via satellite, to 300,000,000 viewers. Total receipts from all sources were estimated at $25,000,000. The promoters made a profit estimated at $1,750,-000 after costs, and Frazier and Ali each received $2,500,000. Frazier kept half of his purse, minus taxes, and as usual, Cloverlay Inc., got 35 percent of it and Manager Durham 15 percent.

In the bout itself Frazier warmed up fairly early, stalking his tall, prancing opponent relentlessly, hammering him with body punches and an occasional hook to the face and enduring some powerful blows himself in return. Throughout its course the fight was close, and sports writers were inevitably nebulous and conflicting in tracing the decisive moments leading up to Frazier's victory. Some saw the trend in Frazier's favor as beginning with Ali's hanging on the ropes in the eighth round. Others marked it from the eleventh round, when Frazier almost brought Ali down with a left hook. Twenty seconds into the fifteenth and final round the Philadelphian sent his opponent sprawling with a wild left hook. Ali was up almost instantly and waited out the referee's mandatory count of eight on his feet. By the end of the fight Ali's left jaw was badly swollen and Frazier's face was a mass of welts and his right eye was all but closed. In his awarding of points, the referee gave eight rounds to Frazier and six to Ali, declaring the remaining round a tie. Another judge gave eleven rounds to Frazier and four to Ali, and the third judge divided the rounds nine-six.

Frazier's ring manner is a crowding, bulldozing style reminiscent of Rocky Marciano. The adjective that Frazier himself most often uses to describe it is "smoking," and his manager has observed: "He's a slugger. He's not a finesse boxer." He enters the ring with a cool, grim confidence that turns, as one observer noted, to "joy" as he warms up to the task of battering his opponent. His most characteristic stance has been described as a "hunch-shouldered, pigeon-toed" crouch, out of which he bobs and weaves, throwing his thumping hooks and lethal crosses. Because both of his fists are powerful, his punching pattern is unpredictable. Among his favorite punches are the left hook, the double hook to the body and chin, and the left hook to the body followed by right cross to the head. In training, he adheres to his schedule with strict discipline, respects and follows the advice of Yank Durham and Eddie Futch, his handler, and spars almost as seriously as he fights in official events. "Getting hit by Joe," one of his sparring partners has said, "is like getting run over by a bus."

Joe Frazier is five feet eleven and a half inches tall, three and three-quarter inches shorter than Muhammad Ali. His physique is thickly muscular and his fighting weight is about 205 pounds. Entering the ring, he wears a regal $300 green satin robe with golden metal decorations custom-made for him by Lew Magram. In 1970 he began cultivating a beard, which he was forced to shave off —except for the mustache—for the fight with Ali. In private life Frazier is a gentle-mannered, laconic, no-nonsense loner, described by a writer for *Time* (March 8, 1971) as "awkward and introspective, given to sullen moods that he calls 'the slouchies,'" but he has become more outgoing since organizing his own rock-blues group, the Knockouts, in which he is lead singer and guitarist. His vocabulary is predominantly hip ghetto street slang. Still a practising Baptist, he reads the Bible daily.

Joe and Florence Frazier, who grew up together in Beaufort, have been married since adolescence. They have five children, a son, Marvis, and four girls, Weatta, Jo-Netta, Natasha, and Jacquelyn. The Fraziers and their pet dogs live in a $100,000 fifteen-room home that Joe owns in the Philadelphia suburb of White Marsh. In the home's gigantic garage are the fighter's six cars, including two telephone-equipped Cadillacs, and motorcycle. Fast driving seems to be the only vice to which Frazier, a teetotaler and nonsmoker, is addicted. Before the fight with Ali, the champ estimated his fortune at $300,000, much of it in real estate and other investments in the Philadelphia area. Deeply attached to his family and his roots, the fighter spends as much of his leisure as possible with his wife and children, and he often visits his mother in Beaufort. Comparing Frazier to Ali on the sub-ject of race relations, Mark Kram wrote in *Sports Illustrated* (March 8, 1971): "He feels just as deeply about his people, but he does not know the lever of political action, does not have the imagination of social combat. He understands only the right of the individual to be an individual, to survive and grow and be free of unfair pressures." After the fight with Ali, Frazier was reportedly considering the advice of Yank Durham that he retire from professional boxing as undefeated champion. If he remains in the ring he is expected to give Ali another chance at the title in 1972.

References

Ebony 23:136+ N '67 por; 66:134+ Mr '71 pors
Look 33:89+ Je 24 '69 por
N Y Times p1+ Mr 9 '71 pors
N Y Times Mag p52+ N 15 '70 por
Sport 45:48+ F '68 por
Time 97:63+ Mr 8 '71 pors

GEBEL-WILLIAMS, GUNTHER

1934- Animal trainer
Address: b. Ringling Bros. and Barnum & Bailey Circus, c/o Solters & Sabinson, 62 W. 45th St., New York 10036

In recent decades a radical change has taken place in one of America's oldest and most cherished institutions, the circus. Once presented almost exclusively "under the big top," in huge canvas tents, circuses are now usually produced in indoor arenas, partly to cut capital costs in the face of mounting overhead. There is also a new frugality in the employment of performers, with greater emphasis on a few key stars. The highest paid of the headliners is Ringling Bros. and Barnum & Bailey's sensational, dashing German-born animal trainer, Gunther Gebel-Williams, of whom Edward Hoagland wrote in *Esquire* (July 1971): "Gebel-Williams . . . constitutes a circus all by himself and is a kind of Nureyev of show business, indeed a man geared for great fame. It's a question of whether he will achieve it, what with the circus' low estate in the world, but in Imperial Rome the crowd's accolade for him would have lapped over the rim of the Colosseum like a tidal wave; he would have been installed in public office."

Golden-haired Gebel-Williams is extraordinary for the daring of his acts, one of which is a pyramid that no other living trainer would dream of duplicating: two natural jungle enemies, an elephant and a tiger, surmounted by himself. What makes him still more extraordinary is the fact that in such feats he controls his animals without chair or blank gun, by quiet voice and touch commands and a strong, confident manner. But his easy authority with the beasts is deceptive. Behind it is not only an uncanny rapport but also a tireless capacity for patient, painstaking work.

Gunther Gebel-Williams, whose original name was Gunther Gebel, was born in Schweidnitz, Silesia in 1934. As Soviet troops approached

GUNTHER GEBEL-WILLIAMS

Schweidnitz toward the end of World War II, he and his mother fled to Cologne, Germany, where Mrs. Gebel found work as a seamstress with the Circus Williams. After three months she left the troupe, but Gunther stayed, and eventually he was adopted by the Williams family.

In his earliest years with the Circus Williams, Gunther learned a variety of tanbark skills, including tumbling, juggling, wire-walking and swinging from a trapeze. His instinct for communicating with and handling animals was beginning to make itself evident, but at that time his work with them was confined to riding horses bareback. In the early 1950's his foster father and stepbrother were killed in circus accidents and young Gebel-Williams was suddenly thrust into a position of adult responsibility. While his foster mother handled the business side of the Circus Williams, he supervised the daily work, and eventually he took over the general management of the troupe, a traditional European one-ring company employing fifty people.

While running the show, Gebel-Williams developed his animal act. From the beginning his chief training instruments were food and voice. "It's not important what you say to them," he once said. "It's the tone and the way it's said. I call them by name, speak in a certain voice, and they know what I mean. They each have a different personality."

After mastering horses—to the point of winning international prizes for his Roman post-riding of them—and then lions (which he later discontinued) and elephants, he moved on to the more difficult tigers. His first step in training was always to develop trust, to make the animals respect him and feel that he understood them. In the case of tigers, when the trust was sufficient he would teach each cat to leap on command, using at first a piece of meat hung from the end of a stick as inducement and, after each leap, indicating approval or disapproval, depending on the quality of the leap, by tone of voice or even an embrace. When he did use a whip, it was only to prod with the butt end. Any extreme roughness on his

part was usually for the sake of the tigers themselves. To break up fights, for example, he would punch aggressors in their noses. "The greatest danger," he pointed out on one occasion, "is that they will kill each other."

Being a basic trainer (as opposed to the performing "tamer," who puts on an act with animals trained by such men as Gebel-Williams), he taught the animals from scratch, obtaining them young and, preferably, jungle-born. (With animals born in captivity, he knew, there is too great a probability that they will have been soured by mishandling.) When he hit his stride, he was training tigers in six months. Combined acts such as those in which tigers jumped on moving horses (normally deathly afraid of the big cats) took much longer.

The elephant-tiger pyramid, for example, took almost two years to perfect. During that time he arranged the daily routines of the two animals so that they would spend as much time together as possible. Thus, they slept next to each other and often took walks together with their master. Finally the elephant would allow the tiger to jump on his back, and the stunt was completed by Gebel-Williams climbing up the elephant and straddling the tiger. Thick padding had—and has —to be kept on the elephant's back, however, because the tiger's inclination to bite into the elephant's hide could not be curbed.

"You cannot tell a wild animal that he has to learn a trick today," Gebel-Williams realized early. "You have to believe that he'll do it tomorrow if you spend enough time with him." He learned that his time regularly spent with his beasts had to include visits to them before and after every show. One reason for the visits was to check on their condition. Another was to reassure them, especially if there were changes in the act. The most important reason was that the animals expected the visits and would become confused if the routine was even slightly changed.

For more than a decade he and his menagerie stunned audiences throughout Europe, and during that time he received many offers from impresarios in the United States. But he refused to leave the Circus Williams, and Ringling Bros. and Barnum & Bailey finally acquired him only by buying his circus, in 1968. He immediately liked the United States, not only because "this is where the money is," but also because of the advantage of having three rings instead of one to work in. Now, while he is putting his elephants and tigers through their paces in the center ring, his horses prance simultaneously in the side rings. Gebel-Williams intends to re-sign with Ringling Bros., or at least remain in the United States, when his present five-year contract expires in 1973.

His starring elephants are Nellie, from India, and Kongo, the only African elephant now in an American circus. When Ringling Bros. and Barnum & Bailey was at the Civic Center in Baltimore, Maryland in March 1971, Gebel-Williams demonstrated his rapport with Kongo to a group of reporters. "He unshackled . . . [the] elephant . . . ," George Nobbe reported in the New York

Sunday News (March 28, 1971). "The animal wandered aimlessly about, and her master walked in the opposite direction. When perhaps sixty feet separated them, Gebel-Williams whirled without warning and shouted the animal's name. Kongo gave a small squeal of delight and trundled toward him. . . . With that sole command, Gebel-Williams made the elephant follow him about the vast storage area and back to her original place."

Reviewing the opening of the 101st edition of "The Greatest Show on Earth" at Madison Square Garden in New York City, Ron Hollander of the New York *Post* (March 31, 1971) described how "an elephant gallumphs across the center ring and launches Gunther Gebel-Williams in a backward somersault onto another elephant's back." Two days before dress rehearsal one of Gebel-Williams' tigers died and another had to be prepared to take his place. The trainer told Norma McLain Stoop, who was reporting on the 101st edition of the circus for *After Dark* (April 1971), that when he put in the new tiger, the jealous veteran cats wanted "to get rid of the interloper . . . even kill him." Yet the act went off perfectly. "You must become a tiger to be able to train tigers," Gebel-Williams said.

Gebel-Williams is a slender, blue-eyed man, muscular but wiry, with a quick, swaying walk and a grin that Edward Hoagland in the *Esquire* article compared to that of "a lapsed angel, a satyr." Hoagland described his face as a "mobile" one, "urchinish," and "inspired." "Its a lean V face, the flat planes cut for mischief and glee, or a lemur's, a tree-dweller's face, big-eyed." Gebel-Williams' expensive sexy costumes, colorful and sequined, are open at the chest, where a large cross pendant on a chain from his neck is visible. His arms bear many scars, the remnants of clawings suffered. He has pointed out that while wild animals may be trained, they can never be tamed. "I don't care how long you work with an animal, how well you think you know him, there's always a chance that one day, when you least expect it, he may revert to his natural instincts and turn on you. A wild-animal trainer who puts total trust in his charges is foolish in the extreme."

Gunther Gebel-Williams, who wed his wife Sigrid about four years ago, was previously married to Jeanette Williams, his stepsister. Both women assist him in his act, usually supervising the horses in the side rings. By Sigrid he has an infant son, Mark Oliver, and by Jeannette a daughter, Tina, who attends school in Germany. With his wife and son, Gebel-Williams lives in spacious quarters on the circus' own railroad train. The trainer relishes money and the luxuries that it buys, such as expensive automobiles, and he enjoys listening to rock 'n' roll music and playing golf. Edward Hoagland wrote of his personality: "He seems almost perpetually elated. . . . He meets people just as easily as wildlife. . . . He is versatile, charismatic, graceful, not driven, not even very ambitious professionally. He is inexhaustible and delights in his work, but his talent exceeds his ambition. This might seem to be his weakness if he were set beside the few greats of the past; his joy and versatility would be his strength."

References

Esquire 76:88+ Jl '71 pors
Life 70:66+ Ap 23 '71 pors
N Y Sunday News S p1 Mr 28 '71 pors
Read Digest 99:133+ N '71 por

GETZ, STAN

Feb. 2, 1927- Jazz musician
Address: b. c/o MGM-Verve Records, 1350 Avenue of the Americas, New York 10019; h. 15 South Broadway, Irvington, N.Y. 10533

For over two decades Stan Getz has maintained his rank as probably the best-known tenor saxophonist in jazz. He first gained prominence in the late 1940's as a member of Woody Herman's "Second Herd," and throughout the 1950's his cool, laconic, melodic improvisations dominated jazz saxophone playing and earned him the nickname of "The Sound." Just when it seemed that Getz's cool style was passing out of vogue in the early 1960's, he attained a mass popularity almost unheard of for a jazz musician with a series of bestselling Brazilian bossa nova recordings, including *Jazz Samba* with guitarist Charlie Byrd and *Getz/Gilberto* with the Brazilian musicians Antonio Carlos Jobim and João and Astrud Gilberto.

The son of Alexander Getz, a tailor, and his wife, Goldie, Stanley Getz was born in Philadelphia, Pennsylvania on February 2, 1927. (His family name had been shortened from Gayetzsky when his parents emigrated from Russia.) At the age of six Stanley moved with his parents and younger brother Robert to the Bronx, New York, where he later attended James Monroe High School. "When I was coming up I played with all kinds of bands —Mickey Mouse groups, mambo bands, dance bands," Getz recalled for Bob Micklin of *Newsday* (November 12, 1968). "Then, after hours, if I wanted to play jazz I went to jam sessions, where we'd play into the next day." In his junior high school band he tried the bass and the bassoon before committing himself to the tenor saxophone. By the time he was fifteen he had appeared with the Bronx All City Orchestra and in a band headed by Dick "Stinky" Rogers. Then, to the disappointment of his high school bandmaster, who had recommended him for a scholarship at the Juilliard School of Music, Getz decided to quit school to go on the road as a sideman with Jack Teagarden's band.

The next few years were restless ones for Getz. After about a year he left Teagarden and played briefly with Dale Jones and Bob Chester and then spent a year (1944-45) with Stan Kenton. Next came stints with Jimmy Dorsey, Benny Goodman, Randy Brooks, Buddy Morrow, and Herbie Fields. In 1947 he moved to California, where he worked with Butch Stone and formed his first group, a trio, which appeared at the Swing Club in Holly-

STAN GETZ

wood. During that period Getz was steadily moving away from the big band swing sound of the 1940's toward the more sophisticated melodic progressions and subtle rhythms of modern jazz, or "bebop" as it was then coming to be called. He also began listening to the saxophone of Lester Young, whose moody, laconic playing had a paramount influence on the development of his style.

Late in 1947 Getz organized the Four Brothers saxophone team (with Zoot Sims, Serge Chaloff, and Herbie Steward) that came to provide the distinctive sound of Woody Herman's band of that period, known as Herman's Second Herd. Getz first reached a mass audience with the band's recording of a piece called Early Autumn, in which he played two short but celebrated solos. After leaving the Herd in 1949, Getz formed his own group, a quartet with Al Haig at the piano, and in 1951 they toured Scandinavia. Following a brief stint as a studio musician at NBC in 1952, he went back to leading his own quintet and cut a now classic recording of "Moonlight in Vermont" with Jimmy Smith.

By the time he was in his early twenties Getz was the acknowledged leader of saxophone playing in the new cool jazz mode, with a host of admirers and imitators. But his career also had its dark side. A drug addict since the age of eighteen, the musician had had to support an increasingly expensive and debilitating heroin habit, and in 1954 he was arrested for trying to steal narcotics from a Seattle, Washington drugstore. Looking back on that period when he and many of his contemporaries were addicted to heroin, Getz told Bob Micklin for the Newsday interview, "None of us knew what we were getting into, what a messy scene it was. We were very young and working hard, staying up all night and looking for false stimulation of one kind or another. So many of us got caught up in this round-robin thing that ends in death or insanity. Dope makes you think you're playing better. It's not true. The best way to play is completely sober, loose and happy . . . or unhappy."

At the time of his arrest Getz made up his mind to stay off drugs. After serving a six-month jail sentence, he resumed his career in 1955 and appeared in The Benny Goodman Story (Universal-International, 1956), a film in which he was featured as one of Goodman's musicians. While vacationing in Sweden later that year he contracted a serious case of pneumonia and pleurisy that required eight months of hospitalization and recuperation. Once his health was recovered Getz returned to the United States to fulfill a busy schedule of appearances and record dates. In reviewing two of the recordings Getz made then (Stan Getz and J. J. Johnson at the Opera House on Verve and The Cal Tjader-Stan Getz Sextet on Fantasy) John S. Wilson commented in the New York Times (August 17, 1958) that Getz had "enlivened" his "floating, other-worldly, trancelike" style with a new "sense of emotional involvement and a vigorously swinging projection." To The Jazz Review editor Martin Williams, however, the finest recording that Getz made during that period was The Soft Swing (Verve, 1957). In a review of that disc reprinted in Jazz Panorama (1962) Williams extolled Getz's "wonderful musicianship, ear, and melodic spontaneity," adding that "he almost rolls around in his rhythmic idiom, teases it, coaxes it with an almost astonishing success."

While on a European tour with Norman Grantz's Jazz at the Philharmonic in the spring of 1958 Getz decided to settle in Denmark. With his Swedish wife, whom he had married two years before, he moved into a villa near Elsinore castle that for the next three years became his home base as he toured Western Europe. Although he found the slower pace of European life congenial, Getz was back in the United States early in 1961, apparently lured home by its jazz. In an interview with Leonard Harris of the New York World-Telegram and Sun (November 26, 1963) Getz explained, "Jazz is the ethnic music of our country. In order to play it, you have to live it. . . . Some Europeans play it pretty well, but they don't feel it the way Americans do."

When Getz played his homecoming engagement in New York at the Village Vanguard in March 1961, John S. Wilson (New York Times, March 23, 1961) detected new depths in his playing: "Once he gets well into a solo, he is more probing and searching . . . less inclined than he once was to string together anticipated stylistic effects." Despite the fact that he was playing at least as well as before, Getz found that his popularity had slipped, mostly because the aggressive and nervous sax style of John Coltrane had come into fashion since his absence. He failed to recapture the last territory of his domain with Focus (Verve), an unusual jazz disc released early in 1962 that received wide critical praise but sold sluggishly. On that record Getz improvised over several pieces written for strings by the jazz composer Eddie Sauter.

But with the release later that year of Jazz Samba (Verve) Getz attained a more widespread popularity than he had ever enjoyed before. The bossa nova ("new wave") had been evolved a few years before by Brazilian musicians playing traditional Brazilian folk music or sambas in a modern jazz style. Its insinuating rhythms and haunting melodies proved singularly compatible to Getz and his collaborator Charlie Byrd, and *Jazz Samba* became one of the best-selling albums in the history of jazz. Reviewing the disc for the Toronto *Globe and Mail* (July 21, 1962) Patrick Scott wrote, "Mr. Getz, in particular, is positively brilliant. His fluent technique, melancholy tone, and bittersweet lyricism . . . are made to order for the intensely melodic subject matter here—alternately brooding and exultant, and all of it contagious." Two songs from the recording, "Desafinado" ("Slightly Out of Tune") and "Samba de Uma Nota Só" ("One Note Samba"), both written by the Brazilian composer Antonio Carlos Jobim, were released separately and became big popular hits.

In the year that followed the release of *Jazz Samba*, bossa nova became a craze in the United States, and scores of albums were put on the market, most of them grossly inferior to Getz's further offerings (*Big Band Bossa Nova*, Verve, 1962 and *Jazz Samba Encore*, Verve, 1963). By the spring of 1964 the public had wearied of the omnipresent bossa nova, but Getz rekindled their interest with *Getz/Gilberto* (Verve), a recording that featured the chief Brazilian innovators of bossa nova, the pianist Antonio Carlos Jobim and the singer guitarist, João Gilberto. Gilberto's wife Astrud made her singing debut on the recording. *Getz/Gilberto* quickly shot up on the best-selling charts, and a single cut from it, "The Girl from Ipanema," sung by Señhora Gilberto, was heard on juke boxes around the nation.

Much of Getz's time during the middle 1960's was devoted to the bossa nova, and he appeared at concerts and on major TV programs that do not normally feature jazz artists. With Astrud Gilberto he even appeared in a teenage rock 'n' roll film, *Get Yourself a College Girl* (MGM, 1964) performing "The Girl from Ipanema." Yet he did not allow the popular success of his Latin music to keep him away from pure jazz entirely. In November 1963, for example, he appeared with Count Basie and the vocalist Jimmy Rushing at the first major jazz concert held at Lincoln Center's Philharmonic Hall, and for the soundtrack of the film *Mickey One* (Columbia, 1965) he improvised saxophone solos to a jazz score by Eddie Sauter. Most recently, however, Getz has apparently adapted a pop-oriented repertoire, and on a typical evening at New York's Rainbow Grill in November 1968, he played jazz ballads, bossa novas, and popular tunes. Reviewing that engagement John S. Wilson (New York *Times*, November 5, 1968) spoke of Getz's "viable, all-purpose style," which he described as "a style of playing that has the melodic appeal and the glossy surface to which a mass audience responds . . . [while] retaining the vitality and creativity that built his reputation in the jazz world before the bossa nova opened new doors for him."

Getz currently records exclusively for MGM/-Verve. Among his discs on the Verve label are *And the Cool Sounds* (1957), *Cool Velvet* (1961), *Stan Getz and Bob Brookmeyer* (1961), *Stan Getz with the Oscar Peterson Trio* (1961), *Au Go Go* (1964), *Getz/Gilberto No. 2* (1966), *Sweet Rain* (1967), *What the World Needs Now* (1968), and *Didn't We* (1969). Other record companies have reissued a number of Getz's early recordings, including *The Brothers*, with Zoot Sims and Al Cohn (Prestige), *The Greatest of Stan Getz* (Roost), *Prezervation*, with Al Haig (Prestige), and *The Stan Getz Quintet at Storyville* (Roost). In 1962 Getz won a Grammy Award for "Desafinado" and in 1964 the National Academy of Recording Artists voted "The Girl from Ipanema" the best record of the year and *Getz/Gilberto* the best jazz album of the year. Getz has won more readers' and critics' jazz polls than any other saxophone player. Throughout the 1950's he was a yearly winner of the *Metronome* Readers' Poll and the *Downbeat* Readers' Poll, and a frequent winner of the *Downbeat* Critics' Poll. As of 1966, Getz had won every *Playboy* Readers' Poll since 1957 and every *Playboy* All Stars All Stars Poll since 1960.

At one time reviewers found Stan Getz almost painfully reserved and introverted onstage, but he has developed a casual and relaxed manner in recent years. The saxophonist is of medium height and build, and one jazz writer described him as "so strikingly handsome that he might easily have achieved success as an actor." In 1956 Getz was married in Sweden to Monica Silfveskiold, whom he had met while she was studying in the United States the year before. They make their home in a large, elegant mansion overlooking the Hudson River in Irvington, New York. With them live their two children, Pamela and Nicholas, and David and Beverly, two of Getz's children by his previous marriage. His oldest son, Steven, is married and plays the drums with his own quintet.

References

    Time 86:58+ S 3 '65 por

    Feather, Leonard. Encyclopedia of Jazz (1960); Encyclopedia of Jazz in the Sixties (1966)

    Panassie, Hugues and Gautier, Madeleine. Guide to Jazz (1956)

    Who's Who in America, 1970-71

GIBSON, KENNETH A(LLEN)

May 15, 1932- Mayor of Newark, New Jersey
Address: b. Mayor's Office, City Hall, Newark, New Jersey 07102

The first elected Negro mayor of a major Eastern city is Kenneth A. Gibson, an independent Democrat who in July 1970 took over the administration of the blighted remains of Newark, New Jersey bequeathed him by the scandal-ridden mayoral regime of machine Democrat Hugh J. Addonizio. As waves of poor Southern blacks migrated to Newark over the past three decades, the relatively affluent whites fled the inner city, with the result that the population of approximately 400,000

KENNETH A. GIBSON

is now more than 62 percent black and 10 percent Spanish-speaking. The New Jersey metropolis has the second highest population density in the country; the highest per-capita street crime rate; one of the most nefarious webs of organized crime and political corruption; the seventh highest number of drug addicts; the second heaviest property tax burden; the highest incidence of venereal disease, new cases of tuberculosis, and maternity deaths; the second highest infant mortality rate; the highest percentage of slum housing; the highest ratio of welfare recipients (one out of every three people); an unemployment rate of 13 percent for the general population and 30 percent for young men; and the rawest, bitterest, most explosive racial confrontation, many observers believe, to be found anywhere in the United States today.

Mayor Gibson, a former city structural engineer, faces the appalling problems of his city with a stolid, technocratic calm, but also with a nearly bankrupt city treasury. The Prudential Insurance Company, the Chamber of Commerce, and other concerned pillars of the Newark business community are trying to assist Gibson with moral support, job training and placement programs, and the like, but if federal and state governments do not come adequately to the aid of Newark and make it a model of urban rehabilitation, its decay could well be an omen of what is in store for all of America's once great cities. "Whatever troubles American cities have," Gibson often says, "Newark will get there first."

The elder of two sons of Willie and Daisy Gibson, Kenneth Allen Gibson was born in Enterprise, Alabama on May 15, 1932. His father was, and is, a butcher. His mother, once a seamstress, is now an aide in a nursing home, and his brother, Harold, is a Newark policeman. Gibson's temperament has been pacific since childhood, as he told Edith Evans Asbury of the New York Times (June 16, 1970): "My mother says that when all the other kids were running around breaking their arms and legs I was sitting still, thinking."

"We never had too much money but we always had enough to eat," Gibson reminisced in an interview with Judith Michaelson of the New York Post (July 4, 1970). "My father had two main principles. One, always take care of your family and two, that he was the boss of the house. He was the authority figure, but we were buddies, too, and we played games together." Willie Gibson instilled in his sons the conviction that "we could do everything we wanted if we tried hard enough."

In the interview with Judith Michaelson, Gibson related how, through hard work and thrift, his father built the family a wooden house with an indoor toilet, a luxury even for whites in the Enterprise community. "His neighbors indicated to him that he couldn't live better than they and so his salary was cut, making it impossible for him to stay." When Gibson was eight the family moved north, to Newark.

In public schools in Newark, Gibson was an honor student. While attending Central High School he added to his family's income by playing saxophone in a dance band and working part time as a porter. After graduating from high school, in 1950, he worked for two years in a factory and spent two more years in the United States Army, with the 65th Engineer Battalion in Hawaii. Meanwhile he had enrolled as a night student in the Newark College of Engineering, and he continued his studies there into the 1960's, while working for the New Jersey State Highway Department. In 1963 he took his degree in civil engineering and became an engineer with the Newark Housing Authority, in charge of the basic engineering in urban renewal projects.

Concurrently, Gibson became prominent in local civil rights and community affairs. He was active in the Urban League, the NAACP, CORE, the YMCA, and the YWCA, and he headed Newark's Business and Industry Coordinating Council, a job-finding organization, and served as vice-president of the United Community Corporation, an anti-poverty agency. The Newark Junior Chamber of Commerce named him Man of the Year in 1964 —the year in which a coalition of Italians and blacks (then only 34 percent of the population) elected Hugh Addonizio mayor.

The leaders of the black community in Newark asked Gibson to run for mayor in 1966 and he agreed because, as he explained later, "the poor and disenfranchised can no longer tolerate being controlled by machine politicians, and politics must become synonymous with social and civil rights." Entering the mayoralty race six weeks before the election and with only $2,000 in funds, he ran, in his own words, not so much a campaign as "a civil rights demonstration." But he took enough of the votes—16,000, or about 20 percent —to force a runoff between Addonizio and Leo P. Carlin, the Republican candidate. Addonizio won the runoff.

As soon as the 1966 election was over Gibson began preparing in earnest for the 1970 mayoralty race, and his determination as a long-term campaigner was reinforced by the riots that wracked the city in 1967, leaving twenty-six persons dead, untold millions of dollars in property damage, and ulcerated relations between Newark's blacks and whites. At the polls on May 12, 1970 Gibson led a field of seven mayoral candidates, tallying more than twice as many votes as the runnerup, Addonizio, but 9 percent less than the clear majority necessary for victory. In the subsequent runoff campaign, the Addonizio forces tried to stigmatize Gibson as a "puppet" of black militant "extremists," notably the poet and playwright LeRoi Jones, also known as Imamu Amiri Baraka, a leader of black separatism in Newark.

From his side, Gibson needed to do hardly more than allude to the widespread loss of credence in the efficiency and integrity of the Addonizio regime. Addonizio and several other city officials were already on trial in federal court in Trenton for allegedly conspiring to extort $1,400,-000 from contractors and actually receiving a quarter of a million dollars in kickbacks from an engineering firm. (Eventually Addonizio was found guilty and sentenced to ten years in prison. The conviction is now being appealed.) Dismissing race as an issue, Gibson asserted that the crux of the mayoral contest was the question: "Who is best qualified and more likely to improve the quality of life in Newark?"

On June 16, 1970, when a record 73 percent of the registered voters turned out for the runoff election, Gibson decisively defeated Addonizio, 55,097 votes to 43,086. It was estimated that ninety-five percent of the balloting Negroes voted for him, and 15 to 20 percent of the whites. Along with Gibson, three black candidates were elected to the nine-man city council. Shortly after the election Gibson said: "One thing my election has done already is to serve notice on organized crime that their license has been revoked."

At his inauguration, on July 1, 1970, Gibson appealed for "unity from all persons interested in the city." On the same day he formally nominated key members of his city government, and before the end of the day the nominations were approved at the first meeting of the new city council. Among the appointments were John L. Reddin, a white police officer of impeccable reputation, as police chief; John P. Caufield, also white, as fire director; William H. Walls, a Negro judge, as corporation counsel; Elton Hill, also black, as assistant business administrator; S. Joseph Frisina, a white campaign worker for Gibson, as deputy mayor; and Raymond Anese, a Puerto Rican who had run unsuccessfully for city council on the Gibson ticket, as the other deputy mayor.

After taking office Gibson revealed that the corruption in the city bureaucracy, as evidenced in attempted bribery and graft, was more pervasive than he had ever dreamed, and he reaffirmed his dedication to extirpating it by all feasible means. Even more compelling was the problem of city finances, because it was estimated that a 1971 budget of $168,000,000 would be necessary just to maintain the status quo in Newark, and existing sources of revenue would provide the city with only about $88,000,000. Rather than raise property tax rates, already almost $10 on $100, Gibson asked the state legislature for increased aid to the city and for enabling legislation for new forms of local taxation.

Meeting in special session in December 1970, the legislature authorized $32,000,000 in incremental aid to Newark and passed the enabling tax legislation. But the city council refused to approve the maximum taxing power granted by the legislature. Instead, in February 1971, it approved a compromise tax package of 1 percent on business payrolls, to be paid by employers, and lesser city taxes on parking lots and sewer assessments. In accepting the compromise, reluctantly, Mayor Gibson pointed out that it would fall far short of bridging the budget deficit of $80,000,-000. The remaining avenue open to him was federal aid, but by October 1971 he had only been able to obtain $15,000,000 in antipoverty funds from the federal government.

Racial polarization in the city was intensified by a teachers' strike that kept about half of the city's 80,000 public school students out of classes for two months in 1971. The predominantly white Newark Teachers Union was demanding a contract providing for binding arbitration-of-grievance procedures and freeing teachers from nonprofessional duties, such as hall and cafeteria supervision. The predominantly black Board of Education refused to approve such a contract, because the feeling in the majority black community is that the teachers in general are suburb-living outsiders who may not have the needs of its children at heart—and if they will not accept the duties as signed by the community, then good riddance to them.

"These people are just going through what the Irish in Boston did under James Michael Curley," one white businessman in Newark commented. "All they want is a share of the power." But Mayor Gibson was almost at his wit's end in trying to defuse the school board-union stalemate. In a letter to the Board of Education and the Teachers Union dated April 10, 1971 he warned that the effort of each side "to achieve total victory can only result in a bitter and total loss." The following day the Mayor said that if the dispute was not speedily resolved he would have to ask the state to take over the Newark school system. But Carl L. Marburger, the New Jersey State Commissioner of Education, commented: "The die is cast. I'm afraid the situation in Newark already is in such terms of black-white, board-union polarization that we couldn't achieve anything." Gibson finally suggested a compromise that both sides accepted on April 18, 1971.

Kenneth A. and Muriel Gibson were married in July 1960. By a previous marriage Gibson has two daughters, Cheryl and JoAnne, and by her first marriage Mrs. Gibson has one daughter, Joyce. At last report the Gibsons were still living in the modest apartment in Newark's Central Ward that they have occupied for years. "I don't go in for fancy trappings," Gibson has said. Temperamentally, the Mayor describes himself as "slow, but awfully persistent," and politically, as a "nominal"

Democrat, a liberal in the tradition of Robert F. Kennedy.

David Gelman wrote in *Newsday* (August 20, 1970): "Gibson is a pleasant looking, brown-skinned man of stocky build and medium height, with brown eyes that harbor just the faintest suggestion of irony. He looks as steady as a rock; everything about him, in fact, seems to say something like, 'Easy does it.'" Others have described the Mayor as "square," "bland," "patient," and "low-key." Serious and laconic, he is not given to small talk, and he doesn't much care what his public image is as long as the focus of his administration is on "the delivery of services to the public." He pointed out to Judy Michaelson in the New York *Post* interview: "I'm an engineer, as you know, by personality, too, and I try to rule out things that are done for dramatic or public relations value."

References

Life 69:42+ Jl 4 '70 por
N Y Post p18 Jl 4 '70 por
N Y Times p41 My 14 '70 por; p50 Je 16 '70 por
Wall St J p14 Ja 27 '71

GIEREK, EDWARD (gye′rɔk)

Jan. 6, 1913- First Secretary of the Polish United Workers Party
Address: b. c/o Central Committee of the Polish United Workers Party, 6 Nowy Swiat, Warsaw, Poland

In what has been called the first successful workers and consumers revolt in the Communist world, demonstrating Polish workers and housewives in December 1970 brought about the downfall of the regime of Wladyslaw Gomulka, First Secretary of the Polish Communist party since 1956. His successor is Edward Gierek, a former miner whose economic management of the heavily industrial southern province of Katowice over the past decade made it the most prosperous area in Poland. By no means a liberal, Gierek is a pragmatic economic expert with little interest in ideology. Since becoming First Secretary on December 20, 1970 he has energetically addressed himself to reviving Poland's moribund economy and dealing with a restless populace that has tired of a standard of living only half that of its Eastern bloc neighbor East Germany.

Edward Gierek was born on January 6, 1913 in Porabka, a village in the Bedzin district of Katowice. After Gierek's father, a coal miner, was killed in a mining accident the family joined a large emigration to the coal mining fields of northern France. At the age of thirteen Gierek quit school to work in the mines. He soon became active in the French trade union movement, and in 1931 he joined the French Communist party. In 1934 Gierek was arrested by the French police for his role in organizing the first sit-down strike in French history. He was deported to Poland as

an "undesirable alien," and soon after was conscripted into the Polish army. In 1937 he left Poland once again, this time emigrating to the coal-mining region of northeastern Belgium, where he took a job as a miner and joined the Belgian Communist party.

During the German occupation of Belgium, Gierek became a full-time Communist party official, and he became active in the underground, organizing a branch of the resistance among Polish miners and factory workers. By the time of the liberation in 1944 he had become head of a separate Polish section of the Belgian Communist party. In 1945 Gierek helped found Belgian branches of both the Union of Polish Patriots, a Stalinist organization, and the Polish Workers party, a more nationalistic Communist party that gained control of postwar Poland. In 1946 Gierek became chairman of the National Council of Poles in Belgium, a position he held until his return to Poland in 1948.

Returning to Poland, Gierek worked in Warsaw for a year as a functionary of the Central Committee of the Polish United Workers party, the name adopted by the Polish Workers party after it merged with the Polish Socialist party in 1948. The next year Gierek was assigned to the party apparatus in Katowice, and by 1951 he had worked his way up to the post of secretary of the party's Katowice province committee. Meanwhile, Gierek studied part time at the Kraków School of Mining and Metallurgy and in 1954 received a degree in mining engineering. Also in 1954 the second congress of the Polish United Socialist party elected Gierek to its Central Committee, naming him head of the department of heavy industry. At the sixth plenary session in March 1956 Gierek was elected a secretary of the Central Committee.

Four months later, a few days after workers rioted in the city of Poznań, the Central Committee hurriedly convened to decide what to do about the public clamor for reform and an end to Soviet-dominated rule. They decided to free Wladyslaw Gomulka, who had been imprisoned in 1951 for his "nationalist deviationism" and who had since become a national hero. They also elected Gierek and two other newcomers to membership on the Central Committee's nine-man Politburo, the party's highest executive body. Like the two others, Gierek was selected because he had lived in the West, had never undergone extended political training in Moscow, and was not generally regarded by the public as a Stalinist.

By October, however, it was clear that such feeble liberalizing gestures would not be enough, and another plenary session installed Gomulka as First Secretary of the party. Among promises of reform, Gomulka set out to solidify his position, and Gierek was one of those removed from the Politburo because he was considered an opponent of the new party head. Gierek returned to his party stronghold in Katowice and in January 1957 was elected a deputy from Katowice to the national Sejm (parliament). He has held that position ever since, serving for many years as a member of the presidium of the Sejm and as chairman of its education and science committee.

Gomulka's new regime did not live up to its liberal promises, despite the heady atmosphere of its early months, and economic stagnation soon brought discontent once more. Hoping to broaden his base of support among party activists, Gomulka, at the third party congress in March 1959, restored many known opponents to high office, among whom was Gierek, who regained his seat on the Politburo. Also in 1959—some sources give 1956 or 1957—Gierek was elevated to the post of First Secretary of the provincial party organization of Katowice.

Often known by the name of Silesia, of which it is a part, Katowice is the most important industrial region in Poland, since it produces 90 percent of the nation's coal (its main export and foreign-exchange earner), half its electricity, most of its metal ores, and about 21 percent of its total industrial product. The province also is the most heavily populated area of Poland, with about 2,500,000 people or 11 percent of the total population. As party head of Katowice, Gierek therefore enjoyed considerable power. Over the next decade he avoided direct involvement in national politics and factional disputes, instead concentrating on the improvement of local economic conditions and the satisfaction of consumer demands. A tough administrator with little patience for intellectuals or theorists, Gierek ran his province autocratically, but with a responsiveness to the people unusual in Polish politicians.

As chief of the Politburo's industrial department, Gierek made the Central Committee pump large amounts of investment capital into Katowice. Under his administration the province's industrial plant underwent considerable expansion and modernization, while non industrial development programs emphasized urban beautification and such highly visible projects as the building of modern apartment houses, schools, sports arenas, parks, and recreational facilities. Gierek attracted competent and energetic young technicians and managers to Katowice from elsewhere in Poland and introduced bureaucratic and procedural reforms to streamline and simplify the machinery of local government. He shrewdly used his influence in the national party to insure that ample supplies of goods of all kinds were available in Katowice even when there were shortages in other parts of Poland. As William Woods wrote in *Poland: Eagle of the East* (1968): "In Warsaw they tell you that whatever the shortages, if good nylon shirts cannot be found in Poznan, or beer in Cracow, or ham anywhere in the country, in Katowice you will be sure to find them all."

Because of its wealth and relative autonomy under his rule, Katowice came to be known as the "Polish Katanga," and Gierek was often called the "Polish Tshombe" or the "king of Silesia." Gierek's critics may have been right in accusing him of holding Katowice's interests above those of Poland, but the power base he built up was, nonetheless, impressive. By the mid-1960's the workers of Katowice province had become the

EDWARD GIEREK

highest paid in all Poland, with many of them building their own homes and buying automobiles, and the Katowice party organization had grown to be the largest in the country (262,000 members in 1968). Compared to other Poles, the inhabitants of Katowice were relatively satisfied with their living standards and economic prospects, and they largely attributed their economic progress to the efforts of Gierek rather than to the national leadership.

Solidly entrenched in Katowice, Gierek became the only major political figure in Poland with a permanent regional power base, and his managerial expertise helped him to emerge as the leader of the young "technocrat" faction of the national party. When widespread student rioting broke out early in 1968 and a government shakeup seemed impending, many observers saw Gierek as the chief threat to Gomulka.

Gierek's part in the anti-"Zionist" campaign of 1967-68, which eventually led to the exile of 15,000 of Poland's 25,000 Jews, was apparently at least partly motivated by his desire to usurp Gomulka. Launched after the Arab-Israeli war of June 1967, the campaign became popular with much of Poland's traditionally anti-Semitic populace, even though Gomulka tried to moderate the trend. Reportedly the first to purge his party organization of Jews, on March 14, 1968 Gierek made a well-received and much publicized speech demanding repressive measures against "Zionists" and other "dirty scum." Four days later Gomulka was repeatedly interrupted during a nationally televised address in Warsaw by shouts of "We want Gierek! Give us Gierek!" from the audience. But Gierek withdrew abruptly into the background, and some sources suggest that Gomulka and Gierek joined forces against a common rival, General Mieczyslaw Moczar, minister of the interior and commander of the secret police. A xenophobic, anti-Semitic hard-liner, General Moczar commanded the loyalties of the "partisan" faction of the party, consisting mostly of older men who had fought during the war and were conservative and fiercely nationalistic.

Over the next two years the authority of the Gomulka regime was eroded by growing public discontent over economic conditions, which were worsening as a result of agricultural failures. Misjudging the extent of the unrest, Gomulka adopted a bonus incentive plan late in 1970 to raise industrial production levels, but it was deeply resented by the workers, who regarded it as a scheme to lower their wages. Workers were already seething when the government enacted a price hike of about 20 percent on food, fuel, and clothing less than two weeks before Christmas. (Most Poles remain loyal to the Roman Catholic church.) Within days rioting broke out in Gdańsk and soon spread to several other northern shipbuilding cities. According to official government reports, forty-four persons were killed in the riots, but other sources have estimated as many as 300 mortalities.

With much of Poland virtually under martial law, an emergency session of the Central Committee was convened on December 20, 1970. The sixty-five-year-old Gomulka, who had been suffering from a heart ailment, was tendered the dignity of resigning "for reasons of health," and Gierek was elected to succeed him. The new government was largely a coalition of Gierek and Moczar supporters, plus a few Gomulka men. General Moczar, a rival too powerful to ignore, was made a member of the Politburo and Central Committee secretary in charge of armed forces and internal security. Reportedly Gierek had met secretly with Leonid I. Brezhnev, Soviet party leader, before taking office, and on December 22 Brezhnev publicly congratulated Poland's new leader on his election. The Eastern bloc countries soon followed suit in recognizing the new regime.

On the eve of his election Gierek appealed over television for national unity and a voluntary restoration of order, promising prompt action to remedy the grievances that had triggered the disturbances and to improve the nation's economy. Although he would not then rescind the unpopular measures that had set off the December riots, Gierek announced a two-year freeze on food prices and a government subsidy for large families and elderly and invalid persons, who were most affected by the price hikes. After Gierek took office the workers returned to their jobs, but during the last week of January 1971 new strikes broke out in the northern cities of Gdańsk, Gdynia, and Szczecin. Gierek flew to Szczecin to meet with shipyard workers, and on January 26 ordered the cancellation of the unpopular bonus incentive program. Two weeks later he sent a delegation to meet with striking textile workers in Lódz, and on February 15 the Gierek government made a second major concession when it announced a rollback in food prices to the pre-December levels effective March 1, 1971.

The price cut was made possible by the Soviet Union's offer to Poland of an estimated $500,000,-000 worth of credits and grain shipments, a sign of Gierek's continuing good relations with the Kremlin. At home the new First Secretary continued to consolidate his position by purging opponents from positions of power in national and provincial party organizations. At a Central Committee plenary session in February the remaining Gomulka supporters were ousted from the Politburo, and Gomulka himself was suspended from membership in the Central Committee because of "serious mistakes in recent years." But Gierek's continuance in power appeared to rest largely on his success with the economy. Shunning any major changes, the Gierek regime has seemed to emphasize making the existing system viable by encouraging workers to increase production with the promise of more housing, better consumer goods, and a higher standard of living.

A tall, burly man with close-cut hair, Edward Gierek has a down-to-earth manner and speaks the Silesian dialect of the miners of his province. He is proud of his familiarity with Western culture, often speaks French with his wife, an ethnic Pole born in France, and reads French newspapers and periodicals regularly. Gierek has been decorated with the Order of the Builder of People's Poland and the Standard of Labor First Class.

References

Midstream 17:22+ F '71
N Y Post p26+ D 21 '70
N Y Times p15 D 21 '70 por
Nat Observer p7 D 28 '70 por
Newsweek 77:21+ Ja 4 '71 por
Washington (D.C.) Post A p1+ D 21 '70
International Who's Who, 1969-70
Wielka Encyklopedia Powszechna (1964)

GINASTERA, ALBERTO (EVARISTO) (hē-nä-stä'rä)

Apr. 11, 1916- Argentine composer
Address: b. Instituto Torcuato di Tella, Centro Latinoamericano de Altos Estudios Musicales, Florida 936, Buenos Aires, Argentina; c/o Boosey & Hawkes, Inc., 30 W. 57th St., New York 10019

Usually regarded as South America's foremost contemporary composer, Alberto Ginastera has been called "the Mozart of the twelve-tone system." Even his earliest music, written in the late 1930's and heavily imbued with the folk music of Argentina, showed his interest in serialism, and many of his mature works, including the Concerto for Piano and Orchestra (1961) and the Concerto for Violin and Orchestra (1963) use that idiom freely. Ginastera has composed ballet music, film scores, instrumental, vocal, and choral works, symphonies, and, most recently, operas. Although many of the Argentine composer's other works have had their premières in the United States, it has been his operas that have made him a popular success there. His first attempt at opera, *Don Rodrigo,* which blends the pageantry and nobility of grand opera with a largely atonal score, became a staple in the New York City Opera's repertory after it opened its first season at Lincoln Center in 1966. His second opera, *Bomarzo,* which was premièred by the Opera Society of Washington in 1967, scored an even bigger hit. Widely publicized for its sensational aspects, it became known in some quarters as "the topless opera." A gothic melodrama of sex and violence, *Bomarzo* stuns audiences visually and its wildly atonal score heightens the eerie, hallucinatory effects of the action. Ginastera's most recent opera, *Beatrix Cenci,* was the first operatic work chosen for production at the new Kennedy Center Opera House in Washington, D.C.

The son of Alberto and Luisa (Bossi) Ginastera, Alberto Evaristo Ginastera was born on April 11, 1916 in Buenos Aires, Argentina. His parents were second-generation Argentines, his father's grandparents having emigrated from Italy and Spain. Ginastera's family had no special interest in music and there were no musicians in the family tree. Although he denies having been a prodigy, the composer revealed his innate musicality at an early age. At five he tried to play the Argentine national anthem on a toy flute, only to burst into tears when he discovered that the flute lacked one of the notes he needed. He began his piano studies two years later, and when he was twelve he entered the Williams Conservatory in Buenos Aires, where he studied composition, piano, and harmony.

Ginastera pursued his academic training until he graduated from secondary school in 1935. The following year he entered the National Conservatory of Music, where he began composing many small pieces. His first major work was a ballet score, *Panambí,* which received the National Prize in 1940. Ginastera graduated from the conservatory with high honors and a professor's diploma in 1938. His graduation piece was a mammoth setting of Psalm 150 for mixed chorus, boys' chorus, and orchestra, which had its first performance in the United States by the Philadelphia Orchestra thirty years later.

In 1941 Ginastera joined the faculties of the National Conservatory and the National Military Academy in Buenos Aires. That same year he received his first international recognition, when Lincoln Kirstein commissioned him to compose a ballet score for his American Ballet Caravan. Before the work, which was entitled *Estancia,* could be mounted, the ballet company was dissolved, but the score was performed in concert in 1943. Ginastera was awarded a Guggenheim Fellowship to study in the United States in 1942, but he postponed his trip because of the war until December 1945. Although he spent most of his fellowship year in New York City, he attended the Tanglewood Music Festival in Massachusetts during the summer. There he met Aaron Copland, who has since become a close friend. In New York Ginastera's Duo for Flute and Oboe had its première performance at a League of Composers concert and the music for the ballet *Panambí* made its North American debut with the NBC Symphony.

By the time Ginastera returned to Buenos Aires in March 1947 he was widely recognized in Argentina and had been awarded numerous prizes

ALBERTO GINASTERA

there. His early works had a strongly nationalistic, folk flavor: *Estancia* has been described as the Latin counterpart of Copland's *Rodeo,* and such compositions of the 1940's as the First String Quartet, the *Obertura para el Fausto Criollo,* the song cycle *Las horas de una Estancia,* and the tone poem *Ollantay* owe much to native Argentine music. Even the later *Variaciónes Concertantes* (1953), which won the Cinzano Bicentennial Prize in 1957, and *Pampeana No. 3* (1954), a pastoral symphony commissioned by the Louisville (Kentucky) Orchestra, retain folkloristic overtones. Yet Ginastera showed an early interest in serial and aleatory writing—*Panambí* has a twelve-tone theme—and, unlike many composers, he evolved gradually and smoothly from a nationalistic to an avant-garde, international composer. By 1962 he could tell Eric Salzman of the New York *Times* (March 11, 1962), "The time for folklore has passed, even for the sophisticated and spiritualized folklore of a Bartók. Of course, composers will still keep their national characteristics. . . . A good composer always has his own personality and that is formed, culturally and spiritually, by his society."

In Ginastera's mature works, many of which have entered the international repertory, his strong personality as a composer is everywhere apparent, revealing his emphasis on rhythms, special sound effects, and instrumental and orchestral sonorities. His String Quartet No. 2 (1958) has become a showpiece for the Juilliard String Quartet; after hearing that ensemble play it at Hunter College in 1966 Harold C. Schonberg of the New York *Times* (October 19) called the composition a "strong, wildly rhythmic . . . handsomely composed, authentically big work." The dazzling young Brazilian pianist João Carlos Martins premièred Ginastera's Piano Concerto in 1961, and it has found favor with many audiences since then. Although Schonberg is not fond of the piece, finding it "very, very effective pianistically, but . . . very, very thin musically" his fellow New York critic Alan Rich (*World Journal Tribune,* October 24, 1966) has called it "the most brilliant essay in the genre produced anywhere since the war." The New York Philharmonic commissioned his Violin Concerto for its first season at Lincoln Center in 1962, but the score was not completed until the following year. After its première at Lincoln Center, with Ruggiero Ricci as soloist, Raymond Ericson of the New York *Times* (October 4, 1963) called the concerto an example of "beautifully intricate workmanship in its unity and coherence" with "wonderful instrumental textures." Although those works vary from the basic tonality of the string quartet to the more pervasive serialism of the other two, they both make fiendish demands on the performer, and Ginastera has said that, to be successful, his works must emerge as virtuoso pieces for the players.

Ginastera's two cantatas have been successfully premièred in the United States. The *Cantata para América mágica* for soprano and percussion orchestra, which the composer has described as "a kind of primitive rite, pre-Columbian ceremony," was extolled by Washington *Evening Star* critic Irving Lowens as "incredibly exciting" when it received its world première at the Inter-American Festival in Washington on April 30, 1961. Three and a half years later *Bomarzo*, a cantata for narrator, baritone, and orchestra, electrified its audience at the Elizabeth Sprague Coolidge Festival of the Library of Congress in Washington. Recalling the cantata, which served as a precursor to the opera of the same name, Schonberg (New York *Times*, February 27, 1966) called it "gut-busting," "a wild work, as far out as any composer is likely to get—serial, aleatoric, athematic."

Despite the dramatic promise of his cantatas, Ginastera was untried as a theatrical composer when he was awarded a 1,000,000-peso commission from the city of Buenos Aires to compose an opera. His lack of experience makes the success of *Don Rodrigo* all the more remarkable. Set in eighth-century Spain, *Don Rodrigo* has for its central figure the last of the Visigoth kings, who, according to legend, lost his throne and the kingdom of Spain because of his illicit love for his ward Florinda. When the new opera premièred at the Teatro Colón on July 24, 1964, John Vincent of the New York *Times* (August 9) felt that "one was witnessing the birth of a work destined to become a landmark similar to [Berg's] *Wozzeck*." Many critics were to compare the opera to Berg's modern masterpiece, for like *Wozzeck*, *Don Rodrigo* is elaborately structured, largely atonal, and composed of a number of sections built on different musical forms. It also makes highly effective use of *Sprechstimme*, or song speech.

The New York City Opera's choice of *Don Rodrigo* to open its first season at Lincoln Center heightened the festivity of the event, for the production, which was staged by Tito Capobianco with a set designed by Ming Cho Lee, was a spectacle of singular brilliance. Most critics admired its power and range of sonorous effects, although some reviewers complained that it lacked expressivity and deep characterization. Alan Rich, on the other hand, maintained that it was "a remarkable demonstration, in fact, of just how much emotional variety and breadth the atonal style can embrace" (New York *Herald Tribune* magazine, March 13, 1966). With the public the opera was such an unqualified success that the company had to schedule two additional performances for the season to meet the demand for tickets. The New York City Opera repeated *Don Rodrigo* at Lincoln Center in 1967 and 1970 and has also performed it in Los Angeles while on tour.

Commissioned by the Opera Society of Washington, Ginastera expanded *Bomarzo* into a full-length opera. In the process he wrote a completely new score that sacrificed none of the excitement of the original. The libretto was adapted by Manuel Mujica Lainez, an Argentine, from his best-selling novel of the same name about a sixteenth-century Duke of Bomarzo who built a gardenful of monstrous stone sculptures. (The garden still stands some miles outside Rome.) Lainez saw Bomarzo as a hunchback, deformed in mind and spirit as well as body, who tries through the grotesque statuary to achieve a kind of immortality. Ginastera has described the opera as a work of "sex, violence, and hallucination," and its gothic horrors, coupled with a score full of serial melodies, aleatory and microtonal passages, and explosive tone clusters, caused a sensation when it had its première at Lisner Auditorium in Washington on May 19, 1967. The reports that filtered back to Argentina so scandalized authorities there that the scheduled August opening of the opera at the Teatro Colón was canceled on moral grounds. *Bomarzo* hardly risked obscurity, however, because Julius Rudel, general director of the New York City Opera and conductor of both *Don Rodrigo* and *Bomarzo*, lost little time in adding it to the adventurous New York company's repertoire. On March 14, 1968 *Bomarzo* opened at Lincoln Center, where it enjoyed as great a success as the first Ginastera opera. Most New York critics found that its sensational aspects had been exaggerated and considered it an improvement over *Don Rodrigo* in its psychological probing.

Columbia Records has released a complete recording of *Bomarzo* as performed by the New York City Opera Company. Other works by Ginastera that have been recorded include the *Cantata para América mágica* (Columbia), the Concerto for Piano and Orchestra performed by Martins and the Boston Symphony (RCA Victor), *Pampeana No. 3* by the Louisville Orchestra (Louisville), the Sonata for Piano by David Bean (Westminster), and *Variaciónes Concertantes* performed by the Boston Symphony under Erich Leinsdorf (RCA Victor). Among Ginastera's more recent instrumental works are the *Concerto per Corda* performed by Eugene Ormandy and the Philadelphia Orchestra in New York in 1967; the *Estudios Symphonicos*, premièred by the Vancouver Symphony in 1968; and a cello concerto and a new piano sonata, heard for the first time at the Hopkins Center Congregation of the Arts at Dartmouth College in the summer of 1968.

Ginastera's third opera, *Beatrix Cenci*, was premièred by the Opera Society of Washington at the Kennedy Center for the Performing Arts on September 10, 1971. Like *Bomarzo*, *Beatrix Cenci* is a violent, hallucinatory work set in Renaissance Italy. After seeing the new opera Louis Snyder of the *Christian Science Monitor* (September 15) wrote, "As Ginastera has proved before, he is a master of theatrical effect, suiting the action to orchestral sound by truly terrifying, ingeniously contrived tonal implication."

Until a production of *Bomarzo* is allowed in Buenos Aires, Ginastera has forbidden Argentine government-supported organizations to perform his works. Despite his unquestioned prestige, the composer's conflict with the puritanical Onganía regime marks only the latest installment in his difficulties with Argentine right-wing governments. During World War II his outspoken liberalism led to his dismissal from the faculty of the National Military Academy by Juan Perón, then Minister of War. After Perón came to power the composer was relieved of the directorship of the Conservatory of Music and Scenic Arts of Buenos Aires, which he had himself founded in 1949. He was restored to his position after the overthrow of the Perón regime in 1955, but left three years later to found and direct the Faculty of Musical Arts and Sciences of the Catholic University of Argentina. He assumed his present post as director of the Latin American Center for Advanced Musical Studies of the Instituto Torcuato di Tella when he established the center in 1963.

A stocky man of medium height who wears thick horn-rimmed glasses, rarely smiles, dresses conservatively, and speaks with deliberation, Alberto Ginastera scarcely cuts the figure of a fiery liberal or avant-garde innovator. Assessing the composer in the New York *Times Magazine* (March 10, 1968), Donal Henahan described him as "a musical Robert McNamara [with] . . . the same squareness of cut, alongside an unexpected liberalism; the same reverence for duty, efficiency and the middle way, alongside intellectual virtuosity and technical brilliance." On December 11, 1941 Ginastera married Mercedes de Toro, a former piano student. They have two children, Alejandro, who works in electronics, and Georgina, who is married to a physician and lives in Paris. The Ginasteras make their home near the center of Buenos Aires. The composer collects African masks and totemic figures, and he is a film buff. During his banishment from academic life by the Perón regime he made his living by writing musical scores for Argentine motion pictures, including *Caballito Criollo* (1954). In his New York *Times Magazine* article Henahan called Ginastera "a Roman Catholic of liberal leanings."

References

N Y Times II p13 F 20 '66 por
N Y Times Mag p30+ Mr 10 '68 pors
Washington (D.C.) Post L p1+ Ap 23 '67
Ewen, David. Composers since 1900 (1969)
Who's Who in America, 1970-71

GINSBERG, MITCHELL I(RVING)

Oct. 20, 1915- Social work administrator; educator
Address: b. Columbia University School of Social Work, New York 10027; h. 372 Central Park West, New York 10025

The dignity of the person on welfare has long been a primary concern of Mitchell I. Ginsberg, who has dedicated his entire professional career to repairing the effects of poverty and eradicating it from the American scene. One of the foremost experts on social welfare in the United States, Ginsberg is at present dean of the Columbia University School of Social Work and was formerly head of New York City's Welfare Department and later of its Human Resources Administration. His bold, exploratory proposals for combating poverty, though often criticized, have made him a leading spokesman for welfare reform. He is particularly noted for his advocacy of a unified national approach to welfare that would emphasize job training and full employment opportunities as the solution to the present crisis. He has also called for increased federal welfare aid to localities and for a national family assistance plan.

A native of New England, Mitchell Irving Ginsberg was born in Revere, Massachusetts on October 20, 1915 to Harry J. Ginsberg, a maintenance worker, and Rose (Harris) Ginsberg. He has one sister. When the boy was ten months old his family moved from Revere to the Dorchester section of Boston's fourteenth ward, and it was in that slum district that Ginsberg grew to maturity. His firsthand experience of poverty had a profound influence on his thinking. In an interview with Judy Michaelson of the New York *Post* (March 15, 1966) he observed, "I drifted into social work, yes, but the concerns I had were always there. My father—he worked in a garage—worked seven days a week, 12 hours a day, for very little money. I always felt something ought to be done."

Ginsberg's boyhood ambition was to become a professional athlete or a sportswriter, and he played baseball enthusiastically until he broke his nose in a collision with another player. Having received excellent grades in elementary school, he was admitted to the Boston Latin School, one of the country's outstanding public secondary schools. The exacting six-year course of study there gave him "a kind of discipline," he reflected many years later, and he won a scholarship to Tufts College, where he majored in history.

While attending Tufts, Ginsberg supported himself by working at jobs provided by the Depression-spawned National Youth Administration. As a sophomore he dug ditches at 30¢ an hour; the next year he earned 40¢ an hour for indexing New York *Times* stories on World War I; and as a senior he was introduced to social work as an NYA basketball coach at Hecht House in Dorchester, again at 40¢ an hour. In addition, Ginsberg was a member of his college baseball and tennis teams, becoming captain of the latter in his senior year. Despite his busy schedule of work

MITCHELL I. GINSBERG

and extracurricular activities, Ginsberg's academic performance continued to be superior. He was admitted to Phi Beta Kappa and in 1937 was awarded a B.A. degree *summa cum laude*.

Unable to find a job compatible with his interest in history, Ginsberg accepted a graduate fellowship and remained at Tufts to work on his M.A. degree in education and psychology, which he obtained in 1938. He also worked part time as a basketball coach at the Roxbury Young Hebrew Association in Boston, and on the advice of that center's executive director he applied for, and received, a national fellowship to Columbia University-affiliated New York School of Social Work (now the Columbia University School of Social Work). It is the oldest of the graduate schools of social work accredited by the Council on Social Work Education.

As a graduate student at Columbia, Ginsberg worked at Cristodora House on Manhattan's Lower East Side. "The poverty there was much worse than in Boston," he has recalled, noting that the experience intensified his conviction that something had to be done. Ginsberg enjoys relating that the director of Cristodora House once called him "the worst social worker since Harry Hopkins," because, as he now admits, he was too eager for change. Ginsberg earned his Master of Social Work degree from Columbia in 1941 and some time later did advanced work at the Center for Human Relations at New York University. From 1942 to 1946 he served in the United States Army as supervisor of the psychiatric social work unit at Camp Carson, Colorado, attaining the rank of technical sergeant.

After returning to civilian life, Ginsberg was employed for varying periods as work group supervisor at the Boston YMHA; program director at the Soho Community House in Pittsburgh, Pennsylvania; program director at Hecht House in Boston; executive director of the Jewish Community Center in Manchester, New Hampshire; and, from 1948 to 1953 an associate in the bureau of personnel and training of the National Jewish Welfare Board in New York City. From 1953 to 1957 he was chairman of the group work committee of the Council on Social Work Education.

In 1953 Ginsberg joined the faculty of Columbia University as an assistant professor of social work, specializing in group work and community relations. He became an associate professor in 1954, a full professor in 1956, assistant to the dean of the School of Social Work in 1958, and associate dean in 1960. During the next few years Ginsberg also served as a consultant to the Community Action Program of the federal Office for Economic Opportunity, as a member of the steering committee of the OEO Headstart Program, as a board member of Mobilization for Youth, and as director of the Peace Corps training project at Columbia University in urban community action (also known as the training project for Colombia and Venezuela).

Early in February 1966 John V. Lindsay, who was just beginning his first term as mayor of New York City, appointed Ginsberg Welfare Commissioner. That post, which paid a salary of $25,000 a year (later raised to $34,000), entailed managerial responsibility for a municipal department that then had some 540,000 clients, 13,000 employees, and an annual budget of $521,000,000. Ginsberg took a leave of absence from Columbia and was sworn in at City Hall on February 14, 1966.

In New York, as in most American cities, both the operations and philosophy of welfare and poverty programs have long been a focus of public attention and political controversy. In the midst of what was commonly regarded as a serious welfare crisis, many New Yorkers welcomed the appointment of Ginsberg because of his excellent credentials. "He has the skills of the trained professional; he retains the compassion that first brought him into the welfare field," a New York *Times* (February 20, 1966) editorial pointed out. "The city will hope that he can devise fresh approaches to one of New York's most urgent challenges."

The job of welfare chief in New York is demanding, tiring, and often frustrating. Even Ginsberg's first day in office, as he remarked to a New York *Times* reporter, was so busy that it seemed like a year, and from that point on he worked long hours, taking few days off and usually eating lunch at his desk. He frequently visited welfare centers and met often with client and employee groups. In July 1967 the press of his duties prevented him from accepting an invitation to visit Israel and reorganize the Jerusalem Department of Social Welfare.

Ginsberg's twenty-two-month tenure as Welfare Commissioner was characterized by a reformist and innovative spirit. One of his first new measures, and certainly the most controversial, was the substitution, in a few selected welfare districts, of a simple affidavit-type declaration of need in place of the expensive, degrading system of regular investigation that was normal welfare procedure. Ginsberg also experimented with a work-incentive program in which a small group of welfare recipients who took jobs were allowed to keep a substantial part of their earnings without losing their welfare eligibility. Several hundred other welfare clients were hired by the department as case aide trainees, while job training and in some cases employment were provided to a few thousand others through vocational rehabilitation and such programs as PREP (Preparation, Retraining, and Education Programs), BEST (Basic Employment Skills Training), TEMPO (Training and Employment for Mothers in Part-Time Employment), and MDTA (Manpower Development and Training).

Other Ginsberg measures included a more liberal policy regarding the dissemination of birth control information; a cash burial allowance instead of public burial in Potter's Field, the establishment of welfare advisory boards, composed mainly of clients, in each welfare district; elimination of arbitrary religious restrictions in the placement of foundlings; enrollment of more than 2,000,000 eligibles in the Medicaid program; and decentralization of Welfare Department operations through the establishment of small neighborhood service centers and the delegation of increased authority to field workers and local supervisors.

Although many of his innovations were successful, especially the affidavit and work-incentive programs, Ginsberg could not implement them on the large scale he desired because he was unable to win approval or enough funds from federal and state welfare authorities. Despite his efforts the New York welfare situation continued to deteriorate, with the number of clients climbing to 765,000 by the end of 1967 and the budget reaching a 1968 total of $917,000,000. Along with new explosions of client dissatisfaction and militancy, there was an increase in employee unrest, strikes, and work stoppages.

Arguing that the welfare problem cannot be solved on the local level, Ginsberg was an outspoken advocate of a federal take-over of the nation's welfare systems. In an appearance before the Senate subcommittee on poverty, employment, and manpower in May 1966, he asserted that America's whole welfare system was "bankrupt" and ought to be "thrown out" and declared: "As long as public assistance does not perform its relief function in such a way as to free the poorest of the poor, rather than lock them in dependency, it has failed as an antipoverty weapon." On other occasions he called for intensive research into the causes and effects of poverty and for a program of guaranteed employment for all, with federal subsidies to induce private industry to hire welfare clients and with the federal government serving as employer of last resort.

In July 1967 Mayor Lindsay created a superagency called the Human Resources Administration, which included the Welfare Department (renamed the Department of Social Services), as well as several formerly independent antipoverty, addiction, youth service, and job training agencies. The following month, when Mitchell Sviridoff, the first HRA Administrator, announced his resigna-

tion, Lindsay offered the post, which paid $40,000 a year, to Ginsberg. To accept the appointment he turned down an invitation to become dean of the Columbia School of Social Work as well as another lucrative offer. He was sworn into office as HRA Administrator on December 5, 1967.

The same problems he had faced at Welfare plagued Ginsberg at HRA, along with an increasing series of new ones. The relief rolls and relief costs continued to rise at a rate that endangered the fiscal stability of the whole city: the 1970 HRA budget was $1,700,000,000, with $1,500,000,000 going to welfare. At the same time the city had to cope with a major upsurge in client demands for increased services and benefits, punctuated by ever more frequent demonstrations by militant client groups. Meanwhile, as the federal and state governments threatened to reduce their allocations for welfare and related programs, Ginsberg had to plan to provide more services to more people with less money than before, while fighting to protect HRA's funds and to keep intact and expand the programs run by the agencies under his direction. As part of his fight, he continued to call for a uniform national welfare policy and for guaranteed employment, and proposed the complete elimination of welfare means tests and the substitution of a national family allowance plan of the kind that is common in many Western nations.

By early 1969 Ginsberg had come under fire for alleged mismanagement and incompetence. Because HRA was still relatively new and encompassed a great diversity of subagencies, no effective overall organizational structure had yet been worked out. In addition to administrative confusion and inefficiency, official investigations revealed several instances of fraudulent accounting practices, misuse of funds, and alleged theft in such subagencies as the Neighborhood Youth Corps.

Although many of the charges stemmed from events that had begun, or taken place entirely, before Ginsberg's appointment, he was still widely held responsible. He ably defended himself against accusations of incompetence, however, and at the same time succeeded in preventing the breakup of HRA by pointing out that if the hunt for wrongdoers in the welfare and poverty structure turned into a general campaign against the welfare and poverty programs, the result would be detrimental to the entire city. To prevent similar occurrences in the future Ginsberg introduced new organizational and auditing measures to streamline operations and safeguard public funds. He also established a welfare research council to study the welfare situation in detail and make major policy and remedial recommendations.

When, in January 1970, Ginsberg was again offered the post of dean of the Columbia School of Social Work, he decided to accept, even though, as he told a New York *Times* reporter, he had found the HRA job the "most exciting professional experience" of his life. Lindsay announced Ginsberg's resignation on January 8, 1970, but Ginsberg agreed to remain at HRA until the end of the year to see the administrative programs he had instituted put into practice and to make the changeover less difficult. On September 1, 1970 he assumed some of the duties of dean on a part-time basis, and in January 1971 he became full-time dean, as well as special assistant on community affairs to the president of Columbia University, William J. McGill. Ginsberg continued his association with HRA in a special advisory capacity.

Ginsberg is a member of the National Association of Social Workers, the American Association of University Professors, the National Conference on Social Welfare, the New York State Welfare Association, the National Association of Jewish Center Workers, the American Public Welfare Association, and the Neighborhood and Regional Planning Board of the Community Council of Greater New York. He was a social work fellow at Adelphi University in 1967. That same year he won the Blanche Ittleson award. In 1966 he received the Michael Schwerner Memorial civil rights award.

A reform Democrat, Ginsberg supported the Presidential candidacy of Adlai E. Stevenson, John F. Kennedy, and Robert F. Kennedy. He was a member of President Richard Nixon's welfare reform task force, but in 1970 he called the Republican administration's proposed welfare legislation only "medium," opposing, for one item, the proposed compulsory work section, because he believes that most people on welfare want to work and do not need to be required to work.

Mitchell I. Ginsberg was married on August 22, 1948 to Ida Robbins, an X-ray technician currently employed at New York's Memorial Hospital. They have no children and live in an apartment in the Park West Village development on Manhattan's West Side. Ginsberg is a thin, gray-haired, professorial-looking man whose characteristic stoop, with his hands stuffed in his pockets, makes him appear less tall than his height of six feet three inches. He is a collector of Lincolniana and an avid baseball, tennis, and basketball fan.

References

Columbia Report p4 Je '70
N Y Herald Tribune p1+ F 11 '66
N Y Post p47 Mr 13 '66; p29 Mr 15 '66 por
N Y Times p1+ F 11 '66 por; p20 Ag 18 '67 por; p59 D 4 '67 por; p20 Ja 9 '70; p38 Jl 10 '70 por
Who's Who in the East, 1970-71

GONZALEZ, EFREN W(ILLIAM)

June 16, 1929- Librarian; organization official
Address: b. Science Information Services, Research and Development Laboratories, Bristol-Myers Products, 225 Long Ave., Hillside, N.J. 07207

The president of the Special Libraries Association for 1971-72 is Efren W. Gonzalez, the manager of Science Information Services in the Research

and Development Laboratories of Bristol-Myers Products, a division of Bristol-Myers Company. Mr. Gonzalez, who began his professional career as a librarian with the Military Sea Transportation Service in 1952, has been in the pharmaceutical library field since 1955. The SLA, with headquarters in New York City, is an association of approximately 7,000 professional librarians and documentalists working in such specialized fields as art, business, education, science, technology, and government.

The only child of Efren and Grace Gonzalez, Efren William Gonzalez was born in New York City on June 16, 1929. His father was an immigrant from Yucatan, Mexico and his mother was a native of Trenton, New Jersey. Gonzalez grew up in the Bronx, where he attended Our Lady of Mercy Grammar School and Cardinal Hayes High School. He early showed a talent for the piano, which he studied under Alexander Semler, and art, which he studied under Leon Helguera, a commercial artist who was a friend of the family.

In high school Gonzalez contributed prose, poetry, and cartoons to the school newspaper, the *Challenger,* and he co-edited that monthly publication in his senior year. In 1947 he graduated from high school and enrolled at Syracuse University with the intention of majoring in journalism. But he soon changed his mind and at the end of his first semester he transferred to Iona College, run by the Irish Christian Brothers, a Roman Catholic order, in New Rochelle, New York. There he majored in philosophy and minored in biology; helped edit the weekly *Ionian;* contributed to the campus literary quarterly; was musical director of a student musical; and participated in student broadcasts over a local radio station. In some of the broadcasts he read news and announcements of campus events and in others he directed, from the piano, his own band in renditions of light jazz compositions and popular songs.

But Gonzalez' most important extracurricular activity at Iona appears, in retrospect, to have been his daily work as a student assistant in the college library. With the encouragement of the librarian, Brother Alexander Thomas, he decided to pursue a career in librarianship, and as soon as he took his B.A. degree, in the summer of 1951, he enrolled in the Columbia University School of Library Service. While working for his master's degree in library science he worked part time reorganizing the library of the Carroll Club, a Manhattan social center for young Roman Catholic working women. His interest in special librarianship was aroused by literature from the Special Libraries Association posted on the bulletin boards of the Columbia library school.

After taking his M.Sc. degree, in June 1952, Gonzalez was hired by the United States Military Sea Transportation Service, Atlantic Area, to restock, from scratch, and standardize all shipboard libraries. He drew up a small standard catalog, purchased titles in bale lots, supervised the assembly-line affixing of stamps, pockets, and cards, and supplied each ship's chaplain (the *ex officio* librarian) with a shelf-list card set. When that job was done, in 1953, he became technical librarian in the material laboratory of the Brooklyn Navy Yard.

Concerning the material laboratory and its library, Gonzalez has written: "This group was a designing and testing facility for the Bureau of Ships, and the library was heavily involved in obtaining and indexing the technical reports issued by government agencies and their contractors. This was when ASTIA was just beginning and the whole area of government reports concerned with scientific and technical investigations was one that had not been encountered at library school. . . . The real meaning of 'special' began to be evident—certainly in the area of types and uniqueness of materials handled. It also became clear how dependent the technical staff was on internal reports, contractor reports, and military specifications in order to achieve success in their own departments."

In 1955 Gonzalez quit his post at the shipyard to become technical librarian at the Nepera Chemical Company in Yonkers, which was closer to his home, and there for the first time he specialized in literature relating to prescription and non-prescription drugs and bulk chemicals. When his supervisor at Nepera moved to Grove Laboratories in St. Louis in 1956, Gonzalez followed him and became technical librarian at Grove. His title was changed to director of technical communications in 1957, and in that position he not only handled books and technical journals but also developed procedures and files to coordinate the technical data generated by internal research and development units in the form of records and reports.

A member of the Special Libraries Association from 1953, Gonzalez served the St. Louis chapter of the SLA in committee appointments, as editor of the chapter's *Bulletin* (1957-58), as an executive board member (1958-59), and as president (1959-60). He also began to serve on committees in the SLA's science-technology and pharmaceutical divisions, and on the association level he was a member (1961-64) and chairman (1962-63) of the convention program committee.

As program chairman, Gonzalez reported at length on the 53d annual convention of the SLA, held in Washington, D.C. in 1962, in *Special Libraries* (September 1962), the association's house organ. His report ended: "This year the convention theme was 'Progress Through Knowledge'. . . . In his televised statement introducing one of the panel discussions, Senator Hubert H. Humphrey called for 'a long-range goal for our information resources.' He underlined the vital need of librarians in effective information management as the international need for scientific knowledge grows. Progress brings change. Change brings the unfamiliar. Are we ready for the Senator's call: 'Let us change the handling of information'?"

Gonzalez was acting convention program chairman in 1964, when the SLA met in St. Louis. The theme of the convention that year was "The Special Librarian as a Creative Catalyst," and joint sessions of the association's fifteen divisions were held to discuss a corollary of the theme: "Creative

EFREN W. GONZALEZ

Organization: The Librarian as a Manager." Gonzalez and F. E. McKenna described the genesis of the two general session programs in an article in *Special Libraries* for October 1964. In 1964-65 Gonzalez was chairman of the SLA's motion picture committee.

Grove Laboratories was acquired by the Bristol-Myers Company in 1958, but the merger of research operations did not take place until 1967. In the latter year Gonzalez was transferred to Bristol-Myers Products in Hillside, New Jersey, as manager of technical communications in the scientific division. In that position he developed lines of coordination among the laboratory, medical, and quality control functions of the division. As manager of Science Information Services in Bristol-Myers' R & D Laboratories, since 1969, he retains his previous duties and is also responsible for the research library and its staff. As he did previously at Grove Laboratories, he is developing at Bristol-Myers a system for the smooth handling of both external scientific literature and internal research reports and experiment records.

After relocating in New Jersey, Gonzalez served on committees of the SLA's New York chapter. He remained active in the association's science-technology and pharmaceutical divisions, and on the association level he was a member of the finance committee (1967-71), the special committee for translations (1968), and the special committee for the reserve fund (1968-69). He was a member of the board of directors for three years, from 1967 to 1970, and during the last two of those years he was secretary of the board. Elected to the presidency of the SLA in 1970, he bore the title president-elect for a full year, 1970-71, in keeping with the tradition of the association. He assumed the presidency when the SLA met in convention in San Francisco, from June 6 to 10, 1971. The theme of the convention was "Design for Service: Information Management."

Efren W. Gonzalez and Rita Ciliotta, whom he met while he was a college student, were married in 1952. They have five children: Efren Thomas, born in 1953, Janet Marie, born in 1954, Barbara

Ann, born in 1955, Lisa Maria, born in 1963, and Lara Elizabeth, born in 1967. The Gonzalezes live in Chatham, New Jersey, where they are parishioners of St. Patrick's Roman Catholic Church. In addition to *Special Libraries,* Mr. Gonzalez contributes to *Unlisted Drugs,* a serial publication of the SLA's pharmaceutical division.

References

Special Libraries 61:102 F '70
Biographical Directory of Librarians in the United States and Canada (1970)

GOOLAGONG, EVONNE

July 31, 1951- Australian tennis player
Address: c/o Victor A. Edwards, 80 Duntroon Ave., Roseville, N.S.W., Australia

Australian tennis player Evonne Goolagong became an instant international celebrity when, on July 2, 1971, a few weeks before her twentieth birthday, she won the women's singles title at the All-England championship tournament at Wimbledon. On that occasion she defeated Mrs. Margaret Court of Australia, who had been the Wimbledon titlist on three separate occasions and was at the time the world's top-rated woman tennis player. Miss Goolagong is one of the few Australians of Aboriginal ancestry to have achieved public prominence and the first among them to compete in championship tennis. Margaret Court, who has announced her impending retirement, has said, with reference to Miss Goolagong, "I think, at last, I have found an Australian to take my place."

Evonne Fay Goolagong, the third of the eight children—four boys and four girls—of Kenneth and Linda Goolagong, was born on July 31, 1951 in the town of Griffith, in the wheat-growing Riverina District of New South Wales, some 300 miles west of Sydney. She spent most of her childhood years in Barellan, a community of some 900 inhabitants about thirty miles from Griffith, in a run-down house at the edge of the town, where the Goolagongs still make their home. Her parents are both part-Aborigine, and she once told Phil Elderkin of the *Christian Science Monitor* (June 7, 1971): "I don't know whether I'm half, quarter, or what. I just know I'm Aboriginal." Her father makes a modest living as a sheepshearer, farm laborer, and mechanic. Although Australia's Aborigines are often subjected to racial discrimination, the Goolagongs, as the only Aboriginal family in Barellan, are accepted as equals by their fellow townspeople.

As a child, Evonne "never cared for dolls," Mrs. Goolagong told John Dunn of *Sports Illustrated* (February 15, 1971). "All she wanted to play with was an old tennis ball. It was her constant companion. She would hold it in her hand and squeeze it all day long. Later she would bounce it and catch it and hit it with a broomstick. She was never without it." By the time she was five, Evonne Goolagong was earning spending money

by retrieving balls at the Barellan War Memorial Tennis Club. After she received a tennis racket as a present, at the age of six, she spent every available moment practising on the local tennis courts. Her dedication greatly impressed the tennis club's president, W. C. Kurtzman, who began to teach her some of the finer points of the game.

In 1961, before she had reached her tenth birthday, Evonne came to the attention of Vic Edwards, one of Australia's best-known tennis coaches and the proprietor of the country's largest tennis school, located in Roseville, a suburb of Sydney. Two of Edwards' assistants had spotted her while conducting a tennis clinic in Barellan, and they reported back to him: "We think we've found a potential champion." Recalling his first impression of her, Colin Swan, one of Edwards' talent scouts, told Harry Gordon, as quoted in the New York *Times Magazine* (August 29, 1971): "She just *flowed* around the court. She was the kind of natural you see once in a long time. She didn't know how to make her shots, of course, but she was always there, in the right place, without even thinking about it." Edwards, who made a special trip to Barellan to see her play, was much impressed. "I decided to leave her alone for a year, to see if she would stick at it," he told a reporter for *Newsweek* (July 5, 1971). "Then I went back to Barellan and found that she had. I was terribly excited." When she was ten, Kurtzman arranged for her to play in a tournament at nearby Narrandera and took her parents along. Upon arriving, he found, to his embarrassment, that the tournament was not for youngsters, as he had thought, but for adults. Unconcerned about the age difference, Kurtzman's tennis prodigy defeated her adult opponent and won the women's singles title in the tournament.

At the age of eleven, Evonne Goolagong began to spend her school vacations at Roseville, where she received intensive coaching from Edwards while boarding with his family. Her travel expenses and her summer clothes were paid for by the townspeople of Barellan. Meanwhile, under Kurtzman's tutelage, she also continued to win local tournaments in her home district. At thirteen she began to attract nationwide attention, and when she won the under-fifteen championship of New South Wales in early 1965 some observers compared her with Wimbledon champion Margaret Smith (now Mrs. Margaret Court), who had also been a prodigy. By that time, according to Edwards, Evonne had already developed a highly effective backhand volley, but she completely lacked the "killer instinct" that characterizes many leading tennis players. Often, after a tournament, she would sympathetically embrace her defeated opponent and try to comfort her.

When Evonne was fourteen, Edwards and his wife, Eva, who have five children of their own, asked the Goolagongs to allow their daughter to stay with them permanently at Roseville. "We left everything to Mr. Edwards," Ken Goolagong told John Dunn in the *Sports Illustrated* interview. "We still do. We know that whatever he decides will be in Evonne's best interests." In addition to giving her intensive coaching in tennis, Edwards—who eventually became her legal guardian—also saw to it that she received a quality education to prepare her for the sophisticated and pressure-filled world in which she would have to move once she achieved tennis stardom. After moving in with the Edwards family, Evonne Goolagong graduated from the Willoughby Girls' High School in Sydney, completed a speech course at Trinity College, and, like Edwards' own daughters, received private instruction in elocution and deportment. In addition, Edwards arranged for her to take a secretarial course at a business school, to enable her to make a living in a field other than tennis, if necessary.

As a high school student, Evonne Goolagong belonged to the school tennis team and was one of six New South Wales representatives in the Pizzey Cup competitions for the Australian interstate championship. In tournaments she often played in partnership with Edwards' daughter Patricia. By the age of sixteen she had won all the Australian state junior titles and national junior titles without losing a set, and between 1968 and 1970 she won forty-four singles and thirty-eight doubles championships on the Australian tennis circuit.

In 1970 Edwards, who now felt that Miss Goolagong was ready for international competition, arranged for her to tour the European tennis circuit. Of the twenty-one tournaments in which she took part, in Great Britain, Holland, France, and Germany, she won seven, including the Welsh and Bavarian titles. Her most notable triumph was her victory over Rosemary Casals in the third round of the British hard-court open championship tournament at Bournemouth, England in April 1970. At Wimbledon two months later she lost in straight sets to Peaches Bartkowicz, 6-4, 6-0, in the second round. Regarding the Wimbledon match, she later observed that she entered it in a state of nervous tension but that it helped her to acquire more poise, self-confidence, and concentration. In December 1970 at Perth, Miss Goolagong was teamed with Margaret Court and Lesley Hunt in successfully defending Australia's possession of the Federation Cup—the women's equivalent of the Davis Cup—against the British challengers.

Evonne Goolagong scored the first major senior singles victory of her career on February 1, 1971, when she defeated her idol, Margaret Court, in the finals of the Victorian Open championships at Melbourne, with scores of 7-6, 7-6. Reporting the encounter for *Sports Illustrated* (February 15, 1971), John Dunn wrote: "From the very beginning of the final match Evonne was in high gear. At no stage did she hesitate to go for winners, even when she was in the most desperate position. Time after time she appeared hopelessly off balance but would save herself with tremendous backhand volleys or fine passing shots. . . . Throughout the match Evonne outplayed Mrs. Court." Following the victory, Edwards predicted that Evonne would be Wimbledon champion by

EVONNE GOOLAGONG

1974. As it turned out, Edwards' estimate missed the mark by three years.

Before entering the Wimbledon competition in late June 1971, Miss Goolagong won the New Zealand and Tasmanian championships and the French Open, and she was a finalist in the Australian Open, which she lost to Mrs. Court. At Wimbledon, where she was seeded third, Miss Goolagong swept to the semifinals with the loss of only one set, to Lesley Hunt. In the semifinals she defeated second-seeded Billie Jean King of the United States, a former Wimbledon champion, in fifty-six minutes, with scores of 6-4, 6-4. A Reuters correspondent, in a dispatch published in the Toronto *Globe and Mail* (July 1, 1971), commented on her performance: "Serving with penetration, hitting her free-flowing ground strokes, particularly a beautiful backhand, deep to the baseline, volleying firmly and moving with great speed, Miss Goolagong played with a maturity and assurance far beyond her years." Mrs. King said of Miss Goolagong after her defeat: "It's a great time in her life and I am really happy for her. I think she's a great person and very humble for her age. She has a great future ahead of her."

On July 2, 1971, before an audience of some 15,000 spectators, including British Prime Minister Edward Heath, Evonne Goolagong defeated Margaret Court—who had been rated the two-to-one favorite—in the Wimbledon finals in sixty-three minutes with scores 6-4, 6-1. Contrasting the styles of the two competitors, sports commentators noted that Mrs. Court appeared hesitant in charging the net, while Miss Goolagong played virtually every shot and seemed at her best under pressure. During the first set, Mrs. Court, after losing the first four games, rallied to win the next three, and was leading, 40-15, in the eighth game. But Miss Goolagong fought back to win that game and hold her service, and in the second set she took an early lead and widened it as the match progressed. With her victory she became the fifth youngest winner of the Wimbledon title in history and the youngest since 1959, when Maria Bueno won it. The silver platter symbolizing the tennis championship was presented to her by Princess Alexandra, president of the All-England Club. "I don't think I've woken up yet," Miss Goolagong said shortly after her victory, which earned her $4,300. "I'm still in a daze. I never thought I'd reach the final, let alone win." She celebrated her triumph that evening with friends at a London discotheque.

After Wimbledon, Miss Goolagong suffered some unexpected setbacks. In the finals of the Irish Open in Dublin on July 10, she lost to Mrs. Court, 6-3, 2-6, 6-3, and the following week, in the North of England championships at Hoylake, England, she lost her quarter-final match to Patti Hogan of the United States, 6-0, 4-6, 6-2. On August 1, 1971 she rallied to win the Dutch Open at Hilversum, defeating Christine Sanberg of Sweden.

As a registered player, Miss Goolagong has, since 1970, held professional status without being committed to any particular organization. Her earnings for 1971 were expected to amount to about $29,000. Edwards, who receives no commission from her, continues to handle her affairs as a labor of love and is content with the added publicity that she brings to his tennis school. She was not entered in the 1971 United States national championships at Forest Hills in New York, because Edwards felt that the strain of an American trip after her European tour would be too great for her, but she plans to compete in the United States in 1972.

Miss Goolagong's visit to South Africa in March 1971 caused considerable controversy, because she was the first nonwhite to compete in championship tennis in that apartheid-ridden country. Although Australian civil rights groups urged her to boycott the event and criticized her for accepting the status of "honorary white" that South African authorities conferred on her, she accepted the invitation on Edwards' advice after being assured that she would be accorded equal treatment. Although she takes pride in her ancestry, Miss Goolagong has at times become annoyed by constant references to her Aboriginal background. "It began to upset me," she has said. "I just want to be myself and be accepted for what I am." On one occasion she jokingly told a British journalist that unless he stopped asking questions about her race she would "point the bone" at him, referring to an ancient jinx imposed by Aboriginal tribesmen on their enemies.

An attractive young woman, five feet five inches tall and well-proportioned, Evonne Goolagong has short, dark, curly hair and a light-brown complexion. Several writers have noted her resemblance to the former child actress Shirley Temple. Her success on the tennis courts has been attributed to her fiercely aggressive style and her great speed, but her outstanding characteristics are her cheerful disposition, warmth, and enthusiasm, which have endeared her to the tennis public. According to Denis O'Brien, who interviewed her for the Australian news magazine the *Bulletin* (February 27, 1971), Miss Goolagong "has an al-most totally ingenuous attitude to the world around her, rarely reads newspapers, smiles a lot, hates saying goodbye to anyone she's come to know well, . . . and stays well within a random interest in the harmless hedonism of her generation—clothes, pop music, parties." As far as boys are concerned, "her career inhibits more than just casual relationships." For recreation she plays golf, and she spends much of her time singing, humming, or listening to popular music on records and on the radio. She remains close to her family and visits her hometown of Barellan about twice a year. "Tennis is my whole life," she says, "and I could not imagine any other."

References

Christian Sci Mon p15 Ap 25 '70 por; p12 Je 27 '70; p19 Je 7 '71 por
Life 71:32+ Jl 16 '71 pors
London Observer p7 Jl 4 '71 por
N Y Times p42 Jl 2 '71 por; p1+ Jl 3 '71 pors
N Y Times Mag p10+ Ag 29 '71 pors
Sports Illus 34:58+ F 15 '71 pors; 35: 14+ Jl 12 '71 por

GOULD, CHESTER

Nov. 20, 1900- Cartoonist
Address: b. Chicago Tribune, Tribune Tower, 435 N. Michigan Ave., Chicago, Ill. 60611; h. Woodstock, Ill. 60098

For forty years America's favorite comic-strip detective, Dick Tracy, has been demonstrating to his readers that crime does not pay. While the square-jawed sleuth and such bizarre adversaries and friends of his as Flattop and B.O. Plenty have become part of United States folklore, the strip's creator is relatively unknown to the general public. Cartoonist Chester Gould conceived the *Dick Tracy* strip in 1931, partly out of indignation over Prohibition-era gang violence in Chicago, where he was then a struggling newspaper artist. Publisher Joseph Medill Patterson, after rejecting cartoon ideas proffered by Gould for ten years, accepted the strip, which began appearing in the New York *Daily News* and other newspapers in October 1931. Since then *Dick Tracy*, while inspiring scores of other crime and adventure comics, has remained the most popular.

Chester Gould, the son of Gilbert R. and Alice (Miller) Gould, was born on November 20, 1900 in Pawnee, Oklahoma. His father was a printer with the weekly Pawnee *Courier-Dispatch* and, later, manager of the weekly *Advance-Democrat* in nearby Stillwater. Fondly remembering his father, Gould told Phil Santora in an interview for the New York *Sunday News* (April 4, 1971): "If God ever created a perfect human being, it was that man." He added that he "never knew anything but perfect happiness" in his rural childhood home. In adolescence he was responsible for a small truck farm.

Gould's artistic ambition manifested itself early. When he was twelve he entered a cartoon contest sponsored by Universal Pictures and won a $5-prize, and at fifteen he invested $20 in a correspondence course in drawing. But his father, who felt that an artist's career offered little security, wanted him to become a lawyer. In compromise, Gould attended Oklahoma A. & M. College (now Oklahoma State University) at Stillwater from 1919 to 1921, majoring in commerce and marketing. While in college he contributed cartoons to student publications and worked as a sports cartoonist for an Oklahoma City newspaper.

In 1921, armed with ideas for cartoons and a total capital of $50, Gould went to Chicago, then considered a Mecca for aspiring journalistic writers and artists. His prime target was Captain Joseph Medill Patterson, co-publisher of the Chicago *Tribune*, who was reputed to have an almost infallible grasp of what the public wanted. While trying to interest Patterson in his cartoon ideas he continued his commercial studies, at Northwestern University's night school. For two years he worked about eighteen hours a day, studying and attending classes, filling a succession of minor art jobs in studios and on such newspapers as the Chicago *Journal* and the Chicago *Herald Examiner*, and drawing cartoons that Captain Patterson invariably turned down.

In 1923 Gould graduated from Northwestern University and began importuning William A. Curley, the managing editor of William Randolph Hearst's Chicago *American*, for a position on the staff of the newspaper. He regularly left cartoons on Curley's desk, but the managing editor was unresponsive. Finally, in 1924, Gould invested $9 in an engraving of one of the cartoons. Taking the editorial page of one issue of the *American*, he pasted a proof of the engraving in the page's cartoon spot, over the drawing by regular cartoonist T. E. Powers, and left the revised page on Curley's desk. "It wasn't my work," Gould later admitted. "It was the maniacal approach that impressed him."

In working for the *American*, he began to wonder if his creative ability were commensurate with his ambition. *Fillum Fables*, a daily strip in which he satirized motion pictures, was syndicated by King Features without much success, and he himself conceded that his next creation, *Radio Cats*, in which felines in human dress made fun of another new entertainment marvel, was "strictly stinkeroo." By 1928 Gould, now a family man, was earning $100 a week, good pay for those days, but his prospects for more than middling success as a cartoonist appeared dim.

Meanwhile Gould continued undauntedly to barrage Captain Patterson with his cartoon ideas, and after Patterson moved east to publish the New York *Daily News*, Gould carried on his campaign by mail. In May 1929 some of the rejects came back with a personal note from Patterson. Encouraged beyond all logic, Gould quit his job with the *American*, drew five comic strips, and went to New York to lay them on Patterson's desk. All five were rejected. Returning to Chicago, Gould looked for employment for months before finally finding a job as an ad illustrator with the Chicago *Daily News* at a salary of $55 a week. While with the *Daily News* he tried his hand at an amazing-fact series of the

CHESTER GOULD

"Believe It Or Not" type, unsuccessfully. When he heard that Patterson needed an editorial-page cartoonist for his New York paper, Gould sent him editorial cartoons daily for four weeks, until he learned that Patterson had hired C. D. Batchelder for the job.

Early in 1931 Gould was working on a new cartoon strip about a policeman named Plainclothes Tracy. The inspiration for it was his personal outrage at such gangsters as Al Capone, whose mobs seemed to be operating with impunity in Chicago. At that time, comic strips were still essentially humorous. The rare instances of police and detective adventure were farcical, as in the burlesque *Hawkshaw the Detective*. In his nascent strip Gould broke the taboo against violence in the comics: one of his samples ended with mobsters—led by "Big Boy," who was obviously modeled after Capone—ready to roast Tracy's feet with an acetylene torch to make him reveal information. Editors of the Chicago *Daily News* to whom he showed the sample drawings found them "atrocious and impossible," and when Gould sent the strip to Patterson he expected it to be rejected as usual.

The answering telegram, dated August 13, 1931, is now framed in Gould's lavish home bar. It read: "Your Plainclothes Tracy has possibilities. Would like to see you when I go to Chicago next. Please call *Tribune* office Monday about noon for an appointment." Gould's interview with Patterson has been recounted in widely differing versions, but all agree that Patterson was responsible for changing Tracy's first name to Dick—a slang term for detective —and that he heavy-handedly revised the plot. As sketched out by Patterson and executed by Gould, the opening strips had Mr. Trueheart—a corner grocer and the father of Tracy's perennial sweetheart, Tess—murdered by gangsters. Tracy's solemn pledge to avenge the old man and his pursuit of the killers marked the genesis of forty years of crimebusting in the comics. Dick Tracy made his debut in the Detroit *Mirror* on October 4, 1931 and the New York *Daily News* began running the strip eight days later.

Although some editors and readers protested Gould's introduction of violence into the comic pages, the *Dick Tracy* comic strip soon attained immense popularity. Tracy's earliest adversaries, such as Redrum (murder spelled backwards) and Steve the Tramp, were unimaginative characters in comparison with the freakish criminals later created by Gould, with names appropriate to their physiques or personalities, from Doc Hump, brought to his deserved end by a rabid dog in 1934, to the current Pouch, a smuggler with a zipper under his chin. In between came the Brow, a foreign spy with a creased forehead who died impaled on a flagpole; the Midget, who was carried about by his wife in a bag and died by scalding in a Turkish bath; Influence, who hypnotized his victims with the aid of special contact lenses; Flyface, a shyster lawyer with flies constantly buzzing around his head; and Mr. and Mrs. Pruneface, B-B Eyes, Breathless Mahoney, Shakey, Oodles, 88 Keys, Mumbles, Itchy, Blowtop, Shoulders, and the Mole. Perhaps the most "popular" of the villains was Flattop, who appeared in *Dick Tracy* in 1944. A dim-witted thug with a head as flat as a tabletop, Flattop derived his name from the World War II slang term for aircraft carrier. When he died, by drowning, fans wired condolences, sent flowers, held mock funerals, and facetiously tried to claim the body.

Although Tracy's associates in the battle against crime—including his young sidekick Junior, Chief Pat Patton (who succeeded Tracy's earlier boss, Chief Brandon), Detective Sam Catchem, and Policewoman Lizz—have often been overshadowed by his more macabre criminal adversaries, Gould has also introduced a colorful sideshow of sympathetic characters who are incidental to the main action of the strip but provide much of its human interest. Probably the most popular of these has been B.O. Plenty, the bewhiskered, tobacco-chewing, malodorous hayseed, who first made his appearance in 1946. At the insistence of fans, Gould had to bring him back again and again. Eventually, B.O. Plenty married an equally unappetizing character, an unkempt hag named Gravel Gertie, and out of their union issued, miraculously, a beautiful daughter, Sparkle Plenty, born with waist-long golden hair. On the occasion of the marriage of B.O. and Gertie, fans sent gifts of tarnished silver, tobacco, and deodorants, to Gould's office, and Sparkle's birth brought a deluge of baby clothes—and added income for Gould in the form of royalties for the Sparkle Plenty doll. With sales amounting to some $3,000,000 during its first year on the market, the doll surpassed even the Shirley Temple doll in popularity.

The fans also took a hand in the long-unconsummated romance of Dick Tracy and Tess Trueheart. "Women sometimes complain that Tracy ought to conquer this eighteen-year hesitancy and marry the girl," Robert M. Yoder wrote in the *Saturday Evening* Post (December 17, 1949), "but he never will." Yoder proved to be mistaken, for on Christmas Day in 1949 Dick and Tess were married. They have since become the parents of a daughter, called Bonnie Braids. Other human interest episodes incidental to Tracy's crime-busting activities include the marriage of Sparkle Plenty, now grown up, to a

struggling young cartoonist; and Junior's marriage to Moon Maid, a celestial creature whom he met in a science fiction episode, a lunar excursion arranged by Tracy's millionaire inventor friend Diet Smith.

Despite his outlandish characters, his occasional journeys into the realm of science fiction, and his tendency, at times, to place his hero in almost hopeless situations, Gould prides himself on a high degree of realism in his depiction of police work. He has taken university courses in crime detection and has familiarized himself with the techniques of the FBI and Scotland Yard. A lagniappe regularly added to his Sunday panels is "Crime Stoppers," a small, boxed-off feature containing a simple hint on crime prevention for laymen. Gould is justifiably proud of his anticipations of technological innovations in police work. The best known is the two-way wrist radio, which Dick Tracy began to use in 1946. and closed-circuit television, which first appeared in the comic strip in 1947. Both of those innovations have since been introduced into actual police work. Among the current prognostications presented by Gould in the strip is a two-way wrist television set.

Gould still maintains an office at the Chicago *Tribune* but he does most of his work in his studio at his home in Woodstock, Illinois, assisted by his brother, Ray Gould, who does the lettering for the strips, and by Rick Fletcher, who draws the backgrounds. He usually works about three months ahead of schedule, and he has a reputation for consistently meeting his deadlines. His drawings, which he and fellow cartoonists sometimes describe as "blueprints" of the action, are admittedly simplistic, and Gould makes no pretense of being a great artist. Describing his drawing technique, Stephen Becker wrote in *Comic Art in America* (Simon & Schuster, 1959): "The elements in each panel are reduced to their essential minimum, and are then blocked in, flatly, squarely and powerfully. . . . Light and shadow are usually ignored, and each panel is drawn as though under a battery of floodlights. . . . The faces and figures are equally simple." Gould himself has ascribed 60 percent of the strip's success to his story line and only 40 percent to the drawing.

Writing in *Holiday* (June 1958), Alfred Bester attempted to analyze Dick Tracy's popularity. "The Morality Play simplicity of names and plot in *Dick Tracy* is characteristic of the strip," Bester observed. "The names clearly describe the characters; the plots are invariably elemental conflicts between good and evil. In Dick Tracy you're never in doubt about 'the good guys' and 'the bad guys'."

Distributed by the Chicago Tribune-New York News Syndicate, *Dick Tracy* was by 1960 appearing in over 500 newspapers with an estimated readership of some 100,000,000, extending to South America and Australia. In Hollywood, Republic Pictures produced three serials based on the strip, in 1937, 1938, and 1939, and RKO made several Dick Tracy features, beginning in 1945. A television series based on Gould's creation, produced by WPIX-TV in New York, was syndicated nationally in the early 1960's. Gould has also received royalties from the sale of a multitude of commercial products with a Dick Tracy theme, including watches, wallets, flashlights, sweatshirts, and bubble gum.

Over the years, Gould has received a number of awards, including one from the Police Athletic League, in 1949, and another from the Associated Police Communications Officers, in 1953. In recognition of Dick Tracy's consistently good grooming, the American Institute of Men's and Boys' Wear awarded Gould a special plaque in 1957. In 1959 the National Cartoonists Society presented him with its Reuben Award as the year's outstanding cartoonist, and his work was featured in the Cavalcade of Comics exhibition presented at the Smithsonian Institution in 1966. Fellow cartoonist Al Capp, the creator of Li'l Abner, has paid Gould the supreme compliment of satirizing Dick Tracy in the "Adventures of Fearless Fosdick," the strip-within-a-strip that is Li'l Abner's own favorite comic. Dick Tracy has also been utilized in the comic strip paintings of pop artists, most notably by Roy Lichtenstein.

In 1970 Chelsea House published an elaborate volume entitled The Celebrated Cases of Dick Tracy, edited by Herb Galewitz, with an introduction by Ellery Queen. In it the reader may observe the changes that Gould's style has undergone through the years and the metamorphosis of his hero from a jaunty young man with a fixed smile to his later appearance as the more mature, square-jawed, eagle-nosed crime-buster. Reviewing the book for the New York Times (December 11, 1970) Walter Clemons found the early Dick Tracy strips "amazingly badly drawn, and therefore fascinating" but saw a marked improvement in Gould's work of the 1940's.

Chester Gould and Edna Gauger were married on November 6, 1926. They have a married daughter, Jean, and a grandson named Tracy Richard O'Connell. The Gould home in Woodstock, some sixty miles east of Chicago, is a remodeled white twelve-room farmhouse with a thirty-foot heated swimming pool, a bar with a revolving floor, and a miniature golf course. It is situated on a 130-acre farm that produces corn, alfalfa, and some livestock. The household includes two schnauzers, called Rocky and Sis. Once described as looking like "a kindly Sunday school teacher," Gould is five feet eight inches tall, has gray hair and blue eyes, and wears horn-rimmed glasses. Once overweight, he is now down to 165 pounds and keeps his weight there by swimming, jogging, and watching his diet. Gould smokes cigars, indulges in an occasional bourbon and water, and enjoys driving in the country and playing poker. He belongs to the National Cartoonists Society, Lambda Chi Alpha fraternity, and the Woodstock Country Club. Thoroughly absorbed in his work, he has no thought of retiring.

References

Coronet 4:122+ Je '66 por
N Y Sunday News mag p3+ D 18 '55 por; mag p4+ Ap 4 '71 por
Newsweek 58:102+ O 16 '61 por
Sat Eve Post 222:22+ D 17 '49 pors
Who's Who in America, 1970-71

GOULD, ELLIOTT

Aug. 29, 1938- Actor
Address: b. c/o Brodsky-Gould Productions, Inc., 152 W. 58th St., New York 10019

The top box-office attraction of an era when film-goers have rejected classically handsome movie stars and improbably heroic heroes in favor of more casual players and characters is Elliott Gould. He has reached stardom by portraying amiable, irreverent, unmistakably urban, and desperately funny young men whose problems strike a responsive chord with many Americans. Those roles include a staid young lawyer experimenting with adultery and wife-swapping in a vain attempt to be a swinger (Bob & Carol & Ted & Alice), a war medic coping with the madness of warfare by playing pranks in his off-duty hours (M*A*S*H), and a graduate student who discovers he is too old for student revolt and too young to join the establishment (Getting Straight). "Gould always seems to be caught up in social—and sexual—tension," observed the writers of a Time cover story on the actor (September 7, 1970) in describing his screen persona. "He embodies an inner need to be hip at the risk of seeming silly, the struggle not to give in to the indignity and/or insanity of contemporary life. The . . . pseudo-hipsters . . . have made Elliott Gould a star for an uptight age. In Gould they see all their tensions, frustrations and insecurities personified and turned into nervous comedy that both tickles and stings with the shock of recognition."

Gould's comic gifts and naturalistic acting technique matured after a long apprenticeship that included an unhappy childhood as a semiprofessional tap dancer and a promising but largely unfulfilled early career in Broadway musical comedy. Until recently he was best known as the husband of the singing superstar Barbra Streisand, from whom he was separated in 1969. After making an auspicious film debut in The Night They Raided Minsky's (1968), Gould hit his phenomenally successful stride with the film, Bob & Carol & Ted & Alice (1969), which won him an Academy Award nomination. Since then he has been in constant demand and has formed his own production company, Brodsky-Gould Productions. The company's first film, Little Murders, based on Jules Feiffer's Off-Broadway comedy hit, was released by Twentieth Century-Fox in 1971.

"Twentieth Century-Fox hasn't gotten around to casting the lead yet for Portnoy's Complaint," a Newsweek writer quipped (March 9, 1970), "but if life is preparation for art, the studio's choice must fall upon . . . Gould." The self-avowed product of a traumatic middle-class Jewish upbringing, Elliott Gould was born Elliott Goldstein on August 29, 1938, the only child of Bernard and Lucille (Raver) Goldstein. He was born in Brooklyn, where he lived in the Bensonhurst section until his adolescence, when he moved with his parents to West Orange, New Jersey. "I don't like to talk about my childhood," Gould told Josh Greenfeld in an interview for Show (February

ELLIOTT GOULD

1970). "It was a terribly unhappy time for me. I didn't grow up with a sense of adventure or curiosity like you're supposed to. I just grew up trying to be nice to my parents."

What Mrs. Goldstein wanted most for her son was a show business career far removed from the garment industry in which her husband worked. (Gould's parents are now divorced and his father is married to his childhood sweetheart.) Anxious to please, Elliott took speech, singing, dance, and drama lessons at Charles Lowe's Broadway show business school for children in Manhattan, where his mother enrolled him at the age of eight. Lowe developed his pupils into a vaudeville act that he booked at temples, hospitals, *bar mitzvahs*, and weddings. Lowe's fledglings also appeared on television, and by the time he was ten Elliott was performing regularly on such local TV shows as *The Bonny Maid Linoleum Versatile Varieties* and occasionally on network shows like the *Colgate Comedy Hour*. The name "Gould" was bestowed on him the first time he appeared on television because his mother thought it sounded better than Goldstein. When he was not performing, his mother kept him busy modeling for photographers and fashion shows. At eleven Gould was tapping out dance numbers at the Palace Theatre as an assistant to a vaudevillian named Jimmy Callahan. "When an entertainer needed a stooge," Gould's father told Mary Cronin for the *Time* cover story (September 7, 1970), "Elliot would be the one they'd choose. He could do a dozen dialects— German, Italian, Jewish, all of them."

After obtaining his early schooling at P.S. 247, Seth Low Junior High School, and a local Brooklyn Hebrew school, Gould enrolled at the Professional Children's School in Manhattan. During his summer vacations he performed at hotels in the Catskill "borscht belt," and one summer he worked in summer stock. According to the *Time* cover story, he did not confine all his acting to the stage: "Friends recall that he would go into a diner, sit next to a little old lady and calmly make a meal out of his paper napkin—complete with salt, pepper and ketchup . . . or call up relatives and con-

found them with some uncanny voice impersonation of the rabbi or the neighborhood butcher. It was the kind of desperately funny behavior that was a frustrated child's plea for attention and a cry for help."

After graduating from the Children's Professional School in 1955, Gould was accepted at Columbia College of Columbia University; according to some sources he studied there for a year. In any case, he began taking ballet lessons and made the Broadway rounds looking for dance chorus work. He landed his first job by telephoning a producer and impersonating an agent who sang the praises of an unknown named Elliott Gould. That earned him $125 a week as a chorus boy in *Rumple*, a short-lived musical that opened on Broadway in November 1957. Over the next few years, he appeared on Ernie Kovacs' television show, in the small part of Earl Jorgensen in the hit 1958 Broadway musical *Say, Darling* and in its 1959 revival at the New York City Center, and in a Jones Beach summer stock production of *Hit the Deck*. Often without work, he lived precariously, especially after he developed a compulsion for gambling. To pay off his gambling debts he once pawned his father's jewelry and for a time sold bogus advertising space in a nonexistent labor union magazine. He also took odd jobs as a department store toy demonstrator, a rug-cleaner salesman, and as a night elevator man at a West Side residential hotel. His prospects brightened when he was cast as the Usher, First Warden, and Priest in *Irma La Douce*, which opened at the Plymouth Theatre on September 29, 1960. During the long run of that David Merrick production Gould succeeded Fred Gwynne as Polyte-le-Mou.

At the suggestion of a stage manager, Gould was auditioned for the leading role in Merrick's next production, *I Can Get It For You Wholesale*, and landed the part. When the musical opened at the Shubert Theatre on March 22, 1962, Gould received mixed reviews. As Harry Bogen, a ruthless heel who cons, lies, and bullies his way to the top in the Seventh Avenue garment trade, Gould struck many critics as too convincingly caddish to engender the necessary sympathy in an audience. And to make matters worse, he was virtually eclipsed by a nineteen-year-old newcomer named Barbra Streisand, who stopped the show in the small part of Miss Marmelstein. Gould, however, was captivated by the talented, eccentric girl as soon as he met her at the auditions, and by the time the show opened he had moved into her small apartment on Third Avenue over a seafood restaurant. They were married on March 21, 1963, three months after *I Can Get It For You Wholesale* ended its run.

A few days after their marriage in Carson City, Nevada, Gould flew to London to appear as one of the sailors in a revival of *On the Town*. When he returned to the United States, he toured with Liza Minnelli in a road company of *The Fantasticks* and in 1964 costarred with Carol Burnett in a CBS-TV special presentation of the musical *Once Upon a Mattress*. His next assignment was the male lead in *Drat! the Cat!*, a feeble spoof on nineteenth-century melodramas that folded after only a week in October 1965. It was a difficult period for Gould, and his wife's success only highlighted his own failures. He spent much of his time managing her career and fending off reporters greedy for details on life with the illustrious Streisand.

In retrospect, however, Gould has called that time an important turning point, for he began to study with Lee Strasberg at the Actors Studio, where he learned, he maintains, to act for the first time, and he entered psychoanalysis. His professional growth was evident when he opened in Jules Feiffer's *Little Murders* on Broadway in May 1967. But, although several critics admired his performance as Alfred Chamberlain, the play's apathetic anti-hero in a New York erupting with senseless violence, they were alienated by Feiffer's black humor and *Little Murders* closed after only a week.

During the summer of 1967 Gould toured with Shelley Winters in Murray Schisgal's *Luv*. He then filmed two pictures. One, "The Confession," has never been released; the other was *The Night They Raided Minsky's* (United Artists, 1968), a look at 1920's burlesque on New York's Lower East Side. After completing *Minsky's*, in which he had a supporting role as the harried young manager of a burlesque house, Gould was involved in an ill-fated theatrical venture, as the lead in Schisgal's *A Way of Life*, which never reached Broadway. Meanwhile, he had signed a contract with Columbia Pictures to appear in the comedy that became the talk of 1969.

Bob & Carol & Ted & Alice deals with the sexual adventures of two couples—married, childraising, financially secure, and fast approaching middle age—who are bent on proving that they can keep up with the latest in hip and swinging lifestyles. The less inhibited Bob and Carol return from a weekend spent at an Esalen-type sensitivity institute and start experimenting with their liberated sexual ideas to the horror and fascination of their square friends, Ted (Gould) and Alice. By the fadeout, all four have had their flings, but none of them can really accept the new morality. Although the sensibilities of some critics were ruffled by the fact that a commercial Hollywood comedy had been chosen to open the 1969 New York Film Festival, most reviewers felt that it deserved the honor. Almost all of them praised Gould's performance as the easygoing, conventional Ted, who is bewildered by his wife and friends and the new demands imposed on him. The Canadian critic Martin Knelman represented the consensus of opinion when he wrote in the Toronto *Globe & Mail* (December 24, 1969), "The performers achieve a marvellous improvisational quality; while they're all good, it's Elliott Gould who walks away with the movie, coming into his own as a light comedian."

The resounding commercial success of *Bob & Carol & Ted & Alice* was matched by Gould's next film, *M*A*S*H*. If the former was a hip, up-to-date specimen of the old Hollywood sex comedy, *M*A*S*H* was a lacerating example of the war service comedy genre, or as the British critic Richard Roud put it, "a *Carry on, Doctor* played for real." Concerned with life at a Mobile Army Surgical Hospital station during the Korean War, *M*A*S*H* juxtaposes the off-duty horseplay and sexual adventures of three young surgeons with their duties of patching up mutilated bodies from the front line. *M*A*S*H* won first prize at the Cannes Film Festival, generally ecstatic reviews, and further glory for Elliott Gould, who as Trapper John played a coolly hip young surgeon determined to undermine the Army's bureaucratic inanities.

Although it also prospered at the box office, Gould's third starring film, *Getting Straight* (Columbia, 1970), did not fare as well with critics. The majority opinion held that it put down both the student activists and the university establishment. But as Harry Bailey, a graduate student caught between university bureaucracy and student revolutionaries, Gould again won commendation. "The insidiousness of this film lies in Gould's presence and performance, because he is simple perfection in his embodiment of the film's anti-hero," wrote Judith Crist (*New York*, May 18, 1970), who classified *Getting Straight* as a campus "freak-show" and later named it one of the ten worst films of the year. Gould suffered his first setback at the box-office with *Move* (Twentieth Century-Fox, 1970), an insubstantial comedy in which he plays a neurotic would-be serious writer who walks dogs and writes pornography. Elliott Gould's fifth starring film, *I Love My Wife* (Universal Pictures, 1970), which opened late in December 1970, received generally lukewarm reviews.

During the summer of 1970 Gould filmed the screen version of *Little Murders* under the direction of Alan Arkin, who staged the play's highly successful Off-Broadway revival in 1969. Gould's next assignment took him to Sweden, where he began work on Ingmar Bergman's first English-language feature film, *The Touch* (Cinerama, 1971). In his first noncomic role, Gould played an American archaeologist in Sweden involved with a Swedish doctor's wife. In partnership with Jack Brodsky, a former Hollywood film publicist, Gould has purchased film rights through Brodsky-Gould Productions to Bernard Malamud's *A New Life* and *The Assistant*, Bruce Jay Friedman's *The Dick*, and Dr. David Rubin's *Everything You Always Wanted to Know About Sex*.

Elliott Gould and Barbra Streisand, who have one son, Jason, agreed to an amicable separation in 1969, and they were divorced in 1971. The motion picture actor spends as much time as possible in New York, where he maintains a duplex apartment in a Greenwich Village townhouse that he has decorated with such trophies of urban life as a large Breyer's ice cream sign and a copper shoeshine stand. Six feet three inches tall and weighing about 205 pounds, Gould has brown eyes and bushy black curly hair. He often sports a large mustache. A sports buff, he follows the New York teams avidly and works out in a gym by playing three-man basketball. Gould does not drink, but he enjoys an occasional cigar and has a passion for sunflower seeds. Interviewers find him likeable and exuberant, a compulsive talker who laces his speech with profanities, sports slang, and nervous one-liners and who loves to discuss his psychoanalysis. The National Association of Theatre Owners named Gould the Male Star of 1970.

References

Fortune 82:109+ O '70 pors
N Y Post p44 Ag 22 '70 por
N Y Times II p15 O 5 '69 por
Washington (D.C.) Post mag p9+ Jl 26 '70 pors

Biographical Encyclopaedia and Who's Who of the American Theatre (1966)
Who's Who in America, 1970-71

GRAHAM, KATHARINE (MEYER)

June 16, 1917- Newspaper company executive
Address: b. Washington Post Company, 1515 L St., N.W., Washington, D.C. 20005; h. 2920 R St., N.W., Washington, D.C. 20007; 870 United Nations Plaza, New York 10017

As president since 1963 of the Washington Post Company, Katharine Graham has directed the newspaper, magazine, television, and radio enterprises of that organization in accordance with family traditions of intellectual freedom, public service, and business acumen. The Washington *Post*, of which she has been publisher since 1969, has become the capital's most influential newspaper and, therefore, one of the most powerful in the United States. Another of the company's important publications is *Newsweek*, whose circulation of some 2,500,000 is the second largest of any American weekly news magazine. Mrs. Graham is a "working publisher," as she has been called in tribute, who relies on the expertise of professionals, allows her editors maximum responsibility, and provides generous budgets to attract some of the top reporting talent in the country.

The fourth in a family of five children, Katharine Meyer Graham was born in New York City on June 16, 1917 to Eugene Meyer, a banker, and Agnes Elizabeth (Ernst) Meyer, an author and philanthropist. She and her brother and three sisters were reared in a manner that encouraged a sense of public responsibility. "Father was very strong," Katharine Graham told Judith Michaelson in an interview for an article in the New York *Post* (November 29, 1969). "There was a great deal of emphasis on not behaving rich and a lot of emphasis on having to *do* something. It never occurred to me that I didn't have to work." In an article in *Vogue* (January 1, 1967) Arthur Schlesinger Jr. wrote that her mother had "long been a force in public affairs, bearing down like a galleon in full sail, all guns firing, on the enemies of education or civil rights or free speech. They were a formidable couple—Eugene Meyer, emphatic and imperious; Agnes Meyer, copious and volcanic."

Mrs. Meyer's devotion to literature, to collecting paintings, and to entertaining celebrities like Paul Claudel and Thomas Mann all contributed to the cultivated atmosphere of Katharine Graham's girlhood home in Washington, D.C. She attended Madeira School, a preparatory school in Greenway, Virginia, where she worked on the student newspaper. In 1935 she entered Vassar College, but the following year transferred to what she considered the more stimulating campus of the University of Chicago, which offered a course in the history of ideas that she recalls as having been "absolutely marvelous." Sharing in the excitement over politics that prevailed at the university, she became a liberal-minded New Dealer. Her father had bought the financially ailing Washington *Post* for $875,000 in 1933 and was spending several millions of dollars to develop it. During her summer vacations Katharine Graham returned to Washington to work on the paper. After earning her B.A. degree in 1938, she went to California to take a job as a reporter for the San Francisco *News*, a Scripps-Howard paper. Her beat was the waterfront.

"The next year my father came out to get me and bring me back to Washington," Mrs. Graham has related, as quoted by Martin Mayer in "Lady as Publisher" (*Harper's Magazine*, December 1968). She then joined the editorial staff of the *Post,* and also, from 1939 to 1945, was employed in the circulation and editorial departments of the Sunday edition of that paper. On June 5, 1940 she married Philip L. Graham, a Harvard Law School graduate and law clerk for Supreme Court Justice Felix Frankfurter. Her work took second place to her marriage. When her husband entered the Army Air Forces for World War II service, she accompanied him from one camp to another until he was sent to the Pacific theatre of operations. She then went back to her job on the *Post*. As she later told Martin Mayer, in the early years of her marriage she had been eager to "learn how to cook and run a house," not knowing even "how to order a tomato on the telephone," but she kept on working because her husband did not want to live off a rich father-in-law.

Major Philip Graham was discharged from the Army in 1945. By January 1946 Eugene Meyer had persuaded him to join the Washington *Post* as associate publisher. Six months later he became publisher. In 1948 Meyer sold all the voting stock of the company for $1 to the Grahams, who assured a continuation of the *Post's* tradition of "virile, strong, and independent" concern for the general welfare. The relationship between Mrs. Graham's father and her husband was a close one. They worked together in acquiring a morning paper, the Washington *Times-Herald,* the *Post's* competitor, which they bought from Colonel Robert R. McCormick in March 1954 for a reported $8,500,000. In March 1961 Graham arranged the purchase by the Washington Post Company of the magazine *Newsweek* from the Vincent Astor Foundation for about $8,000,000. He also expanded the radio and television operations of the company and in 1962 cooperated with Otis Chandler of the

Los Angeles *Times* in establishing an international news service, which now supplies information on world events to more than 300 newspapers in the United States and foreign countries.

Plagued by psychiatric problems for some years, Philip Graham shot himself to death in 1963. Mrs. Graham was then a stylish Washington matron whose time was largely taken up with looking after her Georgetown home and raising her four children, but she had remained deeply interested in the affairs of the company. As pointed out in *Business Week* (May 27, 1967), "She was determined to preserve the family character of the business, and that meant taking the managerial reins herself." In September 1963 on assuming the presidency of the company, the position formerly held by her husband, she expressed her philosophy as a publisher by quoting three sentences from a 1935 statement of her father: "The newspaper's duty is to its readers and to the public at large, and not to the private interests of the owner. In the pursuit of truth, the newspaper shall be prepared to make sacrifice of its material fortunes, if such cause be necessary for the public good. The newspaper shall not be the ally of any special interest, but shall be fair and free and wholesome in its outlook on public affairs and public men."

At the time of Mrs. Graham's election to the presidency the company's holdings consisted of the *Post, Newsweek, Art News* magazine, WTOP Radio and WTOP-TV in Washington, WJXT-TV in Jacksonville, Florida, a 50 percent interest in the Los Angeles Times-Washington Post News Service, and a 49 percent interest in the Bowaters Mersey Paper Company in Nova Scotia, which provides most of the *Post's* newsprint. Later additions to the company were a 45 percent interest in the *Paris Herald Tribune* (now the *International Herald Tribune*), a 50 percent interest in *Book World* (a Sunday supplement), and stations WLBW-TV in Miami and WKCY Radio in Cincinnati.

Arthur Schlesinger Jr. described in his *Vogue* article how Katharine Graham took control of her company: "She studied the operations, asked questions, noted deficiencies, consulted with her staff and with old friends outside, like Walter Lippmann and James Reston, worked out her plans, and, in due course began to make her moves." Probably her most important step was to bring in skilled and experienced newsmen to improve the journalistic quality of the paper. She is said to be an excellent judge of the right man for the right job, and in 1965 in what is considered a major decision she appointed Benjamin C. Bradlee, then Washington bureau chief for *Newsweek*, to the position of managing editor of the *Post*. (He later became executive editor.) Mrs. Graham gave Bradlee a free hand to sharpen the format and to hire top-notch reporters who would turn in probing and perceptive news stories. One of her foremost professional principles is to back up her editors. Although she sometimes questions editorial policy on specific issues, she does not dictate policy. "You want intelligent, large-scale thinkers and writers," she observed to Judith Michaelson, "and

KATHARINE GRAHAM

nobody for whom you have any respect would take an edict from on high."

By 1966 the Washington *Post* had come to rank third in the nation in advertising linage, surpassed only by the Los Angeles *Times* and the New York *Times*. Katharine Graham had raised the editorial budget of the paper to $6,000,000 a year by 1970, doubling the editorial staff and increasing salaries substantially. She also invested some $25,000,000 in a new plant. In a recent financial statement the Washington Post Company reported sales of more than $125,000,000 annually and profits before taxes of more than $10,000,000. By 1970 the daily circulation of the *Post* had exceeded 500,000 and the Sunday circulation had exceeded 650,000, giving it a commanding lead over the *Evening Star* and the *Daily News*, Washington's two other leading newspapers.

The *Post* has also become the competitor of the New York *Times*. In his evaluation of the Washington paper in the *Wall Street Journal* (August 18, 1970) Stanford N. Sesser quoted Mrs. Graham as admitting, "We're never going to be best the way the New York *Times* is best because we have a different situation here. They can write to a highly educated, specialized audience, but we are a mass paper." The *Post*, accordingly, provides many of the features, such as cartoons and a lovelorn column, of a hometown paper. In influence, however, the *Post* has grown considerably since Mrs. Graham moved into the office of the company's president. It is read and consulted by the employees and officials of almost all the important government agencies and departments, by the staffs of diplomatic missions of countries from all over the world, and by the members of Washington's enormous press corps.

Among the *Post's* readers is Vice-President Spiro Agnew, who has deplored the influence of the paper on the nation's capital. "The *Post* supported Mr. Agnew for Governor of Maryland," Sesser recalled in his *Wall Street Journal* article, "but it compared his nomination for the Vice Presidency with the appointment by the Roman emperor Caligula of his horse as proconsul. An Agnew associate says the comment 'was the lowest blow he has ever received in politics.'" In November 1969 in an attack on the news media of the liberal establishment, which he considers subversive, he criticized the Washington Post Company for "monopolization" of vehicles of public information. Replying to his charges, Mrs. Graham asserted, "Vice-President Agnew's remarks about the Washington Post Company are not supported by the facts. The Washington *Post, Newsweek,* WTOP-TV, and WTOP Radio decidedly do not 'grind out the same editorial line.' It is a long-standing policy of the Post Company to enlist in each of their enterprises the best professional journalists we can find and give them a maximum of freedom in which to work. Each branch is operated autonomously. They compete vigorously with one another. They disagree on many issues. We think that the result is journalism of a high caliber that is notable for a diversity of voices on a wide range of public issues." The *Post,* in fact, once ran an editorial criticizing its own news coverage of a story, and at least one of its columnists has attacked another in print.

In behalf of freedom of the press, in 1968 Katharine Graham was one of ten top executives of the nation's largest newspapers, news magazines, and television networks to send a protest to Mayor Richard J. Daley of Chicago on the police treatment of newsmen during the Democratic National Convention. She was also one of the signers of a telegram to Milton S. Eisenhower, chairman of the National Commission on the Causes and Prevention of Violence, requesting that he look into "the subject of police violence aimed at repressing news coverage of such events as the Chicago demonstrations."

In June 1971 the Washington *Post,* along with the New York *Times,* became embroiled in controversy with the United States government over their right to publish excerpts from a classified Pentagon study on United States military involvement in Vietnam that was compiled during the Johnson administration. After first the *Times* and then the *Post* were restrained from publishing the Pentagon papers by court orders issued in mid-June, the United States Supreme Court upheld their action in printing the secret documents on June 30, 1971, in what was considered to be a major victory for freedom of the press.

Since January 1969, when she succeeded John W. Sweeterman, Katharine Graham has held the title of publisher of the Washington *Post,* in addition to the position of president of the company. She attends all important meetings of that paper and usually spends two days a week in New York City attending similar *Newsweek* meetings. According to Donald Robinson's account in *The 100 Most Important People in the World* (1970), when in Washington she leaves for work at about ten or eleven o'clock and is driven to her office in her chauffeured limousine. She usually lunches with a celebrity in her private dining room, often inviting top editors and specialists to join her. A round of evening parties is also part of her working day. She has extensive social connections and her edi-

tors say she is a fine news source. In 1965 she gave a dinner dance in her Georgetown home in honor of the writer Truman Capote. He reciprocated with an elegant party in her honor in the fall of 1966 at the Plaza Hotel in Manhattan, to which he invited more than 500 guests.

Mrs. Graham is a director of Bowaters Mersey Paper Company. She was a member of the First Lady's Committee for a More Beautiful Capital, is on the advisory committee to the John F. Kennedy School of Government for the Institute of Politics at Harvard, and is a member of the public policy committee of the Advertising Council, the governing board of the Business Committee for the Arts, and the Committee for Economic Development. She is a trustee of George Washington University, the American Assembly of Columbia University, the University of Chicago, and St. Alban's School. She is a member of Theta Sigma Phi, the journalism society, and belongs to the Women's National Press Club in Washington, D.C. and the Cosmopolitan Club in New York City. In 1968 she received an honorary degree from Dartmouth University and in 1969, an award for outstanding personal achievement in professional journalism from the American Newspaper Woman's Club. She received a gold medal in 1970 from the National Institute of Social Sciences for her "distinguished services to humanity."

Besides her house in Georgetown, Katharine Graham has a farm in Virginia and a Manhattan apartment in the United Nations Plaza. Her children are Elizabeth Morris (Mrs. Yann R. Weymouth), David Edward, William Welsh, and Stephen Meyer. She is a slim, tall, chic woman with graying brown hair and brown eyes. Playing tennis is one of her favorite recreations. In his *Harper's* article Martin Mayer wrote that she is "a rather lonely widow and by temperament dependent on men." Judith Michaelson, however, who described her as "reserved and rather shy and very patrician," quoted Mrs. Graham as objecting to being called a lonely widow: "I have to *fight* to get two hours to myself. I wish I were lonelier."

References

Bsns W p158+ My 27 '67
Harpers 237:90+ D '68 por
N Y Post p25 N 29 '69 por
Vogue 149:108+ Ja 1 '67 por
Wall St J p1+ Ag 18 '70
Washington (D.C.) Post A p2 S 21 '63 por
Who's Who in America, 1970-71

GREER, GERMAINE

Jan. 29, 1939- Australian writer; educator
Address: b. c/o University of Warwick, Coventry, Warwickshire, England; c/o Diana Crawfurd Ltd., 5 King St., London, WC2E 8HN, England

The current wave of feminism has had a number of widely publicized standard-bearers in the

United States, but the only media "star" to emerge so far outside that country is Germaine Greer, the tart-tongued author of *The Female Eunuch*. In 1964 Miss Greer left her native Australia for England, where, until the publication of her best-selling book, she taught English literature at a Midlands university and enjoyed a modest reputation as an underground journalist and television personality. Since the appearance of *The Female Eunuch* in 1970, she has been given the full celebrity treatment in Great Britain and in the United States, where she made a promotional tour in 1971 to herald the American publication of the book.

Writing in an acerbic and often racy style, Miss Greer argues in *The Female Eunuch* that society has symbolically castrated women by foisting on them a passive, insipid, and "feminine" role that they must renounce to regain their sexuality and natural energies. Because she contends that men too have fallen victim to the present deplorable state of affairs—and because she herself frankly proclaims her own heterosexuality—Miss Greer's book has been acclaimed by men as well as women. *The Female Eunuch* was published by MacGibbon and Kee in Great Britain and by McGraw-Hill in the United States.

The oldest child in a conservative, middle-class family, Germaine Greer was born near Melbourne, Australia on January 29, 1939 and grew up in that city. She often tells interviewers that her mother, Margaret May Mary (Lanfrancam) Greer, gave birth to her firstborn on a cattle station outside Melbourne during a bush fire, but it is not clear whether the family actually lived there. Her father, Eric Reginald Greer, left Australia to fight in World War II shortly after she was born and was gone for six years. After his return her sister, Alida Jane, and her brother, Barry John, were born. Her reports indicate that Miss Greer's childhood was intensely unhappy. "Our society has created the myth of the broken home which is the source of so many ills," she wrote in *The Female Eunuch*, "and yet the unbroken home which ought to have broken is an even greater source of tension, as I can attest from my own bitter experience." She has described her mother as a bored and frustrated housewife who vented her repressed fury on her children by beating them, and her father, who was the advertising manager of a newspaper, as an aloof man who stayed away from the domestic turmoil and nagging at home as much as possible. Germaine ran away from home at seventeen, was forced to return, and left permanently at eighteen.

She was educated on various government scholarships, starting with a junior scholarship to Star of the Sea Convent, in Gardenvale, Victoria, outside Melbourne. After graduating from the convent school in 1956 she attended the University of Melbourne, where she was active in theatre groups, wrote drama criticism, and served on the aboriginal scholarships committee. In 1959 she obtained the B.A. degree with honors in English and French literature. A year later she began graduate work at the University of Sydney, which awarded her the M.A. degree in English with first-class honors in 1961 and made her a senior tutor.

GERMAINE GREER

While a student Miss Greer held jobs as a waitress, a housekeeper, and a hat-check girl. After university she taught for a time in a girls' school in a working-class neighborhood. In 1964 she obtained a Commonwealth Scholarship that enabled her to attend Newnham College of Cambridge University, where she obtained her Ph.D. degree after submitting a dissertation on Shakespeare's early comedies. Around 1967 she obtained a position as a lecturer in English at the University of Warwick, which is located some ninety miles north of London.

While lecturing on Elizabethan and Jacobean drama at Warwick, Germaine Greer indulged in a number of outside activities. She dabbled in acting and appeared for a year on a daffy television show emanating from Manchester, for which she did such things as asking a group of housewives to stage a mock shootout in their supermarket. Since eighteen she had been a fan of jazz and popular music, and in London she mixed easily with rock musicians and underground personalities. She began writing articles for the *Listener* and the *Spectator*, as well as for such underground journals as the pornographic British magazine *Oz*, and she was one of the founders of *Suck*, a pornographic newspaper printed in Amsterdam. In time her repartee and poise before the cameras made her something of a personality on British talk shows.

In an interview with Helen Dudar of the New York *Post* (April 10, 1971), Miss Greer recalled that she was a late starter so far as feminism is concerned. "I was always a freak, which is a terrific advantage," she told the newspaperwoman. "It takes a monster to see what's monstrous in life. But I was no more emancipated than the average black person who's made it and thinks anyone black can." However, she decided to act on a suggestion from her agent that she try writing a book on the failure of women's emancipation.

The result was *The Female Eunuch*, which was published in Great Britain in October 1970 and in the United States six months later. The book is divided into five sections. In the first two, entitled *Body* and *Soul,* Miss Greer discusses the ways in which women are encouraged from earliest childhood to conform to the stereotype of the "Eternal Feminine"—whose essential quality is castratedness—and she rejects that stereotype: "Maybe I couldn't make it. Maybe I don't have a pretty smile, good teeth, nice tits, long legs, a cheeky arse, a sexy voice. Maybe I don't know how to handle men and increase my market value, so that the rewards due to the feminine will accrue to me. Then again, maybe I'm sick of the masquerade. I'm sick of pretending eternal youth. I'm sick of belying my own intelligence, my own will, my own sex. I'm sick of peering at the world through false eyelashes. . . . I'm sick of weighting my head with a dead mane, unable to move my neck vigorously in case I sweat into my lacquered curls. I'm sick of the Powder Room. I'm sick of pretending that some fatuous male's self-important pronouncements are the object of my undivided attention. . . . I'm sick of being a transvestite. I refuse to be a female impersonator. I am a woman, not a castrate."

The concomitant of the stereotype of the Eternal Feminine is the myth of machismo, which deflects male sexual energy into competitiveness and aggressiveness. "The castration of women," Miss Greer writes, "has been carried out in terms of a masculine-feminine polarity, in which men have commandeered all the energy and streamlined it into an aggressive conquistatorial power, reducing all heterosexual contact to a sadomasochistic pattern. This has meant the distortion of our concepts of *Love.*"

The third section of the book, *Love,* deals with that distortion. Like Sartre, Miss Greer believes that love is by nature narcissistic and consists of the recognition of the self in the other. True love, therefore, is possible only between true equals, each of whom is secure in his or her own self-love. Since society has created an inequality between the sexes that has systematically robbed women of their narcissism, it follows that women can rarely love themselves, or, therefore, others. What passes for love in our society are perverted patterns of mutual dependency, the chief forms of which she covers in chapters entitled "Altruism," "Egotism," and "Obsession." Those perversions, however, masquerade under the guise of so-called romantic love, which is followed by the equally pernicious institution of marriage and a frantic search for security. Seeing in the relationship between mother and child a model for the exploitative, possessive relationships that exist between adults, Miss Greer rejects the nuclear family in favor of some sort of extended family structure.

In the fourth section of the book, *Hate,* the author deals with the various ways in which the war between the sexes is waged, and in a chapter entitled "Rebellion," attacks what she considers some of the non-productive tactics embraced by some segments of the women's liberation movement.

Instead of a rebellion Miss Greer proposes a revolutionary change of spirit for women, and in *Revolution,* the concluding section of *The Female Eunuch,* she provides a "peep" at what it would be like if women were truly liberated. Free to embrace their own sexuality—actively, vigorously, and even promiscuously, if desired—women could direct their energy away from repression toward movement and creation, and sex could become "a form of communication between potent, gentle, tender people."

Newsweek hailed *The Female Eunuch* as "women's lib's most realistic—and least anti-male—manifesto," and male book reviewers received it enthusiastically. Christopher Lehmann-Haupt of the New York *Times* (April 20, 1971), for example, called it "a book with personality, a book that knows the distinction between the self and the other, a book that combines the best of masculinity *and* femininity." Feminists were almost equally enthusiastic. Although she regretted that *The Female Eunuch* offered few practical programs for change, Sally Kempton, a member of the New York Radical Feminists, described it in the New York *Times Book Review* (April 26, 1971) as "a great pleasure to read . . . brilliantly written, quirky and sensible, full of bile and insight." Germaine Greer maintains that her book was written neither for men nor for feminists. "The whole idea of the book is to raise consciousness levels," she told Tom Zito of the Washington *Post* (April 22, 1971). "It's really aimed at housewives—the vast majority of women who are so often ignored by the movement." Judging by the brisk sale of the book on both sides of the Atlantic, it appears that Miss Greer has reached the audience she wanted. For several months *The Female Eunuch* topped best-seller lists in Great Britain and in September 1971 it hovered near the top of lists in the United States, where it was chosen as a Book Find Club selection and as a Book-of-the-Month Club alternate. The book has been translated into twelve other languages.

Miss Greer's American publishers, McGraw-Hill, launched her on an exhaustive coast-to-coast tour to promote her book in the spring of 1971, and the mass media were quick to capitalize on her tall, shaggy good looks and ready wit. While in the United States the author appeared on radio and television talk shows and graced the cover of *Life* magazine, which called her a "saucy feminist." At a Theatre of Ideas program held at Town Hall in New York City she waged a battle of the wits with arch male chauvinist Norman Mailer and a few days later made members of the National Press Club in Washington squirm when she discussed "the great vaginal odor story," of how pharmaceutical companies had filled women's magazines with advertisements of "all kinds of things to squirt on women to stop them from being so offensive." Throughout her American tour Germaine Greer was accompanied by a British television crew that filmed her as she was being filmed, taped, and interviewed. She told Tom Zito of the Washington *Post* that the object was to produce a television program, with the working title of "The Media Freaks," that will "show how ridiculous the whole [mass media] thing is."

Germaine Greer has traveled a great deal with some of the money that she has earned from her book and has invested most of the rest. Since the autumn of 1970 she has been on unpaid sabbatical leave from the University of Warwick, but she plans to return to teaching. While lecturing at the university she lives in an apartment in Coventry during the week and travels to London on weekends. Miss Greer is six feet tall, weighs 140 pounds, and has grey green eyes and undisciplined brown hair. She laughs at the press descriptions of her as a beauty, but she is proud of her sex appeal. In fact, she makes no bones about her erotic propensities and likes to call herself a "supergroupie." Although she now opposes marriage, she married an Englishman, Paul du Feu, in May 1968. In her interview with Helen Dudar of the New York *Post* she described him as "a perfectly nice man." "I really liked him, I suppose," she told Miss Dudar, "and I really disliked being his wife. He kept telling me I wasn't doing it right and he'd show me some drudge in carpet slippers pushing a pram and say 'Now that's a wife.'" The couple separated after three weeks, but as of the spring of 1971 they had not divorced. In a recent questionnaire filled out for *Current Biography* Miss Greer listed her political affiliation as "anarchist" and her church affiliation as "atheist."

References

Life 70:30+ My 7 '71 pors
N Y Daily News p44 Ap 12 '71 por
N Y Post p21 Ap 10 '71 pors
Nat Observer p8 Ap 19 '71 por
Newsweek 77:48 Mr 22 '71 por
Washington (D.C.) Post C p1+ Ap 22 '71 por
Greer, Germaine. The Female Eunuch (1971)

GUSTON, PHILIP

June 27, 1913-   Painter
Address: b. c/o Marlborough-Gerson Gallery, 41 E. 57th St., New York 10022; h. Woodstock, N.Y. 27212

To a casual viewer disparity is far more obvious than similarity or continuity in the paintings that typify the various stages of the baffling, exploratory career of Philip Guston—the representational pictures of the 1940's and late 1960's and the intervening abstract expressionist canvases. His one-man exhibition in Manhattan in the fall of 1970, which revealed some affinities between Guston and the Pop artists, has been called the most controversial show of the season. If, however, as at least one reviewer charged, Guston's paintings have followed the fashions in art over the past three decades, many admiring critics see the changes in his work as emerging organically from the preceding stage in an evolving flow. Among the constants in his self-expressive use of diverse idioms are his aesthetic resourcefulness in style and

PHILIP   GUSTON

technique, his sensitivity to the tonal sumptuousness of color and sensuous quality of paint, and his ability to convey ambiguity, or multiplicity of meaning and feeling, to suggest the mystery behind the visible.

Philip Guston was born in Montreal, Canada on June 27, 1913, but has spent almost all of his life in the United States. At the age of six he was taken to Los Angeles, California, where he lived for the next fifteen years. In the absence of general knowledge, there has been considerable speculation about Guston's childhood because much of the content of his paintings is provided by memory. Nostalgia seems mingled with anguish in the recurrent childhood motifs of his work. The urban environment of his early years, also, is reflected in his use of streets and buildings as symbols in pictures characteristic of several stages of his development, including the most recent.

Los Angeles itself influenced Guston in another respect. "Its bizarre character didn't fail to impress him in much the same way it impressed Nathaniel West," Dore Ashton pointed out in her 1960 monograph on Guston. "The scores of absurd and pathetic cults quartered in Los Angeles . . . were never forgotten. To this day, Guston stands off from anything, including art movements, that verge on the sentimental excesses of California cultism."

Having become interested in painting while in high school, Guston attended the Otis Art Institute in Los Angeles for several months during 1930. The necessity to work for a living cut short his formal education in art, but he continued to study on his own in his spare time. When he visited the Arensburg Collection in his teens, Giorgio di Chirico's haunting metaphysical paintings of city streets and architecture and Picasso's monumental classical figures of the 1920's particularly impressed him. At the Los Angeles Public Library he examined and copied reproductions of the work of Signorelli, Mantegna, Piero della Francesca, and Uccello. His absorption of the forms and ideas of those and other masters of the Italian Renaissance became an integral part of the recollected experience that individualizes his painting.

Guston's fascination with large-scale Renaissance frescoes steered him to mural painting, to which he was simultaneously attracted, like many artists of the Depression, by the opportunities it afforded for expressing social protest. One of his earliest pictures was the socially conscious *Conspiracy* (1932), to whose subject or symbolic form, the Ku Klux Klan, he returned some thirty-eight years later. In 1934 Guston visited Mexico to see at firsthand the magnificent wall paintings of José Clemente Orozco, David Alfaro Siqueiros, and other social revolutionists. Then for about a year he worked on murals for the federal Work Projects Administration in Los Angeles.

In 1936 Guston moved to New York City, where he joined the mural division of the local WPA. Among his major assignments was a mural on which he was employed from 1938 to 1940 for the Queensbridge housing project. He won the popular prize for his execution of a mural for the WPA building at the 1939-40 New York World's Fair. On a commission from the Treasury Department's section on fine arts, he had begun work in 1938 on a mural entitled *Reconstruction and Well-Being of the Family*. The picture was intended as a decoration for the Social Security Building, which became the headquarters of the Department of Health, Education, and Welfare in Washington, D.C.

When he could afford to return to easel painting, Guston made the transition by developing sections of one of his Depression murals. In *Martial Memory* (1941) young boys in a slum, with garbage-can tops as shields and sticks of wood as swords, play at wounding each other. Rows of empty windows in the buildings of the background recall di Chirico in their formal structure and ghostly overtones. While the painting may allude to World War II, it suggests secrecy, multiple private and abstract meanings.

Martial Memory became the first in a series of figure paintings ostensibly about childhood, including *Holiday*, whose disturbing sense of fantasy and surrealistic juxtaposition of objects particularly attracted reviewers of his first one-man show in New York City, at the Midtown Galleries in early 1945. In the tender, enigmatic melancholy of another early work, *If This Be Not I* (1945), Guston seemed to Dore Ashton to be responding to a "growing feeling for the sensuous qualities of oil paint" and at the same time to be "peering inward, already searching for what is behind the visible fact."

Other pictures depicting children, boys usually masked or partly masked, are *Night Children* (1946) and *Ceremony* (1948). Discussing the anguished, nightmarish quality of *Ceremony* in the New York *World-Telegram* (July 13, 1948), Emily Genauer wondered if the theme of children at play had a special, personal significance for the artist; he had, after all, explored it in six major paintings. "Perhaps these are not children at all," she said, "but performers in a drama of adult tensions, of human beings bound together in a web, . . . isolated, involved with their own 'games.' " To her and some other critics the children seemed engaged in ritual, and she quoted an admission of Guston, who explained in replying to her question about the repetitiousness of his motif, "I like the ritual quality in any aspect of art or life. This can only give a hint of what I meant. Further than this, I know that I enjoy the ordering of mixed experiences in a picture in such a way that a number of meanings are implied."

Two prestigious prizes may serve as a measure of Guston's success as a representational painter. For *Sentimental Moment*, his figure piece of an unsmiling, raven-haired woman holding a locket in her hand, he won the first prize of $1,000 at the Carnegie Institute's 1945 exhibition of painting in the United States. In 1947 *Holiday* brought him the $1,200 Altman prize, awarded annually by the National Academy of Design for the best work in its exhibition. It was, therefore, his own dissatisfaction with his work, not critical disapproval, that motivated his search for a new idiom.

A 1947 painting, *Porch #2*, concluded Guston's early, overtly figurative period, as the last of the pictures in which children at play appear painfully enmeshed in irreconcilable conflicts. Angular, flattened, distorted and tortured in their formal relationships, Guston's images suggest an intention to have the configurations represent feelings themselves. He made a radical move to abstraction with *The Tormentors* (1947-48), based on a section of *Porch #2*, whose recognizable shapes he transformed into a pattern of flat lines.

In resolving his aesthetic crisis at that particular time Guston was helped financially by a Guggenheim fellowship in 1947, a Prix de Rome and a grant from the American Academy of Arts and Letters in 1948, and a Ford Foundation grant in 1949. He had been teaching art for about six years, from 1941 to 1945 at the University of Iowa and from 1945 to 1947 at Washington University in St. Louis. In the fall of 1948 he went to Europe, where he traveled for about a year in Italy, France, Spain, and England. In exploring European museums, he especially admired the pictures of Titian, Tiepolo, and other Venetian artists who had found pleasure in the medium of painting itself.

Delight in the very gesture of painting—in the celebration of the brush stroke and the textural and luminous properties of pigment for their own sakes—brought together the so-called Action Painters, or the New York abstract impressionists, a dominant force in American painting during the 1950's. Guston became part of that experimental movement when he settled in New York City upon his return from Europe. He supported himself by teaching art at New York University, from 1951 to 1958, and at Pratt Institute in Brooklyn, from 1953 to 1958.

When he began experimenting in abstraction in the late 1940's, Guston produced two or three canvases that faintly suggest urban landscapes. Over the next few years he gradually arrived at a calligraphic style characterized by wispy ribbons of paint in asymmetrical patterns, as in *White*

Painting No. 1 (1951). A vertical-horizontal arrangement of tenuous brush strokes in *Painting 1952* is reminiscent of the plus-and-minus series of Mondrian, to which Guston was perhaps paying tribute.

Rose-hued abstract compositions like *Attar* (1953) and *Zone* (1953-54) and the more varicolored *Summer* (1954) have a quivering, lambent, Monet-like lyricism that led to Guston's being described for a time as an abstract impressionist, rather than an abstract expressionist. "The pictures were diffuse, ambiguous: a surrender to beauty," Dore Ashton observed. But, she went on to say, beneath the shimmering surface of "the many layers of paint, the voices that were later to emerge were rumbling."

In their pensive, subtle loveliness Guston's paintings of the early 1950's seem an offshoot from the main stem of his work, whose more characteristic brooding and dramatic clash began to reassert themselves in larger, heavier areas of color in *The Room* (1954-55) and *Beggar's Joys* (1954-55). Commenting, however, in *Art News* (July 1962) on *Voyage* and *Dial* (both 1956), Frank O'Hara described them as "reticently joyous in their positive assertion of centralized masses, vivid in color, sensuous in paint-handling, detached and lofty as Baroque ceilings." In O'Hara's opinion, *The Clock* (1957), more dusky and foreboding, is one of the artist's masterpieces.

Guston's paintings of 1958, the somber *To Fellini, Dover II,* and *Actor,* further a gradual trend toward compacted, palpable aggregations of color, from the mere flecks of a few years earlier. The two latter pictures are gouaches and, like Guston's oil paintings, achieve much of their vitality and psychological complexity through the half tone, which, Dore Ashton has asserted, is "the chief element distinguishing Guston's style from that of his contemporaries, and framing his originality." Through the half tone, for instance, he is able to capture the fleeting emotions of reverie.

Two important exhibitions of Guston's work— the 1962 retrospective at the Guggenheim Museum in New York, which later traveled throughout Europe, and the 1966 show of eighty more recent paintings and drawings at the Jewish Museum in New York—made apparent the general direction of his development as an abstract expressionist toward larger canvases, blunter gestures, and a melancholy darker tonality. Paintings like *Duo* (1961) and *The Scale* (1961) confirm the observation of H. H. Arnason in *History of Modern Art* (1969) that from the mid-1950's onward "the artist was thinking of color shapes— reds, blues, and greens intertwined with blacks— as personalities engaged in conflicts within the tonal space of the painting."

The main concerns of Guston's abstractions are the aesthetic problems of painting. He was convinced that instead of creating preconceived objects or shapes, the artist must let the form evolve from an empty background through the act of painting. Yet from time to time his canvases afforded a glimpse of representational references, perhaps a tree or a cup. In several paintings after 1958 "he began to articulate motifs that vaguely resembled disembodied heads, balloons in cryptic comic strips, and vestiges of familiar things, such as city streets," Irving Sandler wrote in *The Triumph of American Painting* (1970).

When, therefore, in an exhibition at Manhattan's Marlborough-Gerson Gallery in the fall of 1970 Guston presented a series of some forty cartoon-like paintings and drawings of a city terrorized by hooded Ku-Klux-Klanners, the radical change in his idiom was startling and puzzling, but not unforeshadowed. "I got sick and tired of all that Purity! Wanted to tell Stories," Guston said of his new work, as quoted by Bill Berkson in *Art News* (October 1970). He is indebted to the favorite comic strips of his childhood, such as *Mutt and Jeff* and *Krazy Kat*, in learning to draw in a patently childish way. The clumsiness of his drawings has "an important expressive function," Harold Rosenberg pointed out in the *New Yorker* (November 7, 1970): "It enables him to give a simple account of the simple-mindedness of violence." The compositions are highly sophisticated, in fact, with the concrete objects of the pictures— hooded men, cars, clocks, soles of shoes, electric light bulbs, bottles, cigars—serving as the "props," as Guston has called them, of his complex designs. Rosenberg regarded *By the Window* as "a triumph of formal ordering" in its balancing of forms and distribution of colors.

Although reflecting his involvement in the world of today, Guston's paintings use the Klansmen not to represent a contemporary menace, but to symbolize, some critics have suggested, the oppression and fear of his own private feeling of crisis. Like Claes Oldenburg, James Rosenquist, and some of the other Pop artists, he seems to be choosing, largely for formal purposes, objects and styles from America's recent past that are no longer specifically relevant. A few reviewers of the Marlborough exhibition evaluated Guston's work as that of a Johnny-come-lately to Pop art. After he had charged Guston with having been a "colonizer rather than a pioneer" of the aesthetics of the New York abstract expressionists, Hilton Kramer of the New York *Times* (October 25, 1970) classified the artist in his latest expression as "one of those painters fated to serve a taste instead of creating one." Rosenberg's conclusion in his *New Yorker* critique typified the opposite opinion: "Guston is the first to have risked a fully developed career on the possibility of engaging his art in the political reality. His current exhibition may have given the cue to the art of the nineteen-seventies."

Besides being shown in nearly a score of one-man exhibitions and retrospectives, Guston's work has been represented in more than eighty group exhibitions virtually throughout the world. His paintings are included in the permanent collections of many major American museums. Guston has continued to give some of his attention to teaching. In the spring of 1966 he was artist-in-residence at Brandeis University; during the summer of 1968 he taught at Skidmore College; from 1967 to 1970 he conducted seminars at the New

York Studio School; and in 1969-70 he was guest critic at Columbia University's Graduate School of Fine Arts. He holds an honorary Doctor of Fine Arts degree from Boston University.

During the 1950's Guston began to live and work part of the time in Woodstock, New York, an upstate artists' colony. He now makes his year-round home in Woodstock, where the building of his huge cinder-block studio was completed in late 1967. The gray-haired and powerfully built artist was described nearly a decade ago in *Newsweek* (May 7, 1962) as "tall, handsome, and heavy-browed." At that time he refused with characteristic reticence to be interviewed, insisting, "It's all in the paintings."

Philip Guston was married in 1937 to Musa McKim. In a letter to the editor published in the New York *Times* of December 6, 1970, his daughter, Mrs. Musa Jane Kadish, of Yellow Springs, Ohio, wrote an eloquent, indignant reply to Hilton Kramer's negative review of her father's 1970 show at the Marlborough. "Guston's work has always been, in whatever form it has taken, an intensely personal statement, not always clear and sometimes embarrassingly intimate," she said in part, in defending his sincerity. ". . . I find myself disturbed, fascinated, moved and repelled by [his present] work, by the honesty and humanity of its vision in which the terrifying and ominous rub shoulders with the pathetic and comic. It is really the human condition."

References

Art N 61:71+ Jl '62; 69:44+ O '70 por
New Yorker 46:136+ N 7 '70
Newsweek 59:94 My 7 '62
Time 96:62+ N 9 '70 por

Ashton, Dore. Philip Guston (1960)
Sandler, Irving. The Triumph of American Painting (1970)
Who's Who in America, 1970-71
Who's Who in American Art (1970)

HAMPTON, LIONEL (LEO)

Apr. 20, 1914- Jazz musician; bandleader
Address: b. Lionel Hampton Enterprises, 165 W. 46th St., New York 10036

At the height of the swing era the authorities of a Connecticut town sent in the police to make sure that the jazz musician and bandleader Lionel Hampton would not play his theme number, "Flying Home," at an evening performance in the local theatre. The leaping and stamping of feet that had accompanied an earlier show had threatened to collapse the mezzanine balcony, thus literally bringing down the house.

Since the late 1930's, when he played with the Benny Goodman Quartet, "the Hamp," as Hampton is known to jazz lovers, has specialized in stampeding audiences into pandemonium. His frenetic showmanship, impeccable beat, and dervish-like drive propelled his big band, the temporary home of many jazz celebrities, to the top of the hit charts of the 1940's and 1950's. Since 1965 he has performed with a smaller group, called The Inner Circle, that fluctuates in size from six to eight men. Hampton is a master of the hot musical phrase known as the "riff"—the intricate, inventive pattern that jazz musicians improvise from a given melody—and it was he who introduced the vibraharp or "vibes" into the American jazz idiom.

Lionel Leo Hampton was born on April 20, 1914 in Birmingham, Alabama, the son of Charles and Gertrude (Whitfield) Hampton. (Leonard Feather, the writer on jazz, gives April 12, 1913 as Hampton's birthdate.) He has one brother, who is a law instructor at Prairie View College in Texas. Charles Hampton, the father, had just begun a career as a pianist and singer when the United States entered World War I, and he was sent overseas with the American Expeditionary Forces. Soon he was reported as missing in action. (Years later, after Hampton had grown up, he discovered that his father had not died, but was spending his last years, blind, in a veterans' home.) In her bereavement Gertrude Hampton sent Lionel to the home of her parents, Richard and Lavinia Morgan, in Chicago. Raised as a Roman Catholic, Lionel Hampton attended St. Monica parochial elementary school and St. Elizabeth High School, both in Chicago.

In grammar school Lionel Hampton had been content to beat out his rhythms on his grandmother's pots and pans, but by the time he reached high school his urge to play on real drums, which he could not afford, prompted him to get a job as a newsboy for *The Chicago Defender*. The newspaper, which had a black clientele, sponsored a jazz band for its newsboys, and within a week of obtaining the job Hampton was proudly sitting behind a set of bass drums. Virtually self-taught on both the drums and the vibraharp, Hampton recalled in an interview with Arthur North for the New York *Sunday News* (April 22, 1962) that a little Dominican nun at St. Monica's helped him to learn to play the snare drums by "rapping his knuckles every time he used his left hand to set the beat."

His astute grandmother recognized the direction in which Hampton was headed, and after he graduated from St. Elizabeth High School in Chicago, she sent him to Los Angeles, where one of her friends, Les Hite, had a band. For the next four years Lionel Hampton gained experience in Hite's band, which at that time worked mainly in films, in Eddie Elkins' band, and Paul Howard's "Quality Serenaders." For two years he attended classes in music theory at the University of Southern California. So absorbed was he in music that he was once fired from a job as a soda jerker for breaking too many glasses while tapping out new rhythms.

His reputation as a drummer had so grown among West Coast jazz aficionados that when Louis Armstrong came to Los Angeles to fill an engagement at Sebastian's Cotton Club, he asked Hampton to stand in as his drummer at the club and for recording dates. It was during a recording session with Les Hite's band in Culver City, California, when Armstrong was "fronting" for the group, that Hampton discovered a vibraharp in one of the unused rooms of the studio. He fooled around with it and forty-five minutes later played it on the now famous recording of "Memories of You."

The most difficult problem that Hampton ran into in switching from drums to the vibes was that of using his left hand with the same power as his right. But the versatility of his newly discovered instrument fascinated him, enabling him to play sentimental ballads or hot jazz with equal facility. "The vibraharp," Hampton has said, "was the front door to the electronic age." The instrument that he rescued from obscurity is said to be the only truly indigenous American musical instrument and was perfected only shortly after its discovery by Hampton in the early 1930's. Until then it had been used as a decorative musical instrument, just as chimes were used. "Unlike the wooden-keyed xylophone and marimba," an article in Newsweek (May 15, 1967) has explained, "keys of the vibes are aluminum and the instrument has a sustaining pedal. Its most salient feature is the motor-driven vibrato that provides the characteristic pulsating wah-wah-wah sound and is responsible for its singular bell-like tone. Unchecked by the pedal, it has something of the keening cry of a Siamese cat with sinusitis."

One night in 1936 Hampton was working out on the vibes in the after-hours Paradise Club in Los Angeles when Benny Goodman, "the king of swing," happened by. Out of that encounter eventually developed the Benny Goodman Quartet, with Hampton on vibes, Teddy Wilson on piano, Gene Krupa on drums, and Goodman on clarinet. Hampton moved to New York City, where Goodman was based, and during the next four years the Benny Goodman Quartet set a standard for all succeeding jazz chamber groups. Hampton directed the group's recording sessions (the first took place in August 1936), out of which emerged such memorable performances as "Dinah," "Exactly Like You," "Moonglow," and "My Last Affair." The Benny Goodman Quartet also gained national exposure through their radio programs under the sponsorship of Camel cigarettes. Hampton credits Goodman with being the major influence on his career. "Benny had always been my idol," he has said. "Gladys [Hampton's wife] gave me my first vibraharp, and after that, anything Benny'd play, I'd try to play on the vibraharp."

During his four-year stint with the Benny Goodman Quartet, Hampton made some recordings for RCA Victor with pickup bands and celebrated sidemen that have since become collectors' items. From 1941 until 1947 he recorded for Decca. Hampton can also be heard in all his grunting, groaning, and moaning ecstasy on the MGM, Clef, and Verve labels. With his wife, Gladys, he founded Glad-Hamp Records, Inc.

Plagued by ill health, Goodman broke up his Quartet in 1940, and Hampton, with Goodman's blessing, went out on his own. In the late 1930's the trend in American popular music had moved

LIONEL HAMPTON

towards the big bands, with their blaring, brassy sound, and to organize his own, the Lionel Hampton Orchestra, Hampton combed the United States for unknown, young, and promising musicians, often paying their bus fare. He once even provided shoes when an aspirant arrived barefoot in New York. "Before they'd come to me," Hampton said of some of his early band members in the New York Post (May 18, 1942), "they'd barely had enough to eat. Now they was so anxious to make good, they begged me to rehearse 'em. We'd drive 400 miles for a one-nighter, rehearse, play the job, and start right on to the next town. They didn't sleep for a week. . . . We took a rough stone and made it a shining gem."

Some of the luster of the Lionel Hampton Orchestra, which was organized in September 1940, came from the solo work of such jazz giants as Charles Mingus, Quincy Jones, Illinois Jacquet, Jack McVea, Charlie Parker, Dexter Gordon, Earl Bostic, Fats Novarro, and Dinah Washington. Hampton was one of the first big bandleaders to let a number go on and on until every soloist had exhausted himself. Because of their contributions and Hampton's swinging showmanship and musicianship, the Lionel Hampton Orchestra reached the top of the crowded list of big bands in the 1940's. It gave its first Carnegie Hall concert, for Esquire magazine, in 1945. Both a visual and auditory experience, it was in demand everywhere, from Boston's Back Bay society gatherings to that citadel of black talent, the Apollo Theatre in Harlem. Hampton's reputation for virtuosity on the vibes reached beyond jazz circles to Maestro Leopold Stokowski, who came to the Apollo Theatre expressly to hear him and was so taken by Hampton's sense of rhythm that he reportedly asked the jazz artist if he had ever been to the Belgian Congo. In 1942 the Lionel Hampton Orchestra grossed $40,000; by 1948 it was grossing more than a million dollars a year.

Through the 1950's and on into the early 1960's Hampton continued to lead his band, until it was plainly evident that the days of the big bands were over. Drained by the responsibilities of supervising thirty men, he pared down his group to combo size in the fall of 1965 and christened it "The Inner Circle." "You get yourself a bad crop of cats and they're liable to burn up your loot, and not even want to read the arrangements," he explained during an interview for the New York *Post* (October 3, 1965). "While the sidemen got sloppier, I was giving away my profit and not even pleasing myself or the public the way I wanted to." When The Inner Circle appeared at the Rheingold Festival in New York's Central Park in the fall of 1966, a reviewer for the New York *Times* reported (September 6, 1966): "Eight pieces . . . serve his purposes well. . . . The small group can sustain a riff in lighter, less ponderous fashion. . . . Hampton has only one way of approaching any piece of music. He swings it." Among the establishments where Hampton and The Inner Circle have swung it are the London House in Chicago and Al Hirt's club in New Orleans.

Since the early 1950's, Hampton has made many world tours, bringing jazz to adoring audiences in Israel, Europe, Japan, the Philippines, Formosa, and Okinawa. In 1964 he brought the Lionel Hampton Orchestra to the Antibes (France) Music Festival. His first visit to Israel, which has since become something of a spiritual homeland for him, inspired his only major work, *King David.* The eighteen-minute, four-part symphonic jazz suite had its première under Dmitri Mitropoulos in New York's Town Hall on February 14, 1957. "The music," wrote a reviewer for *Time* (February 25, 1957) "tells in a plaintive harp opening of the Old Testament tribulations of the Jews, blows down the Wailing Wall in a mighty, jumping blast of brass, moves through a lively vibraphone dance to a deafening, full-orchestra crescendo of triumph."

Since leaving the Benny Goodman Quartet, Hampton has been heard on several radio programs. Towards the end of World War II he and his big band provided the music for *What's Your War Job?*, which was sponsored by the War Manpower Commission of the federal government. The first government-sponsored radio show to feature black talent, the program had another claim to distinction in that it offered modified boogie-woogie for the first time on a Sunday morning program. In 1948 Hampton had his own show, under the aegis of the United States Treasury Department, which featured hot jazz, guest stars, and Canada Lee as master of ceremonies. And in 1962 he accepted the post of musical director for a new television station in Washington, D.C.—WOOK-TV —which aims its music and news at a black audience.

As a long-established black celebrity, Hampton is in a strategic position to further the peaceful integration efforts of his race. When he belonged to the Benny Goodman Quartet, he was one of the first black musicians to belong to a predominantly white jazz group. During the 1940's the Lionel Hampton Orchestra was one of the few mixed big bands that played in the American South, but for every white dance it played, the Lionel Hampton Orchestra played a black dance

in the same town. During one engagement in the North, at the Kansas City Auditorium on December 23, 1945, Hampton pulled his band off the stage halfway through the performance to protest the refusal by the management to admit Cab Calloway to the hall of white dancers. His efforts in behalf of the teaching of the black musical heritage in colleges and universities have begun to be vindicated. Two New Orleans schools, the integrated Xavier University and the all-black Dillard University, have asked Hampton to set up courses and have made him a full professor of music. "We need to know more about this music so we'll know more about our history," he says.

On November 11, 1936 Lionel Hampton married Gladys Riddle, who was born in an Indian settlement in Oklahoma and became a seamstress to Joan Crawford and other Hollywood stars. Mrs. Hampton, for many years her husband's business manager, died in 1971. Although reared as a Roman Catholic, in the 1940's Hampton turned to Christian Science, to which he has devoutly subscribed ever since. Other than music, his only interests are baseball, the Bible, the works of Mary Baker Eddy, and his beloved Israel. Hampton holds an honorary doctorate in music from Allen University in Columbia, South Carolina and is a member of Alpha Phi Alpha, the Elks (grand bandmaster), the Friars, and the Grand Street Boys Club of New York City.

Jazz historians have long admired Hampton's compassion, generosity, religiosity, and utter lack of pretense. They agree that he is one of the most emotional performers in the history of jazz. "Sometimes, when I play jazz, it's like a spiritual impulse comes over me," Hampton has said. "Anything I do, I don't know what I'm doing." Speaking of his colleagues, he told George T. Simon in an interview for the New York *Herald Tribune* (August 6, 1961): "None of us does those things on purpose. We got no routine. We just act the way the music and the spirit moves us. That's all. Remember what the Bible says. It says 'Blow the trumpet, beat the cymbals.' That's what we're doin'."

References

Feather, Leonard. Encyclopedia of Jazz (1960); Encyclopedia of Jazz in the Sixties (1966)
Poling, James. Esquire's World of Jazz (1962)
Simon, George T. The Big Bands (1967)

HANKS, NANCY

Dec. 31, 1927- United States government official
Address: b. National Endowment for the Arts, 1800 G St., N.W., Washington, D.C. 20506; h. 930 5th Ave., New York 10028

Among the highest ranking women in the Nixon administration is Nancy Hanks, who as chairman of the National Endowment for the Arts and the

National Council for the Arts is responsible for administering the federal government's first genuine attempt to help subsidize theatre companies, symphony orchestras, museums, and other cultural institutions in the United States. Unlike many European countries with long-established programs of support for the arts, the United States government had neglected its cultural resources, except for the aid given artists during the Depression, until 1965, when the National Endowment for the Arts was created as part of a new National Foundation on the Arts and the Humanities. The endowment agency works closely with the National Council on the Arts, an advisory body that sets agency policy and helps to choose worthy subjects for aid. Before she succeeded Roger L. Stevens as the federal government's national broker for the arts in September 1969, Miss Hanks was associated for thirteen years with the Rockefeller Brothers Fund in New York City as executive secretary of its Special Studies Project. There she directed a pioneering study project on the economic and social problems of the performing arts in America that laid much of the groundwork for the federal program she now heads.

Named for Nancy Hanks Lincoln, the mother of Abraham Lincoln and her distant cousin, Nancy Hanks was born on December 31, 1927 in Miami Beach, Florida. Her parents, who now live in Fort Worth, Texas, are Bryan Cayce Hanks, a corporation lawyer, and the former Virginia Wooding. She had one younger brother, Larry, who was killed in an automobile accident in 1950. The Hanks family lived in Florida but moved to Montclair, New Jersey when Nancy was in high school. She graduated from Montclair High in 1945. She had spent many of her summers in North Carolina at a summer place her parents owned in the Blue Ridge Mountains, and it was perhaps partly because she considered North Carolina her second home that she decided to attend Duke University in Durham. There she majored in political science and took an active part in campus life, joining Kappa Alpha Theta sorority, serving as president of the student government, and once reigning as May queen. During the summer of 1946 she studied geology at the University of Colorado, and two summers later she studied political science at Oxford University in England. Elected to Phi Beta Kappa, she received her B.A. *magna cum laude* from Duke in 1949.

Nancy Hanks first went to Washington in 1951, during the Korean War, accepting what she has recalled as "a rather lowly job as a receptionist" in the Office of Defense Mobilization. After about a year she succeeded in getting a position as a secretary for the President's Advisory Committee on Government Operations, which was chaired by Nelson A. Rockefeller. When Rockefeller was appointed undersecretary of the new Department of Health, Education and Welfare in 1953, he took Miss Hanks along as an assistant. Two years later, when President Dwight D. Eisenhower asked him to set up panels of foreign policy experts in the Special Projects Office of the White House, Rockefeller called on Miss Hanks to be his special assistant.

NANCY HANKS

In 1956 Miss Hanks left Washington for New York City, where she continued to help Nelson Rockefeller set up panels of experts, but this time on a private, non-classified basis for the Special Studies Project of the Rockefeller Brothers Fund. As executive secretary of the project, Miss Hanks directed its staff, helped to select experts for the studies, and handled the publication of their reports. She had already handled the fund's impressive studies on foreign policy, defense, economics, education, and democracy by 1963, when John D. Rockefeller 3d, chairman of the Lincoln Center for the Performing Arts, decided to apply the same methods to exploring the problems of dance, theatre, and music in America. The result was a landmark study entitled *The Performing Arts: Problems and Prospects*, (McGraw-Hill, 1965), which was the first comprehensive treatment of the subject in the United States.

Among other things, the report recommended that state and community arts councils be developed around the country. Convinced of their value, Miss Hanks became a member of the board of directors of the Associated Councils on the Arts, a private, nonprofit organization that promotes the activities of arts councils by organizing conferences, offering consultative services, and publishing books and a quarterly journal on the arts entitled *Cultural Affairs*. Elected president of the ACA in June 1968, Miss Hanks devoted many of her evenings and weekends to the organization's activities while continuing to prepare special studies for the Rockefellers, including one on labor unions.

The National Endowment for the Arts and the National Council on the Arts were established in response to a recognition of the country's cultural needs as elaborated in the Rockefeller study. The council was first set up in the Office of the President in September 1964, but after a year legislation incorporated it into the newly created National Foundation on the Arts and the Humanities. It serves in an advisory capacity to the endowment agency, which handles the dispensing of funds. The first head of the government arts agencies was

Roger L. Stevens, chairman of the Kennedy Center for the Performing Arts. Despite general opinion that he had excelled in that post, Stevens was not reappointed by President Richard Nixon when his four-year term expired in March 1969. The six-month delay that ensued before a new appointment was made led some observers to doubt Nixon's commitment to the arts, but his choice of Nancy Hanks, announced on September 3, 1969, quieted those fears. Her appointment was greeted with enthusiasm in nearly all quarters, including the Washington *Post,* which editorialized on September 7, 1969, "Miss Nancy Hanks is a neat catch as chairman of the National Council on the Arts. . . . For her charm as well as her savvy, she has the respect of the pros in the field. The Nixon administration had erred gratuitously by dismissing Miss Hanks' predecessor, Roger Stevens . . . simply because he was a Democrat. . . . But the appointment of Miss Hanks makes for a good recovery."

Nancy Hanks was confirmed by the Senate early in October and sworn into office a few days later on October 13, 1969. Immediately she was confronted with the task of preparing the 1970-71 budget, which had been delayed while her post lay vacant. When her budget requests were completed, President Nixon went along with her request for a $20,000,000 appropriation, over twice the $9,000,000 appropriated the year before. (During most of the Johnson years, the arts endowment agency had languished on annual budgets of $4,-500,000.) That Congress in a year of tight money ended up by approving $16,400,000, close to the amount requested, was credited both to the administration's firm backing and to Miss Hanks's powers of persuasion on Capitol Hill. According to Marquis Childs, the Washington *Post* columnist, the arts chairman spoke personally to over 200 members of the House and the Senate in making her case for the appropriation.

With increased funding the arts endowment agency has been able to expand its programs. Under chairman Stevens, the main thrust of the agency had been directed toward rescuing institutions, like the American Ballet Theatre and the American National Theatre and Academy, that were in dire financial straits. Miss Hanks, on the other hand, has concentrated on spreading aid on a grass-roots basis throughout the country. In November 1969 she announced that $200,000 in grants would be disbursed to send opera, theatre, dance, and music groups on tour to small communities of the United States. A year later $1,000,-000 was made available to send dance companies on tour around the nation. Money has also been made available to help small communities buy art works and to send art exhibitions on tour. In most of those programs a special emphasis has been put on reaching culturally disadvantaged or economically deprived areas of the United States.

Another emphasis of the arts endowment program under Nancy Hanks has been on bringing the arts to schools and young people. In March 1970 the endowment awarded $700,000 to symphony orchestras and opera companies for free youth concerts and performances in schools. Organizations such as Youth Audiences, Inc., which sponsors live music performances in schools, have also been aided. Another facet of the youth program consists of funding teaching efforts in the arts. Black poets and authors have with federal funding been sent to teach in inner-city schools, and with the United States Office of Education the National Endowment for the Arts has released $750,000 in grants to sponsor teaching programs for professional artists, filmmakers, writers, and performing artists in the nation's schools.

A fast-growing program in the agency has been aid to American dance companies and choreographers. Not long after taking office Nancy Hanks told a press conference, "The United States has become the capital of the dance world and . . . American choreographers and dancers are in constant demand in other nations. We consider . . . grants [to dance] an investment in a great national resource." Along with the $1,000,000 awarded to dance companies for touring in 1970, the federal agency has awarded over $600,000 to the country's three major ballet companies, the American Ballet Theatre, the New York City Ballet, and the City Center Joffrey Ballet, and nearly $150,000 in fellowships to sixteen choreographers, including Merce Cunningham, Eliot Feld, Hanya Holm, Murray Louis, Alwin Nikolais, and Anna Sokolow.

Because of its limited funds, the National Endowment for the Arts had in its early years been able to give little assistance to either American symphony orchestras or to museums, both institutions badly in need of large amounts of money. In 1970, however, the endowment began a sizable program of aid to orchestras, awarding $1,680,000 to thirty-four orchestras in August and $1,820,000 in November. The agency launched an aid program to museums in January of 1971, when it announced that $1,000,000 more than had been granted in all the endowment's previous years of existence, was being awarded to begin a long-range effort to assist museums. Although that money was going only to art museums, the agency planned to help history and science institutions at a later date.

The Nixon administration and Miss Hanks are committed to a policy of encouraging private as well as federal contributions to the arts. Some $2,000,000 of the agency's 1970-71 budget allotment was contingent on the receipt of matching funds from private sources, and many of the endowment's grants are awarded on a matching basis. Miss Hanks has reported that in actual practice each dollar contributed by the agency has generated about $3 of private money. For the 1971-72 fiscal year Miss Hanks requested a budget allotment of $30,000,000.

As chairman of the National Endowment for the Arts and the National Council on the Arts Nancy Hanks earns a salary of $40,000 a year. In Washington she lives in a Georgetown house sublet from New York Senator Jacob K. Javits, and in New York her home is an apartment on Fifth Avenue overlooking Central Park. She also has a small summer house at Southampton, on New York's Long Island. Miss Hanks attends theatre and ballet performances regularly, and she is fond of swimming, gardening, playing golf and tennis, and doing needlepoint. She frequently entertains small gatherings of friends at traditional Southern dinners cooked by her black maid from North Carolina. After interviewing her, Meryle Secrest of the Washington *Post* (October 26, 1969) remarked, "[Miss Hanks has] the kind of smiling reticence that makes her a hard person to know well. This is her style; deceptive, unassuming, she lets other people discover her slowly." Unusually attractive, Nancy Hanks is tall, trim-figured, and fair-complexioned, with dark brown eyes and reddish brown hair. She is a trustee of the Museum of Primitive Art in New York City, Duke University, and Robert College in Istanbul, Turkey. She is a registered Republican and a member of the Capitol Hill Club.

References

N Y Post p31 Ag 19 '68 por; p45 F 8 '69 por; p23 S 27 '69 por
N Y Times p38 S 3 '69 por
Washington (D.C.) Post C p1+ S 4 '69 por; K p1+ O 26 '69 por
Who's Who in the East, 1970-71

HAWN, GOLDIE

Nov 21, 1945- Comedienne; actress
Address: c/o Columbia Pictures, 711 5th Ave., New York 10022

The most popular of the resident zanies on NBC-TV's *Rowan and Martin's Laugh-In* between 1967 and 1970 was a fluffer of lines and spouter of malapropisms named Goldie Hawn, a fey blonde charmer with big bright eyes, a mobile face, and an infectious giggle. Escaping stereotyping, Miss Hawn proved her wider ability as an actress in the role of the kooky paramour in *Cactus Flower* (1969), for which the Academy of Motion Picture Arts and Sciences awarded her its Oscar for best supporting actress. Gene Saks, who directed the film, testified: "Never has a girl, in her first film, been so professional. She was instant relaxation for all on the film." Her next screen credit was the female lead in *There's a Girl in My Soup* (1970), and she is now reportedly planning to star in the film "Butterflies Are Free."

Goldie Jeanne Hawn—who was named after a great-aunt—was born in Washington, D.C., on November 21, 1945, and raised in Takoma Park, Maryland. Regarding her parents, she has said: "My Mom's a Jew from Pittsburgh and my Dad's a WASP from Arkansas." Her father is Edward Rutledge Hawn, a professional musician who used to play the violin, saxophone, and clarinet with society bands at White House and embassy affairs, and her mother is Laura Hawn, a jewelry wholesaler. She has a sister, Patty, eight years her senior.

At her mother's insistence, Miss Hawn studied tap dancing and ballet from the age of three and, in addition, jazz and modern dance from the age of eleven. Her father gave her voice lessons. "I can remember almost all of my childhood," she

GOLDIE HAWN

told Wayne Warga of the New York *Post* (February 15, 1969), "and all the memories are pleasant. There was no conflict, no push, and no competition in my family. When I decided to go into show business no one disagreed." She remembers herself as "always uninhibited," and her mother remembers her as a "charming" child, a "joy to have around," and also as "very industrious," working hard at her dancing lessons. A late bloomer, then not so pretty as her sister, she was seldom distracted by dates. "Boys didn't ask me out," she recalled in an interview with Tom Burke of *McCall's* (October 1969). "I didn't really want to go, but, uh, I wanted them to *ask* me."

As a teen-ager Miss Hawn took part in school and community dramatic productions. After graduating from Montgomery Blair High School in Silver Spring, Maryland she remained in the Washington, D.C. area for a year and a half, studying drama at American University and teaching dancing. Then she danced in choruses at the New York World's Fair's Texas Pavilion and in summer stock musicals and did go-go dancing in Dudes 'n' Dolls, a Manhattan discotheque, and at the Desert Inn in Las Vegas. Her go-go dancing period, especially the Las Vegas part, was, she has said, "the saddest time" of her life, because she is "temperamentally and morally unsuited for Las Vegas and nightclubs." She stayed with it as long as she did because of inertia, or what she calls "this tendency . . . to let things happen." According to Leslie Raddatz in *TV Guide* (June 29, 1968), she was "faced with a major decision" only once, when she was offered "what is euphemistically referred to as 'the easy way'" to success and her response was: "If I have to make it that way, I won't go."

Art Simon, an agent, discovered Miss Hawn when she was dancing in the chorus of an Andy Griffith television special in 1967. He became her manager, signed her with the William Morris agency, and got her the supporting role of Sandy, the wacky neighbor in *Good Morning, World*, a situation comedy about two disc jockeys that ended almost as soon as it was launched on the CBS television network in the fall of 1967.

From the CBS flop Goldie Hawn went to the NBC hit *Laugh-In,* a fast-paced weekly hour of crazy-quilt comedy then in its third week on the air. Like everyone else on the show, she took her turn in the general, rapid-fire mugging, skits, and pratfalls and the puns, tongue twisters, non-sequiturs, and similar one-line jokes, and like the other young women in the company she gyrated occasionally in a bikini. But everything that she did was set off by her own special quality, a combination of Lolita-like sexiness and carefree innocence that made her, as one reporter put it, the most "massively loved" personality on television. "I play a character on *Laugh-In,*" she told Tom Burke in the *McCall's* interview. "The character is not so much stupid as childlike. She's naive, gullible. I'm like her in many small ways."

What charmed millions of viewers more than anything else about Miss Hawn was her upper-register laugh—a natural, spontaneous response to embarrassment or bewilderment—and the show's creators deliberately provoked it. "At first we hired her because she danced and she looked kinda cute," producer George Schlatter told Betty Rollin of *Look* (December 2, 1969). "Then we gave her an intro, and she blew it, and we broke up. Then we told her to do it again, and she blew it again, and then I thought, 'Wait a minute,' and then we started switching the cue cards on purpose. We do awful things to her now—hold up dirty words, pictures—the works."

When she left *Laugh-In,* during the show's 1969-70 run, Miss Hawn had already made her screen debut, in *Cactus Flower* (1969), a Columbia Pictures adaptation of the hit Broadway light comedy about a prosperous dentist (Walter Matthau) who protects his bachelor status by making his mistress (Miss Hawn) think he is already married to his secretary (Ingrid Bergman). The film as a whole received mixed reviews, but the negative ones generally left the cast unscathed, and some singled out Goldie Hawn as the redeeming element. "It is mainly the emerging sweetness and perceptions of this girl's character, as an inquisitive Greenwich kook, that gives the picture its persuasive luster and substance," Howard Thompson wrote in the New York *Times* (December 17, 1969).

In a review of the film for *New York,* Judith Crist called Miss Hawn "an intelligent and sensitive performer" and contrasted her performance with that of Mia Farrow in *John and Mary*: "Goldie Hawn, as cuddlesome a sex kitten as ever had a bit of intelligence and womanly heart to brighten the dumb-blonde stereotype . . . provides all the vitality and youngness and—well, just likeability—that the stylized Miss Farrow lacks." In addition to the Academy Award, Miss Hawn's performance won her the female star of the year award of the National Association of Theatre Owners and fourth place (fifteen votes) in the New York Film Critics Circle balloting for best supporting actress.

In her second motion picture and first starring screen vehicle, *There's a Girl in My Soup* (Columbia, 1970), Miss Hawn gave a restrained performance as a hippie waif who proves to be more than a match for the middle-aged London roué (Peter Sellers) who picks her up. Most critics dismissed the film as a flimsy, smutty farce (although some conceded it was fun to watch), and Roger Greenspun wrote in the New York *Times* (December 16, 1970): "Miss Hawn and Mr. Sellers are handicapped by roles in which any attempt at a characterization must seem an imposition."

Since *Laugh-In* Miss Hawn has performed on television as a guest on the *Dean Martin Show* and as the star of two specials on NBC-TV. After watching *Clairol Command Performance Presents . . . Pure Goldie,* Bob Williams wrote in the New York *Post* (February 16, 1971): "The once crazy *Laugh-In* gal . . . turns out to be some small kind of singer and not too much of a dancer but very much a special TV personality of some engaging quality." The critic for *Variety* (February 17, 1971) was more effusive: "Goldie Hawn . . . has so much going for her she can easily be spun off into at least four primary hunks of corporate assets—as Goldie the Beautiful Blonde, Goldie the Comedienne, Goldie the Singer, Goldie the Dancer. That she can also act, with accent on the handling of lines, is so much velvet, and ditto an ingratiating personality and a built-in sense of presence and timing that give her a computerized headstart in the techniques of underplaying, overplaying, or playing it straight, whichever fits at a particular moment." In the New York Nielsen ratings *Pure Goldie* had greater audience pull (39 percent) than the other shows in the same timeslot, including Carol Burnett's show on CBS (23 percent).

Goldie Hawn and Gus Trikonis, an actor and film producer whom she met when both were in a road production of *Guys and Dolls,* were married in May 1969. They live with several dogs and cats in a brick New England-style house with a swimming pool in Studio City, north of Hollywood. Miss Hawn, apparently unspoiled by success, is, by her own description, "old-fashioned" and "a very domestic person" who "can't wait to have children, and that's the truth." The aspect of show business that "sickens" her is what it does to the femininity of so many "hard, ambitious, aggressive women." "I'm really a very middle-class person," she confessed to Jane Wilkie of *Good Housekeeping* (May 1971). "I mean, the way the middle class lives—with children and nice houses—that's all I ever wanted out of life."

The comedienne, who is five feet six inches tall and weighs about 113 pounds, is a naturally skinny, hearty eater. She has given up smoking, and neither she nor her husband drinks much alcohol. She describes herself as "light and carefree," and one interviewer described her as "a natural, free-wheeling type, but no zany." Frugal, she limits herself to a relatively moderate salary drawn from KMA Inc., (the corporation formed by her, her husband, and Art Simon); collects antiques, but prefers to hunt for them in cheap flea markets; likes to do her own cooking and, sometimes, house cleaning (about which she is compulsive but not fussy); and makes some of her own clothes. She also knits, likes perfumes and rings, and drives a Mark III Continental.

References

Coronet 7:57+ O '69 pors
N Y Sunday News II p18 S 7 '69 pors
Newsday W p12+ Ja 10 '70 pors
Parade p12 Je 14 '70 pors

HEALEY, DENIS (WINSTON)

Aug. 30, 1917-   British Labour politician; Member of Parliament
Address: b. House of Commons, London, S.W. 1, England

DENIS HEALEY

In the opinion of many close observers of British politics, the man most likely to succeed Harold Wilson as leader of the Labour party is Denis Healey. As Secretary of State for Defence in the Wilson government (1964-70), Healey trimmed, tightened, and streamlined Great Britain's military system, effecting greater efficiency with fewer men at a reduced budget. Since Labour's defeat in the general election of 1970, he has been his party's "shadow" Secretary of State for Foreign Affairs, or chief opposition foreign-policy spokesman in Parliament. In the course of his Parliamentary career, which began in 1952, Healey has moved from slightly to the right (by Labour standards), through center (under Wilson), to slightly to the left.

Denis Winston Healey, the son of William Healey, was born on August 30, 1917, at Mottingham in Kent. He has one brother, a lieutenant commander in the Royal Navy. Raised in Kent and Yorkshire, Healey received his secondary education at the Bradford (Yorkshire) Grammar School. Out of youthful—and temporary—pacifist sentiment, he resigned from officers' training at the school, and in 1935 he became active in the Labour movement.

After entering Balliol College, Oxford University, in 1936, Healey became chairman of the university's Labour party, and, like many of his generation, he was a Marxist as an undergraduate. Academically, he established a brilliant record, winning the Jenkyns Exhibition and the Harmsworth Senior Scholarship of Merton College and taking first-class honors in both moderns and humane letters. His education was interrupted by World War II service with the Royal Army Engineers in North Africa and Italy, for which he was decorated with membership in the Order of the British Empire. He completed the work for his M.A. degree immediately upon his discharge—in the rank of major—in 1945.

Healey first ran as a Labour candidate for Parliament, unsuccessfully, in the 1945 general election that swept into office the Labour government of Clement Attlee. Attlee's Secretary of State for Foreign Affairs was Ernest Bevin, then leader of Labour's right-of-center faction. As secretary of the party's international department, beginning in 1946, Healey was a backroom planner for Bevin

and *ipso facto* was in agreement with Bevin's foreign policy views, as he made clear in *Cards on the Table* (1946), one of several pamphlets by him published by the department. During his six years as secretary, Healey attended socialist congresses and conferences regularly throughout Europe and occasionally elsewhere, familiarizing himself with world conditions and polishing his knowledge of several languages.

Not long after Healey visited Canada as a Royal Institute of International Affairs delegate to the Commonwealth Relations Conference, the Canadian Association for Adult Education published his essay *Western Europe: The Challenge of Unity* (1950). The following year Lincolns-Prager issued his *The Curtain Falls*, about socialism in Eastern Europe, and the Fabian Society published *Rearmament—How Far?*, consisting of speeches given by Healey and John Freeman at a Fabian conference in the summer of 1951.

The Labour government fell and the Conservatives began a thirteen-year rule in October 1951. In a by-election four months later Healey won the Parliamentary seat for Leeds East (then South East Leeds) that he still holds. In Parliament and out, he was a close associate of Hugh Gaitskell, the leader of the Labour party from 1955 to 1963. For five years he was a member of Gaitskell's "shadow Cabinet," the group of M.P.'s who formulate opposition policy, lead Parliamentary debate in their areas of special competence, and are expected to form the actual Cabinet when their party regains power. From 1959 to 1961 he was shadow foreign secretary, from 1961 to 1963 shadow Commonwealth and colonial affairs secretary, and in 1963 and 1964 shadow defense secretary.

In addition to his Parliamentary posts, Healey served as British delegate to the Consultative Assembly of the Council of Europe, from 1952 to 1954; British delegate to the Inter-Parliamentary Union Conference in Washington, D.C., in 1953; councillor with the Institute of Strategic Studies, from 1958 to 1961; and British delegate to the Western European Union and the Council of Europe, from 1963 to 1965. With Labour party delegations he visited Moscow in 1959 and 1963, Greece in 1961, Africa in 1962, the Middle East in 1963, Washington, D.C. in 1964 (for talks with members of the Johnson administration), and the Far East, including South Vietnam, also in 1964.

A socialist theoretician as well as a practical politician, Healey served from 1954 to 1961 as a member of the executive of the Fabian Society. He contributed to *New Fabian Essays* (Turnstile Press, 1952), and the Fabian Society published his tracts *A Neutral Belt in Europe?* (1958), *The Race against the H-Bomb* (1960), and *A Labour Britain and the World* (1964). He shared the general, constant view of Labour that national social needs have priority over military ones, but, with Gaitskell, he was wary of the Soviet Union; advocated the establishment of a neutral zone in central Europe, including both Germanys, which would serve as a buffer between East and West; opposed unilateral disarmament, and, asserting that Western Europe was dependent on United States help for its security, approved the basing of United States Polaris submarines in Scotland.

In the contest for party leadership that followed Gaitskell's death, Healey first backed James Callaghan, from the Gaitskell camp, but finally transferred his loyalty to successful contestant Harold Wilson. When forming his government, after Labour's victory in the general election of October 16, 1964, Wilson named Healey his Secretary of State for Defence. During the course of the Wilson government's term every one of the original senior ministerial appointees was replaced except Healey, who remained through the entire period of Labour's Parliamentary mandate as defence minister and member of the Privy Council.

In keeping with Labour's campaign pledge to reduce military spending drastically as a means of making funds available for other purposes, Healey reappraised Britain's defense needs and international commitments, particularly those "East of Suez." He closed British bases in Singapore, Malaysia, and elsewhere in the Near and Far East; cut the strength of the Territorial Army (the home reserve, or national guard) in half; cancelled expensive weapons development and procurement programs, such as the Royal Navy's aircraft carrier program and TSR-2 supersonic bomber project; unified the administrations of the three armed forces within the Ministry of Defence, which he brought under tighter civilian control; and established a Programme Evaluation Group to utilize cost effectiveness procedures similar to those introduced into the United States Department of Defense by Robert S. McNamara, whom Healey personally knew and admired.

To compensate for the cuts in men and arms, Healey put greater emphasis on cooperative European efforts among Western allies, such as NATO, making the British forces in Germany, for example, the best equipped and best trained military contingent in Western Europe. He raised the level of professionalism in the British armed forces, partly through higher pay and bonuses for special duty, such as service in Northern Ireland.

During Healey's tenure as defence secretary, the strength of the British armed forces was reduced from 425,100 to 376,300. By 1968 the cut in the annual defense budget had reached an estimated £400,000 a year—16 percent, or, in terms of total foreign exchange savings, 25 percent. In February 1970 Healey announced an estimated annual defense budget of £2,280,000 (not counting imminent service pay increases) and predicted that by 1972-73 reductions in spending would bring the military budget to less than 5 percent of the gross national product. At the same time, because of increased efficiency and better training, the reduction in military capacity had been estimated at no more than 4 percent.

As a centrist Secretary of State for Defence, Healey drew criticism from the right for his "Little England" defense strategy and from the left for his support of United States policy in Vietnam and his opposition to the use of military force against the racist regime in the breakaway colony of Rhodesia. Since the fall of the Wilson government, in 1970, Healey's tendency, like that of the Labour consensus, has been, at least ostensibly, leftward. He has, for example, for the first time condemned the sale of arms to South Africa and, reversing a position he had held for many years, come out against British entry into the Common Market.

Healey is a muscular six-footer with a friendly face, twinkling blue eyes, and heavy, dark eyebrows. A writer for *Newsweek* (December 6, 1965), described him as "articulate . . . persuasive . . . erudite . . . a rare blend of intellect and action," and Francis Boyd, writing in the *Guardian* (April 3, 1967), described him as a man with a "systematic" mind and "almost boyish vigor" who "enjoys the exercise of power" and has "the physical gusto to give the exercise of power its special savor."

Denis Healey and Edna May Edmunds, a former teacher who now gives lectures to women's organizations, were married in 1945. They have three children, Jenifer (born in 1948), Timothy (1949), and Cressida (1954). Healey lists his preferred recreations as travel, photography, music (both playing the piano and listening to records), and printing. Francis Boyd wrote: "He likes dashing all over the world to international conferences . . . [or] motoring to, say, Yugoslavia, and camping by the wayside. He adores the American way of life, and, when his children were younger, made a point of bringing back from the United States preposterous mechanical toys to play with while ostensibly showing his children how to work them."

References

N Y Times p4 F 23 '66 por
Britannica Book of the Year, 1967
International Who's Who, 1970-71
International Year Book and Statesmen's Who's Who, 1971
Who's Who, 1971-72
Who's Who in America, 1970-71
Who's Who in the World, 1971-72

HENDERSON, FLORENCE

Feb. 14, 1934- Actress; singer
Address: b. c/o Greengrass Enterprises, Inc.,
595 Madison Ave., New York 10022; c/o Katz-
Gallin Assoc., 9255 Sunset Blvd., Los Angeles,
Calif. 90069

During the twenty years since Florence Henderson
arrived in New York from the Midwest as a stage-
struck adolescent, her out-of-town eagerness and
bright-eyed winsomeness have matured into the
radiance of a seasoned performer enormously popular with many different types of audiences. One of
America's finest interpreters of musical comedy, she
has had leading roles in *Fanny* (1954) and in revivals of *Oklahoma!*, *South Pacific*, and other shows.
She has won fans from coast to coast through her
national tour in *The Sound of Music*; through her
appearances on many television programs, including
her own family comedy series, *The Brady Bunch*;
and through her starring performance in *Song of
Norway*, in which she made her film debut in 1970.
For the past four years she has also entertained regularly in a solo act at fashionable supper clubs.

The daughter of a tobacco sharecropper, Florence
Agnes Henderson was born to Joseph and Elizabeth
(Elder) Henderson on February 14, 1934 in the
hamlet of Dale, in a rural section of southern Indiana. She was the tenth and last child in a Roman
Catholic family of Irish descent. With her five
brothers (three of whom are no longer living) and
four sisters, she helped raise tobacco on rented land
in Owensboro, Kentucky, where she spent her childhood. The crop sometimes failed, and during the
Depression Joseph Henderson worked on WPA
projects to provide for his family. Florence attended
grade school at St. Francis Academy in Owensboro,
where pupils had to provide their own books. "One
year my Christmas present was my school reader,"
she recalled in an interview for *TV Guide* (February 7, 1970). During her high school years she had
jobs as a baby sitter and soda jerker.

As if to offset economic hardship, the Hendersons
were fun-loving and close-knit, sharing a natural
musical talent. Florence alone of the children, however, dreamed of a career on the musical stage. She
had been born with a clear, pleasant voice and a gift
for remembering songs, and to those assets she
added determination. Help and encouragement in
developing her talents in singing and dancing came
from the Benedictine teaching sisters at school.
When she was still in grade school, she joined the
choir of St. Bernard's Church in nearby Rockport,
Indiana, where she strengthened her voice by singing in four-part Latin masses, eventually singing
every part. The only professional training she received while still living at home was with the singer
Christine Johnson, who had created the role of
Nettie in the Broadway production of *Carousel* in
1945. Because of lack of money for preparation, a
stage career seemed out of the question. Then, during her senior year in high school, relatives of a
friend—a former theatrical team who had been impressed by Florence Henderson's singing in school
operettas—offered to help her financially.

FLORENCE HENDERSON

At the age of seventeen, in 1951, Florence Henderson arrived in New York City, where she rented
a room at the Barbizon Hotel for Women and enrolled in a two-year course at the American Academy of Dramatic Arts. After her first year, however,
she auditioned, in a bathing suit, for a part in the
musical comedy about a summer resort entitled
Wish You Were Here, wondering naïvely whether a
bathing suit was *de rigueur* for every audition. The
director of the musical, Joshua Logan, cast her in
the role of the New Girl, a one-line part. The show
opened at the Imperial Theatre on June 25, 1952
and ran until the end of November 1953, but long
before its close Miss Henderson had dropped out of
the cast. When Richard Rodgers caught a glimpse
of her in that comedy, he along with Oscar Hammerstein 2d, then casting a road production of their
musical *Oklahoma!*, offered her the role of Laurey,
her first big opportunity on the stage. That tour of
Oklahoma! began in Hartford on August 29, 1952.

During the following summer Miss Henderson
played Resi in the Los Angeles Civic Light Opera
Association's production of *The Great Waltz*. She
then returned to Manhattan to appear in a revival
of *Oklahoma!* at New York City Center for a five-
week engagement, beginning on August 31, 1953.
Delighted with her exhilarating portrayal of Laurey,
Walter Kerr summed up the general opinion of
Broadway critics in his comments for the New York
Herald Tribune (September 1, 1953): "She is the
real thing, right out of a butter churn somewhere.
. . . You not only like this Laurey, you believe in
her; and for as long as *Oklahoma!* finally manages to
run, I never expect to see a better one."

Yet, it was by auditioning in competition with
established stars of the musical theatre, rather than
simply on the strength of her performance as
Laurey, that Miss Henderson won the title role in
Fanny. Joshua Logan, who with S.N. Behrman
adapted the musical play from Marcel Pagnol's
trilogy of comedies about dockside characters in
Marseilles, also cast Ezio Pinza and Walter Slezak
in starring roles. When *Fanny* started its successful
run at the Majestic Theatre on November 4, 1954,
the reviews ranged from lukewarm to ecstatic with

regard to the play itself, but most critics had nothing but praise for the appealing twenty-year-old actress. In a *Variety* poll earlier in the year William Hawkins had chosen Florence Henderson as the most promising young actress of the season. His review of *Fanny* for the New York *World-Telegram and Sun* (November 5, 1954) indicated that her characterization confirmed his estimate: "She has one of the loveliest voices in the theatre. . . . But more exciting, she plays the long and arduous role without a quaver or a false glance."

In meeting the demands of increasingly difficult roles, Florence Henderson had the advantage of continued study. She took voice lessons with Dolf Swing for more than a decade and acting lessons with Mary Tarcai from 1955 to 1959, received coaching in dancing, studied French and Italian, and learned several operatic roles, such as Mimi in *La Bohême*. To prepare for the part that has been called one of the most exacting in the American musical theatre, she took guitar lessons. The role was that of Maria Rainer in *The Sound of Music* by Rodgers and Hammerstein, the hit musical about the singing Von Trapp family of Austria. Miss Henderson portrayed Maria in the 1961-62 road production, reportedly as the choice of Mary Martin, who had created the character in 1959 in the first production of that musical, which was still running on Broadway when the road company set out. Beginning on March 7, 1961, with the opening of the national tour in Detroit, Miss Henderson played to capacity audiences for fifteen months. For her performance in *The Sound of Music* she won the Sarah Siddons Award in 1962.

With José Ferrer as her costar, Miss Henderson portrayed Mary Morgan in *The Girl Who Came to Supper*, a musical comedy by Noel Coward and Harry Kurnitz, based on Terence Rattigan's 1953 British stage comedy, *The Sleeping Prince*. The play, which opened on December 8, 1963 at the Broadway Theatre, deals wittily with an American show girl in London who charms a prince regent from a make-believe Carpathia. Reviewing the musical's pre-Broadway engagement in Boston, Frederick H. Guidry of the *Christian Science Monitor* (October 5, 1963) called Miss Henderson's performance "a marvel of mechanical exactness." But about two months later she captivated most New York critics. "Her charms are legion," George Oppenheimer wrote in a representative review for *Newsday* (December 9, 1963). "She sings enchantingly, dances gracefully and is altogether beguiling as a cocky young American. There is a wonderfully uninhibited naturalness about her and a warmth that makes her doubly endearing." Glowing tributes to Miss Henderson, lush sets, and Coward's sprightly lyrics could not, however, compensate for a rather weak plot that seems responsible for the closing after 112 performances.

New York theatregoers next saw Florence Henderson in the summer of 1964 as the nurse Nellie Forbush in the Lincoln Center revival of *South Pacific*, the Rodgers and Hammerstein musical adaptation of James A. Michener's *Tales of the South Pacific*. Again with professional competence and assertion of individuality she sustained the inevitable comparison with Mary Martin, who had originated the role in its overwhelmingly successful first presentation in 1949.

In 1970 Florence Henderson made her film debut as Nina, the loyal wife of the Norwegian composer Edvard Grieg, played by Toralv Maurstad, in *Song of Norway*, an ABC Picture Corporation release based on the 1944 Broadway operetta by Robert Wright and George Forrest. The producers of that wide-screen color extravaganza, Andrew and Virginia Stone, tried to make the screen version more dramatic and realistic than the stage version by including in Grieg's biography "the other woman." Motion picture critics, by and large, scorched the film as "banal," "second-generation kitsch," and "insufferably sunny-minded" and suggested that Miss Henderson was the victim of inferior scripting. Vast audiences, nevertheless, welcomed the film's wholesomeness as a change from sex-oriented movie fare and enjoyed its musical score and authentic Norwegian scenery.

Seldom at liberty between musical comedy roles, Florence Henderson has filled considerably more than a hundred engagements in special stage presentations, television, and nightclubs. From 1958 to 1962 she starred and toured in the General Motors annual Oldsmobile industrial shows, which are staged like musical comedies. In November 1966 she sang in *Jerome Kern's Theatre*, produced by Lincoln Center of the Performing Arts in New York City to benefit, in part, the theatre's experimental workshop. At the Inner Circle show, entitled *New Faces of 1966*, an annual event presented by New York political writers, she appeared with New York Mayor John V. Lindsay, lending him support in his five-minute song-and-dance routine.

Florence Henderson's strong and well-controlled lyric soprano has a freshness that also characterizes the overall impression she gives as a performer in the entertainment media. Since making an informal television debut as a singer in an off-camera group on the *Ed Sullivan Show* in 1952, she has been seen on every major TV variety program, including the *Dean Martin Show*, the *Jackie Gleason Show*, and the *Jonathan Winters Show*. Among the musical specials on which she has sung are the *Rodgers and Hammerstein Anniversary Show* (1954) and *The Gershwin Years* (CBS, 1961). She was hostess for *Oldsmobile Theatre* (NBC, 1959) and summer hostess for the *Bell Telephone Hour* (NBC, 1964); has performed in dramatic presentations such as *Huckleberry Finn* (CBS, 1957) and *Little Women* (CBS, 1958); and has been a favorite on game shows like *Password* (1963).

Other highlights of Miss Henderson's television work include stints as women's editor on the Dave Garroway *Today* show (NBC, 1959-60) and as the first woman to serve as a summer replacement for Johnny Carson. A born conversationalist, she succeeds on talk shows because of her knack for making others relax and discuss their views freely. Since 1969 Miss Henderson and Robert Reed have been costarring in the weekly family situation comedy *The Brady Bunch* (ABC), about a widow with three daughters who marries a widower with three sons. Although several reviewers lambasted the program, its popularity earned it a second season on the network.

Cheerfulness, crispness, effervescence, and similar traits of Miss Henderson's "girl-next-door personality" have brought her rave notices for her nightclub act. In the late 1950's she had doubled with Bill Hayes in a boy-girl routine, but had then ignored the supper club circuit until 1967, when she introduced her solo show at the Empire Room of the Waldorf-Astoria in Manhattan after break-in appearances at the Salle Bonaventure in Montreal. Since then she has entertained at the Shamrock Hotel in Houston, the Shoreham Hotel in Washington, the Sands in Las Vegas, and other posh night spots. When she played the Plaza's Persian Room in Manhattan in the spring of 1970, a reviewer for *Variety* (March 25, 1970) observed, "She [roams] a wide range and seemingly seeks to explore new horizons and approaches. She tries to eliminate a generation gap by modernizing the standards with a beat and making contemporaries milder, so that the elders can appreciate them for musical values."

Slim, though shapely, Florence Henderson is five feet four inches tall and weighs about 106 pounds. Her eyes are blue and her hair is honey-blond. She and Ira Bernstein, the theatrical producer and company manager, were married on January 9, 1956 and have four children: Barbara Ellen, Joseph Karl, Robert, and Elizabeth. The Bernstein home is a thirty-second story apartment on Central Park South in Manhattan. The older children attend Catholic schools, and at mealtime at home all the members of the family say both a Catholic and a Hebrew grace. Whenever practical Miss Henderson takes her children with her on tour. In 1966 she became the first woman to receive the CARTA Award, given by the Catholic Apostolate of Radio, Television and Advertising.

References

N Y Mirror p22 Ja 12 '61 por
N Y Post p45 Mr 11 '67 por; p19 D 12 '70
N Y Sunday News mag p8 Ap 30 '67 por;
  p74 S 25 '69 por; II p35 O 26 '69 por
N Y Times II p9 Ja 1 '61 por
Biographical Encyclopaedia & Who's Who
  of the American Theatre (1966)

HERNANDEZ, AILEEN C(LARKE)

May 23, 1926- Organization leader; feminist; urban affairs consultant
Address: b. Room 342, 680 Beach St., San Francisco, Calif. 94109

As president of the National Organization for Women (NOW)—oldest, largest, and most "establishment" of the growing number of feminist organizations—Aileen C. Hernandez, a black woman long involved in civil rights and labor causes, sought to change NOW's "embarrassingly elitist and middle-class" image and make it more relevant to the needs of working-class women and women of racial and ethnic minorities. Mrs. Hernandez, who heads a West Coast public relations and management consultant firm, had previously served on the United States Equal Employment Opportunity

AILEEN C. HERNANDEZ

Commission and as assistant chief of the California Fair Employment Practices Commission. She began her career as a union organizer for the International Ladies Garment Workers Union in California. Mrs. Hernandez was elected president of the National Organization for Women in March 1970, succeeding the group's first president, Betty Friedan, who founded NOW in 1966. During the September 1971 annual meeting of NOW, held in Los Angeles, Mrs. Hernandez was elected chairman of the national advisory committee, and she turned over the presidency to her successor, Mrs. Wilma Scott Heide of Connecticut.

Aileen Hernandez was born Aileen Clarke in Brooklyn, New York on May 23, 1926, the only daughter of Charles and Ethel Clarke, both emigrants from Jamaica. She has two brothers, one older and one younger. Mrs. Hernandez has recalled that there was little sex discrimination in her family while she was growing up. Her father worked for an art supply house, and her mother supplemented the family income during the Depression by working in the garment industry. All the children learned to cook, each child was expected to take care of his or her own room, and the brothers, as well as Aileen, were taught simple sewing.

Because she belonged to the token Negro family of the neighborhood, Mrs. Hernandez remembers growing up with "a strange sense that the world was beautiful outside." After graduating as the valedictorian of her class at P.S. 176 in the Bay Ridge section of Brooklyn, she attended Bay Ridge High School, where her class adviser, Martha Caccamo, urged her to continue her education. In 1943 she graduated as class salutatorian, with a scholarship to Howard University.

Howard University is located in Washington, D.C., and Washington in the mid-1940's was very much a Southern city. Mrs. Hernandez remembers waiting for the "Negro taxi," which was always last in line, and has recalled her shock at discovering that in the nation's capital not a single downtown restaurant, hotel, or movie house was open to Negroes. Soon she became an active member of the Howard chapter of the National Association for the Advancement of Colored People and in 1945 and 1946 she was one of those who picketed the National Theatre, Lisner Auditorium, and the Thompson restaurant chain in protest against their segregationist practices. She also supported returning World War II veterans in their efforts to desegregate the city.

On the Howard campus she took part in many extracurricular activities, including the Howard Players, the campus choir, the modern dance group, and the little theatre troupe of the School of Religion. She edited the campus newspaper, *The Hilltop,* in both her junior and senior years and wrote a column on university affairs for the now defunct Washington *Tribune.* In her junior year she was elected to the honor society that was then the equivalent of Phi Beta Kappa in Negro colleges.

In 1947 Miss Clarke received her A.B. degree *magna cum laude* in sociology and political science. That summer she went to Norway under the International Student Exchange program to do graduate work in comparative government at the University of Oslo. After returning to the United States she worked briefly as a salesgirl in Macy's toy department and then took a job as a research assistant in the department of government at Howard University. She left Howard because of illness and, after recuperating in Brooklyn for several months, enrolled as a graduate student in public administration at New York University. During that period she worked as a volunteer in several political campaigns, including the first Congressional campaign of Franklin D. Roosevelt Jr., who later was a fellow commissioner on the Equal Employment Opportunity Commission.

In 1950 the International Ladies Garment Workers Union (ILGWU) established an innovative institute to train labor leaders. Challenged by that program, Aileen Clarke left New York University for a year of training at the ILGWU "labor college." After graduating in 1951 she was assigned to the ILGWU's Pacific Coast Regional Office in Los Angeles, where she worked first as shop organizer and assistant educational director (1951-1959) and then as director of public relations and education (1959-1961). Her activities ranged from planning picnics and dances to organizing legislative mobilizations, political rallies, strikes, and picket lines. She also taught principles of unionism and pre-naturalization classes in English and citizenship to foreign-born union members at the University of California's adult education extension at Los Angeles.

While working for the ILGWU Mrs. Hernandez took graduate courses in nursery and adult education at Los Angeles State College, UCLA, and the University of Southern California. In 1961 she received a master's degree in government from Los Angeles State College with a straight "A" average and was elected to membership in the Pi Sigma Alpha honorary society.

Mrs. Hernandez' union work in southern California gave her a broad acquaintance with the problems of Mexican-Americans, and in 1960 she was invited to tour six South American countries as a specialist in labor education for the State Department. In English and Spanish she lectured on American trade unions, minority groups in the United States, the American political system, and the status of American women.

In November 1961 Mrs. Hernandez left the ILGWU to become a campaign coordinator for Democrat Alan Cranston (now a United States Senator), who was elected California State Controller in November 1962. After the election she was appointed assistant chief of the California Fair Employment Practices Commission, supervising a fifty-member staff assigned to field offices in San Francisco, Los Angeles, Fresno, and San Diego. While with the FEPC, Mrs. Hernandez established a technical advisory committee on testing, which conducts a comprehensive analysis of industrial testing as it affects the hiring of minority group members.

In May 1965 President Lyndon B. Johnson appointed Mrs. Hernandez to the Equal Employment Opportunity Commission, created under the Civil Rights Act of 1964 to enforce the federal law against employment discrimination because of race, color, religion, national origin, or sex. Looking back on her appointment, Mrs. Hernandez told Ida Lewis of *Essence,* a magazine for black women (February 1971), "When people in politics make appointments to commissions they are always trying to balance out various parts of the community. So they sort of hit the jackpot when they get someone who's black, who is a woman, who has a Mexican-American last name, who comes from California, and who's been in the labor movement." For eighteen months Mrs. Hernandez served as the only woman on the five-member commission and was influential in getting the airlines to reverse their policy of firing stewardesses when they marry. In November 1966 she resigned, however, in frustration over the EEOC's lack of progress.

"The commission didn't implement the law and I decided I could do more on my own," Mrs. Hernandez told Frances Cerra of *Newsday* (May 13, 1970). Consequently she returned to California and in San Francisco set up her own public relations and management consultant agency to advise business, government, labor and other organizations in developing programs that use minority groups and women. Her clients have included United Airlines, Standard Oil, United Parcel Service, the National Alliance of Businessmen, the University of California, and the California cities of Richmond, Berkeley, and Los Angeles. In 1969 she became Western representative of and a consultant to the National Committee Against Discrimination in Housing, a national citizens' group that has spearheaded the campaign to achieve open housing and open communities throughout the United States.

When the National Organization for Women was established in Washington, D.C., in October 1966, Mrs. Hernandez, who was then an EEOC Commissioner, reportedly turned down an offer to become the new organization's executive director.

In February 1967, however, she agreed to become NOW's Western vice-president, and at the organization's annual meeting in March 1970 she was elected its second president, succeeding Betty Friedan, NOW founder and author of *The Feminine Mystique*.

A civil rights group for women modeled closely on the NAACP in its structure, NOW seeks to bring women into the mainstream of American life "in truly equal partnership with men." NOW has about 100 chapters across the country, and Mrs. Hernandez told Ida Lewis of *Essence* that "we think we're getting pretty close to 10,000 members." Reformist in approach, the organization has worked primarily to gain equal job opportunities and pay for women and to repeal state and local laws that discriminate against women in such matters as property ownership and unequal punishment for crimes. NOW was one of a coalition of women's groups that sponsored the nationwide Women's Strike for Equality on August 26, 1970. That large-scale demonstration demanded equal jobs for women, free twenty-four-hour day care centers, and free abortions on demand. In the spring of 1970 Mrs. Hernandez testified before a Senate subcommittee on behalf of a proposed "equal rights amendment" to the Constitution, which would eliminate all legally sanctioned forms of sex discrimination. The amendment has been introduced to Congress every year since 1923, but 1970 was the first year that it ever got onto the floor of either House. (It won easy approval in the House of Representatives.)

When Mrs. Hernandez became the president of NOW she vowed to change what she called the organization's "embarrassingly elitist and middle class" image. NOW's membership has been almost totally made up of white, middle-class, professional women. In the past couple of years many of the younger, more radical women have turned to the more radical women's lib groups that have sprung up, and under Mrs. Hernandez NOW made an effort to orient its program more toward black and low-income women. "I'm much more interested in the problems of the mass woman than the professional," she told Frances Cerra of *Newsday* (May 13, 1970), "the women who are trapped in menial jobs, the woman who aspires to become a nurse but never a doctor, an elementary schoolteacher but never a professor. The low-income woman isn't going to run to join NOW, but she's going to relate to our program because she has known for a long time the problems of combining a family with a job."

Mrs. Hernandez sees the women's liberation movement as a natural outgrowth of the black movement, but one with much more radical potential for change. "You could encompass the black revolution in society as it stands with relatively little impact," she told Ida Lewis of *Essence*. "You wouldn't have to change all the institutions if you simply said, yes, from now on . . . black people will be able to do everything that white people are now doing. But if you say that all women will have true equality, this means automatically you're going to have to adjust for a 50 percent infusion into every aspect of society's functions. And you're going to have massive change."

The presidency of NOW is unsalaried, and Mrs. Hernandez continued to run her consultant agency while holding the post. She has been a frequent lecturer on such subjects as civil rights, equal employment opportunity, open housing, and trade unionism, and in 1968 she gave a social science course at San Francisco State College entitled "Government For and Against the People." Mrs. Hernandez was named woman of the year in 1961 by the Community Relations Conference of Southern California and was chosen as one of the ten most distinguished Bay Area women for 1968 by the San Francisco *Examiner*. Howard University has honored her twice: in 1967 she received the Bay Area Alumni Club award for distinguished postgraduate achievement, and in 1968 she received the Charter Day alumni award for postgraduate achievement in the field of labor and public service.

Prominent in many community activities, Mrs. Hernandez is a member of the board of directors of the National Committee Against Discrimination in Housing, the executive committee of Common Cause, the steering committee of the National Urban Coalition, the Task Force on Employment of Women of the Twentieth Century Fund, and the American Civil Liberties Union, the NAACP, the Industrial Relations Research Association, and the American Academy of Political and Social Sciences.

Aileen C. Hernandez was married in 1957 to a Mexican-American garment cutter from Los Angeles. She was divorced in 1961 and has no children. An attractive, well-groomed woman, Mrs. Hernandez was described by Helen Dudar of the New York *Post* (May 16, 1970) as "tall, arrow-postured, terribly assured, terribly fluent, . . . cool and brisk." In her spare time she enjoys golf, deep-sea fishing, cooking for her friends, and, at Christmas, keeping up acquaintance with nearly 1,000 friends through Christmas cards. Mrs. Hernandez lives in the outer Richmond section of San Francisco in an apartment that she shares with her pet dog, a black German shepherd.

References

N Y Post p19 My 16 '70 por
Newsday A p17 My 13 '70 por
Washington (D.C.) Post B p5 Jl 17 '65 por

HIRSCHFELD, ALBERT

June 21, 1903- Artist
Address: 122 E. 95th St., New York 10028

The many hundreds of Albert Hirschfeld caricatures chronicling the New York stage over more than forty years, mainly in the entertainment pages of the New York *Times*, have themselves become part of the heritage of the American theatre. Hirschfeld's commentary on the foibles of the stars of Broadway, and often of the world's vaster stage, transmits the flavor of the play in satiric

ALBERT HIRSCHFELD

wit and assured lines of vigorous and graceful movement. Although sharp and on target, his barbs do not wound, and in *The World of Hirschfeld* (1970) and other collections of his drawings he has supplemented his graphic interpretations with equally good-natured, if sometimes tart, observations in prose on show business and life.

Albert Hirschfeld was born on June 21, 1903 in St. Louis, Missouri, one of three sons of Isaac and Rebecca (Rothberg) Hirschfeld. His brothers, Milton and Alexander Hirschfeld, are no longer living. On a stopover in St. Louis during a trip out west from Albany, New York, his father, a salesman, had met and married a young Russian immigrant, although neither could then understand the other's language.

During his boyhood in St. Louis, Albert took lessons in art, occupying himself with drawing, painting, and sculpting as far back as he can remember. Aware of her son's talent, Mrs. Hirschfeld decided that it should be developed in New York. When Albert was twelve the family moved from St. Louis to Upper Manhattan. Several years later the elder Hirschfeld retired as a salesman and became absorbed in matters of community welfare. Later, from his seventy-third to his ninety-third year, he published a weekly journal. Al Hirschfeld attended public schools and the Art Students League, but at sixteen he was driven by economic necessity to take a job, as an office boy in a motion picture studio in New York. Two years later he became art director for the producer David Selznick, from whose studio he shortly afterward moved to work in the art department of Warner Brothers.

By 1924 Hirschfeld had saved enough money to quit his job and go to Paris, where he spent much of the next few years painting, drawing, and sculpting. During his European sojourn he rounded out his formal training in art with study at the County Council in London and Julienne's in Paris. His early lithograph *Hook Shop, Paris* (1925) was inspired by his observations in Europe, as were the lithographs *Soviet Worker, Moscow* (1927) and *Railway Station, Kharkov, U.S.S.R.* (1928).

Although he had a one-man sculpture show at the Newhouse Gallery in New York in 1928, he had by that time begun to lose interest in both sculpture and painting. Of his work in Paris he wrote in *The World of Hirschfeld* (Abrams, 1970), "Most of my paintings were really drawings in color, and my drawings were really sketches for paintings. . . . My real sense of satisfaction, then as now, was the image in pure line."

The line image, moreover, soon became Hirschfeld's most dependable source of income. On one of his occasional returns to New York during the 1920's he attended a performance of the French actor Sacha Guitry, who was making his debut on the American stage. During the show he sketched a likeness of Guitry on the theatre program. His companion, the press agent Dick Maney, impressed by Hirschfeld's skill, offered to show a copy of the drawing to a friend at the New York *Herald Tribune*. The appearance of the Guitry sketch on the *Herald Tribune*'s drama page the following Sunday marked the beginning of a long association with that newspaper, to which Hirschfeld contributed quite regularly. In 1927 he was theatre correspondent in Moscow for the *Herald Tribune*.

A caricature of the British comedian Sir Harry Lauder was the first of hundreds of sketches that Hirschfeld has created for the New York *Times*. His early relationship with that paper seems somewhat tentative, as well as remote and casual. For about two years, before meeting Sam Zolotow, its drama editor, he received his commissions by telegram and delivered the finished product to the *Times* reception desk. Hirschfeld was soon doing theatre drawings for the New York *World*, the Brooklyn *Eagle*, and the New York *Daily Telegraph*. His chief interests, however, during much of the 1920's and 1930's lay in politics. Besides producing lithographs of social significance, he contributed line drawings of political import to the leftist *New Masses* without pay. A dispute, however, with the *New Masses* editors, who refused to publish his drawing of a Nazified Father Coughlin, led to Hirschfeld's break with that periodical and its doctrine. "I have ever since been closer to Groucho Marx than to Karl," he remarked in *The World of Hirschfeld*.

Charles Dana Gibson and John Held had been early models of Hirschfeld in his humorous drawings. His aesthetic development as a caricaturist was far more decisively influenced in the early 1930's by a trip to the Far East. He had intended to stay for some time in Tahiti and paint, but glowing accounts of life in Bali in letters from his friend the Mexican caricaturist Miguel Covarrubias drew him to that Indonesian island via New Zealand and Australia. Hirschfeld became fascinated with Polynesian art, particularly with huge Javanese shadow puppets.

"His belief that caricature expresses the magic of a child's world," Brooks Atkinson once observed of Hirschfeld (New York *Times*, July 9, 1963), "derives from his belief in the folk art of Javanese puppets." Atkinson also commented on Hirschfeld's admiration for the work of the Japanese print master Hokusai: "The use of black and whites, the easy but graphic perspectives, and the elegance of lines are regarded as classical in the case of Hokusai. They are also classical in the case of Hirschfeld."

Five pictures of the Balinese dance were included in Hirschfeld's 1942 exhibition at Manhattan's Guy Mayer Gallery of lithographs in color and black and white. The exhibition consisted mostly of prints he had made for his book *Harlem* (Hyperion, 1941), for which William Saroyan wrote the text. Blithely satiric, the drawings focused on music and dance in depicting Negro folkways of the time. The book captured the Harlem nightclub atmosphere, just as his earlier work, *Manhattan Oases* (Dutton, 1932), had caught the atmosphere of the speakeasies in the early 1930's.

Drawn into collaboration by a mutual devotion to humor and show business, Hirschfeld and S. J. Perelman began working in the early 1940's on a book for a musical comedy. They were later joined in the venture by Ogden Nash, as lyricist, and Vernon Duke, as composer. "The four of us," Hirschfeld related in *The American Theatre as Seen by Hirschfeld* (Braziller, 1961), "labored a couple of years on this foolproof, tightly knit extravaganza and whelped (from the public point of view) a piece of idiocy titled *Sweet Bye and Bye*." The play never reached Broadway.

Hirschfeld's association with Perelman did, however, prosper in two commissions. One commission sent them to Hollywood to write and draw for *Holiday* magazine. For the other they made a trip that resulted in the best seller *Westward Ha! Or, Around the World in Eighty Clichés* (Simon & Schuster, 1948), in which Hirschfeld's drawings matched Perelman's text in hilarity. Another of Perelman's books that he illustrated was *Swiss Family Perelman* (Simon & Schuster, 1950). He has also illustrated Fred Allen's *Treadmill to Oblivion* (Little, 1954) and Ralph Schoenstein's *My Year in the White House Doghouse* (White, 1969).

In the first book of which he was both author and illustrator, *Show Business Is No Business* (Simon & Schuster, 1951), Hirschfeld satirized the glamor and pretentiousness of the Broadway theatre in prose almost as witty, trenchant, and discerning as his drawings. Some of his caustic caricatures were made to point up particular observations in his text, but most of them had appeared earlier in newspapers and magazines. They included portraits of the critics John Mason Brown and Brooks Atkinson along with those of stars like Ethel Merman, Beatrice Lillie, Ethel Waters, Bobby Clark, and Ray Bolger.

The American Theatre as Seen by Hirschfeld is another collection of his caricatures of stage people, most of which had been drawn for the Sunday entertainment section of the New York *Times*. Hirschfeld grouped his pictures according to the decades since the 1920's and wrote an amusing introduction to each section. The caricatures impart his impressions of many of Broadway's brightest productions, for which he also supplies titles, dates, and names of some of the performers. Besides reflecting the changing spirit and style of the American stage, the sketches show the development of Hirschfeld's artistry over some forty years.

Caricatures of show business people, including personalities from motion pictures and television, also make up the larger part of his handsome, coffee-table, $25 book, *The World of Hirschfeld*. Among the 189 illustrations of that retrospective collection are also early lithographs, a "color portfolio," a group of portraits of celebrities like President Franklin D. Roosevelt, and fanciful sections such as "unlikely casting," which presents Zero Mostel as Peter Pan and Lyndon B. Johnson and Barry Goldwater as the players in *Waiting for Godot*.

Brooks Atkinson in his introduction to *The American Theatre as Seen by Hirschfeld* and Lloyd Goodrich in his introduction to *The World of Hirschfeld* both commented on Hirschfeld's technical skill as a graphic artist. They were particularly interested in the uses he makes of his mastery of perspective and design in capturing total personality, his talent for revealing the uniqueness of his subject in gestures, facial expressions, clothes, and, many times, a role in life or in the play. Goodrich called attention to Hirschfeld's "unerring sense of character," which he regards as a rare and inborn gift.

Hirschfeld himself wrote in his autobiographical preface to *The World of Hirschfeld* that if there were such a word he would be "more comfortable being classified as a 'characterist'" than as a caricaturist. "My primary interest," he explained, "is in producing a drawing capable of surviving the obvious fun of recognition or news value. . . . For the subject which turns me on is people." When Gertrude Stein protested to Picasso that his portrait of her did not look like her, he replied that she would come to look like the portrait. Hirschfeld, somewhat similarly, has remarked, "I consider a successful likeness has been achieved when the subject begins to look like the drawing." Ray Bolger told him that for years he had tried to imitate Hirschfeld's drawings of him. Among Hirschfeld's favorite subjects—persons who lend themselves to being caricatured—are Charlie Chaplin, Carol Channing, Zero Mostel, Bert Lahr, Laurel and Hardy, and Heywood Broun, but the list would run for pages.

For Hirschfeld, caricature is not an art of malice. Although his work is critical, he does not use ridicule to injure an actor or a play. As Atkinson has observed, he is not interested in anatomical distortions or in exaggerations of his subjects' deficiencies: "Instead of burlesquing people, he joins them on their own terms, adding his own gaiety for good measure." There is a professional integrity, or objectivity, in Hirschfeld's work: "My contribution is to take the character—created by the playwright and acted out by the actor—and reinvent it for the reader."

Most of Hirschfeld's theatre drawings begin with his attending out-of-town performances of plays scheduled to open in New York. He draws in the darkened theatre (he has even learned to draw in his pocket), making a series of sketches on which he scribbles in his own shorthand notes about action, fleeting details, and suggestions about a possible overall design of his picture. Later in his studio, seated in a well-worn barber's chair, with his drawing board before him, he transforms his sketches and scribbles into the completed caricature. Commenting on his art in a *National Observer* interview, he said, "There is no lack of talent in caricature, but there is a lack of sponsorship. There's no place to go with it. I seem to be alone with a 40-mile-an-hour gale around me."

For the past twenty-five years Hirschfeld has hidden the name of his daughter, Nina, in the designs of almost every one of his drawings, often in the folds of costumes or curtains, in hairdos, wrinkles, or leaves of trees. The practice began in the fall of 1945 when Hirschfeld celebrated the birth of his daughter by including her name in a drawing he was assigned to do of the musical *Are You With It?* To his picture of the circus background of the show he added a poster of an infant reading a large book. She was billed as "Nina the Wonder Child." For his many fans who delight in searching for the name, whenever "Nina" appears more than once in a picture, he writes the appropriate number after his signature.

Hirschfeld's caricatures have been bought by many private collectors, and his work is in the permanent collections of the Metropolitan Museum of Art, the Whitney Museum of Art, the Museum of Modern Art, the New York Public Library, the Library of Performing Arts of Lincoln Center, the St. Louis Museum of Art, the Cleveland Museum of Art, the Fogg Museum, and other museums. He has executed murals for the American Pavilion of the 1958 World's Fair in Brussels, the Eden Roc Hotel in Miami, the Manhattan Playbill Room, and the Fifth Avenue Playhouse. Among his one-man shows in Manhattan were those at the Heller Gallery in 1960, the Hammer Gallery in 1967, and the Lincoln Center Museum of Performing Arts in 1969. He was awarded a grant from the United States Department of State as specialist for graphic art in South America in 1960.

On an assignment that took him to a Hershey, Pennsylvania summer theatre in the early 1940's, Albert Hirschfeld met the actress Dolly Haas, whom he married on May 8, 1943. He later drew her as she appeared in *Lute Song* in 1946 and in *Crime and Punishment* in 1947. Nina is their daughter. He had earlier married Florence Ruth Hobby, on July 13, 1927; they were divorced in 1942.

A crowded Hirschfeld drawing may include a self-portrait—a bearded man with formidable eyebrows who stands five feet eight inches tall and weighs 170 pounds. In the early 1930's, arriving home from Paris, he was reported in *Variety* to have "sprouted a hanging garden on his chin." Offended by that and other remarks in the news story, Hirschfeld sued *Variety* for $300,000. A jury awarded him six cents, of which he actually received not one penny. His brown eyes are fascinating too. In his foreword to *Show Business Is No Business* Russel Crouse described them as guileless and lamblike—and cunning.

References

Christian Sci Mon p9 My 27 '70
Look 24:64j+ N 8 '60 pors
N Y Times II p1 S 9 '51; p28 Jl 9 '63
Nat Observer p1+ O 24 '66 por
Playbill 6:13+ S '69 por
Toronto Globe and Mail p23 Mr 21 '70
Hirschfeld, Albert. The American Theatre as Seen by Hirschfeld (1961); The World of Hirschfeld (1970)
Who's Who in America, 1970-71
Who's Who in American Art, 1970

HOLTON, (ABNER) LINWOOD (JR.)

Sept. 21, 1923- Governor of Virginia; lawyer
Address: b. State Capitol, Richmond, Va. 23219; h. Governor's Mansion, Richmond, Va. 23219; 3125 Quenham Ave., S.W., Roanoke, Va. 24014

When Linwood Holton, a Roanoke lawyer, was elected Governor of Virginia on November 4, 1969, Republicans hailed their victory as a clear signal of vast changes in the Old Dominion, which had not had a Republican Governor in eighty-four years. The election of Holton, who is closely associated with President Richard Nixon, weakened the domination of Virginia politics by the conservative Democratic Byrd family. While the Republican administration in Washington interpreted the Virginia vote as a hopeful sign for its much-touted "Southern strategy," political observers were more impressed by the success with which Holton had put together a coalition of dissident conservatives, labor, and Negroes, and attributed his election to the increase in urbanization and number of black voters. Governor Holton's main achievement has been to create a new climate in race relations by opening up employment opportunities for blacks and by his moderate stand on court-ordered school desegregation plans in September 1970. Most of his proposals for pollution control, for more effective correctional programs, and for better schools and hospitals have been snagged by lack of money in the state budget. An ebullient and energetic politician, Holton has generated both openness and pragmatism in a state long wedded to tradition. His term of office is four years, and he is prevented by state law from succeeding himself.

Abner Linwood Holton Jr. was born on September 21, 1923 to Abner Linwood and Edith (Van Gorder) Holton in Big Stone Gap, Virginia. His father was president of a coal mine railroad, the Interstate Railroad Company, and his brother, C. V. Holton, is employed by Norfolk & Western Railway. Linwood grew up with his brother and two sisters, Harriet and Louisa, in his native mountain town in the southwestern part of the state, a stronghold of Republicanism in Virginia since Reconstruction days. He got his first taste of politics at the age of twelve when he delivered flyers for a local candidate. In high school he was business manager of the school annual and belonged to the debating society and to the football and track teams. After graduation in 1941 he entered Washington and Lee University, where he majored in commerce, was a member of Omicron Delta Kappa, and served as president of the Interfraternity Council.

By the time he obtained his B.A. degree, in November 1944, Holton was on World War II duty with the United States Navy, having become an apprentice seaman in the Submarine Force in 1943. He was discharged from the Navy with the rank of lieutenant, j.g., in 1946 and from the Naval Reserve with the rank of captain in June 1965. When he had completed his wartime service Holton enrolled in Harvard University Law School. He earned his LL.B. degree in 1949 and later that year was admitted to the Virginia bar. After practising for a time as a member of the Roanoke firm of Hunter and Fox, he became a founding partner of the firm of Eggleston, Holton, Butler & Glenn, also in Roanoke.

Active in the local Republican party, Holton joined a group of young Republicans in ousting an old guard clique in the 1950's, and as a result he became chairman of the Roanoke city Republican committee. Twice he was defeated for a seat in the Virginia House of Delegates: in 1955, when he received 49 percent of the vote, and again in 1957. He was elected vice-chairman of the Virginia Republican Central Committee in 1960, was a delegate to the Republican National Conventions in 1960 and 1968, and served as campaign manager for H. Clyde Pearson in his unsuccessful bid for Governor of Virginia in 1961.

In May 1965 Virginia Republicans tapped Holton to lead the state ticket. Before agreeing to become the gubernatorial candidate he required, among other conditions, that there be indications of both financial and grass roots support within the party. That race marked the first time that many precincts in Virginia had any Republican organization at all, but the campaign was described in the press as a "shoestring effort," with the Republicans spending under $80,000—less than half the budget of the Democratic opponent, Mills E. Godwin. Holton's campaign identified him as a moderate, since he campaigned against Godwin's past anti-integration record, including his support of the $1.50 poll tax. However, in the November election Godwin, who had tried to project a more moderate image himself, won by a margin of 48 percent of the vote to Holton's 38 percent.

During his campaign Holton had turned for help to Richard Nixon. Although considered a political loser at the time, the former Vice-President drew large crowds in his several appearances for Holton. In 1967 Holton returned the favor, becoming one of the six original members of the National Nixon for President Committee. He also served as regional coordinator during Nixon's 1968 campaign for the Presidency. In November Nixon carried Virginia by the same 10 percent margin by which Holton had lost in 1965. Locally the result of Nixon's victory was an expansion of grass roots Republican organization and increased prominence of Holton as a party leader.

LINWOOD HOLTON

At its convention on March 1, 1969 the state Republican party again nominated Holton for Governor. He entered into the campaign with enthusiasm, pushing hard his main theme of the need for a change, to end one-party rule in Virginia, where Republicans had not won a single statewide elected post since 1926, when Harry F. Byrd was first elected Governor. Holton's chances were helped by a bitter struggle in the Democratic party between conservative and liberal forces. William C. Battle finally emerged as the Democratic party's nominee, but the primary left divisions not easily healed. Both candidates were moderates. In sharp contrast to contestants of past Virginia campaigns aimed at white voters only, they both appealed for Negro, as well as labor, votes. Holton's strength was boosted by the endorsement of the state AFL-CIO organization and of the Crusade for Voters, the state's major black voters' organization. Visits from President Nixon and other national political leaders underscored Holton's identification with the Republican administration in Washington. In addition, by stressing his opposition to the Byrd machine Holton picked up dissident conservative support from Democrats to form a coalition that spread across the political spectrum. The campaign was the most expensive one to date in Virginia, with Holton spending close to $400,000 and Battle about $322,000.

Many changes ultimately favoring Holton's candidacy had taken place in Virginia during the 1960's. Of immediate significance was the fact that in 1965 the Supreme Court had ruled that the state's poll tax was unconstitutional, ending the requirement that voters register three years before an election. Black registration drives increased black voting power ten times its 1960 level. Virginia was also rapidly becoming more metropolitan. In 1950 the state was 53 percent rural, but by 1968 the urban corridor in the eastern half of the state included 56 percent of the state's 4,500,000 residents, and personal income had risen 92 percent between 1960 and 1968. While conservatism was still strong, there were signs of turning away from the attitudes of the early 1960's, when the arch-conservative Senator Harry F. Byrd had pushed "massive resistance" to school integration. Industrial growth, particularly in the shipbuilding and naval area around Norfolk, was diversifying an economy that had heavily depended on the tobacco industry. Finally, the Republican party had gradually been gaining strength in the South. During the Johnson administration Republicans had made substantial gains at the state level, and in 1968 Richard Nixon carried eight of the Southern states for the GOP.

Holton won the election on November 4, 1969 by polling more than 52 percent of the vote, in a record turnout of 900,000 voters. His two running mates lost to Democrats, however, and the 100-seat House of Delegates remained overwhelmingly Democratic in spite of Republican gains in the northern Virginia area near Washington. One side of a disagreement as to the source of Holton's support was presented in a political analysis circulated in the White House that attributed Holton's victory to conservative defections from the Democratic party. The effect of the analysis was to uphold those in the administration who urged a Republican "Southern strategy" based on the conservative white vote. That interpretation was rejected by Holton himself. According to a Washington *Post* editorial (November 6, 1969), the election meant a victory for a new image in Virginia politics rather than a personal victory for Nixon, since the greatest margin was piled up by the Democratic J. Sargeant Reynolds in winning the lieutenant governorship. In a later editorial, in May 1970, the *Post* called attention to a study by Professor Ralph Eisenberg, of the Institute of Government of the University of Virginia, that stressed Holton's support among blacks and residents of urban areas, noting that he won 57 percent of the suburban vote and 51.4 percent of the central city vote. Whatever the interpretation of Holton's victory, it symbolized the growing strength of the Republican party in the South.

In his address at his untraditionally festive inaugural on January 17, 1970, and in his subsequent address to the legislature, Holton committed himself to making Virginia a "model in race relations" and to acting to "ensure the quality of our environment." He also underscored Virginia's growth as an urban state and the need to cooperate with the federal government, thus challenging many years of insularity. One of his first acts was to appoint a Negro, William B. Robertson, as an executive assistant to the Governor in charge of consumer protection and business and job development for minority groups. That appointment was followed within the week by a firm order banning racial discrimination in state employment.

As Governor, Holton had power to make over 400 appointments, an authority of particular significance since Democrats had run the state since 1886 and controlled all other elective state offices. Highly selective in his changes, he did not always appoint Republicans or even Virginians. A large number of the appointments were young persons who helped create a youthful image for the new administration. Holton also asked the legislature to take away the appointive power of the judiciary over local political officials, ending a practice that was the bulwark of the Byrd party machinery.

Like many other governors, Holton has found that his thorniest problem is a financial one. In his campaign he had urged a $9 per person rebate to compensate for what he felt was an unfortunate 4 percent tax on food. Because of a tight budget he proposed an alternative plan to give the rebate only to families with incomes under $3,000. Godwin had left behind a $3.8 billion budget, to which Holton quickly added $100,000,000 to pay for new programs. Besides the tax rebate, his proposals included controlling water pollution, mental health services, relocation of the state penitentiary, and park expansion. After failing to get his agencies to make significant budget cuts, Holton tried to increase the cigarette tax from 2½ cents a pack to 5 cents and the liquor tax from 10 to 14 percent. Although the present level of the tobacco tax is one of the lowest in the country, and the increase would only bring it to half the national average of 10 cents a pack, the tobacco industry was strong enough to get the bill defeated in the House. Holton is currently pushing the Nixon administration's revenue-sharing proposal, which he has said is the only real answer to the pressing urban fiscal problems in Virginia. Virginia has long been wary of any cooperation with the federal government that might compromise its jealously guarded state authority. Holton responded to a plea from the cities by providing $4,000,000 for welfare in December 1970, but he was not optimistic about obtaining new taxing authority or state welfare aid from the General Assembly in 1971 to solve urban fiscal problems. While Holton is on friendly terms with many of the Democrats in the Richmond assembly, he has been unable to get important legislation passed.

Because of the conservatism of the state, Governor Holton has not pushed dramatic reform, but instead has concentrated on making the government more efficient. His moderation was highlighted in the summer of 1970 when a federal court ordered that busing of children in Richmond had to be stepped up to achieve more racial integration in the city schools. Although he asked that the plan be set aside until the Supreme Court ruled on it, the court rejected his request. Holton responded by appealing to Virginia parents to comply with the law and then by enrolling his three school-age children in nearby predominantly black schools even though as Governor he could have been exempted from the court order. Predictably, Holton was both criticised for his stance and commended as a courageous new leader in the South.

Holton's political leadership was put to a test when Harry F. Byrd Jr. announced that he was running for the Virginia Senate seat as an independent in November 1970. Many Republicans wanted their party to endorse Byrd rather than nominate its own candidate. Holton, who was aware of Byrd's popularity but disapproved of his conservative position, insisted that the nomination go to a Republican. At the party convention in June the Byrd forces apparently overplayed their hand by bringing in Senator Strom Thurmond and the White House strategist Harry Dent. Reacting angrily, Holton made a strong speech that prompted the convention to endorse his candidate, Ray Garland. The Nixon administration, however, gave no support to Garland, and he lost heavily in the election. The columnist Marquis Childs called the campaign a "lost opportunity" for the Nixon administration to help create "a genuine two-party South." Holton himself retained his optimism about the future of the Republican party and refused to see Garland's defeat as a setback for his own administration or moderate position. However, the precariousness of his coalition was apparent in the overwhelming black support for the Democratic candidate George Rawlings.

On January 10, 1953 Linwood Holton married Virginia Harrison Rogers ("Jinks"), a Wellesley College graduate whose father was a staunch Byrd Democrat. She is an able and enthusiastic campaigner. The couple have four children—Virginia Taylor, Anne Bright, Linwood 3d, and Dwight Carter—who have added unaccustomed liveliness to Virginia's handsome Governor's mansion. Descriptions of Holton inevitably mention his energy and enthusiasm and often his informality. A personable man, he has gray eyes and sandy hair, stands six feet tall, and weighs 185 pounds. His sports are tennis and skiing. He has been president of Roanoke's Washington and Lee alumni chapter and he has served in executive positions with the Chamber of Commerce and the Roanoke Fine Arts Center. An elder of Roanoke's Second Presbyterian Church, he also teaches Sunday school there.

References

Wall St J p10 S 11 '70
Washington (D.C.) Post F p1 N 2 '69
Martindale-Hubbell Law Directory, 1970
Who's Who in America, 1970-71

HORGAN, PAUL

Aug. 1, 1903- Author
Address: b. Wesleyan University, Middletown, Conn. 06457; h. 77 Pearl St., Middletown, Conn. 06457

After four decades of solid but relatively unobtrusive literary distinction, Paul Horgan has finally achieved best-seller status with the novel *Whitewater* (1970), a nostalgic, death-haunted but lyrical evocation of adolescence in a small Southwestern town. The Southwest has been the setting for most of the best of Horgan's thirty-two books, the magnum opus among which is *Great River: The Rio Grande in North American History* (1954), a work of historical nonfiction that won Pulitzer and Bancroft prizes and elicited critical praise for its painstaking scholarship and rich narrative art. (A limited edition of *Great River* is illustrated with the author's own watercolors.) Horgan's reputation was unspectacular until now partly because his very versatility splintered it. Southwest-

PAUL HORGAN

erners thought of him as their regional writer and Roman Catholics as their religious humanist, and, as Lawrence Clark Powell the librarian once remarked, critics found it difficult to type him, so widely did he range "over the whole field of belles lettres—fiction, history, poetry, essays, children's books." Since 1959 Horgan has been at Wesleyan University, where he is now author-in-residence. He is also on the editorial board of the Book-of-the-Month Club.

Horgan is known for his measured, Virgilian style and his painstaking characterization. Calling him a "patrician," John Barkham wrote in the New York *Post* (September 29, 1970): "Time, place, and character are all recalled by an acutely sensitive mind. His sensibilities are those of a generation that valued elegance, symmetry, and morality." And Melvin Maddocks wrote in *Life* (October 9, 1970): "His name modestly guarantees quality—the presence of disciplined if not explosive talents. Horgan has stood for certain unequivocal things. He has been . . . a man with a sense of the past and the makings of a firm moral philosophy."

A second-generation American, Paul Horgan is of English-Irish and French-German descent. His maternal grandfather was Mathias Rohr, a German poet who left the University of Bonn to immigrate to the United States. Horgan was born in Buffalo, New York on August 1, 1903, the second of the three children of Edward and Rose Marie (Rohr) Horgan. His father, a newspaper publisher in failing health, moved the family to Albuquerque, New Mexico when Horgan was twelve and the Southwest was still very much a part of the American frontier. New Mexico in 1915 was still "tierra encantada" (land of enchantment) to the Spanish-speaking descendants of the conquistadores who made up the bulk of the population. Billy the Kid and the wars with the Apache nation were living memories and Pancho Villa was a living fact. Santa Fe, the state capital, had been chartered as a royal city by the Spanish Crown before the Pilgrims landed at Plymouth but boasted a population of less than 15,000, and Albuquerque, the only other municipality of note in a land area larger than all of Italy, was little more than a straggling railroad town. Young Horgan fell in love with the "new world of land," as he has called it, with its vast landscapes, mesas, sandhills, cliffs, and mountains, and with the fascinating history that he was later to help to rescue from oblivion.

After completing his elementary education in Albuquerque public schools, Horgan attended the New Mexico Military Institute at Roswell, New Mexico, where he edited the school literary journal and where he demonstrated a pronounced flair for dramatics, music, and art. While still in school he worked briefly as a reporter and music critic for the Albuquerque *Morning Journal*. In 1922 his father died, and the following year the Horgans moved back East. For three years Horgan studied at the Eastman School of Music in Rochester, New York and worked at the school's theatre, where, according to his own recollection, he "acted, sang, directed, planned and built scenery, wrote, even danced." The multiplicity of his talents posed him a dilemma in the choice of a career. In the end he opted for writing because the latter is, in his view, "the art best able to employ aspects of versatility in other arts."

In 1926 Horgan returned to the New Mexico Military Institute as the institute's librarian, a job compatible with writing and historical research. In developing his craft in the late 1920's he wrote several novels that were never published. His first professionally published work was verse that appeared in *Poetry* magazine. His writing began to appear between hard covers in 1931, when his juvenile historical book *Men of Arms*, illustrated by him, was published by David McKay and a short story of his was included in the *O. Henry Memorial Prize Stories* annual published by Doubleday. Two years later he won the Harper Prize Novel contest with *The Fault of Angels*, a humorous book based on his experiences at the Eastman Theatre.

His first Southwestern novel, *No Quarter Given*, was followed by a spate of fictional works with similar regional settings, including the novels *Main Line West* and *A Lamp on the Plains*, the short story collection *The Return of the Weed*, and the novelette *Far From Cibola*. All were published by Harper & Brothers. During the same period Horgan compiled *From the Royal City* (Villagra Bookshop, Santa Fe, 1936), five accounts of life in Santa Fe written by various hands between 1690 and 1878.

The first book by Horgan to win him serious national attention was *The Habit of Empire* (Harper, 1941), a novel, with lithographs by Peter Hurd, based on Juan de Onate's march of conquest northward into New Mexico in 1599, culminating in the siege of the natural Indian citadel known as the Rock of Acoma. The terse novel of 114 pages was described by the reviewer for *Time* (May 8, 1941) as "an intense mural of hardship, Indian-fighting and Catholic Imperial psychology in colonial New Mexico." The critic added that, although "a little stiff, . . . its leisured 114 pages

should embarrass most space-wasting historical novelists."

When the United States entered World War II, Horgan left his position at the New Mexico Military Institute to become chief of Army Information with the Department of War in Washington, D.C., a post in which he reached the rank of lieutenant colonel and received the Legion of Merit. During the war, he published the novelette *The Common Heart* (Harper, 1942); wrote the play *Yours, A. Lincoln*, produced in New York in 1942; and did the libretto for Ernest Bacon's American folk opera *A Tree on the Plains*, produced in New York in 1943.

On his discharge from the Army, Horgan received the first of two Guggenheim grants. After lecturing for a semester in the Graduate School of Arts and Letters of the University of Iowa for a semester, he returned to Roswell to resume, full-time, his research and writing. In collaboration with the editors of *Look* magazine, he wrote the text for the *Southwest* volume of the *Look at America* pictorial series, published in 1947 by Houghton, Mifflin. In 1952 Longmans, Green published two works of fiction by Horgan, *Devil in the Desert*, the recounting of a Rio Grande legend, and *One Red Rose for Christmas*.

Fourteen years of research and composition went into *Great River*, published in two volumes by Rinehart in 1954. Horgan later explained that in that book he "attempted to bring to the reader a survey of the historical life—pre-Spanish, post-Columbian, pre-technological, and proto-modern—of the American Southwest," placing the events of history against the "qualifying landscape" traversed by the Rio Grande River over its long course. "Three dominant cultures were projected in turn against that land—the Indian, the Latin, and the Anglo-American. . . . I undertook to weave into the more formal, or perhaps more active aspects of Southwestern history various recreations of those elements of belief, custom, group behavior, and social energy that gave to each of the three cultures its own style."

Orville Prescott, reviewing *Great River* in the New York *Times* (October 11, 1954), called it "a labor of love, if ever there was one." Prescott went on: "Mr. Horgan fits his pieces together with loving relish over every detail. And the specific facts he records are always interesting, whether they are facts about the religion and folklore of the Pueblo Indians, the atrocities committed by Coronado's conquistadores, [or] the correct technique of forging a Toledo blade. . . . Paul Horgan writes about such matters with harsh realism and every appearance of objective judgment. But he writes so well, with such skill in capturing the typical emotion of the past, that *Great River* seems almost a romantic book." J. Frank Dobie, writing in the New York *Times Book Review* (October 10, 1954), said: "Paul Horgan is an artist, . . . a master of proportions, perspective, and details. His book is an unfoldment of life with stretches of narrative as vivid as 'Livy's pictured page' and essays as bold as the divagations of Henry Fielding. As a novelist he became long ago a looker down into the wells of human loneliness and he is enough of the painter to be always conscious of color and shadow."

Between 1955 and 1959 the Catholic religious motif dominated Horgan's work, specifically the books of fiction *The Saintmaker's Christmas Eve* (Farrar, Straus, 1955), illustrated by the author, and *Give Me Possession* (Farrar, Straus, 1957); *The Centuries of Santa Fe* (Dutton, 1956), a history of missionaries in the Southwest, illustrated by Horgan; and *Rome Eternal* (Farrar, Straus, 1959), a travel picture book with photographs by Joseph Vadala. *The Centuries of Santa Fe* won the Catholic Book Club's Campion Award.

Horgan's novel *A Distant Trumpet* (Farrar, Straus, 1960), based on the exploits of the United States Cavalry in the Indian country of Arizona in the 1880's, was praised by Paul Engle in the New York *Times Book Review* (April 17, 1960) for its "fine power of fresh detail" and its "feeling for the subtle nuances of human relations," although Engle noted a slight flaw in "the excess comment of the author, heavily emphasizing the obvious." In 1961 Farrar, Straus & Cudahy (now Farrar, Straus & Giroux) published Horgan's *Citizen of New Salem*, a biography of Abraham Lincoln. The same publishers issued the children's story *Toby and the Nighttime* and the nonfiction book *Conquistadores in North American History* in 1963; the fictional work *Things As They Are* in 1964; *The Peach Stone*, a collection of short stories, in 1967; and the novel *Everything to Live For* in 1968. Meanwhile Horgan's *Peter Hurd: A Portrait Sketch from Life* was published by the University of Texas Press, in 1965.

Whitewater, published by Farrar, Straus & Giroux in the autumn of 1970, is the story of two boys and a girl growing up in a Texas town near a lake that symbolizes both death and memory of the past because it preserves, in its depths, the visible ruins of an earlier settlement. Even before the publication of the novel Horgan was certain of $250,000 in royalties from three book clubs (the Book-of-the-Month Club, the Literary Guild, and the Reader's Digest Condensed Book Club) and the Paperback Library. In his review of *Whitewater* in the New York *Post*, John Barkham wrote: "If you recall his last novel, *Everything to Live For*, you will not need to be told that he [Horgan] has a special flair for recording the pleasures and pains of youth. It is this flair that he displays pains of youth. It is this flair that he displays novel we still expect of Paul Horgan, but it is infinitely superior to most of the fiction published these days."

In his *Life* review of *Whitewater*, Melvin Maddocks asked himself the question "Why is a Horgan novel suddenly presumed to have mass appeal?" and answered it: "The air hangs thick with dust, heat, and obsession as well as nostalgia. But in the end *Whitewater* is . . . more hope than desperation. . . . In America's time of troubles, novel readers, like everyone else, need their reassurance—their man of faith and reasonably sound nerves." Two other books by Horgan appeared in 1970: *The Heroic Triad: Essays in the Social*

Energies of Three Southwestern Cultures (Holt, Rinehart, and Winston), a spin-off from *Great River*, and *Maurice Baring Restored* (Heinemann), which the author has called "a labor of homage" to "one of the foundations of my own sensibility." Horgan has, reportedly, been working on a biography of Archbishop Lamy of New Mexico, the prelate who provided the inspiration for the title character in Willa Cather's novel *Death Comes for the Archbishop*.

Supported by his second Guggenheim grant, Horgan became a fellow of the Center for Advanced Studies at Wesleyan University in 1959. He was director of the center from 1962 to 1967, when he became the university's author-in-residence. The latter post requires him to conduct a seminar in advanced fiction writing for upperclassmen. Since July 1969 Horgan has been a judge of the Book-of-the-Month, a position that reportedly pays about $30,000 a year. He is a founder of the Santa Fe Opera Company, and he has served as board chairman of the opera company and president of the Roswell Museum and Art Center and the American Catholic Historical Association. He has been an associate fellow of Saybrook College at Yale University, and he is a member of the National Institute of Arts and Letters. His clubs are the Century, the University (New York), the Cosmos, the Army-Navy (Washington), the Graduate (New Haven), and the Athenaeum (London), and his political party is the Democratic. His honors include thirteen honorary degrees and knightship in the papal Order of St. Gregory.

Paul Horgan is five feet nine inches tall, weighs 165 pounds, and has blue eyes and graying brown hair. A quiet, retiring bachelor, Horgan lives on the Wesleyan campus, in a former coach house filled with 6,000 books and a large collection of paintings and drawings. He himself keeps his hand adept at art. "I love to draw, and to make silly drawings," he confided to Alden Whitman of the New York *Times* (September 1, 1970). He also told Whitman that he is "a virtuoso listener to music, but a fairly conventional one—Beethoven, Mozart, and the like," adding that he is also fond of Aaron Copland. Tennis used to be another of his recreations, when he was younger. Inexperienced as a cook, he usually eats out. "The supreme act of self-respect in any society," Horgan once wrote, in an introduction to a guide to the Roswell Museum, "is to know its own origins, gather all possible evidence for these, and share them with an interested public in a form as appropriate and beautiful as possible."

References

Life 69:12 O 9 '70 por
N Y Post p46 S 29 '70 por
N Y Times p28 Jl 10 '69 por; p30 S 1 '70 por
Contemporary Authors vol 13-14 (1965)
Twentieth Century Authors (1942; First Supplement, 1955)
Who's Who in America, 1970-71

HOVEYDA, AMIR ABBAS (hō-vä-dä')

Feb. 18, 1919- Premier of Iran
Address: b. Office of the Premier, Teheran,
Iran; h. Zafaranieh, Teheran, Iran

The kingdom of Iran has been described by its Premier, Amir Abbas Hoveyda, as "an island of stability and progress" in the "troubled seas of the Middle East." A constitutional monarchy with a population of some 30,000,000, Iran has recently been making rapid strides toward modernization without abandoning its rich cultural heritage that dates back to the founding of the Persian Empire some 2,500 years ago. Dedicated and progressive, Hoveyda is a former diplomat and executive of Iran's largest business enterprise, the National Iranian Oil Company, who became involved in the Shah's reform program while serving as Minister of Finance in the Cabinet in 1964-65. He succeeded to the Premiership in January 1965, following the assassination of his predecessor, Hassan Ali Mansur. Although the ultimate power in Iran resides in Mohammed Riza Shah Pahlevi, Premier Hoveyda wields considerable authority in administering the nation's domestic and foreign policies. He is determined to bring his country up to a social and economic level approaching that of Western nations.

Amir Abbas Hoveyda was born in Teheran on February 18, 1919, one of the two sons of Habib-Ollah (or Habiballah) Hoveyda, a diplomat, and Fatemeh (Afsar-ol-Molouk) Hoveyda. His brother, Fereydoon Hoveyda, a writer and diplomat, is undersecretary of state in Iran's Ministry of Foreign Affairs. After completing his early schooling in Iran, Hoveyda obtained his secondary education at the Lycée Français in Beirut, Lebanon. He then studied at the Université Libre at Brussels, Belgium, where he earned a master's degree in political science and economics, and at the Sorbonne in Paris, where he received a doctorate in history.

In 1942 Hoveyda began his public service career with the Ministry of Foreign Affairs, with which he remained about sixteen years. He became an attaché with the Iranian Embassy in Paris in 1945 and was appointed second secretary with Iran's mission to West Germany two years later. He returned to Teheran in 1951 to serve as deputy director of one of the departments of the Foreign Affairs Ministry. From 1952 to 1956 Hoveyda served in Geneva as director of the liaison department in the office of the United Nations High Commissioner for Refugees. In 1957 he became counselor at the Iranian Embassy in Ankara.

From 1958 to 1964 Hoveyda was a member of the board of directors of the government-controlled National Iranian Oil Company (NIOC). During that period he served successively as assistant to its board chairman, as its general managing director, and as head of its administration and organization. The NIOC—the successor of the now defunct Anglo-Iranian Oil Company—had been founded after the nationalization of the Iran-

ian oil industry in 1951. In October 1954 the NIOC and the Iranian government concluded a twenty-five year agreement with an international consortium consisting of the British Petroleum Company Ltd., and American, French, and Dutch firms. Under its provisions the foreign companies were granted oil concessions in Iran after agreeing to pay 50 percent of all earnings to the Iranian government. During the years that Hoveyda served on the board of NIOC, its facilities for oil exploration, production, and marketing greatly expanded, and additional agreements were concluded with foreign companies.

In the early 1960's Mohammed Riza Shah Pahlevi conceived of a thoroughgoing reform program, known as the White Revolution, to be aimed at modernizing virtually all aspects of Iranian life and undercutting the forces of the revolutionary left, represented by the outlawed Tudeh party. For its formulation, the Shah enlisted the aid of the Progressive Center, a coalition of relatively young, middle-class technocrats drawn from the civil service, business, and the professions. As one of its leading members, Hoveyda was closely associated with the Shah's reforms. Approved by an overwhelming vote in a national referendum in January 1963, the reform program included provisions for extensive land redistribution; nationalization of forests; sale of government-owned industries as backing for land reforms; electoral reforms, including the granting of equal rights to women; profit-sharing for factory workers; and creation of a literacy corps to teach rural Iranians reading and writing skills. Other provisions, which were added later, included formation of a health corps and an agricultural development corps and reforms in the judiciary and the administrative and academic fields.

In 1963 the Shah allowed the national Parliament, which had been temporarily suspended during a period of crisis, to be reopened. To help the Shah carry out his reform program, Hassan Ali Mansur, a close confidant of the monarch and a boyhood friend and brother-in-law of Hoveyda, created a semi-official political party, the Iran-e-Novin (New Iran) party, from the Progressive Center. The party was officially established on December 15, 1963, with Mansur as secretary general and Amir Hoveyda as deputy secretary general and a member of the executive committee. When Mansur was appointed Premier by the Shah in March 1964 he named Hoveyda Minister of Finance in his Cabinet and made him his chief aide.

On January 21, 1965, while on his way to the Majlis, the lower house of Parliament, Premier Mansur was wounded by an assassin's bullet and five days later he died. Four members of Fedayan Islam, a reactionary Moslem group opposed to the Shah's reforms, were arrested for the murder and later executed. Determined that the reform program, begun by Mansur, be continued, the Shah named Hoveyda interim Premier when Mansur was wounded and appointed him to succeed the slain Premier on January 27, 1965. On taking office, Hoveyda pledged that Iran's domestic and foreign policies would remain the same. "Except for the sad absence of Mansur, nothing is changed," he declared. "The same men will carry out the same programs." Along with the Premiership, Hoveyda at first also retained the portfolio of Finance, but he later appointed Dr. Jamshid Amuzegar to succeed him in the latter position. He also relinquished the secretary generalship of the Iran-e-Novin party, which had fallen to him after Mansur's death, because he felt that the Premiership and the top party post should not be occupied by the same man.

Although Hoveyda received an overwhelming vote of confidence in the Parliament four days after he took office, he soon faced serious problems. The problem of internal security, dramatized by Mansur's assassination, was further aggravated when in April 1965 a member of the palace guard made an unsuccessful attack on the Shah, allegedly as part of a leftist plot, causing the Hoveyda government to take repressive measures against extremist groups. Despite increasing oil revenues and the relative success of industrialization under Iran's third economic development plan (1962-68), the country was plagued with a shortage of funds needed for further economic progress. The shortage was largely the result of a sharp reduction in aid from the United States government, which maintained that, in view of its seeming prosperity, Iran was no longer in dire need. Furthermore, the rapid pace of land redistribution placed considerable pressure on the country's rural credit system. To remedy Iran's fiscal problems, Hoveyda introduced a stricter income tax law and, in presenting the national budget for 1965-66, announced steps to stimulate investment, create more employment, stabilize prices, and improve the balance of foreign exchange. The government also negotiated new development loans with the World Bank and the Export-Import Bank.

In foreign affairs, Hoveyda reaffirmed Iran's adherence to the Central Treaty Organization (CENTO), in which it is linked with Turkey, Pakistan, Great Britain, and the United States. In September 1965 he visited Rawalpindi to pledge Iran's support for Pakistan in its dispute with India over Kashmir and to discuss means by which a peaceful settlement of that conflict might be attained. The reduced flow of funds from the United States—which ended its aid program of grants and low-interest loans in June 1966 on the ground that Iran was now a "developed nation"—steered the Hoveyda government in the direction of more cordial relations with the Soviet Union, towards which Iran had been hostile only a few years earlier. In January 1966 Hoveyda negotiated an agreement with the Soviet Union for aid in constructing a steel mill, a machine-tool plant, and a natural gas pipeline, as well as in exploiting Iranian iron mines and coalfields. Under an additional agreement, announced by Hoveyda in February 1967, the Soviet Union agreed to furnish Iran with $110,000,000 worth of military equipment, to be paid for with Iranian natural gas and manufactured goods.

Iran's relations with its Arab neighbors were sometimes tense during Hoveyda's early years as

AMIR ABBAS HOVEYDA

Premier. In the mid- and late 1960's Iran was engaged in an occasionally violent conflict with Iraq over the boundary between the two nations in the Kurdistan region and navigation rights on the Shatt-al-Arab River. In view of Great Britain's announced plans to withdraw from the Persian Gulf region, scheduled for late 1971, the Hoveyda government in the late 1960's pressed its long standing claims to the islands comprising the Sheikdom of Bahrein, arousing some misgivings among neighboring Arab states, notably Saudi Arabia, which considered the area part of its sphere of influence. Iran's generally good relations with Israel, to which it had accorded de facto recognition in 1960, have brought considerable criticism to the Iranian government from such militant Arab states as Syria, Iraq, and the United Arab Republic. After the six-day Arab-Israeli war of June 1967 the Hoveyda government supported a United Nations General Assembly resolution demanding Israeli withdrawal from occupied Arab territory, but it refused to condemn Israel as an aggressor. Trade between the two countries has continued undiminished.

The Hoveyda government's successful reform policies received a popular mandate in the national election of August 1967, in which the Iran-e-Novin party won 183 of the 219 seats in the Majlis, while the two legal opposition parties, the Mardom (People's) party and the Pan-Iranist party, received twenty-eight and five seats, respectively. Meanwhile, the land reform program had been virtually completed, and continued prosperity had enabled the Hoveyda government to exceed some of its economic development goals. The coronation of Mohammed Riza Shah Pahlevi took place with colorful festivities on October 26, 1967. Although the Shah had occupied the throne since 1941, he had postponed his coronation until he was convinced that he had achieved enough social and economic progress to vindicate his position as Iran's sovereign ruler. That vindication was realized in the progressive regime of Premier Amir Abbas Hoveyda, who fulfilled the Shah's expectations of leadership.

In March 1968 Hoveyda introduced Iran's fourth economic development plan aimed at increasing the gross national product by 9 percent annually over a five-year period and projecting public and private investments of about $10.8 billion, much of it from increased oil revenues. The program included among its goals improvements in agriculture, industry, mining, and communications; a 50 percent increase in per capita income; and the virtual elimination of unemployment. Strengthening Iran's ties with both the Soviet Union and the United States, in April of 1968 he received visiting Soviet Premier Aleksei N. Kosygin in Teheran, and in December he made his first state visit to the United States, where he discussed with President Lyndon B. Johnson Iran's defense needs and the prospects for peace in the Middle East, among other topics.

In 1969 Hoveyda introduced measures to deal with the threat of inflation and tried to persuade the members of the international consortium to increase the volume of its production of oil, so that more funds could be made available for Iran's economic development. Iran's need for a strong military defense establishment in view of Great Britain's impending withdrawal from the Persian Gulf was emphasized by Hoveyda in his February 1970 budget message to the Majlis. Also during 1970 the Hoveyda government introduced policy guidelines for fostering industrial growth during the second half of the fourth development plan and shifted the emphasis in its agrarian program from land reform to the encouragement of more efficient methods of agricultural production. On recommendation of the United Nations Security Council the government of Iran in May 1970 relinquished its claim to Bahrein, recognizing its right to become an independent nation. Although Iran's conflict with Iraq continued to flare up anew, diplomatic relations between Iran and the United Arab Republic, suspended since 1960, were restored in 1970. In August 1971 Iran recognized the Chinese Communist government as the "sole legal government of China."

Among reforms introduced by the Hoveyda government in 1971 was a measure curbing the powers of the Civil Service Commission and giving government agencies more control over their own personnel, in the interest of greater efficiency; and a government decentralization plan giving greater authority to provincial and local officials, thereby transferring "the affairs of the people to the people." In February 1971, after months of negotiations, representatives of six Middle Eastern oil-producing countries, led by Iran, signed an agreement with major Western oil companies, substantially increasing oil revenues paid by the companies to the governments. According to the Iran *Tribune* (March 1971), the agreement opened "a new era . . . for the Persian Gulf oil industry" and was a major step toward Iran's "ultimate goal —the independent operation of its oil industry."

In his budget message to the Majlis in March 1971, Hoveyda voiced optimism for his country's future and concluded that Iran was creating its own history in a manner fitting for a nation that would soon celebrate the 2,500th anniversary of its existence as an independent monarchy. "We are moving towards an increasing elevation of our country's international status," he declared, as quoted in *Kayhan International* (March 6, 1971). "We have no doubt that in the very near future we shall be a strong country on a global scale."

Amir Abbas Hoveyda was married in 1966 to Leila Emami (or Leyla Emami-Khoy), who is a graduate of the University of California at Los Angeles. They were divorced in 1971 and have no children. The Premier stands five feet eight inches tall, weighs 172 pounds, and has brown eyes and a fringe of brown hair. He maintains a fifteen-hour-a-day work schedule by taking tranquilizers and keeps in contact with the Shah by means of a telephone "hot line" on his desk. Frowning on paperwork, he has given orders that all reports submitted to him be confined to two pages. "Anything longer than that," he told an interviewer for *Life* (January 14, 1966), "is almost always loaded with baloney." Hoveyda speaks English, French, German, and Arabic and has written articles for various Persian publications. His favorite recreations include golf, reading, and cultivating roses. Among the honors that he has received are Iran's highest civilian award, the Order of Taj, First Class, and the rank of Commander in the French Legion of Honor, as well as decorations from Thailand, Pakistan, Tunisia, Romania, Yugoslavia, Austria, West Germany, and Sweden. He holds an honorary doctorate from the University of Cluj, Romania. Like most of his countrymen, the Premier is of the Moslem religion.

References

International Who's Who, 1970-71
Iran Almanac and Book of Facts, 1969
Who's Who in America, 1970-71

HUSAK, GUSTAV (hōō'säk)

Jan. 10, 1913- General Secretary of the Central Committee of the Communist Party of Czechoslovakia
Address: Secretariat of the Communist Party of Czechoslovakia, Prague, nabr. Kyjevské brigady 12, Czechoslovak Socialist Republic

Following the invasion of Czechoslovakia in August 1968 by armed forces of the Soviet Union and its Warsaw Pact allies that ended the brief period of liberal reforms under Alexander Dubcek, a struggle for leadership began within the Czechoslovak Communist party. From that struggle emerged Gustav Husak, a shrewd, moderate, and pragmatic politician from Slovakia, who succeeded Dubcek as the party's First Secretary in April 1969 and assumed the title of General Secretary in May 1971. A veteran Communist who served in the anti-Nazi underground during World War II and was imprisoned during the Stalinist purges of the 1950's, Husak helped to formulate some of the reforms of the Dubcek regime, during which he served as a vice-premier. In the view of some observers, Husak's orthodox Marxism and his ability to conciliate the U.S.S.R. may eventually permit the achievement of some liberal goals, but within an authoritarian context.

Gustav Husak was born on January 10, 1913 in Bratislava, the capital of Slovakia. He began to work after school at the age of ten. In 1933, as a student, he joined the Slovakian Communist party, and he soon developed a mastery of Marxist theory that won him the admiration of older party members. As a law student at Comenius University in Bratislava he became a well-known speaker for leftist causes and served as chairman of the Association of Socialist Students, a Communist organization. He was also associated with a group of Slovak intellectuals, led by Vladimir Clementis, that centered around the periodical *Dav,* Slovakia's most influential Communist journal before World War II. Like other members of the *Dav* circle, Husak combined advocacy of Communism with a program of Slovak political, economic, social, and cultural nationalism. In an article in *East Europe* (May 1969), Michael Mudry-Sebik, a fellow student at Comenius University, remembers Husak as "an outstanding scholar, diligent and enormously talented in organization and conspiratorial work," who had "little tolerance for political opposition."

After obtaining his law degree in 1937, Husak worked as a lawyer in Vladimir Clementis' law office in Bratislava. At the same time he was active in the underground Communist party organization, and in 1940 he was arrested by the police of the German-backed puppet government of Slovakia. After his release from prison in 1943 Gustav Husak was elected a member of the Slovak Communist party's Central Committee, and the following year he became one of the party's two deputy chairmen. Husak was also the Communist delegate to a series of secret conferences with leaders of non-Communist Slovak resistance groups. From these meetings resulted a unified underground command, the Slovak National Council, which was formally established in December 1943. As the Communist member of the council's presidium, Husak played an important role in the organization and direction of the revolt against the Germans and the fascist Slovak government that began in the fall of 1944 and later became known as the Slovak National Uprising.

After the defeat of Germany and the reunification of Czechoslovakia in 1945, Husak, now a member of the Central Committee of the Czechoslovak Communist party, became a Slovak delegate to the National Assembly and a member of Slovakia's regional governing body, the Board of Commissioners. He served as commissioner of the interior in 1944-45 and as commissioner of transport and technology in 1945-46, and he became chairman of the Board of Commissioners in 1946. In an unsuccessful effort to bring about a Communist takeover of the Slovak governmental apparatus, in October 1947 Husak led the other Communist members of the board in a mass resignation from office. After the Communists gained control of Czechoslovakia in February 1948 Husak

GUSTAV HUSAK

remained chairman of the Board of Commissioners until 1950 and served concurrently, during 1948, as commissioner of agriculture.

Once the Communists were firmly established in Czechoslovakia the party's Stalinist leaders began a period of repression aimed at purging the party membership of such elements as the "national Communists" who, they feared, might conspire to emulate the defection of Marshal Tito's Yugoslavia from the Soviet camp. During the early 1950's Prague was the scene of show trials at which the defendants included Rudolph Slansky, the deposed Communist party chief, and Vladimir Clementis, who had been Foreign Minister. As a long-time associate of Clementis and a member of the *Dav* circle, Husak came under suspicion, and his advocacy of Slovak autonomy was condemned as "bourgeois nationalism."

On May 4, 1950 Husak was removed from the chairmanship of the Slovak Board of Commissioners, although he was allowed, for the time being, to remain on the central committees of both the Slovak and Czechoslovak Communist parties. In 1950-51 he was a department head in the secretariat of the Slovak party organization. On February 6, 1951, however, Husak was deprived of his National Assembly seat, expelled from the party, and arrested on charges of treason and sabotage.

Husak recounted the events following his arrest in an article written in 1968 and published in English translation in *East Europe* (June 1971). Taken to the infamous Ruzyne Prison near Prague and, according to his own account, subjected to severe emotional and physical tortures, Husak was forced to confess to crimes he never committed. He was convicted in 1954, but unlike Slansky, Clementis, and others who were executed, he managed to escape death and received a sentence of life imprisonment.

In May 1960, reportedly because of popular pressure resulting from a resurgence of Slovak nationalism, Husak was released from imprisonment. From 1960 to 1963, while awaiting a review of his trial, he was employed by the Department of Building Works in Bratislava, devoting his spare time to writing a history of the 1944 Slovak National Uprising. In June 1963 his conviction was officially declared illegal and his membership in the Communist party was restored, but he did not return to an active role in politics for several years. From 1963 to 1968 he worked as a researcher in the institute of state and law of the Slovak Academy of Sciences.

While in prison, Husak had developed a passionate hatred for Antonin Novotny, the orthodox Stalinist First Secretary of Czechoslovakia's Communist party. In the autumn of 1967 Husak began contributing a series of articles to *Kulturny Zivot*, the liberal weekly of the Slovak Writers Union, in which he denounced the Novotny regime and called for reorganization of Czechoslovakia as a decentralized federal state, with self-government for Slovakia. One of those articles, published on January 12, 1968—a week after Alexander Dubcek replaced Novotny as party chief—was described by Harry Schwartz in *Prague's 200 Days* (Praeger 1969) as "a plea for genuine democracy in a Marxist state."

Widely identified as one of the most outspoken critics of the Novotny regime, Husak rose to national prominence during the period of liberalization that ensued in the spring and summer of 1968 under Dubcek's leadership. On April 8, 1968 he was named one of the five deputy premiers to serve under Premier Oldrich Cernik. In the beginning, Husak worked in close harmony with his fellow Slovak Dubcek, and he is widely believed to have been one of the main architects of the reformist action program, which Dubcek announced in April 1968. By summer, however, Husak had become an advocate of caution, warning against "ultraradical and anarchist tendencies" and against too speedy a democratization.

In the period immediately following the invasion of Czechoslovakia on August 20, 1968 by the Soviet Union and its Warsaw Pact allies, Husak's public statements were ambiguous, perhaps deliberately so. When on August 22 the liberal leadership of Czechoslovakia's Communist party secretly convened its fourteenth party congress in defiance of the Soviet invasion and chose a predominantly liberal Central Committee and Presidium, Husak repudiated his own election to the new Presidium. He condemned the congress as illegal on the grounds that it had been convened in violation of party statutes and that Slovakia had been under-represented. He thus conciliated the Russians by attacking the Congress while placating liberal elements among his countrymen by apparently emphasizing questions of legality and Slovak nationalism. Along with Dubcek and other Czechoslovak officials, Husak took part in the conference with Soviet leaders that was held in Moscow, August 23 to 27, at which the Czechoslovaks were forced to relinquish many of the reforms instituted under Dubcek.

On August 28, 1968 Husak, who had not held a high party post since 1951, succeeded Vasil Bilak as First Secretary of the Slovak Communist party, and on September 1 he was named to the twenty-one-member ruling Presidium of the Central Committee of the Czechoslovak party. Turning to what he has called the "middle of the road," in the fall of 1968 he began to advocate a policy of "realism," compromise, and friendship towards the Soviet Union. While he did not repudiate the action program of the preceding spring, he asserted that it could only be put into effect gradually and "with due regard for existing conditions." He criticized party liberals, including Dubcek, for their failure to suppress "counter-revolutionary" elements in the period preceding the invasion.

Husak was designated on November 17, 1968 as one of the eight members of the newly organized executive committee of the Czechoslovak Communist party Presidium. According to Harry Schwartz, his speeches at the time seemed to suggest that he was "inviting Moscow to install him in Dubcek's place." Although he had many hardline opponents within the party structure, Husak appeared to be the only candidate for party leadership acceptable to the Russians who at the same time enjoyed a reputation as a moderate, as well as the prestige of having been associated with Dubcek's reforms and with the overthrow of Novotny. Husak strengthened his hand at meetings with Soviet leaders, at Moscow in October, Warsaw in November, and Kiev in December 1968.

In January 1969 a reorganization of the Czechoslovak government was put into effect, establishing a federalized state in which semiautonomous local powers were divided between the 10,500,000 Czechs and 3,500,000 Slovaks. The reorganization plan, which was one of the few surviving elements of Dubcek's otherwise ill-fated action program, is said to have been largely the work of Husak. Under the new federal regime, Husak relinquished his deputy premiership in the state apparatus while retaining his Communist party posts.

Husak attained Czechoslovakia's top leadership position on April 17, 1969, when he succeeded Alexander Dubcek as First Secretary of the Communist party. At the same time, the membership of the party's Presidium was reduced from twenty-one to eleven—removing most of the remaining liberals from the party's top ranks—and its executive committee was abolished. On April 18 Husak took Dubcek's place on the Defense Council, and on June 3 he became head of the party's defense, security, and political organization departments. He relinquished his post as the Slovak party's First Secretary in May, when he was succeeded by Stefan Sadovsky. During the early months of his tenure as party leader Husak worked to normalize relations with the U.S.S.R. and to win Soviet confidence by demonstrating his ability to maintain order among Czechoslovakia's still restive citizenry.

In response to widespread anti-Soviet demonstrations in August 1969, on the first anniversary of the invasion, Husak ordered increased police powers "for the defense of public order" and moved against liberals in the party and the government. On the other hand, he repeatedly denied that there would be a return to Stalinism, and he resisted demands for purge trials made by party conservatives. "We are not butchers, and our party is not a slaughterhouse," he declared in a speech in October 1969. On a visit to Moscow later that month he hailed the 1968 invasion as an "act of international assistance" in defeating "right-wing antisocialist and counterrevolutionary forces."

Threatened by rivals in the party's highest ranks, Husak devoted much of his effort during 1969 and 1970 to consolidating his position and disarming his opponents. His most vehement enemies were orthodox hard-liners who distrusted him as a Slovak and as a reformist associate of Dubcek's, but he also faced opposition from the party's remaining liberals. To combat those factions, Husak, as a centrist, shrewdly packed the Central Committee with his own supporters. By early 1971 more than half of the 115 committee members had been replaced, and about 20 percent of the ordinary members of the party—numbering about 1,650,000 in 1969—had been dropped in a bloodless but nonetheless highly effective purge.

Much of the in-fighting between Husak and his rivals—the strongest of whom was probably the ultraconservative Lubomir Strougal, who had succeeded Oldrich Cernik as Premier of Czechoslovakia in January 1970—took place behind the scenes. One especially dramatic phase of the conflict, however, involving the fate of Alexander Dubcek, was well publicized. The hard-liners in the party pressed for a public trial to discredit the former party leader and eliminate him from the scene. Husak, however, recognized Dubcek's continuing popularity, and perhaps also realized that his arrest and trial might have implications for his own future since he had played an active role in the 1968 liberalization. He therefore appointed Dubcek Ambassador to Turkey in January 1970 and sent him off to Ankara to remove him as a target of the ultraconservatives. Although Dubcek was removed from his diplomatic post and expelled from the Communist party—over Husak's objections—in June 1970, he was permitted to retire from public life without suffering further penalties.

On May 6, 1970 Husak and other Czechoslovakian leaders met in Prague with Soviet officials to sign a twenty-year treaty of "friendship, cooperation, and mutual assistance," in which the Soviet Union's right to intervene in Czechoslovak affairs was formally established. Also during 1970 Husak approached leaders of the Federal Republic of Germany in an effort to settle differences between the two nations. In addition to his role as party chief, in January 1971 Husak was elected chairman of the National Front, an "umbrella organization" representing all legal political groups in Czechoslovakia.

During his first year in power, Western observers had on several occasions predicted Husak's imminent downfall, but by early 1971 he appeared firmly in control of his party and his country. In May 1971 he convened the fourteenth congress of the Czechoslovak Communist party. (The secret session held in August 1968 under that title had been declared illegal.) Husak was reelected party leader by a voice vote of the 1,200 delegates and, in conformity with the Soviet pattern, his title was changed from First Secretary to General Secretary. Addressing the congress, Husak proclaimed a major five-year economic program aimed at eliminating economic grievances and raising living standards through increased agricultural and industrial production and an expanded housing program. Reaffirming Czechoslovak solidarity with the Soviet Union, Husak publicly thanked visiting Soviet Communist party chief Leonid I. Brezhnev for having saved his country from the external and internal perils of imperialism.

After two years in power, Husak arouses little enthusiasm, but many of his countrymen believe that he is by no means the worst leader they might have received in the aftermath of the Soviet invasion and occupation. Comparing the recent political struggle in Czechoslovakia with the religious conflicts of sixteenth-century Europe, Erazim V. Kohak, writing in *Commonweal* (December 26, 1969), classes Husak among "advocates of reform and opponents of Reformation." According to Kohak, Husak "insists on reform—his only reservation is his equally unambiguous opposition to anything that would weaken the party's ties to Moscow or the dominant position . . . of the party in society."

Husak is a former editor of the journal *Nove slovo* and the author of a book on the agricultural problems of Slovakia and one on "the struggle for tomorrow," both of which appeared in 1948. His historical study *Svedektvo o slovenskom narodnom povstani* (Evidence on the Slovak National Uprising), was published in 1964. Husak received the honorary degree of Candidate in Science in 1965. His decorations include the Distinguished Order of the Slovak Uprising, the Military Cross, the Military Medal for Services, and the Klement Gottwald Order. In 1969 he was designated a Hero of the Czechoslovak Socialist Republic and awarded the Soviet Union's Order of Lenin.

Little is known of Gustav Husak's personal life, other than that he is now a widower and that in his 1962 petition for rehabilitation he expressed regret for having neglected his wife and children because of his dedication to duty. Still just as devoted to his work, Husak leads an austere private life. He allows himself few luxuries and chainsmokes Czechoslovakia's cheapest brand of cigarettes. Husak is described in the New York *Times* (September 5, 1968) as "a short, stout man with bushy, graying hair, . . . small tight lips, . . . [and] the look of a severe teacher about ready to discipline his students."

References

East Europe 18:2+ My '69
N Y Times p2 S 5 '68 por; p6 My 26 '71
Newsweek 73:56+ F 17 '69
Time 93:26+ Ap 25 '62 por
Britannica Book of the Year, 1970
International Who's Who, 1970-71
Who's Who in the World, 1971-72

IACOCCA, LEE A(NTHONY) (ī-ə-kŏk'ə)

Oct. 15, 1924- Industrialist
Address: b. Ford Motor Co., American Rd.,
Dearborn, Mich. 48121; h. 571 Edgemere
Court, Bloomfield Hills, Mich. 48013

Undoubtedly the toughest and shrewdest salesman
in Detroit is Lee A. Iacocca, the marketing genius
who sold the American public the Mustang and
such other Ford moneymakers as the Mark III,
the Maverick, and the Econoline truck. After holding several top corporate positions in the Ford
Motor Company, which ranks as the nation's third
largest manufacturer behind General Motors and
Standard Oil, Lee Iacocca was elected president
on December 10, 1970, thus becoming second in
command to Henry Ford 2d, grandson of the
founder and chairman of the board. Iacocca has
spent his entire career with Ford, beginning as
a district salesman in Pennsylvania soon after
World War II. In 1960 he was made general manager of the Ford division, the main nucleus of
power within the company, and in 1965 he was
elected to the board of directors.

Lido Anthony Iacocca was born on October 15,
1924 in Allentown, Pennsylvania to Nicola and
Antoinette (Perrotto), both Italian immigrants.
Nicola Iacocca came to the United States in 1902
at the age of twelve and returned to Italy in 1921
to select a bride. The Iacoccas honeymooned at
Venice's Lido, and when their son was born a few
years later they named him after that famous
beach. As he grew up, Lido began using the
Americanized name Lee. The Iacoccas, who live
in retirement in Allentown, have one other child,
Mrs. Delma Kelechavia.

Nicola Iacocca was a dynamic businessman who
became a millionaire in the real estate business
before the Depression swept away his fortune. At
one time he also ran a car-renting business. Most
of the autos in his fleet were Fords, a fact that
apparently impressed his son, for Lee Iacocca
maintains that by the age of sixteen he knew he
wanted to be a Ford executive. As a boy, Iacocca
attended public schools in Allentown. A bout with
rheumatic fever during his freshman year in high
school forced him to give up athletics, and from
that time on he channeled his competitive energies
into excelling as a student and as a debater. Since
the impairments of rheumatic fever exempted him
from service in World War II, he began commuting to Lehigh University in Bethlehem, Pennsylvania after graduating from Allentown High in
1942. Maintaining an A average, he completed
his undergraduate studies in three years and was
awarded the B.S. degree in industrial engineering
in 1945.

After graduation, Iacocca went to Dearborn,
Michigan as an executive trainee for the Ford
Company, but he soon persuaded the company to
grant him a leave of absence so that he could
accept a Wallace Memorial Fellowship at Princeton University. In 1946 he received a master's
degree in mechanical engineering at Princeton,
after submitting a thesis on torque converters. He
then finished the Dearborn training program he
had temporarily abandoned, accomplishing in nine
months what it had taken his classmates eighteen
months to achieve.

Iacocca's first assignment was as an automatic-
transmission engineer at Ford's Edgewater, New
Jersey plant, but he soon realized that what he
wanted was sales, not engineering. Since the company would not give him a sales job, he quit and
looked for one on his own. After being turned
down at Ford's New York office, he succeeded in
convincing Charles Beacham, the Eastern district
sales manager, to hire him.

For nearly a decade Iacocca worked in sales
and marketing jobs at the Eastern district office
in Chester, Pennsylvania, near Philadelphia. Although he worked long hours, studied the business meticulously, and devised gimmicks to sell
Ford cars and trucks, he received no special recognition until 1956, when he launched a sales
campaign with the slogan "56 for 56" that urged
customers to buy new Fords by paying $56 a
month. The campaign proved so successful in the
Philadelphia area that Robert S. McNamara, then
general manager of the Ford division, adopted the
campaign nationwide and credited it with selling
72,000 extra automobiles. As a result Iacocca, who
was then assistant sales manager of the Chester
office, was made manager of the Washington sales
office. His former boss, Charles Beacham, had in
the meantime moved to the home office as head
of car and truck sales for the Ford division, and
no sooner had Iacocca taken his new position in
Washington than Beacham called him to Dearborn
to become the truck marketing manager of the
Ford division.

Once in Dearborn, Iacocca became a protégé
of McNamara, who was moving upward toward
the company presidency, and the younger man
followed swiftly in his footsteps. In 1957 he was
switched from truck to car marketing, and in
March 1960 he was put in charge of both car and
truck marketing. By that time, however, he was
thirty-five, and he had set his sights on becoming
a vice-president by that age. His disappointment
turned out to be shortlived when, eighteen days
after his thirty-sixth birthday, on November 2,
1960, he was named a vice-president and general
manager of the Ford division, the heart of the
Ford empire.

Although Iacocca enjoyed the sponsorship of
McNamara, he did not hesitate to challenge Mc-
Namara's policies. When McNamara introduced a
safety campaign in 1956 that turned out to be
unpopular, Iacocca remarked that "safety didn't
sell." While McNamara stressed basic transportation, introducing the Falcon, the first of the Detroit compacts, Iacocca recognized the importance
of the youth market and the salability of speed.
For that reason he persuaded Henry Ford 2d to
break with the Detroit auto industry's pact not to
sponsor racing, and he introduced the slogan, "You
sell on Monday what you race on Sunday."

Although Iacocca added some sporty touches
like bucket seats to the Falcon, the first automobile to embody his ideas was the Mustang, one

of the most successful cars in Detroit history. Iacocca envisioned the Mustang as the poor man's Thunderbird, a four-passenger family sedan that a teenage son could drive like a sports car. He began planning it early in 1961 and subsequently won approval from Henry Ford 2d for a $50,-000,000 appropriation for tooling. Over the next few years all the engineering and styling problems were worked out, and meticulous market research studies were completed on the new auto. To the accompaniment of the biggest hoopla since the debut of the Model A, Iacocca introduced the Mustang at the New York World's Fair in April 1964.

Priced at from $2,368 for the basic model to a maximum of $3,500 for all luxury options, 417,800 Mustangs were sold during the model's first year, which stands as a postwar sales record. The success of the Mustang assured Iacocca's continued ascendancy at Ford. On January 14, 1965 he was appointed vice-president of the car and truck group, and on October 11, 1967 he was named executive vice-president of Ford North American automotive operations, the largest of the company's three basic operating units. However, when Ford president Arjay Miller was appointed vice-chairman of the board in 1968, Henry Ford 2d bypassed Iacocca to appoint Semon E. Knudsen, a longtime executive of General Motors, as president. According to insiders, Ford felt that Iacocca needed a few more years of experience before assuming the top position.

On September 11, 1969 Ford summarily fired the former General Motors executive, reportedly because he had been unable to quell dissension among the ranks of Ford executives loyal to Iacocca. Yet Ford was still unwilling to bestow the presidency on his lieutenant, preferring to name Iacocca and the executive vice-presidents of the other two operating units of the company as presidents of their respective units. Although the company was nominally managed by a triumvirate, Iacocca actually wielded the power from the time of Knudsen's ouster. On December 10, 1970 Henry Ford 2d made it official by naming Iacocca president and demoting the other two unit presidents back to the rank of executive vice-presidents.

"Lee is like a Medici prince," a Ford associate commented to George A. Nikolaieff of the *Wall Street Journal* (May 14, 1970). "He has created his own city-state within the company." Many of the Ford executives loyal to Iacocca have been with him since his days in Chester, Pennsylvania, and he is said to be fearless in defending his supporters against the intrigues of corporate politics. Besides loyalty, Iacocca demands hard work from those associated with him, and he has little patience with incompetency. A few years ago he recalled to a reporter for *Time* (April 17, 1964) that when he first became head of the Ford division, "I told a few people, 'Get with it, you're being observed. Guys who don't get with it don't play on the club after a while.' It worked, because all of a sudden a guy is face to face with the reality of his mortgage payments." Department heads were also induced to increase their

LEE A. IACOCCA

productivity by the institution of Iacocca's "black notebook system." Each manager was asked to list his objectives for the next quarter in a notebook that Iacocca graded against his performance.

Perhaps as important to Iacocca's success at Ford as his adroitness in company politics has been his ability to build a durable relationship with Henry Ford 2d, a strong-willed man who has brought about the premature dismissal of a number of Iacocca's predecessors. According to observers, Iacocca combines aggressiveness with deference in his dealings with "Mister Ford," as he is always called within the company. Although they have been known to argue heatedly on many issues, Iacocca has apparently never forgotten whose name is written over the company door. "Mr. Ford is No. 1 in my mind," Iacocca told William Scrrin of the New York *Times Magazine* (July 18, 1971). "Always has and always will be. He hired me, he brought me along, he gave me my opportunities."

While he has not forgotten the youth market, Iacocca has in recent years concentrated his attention on meeting the challenge of foreign economy cars, and he has put on the market two highly successful low-priced Ford models, the Maverick compact in 1969 and the even smaller Pinto in 1970. As of 1971 the Ford company had once more withdrawn its sponsorship from racing events, channeling the funds formerly spent on racing into safety and pollution research. Although Iacocca does not believe that the Detroit auto industry will be able to meet what he regards as the excessively stringent standards of the 1970 Clean Air Act by the 1975 deadline, he has stated that he believes cars will be "virtually pollution-free" by then.

Iacocca serves on the boards of directors of Boston Company, the Detroit Area Council, the Boy Scouts of America, the United Foundation, and the University of Southern California Graduate School of Business Administration. He holds honorary doctorates from Muhlenberg College, Lawrence Institute of Technology, and Babson Institute. He is a member of the National Industrial Pollution Council, Tau Beta Pi, and the Society of Automotive Engineers.

Brash, colorful, and outspoken, Lee A. Iacocca is a favorite with reporters, but away from the office he is a private man who shuns suburban social life for Friday night poker games with old friends and weekends with his family. Iacocca and his wife, the former Mary McCleary, were married on September 29, 1956, several years after they first met at the Ford sales office in Chester, where she was a receptionist. With their two daughters, Kathryn Lisa and Lia Antoinette, the Iacoccas live in a $200,000 home in Bloomfield Hills, a fashionable suburb of Detroit. When he is not working, the auto executive enjoys reading, or keeping in shape with an occasional game of golf or a swim in his large swimming pool. Iacocca is six feet one inch tall, weighs 180 pounds, and has brown hair and brown eyes. He smokes several large, expensive cigars daily. His clubs are the Detroit Athletic and the Orchard Lake Country; his religion is the Roman Catholic, and his political affiliation is with the Republican party, as what he calls a "fairly independent Republican." Iacocca reportedly earns some $550,000 annually in salary and bonuses.

References

N Y Times Mag p8+ Jl 18 '71 por
Newsweek 63:97+ Ap 20 '64 pors
Time 83:92+ Ap 17 '64 pors
Wall St J p1+ My 14 '70 por
Who's Who in America, 1970-71
World Who's Who in Finance and Industry, 1970-71

JACKSON, GLENDA

1937(?)- British actress
Address: b. c/o United Artists Corp., 729 7th Ave., New York 10019; h. 51 Harvey Rd., Blackheath, London, S.E. 3, England

Transcending the stereotype of the glamorous film star, Glenda Jackson was named best actress of 1970 by the Academy of Motion Picture Arts and Sciences for her strong, sensitive, and down-to-earth portrayal of Gudrun Brangwen in the screen version of D. H. Lawrence's novel *Women in Love*. Miss Jackson, who began her acting career in British repertory theatre in the 1950's, won international acclaim when she appeared in the role of the catatonic Charlotte Corday in the Royal Shakespeare Company's production of Peter Weiss's avant-garde psychological drama *Marat/Sade,* presented in London in 1964, on Broadway during the 1965-66 season, and on film in 1967. Her screen credits for 1971 include John Schlesinger's highly rated *Sunday, Bloody Sunday* and the less fortunate *The Music Lovers*, as well as a BBC television series about the life of Queen Elizabeth I. In reviewing *Women in Love* in the *New Republic* (April 18, 1970), Stanley Kauffmann wrote: "Miss Jackson is a very fine actress, but she will probably never be a box-office star because she is not interested in star 'sympathy,' either in the parts she chooses or the way she plays them. She is not an actress in order to be loved but in order to act."

Glenda Jackson was born in Hoylake, near Birkenhead, Cheshire, in England's North Country, about 1937 (several sources suggest that she may have been born in 1939 or 1940), the oldest of the four daughters of a former bricklayer who is now a semiretired jobber in the construction business. During her childhood she spent much of her time at local movie theatres, rarely missing films starring Bette Davis or Joan Crawford, who became—and have remained—her idols. Her early ambition was to become a ballet dancer, but she abandoned that goal when she grew too tall. At sixteen she left school and took a job as a salesclerk at a local drugstore, and as a pastime she joined an amateur dramatic society at the local YMCA. Although her family tried to discourage her from embarking on an acting career, Miss Jackson decided, on an off-chance, to apply for a two-year scholarship with the Royal Academy of Dramatic Art in London and was accepted. "I had no real ambitions about acting," she told Peter Buckley in an interview for *TWA Ambassador* magazine (July 1971), "but . . . I knew there had to be something better than the bloody chemist's shop."

After graduating with honors from the Royal Academy of Dramatic Art, Miss Jackson spent about six years as an actress and stage manager with repertory companies in England and Scotland. About 1958 she met and married Roy Hodges, a fellow graduate of the Royal Academy, who was also struggling to establish himself in the theatre as an actor and director. The early years of their marriage were lean ones, and between acting assignments Miss Jackson worked at such jobs as waitress, receptionist, and file clerk, to make ends meet. Meanwhile, by appearing in some 200 different roles in repertory productions, she continued to enhance her versatile skill as an actress. Her Alexandra in José Ruben's stage adaptation of Dostoyevsky's novel *The Idiot*, presented by the Ikon Theatre Company at the Lyric Theatre in Hammersmith in 1962, elicited some favorable notice from critics, as did her performance as Siddie in Bill Naughton's comedy *Alfie,* which ran for 194 performances at London's Mermaid Theatre in 1963. She also obtained a minor role in the film *This Sporting Life* (Continental, 1963), with Richard Harris and Rachel Roberts.

After auditioning for the Royal Shakespeare Company three times without success, Glenda Jackson was spotted in 1963 by Peter Brook, one of the company's associate directors. Impressed by her imaginative improvisations, Brook signed her to a three-year contract and placed her in his Theatre of Cruelty, an experimental group sponsored by the Royal Shakespeare Company that sought to explore the limits to which the human body could go in sound and motion. "There were twelve of us actors," Miss Jackson told Rex Reed in an interview for the New York *Times* (April 3, 1966). "We'd do exercises, communicate without words, make streams of sound with no relation, just to see how free we could become on the stage. At the end of our study, we did a laboratory evening in a private club. The public was not invited, but everybody in the theatre came: Olivier, Edith Evans, Tynan, Pinter and Osborne and Chris Plummer. It caused a tremendous furor." Her first performance with the group was in a four-minute skit in which she played a nude scene as the London party-girl Christine Keeler and also portrayed Mrs. John F. Kennedy.

In 1964 Peter Brook staged the Royal Shakespeare Company's production of Peter Weiss's symbolic play-within-a-play *The Persecution and Assassination of Marat as Performed by the Inmates of the Asylum of Charenton under the Direction of the Marquis do Sade*—better known under its abbreviated title, *Marat/Sade*. To perform the key role of the insane asylum inmate Charlotte Corday, the fanatical young woman who murders the French Revolutionist Jean-Paul Marat in his bath, Brook chose Glenda Jackson. When *Marat/Sade* opened in London's Aldwych Theatre on August 20, 1964, Miss Jackson, according to *Theatre World Annual* (1966) "made an immediate hit with her sensitive and moving performance." A critic for *Variety* (September 2, 1964) observed that "a fairly inexperienced young actress, Glenda Jackson, . . . rises to heights" with her portrayal of Charlotte Corday and called attention to the finale, "when Mme. Corday, with her hair, whips the back of a half-naked Sade with such telling precision that the audience can almost feel and wince at the laceration."

Imported into the United States by David Merrick, Brook's production of *Marat/Sade* opened at the Martin Beck Theatre in New York City on December 27, 1965. It ran for 145 performances and won the Drama Critics Circle Award and four Tony awards before moving on to Paris for a brief engagement. Although Miss Jackson was nominated for a Tony award and won a Variety poll award as the most promising new actress of the 1965-66 Broadway season, she found her appearance in *Marat/Sade* a harrowing experience. "I loathe and detest everything about this production," she told Rex Reed in the New York *Times* interview. "We all loathe it. . . . It's a play that breeds sickness, with no release for the tension." A filmed stage presentation of *Marat/Sade* with the original cast, released by United Artists in 1967, was generally well received by critics. Describing Glenda Jackson's film performance—which he found worthy of an Academy Award—Rex Reed wrote in his book *Big Screen, Little Screen* (Macmillan, 1971): "Trembling across the sweat-stained floorboards, her face swollen and cracked from the terrors of sleeping sickness and melancholia, her head bobbing like a rotten cabbage on a stick, Miss Jackson gives the kind of performance that should send every American member of the Screen Actors Guild back to drama school." A recording of *Marat/Sade*, featuring Miss Jackson, was released by Caedmon Records in 1966.

Meanwhile, Miss Jackson continued to appear in the Royal Shakespeare Company's productions

GLENDA JACKSON

in England. In the fall of 1964 she played the courtesan Bellamira in Christopher Marlowe's *The Jew of Malta*, and in the spring of 1965 she was in a repertory production of *Love's Labour's Lost*, as the Princess of France. Her powerful interpretation of Ophelia in a production of *Hamlet*, presented at Stratford-upon-Avon under Peter Hall's direction in August 1965, prompted Penelope Gilliatt to suggest in a review that Miss Jackson should play Hamlet, while another critic proposed that the production be billed as "Ophelia." In the 1965-66 season Miss Jackson appeared in Peter Weiss's drama about Auschwitz, *The Investigation*, during its brief London run. Her interpretation of Masha in Anton Chekhov's *Three Sisters* was singled out by critics as one of the outstanding performances of the London theatre's 1966-67 season.

In late 1966 Miss Jackson appeared in Peter Brook's Royal Shakespeare Company production of *US*, a searing indictment of the United States presence in Vietnam, based on documentary sources and presented in the form of a revue. "Before we started doing that thing, I was quite cynical," Miss Jackson recalled in an interview with Guy Flatley in the New York *Times* (February 7, 1971). "But after a while I found myself no longer getting a vicarious pleasure out of my own selfrighteousness, . . . although I continued to disagree with America's position." For a change of pace, Miss Jackson accepted a light comedy role as a lesbian crusader against male chauvinism in David Pinner's play *Fanghorn*, presented at London's Fortune Theatre in November 1967. On the screen she appeared as the wife of a London antique dealer in *Negatives* (Continental, 1968), a "far-out" film, directed by Peter Medak, about people who resort to masquerade to attain fulfillment. The film was generally panned by critics who, while praising Miss Jackson's acting in it, felt that it wasted her talent.

Glenda Jackson's acting career peaked with her Oscar-winning performance in *Women in Love* (United Artists, 1970), the screen adaptation of D. H. Lawrence's novel about the battle of the sexes and relationships among the elite of Great Britain's industrial Midlands in the 1920's. Directed by Ken Russell, and costarring Oliver Reed, Alan Bates, and Jennie Linden, the film was dominated by Glenda Jackson, portraying the sculptress Gudrun Brangwen, an emancipated woman, whom Lawrence was said to have modeled upon the writer Katherine Mansfield. Although critics quibbled about some aspects of the production, they applauded the intelligence, grace, sensuality, and self-assurance of Miss Jackson's performance and the good taste in which her nude sex scene with Reed was presented. "She bursts upon the screen like a young, sturdier version of Katharine Hepburn, with all of her animal magnetism," Arthur Knight wrote in *Saturday Review* (March 21, 1970). "It is a magnificent performance." Her portrayal of Gudrun earned her the Variety Award of Great Britain for the best film actress of 1970, as well as the best actress awards of the New York Film Critics and the National Society of Film Critics in the United States. The Oscar award of the Academy of Motion Picture Arts and Sciences was presented to her in Hollywood on April 14, 1971.

Working again under the agitated direction of Ken Russell, Miss Jackson costarred with Richard Chamberlain in *The Music Lovers* (United Artists, 1971), based on *Beloved Friend*, Catherine Drinker Bowen's biography of Peter Ilich Tchaikovsky. Although critics derided the production as "kitsch," "schmaltz," and "hokum," Miss Jackson, as Nina, the homosexual composer's psychotic wife, won applause for the brilliance and dramatic force of her performance, which included a drunken nude scene, as well as scenes in which she is an inmate of a madhouse. "Glenda Jackson's Nina is perhaps the prize performance," noted a critic for the *Guardian* (February 25, 1971). "I can't think of another actress who could have suggested so much more than was actually written into the part. . . . It was the one absolutely complete portrait in the film."

For her next role, Ken Russell asked her to undertake a hunchbacked, sex-crazed nun in the film version of John Whiting's play *The Devils*, but she turned it down because, as she told Rex Reed in an interview in the New York *Sunday News* (January 24, 1971), she did "not want to play any more slobbering lunatics." (Her rejection of the role—which was later taken over by Vanessa Redgrave—reportedly brought about some ill feeling between her and Russell.) Instead she chose to work under John Schlesinger's direction in the Joseph Janni production of *Sunday, Bloody Sunday* (United Artists, 1971), based on an original screenplay by Penelope Gilliatt. As Alex Greville, a cultured divorcée, she shares the love of a young sculptor, played by Murray Head, with a homosexual doctor, portrayed by Peter Finch. The film was almost universally praised for its depth in exploring human relationships and for its mature and subdued treatment of a sensitive sexual topic. Stanley Kauffmann, in his review in the *New Republic* (October 9, 1971), found Miss Jackson's performance "beautifully modulated, with

humor and sharp slivers of pain and little catlike enjoyments," while Pauline Kael, writing in the *New Yorker* (October 2, 1971), noted that she gave the film a "needed tensile strength" but displayed "a slightly repellent hardness" that was not quite suited to the role.

In early 1971 Miss Jackson starred in the British Broadcasting Corporation television network's six-part biography, *Elizabeth R*, in which she portrayed Queen Elizabeth I from youth to old age. A triumph in England, the series has been acquired for American television. She again plays Elizabeth in her new film, "Mary, Queen of Scots," with Vanessa Redgrave in the title role. Miss Jackson is also scheduled to appear as Charlotte in a forthcoming film about the Brontë sisters, and, in what is perhaps the greatest plum in her acting career, the role of Queen Isabella of Spain in Samuel Bronston's film biography, which began production in Spain in the fall of 1971.

Glenda Jackson and her husband, Roy Hodges, make their home in Blackheath, a middle-class community in southeast London, with their son, Daniel, born in 1969. Hodges, who has left the theatre, now owns an art gallery in Greenwich. Five feet six inches tall and of slight build, Miss Jackson has what Bruce Cook, in the *National Observer* (October 2, 1971), calls a "broad, vaguely Oriental face" that is "easy to like in all its moods." A typical suburban housewife and mother in her private life, Miss Jackson loves cooking, gardening, eating apples, and reading Jane Austen, but dislikes housework, exercise, and traveling by air. She much prefers working in motion pictures to acting on stage or on television. As compassionate as Vanessa Redgrave, she has given benefit performances for humanitarian causes.

References

Christian Sci Mon p15 F 11 '71
Guardian p9 N 28 '69 por
London Observer p3 F 28 '71 por
Look 34:36+ D 29 '70 pors
N Y Post p13 Ja 30 '71 por
N Y Sunday News Mag p12+ F 21 '71 por
N Y Times II p13+ F 7 '71 por
Time 97:53+ Ap 26 '71 pors

KARINSKA, BARBARA

Oct. 3, 1886- Costume maker and designer
Address: b. Karinska, 20 W. 57th St., New York 10019; h. 17 E. 63d St., New York 10021

"There is Shakespeare for literature and Madame Karinska for costumes," the choreographer George Balanchine once said of Madame Barbara Karinska, the costumer of the New York City Ballet. Her singular contributions to ballet were honored in 1962 when she became the first costumer ever to win the Capezio Dance Award, for costumes "of visual beauty for the spectator and complete delight for the dancer." The dance critic Walter Terry has remarked that as a costumer Karinska makes "the garment part of dancing itself." She is the designer and executor of costumes for New York's opera and theatre as well as ballet and on an excursion to Hollywood won the 1948 Oscar for the costumes of *Joan of Arc*.

Barbara Karinska was born Varvara Zhmoudsky on October 3, 1886 in the city of Kharkov in southern Russia. Her family belonged to the upper class; her father, Andrei Zhmoudsky, was a wealthy cloth merchant. As was customary for girls in well-to-do households, she learned the ladylike skill of embroidery at an early age. An inventive child, she rebelled against what seemed to her a lifelessness in her teacher's needlework. Her parents, seeing her talent, allowed her to follow her own bent in embroidery and tapestry-like creations.

When she grew older Karinska became interested in studying law and doing relief work in prisons. She married the editor of a socialist paper in Kharkov, and on the death of her husband not long afterward she took over the editorship. Her socialist views brought her into trouble with Czarist Russian government officials, and she was imprisoned several times, even though her being a woman meant that she was not taken very seriously. At the outbreak of World War I the paper began to lose money and she had to abandon it.

During the war Karinska went to Moscow, where she met and married a lawyer named Karinsky, who held a high office in the Kerensky government. In 1917, while Karinska was vacationing in the Crimea, the Bolsheviks took power in Moscow. Rather than return home to the turbulent city, Karinska, although separated from her husband, remained in the Crimea for about a year. There she became interested in painting and was instructed by several artists. Besides painting, she made pictures by appliquéing chiffon shapes on a chiffon surface. At the end of the year she returned to Moscow to find her husband, who, however, had left the city to look for her. At their Moscow home Karinska did recover her well-hidden jewels.

To earn a living in Moscow after the revolution, Karinska opened an embroidery and dress shop and gave embroidery lessons. Afternoons she held a salon attended by some government officials of the new Bolshevik regime, which at that time encouraged individual enterprise. She exhibited paintings in a gallery and joined other artists in group shows. Because of her increasing reputation, she was offered the title of commissar of art. Pretending that she needed to prepare for that position, she persuaded the government to permit her to go to Germany to study museum administration. In 1928 she left Russia with her daughter, Irena, and her nephew, her jewels safely stowed in the lining of her daughter's hat. Instead of going to Germany, she went to Brussels to join her father and brothers.

Before long Karinska moved on to Paris, where she supported herself and her daughter by selling her jewels and making embroidered scarves and shawls to be sold by Paris shops and Liberty of London. Her income was inadequate, however, and she welcomed the chance to earn some 20

BARBARA KARINSKA

francs when a nightclub performer hired her to remake a costume. Appreciating her workmanship, the nightclub manager and then others in professional entertainment offered her jobs in costume making. Among her clients was Prince Zeretelli, director of an émigré opera troupe, through whom she met Colonel de Basil and René Blum, directors of opera and ballet, and eventually George Balanchine.

Madame Karinska's big break came when she was commissioned by de Basil and Blum to execute the costumes designed by Christian Bérard for *Cotillon*, choreographed by Balanchine. The ballet was performed in a 1932 Monte Carlo presentation and later became part of the repertory of the newly formed de Basil Ballet Russe. Knowing little about the complexities of ballet costumes, such as problems of stress in the bodice, she and a Russian friend, Toussia, began cutting material and kept on cutting until by trial and error they found their own way to make the needed shapes. Even today Karinska experiments in search of the special, perfect cut for each element of her costumes.

Impressed by her first efforts in ballet costuming, de Basil next commissioned Karinska to make costumes designed by André Derain for *La Concurrence* (1932), which Balanchine also choreographed. While in France she had the opportunity to transform the sketches of many great artists, such as Picasso, Matisse, and Chagall, into costumes. Most of her work for about five years was undertaken for the Ballet Russe, but she also had commissions in the French theatre. She was chosen, for instance, to make the costumes designed by Bérard for the Comédie des Champs Elysées' presentation in 1934 of Louis Jouvet's production of Jean Cocteau's *La Machine infernale*.

In 1938 Madame Karinska left France for the United States, which she had visited earlier with the Ballet Russe troupe. Her move from Europe meant little if any departure from the traditions of the Russian ballet. One of her first important projects in New York was executing the costumes designed by Salvador Dali for Léonide Massine's ballet *Bacchanale,* presented at the Metropolitan Opera House by the Ballet Russe de Monte Carlo, recently organized by Massine in a break with de Basil. In 1941 she made the costumes for Anton Dolin's restaging of *Princess Aurora* for the Ballet Theatre in New York. Fourteen years later John Martin commented in *Center* (February 1955) that their "resplendence" was "still fresh in mind."

In New York, Madame Karinska renewed her association with Balanchine, who became artistic director of the Ballet Society in 1946. The following year that company presented his *Renaud,* with costumes designed by Esteban Francés and executed by Karinska. It was for a Balanchine ballet that she herself first designed costumes— *Bourrée Fantasque,* presented in 1949 by the New York City Ballet Company, which developed from the Ballet Society. In his *Center* article Martin described her designs as "chic and witty, beautiful in line, smart and unusual in color, and a perfect complement of the Balanchine-Chabrier music-and-choreography." He then commented on the "extraordinary unity of artistic outlook" of Karinska and Balanchine: "Her dresses, like his dances, are classic abstractions, splendidly unreal, coolly sensuous, with a jeune fille elegance, their formalism airily tinged with waywardness."

While continuing to transform the sketches of others into three-dimensional costumes, Karinska was given increasing opportunities to design. *The Nutcracker* (1954) was the second major New York City Ballet production for which she both designed and executed the costumes. In his enthusiastic review of *Stars and Stripes,* Walter Terry of the New York *Herald Tribune* (January 18, 1958) commented, "Costarring with Mr. Balanchine is a *première couturière étoile* (to coin a phrase), Madame Karinska, who designed the resplendent gaudy and gorgeous costumes and executed them with the authority of a master engineer." Among the other New York City Ballet productions for which she was costume designer were *Liebeslieder Walzer* (1960), *Valses et Variations* (1961), and a restaged *Western Symphony* (1968).

Some of her most ambitious and successful designs were those for Balanchine's full-length *Midsummer Night's Dream,* which had its première in January 1962. Referring to the elegance and beauty of the costumes of the *grand divertissement* and *pas de deux* of the last act, Martin observed in the New York *Times* (January 28, 1962), "Karinska, indeed, may never have created costumes of greater artistry than these. Not only in design, but also in materials and in execution, they are the work of a master." A technicolor film version of the ballet was released through Oberon Productions in 1967.

"To the New York City Ballet I gave my heart," Madame Karinska once said. Her devotion to Balanchine's company, however, has not been exclusive. She has made costumes for many important productions of the Metropolitan Opera Company—from Eugene Berman's designs for *Don Giovanni* (1957), from Cecil Beaton's designs for *Turandot* (1961) and *La Traviata* (1966), and

from Franco Zeffirelli's designs for *Falstaff* (1964), among others. The plays and musical comedies of the Broadway stage for which she has supplied costumes include *Too Many Girls* (1939), *Call Me Madame* (1950), *Can-Can* (1953), *The Girl in the Pink Tights* (1954), *Silk Stockings* (1955), *Candide* (1956), and *Becket* (1960). Visiting Hollywood from time to time, she has also been costumer for several films: *Lady in the Dark* (Paramount, 1944), *Gaslight* (MGM, 1944), *Frenchman's Creek* (Paramount, 1944), *Kismet* (MGM, 1944), and *Kitty* (Paramount, 1945). With the designer Dorothy Jeakins she shared an Oscar of the Academy of Motion Picture Arts and Sciences for the costumes of *Joan of Arc* (RKO, 1948), which starred Ingrid Bergman.

Dancers have high praise for the quality of Karinska's costumes, which show concern even for details not visible to the audience. Careful to study areas of stress and movement, often in planning a costume she makes a doll-type cutout to show positions of action and works the costume to fit the movements. She uses the best materials and will search tenaciously for the right fabric or decoration. As a result of her painstaking, her costumes often last as long as eight years. Especially well known are her tutus, which are layered and cut so as to hang perfectly. She keeps meticulous records of all her costumes with measurements, samples of materials, lists of details, and a sketch so that a costume may be duplicated if that should become necessary.

Discussing Karinska's "passion for accuracy" in an article for *Dance Magazine* (June 1967), Joan Alleman Rubin told what she admits to be a perhaps apocryphal story about her following a design so faithfully that she crocheted black spiders on a costume to match black paint splotches on the sketches. Karinska, as a matter of fact, is not a slavish copier, but an innovative interpreter with a sure knowledge of fabric, sense of color, and ability to imagine how a costume will look in action.

At her workshop on a fashionable block of Fifty-seventh Street in Manhattan, Madame Karinska has a score or more of specialists trained by her over the years in technical skills to meet her standard of perfection. She has made her services as designer and dressmaker available to a small, select group of admirers. Among those favored are Gloria Vanderbilt Cooper, Mrs. Robert Merrill (the wife of the opera singer), and several ballet dancers, including Suzanne Farrell and Patricia McBride. Karinska's daughter, Irena, operates a costume and dressmaking enterprise in Paris under the name Karinska.

Blue and lavender are Barbara Karinska's favorite colors. She has blue eyes, uses blue eye shadow, and often wears dark blue Lanvin suits with blue accessories. Although said to be authoritative and somewhat regal in manner, she has a colorful, vivacious personality. She shares her Manhattan home with her lifelong friend, Toussia, who is also her personal secretary, head seamstress, and business manager. Her house in the East Sixties suggests a European chateau with its antique furniture and tapestry-covered walls. Karinska's hobbies of flower arranging and cultivating many house plants are part of her love of beauty. She has a summer home in Great Barrington, Massachusetts and a country house in Domremy, France, the birthplace of Joan of Arc, to whom she is devoted. Among her recreations is raising sheep, from whose wool she makes blankets. She once had three lambs named Frou-Frou, Tutu, and Blue Grass and two poodles named Bourrée and Fantasque.

References

Center 2:21+ F '55 por
Christian Sci Mon p10 F 17 '69
Dance Mag 41:49+ Je '67 pors
N Y Times p42 Ap 13 '60; II p10 D 31 '61
Newsday A p4+ Je 4 '70 pors
Biographical Encyclopaedia & Who's Who of the American Theatre (1966)
Chujoy, Anatole, and Manchester, P. W., eds. Dance Encyclopedia (1967)

KEACH, STACY

June 2, 1941- Actor
Address: c/o New York Shakespeare Festival, 425 Lafayette St., New York 10003

Stacy Keach, who exploded into theatrical stardom in the title role in *MacBird!* Off Broadway in 1967, has applied his interpretive talent to a range of roles wider than that achieved by most actors twice his age. With the New York Shakespeare Festival he has played Peer Gynt and Falstaff, among other roles, and his Broadway credits include Buffalo Bill in Arthur Kopit's *Indians*. On the screen his most recent portrayal was that of Doc Holliday in *Doc*. The word most often applied to Keach by critics is "masterful," and Julius Novick has written of him: "There is no young actor in this country to match him in classical roles."

Stacy Keach (who has dropped the original Jr. from his name) was born in Savannah, Georgia on June 2, 1941 to Stacy Keach Sr. and Mary Cain (Peckham) Keach. Both parents were actors, and at the time of Stacy Jr.'s birth his father was drama teacher at Armstrong Junior College in Savannah. With his younger brother, James, who is also an actor, Keach was raised in Savannah, in Atlanta, and, after his father became a Hollywood dialogue director and coach, in southern California.

In childhood Keach underwent four operations for a harelip, of which the only remnant is a slight scar on his upper lip. At the beginning of his career his agents advised him to have plastic surgery done but he refused because "the harelip is me." The agents suggested that he would have to limit his aspirations severely, to roles other than leading men or heroes. Again he refused, and his refusal has, obviously, been vindicated.

As a juvenile movie buff, Keach admired Sir Laurence Olivier, Burt Lancaster, Montgomery

STACY KEACH

Clift, Sir Ralph Richardson, Jack Palance, and Lon Chaney Sr. He was especially impressed with Olivier's performances in the films *Hamlet* and, later, *Richard III*. "I realized," he has said, "Olivier was the kind of actor I wanted to be." Growing up, Keach was, by his own account, a "play-actor," "mimicker," and teller of "outlandish stories." In an interview with Meryle Secrest of the Washington *Post* (June 8, 1969) he observed: "One day you realize that everyone around you is . . . playing a part. The professional actor is the one who ritualizes this, I used to have this highfalutin' notion about an actor as someone who has a lot in common with a priest, aspiring to God. I was brought up as an Episcopalian . . . an altar boy. When I was about fourteen or fifteen my faith started to slip. I remember exactly when it happened. It was one Sunday morning when we were going through a new ritual . . . and I did something the priest didn't like. . . . He whispered, 'What is all this Notre Dame s----?' I couldn't believe I'd heard it. I felt like laughing at first, out of nervousness. Afterwards, something was destroyed. I was always searching for some spiritual objective but I could never accept the Christian doctrine that one must lose oneself in a larger being . . . that absorption with oneself was selfish, superfluous."

"All through my youth I was in the environment of show business," he told Miss Secrest. "But I knew I wanted something better than that. I wanted to act the great parts. But my parents discouraged me at every turn. They knew what a rotten life it is if you aren't successful. . . . They wanted me to become a lawyer." Keach compromised and matriculated as an economics major at the University of California at Berkeley, but soon he changed to English and drama. During his undergraduate years he spent two summers as an apprentice actor with the Ashland (Oregon) Shakespeare Festival.

In 1963 Keach graduated from the University of California and enrolled in the Yale University Drama School, where he was a student for one year. In the summer of 1964 he made his first appearance in Joseph Papp's New York Shakespeare Festival in Central Park, as Marcellus and the Player King in *Hamlet*. During the 1964-65 scholastic year he studied at the London (England) Academy of Music and Dramatic Art, and while there he met Sir Laurence Olivier, who gave him the advice that he regards as the most important he has ever received: "If you are really good you can become a character actor and create a charisma." Regarding his sojourn in England generally, Keach told Alex Keneas of *Newsweek* (November 24, 1969): "Watching so much good work destroyed all my illusions about technique. For the first time I realized that craft was finding a simplicity of my own."

After returning to the United States, Keach played Horner in *The Country Wife* at the Repertory Theatre of Lincoln Center in New York City. That experience was, as he recalls it, "disastrous," and he retreated into stock in Williamstown, Massachusetts until his morale revived. About that time, in 1966, Barbara Garson, a young New Leftist, was rewriting *MacBird!*—originally a campus skit, presented at the University of California at Berkeley—for presentation as political cabaret. Superficially a clever parody of Shakespeare, Mrs. Garson's comedy is in substance a statement of the scorn felt by a large segment of the younger generation for American politics as it is now practised. The title character is a boorish, vulgar, grotesque caricature of Lyndon Baines Johnson, who in his stage persona is depicted as plotting the death of John Ken O'Dune (President Kennedy) and thus becoming ruler of "the Smooth Society." In the end, MacBird himself is slain by another political scoundrel, Robert Ken O'Dune, younger brother of John Ken O'Dune.

At first Keach was reluctant to play the title role in *MacBird!*, because Mrs. Garson's outrageous wit, intended for stage performance and effective there, often appeared sophomoric when read silently. He finally accepted the part because of the challenge of delivering Shakespearean verse rhythms in a Southern drawl. When *MacBird!* opened at the Village Gate, a Greenwich Village nightclub, on February 22, 1967, Norman Nadel of the *World Journal Tribune* hailed it as "probably the best political satire around at the moment," but the rest of the New York critics were, to a man, shocked or repelled by it, probably partly because they were, out of habit, applying the good-taste criteria of literary theatre to spirited cabaret. But most of them acknowledged the verve and professionalism of the cast in general and praised in particular Keach's savage, bravura performance, which dominated the play. As Jerry Tallmer later wrote, Keach "was LBJ to the life, ears, nose, hawgdrawl, and bluster."

Keach regards MacBird as "the most effective thing" he has done "conceptually, technically, and professionally." In creating the role he "learned something about . . . the actor's conceptual apparatus . . . a thing not much developed in this country, where we rely mostly on the emotions." For the excellence of his performance, Keach received the Obie and Drama Desk-Vernon Rice awards. At the end of September 1967 he left the cast of *MacBird!* to join the company of *The Niggerlovers*, two plays by George Tabori about white liberal ambivalence regarding the racial problem. The pair of dramas, in which Keach played an old professor and a young business executive, ran for twenty-five performances at the Orpheum Theatre in New York City in October 1967. Two months later Keach created the role of Captain Starkey in Joseph Heller's antiwar moral comedy *We Bombed in New Haven* at the Yale Drama School Repertory Theatre, and with the Yale company he played the title role in *Coriolanus* in May 1968. On the latter occasion Julius Novick observed in the New York *Times* (May 26, 1968): "Not many actors would have [as Keach does] the wit and the art and the physical endowment to show both sides of the character and make the contrast between them so vivid."

In New York Shakespeare Festival productions at the Delacorte Theatre in Central Park, Keach played Falstaff in the summer of 1968 and the title role in Ibsen's *Peer Gynt* the following summer, and at Lincoln Center Repertory Theatre he was Edmund in *King Lear* during the 1968-69 season. On Broadway in 1969-70 he was nominated for a Tony award and won second place among male leads in *Variety*'s poll of New York drama critics for his performance in Arthur Kopit's *Indians*, in which he was a Buffalo Bill Cody tormented by hallucinations about his earlier crimes against Indians and buffalo. The following season he won first place in the supporting actor category in the *Variety* Off Broadway poll for his portrayal of James Tyrone Jr., the persona of Eugene O'Neill's older brother in O'Neill's autobiographical *Long Day's Journey into Night*.

On film Keach may be seen as Blount, the drunken, chess-playing drifter in *The Heart is a Lonely Hunter* (Warner, 1968); as Jake Horner, the young man rendered catatonic by contemporary violence and reanimated by the mad Dr. D (James Earl Jones) in *The End of the Road* (Allied Artists, 1970); as Jonas Candide, who circuit-rides a rural Southern prison system with a portable electric chair, sweet-talking his victims into acceptance of their fate in *The Traveling Executioner* (MGM, 1970); and as the title character in *Doc* (United Artists, 1971), a deglamorization of legendary Western "hero" John "Doc" Holliday. Critics generally have given his starring vehicles on the screen bad or mixed reviews while praising his performances in them.

On television Keach narrated *The Century Next Door* (WCBS-TV, New York, July 1970), a documentary about life in New York City one hundred years ago, and he and his brother played the title parts in *Orville and Wilbur* (Public Broadcasting System, June 1971), a biography of the Wright brothers. In 1971 Keach and Hal Dubin formed Praxis Productions, the first completed project of which was *The Repeater*, a twenty-minute film shot on location in Kilby Prison in Alabama, as was *The Traveling Executioner*. *The Repeater* has been shown on National Educational Television as part of NET's *American Dream Machine* series. With his friend Harris Yulin, Keach often shoots 8 and 16mm footage in and around New York City, where he lives.

Stacy Keach is six feet tall, weighs 170 pounds, has deep-set light blue eyes, high cheekbones, and fine hair that curls at the neck and is thinning in front. In conversation he speaks softly, occasionally interjecting a muted, abortive laugh, which Meryle Secrest described as "his substitute for anger." Off stage Keach dresses for comfort more than appearance, smokes cigarettes, reads the *I Ching*, has a mild interest in astrology, and, according to one observer, is "gregarious, extroverted, and slyly funny." On stage he has become more and more inner-directed. "I've reached the point," he told Alex Keneas in the *Newsweek* interview two years ago, "where my feelings emerge without my having to think about manifesting them."

Keach was married—"on and off," as he says—to a Berkeley classmate for three years. "I just couldn't cope with it [the marriage] and be an actor too," he told David Freeman in an interview for an article in *New York* (July 7, 1969). When working with Judy Collins (better known as a folk singer than an actress) in *Peer Gynt* he became a close friend of hers. It was at her suggestion that he began going to Encounter group sessions, where he discovered the significant question he must ask himself about his motivation in acting: "Am I running away from myself or trying to discover who I am?" He works at his acting compulsively, with total commitment, and he admires others who give their "all each time . . . risk the whole thing every time out" Olivier, Michael Redgrave, Albert Finney, Toshiro Mifune, and the late Janis Joplin ("pure raw energy in action").

What William Wolf in *Cue* (April 25, 1970) called "that extra measure of electricity behind the technical talent readily visible in a Keach performance" is kept vibrant by an involvement in reality. Keach, who tries to concentrate on his work in such a way as not to sacrifice his personal life, told Wolf: "I think the way you remain open and vulnerable to living experience has something to do with it [being a great actor]. Also being able to have good friends, be happy, and appreciate life." Joseph Papp has said, "Stacy's real uniqueness as an actor is his humanity. He always gives the stage to another actor," and an actress who has worked as an extra in New York Shakespeare Festival productions has testified, "Stacy will share everything with you. . . . He is sort of a father figure even though he's our age. When he makes a decision, we all accept it. He is also a very private person. We know when he wants to be alone." Keach finds what he calls "the political games" of the theatrical world, especially Broadway, "horrible," but he believes that "if your ego is easily bruised there is something wrong with your powers of endurance. . . . It's important to sustain openness, generosity, the ability not to get uptight."

References

N Y Sunday News II p28 N 16 '69 por
N Y Times II p1 O 19 '69
Who's Who in America, 1970-71

KEELER, RUBY

Aug. 25, 1910- Dancer; actress
Address: b. c/o Gloria Safier, 667 Madison Ave., New York 10021

Throughout her career in entertainment, Ruby Keeler has always been at the right place at the right time. As a youngster, she tap-danced her way to the top in the New York speakeasies of the Prohibition era, emerging from their smoke-filled interiors to the glitter of Broadway. She quickly rose from chorus girl to Ziegfeld girl and on to a sizable part in Ziegfeld's *Whoopee!* (1928). Her marriage to Al Jolson in 1928 took her to Hollywood, where she was cast as *the* ingenue of the 1930's. She frolicked in the joys of romance in such Busby Berkeley dance spectaculars as *42nd Street* and *Footlight Parade*, which captured the good-natured, warm-hearted, sparkling charm that she, more than anyone else, personified. Soon after her divorce from Jolson in 1940, she retired from the screen, and during thirty years of her marriage to John Lowe she virtually disappeared from public view. Missed but never wholly forgotten, in 1971 the once reigning favorite of Hollywood's Golden Era captivated Broadway audiences again in the "new 1925 musical," *No, No, Nanette*.

Ruby Keeler, the second of six children of Ralph and Elnora (Lahy) Keeler, was born on August 25, 1910 in Halifax, Nova Scotia, Canada. When she was three, the family left Nova Scotia to settle in an East Side tenement in New York City, where her father drove a truck for the Knickerbocker Ice Company. She attended the parochial grammar school of the St. Catherine of Siena Roman Catholic Church, where she participated in "drill," a class in rhythmic exercises conducted by Helen Guest. Miss Keeler's formal dance training scarcely progressed beyond those schoolgirl exercises, although she was briefly enrolled in a dance school where she studied rudimentary ballet. She learned the popular dances of the 1920's and performed them at community functions. Her parents enrolled her in the Professional Children's School, and in 1923 she landed her first professional job, in the chorus of George M. Cohan's *The Rise of Rosie O'Reilly*.

High-spirited and serious-minded, Ruby Keeler competed with professionals to win a Nils Thor Granlund dance contest. She was only thirteen, but impresario "Granny," who marketed much of the talent for New York's hot spots, placed her in the Texas Guinan show at the El Fey Club. In the glamorous, almost mythical world of F. Scott Fitzgerald and Michael Arlen, gangsters and Broadway producers, Ruby Keeler tapped and smiled, hoofed and winged her way through the saloons, cigar smoke, and booze of Prohibition.

RUBY KEELER

For the young performer it was a training ground to expand her technique.

On Broadway before long, she joined the chorus of *Bye Bye Bonnie*, a 1927 musical in which her specialty number, "Tampico Tap," received favorable comments from the critics. The producer Charles Dillingham featured her in *Lucky* (1927). An instant failure, the show closed overnight, but Dillingham engaged Miss Keeler for *The Sidewalks of New York* (1927). Broadway audiences and critics took notice; Richard Watts Jr., writing in the New York *Herald Tribune* (October 4, 1927), mentioned the "excellent dancing by Ruby Keeler." Florenz Ziegfeld signed her as chief tap dancer for *Whoopee!*, the 1928 musical starring Ruth Etting and Eddie Cantor. During the summer months before the show went into rehearsal, Miss Keeler visited the West Coast to perform for the Loew's theatre chain in prologue shows. When she stepped off the train, an admirer who had seen her back East was waiting to be formally introduced. William Perlberg, a West Coast agent, performed that service for Al Jolson. Their meeting became legendary, but Miss Keeler described it accurately and succinctly for Ronald L. Bowers in *Films in Review* (August-September 1971): "The introductions were perfunctory and everybody went their separate ways. And that's the true story of how I met Jolson."

Several months later Ruby Keeler became the fourth Mrs. Al Jolson, to the delight of the columnists. Because of the difference in their religions—Miss Keeler is a Roman Catholic and Jolson was a Jew—the marriage was performed by a justice of the peace in Pittsburgh on September 21, 1928. Although the Jolson name generated considerable publicity for the young dancer, making her a national celebrity, Jolson at various times exerted a negative influence on her career. After a short honeymoon, she returned to the out-of-town tryouts of *Whoopee!*, and although she earned good notices for her featured part, she left the long-running show before its New York opening. At Jolson's insistence, she returned with him to California.

Ziegfeld held no grudge against Miss Keeler for dropping out and offered her a large part the following year in *Show Girl*. With Jolson's approval she opened with the show in New York on July 2, 1929. Her two important numbers were warmly received. Jolson, always the consummate showman, added a minor footnote to Broadway history when he rose from his seat in the orchestra to serenade his wife. The film version of his life suggests that Jolson was rushing to the aid of his fainting wife, but Miss Keeler corrected that fiction in a New York *Times* (January 10, 1971) interview with Guy Flatley: "Al did stand up in the audience and sing . . . but just because Al liked to sing, and when he felt like singing, he sang." Not yet twenty years old, she precipitously left *Show Girl* and went to Hollywood to live full time as Mrs. Al Jolson.

The years between the end of Ruby Keeler's Broadway career and her entrance into films are not well documented. In 1928, while in Hollywood, she had done a two-minute promotional short for Fox to test the effectiveness of new Movietone equipment in reproducing the sound of tap dancing. That performance was hardly a movie debut. Now that Jolson was at the summit of his screen popularity, the columnists reported that Ruby Keeler kept receiving and turning down movie offers. She has denied in press interviews, however, that producers urged her to go into pictures until a test she had been persuaded to do for a Jolson film was seen by Darryl F. Zanuck of Warner Brothers, who signed her for the ingenue role in *42nd Street* (1933), her actual film debut.

It was not the separate elements of the film but their mixture, with Ruby Keeler as the catalyst, that made *42nd Street* unique. Other films had used Busby Berkeley dance routines, and the plot of the upstate fledgling suddenly called upon to fill the prima donna's shoes was already hackneyed. Yet, new in scale and refinement, the film made history. Her years of training in clubs and on Broadway had made Miss Keeler a remarkably flexible performer. Busby Berkeley saw his chance to create dance numbers for her far more complex than anything yet put on film. His two important pieces for Miss Keeler are the title number, during which she taps on the roof of a taxi, and a soft-shoe routine for the now famous "Shuffle Off to Buffalo."

Ruby Keeler delighted the critics. Richard Watts Jr. of the New York *Herald Tribune* called her "one of the best of all possible tap dancers." The reviewer for the Los Angeles *Times* summed up the nation's enthusiasm: "The surprise among the players is of course, Ruby Keeler, whose hesitant, clear speech and demurely fresh appearance make her a far more effective and appealing personality in her screen debut than her husband, Al Jolson, in spite of his importance as a revolutionary tradition." Ruby Keeler and her partner in *42nd Street*, Dick Powell, became the favorite young couple of the decade. All style and no substance, that movie set the pattern for film musicals for years to come. Today it is studied by anyone seriously interested in the history of film and continues to have a wide appeal for less specialized moviegoers.

Among the succession of musical hits starring Miss Keeler and Dick Powell as dance partners was Berkeley's *Gold Diggers of 1933*, in which Miss Keeler displayed lively tapping in the "Pettin' in the Park" number. Visual extravagance and the performance of the seemingly impossible dominated the screen. For the "Shadow Waltz" number in *Gold Diggers*, Berkeley achieved a spectacular effect in which girls, strapped with electric wires, played lighted violins while Dick Powell sang in the foreground. In Ruby Keeler's next picture, *Footlight Parade* (1933), Berkeley had her dance on top of a bar. *Dames* (1934), in which Powell serenaded Miss Keeler while her visage was multiplied and rotated upon the screen, was Miss Keeler's last film under Berkeley's supervision. She also changed studios, from Warner Brothers to First National, for *Flirtation Walk* (1934), a West Point musical that kept the Keeler-Powell team intact. Miss Keeler remarked to John Gruen in an interview for *Close-Up* (1968), "For several years I was destined to be Dick Powell's screen partner, and, I guess in those sad Depression days, Dick and I did bring a bit of sunshine into people's hearts."

The year 1935 was a promising one for the Jolsons. Eager audiences awaited the release of *Go Into Your Dance* (First National), the film that united husband and wife as costars. Directed by Bobby Connally and featuring Patsy Kelly, it had a more solid plot and characterization than the usual musical and depended heavily upon the talents of its two stars. Kate Cameron of the New York *Daily News* commented, "Romantics of the picture-going world can gorge themselves as that skilled pair of entertainers sing, dance, and make love to each other." In their only film together Miss Keeler portrayed a naïve dancer who helps a talented entertainer, played by Al Jolson, to make a comeback. On the screen the couple worked well together, and the "I'm a Latin from Manhattan" number highlighted the special abilities of both performers.

Miss Keeler's last two films with Dick Powell, *Shipmates Forever* (First National, 1935) and *Colleen* (Warner, 1936), were not altogether successful. *Shipmates* was basically a briny version of *Flirtation Walk*, with the background changed from West Point to Annapolis. *Colleen* appeared "faded" to the reviewer of the New York *Times;* the public was, in fact, beginning to tire of the lavish musical. "In my day," Ruby Keeler recalled in 1950, "musicals didn't get better—they just got bigger." *Ready, Willing and Able* (Warner, 1937) contains one of her best numbers. The finale called for her and her partner, Lee Dixon, to dance on the keys of a giant typewriter. The routine remains Ruby's favorite screen dance. Robert Roman quoted her in *Dance Magazine* (December 1970) as saying, "I suppose you might call it one of the last of the real rhythm dance numbers. They just don't do it that way anymore."

RKO produced Miss Keeler's next picture, *Mother Carey's Chickens* (1938), a departure from the lavish musicals that had made her a star. Her straight dramatic role and the nostalgic mood of the film, based on a novel by one of her favorite authors, Kate Douglas Wiggin, provided an escape from her much-publicized domestic troubles. The conflict in their careers had always been a strain between Ruby Keeler and Al Jolson, but more important was the conflict of their personalities. Despite her stardom, Miss Keeler remained a shy woman who, unlike her husband, disliked parties and crowds. The differences in their ages (Jolson was twenty-five years her senior), religion, and tastes proved insurmountable. Miss Keeler and Jolson separated in 1939, and their divorce became final on December 27, 1940. She made one last film, *Sweetheart of the Campus* (1941), this time for Columbia, but perhaps because of miscasting, it was not among her triumphs.

On October 29, 1941 Miss Keeler married John Homer Lowe, whom she had met several months earlier. A prominent California broker, he offered Miss Keeler the long-awaited opportunity to settle down and raise a family. Her retirement from show business was for a time complete. But by 1950 Miss Keeler was making guest appearances on TV. When she performed on Ken Murray's *Television Review*, a *Variety* reporter called her "Murray's ace lure." In 1963 Jerry Lewis featured her in two specialty numbers that created amazement in the press that "this star of 30 years ago was so lithe." She returned to the stage during 1968 for a three-week run of a revival of *Bell, Book and Candle*.

The fad of "sentimental nostalgia" had led in 1965 to a Busby Berkeley film festival at the Gallery of Modern Art in New York, at which Ruby Keeler was present. Neither she nor Berkeley had any conception of the popular culture movement with its quixotic flirtations with the stars of yesterday. She was ingenuously delighted by the tribute to the Berkeley musicals, but found that she had become "the queen of campy satire."

In 1970, therefore, when Harry Rigby offered her the role of Sue in the revival he was planning of the 1925 musical *No, No, Nanette*, Miss Keeler thought it a joke. She had seen the Bernadette Peters impersonation of herself in *Dames at Sea*, a 1969 satire of the film musicals of the 1930's. When she found that Rigby did not intend to ridicule the old musicals and that Busby Berkeley had been hired as production supervisor, Miss Keeler decided to take the part because, as she told M. J. Wilson of Newsweek Feature Service, "there was a feeling of warmth of participation, of warm nostalgia, not cruelty about this show." She left no doubt that although she is Ruby Keeler, she no longer fits her movie image. A very much composed and dignified grandmother, she made what John Schubeck of WABC-TV called "the entertainment comeback of the Century."

No, No, Nanette opened to rave reviews at the 46th Street Theater on January 19, 1971. The creation of Vincent Youmans (music), Otto Harbach and Frank Mandel (book), and Irving Caesar and Otto Harbach (lyrics), it was adapted and directed by Burt Shevelove and choreographed by Donald Saddler. The plot includes all the familiar elements of the musicals of the 1920's, sufficiently complicated and extended to accommodate the spectacular production numbers. As Sue, Miss Keeler plays a Bible publisher's wife piqued by his innocent involvement with three young girls. She is featured in two dance numbers, "I Want To Be Happy" and "Take a Little One-step," which was restored to the show for her from the London production of forty years ago. Richard Watts, her old admirer, wrote in the New York *Post* that the dancing and songs were vital to *No, No, Nanette* and that "Ruby Keeler can still do a tap dance or a soft-shoe number that is a joy." Critics unanimously agreed that Ruby Keeler made the show work. Richard Philips observed in *After Dark* (March 1971), "She doesn't miss a trick, dancing across that stage, her brows knit with merriment and concentration and her mouth in a wide O of wonder—it's really me and the gang's all here for a nifty fun fest. Her dancing is a consummate pastiche of the period; tap today has lost some of the athletic quality which characterizes Miss Keeler's performance." Helen Gallagher and Patsy Kelly, an old friend of Miss Keeler's, won Tony awards for their roles in the show. *No, No, Nanette* also brought Tony awards to Saddler as best choreographer and to Raoul Pène du Bois as best costume designer.

Ruby Keeler, whose hair is now silver, still has the bright blue eyes and trim figure that Busby Berkeley and her fans admired almost forty years ago. Although she had not continued dance practice, playing tournament golf and swimming kept her in shape, and she had little trouble holding her own with the young Berkeley girls. Her sister Gertrude and her son John accompanied her to New York, and John joined *Nanette* as an assistant stage manager. She has three other children— Teresa, Christine, and Kathleen—by her marriage to Lowe, who died in 1969. During her first marriage, in 1935 she and Jolson adopted an infant boy whom they named Al ("Sonny Boy") Jr. He later changed his name to Peter. On May 14, 1971 the Catholic Actors Guild presented Miss Keeler with the George M. Cohan Award, an especially moving tribute because it was a Cohan production that first brought her to the Broadway stage.

References

After Dark 44:62+ D '70 pors
Dance Mag 44:62+ D '70 pors
Films in Review 22:405+ Ag-S '71 por
Look 35:70+ F 9 '71 pors
N Y Times p56 Je 25 '70 por; II p1+ Ja 10 '71 pors
Newsweek 76:63 Ag 3 '70 por
Toronto Globe and Mail p25 N 7 '70 por
Washington (D.C.) Post B p1+ Jl 10 '70 pors
Gruen, John. Close-Up (1968)
Who's Who in America, 1970-71

KELLY, JOHN B(RENDEN), JR.

May 24, 1927- Former athlete; organization official; business executive; municipal official
Address: b. John B. Kelly Inc., 1720 Cherry St., Philadelphia, Pa. 19103; h. Plaza Apts., 18th and Parkway, Philadelphia, Pa. 19103

In the latter half of the nineteenth century unscrupulous promotion practices and spreading venality fouled the integrity and threatened the continued existence of athletic amateurism, or the enjoyment of sport for sport's sake, in the United States. Colleges had their own regulating mechanism, eventually formalized on a national level in the National Collegiate Athletic Association. To the rescue of nonprofessional athletes in or outside of college came the Amateur Athletic Union, a regulatory federation founded by dedicated sportsmen in 1888. The AAU quickly put amateurism's house in order, and it has stood guard over it ever since. That guard had grown rigid in recent decades, according to an increasing number of critics within the organization, but those critics see hope for rejuvenation in the AAU's current president, progressive-minded, relatively young John B. Kelly Jr. Kelly, son of the late millionaire masonry contractor John B. Kelly Sr. and brother of Princess Grace of Monaco, is a former world champion sculler, a Philadelphia city councilman at large, and the president of John B. Kelly Inc., the Philadelphia-based company founded by his father. His term in the AAU presidency, begun in December 1970, is for two years.

John Brenden Kelly Jr., known to friends as Jack or Kell, was born in Philadelphia, Pennsylvania on May 24, 1927. His mother, the former Margaret Majes, was a physical education instructor. He has two sisters in addition to Princess Grace: Margaret, who is older than he, and Elizabeth, who, like Grace, is younger. In 1920 Kelly Sr., an Olympic champion sculler, was denied entrance to the Diamond Sculls of the Royal Regatta at Henley-on-Thames, England, the crowning event in rowing, because at that time only bona fide "gentlemen" were eligible, and he had once been a menial laborer, a bricklayer. Determined that his son would some day avenge the insult and vindicate the family honor by winning the Henley race, he began training him in rowing when he was seven years old, on the Schuylkill River. Later, for Jack's sake, he bought the Vesper Boat Club in Philadelphia and replenished its fleet.

Kelly was educated at Pennsylvania Military Prep School, William Penn Charter School, and the University of Pennsylvania, where he majored in economics and took his B.A. degree in 1950. An all-round athlete, he was a football star at William Penn Charter School, and he made center on the University of Pennsylvania team, but the extraordinary Chuck Bednarik outshone him in that position and his father persuaded him to quit football, in which he could only hope to be second best, in order to put all of his energy into becoming the world's best sculler. Between secondary school and college Kelly was a seaman in the United States Navy for a year (1945-46). He did another tour of duty with the Navy in 1951 and 1952, as an ensign, and for fourteen years thereafter he was a lieutenant junior grade in the Navy Reserve.

In more than thirty races in the mid-1940's Kelly was beaten only twice. In the late 1940's he won the Canadian (1947), United States (1948 and 1949), European (1949), Belgian (1949), and Swiss (1949) single sculls championships. But the victories of which he and his father were proudest were those in the Royal Henley Regatta that father and son had been anticipating for years. Wearing a replica of the green cap that his father had once worn, Jack Kelly finished eight lengths ahead of Carl Fronsdal of Norway to take the mile-and-a-quarter event in July 1947, and two years later he again finished first at Henley, about 100 yards ahead of compatriot Jack Trinsey. His time in the second Diamond Sculls victory was eight minutes and twelve seconds, thirty-seven seconds faster than his clocking in 1947. He was awarded the Sullivan Trophy as the outstanding American amateur athlete of 1947.

Kelly won the United States singles title for the third time in 1950, and he took the title in each of the five consecutive years beginning in 1952. In the 1950's he also took the Mexican (1953) and Pan-American (1955) singles crowns and shared in the Pan-American doubles championship (1959). The Vesper Club's eight-oared crew, captained by Kelly, won the United States and Canadian championships and finished second in the European championships in 1958.

The only major single sculls prize never attained by Kelly was an Olympic gold medal. In the Olympiad in London in 1948 he was defeated in the semi-finals, at Helsinki in 1952 he lost in the repechage (the second trial heat), and at Melbourne in 1956 he finished third in the final race, winning a bronze medal. In the 1960 Olympics, in Rome, he entered only the double sculls, with Bill Knecht. With Knecht suffering from dysentery and Kelly barely recovered from the illness, they finished fourth in the repechage.

In the meantime Kelly had begun working his way up the ranks in his father's company, from apprentice bricklayer through journeyman to executive positions. (As an apprentice he finished first in a Pennsylvania state bricklaying contest, out of a field of twenty apprentice finalists.) Following the death of his father he retired from sculling competition, after the 1960 Olympics, in order to devote himself more fully to directing company affairs and building up and coaching Vesper Club rowing and swimming teams. At the same time he began his climb up the ladder of leadership of the Amateur Athletic Union.

Elected a fifth vice-president of the AAU in 1961, Kelly moved up a notch in the association's hierarchy every two years. His assumption of the presidency was ratified on December 5, 1970, by a vote of the delegates to the eighty-third annual convention of the AAU, held in San Francisco. The convention was marked by the appearance of

JOHN B. KELLY JR.

a group of track and field athletes, led by Olympian Hal Connolly, who had been disqualified as amateurs because each was a professional in one or another sport. Calling themselves the UAA (United Amateur Athletes) "because we're just the opposite of the AAU," they presented several demands, the chief of which was the rescinding of the AAU rule depriving them of amateur status even in sports other than their professional specialties.

In his presidential acceptance speech Kelly agreed with the UAA group that the present rule is "ridiculous," that it "encourages athletes to lie and cheat in order to compete" or penalizes them by requiring abandonment of their livelihoods for long periods before and during amateur competition. He promised to seek a realistic definition of amateurism and predicted that the trend in the future will be toward open-competition events, in which professionals may compete alongside amateurs.

In his acceptance speech Kelly called generally for a reassessment of AAU policy to the end of making it more realistically flexible, in keeping with "the age of Aquarius," as long as changes are made with the sanction of the International Amateur Athletic Association and the International Olympic Committee. He promised to work toward giving young athletes a greater voice in association policy; giving the AAU committees concerned with specific sports greater autonomy; changing the name of the association to the American Athletic Union (because the adjective "amateur" has the connotation of "unskilled" in many minds); creating a "sports corps" of athlete volunteers to teach skills and training methods to young people in disadvantaged areas; and expanding the financial base of the AAU by greater television coverage of events in such fields as wrestling, gymnastics, and basketball. (The AAU already has a television contract with the CBS network.)

Kelly also broached a rapprochement with the National Collegiate Athletic Association, and Walter Byers, the executive director of the NCAA, responded by saying that Kelly's statement was "reassuring." The two associations had been feuding for years over jurisdiction in some sports and over the right to represent American sports in international amateur organizations.

The organizations in which Kelly is an officer are many and varied. He is a director of the National Rowing Foundation, the United States Rowing Society, the University of Pennsylvania Varsity Club, the University of Pennsylvania Museum, Americans for the Competitive Enterprise System, Equity Concepts Inc., the Lincoln National Bank, the Paramount Life Insurance Company, and the Hero Scholarship Fund, and the president of the John B. Kelly Foundation and the Philadelphia Athletic Club. He has chaired the Non-Partisan Register and Vote Campaign, the Philadelphia Youth Fitness Committee, and the Easter Seal Committee, and he is a member of the Philadelphia Mayor's Sports Advisory Council, the executive committee of the Philadelphia 1976 Bicentennial Corporation, the Philadelphia Historical Commission, and the United States Olympic Committee.

John B. Kelly Jr. and Mary G. Freeman, married on March 4, 1954, are now separated. They have six children, Ann, Susan, Maura, Elizabeth, John B. 3d, and Margaret. Kelly, who has been compared to Superman's alter ego, Clark Kent, in appearance, is six feet one inch tall, weighs 195 pounds, and has brown hair and blue eyes. His sense of humor was typified by his performance at the AAU inaugural banquet, when he tore off his shirt, Clark Kent style, and emerged with muscles flexed beneath a Superman tee shirt. Kelly, who has no significant recreations outside of sports, regularly works out at the Philadelphia Athletic Club and rows at the Vesper Club, of which he is secretary-treasurer. His religious affiliation is Roman Catholic and his political affiliation is Democratic. He was named Man of the Year 1956 by the Catholic War Veterans and in 1960 and 1961 he was named Outstanding Young Man of the Year by the Philadelphia Junior Chamber of Commerce. His other honors include the Philadelphia Zionist Award, the Jewish War Veterans Brotherhood Award, and election to the Pennsylvania and the Helms Sports Halls of Fame.

References

Amateur Athlete 42:6+ Ja '71 pors; 42:4+ F '71 pors
N Y Times p40 Je 27 '56 por; p22 Ag 31 '60; p69 D 7 '70 por
Sports Illus 34:32+ My 10 '71 pors

KEMENY, JOHN G(EORGE) (kem'en-ē)

May 31, 1926- Educator; mathematician; philosopher
Address: b. Office of the President, Parkhurst Hall, Dartmouth College, Hanover, N.H. 03755; h. 14 Webster Ave., Hanover, N.H. 03755

In 1970 the brilliant mathematician-philosopher John G. Kemeny agreed to succeed the retiring John Sloan Dickey as president of the small but prestigious Dartmouth College, with the proviso that he be allowed to continue teaching at least one undergraduate class. Kemeny, a pioneer in promoting the new math and the use of computers in general education, has been teaching at Dartmouth since 1954. As chairman of the Department of Mathematics there, from 1955 to 1967, he revolutionized the curriculum, and at the time of his appointment to the presidency he was in the process of planning interdisciplinary and other innovations in curricula for the 3,800-student college as a whole. As president he continues to lower the administrative walls that fragment faculties and separate science from the humanities. In a time of general campus discontent Kemeny enjoys an unusual popularity with students, apparently because he shares their sensitivity to urgent contemporary social and political issues, and because he makes himself accessible to them and hears them out. It is his belief that students "really don't want final decision-making authority on most campus matters—they want to be heard."

John George Kemeny was born in Budapest, Hungary on May 31, 1926 to Tibor Kemeny, a commodities export-import broker, and Lucy (Fried) Kemeny. With his sister, Kemeny grew up in Budapest until 1940, when a Nazi invasion of Hungary appeared imminent and the Kemenys fled the country, immigrating to the United States, and settling in New York City. At that time Kemeny knew Latin and German in addition to his native tongue, but he could not speak English. Mastering the language quickly, he led his class scholastically at George Washington High School in Manhattan.

In 1943 Kemeny graduated from high school and entered Princeton University to major in mathematics and minor in philosophy. His college studies were interrupted early in 1945, when he was inducted into the United States Army and assigned to work under mathematician John von Neumann in the computing center of the theoretical division of the Manhattan (atomic bomb) Project at Los Alamos, New Mexico. At the center he vied with eighteen IBM computers in solving key differential equations.

After the war Kemeny returned to Princeton, where he was president of the German Club and the Roundtable and a member of the Court Club and the fencing team. In 1947 he received his B.A. degree *summa cum laude*, Phi Beta Kappa, and at the top of his class. While working for his doctorate at Princeton he assisted Professor Alonzo Church in mathematics research (1947-48) and Professor Albert Einstein in advanced unified field theory (1948-49). He was considering joining the United World Federalists as a full-time staff member, but Einstein dissuaded him by pointing out that "the way to have [political] influence is to become preeminent in your field."

Kemeny's dissertation for his Ph.D. degree was an analysis of the new "type" and "set" theories in mathematics. Immediately after taking the degree, in 1949, he joined the Princeton faculty as an instructor in mathematical logic. Two years later he moved to the Department of Philosophy as an assistant professor, and in 1952-53 he was bicentennial preceptor in philosophy. He went to Dartmouth College in 1953 with an appointment as professor of mathematics and philosophy and with the understanding that he was to rebuild the mathematics department, many of whose members were nearing retirement simultaneously.

As chairman of the Department of Mathematics, from 1954 to 1967, Kemeny recruited an outstanding faculty and reshaped the curriculum. Traditional math courses for freshmen and sophomores, he had observed, by their stress on monotonous drills and the solving of problems whose solutions are already available in reference tables, tended to bore gifted students—driving them from further study in math and to demoralize average ones. Accordingly, he drastically reduced calculus drills in favor of efficient use of reference material, and he introduced into first-year classes the basic ideas of differential calculus (in addition to the usual integral calculus) and into sophomore classes the use of modern, finite mathematics in solving problems of probability, logic, set theory, games theory, partitions, and the like. Thus he made it possible even for the students not specializing in math to see the new frontiers in mathematics and to appreciate the excitement of exploring them. For gifted prospective specialists he set up a challenging honors program on the undergraduate level, and on the graduate level he established Dartmouth's first doctoral program in math, an experimental program designed to prepare students not only for independent research—as most university and college math departments were doing—but also for university and college teaching.

Also, with Professor Thomas E. Kurtz, Kemeny made computer use an integral part of general learning on the Dartmouth campus. The two men invented BASIC, a simplified computer language easily mastered by undergraduates, and under their supervision a campus-wide computer timesharing system was set up, with sixty terminals, or teletype consoles, in classroom buildings linked to the college's Kiewatt Computation Center, containing a General Electric 635 computer. Following the Dartmouth example, other colleges and universities began to investigate the general educational uses of computers and to borrow the BASIC code. Kemeny helped to set up a cooperative computer link between Dartmouth and some twenty-four high schools and twelve other colleges in New England. The math courses and programs Kemeny established at Dartmouth became models for new curricula at other schools, and through his influence as a lecturer and officer of the Mathematical Association of America he played an important role in effecting the adoption of the new math by American educational institutions generally, on all levels. In acknowledgment and aid of the work of Kemeny and his associates, the Alfred P. Sloan Foundation financed the building of Dartmouth's Albert Bradley Center for mathematics study and research.

At one point in his tenure as chairman of the Department of Mathematics, Kemeny was also

JOHN G. KEMENY

simultaneously a teacher of philosophy and a member of the steering committee for an honors program interrelating math and the social sciences. In 1967 he resigned his chairmanship—but not his classes—to become Coordinator of Educational Plans and Development, in charge of revamping the various curricula of the entire college, and he held that post until his appointment to the presidency. At the same time he was chairman of the college's committees on coeducation and equal opportunity. (Dartmouth was then beginning to adjust to a new policy calculated to increase the matriculation of blacks. As for women students, Dartmouth announced in November 1971 that it would adopt coeducation in 1972.) He was, simultaneously, the first holder of the Albert Bradley Third Century Professorship—established in 1969 to encourage innovation in teaching. In the professorship, he created an experimental interdisciplinary course on the possible uses of the computer in solving the problems of contemporary technological society and bettering the lives of individuals in that society.

Kemeny's appointment to the Dartmouth presidency followed a year during which the Ivy League school was torn by anti-ROTC and prominority disturbances similar to those erupting on campuses across the United States. At a press conference held on the day of his appointment, January 24, 1970, Kemeny announced among other plans, that Dartmouth would expand its services to the surrounding New Hampshire community in the areas of culture, medical care, and environment protection and that it would accelerate its efforts to help disadvantaged students, particularly Negroes, poor whites from northern New England, and American Indians. (The college was founded in 1769 primarily for the education of Indians, but only three native Americans were enrolled in 1969. There is now in operation at the school a scholarship program calculated to insure the enrollment of about fifteen of them every year, and an Indian center has been established on campus.)

At his inauguration, on March 1, 1970, Kemeny set four immediate general priorities for his administration: "a decent standard of living for all who serve the institution," including clerical and maintenance employees; "improvement of the quality of student life"; continuous adaptation of educational programs to "an age of rapid change"; and the physical facilities necessary for the implementation of the first three priorities. Among individual priorities, he cited as among "the most urgent" the finding of ways to make students from disadvantaged backgrounds "feel a part of the Dartmouth family" and to resolve the co-education question. A student leader later observed that when Kemeny assumed office "we felt there was hope again that students could find meaningful leadership from their president."

Student protest against the war in Vietnam, dampened by the Nixon administration's vague commitment to ending the war, was rekindled when the United States invaded Cambodia at the end of April 1970, and it reached white heat when National Guardsmen killed four students at Kent (Ohio) State University on May 4, 1970. Within hours of the Kent killings, Kemeny joined a number of other college and university presidents in addressing to President Nixon a plea "to consider the incalculable dangers of an unprecedented alienation of America's youth," and in unison with a student "strike call," he suspended all regular academic activities on the Dartmouth campus for the remainder of that week (Tuesday through Friday). When he addressed the students at the end of "strike week" he was given what the *Dartmouth Alumni Magazine* (June 1970) described as "a thunderous standing ovation."

Kemeny is the author of *A Philosopher Looks at Science* (Van Nostrand, 1959) and *Random Essays on Mathematics, Education, and Computers* (Prentice-Hall, 1964), and he is the coauthor of some nine books, including *Introduction to Finite Mathematics* (Prentice-Hall, 1957), *Finite Mathematical Structures* (Prentice-Hall, 1959), *Finite Markov Chains* (Van Nostrand, 1959), *Mathematical Models in the Social Sciences* (Ginn, 1962), *Finite Mathematics with Business Applications* (Prentice-Hall, 1962), *Denumerable Markov Chains* (Van Nostrand, 1966), and *Basic Programming* (John Wiley, 1967). *Introduction to Finite Mathematics* has sold more than 200,000 copies in English and has been translated into several other languages.

The Dartmouth president is a consultant to the Rand Corporation, a trustee of the Foundation Center and the Carnegie Foundation for the Advancement of Teaching, an associate editor of the *Journal of Mathematical Analysis and Applications*, and a member of the American Mathematical Society, the American Philosophical Association, and the Association for Symbolic Logic. In the Mathematical Association of America he has been a national lecturer, a member of the board of governors, and the chairman of several panels, and he has filled equally important positions with the Educational Testing Service, the National Examination Board, the National Research Council,

and the National Science Foundation. His honors include two honorary degrees.

John G. Kemeny and the former Jean Alexander were married on November 5, 1950. They have two children, Jennifer and Robert. In addition to their home in Hanover, the Kemenys have a wood farm in Lyme, New Hampshire. Kemeny is five feet ten inches tall, weighs 185 pounds, has brown hair and brown eyes, wears a mustache, and prefers turtleneck sweaters to shirts and ties. He smokes two packs of cigarettes a day. By birth he is a Jew—the first Jew to head an Ivy League college—but he does not formally practise Judaism. In politics he is a Democrat. He has been a naturalized citizen of the United States since 1945. Kemeny retires late, usually about two in the morning. Except for spectator sports and reading, his recreations are in, or related to, his work. He considers teaching a recreation, and his favorite hobby is playing with computers. A game that he often plays is a computerized football contest between Dartmouth and one of its Ivy League rivals. He has computer terminals in both his home and his office, and he predicts that by 1990 such electronic keyboards will be as common as telephones and that their use will raise the intellectual level of the average home to "the pre-television level."

References

Dartmouth Alumni Magazine 62:20 Je '70 por
N Y Times p1+ Ja 24 '70 por
Newsweek 75:75 F 2 '70 por
Time 95:66 F 9 '70 por
Who's Who in America, 1970-71

KIRKPATRICK, RALPII

June 10, 1911- Harpsichordist
Address: b. c/o Herbert Barrett Management, 1860 Broadway, New York 10023; Yale School of Music, New Haven, Conn. 06520; h. Old Quarry, Guilford, Conn. 06437

The current revival of interest in baroque music can partly be attributed to Ralph Kirkpatrick, who is generally acknowledged to be the world's greatest harpsichordist and an eminent scholar on seventeenth and eighteenth century keyboard music. Kirkpatrick began playing baroque music in recitals in America and Europe in the 1930's and has since played in most of the major music capitals of both continents. An unmannered performer, he articulates the complexities of baroque music with virtuosity, intellectualism, and subtlety of shading. Although he has mastered an extensive repertoire that includes the keyboard works of Mozart, Purcell, Handel, Couperin, and Rameau, Kirkpatrick is best known for his performances of Scarlatti and Bach and in 1967 completed the prodigious task of recording the entire clavier works of Bach for Deutsche Grammophon Gesellschaft. He regards himself as an amateur scholar, but Kirkpatrick is highly respected for his scholarship, especially for his definitive critical biography of Domenico Scarlatti, published in 1953. He has served on the faculty of Yale University since 1940.

Descended from early New England settlers, Ralph Kirkpatrick was born on June 10, 1911 in Leominster, Massachusetts to Edwin Asbury Kirkpatrick, a psychologist, and Florence May (Clifford) Kirkpatrick. He has two sisters, Marian and Alice, and a brother, Clifford, who is professor emeritus of sociology at the University of Indiana. Recalling his early life, Kirkpatrick told Hubert Saal of *Newsweek* (November 24, 1969), "My father had an undiscouraged belief in human perfectibility. . . . I grew up thinking anything was possible if you were willing to work hard enough." He began studying the piano at the age of six under the instruction of his mother and continued to study that instrument through his years at Leominster High School, from which he graduated in 1927. As a scholarship student at Harvard, Kirkpatrick gave piano lessons and toured as a piano soloist and accompanist with vocal ensembles. But his interest in the piano waned once he began playing a harpsichord that was donated to the music department in 1929, and a year later he gave his first public harpsichord performance, in Cambridge, Massachusetts. After receiving the B.A. degree in fine arts in 1931, Kirkpatrick left for Europe to study on a two-year John Knowles Paine traveling fellowship in music from Harvard.

In Paris Kirkpatrick conducted research on old music at the Bibliothèque Nationale, learned music theory under Nadia Boulanger, and studied the harpsichord with Wanda Landowska. During the summer of 1932 he studied early keyboard music and instruments with Arnold Dolmetsch in England and then went to Germany, where he studied with Günther Ramin and Heinz Tiessen. In January 1933 he made his European debut with a harpsichord recital in Berlin, followed by other performances in Germany and Italy. During the summers of 1933 and 1934 he was on the faculty of the Mozarteum Academy in Salzburg, Austria.

Kirkpatrick began playing concerts in the United States after his return from Europe in 1934, but he took another year off in 1937-38 to examine manuscripts and early editions of seventeenth and eighteenth century chamber music in European libraries as a Guggenheim fellow. In 1938 he inaugurated a festival of baroque music in the ballroom of the Governor's Palace in Williamsburg, Virginia, where he directed annual festivals for the next seven years. After hearing Kirkpatrick play the harpsichord at a Williamsburg festival performance in 1939, Carleton Sprague Smith wrote in the New York *Herald Tribune*, "Ralph Kirkpatrick is undoubtedly the ablest harpsichordist in this country today. Few musicians possess thorough scholarship, virtuosity in abundance and true musicianship—in short, a complete mastery of their métier."

During the 1940's Kirkpatrick toured the United States, making solo recitals and appearing with chamber music ensembles. In 1944 he began making annual tours with major orchestras across the United States, and after World War II he extended

RALPH KIRKPATRICK

his tour itineraries to Europe. But he also devoted a major segment of that busy period to his research into the life and works of Domenico Scarlatti, the eighteenth-century Italian harpsichord virtuoso and composer. The result was *Domenico Scarlatti* (Princeton University Press, 1953), which is now considered the definitive critical biography of the enormously productive composer. Kirkpatrick included in the book a numbered list of Scarlatti's works that superseded an earlier cataloguing and quickly became standard. Although he delved into the archives of libraries across Europe in pursuit of information on Scarlatti, he gained some of his most valuable source materials by flipping through the pages of a telephone book in Madrid, where the composer spent the last three decades of his life. Kirkpatrick discovered three generations of Scarlattis living in Madrid, who provided him with a wealth of unpublished documents to further his research.

Paying tribute to his stature as a harpsichordist, in 1956 Deutsche Grammophon Gesellschaft, the German recording company, selected Kirkpatrick to record the entire canon of Bach's keyboard music (excluding those works written for the organ) for their Archive series. In deference to his scholarship, the company gave Kirkpatrick the authority to decide what compositions not firmly authenticated as Bach's would be included. When it was completed in 1967 the series consisted of twenty long-playing discs. Some of the pieces, including the Inventions and Sinfonias, were played on the clavichord, and Kirkpatrick recorded the entire *Well-Tempered Clavier* on both the harpsichord and the clavichord. Musicologists have debated over whether the composer had in mind the harpsichord or the clavichord when he wrote that giant opus, but in an interview with Roy McMullen of *High Fidelity* (September 1965) Kirkpatrick conjectured that Bach may have been indifferent to which instrument was used. "I think that Bach, particularly in the latter part of his life, often wrote music that was purely abstract—that was beyond the idea of actual performance," Kirkpatrick told McMullen.

Recording sessions for the Bach series were held at Deutsche Grammophon studios in Zurich, several German cities, and Paris. The chief technical problem was presented by the soft-voiced clavichord, an early forerunner of the modern piano. Although the clavichord offers a considerably wider range of dynamic shading than the harpsichord, it soon became evident that its range could not be captured on tape unless its sounds were amplified at a rate six times as great as for the harpsichord. That meant, of course, that any faint sound within the studio or distant noise in the street was also likely to be picked up. Kirkpatrick searched the streets of Paris around the recording studio to locate workmen whose labors were being recorded along with Bach's fugues. One of the best solutions to the noise problem improvised by Deutsche Grammophon technicians was to isolate Kirkpatrick and his clavichord in a tiny makeshift room constructed of sections of a rehearsal stage propped up with chairs.

The delicate tones of the clavichord also present problems in the recital hall, but Kirkpatrick surmounted them in January 1961 at Carnegie Recital Hall, when he held the first public recital of clavichord music ever heard in New York City. For that all-Bach concert, which consisted of Little Preludes, several Preludes and Fugues from the *Well-Tempered Clavier,* and the fifth and sixth French Suites, Kirkpatrick arranged for unobtrusive electronic amplification of the clavichord, and he asked the audience to refrain from applause between numbers. His success was attested to by fellow harpsichordist Igor Kipnis, who wrote in the New York *Times* (January 16, 1961): "Kirkpatrick's marvelous sense of rhythmic freedom, the occasional rhythmic alterations, the subtle use of the 'bebung' (a method of gently alternating pressure on an already depressed key in order to produce vibrato), the improvisational but not obtrusive ornamentation . . . , all combined with the expressive quality of the clavichord to provide a stimulating and enchanting evening."

Long familiar to audiences at Carnegie Hall, Kirkpatrick began appearing at Lincoln Center's Philharmonic Hall after it was completed in the early 1960's. Some of his performances there have included a one-evening recital of the entire Book I of the *Well-Tempered Clavier* in 1963; a concert with several other musicians of chamber music by the eighteenth-century French composer Jean-Philippe Rameau that he assembled and directed in 1965; and a Mozart program in which he played the eighteenth-century and modern pianos as well as the harpsichord in 1966. For the opening of the smaller and more intimate Alice Tully Hall at Lincoln Center in 1969 Kirkpatrick presented three programs of harpsichord music, playing Bach, Scarlatti, and François Couperin. Although most New York critics have had nothing but unreserved admiration for Kirkpatrick's clean, pure, logical style of playing, a few find it rather too dry or pedantic. One of those is the New York *Times* critic Harold C. Schonberg who, while acknowledging the harpsichordist's intelligence and technical mastery, complained in a review (October 16, 1969), "Mr.

Kirkpatrick is an artist so anxious to avoid romanticism in the Landowska manner that he leans over backward in the opposite direction."

Such occasional critical rebuffs have not diminished Kirkpatrick's stature as an international artist. He has been accorded the honor of invitations to play Scarlatti in his native Italy, Mozart and Haydn in Vienna, and French music at Versailles. In Germany he has performed Bach at the Bach Festivals in Munich and in Leipzig, where he played the Concerto in D minor with the Gewandhaus Orchestra at the composer's grave in the Thomaskirche. When his 1970 concert season was completed, he had toured France, East and West Germany, and Italy, as well as the United States.

As the first Ernest Bloch Professor of Music at the University of California at Berkeley, in the spring of 1964 Kirkpatrick taught an undergraduate course on the *Well-Tempered Clavier* with Joseph Kerman. He also performed the entire work on both the harpsichord and clavichord in a series of ten concerts, conducted a workshop on it for pianists and harpsichordists, and delivered six formal lectures. After serving for many years as an instructor in harpsichord at Yale University, Kirkpatrick was made an associate professor of music there in 1956 and a professor in 1965. During recent years, however, the heavy schedule of his appearances has forced him to cut down his academic commitments at Yale.

His university experience has fortified Kirkpatrick's conviction that the revival of interest in early music began with the young. A few years ago he told William Bender of the New York *Herald Tribune* (October 27, 1963): "I don't know how it happened, but the taste of the younger generation changed. I remember waking up one day shortly before World War II and realizing that the whole Romantic era was dead. You used to hear people say they had been 'shattered' by a musical experience. Not any more. There seems to be a need for being restored, and this is exactly what the music of, say, the eighteenth century does."

Among the recordings by Kirkpatrick that are currently available, in addition to the Bach Archive series, are *Sixty Sonatas* by Scarlatti (Columbia Masterworks) and *Harpsichord Recital* with pieces by Purcell, Couperin, Rameau, Handel, Bach, and Scarlatti (Deutsche Grammophon). He has also recorded the piano concertos and sonatas of Mozart. Kirkpatrick's research has led him to publish three new editions of Baroque music: *Bach: Goldberg Variations* (G. Schirmer, 1938); *Scarlatti: Sixty Sonatas* (G. Schirmer, 1953); and *Clavier Büchlein vor Wilhelm Friedemann Bach* (Yale Univ. Press, 1959). His most recent enthusiasm is the keyboard music of the Elizabethan composers, particularly William Byrd. Kirkpatrick by no means limits his attention to early music, however, and he has performed in the premières of work by Igor Stravinsky, Darius Milhaud, Walter Piston, Henry Cowell, Quincy Porter, and Elliott Carter.

Ralph Kirkpatrick's interests outside music range from English, French, German, and Italian literature of all periods to early churches and contemporary painting. He is also a collector of books and prints. At his house in Connecticut, Kirkpatrick enjoys cutting wood and other outdoor work, and he likes to go for an occasional swim. Nonetheless he admits to being a bit overweight, a condition that may be related to his proficiency in gourmet cooking. Kirkpatrick is five feet ten inches tall, gray-haired, blue-eyed, and bespectacled. Politically he considers himself a liberal. For his work on Scarlatti, Kirkpatrick was awarded the Italian Order of Merit in 1954, and he has received an honorary doctorate from Oberlin College. He is a member of the American Musicological Society, the Music Library Association, the American Academy of Arts and Sciences, the American Philosophical Society, and the Century Association. Although his scholarly pursuits have earned him nearly as much renown as his performances, Kirkpatrick maintains that he is only an amateur scholar. On a questionnaire completed for *Current Biography* he explained that his status as an amateur is "as jealously guarded with respect to any form of scholarship as professional status is striven for in performance."

References

> Newsweek 74:33+ N 24 '69 por
>
> Blom, Eric, ed. Grove's Dictionary of Music and Musicians vol 4 (1954)
>
> Ewen, David, ed. Living Musicians (1940)
>
> Slonimsky, Nicolas. Baker's Biographical Dictionary of Musicians (1958)

KLEIN, HERBERT G(EORGE)

Apr. 1, 1918- United States government official; journalist
Address: b. The White House, 1600 Pennsylvania Ave., N.W., Washington, D.C. 20500; h. 4917 Crescent St., Chevy Chase, Md. 20015

The man largely responsible for the public image of the administration of Richard Nixon is the veteran journalist Herbert G. Klein, a long-time friend and associate of the President. To avoid charges of a "credibility gap" that had been leveled against his predecessor, Lyndon B. Johnson, Nixon created the post of director of communications for the executive branch after his election as President in November 1968, and appointed Klein to occupy it. Klein, whose friendship with Nixon dates back to 1946, and who served as his press aide in all of his subsequent political campaigns, has had a distinguished career as a journalist with the Copley newspaper chain in California and was editor of the San Diego *Union* at the time of his appointment. As director of communications Klein is a member of Nixon's White House staff and works closely with Presidential press secretary Ronald L. Ziegler. Klein's chief responsibilities are to coordinate news emanating from the executive departments and to keep open the channels of communication between the administration and the public.

Herbert George Klein was born on April 1, 1918 in Los Angeles to George J. and Amy (Cordes)

HERBERT G. KLEIN

Klein. He has a brother, Kenneth F. Klein; his sister, Eleanor Schmierer, is no longer living. Klein became interested in current events at an early age, and after graduating from Roosevelt High School in Los Angeles in 1935 he enrolled as a journalism major in the University of Southern California, where he became sports editor of the student newspaper, the *Daily Trojan*. After obtaining his B.A. degree in 1940 he became a reporter for a weekly newspaper in Temple City, California. For a time he also worked as a reporter for the trade magazine *Iron Age*. Having decided to cast his lot with the growing Copley newspaper chain, later that year he took a $13-a-week job as a copyboy with the Alhambra (California) *Post-Advocate* and was made a reporter the following year.

In 1942 Klein entered the United States Naval Reserve and was commissioned an ensign. Assigned to communications and public relations near Boston and San Diego, he eventually rose to the rank of commander. In 1946 he went on inactive status with the reserve and returned to the *Post-Advocate* as a political reporter and news editor. That year he covered the Congressional campaign between Richard Nixon, who was making his first bid for elective office, and the incumbent Democrat Jerry Voorhis. Klein and Nixon immediately became friends, and when Nixon, who won the 1946 race, ran for reelection in 1948, he persuaded Klein to act as an unpaid publicist in his campaign. After that, Klein was on the payroll in all of Nixon's campaigns. In 1950 he was a publicist in Nixon's Senate race. When Nixon ran for Vice-President with General Dwight D. Eisenhower in 1952, Klein was publicity director in California for the Eisenhower-Nixon committee. In 1956, when the Eisenhower-Nixon team ran for reelection, Klein was assistant press secretary to the Vice-President, and at the January 1957 inauguration he served as press secretary. According to *Time* (June 1, 1959), when he was carrying out those assignments, "Klein earned increasing respect from political reporters as a pressman's press secretary."

Between election campaigns Klein continued to advance through the ranks of journalists. In 1950 he moved to the San Diego *Evening Tribune,* another link in the Copley chain, as a feature writer, and in 1951 he became an editorial writer. The following year he joined the San Diego *Union* as chief editorial writer, and he was its editorial page editor, associate editor, and executive editor, before becoming editor in 1959. A staunchly Republican paper, the *Union*—which has been considered the key paper among the fifteen that make up the Copley chain—boosted its circulation from some 88,000 to about 125,000 during Klein's editorship, from 1959 to 1968. According to the New York *Times* (June 18, 1960), Klein's major asset as editor was his "quietness and restraint—blended with an ability to mollify and get along with people." In those days the *Union* was staffed by ultra-conservative managers and liberal employees, a combination that made Klein's moderate conservatism and his talents as a peacemaker all the more valuable. During that period, Klein also earned a reputation as an ardent advocate of freedom of information.

In May 1959 Klein took a leave of absence from the *Union* to join Nixon's seventeen-member office staff as a $16,000-a-year special assistant to the Vice-President. His first assignment was to accompany Nixon in the summer of 1959 on his goodwill trip to Moscow. Its highlight was the now famous "kitchen debate" between Nixon and Soviet Premier Nikita S. Khrushchev. It was at Klein's soft-spoken but firm insistence that the Soviet authorities rescinded their censorship directive limiting the number of correspondents that could accompany the Vice-President, and permitted the Nixon party to travel with relative freedom.

During Nixon's unsuccessful 1960 Presidential campaign against John F. Kennedy, Klein again served as his press secretary. Relations between the press and the Vice-President were anything but harmonious at the time, and Nixon charged journalists with deliberate slanting of the news. Reporters in turn, complained that Nixon was not accessible to newsmen, and some of them blamed Klein for the bad press he received. Reflecting on the campaign later, Klein remarked that on the whole press coverage had been fair, except that a few reporters had slanted their stories against Nixon. Klein also was Nixon's press secretary during his unsuccessful bid for the governorship of California against Edmund G. Brown in 1962.

For his 1968 Presidential campaign Nixon again talked Klein into handling press relations. As manager for communications, Klein did not travel with the Nixon team but coordinated press relations and media organization from his office. After Nixon's election on November 5, 1968 Klein agreed to remain on his staff. He asked, however, that, instead of being named press secretary, he be made responsible for overseeing and coordinating press relations for the entire executive branch. Other Presidential press secretaries had tried to bring that about in the past, but it turned out that they spent most of their time in daily briefings

with the Washington press corps. Realizing the importance of separating the two functions, Nixon appointed Ronald Ziegler, a young California advertising executive, as his special assistant in charge of press relations. On November 25, 1970 he named Klein to the newly created $42,500-a-year post of director of communications for the executive branch. As one of several top assistants on the President's White House staff, Klein exercises a policy-making role. He formulates information policy for the executive branch and coordinates the public relations of the White House, the executive departments, and the Republican National Committee. Aware of the public relations problems faced by the Johnson administration, Klein said soon after his appointment: "Truth in government is to become the hallmark. We expect to eliminate any possibility of a credibility gap."

Some observers feared that Klein's powers might lead to "centralized control of information" or censorship of news unfavorable to the administration. An article in *Newsweek* (December 9, 1968) suggested that Klein "seemed to be assuming a function . . . [of] keeping the lid on bad news and making certain good news gets spread around —often with the President's name on it." In an editorial in the New York *Times* (November 27, 1968) Klein's position was compared to that of a "minister of information." It pointed out that in the United States, where European-style parliamentary government did not exist, the Washington press corps performed a "quasi-parliamentary function" by questioning the President and other members of the administration. The editorial expressed the hope that Klein's position would not infringe upon that function.

Klein has reassured the public and the press that he will not act as a censor and that his position gives him no special veto powers. Admitting that some news has to be withheld in the public interest—which is clearly defined in the 1967 Freedom of Information Act—or in the interest of the national security, he insists that there will be a free "flow of information" as far as the administration is concerned.

Despite their misgivings about the potential dangers to the democratic process inherent in his position, newsmen generally rated Klein, during his early months in office, as impartial, honest, and efficient. They pointed out that he had done much to keep the channels of communication open; that he persuaded reluctant Cabinet members and other officials to appear for press interviews and on television; and that he induced government agencies to release information previously withheld from the public. At a meeting of the American Society of Newspaper Editors in April 1969 Samuel J. Archibald of the University of Missouri Freedom of Information Center observed that in recent months "some dents have been made in news barriers at the federal government level," and added: "Herb Klein is the most qualified man ever put in the federal government's top information post."

Klein, who compares his office to "a public relations firm which is the consultant to a number of corporations," coordinates the news of the various executive departments, with the exception of State and Defense. He attends the daily early morning meetings of White House staff officials, as well as Cabinet and Urban Affairs Council meetings, and Republican Congressional leadership sessions. His staff, which in late 1969 numbered fourteen members, includes four senior assistants, who keep informed on the policies of the various government departments. Klein, who counsels departments in the issue of press releases, uses the information he gathers in his contacts to help compile the briefing book to which Nixon refers in preparing for press conferences.

Klein also promotes the policies of the Nixon administration. In preparing for Presidential news conferences, he and Ziegler distribute "fact sheets" and set up "background" sessions for newsmen, to present the administration's version of news events. To ensure that the flow on information to the public is not limited by the interpretations given to news events by the White House press corps, Klein has taken the initiative in mailing press releases and advance copies of major speeches to newspapers, editorial writers, and broadcasting stations throughout the country. In the summer of 1970 he arranged the first of a planned series of regional briefings of select groups of journalists and television executives by the President and high-ranking administration officials. During the 1970 election campaign Klein played a key role in coordinating speeches by administration officials in behalf of candidates in various parts of the United States. He was criticized in November 1969, when it was learned that he had telephoned television stations to inquire about the kind of editorial opinion they planned to present on forthcoming Nixon speeches. Denying charges that this was an attempt to influence the news, he explained that local television executives had asked that the White House keep itself informed on local opinion, and that phone calls were the only way to tap local broadcasting opinions.

Levying on his journalistic expertise, Klein tries to get the maximum political mileage for the administration from a news event. For example, he persuaded Postmaster General Winton M. Blount to make his announcement on the 1969 postal reform measures at the White House, thereby according them a greater amount of public exposure. Similarly, he convinced Nixon to give key legislative proposals maximum public visibility by giving White House briefings on Presidential statements. In the summer of 1969 he planned a nationwide tour by administration officials whose purpose was to interpret the president's welfare program to the public.

On occasion Klein has spoken out on his own. In November 1969, after Vice-President Spiro T. Agnew charged the television industry with unfairly slanting news commentaries against the administration, Klein allied himself with the substance, if not the brio of the Vice-President's assertions. In a talk before hundreds of radio and television executives he said that Agnew "was doing an outstanding job in raising questions which

should be debated," and that the criticism should be extended to all news media. On other occasions he has said that although he felt that the press was basically fair-minded and highly professional, it was often inadequate in presenting the views of the "silent majority" while giving undue coverage to a violent minority. In May 1970 he appeared on the *Dick Cavett Show* on ABC-TV to explain the government's military activities in Cambodia. That June he was one of a delegation of high government officials sent by Nixon on a fact-finding tour of the war zones of Cambodia and South Vietnam.

Much of Klein's effectiveness derives from his intimacy with Nixon and his ability "to speak virtually with the President's voice." Although some observers have suggested that Ziegler may exert more influence on the administration because of his closer daily contact with Nixon, others, pointing out the long friendship between Nixon and Klein, feel that Klein carries more clout. R. W. Apple Jr. noted in the New York *Times* (November 26, 1968) that Klein, through his low-key, easygoing manner, helps Nixon to relax his tensions, and "brings to the relationship an emotional non-complexity, a calm, and a perspective that Mr. Nixon values highly."

Klein has been a juror on the Pulitzer Prize committee. He was a director of the American Society of Newspaper Editors from 1966 to 1968, and he has been a member of the National Editorial Writers' Association, the Associated Press Managing Editors' Organization, and United Press International Editors. He has been an officer of Sigma Delta Chi, the national journalism society, and of Delta Chi fraternity. In California he was active in the American Legion, the Convention and Visitors Bureau of San Diego, the Alhambra Rotary Club, and the La Jolla Lamplighters. He is a past president of the Alhambra Junior Chamber of Commerce, and he has served on the boards of directors of the San Diego chapter of the American Red Cross, the San Diego-Yokohama Friendship Society, and the Kiwanis Club. He is an elder of the Presbyterian church, and he serves as a member of the board of the National Presbyterian Center.

Herbert G. Klein was married on November 1, 1941 to Marjorie Galbraith of Long Beach, California, who was his fellow student at the University of Southern California. They have two married daughters Joanne (Mrs. Robert E. Mayne) and Patricia (Mrs. H. Thomas Howell). Klein is five feet eleven inches tall, weighs 190 pounds, and has green eyes and wavy brown hair. He dresses casually and has been described as self-effacing, but efficient. According to the New York *Times* (November 26, 1968), he "is more than anything else a family man in his spare time" who "likes to praise his wife." His favorite recreations are golf, skin-diving, tennis, and football, and he used to keep a string of lobster pots near his oceanside home in La Jolla. According to *Time* (December 6, 1968), Klein's "notable talent is neither writing nor editing, but getting along with people."

References

N Y Post p31 Ag 8 '68 por
N Y Times p11 Je 18 '60 por; p35 N 26 '68 por
Time 92:30+ D 6 '68 por
Who's Who in America, 1970-71
Who's Who in American Politics, 1969-70

KUNSTLER, WILLIAM M(OSES)

July 7, 1919- Attorney
Address: b. Law Center for Constitutional Rights, 588 9th Ave., New York 10036

The corporation lawyer who identifies with the company he represents has his radical counterpart in William M. Kunstler, the legal paladin of "the Movement," that amorphous configuration of disparate New Left, antiwar, black liberation, and similar counter-culture groups in the United States. Kunstler's commitment as a controversial and courageous "people's lawyer," specializing in protecting the rights of political dissenters, civil disobeyers, the militant poor, and other unpopular clients, began in the early 1960's, when he went to the aid of civil rights defendants in courtrooms throughout the South. His "radicalization" took place during his defense of the Chicago Seven, accused of conspiracy to incite violence during the 1968 Democratic Convention. Other clients of Kunstler have ranged from Black Panthers through campus rebels to the Catonsville Nine, the Roman Catholic peace militants, led by Fathers Philip and Daniel Berrigan, convicted of napalming Selective Service files. The current headquarters for Kunstler's Movement work is the Law Center for Constitutional Rights, founded by him in collaboration with Arthur Kinoy, Morty Stavis, and Ben Smith in 1969. The attorney is an associate professor of law at New York University Law School, whose faculty he joined in 1950, and a lecturer at Pace College and the New School for Social Research.

William Moses Kunstler was born into a middle-class Jewish home in New York City on July 7, 1919. His mother was the former Frances Mandelbaum and his father was Dr. Monroe Bradford Kunstler, a general practitioner. "My father was a fanatic doctor . . . ," Kunstler has recalled, in an interview with Kenneth Gross of *Newsday* (March 21, 1970). "I spent the early years of my life walking around angry at him because he wasn't around. He was out being a doctor. I never understood what that meant until after he was dead." Growing up, Kunstler was closer to his grandfather, Dr. Joseph Mandelbaum, physician to the New York Giants and to Mayor Fiorello H. La Guardia, a warm person who had an easy rapport with children. The attorney has a younger brother, Michael, his law partner, and a sister, Mary I. Horn.

Kunstler attended P.S. 93, P.S. 166, and De Witt Clinton High School, all in New York, and Yale University, where he majored in French, was a varsity swimmer, and took his B.A. degree with a Phi Beta Kappa key in 1941. Just before his graduation from Yale he and fellow student William Stone privately published a collection of their poems, *Our Pleasant Vices*. During World War II, serving as a signal intelligence officer with the United States Eighth Army in the Pacific, Kunstler earned the Bronze Star and the rank of major.

Although he was more interested in writing than in law, Kunstler matriculated at the Columbia University School of Law when he was discharged from the Army, in 1946. "Initially, I went to law school because it offered status, prestige, and the promise of a reasonably high income—all the wrong reasons," Kunstler has said. "Today I realize that the profession offers the possibility of the truly dedicated life in which the worker-lawyer is the equivalent of the worker-priest." While working for his law degree he taught a course in writing in the School of General Studies at Columbia and reviewed books for the New York *Times*, the New York *Herald Tribune*, and other publications.

In 1948 Kunstler received his LL.B. degree and was admitted to the New York bar. After detouring from law for a few months as an executive trainee at R. H. Macy & Company, a Manhattan department store, he became a partner with his brother in the firm of Kunstler & Kunstler (now Kunstler, Kunstler & Hyman). Through the 1950's Kunstler's work was, with few exceptions, in marriage, estate, and business law. The exceptions were some American Civil Liberties Union cases, the most important of which was his defense of William Worthy, a reporter for the Baltimore *Afro-American* to whom the United States Department of State denied passport renewal after he visited China in violation of a department ruling in 1957. "I guess I had these libertarian tendencies . . . ," he recounted to Lawrence Mosher in an interview for the *National Observer* (March 16, 1970). "I lost the Worthy case, but it gave me a taste for a certain kind of law where you are dealing with national issues, constitutions, and the rights of individuals. But I still hadn't become a flaming crusader."

Between May and August 1961 the Congress of Racial Equality mounted the "freedom rides," public transportation tours of the Deep South by integrated groups challenging racial segregation in interstate travel and travel facilities. Waves of freedom riders (numbering, all told, in the hundreds), violently harassed in Montgomery and Birmingham, Alabama, were arrested en masse as they arrived at the bus, rail, and air terminals of Jackson, Mississippi. At the request of the ACLU, Kunstler went, not very enthusiastically, to the Mississippi capital in the middle of June to give "moral support" to Jack H. Young, the black CORE lawyer who was defending the riders. In witnessing the bravery of the civil rights protesters arriving in Jackson, he came to the sudden realization that "only by personal involvement can one justify his existence, either to himself or to his fellows." He immediately offered his services to CORE and the offer was gratefully accepted.

Looking for a new gambit by which to thwart the "railroading" of freedom riders in local courts, Kunstler found one in a dormant "removal" statute passed by the Reconstruction Congress in 1866 to protect ex-slaves from courts controlled by their former masters. On the basis of that law, Kunstler filed petitions for the removal of some of the cases from state to federal courts, thereby forestalling precipitate local execution of fines and jail sentences or forfeiture of bail bonds. The removal ploy was typical of Kunstler. Some lawyers hostile to him have complained that he is an impatient "grandstander" who pays too little attention to legal proprieties and technicalities, but none has dared question his bold creativeness in preparing his cases and his provocative art in presenting them.

Later in the 1960's Kunstler served as special counsel for Martin Luther King and King's Southern Christian Leadership Conference; as a member of the legal advisory staff of the Council of Federated Organizations, the coalition that directed the massive voter registration drive in Mississippi; as general counsel for the Mississippi Freedom Democratic party; as counsel for the Student Nonviolent Coordinating Committee; and as a director of the Gandhi Society for Human Rights, dedicated to providing "front-line emergency legal assistance in lower courts, particularly where nonviolent demonstrations involve mass arrests and imprisonment."

In 1962 and 1963 Kunstler successfully appealed the conviction of the Rev. Fred L. Shuttlesworth and other Negroes who had challenged segregated seating on buses in Birmingham, Alabama, and during the same period he and William Higgs tried, unsuccessfully, to win a court ruling favorable to Dewey Greene, a Negro student denied admission to the University of Mississippi. Three years later, he defended Stokely Carmichael after Carmichael was arrested for civil rights agitation in Selma, Alabama, and he contested the constitutionality of federal grand jury selection in the Southern District of New York, on the ground that the method used "regularly, systematically, and intentionally" excluded Negroes, Puerto Ricans, and members of other ethnic minority groups. In 1967 he appealed the rape-and-robbery conviction of Thomas Carlton Wansley, a Lynchburg, Virginia Negro; represented Adam Clayton Powell in Powell's fight against his exclusion from Congress; and, in one of his greatest coups, won a federal court ruling against the *de facto* segregationist "track system" of assigning pupils to classes in the public schools of Washington, D.C. He was defense attorney for the Roman Catholic peace militants, including the Berrigans, convicted of destroying Selective Service records in 1967 and 1968, and in January 1969 he helped to win the release from federal prison of Morton Sobell, convicted of conspiring in espionage with the Rosenbergs. Kunstler is also defense attorney in the still unresolved case of H. Rap Brown, the black militant accused of inciting a riot in Cambridge, Maryland in 1967.

Kunstler's most famous—or, to his enemies, notorious—defense was that of the Chicago Seven.

WILLIAM M. KUNSTLER

The conspiracy trial, conducted from September 1969 to February 1970, was a raucous affair, characterized by observers on both the left and the right as a "mockery" of the judicial process. The defendants regularly breached courtroom decorum, Judge Julius J. Hoffman was extraordinarily punitive, and Judge Hoffman and Kunstler sparred ferociously. Their sharpest confrontations occurred when the judge refused to permit Ramsey Clark, former Attorney General of the United States, and the Rev. Ralph Abernathy, Martin Luther King's successor as head of the Southern Christian Leadership Conference, to testify for the defense. After the Abernathy ruling Kunstler told the judge: "I have sat here . . . and watched the objections denied and sustained by your honor and I know that this is not a fair trial . . . and these men are going to jail by virtue of a legal lynching." When the civil rights leader arrived in the courtroom, Kunstler embraced him, in violation of the judge's admonition that no one indicate Abernathy's presence to the jury.

The jury in Chicago found none of the defendants guilty of conspiracy and only five guilty of incitement, but Judge Hoffman handed down his own convictions before the verdicts were announced, while the jury was out deliberating. He found not only all seven defendants but also Kunstler and cocounsel Leonard I. Weinglass guilty of contempt on a total of 160 counts and sentenced them to a total of fifteen years and twenty-five days in prison. Twenty-four of the counts were against Kunstler, who was sentenced to four years and thirteen days in federal prison. (The sentence is still being appealed.)

The board of directors of the American Civil Liberties Union immediately issued a statement expressing "gravest concern" over "the extraordinary and unconstitutional use of summary contempt power at the end of a trial." The American Bar Association did not comment on either Judge Hoffman's or Kunstler's conduct during the trial, but the *American Bar Association Journal* (June 1970) editorially excoriated the defense attorney for declaring himself to be at the service of none but "those whose goals I share." In reply to the editorial, Kunstler pointed out that the American Bar Association was just as selective as he regarding clientele. "The ABA formula of a lawyer for hire specifically excludes those who most need legal help," he told one reporter, and another quoted him as adding, "If more members of the ABA were available for such work, then perhaps I would be able to be more catholic in my selection of clients." Shortly after the close of the Chicago conspiracy trial, Kunstler joined the team of lawyers preparing the defense of Bobby Lee Williams, a Black Panther accused of assaulting a police officer with intent to kill in Elizabeth, New Jersey.

Writing has always been Kunstler's favorite avocation. For Oceana's Legal Almanac series he wrote *The Law of Accidents* (1954), *First Degree* (1960), and *And Justice for All* (1963), and he is the author of *Beyond a Reasonable Doubt* (Morrow, 1961), about the Caryl Chessman case; of *The Case for Courage: The Stories of Ten Famous American Attorneys Who Risked Their Careers in the Cause of Justice* (Apollo, 1962); of *The Minister and the Choir Singer* (Morrow, 1964), about the 1922 Hall-Mills murder case; and of *Deep in My Heart* (Morrow, 1966), an autobiographical account of the civil rights struggle. In the late 1950's he wrote and narrated the scripts for *Famous Trials*, a program broadcast over radio station WEVD in New York City. According to reviewers, in his textbooks he is able to make dry material "readable" and in his popularized narratives he is "lucid, straightforward" and "sound in historical research, deft in characterization, and skillful in . . . treatment of trial procedure and substantive law."

Kunstler is an angular, loping 175-pound six-footer with long, dark-brown, graying hair. He appears to some observers as "Lincolnian," especially in his manner of stooping at the speaker's lectern. According to Kenneth Gross in the *Newsday* article, the hint of a lisp sometimes creeps into his private speech, but his public voice is a resonant baritone, strong but generally gentle and low-keyed until he reaches a point of anger or emphasis. Victor S. Navasky of the New York *Times Magazine* (April 19, 1970) described his courtroom style as "loose, honest, risk-taking" and his rhetoric generally as taking on "the coloration of the leftmost person in the room." Kunstler makes a practice of hugging all the men and kissing all the women he meets as friends or allies. "I cannot trust anyone who won't let you touch them," he explained to Navasky.

William M. Kunstler and Lotte Rosenberger—a fifth cousin who, as a child, had emigrated from Germany to escape concentration-camp incarceration—were married on January 14, 1943. They have two children, Karin (Mrs. Neal Goldman) and Jane. When his busy itinerary permits, Kunstler and his wife live in an eleven-room home he owns in Mamaroneck, Westchester, New York. But he rents out the top floor of the house to help with the upkeep, and his life style is no longer completely in tune with suburban affluence. "You have to learn to live simply," he advised a law student recently. "You have to learn to do without. Just get enough to live on. Animals that overeat die. I stopped a profitable law practice when I was forty years old. I decided then that you have to get off the economic escalator." When defending such clients as the Chicago Seven, Kunstler not only accepts no fees but personally raises funds for the defense. The Law Center for Constitutional Rights supplies him with about $100 a week in addition to lodging and travel expenses, and speaking and lecture honorariums bring his annual income up to approximately $20,000 a year. Kunstler has been urged by friends in the Movement to switch to the "hip life" completely, and he has considered becoming a live-in commune lawyer, but so far he thinks he "probably won't." Admitting that he has not been entirely successful in freeing himself from his middle-class conditioning, he confessed to Kenneth Gross of *Newsday* that accustoming himself to using such militant gestures as the clenched fist salute and the slogan "right on" was "not an easy thing . . . for a man of my background." But he told Lawrence Mosher in an interview for the *National Observer* (March 16, 1970) that he likes "the communal life, sitting around with young people, listening to rock music." He also enjoys listening to other forms of music, such as classical, swing, and opera, and swimming is another of his recreations. His honors include the New York Bar Association's Press Award (1957) and the Civil Rights Award (1963). Kunstler takes the more threatening of the crank calls and letters he receives seriously but philosophically, with fatalistic resignation: "In this country you live with that always." In recent years he has been given more publicity in the press than the celebrated lawyers F. Lee Bailey, Louis Nizer, and Melvin Belli all put together.

The Movement lawyer has no religious or political affiliations. In the 1968 Presidential election he intended to register a protest vote for black antiwar candidate Dick Gregory, but in the voting booth, as he has recalled, he was "overwhelmed" with "fright" at the specter of Richard Nixon becoming President and cast his ballot for Hubert Humphrey. His world view is pragmatic utopian, based not so much on any systematic, reasoned social philosophy as on spontaneous identification with the oppressed. Contradicting the assertions of some of his critics, he has constantly reiterated that he disapproves of violence as a means of social change while understanding the disillusionment and alienation that drive some men and women to it. In his speeches he often points out that the Movement tried peaceful "protest" in the 1960's; that it has gone on to disruptive "resistance"; and, if that fails, that the next step might, logically, be "rebellion." In an address to the Conference on Business Responsibility and the American Crisis organized by prominent business executives in New York City in June 1970, he warned: "Unless there is some shift in economic policies, some reconsideration of the concept of private property, and some unequivocal act that would hasten the end of the Vietnam war, Armageddon is at hand."

References

N Y Times p38 S 7 '68 por
N Y Times Mag p30+ Ap 19 '70 pors
Nat Observer p1+ Mr 16 '70
Newsday W p12+ Mr 21 '70 pors
Wall St J p1+ N 28 '69
Washington (D.C.) Post G p15 Ap 5 '70;
   B p1+ Ap 12 '70 pors
Kunstler, William M. Deep in My Heart
   (1966)
Who's Who in America, 1970-71

GREGORIO LÓPEZ BRAVO

LÓPEZ BRAVO, GREGORIO

Dec. 19, 1923- Foreign Minister of Spain
Address: b. Ministry of Foreign Affairs, Madrid,
Spain

For more than three decades Generalissimo Francisco Franco bolstered his exercise of virtually absolute power in Spain by filling important government posts with members of his own Falangist party. Now, as if preparing the regime that will rule after his departure, he has begun to turn to bright, pragmatically minded, relatively young men outside of party ranks. Among those the aging Caudillo has chosen for positions of leadership in a post-Franco era is Gregorio López Bravo, who succeeded Fernando María Castiella as Minister of Foreign Affairs on October 30, 1969. López Bravo, a marine engineer by profession and a former Minister of Industry, is a technocrat, an expert public servant less concerned with politics, ideology, or tradition than with reasonable, practical, and efficient ways to achieve social and economic progress. Trying to bring Spain out of its isolationist shell and back into the mainstream of world affairs, he has negotiated important agreements with the United States and the nations of the Common Market, made unprecedented diplomatic overtures to the Soviet Union, and cemented ties with many countries of Africa and Latin America. Above all, he seeks "the complete incorporation of Spain into Europe."

Of upper middle-class background, Gregorio López Bravo—whose family name is given as López Bravo de Castro in some sources—was born in Madrid on December 19, 1923, the son of Sotero López and of the former Consuelo Bravo. After earning his doctorate in naval engineering at the Escuela de Ingenieros Navales in Madrid, in 1946, he was successively a marine engineer and managing director of two shipbuilding firms. He entered the service of the Spanish government on August 13, 1959 as director-general of foreign commerce, a post in which he remained until December 9, 1960, when he was named director-general of the Instituto Español de Moneda Extranjera (Spanish Institute of Foreign Currency).

On July 11, 1962 López Bravo was appointed by Franco to the Cabinet post of Minister of Industry, and during his seven years in that office he worked for closer economic cooperation with the United States and Western European countries. In an effort to promote the development of free-enterprise industry he introduced legislation aimed at limiting the powers of the National Institute of Industry, a state-owned holding company, founded in 1941, that controlled much of Spain's industrial production. In announcing the new legislation in November 1963 he explained that under its provisions the special privileges that had made the institute strong would be extended to private industries in areas of production where rapid growth was considered desirable and that the National Institute of Industry would have to curtail its activities wherever and to whatever degree demanded by the "interest and welfare of the community." As Minister of Industry he traveled extensively, paying official visits to the United States, Latin America, Europe, Asia, and North Africa.

Generalissimo Franco announced a sweeping reconstruction of his government on October 29, 1969, involving the replacement of thirteen of the nineteen Cabinet ministers. In the years that followed the Spanish Civil War the government of Spain had been largely in the hands of the military and of members of Franco's own Falange party, but more recently Franco had begun to rely increasingly on the younger, more forward-looking —and essentially nonpolitical—technocrats to fill key economic and administrative posts in the government. Many of these technocrats, including López Bravo, belong to Opus Dei, a highly influential Roman Catholic lay order whose 22,000 members, drawn largely from Spain's intellectual, professional, and business elite, have taken vows to serve God not in the monastic tradition of retreat from the world but rather in normal "worldly" vocations.

In an obvious move to entrust the future of Spain largely to the technocrats, Franco chose a majority of the ministers in his new Cabinet— which was sworn into office on October 30, 1969 —from among members of Opus Dei. In an article in the London *Observer* (November 2, 1969), William Cemlyn-Jones called Franco's choice of López Bravo as Minister of Foreign Affairs "the most surprising and significant appointment" and referred to the new Foreign Minister as "a typical product of the new, prosperous, and influential middle class—a class which scarcely existed in Spain during the 1930's." Richard Eder, writing in the New York *Times* on the same date, pointed out that under the previous Foreign Minister, Fernando María Castiella, Spain's foreign policy had centered around the diplomatic campaign to wrest Gibraltar from Great Britain. He noted that López Bravo had privately deplored Castiella's neglect of what he regarded as more vital matters, such as the establishment of closer ties with the United States and Western Europe and diplomatic approaches to the countries of Eastern Europe, Latin America, and other parts of the world.

Soon after taking office, López Bravo took the initiative in healing the relations between Great Britain and Spain, which had been deteriorating for three years. While insisting that Spain did not intend to relinquish its claims to Gibraltar, he indicated that a peaceful settlement of the dispute was possible. "Gibraltar is one of the compass points of our foreign policy, but it is not magnetic north," he declared in an explanation of the thaw in relations between Spain and Britain.

In late December 1969 López Bravo embarked on an extended tour designed to expand Spain's circle of friends around the world. In Manila, where he attended the second inauguration of Philippine President Fernando Marcos, he conferred with United States Vice-President Spiro T. Agnew and met with officials of the Mexican government, which has never recognized the Franco regime. On January 2, 1970 he stopped off in Moscow—thus becoming the first Spanish Cabinet member to visit the Soviet capital in thirty-five years—and engaged in secret talks with Soviet officials. The topics discussed were not revealed, but Kremlin watchers assumed that they included the reestablishment of diplomatic and trade relations between Spain and the Soviet Union, which had been broken off at the time of the Spanish Civil War.

From the Soviet Union López Bravo went to Brussels to discuss Spain's relations with the European Economic Community, and thence he went to Cairo, where he affirmed Spain's support of the Arab cause in the Middle Eastern conflict. He indicated, however, that friendship with the Arab countries did not preclude friendly relations with Israel and suggested that Spain might extend diplomatic relations to the Jewish state if such a move appeared conducive to peace in the Middle East. Before the end of January 1970, López Bravo conferred with Pope Paul VI and Vatican officials in Rome, presumably on such issues as the concordat between the Spanish government and the Vatican. The concordat, which gives Franco veto power in the naming of Spanish bishops, is now being studied by both sides preparatory to revision. In the first official visit of a Spanish foreign minister to France in thirty-three years, López Bravo met with President Georges Pompidou and other government officials in Paris. In a joint communique, issued on February 11, Pompidou and

López Bravo pledged cooperation in cultural, scientific, commercial, industrial, and agricultural affairs and in efforts to strengthen relations between Spain and the European Economic Community. The visit also resulted in an agreement for Spain's purchase of thirty French jet fighter planes. López Bravo has pointed out that his intensified activity on the international scene represented a "change of style" rather than any fundamental change in Spanish foreign policy. "I will go to any country if it is in the interest of Spain to do so," he has said. Spain's new style of diplomacy bore fruit when, on March 12, 1970, after eight years of negotiations, the Franco government signed a six-year preferential trade agreement with members of the European Economic Community, to take effect in October 1970.

Diplomatic relations between the United States and Spain had become somewhat strained in the two years before López Bravo became Foreign Minister, partly as a result of opposition in both countries to the continued presence of American military bases in Spain. Negotiations for the renewal of the 1953 mutual defense agreement between the two powers were deadlocked in 1968 and 1969, and the agreement was due to expire in September 1970. On March 18, 1970 López Bravo went to Washington, D.C. to start exploratory talks with President Richard Nixon and other officials about the future of the American bases. On August 6, 1970, after months of negotiations between López Bravo and United States Secretary of State William P. Rogers, the two governments signed a five-year agreement that reaffirmed the right of the United States to continue to use three air bases and one submarine base in Spain. In return, Spain was to receive $120,000,000 in loans and about $60,000,000 in grants from the United States, to be used in part to finance the purchase of Phantom jet fighters and other aircraft. The agreement also provided for cooperation in cultural, scientific, and other areas, and it called for the establishment of a joint defense committee to coordinate "reciprocal defense support" of the two governments. Foremost among the opponents of the agreement in the United States was Senator J. William Fulbright, chairman of the Senate Foreign Relations Committee, who objected in particular to the fact that it took the form of a presidential agreement, rather than a treaty subject to Senate ratification. The agreement brought Spain into closer coordination with the North Atlantic Treaty Organization, although its membership in NATO continued to be blocked by some member nations that objected to Franco's authoritarian regime.

In June 1970 López Bravo went to Mauritania to discuss the status of the Spanish Sahara, one of Spain's few remaining possessions in Africa. Although no agreement was reached, López Bravo declared that Spain would act "according to the line laid down by the U.N." and that his country recognized "the inalienable right of the people of the Sahara to determine their own future." Addressing the United Nations General Assembly on October 16, 1970, López Bravo expressed the view that the world organization in its twenty-five years of existence had not achieved its purpose of preserving international peace and security. Asserting that small and medium-sized nations should play a more significant role in the solution of major problems, he pointed out that Spain, as a geographical, cultural and historical crossroads, could serve as a meeting ground for many conflicting viewpoints.

During Lopez Bravo's visit to the United Nations, he and Soviet Foreign Minister Andrei Gromyko conferred for some ninety minutes, discussing, among other matters, ways of facilitating the return home of Spanish Civil War exiles in the Soviet Union. López Bravo later said, as quoted by James Odgers in the Washington *Post* (December 13, 1970), that the discussions had enabled him and Gromyko "to meditate very profoundly on the method and pace at which our bilateral relations should evolve." He added that Spain planned to continue its gradual expansion of consular and commercial relations with Eastern Europe.

During López Bravo's first year as Foreign Minister a major financial scandal erupted in Spain over the misappropriation by the Matesa Company, a manufacturer of textile machinery, of large sums of money lent by the government to help the firm increase its volume of exports. López Bravo's name was mentioned in connection with the incident only because he had been Minister of Industry at the time the loans were made. A government investigation failed to turn up any evidence that he might have been implicated in the scandal. While eighteen persons, including two former Cabinet ministers and the president of the Bank of Spain, were indicted, López Bravo was formally exonerated by a ruling of the Spanish Supreme Court in February 1971.

López Bravo accompanied Prince Juan Carlos, the designated successor to Franco, on a state visit to the United States in January 1971. Two months later he visited Morocco and announced that the two countries had agreed to consult on all questions involving peace and security in the Mediterranean and the Straits of Gibraltar. Having designated 1971 as "the Hispano-American year for Spanish foreign policy," he embarked in March on a tour of Argentina, Chile, Uruguay, Paraguay, and Brazil. As he left Spain, he called for a "bold, realistic, and modern policy toward Latin America," and he announced that he planned to visit almost every Latin American country during the year, including Cuba, with which Spain maintains diplomatic, economic, and cultural relations despite ideological divergences.

Gregorio López Bravo and María Ángeles Velasco Schmidt were married in 1948 and have nine children. López Bravo is of medium height, has dark wavy hair, and has been described as having the appearance of a bullfighter. He speaks English fluently. William Cemlyn-Jones portrays him in the London *Observer* (November 2, 1969) as "brilliant, energetic, likeable, and efficient." As a Cabinet member, López Bravo holds the title Procurador (attorney) within Spain's partially elected parliament, the Cortes. A former chairman of the Association of Naval Engineers and of the Institute of Civil Engineers in Spain, López Bravo has also served as counsellor to the National Institute of Engineers and director of the Atomic Energy Board. He is a member of the Institute of Naval Architects of the United Kingdom and of the Association Technique Maritime et Aéronautique of France.

References

London Observer p23 N 2 '69 por
Washington (D.C.) Post B p2 N 2 '69 por
International Who's Who, 1970-71
Who's Who in Spain, 1963

LORD, JOHN WESLEY

Aug. 23, 1902- Methodist bishop
Address: b. 100 Maryland Ave., N.E., Washington, D.C. 20002; h. 2020 Plymouth St., N.W., Washington, D.C. 20012

In 1970-71 the Council of Bishops of the United Methodist Church, the second largest Protestant denomination in the United States, was headed by Bishop John Wesley Lord. A bishop since 1948, Lord has since 1960 presided over the Methodist Church's Washington Area, a jurisdiction embracing the District of Columbia, Delaware, most of Maryland, and a small portion of West Virginia. In the course of his career Bishop Lord has grown increasingly progressive and daring in his stands on such issues as social and racial justice and peace. Beginning in 1966, he set a controversial precedent by assigning black pastors to white parishes in St. George's County, Maryland. An outspoken critic of American policy in Indochina, he helped Dr. Benjamin Spock to set up the Committee of Responsibility, dedicated to saving burned and maimed Vietnamese children, and he has served as director of Concerned Citizens for Peace in Vietnam and as a leader of the Peace Mobilization. At the end of his one-year term as president of the Methodist bishops, Bishop Lord was succeeded by Bishop Paul Harding Jr. of Columbia, South Carolina, in April 1971.

Named after the founder of Methodism, John Wesley Lord was born in Paterson, New Jersey on August 23, 1902 to John James Lord, a letter carrier, and Catherine (Carmichael) Lord. From his father, a religious man with old-fashioned ideals of honesty, dedication to work, and "inner integrity of soul," Lord learned, as he has said, "the meaning of honor in all of life's relationships." As a child, Lord delivered newspapers after school. According to Kenneth Dole of the Washington *Post* (April 25, 1970), his awareness of and antipathy toward racial injustice dates back to the time when he was eight years old and "his family was denied lodging in the Northfield (Massachusetts) Inn, at a Moody [Bible Institute] vacation conference, because a Negro teacher accompanied them."

After graduating from Montclair (New Jersey) State Normal School, in 1922, Lord taught school for two years before entering Dickinson College in

BISHOP JOHN WESLEY LORD

Carlisle, Pennsylvania, where he took his B.A. degree in 1927. While studying at Drew Theological Seminary in Madison, New Jersey he served as assistant pastor at the Emory Methodist Church in Union, New Jersey. In 1930 he received his Bachelor of Divinity degree from Drew, and during the following year he did graduate work in philosophy at the University of Edinburgh, Scotland.

Lord was pastor of Union Community Church in Union, New Jersey from 1931 to 1934; of the First Methodist Church in Arlington, New Jersey from 1935 to 1938; and of the First Methodist Church in Westfield, New Jersey from 1938 to 1948. During his pastorate in Westfield, Kenneth Dole relates in his Washington *Post* article, he "was called a 'Negro lover' because he invited a Negro dentist and his wife to join the congregation." Meanwhile, in 1943, he took his doctorate in divinity at Dickinson College.

The Northeastern Jurisdictional Conference of the Methodist Church, in session at Albany, New York, elected Lord a bishop on June 18, 1948, and he was consecrated two days later in Trinity Methodist Church, Albany. From 1948 to 1960 he was resident bishop in the Methodist Church's Boston Area, and while in Boston he received an S.T.D. degree from Boston University, in 1949. In the same year he was given an LL.D. degree by Dickinson College.

At the 1960 session of the Northeastern Jurisdictional Conference, held in Washington, D.C., Lord was named bishop of the Washington Area. In March 1962 Bishop Lord headed a National Council of Churches mission to military personnel on Okinawa. In public statements during 1962 he supported Virginia's voluntary sterilization program, which had been attacked by Roman Catholic Archbishop Patrick A. O'Boyle, and he opposed the Jewish Community Council's request that all religious observances be barred from public schools in the Washington area.

Presiding at the Baltimore Conference of the Methodist Church in June 1963, Lord proposed that the conference provide financial support for churches serving inner-city neighborhoods. In an article in the Methodist monthly *Together* for September 1963 he asserted that parents cannot, in good conscience, leave their children's entire religious and spiritual training to agencies outside the home, and he advised pastors to set up classes to help prepare parents for conducting family prayers and Bible readings.

Testifying before a House of Representatives committee in May 1964, Bishop Lord advised against changing the First Amendment to permit prayer in the public schools. In *Together* (January 1965) he expressed hope for the development of contraceptives that would be acceptable to Roman Catholics as well as Protestants. Later in 1965 he was among the prominent clerics who went to Selma, Alabama to participate in the civil rights march there. Lord was in the front rank of the march, arm-in-arm with Dr. Martin Luther King.

The first black pastor to be appointed to a white church in the greater Washington area was the Rev. Harold G. Johnson Sr., who was assigned by Bishop Lord to the Bells United Methodist Church in Camp Springs, Maryland in 1966. In the years following, Lord made other such controversial appointments, including the assignment of the Rev. Dr. Edward G. Carroll to Marvin Memorial United Methodist Church in Silver Spring, Maryland." "Enrollment has fallen off at some churches," Kenneth Dole reported in the Washington *Post*, "but the withdrawal rate has leveled off." Lord has commented: "The quality of the fellowship has deepened. Let's say it honestly, it is more Christian."

In a talk at Howard University in March 1966 Bishop Lord deplored inhumane conditions and procedures in American prisons and suggested a concrete program of penal and rehabilitation reforms, including conjugal visits when merited and feasible, a reduction in the volume of commitments of petty offenders, such as alcoholics, and increased use of probation. "The health of any society may be measured by its treatment of . . . [the] penal population," he pointed out. In November 1966 Lord gave his approval to the "Church-o-Theque," a controversial worship service, utilizing contemporary pop styles of music, at the Mount Vernon Place Methodist Church in Washington.

Lord joined with eleven other clerics of various denominations in December 1966 in sending President Johnson an open letter criticizing American bombing of Hanoi, North Vietnam. After condemning the "cruel" and "indiscriminate" killing of civilians, the letter asked: "How can your call for negotiations and a peaceful settlement be taken seriously when the United States forces escalate their actions at a time like this? The world looks upon this as an act of bad faith." Lord again spoke out against American conduct in Vietnam in a sermon in September 1967: "There is much wishful thinking but little real and passionate devotion to the things that make for peace. We have a desire for peace but it is qualified by all manner of ifs and buts which no one has the serious disposition to eliminate. . . . I must dissent when my country pursues a course of action that violates both the political and spiritual conditions upon which lasting peace among the nations becomes possible." Among the delusions that Americans must renounce before they can contribute to peace in the world, he said, is the proposition that the American way of life is the best way for the whole world. Five months later Lord and other members of Clergy and Laymen Concerned About Vietnam charged that American and Allied forces in Vietnam have violated international rules for the conduct of war.

On May 26, 1967 Bishop Lord was elected chairman of Washington's Interreligious Committee on Race Relations. In assuming the chairmanship he asserted that social service is not enough to cure such social problems as poverty. The poor will remain without "hope and faith," he said, until basic changes are made in the social structure. "I want ICRR to be the catalyst to bring about those changes." During the electoral campaigning the following year the committee, which is composed of fifty-five of the capital's religious and civic leaders, urged voters to ignore appeals to fear and "emotional calls for law and order."

In January 1968 Bishop Lord was a member of a group of Roman Catholic, Jewish, and Protestant clergymen who made a twenty-two-day tour of seven countries in the cause of peace. The high point of the trip was the International Interreligious Symposium of Peace, held in New Delhi, India from January 10 to 14, where the group met with Moslem, Buddhist, Hindu, and Shinto leaders. Indirectly responding to Pope Paul's encyclical on birth control, *Humanae Vitae*, in November 1968, Bishop Lord declared that married couples are acting immorally if they do not use artificial birth control when that is the responsible decision and, conversely, if they block birth artificially when childbearing is clearly the responsible choice. "Sheer common sense and a knowledge of the kind of world in which we live as well as spiritual and moral considerations determine the Protestant attitude," he said.

"The Intellectual Burden of Peace," a sermon delivered by Lord at the centennial of the Metropolitan United Methodist Church in Washington in 1969, refined the Bishop's thoughts on war and peace. In it he pointed out that those who go beyond mere wishful thinking and undertake the mental effort of analyzing what peace requires will come to the conclusion that nations must surrender sovereignty sufficiently to "take the next natural step in the development of civilization, the establishment of a world community."

In another talk in 1969, before a meeting of the Eastern Shore Methodists, Lord reminded his audience that Methodism, at its origin, was a movement of unpropertied poor that frightened the British establishment just as the rebellion of youth is shaking up society today. "You cannot keep things as they are," he said, "You cannot prevent change. . . . God punishes those who won't change." He went on to say that John Wesley "insisted upon salvation, and the full work of God in the individual, but Wesley then expected an individual so changed to go and change the society that had exploited him and caused him to lose human dignity."

As president of the Council of Bishops of the United Methodist Church, Lord presided at a national Methodist conference in St. Louis in April 1970. The conference, attended by 100 bishops and 970 delegates representing the 11,000,000 members of the denomination, was marked by hostility between traditionalists and a faction of dissidents who wanted the church to put $2,000,000 into "projects and programs relating to the needs of black young people."

At a press conference held jointly with three other major Protestant leaders in Washington in May 1970, Lord accused President Nixon of indifference to the moral dimensions of the war in Indochina and noted the President's failure to follow the custom of his predecessors of consulting with church leaders on major issues. The following month, in an extraordinary ecumenical gesture, Lord ordained thirty-seven Methodist deacons and sixteen Methodist elders in a ceremony at the Washington Episcopal Cathedral in which he was assisted by Episcopal Bishop William F. Creighton of Washington.

John Wesley Lord and Margaret Farrington Ratcliffe were married on April 29, 1931. They have a daughter, Jean Phillips Lord (Mrs. Arnold C. Cooper). Bishop Lord is a trustee of Sibley Memorial Hospital in Washington and of several colleges and universities, including Western Maryland College in Westminster, Maryland; a member of the general board of the National Council of Churches, the Commission on Ecumenical Affairs, the National Council for a Responsible Firearms Policy, and the United States Interreligious Committee on Peace; vice-president of the board of visitors of Harvard Divinity School; and chairman of the board of governors of Wesley Theological Seminary in Washington. Morgan State College gave him an S.T.D. degree in 1966. Lord is a Republican, a 33d degree Mason, and a member of Phi Kappa Sigma and Tau Kappa Alpha. Kenneth Dole in his Washington *Post* article described the Bishop's voice as "resonant" and "kindly," and Dole ended the article by calling Lord "a continually changing man, but always committed to honor."

References

Washington (D.C.) Post B p4 Je 19 '60; B p6 Ap 19 '69; B p7 Ap 25 '70 por

Who's Who in America, 1970-71

LOWENSTEIN, ALLARD K(ENNETH)

Jan. 16, 1929- Attorney; organization official
Address: b. 3115 Long Beach Rd., Oceanside, N.Y. 11572; Americans for Democratic Action, 1424 16th St., N.W., Washington, D.C. 20036

In May 1971 former New York insurgent Democratic Congressman Allard K. Lowenstein was elected national chairman of Americans for Democratic Action, a liberal political action and education organization in the New Deal tradition. The restlessly energetic Lowenstein, a tireless political strategist with a flair for building bipartisan grass-

ALLARD K. LOWENSTEIN

roots coalitions, was the chief architect of the successful "Dump Johnson" movement of 1967 and 1968. Much of his energy as ADA chairman is being spent in a drive to register newly enfranchised eighteen-to-twenty-one-year-old voters. "If we—and many others—do our work well," he has explained, "we will not only elect a new President committed to peace abroad and social and economic justice at home; we will at the same time have repudiated both the cynicism of those who believe that the voters will not vote and the nihilism of those who believe that they should not vote." Outside of politics, Lowenstein is an attorney, best known for his work in civil rights cases, and a teacher of political science. During the academic year 1970-71 he was scheduled to teach a weekly course on public policy at Yale University and conduct a lecture series at Harvard University.

Allard Kenneth Lowenstein was born in Newark, New Jersey on January 16, 1929, and he grew up in Harrison and Scarsdale, Westchester County, New York. His father was Gabriel Abraham Lowenstein, a physician and biochemist who taught at the Columbia University College of Physicians and Surgeons before becoming a New York City restaurateur. His mother was Augusta (Goldberg) Lowenstein. Both parents are dead. Lowenstein has two brothers, Bertrand, a physician, and Larry, who followed his father into the restaurant business, and a sister, Mrs. Dorothy DiCintio.

In childhood Lowenstein followed with intense partisanship the day-to-day progress of the Loyalist, or anti-Franco, army in the Spanish Civil War and the Allied forces in World War II. "I felt we should have been fighting Hitler earlier and wanted very much to get into it," he has recalled. On one occasion, when he was sixteen years old, he tried, unsuccessfully, to run away from home and enlist in the United States Army.

Lowenstein was educated at the Horace Mann School in New York City, the University of North Carolina (B.A., 1949), and the Yale Law School (LL.B., 1954). As vice-president of the student legislature at the University of North Carolina he assisted university president Frank Graham in his efforts to integrate the campus. When Graham became a United States Senator, Lowenstein went to Washington as his special assistant, in 1949.

During the early 1950's Lowenstein presided over the National Student Association and chaired a national organization of student volunteers for Presidential candidate Adlai Stevenson. Following two years of service with the United States Army in Germany, he became educational consultant to the American Association for the United Nations, where he formed a close working and personal relationship with Eleanor Roosevelt, one of his idols. In 1958, the year he was admitted to the New York bar, he worked as foreign policy assistant to Senator Hubert H. Humphrey.

In 1959 Lowenstein toured South-West Africa, an international territory under the jurisdiction of the Republic of South Africa, to investigate racial oppression there in the hope of "arousing the conscience of the world." In a report to the United Nations Trusteeship Council he described the condition of blacks in the territory as even more wretched than in South Africa itself and recommended the imposition of economic sanctions against the government. His impassioned, pessimistic narrative of his journey, *Brutal Mandate*, was published by Macmillan in 1962. Reviewing the book in the New York *Times* (July 16, 1962), Orville Prescott called Lowenstein "a capable writer, . . . a fiery idealist, a zealous crusader for social and political righteousness."

Lowenstein managed the successful 1960 Congressional campaign of pioneer Reform Democrat William Fitts Ryan in Manhattan's Twentieth District. In 1961-62 he taught political science and served as assistant dean of men at Stanford University, and during the following two years he was on the faculty of North Carolina State University. At both universities he was a controversial figure— at Stanford because he supported the student side in a campus power dispute and at North Carolina State because State authorities objected to his encouragement of local civil rights demonstrators. As a lawyer Lowenstein donated his services to jailed civil rights workers in the deep South in the early 1960's. He also recruited student volunteers for voter registration drives in Mississippi; helped organize the Mississippi Freedom Vote, the forerunner of the Mississippi Freedom Democratic party; and served as an adviser to Martin Luther King and the Southern Christian Leadership Conference.

In 1967-68 Lowenstein taught political science at the City University of New York. He was a civilian observer of the elections held in the Dominican Republic in 1966 and in South Vietnam in 1967. After his return from Vietnam he founded the Conference of Concerned Democrats and the Coalition for a Democratic Alternative, organizations opposed to Lyndon B. Johnson's war policy and dedicated to blocking his renomination for President. To muster support for an alternative candidate he visited hundreds of cities and campuses across the United States. His call rallied an "army" of young people, ready to serve as volunteers for a Democratic peace candidate.

After failing to persuade Senators Robert F. Kennedy and George McGovern to challenge Johnson in the Democratic primaries, Lowenstein announced, in November 1967, that his group would support the candidacy of Senator Eugene McCarthy. Later Kennedy entered the race and sought to retrieve Lowenstein's backing, but Lowenstein, suppressing his empathy for Kennedy, loyally kept his forces in the McCarthy camp.

In the Democratic preference primary in New Hampshire on March 12, 1968 the relatively unknown McCarthy scored impressively against the President, receiving 28,721 ballots (only 300 less than Johnson) and picking up twenty of the state's twenty-four Democratic National Convention delegate votes. On March 31 President Johnson announced that he would not seek reelection. Later Lowenstein reminded a group of his student followers what they had accomplished: "[We ended] the inevitability of Lyndon Johnson's election. . . . We did it without a major name, money, or the mass media. We showed that the system is not so resistant to change but that it is badly corroded."

Before the 1968 Democratic National Convention in Chicago, Lowenstein formed the Coalition for an Open Convention for the purpose of opposing the nomination of Hubert Humphrey, the administration's candidate, and putting a forthright peace plank in the party platform. At the tumultuous convention itself, in August 1968, he was among the more conspicuous and vociferous of the leaders of the dissenting minority. The dissent was effectively stifled, a strong peace plank was blocked, and Hubert Humphrey received the nomination according to plan. After the Johnson administration stopped the bombing of North Vietnam, Lowenstein supported Humphrey in his unsuccessful race against Republican Presidential candidate Richard Nixon.

After moving to Long Beach, Long Island, in Nassau County's Fifth Congressional District, he ran for Congress there, and in the June 1968 primary he defeated Albert Vorspan for the Democratic nomination. The following November, running on both the Democratic and Liberal tickets, he faced Conservative-Republican Mason L. Hampton, who was favored to win in the predominantly Republican district. During the campaign Lowenstein's young volunteers canvassed almost every home in the district, persuading voters that their candidate was far from being the radical depicted by his opponent. In his speeches Lowenstein stressed national issues, calling the Indochina war "morally, politically, and economically indefensible" and asserting that "national priorities must be reordered to allow us to take care of our urgent needs—housing, education, job training, transportation, pollution, and conservation."

At the polls on November 5, 1968 Lowenstein upset Hampton, 99,193 votes to 96,427. As a member of the Ninety-first Congress he was cautiously quiet, as freshmen Representatives are expected to be, but he voted just as he had promised in his campaign—liberally and with a view to the national interest. His legislative record included courageous (because unpopular) votes against the District of Columbia anti-crime bill, a proposal to cut off aid to students involved in campus disorders, an anti-pornography measure, and nearly a score of military appropriation bills, including one for the Safeguard antiballistic missile. He voted for tax relief, reform of military conscription, and abolition of the House Un-American Activities Committee. His committee assignment was on the House Committee on Agriculture.

In the House, Lowenstein allied himself with a bipartisan group of young Representatives seeking fundamental changes in archaic House rules and customs, and with Republicans Paul N. McCloskey Jr. and Donald W. Riegle Jr. and Democrat Donald Fraser he set up a coordinating center for strategy in planning and pushing peace legislation. Among his constituents he held community hearings to keep abreast of opinions on local and national issues, and he set up advisory councils on such problems as housing, jet noise, transportation, and wetlands preservation.

While in Congress, Lowenstein visited numerous trouble spots abroad, including Indochina and Biafra (to make arrangements for flights to carry food to the starving), and strife-torn campuses at home. On the campuses he condemned indiscriminate use of violence by the police and military without condoning the violence encouraged by such militant groups as the Students for a Democratic Society. "If the disaffected say the alternative to Nixon is bombs in Greenwich Village, then the country will turn right to oppression," he said on one occasion. "People will say, 'I'd rather have my phone tapped than be blown up.' Only they won't tap just the phones of the extremists."

In 1970 the Republican-controlled New York State legislature gerrymandered the Fifth Congressional District to exclude the Jewish and liberal Democratic Five Towns area and substitute for it Catholic and conservative Republican Massapequa. In the November 1970 election Republican-Conservative Norman F. Lent defeated Lowenstein by some 8,000 votes, out of more than 180,000 cast. After leaving the House of Representatives, Lowenstein joined the faculty of the Yale University School of Urban Studies.

In April 1971 Lowenstein, with Republican Representatives McCloskey and Riegle, began a national nonpartisan voter-registration drive among young people. "The right to vote has been extended to 25,000,000 young men and women," Lowenstein explained, "and this fact alone all but assures a repudiation of the Nixon-Johnson coalition—if the great majority of these potential voters can be persuaded to register and vote. But widespread despair and cynicism must be overcome. Simpler procedures for registration must be worked out and publicized. To achieve these goals, bipartisan rallies and organizational meetings will be held in cities across the country." Riegle said: "Unless there is a substantial shift in the course pursued by President Nixon at home and abroad, I, along with other Republicans, will oppose his renomination in 1972." The voter registration drive has been bolstered with money from the Joseph Rauh Civil

Rights-Civil Liberties Fund of Americans for Democratic Action. Lowenstein was a vice-chairman of the Americans for Democratic Action before his election to the chairmanship of the organization on May 2, 1971.

Allard Kenneth Lowenstein and Jennifer Lyman were married on November 25, 1966. They have three children: Frank Graham, Thomas Kennedy, and Katherine Eleanor. Lowenstein is five feet eleven inches tall, weighs about 170 pounds, and has dark, thinning hair and brown eyes. Unconcerned about his wardrobe, he wears casual clothes when feasible, and his suits and coats often have a rumpled look. A lifelong amateur athlete, he abstains from tobacco and alcohol. Lowenstein's interest in Spain has never abated. He speaks Spanish, visits the country occasionally, and maintains ties with Loyalist veterans.

While ebullient in temperament and intense in his beliefs, Lowenstein is usually gentle in manner and has a sense of humor of which he himself is often the butt. The articulate ADA chairman, who confesses to being a "talker," speaks softly—and, if the occasion demands, endlessly. His enemies characterize him variously as "pushy" and "naive," but neutral and friendly observers have described him as "idealistic," "energetic," "forceful," "resilient," and—in reference to his teaching—"inspired and inspiring." Eleanor Roosevelt once wrote of him: "He is a person of unusual ability and complete integrity. I think he will always fight crusades because injustice fills him with a sense of rebellion." And in March 1968 Robert F. Kennedy wrote to Lowenstein: "For Al, who knew the lesson of Emerson and taught it to the rest of us: 'They did not yet see, and thousands of young men as hopeful, now crowding to the barriers of their careers, do not yet see, that if a single man plant himself on his convictions and then abide, the huge world will come round to him.'"

References

ADA World 26:1+ My-Je '71 pors
Harper 237:47+ D '68 pors
Look 34:36+ Ag 25 '70 por
N Y Post B p4 My 19 '68 por; p3 My 2 '69
N Y Times p14 Jl 1 '68 por
New York 1:28+ Ag 12 '68 por
New Yorker 45:31+ Ja 10 '70; 46:51+ N 21 '70
Newsday W p3+ N 9 '68 pors
Washington (D.C.) Post B p4 My 19 '68
Who's Who in America, 1970-71
Who's Who in American Politics, 1969-70

LUDWIG, CHRISTA

Mar. 16, 1932(?)- Opera and concert singer
Address: b. c/o Maurice Feldman, Suite 1404, 745 5th Ave., New York 10022; h. Seefeldstr. 11, Lucerne, Switzerland

In the forefront of contemporary classical vocalists stands Christa Ludwig, a versatile "dark" soprano whose voice remains warm and secure throughout the range of both the high and mezzo registers. Miss Ludwig, a member of the Vienna State Opera since 1955, performs several months annually with the Metropolitan Opera Company in New York City, and she is much in demand in other major opera houses and concert halls throughout the world. In her Wagnerian, Straussian, and other operatic roles her superb voice—at once highly controlled and unpretentious—is enhanced by a strong, sensuous stage presence and a consummate acting skill, especially in comedy. And as a singer of lieder she has, in the words of critic Robert Lawrence, "qualities of tone, musicianship, imagination, bound by a charismatic thread, [that are] rarely met with in a single artist."

Christa Ludwig is the daughter of the Austrian tenor, stage director, and opera manager Anton Ludwig and the famous German contralto Eugenie Besalla Ludwig. Miss Ludwig, who celebrates her birthday on March 16, was born in Berlin, Germany. The year of her birth as given by conflicting sources ranges from 1928 to 1935. She has a stepbrother, Heinz, an architect and stage designer, and a stepsister, Annemarie, a former singer. Another stepbrother, Rudi, an actor, was killed in World War II.

Her mother was her one and only voice teacher and coach and remains her closest critic, as Miss Ludwig noted in an interview with John Gruen for the New York *Times* (January 31, 1971). After referring to her experience with psychoanalysis, she said: "I've been told I have a mother complex. I think that's complete nonsense, of course. But it's true, perfectly true, that I have a wonderful mother from whom I've learned everything."

Miss Ludwig's voice matured early. At seventeen she made her operatic debut in Frankfurt, singing the mezzo-soprano role of Prince Orlovsky in Johann Strauss's *Die Fledermaus*. In short tenures at various German opera houses she added to her budding repertoire such roles as the title parts in Honegger's *Antigone* and *Judith* and Marina in Moussorgsky's *Boris Godounov*. William Mann, writing in *Opera* (October 1955), reported her to be "a fulsome female counterpart to Boris," with pure "rather than contrived" high notes and "confident" acting.

In 1955 Miss Ludwig joined the Vienna State Opera, which has since remained her home base. Early in her tenure with the Vienna company she met Walter Berry, when he was cast as Figaro and she as Cherubino in a production of *The Marriage of Figaro*. When she sang her first Carmen, in 1957, Berry again performed opposite her, as Escamillo. They were married shortly afterward, on September 29, 1957, and two years later a son, Wolfgang, was born to them. During the years of their marriage the couple maintained three homes: a house in the Vienna woods, overlooking the Danube, where the ménage included Miss Ludwig's mother (who also traveled with the couple), Mr. Berry's mother and father, several servants, and some dogs and cats; an apartment in New York; and another apartment in Lucerne, Switzerland, used only occasionally, for holidays, weekends, or stopovers.

When Miss Ludwig made her Metropolitan Opera debut, in the role of Cherubino in 1959, Howard Taubman of the New York *Times* (December 11, 1959), who had previously heard her sing Wagner, thought that the part did not suit her. "The German mezzo has a voice of size and quality, and she brings a full-blooded style to such parts as Maddalena and Fricka. But her Cherubino lacks lightness and flexibility." As he wrote in the *Times* sixteen days later, Taubman was much more impressed with her in her second Met role, that of Octavian in *Der Rosenkavalier:* "Her opulent mezzo was firmly controlled. Her top tones were accurate. Her bearing as the young Cavalier of the Rose was admirable." Later in the same Met season Miss Ludwig sang Amneris in *Aida,* with, as another *Times* critic noted, "the power and sonority the role calls for" (January 15, 1960). In December 1960, when she sang Dejanira in an America Opera Society concert production of Handel's *Hercules,* Raymond Ericson of the *Times* (December 3, 1960) called her voice "a lovely one . . . even in texture from its lowest to its highest notes."

In 1961 Angel Records released a recording of Bellini's *Norma* in which Maria Callas interpreted the title role and Miss Ludwig sang the part of Adalgisa. "Miss Ludwig brings warmth to all her duties," John W. Clark noted in reviewing the album for *Musical America* (October 1961) and went on to say that Miss Ludwig had "a better-than-suitable diction, and a very well disciplined scale in the two famous duets with Norma. . . . I also enjoy her dramatic urgency, in her own scenes and in ensemble." Among the outstanding singers assembled for Otto Klemperer's 1962 Angel recording of Bach's *St. Matthew Passion* Raymond Ericson of the New York *Times* (November 25, 1962) singled her out for special praise. "The voice has a richness and purity that give pleasure in themselves, aside from the singer's fine style." In the Angel recording of Mozart's *Cosi fan tutte* (1963), she sang Dorabella with a voice that, as Alan Rich of the *Times* (April 21, 1963) observed, "seems to grow more luscious with every record she makes."

In 1963, as a guest performer in Tokyo with the Deutsche Oper of Berlin, Miss Ludwig sang Leonore in Beethoven's *Fidelio.* In March 1965 she and Walter Berry sang Iphigenia and Agamemnon, respectively, in an American Opera Society production of Gluck's *Iphigenia in Aulis* at Carnegie Hall in New York City. In the same month, also at Carnegie Hall, the couple gave their first New York recital, a program of lieder and duets. "Of the two," John Gruen wrote in the New York *Herald Tribune* (March 6, 1965), "it was Miss Ludwig who offered that rare commodity known as soul. Her voice, a rich, sinuous, and beautifully controlled instrument, has the capability to evoke great sentiment and depth of feeling."

When Walter Berry made his Metropolitan Opera debut, as the impoverished dyer Bakar in Richard Strauss's *Die Frau ohne Schatten* in 1966, Miss Ludwig sang the dyer's sensuous wife. "The

CHRISTA LUDWIG

singing, which requires a display of vocal acrobatics that few performers can successfully negotiate, was excellent," a reviewer reported in *Time* (October 14, 1966). "Loudest bravas went to Christa Ludwig, whose lusty soprano and hip-swinging histrionics had bite and conviction." Two months later at the Met, Berry and Miss Ludwig sang, respectively, Telramund and Ortrud in Wagner's *Lohengrin.* On that occasion Alan Rich wrote in the New York *World Journal Tribune* (December 9, 1966): "Miss Ludwig is such a magnificent singing actress that, even with the simplest of gestures, and standing for the most part very still, she has it in her to create a genuine and overwhelming personage." The 1966 Bayreuth Festival production of Wagner's *Tristan und Isolde,* with Christa Ludwig as Brangaene, was recorded in performance by Deutsche Grammophon and the recording was released late in the year.

In September 1967 the Vienna State Opera took to Expo '67, the World's Fair in Montreal, Canada, five productions, including *Der Rosenkavalier,* in which Miss Ludwig sang Octavian, and Alban Berg's *Wozzeck,* in which she sang Marie. Two months later she and her husband performed in Wagner's *Die Walküre* at the Metropolitan, as Fricka and Wotan respectively. When Miss Ludwig gave her first solo recital at the Museum of Modern Art in November 1968, Donal Henahan wrote in the New York *Times* (November 15, 1968): "In the overwhelming majority of instances . . . by the time a singer has matured enough to sing lieder with intelligence and emotional depth, the voice is in tatters. Now and then . . . there comes along a great artist whose voice lasts into late maturity or whose maturity comes early. Christa Ludwig . . . is one of the latter sort of lieder singer. . . . Her all-Brahms recital . . . was a tour de force in every way, for in neither vocal finesse nor as a song interpreter does the Viennese mezzo-soprano have many peers. Vocally, her program was a model of the lieder craft: no faking, no talking through the difficult passages, no substitution of charm for voice."

During the Metropolitan's 1968-69 season, Miss Ludwig demonstrated that she is one of the rare singers able to perform both the soprano role of Marschallin and the mezzo-soprano role of Octavian in *Der Rosenkavalier*. The following season at the Met she again proved that she is, in the words of Winthrop Sargeant of the *New Yorker* (February 7, 1970), "the best of all contemporary Octavians." On December 2, 1969 Miss Ludwig devoted a Carnegie Hall recital to Rückert songs, Mahler's *Lieder eines fahrenden Gesellen*, and some works by Schumann. "Her voice sounded particularly well—supple, fresh, and warm—and the discipline she imposes upon it, in terms of breath control, long *legato,* and a crisp enunciation, is little short of fantastic . . . ," a critic reported in *High Fidelity and Musical America* (February 1970). "Her main (and almost only) fault as a recitalist is a tendency toward comfortableness, toward a placidity which does not illuminate the anguish—the individuality—of each separate work."

Walter Berry and Christa Ludwig were divorced in June 1970. In a Viennese newspaper article that summer Berry was quoted as saying that one of the points of friction between them was the nature of their travel accommodations. While he would have preferred small hotel rooms, she insisted on large suites or whole floors. "That comment in the Vienna paper about my wanting a lot of space—well, it's true . . . ," Miss Ludwig later told John Gruen in an interview for the New York *Times* (January 31, 1971). "And we are such different types. I need quiet, and I need time for concentration. Walter likes to go out and be with friends and talk and laugh. The thing is, everybody should do what he likes. As things stand now, it has all worked out for the best, and Walter and I now love each other very much." At another point in the interview she said: "When Walter and I divorced I lost a husband but I gained a very good friend."

After the divorce, Berry and Miss Ludwig continued to sing together on occasion. At the Metropolitan Opera on January 16, 1971, for example, they returned to their familiar roles in *Die Frau ohne Schatten*. Among Miss Ludwig's other Met roles in the 1970-71 season was that of Kundry in Wagner's *Parsifal*. According to critics, her "inspired" performance brought that long, "sleepy" production "to life" and became "the high point of Miss Ludwig's career here." After her last Met appearance of the year, in March, she was scheduled to return home to Vienna for a spate of performances, including a role in the première of Gottfried Von Einem's *Die Besuch der alten Dame* (*The Visit*), based on the play by Friedrich Dürrenmatt. Her itinerary later in 1971 took her to La Scala in Milan, Covent Garden in London, the Hollywood Bowl in Los Angeles, and opera stages in San Francisco, Rome, and Paris.

The two most ambitious ventures in recording history were recordings of the complete four-opera, fifteen-hour cycle of Wagner's *Der Ring des Nibelungen.* The first was a Decca Ltd. recording, with music by the Vienna Philharmonic Orchestra under Georg Solti, completed in 1965. The second was a Deutsche Grammophon recording, with music by the Berlin Philharmonic under Herbert von Karajan, completed in 1970. Christa Ludwig participated in both projects, singing several roles, including Waltraute in *Götterdämmerung* and Fricka in *Die Walküre*. "I have never heard so convincing an interpretation of the part [of Fricka] . . . ," Alec Robertson wrote in *Gramophone* (September 1966). "Ludwig conveys those turbulent emotions most powerfully and always with dignity, indeed, nobility." And Paul Hume wrote in the Washington *Post* (September 27, 1970): "Clearly Christa Ludwig is the world's reigning Waltraute. . . . She is magnificent." The Berry-Ludwig recital discography includes a 1968 Seraphim recording of songs by Beethoven, Haydn, Strauss, and Wolf, a 1969 Deutsche Grammophon LP of songs by Wolf, and a 1970 Columbia album of Mahler songs. Reviewing the last mentioned recording in the *Saturday Review* (January 31, 1970), Robert Lawrence said: "Beyond the question of technique, there is the Ludwig spirit, lyrical *in excelsis.*"

Christa Ludwig is five feet seven inches tall and has brown hair and eyes that have been described as "dancing." After interviewing the singer in her Manhattan apartment, on Central Park West, John Gruen described her in detail in his New York *Times* article: "Christa Ludwig greets me with a dazzling smile. . . . Her tall, well-built figure immediately suggests health and generosity of spirit. Her walk . . . is at once sensual and vital —a walk that invariably lends a special sexiness to her performances. Her face is not beautiful in the conventional sense. It has a pixieish quality— a trusting face . . . with intelligent brown eyes and flawless skin. . . . Her voice is tinged with a soft German accent. When she laughs, there is music in the room." Elsewhere in his article Gruen observed: "Her surface calm—her open, friendly charm—would indicate that her decision in favor of solitude and unrelenting work totally agrees with her. And yet . . . an ephemeral wavering of the voice, a slight trembling of the hand . . . offers room for doubt."

Miss Ludwig's favorite recreations are swimming, walking, reading, listening to music, cooking, weaving, and dabbling in archeology. She is a Roman Catholic and a member of Sigma Alpha Iota. Her honors include the title of "Kammersängerin," bestowed by the Austrian government in 1963, the Mozart Medal of the Mozart Society of Vienna, and, in the United States, the 1968 Grammy Award for best classical vocal soloist, given by the National Academy of Recording Arts and Sciences for her Angel recording of "Shepherd on the Rocks" and other songs by Schubert, Brahms, Ravel, Saint-Saens, and Rachmaninoff. Her son Wolfgang lives in Vienna with Miss Ludwig's mother.

References

N Y Times II p15 O 30 '66; p51 Mr 24 '69; II p19+ Ja 31 '71 por
International Who's Who, 1970-71

McCLOSKEY, PAUL N(ORTON), JR.

Sept. 29, 1927- United States Representative
from California; lawyer
Address: b. 1511 Longworth House Office
Building, Washington, D.C. 20215; 141 Borel
Ave., San Mateo, Calif. 94402; h. 1113 Lang-
ley Lane, McLean, Va. 22101

Among the challengers of President Richard
Nixon's expected bid for reelection in 1972, the
only Republican to have declared his candidacy
as of late 1971 is Representative Paul N. ("Pete")
McCloskey Jr. of California. His maverick campaign against the President, begun in February
1971, is reminiscent of Democratic Senator Eugene J. McCarthy's "Dump Johnson" campaign of
1968. It was motivated by McCloskey's dissatisfaction with the Nixon administration's failure to
end the war in Southeast Asia and with what he
considers its duplicity in dealing with Congress
and the American people. A lawyer and a Marine
Corps hero of the Korean war, McCloskey defeated the former child actress Shirley Temple
Black and several other candidates in 1967, in
a special election in California's Eleventh Congressional District. Since entering Congress, Mc-
Closkey has intensified his antiwar campaign and
has deepened his lifelong concern with conservation.

Paul Norton McCloskey Jr., the younger of the
two children of Paul N. and Vera (McNabb)
McCloskey, was born on September 29, 1927 in
San Bernardino, California. His sister, Virginia, is
the wife of Dr. Walter J. Hartzell Jr. A fourth-
generation Californian, whose great-grandfather,
John Henry McCloskey, sailed in 1853 from Ireland around Cape Horn to San Francisco, he is
also a third-generation member of the state bar of
California; his father and both grandfathers were
practising attorneys. McCloskey grew up in South
Pasadena, "amid clean air and open space," and
he recalls that it was "one of the privileges of all
times to live in California, hiking and fishing and
back-packing." The senior McCloskey greatly influenced his son, passing along to him his nickname, "Pete," his love of competitive sports, his
stern sense of duty, and his allegiance to the Republican party.

After recovering from a serious case of nephritis
at the age of eight, Pete McCloskey entered Southwestern Military Academy in San Marino, California, where he became keenly interested in Civil
War history. Later, at South Pasadena-San Marino
High School, he took part in interscholastic baseball and student politics. Graduating in 1945, two
months before the end of World War II, he joined
the Navy's V-5 pilot training program, which provided an accelerated college course and aviation
training. After nine months of study at Occidental
College and the California Institute of Technology,
he grew restless and, requesting active duty, he
was assigned to the Great Lakes Naval Training
Station, where he served as a seaman first class
for ten months, until his discharge from the
service in 1947.

PAUL N. MCCLOSKEY JR.

Entering Stanford University in 1948 with advanced standing, McCloskey joined Phi Delta
Theta fraternity and supplemented his G.I. benefits by working as a laborer, athletic coach, and
semiprofessional baseball player. He graduated
with a B.A. degree in 1950. Inspired by friends
who were former United States Marines, he joined
a Marine Corps platoon leader training program
and was commissioned a second lieutenant. In
February 1951 he was sent to Korea where, as a
platoon leader with the Fifth Marine Regiment,
he was wounded while successfully leading a bay-
onet charge up Hill 566. Awarded the Navy Cross
for "daring initiative, aggressive determination,
and inspiring leadership," he also received the
Silver Star and a Purple Heart. After his return
to California in early 1952, he resumed his studies
at Stanford Law School, where he became a member of the legal fraternity Phi Delta Phi, worked
as a law librarian, and obtained his LL.B. degree
in 1953.

After his admission to the state bar McCloskey
served as deputy district attorney for Alameda
County during 1953-54. In 1955 he joined the
firm of Costello & Johnson in Palo Alto, and the
following year he helped found the firm of Mc-
Closkey, Wilson, Mosher & Martin there. Often
working without fee, he represented juveniles,
members of minority groups, sexual deviates, and
others who had difficulty finding legal counsel and
won many of his cases by means of exhaustive research and a forceful courtroom manner. In 1965
he established a partnership with Lewis Butler,
a San Francisco lawyer specializing in conservation cases.

The Marine Corps continued to hold a strong
attraction for McCloskey, although he distrusted
the brass and had a distaste for military pomp.
From 1952 to 1960 he was on active reserve with
the Seventh Infantry Battalion; from 1960 to 1967
he held ready reserve status, and during that period he attained the rank of lieutenant colonel.
Having become a counter-insurgency expert
through research on guerrilla warfare, he played
a key role in Operation Silver Lance, the Ma-

rines' most extensive military maneuvers since World War II, staged at Camp Pendleton in 1965.

In 1963 Charles Daly, a fellow Marine veteran then on the White House staff, added McCloskey's name to a list of attorneys to be invited to a White House Conference on Civil Rights. After hearing President John F. Kennedy's address to the conference, McCloskey resolved that he would enter politics with the aim of reshaping the Republican party to help it regain its liberal tradition. Although in the 1960 Presidential campaign he had been co-chairman of Young Lawyers for Nixon-Lodge, in 1964 he refused to endorse Barry M. Goldwater's Presidential candidacy and supported the Democrat Pierre Salinger against the conservative Republican George Murphy in the California Senate race. A founder of the California Republican League, a moderately liberal group created to combat extreme rightist elements in the party, McCloskey served as chairman of its critical issues conference in 1967.

From 1965 to 1967 McCloskey acted as special counsel for a conservation group known as Save Our Skyline in litigation against Stanford University, the Pacific Gas and Electric Company, and the Atomic Energy Commission. Its aim was to block plans for construction of high-tension powerlines, designed to feed an accelerator built by the university, across the exclusive township of Woodside in San Mateo County. The legal battle, which took him twice to Washington, D.C. to testify before the Atomic Energy Commission and the Joint Atomic Energy Committee, brought him the publicity, local recognition, and organized support he needed to enter politics.

Although McCloskey had considered challenging J. Arthur Younger, who had represented California's Eleventh District in Congress for seven terms, in the 1966 Republican primary, he decided to postpone his first bid for elective office. The following year however, when Younger's terminal illness caused the seat to be vacated, McCloskey became a leading contender, publicly announcing his candidacy on June 2, 1967. The contest for the Congressional seat eventually included six Democratic and four Republican candidates—the most celebrated of them Mrs. Shirley Temple Black, who was favored to win the special election, scheduled for November 14, 1967, by a large margin.

The war in Indochina loomed as an issue in the election campaign and greatly affected McCloskey personally. In 1965, after a friend had returned from Vietnam as an amputee, McCloskey applied for active duty as a battalion commander but was rejected. He then applied for work in Vietnam with the Agency for International Development and was accepted for a two-year tour of duty. Reconsidering the needs of his family, he decided to stay at home. His early campaign literature briefly indicated support of President Lyndon B. Johnson's Indochina policies, but on September 12, 1967 he released what has been called his "dove bombshell," a nine-page statement in which he called for immediate efforts to negotiate with the Hanoi government for an end of the war on the basis of the 1954 Geneva Accords. While rejecting a unilateral troop withdrawal, he advocated a gradual de-escalation over a two-year period in the event negotiations failed.

In the November election, McCloskey received a plurality of 34.4 percent, defeating Mrs. Black—who had represented a conservative Republican position and supported the administration on the war—by a vote of 52,878 to 34,521. The leading Democratic contender, San Mateo City Councilman Roy A. Archibald, also a war critic, received 15,069 votes. A runoff election, held on December 12, 1967 between the top candidates of the two parties, resulted in 66,314 votes for McCloskey, 44,370 for Archibald, and 3,998 write-in votes for Mrs. Black. A waiver of House rules permitted McCloskey to be sworn in as a member of the Ninetieth Congress on December 14, 1967, before the election results were official, enabling him to assume his duties before the Congressional recess. In the House of Representatives, McCloskey was appointed to the subcommittee on conservation and natural resources of the Government Operations Committee, and to the fisheries and wildlife conservation, merchant marine, and maritime education and training subcommittees of the Merchant Marine and Fisheries Committee.

Initially a supporter of Richard Nixon, McCloskey was a member of the Republican "truth squad" during the 1968 Presidential campaign. His voting record indicates that during the Ninety-first Congress he supported President Nixon 71 percent of the time, despite the fact that he opposed the administration on such key issues as the Safeguard antiballistic missile, the supersonic transport plane, and military appropriations for Southeast Asia. McCloskey, who considers himself a fiscal conservative, has admitted that he often votes with the party leaders because of what he feels is a lack of expertise on his part. At the same time, he has maintained his liberal credentials. Americans for Democratic Action gave him a score of 64 percent for 1970, while the liberal Republican Ripon Society rated him at 100 percent.

Supported by an alliance of liberal Republicans, Democrats, and independents, McCloskey has experienced some difficulty in winning the Republican primaries in his home state. In the 1968 primary his margin of victory over former Congressman Robert B. Barry was only about 3,000 votes, but he went on to defeat his Democratic opponent, Urban Whittaker, in the November election by a vote of 166,252 to 40,957. His 1970 margin of 144,104 to 39,197 over Democrat Robert E. Gomperts was the second-highest among Republican Congressional candidates in the United States.

Conservation is, in McCloskey's view, the most vital domestic issue. He has sponsored a number of pollution control bills, and in 1969 he was co-author of a report urging a total ban on environmental testing of chemical and biological warfare agents. He and Democratic Senator Gaylord Nelson of Wisconsin served as honorary co-chairmen of the Environmental Teach-In group, which organized the nationwide activities for Earth Day,

April 22, 1970. On the question of military strength, McCloskey believes that the United States should maintain parity with the Soviet Union. An advocate of the military draft, as opposed to an all-volunteer army, McCloskey said in testimony before the House Armed Services Committee in March 1971: "There are men who love to kill, but it seems to me the nation is far safer when its army is made up of reluctant citizen-soldiers than by men who take pride in being professional killers."

On the other hand, McCloskey's growing conviction that the United States is acting both illegally and immorally in Indochina has caused him to step up his opposition to American military involvement there. In January 1968 he returned from his first visit to Vietnam "with grave doubts that what we do there is right." Between March 1969 and November 1970 he wrote five progressively strident letters to President Nixon, urging him to admit the error of United States policy and to start troop withdrawals, but he failed to receive any direct reply. With eight other members of Congress, McCloskey supported the national student anti-war protest of October 1969. He teamed with Representative Donald Riegle of Michigan in drafting a motion to repeal the Gulf of Tonkin Resolution of 1964 and became a leader in the efforts to obtain House passage of the Senate's McGovern-Hatfield and Cooper-Church amendments, aimed at disengaging United States forces from Southeast Asia. Returning from his second Indochina trip, in early 1970, he strongly criticized the Nixon administration's "Vietnamization" policy.

In a speech delivered at Stanford University on February 10, 1971, following the United States military incursion into Laos, McCloskey suggested a "national dialogue" to discuss the impeachment of President Nixon as a possible legal means of inducing him to change his war policy. Eight days later, speaking on the floor of the House, he declared that although he did not at this time advocate impeachment, "a reasonable argument can be made that the President's recent decision to employ American air power in the neutral countries of Laos and Cambodia exceeds his constitutional powers." Later that day he told reporters that unless the President reversed his policy, or unless a more qualified candidate came forward, he would challenge him in the 1972 Presidential primaries. Official Republican reaction to McCloskey's declaration was typified by California Governor Ronald Reagan's statement that "the young man doesn't know what he is talking about."

The drive to "Dump Nixon" gathered momentum during the spring of 1971, with rallies of youthful supporters, and the opening by McCloskey and Riegle of a small campaign headquarters in Washington. During a trip to Laos in April, McCloskey accused the American Ambassador of a policy of deliberately destroying Laotian villages, and he later testified before the Senate Judiciary subcommittee on refugees that the State Department was concealing the extent of United States bombing. On July 9, 1971 McCloskey officially announced that he intended to enter primaries in California, New Hampshire, and possibly other states, with the intention of heading a slate of nominees to the 1972 Republican National Convention pledged to ending the Indochina war, once the return of American war prisoners was assured. "We seek in addition to ending the war to restore truth in government, to achieve a return to the historical Republican moral commitment on social issues rather than the present 'Southern strategy,' and a restoration of judicial excellence," McCloskey said after his announcement. McCloskey's campaign has met with silence from the White House, and he has received little support from prominent Republicans.

From 1964 to 1967 McCloskey lectured on legal ethics at the Santa Clara and Stanford university law schools. He wrote a textbook, *The United States Constitution* (Addison-Wesley, 1964), which he has designated his "personal rebuttal to the John Birch Society." McCloskey was president of the Palo Alto Bar Association in 1960-61 and of the Conference of Barristers of the State Bar of California in 1901-02, and a trustee of the Santa Clara Bar Association from 1965 to 1967. In 1966-67 he served as an arbitrator with the American Arbitration Association. He was president of the Stanford Area Youth Plan from 1960 to 1966 and of the Palo Alto Fair Play Council in 1965, and director of the Family Service Association from 1961 to 1965. His interest in conservation led him to join the Committee for Green Foothills, the Planning and Conservation League for Legislative Action, and the Sierra Club. The Palo Alto Junior Chamber of Commerce named McCloskey Young Man of the Year for 1961.

Paul N. McCloskey Jr. married Caroline Wadsworth of Altadena, a fellow Stanford student, on August 6, 1949. They have four children—Nancy, Peter, John, and Kathleen—and they live in a hillside house in Portola Valley, near Palo Alto. Although McCloskey is listed in some sources as a Presbyterian, the family claims no formal religious affiliation. Rugged, square-jawed, and of military bearing, Pete McCloskey wears his dark hair in a crew cut and is said to have the "Kennedy charisma." He enjoys back-packing and fishing in the High Sierras. Friends know him as competitive and somewhat impetuous, with a Victorian belief in the concepts of duty, honor, and loyalty. "He's not a knee-jerk liberal by a long shot," one acquaintance has said, as quoted in the Washington *Post* (May 8, 1971). "But he has guts, brains, and a sense of mission."

References

Cong Q 29:1227+ Je 4 '71
N Y Post p22 Ap 24 '71 por
N Y Times p2 Ap 12 '71 por
N Y Times Mag p28+ Ap 18 '71 pors
Congressional Directory, 1971
Minott, Rodney G. Sinking of the Lollipop; Shirley Temple vs. Pete McCloskey (1968)
Who's Who in America, 1970-71
Who's Who in American Politics, 1969-70

McGANNON, DONALD H(ENRY)

Sept. 9, 1920- Broadcasting executive
Address: b. Westinghouse Broadcasting Co.,
Inc., 90 Park Ave., New York 10016

In the American broadcasting industry one of the
most forceful voices is that of Donald H. Mc-
Gannon, president and board chairman of the
Westinghouse Broadcasting Company (Group W).
A foe of huckstering in television and a gadfly
of the major networks, McGannon has consistently
championed imaginative and public service-orient-
ed programming. Group W now embraces twelve
radio and television stations (the maximum permitted under the law) in nine major cities: WBZ,
WBZ-TV (Boston); WINS (New York); KYW,
KYW-TV (Philadelphia); WJZ-TV (Baltimore);
KDKA, KDKA-TV (Pittsburgh); WOWO (Ft.
Wayne); WIND (Chicago); KPIX (San Francisco); and KFWB (Los Angeles). In addition to
owning and operating those stations, Westinghouse
produces and syndicates such well-known television programs as the *David Frost Show*, operates a
worldwide news service, and runs cable-television
businesses.

In 1951 McGannon abandoned a promising law
career to join the fledgling television industry as
an executive for the DuMont Television Network. He moved to the Westinghouse Broadcasting Company, an offshoot of the Westinghouse
Electric Corporation, in January 1955 as vice-
president and was elected president that November. To launch Westinghouse into the education
and training field, McGannon founded the Westinghouse Learning Corporation in 1967. In a reorganization of the parent company in 1969 the
broadcasting executive was named a vice-president of the Westinghouse Electric Corporation
and president of its broadcasting, learning, and
leisure time group.

Donald Henry McGannon was born in the
South Bronx on September 9, 1920 to Robert E.
McGannon, a New York City fire department captain, and Margaret (Schmidt) McGannon. The
family regularly spent their summers in Norwalk,
Connecticut, where Donald, his father, and a
brother built six houses with their own hands.
Each house was constructed during the summer
and sold in the fall. Donald worked a newspaper
route while attending parochial schools in the
Bronx and financed his undergradute education
at Fordham College by selling coal and fuel oil.
Because his father wanted him to be a lawyer,
after obtaining his B.A. degree in 1940, at nineteen, he enrolled at Fordham Law School. Mc-
Gannon's studies were soon interrupted by World
War II, however, and he joined the Coast Artillery Corps of the United States Army in 1941.
Discharged with the rank of major in 1946, he
returned to Fordham and was awarded the LL.B.
degree in 1947. McGannon immediately set up
practice with two other young lawyers in a small
Park Place office in New York City, but he moved
to Norwalk to join the law firm of Paul Connery
later in 1947.

McGannon was soon well established in the
legal profession and in 1950 he opened his own
office in Norwalk. In 1951 McGannon's older
brother introduced him to Chris J. Witting, then
director of broadcasting for the DuMont Television Network. The two men established an immediate rapport, and, after a few meetings,
Witting induced McGannon to give up law and
become one of his assistants. The television industry was new and growing, McGannon was an
eager and fast learner, and in 1952 he became
general manager and assistant director of the
network. He retained that position until January
1955, when, a few months before DuMont gave
up television, he joined the Westinghouse Broadcasting Company (WBC) as vice-president and
general executive. Witting had become head of
WBC in 1953, and when he moved up to the
vice-presidency of Westinghouse Electric later in
1955, McGannon became president of WBC.

Unlike the networks, which are primarily sup-
pliers of programs to their affiliated stations, the
Westinghouse Broadcasting Company is fundamentally a broadcasting organization that owns
and operates radio and television stations. In addition it produces taped programs that are supplied to its own station, and frequently to other
stations. While a network pays its affiliates to
carry its programs because it gets its revenues
from selling network advertising time, Westinghouse subscribers pay the company for the programs and then sell their own advertising. In
1963 McGannon announced that Westinghouse
would henceforth be known as Group W, not
WBC, to emphasize its distinct character as neither a network nor an aggregate of individual
stations but as "a third force in broadcasting"
made up of stations with "a common philosophy
about broadcasting."

As part of that philosophy, the stations of
Group W program more adventurous educational
and cultural fare than is normally found on commercial television. Westinghouse has syndicated
a number of popular entertainment programs, including the *Merv Griffin Show* (now a CBS network presentation); its current variety programs,
the *Mike Douglas Show* and the *David Frost
Show*; and color specials starring Griffin, Douglas,
or Frost. But its documentaries on national and
international affairs and its classical music series
are even more characteristic. After the first Sputnik, Westinghouse presented a series of children's
programs on mathematics entitled *Adventures in
Numbers and Space* that starred Bil Baird and
his puppets. Four years later the company joined
with National Educational Television and broadcasters in Great Britain, Australia, and Canada to
produce and distribute throughout the world a
series of TV documentaries to promote international understanding. In 1963 Westinghouse offered a pretaped TV debut of *The Advocate* on
the same night the play opened on Broadway,
and two years later it presented *Postmark Zero* a
few days after its Broadway debut.

McGannon delivered his first jolt to the networks immediately after he became president of

Westinghouse, when he severed the network affiliations of the company's five radio stations, four of which carried NBC programs. Pointing to the increased demand for local advertising, he contended that the local stations were losing money by carrying network shows. Convinced that radio listeners wanted local service, not network, programs, he set out to upgrade the standards of news reports on Westinghouse radio. To avoid "rip and read" news—items read right as they come off the wire services—McGannon staffed each station with local reporters and rewrite men and encouraged the programming of local interpretive and editorial news presentations. He also established a Washington news bureau to search out and prepare news specifically slanted to the markets serviced by each station. In 1965 McGannon created one of the first all-news radio stations in the country at WINS, which had formerly been one of many New York City rock 'n' roll stations. Since that time Westinghouse has converted KYW, Philadelphia, and KFWB, Los Angeles, to all-news. Group W's news service now includes staffed bureaus in Europe and Southeast Asia as well as in Washington.

For a number of years McGannon has carried on a running battle with the networks over the number and quality of network commercial breaks. In 1966 Group W's Baltimore station, WJZ-TV, refused to carry ABC's *Batman* series because it contained four rather than the usual three one-minute commercial breaks. McGannon wrote a letter to the president of the network strongly urging him to abandon that practice in future programming. A year later he threatened not to carry NBC's Tuesday and Saturday prime time movies if the network carried out its plan to increase the number of one-minute commercial breaks from fourteen to sixteen. Even though McGannon had once served as chairman of the National Association of Broadcasters' Television Code he decided to withdraw Group W's TV stations from the code in 1969, because he felt that it was allowing too much laxity to networks in the advertising of intimate feminine products and in the "piggy-backing" of commercials. ("Piggy-backing" refers to the practice of inserting two or more commercial messages into the time slot allotted for one commercial.) When CBS and NBC announced rate hikes for affiliates and increased time for commercials later that year McGannon complained to the Federal Communications Commission. His testimony to the FCC had a considerable influence on the commission's 1970 decision to cut back the number of prime time hours allotted to network programs from four hours to three, effective in the fall of 1971.

McGannon directs the activities of all Group W subsidiaries, serving as chairman of the boards of Group W Productions, Inc., Group W Program Sales, Inc., Seven-Up Bottlers of Fairfield County, Inc., Seven-Up Bottlers of Puerto Rico, Inc., and the company's cable television interests: Clearview of Georgia, Inc., Florida Antennavision, Inc., Clearview of Florida, Inc., Micro-Relay, Inc., and CATV Enterprises, Inc. In 1967 he founded and

DONALD H. McGANNON

became board chairman of the Westinghouse Learning Corporation, a subsidiary of Westinghouse Electric. Among the new corporation's activities are running Job Corps training centers, designing high school buildings, and creating and selling Project PLAN, a computer-run education program that allows children to learn at their own speeds. When the Westinghouse Electric Corporation was reorganized in 1969 McGannon became one of the four top men in the organization as president of its broadcasting, learning and leisure time group.

Since 1956 Group W under McGannon's leadership has sponsored six Public Service Programming Conferences for radio and television broadcasters from around the nation. At the most recent conference, entitled *The Unfinished American Revolution,* Hubert H. Humphrey was the featured speaker, and experts on race relations, transportation, crime, housing, and air and water pollution met with the broadcasters to discuss problems of urban America. A pioneer in the recruitment of minority groups for careers in radio and television, McGannon helped to set up the Broadcast Skills Bank in conjunction with the Urban League in 1965. In recognition of his services to broadcasting McGannon has received the CARTA Award of the Catholic Apostolate of Radio, Television and Advertising (1962), the Distinguished Service Award of the National Association of Broadcasters (1964), and the Trustees Award of the National Academy of Television Arts and Sciences (1968).

The Westinghouse executive has been active in many civic activities outside the broadcasting industry. A former member of the Connecticut Democratic State Committee, he is chairman of the Connecticut Commission for Higher Education, a trustee of the National Urban League, and a member of several governmental agencies and groups. He is a director and founder of Sacred Heart University in Bridgeport, Connecticut and a trustee or adviser of New York University, the New York Law School, Georgetown University, Ithaca College, Fordham University, Emerson College, and Marymount College. He is a member and former chairman of the National Book Committee, chairman of the American Heritage Foundation, a trustee of the American Film Institute, a director of the Advertising Research Foundation, and an associate member of the Foreign Policy Association.

On August 22, 1942 Donald H. McGannon married Patricia H. Burke. With their thirteen children the McGannons live in a large Victorian house in New Canaan, Connecticut. Retaining the construction skills that he learned as a youngster, McGannon several years ago built a fireplace in the house and supervised the construction of a swimming pool and a hardtop driveway on the grounds. Tall and well built, McGannon dresses conservatively and seems easygoing and affable despite his relentless drive and energy. A faithful Roman Catholic, he is a Knight of the Order of Malta and other honorary papal orders. McGannon holds honorary doctorates from half a dozen universities, including Fordham, St. Bonaventure, and Fairfield.

References

N Y Sunday News II p15 F 7 '65 por
Printers Ink 253:80+ D 9 '55; 264:42+
S 26 '58

Who's Who in America, 1970-71

McGILL, WILLIAM J(AMES)

Feb. 27, 1922- University president; psychologist
Address: b. Office of the President, Columbia University, New York 10027; h. 60 Morningside Dr., New York 10027

The sixteenth president of Columbia University is William J. McGill, a leading research psychologist and former chancellor of the University of California at San Diego. As San Diego chancellor from 1968 to 1970, Dr. McGill served a stormy apprenticeship in university administration, battling both radical student disrupters and Governor Ronald Reagan. But his record so impressed the selection committee at Columbia University that they chose him to succeed interim president Andrew W. Cordier, effective September 1, 1970. (Columbia had been without a permanent president since 1968, when Grayson Kirk resigned in the wake of bloody clashes between students and police that closed the university for six weeks.) McGill had been a psychology professor at Columbia for nine years, part of the time as department head, until 1965, when he went to San Diego to set up the new university's psychology department.

A Roman Catholic, William James McGill is the first non-Protestant president in Columbia's 217-year history. He was born in New York City, in his grandmother's house at 133d Street and Third Avenue, on February 27, 1922. His family later moved to the Bronx. McGill's father, William E. McGill, was a musician born in Liverpool, England, who earned his living as an arranger

and copyist for network radio before his death in 1967. McGill's mother, Edna (Rankin) McGill, lives in the Fordham section of the Bronx.

A scholarship student, McGill attended Cathedral Boys High School in New York City, from which he graduated in 1939. "It was a school for poor, bright boys, and it was there that every line of my life was laid down," he later told an interviewer. Working his way through Fordham College by selling neckties at Macy's, McGill earned an A.B. degree in 1943 in psychology and was elected to Phi Beta Kappa. After graduation, he worked for three years as a controls engineer in a Bronx concern and then returned to Fordham for graduate studies in experimental psychology. Specializing in the statistical analysis of human behavior, McGill completed his master's degree in 1947 at Fordham and his doctorate at Harvard University in 1953.

While a graduate student McGill had been an instructor at Fordham, a teaching fellow at Harvard, and an instructor at Boston College. In 1951 he joined the staff of the Lincoln Laboratory at the Massachusetts Institute of Technology, where he did research on a computer air defense system. He was named an assistant professor of psychology at M.I.T. in 1954.

In 1956 McGill returned to New York City to become an assistant professor of psychology at Columbia. He was promoted to associate professor in 1958 and professor in 1960. In 1959 he began teaching in the graduate faculty of pure science as well, and from 1961 to 1963 he was chairman of the Columbia department of psychology. McGill has recalled that his dissatisfaction with Columbia began while he served as department head, a position that he discovered had only limited powers. "I couldn't convince the senior men to interest themselves in any new developments in my discipline, such as the informational sciences, or to recruit young men I knew were available," McGill once told an interviewer, as quoted by Kenneth Lamott in the New York *Times Magazine* (August 23, 1970).

McGill remained at Columbia until 1965, when he was asked to help establish the psychology department at the newly opened branch of the University of California at San Diego. Convinced that both Columbia and New York City were on the wane and that "the center of gravity was shifting westward," McGill accepted the post. In addition to teaching at San Diego he served as a member and chairman of the committee on educational policy and as a member of the academic council of the academic senate and of the chancellor's senate council. In 1968 he was elected chairman of the state-wide academic senate, but he relinquished the post that summer when he was named chancellor of the University of California at San Diego.

Immediately after McGill was appointed chancellor in July 1968 he became embroiled in controversy over the reappointment of San Diego's Marxist philosophy professor, Herbert Marcuse, a hero of the New Left. Despite much conservative opposition from within and without the university system, McGill insisted on the right to reappointment of Marcuse, whose contract had to be renewed annually since he was over the official retirement age. "There will be no inquisition aimed at political heretics while I am chancellor," McGill told the academic senate.

The Marcuse affair, McGill's later defense of San Diego alumna Angela Davis' right to teach at UCLA, and his unequivocal libertarian stand on other cases of academic freedom brought him into conflict with Governor Ronald Reagan, Superintendent of Schools Max Rafferty, the American Legion, the Board of Regents, and the citizenry of La Jolla, the conservative suburban community where the San Diego campus is located. But critics emerged from the left as well as the political right, because, although he accepted the validity of student protest and demonstration, McGill was not willing to let violent student radicals disrupt his campus. During his chancellorship two student strikes and four sit-ins took place on the San Diego campus. McGill's tactics for handling such disturbances were firm but restrained, and he never called in the police. One of his most successful techniques was the serving of legal documents to troublemakers that banned them from the campus for two weeks. Often he prevented outbreaks by confronting angry or disturbed students and discussing their grievances. Whenever feasible, their demands were met. For example, McGill directed plans for the creation of a new university school that would stress the study of minority peoples. Scheduled to open in September 1971 with liberal admission standards, the school was expected to have an enrollment one-third black, one-third Mexican-American, and one-third "other."

As an academic, McGill had left Columbia in 1965 because he believed it was running "downhill"; a few years later, as a university administrator, he must have found it one of the most challenging of institutions. In 1968 the large urban university was rocked by dissent arising largely from student unhappiness over the university's relations with the Harlem community that it abuts and over its indirect support of the Vietnam war through its military research contracts. In April radical S.D.S. (Students for a Democratic Society) members and their supporters seized five buildings and held them for several days, until some 1,000 policemen were called in to oust them. As a protest against the use of police, a general student-faculty strike was declared that closed down the university for the remainder of the term.

That August, Grayson Kirk, its president, resigned, and the board of trustees quickly named Andrew W. Cordier, dean of the School of International Affairs and former Under Secretary General of the United Nations, as acting president. A year later Cordier was appointed president, but with the understanding that his tenure would be temporary because he wished to return to his post as dean. Meanwhile, a student-faculty panel chosen by the board of trustees searched for eighteen months before it found a permanent president for Columbia. In August 1969 a formal offer was rejected by Alexander Heard, the chan-

WILLIAM J. MCGILL

cellor of Vanderbilt University. Finally, on February 2, 1970, the university announced the appointment of McGill.

Late in the summer of 1970 McGill took up his duties at Columbia. That September the fall term began without incident, and near the end of the month the new president issued a set of guidelines for campus political activities during the coming Congressional election campaign, designed to protect the tax-exempt status of the university by forbidding the free use of campus facilities for campaigning.

The gravest problem facing President McGill when he took office on September 1, 1970 was that of the university's finances. Since 1965 Columbia's budget had doubled, largely because of inflation, and the projected budget deficit for the 1970-71 school year was $15,300,000. In September McGill instituted a thoroughgoing analysis of the university's finances and issued a memorandum to all heads of schools asking for a 10 percent cutback in administrative costs for 1970-71. By the end of the year the president had cancelled his own traditional inaugural ceremony as a token austerity measure, allocating the saved $18,000 to financial aid to students, and he had decided to phase out the theatre arts division of the School of Arts. On January 10, 1971 he announced a five-year austerity program designed to balance the university's budget by 1973. With its cuts in administrative services and academic programs, the plan temporarily halted Columbia's growth.

In February 1971, when militant students tried to disrupt classes in political and Puerto Rican history and wrecked several offices in the School of International Relations, President McGill swiftly condemned the disturbances as infringements on academic freedom. His condemnation came after the university senate failed to denounce the disruptions. "I did not spend the last three years in bitter public struggle defending the teaching rights of Linus Pauling, Herbert Marcuse, and Angela Davis, only to watch such rights trampled at Columbia," McGill wrote in a letter to the president of the senate.

Despite his distress of such acts of what he calls "self-righteous moralism" by student militants, McGill remains optimistic about the upheaval on today's campuses. He sees youth culture as a still poorly defined reaction, taking the form of romantic alienation and protest, against the depersonalization of modern technological society. Yet McGill believes that their movement is of the utmost importance and that the present era may be looked back upon as a turning point in history comparable to the Renaissance or the Industrial Revolution. He has said that radical student revolutionaries are not much of a problem in themselves: what is to be feared is the possible repression from conservative forces in the community if militants gain influence over masses of discontented students.

In testimony before the President's Commission on Campus Unrest and elsewhere, McGill has estimated that from a third to a half of the present student population are alienated. Since he believes that the leading cause is the pressure exerted on them to stay out of the work force and remain in school for ever lengthening periods, he has called repeatedly for major reforms in the national educational system to provide freer movement between university and professional life. He advocates core curriculum studies of varying lengths of time geared to career needs with provision for the student's reentry into college after periods of work experience.

As an academic, McGill is regarded as one of the nation's leading quantitative psychologists on the strength of his contributions to mathematical psychology, information processing, and the study of sensory mechanisms. A Columbia psychologist has described him as "perhaps the world authority on reaction time." The author of over thirty-five professional studies and reviews, McGill has served as associate editor of the *Journal of the Mathematical Society* and *Perception and Psychophysics* and as consulting editor of the *Psychological Bulletin* and *Psychometrika*.

McGill is a member of the Society of Experimental Psychologists, the governing board of the Psychonomic Society, the board of trustees of the Psychometric Society, the American Statistical Association, the Biometric Society, the Society of Experimental Psychologists, the New York Academy of Sciences, and Sigma Xi. He is a fellow of the American Psychological Association and the American Association for the Advancement of Science. McGill has received honorary degrees from Columbia University, Fordham University, and the Catholic University of America, a Fordham achievement award, and an American Civil Liberties Union award for his contribution to academic freedom.

On June 14, 1948 William J. McGill married Ann Rowe of Boston. They have two children, a daughter, Rowena (Mrs. Thomas B. Springer), and a son, William. The McGills live at 60 Morningside Drive, the official residence of all Columbia presidents since the turn of the century. Interviewers have found McGill to be a vigorous, articulate, and open man with a sense of humor. He is stockily built, has white crew-cut hair, and favors tweed jackets and striped ties. In his spare time he tinkers with radio equipment.

References

N Y Times p1+ F 3 '70 por
N Y Times Mag p26+ Ag 23 '70 pors
International Who's Who, 1970-71
Who's Who in American College and University Administration, 1970-71

McINTIRE, CARL

May 17, 1906- Protestant clergyman
Address: b. Twentieth Century Reformation Center, Collingswood, N.J. 08108

American Protestantism's self-styled "number one anti-Communist" is the Rev. Carl McIntire, a firebrand radio evangelist who preaches an amalgam of fundamentalist Christianity and hawkish patriotism. McIntire, a former Presbyterian minister, founded the schismatic Bible Presbyterian Church "for Bible-believing Presbyterians" in 1936, and twelve years later he organized the International Council of Christian Churches to counter the "liberalism and apostasy" of that "ecumenical monster," the World Council of Churches. Since 1957 his daily radio program the Twentieth Century Reformation Hour, has been alerting Bible Belt listeners to the dangers of loose interpretation of Scripture; the theological "modernism" of mainstream Protestantism, with its "social Gospel"; the lust for power of the "fascist" Roman Catholic Church; government-imposed socialization of life in the United States; any and every form of external coexistence with Communism; and the infiltration of Communist influences internally, in church, state, school, and family. In recent years McIntire has mounted in Washington, D.C. a series of Vietnam war pep rallies called Marches for Victory. In terms of real estate, the archconservative preacher's bastions are in Collingswood, New Jersey, Cape May, New Jersey, and Cape Canaveral, Florida. Among the institutions he operates are a seminary and several colleges dedicated to training "Christian warriors" for the "holy war against Communism." Rejecting the political label of "extreme right-winger" that some critics would impose on him, McIntire categorizes himself as "the servant of the Lord in a very Holy Cause."

Carl McIntire, the son of a Presbyterian minister, was born in Ypsilanti, Michigan on May 17, 1906. During his childhood the family moved to Oklahoma, where his grandmother had been a missionary to the Choctaw Indians, and he grew up in Durant in that state. "Young Carl, in the true Scottish Presbyterian tradition, was reared on oatmeal and the Shorter Catechism," his official biography states. "The Bible was read every day and the family would pray together."

McIntire prepared for a career in law before "God called" him "to help mankind." He did his undergraduate studies at Park College in Parkville, Missouri, a liberal arts school related to the

Presbyterian Church. In 1927, upon taking his degree at Park, he enrolled at Princeton University, as his father had done before him. At Princeton he enthusiastically lined up behind one of his professors, fundamentalist theologian J. Gresham Machen, in dissenting from "modernist" trends in the curriculum of the Princeton Theological Seminary. When Machen left Princeton to found Westminster Seminary in Chestnut Hill, Pennsylvania, McIntire followed him, in 1929.

After taking his divinity degree at Westminster Seminary, in 1931, McIntire was ordained in the Presbyterian Church U.S.A. (now the United Presbyterian Church U.S.A.). As a Presbyterian minister he loudly criticized the church's liberal missionaries, protested what he alleged to be its discrimination against conservative missionaries, withheld financial support from its national office, and refused to resign from a rump foreign mission board. In 1935 an ecclesiastical court found him guilty of "sowing dissension within the church," as Rev. Dr. Kenneth G. Neigh, general secretary of the Board of Missions of the United Presbyterian Church, has recounted, and "his ministerial credentials were withdrawn."

Soon after his unfrocking, McIntire made his Bible Presbyterian Church in Collingswood, New Jersey the nucleus of a splinter denomination of the same name, which now embraces fifty-five congregations throughout the United States. In 1941 he formed his conservative alternative to the National Council of Churches, the American Council of Christian Churches, which now contains about fifteen small fundamentalist denominations with a total membership, according to widely differing estimates, of between 500,000 and 1,500,000. In the 1960's the A.C.C.C., seeking a more "responsible" public stance (but no change in basic positions), began to reject its flamboyantly militant founder, and in 1969 the membership voted him off the organization's executive board. He remains president of the International Council of Christian Churches, founded by him in 1948 and now numbering at least sixty-four member denominations around the world.

In the late 1950's and early 1960's McIntire devoted most of his nationally conspicuous energies to combatting the amelioration of Soviet-United States relations. For example, he led a protest in Washington, D.C. against an official government reception planned for Soviet Premier Nikita S. Khrushchev—"an act offensive to our God and a violation of His holy law"—in September 1959; participated in a rally in Rio de Janeiro, Brazil in June 1960 against the inclusion of two delegates from the Soviet Union in the tenth international congress of the World Baptist Alliance; challenged the Russian Orthodox Church's application for membership in the World Council of Churches in November 1961; and led protest rallies when a delegation of Soviet churchmen visited the United States as guests of the National Council of Churches in February and March 1963.

For his 1,800-member congregation in Collingswood, New Jersey, McIntire built a new, large,

REV. CARL McINTIRE

$600,000 brick church in 1960. A few blocks down Haddon Avenue from the church is a three-story building, a former school, renamed the Twentieth Century Reformation Center. The center houses McIntire's office; a reception room; a library; the I.C.C.C. office; a mail room; a computer room, where a mailing list is filed on IBM cards; and the studio where McIntire tapes his extemporaneous daily thirty-minute broadcasts for distribution to several hundred radio stations in the Bible Belt of the South, the Midwest, and the Southwest. Behind the center is the printing plant where the weekly Christian Beacon (circulation about 134,000) and McIntire's tracts are run off. Across the street is the Reformation Bookstore, and behind the bookstore are the offices of International Christian Relief, the I.C.C.C.'s philanthropic arm, which distributes food, clothing, and medicine in mission lands. McIntire's denomination also operates a small high school in Collingswood, Faith Christian High School.

A total of almost 100 persons, many of them elderly women and all of them recruited from McIntire's flock, man the varied operations. Hugh R. Tashereau reported on the ambience of the Collingswood congregation in a letter to the Washington Post (January 3, 1964): "Whether aware of it or not, these people live in a sealed community, a shut-off world wherein one voice, that of their pastor, speaks for all and of all. In the many homes I have visited, I have looked for but never seen any evidence of newspapers or other regular means of communication."

In 1963 McIntire purchased the Admiral Hotel, a seaside resort hotel in Cape May, New Jersey, renamed the Christian Admiral, and turned it into a Bible conference center and vacation hotel for his followers. Behind the hotel he built the small administration building of Shelton College, a fundamentalist Bible school with a faculty of twenty-nine and an enrollment of 165 or so, and a short distance down the beach he bought a second hotel, Congress Hall, for dormitory and additional conference space. Other acquisitions, of beachside cottages and houses, brought the assessed value off McIntire's property in Cape May to $1,500,000. As many as 50,000 guests at a time, paying a minimum of $11 a day, have attended conventions in Cape May.

McIntire is the president of Faith Theological Seminary in Elkins Park, Pennsylvania, across the state border from Collingswood. The seminary owns radio station WXUR in Media, Pennsylvania, which used to carry McIntire's broadcasts live. In the late 1960's major civic and religious groups, led by the Greater Philadelphia Council of Churches, complained to the Federal Communications Commission that the station was serving as an outlet for sentiments that were, as one clergyman described them, "highly racist, anti-Semitic, anti-Negro, anti-Roman Catholic." In July 1970 the F.C.C. announced that WXUR's license would not be renewed, because of consistent violation of the fairness doctrine, which requires a station to provide persons it attacks with time for reply.

Another serious blow was dealt to McIntire in January 1971, when the New Jersey State Board of Higher Education stripped Shelton College in Cape May of its accreditation because of "substantial academic deficiencies coupled with a lack of institutional integrity and administrative competence" and a lack of "candor in dealing with the public, students, and the state." But McIntire parried quickly and with aplomb. In the February 25, 1971 issue of the *Christian Beacon* he announced that Shelton would continue to operate despite the loss of its power to grant degrees. It would do so, he explained, as part of a three-college conglomerate that would include a small California campus with degree-granting power: Linda Vista Baptist Bible College in El Cajun, recently acquired by McIntire and renamed Southern California Reformation College.

The third campus in the conglomerate is to be established in Cape Canaveral, Florida, where McIntire acquired title to a multi-million-dollar real estate package in February 1971. The property, dubbed the Reformation Freedom Center by the preacher, is on a 300-acre tract of land at the gates of the Kennedy Space Center and extending from the Atlantic Ocean to the Banana River. It includes the former Cape Kennedy Hilton, a 200-room convention center renamed the Gateway to the Stars Freedom Center Hotel; a 2,500-seat conference center; three office buildings; and a luxury apartment development. Like the Cape May complex, the Reformation Freedom Center in Cape Canaveral will have a religious museum, anti-Communist seminars and other religio-patriotic educational services, and retirement facilities for the faithful.

The welcome accorded McIntire in the space-center town has been mixed. Roger W. Dobson, the president of the local Chamber of Commerce, was among those with a positive response: "We were down to about 4,000 population in the 1970 census from a peak of 7,000 before the space cutbacks. Now we expect the population to double in the next couple of years. He will not only bring people and business but strengthen the moral fiber

of the area." The Rev. James Dale, minister of the Rockledge United Methodist Church, was of another mind: "Here in this place in which mankind produced a scientific feat that captured the imagination of the whole planet, we are now witnessing . . . a throwback to the dark ages."

To signal the beginning of a "spiritual revival" that would "turn this nation from revolution, hippiedom, and slavery," McIntire conceived and helped mount "Victory in the Sky," the launching on July 4, 1970 of 113,000 red, white, and blue balloons from 120 locations throughout the United States. In Washington, D.C. in 1970 and 1971 he organized several of the pro-Vietnam war demonstrations that he calls Marches for Victory. Vice-President Ky of South Vietnam was to have been the main speaker at one of the rallies, in October 1970, but he backed down, probably at the urging of the White House. In July 1971, when President Nixon announced his intention to visit China, McIntire and seventy-five of his followers, armed with Bibles and United States flags, held a protest demonstration on the steps of the Capitol in Washington.

"The fear we have against full war," McIntire explained after one of his Marches for Victory, "is a fear that has been instigated by Communist propaganda. But that fear has no weight with men of God. After all, the Bible tells us that Christ is coming back to carry the dead away. Now, with him coming back, how could it be possible that the world is going to be blown up?"

McIntire is a big man, over six feet tall and bulky, who moves, according to Paul W. Valentine of the Washington *Post* (October 2, 1970), "with the immense precision of an elephant, his frame hidden in a floppy blue suit." He has what has been described as a "jowly" face, with a sharp Roman nose and clear light-blue eyes, surmounted by wavy, graying hair. Interviewers and other close observers of McIntire testify that he is a "personable, pleasant conversationalist" with a "hearty" hello and a heartier handshake, a calm voice, soft though resonant, and "the polished grace of a successful businessman." Paul W. Valentine described him on the stump: "McIntire . . . stares intensely at his audience. . . . He hacks the air briefly with his right hand. His lips move with an economy of motion. Words in a flat, steady Oklahoma accent issue from a small mouth. His face, transfixed with a kind of flaccid energy, is interrupted only occasionally by a terse smile."

Carl McIntire and his wife, the former Fairy Davis, have been living in the same house in Collingswood for thirty-two years. They have three grown children, two daughters and a son. The son, Thomas Carl McIntire, assists his father in his ministry and is generally considered to be his heir apparent in the leadership of the Twentieth Century Reformation. Carl McIntire does not smoke or drink alcoholic beverages or coffee and, with the exception of fishing, he seeks no recreation outside of his work. He does insist, however, that nothing deprive him of the refreshment of his nightly, sound sleep. The circle of McIntire's personal friends extends abroad, to include such men as the Rev. Ian Paisley, the Protestant Northern Irish M.P. and anti-Catholic leader. The title "Dr." with which McIntire is often addressed by his followers derives from two honorary doctoral degrees he has received, from Bob Jones University and the Toronto Baptist Theological Seminary. McIntire's various enterprises are financed by several million dollars contributed annually by his followers, (usually in small donations mailed weekly or monthly), but the doughty preacher himself receives no income other than his $15,000 salary as pastor of the Bible Presbyterian Church in Collingswood. McIntire is registered as a Republican.

References

N Y Post p27 Mr 31 '64 por
N Y Times p36 O 3 '70 por; p15 Mr 13 '71 por
Nat Observer p5 O 31 '66 por
Newsday A p4 Ap 17 '70 pors
Turner, William W. Power on the Right (1971)

McKAYLE, DONALD (COHEN)

July 6, 1930- Choreographer-director
Address: b. c/o William Morris Agency, 151 El Camino, Beverly Hills, Calif. 90212; h. 3839 Davana Rd., Sherman Oaks, Calif. 91403

One of America's most distinguished black choreographers, the versatile Donald McKayle is equally at home in the concert dance field, the legitimate theatre, and television, films, and nightclubs. His choreography for the musical version of Clifford Odets' *Golden Boy*, starring Sammy Davis Jr., carried "a stupendous theatrical impact," according to one critic, and in 1963 he received the Capezio Dance Award for his "translation of American folk material into theatre dances of interracial cast which faithfully reflect life in our land."

Throughout his career Donald McKayle has worked to gain recognition for black artists, as artists, and has explored the themes of his cultural identity to find their universal message. He has written: "One cannot help but be moved by these forces, no matter what one's birthright, and they become national and international treasures, for art knows no boundaries." He has fought against the injustices and prejudice suffered by Negro dancers and choreographers in the theatre, ballet, and concert dance fields, but he has always maintained an integrated company. "The need to categorize I consider a point of contention," he has said. "To me, one's alliance is determined by the manner of one's work."

Donald Cohen McKayle was born in New York City on July 6, 1930. With his West Indian parents, Philip Augustus McKayle, a machinist, and Eva Wilhemina (Cohen) McKayle, and his brother, Philip Jr., he grew up and attended school in the Bronx. After graduating from De Witt Clinton High School in 1946 he enrolled at City College

of New York, but left after his sophomore year to take dance classes and perform full time. McKayle decided to make dance his career after seeing his first dance concert, a performance by Pearl Primus. He began studying during his last year in high school as a scholarship student at the New Dance Group. Although his teachers have included Martha Graham, Merce Cunningham, Nenette Charisse, and Karel Shook, his most enduring loyalty has been to the New Dance Group, a school where egalitarian policies and all varieties of dance have been stressed.

Donald McKayle made his debut as a dancer in the spring of 1948, appearing in the works of Sophie Maslow and Jean Erdman at the Mansfield Theatre. For several years he appeared with other choreographers, including William Bales, Anna Sokolow, and Mary Anthony, and with Martha Graham during her 1955 tour of the Orient. He also danced in the Broadway shows *Bless You All* (1951), *House of Flowers* (1955), *Copper and Brass* (1957), and *West Side Story* (1957). Commenting on his performing style in 1954, dance critic Walter Terry said that he commanded attention "through the beauty of his movement, through a gentle but emotionally charged presence, and through a quality which I can best describe by saying that it was rather like an invitation to join him in the wonders of motion."

Like many modern dancers, McKayle started to choreograph almost as soon as he began performing. Along with Esta Beck, who later became his wife, he gave four pieces in a Stage for Dancers concert at the Henry Street Playhouse in the fall of 1950, sharing the program with choreographers Lucas Hoving, Rena Gluck, and Miriam Cole. Among McKayle's works at that concert was *Saturday's Child*, based on a poem by Countee Cullen that was spoken by the choreographer himself. The piece demonstrated what were to remain two of his strongest qualities as an artist: an appreciation of his many-faceted black heritage, and an ability to create universally sympathetic characterizations out of that background. *Dance* magazine critic Doris Hering commented on that "bitter poem of an underprivileged child" in July 1951: "It gave one the feeling that Mr. McKayle had grasped the one stabbing moment of articulateness in an otherwise silent and beaten being."

McKayle had begun work on his celebrated *Games* in 1950, and after some revision it had its official première at the Hunter College Playhouse in May 1951, in a joint concert with Daniel Nagrin. Inspired by the street games and violence of the choreographer's own childhood, "the shadowed happiness of little city children," *Games* was divided into three sections: Play, Hunger, and Fear. McKayle had discovered that those three themes dominated the songs and games of children, transcending historical periods and geographical boundaries. Instead of dancing in *Games*, McKayle, with a female partner—originally June Lewis and later Shawneequa Baker and others—leaned out of a sketchy prop window and sang the familiar rhymes. Margaret Lloyd of the *Chris-*

DONALD MCKAYLE

tian Science Monitor (December 8, 1956) called *Games* "a minor masterpiece." It is still performed at McKayle company concerts, and in the fall of 1969 it entered the repertory of Eliot Feld's American Ballet Company.

Using Negro spirituals, early in 1952 McKayle choreographed another of his documentary works, *Her Name Was Harriet*. Based on the life of Harriet Tubman, the escaped slave and heroine of the pre-Civil War Underground Railroad movement, the dance had both a dancer and a singer portraying the main character. Critic Robert Sabin, writing in the *Dance Observer* (March 1952), found the dance "uneven," but said it revealed McKayle's "warmth, a deep humanity, and a creative imagination that never seems to fail him."

Nocturne, set to music of the eccentric New York street musician and composer, Moondog, and first performed at Jacob's Pillow in the summer of 1953, was a sinuous, pure-dance work for nine dancers. With its tranquility, it represented a point of departure for McKayle, most of whose previous works had been outcries against social injustice. It has been performed by the Batsheva Dance Company of Israel and the Repertory Dance Theatre of the University of Utah.

McKayle based his next important concert work, *Rainbow Round My Shoulder*, on the Southern institution of the prison chain gang. Seven men toiled in powerful and sweaty sequences of movement, pausing to dream of their girl friends, wives, or mothers. Symbolizing the chain gang's lost freedom, the female dream figure was played by Mary Hinkson. Like *Games*, *Rainbow Round My Shoulder* ended in a crescendo of violence, when one prisoner tried to escape and was shot. At the dance's première, which took place on May 10, 1959 at the 92d Street YM-YWHA in New York City, the black folksinger Leon Bibb sang the accompanying work songs.

His lifelong fascination with jazz led McKayle to choreograph *District Storyville* (1962), a narrative work set in New Orleans' famed red-light district, where jazz was born in street funeral processions and brothels. To Walter Terry of the

New York *Herald Tribune* (April 23, 1962) it was "fast, funny, hot and lowdown," and "an irresistible work of music-theater." Composed by Dorothea Freitag, the score was a pastiche of early music by Sidney Bechet, Duke Ellington, and Jellyroll Morton. Requiring a full evening to perform, *Reflections in the Park* (1964) represented a collaboration between the choreographer and the jazz musician Gary McFarland, in which McKayle tried to make "a contemporary statement of love, dreams, cruelties, and fantasies in the heart of a big city." Carmen de Lavallade and Gus Solomons Jr. were the couple who on their stroll through the park encountered a variety of characters and situations. In the New York *Herald Tribune* (March 7, 1964) Walter Terry wrote: "Each vignette is expertly drawn in dance terms. . . . To project these scenes, these incidents, these contrasting (yet curiously related) feelings, Mr. McKayle has come up with quite probably the best movement patterns he has ever invented."

Whatever his other commitments, Donald McKayle has always managed to devote some of his time to the legitimate theatre. In 1959 he was called in as director to salvage the all-Negro Harold Arlen-Johnny Mercer musical *Free and Easy*, which was foundering after its European opening. He had already staged nightclub sequences for Rita Moreno, Helen Gallagher, and Harry Belafonte. He choreographed incidental dances for the 1962 summer season of the New York Shakespeare Festival, and the following year he directed the gospel show *Trumpets of the Lord*. About that time, when he was reaching his peak as a concert choreographer, he was drawn increasingly into more lucrative assignments for Broadway, television, and films, but although he was to become in great demand in his second career, he never abandoned concert dance.

For his staging of the dances and the much acclaimed prize fight scene in the Sammy Davis Jr. show *Golden Boy* (1964), McKayle was nominated for an Antoinette Perry Award. In the years that followed he choreographed *A Time for Singing* (1966), *I'm Solomon* (1968), and in London *The Four Musketeers* (1967). His long list of television credits includes shows for Bill Cosby, Leslie Uggams, Dick Van Dyke, and specials dealing with soul music, jazz, and the 1920's. McKayle also staged the dances for the perennial Christmas opera *Amahl and the Night Visitors* (1964), and has mounted most of his own concert works for television. He did his first film choreography for the 20th Century-Fox version of James Earl Jones's stage hit *The Great White Hope*.

In 1967 McKayle produced another ambitious full-length concert work, *Black New World*, incorporating *Rainbow*, *Storyville*, and his Harriet Tubman piece, retitled *They Called Her Moses*, and some of his new material. *Black New World* reviewed the history of the Negro in America from slavery to the contemporary *Freedom Rock*. Although Walter Terry in the New York *World Journal Tribune* (February 9, 1967) pronounced it "a stunning job of balancing dignity with high jinx, tragedy with boisterous comedy, nobility with lowdown razzmatazz," Doris Hering of *Dance Magazine* (April 1967) chided the choreographer for allowing "the humanity of his characters to disintegrate before our eyes," with sections resembling a nightclub act. *Black New World* spent much of the following year on tour in Europe, playing at a number of festivals and at London's Strand Theatre.

In turning to more abstract themes in his concert work of recent years, McKayle has encountered almost unanimous disapproval from the critics. His *Daughters of the Garden,* to music of Ernest Bloch, was originally choreographed when he was teaching at Israel's Batsheva Dance Company in 1964, and later was mounted for the Harkness Ballet as well as for his own company under the title *Daughters of Eden.* According to Jean Battey of the Washington *Post* (May 8, 1965), it was derivative of the Martha Graham style of movement, leading her to believe that "McKayle's forte seems to lie not so much in the realm of pure movement as in capturing the spirit of real, contemporary people through his choreography." First exhibited at a 1968 concert at the Brooklyn Academy of Music, his new quasi-Graham pieces, *Wilderness* and *Incantation,* ventured into a maze of symbolic complexities that reviewers found incomprehensible. When *Burst of Fists,* to music of Howard Roberts, was shown at performances of the McKayle company during the New York City Center's 1969 American Dance Season, Don McDonagh of the New York *Times* (May 23, 1969) vetoed it as "disappointingly banal." His earlier, less self-conscious works continued to be impressive, however, and *Games, Rainbow Round My Shoulder, Saturday's Child,* and *I'm On My Way from Black New World* were shown at Clark Center for the Performing Arts in New York's West Side YWCA in June 1968.

Although Donald McKayle has created a number of unsatisfactory dances, his successful ones have been memorable enough to place him in the front rank of American choreographers. His company was chosen to perform at the 1960 Festival of Two Worlds in Spoleto, Italy, and he was one of four choreographers selected in 1964 to do a work for the short-lived but prestigious American Dance Theatre's first season. In 1965 he acted as an ex officio cultural adviser to the government of Tunisia, and he has served on the boards of the New Dance Group, Clark Center, the Dance Circle of Boston, the Society of Stage Directors and Choreographers, and the National Center of Afro-American Artists. McKayle is a founding member of the Black Academy of Arts and Letters, and he has taught at many major studios and colleges.

In the spring of 1970 Donald McKayle moved to Los Angeles after living all his life in New York City. The composer and accompanist C. Bernard Jackson, who had written the scores for two spectacularly unsuccessful McKayle dances, *Arena* and *Blood of the Lamb* in 1963, had become director of the Inner City Cultural Center in Los Angeles, and invited McKayle, together with dancers Janet Collins and Jaime Rogers, to head a new company with headquarters at the Center. Jackson told an interviewer from *Dance Magazine* (June 1970) that the company's aims would be to perform the works of contemporary choreographers and to explore and preserve the heritage of California's minority groups. At the end of 1970, the Inner City Repertory Dance Company was training dancers and planning for a spring debut.

Donald McKayle is tall and handsome, with a powerful build and a smile of epic proportions. By his 1954 marriage to the dancer Esta Beck he has two daughters, Gabrielle and Liane. The couple were divorced several years later, and in May 1965 McKayle married Leah Levin, who dances professionally under the name Lea Vivante. They have a son, Guy Eylon.

References

Dance Mag 37:30 F '63 pors
Chujoy, A., and Manchester, P. W., eds. Dance Encyclopedia (1967)
Cohen, Selma Jeanne, ed. The Modern Dance (1965)
Sorell, Walter, ed. The Dance Has Many Faces (1966)
Who's Who in the East, 1968-69

McMAHON, WILLIAM (mək-mä'un)

Feb. 23, 1908- Prime Minister of the Commonwealth of Australia
Address: Parliament House, Canberra, A.C.T. 2600, Australia

A veteran public servant, William McMahon became the twentieth Prime Minister of the Commonwealth of Australia on March 10, 1971, following his election as leader of the Liberal party. He succeeded John G. Gorton, who resigned as a result of a dispute within government ranks. A member of the Australian Parliament since 1949, McMahon has headed several ministries and served with distinction as Treasurer from 1966 to 1969, and as Foreign Minister from 1969 to 1971. As Prime Minister, McMahon is faced with the formidable task of rebuilding the coalition of Liberal and Country parties, which appeared to have reached its lowest ebb after twenty-two years in power. Since taking office, he has tried to restore Australia's ailing economy and to reorient the nation's foreign policy in view of the winding down of the Vietnam conflict.

William McMahon, the son of William Daniel and Mary McMahon, was born in Sydney on February 23, 1908. His family, one of the oldest and most affluent in Australia, was in the transport business. When he was still a child his parents died, and he was brought up by relatives. He was educated at Sydney Grammar School and at St. Paul's College, University of Sydney, and he reportedly studied theology before deciding on a law career. After attending night classes and obtaining his LL.B. degree from the University of Sydney, McMahon practised until 1939 as a solici-

WILLIAM MCMAHON

tor with Allen, Allen & Hemsley, one of Sydney's oldest law firms. In April 1940 he enlisted in the Australian Army and was appointed a lieutenant in the First Infantry Battalion. During his five-and-one-half years in the army he rose to the rank of major, and after his return to civilian life in 1945 he spent sixteen months traveling in England, France, Canada, and the United States. He then returned to the University of Sydney where he completed a four-year course in economics in two years. He graduated with distinction, earning the bachelor of economics degree, as well as a prize for proficiency and a public service award.

McMahon entered politics in the elections of December 1949, which marked the beginning of the coalition of the Liberal and Country parties under Prime Minister Sir Robert Menzies. As the candidate of the right-of-center Liberal party for the new seat of Lowe, New South Wales in the House of Representatives, McMahon defeated the Labor party candidate, John Burton, a former Minister of External Affairs. He has since been reelected eight times, most recently in 1969. Entering the Menzies government as a junior minister in 1951, McMahon served until 1954 as Minister for the Navy and Minister for Air. From 1954 to 1956 he was Minister for Social Services and from 1956 to 1958 served as Minister for Primary Industry. He was elevated to Cabinet rank in 1958, when he was named Minister for Labor and National Service, and he remained in that post until 1966, when he was appointed Treasurer. From 1964 to 1966 McMahon also served as vice-president of the Executive Council, a body of Cabinet ministers under the chairmanship of the Governor General that deliberates on measures requiring the assent of the British Crown. He was appointed a Privy Councillor in June 1966.

In addition to his regular ministerial posts, McMahon served as acting Minister of Trade and acting Minister in charge of the Australian Commonwealth Scientific and Industrial Research Organization (CSIRO) in 1956, and as acting Minister for National Development in 1959. In 1960

and 1961 he was acting Attorney-General and in the latter year he also served as acting Minister for Territories. He was acting Minister for Labor and National Service in 1957 and again in 1966, 1968, and 1969.

Over the years, McMahon made a number of trips abroad in connection with his ministerial duties. In late 1952, while heading the Navy and Air ministries, he visited Korea and Japan. In the winter of 1957-58 he led the Australian delegation to the Commonwealth Parliamentary Association conference in New Delhi. He attended conferences of the International Labor Organization in Geneva in 1960 and 1964 and presided over the I.L.O. Asian Regional Conference in Melbourne in 1962. In 1964 he visited the United States, England, and the European continent to study labor and industrial developments. As a Cabinet minister McMahon reportedly took part in the decisions, in late 1964 and early 1965, that led to Australia's military involvement in the Vietnam conflict.

When in January 1966 Harold E. Holt succeeded retiring Sir Robert Menzies as Liberal party leader and Prime Minister, McMahon was elected deputy party leader and appointed Treasurer in the Holt Cabinet. As Australia's chief spokesman in economic affairs at a time when the country's mineral wealth was beginning to make an impact on the world market, McMahon displayed considerable talent, and he soon won recognition as the "most effective Treasurer" in Australian history. As Treasurer he attended meetings of the Commonwealth Finance Ministers at Montreal in 1966, Trinidad in 1967, and London in 1968. A member of the board of governors of the International Monetary Fund and World Bank from 1966 to 1969, McMahon took part in its meetings at Washington in 1966 and 1968 and Rio de Janeiro in 1967. He served as chairman of the board of governors meetings of the Asian Development Bank at Manila in 1968 and at Sydney in 1969. McMahon visited Switzerland and West Germany in September 1968 for discussions with banking authorities on the question of raising loans.

In January 1968, a few weeks after the presumed death by drowning of Prime Minister Holt, McMahon tried unsuccessfully to attain the leadership of the Liberal party and the Prime Ministership, which automatically goes to the leader of the ruling party. Although McMahon was considered the most likely contender, his candidacy was vetoed by the Country party leader, John McEwen, who had become interim Prime Minister following Holt's disappearance in December 1967, and whose approval was required under a coalition agreement between the Liberal and Country parties. Because of McEwen's opposition—reportedly as a result of a personal feud—McMahon was removed from consideration, and John G. Gorton, then Minister for Education and Science and government leader in the Senate, was elected as a compromise candidate. When Gorton formed his first Cabinet in February 1968 he reappointed McMahon Treasurer.

After the Liberal-Country party coalition had suffered a setback in the October 1969 election, Gorton was faced in early November by challenges for the party leadership from McMahon and Minister for National Development David Fairbairn, but he defeated both challengers. On November 11, 1969 Gorton removed McMahon as Treasurer and appointed him Minister for External Affairs. The appointment was viewed as a demotion and as an act of reprisal by the Prime Minister against McMahon's efforts to wrest control of the Liberal party from him. McMahon soon upgraded his new position, however, and remained a key figure in government. He reorganized the department along lines of greater efficiency, renaming it the Department of Foreign Affairs and changing his own title to that of Minister of Foreign Affairs.

As Foreign Minister, McMahon tried to maintain Australia's good relations with its neighbors in Asia and the Pacific. In April 1970 he took part in a session of the Economic Commission for Asia and the Far East at Bangkok, and in September he headed the Australian delegation at the opening of the United Nations General Assembly. Outspokenly pro-American and anti-Communist, he supported United States policies in Southeast Asia and the use of Australian troops in the Vietnam war. Among other actions, during 1970 he protested French nuclear weapons testing in the Pacific, announced a three-year, $60,500,000 economic aid program for Indonesia, established a special interdepartmental committee to study relations between Australia and Japan, and urged Great Britain to maintain a military presence in Southeast Asia in cooperation with Australia, New Zealand, Malaysia, and Singapore. At the Commonwealth of Nations conference at Singapore in January 1971, McMahon averted an open rift between Australia and several African and Asian countries after Gorton had indicated his support for a British plan to sell arms to South Africa.

The Liberal-Country party coalition government was faced with a major crisis in March 1971, when Defense Minister Malcolm Fraser resigned, charging that the Prime Minister had sided with the military establishment against him in a dispute over policies affecting the civic-action program of Australian forces in South Vietnam, and declared that Gorton was no longer fit to lead the country. A secret ballot among the Liberal party's members of Parliament resulted in a tie, with thirty-three supporting the Prime Minister and thirty-three voting against him. In a second ballot Gorton, who had previously abstained, cast his vote against himself, declaring that he no longer had the confidence of the party, and announced his resignation. McMahon, who had been reelected deputy leader of the Liberal party in November 1969, then declared himself a candidate for the party leadership and easily defeated B. M. Snedden, the Minister of Labor and National Service, for the post.

Sworn in as Prime Minister on March 10, 1971, McMahon became the oldest Australian ever to occupy that office. Commenting on the change in Australian leadership, Bruce Grant wrote in the Washington *Post* (March 11, 1971): "After the public battering of the last three years the Liberal party will now support with relief a man who fits the party's public image." On the other hand, a correspondent for *Time* (May 24, 1971) suggested that McMahon was "likely to prove a transitional figure."

Calling himself "a party man from the top of my head to the soles of my feet," McMahon shortly after his inauguration promised to rebuild unity in the Liberal-Country party coalition—which at the time had only a seven-seat majority in the 125-member House of Representatives—and began strengthening its position for the national elections scheduled for November 1972. To allay tensions caused by the recent crisis he supported Gorton's election as deputy party leader and appointed him Minister of Defense. (Later, however, in August 1971, the Prime Minister forced Gorton to resign his Cabinet post.) Responding to charges that his predecessor had concentrated too much power in the Prime Minister's hands, McMahon instituted changes in the organization of government aimed at vesting more authority in the Cabinet as a whole. Five days after taking office McMahon survived a motion of no confidence, introduced by Gough Whitlam, the leader of the opposition Labor party, who had hoped thereby to bring about an immediate general election.

Although McMahon had announced at the time of his inauguration that his government would be "very anti-Communist and very antisocialist," he has already adopted a more liberal policy toward Communist nations. He soon authorized the establishment of a Soviet trade office and shipping agency in Sydney, as well as the sale of Australian sugar cane harvesting equipment to Cuba. In view of a recent thaw in relations between the United States and Communist China and initiatives taken by the leadership of the Australian Labor party to establish contacts with the Peking government, McMahon announced in May 1971 that Australia would seek a "dialogue" and a possible normalization of relations with the Chinese People's Republic. In an article in the *Far Eastern Economic Review* in June 1971 he suggested that a "two-China policy"—under which Communist China would be admitted to the U.N. while the Nationalist regime on Taiwan would retain its seat—might be feasible. Writing in the *Christian Science Monitor* (March 16, 1971), Maximilian Walsh suggested that the clues to McMahon's defense and foreign policies were to be seen in "his personal pride in professionalism and his inclination to see most political questions as having their roots in economics."

While reaffirming Australia's support of the Saigon government in Vietnam—an issue on which Australian public opinion appeared to be about equally divided—McMahon has also pursued the gradual disengagement, begun under Gorton, of Australian forces from Indochina, in line with United States Vietnamization policy. On becoming Prime Minister, McMahon had declared that "the policy on Vietnam has been more firmly pressed by me than by any other person" and that "this policy will continue," but added that "all policies are open to review." After the New York *Times*, in June 1971, published the "Pentagon papers"—a series of secret documents dealing with the process by which the United States and other countries, including Australia, became militarily involved in Vietnam—McMahon called for an urgent high-level inquiry into the circumstances under which Australia committed armed forces to that conflict in response to charges by Labor party leader Whitlam that Australia had been "conned" by the United States into taking part in the Indochina war.

A major problem facing McMahon's government has been inflation, which accounted for a 7.6 percent increase in living costs during 1970. Furthermore, despite continued economic growth, Australia has experienced a sharp decline in wool prices and has run into marketing problems for other important products. As one of his first steps after taking office, McMahon ordered a complete review of the nation's economy and also announced plans to reexamine the system of distribution of federal funds to the states, which for some years had been a source of dissatisfaction among state governments. Another issue dividing Australians has been the country's racial policies. They continue to meet much criticism, although in recent years the previously all-white immigration policy had been somewhat liberalized and some improvements had been made in the lives of Australia's approximately 120,000 Aborigines. The race issue was brought into focus when an all-white South African rugby team that visited Australia in June 1971 with the approval of the McMahon government was greeted by widespread anti-apartheid demonstrations.

William McMahon had remained a bachelor until December 1965, when he married Sonia Rachel Hopkins, the daughter of a textile merchant and a member of one of Sydney's wealthiest and most socially prominent families. They have two children, Melinda Rachel and Julian Dana William. Mrs. McMahon, who is twenty-five years younger than her husband and has been described as the "most glamorous Prime Minister's wife that Australia ever had," is a former model and has also worked as an occupational therapist, a film producer's assistant, and a staff member of the Australian News and Information Bureau in New York. In addition to their official residence in Canberra, the McMahons have a home in Bellevue Hill, a suburb of Sydney.

Known to his fellow Australians as "King Billy," McMahon has, according to a profile in the New York *Times* (March 11, 1971), "sharp, probing blue eyes" and "bushy white sideburns falling below the earlobes to set off a high, balding pate." His height is about five feet seven inches. A boxer in his younger years, he still plays squash and golf, and he is fond of reading, music, ballet, and the theatre. He is of the Anglican faith, and his clubs include the Union, the Royal Sydney, the Elanora Country Club, the Melbourne, Tattersalls in Sydney, and the Commonwealth in Canberra. A compulsive worker, McMahon has been called the "quiet Australian" because of his tranquil nature. Asked to express his feelings about attaining the Prime Ministership, he calmly replied: "I have taken it in a composed way because I have been here for a long time."

References

N Y Times p14 Mr 11 '71 por
Time 97:26 Mr 22 '71 por
International Who's Who, 1970-71
International Yearbook and Statesman's Who's Who, 1971
Who's Who, 1971-72
Who's Who in Australia, 1965

McNAIR, BARBARA

Mar. 4, 1939- Singer; actress
Address: b. c/o Kal Ross, 8721 Sunset Blvd., Los Angeles, Calif. 90069

Sultry, tawny Barbara McNair, long a reigning thrush in the big nightclub and sophisticated supper club circuits, has in recent years been applying her talent increasingly to acting as well as singing. She starred in the musical *No Strings* on Broadway in 1963, began playing dramatic roles on television the following year, and made her Hollywood acting debut in 1968, in *If He Hollers, Let Him Go!* Her most recent featured film role was in *They Call Me Mister Tibbs!* As a singer, known for her disciplined voice, flashing smile, and warm personality, she still performs in clubs, mostly in Las Vegas, and on television she has starred in syndicated variety shows packaged by Four Star International. While versatile, she usually avoids rock 'n' roll numbers in favor of standard pop songs and show tunes. One of her biggest recent hits was "You Could Never Love Him," recorded on the Motown label. Critics and other observers have described Miss McNair as "regal," "stunning," "fresh," and "joyous."

Barbara McNair was born in Racine, Wisconsin on March 4, 1939 to Horace McNair, a foundry foreman and a sandblaster, and Claudia (Taylor) McNair, who later went to work as a cook in a home for retarded children. In addition to two full siblings, Jacqueline McNair Gaither and Horace McNair, the singer has a half brother, Samuel Moseley, and a half sister, Juanita Moseley. Juanita lived and traveled as companion and aide to Barbara for many years.

Miss McNair began taking voice lessons in Racine when she was ten, and later she studied at the Chicago Conservatory of Music. Her show business aspirations were inspired by Hollywood musicals and whetted by the entertainers, particularly Billy Daniels and others from the nightclub circuit, whom she saw on television. She told Blaik Kirby of the Toronto *Globe and Mail* (March 7, 1970): "I used to see people on TV and say, 'My goodness, how many people know that they exist.'" She added that a statement that she once read in a magazine article by Gore Vidal was one of her cherished mottoes: "In the sea of humanity, to keep one's head above the water."

Her parents encouraged her musical ambitions, but the father constantly preached "security" to her—the wisdom of having a mundane skill to fall back on, if need be, for a livelihood. Accordingly, she worked diligently at her secretarial courses in

BARBARA McNAIR

high school and became excellent at stenography and typing (120 words per minute). Following graduation, she matriculated in the music department of the University of California at Los Angeles, paying her way by working as a playground director. After a year she left UCLA because the traditional courses offered were not helping her to prepare specifically for a show business career.

With her sister Juanita, Miss McNair moved to New York City, where she lived at the Harlem YWCA and worked as a typist with the National Federation of Settlements before obtaining a booking at Max Gordon's Village Vanguard in Greenwich Village. In that debut engagement she learned, painfully, that handling nightclub audiences is no easy matter. "People talked and smoked and drank—while I sang," she recounted in an interview with Joseph Wershba of the New York Post (July 22, 1963). "People never did that in Racine. I was shocked. I went back to regular employment." But not for long. After winning one of the competitions in Arthur Godfrey's television series Talent Scouts, a weekly showcase of new talent, she sang on Godfrey's daily network radio show for a week and then reentered the nightclub world. From the Purple Onion, a Manhattan basement room for neophytes, she went to the Upper East Side's prestigious Blue Angel and from there to Miami Beach, to begin her search for fame and fortune in the "commercial" circuit that includes the big Hollywood and Las Vegas clubs.

The late Richard Kollmar, a booster of Miss McNair ever since he saw her perform at the Purple Onion, was one of the producers of The Body Beautiful, a musical with a prizefighting theme that ran on Broadway for less than two months early in 1958. Through Kollmar she was cast in a supporting role, and she drew good notices (in contrast with the panning the show itself took), especially for her exhilarating rendition of "Fair Warning." Three seasons later she was in another musical, I'm With You, starring the late Nat King Cole, which closed during its tryout tour.

Recalling the years when she was struggling for recognition in an interview with Earl Wilson

(New York Post, January 6, 1968), Miss McNair said: "I made a terrible rock 'n' roll record called 'Bobby' that sold 200,000 more than any other record I made. I had to go on TV with it—and I was embarrassed. I only did it because they let me record 'Til There Was You.'" In the late 1950's and early 1960's she appeared occasionally on the television shows hosted by Jack Paar and Arlene Francis and very often on Garry Moore's show, and later she performed on Hollywood Palace, the Ed Sullivan Show, and Carol Burnett and Red Skelton's programs. During the 1962-63 season she had her own local program, over WABC-TV in New York City.

In May 1963 Warner Brothers released the motion picture Spencer's Mountain, in which Miss McNair appeared in one scene in a nondramatic role, as the singer of "America the Beautiful" at a high school graduation ceremony. The following month she replaced Diahann Carroll as the feminine lead in the Broadway hit No Strings, a musical play about a love affair in Paris between a black high fashion model and a white expatriate American writer, with music by Richard Rodgers. Norman Nadel, writing in the New York World-Telegram and Sun (July 16, 1963), compared her performance with that of her predecessor: "Both sing well. . . . The difference shows up more in her [Miss McNair's] personality. Miss Carroll was ice and fire. Miss McNair is fire—sometimes a remote fire, as the script dictates—but never ice. . . . With Miss Carroll, elegance was foremost. With Miss McNair, it is effervescence." She remained at the head of the No Strings company when, in the late summer and fall of 1963, it made a national tour that was plagued by audience hostility to the show's interracial theme, especially in cities bordering the South.

Her first straight dramatic role was in a psychiatry-oriented teleplay about racial integration presented in 1964 in the network series The Eleventh Hour, and her performance there led to acting credits in the series Hogan's Heroes, Dr. Kildare, and I Spy. As she later observed, she became "hooked" on acting. "I love singing, but it's hard to really develop a mood in a song; it's too short. I feel freer [in acting] . . . ; I can get down to the bottom pit of emotion."

In 1964 Warner Brothers Records released I Enjoy Being a Girl, an album in which Miss McNair rendered, in addition to the title song, "On Second Thought," "The Friendliest Thing," "Stairway to Paradise," and "The Other Side of the Tracks." The latter was at that time the most popular of her renditions, both as a single disk and as part of her nightclub repertoire. A correspondent for Variety (July 22, 1964) reporting from the Crescendo in Los Angeles, described her as delivering it "in a clipped, sharp jazz style that shows innate musicianship and a definite knowledge of lyrics and phrasing." He went on to observe her versatility in giving "a solid belt" to "The Lady Is a Tramp," and a "sensitive" interpretation to the moody dramatic ballad "Irma La Douce." Miss McNair has included in her act impressions of Pearl Bailey, Carol Channing, and others.

Among the clubs played by Miss McNair in 1964 were the Copacabana in New York, the Eden Roc in Miami Beach, and the Shamrock in Houston. When she "arrived" at the Persian Room of the Hotel Plaza in New York City, the summit of supper clubs, on December 22, 1965, a critic for *Variety* (December 29, 1965) found the "heavy-beat, over-energetic" numbers in her repertoire not cosmopolitan or "cerebral" enough for the Plaza clientele but he conceded the singer her due: "The dazzling distaffer has the vocal ability to handle almost any type of song . . . and knows the value of enhancing the lyrics with good timing, excellent diction, and a sense of drama."

John S. Wilson of the New York *Times* (January 1, 1966) was unqualified in his positive assessment of her Plaza performance: "She is a highly knowledgeable performer who projects an aura of beauty, a warm personality, and an appealing sense of fun. And she shows a discipline in the light and strong sides of her singing that keeps her program in fine balance. Miss McNair has the voice and imagination to find fresh values in her songs." He noted that she gave a "gentle simplicity" to "How to Handle a Woman," muted the wistfulness of "Yesterday," and interpreted "Don't Rain on My Parade" with "dramatic power." About the time of her debut at the Persian Room, Miss McNair signed with Motown Records, which released her album *Here I Am* in 1967 and issued *The Real Barbara McNair* three years later.

As Miss McNair has observed, in an interview with Jo Ann Harris for an article in the Washington *Post's* TV Channels (September 21, 1969), her career was "going along nicely" but "wasn't spectacular" until October 1968, when the Cinerama Corporation released the Forward Films production *If He Hollers, Let Him Go!* and *Playboy* magazine ran a spread of stills from the motion picture. In the film she portrayed Lily, a nightclub singer who is the girlfriend of James Lake (Raymond St. Jacques), a black escapee from a Southern jail who becomes involved against his will in a psychotic white man's plot to kill his rich wife. Miss McNair herself considered the movie "dreadful," and, like other critics, Howard Thompson of the New York *Times* (October 10, 1968) panned the movie, calling it a "lurid, cliché-flapping melodrama with painfully embarrassing racial trimmings . . . contrived, unconvincing, and dishonest." Thompson added: "The sole brightness is the screen debut of Barbara McNair, the beautiful young singer, who does very well in two scenes (one of them involving some brief but unstartling nudity)." Miss McNair told Jo Ann Harris that she weighed the pros and cons carefully before allowing the nude shots of her to be reproduced in *Playboy.* "I considered the publicity I'd get from the article and decided that I'd either take this gamble on my career or give it up completely. . . . I found that it helped my career immensely. In this business, sensationalism counts."

The tangible fruits of the "sensationalism" included her own weekly television variety and interview program, *The Barbara McNair Show,* syndicated to thirty stations for twenty-six weeks in 1969-70 and rerun in some localities thereafter; *On Stage With Barbara McNair,* a syndicated television special costarring Duke Ellington, that was distributed for broadcast in the same season; and a spate of starring or featured screen roles.

The film roles were the paramour of a jet-set Mafioso whom the mob won't let go straight in *Stiletto* (Avco Embassy, 1969), a glossy, fast-paced, mediocre cops-and-Cosa Nostra thriller; one of a trio of nuns in lay clothes helping a physician (Elvis Presley) run a ghetto clinic in *Change of Habit* (Universal, 1969), a saccharine but warm slice of Pollyannaism; a singer-paramour in *Venus in Furs* (Marican International, 1970), an abominable, opaque psycho-sex exploitation film—not based on Leopold von Sacher-Masoch's classic—about a spaced-out musician (James Darren) haunted by the spectre of a woman killed at an orgy (Maria Rohm); and the nice middleclass wife of a black San Francisco police detective (Sidney Poitier) in *They Call Me Mister Tibbs!* (United Artists, 1970), a murder mystery with token social and political overtones.

Critics in *Variety* (October 22, 1969 and May 6, 1970) observed that Miss McNair was "excellent" as the nun in *Change of Habit* but that in *Venus in Furs,* "with [Jess] Franco directing his own dialogue, neither Darren nor Miss McNair have a chance." Her best scene in *Venus in Furs,* according to the reviewer of that movie, "was a good lowdown delivery of 'Let's Get Together' while writhing on a nightclub floor." In reviewing *Stiletto,* critics in general spared Miss McNair the animadversions they hurled at the film, commenting only on her beauty, and they had nothing derogatory to say about her handling of the onedimensional characterization assigned her in *They Call Me Mister Tibbs!*

Miss McNair has been married, and divorced, twice. During her second marriage—to Jack Rafferty, a San Francisco press agent and nightclub owner of Irish descent—she lived in San Francisco. Previously she had lived with her sister in a home that she owned in the Bronx, New York, and she now resides in Las Vegas. She describes herself as "not neat" and as a night person who "functions better after dark." She is candid in expressing her opinions in interviews, whether the subject be politics, race, or other entertainers. She is an antiwar Democrat who found her tour of Vietnam with the Bob Hope troupe at Christmas 1967 "very depressing." Racially, despite the lightness of her skin and her Caucasian-like features, she identifies "with blackness," as she told an interviewer for *Jet* (September 4, 1969). "But . . . I don't want someone else's way of how I am to project myself as a black person forced on me. I want to do it the way that is me." Elsewhere she has observed that, while the entertainment world is a naturally visible area of racial conflict, "the white man in show business is becoming aware of the Negro as a Negro, as living a total life as human beings, not as problem human beings."

Barbara McNair, whose beauty is patent, is the first Negro to be included in the "ten most beautiful" list of the International Cosmetologists Society. She is five feet three inches tall, weighs 115 pounds, has dark brown hair and eyes, and prefers tailored clothes in her private life. Interviewers report that she is a warm, "sentimental" person with a sense of humor, a natural "out-loud" laugh, and who is free from the hypersensitivity, aggressiveness, and temper tantrums to which so many in her profession are given. "People lecture me to be more pushy," she told Sidney Skolsky (New York *Post*, November 9, 1968), and in an interview with Blaik Kirby of the Toronto *Globe and Mail* (March 7, 1970) she said: "I never drive myself. It [success] always happens to me. I'd never sell my soul for this business. I've always managed to have one fine time in life. Whatever I do I like to do well, but I'm not compulsive. I put this business in its place. . . . I was once told, long ago, that I'd never make it in this business because I was too sane. . . . But I didn't let that deter me."

References

N Y Post p23 Jl 22 '63 por
N Y Sunday News II p42 Jl 14 '63; mag p4 F 20 '66 por
Biographical Encyclopaedia & Who's Who of the American Theatre (1966)
Who's Who in America, 1970-71

MAURER, ION GHEORGHE (mou'rər yôn gā-ôĭ'gā)

Sept. 23, 1902- Chairman of the Council of Ministers of the Socialist Republic of Romania
Address: b. Council of Ministers, Piata Victoriei, Bucharest, Romania

One of the most dramatic political developments in Eastern Europe in the last decade has been Romania's assertion of a high degree of national autonomy within the Soviet bloc. Under the leadership of Gheorghe Gheorghiu-Dej, and, since his death in 1965, under his successor, Nicolae Ceausescu, the Romanian Communist party has maintained an orthodox Communist regime at home, followed a middle path in the ideological conflict between Moscow and Peking, and jealously guarded Romania's right to become economically self-sufficient—a goal that is reflected in Romania's profitable trade relations with the non-Communist nations of Western Europe and in its high growth rate. The man who, perhaps more than any other Romanian leader, embodies the sophisticated policies that have characterized Romanian diplomacy in recent years, is Ion Gheorghe Maurer, a lawyer, who rose through the government and party ranks after World War II as a protégé of Gheorghiu-Dej and has served since 1961 as Chairman of Romania's Council of Ministers—a position equivalent to that of Premier. A shrewd, resourceful man devoted to Romania's national interests, Maurer has become the spokesman for his country's independent course and has re-

ION GHEORGHE MAURER

presented Romania in the major capitals of the world.

Ion Gheorghe Maurer was born in Bucharest on September 23, 1902 into a family of intellectuals of modest means. His father, a teacher, was a member of the ethnic German minority of Transylvania, a region of Hungary until 1918, when it became part of Romania. From his mother, a Frenchwoman, Maurer acquired an abiding appreciation of French literature and history as well as a fluency in French. After obtaining his secondary education at a military college in the city of Craiova in southwestern Romania, Maurer studied at the University of Bucharest, which conferred a law doctorate on him in 1923. Later he undertook graduate studies at the Sorbonne in Paris.

From 1924 to 1927 Maurer served successively as judge and public prosecutor in the county of Tirnava Mare in Transylvania. He left the judiciary in 1927 to enter law practice in the Transylvanian town of Sighisoara. Among his early cases was one in which he acted as defense attorney for a group of workers prosecuted for trade union activity. Maurer returned to Bucharest in 1932 to become legal counsel for several large banking houses. Meanwhile he had become active politically, first as a Liberal, and then as a member of the National Peasant party. As his interest in politics developed he abandoned business law and soon became well known as a defense attorney for activists of the labor movement and the radical left.

In 1933 Maurer defended Gheorghe Gheorghiu-Dej and several other Communists who had been arrested for organizing a railway strike. Although he lost the case, it marked the beginning of a lifelong friendship and political association between Maurer and Gheorghiu-Dej. As defense counsel and legal adviser to the Communists, Maurer maintained communications between Gheorghiu-Dej in prison and the party organization. He reportedly joined the Communist party in 1936, about which time he also became secretary of the Anti-Fascist Legal Bureau, an organization that provided for the legal defense of leftists accused of political offenses. During the late 1930's, with most of its leaders in prison, the

Romanian Communist movement went underground, and little is known of Maurer's activities at that time. In 1938, after King Carol II formed his short-lived anti-fascist coalition called the National Renaissance Front, Maurer reportedly served for a brief period as administrator, or publisher, of *Romania,* an official government newspaper.

Sources vary as to Maurer's activities during World War II. He reportedly was arrested in 1940 or 1941 by the secret police of Ion Antonescu's fascist dictatorship and interned in a prison camp at Tirgu Jiu. Another account places the date of his arrest in 1943 and indicates that for the preceding three years he had practised law while remaining aloof from politics. According to still another source, Maurer was arrested on two separate occasions, and after his second release, in 1943, he was sent to the Crimean front as a lieutenant in the Romanian army, then still fighting on the side of the Germans. Most sources agree that sometime during the war Maurer became active in the anti-fascist underground resistance movement in Romania. In 1944 he reportedly became an aide to General Emil Bodnaras, a Romanian army officer who had returned home after a decade in the Soviet Union to help organize the Romanian Communist movement for the postwar period.

In 1944 Maurer, according to some accounts, saved Gheorghiu-Dej, Nicolae Ceausescu, and fourteen other Communist leaders from possible execution by the Nazis by engineering their escape from Tirgu Jiu prison. He is said to have accomplished this feat by simply entering the prison disguised as a Romanian (or German) officer and marching off with the prisoners. Maurer is also credited with having taken part, along with General Bodnaras, in the organization of the coup of August 23, 1944, in which King Michael, aided by liberal and leftist elements, overthrew Antonescu's government and instituted an anti-fascist regime. The extent of his participation is uncertain, however, since most Western historians agree that the Communists played a relatively minor role in the coup.

Maurer entered government service in the post-liberation coalition government of General Constantin Sanatescu in November 1944 as secretary general of the Ministry of Communications headed by Gheorghiu-Dej. When the latter became Minister of Communications and Public Works in the Communist-dominated coalition government of Petru Groza in March 1945, he appointed Maurer undersecretary to the ministry. Meanwhile, Maurer had also moved up in the ranks of the Romanian Communist party, and at its national conference in October 1945 he was elected a member of the party's Central Committee. In 1946 Maurer was a member of the Romanian delegation to the Paris peace conference and to its Balkan Economic Commission.

In the parliamentary elections of November 19, 1946, in which the Communists greatly increased their strength, Maurer was elected to the Chamber of Deputies as a candidate of the Bloc of Democratic Parties. Later that month, when Gheorghiu-Dej became Minister of National Economy, Maurer moved with him as his undersecretary. He continued in the post after that ministry was reorganized, in April 1947, as the Ministry of Industry and Commerce. On March 29, 1948 Maurer was elected a deputy to Romania's new legislature, the Grand National Assembly, as a candidate of the Front of People's Democracy, and he has since been regularly reelected. When in April 1948 the Ministry of Industry and Commerce was divided into two Cabinet departments, Maurer was appointed deputy minister in the new Ministry of Industry.

In October 1948 Maurer was removed from office. His official biographical statement gives no indication of the circumstances, but a Reuters dispatch in the New York *Times* (July 15, 1957) suggests that he had come into disfavor because of his association with Lucretiu Patrascanu, a leading Romanian "national Communist" who was arrested in 1948 during a period of Stalinist repression and was executed in 1955. It was rumored at the time in the West that Maurer was also arrested, but those rumors were later dispelled. According to David Floyd, writing in *Rumania: Russia's Dissident Ally* (Praeger, 1965), Maurer remained in disfavor from 1948 until 1956. During that period he lost his Central Committee membership and was assigned to various unimportant functions. From 1948 to 1951, according to his official biography, he engaged in undefined "active work" for the party's central organization, and from October 1952 to December 1953 he held the office of First State Arbiter, a minor judicial post. In 1954 he was named director of the Institute of Legal Research of the Romanian Academy, and he remained in that position until October 1958.

As a protégé and trusted associate of Gheorghiu-Dej—who had become First Secretary of the Romanian Communist party in 1955—Maurer rose rapidly through the ranks following his restoration to favor. In 1956 he went abroad on several diplomatic missions, and on July 14, 1957 he was appointed Foreign Minister, a post he retained until the following year. In addition he served from March to December 1957 as vice-president of the Grand National Assembly. In January 1958 Maurer was elected, upon recommendation of Gheorghiu-Dej, to succeed the late Dr. Petru Groza as President of the Presidium of the Grand National Assembly, or titular head of state, a position he held until 1961. At the eighth congress of the Romanian Communist party, in June 1960, Maurer was reinstated to full membership in the party's Central Committee, and for the first time he was elected to its ruling nine-member Politburo, replacing Constantin Pervelescu.

The Grand National Assembly elected Maurer on March 21, 1961 to his present post of Chairman of the Council of Ministers, or Premier. On the same date, in a major overhaul of the state apparatus, the Presidium of the Grand National Assembly, which had been headed by Maurer, was replaced as the chief executive organ by a seventeen-member State Council, with Gheorghiu-Dej as president. Maurer was named one of its three vice-presidents, and he remained in that post until August 1965. At the ninth party congress, in July 1965, Maurer was elected to the new seven-member Permanent Presidium of the Central Committee, which replaced its Politburo, and he was also named one of the fifteen members of the Central Committee's executive committee, which was created at that time. Reelected Chairman of the Council of Ministers in March 1969, Maurer at the same time became a member of Romania's newly organized Defense Council.

Although the top leadership positions in the Romanian government and Communist party organization are held by Nicolae Ceausescu—who succeeded Gheorghiu-Dej as the party's First Secretary at the latter's death in March 1965 and became President of the State Council in December 1967—Maurer, who is second in command, has been the foremost spokesman for Romania's independent economic and foreign policy and is, according to David Floyd, his country's "principal negotiator with the outside world on all political matters." It was Maurer, who, in an article in the *World Marxist Review* in November 1962, first openly declared Romania's economic and political independence of the Soviet Union. In cautious but clear language he rebuked both the Russians and the Chinese for their "unfraternal" differences and he exposed Soviet Premier Nikita Khrushchev's scheme for "integration" that would have enabled Russia to dominate the national economies of Eastern European countries through the Council for Mutual Economic Aid (Comecon), the Communist bloc's counterpart of Western Europe's Common Market.

One of Maurer's earliest and most striking gestures to the West was his widely publicized state visit to Paris in July 1964, which he undertook without consulting the Soviet government. As the first visit to a Western capital by the head of any Eastern bloc government other than the Soviet Union, this was, as Ghita Ionescu observed in *The Break-up of the Soviet Empire in the East* (Penguin, 1965), a "spectacular demonstration of the new Romanian prestige and nonconformism." The visit brought about an agreement between France and Romania to expand their cultural, scientific, and economic relations. Furthermore, Maurer's talks with President Charles de Gaulle, who was at the time trying to establish an independent diplomacy for his own country, did much to restore the traditional friendship that had existed until World War II between France and Romania—which has long considered itself an island of Latin culture in a Slavic sea.

Refusing to go along with Soviet moves to isolate Communist China, Romania has established cordial relations with other dissident Communist countries like Yugoslavia and Albania. At the same time, to enhance Romania's prestige, Maurer has tried to act as an "honest broker" in the Sino-Soviet ideological conflict. In March 1964 he led a delegation to Peking and afterward met with Khrushchev in Moscow in an attempt to mediate the differences between the two powers. Although unsuccessful in that and subsequent efforts, in September 1969, while attending Ho Chi Minh's funeral in Hanoi, he succeeded in arranging a diplomatic conference between Russian and Chinese representatives. In November 1965 he offered to act as an intermediary to bring about direct peace talks between the United States and North Vietnam, and in the summer of 1967, when he visited Peking shortly after a secret meeting with President Lyndon B. Johnson in Washington, D.C., he acted as an unofficial emissary in an attempt to open communications between the United States and Communist China.

Perhaps Romania's most dramatic difference with the Soviet Union occurred shortly after the Arab-Israeli War of June 1967. Alone among the nations of the Soviet bloc, Romania refused to join Russia in condemning Israel as an aggressor. In a speech to the emergency session of the United Nations General Assembly on June 23, Maurer supported Israel's demand for direct negotiations between the belligerents and called for a "lasting, peaceful settlement" based on "a spirit of realism and mutual respect." Maurer further demonstrated his country's independence from the Soviet Union when, during a visit to the Hague in July 1967 he suggested that Europe might be a safer place "if NATO and the Warsaw Pact were both scrapped." He denied, however, that Romania had any intention of leaving either the Warsaw Pact or Comecon.

The invasion of Czechoslovakia by the Soviet Union and four of its Warsaw Pact allies in August 1968, ending the liberal reforms instituted in that country by Communist party chief Alexander Dubcek, brought further tensions between Moscow and Bucharest. To demonstrate their sympathy, Maurer and Ceausescu, together with President Tito of Yugoslavia, had paid a friendly visit to Czechoslovakia shortly before the invasion. Referring to the Soviet argument that the invasion was determined by Czechoslovakia's drift away from the socialist camp, Maurer declared in a speech on September 1, 1968 that Romania was "building socialism in such a way that it could never be said that we have drifted away from it." He added that "the Romanian people cannot conceive and would not accept living otherwise than free, sovereign, and masters of their destiny." For some months after the invasion there were rumors that Romania might meet the same fate.

Despite frequent tensions, Maurer has consistently pointed out that Romania considers itself a loyal member of the Soviet bloc, and he has tried to dispel rumors of a possible split between Romania and the Soviet Union. On July 7, 1970 he and Soviet Premier Kosygin met in Bucharest to sign a twenty-year treaty of friendship, cooperation, and mutual assistance, extending a pact that had originally been concluded in 1948. The two nations agreed to adhere to the Warsaw Pact in response to NATO, to recognize national sovereignty and the inviolability of frontiers, and to resolve disputes by peaceful means. The pact was widely regarded as a sign of Soviet recognition of Romania's aspirations for a more independent status. "On balance," wrote Charlotte Saikowski in the *Christian Science Monitor* (July 9, 1970), "the pact seems to fortify Bucharest's hand. The national-minded Romanians by and large have preserved their principles of independence." Later that year Maurer concluded similar treaties with Poland and Bulgaria.

A member of the Academy of the Socialist Republic of Romania and of the Romanian Academy of Social and Political Sciences, founded in 1970,

Maurer has served since 1966 as honorary president of the Association for International Law and International Relations of the Socialist Republic of Romania. The University of Teheran has conferred an honorary doctorate on him. Maurer holds a number of decorations, including the Order of Labor, the Order of "the 23d of August," and the Order of the Star of the Republic. He obtained Romania's highest national distinction in 1962, when he was named a Hero of Socialist Labor.

Ion Gheorghe Maurer has been married twice. His first marriage, the outcome of a college romance, ended in divorce. With his second wife, Elena, a native of Bessarabia, whom he married after World War II, he has one child. (According to one source, he has a son named Jean, while another source states that he has a daughter.) Almost six feet tall and gray haired, Maurer is a suave, sophisticated, dynamic man. A profile in the New York *Times* (July 28, 1964) describes him as "far from the rough-and-ready Communist stereotype" and as "a well-dressed, well-traveled diplomat, at ease with women and as comfortable in the salons and nightclubs of Bucharest as he is in its council chambers."

References

N Y Times p2 Jl 28 '64 por
International Who's Who, 1970-71
Who's Who in the World, 1971-72

MAX, PETER

Oct. 19, 1937- Artist; business executive
Address: b. Peter Max Enterprises, 325 E. 75th St., New York 10021; h. 118 Riverside Dr., New York 10024

In aspiring to do visually, in the graphic arts world, what the Beatles have done in music, Peter Max has become an acknowledged pop culture hero of American youth. His combinations of motifs and techniques of classical, Art Nouveau, Op, pop, and other types of art achieve a highly personalized, exuberant, and psychedelic style that has been described as "crisp electricity." Drawn with crayon or felt pen, his designs vibrate with somewhat lopsided blue and pink and yellow flowers, skies studded with stars and rainbows, smiling lips, and other tokens of euphoria. Unlike most artists, Max has a talent also for salesmanship and has proved himself an entrepreneur of exceptional acumen. About the time that he turned thirty he headed a business in New York City grossing well over a million dollars a year, owned 50 percent of five companies, and employed more than thirty artists. Millions of posters have been made from his drawings, and his flamboyant designs have decorated the Manhattan classified telephone directory, city buses nationwide, clothing and clothing accessories, and scores of household articles.

Accounts of Peter Max's early life seem almost as fanciful as his paintings. The only child of Jacob and Sala Max, he was born in Berlin, Germany on October 19, 1937. (Some sources give 1939 as the year of his birth.) Soon afterward the family fled to Shanghai to escape Nazi persecution and the turmoil of World War II in Europe. They remained for about ten years in the Orient, where Jacob Max made a comfortable living as a pearl merchant. Peter attended an English school and spent much of his time observing and talking with the Buddhist monks at a pagoda near his home. Their painting may have inspired him to become an artist. The Max family is also said to have lived for a year in Tibet before moving, in about 1950, to Israel. There Peter became interested in astronomy, a study that later enormously influenced the content of his work.

After sojourning in Rome and Paris, the Max family moved to the United States in 1953 and settled in Brooklyn, where Peter completed his general education at Lafayette High School. For about five years he studied at the Art Students League, the Pratt Graphic Arts Center, and the School of Visual Arts to prepare for a career in commercial art. In 1962 Peter Max and a partner, Tom Daly, opened the Daly-Max Studio, a graphic arts business that brought them into contact with Madison Avenue advertising agencies. Within two years the firm had won more than sixty awards in typography and illustration for book jackets, record covers, and other items.

Somewhat abruptly, however, Max withdrew in 1965 from his flourishing partnership with Daly, feeling that he had been diverted too far from pure design to production. He retreated to a large Riverside Drive apartment overlooking the Hudson for a two-year sabbatical, during which he accepted only a few choice commissions. That period of creative refreshment strengthened the Far Eastern influences that had permeated his early commercial designs. "I read I Ching and explored the thinking of the Eastern mystics," he recalled in an interview with Eugene Boe for *Cue* (October 4, 1969), "and this opened my mind and gave me the key to who I was, relative to my evolution and Mother Earth." In 1966 Max visited France to work on designs for Conrad Rooks's avant-garde film *Chappaqua*. After meeting in Paris Rooks's guru, the Hindu holy man Swami Satchidananda, Max began the practice of Yoga, a discipline that helped shape his art.

When Max emerged from his seclusion at the end of about two years, he was prepared to transform the world with thousands of drawings, patterns, and experimental ideas for household and other products ranging from stationery to furniture. Some of the basic elements of his style appeared with amusing effect in his 1967 interior design of the Manhattan restaurant Tin Lizzie Steak House. He developed a mood of nostalgia through a combination of themes of the turn of the century and early twentieth century: paisley wallpaper of Art Nouveau origin, stills from Charlie Chaplin movies, a photograph of Shirley Temple from the 1930's, John Held cartoons, old sheet music, and several large Max canvases. In the center of the room he placed a flower-bedecked 1915 Ford and scattered around penny arcade machines, bentwood chairs, and wicker pieces.

By mid-1967 Max's designs were being applied to tableware, glassware, book covers, shower curtains, upholstery fabrics, rugs, and other wares, most of them mass-produced. His biggest sellers were mod posters that celebrated love and joy in smiles, stars, lettered messages, and psychedelic explosions of warm colors. In his posters he made particularly striking use of a device of his own invention called the "panopticon," the hallmark of much of his design. "A montage of forms, repeated over and over again, the panopticon creates the visual effect of designs viewed through a kaleidoscope," as the device was described in *Interior Design* (June 1967).

The Peter Max poster fad started building in 1967 when young people began asking for copies of those he had made for local stores. The posters were being printed by the Security Printing Company of New York, whose co-owner, Denton Stein, brought the artist into the poster business. "We set up Peter Max Posters as equal partners," explained Stein, who was quoted in *Business Week* (March 16, 1968). "We had always been job printers; suddenly we had sales representatives and sold a half-million posters in eight months. This year we'll sell a million more." Posters were sold in twenty-five different Max designs at $2 each in bookstores, department stores, and novelty shops throughout the United States. Orders came in, too, from Japan and European countries. One of Max's customers was the New York City department of parks, which commissioned a Halloween poster.

In the fall of 1968 Max won a commission from Metro Transit Advertising Company to brighten up New York City buses with his vividly colored posters. Metro, which owns advertising franchises on buses, streetcars, and subways in ten major American cities, gradually extended Peter Max's mobile one-man art show to tens of millions of passengers of local transit vehicles across the country. "I'm bringing art to the people where the people are," Max declared. "Now they don't have to go to galleries and see paintings on a wall. Transit Art moves—it's a new way of looking at art."

Among the growing list of Max-designed items on sale in 1968 were clocks with numberless faces manufactured by the General Motors Company. He moved into the home furnishings market also with designs for mugs, ashtrays, towels, napkins, place mats, tablecloths, trivets, and other products. Max planned to expand his catalogue to some seventy articles by the end of the following year and to include clothing accessories such as psychedelic scarves bearing his signature. Besides providing patterns and ideas for the five producing companies that make up Peter Max Enterprises, by 1969 he had granted manufacturing licenses to scores of other companies.

Peter Max's office listed twenty-five firms that in 1971 were producing and marketing posters and other wares of his creation. The list included Crown Publishers, publisher of *The Peter Max Poster Book* (1970); William Morrow & Company, publisher of the Peter Max Library (1970),

PETER MAX

a series of Max-illustrated books containing the words of Swami Satchidananda; and Franklin Watts, Inc., publisher of a line of Max's children's books, including *The Peter Max Land of Yellow* (1970). Other firms on the list manufactured Max-adorned dresses, body stockings, curtains, drapes, bedspreads, plastic pillows and tote bags, calendars, sleeping bags, umbrellas, trays, cans, picture frame mats, stationery, gift wrappings, puzzles, ties, tee shirts, sweat shirts, sheets and pillow cases, and a school ensemble containing a looseleaf notebook and spiral-bound pads. Among the Peter Max specials soon to be marketed were belts, bank checkbooks, sleep wear, swim wear, watches, and men's shirts. His projects include ambitious plans in film making.

Admirers of Peter Max have predicted that he will become as well known to the American public as Norman Rockwell and Walt Disney. He has widened his reputation in recent years while promoting the sale of his products through personal appearances at stores in large cities and interviews on radio and television and in newspapers. A traveling art show, "The World of Peter Max," opened at the M. H. De Young Memorial Museum in San Francisco in March 1970 and later was shown in several other cities across the country. Also during that year the London Arts Gallery mounted a Peter Max fine arts show, a five-year retrospective of the artist's work, including acrylic paintings and plexiglass sculptures. In May 1970 CBS-TV presented a special called "Fifth Dimension of the Cosmic Universe of Peter Max."

"It's not me covering the world; it's some great cosmic force through me," Peter Max has asserted in press interviews. He once explained, "I'm really dealing with the future now and what makes it all revolve—man around earth, earth around sun, sun around the Milky Way. It's Cosmic Art" (quoted in the Washington *Post*, June 28, 1969). His art for the masses is geared largely to the demands of the youth market; his fresh, bold look suits the "U-25 taste"—"under twenty-five, not just chronologically, but spiritually." He conveys his Yoga-inspired themes of peace and brotherhood lightheartedly through symmetrical, rhythmical patterns of flowers, faces, butterflies, doves, checkerboards, rainbows, stars and planets, and running and flying youthful figures. Both flowing and sharply geometrical, his forms, of bright merging colors, undulate and swirl and sometimes zoom.

In 1963 Peter Max married Elizabeth Ann Nance, a former beauty queen from North Carolina. The astrology-minded couple named their first child, born in 1964, Adam Cosmo and their daughter, born in 1966, Libra Astro. The Maxes live in the same Riverside Drive apartment that the artist formerly used also as a studio. A so-called "hippie millionaire," Max wears colorful mod clothes and once owned a chauffeur-driven 1952 Rolls Royce decorated with pink, blue, and yellow decals. He is a slim man of slightly below average height and has brown eyes, black shoulder-length hair, oversize teeth, and a walrus moustache.

Neither Peter Max nor his wife drinks alcoholic beverages or smokes, and both are vegetarians. He once refused a lucrative contract in advertising for a cigarette company and instead made posters free of charge for the American Cancer Society. "Outwardly, at least," Eugene Boe wrote in his *Cue* article, "this is a gentle and serene man who seems like a good exponent of the spiritualism he espouses. . . . The tenet of peace and love certainly prevails within his working commune." Industrious and energetic, Max attributes his stamina to weekly lessons with Swami Satchidananda, whom he persuaded to move to New York and helped to establish the Integral Yoga Institute. His involvement with Yoga is central to his work, as Peter Selz pointed out in the catalogue of "The World of Peter Max" exhibition: "Peter Max has set out to create a tangible and simple fusion of East and West by applying the joy of Eastern Yoga teaching to the whole range of technological systems of the West with the hope of redecorating the world."

References

Bsns W p78+ Mr 16 '68 por
Cue 38:25 O 4 '69
Interior Design p118+ Je '67 por
Life p34+ S 5 '69 pors
London Observer p23 S 6 '70 por
N Y Times p42 F 20 '68 por
Newsday p120 My 15 '69 por
Newsweek 73:112 Ap 14 '69 por
Washington (D.C.) Post F p1+ N 1 '69

MAZZO, KAY (mä'sō)

Jan. 17, 1947- Ballerina
Address: b. New York City Ballet, New York State Theatre, Broadway and 64th St., New York 10023; h. 155 W. 68th St., New York 10023

The New York City Ballet's youngest principal dancer, Kay Mazzo, brings a simple lyricism,

KAY MAZZO

serenity, and authority to her leading roles in *Jewels, Dances at a Gathering, Agon, The Brahms-Schoenberg Quartet, A Midsummer Night's Dream,* and *Don Quixote,* among other productions in the Manhattan company's repertoire. At the beginning of her career Miss Mazzo was identified with the nymph in Jerome Robbins' *Afternoon of a Faun,* which she first danced as the "baby ballerina" with Robbins' troupe Ballets USA in 1961. She joined the New York City Ballet in 1962 and became a regular soloist in 1965 and a principal four years later. Balletomanes generally regard her as the successor to Suzanne Farrell, the New York company's unofficial prima ballerina until she quit the troupe in 1969, reportedly over differences with its director and chief choreographer, George Balanchine.

Of Italian and Yugoslavian descent, Catherine Mazzo was born in Chicago, Illinois on January 17, 1947, the only child of Alfred and Catherine (Hengel) Mazzo. Her father is a sales representative for a paper company and her mother, a piano teacher. On the advice of the family doctor, frail, six-year-old "Peanut," as Miss Mazzo was nicknamed, enrolled in dance classes to improve her health. After three years of ballet, jazz, character, and tap lessons with a Chicago teacher named Bernadene Hayes, Kay was chosen by the New York City Ballet to be one of the children in Balanchine's *The Nutcracker* during the company's Chicago performances. She repeated the role when the company returned to Chicago the following year, and by that time her chief ambition in life was to become a permanent member of the New York City Ballet.

When she was eleven Miss Mazzo accompanied her father on a business trip to New York City and sampled the lessons at the School of American Ballet, the New York City Ballet's training school. The following summer she returned for a full course, and when she was thirteen her family moved to New York and she became a full-time student in the school. Progressing rapidly, she was accepted as an apprentice with the New York City Ballet within two years, in 1961.

That same year, 1961, Jerome Robbins was reorganizing his Ballets USA company, and for a lark Miss Mazzo went along with some friends to the auditions. To her surprise, she survived the initial audition and the subsequent eliminations. With the permission of the New York City Ballet, she joined the Robbins company and appeared with it on a European tour, accompanied by her mother, and in a brief Broadway season. She danced in much of the company's ballet-jazz repertoire, but it was her performance in Robbins' duet, *Afternoon of a Faun*, that created a sensation in Paris, Copenhagen, Spoleto, and the other cities on the Ballets USA itinerary. She was televised dancing the role in London and Berlin, and later she gave a command performance at the White House for President John F. Kennedy and the Shah of Iran.

After Ballets USA disbanded, late in 1961, Kay Mazzo resumed classes at the School of American Ballet, and three months later she joined the New York City Ballet's corps de ballet. In her second season with the company she was given her first solo, in Todd Bolender's *Creation of the World*, and late in 1963 she made her first New York City Ballet appearance as the nymph in *Afternoon of a Faun*. When she performed in another Robbins ballet, *Interplay*, a year later, Walter Terry reported in the New York *Herald Tribune* (September 20, 1964), "Pert little Kay Mazzo . . . was right at home and danced both the ballet's spritely measures and its romantic blues passages with great charm."

Balanchine picked Miss Mazzo for the tragic lead in *La Valse*, one of his more successful works, in the autumn of 1964, and when she performed the role of the doomed girl Allen Hughes wrote in the New York *Times* (October 7, 1964), "Miss Mazzo has a small round face with an expression that is usually either pert or wistful. . . . Because she also maintains good, authoritative carriage of the upper part of her body, she makes you know that she is somebody and that she is doing something important."

Meanwhile, Miss Mazzo was making occasional appearances elsewhere when not engaged at Lincoln Center. For example, she performed in Robbins' *Opus Jazz* to celebrate President Kennedy's birthday at Madison Square Garden, in his *Tchaikovsky Pas de Deux* with the Mobile (Alabama) Civic Ballet, and in his *Pas de Dix* and *Minkus Pas de Trois* in a company headed by Maria Tallchief and Royes Fernandez at Jacob's Pillow. In a dance tribute to the memory of President Kennedy, sponsored by the Dallas Civic Opera Guild in the autumn of 1964, she danced with Jacques d'Amboise in *Meditation from Thais*, and the two dancers performed the same work on the television program *Hollywood Palace* in January 1965.

In the New York City Ballet, after creating the lead in John Taras' *Shadow'd Ground* and adding Balanchine's *Liebeslieder Walzer* to her repertoire, Miss Mazzo was promoted to the rank of soloist in the spring of 1965, but for several years she remained overshadowed by the company's older soloists. After seeing her as the Marzipan Shep-

herdess in *Nutcracker* Clive Barnes complained in the New York *Times* (January 9, 1967), "One would really like to see her given the chance to do more." Looking back, Virginia Lee Warren observed in *Dance Magazine* (January 1970) that "critics were slow to acclaim her, but dancers have always loved her."

In the New York *Times* for April 17, 1967 Clive Barnes reported that in the third movement of Balanchine's ultra-modern *Episodes* Miss Mazzo gave "its complexities a touchingly lean and tender look." Barnes was less happy with her performance in the ballerina role in John Taras' *La Guirlande de Campra*, however, noting that she possessed a "naturally patrician look . . . . [that] here . . . proved almost too serene, too unwavering in expression." When Miss Mazzo debuted as Balanchine's Firebird almost two years later, Anna Kisselgoff of the New York *Times* (January 20, 1969) had a similar complaint: "The beauty of her style of dancing is most apparent in its lyricism, and her technique in the difficult pas de deux . . . was flawless. Yet her characterization lacked the required dazzle."

The turning point in Miss Mazzo's career occurred in the spring of 1969, when Suzanne Farrell, protégé of Balanchine, departed from the company in mid-season. On May 18 she stepped into a role that had been closely identified with Miss Farrell, the lead in the Diamonds section of Balanchine's *Jewels*. (She had previously danced the lead in the Emeralds section.) Barnes asserted in the *Times* (May 20, 1969) that he generally preferred Miss Mazzo. "She hasn't the singing, instinctive musicality of Miss Farrell. . . . Yet she does have her own, quieter qualities, and her dancing has a pleasingly secretive passion. She has a warmth and feeling, and, most of all, a touching vulnerability." Other Farrell roles that have been assigned to Mazzo include the girl in *Serenade*, the lead in the second movement of *Symphony in C*, Titania in *A Midsummer Night's Dream*, Terpsichore in *Apollo*, and Dulcinea in *Don Quixote*.

On the whole, Miss Mazzo's performances have received favorable comparison with the former star's, but such comparisons justifiably annoy her. "It's illogical to dissect an individual's performance with analogies. I am whatever I am at the moment of the ballet. It makes me uncomfortable to be compared with anyone. But more than that, it makes me mad," she told Barbara Gail Rowes of the Washington *Post* (July 26, 1970). Nonetheless, such comparisons are probably inevitable. Although the New York City Ballet ostensibly eschews the star system, in fact Balanchine has over the years favored a series of ballerinas, giving them the best parts and creating new ballets for them. Suzanne Farrell enjoyed such status, and Miss Mazzo is her heir presumptive. Despite the pressure that the situation has put on the dancer, Miss Mazzo is apparently able to take it in her stride. As she explained to Hubert Saal of *Newsweek* (February 22, 1971), "Success is a public word. No one here thinks, 'Oh, if I do well in this new part it will make me famous or successful.'

What we think about is learning it correctly, doing it well, putting yourself into it. Success is just the joy of dancing."

Among the roles that Miss Mazzo has added to her repertoire in recent years are the Sugar Plum Fairy in *Nutcracker,* the beautiful sleepwalker in Balanchine's *La Sonnambula,* a dancer in Robbins' *Dances at a Gathering,* and leads in Balanchine's *Donizetti Variations, Brahms-Schoenberg Quartet, Who Cares?, Agon,* and the *Haydn Concerto.* In May 1971 she made what Clive Barnes called "a distinguished and assured debut" as Odette in Balanchine's version of *Swan Lake.* "Miss Mazzo is a dancer of line rather than music," the critic wrote in the New York *Times* (May 17, 1971); "her long neck, graceful arms and well-placed body are her sovereign assets."

On stage dark-haired, brown-eyed, delicate Kay Mazzo appears smaller than her actual size, which is five feet five and one-half inches and 104 pounds. Her real-life personality, however, is strikingly similar to the serene and refined image that she projects in performance, according to interviewers. At her father's insistence, Miss Mazzo persevered in her secondary school studies at the Rhodes School, a mid-Manhattan private school, despite the pressures that commutation between there and Lincoln Center put on her time. She received her diploma in 1968. In June of that year she was married to Jordan Benedict, an architecture student, but they separated a few months later and were divorced in 1971.

"I objected—and I still do . . . to the exclusive commitment to dance," Miss Mazzo told Hubert Saal of *Newsweek* (February 22, 1971). "So a few years ago I started a program of normalcy. . . . I even took up cooking. . . . I tried taking a course in literature. I did everything I could to meet people outside the dance. But there's no way, no time or energy left after twelve hours in the theater. . . . If you've got a problem, if your heart's breaking, just go and take class and rehearse and perform and forget. . . . I've given up on normalcy." With her two cats Kay Mazzo lives in an apartment a few blocks from Lincoln Center. She is a Roman Catholic.

References

Dance Mag 40:46+ Jl '66 pors; 44:60+ Ja '70 pors
Dance World (1970)
Newsweek 77:99+ F 22 '71 por
Washington (D.C.) Post G p1+ Jl '70 por

MEDEIROS, HUMBERTO S(OUSA) (mä-dā'rōs)

Oct. 6, 1915- Roman Catholic prelate
Address: b. Chancery of the Archdiocese of Boston, 2121 Commonwealth Ave., Brighton, Mass. 02135

From a small, impoverished diocese in southern Texas a little-known bishop, Humberto S. Medeiros, moved in September 1970 to the archdiocese of Boston, which ranks with New York and Chicago among the country's largest, to replace as archbishop one of the most illustrious princes of the Roman Catholic church in America, Richard Cardinal Cushing. Pope Paul VI's designation of Medeiros, a Portuguese immigrant, was hailed by advocates of a progressive, community-involved church because during his four-year episcopacy in Brownsville, Texas he had built a solid reputation in social activism as a defender of human and civil rights of minority groups, particularly the Mexican-American migrant farm workers.

Born on October 6, 1915 in the village of Arrifes, not far from Ponta Delgadas, capital city of the island of São Miguel in the Portuguese Azores, Humberto Sousa Medeiros is the son of Antonio Sousa and Maria de Jesús Sousa Massa (Flor) Medeiros. In 1931 he migrated to the United States with his family, settling in Fall River, Massachusetts, where he was naturalized nine years later. After their arrival in New England, his father became a millworker and Humberto took a job sweeping floors in a textile mill for 62 cents a day. Experienced at first hand with the plight of the unskilled minority worker and perhaps mindful of his own disadvantaged early years in Massachusetts, Medeiros mentioned particularly "the poor, the deprived, and the oppressed" in his first greeting to the people of the Boston archdiocese when he was named archbishop in September 1970.

During his free time while employed at the mill, Medeiros learned to speak English. He was twenty-one years old when he graduated from B.M.C. Durfee High School in Fall River. Soon afterward he studied for the priesthood at Catholic University in Washington, D.C., which awarded him his M.A. degree in 1942 and his Licentiate in Sacred Theology in 1946. Ordained at the university on June 15, 1946, he returned to Massachusetts to begin a succession of assignments as assistant priest, at St. John of God parish in Somerset in 1946, at St. Michael's parish in Fall River in 1946-47, at Our Lady of Health parish in Fall River in 1947, and at Mt. Carmel parish in New Bedford in 1949. He also served as chaplain at the St. Vincent de Paul Health Camp in 1948-49.

Research undertaken by Medeiros in 1949 and 1950 at Catholic University and the North American College (Gregorian University) in Rome contributed to his qualifying for a Doctorate in Sacred Theology, conferred in 1952 by Catholic University. Meanwhile, he had been named assistant priest at Holy Name parish in Fall River in 1950 and assistant chancellor of the diocese in 1951. During the next three years at that chancery he held the additional offices of chaplain of the Sacred Hearts Academy in Fall River and of vicar for religious, a position of service to members of religious orders—priests, brothers, and sisters—working within the diocese.

From 1953 until 1966, during the episcopacy of the Most Reverend James L. Connolly, Father Medeiros was vice-chancellor and later chancellor of the Fall River diocese. A notable event of that period was his receiving, in 1958, the papally conferred rank of domestic prelate and with it the title of Right Reverend Monsignor. In 1960 he was chosen pastor of the parish, St. Michael's, where he had served as assistant priest in the year following his ordination. He remained at St. Michael's until 1966, when after having been elevated to the bishopric by Pope Paul VI, he was selected to succeed the Most Reverend Adolph Marx, first bishop of Brownsville, Texas, who had died the preceding year.

The diocese of Brownsville, which covers a four-county area in the Rio Grande Valley of Texas, has a Catholic population of 250,000, mostly migrant farm workers. Upon taking up his duties there, Bishop Medeiros introduced the custom of opening his office three mornings a week so that he would be accessible to his flock. He ended the segregated practice by which the Anglos in a town went to one church and the Mexican-Americans to another. Adapting his life-style to that of his people, he traded in the episcopal limousine for an ordinary sedan and settled himself in one room of the bishop's mansion to make the others available to traveling priests. He distinguished himself by an unusually close involvement with the workers, journeying thousands of miles during the summer months to minister to them in their harvest labors. "I was the one who came back enriched," he said during a press conference in September 1970. "In our valley most of the people are so poor, but they are still a joyful people. . . . They have no despair."

A champion of the rights of the migrant laborers, Medeiros supported their efforts to gain a minimum wage of $1.25 an hour and to secure improved working conditions. When the workers went on strike in 1966, he defended them as victims of an economic system dominated principally by the profit motive, without sufficient regard for social obligations to employees. As quoted in the New York Times (September 9, 1970), Bishop Medeiros asserted, "When the migrant farm workers of America ask for a living wage, they do not ask for charity. What they demand is theirs by natural right. We have no time to waste. We must hurry to bring about the needed reforms for situations existing whose injustice cries to heaven."

Prisoners in the Cameron and Hidalgo County jails also benefited from Bishop Medeiros' special regard for human rights. At Christmas and Easter he customarily visited the jails to talk with the inmates, share their meals, and offer mass. "I want to be with those who need me," he once explained. Some Anglos in the diocese resented his mingling with the Spanish-speaking poor and his activities with militant groups in behalf of civil rights. In reply to name-calling, he asked, as reported in Newsweek (September 21, 1970), "If Christ lived today, do you think he would cut himself off from the Mayos [the Mexican-American Youth Organization] or from the Black Panthers? I am not going to stop these contacts even if I am called a Communist."

During his tenure in Brownsville, Bishop Medeiros multiplied the services of the diocese, which became the sponsoring agent for housing developments to accommodate Mexican-Americans. When he had arrived in Brownsville, there were forty parishes and eighty-one priests; four years later the parishes numbered fifty-eight, served by 111 priests.

ARCHBISHOP HUMBERTO S. MEDEIROS

Although he has maintained that the church should be modest in its building, he added thirty-nine parish houses and churches to the diocesan system that he directed.

Joining with prelates outside his own diocese, Medeiros fought for the working man as a member of the ad hoc committee on farm labor of the National Conference of Catholic Bishops, a group that helped to settle the prolonged dispute between Cesar Chavez' union and the California grape growers. He also served as chairman of the American Bishops' United States Catholic Conference subcommittee on allocations for Latin America. In recognition of his achievements in social justice, Critic magazine, a progressive Catholic journal, named Bishop Medeiros one of twelve bishops who showed the greatest promise for the future of the Catholic church in the United States.

The archdiocese of Boston, to which Medeiros was transferred after four years in Brownsville, has nearly 2,000,000 communicants and some 1,400 priests. Because of the burdensome administrative responsibilities that his new post entails it was suggested in the press that Bostonians would be unlikely to enjoy as close an association with Medeiros as the people of Brownsville, where he performed his pastoral duties in an outgoing and personal manner.

Boston's priests and Catholic laymen responded favorably in general to the selection of Medeiros as successor to Cushing, who had retired on September 8, 1970, although many observers registered surprise at the choice of a Portuguese-born prelate to head what has been termed a "bastion of Irish Catholicism." Others regarded the appointment as an indication of the church's sensitivity to the sizeable Portuguese population in southeastern Massachusetts and to the large influx in recent years of Puerto Ricans and Cubans. Commenting on the choice of a member of an ethnic minority to lead the archdiocese, Msgr. John Tracy Ellis, a foremost historian of the American Catholic church, said, "A decade ago this would have been unthinkable. It's a sign of healthy maturing of the church and a compliment to the common sense of its leaders."

On October 7, 1970 at a ceremony in Boston's Holy Cross Cathedral presided over by Richard Cardinal Cushing, Archbishop Luigi Raimondi, Apostolic Delegate from the Vatican to the United States, formally installed Medeiros as archbishop of Boston. With characteristic humility, Archbishop Medeiros delivered a homily on the occasion asking for the support and cooperation of the faithful of the archdiocese: "I cannot rely on any power of my own. Even if I come to you full of hope and confidence in the Lord Jesus and in His Church, I must admit that it is not without 'great fear and trembling.' Personally I feel too weak and too small for the task entrusted to me by the Holy Father, but I believe I can do all things in Him who is our strength."

Very soon after his arrival in Boston, Archbishop Medeiros indicated that he would continue to further the interests of his predecessor, Cardinal Cushing (who had died on November 2, 1970), in exceptional children, the aged, the infirm, and the imprisoned. To become known to as many people as possible, he attended ecumenical services and liturgical rites throughout the archdiocese, visiting hospitals and other institutions, as well as various youth and ethnic groups.

In an interview with Louis Garinger of the *Christian Science Monitor* (November 11, 1970), the Archbishop expressed a positive attitude toward the restlessness of young people, seeing hope in their dissatisfaction with contemporary society and in their quest for new values. "Now even though some of our youth are disoriented," he said, "if they are seeking for what is good and true, I am sure the Lord will not disappoint them. Maybe they are not calling it God, but it is God they are searching for." Regarding the ecumenical effort of his church, he is firmly convinced of the value of interchurch cooperation, but maintained in the interview for the *Christian Science Monitor,* "There is no point in my watering my belief to suit you or you watering yours to suit me. I am not selling my conscience to you, nor am I trying to buy your conscience."

A few months after taking up his official duties in New England, the Archbishop sparked a controversy discouraging to the ecumenical cause when he described the attempt to liberalize abortion laws as "a new barbarism" and "a step backward." His remarks occasioned immediate and sharp reaction from Protestant and Jewish leaders and created concern in some quarters that interfaith relations had been harmed considerably, possibly not so much by the Archbishop's view, which is the official Catholic stance on the issue, as by what the Rev. Robert N. West, international leader of the Unitarian Universalist Association, called "frantic and fanatic name-calling."

On topics such as the importance of Catholic schools, priestly celibacy, and the ordination of women, the Archbishop holds traditional views, endorsing the policies of Pope Paul VI. Asked about his views on the Vietnam war in a press conference shortly after his appointment, Archbishop Medeiros replied, "I wish it had ended yesterday. But I do not know how to end it. . . . It is our government which has to make the decision on how to end it."

But he favored church involvement in political affairs "whenever there is a moral issue."

Archbishop Medeiros has a round, pleasant face with bushy eyebrows. Modest and somewhat self-effacing, he presents a contrast to the ebullient, flamboyant Cardinal Cushing, but he is said to resemble his predecessor in his simple piety and the vigorousness of his convictions. He is an optimistic, practically oriented man who obviously prefers engagement in social action to theoretical controversy. At the basis of his spirituality lies a reliance on Scripture, which he believes holds the answers to the problems besetting the contemporary world. Hopeful of an increasing receptiveness to the Gospel message, the Archbishop told Garinger of the *Christian Science Monitor* that the church is "always in need of renewal because every member is. I have to be renewed everyday. The Lord Jesus Christ is making us new creatures all the time." Because of his faith in an evolving society, Archbishop Medeiros dedicates his strength to whatever action he feels will serve that new creation. Appropriately, his episcopal motto is *Adveniat Regnum Tuum* or May Thy Kingdom Come.

References

Christian Sci Mon p8 N 11 '70 por
N Y Times p1+ S 9 '70 por; IV p12 S 13 '70; p30 O 8 '70 por
Nat Observer p5 S 14 '70
Newsweek 76:82+ S 21 '70 por
Time 96:61 S 21 '70 por
Washington (D.C.) Post A p1+ S 9 '70 por
American Catholic Who's Who, 1970-71
Who's Who in America, 1970-71

MÉDICI, EMÍLIO GARRASTAZÚ (mā'dē-sē)

Dec. 4, 1905- President of Brazil
Address: Palácio da Alvorada, Brasilia, Brazil

Once described as "the epitome of the professional soldier—quiet, dignified, aloof from politics," General Emílio Garrastazú Médici became the twenty-seventh president of Brazil in October 1969, after a military junta chose him to succeed the ailing Arthur da Costa e Silva. He is the third chief of state of South America's largest and most populous nation since a military coup toppled the civilian government of President João Goulart in 1964. Although Médici did not aspire to the presidency, he accepted the office because he was convinced that his country—despite its immense social, political, and economic problems—has a "destiny of greatness" and that it contains within its borders "all the resources necessary to the promotion of . . . humanized development." Since taking office, Médici has done little to implement his early promise to return Brazil to democratic rule or to restore the basic constitutional liberties suspended in December 1968. At the same time, he has concentrated his efforts on programs designed to bring economic prosperity to his country.

Emílio Garrastazú Médici was born on December 4, 1905 in the town of Bagé, in the cattle country of Rio Grande do Sul, Brazil's southern-most state, to Emílio and Julia (Garrastazú) Médici. His mother was of Basque ancestry, and her maiden name, which in the Basque language means "persistence," is said by some of Médici's colleagues to characterize his personality. His father was descended from Italian immigrants who settled in southern Brazil in the nineteenth century. Médici decided upon a military career early in life, and at the age of twelve he entered military school in Pôrto Alegre, the capital of Rio Grande do Sul. In January 1927 Médici became a cadet at the Realengo Military Academy in Rio de Janeiro, and after completing his officers' training there, he was commissioned a second lieutenant in the cavalry on July 14, 1927.

Médici spent the early years of his military service in Rio Grande do Sul, which is part of Brazil's third military region. Still assigned to the cavalry, he was promoted to the rank of first lieutenant on July 18, 1929, and to captain on October 2, 1934. In the latter year he went to Rio de Janeiro to study at the School of High Command and the General Staff Preparatory School. He attained the rank of major on June 24, 1943, and became a lieutenant colonel on June 26, 1948. After serving for a time as commander of a cavalry regiment at Campo Grande in the state of Matto Grosso, Médici returned to Rio Grande do Sul, where he became an intelligence officer on the staff of General Arthur da Costa e Silva, then commander of the third military region, with whom he formed a lasting friendship. Promoted to the rank of colonel on July 25, 1953, Médici then became Costa e Silva's chief of staff, and he remained in that post for several years. A Brazilian officer who knew both men during that period has recalled that Médici's calm and imperturbability complemented his commander's more fiery temperament, and remarked as quoted in the New York *Times* (October 8, 1969): "When people left [Costa e Silva's] office burning mad, it was Médici who took them aside and calmed them down."

On July 25, 1961, Médici was promoted to brigadier general, and about that time he was appointed chief of staff of the army high command in Rio de Janeiro. Later he became commander of the National Military Academy at Agulhas Negras near Rio, and he was serving there when on March 31, 1964 a junta of high-ranking Brazilian army officers initiated the coup that resulted in the overthrow of the government of President João Goulart. Médici played no part in the coup, although as a conservative he sympathized with the goals—if not the methods—of the rebels. As a professional soldier, however, he was disturbed by the disunity and the potential for bloodshed that the coup created in the ranks of the army. When a column of loyalist troops from Rio de Janeiro were reportedly about to engage an insurgent column from São Paulo on the Rio-São Paulo road, Médici interposed the cadet corps under his command between the two opposing forces to prevent a clash. His action led to negotiations that resulted in the peaceful reunification

EMÍLIO CARRASTAZÚ MÉDICI

of the army. Soon afterward, Médici declared his support for Brazil's new military government, headed by President Humberto Castello Branco.

From 1964 to 1966 Médici served as military attaché to the Brazilian Embassy in Washington, D.C., and in July 1965 he was promoted to major general. After Costa e Silva was elected president in October 1966, Médici returned to Brazil and left the army to become civilian head of the national intelligence service. During his two years as intelligence chief Médici remained almost unknown to the Brazilian public, but he is said to have greatly increased the efficiency, effectiveness, and scope of the service, while gaining considerable insight into Brazil's social problems.

Médici returned to the army in March 1969 with the rank of lieutenant general and took command of the third military region, encompassing his home state of Rio Grande do Sul and the adjoining states of Paraná and Santa Catarina. As commander of the Third Army, Médici was said, according to a correspondent for *Le Monde* (October 15, 1969), to have "helped his great friend Costa e Silva circumvent several pointless crises and surmount numerous problems by firmly but discreetly making his position clear." According to some reports, Médici was Costa e Silva's choice as his successor. As events developed, however, the president was unable to play any part in choosing the man who would succeed him in office; in late August 1969 he was felled by a stroke that led to his death a few months later. Pending the selection of a new chief of state, the government was taken over by a military junta consisting of the three armed forces ministers.

In choosing a new president, Brazil's military leaders bypassed Costa e Silva's civilian vice-president, Pedro Aleixo, who would have been constitutionally eligible to succeed to the presidency. After Costa e Silva became incapacitated, the more than 100 generals on active duty were consulted, and from their recommendations a candidate list was compiled from which the ten generals of the Army High Command were to make their choice. As a member of the High Command,

Médici attended the earliest meetings on the presidency. He withdrew when it became evident that he was a leading candidate, indicating that he did not want to be president and that he preferred the uncomplicated routine of army life. Ironically, the very sincerity of those feelings seems to have influenced the High Command in his favor. As a nonpolitical general lacking ambitions for personal power, and as a moderate who might appeal to all shades of military opinion and to large segments of Brazil's restive populace, Médici appeared to be, as Joseph Novitski suggested in the New York *Times* (October 6, 1969), "the least controversial candidate to fit a compromise description of the desired qualities of the next President worked out in abstract by the army's ranking generals." According to an editorial in the *Christian Science Monitor* (October 13, 1969), the choice of Médici as president was "a move to provide Brazil with a head of state whose accession will not rock the boat any more than it has already been rocked."

After the only other important contender for the office—Major General Afonso Albuquerque Lima, a "hard-line" nationalist—was eliminated from consideration, the generals of Army High Command announced on October 7, 1969 their choice of Médici for the presidency. Ten days later he was officially nominated by the government party, the Aliança Renovadora Nacional (ARENA). A special session of the Brazilian Congress, meeting on October 25, elected Médici to the presidency by a vote of 293 to 0, with the members of the Movimento Democrático Brasileiro (MDB)—Brazil's only legal opposition party—abstaining. Admiral Augusto Hamann Rademaker Grunewald, a "hard-liner," was elected vice-president.

Sworn in on October 30, 1969 for a term scheduled to expire on March 15, 1974, Médici named ten new ministers to his Cabinet while retaining five who had served under Costa e Silva. At the time of his inauguration, a series of fifty-eight amendments to the 1967 constitution became effective, codifying the increased executive powers contained in the Fifth Institutional Act, under which the constitution had been suspended in December 1968. Although Médici, as president, assumed theoretically absolute powers to rule by decree, there was some question as to the actual extent of his power. Costa e Silva had the same absolute power in theory, but in practice he often had to defer to the "hard-line" generals who had put him in office.

Shortly after his nomination Médici had made a nationally televised address in which he promised to try to bring about the restoration of democracy in Brazil before the end of his term. At his first formal press conference, on February 27, 1970, however, Médici denied having made any definite commitment to restore democracy. "When I assumed the presidency . . . , I said I hoped to restore the democratic system . . . before the end of my term," he told reporters. "I did not say I would restore it." The attainment of democracy, he asserted, "calls primarily for a profound change in the mentality of those who participate in the political process." Speaking at the War College a few days later, Médici declared that the "revolutionary state" would continue "as long as it takes to implant the political, administrative, juridical, social, and economic structures capable of raising all Brazilians to a minimum level of well-being."

At first Médici was relatively moderate in handling political opposition, but by mid-1970 his regime had become sharply repressive in its treatment of dissent. Although in December 1969 Médici had repudiated the use of torture on political prisoners, such methods reportedly continued to be used on a wide scale despite protests from foreign and domestic sources, and from the Vatican. Censorship was extended and made more stringent, preventive detention was applied, and many scientists, educators, journalists, and politicians were deprived of their political rights. To justify those harsh measures and establish a basis for further repression in the future, Médici and his aides proclaimed a relentless "war against subversion" and called attention to alleged Communist infiltration of Brazilian institutions.

Although Médici did not permit the formation of a third political party, he allowed a national election—Brazil's first in four years—to be held on November 15, 1970. It was prefaced by Operation Cage, a mass crackdown on dissidents of all shades, resulting in thousands of arrests within a few days. The election, in which ARENA increased its majority of congressional seats from two-thirds to three-fourths, was viewed by Médici as a step toward the restoration of democracy. Although some 400,000 voters, mainly in the Rio de Janeiro area, cast blank ballots—the only way they could register political opposition—the generally high voter turnout was interpreted as a sign of public satisfaction with Médici's policies.

Médici's economic development program, which he announced at his new government's first full Cabinet session in January 1970, projected a broad range of goals in all spheres of Brazilian life and was designed to enable Brazil "to overtake, in record time, the level of development of the industrial countries." According to Joseph Novitski, writing in the New York *Times* (January 11, 1970), the plan showed that Médici intended "to continue the balancing act between inflation control and economic development that has marked Brazilian governments since the military assumed a dominant role in 1964." Much of Médici's economic success has resulted from an increasing flow of foreign capital into Brazil from investors who because of the president's firm commitment to the free enterprise system felt reassured that their properties would be secure from nationalization.

With a 7 percent economic growth rate and a 30 percent increase in exports, 1970 was an unparalleled boom year, at least for Brazil's urban workers. In March 1971 Médici announced plans for economic and social measures aimed at correcting the economic imbalance between urban and rural populations, including a social security program for peasants and farm workers. Like most of his predecessors, Médici recognizes that Brazil's economic future lies in the underpopulated, undeveloped, and potentially rich jungles of the Amazon delta, and he has devoted much of his effort to the opening of this vast area for economic development through such measures as the construction of a 2,480-mile trans-Amazon highway, scheduled to be completed in 1974. In July 1971 Médici announced an extensive agrarian reform and rural modernization program for Brazil's impoverished northeastern region. The $800,000,-000 program would include compensated expropriation of large, under-utilized landed estates for redistribution to peasants, as well as technical assistance to small farmers. Various programs already underway were incorporated in a master development plan that President Médici presented to Congress in September 1971. The goals of the three-year project extend beyond the end of his administration in 1974. Within a generation, according to the plan, Brazil will be a fully developed industrialized country.

In his efforts to maintain order on the domestic scene, Médici has been much less successful. Leftist urban guerrillas, supported by university students and progressive elements in the Roman Catholic clergy, have continued to wage war on the government by means of such acts as kidnappings of foreign diplomats. On the other hand, right-wing vigilante "death squads" have staged gangland-style executions of petty criminals and political dissenters, often with the tacit approval of government authorities. Nevertheless, in an address to Congress on March 31, 1971, marking the seventh anniversary of the 1964 coup, Médici expressed his satisfaction with Brazil's existing political system, which he described as "democratic order," and he declared that he did not anticipate any changes in it for the foreseeable future.

Emílio Garrastazú Médici was married in 1931 to his home-town sweetheart, Scila Gaffrée Nogueira. They have two sons and four grandchildren. Heavy-set, and dignified in appearance, the president is about six feet tall and has been described as "a man of few smiles and friends." In addition to his native Portuguese he speaks Spanish and English. He leads a quiet life, and his recreational activities consist mainly of nightly gin rummy games with his wife and watching his favorite soccer team, the Flamengo club of Rio de Janeiro, which is sometimes called "the team of the people." Among the decorations he holds is the Grand Cross of the Order of Military Merit, the Order of Naval Merit, the Order of Aeronautical Merit, the Military Medal, the Passador de Platina, the War Medal, the Medal of the Pacificador, and the Merit Medal of Santos Dumont.

References

N Y Times p16 O 8 '69 por
Nat Observer p9 O 13 '69
Britannica Book of the Year, 1971
Dictionary of Latin American and Caribbean Biography, 1971-72
International Who's Who, 1970-71

MILLETT, KATE (mil'et)

Sept. 14, 1934- Author; feminist leader
Address: b. c/o Doubleday & Co., Inc., 277 Park Ave., New York 10017

For those who think of philosophers as septuagenarian males, the youthful, profane, and free-wheeling Kate Millett must come as something of a surprise. Miss Millett found herself generally acknowledged as the "principal theoretician" and "new high priestess" of the women's liberation movement with the publication of her book *Sexual Politics* in the summer of 1970. A former teacher of English literature and philosophy at Barnard College, Miss Millett now gives a course in the sociology of women at Bryn Mawr College. She is also a sculptor whose work has been described as "whimsical" and "sardonic."

In *Sexual Politics; A Surprising Examination of Society's Most Arbitrary Folly* (Doubleday, 1970) Miss Millett advances the thesis that relations between the sexes are political with "politics" broadly defined as "power-structured relationships" or "arrangements whereby one group of persons is controlled by another"; that under the patriarchal system, the only one known to recorded history, men as a class have controlled and dominated women as a class; and that while sex differences (male-female) are physiological and apparent at birth, gender differences (masculine-feminine) are culturally conditioned. According to her, in our male-dominated society men "learn" to be aggressive, domineering, and achievement oriented and women learn such traits appropriate to a "dependency" class as passivity and submissiveness. If there *are* biologically determined differences in the psychological make-up of men and women, she asserts, they cannot be determined "until the sexes are treated . . . alike."

The second of three daughters, Katherine Murray Millett was born in St. Paul, Minnesota on September 14, 1934. The family background was Irish Catholic. One of her sisters is Mallory Millett Jones, an aspiring actress who is also active in the women's liberation movement. Kate Millett's father, a contractor, deserted the family when she was fourteen. Faced with supporting three growing children, the mother looked for work. Miss Millett recalled in an interview with Helen Dudar of the New York *Post* (August 1, 1970): "My mother had a college degree and do you know what she was offered for her first job? Demonstrating potato peelers. . . . Then she got a job selling insurance. Men get wages until they can earn commissions. My mother had to live on straight commission and the first year it was $600. Yeah, we went hungry. We lived on fear largely."

Kate Millett attended parochial schools—but with a dwindling faith, and, finally, rebelliousness—and the University of Minnesota, where she received her B.A. degree in English, *magna cum laude* and Phi Beta Kappa, in 1956. Her increasingly apparent tendency to flout convention disturbed a rich aunt, who offered to send her to Oxford University for graduate study. She accepted the offer,

KATE MILLETT

because "it was that or Woolworth's." At St. Hilda's College, Oxford, Miss Millett studied English literature for two years, earning first class honors in 1958. Returning to the United States, she began to teach English at the University of North Carolina but in mid-semester she quit and moved to New York City with the intention of devoting herself to painting and sculpting. She rented a loft on the Bowery for her combined studio and living quarters, and to support herself she worked successively as a file clerk in a bank and as a kindergarten teacher in Harlem.

From 1961 to 1963 Miss Millett was in Japan, where she sculpted and taught English at Waseda University in Tokyo. While in Japan she had her first one-woman show, at the Minami Gallery in Tokyo. The show was an exhibit of "chug" sculpture, which involves the assemblage of found metal objects. After returning to the Bowery in New York City she concentrated on furniture sculpture, also known as pop furniture or, as she prefers to call it, "common objects." Typical pieces were chairs with human-like legs, a bachelor chest made to look like a four-legged pygmy, a bed with two pair of protruding feet, and a piano with fists poised over the keyboard. There was a well-publicized show of her "suite of furniture" at the Judson Gallery in Greenwich Village in March 1967. The following year she returned to academic life, working for her Ph.D. degree in English and comparative literature at Columbia University while teaching English in the university's undergraduate school for women, Barnard College.

Meanwhile, her political career had begun to develop. Soon after returning from Japan she joined the Congress of Racial Equality and the peace movement, and about the beginning of 1965 she learned of the nascent new phase of the campaign for civil rights for women. "All my life," she recalled, as quoted in *Time* (August 31, 1970), "guys said I was neurotic. I didn't accept my femininity, they said. . . . And I thought . . . this [the women's liberation movement] is for me." When Betty Friedan founded NOW (the National Organization for Women) in 1966, Miss Millett became chairman of the organization's education committee, and in that position she wrote "Token Learning," a privately distributed critique of the quality of education in women's colleges. At Columbia she was not only a fiery organizer for women's liberation but a militant champion of various other progressive causes, including abortion reform and student rights. Apparently because her agitation made her anathema to the administration, she was relieved of her teaching post at Barnard College on December 23, 1968. "I was too much of a middle-class threat," she told Marie-Claude Wrenn in an interview for *Life* (September 4, 1970). "I wore sunglasses to faculty meetings and took the student side during the strikes."

In its original, or germinative, form, *Sexual Politics* was a short manifesto read by Miss Millett to a women's liberation meeting at Cornell University in November 1968. "It was a fiery little speech directed at girls, witty and tart and stuff like that—at least I thought it was," she recalled in an interview for *Time* (August 31, 1970). "I used to listen to it rhapsodically on tape. It needed a job of editing, but at the time I thought it was glorious." In February 1969 she began to develop the brief document into her doctoral thesis. "I was trying to trace the reasons why the first phase of the sexual revolution started, and how it changed, through the currents of literature . . . showing how literature reflects certain sides of our life, the way diamonds reflect light, or the way a broken bottle does. From culture criticism it got bigger and bigger until I was almost making a political philosophy. . . . I was really afraid to write this book. . . . I used to go crazy with terror about it." But she worked on the manuscript ceaselessly, with undivided attention, for months, finished it in September 1969, polished it, and successfully defended it for her Ph.D. in March 1970. She was awarded the degree "with distinction."

The dissertation was published as a book in August 1970. Before the end of the year *Sexual Politics* went through seven printings and sold 80,000 copies. Paperback rights were sold to Avon Books. Most of the reviews of the book were by men, many of whom were, as Helen Dudar observed in her New York *Post* article, "by turns respectful, skeptical and . . . unnerved by the whole strange affair of women organizing to change their status." Kate Millett told Miss Dudar that the reviews were of little use to her. "What I get is . . . their neurotic reactions. You expect to learn from criticism." One female reviewer, Muriel Haynes, writing in the *Saturday Review* (August 29, 1970) called *Sexual Politics* "a persuasive synthesis of the interacting elements . . . that have kept the uniquely hardy old party we know as patriarchy so long in office," and another, Barbara Hardy, reviewing the book in the New York *Times Book Review* (September 6, 1970), called it "a rare achievement . . . a piece of passionate thinking on a life-and-death aspect of our public and private lives."

Sexual Politics is divided into three sections. The first, which deals with the theory and instances of sexual politics, establishes the fundamental thesis that sex is a political category with status implications. "What goes largely unexamined, often even unacknowledged in our present social order is the birthright priority whereby males rule females." In monogamous marriage and the nuclear family as we know it, Miss Millett maintains, women (and children) are treated primarily as property belonging to the male. Lower-class women are exploited and reduced to a source of cheap labor and middle- and upper-class women are forced into a parasitical existence, dependent for food and favor upon the ruling males. When the system is most successful, she says, it results in an "interior colonization" —the creation of a slavelike mentality in which women are devoted to their masters and the institutions that keep them in bonds.

In the second part Miss Millett discusses the historical background of the subjugation and liberation of women. The section begins with an account of the first phase of the sexual revolution, which started about 1830 and ended, abortively, in reform rather than revolution, when women in the United States gained suffrage. Going on to analyze the counterrevolution, she specifies Sigmund Freud as its archvillain. She dismisses as "a male supremacist bias" Freud's theory that "penis envy" is the basis for women's masochism and passivity and that "fear of castration" is the basis for men's greater success at repressing instinctual drives and therefore attaining higher cultural achievement. She also examines and rejects functionalism and Eric Erickson's relatively "benign" theory of womb envy, among other versions of anatomy-is-destiny thought.

In the third and final section she examines four major modern writers insofar as they reflect the sexual politics of our society. D. H. Lawrence, according to Miss Millett, sees women at their most womanly as willing subjects and sacrifices to male creative power. Henry Miller sees women only as sexual partners, and sees the ideal sexual partner not as a person but as an object, a genital playground designed solely to fulfill male needs. Norman Mailer is a "prisoner of the virility cult," to whom sexuality means sadism, violence, and usually sodomy as well. Only in Genet, the French chronicler of the homosexual underworld, does she find a sympathetic understanding of the position of women. She sees in the hatred and hostility directed at Genet's homosexual "queens" a mirror image and intentional parody of relations between the sexes in heterosexual society. (Elsewhere Miss Millett says that the one nineteenth-century male writer who was able to see that "sexual politics is a mental habit buried deep in our culture" was the novelist George Meredith.)

Before the publication of *Sexual Politics*, in September 1969 Kate Millett had been rehired by Barnard to conduct an experimental communal school of philosophy in which some thirty-five students and faculty members lived and worked together in an off-campus hotel. She was "phased out" of that position the following semester when the program was transferred to the general faculty.

Since the publication of her book Miss Millet has been involved in a wide range of feminist activities. In 1970 she partially financed and directed an all-woman crew in the production of a low-budget documentary film about the lives of three women (one of them her sister Mallory). Although *Three Lives* was intended for college and other noncommercial audiences, it was premièred by Impact Films at a commercial New York City theatre late in 1971 and received generally excellent reviews. Currently she is teaching a course on the sociology of women once a week at Bryn Mawr College, and she and her publishers are planning a second book, tentatively titled "Yak," an allusion to her talkativeness. The academic tone of *Sexual Politics* will, she has said, be absent from any further writing that she does. "My style is more run-of-the-mouth Americanese, like Henry Miller. I use lots of four-letter words."

Miss Millett is an activist in or supporter of a full range of women's liberation groups, from NOW to the Radical Lesbians. Helen Dudar in her *Post* article called her association with the latter group "a blunt defiance of a culture that makes labels." Miss Dudar quoted her: "It's society that created the categories homosexual and heterosexual. We're sexual, and we're going to love people who are loveable no matter what color, gender, or anything else they are." Miss Millett has been involved in attempts to organize prostitutes, and in August 1970 she took part in the symbolic seizing of the Statue of Liberty in celebration of passage of the Equal Rights Amendment (prohibiting discrimination because of sex) by the House of Representatives.

Kate Millett is married to Fumio Yoshimura, a Japanese sculptor whom she met during her sojourn in Japan. "She was a very ordinary American liberal when I met her," Yoshimura has said, and she refers to Yoshimura as her "friend and lover." The two lived together without the intention of marrying until 1965, when Yoshimura was threatened with deportation unless he had an American wife. The couple, who have no children and, according to last report, intend to have none, live together in the Bowery loft that also serves as their studio. Millett's favorite contemporary writer is Samuel Beckett, and in late 1970 she was reading the works of Gandhi and Erik Erikson's *Gandhi's Truth*. She told Philip Nobile in an interview for the Washington *Post's Book World* (November 22, 1970) that she was experiencing "a creeping pacifism." "I get more and more committed to that as a way of life."

Miss Millett has what Marie-Claude Wrenn described in her article as an "Irish temper," but it cools quickly. Looking back on her bristlingly angry book, she told Miss Wrenn: "I had to overstate my case and find the most brutal episodes. I hope I pointed out to men how truly inhuman it is for them to think of women the way they do, to treat them that way, to act that way toward them. All I was trying to say was, look, brother, I'm human." Elsewhere she has said that she is sanguine about the prospect of the second stage of the feminist movement culminating in a sexual revolution, "if we stay nonviolent, if we make it people's liberation, and if we ally ourselves with people who don't have a great enough part of the system."

References

Life 69:22 S 4 '70 pors
London Observer p44 Mr 21 '71 por
N Y Post p17 Ag 1 '70 por
N Y Times p30 Jl 20 '70; p30 Ag 27 '70 por
Time 96:19 Ag 31 '70 por

MINGUS, CHARLES

Apr. 22, 1922- Jazz musician; composer
Address: c/o Susan Graham, 120 E. 10th St.,
New York 10003

Although he has been away from the limelight in
recent years, Charles Mingus remains one of the
most distinguished and colorful personalities in
the world of jazz. A virtuoso of the bass, which
he began playing with some of the leading jazz
combos in the 1940's, Mingus increased the musical importance of that instrument, and his unique
compositions have been widely acclaimed. Commenting on Mingus as a composer, Robert Oster-
mann wrote in the *National Observer* (September
6, 1965): "You can't place him in the so-called
mainstream of modern jazz, or in the avant-garde,
because he's on the move to another position while
you make up your mind."

Charles Mingus was born on April 22, 1922 in
Nogales, Arizona. Before he was a year old, the
Minguses moved to Los Angeles, settling in the
Watts area, now a black ghetto. His mother died
when he was three or four, and his father, an
Army man, remarried soon thereafter. His two
older sisters both received musical training, and
his late stepbrother was a guitarist who specialized in Spanish music. While attending school in
Watts, Charles was made aware of his racial heritage by the prejudice he found there. He remembers one woman teacher who hurled racist epithets at him, slapped him, and stifled his
motivation to learn. "They were thinking of sending me to a dumb school," Mingus told Nat Hentoff, as quoted in *The Jazz Life* (Dial, 1961).
After visiting the school and checking the I.Q.
records, his father told him: "Even by a white
man's standards you're supposed to be a genius."
On that same occasion, the father informed the
school authorities that if the boy were ever slapped
again he would return the attack tenfold.

Mingus' first encounter with jazz came when,
at about the age of eight, he heard a Duke Ellington recording on the radio. Before that, his musical horizons had been limited to the blues type
of gospel singing that he heard at the Holiness
church to which his stepmother belonged, and the
more sedate hymns sung in the Methodist church
attended by his father. When he was about six,
he was given a trombone, but the inadequate instruction he received from his teacher led him to
believe that he lacked the talent to master that
instrument. Nevertheless, he continued to practise, and occasionally he and his sisters gave musical recitals at the Methodist church.

About four years after he had begun to play
the trombone, Mingus met Britt Woodman, later
a trombonist with Duke Ellington's band. Woodman was only two years older than Mingus, but
he had already begun to play professionally.
When, at Woodman's suggestion Mingus took up
the cello, the schooling he received in that instrument was again substandard. He gained some
practical experience with his school band and
with the Los Angeles Junior Philharmonic, but in
high school his mastery of the cello did not measure up to required standards, and he had to leave
the school orchestra after a short time.

Mingus then decided to join the high school
jazz band, which then included such future jazz
stars as Woodman, Buddy Collette, and Chico
Hamilton. Because the cello is unsuitable for jazz,
Mingus followed Collette's advice and took up
the bass. Collette introduced him to Red Callen-
der, a professional jazz musician, who schooled
him in the rudiments of bass playing. Later,
Mingus studied for five years with H. Rheinschagen, a bassist who at one time played with
the New York Philharmonic. Under Rheinschagen's
tutelage he acquired the self-discipline and technique that enabled him to master the instrument.
Mingus was increasingly inspired by such jazz
giants as Ellington, Art Tatum, and Charlie
(Bird) Parker, but he was also influenced by
Ravel, Debussy, and Richard Strauss. At nineteen
he composed *Half-Mast Inhibition,* an orchestral
work considered avant-garde at the time.

Mingus' unique contribution to jazz has been
his expansion of the melodic function of the bass.
Traditionally that instrument had served a rhythmic function, replacing the tuba when New Orleans jazz moved indoors. Jimmy Blanton, a young
bassist with Ellington's band, by moving in that
direction before his death in 1942 at the age of
twenty-one, had demonstrated that a more subtle
melody could be produced with a bass. It remained for Mingus to bring the bass to the point
where it could be compared to the guitar—with
the drum providing the essential rhythm. Mingus'
distinctive method is to play slightly "out in front"
of the beat, rather than "on" it—or "behind" it,
as Miles Davis tends to do. The result is an almost frenetic rhythmic tension.

Beginning his professional career about 1940,
Mingus performed with Lee Young before he
joined Louis Armstrong, with whom he remained
from 1941 to 1943. He spent the years 1946
through 1948 with Kid Ory, Alvino Rey, and
Lionel Hampton, in that order. With Hampton
he made his recording debut in a bebop album,
released in 1947 by Decca, that included his composition *Mingus Fingers.* Also in the late 1940's
Mingus—along with Parker, Bud Powell, Max
Roach, and Dizzy Gillespie—made the recording
Jazz at Massey Hall, now a classic. After appearing with the Red Norvo trio in 1950-51 Mingus
temporarily quit music and settled in New York
City, where he went to work for the post office.
It was Parker who sought him out and persuaded
him in December 1951 to return to music, especially encouraging him to continue to write.

Following a stint with the Billy Taylor trio in 1952-53, Mingus appeared with other groups, including those of Parker, Gillespie, Tatum, Powell, and Stan Getz. In 1953 he tied for the New Star award in *Down Beat*'s critics' poll. Meanwhile, in 1952 Mingus and Max Roach had started their own recording company, the now defunct Debut Records, partly for the purpose of recording a series of Jazz Workshop concerts presented by Mingus beginning in the summer of 1953.

By 1956 Mingus had considerably matured as a composer. Many of his works were written in cooperation with sidemen in the groups he led. He expanded upon the concepts laid down by Parker—who died in 1955—but he refused to be boxed in by any limitations. "I remember Fats Navarro telling me, 'That's not it, Mingus, that's what they *used* to do,'" he told Nat Hentoff. "Well, I'm not going to worry about that sort of thing any more. I'm going to be *me*. If Bird were to come back to life, I wouldn't do something because *he* did it. I'd have to feel it too."

Commenting on Mingus' style, Leonard Feather noted in the 1960 edition of his *Encyclopedia of Jazz:* "His music aimed always at the further extension of the horizons of jazz and sometimes experimented with atonality and with a wide range of dissonant effects, some of which the more conservative listeners found hard to appreciate at first. Some elements offer a sharp and piquant contrast, with clearly defined folk music roots and a savage, shouting, blues-derived intensity." One jazz aficionado, contrasting Mingus' tight rhythmic control with that of other jazz groups, noted that "when a Mingus group deals with dissonance and atonality, it does not sound as if the musicians had recorded in separate rooms on different days."

Mingus has taken new and untried musicians and helped them to tap their potentialities. He never hesitates to criticize an errant sideman, even before an audience. As pianist Mal Waldron once put it, "He makes you find yourself." Another musician who worked with Mingus has said: "When you're with Mingus there is no place to hide. You really have to face who you are. . . . If you can meet that test, you leave Mingus with a confidence that is part of you for the rest of your time in music." According to Whitney Balliett, writing in the *New Yorker* (November 9, 1957), "Mingus, as a jazz composer, daringly asks of his musicians even more than the classical composer asks of his—that they carry both the letter and the spirit of the basic patterns of his composition over into their own improvisations instead of conventionally using them as a trigger for their own ruminations."

Over the years, Mingus has taken part in music festivals. In 1957 he was commissioned by Brandeis University to write a jazz composition, *Revelations*, for its fourth Festival of the Creative Arts. It was described by one jazz musician as "a powerful piece which begins with an almost Wagnerian brooding-like intensity, . . . revealed some beautiful dissonances . . . [and] reached its climax with a kind of centrifugal force." In the summer of 1960 Mingus, with Max Roach and several others, broke away from the Newport (Rhode Island) Jazz Festival in which they had been scheduled to appear, in protest against its growing commercialism and tendency to cater to mass tastes. Setting up a rival festival at nearby Cliff Walk Manor, they drew large crowds and received excellent reviews. An LP album, *Newport Rebels*, resulted from that venture, but efforts to make it into a permanent institution were unsuccessful. The participation of the Charles Mingus Sextet in the 1964 Monterey Jazz Festival was, in the view of critic Ralph J. Gleason, one of the outstanding events in the festival's seven-year history. Reviewing the album *Mingus at Monterey* in the San Francisco *Chronicle* (January 24, 1965), Gleason contended that Mingus had established himself "on a plane with Duke Ellington."

CHARLES MINGUS

With the upsurge in the popularity of jazz in the late 1950's and early 1960's, new jazz clubs blossomed from coast to coast, giving musicians more showcases for their talents and providing them with greater economic security. But there was another side to the picture: jazz had become a fad, attracting uninterested and noisy audiences. Most musicians suffered the situation in silence, but Mingus became known as "jazz's angry man." Sometimes he stopped suddenly and without warning during a performance to insist that the audience listen to the music. Once he stopped in the middle of a number to deliver what has been described as one of his milder lectures to an especially rowdy crowd, telling them: "You're here because jazz has publicity, jazz is popular, . . . and you like to associate yourself with this sort of thing. But it doesn't make you a connoisseur of the art because you follow it around. You're dilettantes of styles." On the other hand, he sometimes responded to applause with words of appreciation.

Resenting racial discrimination in all its forms, Mingus once said, as quoted in *Time* (October 2, 1964): "Don't call me a jazz musician. The word jazz means nigger, discrimination, second-class citizenship, the back-of-the-bus bit!" Despite his strong race-consciousness, his combos have been almost invariably integrated. An article in *News-*

week (December 10, 1962) quoted Mingus as paying tribute to his sideman Don Butterfield, calling him the "best damned jazz tuba player in the country," and adding: "I don't mention that because he's white, either. He's colorless, like all the good ones." For some years, Mingus has repeatedly announced plans to settle in Europe, where he has often been more appreciated than in the United States.

Pianist Billy Taylor has commented on the complexity of Mingus' personality: "Of course he's resentful, of course he's bitter. He wants fame and recognition for what he's done, and he sees other people, not as talented as he is, getting credit for his accomplishments. He's like a lot of big men. He's very emotional and very direct.... His music is so well thought out and organized, but he doesn't act that way in his personal life." But Michael Weisser, writing in *Down Beat* (February, 1964) noted that "Mingus' anger, controlled, greatly contributes to the tension of his music. The fact that he has continued to be creative long after other top musicians have succumbed to success should inform his critics to listen to what he is playing as well as what he is saying."

After two years of self-imposed retirement, Mingus appeared at the Village Vanguard in New York City on June 17, 1969. According to Whitney Balliett of the *New Yorker* (June 28, 1969), Mingus was in excellent form, firmly in control, and looking "like a seventy-year-old philosopher summoned to his alma mater for an honorary degree." In the summer of 1970 he appeared at New York's Top of the Gate, and that fall he went on an extended European tour that included an engagement at Ronnie Scott's Club in London. He was scheduled to go on a six-week tour of Japan in early 1971. According to his agent, Susan Graham, Mingus has been offered a teaching chair at the University of Buffalo, and he plans to begin to teach musical theory there in the near future.

Mingus has recorded for the Atlantic, United Artists, Columbia, MGM, RCA-Victor, Prestige, Bethlehem, Jubilee, Candid, Savoy, Impulse, Limelight, and other labels. Among his most popular albums are *Charles Mingus Presents Charles Mingus, Mingus Ah Um, Mingus, Mingus, Mingus, The Clown, Pithecanthropus Erectus, The Black Saint and the Sinner Lady,* and *Mingus Plays Piano.* His own favorite, recorded in 1957 but not released until 1962, is *Tijuana Moods,* which he has called "the best record I ever made." Before the combination of jazz and poetry readings reached the apex of popularity in the late 1950's, Mingus recorded an album with Langston Hughes and played in clubs with such poets as Kenneth Patchen.

Early in his career Mingus became involved in motion pictures, appearing in *Road to Zanzibar* (Paramount, 1941) with Bing Crosby and Bob Hope, and *Higher and Higher* (RKO, 1943) with Frank Sinatra. Later, he wrote the score for John Cassavetes' film *Shadows* (Lion-International, 1960). With Dave Brubeck he wrote the music for *All Night Long,* a British film about jazz musicians, based on *Othello.* In 1968 he was the sub-ject of a documentary film, *Mingus,* produced and directed by Thomas Reichman and released by Inlet Films. He has appeared on television shows, including a CBS series with Mel Tormé. Mingus' long-awaited book, *Beneath the Underdog,* on which he has been working from time to time since the 1950's, was published by Alfred A. Knopf, Inc. in May 1971. One of the editors at Knopf has said: "It's a very hard book to label. There are scenes taken directly from his childhood and from his musical background. There are interpretive accounts of realities and surrealities. It's neither all true nor all fiction, not an autobiography or a novel. I guess it's Mingus."

Charles Mingus reportedly has been married and divorced three times and has six children. In an interview with Jerry Tallmer in the New York *Post* (July 9, 1964) he referred to his son Charles Mingus Jr., a painter. Tallmer noted that a weight loss of some eighty pounds now placed Mingus at about 180 and made him look twenty years younger. While Mingus had formerly been "bearded, brooding, monolithic, a giant Buddha of intricate music and somber moods," he was now (in 1964), according to Tallmer, "tough, taut, clean-shaven and more whimsically caustic than somber." Balliett noted in his 1969 review that "Mingus has astonishingly intelligent eyes, and he invariably gives the impression that he *sees* every sound and texture and smell within a hundred yards." Disdainful of the diminutive of his given name, by which he had been known early in his career, Mingus has said, "Don't call me Charlie, that's a slave name, that's what you would name a dog."

References

New Yorker 45:76+ Je 26 '68
Mingus, Charles. Beneath the Underdog (1971)
Feather, Leonard. Encyclopedia of Jazz (1960)
Goldberg, Joe. Jazz Masters of the Fifties (1965)
Hentoff, Nat. The Jazz Life (1961)
Panassie, Hugues and Gautier, Madeleine. Guide to Jazz (1956)
Who's Who in America, 1970-71

MONOD, JACQUES (LUCIEN) (mo-nō')

Feb. 9, 1910- French molecular biochemist
Address: b. Institut Pasteur, 25 Rue du Docteur Roux, Paris 15, France; h. 16 Rue Thibaud, Paris 14, France

France, whose tightly centralized, tradition-bound university system tends to discourage fresh approaches in pure research, has produced Nobel laureates in science only twice in the past thirty-six years. The first instance was in 1935, when the Joliot-Curies won the Nobel Prize in chemistry. The second was in 1965, when Jacques Monod and two of his colleagues at the Pasteur Institute, long a haven for brilliant mavericks, shared the award in medicine and physiology. Monod and his associates were cited for fathoming one of life's deepest secrets, the complex mechanism by which genes manufacture the proteins necessary for the differentiated development of every living thing, and for thereby setting the direction of today's awesome revolution in genetics. Monod, the foremost living French scientist in his field, has been a staff member of the Pasteur Institute since 1945 and director of the institute since April 1971. He is also an existentialist humanist, a philosopher of science whose views may be consulted in his book *Le Hasard et la Nécessité* (1971), which enjoys the rare distinction of being at once an instant bestseller in France and a work treated in the intellectual community there and internationally with a respect at least distantly comparable to that accorded the meditations of the late Teilhard de Chardin, with whose teleological evolutionary theory Monod disagrees. In October 1971 Monod's book was published in the United States by Random House under the title *Chance and Necessity*.

Jacques Lucien Monod was born on February 9, 1910. His birthplace was Paris but he considers himself less a Parisian than a native of the south of France, where he grew up. His mother was an American of Scots descent, the former Charlotte Todd MacGregor of Milwaukee. His father was Lucien Monod, who, as a painter, was an anomaly in a family known for a century and a half for its physicians, Huguenot clergymen, teachers, and civil servants. Describing his father as a man "in whom artistic sensibility was combined with prodigious erudition and passionate love of the works of the mind," Monod once expressed his filial debt thus: "He fostered a positivist faith in the joint progress of science and society. It is to him, a reader of Darwin, that I owe my early interest in biology." Another important formative influence on Monod was Dor de la Souchère, his Greek teacher at the Lycée de Cannes and the founder and curator of the Antibes Museum.

In 1928 Monod took his baccalaureate degree and matriculated as a student of natural science in the Faculté des Sciences of the University of Paris, where he earned his licencié ès sciences degree in 1931 and his docteur ès sciences degree ten years later. Interested in studying the origins of life, he began to concentrate on genetics, and specifically on the chemical processes involved in the development of bacterial cultures, early in his doctoral work.

Monod was an assistant in the Faculté des Sciences for ten years, beginning in 1934, and on leave from the university he spent the year 1936-37 in the United States, working under geneticist Thomas Hunt Morgan at the California Institute of Technology on a Rockefeller Foundation fellowship. During World War II he fought in the Resistance as an officer in charge of an underground military unit and after the liberation of France as an officer in the regular French army, winning the Croix de Guerre, the Legion of Honor, and the American Bronze Star.

JACQUES MONOD

The rigid, government-controlled administrative structure imposed on French universities by Napoleon Bonaparte at the beginning of the nineteenth century has retarded scientific research in France ever since. When Monod was a graduate student and assistant at the University of Paris, the Faculté des Sciences was, as he has said, "twenty years or more behind contemporary biological knowledge," ignorant of the new science of genetics because it had no disciplinary category in which to accomodate it. "My teachers, who were not ill-disposed toward me, gave me to understand that I hadn't any future in the university because what I was doing was at the border between microbiology and biochemistry."

In 1945 Monod left the Faculté des Sciences and took refuge in the Pasteur Institute, one of dozens of research and teaching units within the complex known as the Centre Nationale de la Recherche Scientifique. Virtually from its founding, in 1888, the institute had been a home for those orphans of the French university system devoted to, in Monod's words, scientific "disciplines which, having nothing traditional about them, could find no place in traditional sectors." At the institute Monod headed the microbic physiology laboratory for nine years, until 1954, and the cellular biochemistry department for seventeen years, until his appointment as director.

Monod's Pasteur Institute colleagues André Lwoff and François Jacob were the other members of the team cited by the Nobel Prize committee for making important discoveries about the way that cells carry out their life chemistry. Monod's contribution to the discoveries was chiefly in the area of protein metabolism, especially the synthesis of the bacterial enzyme B-galactosidase. Lwoff's was in virus infestation, particularly in lysogenic bacteria, and Jacob's was in enzymatic induction and repression.

Lwoff was an old friend with whom Monod had already worked unofficially in enzymatic adaptation experiments. When the two were collaborating in the postwar years it was already known that genes, arranged in chromosomes in the nucleus of every cell in every living organism, are the genetic templates according to which the cell reproduces and the plant or animal develops in one way rather than another. And scientists elsewhere were in the process of discovering and elucidating the stuff of genes, a nucleic acid known as DNA (deoxyribonucleic acid), the chemical bearing the genetic code. But little was known about the complex chemical interactions by which the hereditary information is translated into the production of necessary enzymes and other proteins.

Experimenting with phage viruses infesting sewage bacteria, Lwoff and Monod were by 1950 able to demonstrate that when some viruses infect a cell they do so as aliens, commandeering the cell's genetic machinery—and in the process destroying the cell—without becoming part of it, while others, called proviruses, integrate themselves into the nucleus of the cell and, encoded in the DNA, are passed on from generation to generation as the cell reproduces. In concentrating on the inducible bacterial enzyme B-galactosidase in his work with Lwoff and, later, with Germaine Cohen-Bazire, Monod confirmed and extended a discovery that George W. Beadle and Edward L. Tatum had earlier made about enzymes, the catalysts that control chemical reactions in living organisms: each of the thousands of enzymes in a cell has its own production-regulating gene. The unanswered question remained: How is the production triggered and halted?

Beginning in the mid-1950's, American scientists identified *in vivo* a nucleic acid, RNA (ribonucleic acid), that mimicked the DNA code. But the precise role of this DNA-like substance remained unknown until Monod and François Jacob discovered it in the course of a three-year collaboration (1958-61), during part of which they were assisted by Arthur Pardee. Monod and Jacob named this nucleic acid having a base sequence complementary to the DNA helix "messenger RNA," and they described it as the agent that carries the code to the ribosomes and there directs the production of proteins. They also introduced the concept of the operon, or working gene cluster, a concept that paved the way for, and was reinforced by, the work of Marshall W. Nirenberg and others who later definitively cracked the genetic code.

The operon concept explains the strange, salutary fact that while a current of RNA constantly carries the DNA's protein-making instructions, the instructions are not carried out ceaselessly, to the point of chemical chaos, but intermittently, as needed. Monod and Jacobs' explanation was that repressor instructions are also encoded in the DNA and also transmitted constantly via RNA, and those cancel out the structural message. They pictured the operon, or gene cluster, as a circuit with a negative feedback safeguard, analogous to a thermostat. In the circuit are three genes: complementary regulator and structural genes and, between them, a common operator gene. As long as the operator is receiving the repressor signal sent out by the regulator, it is inhibited from activating the structural gene, and no protein production takes place. But as soon as there is a pertinent enzymatic threat from within or without the cell a chemical substance called a metabolite intrudes into the flow of the repressor message to the operator, blocking contact. The operator is then free to let the structural gene carry out the positive message and make the protein necessary for adaptation to the threat. Thus is life normally sustained under hostile, changing conditions. But it is also, ironically, the way that a quiescent virulent intruder into the gene structure may become activated.

In allocating funds among the various research facilities within the CNRS, the French Ministry of Education has customarily favored those projects with evident applicability to medicine or industry, and during the long years that the Pasteur Institute scientists were earning their Nobel Prize the immense possible implications of their work for the control of heredity and disease—particularly cancer—were not as clear as they are today. Consequently they carried out their epochal research with little help from the French government, in, as Monod has recalled, "a small, sordid, and stuffy" attic room. In an interview published in *Le Nouvelle Observateur* (October 20, 1965), Monod expressed his gratitude for the financial grants from governmental and private agencies in the United States without which the achievement would have been impossible. While praising the attitude toward scientific research in the United States as a "universal conception that is spontaneous, natural," he denounced "the scientific chauvinism so strong in France, as also in Germany and England." Noting that the French government had recently approached the Pasteur Institute with offers of more generous help in return for assurances of the practical applicability of the research carried out, he commented: "We refused. These people don't know what research is. We don't have to justify research. It is as plain as the nose on your face." Monod wants independent public universities with comprehensive departments of study rather than small-staffed institutes, and he would like to see put into effect a program of post-doctoral studies for enrichment in related scientific fields.

In an address at a symposium on "The Place of Value in a World of Facts" in Stockholm, Sweden in September 1969 Monod declared that the value systems of the past, from mythology through religion to rationalism and Marxist dialectical materialism, have been invalidated by modern science. If our society is to survive, he said, it must stop paying lip service to empty, inadequate faiths in which "no one really believes" and find a new moral standard that will be "axiomatic," transcending science—which is not competent to arbitrate value—but analogous to science's method of finding truth through "logic confronted by experience." Otherwise, he warned, society would be incapable of living up to the promise offered by contemporary science or facing the menace presented by it. Regarding the menace, Monod has elsewhere expressed his concern over such matters as genetic engineering, and he has suggested that scientists as responsible individuals and as a group must confront the possibility that occasions may arise when they will have to decide that, for the sake of humanity, a dangerous discovery must be suppressed on their own initiative.

When *Le Hasard et la Nécessité* was published at the beginning of 1971 it quickly became a popular success, and 155,000 copies were in print by March. In the book-length meditation on the philosophical implications of the revolutionary discoveries made about basic life processes by scientists such as himself in recent decades, Monod stated his conviction that life began by the chance collision of particles of nucleic acid in the "prebiotic soup," and that human evolution came about by a paradoxical combination of free, unpredictable mutations and the kind of necessity, or inexorable natural selection, of which Darwin spoke. "Chance alone is the source of all novelty, all creation in the biosphere. Pure chance, only chance, absolute but blind liberty at the root of the prodigious edifice that is evolution: this central notion of modern biology is today . . . the only one conceivable." Echoing his old friend the late Albert Camus, he concluded: "Man knows at last that he is alone in the indifferent immensity of the universe. . . . His duty, like his fate, is written nowhere. It is for him to choose between the kingdom and the darkness."

Jacques Monod and Odette Bruhl, an archaeologist and museum curator, were married in 1938. They have two sons, one a geologist and the other a physicist. Monod is a short, trim, handsome man who looks much younger than his years. In 1969, when he was fifty-nine, one journalist compared his appearance to that of "a matinee idol of thirty-five." The French biochemist speaks fluent English, with only a slight accent. His recreations are sailing, mountain climbing, and playing the cello, at which he is excellent. In recent years Monod has held professorial posts at the Sorbonne and the Collège de France in addition to his position at the Pasteur Institute, and he is an adviser to the Salk Institute in California. His honors include several honorary degrees and the Leopold Mayer Prize of the French Academy of Sciences (1962). He is a member of the American Academy of Arts and Sciences and Deutsche Akademie der Naturforscher Leopoldina and a foreign member of the Royal Society and the National Academy of Sciences.

Politically, Monod was once a Communist, but he broke from the party when Stalin insisted that all members accept Lysenko's now discredited genetic theory. Sympathizing with the youthful New Left, he joined his students in street demonstrations during the campus rebellion of the spring of 1968. For the precarious period that mankind faces in the immediate future, Monod advocates a stable-state society, characterized by limited population growth and supervised by a form of world authority. He believes that nationalism, like war, is part of the "darkness" rather than the "kingdom."

References

N Y Times p36 O 15 '65 por
Science 150:462+ O 22 '65 por
McGraw-Hill Modern Men of Science (1966)
Sourkes, Theodore L. Nobel Prize Winners in Medicine and Physiology, 1901-65 (1966)
Who's Who in America, 1970-71
Who's Who in France, 1969-70
World Who's Who in Science, 1968

MOORE, MARY TYLER

Dec. 29, 1937- Actress
Address: b. 1040 North Las Palmas, Hollywood, Calif. 90038; h. 703 North Beverly Drive, Beverly Hills, Calif. 94710

As the bright, ebullient housewife in the CBS situation comedy series the *Dick Van Dyke Show*, Mary Tyler Moore won three Emmy nominations and two Emmies and reigned for five years (1961-66) as, in the words of Joanne Stang of the New York *Times*, "the virtually uncontested popularity queen of weekly television." But public appreciation of her natural talent as a comic actress was somewhat obscured by the illusion that Dick Van Dyke was "carrying" her. That misconception has been forever laid to rest now that Miss Moore stars in her own CBS series, the *Mary Tyler Moore Show*, a half-hour weekly spoof on TV production itself. In that show, which made its debut in 1970, she is able to give fuller vent to the irony that belies her much-touted "wholesome" physical beauty and to employ to better advantage the fine sense of timing that comes from her training in the dance.

Mary Tyler Moore was born in Brooklyn, New York, on December 29, 1937, the oldest of the three children of George Tyler and Marjorie (Hackett) Moore. Raised a Roman Catholic, she attended St. Rose of Lima Grammar School in Brooklyn until, when she was eight, the family moved to Los Angeles, California, where her father became an executive with the Southern California Gas Company. Alluding to the "happy home" in which she was raised, Miss Moore told Joanne Stang in an interview for the New York *Times* (May 9, 1965): "I know that everyone successful in this business is supposed to have some neurosis that provides that extra push. In that area I guess I am deprived. . . . I've never felt neglected or suffered from a loss of love."

In Los Angeles Miss Moore attended St. Ambrose Grammar School and Immaculate Heart High School, and she studied dancing throughout childhood and adolescence. In a statement made to *Current Biography* in 1970, Miss Moore said that the chief factor in her choice of a career was "a love of ballet and all forms of make-believe." As soon as she graduated from high school, in 1955, an uncle and aunt with show business connections helped her get her first job, as a singing and dancing pixie in television commercials for

MARY TYLER MOORE

comic actress and some recognized her forte, which is timing. Analyzing her popularity with women as well as men in the home audience, Joanne Stang wrote in her New York *Times* article: "Miss Moore has made housewifery a highly palatable pastime. . . . She is neither drudge nor harpy and, while pert, not 'cute' enough to make one gag. The ladies are grateful to find one of the sorority portrayed with ginger, and they sense—quite accurately—that anyone who *seems* so nice must really be so."

Beginning in 1962, the *Dick Van Dyke Show* ranked consistently among the top fifteen network programs on television, and toward the end of its tenure it reached seventh place in the rankings. In both 1963 and 1964 the National Academy of Television Arts and Sciences honored the show with three Emmy awards, for outstanding humor, writing, and direction, and in both 1964 and 1965 Van Dyke and Miss Moore won the Emmy awards for the best acting in a regular television series. In 1965 Miss Moore also received the Foreign Press Golden Globe Award for best female television personality of the year.

Production of the Dick Van Dyke Show ended in 1966, when Van Dyke left the cast to venture into motion pictures. (Reruns of the series have been syndicated to local television stations around the country.) Producer David Merrick chose Miss Moore to star as Holly Golightly in *Breakfast at Tiffany's*, a musical stage version of Truman Capote's novel, but there were difficulties with the book and the show closed in December 1966 after four preview performances at the Majestic Theatre in New York.

From Broadway, Miss Moore went to Hollywood, where she had already made one film, *X-15* (United Artists, 1961), which she has called "the worst picture in film history." Under contract to Universal Pictures, she played Julie Andrews' prim, Mary Pickford-like roommate in *Thoroughly Modern Millie* (1967), an "unappealing role," as Paul D. Zimmerman noted in *Newsweek* (April 10, 1967), that she managed to "survive"; she was miscast as a hippie who turns chic when a tropical bird infects all of New York City with a euphoria-creating virus in *What's So Bad About Feeling Good?* (1968); and she played a nun in lay clothes helping a dedicated physician (Elvis Presley) in a Puerto Rican-Negro ghetto in *Change of Habit* (1969). Donald J. Mayerson of *Cue* (January 31, 1970), while acknowledging that *Change of Habit* was "simplistic," with a "Pollyanna approach to the urban crisis," nevertheless found it to be "gentle and warm," and according to the reviewer for *Variety* (October 22, 1969) Miss Moore delivered "a spritely performance."

An hour-long music-and-comedy special starring Dick Van Dyke and Mary Tyler Moore, aired over the CBS television network on April 13, 1969, drew such a strong response from viewers that all three major networks offered Miss Moore series contracts. She accepted the CBS offer, a multimillion-dollar contract that gave her part ownership of the production and a free hand in its con-

Hotpoint appliances. Those and other commercials brought her an income of $10,000 in her first year as a professional, and they led to assignments in the chorus of the *Eddie Fisher Show* and other television programs.

In her first continuing dramatic role on network television, that of the sultry-voiced secretary to the private detective (David Janssen) in *Richard Diamond* in 1959, Miss Moore was invisible to the home audience, except for her hands and legs. That thirteen-week assignment was frustrating and low-paying, but under its impetus she found regular employment as an actress in teleplays—some sixty-five in all—in such series as 77 *Sunset Strip, The Deputy,* and *Hawaiian Eye.*

When Miss Moore auditioned for the role of Danny Thomas' daughter in the situation comedy series *Make Room for Daddy,* the aquiline-nosed comedian rejected her, for physiognomic reasons. ("With a nose like yours, my darling, you don't look like you could belong to me.") But Thomas remembered her when he and Carl Reiner, his partner in Calvados Productions, were casting for the *Dick Van Dyke Show,* a half-hour weekly situation comedy series based loosely on Reiner's experiences as a television comedy writer. Thomas and Reiner signed her for the female lead, Laura Petrie, the wife of the writer, Rob Petrie (Dick Van Dyke). They cast Rose Marie and Morey Amsterdam as Rob's professional colleagues, and Richard Deacon was also signed as a regular in the cast. The scripts written by Reiner, Bill Persky, and Sam Denoff were essentially misadventures, often zany but rooted in the probable, that revealed the all-too-human fallibility of the Petries without detracting from their image as a warm, loving, and lovable couple.

The *Dick Van Dyke Show* was a success from its debut, in September 1961, and Mary Tyler Moore was an integral ingredient in that success. Some critics were distracted by her "pert" personality, "luscious" figure, and "wholesome" beauty, but once the obeisances to Venus were paid most reviewers acknowledged her ability as a nimble

ception. The show created for CBS, with her consultation, by James L. Brooks and Allan Burns was the *Mary Tyler Moore Show*, about Mary Richards, assistant producer of a news show at a Minneapolis television station. The performers signed to support Miss Moore in the series were Ed Asner (who plays Grant, the bibulous head producer), Ted Knight (who plays Ted Baxter, the egocentric news anchorman), Valerie Harper, and Gavin McLeod.

The *Mary Tyler Moore Show* premièred on Saturday, September 19, 1970 at 9:30 P.M. Eastern Standard Time. Two weeks after its debut Marvin Kitman of *Newsday* (October 6, 1970) described it as "tightly written, amusing," and two months later John Leonard wrote in *Life* (December 18, 1970): "Much, justifiably, has been made of Miss Moore's extravagant gestures, superb sense of timing, comic instinct, repertoire of tricks, voice that scales the escarpments of hysteria in ten seconds flat. She's wonderful. But the really subversive thing about the show is that she's over thirty without being either a widow or a nurse. Her only magical power is a withering irony that exposes most of the men around her as jerks. . . . If the *Mary Tyler Moore Show* ever goes into weekday reruns, vampirized homemakers may get their consciousness raised to the point where they will refuse to leave their brains in the sugar canister any longer." The show is filmed at the General Services Studios in Hollywood with three cameras and a live audience. The star has often said that she finds television work much more satisfying than movie making, with its fragmented operations in which the actors are often bewildered pawns of directors.

Mary Tyler Moore married Grant A. Tinker, a television executive at Twentieth Century-Fox, on June 1, 1963. By a former marriage, to Richard Meeker, a television account executive, she has a son, Richard. Regarding her present husband, she has said: "I don't want to be anyplace without him." At last report the Tinkers were living with Richie and three dogs in a Beverly Hills mansion leased from George Montgomery but they were looking forward to having a house of their own overlooking the Pacific. In the meantime they were spending their weekends in a small seaside apartment. "I like the outdoor life," Miss Moore has said. Her favorite outdoor recreations are swimming, ice skating, horseback riding, and water skiing, and in her sedentary leisure she likes to curl up with a book, usually a bestseller. She does not enjoy household chores, which she leaves, as she has said, to "a lady who cooks much better than I do." "I'd much rather sit down over a cocktail at the end of the day than struggle in the kitchen." Her preferred clothing is casual—slacks, sweaters, sneakers.

The brunette actress was described by a writer for *Newsweek* (August 1, 1966) as "tall and well proportioned [five feet seven, 123 pounds], with slim legs, a wide sensuous mouth, and a pert nose. After interviewing her, Agnes Murphy wrote in the New York *Post* (July 15, 1967): "Her coffee brown eyes sparkle, grow thoughtful, flash, and can probably glower as her mood changes." And after he talked with her, Rollie Hochstein reported in *Good Housekeeping* (April 1967): "While Mary looked and talked like a sunny neighbor, she also has been notably hard-headed, hard-driving, and career-minded."

References

Good H 172:59+ Ja '71 por
N Y Post p56 Ap 15 '67 por; p43 Jl 15 '67
N Y Times II p17 My 20 '62 por; II p15 My 9 '65 por
N Y World Journal Tribune mag p20+ Mr 19 '67 por
Newsweek 68:78 Ag 1 '66 por
TV Guide p34+ S 19 '70 por
Who's Who of American Women, 1970-71

MOORER, THOMAS H(INMAN)

Feb. 9, 1912- United States military official; Naval officer
Address: b. Office of the Chairman of the Joint Chiefs of Staff, The Pentagon, Washington, D.C. 20301; h. 402 Barbour St., Eufala, Ala. 36027

The most technologically advanced armed forces of any country are only as good as the men who must man the weapons, according to one of the Navy's leading strategists, Admiral Thomas H. Moorer, the former naval aviator and fleet commander who is now Chairman of the United States Joint Chiefs of Staff, the highest military post in the nation. Moorer, a World War II hero in the Pacific and much bemedalled former Chief of Naval Operations, has asserted, "No matter how complex or how awesome you build the weapons of war, man is still the vital element of our defense. Men make decisions; men fight battles, and men win wars." Admiral Moorer has championed the aircraft carrier as one of the most crucial components of United States defense strategy throughout his career.

Of Dutch and English ancestry, Thomas Hinman Moorer was born in Mount Willing, Alabama on February 9, 1912, the son of Dr. Richard R. Moorer, a dentist, and Hulda (Hill Hinson) Moorer. He has two brothers, Dr. William D. Moorer, a dentist, and Captain Joseph P. Moorer of the United States Navy, and a sister, Mrs. E. A. Wilkinson. In 1927 Thomas Moorer graduated from Cloverdale High School in Mount Willing, where his favorite subject was history, as a fifteen-year-old class valedictorian. Interested in technology and drawn by a "natural attraction" to military service, Moorer applied for admittance to the United States Naval Academy in Annapolis, Maryland, but because of his youth, he was not admitted until June 1929, when he was seventeen years old.

As a midshipman, Moorer majored in engineering and he was a lineman on the varsity football team for three years. After his graduation and commission as an ensign in June 1933, he served

ADM. THOMAS H. MOORER

for six months as a junior officer in the gunnery department aboard the cruiser USS *Salt Lake City*. In December 1933 he was transferred to the Navy Yard in New York, where he helped to fit out the cruiser USS *New Orleans* and then served aboard that ship in its gunnery and engineering departments until June 1935.

For the next year Moorer took flight training at the Naval Air Station in Pensacola, Florida, receiving his wings and a promotion to lieutenant (j.g.) in July 1936. The following month he was assigned to Fighting Squadron One-B, based briefly on the aircraft carrier USS *Langley* and later on the USS *Lexington*. In July 1937 he was transferred to the USS *Enterprise*, where he served with Fighting Squadron Six. Moorer was assigned to Patrol Squadron Twenty-Two, a unit of Pacific Fleet Air Wing Two, in June 1939. Transferred to Fleet Air Wing Ten, he was with that squadron at Pearl Harbor, Hawaii when the Japanese attacked on December 7, 1941. By then a full lieutenant, Moorer was one of the first American pilots to get his plane into the sky after the attack.

Moorer's squadron was sent to the Southwest Pacific, and on February 19, 1942, during the Dutch East Indies campaign, his twin-engine Catalina PBY was attacked by nine Japanese fighter planes, north of Darwin, Australia. With one engine destroyed and large chunks torn out of its fuselage and gas tank, the PBY burst into flames. Moorer brought the almost controlless plane down to the surface of the water at the dangerous speed of more than one hundred miles an hour. "I struck the water at great force," he later recalled, "but after bouncing three times I managed to complete the landing."

The eight-man crew, four of whom were wounded, including Moorer, who had a piece of shrapnel lodged in his hip, paddled away from the burning wreckage in life rafts. Two hours later they were picked up by a Philippine freighter laden with ammunition and supplies. Moorer and his crew had hardly boarded the freighter when it came under attack by twenty-seven Japanese dive bombers. After several direct hits, the ship began to sink and Moorer ordered his men overboard, taking command of one of the two lifeboats that the Filipinos managed to get over the side.

Although wounded, Moorer navigated the two lifeboats to an uninhabited island where he drew a huge "SOS" in the sand. Two days later the castaways were rescued by a Royal Australian Air Force plane. In addition to receiving the Purple Heart because of his wounds, Moorer was awarded the Silver Star for his "extremely gallant conduct" and his "courage and leadership" during the incident. Three months later, after he successfully flew supplies to a beleaguered garrison and evacuated eight seriously wounded men from the island of Timor, in the southern Malay Archipelago, Moorer was awarded the Distinguished Flying Cross.

Moorer returned to the United States in July 1942, only to leave the next month for the United Kingdom, where he temporarily served as a mining observer for the Commander in Chief of the United States Fleet. Promoted to the rank of lieutenant commander in October 1942, he served in the United Kingdom until March 1943, when he assumed command and fitted out Bombing Squadron One Hundred Thirty-Two, which operated in Cuba and Africa from its home base at Key West, Florida. In March 1944 Moorer was detached from that command to serve as gunnery and tactical officer on the staff of the Air Force Commander of the Atlantic Fleet. He remained in that post until July 1945, during which period he was promoted to the rank of commander.

For his work on the staff of the Commander Air Force, Atlantic Fleet, Moorer was awarded the Legion of Merit. The citation read that he "planned and supervised the development and practical application of tactics, doctrines, and training methods relating to anti-submarine warfare and gunnery; supervised many experimental and developmental projects; and coordinated information on enemy tactics and countermeasures. . . . By his outstanding executive ability, Commander Moorer contributed materially to the combat effectiveness of aircraft in anti-submarine warfare. . . ."

In August 1945 Moorer was transferred to Japan, where he was assigned to interrogate Japanese officials for the Strategic Bombing Survey of the Office of the Chief of Naval Operations. In May 1946 he returned to the United States, where for the next two years he served as executive officer of the Naval Aviation Ordnance Test Station, Chincoteague, Virginia. He next saw sea duty as operations officer of the aircraft carrier USS *Midway* from July 1948 to November 1949, when he was assigned to the staff of the commander of Carrier Division Four, Atlantic Fleet, as operations officer, a post he held until July 1950.

For a year, beginning with August 1950, Moorer served as experimental officer of the Naval Ordnance Test Station in Inyokern, California. Having been promoted in the meantime to the rank of captain, in the following year he went to Newport, Rhode Island, where he attended the Naval War College. In August 1953 he was again assigned to the staff of the Commander Air Force, Atlantic Fleet, where he served as plans officer.

In another and more prestigious desk assignment, Moorer was ordered to report to the Navy Department in Washington, D.C., in May 1955, to serve as aide to the Assistant Secretary of the Navy (Air), but a year later he was back on sea duty as commanding officer of the USS *Salisbury Sound*. After President Dwight D. Eisenhower approved the selection of Moorer for the rank of rear admiral in July 1957, he reported to the Office of the Chief of Naval Operations in Washington, serving as special assistant in the Strategic Plans Division. Specializing in matters relating to war games, from January 1958 until July 1959 he was assistant Chief of Naval Operations, after which assignment he became commander of Carrier Division Six.

Once again assigned to the office of the Chief of Naval Operations in November 1960, Moorer directed the long range objectives group. While in the Pentagon he sometimes nettled Robert McNamara, then Secretary of Defense, and his aides (whom he christened "the numbers-racket people") by presenting them with analogies. One of his favorites was: "Arnold Palmer played golf the other day. In terms of your weapons-analysis system he used his 5 iron three times, his driver 18 times, and his putter 38 times. Well, according to your system, if he wants to play even better golf, he should go out and get more putters." In October 1962 Moorer was advanced to the rank of vice-admiral and placed in command of the Seventh Fleet. For his work with the Seventh Fleet he was awarded the Distinguished Service Medal. On June 26, 1964 he was made a full admiral and named Commander in Chief of the Pacific Fleet.

When, in April 1965, Moorer took charge of NATO's allied command, the United States Unified Atlantic Command, and the United States Atlantic Fleet, the takeover marked the first time an American naval officer had been given command of both the Pacific and the Atlantic fleets. During the crisis in the Dominican Republic in 1965-66, Moorer was awarded a Gold Star in lieu of a second Distinguished Service Medal. The citation praised Moorer for directing military operations "with utmost professionalism, judgment, and diplomacy, resulting in a cease-fire, politico-military stabilization of the situation . . . and finally the orderly and peaceful withdrawal of U.S. forces." He was also cited for revising NATO's maritime strategy, for developing the concept of a standing naval force for the Allied Command Atlantic, and for helping to establish the headquarters of the Iberian Atlantic Command.

On June 3, 1967 President Lyndon B. Johnson named Thomas H. Moorer to succeed Admiral David L. McDonald as Chief of Naval Operations and to serve as the representative of the Navy Department on the Joint Chiefs of Staff. After Senate confirmation, Moorer became the eighteenth Chief of Naval Operations on August 1, 1967. He took over the post during a critical period in American history, while the war continued in Vietnam and while Navy technology explored beneath the seas and extended into outer space. In 1968 the growing presence of the Soviet Navy began to make itself felt when a large Russian task force appeared in the Mediterranean, the Red Sea, and the Indian Ocean.

To counter the new Soviet threat, Moorer called for the modernization of aging United States naval forces and promoted the "multiple-buy" system, thus assuring a steady, yearly input of new ships for the fleet. Under Moorer's leadership, nuclear submarine construction entered a new phase, and programs were instituted for faster "hunter-killer" and electric-drive "quiet" types to carry the latest equipment for undersea warfare. Pointing to the dramatic Russian buildup, Moorer warned that American indifference to the Soviet threat could lead to the United States's becoming a second-rate power, and he called for a new emphasis on defense. In a recent speech while accepting the Hawks Award from American Legion Air Service Post 501 in New York City, Moorer said: "Now I think that we do have domestic problems. People are talking about the rearranging of priorities. But I can only say that no matter what problems we have, unless we provide for the defense of the country, then all other problems become moot."

President Nixon reappointed Moorer Chief of Naval Operations in June 1969, in recognition of the same superior performance in office that won him a Gold Star that same year for his "forceful and aggressive leadership . . . during a period of increasing worldwide commitments and continuous combat operations against enemy forces in Southeast Asia." So confident was Nixon of Moorer's capabilities that on April 14, 1970 he appointed Moorer to succeed General Earle G. Wheeler as chairman of the Joint Chiefs of Staff, the nation's highest-ranking military office. The Joint Chiefs, consisting of a chairman and the heads of the Army, Navy, Air Force, and Marine Corps, advise the President and the Secretary of Defense on the nation's defense needs. Confirmed by the Senate in June 1970 by a vote of 78 to 2, Moorer became the first naval officer in thirteen years to serve as Chairman of the Joint Chiefs of Staff. In that post he was called to testify before the House Armed Services Committee in March 1971 on the administration's $76 billion defense spending request. He cautioned again that within several years the United States could fall into a position of "strategic inferiority" to the Soviet Union.

Thomas Hinman Moorer married Carrie Ellen Foy of Eufala, Alabama, who is known as one of Washington's most popular and gracious hostesses, on November 28, 1935. They have three sons, Thomas Randolph, Richard Foy, and Robert Hill, and a daughter, Mary Ellen (Mrs. David Butcher). The Moorers live in historic Admiral's House, the hospitable, rambling Victorian mansion originally built in 1893 for the superintendent of the Naval Observatory. Six feet tall and weighing 195 pounds, Moorer has brown eyes and receding brownish-gray hair. Hunting, fishing, chess, bridge, and golf are his favorite recreations. Newsmen have often described him as soft-spoken, affable, low-keyed, and noncontroversial, and as an organization man with a quiet sense of humor and more than his share of small-town Southern charm. His colleagues see him as "the man you always send for when you have a tough job" and have called him "damned competent but not flamboyant." One of his Pentagon associates has said: "The big thing about Tom Moorer is that he is steady. He uses the 'soft sell' approach, and does it effectively. But he does his homework, and always seems to know what he is talking about."

Among the organizations to which Moorer belongs are the United States Naval Institute, the Naval Historical Foundation, the Alfalfa Club, the Navy Relief Society, the Alabama Academy of Honor and the Navy Mutual Aid Association. He holds an honorary Doctor of Laws degree from Auburn University and the Stephen Decatur Award of Operational Competence from the Navy League. Moorer is an independent in politics. A Protestant, in April 1970 he testified in the United States District Court in Washington in support of compulsory chapel attendance at the nation's three military service academies. "An atheist could not be as great a military leader as one who is not an atheist," Moorer said. "I don't think you will find an atheist who has reached the peak in the Armed Forces."

References

N Y Times p2 Ag 16 '68 por
Time 85:21 F 26 '65 por
Washington (D.C.) Post A p1 Ap 15 '70
International Who's Who, 1970-71
U.S. Navy Biographical Dictionary, 1964
Who's Who, 1969-70
Who's Who in America, 1970-71

MORRIS, ROBERT

Feb. 9, 1931- Sculptor
Address: b. c/o Leo Castelli Gallery, 4 E. 77th St., New York 10021

An art theorist who investigates his concepts in his own work, Robert Morris has severely disturbed traditional ideas about sculpture with "minimal" objects and random constructions of gigantic scale that fuse process with product and call not simply for visual perception but kinesthetic response to mass, weight, and scale. "He has taken us as far from the past as any other sculptor at this time," Samuel Wagstaff, curator of contemporary art of the Detroit Institute of Arts, recently said of Morris, whose influence has also been felt in "soft" sculpture, "earthworks," and other idioms that appeared in the 1960's. In exploring the processes of perception, he has experimented in the dance, as well as sculpture, and to a lesser degree in film and tape recording.

The son of Robert and Laura Pearl Morris, Robert Morris was born on February 9, 1931 in Kansas City, Missouri, where his parents still operate a dry cleaning business. He began to paint at the age of eight or nine. From 1948 to 1950 he studied at the University of Kansas City and the Kansas City Art Institute. During a later, ten-year residence on the West Coast he attended the California School of Fine Arts in San Francisco in 1951 and Reed College from 1953 to 1955. The hiatus in his study occurred when he was sent to Korea with the United States Army Corps of Engineers to work on airfield construction.

In contending during the 1950's with what he believed to be fundamental artistic problems, Morris became disenchanted with painting as a suitable means of achieving his objectives. He has described his work of that decade as abstract expressionism in the style of Clyfford Still and of Jackson Pollock, in whose canvases form emerges from the act of painting itself. Marcia Tucker observed in her survey for Morris' sculpture exhibition at the Whitney Museum of American Art in 1970 that by the mid-1950's he had begun to show a concern for the process as well as the product of an artistic effort. The influence of Pollock could be seen in the "overall patterning, loose brushwork and understated color." Morris held one-man shows at the Dilexi Gallery in San Francisco in 1957 and 1958, but the following year he gave up painting, frustrated by the irrelevancy in his own work between the process and the finished picture.

Shortly after he had moved to New York City in 1961, Morris enrolled in Hunter College, taking graduate courses in art history during 1962 and 1963. At about the time he left California he became involved in working in three dimensions, creating "objects." As its title suggests, his first sculptural piece, *Box With the Sound of Its Own Making* (1961), is a walnut box containing a three-hour tape recording of the sounds made when the box was being fabricated. Morris had once complained, as quoted in *Newsweek* (January 19, 1970), that painting "couldn't contain the time that went into doing it." In *Box*, however, he succeeded to a degree in merging past and present as well as process and product.

Some of the other constructions of what has been called Morris' neo-Dada period focus attention on the nature of an object by references, at times paradoxical, to its function. In *Metered Bulb* (1963) a bulb provides light for the meter that measures its consumption of electrical power. Another witty 1963 composition, untitled, consists of a padlocked cabinet bearing the inscription "Leave Key on Hook Inside Cabinet." The products of that early phase of Morris' career have been compared to compositions of Marcel Duchamp and Jasper Johns, and in his own writings Morris has acknowledged antecedents in Duchamp. In an essay, however, on Morris' work for a retrospective at the Corcoran Gallery in late 1969, Annette Michelson noted that except for an initial indebtedness Morris' relationship to Duchamp is "essentially analogous to that of a composer returning to a master's themes as to a repertory of sources for profoundly innovative variations."

Among the different artistic expressions that Morris explored in the early 1960's was the dance. While still in California, he had taken part in theatrical improvisations and in that hybrid art form, the so-called "happening." During the years from 1963 to 1965 he created five avant-garde dance pieces, *Arizona, 21.3, Site, Weatherman Switch,* and *Check,* which have been presented in New York, Buffalo, Ann Arbor, Stockholm, and Düsseldorf. In several works seen in New York, Morris was choreographer, designer, and principal performer. *Waterman Switch,* presented at the Judson Memorial Church in New York in March 1965, provoked lively comment, not all of it critically favorable. In it Morris and Yvonne Rainer, to whom he was then married, moved slowly across the stage in a face-to-face embrace, costumed only in mineral oil. Movement in that dance, as in some others, was kept to a minimum, but by making movement an object, Morris reduced the effect of nudity. In an interview with E. C. Goossen in *Art in America* (May-June 1970), Morris explained that his interest in the dance was part of his general involvement with "that relationship toward things that has to do with the body's response, that set of relationships toward mass and weight as well as scale." Although he no longer performs or choreographs, he continues to design, having created settings for productions of the Merce Cunningham Dance Company.

In keeping with his tendency toward simultaneous, rather than successive, developments in various idioms, in 1961 Morris produced his first unitary object, an eight-foot plywood column. That piece and other large structures, such as boxes and arches, of rigid, extremely simplified forms were soon to be called "minimal" or "primary," having anticipated the minimal sculpture movement, of which Morris is a recognized pioneer. His December 1964 show at the Green Gallery in New York was devoted to a display of gray plywood geometric structures, each devoid of internal relationships, which Morris felt would have diminished the relationship of the object to the surrounding space and to the spectator. Writing later in *Artforum* magazine (October 1966), he asserted that "the better new work takes relationships out of the work and makes them a function of space, light, and the viewer's field of vision."

Shape is the most important element of sculpture for Morris. In 1965 he began work on a group of plywood L-beams, which because of their shape can be placed in a number of different ways, each way producing a different aesthetic effect. He has also formed geometric structures from plexiglass, fiberglass, aluminum, metal mesh, and other materials. Commenting on the most minimal of Morris' sculptures, a plywood rectangular solid made in 1966, Marcia Tucker pointed out, "This piece, like so many others, forces us to confront the complex question of how one perceives things, that is, how we are involved with the work, how we react to it and to what extent our involvement lends it meaning."

Morris is also interested in the ways that scale and surface influence, or alter, perception. Color, like internal relationships, is rejected in his minimal work, except for the flat gray of his plywood pieces that does not interfere with the effects of the play of light on form. Color, he believes, does

not contribute to the essential character of sculpture in filling space. It is, moreover, nontactile and therefore presumably not necessary to the haptic response that Morris intends his sculpture to evoke in the viewer.

Although Morris continued to execute minimal sculptures, in 1967-68 a shift appeared not only in the physical nature of his work, but perhaps also in its underlying sensibility. During the summer of 1967 he made the first of a group of large-scale felt pieces—shredded felt heaped at random on the floor and ribbons of felt draping the wall or falling in tangles to the floor. When some of his felt sculptures were shown at the Leo Castelli Gallery in New York in April 1968, he told Grace Glueck of the New York *Times* (April 28, 1968) that he was attracted to the new medium because of the "physicality, the presence" of the material and the fact that the form it takes is not "preconceived." An admirer of the soft sculpture of Claes Oldenburg, Morris explained his fascination with the role of gravity in shaping a work: "Everytime you hang the same felt piece, the action of gravity changes it. You can't visualize the outcome."

A few months after Morris' felt sculptures were shown in New York, his first "earthwork"—a mound of earth mixed with felt chips and other bits of seeming junk—was included in a group show at the Dwan Gallery in Los Angeles, in October 1968. In the same year Morris received a $10,-000 commission from the students at Northwestern University to landscape a landfill between the campus and Lake Michigan. A project undertaken at the Castelli warehouse in New York the following year consisted of earth, water, paper, grease, wood, felt, electric lights, photographs, and other media. Morris altered it daily, first by the addition of elements and then by their subtraction until in the final state little remained but threads and photographs of the work in progress. In a recent series of lithographs he presented his ground plans for ten projected earthworks in Missouri.

Related to his earthworks in both concept and chronology are Morris' "scatter" pieces, which also eliminate the figure-ground distinction usually observed in sculpture. An example is a 1968-69 work consisting of a large room scattered with pieces of felt, various metals, and rubber. The haphazard assemblage of heterogeneous items gives the effect of homogeneity; the viewer perceives the whole of the work, not its separate parts. One of his open-air pieces, "outside the structuring factor of the room," is a 1970 arrangement of steel, timbers, and huge concrete boulders executed for the Detroit Institute of Arts.

The development of Morris' innovative work in sculpture was surveyed in all its variety and complexity in a retrospective exhibition organized jointly by the Corcoran Gallery of Art in Washington and the Detroit Institute of Arts and shown in both cities in late 1969 and early 1970. In January 1970 he was represented in the Museum of Modern Art's "Spaces" exhibition, a show that called upon the spectator to experience particular aesthetic concepts with all his perceptive faculties, rather than simply to perceive visually "collectible" art objects. Morris' contribution was a slightly refrigerated room containing a landscape *trompe l'oeil*, a vista of mountaintops achieved by perspectival planting of tiny spruce trees. The work was destroyed after the show.

The new works of Morris exhibited at the Whitney Museum of American Art in New York in April-May 1970 included geometric pieces and imposing "spill" constructions. The largest of the latter was a ninety-six-foot-long stack of massive concrete blocks, steel pipes, and heavy wooden beams. That random aggregation, one of many that have led to Morris' being called "the prophet of the New Disorder," was installed with the help of a crane over a period of several days. The public was allowed to watch the less dangerous phases of the installation at the Whitney as part of experiencing the process of art.

Grace Glueck, who reviewed the Whitney show in the New York *Times* (April 11, 1970), acknowledged that Morris' spill pieces did carry out his theories—"the 'positive value' of huge and public scale; the spectator's forced confrontation with unaltered materials; and the avoidance of 'preconceived ideas,' such as composition and the relationship of parts." She recognized the "exciting expressive power" of his work, with "the massive, unsettling scale overwhelming the space of the room." At the time of Morris' show in Detroit, on January 25, 1970, another art critic of the New York *Times,* Hilton Kramer, had described his own "experience as a participant in the artist's particular *mise en scène*" as "simply too thin, too commonplace, too utterly sterile, to permit either a recapitulation or an analysis." He summed up what he considered to be the standard criticism of minimal and related movements: "the triumph of ideas over art."

By posing challenging questions, all of Morris' work, including his essays in *Artforum,* has stirred widespread critical debate. "Some critics have condemned its preciosity and consider it a sabotage of the artistic process," Martin Friedman wrote in *Art International* (December 1966). He pointed out, however, that Morris sees his work as representing more than "a dialectical position and not only rebels against what he considers a dead tradition of sculpture but by his production offers a positive, if radical, alternative." In defending Morris against the charge that he is "concerned only with ideas for which the sculpture serves as illustration," Marcia Tucker has argued that his transcendence of established forms and methods in sculpture defies usual critical analysis and must be appreciated in terms of the nature of human experience.

On May 18, 1970 Morris closed his show at the Whitney Museum, which had been scheduled to run until May 31. The closing, he explained, was intended to underscore the need that he and others felt "to shift priorities at this time from art making and viewing to unified action within the art community against the intensifying conditions of repression, war and racism in this country." Morris was chosen chairman of a group—the New York Strike—organized to stage a strike against museums and galleries, stop collaboration with the federal government on artistic activities, and attempt to politicize gallery and museum visitors. A strike on May 22 succeeded in closing some 100 museums and galleries. One of those that stayed open, the Metropolitan Museum of Art, was the target of an orderly sit-in by nearly 500 artists, students, and teachers led by Morris.

As a steering member of the emergency cultural government committee of the New York Art Strike, Morris helped to engineer the withdrawal in June 1970 of about half of the artists whose graphics had been chosen for exhibition in the United States pavilion at the Venice Biennale. In protest against certain foreign and domestic policies of the federal government, the committee intended to "challenge the United States government for the loyalties of American artists in each and every upcoming international art event in which government sponsorship is a criterion for participation." Toward the end of the year, however, Morris had decided to curtail his political activity in favor of spending more time on his sculptural efforts, especially on the preparations for an exhibition at London's Tate Gallery that opened in April 1971. He has continued to challenge certain art institutions, most recently with the formation of the Peripatetic Artists Guild, which would enable artists to work under commissions for rates based on time spent, in refutation of the long-standing gallery system.

Robert Morris' work has been represented in more than sixty group shows in the United States and abroad. He has taught since 1964 at Hunter College and has conducted seminars at Yale University and the University of Wisconsin. His awards include a 1966 prize of the Chicago Art Institute and a Guggenheim International Award for 1967. According to David L. Shirey of *Newsweek* (January 19, 1970), Morris "usually wears Levis, a bolero vest, puffs on a stogie and is a dead ringer for the young Buster Keaton." He lives in a spacious, white-walled loft apartment in lower Manhattan, near the so-called "SoHo" district, which has become known recently as a home for artists and reasonably adventurous galleries. His apartment does not actually function as a studio, since the scale of most of his current work requires something more nearly the size of a large warehouse.

References

Art in Am 58:104+ My-Je '70 por
N Y Post p37 Je 4 '70 por
N Y Times II p27 Ja 25 '70
Newsweek 75:94 Ja 19 '70
Time 91:74 My 17 '68 por

Tucker, Marcia. Robert Morris (1970)
Who's Who in America, 1970-71

MORTON, ROGERS C(LARK) B(ALLARD)

Sept. 19, 1914- United States Secretary of the Interior
Address: b. Department of the Interior, C St. between 18th and 19th Sts., N.W., Washington, D.C. 20240; h. "Presqu'ile," R.D. 1, Easton, Md. 21601

When designated Secretary of the Interior in November 1970, Rogers C. B. Morton at last achieved the office to which he seems to have been directed by a series of successful careers in business, farming, government, and politics. An affable man of towering stature, he had built up his influence within the Republican party from a background of family distinction, personal wealth, and business acumen through four terms in the United States House of Representatives from Maryland's Eastern Shore. A congenial political relationship with President Richard Nixon led to his appointment as chairman of the Republican National Committee in April 1969. Morton's enthusiastic acceptance of the Cabinet post of Secretary of the Interior reflected his lifelong enjoyment of outdoor life. He foresees a growing role for the Interior Department in conserving and preserving the nation's natural resources and a more dedicated mission to manage the use of those resources for the national benefit, including the often-competing economic, social, and environmental interests.

A descendant of the American Revolutionary frontier leader General George Rogers Clark, Rogers Clark Ballard Morton is a seventh-generation Kentuckian. He was born on September 19, 1914 in Louisville, Kentucky to Dr. David Cummins and Mary Harris (Ballard) Morton. His wealthy and socially prominent family had long been active in Republican politics, and his older brother, Thruston B. Morton, became a Senator from Kentucky, serving from 1957 to 1968.

During Morton's childhood the family used to leave their gracious home in Kentucky to spend the winter months at Eau Gallie on Florida's inland waterway. He later prepared for college at Woodberry Forest School, near Orange, Virginia, and then, as his brother had done seven years earlier, he entered Yale University. A basketball

ROGERS C. B. MORTON

player in college, as in secondary school, Morton once scored 30 points in a game against the Columbia University team, in the days when that was an impressive number. Trips out West, including camping adventures, during his student years reinforced his early love of the outdoors. In the summer of 1933 he worked for several weeks on a ranch near Yellowstone National Park.

After graduating from Yale with the B.A. degree in 1937, Morton studied for a year at the College of Physicians and Surgeons at Columbia University, but eventually decided against following his father in a medical career. He served for a time in the Navy, until being discharged because of a back ailment. When the United States entered World War II, he enlisted in the Army as a private in the field artillery and was sent to officers' candidate school and then to the European Theatre of Operations. He attained the rank of captain before leaving the service in 1945.

Since 1939 Morton had been engaged in the management of Ballard & Ballard Company, the family flour milling and processing firm. Returning to Louisville after the war, he assumed the vice-presidency of the company, and the following year was named president. He remained in that office until 1951, when the firm merged with the Pillsbury Company. Retaining an administrative association, he held the posts of vice-president of Pillsbury until 1953 and of director and member of the executive committee from 1953 to January 1971. Prominent in Louisville community affairs after the war, he served as a trustee of the University of Louisville, as a member of the board of the Children's Hospital, and as finance chairman of the local Republican organization.

In the early 1950's Morton and his family moved from their farm in Oldham County, Kentucky to a thousand-acre farm in the Chesapeake Bay region of Maryland. He had searched for a new place to settle by sailing on the forty-nine-foot yacht, owned jointly with his brother, from Florida up the inland waterway and found he preferred Maryland's Eastern Shore. Morton raised cattle and began a commercial cattle-feeding business. In Maryland he also cultivated his interest in politics, for which he had shown a flair when managing the early campaigns in Kentucky of Thruston Morton, who had first been elected to Congress in 1946. At a disadvantage in a traditionally Democratic territory, in 1960 Rogers Morton organized the unsuccessful election attempt of Edward T. Miller, the Republican Congressional nominee from Maryland's First District. Becoming a Republican candidate himself in 1962, he won a seat in the House of Representatives in the Eighty-eighth Congress and was reelected with considerable margins four times.

The committees on which Morton served during his first three terms in the House were the Interior and Insular Affairs, the Merchant Marine and Fisheries, and the Select Committee on Small Business. As ranking minority member of the territorial and insular affairs subcommittee of the Interior Committee, he was one of two Representatives appointed in 1965 to the United States—Puerto Rico Commission on the status of the Commonwealth of Puerto Rico. In 1969, when the Ninety-first Congress convened, he relinquished his other House assignments to become a member of the powerful, tax-writing Ways and Means Committee.

Representative Morton's voting record appears to be one of distinct moderation both in reflecting the conservativeness of his Maryland district and in adhering to party policies. After considerable hesitation he voted for the 1964 Civil Rights Act, probably against the wishes of most of his constituents, but in 1968 he opposed a civil rights-open housing bill favored by President Nixon. During the Ninetieth Congress his votes showed more than 50 percent agreement with the positions of the conservative coalition of Republicans and Southern Democrats and during the Ninety-first Congress, more than 60 percent agreement with the stand on issues taken by Nixon. As revealed in the voting studies of the *Congressional Quarterly Almanac* he was by no means among the high scorers in the consistency of his support during those four years.

On environmental and conservation measures Morton's record is somewhat uneven. His opponents point, for example, to his refusal to endorse the use of federal funds for highway beautification. On the other hand, he drafted the legislation that established the Assateaque Island National Seashore in Maryland and Virginia in 1965; helped to develop laws for preserving estuarine areas; and sponsored an oil-pollution-control bill. In the Ninety-first Congress he was a sponsor in the House of Nixon's major environmental program.

An avid partisan politician, Morton had quickly established himself in the House Republican organization by running candidate schools for G.O.P. Congressional hopefuls, starting a program to send young Congressmen to speak on college campuses, and by proving himself a successful fund-raiser for the House Republican Campaign Committee. After Barry M. Goldwater's defeat in the 1964 Presidential election, Morton worked to revive the party by touring the country to speak to local groups. From the start of the political maneuvering for the 1968 Presidential election, he backed Nixon. Although Morton declined to serve as his national campaign manager, he became floor manager on the efficient team that won the nomination for Nixon at the G.O.P. convention in Miami in August. Morton also made the nominating speech for Spiro T. Agnew, the candidate for Vice-President. After the convention Morton was on Nixon's Key Issues Committee, whose twenty-five members met regularly to discuss campaign matters and advise the President-elect and his running mate.

The month following Nixon's Presidential inauguration, Ray C. Bliss offered his resignation as chairman of the Republican National Committee, to become effective in mid-April 1969. Rogers Morton was named as Nixon's personal choice for the post. The national committee of both major political parties officially governs the party under the leadership of the national chairman. When the party has a President in office, the President becomes the actual leader, the chairman acts as the chief spokesman for Administration policies. Morton accepted the position under the condition that he be able to select his own staff, to which the President agreed. His success blocked an attempt by an old associate of Nixon, Murray Chotiner, to assume a powerful place in the party headquarters, and added to Morton's political stature. Assuming the chairmanship after being unanimously elected by the national committee on April 14, he insisted on serving without pay. He retained his seat in the House of Representatives and his membership on the Ways and Means Committee.

The new chairman began his task of regaining control of the Congress for the Republicans in the 1970 mid-term elections with a determination to change the party image, to transform the G.O.P. into the "swinging, action party of the day." He recruited new people for top positions and planned a reorganization of the committee's structure. He pledged to work for deeper involvement in the affairs of state and other local G.O.P. units, to abolish traditional divisions in the headquarters that had catered to minority and ethnic voting blocs, and to broaden the party's base of support by becoming "massively involved with millions of young people . . . black people . . . poor people." Within minutes of his election, he announced in a news conference that he would lead a party campaign in support of the Administration's antiballistic missile (ABM) proposal, for "good political purpose." His proposal drew sharp criticism from Republican ABM opponents who saw it as a loyalty test to suppress dissent within the party, from the Democrats who threatened to launch an anti-ABM information campaign, and, within the week, from the President himself, who implied a rebuke when he stated that he did not consider the ABM issue to be a partisan question. Following that somewhat clamorous initiation into his job, Morton worked closely with the White House in supporting the President's Vietnam war policies and some of Vice-President Agnew's more controversial statements concerning television news coverage.

In December 1969, after much speculation in the press to the contrary, Morton in a joint appearance with Nixon, announced that he would not run in Maryland's 1970 Senate race, but would campaign to remain a Representative. His refusal was analyzed as an indication that G.O.P. strategists had decided that Democratic Senator Joseph D. Tydings was unbeatable, in a state where voter registration was almost three-to-one Democratic, and that Morton's seniority in the House and his place on the Ways and Means Committee were too valuable to risk.

After an undistinguished Republican showing in the 1970 elections had increased the friction between elements of the White House political staff and members of the national committee, Morton resigned the chairmanship. In late November he was designated as Nixon's choice to replace Walter J. Hickel as the Secretary of the Interior, a post that had eluded him after Nixon's 1968 victory when the President honored a pledge to give the job to a Westerner. Morton was officially nominated to the Cabinet post by the President on January 25, 1971. The Senate Interior Committee, which was friendly toward him, unanimously approved the nomination after two days of hearings. Morton told the committee that he was resigning his directorship of the Pillsbury Company, which had been charged with alleged price-fixing, and of the Atlas Chemical Company, a large producer of explosives, with which he had been associated since 1959.

Although the League of Conservation Voters found much fault with Morton's voting record in environmental issues, he had vowed upon his designation as Secretary of the Interior "to purify our environment." At the Senate hearing on his nomination, he asserted, "The priority of our environment must be brought into equity with that of our economy and our defense. Otherwise, at some point in time, . . . there will be no economy to enjoy, and practically no reason for defense." He was sworn into office on January 29, 1971.

The Department of the Interior encompasses a large number of diverse agencies dealing with natural resources such as oil, gas, and water; peoples, including the American Indian and the population of the Trust Territory of Micronesia; and land in the national parks and forests and wilderness areas. Morton was immediately faced with issues including government clearance for the controversial trans-Alaska oil pipeline, development of United States-owned mineral resources, and the creation of parks in or near urban areas. In February he announced that he was a "long way" from a decision on the pipeline and in October he reported that the issue was still under study —a boost for environmentalists opposed to the project. In early March the Administration disclosed a plan to reorganize the department to make it more responsive to White House policies. Morton explained that his aim was to control all programs within the department and prevent agencies from acting independently through chan-

nels to Congress and contacts in their particular fields, such as gas and oil. His program looked toward a balanced utilization of natural resources and a "vigorous program" of park development. He has expressed an intention to give the American Indians increased opportunity and responsibility for their development. The new secretary's Eastern background, political expertise, and belief in the committee system have been seen as probable assets in gaining legislative approval for his ideas.

Rogers C. B. Morton and Anne Prather Jones, of Louisville, were married on May 27, 1939. They have a son, David C., who is an architect, and a married daughter, Mrs. Anne Jones McCance. The Mortons own an award-winning restored Washington, D.C. town house, a beach house in the Bahamas, and a spacious old house at their Maryland farm, of which they have retained 165 of the original 1,000 acres. Morton, who used to say that his middle initials stood for "Chesapeake Bay," has been called a "jolly giant," standing six feet six and a half inches tall and weighing about 250 pounds. He has a shaggy white head of hair. His accomplishments include carpentry, boating, outdoor sports, and piloting his own plane. "He also has a lightning mind for repartee," a friend of his told a staff writer for the Washington *Star* (December 14, 1970), "is a first class raconteur and has a magnificent sense of humor." Among his clubs are the Pendennis in Louisville and the Chesapeake Bay Yacht. As a descendant of an American Revolutionary war officer, Morton is a member of the Society of the Cincinnati. He has served on the board of visitors of the United States Naval Academy and since 1962 on the board of visitors and governors of Washington College of Maryland. The family's church is the Episcopal.

References

Louisville Courier-J p1+ D 29 '70
N Y Post p47 Mr 11 '69 por
N Y Times p19 F 27 '69 por; p35 N 27 '70 por
Time 96:46+ D 14 '70 por
Wall St. J p3 N 27 '70
Washington (D.C.) Post H p1+ Ag 10 '69
Washington (D.C.) Star D 14 '70
Congressional Directory (1971)
Who's Who in America, 1970-71
Who's Who in American Politics, 1969-1970

MOSS, FRANK E(DWARD)

Sept. 23, 1911- United States Senator from Utah; lawyer
Address: b. New Senate Office Bldg., Washington, D.C. 20510; h. 1848 Wasatch Dr., Salt Lake City, Utah 84108

The success of Senator Frank E. Moss, a self-styled liberal Democrat, in winning election three times as Senator from the predominantly conserva-

FRANK E. MOSS

tive Republican state of Utah, is primarily due to his many legislative accomplishments on behalf of his home state. After spending eighteen years in elected offices in Utah, he won a three-way race for the Senate in 1958, partly because of a split in the Republican vote. In 1970 he survived a determined effort by the Nixon administration to defeat him. Willing to do the hard work in preparing legislation, Moss has focused on issues important to his state, such as development of natural resources, but has also been a leader in handling problems of national concern like those involving consumer protection, pollution, and law and order. Over the years an impressively large number of Moss-originated bills have been either enacted into law or incorporated into other laws. On January 21, 1971 he was elected to the third-ranking position of leadership in the Senate, the secretary of the Democratic conference.

A descendant of pioneering Mormons, Frank Edward Moss was born in Salt Lake City, Utah on September 23, 1911 to Maud (Nixon) and James Edward Moss, a Utah educator. He attended public schools, graduated from Granite High School in 1929, and obtained his B.A. degree *magna cum laude* from the University of Utah in 1933. Enrolling in the George Washington University Law School in Washington, D.C., he served as editor of the *Law Review* in 1936-37 and was awarded his Juris Doctor degree *cum laude* in 1937.

During the next two years, from 1937 to 1939, he remained in Washington as a member of the legal staff at the Securities and Exchange Commission. He then returned to Utah to open a private law practice in Salt Lake City, where in 1940 he was elected to his first public office, as a city judge. After the United States' entry into World War II, he served with the Army Air Corps in the judge advocate general's department in Europe. (He is at present a colonel in the United States Air Force Reserve.) At home in Utah following his discharge from the service in 1945, he was reelected city judge of the Salt Lake City court, an office he held until his resignation in

1950. Then for eight years he served as county attorney in Salt Lake County, a post to which he was elected in 1950 and again in 1954. During those years he practised law in the Salt Lake City firms of Moss & Hyde from 1951 to 1955 and Moss & Cowley from 1955 to 1959.

In his first bid for statewide office Moss failed to win the gubernatorial nomination at the Democratic primary convention of 1956. Two years later, however, he made what was described in the *Congressional Quarterly Almanac* (1958) as a "surprisingly strong showing—for a Democrat from Utah," by drawing 37,000 votes in the party primary for nomination to the United States Senate. As a whole, the Democratic ticket chalked up 51 percent of the primary vote, as compared to its 40 percent in 1956. Moss's opponents were the incumbent Republican Senator Arthur V. Watkins and former Governor J. Bracken Lee, an outspoken foe of the income tax. According to the New York *Times* (November 6, 1958), the three-way contest was "one of the most bitter campaigns in recent Utah history."

Making a strong appeal to the labor vote in his drive for office, Moss concentrated on the industrializing areas of the state. He criticized the G.O.P. for not supporting the Kennedy-Ives labor reform bill and was able to tap out-of-state funds from party and labor sources. In the election on November 4, 1958 Moss received 38.7 percent of the vote, with Watkins getting 34.8 percent and Lee 26.5 percent. The split in the Republican ranks contributed greatly to Moss's lead, but a reporter for the New York *Times* (November 6, 1958) found, "There is no doubt the general pro-Democratic trend, sparked by labor leadership and the Utah party's 'liberal group,' was a dominant factor in the Moss victory."

Over more recent years, however, Utah, with a population that rose from just under to just over 1,000,000 during the 1960's, has clearly remained in the Republican column, a fact that has made Moss fairly vulnerable. Since 1952 the state has always cast its electoral votes for Republican Presidential candidates, with the sole exception of Senator Barry M. Goldwater in 1964. In that year Moss faced his first reelection campaign. While he was unopposed in the primary, early polls in April gave him little chance of winning. Identifying himself as a "Johnson man," he defeated the staunchly conservative Ernest Wilkinson by 228,-210 votes to 169,492. Some political observers named Moss among the candidates who in the Democratic landslide rode in on Johnson's coattails. The 1970 election was a much more unequivocal indicator of Moss's popularity. The Republicans tried manfully to unseat him and to elect Representative Lawrence J. Burton to the Senate by sending in nationally prominent Republicans to campaign for him. Mindful of the heavy anti-tobacco Mormon constituency in Utah, Moss emphasized the strenuous campaign he had been waging against cigarette advertising on TV. He defeated Burton with 56.1 percent of the vote.

In an interview for the *U.S. News and World Report* (December 26, 1958), soon after his first election to Congress, Moss described himself as a "liberal Democrat" with a "twinge of conscience." He indicated that he would proceed cautiously in many areas of domestic legislation and also in tune with the dominant "cold war" philosophy of the period, which advocated that the United States maintain a strong defensive posture in foreign affairs. Thus he was against lowering the defense budget, but wanted more careful scrutiny of the use made of foreign aid money, preferring development aid over military assistance. He also expressed his concern over federal deficit financing and his reluctance to transfer problems too hastily from state to federal jurisdiction. At the same time he recommended a federal ban on state right-to-work laws and argued for federal aid in helping the West develop its resources, both because the states lack the money and because of the benefits accruing to the entire nation from such development.

Senator Moss's voting record has been consistent with those initial concerns. According to vote profiles in the *Congressional Quarterly Almanac,* during his first term in office he voted with his party more than 80 percent of the time and supported the conservative coalition only from 12 to 14 percent. During 1962, when John F. Kennedy was President, he ranked among the Democratic Senators who voted most consistently with their party majority. In the Eighty-ninth and Ninetieth Congresses he supported President Lyndon B. Johnson 66 percent of the time on all issues, but on foreign policy alone his percentage increased to 81. After visiting Africa in 1960, he criticized the Eisenhower administration for not identifying with the self-determination efforts of the African nations and urged that more technical help be given them. That same year he came out for increasing funds for defense, voting to restore $294,000,000 deleted by the House from the defense budget for the Bomarc B antiaircraft missile. Moss also supported the 1962 Trade Expansion Act and the 1963 Nuclear Test Ban Treaty. His description of himself as a "cautious liberal" is in keeping with the voting score of 70 given him by the Americans for Democratic Action toward the end of his second term.

The key to Moss's effectiveness as a Senator has been his hard-working attention to the concerns of his home state, as brought out by radio-TV commentator Joseph McCaffrey: "He is smart, articulate and a hard worker, a parlay which is hard to beat in any field. But Senator Moss is not as widely known nationally because his primary concern is his home State of Utah. While some members of the Senate herald their presence with a shower of press releases, Moss works quietly, concentrating on the basic issues confronting his state." Because of Utah's vast underdeveloped lands, Moss sought and was granted membership on the Senate Committee of Interior and Insular Affairs. He was made chairman of the subcommittee on minerals, oil and gas, and is a member of the subcommittees on water and power, and parks and recreation. He was also named to the Commerce Committee, and is chairman of the con-

sumers subcommittee, vice-chairman of its natural resources subcommittee, and a member of the aviation, communications and surface transportation subcommittees. He is also on the Post Office and Civil Service Committee and on the Special Committee on Aging, serving as chairman of the latter's subcommittee on long term care and housing for the elderly.

President Kennedy once said, "Senator Moss has preached the doctrine of the wise use of water with, I think, more vigor than almost any other member of the United States Senate." During his first year in Congress Moss represented the Interior Committee as part of a nine-man delegation visiting the Soviet Union for thirty-one days to inspect dams and hydroelectric power facilities. The Senators praised the technical advancement of the Russians, who they believed could easily overtake the United States in water development efforts. In search of ways to import water into water-short areas, Moss has been the principal spokesman for the North American Water and Power Alliance, which has proposed a plan to bring in water from Alaska and northern Canada to the intermountain region. He has also pushed the Central Utah Project to divert a large part of the Colorado River water for use in populated areas of Utah and has annually sponsored appropriations to study and promote the project, which is being funded step by step. He has introduced and steered to passage several water-related bills, such as the Dixie Project in the Eighty-eighth Congress to authorize multipurpose development of certain rivers in Utah, assistance to small reclamation projects in the Eighty-ninth Congress, and flood control projects in the Ninetieth Congress.

Out of his concern for water problems Moss wrote *The Water Crisis* (Praeger) in 1967, a study on the politics of water and a realistic treatment of the way in which various jurisdictions, local and federal, compete for influence, thereby compounding the crisis of water shortages. He points out that state and local governments have crippled federal planning efforts and the law has become a delaying device. While documenting the infighting among federal agenices and lamenting that "no one is in charge of the federal effort," Moss is primarily interested in solutions and prescribes more planning by all agencies working together at all levels of government.

Water development inevitably means building dams, which in turn usually runs counter to the interests of conservationists. Moss was criticized in an editorial in the New York *Times* (June 10, 1960) for his opposition to the erection of structures to protect Rainbow Bridge National Monument from possible water backup from the Glen Canyon Dam. Although Moss has sponsored many projects dear to the hearts of conservationists, he has also argued against what he calls "stand pat conservationists" who put their cause above needed development projects. His work in pushing through the Canyonlands National Park bill, passed in the Senate on August 2, 1963, is an example of his position. Conservationists commended him for sponsoring the 258,600-acre-park measure, but they criticized him for not banning mineral, oil, and gas exploration and for not making the park larger, to include nearby natural attractions. In 1970 Moss did introduce a bill to expand the park by 100,000 acres. For the advancement of parks elsewhere he sponsored legislation expanding the Golden Spike National Historical Site and lended support to national parks on Cape Cod and the Indiana dunes. He sponsored bills to provide access to parks in order to facilitate their development and coauthored the Multiple Use Act in 1964 to enable the Bureau of Land Management to determine the best use of public lands, for wilderness areas, recreation, or industrial development.

Moss has pursued a balance between developing the country's resources and protecting the environment in a variety of ways. He has promoted legislation to develop such resources as oil shale and oil production from tar sands, to protect the rights of independent prospectors of phosphate, and to stimulate research leading to the upgrading of western coal. He was also a cosponsor of a coal mine safety bill that was passed in December 1969. He introduced legislation to further regional development in the Western states, most notably through the Four Corners Regional Development Commission, which has brought millions of dollars in public works and money and technical assistance grants to the area. At the same time Moss has been one of the leaders in warning against pollution. For several years he has urged the establishment of a separate Department of Natural Resources and Environment to coordinate programs. He was a cosponsor of the Environmental Quality Education Act and has pressed for many specific bills to increase research and enforce standards.

"A leading champion of the consumer in Congress," as he was described in the New York Times, Moss cosponsored the original truth-in-lending bill in 1960, proposed the creation of an independent consumer council, and wrote the Toy Safety Act in 1969. As a result of hearings that he conducted in July 1969 on consumer reaction to the Fair Packaging and Labeling Act, he drafted a bill covering product guarantees and began preparation of another relating to door-to-door sales. With Senator Philip Hart of Michigan he introduced a bill to place federal inspectors in fish-processing plants, and he has presented a bill to require "child resistant" packaging of poisonous products.

One of his most newsworthy achievements was the ban on all cigarette advertising on TV, a measure on which he had worked since 1959 and which finally went into effect on January 1, 1971. Senator Frank Church pointed out in the Senate on March 1, 1970, "Seldom does a Senator take up a cause and, almost singlehandedly, bring his colleagues to his way of thinking and steer his vision into law. Senator Frank E. Moss of Utah did just that on the cigarette advertising bill." In a later attack on the use of tobacco, Moss led five other Senators in July 1971 in an effort to strip from the agricultural appropriations bill all tobacco export subsidies.

To help meet the needs of the elderly, Moss fought for the adoption of Medicare, amended a bill in order to raise the standards of nursing homes under Medicaid, and cosponsored the January 1, 1970 increase in Social Security benefits. On behalf of Indians he has worked to resolve disputed land ownership, to reimburse Indians for tribal funds used for irrigation, and to allow for more flexibility in how oil and gas funds from Indian reservations are used.

Recalling his years spent as a prosecutor in Salt Lake County, Moss has favored legislation to provide federal assistance to local areas to improve their effectiveness in fighting crime. He was the chief Senate sponsor of the Law Enforcement Assistance Act of 1965 and was responsible for an amendment to the Safe Streets Act of 1968 to increase aid in upgrading local police forces. In the area of transportation he has urged the adoption of a national master transportation plan and has asked for a halt on discontinuance of passenger train service until such a plan can be formulated.

On another issue affecting the entire nation, Moss came out for controls on contributions to political campaigns in 1961, recommending a $10,000 ceiling on contributions by a single person and a tax credit plan to increase the number of contributions. With increasing demonstrations by students against the Vietnam war, on September 10, 1969 Moss called for the retirement of General Lewis B. Hershey, head of the selective service system, as a "meaningful gesture to the nation's young that their government is beginning to respond."

Frank E. Moss married Phyllis Hart on June 20, 1934. They have one daughter, Mrs. Marilyn Moss Armstrong, and three sons, Edward, Brian, and Gordon. The Senator's friends often call him Ted. He is an active lay official of the Church of Jesus Christ of Latter-Day Saints. He belongs to the Salt Lake County, Utah, and American Bar associations; served as president of the Utah Association of County Officials in 1955-56, and twice was president of the National Association of District Attorneys, from 1956 to 1958. Elected to the Order of the Coif, he is also a member of Phi Kappa Phi and Phi Delta Phi. In the past he served as director of the Utah Association for the United Nations, vice-president of the Air Reserve Association of the United States, director of the Utah Cancer Society, and president of the Salt Lake Lions Club. His awards include the Bronze Medal for Distinguished Service to the Aging, presented in December 1969 by the American Association of Homes for the Aging. With hunting as his sport, he has worked in Congress to protect the rights of sportsmen in matters of gun-control legislation.

References

Biographical Directory of the American Congress, 1774-1961 (1962)
Congressional Directory (1970)
Congressional Quarterly Almanac (1958)
Who's Who in America, 1970-71
Who's Who in American Politics, 1967-68

MUHAMMAD, ELIJAH

Oct. 7, 1897- Black Muslim leader
Address: b. Muhammad's Mosque No. 2, 2548
Federal St., Chicago, Ill. 60616; h. 4847 Wood-
lawn Ave., Chicago, Ill. 60615

Like Marcus Garvey before him, Elijah Muhammad preaches that the only salvation for the black
man in the United States is withdrawal into his
own autonomous nation, away from a white social
and economic system that is—in Muhammad's view
—rigged against him. Tough-minded Muhammad
claims to be the divinely appointed "Messenger"
of Allah, and thousands of poor, alienated blacks
have accepted his message, changing their lives
to join the Nation of Islam, with its stern morality, strict authoritarianism, pacifism (except in
self-defense), racial dignity, and program of economic self-improvement. Working toward the day
when they hope to have their own self-subsisting
nation, either in territory set off for them within
the United States or acquired elsewhere with the
help of the American white community (which,
in their view, owes the descendants of slaves compensation for 400 years of oppression), the Black
Muslims have set up many business enterprises,
schools, farms, and other institutions, and the
wealth of the still relatively small group is estimated at more than $10,000,000. As the late Louis
E. Lomax pointed out in his book *The Negro
Revolt* (1962), Muhammad's demand for a separate state enjoys the "symbolic support" of many
blacks who are not Muslims. "Many Negroes
feel . . . that white people will never yield, that
we will spend the remainder of our days waging
a major war over a morsel. This results in a
strange kind of withdrawal from the American
community." While many critics have expressed
fear that the militant rhetoric of the Black Muslims may inspire violence, others have pointed out
that it is a creative channel for the pent-up aggressiveness of downtrodden men and women who
have reason to be bitter at their lot.

One of thirteen children, Elijah Muhammad
was born Elijah (or Robert, according to some
sources) Poole on October 7, 1897 to two former
slaves, Wali and Marie Poole. His birthplace was
a small piece of cotton land—part of a white man's
plantation—just outside of Sandersville, Georgia,
out of which his sharecropper father eked a precarious living. Wali Poole was also a Baptist
preacher. Because he had to work as a field hand,
Muhammad attended school only until he was
nine. Looking back on his childhood and adolescence in Georgia, he has said: "I saw enough of
the white man's brutality . . . to last me 26,000
years."

The Muslim leader's light beige skin is living
evidence of the sexual sin of some hypocritical
white slave master. Referring to that distant crime,
Ralph McGill wrote in a syndicated column published in *Newsday* (March 3, 1965): "Young
Poole . . . came to hate that white man who, somewhere in the past, had coerced a slave woman. . . .
We have here a lesson that needs no elaboration.

ELIJAH MUHAMMAD

Some of man's most casual acts are like stones
dropped into a large pool. It is a long time before
the ripples reach the shore."

At sixteen Poole left home and began wandering the United States, working on railroad gangs
and doing other odd jobs. In 1923 he settled in
Detroit with his wife, the former Clara Evans, and
became an assembly-line worker in the Chevrolet
automobile plant. It was in Detroit in 1930 that
he encountered "Allah," in the person of one W. D.
Fard, a light brown-skinned peddler of silks from
"Mecca" who carried from door to door in the
city's black community, along with his wares, the
news of the "Lost-Found Nation of Islam in the
Wilderness of North America." He has recalled,
regarding Fard: "He didn't have to tell me that
he was Allah. When I first met him, I knew him.
I recognized him. And right there I told him that
he was the one the world had been looking for
to come."

When Fard mysteriously disappeared in 1934,
Poole changed his name to Muhammad and announced that the "Master" had designated him
his "Messenger," or "Apostle," the custodian of
his revelation. "He put me over the whole thing,
the whole nation. He made me the head of the
black man in America." But there were rivals for
the position claimed by Muhammad. "I had to
leave Detroit," Muhammad has recalled, as quoted
by Hans J. Massaquoi in *Ebony* (August 1970).
"The enemies, hypocrites, united together to drive
me out and I had to come here [to Chicago] and
later they came here. They united to drive me out
of here and kill me and I fled to the East Coast,
where I stayed seven years." During those seven
years he traveled much and recruited constantly,
building up small groups of followers in numerous
cities.

Working inconspicuously, Muhammad was practically invisible to the white power structure—
until the United States entered World War II,
when he was arrested for openly sympathizing
with the Japanese and encouraging young blacks
not to serve in the United States's armed forces.
Aquitted of sedition, he was found guilty on the

technicality that he himself, then forty-five years old, had refused to comply with the Selective Service Act. For that crime he served four years, from 1942 to 1946, in the federal penitentiary at Milan, Michigan.

His imprisonment appeared a martyrdom to his followers, and it so enhanced his position in the Nation of Islam that he was, on his release, able to return to Chicago as undisputed leader of the cult. Black Muslim membership grew slowly in the immediate postwar years and rapidly after 1954. Many of the converts, then as now, were inmates of prisons. Among the latter was Malcolm X (né Little), a natural leader who became a close lieutenant of Elijah Muhammad after his release from jail in 1953.

The growth of separatist sentiment among uneducated, economically desperate blacks in the 1950's went largely unnoticed in the white community because it paralleled the development of the more conspicuous integrationist civil rights movement, which attracted middle and upper-class Negroes who had a stake in the status quo. The Black Muslims looked with scorn or ridicule on those civil rights leaders, such as Martin Luther King, who hoped to achieve justice and equality in the United States by applying the technique of passive resistance used successfully by Gandhi in India. Malcolm X expressed the Muslim view graphically and succinctly: "There is a big difference in the passiveness of King and the passiveness of Gandhi. Gandhi was a big dark elephant sitting on a little white mouse. King is a little black mouse sitting on top of a big white elephant."

Those in the white, or white-oriented, community who *were* aware of the Black Muslims dismissed them as pitiable, or at least ineffectual, rhetoricians of separatist militancy. As Hans J. Massaquoi observed in his *Ebony* article, that attitude suddenly changed in the early 1960's, when Elijah Muhammad, perhaps because his health was then beginning to decline, allowed the brilliant spellbinder Malcolm X to come to the fore. "As chief spokesman of the Messenger, brother Malcolm was soon accorded the respect and coverage due the most militant and most revolutionary personality of his time. While Malcolm defiantly offered to meet white violence with black violence, the number of Muslim followers and sympathizers swelled—but so did the number of Muslim enemies. Before long, white hysteria about the 'subversive' sect had spread like the croup. Muslim shootings and killings by trigger-happy police became the order of the day, offering a preview of what was in store for another, yet to be born, black militant group [the Black Panthers]."

Massaquoi went on: "The most crucial blow Muhammad and his movement has suffered so far has been brother Malcolm's defection and subsequent assassination in 1965, events which tore the movement into two hostile camps. Although the two convicted assassins have been vaguely identified as Muslims, Muhammad has steadfastly denied official Muslim involvement in the killing. There are still many young black militants who, having chosen Malcolm as their idol, are plagued by doubts about the Muslims' role in their martyr's death. But most of the suspicion and innuendos have subsided and Black Muslim popularity among the young is again on the rise." (The recruitment of world-champion prize fighter Muhammad Ali, né Cassius Clay, has been the most impressive single example of the Black Muslims' appeal.)

The membership of the Nation of Islam has not been officially counted, but estimates run between 50,000 and 250,000, if one includes non-dues-paying adherents. The actual number of active members of mosques is only about 10,000. Forty-nine major mosques are listed in *Muhammad Speaks*, the movement's weekly tabloid newspaper. There are reported to be some thirty minor groups in addition to that number, and two dozen federal prisons have Black Muslim contingents. In most mosques, services are held three times weekly. Members able to do so contribute at least 10 percent of their income to the support of their mosque, and those who are not able contribute their time and energy to such work as selling *Muhammad Speaks* on street corners.

The "revelation" promulgated by Elijah Muhammad may seem nonsense to those who approach it without the key of faith. In gist, he teaches that the tribe of Shabazz, embracing all nonwhite peoples of the world, was the original humanity created by God, or Allah, and that the white race was a later, evil mutation. But whites were given their chance, and after 6,000 years of probationary rule, have proved themselves hopeless "devils," morally depraved and intellectually inferior. The era of white dominion is destined to end in the 1970's, by self-genocide through war. Blacks should therefore prepare themselves for the day of their autonomy by "waking up, cleaning up, standing up." "Every white man knows his time is up. I am here to teach you to be free . . . from the white man's yoke."

The Black Muslim credo is put in simpler, more concrete terms in the manifesto published regularly in *Muhammad Speaks*. "We believe in the One God Whose proper Name is Allah. We believe in the Holy Qu-ran [the Black Muslim version of the Koran] and in the Scriptures of all the prophets of God. We believe in the truth of the Bible, but we believe that it has been tampered with and must be reinterpreted so that mankind will not be snared by the falsehoods that have been added to it. . . . We believe in the resurrection of the dead, not in physical resurrection but in mental resurrection. We believe that the so-called Negroes are most in need of mental resurrection: therefore they will be resurrected first. Furthermore, we believe that we are the people of God's choice, as it has been written, that God would choose the rejected and the despised. We can find no other persons fitting this description in these last days more than the so-called Negroes in America."

In the same manifesto, Elijah Muhammad proclaims the political and economic aims of the Black Muslims: "We want freedom. . . . We want justice applied equally to all, regardless of creed or class or color. We want equality of opportunity. . . . We want every black man and woman to have the freedom to accept or reject being separated from the slave masters' children and establish a land of their own. . . . As long as we are not allowed to establish a state or territory of our own, we demand . . . equal employment opportunities—now! We do not believe that after 400 years of free or nearly free labor, sweat and blood, which has helped America become rich and powerful, that so many thousands of black people should have to subsist on relief or charity or live in poor houses."

The monolithic Nation of Islam demands of its members a military discipline in community affairs and an almost puritanical morality in private life. Muslims render unswerving obedience to their leaders, and especially to Elijah Muhammad. They pray five times a day, eat once a day, and abstain from pork, smoking, alcohol, profanity, gambling, and dope. To counter the ingrained white stereotype of the black man, they also forego music (except religious chanting) and dancing. They strive for somber propriety, eschewing loud talk and laughter and adhering to a ritualistic politeness. They dress neatly, the men in white shirts and dark suits and ties and the women (who use no conspicuous cosmetics) in long white robes and kerchiefs. In sex, promiscuity is forbidden, and all are urged to marry, preferably within their faith, and never outside of their race. Muhammad frowns on both birth control and bottle (as opposed to breast) feeding of babies as white men's tricks. Black Muslims generally renounce their legal surnames ("slave names"), using instead the letter X (meaning "true identity unknown"). Aside from draft resistance (which is optional with individuals) they are painstakingly law-abiding, under penalty of expulsion, but they do not vote or otherwise collude with the political apparatus in the United States.

For the education of their children, the Muslims have a nine-grade school in Detroit and a twelve-grade school in Chicago, and adult education classes are conducted weekly at all the mosques. Home economics is taught to the women and physical culture and self-defense techniques to the men. (The most physically fit of the men are inducted into the judo-trained Fruit of Islam, the elite guard that protects Muslim leaders, maintains order at public meetings, and responds to emergencies requiring a show of force.) The basic skills, such as reading, writing, and mathematics, are also taught, to those deficient in them. All classes are sexually segregated. Courses in civilization are taught to all.

In keeping with Muhammad's slogan "Build black, buy black," the Black Muslims operate and patronize dozens of their own business enterprises in Chicago, Washington, D.C., New York, and elsewhere. The enterprises include grocery stores, apartment houses, factories, farms, cleaning establishments, restaurants, bakeries, and service shops for office machines, Venetian blind repair, and so on. For their economic contribution to the black community, the Nation of Islam was cited at the annual award luncheon of the Society of Afro-American Policemen in 1969. At that luncheon, New York State Senator Basil Patterson also asserted that the Muslims had "done more to rehabilitate narcotics addicts than any corrective agency in the country."

On the subject of black initiative in the economic order, Muhammad wrote in *Message to the Black Man* (Muhammad's Mosque No. 2, 1964): "Unite to create a future for yourself. . . . Stop buying expensive cars, fine clothes and shoes before being able to live in a fine home. . . ." In the same book he said: "Observe the operations of the white man. He is successful. He makes no excuses for his failures. He works in a collective manner. You do the same." And: "Separate yourselves from the 'slave master'. . . . Make your own neighborhood a decent place to live. Rid yourself of the lust of wine and drink and learn to love self and your kind before loving others." In addition to *Message to the Black Man*, Muhammad has written *How to Eat to Live*.

The Honorable Elijah Muhammad, as he is officially known within the Nation of Islam, is a small (five feet six), frail man with delicate features of a slightly Oriental cast. His face, with its thin, pursed lips, generally suggests saturnine repose or inscrutability, but his eyes, as one observer noted, can "glower with Messianic fervor," and his smile is prepossessing. In his public appearances he wears a black bow tie and black velvet fez, embroidered with stars and crescent, usually along with a slightly lighter suit. Because his voice is soft and reedy, it makes an ironic counterpoint to the fierce message it delivers. In his speeches he has what observers have called "imperfect syntax" and "the style of an uneducated Southern preacher," but he can be electrifying. Alfred Balk and Alex Haley, in an article in the *Saturday Evening Post* (January 26, 1963), described him on the platform: "The tiny Muhammad sat impassively. Then, as he rose to speak, he seemed transformed. His movements became abrupt, jerky. He stared piercingly at his audience, spitting out his words in harsh, thin tones."

The Muslim leader has six sons and two daughters, who assist their father in his work. (Two of the sons defected in the mid-1960's, but they apparently later returned to the movement.) His daughter Ethel Sharrieff leads the Black Muslim women's corps, and her husband, Raymond Sharrieff, is the Supreme Captain of the Fruit of Islam. Muhammad's chief residence is a nineteen-room mansion on the South Side of Chicago, but in the winter he lives in a four-bedroom house in Phoenix, Arizona, for reasons of health. (He suffers from asthma and bronchitis.) He fasts regularly, often for several days at a time. In an article in the New York *Post* (April 9, 1964), Helen Dudar wrote: "No one who has dealt with Elijah Muhammad at any length doubts his belief in his divine mission."

References

Ebony 25:78+ Ag '70 pors
Life 54:23+ My 31 '63 pors
Time 77:14 Mr 31 '61

MURPHY, FRANKLIN D(AVID)

Jan. 29, 1916- Publisher; educator; physician
Address: b. Times Mirror Co., Times Mirror
Square, Los Angeles, Calif. 90053; h. 419
Robert Lane, Beverly Hills, Calif. 90210

With his appointment to the post of chairman of
the board of directors and chief executive officer
of the Times Mirror Company, in September 1968
Franklin D. Murphy embarked on the third major
career of his many-sided, productive life. As a
physician, he had specialized in internal medicine,
had served from 1948 to 1951 as dean of the University of Kansas School of Medicine, and had
established a statewide health care system that
became world famous in medical circles. As a university chancellor, he had led the already immense
University of California at Los Angeles through
eight years of unprecedented growth, maintaining
relative tranquility in a time of rising student unrest at UCLA's affiliated campus, the University
of California at Berkeley. As chief of the Times
Mirror Company, Murphy presides over an ambitious publishing-printing conglomerate ranking in
size below only Time, Inc., and McGraw-Hill Book
Company. In addition, Dr. Murphy's memberships
or officerships in many governmental, cultural,
academic, and professional boards and commissions may be said to constitute a full-time occupation of public service.

Franklin David Murphy was born on January
29, 1916 in Kansas City, Missouri, the oldest of
three children of Franklin Edward Murphy, a physician, and his wife, the former Cordelia A. Brown,
a concert pianist. His father, a founding faculty
member of the University of Kansas School of
Medicine, transmitted to his children a sense of
satisfaction and pleasure in learning. Also a physician, Franklin Murphy's brother, Dr. George E.
Murphy, is associate professor of pathology at
Cornell Medical College in New York City; his
sister, Mrs. Cordelia M. Ennis, lives in California.

At his preparatory school in Kansas City, the
Pembroke Country Day School, Murphy played
football and earned virtually a straight A average.
He enrolled in the University of Kansas in 1932,
majored in zoology, and graduated with a B.A. degree and a Phi Beta Kappa membership in 1936.
During the academic year 1936-37 he studied
physiology at the University of Göttingen, in Germany, on a University of Kansas exchange fellowship. Then after three years at the University of
Pennsylvania School of Medicine, he graduated at
the head of his class, obtaining his M.D. degree
in 1941.

While engaged from 1941 to 1944 in postgraduate work in internal medicine at the University
of Pennsylvania, Dr. Murphy served during the
first year as an intern at the university hospital
and during the next two as resident physician and
assistant instructor in medicine. In 1944 he entered
the United States Army and was assigned to research projects on tropical diseases, particularly
malaria. He was separated from the Army in the
rank of captain in 1946, with an Army Commen-

dation Ribbon and Citation for his research in
tropical diseases.

His military service completed, Dr. Murphy
opened a private practice in internal medicine in
Kansas City. He was concurrently a part-time instructor at the School of Medicine of the University of Kansas, of which in 1948 he became dean
and associate professor of internal medicine. During his three years as dean, Dr. Murphy acquired
unprecedented sums in gifts, grants, and legislative appropriations to expand and improve the
medical school and its hospital. A multimillion dollar building program was launched; the school's
faculty was upgraded and salaries were increased;
the student body was expanded by 25 percent;
research activity was greatly accelerated; and a
system of full-time clinical instruction was instituted. Dr. Murphy initiated a project that came
to be known as the Kansas Rural Health Plan,
a model statewide system that brought what some
observers have called the "best medical protection
in the world" to a state then facing a medical
care crisis, with acute and mounting shortages of
hospitals and physicians.

Under Murphy's plan, small towns were encouraged to build minimal facilities for medical practice and then to lease or sell such facilities to a
doctor on terms geared to his ability to pay, thus
reducing the initial investment required of a young
physician setting up an independent rural practice. To combat the professional isolation that his
students feared would accompany it, Murphy developed a strong program of continuing postgraduate instruction, centered at the university and
reaching throughout the state in a network of
"mobile medical schools." The education of a
doctor, Murphy insisted, is a forty-year program.

On September 1, 1951 Dr. Murphy took office
as the tenth chancellor of the University of Kansas, succeeding Chancellor Deane W. Malott, who
became president of Cornell University. As chancellor, Murphy continued his vigorous campaign
to win educational appropriations from the state
legislature, and under his leadership Kansas became one of the most rapidly improving Midwestern universities of the 1950's.

Chancellor Murphy's activities during his years
at Kansas extended beyond academic duties to include membership and chairmanship in many governmental and private organizations. In addition
to being president of the State Universities Association, he was appointed chairman in 1954 of a
committee to study federal health spending for
the Commission on Intergovernmental Relations
and chairman in 1956 of the American Council on
Education. He served in 1957 on the Federal Commission on Government Security. In 1948 he
joined six other American university heads in making a privately funded study of higher education
in the Soviet Union and in 1959 was chairman of
the United States advisory commission on educational exchange under the Department of State.
He was a trustee of the Menninger Foundation,
the Kress Foundation (of which he later became
president), and the Carnegie Foundation for the
Advancement of Teaching; and a member of the

State Commission for the Eisenhower Library, the Eisenhower Exchange Scholarship Program, and from 1950 to 1954 a special medical advisory group for the Veterans Administration.

In 1960 Dr. Murphy left the University of Kansas to succeed Vern O. Knudsen as chancellor of the University of California at Los Angeles, second largest of the nine divisions of the huge state university. He assumed command of a 411-acre campus with twelve colleges and sixty-one departments and an enrollment of 17,000 regular students with an additional 10,000 in extension courses. In his inaugural address in September 1960 Murphy promised to lead the university to "major scholarly distinction in worldwide terms." By 1966 UCLA had attained its planned enrollment of about 27,000 full-time students, thereby catching up with the prestigious campus at Berkeley. During those six years it had also more than tripled its research grants, more than doubled its total annual budget to $85,000,000, and added ten new interdisciplinary study centers and thirty-one new buildings. "Buildings don't make the university any more than clothes make the man," Murphy told a reporter for *Time* (October 21, 1966), "but in these days you can't do sophisticated research in tents." The expansion of research had been one of the priorities of Murphy, who believes that a university has a dual function: teaching and research.

The Los Angeles campus, unlike Berkeley's, remained fairly free of the kind of violent demonstration staged by students at many American colleges and universities during the 1960's. More conservative and more accessible to students and teachers than Clark Kerr, then the University of California president, Murphy combined firmness with flexibility and wide-open channels of communication in meeting dissent. "You can't substitute memos and bulletins for the courtesy of a dialogue and an explanation," he asserted, as quoted in *Time* (October 21, 1966). At UCLA, Murphy encouraged greater student participation in curriculum changes and student affairs, but opposed capitulation to the demands of those who "yell and snarl at the people of California." Instead of arresting students engaged in political solicitations on campus, an issue that triggered disruption at Berkeley, he allowed them to continue while their case was heard by the campus review board—then cast the tie-breaking ballot against their activities, stating, "I believe that the university should be a market place of ideas, but we won't tolerate anything here that interferes with our operation."

Just as Dr. Murphy's accomplishments as dean of the medical school at Kansas included better health care for the whole state, so his concerns at UCLA extended to the problems of Los Angeles, and of American cities in general. On moving to that city in 1960, Murphy predicted that Los Angeles would rank within ten years with London, Paris, and New York as one of the world's four great cities. In one attempt under Murphy to put its resources at the service of the city, the university set up an experimental urban studies

FRANKLIN D. MURPHY

center, which used an interdisciplinary approach to such problems as the integration of public and private welfare services in the Watts section of the city. As a cultural center for the city, in 1965 alone the university attracted 500,000 Los Angeles residents to concerts, lectures, and stage performances on campus.

During his last years at UCLA, Murphy's efforts were frustrated in part by the financial squeeze imposed on the University of California by the administration of Governor Ronald Reagan. When the university's request for a $278,000,000 state appropriation was cut to $231,000,000 in 1967, Murphy told the regents: "I do not intend to preside at the liquidation or substantial erosion of the quality which fifty years of effort have created." As reported in *Time* (September 27, 1968), he complained, "It's a demeaning thing to run around with a tin cup, pleading with people to help me help their children." He also criticized the power of the board of regents, whose members, he maintained, lacked experience in education, and he called the job of chancellor a "physical, emotional, and creative drain."

On February 16, 1968, denying that his decision was motivated by growing friction with the Reagan administration, Murphy resigned from the University of California to become chairman of the board of directors and chief executive officer of the Times Mirror Company the following September. "I believe I have made my maximum contribution to higher education," he wrote in his letter of resignation. "On the other hand, I find in the opportunity presented me by the Times Mirror Company a new and extraordinary potential for personal satisfaction, since a great publishing company like a great university is ultimately in the business of communication and education."

The Times Mirror Company controls many diversified publishing and industrial enterprises. According to *Fortune* (September 1, 1968), at the time that Murphy became chairman it was the largest publisher of paperback books, the largest publisher of Bibles, one of the two largest producers of road maps, and one of the largest printers of telephone books. Its core enterprise, the Los Angeles *Times*, had been transformed during the 1960's from a conservative, rather provincial publication to a growing, influential newspaper with an editorial staff of 450, a daily circulation exceeding 950,000, the largest advertising volume in the world, and a flexible political position more compatible with Murphy's own moderate Republicanism.

The man responsible for revitalizing the Los Angeles *Times* was Otis Chandler, heir to the eighty-two-year family control of the enterprise. It was his decision to continue to concentrate on the newspaper itself when his father, Norman Chandler, then sixty-eight, retired from the chairmanship. That retirement created the vacancy filled, somewhat unexpectedly, by Murphy, who was regarded as an outsider with academic rather than business experience, although he had been elected to the board of directors of the Times Mirror Company in 1965. On accepting the post, Murphy announced that the company would be managed by a "three-man team": Otis Chandler, in charge of the newspaper and forest products division; the company president Albert Casey, in charge of "acquisitions and other subsidiaries"; and Dr. Murphy, handling "the knowledge industry end of the company and providing overall guidance." Prospective acquisitions in the knowledge industry covered the fields of magazines, newspapers, radio, television, computerized information retrieval systems, and classroom technology. The company now owns an interest in a cable television company. In April 1970 it acquired Harry F. Guggenheim's 51 percent controlling interest in *Newsday*, a Long Island newspaper with a daily circulation of 440,000, the largest of any suburban paper in the country. Three months later it bought the Dallas *Times Herald* and its broadcast properties.

Murphy's business interests before he joined the Times Mirror executive team included membership on the board of directors of the Ford Motor Company, Hallmark Cards, Norton Simon, Inc., Bank of America, and McCall Corporation (he resigned from McCall upon assuming the Times Mirror chairmanship). His cultural activities include membership in the American Academy of Arts and Sciences and on the board of trustees of the National Gallery of Art and the Los Angeles County Museum of Art. He is also a member of the Urban Institute, the President's Foreign Intelligence Advisory Board, American Board of Internal Medicine, and American College of Physicians.

Among his former memberships were those on the board of visitors to the Air University of the United States Air Force, medical advisory commission of the American Legion, council on medical education and hospitals of the American Medical Association, and the committee on educational interchange policy of the Institute of International Education, National Council of the Boy Scouts of America, and board of governors of the American Red Cross. His Greek-letter societies, in addition to Phi Beta Kappa, are Sigma Xi, Nu Sigma Nu, Alpha Omega Alpha, and Beta Theta Pi. In 1949

he was selected as one of the ten outstanding young men in the nation by the United States Junior Chamber of Commerce. He holds honorary doctorates from more than a dozen colleges and universities, including the University of Pennsylvania, the University of Notre Dame, the University of Judaism, and Hebrew Union College. His church is the Episcopal.

On December 28, 1940 Franklin D. Murphy married Judith Joyce Harris, also of Kansas City, a graduate of Vassar College. They have four children: Judith Joyce (now Mrs. Walter Dickey), Martha Alice (now Mrs. Craig Crockwell), Carolyn Louise, and Franklin Lee. Dr. Murphy is five feet ten inches tall, weighs 160 pounds, and has blue eyes and graying brown hair. He was described in the *Christian Science Monitor* as "a ruddy, genial man of great enthusiasms." Reading and listening to music are his recreations, and his tastes in both tend to be comprehensive, with a preference for the work of classical composers.

References

Christian Sci Mon p1+ N 2 '65 por
Fortune 77:99+ S 1 '68 por
Los Angeles Times I p1+ S 18 '60 por
N Y Times p13 F 17 '68 por
Newsweek 56:106 Jl 25 '60
Time 88:98 O 21 '66 por
Today's Health 44:24 Je '66

International Who's Who, 1970-71
Who's Who in America, 1970-71

NEARING, SCOTT

Aug. 6, 1883- Social scientist; farmer
Address: b. Social Science Institute, Harborside, Me. 04642

In one of those perennial recurrences of the Joseph in Egypt archetype, the society that rejected Scott Nearing as a political heretic half a century ago has come begging at his door for some of his ecological wisdom. Nearing, now nearly ninety years old, was an established academic social scientist when the hysteria regarding "Bolshevism" broke out in the United States during World War I. As a nationally known radical pacifist, collectivist critic of a social and economic order that he regarded as acquisitive and predatory, he was blacklisted in university and publishing circles. Bereft of professional status and livelihood, Nearing four decades ago became a homesteader in rural New England, and there he and his wife, Helen, both vegetarians, have made a success of self-subsistent organic farming. Today youthful communards opting out of the urban jungle look upon the Nearings as prophetic pioneers and seek back-to-the-land guidance in their books, especially *Living the Good Life; How to Live Sanely and Simply in a Troubled World*. The latter, originally published in 1954 by the Social Science Institute, the intellectual adjunct of the couple's farming experiment, was reissued by Schocken

Books in 1970. Nearing and his wife have collaborated on five books, and he alone has written some fifty, including *Economics for the Power Age* (John Day, 1952), *Socialism in Practice* (New Century, 1962), and *The Conscience of a Radical* (Social Science Institute, 1965).

Scott Nearing was born in Morris Run, Pennsylvania on August 6, 1883 to Louis Nearing, a merchant, and Minnie (Zabriskie) Nearing. He had two brothers, Guy and Max, and three sisters, Mary, Dorothy, and Beatrice. After graduating from Central Manual Training High School in Philadelphia, in 1901, he studied oratory at Temple College (now Temple University) and economics at the University of Pennsylvania. He took his B.S. degree at the University of Pennsylvania in 1905 and his Ph.D. degree there four years later.

From 1906 to 1914 Nearing was an instructor in economics at the University of Pennsylvania. During that period he also taught at Swarthmore College and published, among many other books, *The Solution of the Child Labor Problem* (Row, Peterson, 1911) and *Wages in the United States* (Macmillan, 1914). With Frank D. Watson he wrote the textbook *Economics* (Macmillan, 1908), and he collaborated with his first wife, Nellie Seeds, on *Women and Social Progress* (Macmillan, 1912).

In 1914 Nearing was promoted to assistant professor of economics in the University of Pennsylvania's Wharton School of Finance. In a nationally publicized academic freedom case, he was dismissed by the university the following year because his crusade against the exploitation of child labor had stepped on some influential political toes. He taught at the Rand School of Social Science in New York City in 1916, and during the following academic year he was professor of social science and dean of the College of Arts and Sciences at the University of Toledo in Ohio.

When the Rand School published *The Great Madness* (1917), a thirty-two-page tract by Nearing against United States intervention in World War I, a federal grand jury indicted the author for inspiring resistance to military recruitment. At his trial Nearing was acquitted, but the stigma of the indictment stuck. The University of Toledo dismissed him; his textbooks, including *Elements of Economics* (Macmillan, 1918), written with Henry R. Burch, were withdrawn from curricula; and mass circulation magazines stopped publishing articles by him. He sought refuge in Communism, but the Communist party eventually rejected him because of his individualism generally and, specifically, his deviation from Lenin's theory of imperialism.

His point of view, however, remained essentially Marxist, as indicated in such books as *Dollar Diplomacy* (Huebsch, 1925; Monthly Review Press, 1969), a study of the collision of United States political and economic policies abroad with the aspirations of emerging nations, written in collaboration with Joseph Freeman; *Education in Soviet Russia* (International, 1926); *Whither China?* (International, 1927); *Black America* (Vanguard,

SCOTT NEARING

1929); *Must We Starve?* (Vanguard, 1932); and *Fascism* (Open Road, 1933). During the 1920's and 1930's he was a correspondent for the Federated Press.

In 1932 Scott and Helen Nearing bought sixty-five acres of eroded land on a mountain slope in Pike Valley, Vermont. There, with their own hands and without machinery, they built a fieldstone house, methodically revivified the soil by organic means, and developed a 4,200-bucket maple "sugarbush" by which they supported themselves. In *The Maple Sugar Book; Together with Remarks on Pioneering as a Way of Living in the Twentieth Century* (John Day, 1950; Schocken, 1971) they gave a detailed account of their maple sugar and syrup making and also a scholarly history of sugaring in general. Reviewing *The Maple Sugar Book* along with *Living the Good Life* in the Washington Post (June 3, 1971), Lloyd Ferris testified that the books "caught me as no other books have ever done. In one day my conventional goals were shaken to pieces and a vision took their place." While in Vermont, Scott Nearing also wrote, among other books, *United World* (Island Press, 1944), which suggested a program for a world federation, *The Tragedy of Empire* (Island Press, 1945), about imperialism and its alternatives in an industrial age, and *Democracy Is Not Enough* (Island Press, 1945), about the economic basis for democracy.

To escape the encroachment of ski resort developers and curious tourists, the Nearings quit their Vermont home in the early 1950's, after nineteen years there, selling the place to novelist Pearl Buck and moving to their present farm, located on 100 acres of timberland in Harborside on the Maine Coast. On five cleared acres they grow the vegetables for their table and the blueberries that they sell or barter as well as eat. Their residence is a century-old clapboard house, and they are in the process of building a stone house on a ledge where their land overlooks the sea. Visitors to the farm include gardening clubs, ecology crusaders, prospective homesteaders seeking encouragement or advice, and people interested in the Social

Science Institute, which offers lectures and discussions by Scott Nearing on international affairs, social engineering, and other subjects. Recent lectures delivered by Nearing before college and other groups include "China and Its Communes," "The Myth of National Security," "Social Decay in the United States," and "The Choices Before Us."

Nearing is five feet eight inches tall and weighs 160 pounds. Robert Taylor of the Boston *Sunday Globe* (November 1, 1970) described Nearing's appearance after a visit to the farm at Harborside: "He still appeared athletic; incredibly so; tanned, fit. . . . A shock of silvery hair enhanced a fleeting resemblance to Justice Douglas." Nearing, who has no political affiliations but still considers himself committed to socialism, summed up his view of the United States in the current world political context for Taylor: "The American Empire arrived on the world scene too late. The conquest of Asia, which began with the landing of American troops in the Philippines in 1899, is still going on. The West has been slipping for seventy years; a society is not a success that only makes rich people richer. The question an individual has to answer is 'Where do I stand in the process of disintegration?' Those who rely on the marketplace will degenerate into mindless consumers. Everybody ought to do some work with their hands instead of becoming parasitic to a post-industrial economy."

Scott Nearing's marriage to Helen (Knothe) Nearing was solemnized in 1947. Mrs. Nearing, a concert violinist when she met her husband, also plays the organ and the block flute. By his previous marriage to Nellie Seeds, who died in 1946, Nearing has two sons, John and Robert. The Nearings, who have no telephone or television, enjoy walking, reading, music, and conversation with friends. Out of respect for life they not only refrain from hunting and fishing but keep no animals, because they regard even the status of pets as bondage. The saddest month of the year for them is November, when hunters come and kill the deer on their land. "We usually go away," Nearing told Joan Cook in an interview for the New York *Times* (April 26, 1971). "We don't like to stay and see our friends killed." Winters the Nearings usually travel. In recent years they visited Canada, Western Europe, the Soviet Union, China, and various countries in Asia. In earlier travels Nearing visited Cuba, Mexico, South America, and Israel, among other places. His chief purpose in traveling is to observe political, social, and economic conditions, and his trips provide the material for such of his books as *Socialism in Practice* (New Century, 1962), about Eastern Europe, and such collaborations with his wife as *The Brave New World* (Social Science Institute, 1958), about China. (The couple's passports were revoked when they violated Department of State regulations by going to China in 1957). Nearing is a regular contributor to *Monthly Review* and he occasionally contributes to *Organic Gardening*. He has recently been working on an autobiography that he is planning to publish under the title of "The Making of a Radical."

While the Nearings might have wished their rural experiment could have been broader, to include full realization of their cooperative ideal regarding the distribution of goods, they have at least demonstrated that it is possible for a couple or a family group, with a minimum of health and capital and a willingness to work, to liberate themselves completely from the wage-slave labor market and almost completely from the commodity market and, in their words, "live with nature, make themselves a living that will preserve and enhance their efficiency, and give them the leisure in which they can do their bit to make the world a better place." In his introduction to *Living the Good Life* Paul Goodman observed: "The eccentric ideas of the Nearings and others are no longer out in left field. History, alas, has caught up with them. With a few more years of power failures, transit strikes, epidemics of heroin overdose, water shortage, unacceptable levels of air pollution, and crashing airplanes, hundreds of thousands of New Yorkers will regard Scott and Helen Nearing as uncanny prophets."

References

Washington (D.C.) Post B p1+ Je 3 '71 pors

Nearing, Scott and Helen. Living the Good Life (1970)

Who's Who in America, 1970-71

NE WIN (nä win)

May 24, 1911- Burmese statesman; army officer
Address: b. Office of the Chairman of the Revolutionary Council, Rangoon, Burma

Nearly a decade ago in a lightning coup General Ne Win substituted military dictatorship for parliamentary democracy in Burma by ousting Prime Minister U Nu and monopolizing power for himself as chairman of the Revolutionary Council and Minister of Defense. A nationalist who had fought along with U Nu in Burma's struggle for freedom from the British, Ne Win appeared to assume political leadership in 1962 only with reluctance. In transforming Burma into a police state he has introduced a system of nationalization known as the "Burmese Way to Socialism" and has pursued a xenophobic foreign policy of complete nonalignment. With the support of the army he has preserved a high degree of stability, although threatened by economic decline, rebellion among tribal and ethnic groups, fear of domination by Communist China or other foreign powers, and, recently, a dissident movement led by U Nu.

Born on May 24, 1911 in Paungdale, Prome District of central Burma, the first child of U (Mr.) Po Kha and Daw (Mrs.) Mi Lay, Ne Win was named Shu Maung—"apple of one's eye." According to one source, the name "Shu" is not distinctively Burmese and suggests a Chinese ancestry on one side of the family, as has often been reported. His father came from a provincial family of modest circumstances and held the job of revenue surveyor for the Paungdale area, a government position ranked at the lower level of the civil service scale. He also managed the family estate, whose lands Shu Maung helped to cultivate in boyhood.

After attending the middle school in Paungdale, Shu Maung was sent by his parents to the National High School in Prome. At school he was not distinguished for either his academic or athletic prowess, but he was credited with a keen and questioning mind and with sportsmanship in football, hockey, and tennis. He showed no interest in the local political leaders of the nascent Burmese independence movement who sought his father's support, nor did he aspire, as did most of his colleagues, to enter the prestigious civil service. Instead, he hoped to become a doctor and in June 1929 enrolled in the intermediate science course at Rangoon University.

While in college Shu Maung developed his athletic skills by playing on the football team and winning trophies for intramural hockey. He avoided campus political debates for the diversions of Rangoon, but polished his English and studied literature. After he had failed his biology examination in 1931, he withdrew from the university. Continuing to live in Rangoon, however, he maintained contacts in both academic and social circles and eventually took a clerical job at the Churchill Street Post Office.

Shu Maung soon began to share the growing discontent of many young Burmese with their lot and the tendency to identify British colonialism as the source of their own and Burma's troubles. He joined the Dobama Asiayone (Our Burma Association), the Burmese nationalist society organized at the university in 1930, and along with other members adopted the title "Thakin" (literally "Master"), which until then had been reserved for the British. Through that association Shu Maung became involved with Burma's independence movement and with its two most prominent leaders, Aung San and U Nu, in the effort to free the country from its status as a self-governing unit within the British Commonwealth. So long as the Thakins confined themselves to protest and demonstration, Shu Maung remained in the background, providing intelligence gathered through his job at the post office and his social connections. But when the Japanese offered the Thakins military training, he was among the first of the nationalists to volunteer.

During the summer of 1941 Shu Maung and others of the now-famous Thirty Companions were smuggled out of Burma aboard a Japanese freighter. Upon arrival in Hainan, the group began intensive training under the most spartan conditions and rigorous discipline. Impressed by the vigor with which Shu Maung responded to the strenuous regimen, the Japanese chose him for the exclusive "San-pan," or third class, selected after basic training for the highest command levels. Aung San, who had recruited the group and was informally recognized as its leader, agreed, declaring that Shu Maung would be his right hand in Burma's drive for independence.

GEN. NE WIN

Along with other members of an advance team, in October 1941 Shu Maung was infiltrated into Bangkok, and on the following December 26 the Burma Independence Army (BIA) was formed. That night at Aung San's suggestion each of the Thirty Companions chose an auspicious name to dedicate himself to his new mission. Shu Maung became Ne Win, meaning "brilliant as the sun." The companions also adopted the traditional Burmese title "Bo," designating a leader of fighting men.

In December 1941 also the Japanese began their invasion of Burma, which became a key battlefield in World War II because of the strategic importance of the Burma Road as an Allied supply line to China. Returning to Rangoon in February 1942, Ne Win devoted himself to recruiting, persuading Burmese Army units to defect from the British, and preparing for the take-over of the city as the British withdrew. The arrival of the BIA was followed closely by that of the Japanese Fifteenth Army, and it was the flag of the rising sun, not the Burmese tricolor, that then flew from Government House. Ne Win later recalled, as quoted by Maung Maung in *Burma and General Ne Win* (1969), "Doubts began to awaken in Burmese minds when the Japanese . . . broke their promise for declaring Burma's independence and handing over the administration of the town to the Burmese themselves."

Major Ne Win took part in only a few actions against the British. He spent much of the war years organizing the new Burmese Army, supervising the selection of some 3,000 out of 23,000 volunteers, and coming to know each soldier personally. When the Japanese set up an "independent" Burmese government in August 1943, Aung San became Minister of War and Ne Win, then a colonel, became Commander in Chief of the Army. During the next two years, as plotting against the Japanese began, the Burmese expanded their army. In December 1944, when British forces returned, the Burmese Army under Ne Win dispersed into the Irrawaddy Delta. It later waged a bitter guerrilla campaign against the Japanese until British authority was restored in August 1945. For his part in the resistance Ne Win received the United States Legion of Merit.

Burma gained its independence as a sovereign nation, completely outside the British Commonwealth, on January 4, 1948. Independence unleashed political and ethnic tensions that resulted in the assassination of Aung San and other statesmen and the growth of guerrilla warfare in the countryside. For nearly a decade, from 1948 to 1958, Prime Minister U Nu, who did not interfere with the army, and Ne Win, a general and Defense Minister, who was not then concerned with politics, were able to maintain a semblance of order. During that period Ne Win also served briefly as Deputy Prime Minister. In 1958, however, U Nu's political apparatus split and he was forced to offer amnesty to Communist rebels in return for their support. His opponents sought the support of rightist elements and secessionist groups. On September 26, to avoid civil war, Ne Win moved to take over key positions throughout the country, agreeing at U Nu's request to form in October a caretaker government for six months to restore sufficient order for new elections to be held.

The first Ne Win government was sworn in on October 29, 1958. With no consideration for the interests of any political group, army troops restored public services and the flow of commerce, cleaned up Rangoon, and resettled hordes of refugees who had camped in the capital. Ne Win introduced popular government in some of the tribal areas and also made several foreign policy adjustments, such as renewing acceptance of United States aid and signing nonaggression and border treaties with the government of Red China. At the end of six months he was persuaded to remain in office for about a year. He then fulfilled his promise by holding elections, in February 1960, to give Burma, as he put it, "a second chance at democracy."

Although he had swept the elections, in his second assay at democracy U Nu soon ran into the earlier difficulties. Attempting to consolidate political support, he alienated religious minorities; attempting to accommodate secessionist elements, he encouraged demands for autonomy. In late February 1962 secessionist leaders arrived in Rangoon to press their demands. Fearing that the country was once more on the brink of disaster, Ne Win moved again, this time on his own initiative. On the night of March 1, 1962 he supervised the army take-over of Rangoon and the arrest of U Nu, his Cabinet, and the tribal leaders. The following morning he informed the people that he would give Burma a government appropriate to its needs.

During the next few months, as Ne Win moved rapidly toward that goal, martial law was declared, the legislature and the supreme court were dissolved, and the constitution was abolished. In their places Ne Win established a Revolutionary Council of seventeen (later thirteen) members, with himself as chairman. Some of the members, along with one nonmember, formed a council of ministers, or military Cabinet. On April 30, 1962 Ne Win issued a twenty-eight-point manifesto outlining the Burmese Way to Socialism, which promised to remove the evils of the "pernicious" economic system, but the key to which lay in what has been described as "political and economic mysticism." Simultaneously, as part of the nationalistic effort to free Burma from alien influences, the Ford and similar foundations were asked to end their programs in Burma and contacts with foreign diplomats were restricted. The Revolutionary Council's proposal of a one-party system led to the formation of the Burmese Socialist Program party a few months later.

Open resistance to Ne Win's new regime came first from students of Rangoon University, whose campus the army invaded in July 1962. In a warning to other dissident groups Ne Win vowed to meet "sword with sword, spear with spear." During 1963 he drastically curtailed economic, political, and diplomatic activity. In February he forced the resignation of Aung Gyi, his most likely successor, who had been identified as the most moderate of the Revolutionary Council members. In the same month foreign banks and trading companies were nationalized, and by the end of the year most business enterprises were either controlled or directed by the government. Although he pursued limited aid agreements with the United States and the Soviet Union, Ne Win placed even further restrictions on association with diplomats and permitted foreign correspondents to remain in Burma for only seventy-two hours and then only in transit. In August he began a wave of political arrests and in November broke off talks with Communist rebels, arresting over 400 of their leaders. By December, according to reports in the Western press, Ne Win appeared in public only with a pistol in his lap and a cordon of troops.

The sources of Ne Win's economic and political views, according to his biographer Maung Maung, were his prewar readings of Marx and Stalin, whose concepts he regarded with enough reservations to produce what another observer has termed an "outdated Fabian socialism." His social and religious views are strongly rooted in Buddhism and Burmese traditions and culture. But overshadowing those influences remain the selfless discipline and pragmatism of the soldier: "I don't care how you do it, but get the job done," he once told one of his ministers, as reported in the Christian Science Monitor (October 7, 1963).

With his direct, aggressive approach, Ne Win could neither ignore nor make excuses for the economic and political doldrums in which Burma remained. In November 1965 his military government invited the public to air its grievances in letters to the press, and the following month he publicly admitted that Burma was in an economic "mess." During 1966 Ne Win began to ease economic controls and to relieve some political tension, in the fall releasing U Nu and most other major political prisoners from detention.

Having developed out of considerations of the sovereignty and security of strategically located Burma, Ne Win's views on foreign policy are said to be reinforced by an early admiration of the policies of the Tokugawa shogunate that isolated—and thus saved—Japan from the perils of international politics. Rather than a positive nonalignment, therefore, he has adopted a sort of negative noninvolvement. In contrast to his neighbors, Ne Win has tended to discourage foreign aid: "Unless we Burmans can learn to run our own country, we will lose it," he explained to Harrison E. Salisbury in an interview for the New York *Times* (June 20, 1966). So strictly does Ne Win adhere to his policy of neutrality that his visit to Washington in 1966, on one of several trips he has taken to the United States, was regarded as a ceremonial balancing of his visits to Peking and Moscow in 1965. With a rare aversion to international prestige, he once reportedly turned down the Magsaysay Award because of the publicity involved. (The Magsaysay Award was set up in 1957 by the Rockefeller Fund to perpetuate the ideals of the late Ramón Magsaysay, the president of the Philippines.)

General Ne Win is stocky in build and taller than most of his compatriots, standing five feet ten and a half inches. He has two sons by his first wife, whom he married in the 1930's and divorced in 1952, and two more by his second wife, Daw Khin May Than, known as Kitty to her friends. She is the daughter of a prominent Burmese surgeon and in 1947 studied nursing in the United States. Madame Ne Win reportedly has five daughters by a previous marriage. Although he has sold his horses and has outlawed racing, once a favorite sport of his, Ne Win remains a soccer and tennis enthusiast and shoots a round of golf in the 80's. Many Western political observers have commented on his modesty and aloofness and his apparent indifference to wealth and personal glory. "His whole personality," T.D. Allman wrote in the *Guardian* (November 28, 1970), "—inflexible, dedicated, austere—conveys a totally unemotional approach toward his life, work, and country."

References

N Y Times p46 Mr 9 '62; p1+ Je 20 '66 por; p4 S 9 '66 por
N Y Times Mag p27+ F 27 '66 por
Sr Schol 84:6+ Ap 17 '64 por
Washington (D.C.) Post E p2 S 4 '66 por
Asia Who's Who (1960)
Hanna, Willard S. Eight Nation Makers (1964)
International Who's Who, 1970-71
Maung, Maung. Burma and General Ne Win (1969)
Trager, Helen G., ed. We the Burmese (1969)

ODISHAW, HUGH

Oct. 13, 1916- Scientific administrator
Address: b. National Academy of Sciences, 2101 Constitution Ave., Washington, D.C. 20418; h. 10410 Stable Lane, Potomac, Md. 20854

Hugh Odishaw, who enjoys a reputation as a skillful and innovative scientific administrator, is a

HUGH ODISHAW

member of the executive staff of the National Academy of Sciences, the influential organization that acts as unofficial adviser to the United States government on matters of science and technology. There he is executive secretary of the division of physical sciences, which functions under the National Research Council to encourage wide participation by scientists and engineers in service to the nation. From 1953 to 1963 Odishaw was executive director of the United States National Committee for the International Geophysical Year, an administrative division created by the Academy to sponsor American participation in the worldwide research project dedicated to the earth sciences. Odishaw is still a director of the IGY World Data Center-A, which keeps the records and collates the information contributed by American researchers, and he was once executive director of the Space Science Board, which cooperates with foreign scientific bodies in the peaceful exploration of space.

A native of Canada, Hugh Odishaw was born on October 13, 1916 in North Battleford, in the province of Saskatchewan to Abraham and Miriam (Davojan) Odishaw. His parents settled in the United States in 1922, when Hugh was six, and he was reared and educated there. After graduating from high school he enrolled at Northwestern University as a liberal arts major and obtained his B.A. degree in 1939. He studied at Princeton University for a year, after which he returned to his alma mater for further graduate work in the humanities and the physical sciences. When Odishaw received the M.A. degree from Northwestern University in 1941, he was appointed an instructor of English and mathematics at the Illinois Institute of Technology. While teaching there he took courses to strengthen his background in technology and the applied sciences and he earned a B.S. degree from the Illinois Institute of Technology in 1944.

In 1944 Odishaw joined the Westinghouse Electric Corporation as a researcher in the radar laboratory. The company had World War II defense contracts and was deeply involved in developing radar and other related radio detecting and ranging devices. Although he remained at Westinghouse for only one year, Odishaw acquired a solid background in radar research and in 1945 he was appointed to direct the activities of the European Theater Radar Study Group at the Radiation Laboratory of the United States Office of Scientific Research and Development, in Washington, D.C. From 1946-53 Odishaw was assistant to the director of the National Bureau of Standards, the leading federal agency for research in the physical sciences. Founded in 1901, the Bureau provides information for business, industry, and the sciences, and its research covers such diverse subject areas as analytical and inorganic chemistry, applied mathematics, atomic and radiation physics, metallurgy, and weights and measures.

In 1951 an international union of scientists proposed that a cooperative scientific project be established to explore the earth and its environment as interrelated physical systems. Two years later definite plans for the International Geophysical Year (IGY) were formulated, bringing together approximately 60,000 scientists from sixty-six nations. The United States Congress authorized the National Academy of Sciences to establish an administrative unit to supervise American participation in the IGY program. The United States National Committee for the IGY was created as just one of many participating scientific groups, and Hugh Odishaw was appointed the executive director as well as a staff member of the National Academy of Sciences. As such, he was responsible for organizing and coordinating all the research programs developed by the American scientific community and defining goals for the scientific disciplines taking part in the IGY. Although funds and research facilities were contributed by each participating nation, the IGY remained non-political, with each country pledging international cooperation and a free exchange of scientific data. To Odishaw the IGY represented "the single most significant peaceful activity of mankind since the Renaissance and the Copernican Revolution."

The period of scientific investigation for the International Geophysical Year ran from July 1, 1957 to December 31, 1958. That time period was selected because it coincided with the eleven-year cycle of maximum sunspot activity, thus allowing scientists to identify and study such related solar phenomena as solar flares, cosmic rays, and magnetic storms that disturb the earth's environment. The grandeur and scope of the program held out the bright prospect that scientists would make significant strides in expanding man's knowledge and mastery over the universe. Odishaw, who once told a reporter for the Washington *Post and Times Herald* (November 6, 1955) that it seemed inconceivable that some startling discovery would not be made, believed that the interest aroused by the IGY and the additional government funds voted for the program would benefit the entire scientific community and stimulate special research in usually neglected areas, such as the Pacific and the North and South Poles.

A major project of the IGY was an investigation of the shape and structure of the earth. Geophysicists used new seismic techniques and instruments to study the stresses and strains within the earth's crust, thus encouraging Odishaw to predict that the measurements would provide information for more accurate earthquake predictions. Seismologists observed irregularities and regional geographic variations in the subcrust of the earth similar to those appearing in the earth's crust, such as flat plains or mountain peaks. Other IGY projects calculated the distribution of the earth's mass and measured the tides that affect the earth's solid surfaces daily. Odishaw also supervised the preparation of more precise tables of the earth's longitudes and latitudes to aid sea and air navigation and make possible more accurate satellite and missile launchings.

A second research area planned for the IGY brought together meteorologists, oceanographers, and glaciologists to study the earth's heat and water supply. Of special interest to scientists was the complex interrelationship governing the earth's ice cover, seas, and lower atmosphere and influencing weather and climate, ocean currents, and the ocean's food supply. Odishaw reported that oceanographers recorded three major countercurrents in the oceans that directly affected man's environment. Scientists also observed an exchange of waters between the southern and northern hemispheres, coinciding with the seasons. One of the practical results of oceanographic research, according to Odishaw, was the discovery that millions of miles of ocean bottom in the southeast Pacific contained manganese, nickel, and cobalt mixed with copper, valued at approximately $500,000 a square mile.

Odishaw has emphasized the importance of weather studies conducted by IGY meteorologists, who used radio-equipped balloons to map air currents, temperature, pressure, and humidity. High-reaching balloons were sent aloft to test for nuclear debris. The IGY established drifting ice stations to gather information in the Arctic and sub-Arctic regions, and under international impetus the United States set up its first comprehensive program in glacial research. Glaciologists revised their estimate of the total amount of ice and snow in the world by 40 percent, casting new light on the earth's heat and water balance. Scientists discovered that the 6,000,000 square miles of Antarctica consisted of a complex island chain buried under ice, not a solid land mass as once believed.

The IGY solar research program achieved an impressive array of firsts. In 1955 Odishaw announced that the United States would send up satellites equipped with tracking devices and cameras to gather data on the nature of the upper atmosphere. The seven satellites sent into orbit—four by the United States and three by the Soviet Union—proved invaluable tools for observing and measuring the earth from altitudes previously unattainable. Odishaw views those launchings as "pioneering and historic events" that make the Space Age a reality. IGY researchers collected new evidence on the origin and behavior of cosmic rays, those electrically charged particles that bombard the earth from all directions. Scientists identified the Van Allen radiation belt at a height of 250 miles, increasing in intensity with altitude to an undetermined level. IGY researchers proved the existence of the "electro-jet," an equatorial electric current previously considered only in theory. Estimating that IGY projects contributed to national defense, military strategy and airline safety, Odishaw commended them for "opening new horizons on earth and beyond earth so that it appears that another renaissance can be ours."

When the IGY ended in December 1958 and all its information was made public, Odishaw reported that an "unprecedented storehouse of facts" about the earth and its environment had been recorded at World Data Centers in the United States, the Soviet Union, and western Europe. He expressed satisfaction with its accomplishments, which "fulfilled all expectations . . . exceeded our hopes . . . and served as a prologue to the future." All the primary scientific objectives of the IGY had all been achieved, a spirit of cooperation between East and West had been maintained throughout the program, and the two leading participants, Russia and the United States, tried to conciliate their differences and eliminate strife. Odishaw and his American colleagues played down the "space-race" aspect of the satellite program, and although the Soviets led in satellite launchings, the Americans held their own by sending aloft moon rockets that penetrated more than 70,000 miles in space. Shortly after the IGY began, a Russian observation station reported sighting a solar flare not visible elsewhere, and American astronomers prepared to watch for the magnetic storms and auroral displays that followed. When Sputnik III collected tape recordings on space radiation measurements, Russian scientists gave Odishaw a telemetry code with which to analyze the data. Odishaw summed up the IGY enterprise as a "human engagement, which achieved international cooperation in a period of sharp and perhaps unparalleled political unrest."

Because of the unqualified success of the IGY, many nations planned to continue cooperative international studies through 1959 and beyond. The International Geophysical Cooperation-1959 (IGC-59) was established with various subcategories in each scientific specialty. The National Academy of Sciences formed a new national committee called the Space Science Board and named Hugh Odishaw as its executive director. He continued to serve as executive director of the IGY national committee, while completing the projects and evaluating the data as director of World Data Center-A in the United States. He coordinated the national program of the Space Science Board within guidelines established by the international organization and directed the activities of national space committees dealing with government agencies. Since 1964 Odishaw has been executive secretary of the division of physical sciences of the National Academy of Sciences-National Research Council.

Early in his career Odishaw contributed articles to scientific journals on various aspects of radar and on standards and measurements. He is the author of many papers on the progress and achievements of the IGY and post-IGY programs. Odishaw is on the editorial boards of the American Geophysical Union and the International Science and Technology journal. He collaborated with a group of editors on *Antarctica in the International Geophysical Year* (1956) and with S. Ruttenberg on *Geophysics and the IGY* (1958), both published by the American Geophysical Union. Odishaw and E. U. Condon edited *The Handbook of Physics* (McGraw-Hill, 1958), which critics praised as "a detailed and comprehensive volume . . . recommended to students and working scientists." *Science and Space* (McGraw-Hill, 1961), compiled by Odishaw and L. V. Berkner, is a collection of reports written by recognized specialists for the Space Science Board. In compiling *The Challenges of Space* (Univ. of Chicago Press, 1962) Odishaw drew on his experiences to describe space efforts and to summarize the national and international space programs. In 1964 Odishaw edited the two volumes of *Research in Geophysics* (MIT Press), and in 1967 he was joint editor, with E. U. Condon, of *The Earth in Space* (Basic Books).

Odishaw belongs to the data and publications group of the Committee on Space Research (COSPAR) of the International Council on Scientific Unions and he is the Academy's representative for World Data Center-A to the International Geophysics Committee. He has been honored with fellowships in both the American Geophysical Union and the Royal Society of Arts. He is a member of the American Association for the Advancement of Science, the American Physical Society, the American Institute of Electrical Engineers, and the History of Science Society. Odishaw holds a distinguished public service award from the United States Navy, a distinguished alumni award from the Illinois Institute of Technology, and an honorary doctor of science degree from Carleton College.

In 1958 Odishaw married Marian Lee Scates. They have three daughters, Marian Louise, Tracy Lee, and Courtney Lee, and one son, Geoffrey Scott. Odishaw is a Presbyterian.

References

American Men of Science 11th ed (1966); Supplement 6 (1970)
Who's Who in America, 1970-71

OTTO, FREI (PAUL)

May 31, 1925- German architect; university professor
Address: b. Institut für Leichte Flächentragwerke, Technische Hochschule, Stuttgart, Federal Republic of Germany; h. Bergstrasse 19, 7251 Warmbronn, Federal Republic of Germany

In the view of the German architect Frei Otto, "like nutrition, the art of building is in a bad way in many countries—it is underdeveloped." A possible solution to the problem stated by Otto may

FREI OTTO

be found in his own work. A pioneer in light-weight construction, he is internationally renowned for his tensile and pneumatic structures, utilizing a minimum of material to span a maximum amount of space. Deriving much of his inspiration from nature, Otto has since the early 1950's designed a wide range of lightweight structures, including exhibition tents—most notably the German pavilion for Montreal's Expo 67—as well as sports arenas, retractable roofs for outdoor theatres, covers for docks and construction sites, and giant envelopes intended to house entire cities. The noted Mexican architect Felix Candela has said of Frei Otto's work: "His structures display that quality of logic and common sense which is so rare in other contemporary work, and moreover have the advantage of possessing . . . simple and unsolicited beauty which reveals the touch of the expert and yet is also pleasing to the man in the street."

Frei Paul Otto, the son of Paul Karl and Eleonore (Oehler) Otto, was born on May 31, 1925 in Siegmar, an industrial town in Saxony, and spent his boyhood in Berlin. Even as a child he had an eye for natural phenomena, and—inspired by his father and grandfather, who were sculptors—he developed a talent for constructing things. Fascinated by the floating property of a pheasant feather, he began to construct paper and balsa wood models of swept-wing and slotted-wing airplanes, and by the time he was ten he was designing fin propulsion systems and ornithopter aircraft. At fifteen he began building and flying gliders and familiarized himself with the principles of aerodynamics. In 1942 Otto designed a two-engine swept-wing plane, capable of slow and fast flight. During school vacations that year, he received training as a stonemason.

After completing his secondary education and passing his Abitur in 1943, Frei Otto was drafted into the German air force, where he continued to work at aircraft design and saw action as a fighter pilot. As a prisoner in a camp near Chartres, France from 1945 to 1947, Frei Otto found time to study structural engineering theory while work-ing on such civil engineering projects as the reconstruction of housing, war cemeteries, and waterworks. Because of the dearth of construction materials resulting from wartime conditions, Otto was faced with the challenge of obtaining maximum use from a minimum of material. His projects at the prison camp, including the design of low-volume lattice girders, were important steps in the development of the principle of "minimal" construction that characterized much of his later work.

Back in Germany after his release from imprisonment, Otto entered the Technische Universität of Berlin in 1948 to study architecture under professors Hans Freese, Hellmuth Bickenbach, and Gerhard Jobst. There he delved more deeply into the problem of economy in construction. During 1949 he did research in the development of new building materials and the use of rubble in construction. A study tour in the United States in 1950-51, which enabled him to make the acquaintance of such great architects as Frank Lloyd Wright, Ludwig Mies van der Rohe, Eero Saarinen, and Richard Neutra, marked a highlight in Otto's professional development. The tour included two months of study at the University of Virginia and four months of travel, during which he studied urban planning, the history of American cities, residential building construction, and new types of structures. Some drawings for the design of the first suspended roof, intended for an arena in Raleigh, North Carolina, that he saw in the engineering consultants' office of Fred N. Severud in New York City, provided a major impetus for his future work. On his return to Germany in 1951 he executed his first designs for suspended roofs—for a concert hall, auditoriums, and multistory buildings. Other 1951 projects included designs for a Protestant church, an office building, and a prestressed arch bridge.

In 1952, after submitting as his project a plan for a housing development for a Berlin suburb, Frei Otto graduated *summa cum laude* from the Technische Universität with the degree of Diplom-Ingenieur, which qualified him to practise architecture on his own. Continuing his architectural studies on a graduate level, Otto submitted his doctoral dissertation, "Das hängende Dach" ("The Suspended Roof"), in October 1953. The work included documentation of his studies on suspended roofs, discussion of prestressed and non-prestressed tension structures, an experimental study of deformations by optical techniques, and data on wind-tunnel tests. In connection with his doctoral work, Otto undertook preliminary projects involving membranes, cable networks, and giant envelopes, which he was to develop more fully in later years. In 1953 he sketched a design for a 1,800-foot cable-network roof to protect the construction of a dam in a Swiss Alpine valley. His projects for that year also included a design for a mission church in East Africa; and plans for an ecclesiastical college in Berlin-Zehlendorf, for which he won first prize in a town-planning competition. The Technische Universität awarded Otto the degree of Doktor-Ingenieur in 1954, and in the same year the Bauwelt-Verlag in Berlin published *Das hängende Dach*, which was later also published in Spanish, Polish, and Russian translations.

In 1954 Otto became associated with Peter Stromeyer, a partner in L. Stromeyer and Company of Konstanz, Europe's leading tent manufacturer, for whom he created a number of new designs over the next few years, including garden shelters, sun and wind screens, camping tents, canopies, and undulating aircraft hangar tents. The first of his tent designs to be constructed was a cable-mast supported saddle-shaped bandstand roof with a simple four-point surface, displayed in 1955 at the Federal Garden Exhibition in Kassel. For the Federal Garden Exhibition in Cologne two years later, Otto created somewhat more complex tent designs, including an entrance archway and a star-shaped dance pavilion, and for Interbau, the national building exhibition in Berlin in 1957, he designed cafe tents and a roof membrane for the "city of tomorrow" exhibition hall. To expand his research facilities, in 1957 Otto, along with several associates, founded the Entwicklungsstätte für den Leichtbau (Development Center for Lightweight Construction) in Berlin.

From 1959 to 1961 Otto was largely preoccupied with research on pneumatic membrane structures, whose shape and stability are maintained by air or gas pressure. To gain a better understanding of the principles in their design, Otto devoted some time to the study and observation of soap bubbles. Among the projects he designed along those lines are water towers, oil storage tanks, grain silos, and greenhouses. More recently, using similar principles, Otto conceived of a giant envelope, to encompass an Arctic city of 45,000 inhabitants, that would be stabilized by the pressure generated by the city's air conditioning system.

During the early and mid-1960's, Frei Otto and his associates worked on a variety of projects, including open-air theatres for Nijmegen, Holland, Wunsiedel, Germany and Cannes, France; covers for a dock in the port of Bremen and a construction site in England; tents and pavilions for the 1963 International Horticultural Exhibition in Hamburg; and pavilions for the 1964 Swiss National Exhibition in Lausanne. In 1962 and 1963, after studying such natural objects as egg shells, diatoms, and skeletal structures of plants and animals, Otto concentrated on the design of shell structures, lattice domes, and space frames with rigid joints. An example of the latter is a bell tower for a Protestant church in Berlin-Schönow, executed in 1963 by Frei Otto and Ewald Bubner.

Concurrently with his work in architectural design, Otto has been active as a teacher and lecturer. In 1958 he came to the United States as a visiting professor at Washington University in St. Louis, where he conducted a seminar on lightweight structures, and the following year he was a visiting lecturer at the Hochschule für Gestaltung in Ulm. As a visiting professor at Yale University in 1960, he conducted a study of ramified

compression structures and worked on the design of an assembly and exhibition hall for Chicago. In 1961-62 he worked as an assistant to Professor Peter Poelzig at the Technische Universität in Berlin. During 1962 he also was a visiting professor at the University of California in Berkeley, at the Massachusetts Institute of Technology, and at Harvard University, and he conducted a seminar at the Universidad Nacional del Zulia in Maracaibo, Venezuela. In 1964 Otto founded the Institut für Leichte Flächentragwerke (Institute for Light Surface Structures) at the Technische Hochschule in Stuttgart, which by providing him with all the facilities he needed for his projects, enabled him to work under more favorable circumstances than ever before. Otto serves as director of the institute and also holds the title of honorary professor. In 1966 he was a visiting professor at the National Design Institute in Ahmadabad, India.

Otto's most elaborate achievement to date is his design of the structure of the highly acclaimed German Pavilion for Montreal's 1967 world exposition, Expo 67. His chief collaborator on the project was Rolf Gutbrod, who designed the interior. The pavilion's huge, tent-like roof, constructed of steel mesh, covers a translucent, prestressed plastic membrane suspended from eight large masts of varying heights. It covers an area of 110,000 square feet and encompasses a volume of 1,864,000 cubic feet. The tent was intended to provide a "roofed landscape" with peaks and valleys, harmonizing with the exposition's theme, "Man and His World."

Among Frei Otto's most recent projects are the tent-like Indian pavilion for the 1970 world exposition at Osaka, Japan; a large automatically retractable membrane roof, covering the open-air theatre in the ruins of the medieval monastery at Bad Hersfeld, Germany; similar retractable roofs for swimming pools and skating rinks in France; and automatic umbrella-type roofs for the 1971 Federal Garden Exhibition in Cologne. In collaboration with Rolf Gutbrod, Otto has been working on the design for a congress center for Mecca, Saudi Arabia, complete with a hotel, a restaurant, conference halls, and a mosque. The elaborate Olympic stadiums in Munich, for which Otto has designed cable-net roof structures in collaboration with Fritz Leonhardt and others, are scheduled for completion for the 1972 Olympic Games.

In the summer of 1971 the Museum of Modern Art in New York City mounted a retrospective photographic exhibit of Frei Otto's work. Ludwig Glaeser, the curator of the museum's department of architecture and design, observed: "During the millennia in which man had to rely on gravity to give buildings stability, the enormous amounts of material used were disproportionate to the actual loads that vaults and domes had to carry. . . . Frei Otto arrived at structural solutions that, for the first time, reversed this ratio." Reviewing the exhibit in the New York *Times* (August 15, 1971), Ada Louise Huxtable called Otto's work "a remarkable synthesis of architecture, engineering, invention and art," but warned against overestimating its significance. "These are noteworthy structures, made possible by the unique technology of this century, developed by a man of genius, suitable for some striking and particular uses," she wrote. "They don't have to be universalized or justified with false pragmatism. For a variety of genuinely pragmatic reasons we are not going to be living under them or covering our cities with them. Why can't we admire them on their own terms?" Aware of the limitations of his work, Otto, unlike some architects, does not insist that his creations be preserved for eternity and is willing to see them demolished once they have served their functions. "Every building must die, as does man," he has said.

In addition to his architectural projects, Frei Otto has also created sculptures, furniture of heavy fabric and laminated material, children's toys, water fountains, and a horizontal sundial. He has contributed some 200 articles, most of them in German, to professional journals. His major work is *Zugbeanspruchte Konstruktionen*, published by the Ullstein Verlag. The first volume, on which he collaborated with Rudolf Trostel, deals with pneumatic structures and appeared in 1962. The coauthor of the second volume, which was published in 1966, is Friedrich-Karl Schleyer; it deals with structural systems, analysis of cable networks, and related topics. The two volumes were published in English translation as *Tensile Structures* (M.I.T. Press, 1967-69). Conrad Roland's comprehensive study of Otto's work, *Frei Otto: Spannweiten* (1965), was translated into English by C. V. Amerongen under the title *Frei Otto: Tension Structures* (Praeger, 1970).

Frei Otto and Ingrid Smolla were married on May 28, 1952. They have three daughters: Angela, Bettina, and Christine; and one son, Dietmar. Otto is about five feet eight inches tall, weighs 152 pounds, and has brown eyes and gray hair. He is a Protestant. In 1967 he received the Kunstpreis für Architektur, awarded by the city of West Berlin, and he was corecipient, with Rolf Gutbrod, of the Auguste Perret Prize of the Union Internationale des Architects. Otto is a member of the Bund Deutscher Architekten and of the Academy of Arts in Berlin. He was made an honorary fellow of the American Institute of Architects in 1968.

References

Roland, Conrad. Frei Otto: Tension Structures (1970)
Wer ist Wer? (1969-70)
Who's Who in America, 1970-71

OWINGS, NATHANIEL A(LEXANDER) (ō'ingz)

Feb. 5, 1903- Architect; planner; conservationist
Address: b. Skidmore, Owings & Merrill, 1 Maritime Plaza, San Francisco, Calif. 94111; h. Big Sur, Calif. 93920; "Festina Lente," Route 1, Box 231, Sante Fe, N. Mex. 87501

If the cities of the future, with their inevitable higher population density, are to be triumphs of design and technology, rather than slums, the architects and planners of today may have to come to share the conviction of Nathaniel A. Owings that the problems of environmental control should be their professions' paramount concern. Owings is the founding partner of Skidmore, Owings & Merrill, which developed from the team he formed with Louis Skidmore in 1936 and which has since won more top awards for quality of design from the American Institute of Architects than any competitor. His diversified, decentralized architectural-engineering firm, with offices in five cities across the country, has countered the urban crisis with bold new architectural concepts like those of the Crown Zellerback building in San Francisco and the John Hancock building in Chicago. Owings, the author of *The American Aesthetic* (1969), has also directed expert team planning in redevelopment projects in several cities, including Washington, D.C., where he served as chairman of the President's commission on the redesigning of Pennsylvania Avenue.

Primarily of Welsh descent, with traces of Scottish and Irish extraction, Nathaniel Alexander Owings was born to Nathaniel Fleming and Cora Nima (Alexander) Owings on February 5, 1903 in Indianapolis, Indiana. His younger sister, Eloise, is Mrs. Louis Skidmore. Earning his living as a specialist in selecting, importing, milling, and selling fine woods for furniture making, his father provided a comfortable home for the family in Indianapolis. That beautifully planned city reinforced what Owings thinks of as his inborn taste for elegance of style and in part accounts for his concern for preserving the excellence in America's cultural heritage. He also loved rural Indiana, often visiting his cousin's farm in Rush County. When Nathaniel was thirteen years old, his father died. His resourceful mother became a CPA through correspondence courses and worked as a bookkeeper to liquidate, with her son's help, her husband's debts and to support the family.

In boyhood Nathaniel Owings was devoted to scouting, and he became an eagle scout. After his graduation from Arsenal Technical High School in Indianapolis in 1920, he attended, on a Rotary Club scholarship, the International Scout Jamboree in London and then made a tour of France. Once having seen the cathedrals of Europe, particularly Notre Dame, Chartres, and Mont-Saint-Michel, Owings made up his mind to be an architect. "There is a miracle," he has remarked, as quoted in *Time* (August 2, 1968), "in discovering what you want to do and never questioning it again. It happens rarely."

To prepare for his career Owings enrolled in the University of Illinois as a student in architectural engineering in 1921. At the end of his first year he became ill, and when he was ready to resume study some months later, he entered Cornell University. There he waited on tables to meet part of his expenses, which included those accruing from his enthusiastic enjoyment of campus life. In 1927 he was awarded the B.S. degree in both architecture and engineering. During the year of apprenticeship following his graduation he was employed as a draftsman for the New York City architectural firm of York and Sawyer. Assigned to a team designing the public washrooms for the Commerce Department Building in Washington, D.C., he did so good a job that he was put to work on planning details for the main entrance.

Owings' hero among architects was Raymond Hood, whose RCA building for Rockefeller Center impressed him greatly. Hood was a member of the architectural commission for the 1933 Century of Progress Exposition at Chicago, and through his association with Hood, Owings was put in charge of concessions design and was made development supervisor at the Chicago fair. When the deepening Depression caused a retrenchment in construction and a discarding of many of the expensive plans of the country's foremost architects, Owings worked with Louis Skidmore, chief designer of the fair, to build the pavilions for more than 500 exhibits at minimum cost, using lightweight, mass-produced materials, such as beaverboard. In finding solutions to the problems of the Chicago fair, Owings discovered that he had a flair for drawing up large-scale plans and devising means of realizing them.

Skidmore and Owings formalized their partnership in Chicago in January 1936. John O. Merrill, an architectural engineer, joined the firm as a limited partner in 1939, and, along with four other architectural specialists, became a general partner in 1949. Almost from the beginning the firm operated under a decentralized arrangement, with Owings overseeing the Chicago office and Skidmore, the New York office. Skidmore, Owings & Merrill later acquired three additional offices, in San Francisco, Washington, D.C., and Portland, Oregon. Decentralization, along with the policy of hiring talented men in many special fields, such as site surveying, and fluidity in assignment of personnel, enabled the firm to handle a large volume and variety of work at one time.

Among the first commissions of the Skidmore and Owings partnership were designs for several buildings of the New York World's Fair of 1939-40, a hospital in Petoskey, Michigan, and a paper mill for Kimberly-Clark in Neenah, Wisconsin. When the United States became involved in World War II, the architects were prepared to undertake extensive government projects connected with the defense effort. After designing the reception center and welfare building at the Great Lakes Naval Training Station in Illinois in 1942, the firm was commissioned to build the secret town of Oak Ridge, Tennessee, where the atomic bomb was to be developed.

The largest of half a dozen or so wartime projects that Skidmore, Owings & Merrill carried out for the federal government, the construction of Oak Ridge involved town planning, surveying, and road building, with provisions for future development, as well as the designing and furnishing of all community facilities, such as hospitals, schools, and housing for some 75,000 residents. Although hampered by security restrictions, the

NATHANIEL A. OWINGS

firm fulfilled its basic assignment in about two years, from 1943 to 1945. It received a Manhattan District Award for an achievement that was described in *Architectural Forum* as "the best job of emergency planning to come out of the war."

In the postwar construction boom Skidmore, Owings & Merrill returned to private building with many choice commissions throughout the United States. They included the plants for the H. J. Heinz Company in Tracy, California (1946) and Pittsburgh (1949-52); the Terrace Plaza Hotel in Cincinnati (1946-48); the Lake Meadows Apartment buildings in Chicago; the Ford Motor Company's central staff offices in Dearborn Michigan; the Veterans Administration Hospital in Brooklyn (1950); and New York University Bellevue Medical Center in New York City. The Museum of Modern Art presented the designs of those and other buildings in an exhibition of the architecture of Skidmore, Owings & Merrill in the fall of 1950. An accompanying bulletin pointed out that its work is "persistently characterized by the idiom of the firm rather than that of any individual within the firm" and that its team of architects "produces with originality, efficiency and craftsmanship visually exciting architecture which records the esthetic and technological experiences of our civilization."

An outstanding illustration of the "clear pattern of modern architecture" attributed to the firm in the museum's bulletin is New York City's spectacular Lever House. In the Bauhaus tradition of Walter Gropius and Mies van der Rohe, Lever House rises as an uncluttered, geometric tower, a rectangular twenty-one-story structure with walls of glass and stainless steel. It opens the city by occupying only a small part of the block, reserving 75 percent of its site for a plaza. As reported in *Time* (August 2, 1968), "The bold positioning of horizontal slab and vertical shaft . . . was revolutionary. More than any other, it set the style of office buildings in the 1950's and 60's." Imitations of Lever House by other architectural firms, however, have frequently been unsatisfactory.

Modular glass walls, again, were a striking feature of the designs for the $152,500,000 Air Force Academy near Colorado Springs, for which Skidmore, Owings & Merrill was commissioned in 1954. The firm had the additional responsibility of supervising the construction of some forty general contractors on the 17,900-acre site. Owings' chief role in the project was to maintain liaison with members of a Senate appropriations subcommittee and Air Force officers, some of whom objected to what they considered radically ultramodern designs in the original plans, such as those for an accordion-like chapel.

Many of the firm's commercial buildings have also provoked controversy, including architectural landmarks such as the Chase Manhattan Bank in downtown Manhattan and the Alcoa building in San Francisco, which is braced by cross girders against earthquakes. Similarly fortified against strong winds, the John Hancock skyscraper of offices and apartments stands 100 stories tall on Chicago's Gold Coast, a complete community in itself. Besides other office buildings, like the Main Place complex in Dallas and the Georgia-Pacific Corporation in Portland, Oregon, Skidmore, Owings & Merrill has recently designed many buildings of diversified purpose, including the School of Art and Architecture building of the University of Illinois, the Oakland-Alameda County Stadium in California, the Mauna Kea Hotel in Hawaii, and the Qantas Hotel in Sydney, Australia.

Owings has named among the most significant assignments he has ever undertaken that of chairman of the Temporary Commission on Pennsylvania Avenue, to whose preceding advisory council he was appointed by President John F. Kennedy in 1962. With the support also of the administrations of Presidents Johnson and Nixon, Owings supervised the drawing up of a master plan for a vast remodeling of Pennsylvania Avenue in Washington from the White House to the Capitol, making it the imposing ceremonial boulevard it was intended to be in Pierre L'Enfant's original plan for the nation's capital in the late eighteenth century. If Congress appropriates funds for the project, the renovation of Pennsylvania Avenue could be completed in time for Washington's celebration of its bicentennial year, 1976. In a related but far less ambitious commission Owings began in the spring of 1965 to design a comprehensive revitalization of the Washington Mall, which seems to many Washingtonians and tourists to be lacking in interest and beauty.

While working on Washington redevelopment problems, Owings involved his firm in what he ranks as probably his most important job—the designing of an eighteen-mile strip of highway Interstate 95 through the center of nearby Baltimore. He brought to the city an urban design concept team of architects, engineers, and traffic and transit specialists to solve the problem of movement while preserving historical, residential, and recreational areas. Owings considers himself a neutral in the age-old urban battle between mobility and place-space, a planner who sees to it that everybody gets a fair deal in meeting the "intrusion of technology"—both those for transportation interests and those for "fixed things."

In an interview for Baltimore magazine (April 1969) Owings noted that he was a member of the Secretary of the Interior's Advisory Board on National Parks, Historic Sites, Buildings and Monuments: "So one of my great interests is in historic buildings and the preservation of the quality of the past." During the late 1960's, for instance, when the projected widening of a New Mexico highway threatened to destroy the aesthetic setting of the ancient adobe Church of San José de Gracia de Las Trampas, he helped lead a successful fight to divert the path of the highway and then to restore the decaying historic church to its original beauty. Owings' role in resolving conflicts of interests, on a modest scale in Las Trampas and on a vast scale in Washington and Baltimore, exemplifies what he recognizes as a new dimension in planning, a political task—"the art of getting things done" by appealing to human reasonableness.

The responsible concern of the architect in the enormous problems of environmental control has claimed increasing attention and endorsement from Owings. "I have a conviction," he wrote, "that whatever his other needs may be, man, in order to be happy, is compelled to express his love of beauty. . . . Men and termites form societies of builders, but of all the known building creatures on this planet, only man seems to create beauty consciously in what he constructs. It is in service to this vital difference that this book has been written."

Owings' book is The American Aesthetic (Harper & Row, 1969), illustrated with aerial photographs by William A. Garnett, with whom he flew across much of the country to document his proposals for a new aesthetic inspired by America's landscape in combination with its industrialization. The solution to the nation's multifarious ecological problems, such as those resulting from urban blight and the misuse of natural resources, is not, he argues, an extension of suburban erosion of rural areas or urban dispersal through satellite cities, but rather environmental planning that provides for both open spaces and high-density core cities: "Sharply defined, the city must stand in the clear, clean air of the open country around it."

Owings, who is at present chairman of the board of control of the Urban Design Concept Team, has directed redevelopment planning in Chicago and San Francisco as well as Washington and Baltimore. In 1970 Ball State University presented him with an honorary LL.D. degree and an accompanying citation that read in part, "While others predict the demise of America's great cities . . . you plan courageously for another kind of America, bringing into focus and adding perspective to the needs of a growing population living more closely together in an orderly and esthetically pleasing environment."

A fellow of the American Institute of Architects, Owings is also chairman of its newly formed national human resources council. He is a trustee of the American Academy in Rome, an academician of the National Academy of Design, and an associate of the National Academy of Art. His clubs are the Century Association in New York, the Family Club in San Francisco, the Metropolitan Club in Washington, the Commercial Club of Chicago, the Wayfarers Club in Chicago, and the Arlington Club in Portland, Oregon.

By his first marriage, to the former Emily Huntington Otis, on September 5, 1931, Nathaniel A. Owings has a son, Nathaniel, and three daughters, Emily, Natalie, and Jennifer. The marriage ended in divorce in 1953, and on December 30, 1953 Owings married Margaret Wentworth, the artist, writer, and conservationist. Her daughter by a former marriage is Anne Wentworth Osorno. After his marriage to Margaret Wentworth, Owings bought a fifty-five-acre site on the Big Sur coast near Carmel, California. Here he built his first house, "Wild Bird," on a cantilevered concrete ledge some 600 feet above the Pacific. In the early 1960's he led a community movement to preserve the rugged beauty of Big Sur by zoning laws regulating the building of new houses, touring facilities, and highways. Owings also has a vacation home in New Mexico.

The urban affairs specialist Daniel P. Moynihan, who served on the Pennsylvania Avenue planning committee, once said of Owings, as quoted in *Time* (August 2, 1968), "He is ebullient, competent and devoted—and also a randy rogue, a bandit and a buccaneer. His great ability is to get other people to do good work." Much of his persuasiveness had been attributed to his personal charm, patience, shrewdness, and energy. He is a dapper man, standing five feet eleven inches tall and weighing 165 pounds; he has brown eyes and dark-brown hair. His recreations are horseback riding, travelling all over the world to investigate historic sites, and hiking in wilderness areas.

References

Baltimore p19+ Ap '69 por
Fortune 57:137+ Ja '58 por
Time 74:38+ D 28 '59; 92:39+ Ag 2 '68 pors
Washington (D.C.) Post G p9 Ap 7 '66 por
Washington (D.C.) Star mag Jl 30 '67 por
International Who's Who, 1970-71
Who's Who in America, 1970-71

PAISLEY, IAN (RICHARD KYLE)

Apr. 6, 1926- Northern Ireland political leader; member of the British Parliament; Protestant clergyman
Address: b. House of Commons, London, S.W. 1, England; h. Beersbridge Rd., Belfast, Northern Ireland

A key figure in the turbulent politics of Northern Ireland, the Reverend Ian Paisley has emerged in

IAN PAISLEY

recent years as the leading spokesman for militant Protestants in their centuries-old and often violent struggle with Ulster's Roman Catholic minority. The self-styled moderator of the Free Presbyterian Church of Ulster—a dissident sect that he founded in 1951—Paisley was elected to the Ulster Parliament in April 1970 and became a member of the British House of Commons two months later. Asserting that Northern Ireland is in a state of war, the fiery fundamentalist minister is convinced that the Roman Catholic Church is a threat to Ulster's freedom. "You cannot talk peace until the enemy surrenders, and the enemy is the Catholic Church, which has never accepted the Northern Ireland Constitution," he has said. "We will keep Ulster Protestant and we will keep Ulster free."

Ian Richard Kyle Paisley was born in Armagh, Northern Ireland on April 6, 1926, the younger of the two sons of the Reverend J. Kyle Paisley. His mother, a former governess, is a native of Edinburgh, Scotland. Paisley may have inherited his religious zeal from his father, a Baptist minister, who split with his denomination and established a church of his own in Ballymena, County Antrim. Growing up in Ballymena, where he was said to have spent "a strict and separate childhood," Paisley attended the Ballymena School before entering Ballymena Technical College in 1939. After graduating he tried farming for a time.

Soon, however, he "felt a definite calling" to enter the ministry and went to South Wales, where he enrolled in the Barrie School of Evangelism of the Reformed Presbyterian Church—a small sect that had broken with the mother church in the seventeenth century. On completing his studies there he tried unsuccessfully to enroll in the theological college of the Northern Ireland Presbyterian Church before being accepted by the Theological Hall of the Reformed Presbyterian Church of Ireland. Paisley was ordained to the Christian ministry in August 1946 while serving with the Evangelistic Mission Hall, an independent institution founded by members of one of Belfast's Presbyterian congregations. His ordination, which was performed by his father, was, according to Presbyterian Church sources, not in conformity with traditional church practice.

In 1951 Paisley was invited to conduct a mission at a Presbyterian church in County Down that was temporarily without a minister. When the presbytery objected, a group of Paisley's followers split off, and formed their own sect, the Free Presbyterian Church. Paisley thereupon changed the name of his chapel to the Free Presbyterian Church of Ulster, giving himself the title of moderator. Although a 1961 census showed that Paisley's church had at the time a little over 1,000 members, a survey conducted by Lancaster University in 1968 indicated that he could muster the support of as many as 200,000 Ulster Protestants. According to an Associated Press estimate the membership of his church was about 20,000 in January 1969. By 1970 there were more than thirty Free Presbyterian churches operating throughout Northern Ireland, most of them housed in small buildings of the mission hall type. In October 1969 Paisley opened the new $420,000 Martyrs Memorial Free Presbyterian Church of Ulster on Ravenhill Road in Belfast. The church, which he claimed was "the largest Protestant church to be opened in the United Kingdom since the turn of the century," serves a congregation of some 600 families and had a net income of about $145,000 during its first year.

To disassociate themselves from Paisley, spokesmen for the Presbyterian Church—which, with 29 percent of the population constitutes the largest body of Protestants in Northern Ireland—issued a statement, quoted in the London *Times* (January 29, 1969), attacking the Free Presbyterian Church. "This body has repeatedly sought to take advantage of local dissatisfaction or disputes," the statement read. "A virulent campaign has been sustained against . . . the major Protestant churches for advocating moderate policies and better ecumenical and community relations. Considerable appeal has been made also to political as well as theological fears by mob oratory. . . . While Mr. Paisley's own church body remains relatively small . . . the attention he has received . . . [for] his more outrageous statements and activities, has built him up as a public figure out of true proportion."

The "outrageous statements and activities" concerned Paisley's virulent anti-Roman Catholic campaign. Northern Ireland, with a population of about 1,000,000 Protestants and some 500,000 Roman Catholics is a part of the United Kingdom. Religious strife has simmered since 1690, when William of Orange led English troops to Londonderry to defeat the remaining Roman Catholics loyal to King James II at the Battle of Boyne. Ulster has been under Protestant domination ever since, and the Catholic minority has become increasingly dissatisfied with what it considers gross discrimination in such areas as employment, public housing, the dissemination of welfare funds, and the franchise to vote in local elections. Friction between Protestants and Catholics has intensified since the six northern counties of Ireland chose to remain with the British Crown instead of join-

ing with the predominantly Catholic south of Ireland in forming the Irish Free State in 1922 and the Republic of Ireland in 1948.

Paisley found a ready audience for his anti-papal sermons among Ulster's urban working-class Protestants, who feared that their centuries-old ascendancy over the Catholics was slipping away, and in the country districts, where Catholics were often in the majority. Protestant farmers, believing that the Catholics threatened their homes and lands, rallied to the firebrand churchman when he told them: "We must let the forces of popery know that we Protestants are here to stay and that we will remain in control."

In 1962 Paisley went to Rome to protest against the participation by Protestant observers in an ecumenical council meeting at the Vatican. A few years later, incensed because the Archbishop of Canterbury was about to visit the Pope, Paisley boarded the Archbishop's Rome-bound aircraft. He was detained by the Italian police on arrival and put on a return flight to London. Paisley later said that the Archbishop was "slobbering on his slippers" when he called on the Pope. Preaching at rallies more than a dozen times a week, Paisley concentrated his attacks on the Pope, whom he called "Old Red Socks," and on the Roman Church, which he dubbed the "Scarlet Woman," but denied that he harbored ill will toward individual Catholics. "No one . . . need fear Ian Paisley—Protestant or Catholic, Orangeman or Hibernian," he said at one of his rallies, as quoted in the Dublin magazine *This Week* (May 1, 1970). "I will fight for justice for all." As one of his supporters has explained, Paisley hopes to see Roman Catholics "brought into the light of the Gospel."

Moderate politicians such as Captain Terence O'Neill—Northern Ireland's Prime Minister from 1963 to 1969—have also been among Paisley's favorite targets. Infuriated because the Ulster Prime Minister had conferred with Prime Minister Sean Lemass of the hated Irish Republic in early 1965, Paisley intoned from the pulpit of his Belfast church: "We call upon Thee, O Lord, to rid us of the arch-traitor, the Prime Minister Captain Terence O'Neill."

Sentenced to prison for three months in July 1966 for refusing to obey a court order to keep the peace after he had been found guilty of leading a march through a Roman Catholic area of Belfast that ended in bloody rioting, Paisley was given a hero's welcome by his admirers when he was released. He continued to gather support during the late 1960's, leading rallies, marches, and demonstrations throughout Northern Ireland. Although from the pulpit he decried violence, the demonstrations usually ended in rioting between his supporters and members of the militant Roman Catholic civil rights movement. In January 1969 he was again convicted of unlawful assembly and sentenced to three months in prison. He was freed on bail, however, when he announced he would run for the Ulster Parliament as a candidate from the rural constituency of Bannside, a seat that had been occupied by O'Neill for twenty-three years.

Running on a Protestant Unionist ticket, Paisley waged a heated campaign. He denounced O'Neill —the incumbent candidate of the ruling Unionist party—for his moderate position toward the Catholic civil rights movement, which, he charged, was a front for the illegal Irish Republican Army. He accused the Prime Minister of aiding the Catholic hierarchy in its attempt to subvert the Constitution and take over the country. O'Neill, a lackluster campaigner, managed to win the general election—held on February 24, 1969—with 7,745 votes, but Paisley demonstrated considerable strength by garnering 6,331 votes. A third candidate, representing the Catholic civil rights movement, received 2,310 votes.

The following month, Paisley returned to prison to finish serving his sentence, having refused an offer by a judge to suspend the sentence if the militant Protestant leader would promise to keep the peace. Released on May 6, 1969 in an amnesty declared by James Chichester-Clark—who had become Prime Minister of Northern Ireland a few days earlier, when O'Neill stepped down—Paisley urged Ulster Protestants to get together and "give the new Prime Minister a fair chance." He refused, however, to rule out further anti-Catholic demonstrations. "I am more convinced than ever that the civil rights movement is a front organization for subversive elements who are against law and order, against the constitution, against the flag, and against the Queen," the Protestant leader said after he stepped through the gates of Belfast prison.

During the summer of 1969 Northern Ireland was racked by some of the worst riots in its history. Areas of Belfast and Londonderry became virtual battlegrounds between Catholics and Protestants. In August 1969 Prime Minister Chichester-Clark was forced to ask British Prime Minister Harold Wilson to send aid. Wilson dispatched 6,000 British troops, who managed to restore order after a week of bloody violence in which eight people died and nearly 800 were injured. Angered because Chichester-Clark had asked Wilson for aid, Paisley charged the Ulster government with having "capitulated to the Roman Catholic Church." On two occasions, however, Paisley was credited with having averted renewed major violence when, at the request of police, he persuaded crowds of his own supporters to disperse.

In early September Paisley went to the United States to follow the trail of Bernadette Devlin, a young, dynamic leader of Northern Ireland's Catholic civil rights movement and a member of the British Parliament, who had gone to America to plead the Catholic case and raise money for victims of the riots. Paisley, who called Miss Devlin "the nearest thing to a Communist in the Roman Catholic Church that I can see," declared that the purpose of his trip was to dispute whatever claims she might make about the situation in Northern Ireland.

Defying a government ban on outdoor demonstrations, Paisley on September 30 led more than 3,000 of his followers in a protest outside Stormont—the Ulster Parliament—against concessions by the government to the Catholic population. Less than a week later new violence flared in Belfast and British troops had to use tear gas to disperse a crowd of Paisley's followers after five hours of street fighting. Meanwhile, an official commission of inquiry headed by Lord Cameron, had been investigating the situation in Northern Ireland and released its report on September 11, 1969. While blaming the Catholic civil rights movement for much of the rioting, the Cameron Report, obviously referring to Paisley, also assailed those who "by their appeal to sectarian prejudices and bigotry have assisted to inflame passions and keep alive ancient hatreds."

Continuing to try to gain a political platform for his views, Paisley again was a Protestant Unionist candidate in a by-election on April 16, 1970 for the Bannside seat which had been vacated when O'Neill was elevated to the House of Lords after resigning as Ulster's Prime Minister. Campaigning on a platform to end the moderate reforms granted by the government to the Catholics, Paisley defeated the Unionist candidate, Dr. Bolton Minford, by a vote of 7,981 to 6,778. A Labour party candidate received slightly over 3,500 votes. Soon after his victory, Paisley called on Prime Minister Chichester-Clark to resign. "If not," he said, "I will make it so hot for him that he will want to retire." Attributing his victory to "the intervention of Almighty God," Paisley took his seat in the Stormont Commons on April 21, 1970.

Less than two months later Paisley gained a foothold in the British Parliament when, as a Protestant Unionist candidate, he successfully contested the House of Commons constituency of North Antrim in the general election of June 18, 1970. He defeated the official Unionist candidate, who had occupied the seat for eleven years, by 2,679 votes. "Of course my election will help peace in Northern Ireland," Paisley said at the conclusion of his campaign. "I will be in the House of Commons to answer the lies and slander of Bernadette Devlin." He also asserted that his victory was tantamount to "marching orders" for Ulster Prime Minister Chichester-Clark.

In 1966 Paisley received an honorary doctorate of divinity from Bob Jones University, a fundamentalist institution in Greenville, South Carolina. He is also said to hold degrees from the Pioneer Theological Seminary in Rockford, Illinois and the Burton College and Seminary at Manitou Springs, Colorado. Paisley acts as chairman of the Ulster Constitution Defence Committee, and his name has been associated by his opponents with the outlawed Ulster Volunteer Force. He is editor of the *Protestant Telegraph*, a Belfast weekly, and author of the book *An Exposition of the Epistle to the Romans; Prepared in the Prison Cell* (Marshall, Morgan & Scott, 1968). Among his many polemical pamphlets is one entitled *A Startling Exposure: Billy Graham and the Church of Rome* (1970), an attack on the popular American evangelist.

The Reverend Ian Paisley and his wife, Eileen, have three daughters, Sharon, Rhonda, and Cherith, and twin sons, Kyle and Ian. The family lives in a

Victorian semidetched home in Belfast. Mrs. Paisley is a member of the Belfast City Council. The hefty, barrel-chested, blue-eyed cleric, who has been labeled "the big fella," is six feet four inches tall and weighs 220 pounds. Described by admirers as "brilliant and erudite," Paisley is said by them to have "bottomless wells of energy" and a sense of humor. Commenting on his oratorical style, Alfred Friendly wrote in the Washington *Post* (April 12, 1970) that his "words stream out in a loud unvarying pitch without subtleties of shading or structure." A devoted family man, Paisley does not smoke, drink, or attend motion pictures. His friends call him "the good doctor," while to his opponents he is "the clergyman in jackboots," "the bloated bullfrog," a quasi-fascist, and the devil incarnate. Although Paisley has denied that he has ambitions to become the Prime Minister of Northern Ireland, he told a correspondent for *Newsweek* (April 27, 1970): "If the people called me in their hour of need, how could any man refuse?"

References

Guardian p9 Je 29 '66 por
London Observer p17 Jl 10 '66 por
N Y Post p55 S 10 '69 por
Newsweek 74:28+ S 1 '69 por
Washington (D.C.) Post E p2 Jl 24 '66 por;
A p21 Ap 12 '70 por

PASTRANA BORRERO, MISAEL

Nov. 14, 1923- President of Colombia
Address: b. Palacio San Carlos, Bogotá, Colombia

Misael Pastrana Borrero, a lawyer and former business executive, succeeded Carlos Lleras Restrepo for a four-year term as President of Colombia on August 7, 1970, after defeating former dictator Gustavo Rojas Pinilla in a close race. Pastrana, a Conservative, served in several Cabinet posts in the 1960's and was Colombia's Ambassador to the United States in 1968-69. He is the last President to be elected under Colombia's unique National Front agreement, which provided for a coalition of the country's two leading political parties, the Liberals and the Conservatives. Since assuming office, Pastrana has tried to maintain a delicate balance between conservative landowners and industrialists on the one hand and militant workers, peasants, and students on the other, while implementing his predecessor's social and economic reforms, aimed at raising the living standards of Colombia's 21,000,000 people.

Misael Pastrana Borrero, the son of Misael Pastrana and Elisa Borrero de Pastrana, was born on November 14, 1923 in the city of Neiva in southwestern Colombia. His father was active in local politics and served as a senator from the department of Huila. Although not wealthy, the family has been identified with Colombia's political elite. As a boy, Pastrana showed little inclination for a public service career. He obtained his primary education in Neiva and then attended a Roman Catholic boys school in Bogotá, the national capital, before entering the Pontifica Universidad Javeriana there for the study of law and economics.

After receiving his doctorate from the university, Pastrana briefly practised law and also served as a judge. He underwent his first experience in diplomatic service when he was sent to Rome as secretary to the Colombian Embassy at the Vatican. While in Rome, he rounded out his education by studying at the Ferri Institute. In 1948 he returned to Colombia, where he became secretary to the President and Conservative party leader Mariano Ospina Pérez. His admiration for Ospina Pérez helped stimulate his interest in public affairs, and he was particularly impressed by the President's actions in overcoming the national crisis that arose from the assassination of the popular Liberal leader Jorge Eliécer Gaitán in April 1948.

When Ospina Pérez left the Presidency in 1950, Pastrana returned to private life, resuming his law practice and associating himself with several business enterprises. He remained aloof from politics until 1957, when a National Front (Frente Nacional) coalition agreement was concluded between the leaders of the Liberal and Conservative parties, aimed at ending the bitter interparty struggle that had resulted in the deaths of some 200,000 Colombians in the late 1940's and the 1950's. The National Front alliance, which ended the dictatorship established by General Gustavo Rojas Pinilla in 1953, provided for the quadrennial alternation of the Presidential candidacy between Liberals and Conservatives for a sixteen-year period beginning in 1958 and for the equal division of other, lesser candidacies among the two parties during that period.

As a member of the Conservative party within the framework of the National Front, Pastrana has exemplified the spirit of interparty understanding and compromise behind that coalition. His interest in economic development and social reform brought him in 1960 into the Cabinet of Liberal President Alberto Lleras Camargo, where he served successively as Minister of Development, Minister of Public Works, and Minister of Finance and Public Credit. In 1962, when it was the Conservative party's turn to put up a candidate for the presidency, Pastrana's name was mentioned, but the nomination went to Guillermo León Valencia, who won the election. He was succeeded by the Liberal Carlos Lleras Restrepo in the 1966 elections, in which Pastrana was the unsuccessful candidate for the Senate from the department of Huila.

When Lleras Restrepo took office as President in 1966 he appointed Pastrana his Minister of Government (or Minister of the Interior). Among his achievements in that post was his successful promotion of a constitutional amendment for the modernization of the government administration and for more efficient planning of public expenditures. The measure was approved by the national Congress in late 1968, after much discussion. In 1968-69 Pastrana was Colombia's Ambassador to the United States. He has also served as secretary general of the Ministry of Foreign Affairs of Colombia and as an alternate member of the Colombian delegation to the United Nations and to the Organization of American States.

Responding to a request from Conservative party leaders that he seek candidacy in the 1970 Presidential election, Pastrana returned home from Washington in September 1969. Under the provisions of the National Front agreement, the party whose turn it was for the Presidency—in this case the Conservatives—had to choose its candidate first and then submit the name to the other party for approval. Although Pastrana enjoyed the backing of the party leadership, many Conservatives had misgivings about his candidacy, partly because he had served in the Cabinets of two Liberal presidents. At the Conservative party convention in early November, Pastrana won a narrow first-ballot victory over former Foreign Minister Evaristo Sourdis, but since his vote fell short of the required two-thirds, a second ballot was taken, which resulted in a tie. The stalemate was then resolved by the Liberal party which, at its convention on December 5, 1969, approved of Pastrana by an overwhelming majority.

Although in the three preceding Presidential elections the National Front candidates had won hands down, in 1970 the situation was complicated by the emergence of former dictator Rojas Pinilla as a candidate. Rojas—whose most vocal supporter on the Congressional level was his daughter, Senator María Eugenia Rojas de Moreno Díaz—admittedly set out to disrupt the National Front and to restore the type of government he had piloted in the 1950's. His organization, the Alianza Nacional Popular (ANAPO), which he had to register as a Conservative party to qualify as a Presidential candidate, commanded a broad base of support among Colombia's urban poor, who claimed that their economic needs had been shortchanged by the National Front governments. It also included such diverse elements as military men, students, and dissidents from the Liberal and Conservative parties.

As the official candidate of the Conservative party, Pastrana faced additional opposition from dissident elements within Conservative ranks, represented by his convention rival, Sourdis, who was bolstered by strong regional support along Colombia's Caribbean coast; and by former Labor Minister Belisario Betancur Cuartas, who could count trade union spokesmen and disaffected Liberals among his supporters. Under the provisions of the National Front agreement, all four candidates were on the ballot as Conservatives. An added factor in the election was the urging, by forces of the extreme left, of citizens to abstain from voting.

A somewhat drab candidate compared to the flamboyant General Rojas, Pastrana began his campaign in January 1970 with a promise to continue his predecessor's social and economic reforms. In the election of April 19, 1970, in which some 43 percent of the eligible voters abstained, Pastrana defeated Rojas by a narrow margin. The final vote,

MISAEL PASTRANA BORRERO

after a recount, was 1,614,419 to 1,557,782, with the other two candidates receiving about 700,000 votes between them.

Refusing to accept the election results, the Rojas forces staged such violent demonstrations that outgoing President Lleras Restrepo was forced to call out troops and suspend civil rights. For three weeks after the elections the former dictator and his daughter were placed under house arrest. The unrest continued to flare up here and there in the months that followed, and at the time of Pastrana's inauguration the country was in a state of siege, with troops and tanks patrolling Bogotá. The supporters of Rojas boycotted the inauguration ceremony, having decided that, in view of their relatively favorable showing in the elections, they would concentrate on parliamentary activities. "Pastrana was declared winner by fraud and we will not accept him," Señator Rojas de Moreno Díaz declared at the time, as quoted in the Washington Post (August 8, 1970). "We will cooperate in the legislature, which is separate from the executive."

Addressing dignitaries from some fifty countries at his inauguration on August 7, 1970, Pastrana called for the establishment of a new "social front," mobilizing the entire nation for the fight against "misery, . . . ignorance, sickness, unemployment, and sadness." Like that of his predecessor, Pastrana's thirteen-man cabinet is composed of six Conservatives, six Liberals, and one unaligned member. Although the National Front failed to obtain a majority of the seats in either house of Congress, a post-election agreement with the Sourdis and Betancur forces enabled Pastrana to establish a working Congressional majority.

To cope with Colombia's pressing economic and social problems, the Pastrana government has drawn up a long-range development program, aimed at reducing unemployment, increasing the gross national product, diversifying the economy, stimulating exports, attracting overseas investments, stabilizing wages and prices, and promoting tourism. The program calls for implementation of agrarian reform, improvement of urban areas, and a fight against poverty through education and other means. Pastrana's policies have been welcomed by the United States government, which had strongly supported the reforms instituted by President Lleras, and which hopefully looks upon Colombia as a bulwark of democracy on the South American continent.

Although Colombia has had a land reform program since 1961 its implementation has been lethargic, because of the resistance of the large landowners and their representatives in the Congress, many of whom belong to Pastrana's own Conservative party. In the months preceding Pastrana's inauguration, the outgoing Lleras government paved the way for extensive land redistribution by expropriating some 60,000 acres from large landowners in the Cauca Valley, one of Colombia's richest agricultural regions. Some landless peasants were impatient with the government's pace of land reform and invaded farmlands on their own, forcing Pastrana to remove them.

Diversification of Colombia's economy, once almost exclusively dependent on coffee, has progressed, thanks to the aid and advice of the United States Agency for International Development. Such products as shoes, textiles, glassware, furniture, shrimp, and cut flowers are now exported from Colombia to the United States, and the market has expanded to Europe and to other Latin American countries. Paradoxically, those Colombian exports are threatened by mounting pressure in the United States for import restrictions.

Pastrana's enthusiasm for the Andean Pact—a trading partnership that includes Colombia, Ecuador, Peru, Bolivia, and Chile—displeases some industrialists in the Conservative party, who fear the nationalization policies of some of its member nations and feel that the bloc's announced plans to buy out foreign investors would prove too costly for Colombia's economy. Pastrana believes that adherence to the pact need not lead to state control, and that private industries owned by Colombians, possibly in partnership with foreigners, could flourish under it. While favoring foreign investments, Pastrana feels, however, that foreign capital should not compete with national capital, and that such investment must lead to the genuine economic and technological development of the nation.

Pastrana has also been under attack from members of labor unions, peasant organizations, and militant student groups, who feel that his government has been moving too slowly to implement reforms. In February 1971, following peasant invasions of landed estates and a strike by teachers, student riots broke out in Cali. Pastrana imposed modified martial law, declaring that "an overwhelming silent majority . . . wants order, justice, peace, and freedom." A twenty-four hour general strike, called in March by the Union of Colombian Workers, was declared illegal by the government and fizzled out. After putting down additional student uprisings in April, Pastrana asserted: "We have dominated a difficult situation. Subversion has been left behind." A split between the traditionalist and progressive factions within the Conservative and Liberal parties led to the resignations, on June 1, 1971, of eleven Cabinet members in an apparent move to enable Pastrana to readjust differences within his National Front coalition.

Because of the growing disunity within the traditional political parties and the increasing strength of the alienated, observers are concerned for the future of Colombia's democratic institutions after the National Front agreement and Pastrana's presidential term expire in 1974. Some optimism was expressed by the conservative William F. Buckley, who wrote in the New York *Post* (January 28, 1971), following an interview with Pastrana: "Colombia is one of the best bets in Latin America. It is basically conservative, basically democratic, basically enlightened. . . . With a market for her exports, the control of her incredible population rise, and resistance to the socialist alternative, she should make it."

Among the private business organizations with which Pastrana has been associated is the Corporación Financiera Nacional, of which he was founder and executive vice-president. From 1963 to 1965 he was president of the United States-controlled textile corporation Celanese Colombiana, previously headed by Carlos Lleras Restrepo. He is the founder of the Centro Colombiano de Estudios.

Misael Pastrana Borrero is married to the former María Cristina Arango, the daughter of the Liberal politician and former Presidential candidate Carlos Arango Vélez, who was Colombia's Ambassador to the Vatican at the time when Pastrana was secretary at the Embassy there. They have four children, Juan Carlos, Andrés, Jaime, and María Cristina, and they make their home in a new development on a hillside near downtown Bogotá. Pastrana, whose hands and face are scarred as a result of an accident that he suffered in his youth, is described in a profile in the New York *Times* (August 8, 1970) as a "quietly elegant man" who is remembered by his former business associates as "an intelligent, personable executive with a sharp eye for detail and the ability to decide quickly."

References

N Y Times p5 Ag 8 '70 por
Visión p28+ Ag 14 '70 por
International Who's Who, 1970-71

PENDERECKI, KRZYSZTOF (pen-dər-ets' kē)

Nov. 23, 1933- Polish composer
Address: b. c/o Belwin-Mills Publishing Corp., 16 W. 61st St., New York 10023

At a time when the musical avant-garde is often accused of being uncommunicative and overly abstract, Polish composer Krzysztof Penderecki believes that music "should speak for itself, going straight to the heart and mind of the listener."

Since the early 1960's, Penderecki has gained increasing prominence, largely on the basis of works centered on themes of martyrdom, injustice, and persecution. His choral composition *Passion and Death of Our Lord Jesus Christ According to St. Luke* (1966) brought him international acclaim. Penderecki's 1969 opera, *The Devils of Loudun,* was criticized by some reviewers as failing to realize the composer's potential, but it created considerable impact because of its dramatic power and its graphically explicit production. Although Penderecki avoids the extensive use of electronic devices and formula serialism and has been criticized as an over-praised and sensation-mongering "backslider" by some radical spokesmen of the avant-garde, his compositional techniques, if somewhat monotonous, are often innovative and effective.

Krzysztof Penderecki was born into a Roman Catholic family on November 23, 1933, in Debica, near Krakow, in southern Poland. As a child he witnessed some of the devastating effects of the German occupation of Poland, and he has acknowledged that his impressions of those years have influenced the dramatic themes of many of his works. Religion, rather than music, dominated his early life. "Until I was fifteen I was perhaps overly devout," Penderecki told an interviewer for *Newsweek* (March 17, 1969). "I had begun reading Augustine and Aquinas. My mother wanted me to go into the church. In our town the church was absolutely the center of life. People would kiss the shoulder of the priest as he walked by."

In Krakow, where he had gone in 1951 for his higher education, Penderecki concentrated on art, literature, and philosophy and became interested in cybernetics. There he taught himself to play the violin as a hobby and made his first informal attempts at composition, in the style of traditional violin literature and of the pre-Bach polyphonists. By 1953 his musical interests had developed to the extent that he began to take composition lessons with Franciszek Skolyszewski, and the following year he entered the State School of Music in Krakow.

Among the major influences on Penderecki's musical development was that of Artur Malawski, one of his principal teachers at the State School of Music. Malawski, who died in 1957, was an adventurous composer who remained aware of musical tradition. Acknowledging his indebtedness to Malawski some years later, Penderecki said, as quoted in *Music and Musicians* (September 1969): "The general principles at the root of a work's musical style, the logic and economy of development, and the integrity of a musical experience embodied in the notes the composer is setting down on paper, never change. The idea of good music means today exactly what it meant always." After Malawski's death, Stanislaw Wiechowicz succeeded him as Penderecki's principal teacher at the State School. As a student, Penderecki composed some conservative works for small ensembles, including a string quartet, in 1955, and a set of three miniatures for clarinet and piano in 1956. He obtained his diploma from

KRZYSZTOF PENDERECKI

the State School of Music in 1958, after submitting as his graduation composition the "Epitaph on the Death of Malawski," for timpani and strings.

Penderecki benefited from the more liberal policies instituted in Poland in 1956 under Communist party chief Wladyslaw Gomulka, which to some degree freed Polish artists from the Stalinist strictures of Socialist Realism. One result of that liberalization was the creation, in 1958, of the Experimental Studio of Polish Radio and Television, which encouraged experimental composers, Penderecki among them. His first published work, *Psalms of David,* for choir and percussion, appeared in 1958, reminding critics of Stravinsky's *Symphony of Psalms* and the early works of Carl Orff. In 1959 Penderecki was encouraged to enter anonymously three of his works—the *Psalms of David, Emanations,* and *Strophes* in a competition sponsored by the Polish Composers Association to encourage young composers of avant-garde works. The competition marked his first real impact upon the musical public: *Strophes*—a composition for soprano speaker and ten instruments —won first prize; his other two entries captured the second and third prizes. When *Strophes* was performed later that year at the Warsaw Autumn Festival it drew much applause but also elicited negative reactions from some of the more conservative members of the audience.

Many of the characteristics that distinguish Penderecki's later compositions were adumbrated in *Strophes,* including unconventional pictorial notation; free progression unhindered by normal tempo and meter; partially controlled aleatory structures; and abnormal sounds evoked from both voices and instruments. In *Strophes,* as in many of his later compositions, Penderecki set his music to unusual texts, including Menander, Sophocles, Isaiah, Jeremiah, and Omar Khayyam. Another characteristic of some of his early works was his experimentation with serialism, although he rejected the twelve-tone method of composition as too confining for his needs. He told Donal Henahan in an interview in the New York *Times* (February 23, 1969) that his work is "a direct reaction against the Webern style as practiced and promulgated at Darmstadt." Harold C. Schonberg of the New York *Times* has noted that Penderecki is anything but a doctrinaire modernist and that he is largely unaffected by the prevailing esthetic of much of contemporary music.

Penderecki extended his experiments with serialism, unconventional time systems, and unusual instrumental sonorities and nonverbal choral sounds in such early works as *Anaklasis* (1960) for strings and percussion; and *Dimensions of Time and Silence* (1960) for chorus and orchestra. Stefan Jarocinski, writing in *Musical Quarterly* in 1965, described the latter as "varicolored lines and structures . . . joined by means of permeation; the mixed chorus . . . takes over the function of percussion and also serves to produce rustling effects by an appropriate combination of whistling and sibilants."

His nine-minute *Threnody for the Victims of Hiroshima* (1960) was the first of Penderecki's compositions to gain international recognition and remains one of his best-known and most widely performed works. Scored for fifty-two stringed instruments, it is characterized by dense tone clusters and microtones in extremely high registers. Soon after its première at the Warsaw Autumn Festival, Everett Helm referred to Penderecki in the New York *Times* (October 8, 1961) as the "enfant terrible of Polish music" and pointed out that he had dispensed with the "concept of exact pitch and intervals as an organizing factor in composition—thus with anything resembling melodic or harmonic relationships." *Threnody* earned Penderecki a UNESCO award, as well as the Fitelberg prize and the Polish Ministry of Culture award.

Penderecki further demonstrated his flair for the unorthodox in *Polymorphia* (1961), which he composed for forty-eight strings with the aid of encephalographs of mental patients at a Krakow medical center where he was working as a volunteer. While the patients listened to a tape of *Threnody*, Penderecki recorded their brain waves and used the graphs as the basis for the musical line in the second half of *Polymorphia*. Wedding unconventional techniques to traditional religious themes, he composed *Psalmus for Magnetic Tape* (1961); *Stabat Mater* (1962), later incorporated into the *St. Luke Passion*, for a capella chorus; and *Canon* (1962) for fifty-two stringed instruments, which won him the Krakow Composition Prize. Among his other notable orchestral works are *Fluorescences* (1962), *Sonata for Cello and Orchestra* (1964), and *De Natura Sonoris* (1966). The two-hour oratorio *Passion and Death of Our Lord Jesus Christ According to St. Luke* assured Penderecki's international fame and is generally considered to be his masterwork. Commissioned by the West German Radio for the 700th anniversary of the Münster Cathedral, the *Passion* was first performed there in March 1966 and was greeted with superlatives in Europe, the United States, and Latin America. The work had its American première in Minneapolis on November

2, 1967, when it was presented by the Minneapolis Symphony (now the Minnesota Orchestra) under Stanislaw Skrowaczewski, who also conducted its New York première at Carnegie Hall on March 6, 1969. The government of the West German state of North Rhine-Westphalia conferred its grand prize on Penderecki in 1966 for the *St. Luke Passion*. In the same year he also received Poland's Pax Prize and the Jurzykowski Prize of the Polish Institute of Arts and Sciences.

The *Passion* is perhaps the most notable example of what several critics have described as Penderecki's "eclectic" style, incorporating Gregorian chant, folk music, nonverbal choral sounds, and modified serialism. Although it contains dissonant and atonal passages, it also includes sections with conventional key structures. Schonberg suggested in the New York *Times* (March 16, 1969) that the audience at the New York première of the *St. Luke Passion* may have witnessed a "birth of neo-romanticism" for the 1970's. In the same article he cited Penderecki's *Capriccio for Violin and Orchestra* (1968), in which "aggressive modernism was tempered with a kind of nostalgia that looked back to such virtuoso nineteenth-century composers as Vieuxtemps and Wieniawski." Other critics have discerned "neoclassical" elements in Penderecki's work. Those views have reinforced the widely held opinion that Penderecki is not indebted to any single movement, but that, as a critic for *Time* (October 14, 1966) suggested, he "fashions the music to suit the subject, forges a style that is uniquely his own by freely incorporating any and all musical modes into a modern context."

The religious motif has remained prominent in Penderecki's work. His *Dies Irae,* scored for solo voices, chorus, and orchestra, was commissioned as part of a memorial for the victims of Auschwitz and was first performed on the site of the former Nazi death camp (now the Polish city of Oswiecim) in 1967. Some critics have suggested that the *Dies Irae* rivals the *St. Luke Passion* in its dramatic impact. The Cathedral of Altenberg, near Cologne, Germany was the scene of the April 1970 première of *Utrenja*, a forty-minute composition on a grand scale, for soloists, orchestra, and two separate choruses, based on the Old Slavonic morning prayer describing the entombment of Christ. A sequel to the *St. Luke Passion,* both thematically and musically, *Utrenja* is basically atonal, with massed tone clusters and with instruments and voices surviving in microtones. It has some aleatory sections.

Explaining his concentration on religious themes, Penderecki once remarked to Bernard Jacobson of *High Fidelity* magazine: "I am a Catholic, but membership in a given church is not really the point. It's rather that I am very much concerned with . . . Auschwitz, Hiroshima . . . and the implications of the Passion. . . . And I am concerned with these things in an essentially moral and social way." According to Penderecki, the Communist Polish government makes no effort to discourage composers who want to express themselves in a religious context.

The adventurous Hamburg Opera Company commissioned Penderecki's first opera, *The Devils of Loudun*, with a German libretto by the composer based on John Whiting's play *The Devils*, which had in turn been inspired by Aldous Huxley's 1952 historical study. In a framework of what has been described as a "study in paranoia and sexual hysteria plus political villainy," the libretto sketches the story of a prioress in seventeenth-century France, whose unfulfilled desires for a worldly priest lead to charges that he infected a community of nuns with impious desires and caused them to be possessed by devils. Abetted by political and ecclesiastical machinations, the community ultimately brings about the torture and execution of the priest. The opera had its première in Hamburg on June 20, 1969, under the direction of Konrad Swinarski, and two days later another production was staged in Stuttgart by Günther Rennert. Its American première—and its first production in English—was presented by the Santa Fe (New Mexico) Opera Company on August 14, 1969 under Swinarski's direction.

In view of the high expectations aroused by the surcharged dramatic intensity of Penderecki's previous work, *The Devils of Loudun* proved something of a critical disappointment. Reviewers took the composer to task for failing to provide dramatically arresting music or dramatic movement and for including too much undistinguished "background music" and monotonous *Sprechgesang*. But, as quoted in *Newsweek* (August 25, 1969), Penderecki himself acknowledged that "the whole intention was not to make the music overpowering. It is music theatre more than opera."

Penderecki was professor of composition at the Krakow State School of Music from 1958 to 1966, and at the Folkwang Hochschule für Musik in Essen, West Germany in 1966-67, but he seems to have lost interest in teaching. He travels extensively and has lived in West Berlin—where he worked under a grant from the West German government—and in Vienna. He first visited the United States in 1967, for the première of the *St. Luke Passion*. In 1971 Philips Records released a complete album of *The Devils of Loudun*. A number of Penderecki's other works have been recorded—under the Philips, Nonesuch, and other labels—including the *St. Luke Passion*, *Threnody for the Victims of Hiroshima*, *Dies Irae*, *Capriccio for Violin and Orchestra*, *Pittsburgh Overture*, *De natura sonoris*, *Psaumes* (1958), *Anaciasis* (1960), *Fluorescenses* (1961), *Stabat Mater* (1962), and *Sonata for Cello and Orchestra* (1964).

Krzysztof Penderecki and his second wife, Elizabeth, an actress, have a son Lukasz, who was born a week after the European première of the *St. Luke Passion*. A scholarly-looking, bearded man, Penderecki wears dark-rimmed glasses and, unlike some other members of the avant-garde, dresses conservatively in custom-tailored suits. In addition to his native Polish, he speaks German but has to rely on interpreters when communicating in English. Between trips abroad, Penderecki regularly returns to Poland for periods of complete isolation and concentrated work.

References

Music and Musicians 18:34+ S '69 por
N Y Times II p19+ F 23 '69 por
Sat R 51:63+ F 24 '68 por
Ewen, D., ed. Composers Since 1900 (1969)
International Who's Who, 1970-71

PERELMAN, S(IDNEY) J(OSEPH)

Feb. 1, 1904- Writer
Address: b. c/o Simon and Schuster, 630 5th Ave., New York 10020

One critic has dubbed S. J. Perelman America's "lampoonist laureate," but Perelman prefers to think of himself as "a *feuilletoniste* . . . a writer of little leaves"—those scrupulously written, meticulously polished, and sportive essays that he has been contributing to magazines for four decades. One example is his famous *New Yorker* series "Cloudland Revisited," which takes a parodistic look backward at the more lurid motion pictures and bestsellers of his salad days. The salient characteristic of Perelman's surreal causeries is the tension between the experience of an erudite, cranky mind with sharp powers of observation and recall (especially for words, the more arcane the better), and the unpredictable flights of a baroque imagination. Citing Perelman's "profound gift for derangement," Gilbert Millstein has credited him with being "unflagging in his dismemberment of the cliché, ever-zealous to enshrine outdated slang, sedulous in his absorption of who knows how many thousands of absurdities and fatuities ground out in dead earnest by thousands of anonymous others and by him reworked into the most allusive nonsense. He is a veritable compendium of the worst that has been thought and said."

Regularly published in book form, Perelman's pieces now fill a score of volumes, including the collection *The Road to Miltown, or Under the Spreading Atrophy* (1957) and the multi-collection *A Child's Garden of Curses* (1951). In addition, the humorist has written for Broadway, television, and Hollywood, where his best-known achievements have been Marx Brothers comedies and the Oscar-winning script for *Around the World in Eighty Days* (1956). Since 1970 he has been living in London, as a self-styled "resident alien."

Sidney Joseph Perelman was born in Brooklyn, New York on February 1, 1904 to Joseph Perelman, who had immigrated to the United States twelve years before, and Sophia (Charra) Perelman. He grew up in Providence, Rhode Island, where his father, an engineer manqué, worked as a machinist, tried raising chickens (unsuccessfully), and ran a dry goods store. "My chief interest always was to be a cartoonist," Perelman revealed in an interview with William Zinsser for the New York *Times Magazine* (January 26, 1969), "and I began very early to draw cartoons in my father's store on the long cardboard strips around which the bolts of Amoskeag cotton and ginghams were stored."

Perelman also began very early to carry home from the Providence Public Library armloads of

S. J. PERELMAN

books, starting with Horatio Alger and moving upwards through Sax Rohmer to Charles Dickens. "I must have developed a fondness for whatever Dickens I read," he remarked to Myra MacPherson of the Washington *Post* (October 18, 1970). "My names and titles spring out of my lifetime devotion to puns." The first humorist to influence him, as he told William Zinsser in the interview for the New York *Times Magazine* (January 26, 1969), was George Ade. "Ade's humor was rooted in a perception of people and places. He had a cutting edge and an acerbic wit that no earlier American humorist had. Generally speaking, I don't believe in kindly humor. . . . One of the most shameful utterances to stem from the human mouth is Will Rogers' 'I never met a man I didn't like.' The absolute antithesis is Oscar Wilde on the foxhunting Englishman: 'The unspeakable in pursuit of the uneatable.' . . . Wilde's remark contains, in briefest span, the truth; whereas Rogers' is pure flatulence." After Ade, Perelman absorbed the humor of Stephen Leacock and Ring Lardner, and later his development as a humorist was influenced by Robert Benchley, Donald Ogden Stewart, Frank Sullivan, Flann O'Brien, and James Joyce, whom he considers *"the* great comic writer of our time."

In 1921 Perelman graduated from Classical High School in Providence and entered Brown University, also in Providence. At the university he joined the staff of the campus humor magazine, the *Brown Jug,* as a cartoonist, and later he became editor of the publication. In his cartooning he emulated John Held Jr., the recorder of the "flapper" life style, and his editorials—his first serious attempts at writing of any kind—reflected the influence of H. L. Mencken, whom he had just then begun to read. "H. L. Mencken was the Catherine wheel, the ultimate firework . . . ," Perelman later observed. "With his use of the colloquial and the dynamic, the foreign reference, and the bizarre word like *Sitzfleisch* he brought adrenalin into the gray and pulpy style of the day." Perelman's enduring friendship with the late novelist Nathanael West began at Brown, where West was one year ahead of Perelman.

Upon graduation from Brown, Perelman was hired as a cartoonist by *Judge,* then a popular weekly humor magazine. In addition to two cartoons a week—bearing such captions as "I've got Bright's disease and he's got mine"—he eventually contributed regular humorous pieces to *Judge.* But in his writing, as he later observed, he was only "beginning to develop a sense of parody and of lapidary prose." His characteristic style in written humor did not emerge until he moved from *Judge* to *College Humor,* in 1929. Horace Liveright published Perelman's first collection, *Dawn Ginsbergh's Revenge,* in 1929, and the following year Liveright issued *Parlor, Bedlam, and Bath,* written by Perelman in collaboration with Quentin T. Reynolds. On July 4, 1929 Perelman married Laura West, the sister of Nathanael West. Three years later the Perelmans, along with Nathanael West, settled on a ninety-one-acre farm near Erwinna in Bucks County, Pennsylvania that they and West purchased from Mike Gold.

Recruited by the Marx Brothers, Perelman collaborated in the writing of the scripts for the films *Monkey Business* (Paramount, 1931) and *Horsefeathers* (Paramount, 1932). Perelman's hand was evident in such pieces of dialogue as that in *Horsefeathers* when Groucho Marx, told by his secretary that "Jennings is waxing wroth outside," replies, "Well, tell Roth to wax Jennings for a while." He worked intermittently in Hollywood for eleven years, mostly on films that he would rather forget, such as *Sweethearts* (MGM, 1938) and *Ambush* (Paramount, 1939). He remembers the movie capital of the U.S.A. with "revulsion," as "a dreary industrial town controlled by hoodlums of enormous wealth."

During his Hollywood years Perelman also wrote, with much more psychic income, for Broadway. In the early 1930's he contributed sketches to the revues *Third Little Show* (1931) and *Walk a Little Faster* (1932), and with his wife he wrote the comedies *All Good Americans* (1934) and *Night Before Christmas* (1941), both of which had short runs. Later he wrote the book for Kurt Weill's successful musical *One Touch of Venus* (1943), with Ogden Nash, and with Al Hirschfeld, *Sweet Bye and Bye* (1946), which never got beyond Philadelphia during the pre-Broadway tryout.

His first collection to contain pieces originally written for the *New Yorker*—beginning in 1931— was *Strictly from Hunger* (Random House, 1937), in the foreword to which Robert Benchley conceded to Perelman the mantle of leadership in "the dementia praecox field." In reviewing Perelman's *Look Who's Talking!* (Random, 1940), a writer for *Time* (August 12, 1940) called the author a "screwball wit" with "an exquisite sense of cliché and mimicry and a nihilism that delights in knocking over-crystallized words, objects, and gestures into glassy pieces that cut each other." In quick succession Random House published Perelman's *The Dream Department* (1943), *Crazy Like a Fox* (1944), and *Keep It Crisp* (1946), and Harcourt, Brace issued his *Acres and Pains* in 1947.

Under the pseudonym of Sidney Namlerep, Perelman wrote his own introduction to *The Best of S. J. Perelman* (Modern Library, 1947). Of Perelman, "Namlerep" wrote: "In his pages proliferate all the weird grammatical flora tabulated by H. W. Fowler in his *Modern English Usage*—the elegant variation, the Facetious Zeugma, the Cast-Iron Idiom, the Battered Ornament, the Bower's-Bird Phrase, the Sturdy Indefensible, the Side-Slip, and the Unequal Yoke-fellow."

Al Hirschfeld and Perelman circled the globe together to illustrate and write, respectively, *Westward Ha!, or, Around the World in Eighty Clichés* (1948), the first of Perelman's books issued by Simon and Schuster, who have remained his publishers ever since. Hirschfeld also illustrated Perelman's *Listen to the Mockingbird* (1949) and *Swiss Family Perelman* (1950). The humorist's *Ill-Tempered Clavichord* was published in 1952 and three years later thirty-six pieces described by the author as "otherwise unavailable" were brought together in *Perelman's Home Companion*.

After some thirteen years away from Hollywood, Perelman returned to it to write the script for *Around the World in Eighty Days* (United Artists, 1956), which won him an Academy of Motion Picture Arts and Sciences award. In the late 1950's the humorist did a few scripts for network television, including the libretto for *Aladdin,* a musical fantasy, and a travelogue about London narrated by Elizabeth Taylor. His most conscientious and best-reviewed creation for television was *Malice in Wonderland,* an hour-long comic playlet written for the NBC Sunday afternoon showcase *Omnibus* (January 18, 1959). In that freewheeling spoof, as critics observed, he "savagely," "delightfully" reduced to absurdity the mores of Hollywood. "In a medium where humor normally is so dismally bland," Jack Gould wrote in the following morning's New York *Times,* "the Perelman sting and substance were sublime."

The raw material for Perelman's contributions to magazines—principally the *New Yorker* and *Holiday*—in the late 1950's and early 1960's ranged from an African safari to a search for black-market sturgeon in London. Reviewing a collection of thirty-four of the pieces, *The Rising Gorge* (1961), Gilbert Millstein of the New York *Times* (December 10, 1961) called them "cunningly buffed bits of moonstone strung out on wire of purest fool's gold," and he proffered a choice sample kickshaw, an aside by the author in a conversation with his wife: "The only response she got was an indulgent chuckle from behind my newspaper, which was rather unaccountable, since I lay dozing a good ten feet away from it."

In his play *The Beauty Part* Perelman set out, as he explained to interviewers, to lampoon the "cultural explosion" that seems to make it "incumbent on everyone to express themselves in words or paint" or "to leap around in homemade jerseys." The comedy, starring Bert Lahr, opened auspiciously at the Music Box Theatre on Broadway on December 26, 1962, but a New York City newspaper strike blacked out reviews and publicity and it closed prematurely, on March 9, 1963.

Reviewing the book *Chicken Inspector No. 23* for the New York *Times* (September 21, 1966), Martin Levin found Perelman's "capacity for outrage unquenched" and his "matchless sense of the ridiculous" undiminished. "The only thing that works against him is the spirit of our grotesque times. It is not easy to satirize the absurd when the absurd has become official. Grossness is so much a part of our way of life that it sometimes defies comic extension." Against the "spirit of our grotesque times," Perelman has continued to hold his own, if Eudora Welty is correct in her assessment of Perelman's next collection, *Baby, It's Cold Inside* (1970): "Back of some of these pieces, and not very far, lies deep sadness, lies outrage. What an achievement Mr. S. J. Perelman makes today, that out of our own sadness and outrage we are brought, in these little leaves, to laugh at ourselves once more."

During the summer of 1970, a few weeks after the death of his wife, Perelman sold his farm, and the following October he moved to London. Before emigrating, he told a reporter for the New York *Times* (September 18, 1970): "The fact that I think it's volcano time in this country is not responsible for the move, though I'm just as appalled as everyone about the conditions. . . . I've had all the rural splendor I can use, and each time I get to New York it seems more pestilential than before." The objects of his disaffection included "insanity and violence," "twice-breathed air," the political climate ("all the way down from the co-author of the Mundt-Nixon bill . . . to every hard-hat and red-neck in the country"), and incivility. Life in London seemed to him much more "rational." "The obvious good manners and consideration of people there toward each other may be only selfish, but it's good enough for me." Early in his expatriation, Perelman embarked on an eighty-day world tour, in deliberate emulation of Jules Verne's traveler, Phileas Fogg. The *New Yorker* and Simon and Schuster planned to publish his account of the journey in serial and book form, respectively.

Of Perelman's ingenious syntax Melville Maddocks has written, in the *Christian Science Monitor* (September 1, 1966): "The Perelman style—its eminent reasonableness, its barely-mock dignity, its subtly staged collisions between gentility and slang—allows him to keep cover until the last possible moment. Round and round the half-crouching sentences spiral until the reader feels like a besieged straight man in a Marx Brothers movie." The insouciant look of Perelman's work is grossly deceptive. Believing that "easy writing makes hard reading," he writes draft after draft before he is satisfied with a manuscript, spending between two weeks and "a lot longer" than a month on a short piece, as he revealed to Martha MacGregor in an interview for the New York *Post* (September 12, 1970). Also believing that "by definition a writer must be a reader," he spends much of his leisure reading. Among his favorite authors are V. S. Pritchett and Edmund Wilson, whom he respects as authorities on English style, E. M. Forster, Henry David Thoreau, and Raymond Chandler. His literary friends have included Somerset Maugham, T. S. Eliot, Aldous Huxley, and F. Scott Fitzgerald. Photographs of Maugham, Joyce, and the late C. S. Lobrano, his favorite editor at the *New Yorker*, and a watercolor by Stuart Davis adorn the wall of his workroom. Among his favorite motion pictures are those of W. C. Fields.

Brooks Atkinson once described S. J. Perelman as "a slight, immaculately groomed gentleman with a doleful look," and another observer has called his look "owlish." Perelman wears a neat mustache and a pair of oval, steel-rimmed glasses that he picked up in Paris in 1927. In general appearance he is tweedy but dapper, as elegant in his choice of wardrobe as he is in his choice of words. While he is soft-spoken and reserved in manner, those who know him testify that he is "a full-time wit" who converses in "multiple fascinating directions." Perelman has two children, Adam and Abby Laura. Pointing out that he is not "a happy laughing kid" but a "crank," the humorist has said: "I'm highly irritable and my senses bruise easily, and when they are bruised I write."

References

> Cue 31:15 D 15 '62 pors
> Life 52:85+ F 9 '62 pors
> N Y Times Mag p26+ Ja 26 '69 pors
> Washington (DC) Post E p1+ O 18 '70 pors
> Twentieth Century Authors (1942; First Supplement, 1955)
> Writers at Work: The Paris Review Interviews 2d series (1963)
> Who's Who in America, 1970-71

PEROT, H(ENRY) ROSS (pə-rō')

June 27, 1930- Industrialist; philanthropist
Address: b. Electronic Data Systems Corp., Exchange Bank Tower, Dallas, Tex. 75235; h. 10444 Strait Lane, Dallas, Tex. 75229

Self-made Texas multimillionaire H. Ross Perot, a paragon of the Protestant ethic, has dazzled Wall Street with his business acumen and captured headlines with his patriotic zeal in behalf of United States prisoners of war in North Vietnam. Perot's fortune is based on his near total ownership of the Electronic Data Systems Corporation, a rapidly expanding computer service company that he founded in Dallas in 1962. Through one of the sharpest underwriting deals in financial history, Perot became a billionaire within a few months of offering a small portion of E.D.S. stock to the public in September 1968. Wall Street vagaries have since reduced his resources somewhat but not his determination to spend them on projects that he believes in. Far from the stereotype of the Texas right-winger, Perot espouses an essentially nonpolitical faith in initiative, hard work, old-fashioned reverence for home, country, and religion, and a profound disdain for bureaucracy. Although his philanthropies have included large contributions to the Boy Scouts and to ghetto pub-

lic schools, he is best known for his ventures into international diplomacy to aid the American POW's, and especially for his unsuccessful attempt to fly to Hanoi in December 1969 with Christmas packages for the prisoners. In the world of finance Perot's most recent coup was his takeover of F. I. du Pont, Glore Forgan and Company, New York's third largest brokerage house.

Henry Ross Perot was born on June 27, 1930 in the east Texas city of Texarkana. His father, now deceased, was Gabriel Ross Perot, a cotton broker and part-time horse trader who kept his family living fairly comfortably in a three-bedroom red-brick house in Texarkana. "Dad's business was talked morning, noon, and night in that house," Bette Perot, the millionaire's sister and director of his private foundation, told Terence Shea of the *National Observer* (September 14, 1970). "Dad was a real trader, and Ross learned many lessons just listening. He absorbed everything."

When he was six Perot went to work for his father, breaking horses to the saddle for a dollar or two apiece. (His nose still shows the results of the falls he took.) But his real talent was for selling, whether Christmas cards, used saddles, or the *Saturday Evening Post*. At the age of twelve he worked out a deal with the circulation department of the Texarkana *Gazette* whereby he would establish a paper route in the town's black slum area and in return would earn 70 percent rather than the customary 30 percent of subscription fees collected. Setting out each morning at 3:30 on horseback, he covered twenty miles before school each day, and he was soon making $40 a week. The circulation department tried to renege on his added percentage, but he successfully countered that effort by going directly to the owner.

As a Boy Scout, Perot rose to the rank of Eagle Scout. In school he was a mediocre student until the eleventh grade, when the teacher told him he was not as bright as his classmates and thus prodded him into earning straight A's. After high school he attended Texarkana Junior College as a pre-law student, but his real ambition was to study at the United States Naval Academy and go to sea. In 1949 he succeeded in obtaining an appointment to Annapolis.

At Annapolis Perot was only a middling student, graduating 454th in a class of 925, but his classmates voted him the best all-around midshipman and life president of the class. After receiving his commission, in June 1953, Perot boarded the destroyer USS *Sigourney* en route to Korea, but the Korean war ended before the ship arrived. Ensign Perot's next assignment was as assistant navigator aboard the aircraft carrier USS *Leyte*. "I loved the Navy, loved the sea, loved ships," he told Fred Powledge of the New York *Times Magazine* (February 28, 1971). "But I always find that whatever I'm doing, I'm thoroughly involved in it. In the Navy, the promotion system and the seniority system and the waiting-in-line concept were just sort of incompatible with my desire to be measured and judged by what I could produce." Perot decided not to sign up for another hitch and was discharged in 1957 with the rank of lieutenant.

While serving aboard the *Leyte*, Perot had been invited by a visiting executive from the International Business Machines Corporation to look him up after his discharge. Perot did so, and obtained a job selling computers in Dallas. In his fifth year with I.B.M. he sold his year's quota in the first three weeks of January, and his initiative was rewarded with a desk job in the corporation's Dallas office. While in that job he came across Henry David Thoreau's observation, "The mass of men lead lives of quiet desperation," and he took it as a personal warning that he must not allow his initiative and individuality to be stifled in a corporation trap. When I.B.M. offered him an administrative position in White Plains, New York, he decided to quit and strike out on his own.

While working for I.B.M., Perot had observed that companies leasing hardware from the corporation often had trouble learning how to utilize it. He decided that there was need for a service organization that would design, install, and operate electronic data processing systems for clients on a contract basis. On his thirty-second birthday, June 27, 1962, he founded Electronic Data Systems with $1,000 in savings and with his wife, his sister, and his mother as charter directors. Determined not to go into debt buying capital equipment, he initially used a computer owned by a Dallas insurance company, buying unused time on it at wholesale rates and then selling it retail to another firm. His staff, at first consisting of himself and a secretary, was soon expanded to include two former I.B.M. salesmen and an ex-I.B.M. systems engineer. All three are now multimillionaire vice-presidents of E.D.S. The first customers serviced by E.D.S. were insurance firms, and medical insurance claims have continued to provide the bulk of the company's business.

During the 1960's, E.D.S. doubled its business annually, branch offices sprang up in major cities throughout the United States, and the number of employees grew to 1,700. When Perot decided it was time for his company to go public, in 1968, he handled the stock offering as shrewdly as he had built up the firm. First he recapitalized E.D.S. so that nearly 12,000,000 shares were in existence, each with a par value of 20¢. Of the new shares, however, he offered only 650,000 for sale, and he shopped carefully among Wall Street underwriters for the firm that would guarantee the highest price. He finally chose R. W. Presspich and Company, which brought out E.D.S. at $16.50 a share, representing a near record price-to-earnings ratio of 118 to one. At the close of trading the first day, September 12, 1968, E.D.S. was selling at $23 a share. Since Perot had kept more than 9,000,000 shares for himself, his net worth at sunset was over $200,000,000. By the first week of October, E.D.S. stock was quoted at $33, and at the height of the bull market in 1969-70 it hovered around $150, making Perot, on paper at least, a billionaire.

In frantic over-the-counter trading on April 22, 1970, the value of E.D.S. stock dropped to $100 a share, causing Perot a paper loss of almost half a billion dollars. But Perot has a detached attitude toward his wealth. "The day I made Eagle

H. ROSS PEROT

Scout was more important to me than the day I discovered I was a billionaire," he once told a reporter. Uninterested in a life of personal luxury and determined not to leave his children so much money as to deprive them of the same chance at personal initiative that he had, he directs his money toward projects that he considers deserving. One such is the United States government, to which he pays taxes even on the tax-exempt money he puts into the Perot Foundation, the nonprofit corporation he established in April 1969 to handle his philanthropies. Among the foundation's beneficiaries are the Dallas public school system, which is receiving $2,500,000 over a three-year period, two-thirds of it for a ghetto elementary school, in addition to $72,000 for a high school leadership program; the Boy Scouts of Dallas, who are receiving $1,000,000 to help them extend their work to black and Mexican youth; and a Dallas Roman Catholic high school, which is receiving $150,000 because Perot, a Presbyterian, heard that it was a good school.

But Perot's most publicized project has been his effort to free United States prisoners of war in North Vietnam, an effort that has cost him an estimated $2,000,000. That crusade began in the fall of 1969, when the wives of four POW's wanting to go to Paris to ask North Vietnamese officials there for news of their husbands petitioned Perot to subsidize the trip. He did so, and the four women went to Paris, to no avail. The matter might have ended there, but the Texas philanthropist, deeply touched by the plight of the prisoners and their families, directed a team of E.D.S. experts to devise a campaign to help the prisoners.

The E.D.S. group quickly set up an organization called United We Stand, which spent $1,000,000 on newspaper and television advertising to publicize the POW problem and to urge public support of President Nixon's Vietnam policies. (In Perot's opinion, the fastest way out of Vietnam is for United States citizens to unite behind the government.) Within a few weeks United We Stand had collected twenty-six tons of mail, food, clothes, and medicine for the Americans held in North Vietnam.

Perot chartered two planes and with his cargo set off for Hanoi in December 1969. He was never allowed to land there, despite his personal pleas to North Vietnamese diplomats in Bangkok and Vientiane and even, by telephone, to Soviet party chief Leonid Brezhnev. Nor were Perot's later attempts successful. In January 1970 he offered $100,000,000 as ransom for the prisoners, but the offer was ignored. Three months later he flew with many prisoners' wives to Vientiane and to Paris in a vain attempt to meet with North Vietnamese officials to discuss release of the prisoners. Late in 1970 he planned another Christmas trip to Hanoi, but was foiled when the Soviet airliners he chartered canceled the flight.

Ostensibly his missions have been failures, but Perot contends that they have had the following salutary effects: they woke the American people to the plight of the prisoners; put the fate of the POW's on the agenda of the Paris peace talks; made the North Vietnamese more humane in their treatment; and increased the flow of mail to the prisoners and the number and size of the packages they are allowed to receive.

Despite his personal opinions about Vietnam policy, Perot does not condemn war protesters. "It's the ones who haven't committed themselves [on the war issue] who have given aid and comfort to the North Vietnamese," he told Christopher S. Wren of *Look* (March 24, 1970). To stimulate a sense of participatory democracy in more citizens, Perot has long cherished the idea of establishing what he calls an "electronic town hall," consisting of network television programs devoted to bipartisan discussion of national issues. Viewer opinions would be elicited, compiled by computer, and made available to legislators.

Perot's adventures in public service have inspired speculation about possible political motives on his part, but he scoffs at the suggestion that he might be interested in seeking political office. In an interview with William McAda of the New York *Sunday News* (February 22, 1970) he declared: "I would make a very bad politician. I have no patience for the red tape and inactivity." He is also regarded in some circles as an agent of the Nixon Administration. Indeed, he was a substantial contributor to the President's 1968 campaign; he allowed a number of his employees to take sabbaticals to work in the campaign; and he is an old friend of Attorney General John Mitchell. But he claims that he is a "nonextremist," aligned with neither Democrats nor Republicans, and that his United We Stand project would have backed Humphrey's policies had he been elected President. There seems to be no evidence that Perot has received any encouragement for his prisoner-of-war crusade from Washington beyond the expediting of visas and other such routine cooperation. As one administration official told Kent Biffle of *Newsweek* (April 13, 1970), "The [State] Department looks on him as a rich but eccentric uncle. One may secretly admire his eccentricity, but one doesn't want to get too close for fear of what he might do next."

An unabashed moralist of the old school, H. Ross Perot makes clear to all new E.D.S. employees that marital infidelity will mean summary dismissal. He does not insist that his employees emulate his abstinence from liquor and cigarettes, but he does require male employees to dress as he does, in conservative dark suits and white shirts, and even messenger boys must wear a tie. The byword of the company is efficiency: supervisors are trained to look for and remedy any waste of time or motion. Perot is a small, wiry man, five feet six inches tall and weighing 130 pounds, who wears his blond hair close-cropped. Modest in his tastes, he buys his suits from the rack, drives a five-year-old Lincoln, and dines on cheeseburgers as often as on steaks. Since 1956 he has been married to the former Margot Birmingham. Mr. and Mrs. Perot and their four children—three daughters and Ross Jr.—live comfortably but unostentatiously in an exclusive suburb of north Dallas. Perot regards his family as central in his life and scrupulously keeps his wife and children out of the public eye. "If I could do one thing, I would try to construct a strong family unit for every family [in the United States] on the basis of love, understanding and encouragement," the millionaire philanthropist told William McAda in the *Sunday News* interview. "All the other problems then would disappear."

References

Fortune 78:168+ N '68 por
Look 34:28+ Mr 24 '70 pors
N Y Sunday News p136+ F 22 '70 pors
N Y Times p41+ N 28 '69 por
N Y Times Mag p16+ F 28 '71 pors
Nat Observer p22 S 14 '70 por
Newsweek 75:68+ Ap 13 '70 pors
Who's Who in America, 1970-71

PLUNKETT, JIM

Dec. 5, 1947- Football player
Address: b. New England Patriots Football Club, 78 Lansdowne St., Boston, Mass. 02215

In the 1971 professional draft of college players the New England Patriots of the American Conference of the National Football League got the prime choice, Heisman Trophy winner Jim Plunkett, Stanford University's slinging quarterback. Plunkett led the Stanford Indians, previously a feckless, middling team, to a three-year record of 22 wins, 8 losses, and 2 ties, climaxed by victory in the Rose Bowl. In the process he established himself in third place in all-time rankings of major-college passers and set a new career mark in total offense in the National Collegiate Athletic Association.

The strapping Plunkett has an overarm delivery that makes interception difficult, and his powerful thrusts are deadly accurate up to sixty yards and effective, on occasion, up to ninety-six yards. In addition, he has speed and agility in shaking tacklers, a strong will to win, a keen eye for anticipating defensive moves, and a poise that enables him to stay "in the pocket" under pressure and to aim his throws without panic from that situation. "Plunkett is the best drop-back passer I've seen in college football," coach Tommy Prothro of U.C.L.A. has said. Like veteran Patriot quarterback Joe Kapp, Plunkett is of Mexican descent, and much of his spare time has been spent in giving career and life guidance to Chicano children through group talks and personal counseling.

Jim Plunkett's Mexican ancestry has a German-Irish admixture in the paternal line. The youngest of three children and only son of William and Carmen Plunkett, he was born in San Jose, California on December 5, 1947. His father, a blind news vendor, died in 1969. His mother, who is also sightless, still lives in San Jose. The parents, while bilingual, spoke only English to their children, and Plunkett grew up without learning to speak or understand Spanish. Because the family's income was meager, Plunkett earned his own spending money in childhood. As soon as he could count change he began selling newspapers, and later he worked in a gas station.

A quiet, nongregarious homebody who was big for his age, Plunkett found in sports a congenial outlet for his youthful energies. Despite the handicaps of a childhood bone disease and a tendency to obesity, he was an all-around San Jose schoolboy athletic star from the time he was a fifth-grader at Mayfair Elementary School. At Lee Matheson Junior High School he excelled at basketball, wrestling, track, and baseball and discovered his ability as a passer in football. He was the sparkplug quarterback with the junior varsity football team at Overfeldt High School and with the varsity at James Lick High School, where he transferred in 1964. In the latter year he paced James Lick High to the Mt. Hamilton League title and in 1965 to an undefeated season. In both years he was named to the All-League team, and in 1965 he also made the North Shrine All-Star team.

Many colleges and universities offered Plunkett football scholarships when he graduated from high school in 1966. He chose Stanford University in Palo Alto, California for two reasons: it had a good reputation academically, and it was close to his home. Just before he entered Stanford he underwent surgery for a thyroid tumor. The growth turned out to be benign, but recuperation from the operation delayed Plunkett's entrance into the freshman lineup at Stanford and when he finally did leave the bench his performance was below his standard. At the same time he fell behind his class academically—a full year behind, in effect. Later Plunkett, a political science major with an IQ described as "very superior," established and maintained a B average.

When Plunkett moved up to the Stanford varsity in 1967, Coach John Ralston wanted him to switch from the quarterback position to defensive end, but Plunkett refused. Having three other quarterbacks, Ralston kept Plunkett "red-shirted"—active in practice but benched during games—throughout the 1967 season. By that device he delayed for one year the beginning of the official counting of Plunkett's eligible playing time. (N.C.A.A. rules state

JIM PLUNKETT

that no one may play for a college varsity team more than three years.)

In 1968, his first year in the varsity lineup, Plunkett succeeded in completing 142 out of 268 passes for 2,156 yards and 14 touchdowns. The yards he gained aerially set a record in the Pacific Eight Conference and his total offense yardage (distance covered in the air and on the ground) ranked tenth in national standings. During the season he cracked some ribs, and he played the last few games with an injured right knee, from which surgeons removed damaged cartilage at season's end. The following year, completing 197 out of 336 passes, Plunkett set new Pacific Eight records for passing yardage (2,673 yards), touchdown passes (20), total offense yardage (2,786 yards), and total offense in a single game (416 yards, against Purdue). Nationally, he ranked fifth in passing and third in total offense.

When his class graduated (without him) in 1970, Plunkett became eligible for the pro draft. He was tempted to announce his availability for the draft, because his mother needed financial help, and as a college athlete he was barely able to support himself by supplementing his scholarship with summer construction jobs. But he rejected the temptation, out of loyalty not only to Stanford but also to the Chicano children he was counseling. "How could I tell them not to drop out of high school," he later explained, "if it looked like I was dropping out of Stanford?"

In 1970 Plunkett sparked the Indians to an 8-3 season, the Pacific Eight championship, and a trip to the Rose Bowl. Completing 191 out of 358 passes for 2,715 yards and 18 touchdowns and gaining an additional 183 yards and 3 touchdowns on the ground, he bettered most of the conference records he himself had already set. His three-season totals with Stanford were 530 out of 962 passes completed for 7,544 yards and 52 touchdowns, and his career record of 7,887 yards in total offense was by far the highest in the history of the N.C.A.A. On November 24, 1970 the Downtown Athletic Club in New York City awarded Plunkett the Heisman Memorial Trophy, bestowed annually on the college football player judged best in a poll of sportswriters.

In the Rose Bowl at Pasadena, California on New Year's Day 1971 the Stanford Indians upset unbeaten Ohio State, the ten-point favorite, 27-17. Plunkett, who completed 20 of 30 passes for 265 yards and ran 49 yards on the ground on four effective quarterback draws, was named Player of the Game. Eight days later, as starting quarterback in the all-star game in the Hula Bowl in Honolulu, he led the North team to victory and was again chosen Player of the Game.

Representatives of the twenty-six teams in the National Football League meet annually to choose, in turn, the college-departing players they would like to add to their rosters. The choices are made in order of team strength, with the lowest ranking professional team having first choice. In the pro draft meeting held late in January 1971, the Boston Patriots (now known as the New England Patriots), by virtue of their abysmal 1970 record of 2-12, had first pick, and they chose Plunkett. The lustre that Plunkett immediately added to the Patriots' image was evident in the team's ticket sales. By the middle of February, 32,000 season tickets were sold, and the Boston front office predicted that it would sell another 45,000 before the Patriots' new Schaeffer Stadium opened in suburban Foxboro, Massachusetts in August 1971. (In 1970 the team had sold only 24,000 season tickets, and in 1969 only 9,000.) Even before the Patriots actually chose Plunkett the market value of the club's stock rose by $1,500,000 in anticipation of the choice.

Jim Plunkett is six feet two and one-half inches tall and weighs 212 pounds. He has a swarthy complexion, deep-set eyes, a broad nose, high cheekbones, and large, tough hands. His voice is soft and his manner has been described as "passive" and "often solemn." Closely attached to his roots, he visits his mother as often as possible and does not relish the thought of moving across the continent to Boston. The Patriots' low rank in the NFL doesn't discourage him. "I don't think that way ...," he told Arnold Hano of *Sport* (May 1971). "Sure it's nice to join a team with a winning tradition. But maybe we can build a winner at Boston."

References

N Y Times p42 N 25 '70 por
Newsweek 76:72 O 12 '70 por
Sport 51:57+ My '71
Sr Schol 97:18 N 2 '70 por
Time 96:78 D 7 '70 pors

POLYANSKY, DMITRY S(TEPANOVICH)

Nov. 7, 1917- Soviet official
Address: U.S.S.R. Council of Ministers, Manezhnaya Square, Moscow, U.S.S.R.

A rare phenomenon in Soviet politics, Dmitry Polyansky, First Deputy Premier of the U.S.S.R., is a man who has worked within the party hierarchy of two successive regimes without surrendering his independence. Although he rose rapidly under Khrushchev as his protegé, he increasingly criticized Khrushchev's agricultural policies over the years and eventually condemned them as misguided. He has, on occasion, protested the present regime's management of domestic affairs. As one of the youngest, most dynamic, and most able of the Soviet leaders, he is regarded by many observers as a likely contender for the position of Premier. Polyansky is currently the Soviet official chiefly responsible for agricultural policy.

Polyansky's background and training make him a likely man for that responsibility. The son of Ukrainian peasants, he was born in the village of Slavyanoserbsk (Province of Lugansk, Donets Basin), November 7, 1917, during the Bolshevik Revolution. There he attended secondary school, joined the Komsomol in 1931, and after completing school the following year went to work in a *sovkhoz* (state farm). His formative years coincided with a period of radical change in social and political values in the Soviet Union—the initial stages of forced collectivization, when resistance by the peasants, particularly in the Ukraine, was at its height. Thus Polyansky acquired a firsthand familiarity with the problems that plagued Soviet agriculture both before and after the transition to a new economy.

In 1935, after spending several years in a *sovkhoz*, Polyansky enrolled in the Kharkov Agricultural Institute. As a student, he busied himself in the Komsomol, rapidly advancing in its ranks and attracting the favorable notice of local party leaders. In 1939 he became a full member of the Communist Party, and on graduating from the Kharkov Agricultural Institute that year, he became head of the peasant youth department of the Kharkov Oblast Komsomol committee.

Little is known about Polyansky's activities from 1939 to 1942, except for the fact that after serving in the Red Army he attended the Higher Party School of the CPSU Central Committee. He graduated in 1942. Until the war ended, Polyansky worked as an administrator supervising the production and shipment of grain to the front lines, first serving as head of the political section of the Khoroshensk machine and tractor station in Altay; then as first secretary of the Karasuk regional committee of the CPSU. Some observers have interpreted those posts, along with Polyansky's brief term of military service and early candidacy for the Higher Party School, as indications that even at that stage of his career he had ingratiated himself with members of the higher echelons of the party apparatus. The fact that he was promoted in 1945 to executive rank within the CPSU Central Committee appears to confirm this. In his book *Power in the Kremlin* (Viking, 1967) the noted Sovietologist Michel Tatu contends that Polyansky's work as personnel board organizer and inspector for the Central Committee during 1945-49 indicates that he had become a pivotal figure in the party organization.

Party backing and Polyansky's organizational skill led to the key offices he held in the Crimea from 1949 to 1955. Elected second secretary of the Crimean Oblast CPSU Committee in 1949, he moved on in 1952 to become Chairman of the Crimean Oblast Executive Committee, and in the last three years he headed the Crimean Oblast Party Committee. Polyansky played an important role in the restoration back to health of the economy in the Crimea, an area devastated both by World War II and by a massive deportation of the native Tartar population.

When Khrushchev assumed control of the party in 1955, Polyansky's name began to figure more largely in news dispatches from the Soviet Union, leading many observers in the West to regard him as one of Khrushchev's "lieutenants." With the benefit of hindsight, experts on Soviet affairs have now begun trying to sift fact from legend in an effort to determine precisely what Polyansky and other officials owed to Khrushchev. Their studies make Polyansky's denunciation of Khrushchev in 1964 seem more explicable. One of the legacies of Stalin's regime, the gross imbalance between agricultural and industrial output in the Soviet Union prompted Khrushchev to institute his "virgin lands" project in 1954, involving the cultivation of vast stretches of arid land in Asiatic Russia. A year later, when only dubious results had been achieved, he selected Polyansky to head the project in the Urals, appointing him first secretary of the Orenburg Oblast Committee. From that position Polyansky rose rapidly to power. At the twentieth Party Congress in 1956, he was elected a member of the CPSU Central Committee, and the following year he was appointed first secretary of the CPSU Committee in the Krasnodar, one of the chief agricultural regions of the Soviet Union. In 1958 he succeeded Kozlov as head of the Russian Republic, the largest republic in the Soviet Union. During that year he also became an alternate member of the Central Committee Presidium, the highest organ of the Soviet political system. When he achieved full membership in 1960, he was the youngest man in the Presidium, while retaining his post as head of the Russian Republic.

Observers in the United States had a chance to judge the man and his style when Polyansky headed a Soviet delegation in January 1960 for a three-week tour of that country. Since the visit was intended as a kind of cultural exchange of high-level officials, in a Soviet response to a tour of the U.S.S.R. by American governors the previous year, Polyansky's conduct did little to lessen international tensions. Dispensing with the amenities, he had scarcely disembarked when he launched into a political speech, reminding newsmen that the Soviet Union had undertaken unilaterally to reduce its armed forces. Yet if his outspoken criticism of the United States seemed disconcerting, Polyansky impressed observers as belonging to an entirely new breed of Soviet politician, and as a man with a genuinely inquiring mind. No less refreshing was his pungent wit, only slightly less epigrammatic and memorable than Khrushchev's.

Although Polyansky obviously arrived with certain preconceptions about the United States, he appeared to be sincerely interested in a competition between the two powers that would be based on the merits of the two political systems, not their armed strength. Even during a vehement de-

DMITRY S. POLYANSKY

bate on civil rights with Emmanuel Celler, the chairman of the House Judiciary Committee, he seemed less like an intractable critic than a man with a flair for polemics, who thoroughly relished his role as provocateur. Most American commentators agreed that his visit adumbrated an end to the fear and mistrust characteristic of the Soviet Union's approach to competing ideologies.

As part of a major shift in the party hierarchy, Polyansky was promoted to full membership in the Presidium, along with Kosygin and Podgorny, in May 1960. The reshuffle was interpreted not as a purge but as an emphasis on more effective party and government leadership, particularly in domestic affairs. As with any significant change in the Kremlin, however, it touched off a flurry of speculation in the West. In a New York Times editorial (May 7, 1960) C. L. Sulzberger noted that if Kozlov seemed the man most likely to succeed Khrushchev in the near future, Polyansky appeared an equally likely candidate for the succession to follow—the "man of the day after tomorrow." If Polyansky were to become Premier, Sulzberger added, he predicted "major and revolutionary shifts" in Soviet policy. Obviously Sulzberger could not have foreseen Khrushchev's ouster in 1964, nor Kozlov's death the following year, but his remarks testify to the stature Polyansky had achieved by 1960.

At a Central Committee meeting in January 1961, Polyansky set forth the details of a plan for a radical reorganization of Soviet agriculture. Signs of friction between him and Khrushchev became apparent when the Premier curtly interrupted Polyansky several times during his summary of the 1960 agricultural output. Although the reforms that Polyansky outlined were more or less engineered by Khrushchev himself, Polyansky's insistence that collective farms not be converted into state farms (agricultural factories operating with hired labor) represented the continuation of a policy debate begun by the two men the year before. In November 1961 the dispute was resolved in Polyansky's favor, when Khrushchev himself acknowledged the futility of having the state absorb the debts of collective farms that were operating at a deficit. Despite their differences, Polyansky was still regarded as a "Khrushchevite," an impression reinforced when he led the attack on Marshal Voroshilov, a man whom Khrushchev had labeled as an "anti-party reactionary." However, as Soviet experts were quick to point out, the "anti-party" campaigns of 1957 and 1961 were part of a broader Kremlin strategy, and participation in them did not necessarily represent unequivocal allegiance to Khrushchev. Polyansky's willingness to challenge Khrushchev publicly on crucial issues of domestic policy indicated that, in his case at least, the term "Khrushchevite" decidedly needed qualification.

Indeed, when Khrushchev was overthrown in October 1964, Western observers realized that they had seriously underestimated the degree of party opposition to him in the years preceding his fall from grace. Although the full details of that event may never be disclosed, in retrospect signs of discontent could be discerned as far back as 1962. Polyansky's disagreements with Khrushchev stemmed from an even earlier date, and when the latter appointed him Deputy Chairman of the U.S.S.R. Council of Ministers in 1962, there was still no evidence that the rift had healed. Khrushchev's policies continued to irritate the party hierarchy, and by the time of his ouster, resentment was virtually unanimous. As for Polyansky's role in the removal, Soviet analysts emphasize that his criticism of Khrushchev over the years represented a minimal contribution to a "cult." By choosing Polyansky and Suslov as spokesmen for the denunciation, party officials vented their major grievances against Khrushchev: his mishandling of relations with foreign Communist parties and his mismanagement of economic affairs.

In 1965 Polyansky was promoted to First Deputy Chairman of the U.S.S.R. Council of Ministers, and on November 6, at a celebration commemorating the forty-eighth anniversary of the Bolshevik Revolution, he delivered the annual Kremlin policy statement. The choice of him as speaker reflected both his prestige in the government and its increasing emphasis on collective leadership. Polyansky's discussion of international affairs followed the Party's new ideological strategy: a more intransigent position towards Communist China and a critical, though milder, approach towards United States foreign policy.

When Polyansky headed a delegation to Canada in the summer of 1966 he became the highest-ranking Soviet official to have visited that country. If, as he said, his intention was to liven up "Soviet-Canadian contacts, especially in the fields of trade, culture, and exchanges of specialists," he more than succeeded. During his stay he arranged for the purchase of $800,000,000 worth of Canadian wheat and flour, the establishment of passengership service between Montreal and Leningrad, and a direct air-link from Montreal to Moscow.

Equally effective was the impression he made on the Canadian public. Whether discussing problems of soil erosion with farmers in Saskatchewan

or foreign policy with officials in Ottawa, Polyansky charmed people by his wit, ebullience, and disarming informality. He candidly admitted the superiority of Canadian agricultural techniques to those of the Soviet Union and expressed eagerness to learn more about them. Only once, during a clash with External Affairs Minister Paul Martin over United States intervention in Vietnam, was the unanimous enthusiasm for him momentarily dispelled. Summing up the visit in the July 4 Toronto *Globe and Mail* (July 4, 1966), Bruce West described Polyansky in terms that were strikingly reminiscent of those that Sulzberger had used in 1960. If Polyansky one day became Premier, West concluded, "there might be a startling and lively change in the stolid face Russia has traditionally presented to the rest of the world."

Polyansky has proved as outspoken in his criticism of the current leadership as he was of Khrushchev. Disturbed by the government's failure in 1967 to allocate sufficient funds to improve Soviet agriculture, he voiced his disagreements in *Kommunist*, the Party's leading ideological journal. His article was an implied thrust at Kosygin for diverting agricultural funds to the consumer-goods industry. Citing the crude techniques used by farm workers and the substandard living conditions at many of the state and collective farms, Polyansky warned that the fate of the entire economy hinged on the reform of agriculture. In time his view seems to have prevailed. At the third All-Union Kolkhozniks' Congress in November 1969 Polyansky delivered a speech entitled "The New Model Kolkhoz Statute" in which he outlined ways to transform the collective farms into profitable enterprises. Since then he has been the leading authority on Soviet agricultural management.

Polyansky was a deputy to the U.S.S.R. Supreme Soviet at the 1954, 1958, 1962, and 1966 convocations. He has twice been awarded the Order of Lenin.

References

Conquest, Robert. Russia After Khrushchev (1965)
Prominent Personalities in the USSR (1968)
Tatu, Michel. Power in the Kremlin (1967)

PRESCOTT, ROBERT W(ILLIAM)

May 5, 1913- Airline executive
Address: b. Flying Tiger Corp., 7401 World Way West, Los Angeles International Airport, Los Angeles, Calif. 90009; h. 1640 Carla Ridge, Beverly Hills, Calif. 90210

The founder and president of the Flying Tiger Line, the world's oldest and largest all-cargo airline, is Robert W. Prescott, a veteran of General Claire L. Chennault's legendary Flying Tigers, the crack corps of swashbuckling American mercenaries who flew for China against the Japanese early in World War II. Later in the war Prescott flew cargo into China, and in 1945 he founded the Flying Tiger Line with the financial backing of a group of California businessmen. With the motto, "We'll fly anything, anywhere, anytime," the enterprise lived on while hundreds of other young airlines died in the postwar years, but its survival remained precarious until the mid and late 1960's, when it was buoyed by military contracts in Vietnam, a license from the Civil Aeronautics Board to fly the first all-cargo route across the Pacific, and, more fundamentally, a landmark C.A.B. decision favorable to all-cargo carriers. Taking into account projected growth in the world economy and the increasing demand for cargo transport by air, Prescott has confidently predicted that the company will continue to flourish even as the war in Vietnam draws to an end and that it will grow to ten times its present size by 1980.

Robert William Prescott was born in Fort Worth, Texas on May 5, 1913, the seventh of eight children of George Washington Prescott, a truck driver, furniture salesman, and auctioneer, and Una (Stewart) Prescott. After graduating from high school Prescott drove a truck and held various other jobs in the Fort Worth area until 1934, when he left for California. After failing to gain admission to the California Institute of Technology as an engineering student, he took an associate bachelor of arts degree at Compton Junior College, in 1936, and studied law for a year and a half at Loyola University in Los Angeles. He worked while studying, mostly as a truck driver.

Prescott joined the Navy in 1939, and after completing training at the United States Naval Flying School in Pensacola, Florida he taught at the school, in the rank of ensign, for a year. In September 1941 the Navy permitted him to resign his commission to join General Chennault's American Volunteer Group, popularly known as the Flying Tigers. The group, consisting of three P-40 fighter squadrons, was more attractive to many adventurous flyers than the United States military service air forces because of its glamorous image and high rate of pay—$600 a month plus a $500 bonus for every Japanese plane shot down. Prescott was credited with downing six Japanese fighter planes over the rice paddies of Burma while with the Flying Tigers.

So effective were Chennault's Flying Tigers against the Japanese that the United States Army wanted the General to organize a similar force for them. In April 1942 Chennault was called to active duty in the Army and three months later the Flying Tigers were disbanded. Returning to the United States, Prescott went to work for Trans World Airlines as an intercontinental pilot, and while with Trans World he copiloted the plane that carried Joseph E. Davies to Moscow to confer with Stalin on United States-Soviet war plans. After a few months with Trans World he flew as a captain for the China National Aviation Corporation, completing over 300 missions carrying military supplies from India to China.

By the time he returned again to the United States, late in 1944, Prescott was dreaming of founding his own airline. On his honeymoon in Acapulco he met a group of Los Angeles businessmen, headed by Samuel B. Mosher, who were con-

ROBERT W. PRESCOTT

sidering establishing an air freight line along the west coast of the United States and Mexico. He convinced them that a transcontinental route across the United States would be more successful, and they agreed to match whatever capital he could raise.

Contacting other veterans of the American Volunteer Group, Prescott rounded up nine who were willing to join him in the airline venture. Together they raised $89,000, and that sum was matched by the California businessmen. With fourteen Budd Conestoga planes bought from Navy surplus, the nation's first all-cargo airline went into operation on June 25, 1945 in a two-car garage at the Long Beach (California) Municipal Airport. At first the line was called the National Skyways Freight Corporation, but everyone knew it was operated by former Flying Tigers, and its planes were painted in Flying Tiger style, with tiger-shark heads on the snouts. Prescott soon changed the name to Flying Tiger Line Inc.

About 300 cargo airlines were established in the postwar years, most of them by former war pilots using military surplus aircraft. But the attrition rate was high, and today there are only two all-cargo airlines besides the Flying Tiger Line in the United States: Airlift International Inc. and Seaboard World Airlines Inc. The survival of Prescott's line, in the beginning at least, was attributable to the determination and resourcefulness of its operators. Each "Tiger" was not only a pilot and freight handler but also a salesman, hustling business in air terminal lobbies with anybody who had cash. In those days they would hire themselves out for almost anything, from publicity stunts to unusual charter passenger flights, and their cargoes ranged from corpses and fresh-cut flowers to Elsie the Borden Cow and Roy Rogers' horse. On the ground they supplemented their flight income by providing repair and maintenance services for aircraft belonging to foreign airlines.

In 1947 Prescott's airline carried supplies to the occupation forces in Japan under General Douglas MacArthur, and two years later it participated in the Berlin airlift. In 1949, after a long legal battle,

Prescott won a certificate from the Civil Aeronautics Board that allowed his airline to fly the nation's first regularly scheduled transcontinental all-freight flights. The route awarded stretched across the Northern United States, connecting such Eastern cities as Boston, New York, and Hartford with Los Angeles, San Francisco, and Portland, Oregon. The award marked a decisive victory over Prescott's cargo-carrying competitors because most customers preferred regular flights, and the Flying Tiger Line showed a profit for the first time in 1949.

From 1950 to 1954 the Flying Tiger Line carried supplies to United States forces in Korea, under the largest military freight contract then held by any civilian company flying the Pacific. But, military contracts aside, the air-freight business remained a precarious way to make money. The Flying Tiger Line had some difficult years in the late 1950's, and in the fiscal year 1959-60 it suffered a net loss of $998,668.

The woes of air freight handlers continued into the 1960's. It has been said that the air cargo industry was established too early for its own good, because postwar airplanes lacked the speed and cargo capacity to lure customers away from other modes of transportation for their goods. But when efficient jet aircraft finally became available during the 1960's, the air cargo carriers all too often lacked the financial resources to buy them. The large combination carriers, on the other hand, were licensed by the C.A.B. to transport both passengers and cargo, and by the mid-1960's they were threatening to drive the cargo carriers out of business with their new jet freighters.

Prescott led the fight of the air cargo industry against the combination airlines. In the fall of 1963 the all-cargo lines petitioned the C.A.B., urging it to forbid the combination carriers to operate all-cargo flights. They proposed that the board authorize the all-cargo lines to sell freight space wholesale to the passenger lines, which would act as retail space sellers. Prescott, meanwhile, sent a letter to the heads of some 15,000 business concerns that used passenger lines extensively informing them that the major airlines were charging them exorbitant passenger rates to offset losses they were sustaining in freight hauling.

Prescott also tried, as he had before, to obtain a price cut in air mail rates, to the end of taking more mail business from the passenger lines. In April 1964 he placed an advertisement in newspapers in the form of an open letter to the Postmaster General from the Flying Tiger Line. "We are one of your airmail contractors . . . ," the letter read. "We are sure we are charging you too much. In 1958 we filed an offer with the Civil Aeronautics Board to cut our rate by almost 50 percent. This still has not been acted upon." In another advertisement he pointed out that under present mail rates it cost $4,200 to ship 10,000 pounds of mail cross-country, while it cost only $1,700 to ship 10,000 pounds of lobsters over the same route. To dramatize that point he delivered a thousand live lobsters and an equal number of miniature airmail sacks to Capitol Hill.

His campaign for lower mail rates strengthened the credibility of his argument that all-cargo lines were willing and able to handle freight more efficiently and economically than combination lines. Persuaded, the C.A.B. in 1966 ruled that the all-cargo lines would henceforth have the exclusive right to sell blocked space, that is, a consistent amount of space sold to volume shippers on specified regular flights at discount rates.

In 1966, when swelling Vietnam war contracts were fattening the Flying Tiger Lines' profit figures, Prescott placed the largest fleet order ever made for jet freighters, contracting to buy at a cost of $206,000,000 seventeen of the largest and most efficient model currently available, the Boeing "stretched" DC-8-63. The planes were ready to be put into use in 1969 when the Flying Tiger Line was awarded the lucrative mail and freight route from the West Coast to Japan, Korea, Okinawa, Hong Kong, Taiwan, the Philippines, South Vietnam, and Thailand.

To strengthen the Flying Tiger Line's management, Prescott in 1967 succeeded in hiring Wayne M. Hoffman, then executive vice-president of the New York Central Railroad, as the company's chairman of the board. Hoffman is in charge of pricing and marketing, while Prescott concentrates on air operations. In 1970 the company was reorganized into a holding company, the Flying Tiger Corporation, of which the Flying Tiger Line is the chief holding. The corporation also owns the North American Car Corporation, a railroad car leasing company.

While major airlines in the United States generally were trying to recover from record losses in 1970, Flying Tiger reported record profits of $10,528,000, and Prescott and Hoffman have good reason to be optimistic about the future. Although only about 1 percent of the world's cargo is transported by air at present, that figure is expected to jump to 7 percent by the end of the century, and the airline executives predict that cargo tonnage will be 200 times greater by then.

The brash flamboyance and vigor of the World War II fighter pilot has never left Bob Prescott. He credits his success in business largely to his ability to be flexible and think intuitively, and he has been described as a "rough-and-tumble" talker who uses "colorful" language. For relaxation he likes to play golf and to pilot his private plane, a Cessna. On July 16, 1962 Robert W. Prescott married Dr. Anne-Marie Bennstrom. He has three children, French, Kirsten, and Peter, by a previous marriage, to Helen Ruth Verheyden. Separately from the Flying Tiger Corporation, Prescott owns a controlling interest in a chain of restaurants called the Hungry Tiger. He is active in Democratic politics.

References

Forbes 99:34+ Ja 15 '67 por
N Y Times III p3 N 13 '60 por
Nations Bsns 58:65+ O '70 pors
Who's Who in America, 1970-71
Who's Who in Finance and Industry, 1970-71

PRINCE, HAROLD

Jan. 30, 1928- Producer; director
Address: b. 1 Rockefeller Plaza, New York
10020

Stepping up from stage manager to producer at
the age of twenty-six, Harold Prince was dubbed
the "Boy Wonder" of Broadway when he cosponsored *The Pajama Game* in 1954. He followed
that smash musical with a string of hits, including
*West Side Story, A Funny Thing Happened on
the Way to the Forum,* and *Fiddler on the Roof.*
Since 1962, having learned the art of directing
from George Abbott and Jerome Robbins, he has
staged as well as produced many of his shows,
some of them award winners. With *Cabaret, Zorbá,
Company,* and *Follies* he has proved himself a
talented, sensitive director who has enlarged
the musical play as a theatrical form by treating
challenging themes of underlying seriousness that
stimulate intellectually as well as entertain.

A native New Yorker, Harold Smith Prince was
born in Manhattan on January 30, 1928, the only
child of Milton A. and Blanche (Stern) Prince.
From his father, a Wall Street stockbroker with
Stanley Heller & Company, he probably acquired
the head for business and finance that contributed much to his success as a producer. His
mother was an avid theatregoer who knew several
people in the entertainment world and who encouraged her son's early enthusiasm for the stage.
He has recalled that the first play he saw was a
Mercury Theatre production of *Julius Caesar* starring Orson Welles. "Theatre was always part of
my life," he told Robert Wahls in an interview
for the New York *Sunday News* (June 9, 1963),
"and Saturday matinees and second balconies were
a passionate hobby all through my school days."

In 1944 Hal Prince graduated from Franklin
School, a preparatory school on Manhattan's West
Side. Then attending the University of Pennsylvania, he majored in English and became an
energetic member of the Penn Players, for whose
productions he wrote, acted, and directed. He also
founded and managed the campus radio station.
When he had earned his B.A. degree in 1948, he
began his career in the New York theatre by applying for employment in the office of a distinguished craftsman of the stage, the producer, director, and playwright George Abbott. Impressed
by Prince's eager willingness to work, Abbott
hired him to perform odd jobs and write several
television scripts, at apprentice's wages.

Prince's first noteworthy Broadway assignment
was as assistant stage manager for Abbott's presentation of *Touch and Go,* a musical that opened
at the Broadhurst Theatre in 1949. He was also
stage manager for the revue *Tickets, Please,* produced by Arthur Klein at the Coronet Theatre in
April 1950, before he was drafted into the United
States Army and sent to Germany with an artillery unit. Although he resented military service
as an intrusion upon his career, with characteristic good humor he wrote a GI's guidebook entitled "Where a GI Should Go in Europe." On

HAROLD PRINCE

his arrival home in 1952, he resumed employment
with George Abbott as assistant stage manager for
the musical *Wonderful Town,* which had its première at the Winter Garden on February 25, 1953.

While *Wonderful Town* was running, Prince
and Robert E. Griffith, who had worked together
stage-managing Abbott's shows, decided to produce a musical themselves. Griffith, a seemingly
relaxed, family man in his forties, was the antithesis of the energetic, nervous Prince, but their
opposite qualities blended in a highly successful
partnership. Griffith discovered the material for
their first musical in Richard Bissell's novel *7½
Cents,* and the quick-acting Prince read the book,
contacted the agent, and obtained an option on it
within twenty-four hours. Although Abbott regretted losing two of his staff, he agreed to direct
the projected show along with Jerome Robbins
and also wrote the script with Bissell. Prince disclosed to Herbert Mitgang, in an interview for
the New York *Times* (June 5, 1960), the difficulties they had raising money: "In 1954 none of
the smart money would support us. We couldn't
even get some of the big investors like Howard
Cullman to come to an audition. But we had
dozens of auditions, and there were others in the
theatre with faith in the show. Our backers even
included kids in the chorus and dressers backstage." From 164 investors he raised the required
$250,000. He also co-opted a third producer,
Frederick Brisson, husband of Rosalind Russell,
who helped finance the show and remained in the
partnership until 1957.

The Pajama Game, based on the *7½ Cents* story
about labor troubles in a pajama factory, opened
at the St. James Theatre on May 13, 1954 to enthusiastic reviews. Walter Kerr described it in the
New York *Herald Tribune* (May 14, 1954) as
a "bright, brassy, and jubilantly sassy show" that
takes "a whole barrelful of gleaming new talents,
and a handful of stimulating ideas as well, and
sends them tumbling in happy profusion over the
footlights." After it had achieved the unusual feat
of making a profit before reaching New York, the
show ran for 1,063 performances on Broadway

and was revived at the New York City Center in May 1957. By 1965 it reportedly had earned $1,850,000. Prince received the 1955 Tony (Antoinette Perry Award) as producer of the best musical, while the show itself won seven Donaldson Awards, the New York Drama Critics Award, and the Evening Standard Award. Warner Brothers filmed *The Pajama Game* in 1957 with Prince as associate producer.

The songwriters who had collaborated on *The Pajama Game,* Richard Adler and Jerry Ross, rejoined Abbott as coauthor and director to create another hit for Prince and his partners, *Damn Yankees,* a musical about baseball. It began a 1,019-performance run at the 46th Street Theatre on May 5, 1955. Prince, who won his second Tony for the stage production of *Damn Yankees,* again took over the job of associate producer for Warner Brothers' film version, released in 1958. *New Girl in Town,* the Prince-Griffith-Brisson musical adaptation of Eugene O'Neill's *Anna Christie,* followed *Damn Yankees* at the 46th Street Theatre for a shorter run, beginning on May 14, 1957.

For years producers had been turning down *West Side Story,* a musical tragedy about teen-age gang warfare in Manhattan's Puerto Rican community, which had evolved from Jerome Robbins' idea for a contemporary treatment of the theme of *Romeo and Juliet.* Then in the spring of 1957 Stephen Sondheim, who had written the lyrics for Leonard Bernstein's score, aroused the interest of Prince and Griffith in their project. Although some of their usual investors hesitated to back a show that they considered somewhat pretentious, the producers raised the necessary $300,-000 in a week. Contrary to predictions, *West Side Story* not only proved to be an immediate box office hit but is regarded as a masterpiece of the American musical theatre. It played at the Winter Garden from September 26, 1957 to June 27, 1959 and in the spring of 1960 reopened there for another long run. In London critics voted it the best musical of 1958 for the Evening Standard Awards.

Resuming their association with Abbott as director and coauthor, Prince and Griffith produced two more musicals, *Fiorello!,* at the Broadhurst Theatre on November 23, 1959, and *Tenderloin,* at the 46th Street Theatre on October 17, 1960. The former, a portrait of the colorful New York mayor, Fiorello La Guardia, won the Pulitzer Prize and the New York Drama Critics Award, among other honors. A less distinguished effort, perhaps, *Tenderloin* seemed to some critics a pale shadow of *Fiorello!* in duplicating the formula of a nostalgic New York setting and historical characters. Prince and Griffith followed *Tenderloin* with their first commercial failure, a nonmusical spy play called *A Call on Kuprin,* which closed at the Broadhurst in the spring of 1961 after twelve performances.

Soon afterward, on June 8, 1961 Griffith died suddenly. "I had no buffer when Bobby died. I was lost at first," Prince told Robert Wahls of the New York *Sunday News.* "For the first time

in years, we had no shows running, nothing that had to be attended to immediately. . . . Life had never presented me with reality in such an inescapable and dramatic way." By the end of six weeks' vacation in Europe, he had made up his mind to continue his work in the theatre alone. On December 21, 1961 his handsome production of the light-hearted comedy *Take Her, She's Mine* opened at the Biltmore Theatre, and on May 8, 1962 *A Funny Thing Happened on the Way to the Forum* reached the Alvin Theatre for a run of over two years. The latter, a musical burlesque based on plays of Plautus and starring Zero Mostel, had disappointed audiences at pre-Broadway performances in Washington, D.C. Prince's industry and ingenuity in transforming his show into a popular hit earned him another Tony.

Prince's ambitions to be a director were realized in 1962, when he replaced Word Baker, who resigned from *A Family Affair.* In the two weeks preceding the musical's opening at the Billy Rose Theatre on January 27, Prince changed eighty of the script's 110 pages. His doctoring failed to disguise the weakness of the material, however, and the show ran for only sixty-five performances. Encouraged by Abbott's praise of his work, he then directed a production of Thornton Wilder's *The Matchmaker* for a five-week tour sponsored by the New York State Council on the Arts in the fall of 1962. *She Loves Me,* the first show both produced and directed by Prince, opened at the Eugene O'Neill Theatre on April 23, 1963 and ran for 302 performances. Many critics felt that the musical play deserved greater prosperity and congratulated Prince on the delicacy and intimacy he imparted to his love story.

Among the phenomenally successful productions of Prince is a musical of authentic Eastern European Jewish flavor, *Fiddler on the Roof,* based on stories by Sholom Aleichem. On September 22, 1964 at the Imperial Theatre *Fiddler,* staged by Robbins, began one of the longest runs in Broadway history. It won nine Tony awards, has been performed in a score or more of countries abroad, and by 1970 had amassed box office receipts in the United States alone totaling some $30,000,000, from an initial investment of $380,000. Prince's next two musical productions, *Flora, the Red Menace* in 1965 and *It's a Bird. . . . It's a Plane. . . . It's Superman* in 1966, were commercial fiascos. He also directed *Baker Street,* a Sherlock Holmes "musical adventure," for the producer Alexander H. Cohen in 1965.

With *Cabaret,* Prince introduced in his musicals what may be called the Brechtian approach, the use of songs primarily to comment on the action or situation rather than to aid the flow of the plot. *Cabaret,* adapted from *I Am a Camera,* the stage version of Christopher Isherwood's *Berlin Stories,* conveys through the atmosphere of a Berlin nightclub the decadence of Germany in 1929-30. It opened at the Broadhurst on November 20, 1966 to mixed reviews, varying from "vulgar" and "disappointing" to "sparkling" and "excellent," but box office proceeds testified to the unequivocal delight of audiences. The eight Tony Awards given to *Cabaret* included the one for direction. Reaffirming his status as a leading Broadway director, that award is one of Prince's most prized possessions. He also staged the national production and London production of *Cabaret*.

The music and lyrics for *Cabaret* were written by John Kander and Fred Ebb, who also collaborated on *Zorbá*, derived from the novel *Zorbá the Greek* by Nikos Kazantzakis. With few exceptions, one of them being Walter Kerr of the New York *Times*, critics gave *Zorbá* glowing notices when it opened at the Imperial Theatre on November 17, 1968. Clive Barnes, another critic of the New York *Times* (November 18, 1968), credited Prince, as producer and director, with the "exquisite style and finesse" of the musical. "Prince is one of the very few creative producers on Broadway," he observed, "—a man who can put his own imprint on a show." When three principals of *Zorbá* fell ill during the summer of 1969, Prince cut short its New York run and sent it on a long tour, intending to recast and restage it for a later Broadway presentation.

Company, the most controversial, unorthodox, and perhaps most extravagantly praised of Prince's productions, premièred at the Alvin Theatre on April 26, 1970. The caustic, ironic, and episodic book of George Furth and the music and lyrics of Stephen Sondheim focus on the tribulations of five married couples as seen through the eyes of their uncommitted friend, a New York bachelor. A critic for *Time* (May 11, 1970) described *Company* as "a landmark musical, one of those few shows that enter the permanent lore of the theater by altering the vocabulary of dramatic possibilities." He went on to say, "Prince surpasses himself in staging this show and invests each scene with an electric tingle of surprise, delight and authority." *Company* was chosen for the New York Drama Critics Circle Award as the best musical of 1970 and for seven awards in the critical poll run by *Variety*, including that of best director. On April 4, 1971 Prince's latest Broadway production, *Follies*, opened to generally enthusiastic reviews.

Prince made his screen directorial debut in the gothic tale *Something for Everyone* (Cinema Center Films, 1970), drawn from Harry Kressing's *The Cook*, a novel about a degenerate social climber who tries to get control of the Bavarian castle of an impecunious aristocratic family. Filmed in Bavaria with Michael York and Angela Lansbury in the leading roles on a $2,000,000 budget, the movie was applauded for its dazzling settings and polished style. Most reviewers found it flawed, if amusing, though they could not agree on where its weakness lay.

In 1958 Prince was caricatured by Richard Bissell in *Say, Darling* in the character of Ted Snow, a brash young producer brimming with baroque ideas for setting serious themes to popular music. At first Prince resented the depiction as absurd and slanderous, but he has admitted that in his early twenties he was impatient and overambitious, afraid of being a failure. "My tempo is even faster than New York's tempo," he once re-

marked. Intense and enthusiastic about his work, he is able to absorb himself completely in his current production and to inspire the whole company with his dynamism. Throughout his working life he has shared an office with Abbott.

Many of Prince's shows employ the same craftsmen of the performing arts, a measure of the respect and liking he generates in people of the theatre. He attributes the relatively low cost of his productions to his training in stage managing, maintains that he knows the price of every item in every scene, and generally avoids casting highly paid stars. Most of his backers have been with him since *The Pajama Game*, and only friends and favorite employees may join their ranks. As president of the League of New York Theaters, to which he was elected in 1964, Prince helped put into effect a new code of theatre practices to give the public a fairer deal and also presided over negotiations with Equity to safeguard the rights and salaries of actors. He resigned his office in 1965 to take part in John V. Lindsay's mayoralty campaign. In October 1969 Prince canceled a performance of *Fiddler on the Roof* to support the nationwide moratorium protesting the Vietnam war. His social consciousness is reflected in much of his work.

On October 26, 1962 Harold Prince married Judith Chaplin, daughter of the Hollywood producer Saul Chaplin. They have two children, Charley and Daisy. Prince is a slim man of medium height, with close-cropped graying hair. In recent years he has acquired a mustache and beard. His clubs are the Coffee House and the Lambs, and his recreations are walking, playing tennis, and swimming. A multimillionaire, he has a house on Manhattan's Upper East Side and another home at Pollensa on Majorca.

References

After Dark 11:38+ Ja '70 por
N Y Post Mag p2 Ap 1 '67 por
N Y Sunday News II p10+ Je 9 '63 por
N Y Times II p1+ Ap 21 '63; p31 Je 9 '64 por; p58 N 4 '68 por; II p1+ N 24 '68 por
Newsweek 72:105+ D 2 '68 por
Biographical Encyclopaedia & Who's Who of the American Theatre (1966)
Newquist, Roy. Showcase (1966)
Who's Who in America, 1970-71
Who's Who in the Theatre (1967)

QUAYLE, ANTHONY

Sept. 7, 1913- British actor; director
Address: h. 22 Pelham Crescent, London, S.W. 7, England

During his career of forty years in the theatre Anthony Quayle has earned a reputation as one of the English-speaking world's most distinguished classical actors, and he has been equally successful on the popular stage, on television, and in films. The British actor launched his career by

ANTHONY QUAYLE

playing bit parts with the Old Vic, soon added directing to his accomplishments, and from 1948 to 1956 served as the chief administrator of the Royal Shakespeare Theatre at Stratford-upon-Avon, simultaneously performing in or staging over a score of Stratford productions. Since 1956 he has appeared in many dramatic roles in the West End, and in New York he has been celebrated for his performances in the title roles of *Tamburlaine the Great* (1956) and *Galileo* (1967). Most recently, he kept London and New York theatregoers on the edge of their seats with his portrayal of an eccentric mystery writer in the ingeniously plotted British thriller *Sleuth*, the New York cast of which he left on September 25, 1971. An Academy Award nominee in 1970 for his supporting role in the historical film *Anne of the Thousand Days,* Quayle has appeared in many motion pictures, and he starred in a British TV detective series entitled *Strange Report* that was shown in the United States by NBC in 1971.

John Anthony Quayle was born on September 7, 1913 in Ainsdale, Lancashire, England to Arthur and Esther (Overton) Quayle. Although Arthur Quayle was an attorney, his one passion in life, according to his son, was the theatre. In an interview with Roberta Brandes Gratz for the New York *Post* (May 10, 1967) the actor recalled, "My family was all doctors with a certain amount of law. . . . I was supposed to go into the family drug business but I had absolutely no aptitude for chemistry or physics. In school I knew I would only be good at acting or writing. I guess my father sowed the seed for it. He adored the theater."

After completing his secondary education at the Rugby School in 1930, Quayle attended the Royal Academy of Dramatic Art for a brief time, but he quit in 1931 to take a job as a straight man to a music hall comic. Quayle's vaudeville days ended later that year when Sir Tyrone Guthrie, who had seen him perform at the Royal Academy, helped him to get a small part in *Robin Hood,* which opened in the West End on December 28, 1931. Quayle told Robert Berkvist of the New York

Time (March 14, 1971) that both Guthrie and Sir John Gielgud encouraged him in his gravitation toward classical roles. "Besides," he told Berkvist, "I wasn't asked to be a handsome young man in films because I wasn't a handsome young man."

In September 1932 Quayle joined the famed Old Vic Company, with which he played a variety of small parts over the next few years. He added to his repertoire each succeeding season by performing in revivals in the West End. In December 1936 he made his debut on the other side of the Atlantic when he appeared as Mr. Harcourt in a Broadway production of *The Country Wife.* Returning to England and the Old Vic in 1937, Quayle was Laertes and Horatio in *Hamlet,* Demetrius in *A Midsummer Night's Dream,* and Cassio in *Othello.* From January to April of 1939 he toured with the Old Vic on the Continent and in Egypt.

Quayle was one of the early enlisters in the British Army during World War II, serving in the Royal Artillery from 1939 to 1945 and rising to the rank of major. For six months he engaged in a perilous mission behind enemy lines in Albania, working with the British Special Operations Executive and the American O.S.S. to organize partisan forces in guerrilla operations against the German Army. Most of the rest of the war he spent as a member of the headquarters staff on Gibraltar, where he had the opportunity to meet Winston Churchill, General George C. Marshall, Dwight D. Eisenhower, and Charles de Gaulle.

Assigned to providing entertainment for the troops on Gibraltar, Quayle wrote and staged pantomimes and revues and directed several plays. His work was seen by John Perry, a London theatre manager then with the RAF, who after the war invited him to direct Rodney Ackland's dramatization of *Crime and Punishment* in the West End. It was a prestigious directing debut for Quayle, since the production starred Gielgud, Edith Evans, and Peter Ustinov and became a considerable success after it opened on June 18, 1946. Quayle went on to direct London productions of *The Relapse, Harvey,* and *Who Is Sylvia?* Meanwhile, his reputation as an actor was enhanced by his West End performances as Enobarbus in *Antony and Cleopatra* in 1946 and as Iago in the 1947 production of *Othello* starring Jack Hawkins.

In 1948 Quayle joined the Shakespeare Memorial Theatre Company (now the Royal Shakespeare Theatre) as a director and actor, and in October of that year he became director of the theatre. During his eight years with the Stratford company he twice took it on tour to Australia (1949, 1953), produced the entire cycle of Shakespeare's chronicle plays, and recruited such prominent actors as John Gielgud, Margaret Leighton, Ralph Richardson, and Michael Redgrave for appearances with the unsubsidized company for only a fraction of their usual fees. Among the roles that Quayle played at Stratford were Iago; Claudius; Petruchio; Henry VIII; Antony; Falstaff in *Henry IV, Parts I and II,* and in *The Merry Wives of*

Windsor; Coriolanus; Othello; Bottom in *A Mid-summer Night's Dream;* Pandarus in *Troilus and Cressida;* and Aaron in *Titus Andronicus.* Among the plays that he directed were *The Winter's Tale, Troilus and Cressida, Macbeth, Julius Caesar, King Lear* with John Gielgud, *Richard II, Henry IV, Part I* with John Kidd, *Henry V, Othello,* and *Measure for Measure.*

A few months before he left the Shakespeare Memorial Theatre Quayle starred in Tyrone Guthrie's Stratford (Ontario) Shakespeare Festival production of *Tamburlaine the Great* by Christopher Marlowe, which played first in Canada and then, in January 1956, at the Winter Garden in New York City. The turgid Elizabethan drama, which Wolcott Gibbs (*New Yorker,* January 28, 1956) characterized as "a dark and shapeless mélange of unrelated violence," proved too inaccessible to modern audiences to achieve commercial success, but every aspect of the mammoth production, including Quayle's bravura performance as the bloody Oriental tyrant, received high critical praise. A typical reaction was that of Wolcott Gibbs who wrote that, as Tamburlaine, the British actor combined "a chilling and almost lunatic savagery with a kind of barbaric grandeur."

In October 1956 Quayle opened in the West End production of Arthur Miller's *A View from the Bridge,* winning critical applause in the role of Eddie. After he left that production he played Aaron in *Titus Andronicus* at the Paris Festival in May 1957, toured Eastern Europe with the play, and began a West End run with it in July.

Returning to Broadway in May 1958, Quayle costarred with Katharine Cornell in *The Firstborn,* Christopher Fry's verse drama about the deliverance of the Jews from Egypt. Although most critics found the play inferior to Fry's other works, they had nothing but praise for Quayle's efforts, as both actor and director. "Mr. Quayle is the dominant influence in the production," wrote Brooks Atkinson in the New York *Times* (May 1, 1958). "As actor, he portrays a fanatical, clear-headed Moses who understands his mission and submits to God, but also has misgivings. . . . As director . . . he has breathed life into a rather colorless script and made something bold and beautiful out of a well-loved Bible story." After a limited engagement in New York, the production toured Israel.

Over the next few years Quayle appeared in a number of London productions, including *A Long Day's Journey into Night* (1958), *Look After Lulu* (1959), *Chin-Chin* (1960), *Power of Persuasion* (1963), *The Right Honourable Gentleman* (1964), and *Incident at Vichy* (1966), but he did not return to the New York stage until 1967, when he starred in the Lincoln Center Repertory Theatre's production of Bertold Brecht's *Galileo.* The play marked the first genuine critical success for the struggling young repertory company, and Quayle's performance was given much of the credit for it. "Mr. Quayle is the best actor who has so far been seen at the Vivian Beaumont," wrote Calvin Trillin in the *New Yorker* (April 22, 1967). ". . . Quayle makes the astronomer a highly sympathetic character, and when, under the pressures of church and state, he denies what are to him self-evident facts of astronomy, he becomes a figure of almost tragic dimensions."

After his triumph as Galileo, Quayle returned to London to direct a production of *Lady Windermere's Fan.* He was back in New York early in 1968 to stage a revival of Giraudoux's *Tiger at the Gates* for the Lincoln Center Repertory Theatre. That production got a chilly reception from the critics, as did *Halfway Up the Tree,* a tepid comedy by Peter Ustinov that played on Broadway for a short time later that year with Quayle in the leading role.

Early in 1970 Quayle opened in the West End in Anthony Shaffer's *Sleuth,* an entertaining and suspenseful melodrama about a middle-aged detective-story writer's attempts to get revenge on his wife's young lover. Acclaimed as the best play of its genre in decades, *Sleuth* scored a smash success in London and in New York, where it won a 1970 Tony Award after opening at the Music Box Theatre on November 12, 1970. The play afforded Quayle an opportunity to turn in a virtuoso performance, and he stayed with it in London for nine months before leaving to star in the Broadway production. "Mr. Quayle, grizzled, quizzical and outrageously eccentric, plays a man given to jokes with a pleasantly grim, slightly paranoid seriousness," wrote Clive Barnes in the New York *Times* (November 13, 1970) after opening night. He characterized Quayle's performance as "absolutely outstanding," and his fellow critics fully agreed with him.

Despite Quayle's unintermittent success with the critics, *Sleuth* marked his first major success at the box office, and he has often depended on film and television assignments to supplement his income. "I had to do all sorts of crap," the actor reminisced to Jack Leahy of the New York *Sunday News* "I was in Tarzan films, and 'Fall of the Roman Empire,' and one dreary thing after another." Among the films of greater distinction in which he has been featured are Hitchcock's *The Wrong Man* (Warners, 1957), *The Guns of Navarone* (Columbia, 1961), and *Lawrence of Arabia* (Columbia, 1963). In 1970 he received an Academy Award nomination as best supporting actor for his portrayal of Cardinal Wolsey in *Anne of the Thousand Days* (Universal, 1970). On British and American television he has appeared on many dramatic programs, including the Hallmark Hall of Fame and Producer's Showcase in the United States. In 1968 Quayle filmed a television adventure series in London entitled *Strange Report,* in which he starred as a private detective named Adam Strange. The series, which consisted of sixteen hour-long segments, enjoyed considerable popularity in Europe and in the United States, where it was telecast by NBC in 1971.

In May 1971 Anthony Quayle told Leahy of the *Sunday News* that after leaving the cast of *Sleuth* in September he planned to sail his forty-foot ketch from England to Malta, a 2,000-mile trip that he estimated would take three months. An ardent sailor, Quayle usually spends his vacations sailing with his family. Since June 3, 1947 he has been married to Dorothy (Hyson) Quayle, a former American actress, and they have a teen-aged son named Christopher and two adult daughters, Jennifer, an actress, and Rosanna, a teacher. (His first marriage, to Hermione Hannen, ended in divorce.) A modest, kindly man who has been described as a good listener as well as a good talker, Quayle calls himself "a very private person." Of imposing figure, he is six feet one inch in height and weighs 180 pounds, and he has blue eyes and gray hair. When he is not sailing or working, he enjoys raising roses and reading history and biography. Some years ago he wrote two novels based on his wartime experiences that were best-sellers in England. The first was *Eight Hours from England* (Heinemann, 1945; Doubleday, 1946), which was about a British officer in Albania, and the second was *On Such a Night* (Heinemann, 1947; Little, Brown, 1948), set on a British-controlled island in the Mediterranean. In 1952 the Order of Commander of the British Empire was conferred on him.

References

Guardian p8 Jl 6 '70 por
N Y Post p46 My 10 '67 por
N Y Sunday News p6+ My 2 '71 pors
N Y Times II p15 Mr 14 '71 por
TV Guide 19:20+ Ap 3 '71 por
Biographical Encyclopaedia & Who's Who of the American Theatre (1966)
Who's Who, 1971-72
Who's Who in the Theatre (1967)

REDFORD, ROBERT

Aug. 18, 1937- Actor
Address: b. c/o Gottschalk and Frankfurt, 200 Park Ave., New York 10017; h. Box 837, Provo, Utah 84601

The rugged individualists of American myth, as projected through a contemporary sensibility, are the favorite roles of Robert Redford, who became a box-office star as an Old West gunslinger born too late in *Butch Cassidy and the Sundance Kid* (1969). Since then he has portrayed a fiercely competitive Olympic skier in *Downhill Racer* (1969), a sheriff reluctantly committed to hunting down an Indian outcast in *Tell Them Willie Boy Is Here* (1969), and a swaggering but mediocre motorcyclist in *Little Fauss and Big Halsy* (1970). Before hitting his present stride Redford had best been known as the staid, young, Ivy-League lawyer of Neil Simon's hit comedy *Barefoot in the Park,* a role he created on Broadway in 1963 and repeated in the 1967 film.

Charles Robert Redford Jr. was born on August 18, 1937 in Santa Monica, California to Charles Redford, an accountant, and Martha (Hart) Redford. He has one brother, William. As a student at Van Nuys High School in Santa Monica Redford won a gold key *Scholastic* magazine art award and excelled in football, tennis, and baseball. "I was in competitive sports from the time I was

eight," he recalled in an interview with Joseph Gelmis of *Newsday* (December 20, 1969). ". . . I never knew the sheer joy and fun of just going out and kicking a ball around. I was always in a uniform, playing to win. I was fiercely competitive, and I liked winning." He was also in a gang that raced hot rods, fought in the streets, and occasionally broke into mansions in Bel Air. "We never stole anything much, we just did it for kicks," he told Tom Burke of the New York *Times* (October 26, 1969). "As a generation, we were bored. Not like today's kids, who are doing beautiful things. We had no clear image of ourselves."

Redford graduated from high school in 1955 and, following his mother's death, entered the University of Colorado on a baseball scholarship to major in art. At the beginning of his sophomore year he quit, however, and worked in the California oil fields until he had money enough to leave for Europe. For thirteen months he hitchhiked through the Continent, lived in Florence and Paris, and painted. "Finally you come to live by your wits, like Henry Miller used to write about," Redford told Gelmis of *Newsday*. "And it all gets pretty interesting, pretty interesting. And that's when you begin to think of the years that were wasted banging a ball around a ball park."

With $200 he raised from an art show in Florence, Redford returned to the United States in 1958 and soon enrolled at the Pratt Institute in Brooklyn to study art. He also began studying at the American Academy of Dramatic Arts, although he had no clear idea of becoming an actor. "I'd never been in a play in my life," he told Tom Burke in the *Times* interview. "Acting seemed ludicrous to me, but people kept telling me I could do it. I hated the Academy until one day in movement class, when we had to put choreography to a poem. I was damned if I was going to. But the teacher kept calling on me, and I finally got up without even thinking and went right into 'The Raven,' the only poem I knew by heart, and I just *went wild!* I used the entire room, I was all over it, doing flips and twists, running out into the hall, grabbing people out of their chairs. I got to the end and the teacher said, 'Fine, now do it again.' And I did it again! I was suddenly so free I could do *anything!*"

Redford launched his acting career on Broadway with a walk-on part as a basketball player in *Tall Story* (January 1959) and a small role in Dore Schary's *The Highest Tree* (November 1959). For the next few years his was a familiar face on television dramas, in which he often played a young neurotic or killer. Among his TV credits are *Twilight Zone* (CBS), *Alfred Hitchcock Presents* (CBS), *The Untouchables* (ABC), and *The Virginians* (NBC). Redford was acclaimed for his performances in the CBS *Playhouse 90* play entitled *In the Presence of Mine Enemies* and in Sidney Lumet's production of *The Iceman Cometh* for WNTA's *Play of the Week*. In 1963 he was nominated for an Emmy award for his performance in *Voice of Charlie Pont* on *Alcoa Première* (ABC).

Redford made his movie debut in *War Hunt* (United Artists, 1962), a taut anti-war drama in which he played opposite John Saxon. The film and the performers received excellent reviews, but *War Hunt* was low-budget and received little promotion or public attention. After finishing the film, however, Redford found a suitable vehicle for his talents back on Broadway in the comedy *Sunday in New York*, which led to a starring role opposite Elizabeth Ashley in *Barefoot in the Park*, Neil Simon's comedy about the domestic squabbles of a young married couple in New York. *Barefoot in the Park* opened on October 23, 1963 and ran for four years; Redford left after eight months. "I prefer movies to plays," he explained to Gelmis in the *Newsday* interview, "because I'm only good for about two and a half months. That's the limit of my endurance. . . . My perversity came out [in *Barefoot*]. I created accidents and problems to break the monotony. . . . If you came on with one shoe off one night, at least it made life happen on stage. Otherwise, it got pretty plastic after a while."

After his adventures in *Barefoot*, Redford made four disappointing films, *Situation Hopeless—But Not Serious* (Paramount, 1965), based on a novel by Robert Shaw; *The Chase* (Columbia, 1966), directed by Arthur Penn; *This Property Is Condemned* (Paramount, 1966), from a play by Tennessee Williams; and *Inside Daisy Clover* (Warner Brothers, 1966), from the novel by Gavin Lambert. For each of his performances Redford received some favorable notices, but the pictures themselves were such failures that they did nothing to further his career. Frustrated and bored, Redford left everything, packed up his wife and children, and once again went to Europe.

A year later Redford returned to the United States to recreate his stage role in the film version of *Barefoot in the Park* (Paramount, 1967). His first successful film, *Barefoot in the Park* might easily have typecast him as a bland young juvenile in light comedy, and a *Variety* reviewer nominated him as the probable successor to Cary Grant. But Redford resisted stereotyping, and when he disapproved of the final script of the next film his studio wanted him to do (*Blue*, Paramount, 1968) he walked out a week before production was to begin. The result was a lawsuit and a year of unemployment.

When Redford returned to the screen it was with a determination to appear only in films that he thought worth doing, films, he told Louise Sweeney of the *Christian Science Monitor* (December 8, 1970), "about specifically, intrinsically American guys, with their roots solidly in the American scene or tradition." The first result of that resolution was *Butch Cassidy and the Sundance Kid* (Twentieth Century-Fox, 1969), a slick, but interesting entertainment based on the real-life adventures of the Old West's last two famous bandits, who fled the United States in 1904 for Bolivia, where they hoped to find less carefully guarded banks. In many ways the film resembled *Bonnie and Clyde*, except that its two robbers, played by Redford and Paul Newman, were lov-

ROBERT REDFORD

able bumblers endowed with humor and high spirits as well as good looks. "They're a pair of nice guys," wrote Judith Crist in *New York* (September 29, 1969). "Newman's Butch is a charming and agreeable chap with a high sense of comedy; Redford's Sundance is a quiet man, deadpan, but a man of sentiment behind the shaggy mustache and sharpshooter's squint. And under the laughter there's an awareness of doom, that their day is passing, that beautiful old robbable banks are being uglified with tough steel, that they're too old for ranching, let alone rustling, and the big time isn't around."

The spectacular success of *Butch Cassidy and the Sundance Kid* led to the release by Paramount two months later (in November 1969) of *Downhill Racer*, long a pet project of Redford's and produced by him and Richard Gregson. An unsentimental look at the world of amateur competitive skiing, the film starred Redford as an ambitious young man from a dingy little town in Colorado who aspires to be an Olympic champion. Much of the ski footage was shot at the Olympic races at Grenoble in 1968. "Although its medium is skiing (brilliantly photographed for speed and danger . . .), the real subject of the film is competition," wrote Roger Greenspun of the New York *Times* (November 7, 1969). ". . . In *Downhill Racer* not to win is to lose—in ski racing and in every other facet of life it observes." *Downhill Racer* was generally rated as one of the best sports films ever made and Redford won universal praise. "Redford is a remarkably suggestive actor," Miss Crist wrote in *New York* (November 10, 1969), "a glance in the mirror, the flick of his head, a moment's hesitation revealing depths within; with a gesture he discards the kid-with-ambitions veneer and reveals the sophisticated in-fighter beneath, a moment later bringing a poignancy to the man who has learned a little the hard way but comes upon his major truth in a flash."

A third film with Redford was released in the last weeks of 1969, *Tell Them Willie Boy Is Here* (Universal). The film was written and directed by Abraham Polansky, who returned to Hollywood after nearly twenty years on the infamous political blacklist. Based on an actual event of 1909 in Southern California, the screenplay had to do with the hunting down and killing of a young Paiute Indian by a sheriff who was driven more by the hatred and paranoia of his fellow whites than by the Indian's crime. To some reviewers the film was a masterpiece; others found it a pretentious and overly didactic parable on American race relations. The notices were unanimous for Redford as the sheriff, however. "Redford's 'presence' is magnificent," wrote the *Variety* critic (October 22, 1969), "always suggesting the classically-structured, powerful-but-weak American."

Like *Downhill Racer, Little Fauss and Big Halsy* (Paramount, 1970) was largely a study of competition, but in that film Redford played not a winner but a loser, a womanizing con man who tries to hide his mediocrity by building up a spurious facade as a winner. By the end of the film Redford has lost the big motorcycle race, his girl friend, and his only friend, Little Fauss (Michael J. Pollard). Most critics thought the film suffered from poor direction (by Sidney J. Furie) and tried to exploit too many of the popular subjects and motifs of such films as *Downhill Racer, Easy Rider*, and *Bonnie and Clyde*, but Paul D. Zimmerman of *Newsweek* (October 26, 1970) found it "considerably more than another bike picture." "For all this surface trendiness," Zimmerman wrote, "*Fauss and Halsy* uses its conventions, not for their own sake, but as a way of examining the values of American life. And it explores these values the hard way—by getting beneath the skin of its protagonist. Robert Redford plays Halsy, and if you want to label this movie, then call it a Redford movie. For Halsy is independent, lonely, running, remote, obsessed—all the qualities we have come to expect from a Redford hero."

Since September 12, 1958 Robert Redford has been married to Lola Jean Van Wagenen, and they have three children, Shauna, David James, and Amy Hart. Like his Mormon wife, Redford neither smokes nor drinks. The Redfords maintain a cooperative apartment on the Upper West Side of Manhattan, and they spend about three months a year at their Utah mountain lodge, which the actor designed and built with a friend's help.

Redford is six feet tall, weighs 170 pounds, and has blue eyes and reddish blond hair. Like the characters he plays on screen, he is adamantly individualistic, and he has struck some interviewers as cool and remote. Movie critic Richard Schickel, a longtime friend, provides a more intimate view of the actor, however. In an affectionate portrait of Redford for *Life* (February 6, 1970) he characterized him as a perennial adolescent who has a way of making even his contemporaries feel old and has long referred to himself, "in his many self-satirical moments, as 'the Kid.'" "All he ever does (without meaning to) is remind you of pleasures postponed, risks untaken, life not lived quite as fully as you intended when you used to think of yourself as 'the Kid,'" Schickel

observed ruefully. Still a sports enthusiast, Redford skis, water-skis, rides horses, and drives motorcycles and racing cars. (According to Schickel, most of Redford's friends have suffered bangs, bruises or an occasional fracture while being good-naturedly goaded on to test their daring at Redford's Utah retreat.) He has bought up the land around his Utah home and is developing a winter resort there that he calls Sundance. Some ski lifts are already completed, as well as stables, an outdoor theatre, and a lodge, and in the planning stage are condominiums, a boutique, restaurants, and a movie theatre. Redford makes no effort to hide his distaste for Hollywood, and he claims to have no longtime commitment to an acting career. "I'll stay in acting until I get bored with myself or until I no longer enjoy it," he told an AP interviewer (Toronto *Globe and Mail*, September 14, 1970). "Then I'll get into something else. It won't be a traumatic thing."

References

Christian Sci Mon p13 D 8 '70 pors
N Y Times II p17+ O 26 '69 por
Newsday Wp8+ D 20 '69 pors
Biographical Encyclopaedia & Who's Who of the American Theatre (1966)

REESE, DELLA

July 6, 1932- Singer
Address: c/o Lee Magid, Inc., 5750 Melrose Ave., Hollywood, Calif. 90038

One of the most engaging and personable of today's popular singers is Della Reese, whose warm, relaxed manner and vibrant song delivery have made her a favorite with nightclub and television audiences. A former gospel singer, Miss Reese brings to jump tunes, blues, and even romantic ballads the kind of powerful voice, rhythmic excitement, and fervor associated with gospel singing. She has headlined at top supper clubs from the Copacabana in New York to Cocoanut Grove in Hollywood, and on television she has made hundreds of guest appearances, filled in for Johnny Carson on the *Tonight Show*, and in 1969-70 hosted her own syndicated variety show entitled *Della*. Her songs may be heard on the Jubilee, RCA, ABC, and Avco Embassy labels.

The youngest in a family of five girls and one boy, Deloreese Patricia Early was born on July 6, 1932 in Detroit, Michigan. Her parents were Richard Early, a factory worker, and Nellie Early, a domestic. Mrs. Early was a devout churchgoer, and at the age of six Deloreese was given the opportunity to sing in the junior choir of the Baptist church she attended. Soon she was a featured singer. "I was very small, and I could carry a tune and remember the words," Miss Reese told Dick Kleiner in an interview for the New York *World-Telegram and Sun* (December 18, 1959). "So they had me go on at the end, just before they passed the plate. I was a shill—but for a good cause." When Deloreese was thirteen, Mahalia Jackson came to Detroit for a concert, and she chose the girl to fill in for an ailing soprano in her group. Impressed by the girl's vocal power and verve, Miss Jackson gave her a spot in her gospel choir. For the next five summers Deloreese toured with the queen of the gospel singers between sessions at Miller and North Eastern high schools in Detroit.

Intending to major in psychology, Miss Reese entered Wayne University in Detroit in the fall of 1949, but the death of her mother and the illness of her father forced her to drop out of college at the end of her freshman year to earn a living. "There was no slow transition from adolescence to adulthood for me," Miss Reese told Jack Leahy of the New York *Sunday News* (September 8, 1963). "When my mother died, I immediately became a woman. . . . I had to get out and start making my own way of life."

After moving out of the family home into a small rented room she took a succession of jobs, working briefly as a switchboard operator, a receptionist, and even as a taxicab driver. Meanwhile, she sang with the Meditation Singers, a gospel group she had formed at Wayne State, and occasionally with other well-known performers such as the Clara Ward Singers, the Roberta Martin Singers, and Beatrice Brown's Inspirational Singers. But singing for a living did not occur to her at the time. "I was interested in singing, but I thought of it as something to do when you didn't have anything else to do," she told Don Nelson of the New York *Sunday News* (December 29, 1957). "As far as I was concerned, a regular job in business was still the best." Furthermore, she saw little possibility of making a livelihood as a singer. Gospel singers were lucky to make enough money to cover expenses, and popular singers had to entertain in nightclubs, places that she, like her mentor Mahalia Jackson, felt were compromising to a person of religious beliefs. When she finally decided to try pop singing, it was partly because of the encouragement of the Reverend E. A. Rundless of Detroit's New Liberty Baptist Church, who said to her: "It's not so much what you do as how you feel inside. If you feel that you can do a good job, why not try?"

In or around 1951 she got a job as a hostess-singer at a combination bowling alley-nightclub, and shortly afterward she obtained her first professional engagement at a Detroit nightclub. A newspaper ran a contest in which its readers were invited to vote for a favorite local singer, who would win a one-week engagement at Detroit's Flame Showbar. Miss Reese rallied all her friends, won the contest, and stretched that one victorious week into eighteen. At that time she was married to Vermont Adolphus Bon Taliaferro, a Detroit factory worker, and to make her name fit on the marquee, she shortened it to Pat Ferro. At the end of her run she decided to split her first name; Della Reese has been her professional name ever since.

Among those who caught her act at the Flame Showbar was Lee Magid, a theatrical agent from New York City. When she later sent him a copy of a record she had made on a local label, Magid became her manager and obtained a job for her

DELLA REESE

in New York as a vocalist with Erskine Hawkins' orchestra at a salary of $65 a week. (Magid, who is now based in Hollywood, remains her manager.) Her nine months with the orchestra, in 1953, taught her singing discipline, because Hawkins allowed her only three songs, "Sincerely," "Teach Me Tonight," and "Let Me Go, Lover." To provide some relief from the monotony, she mastered several styles of delivery, singing the songs as jump tunes, blues, or Latin numbers.

In 1954 Jubilee Records signed Miss Reese to a recording contract, and her first release for them, "In the Still of the Night," sold 500,000 copies. Three years later she had her first big hit, "And That Reminds Me," which sold over a million copies to earn her a Gold Record and the *Billboard*, *Variety*, and *Cash Box* awards as the Most Promising Girl Singer of 1957. Around that time she also made her national television debut, on the *Jackie Gleason Show*, followed by several appearances with Ed Sullivan, many nightclub engagements, and a singing role in *Let's Rock* (Columbia, 1958), a youth-slanted film starring Julius La Rosa.

Soon after signing with RCA Victor in 1959, Miss Reese recorded a ballad entitled "Don't You Know?," which won her a second Gold Record. In 1960 she became the first black singer ever to deliver "The Star-Spangled Banner" at professional baseball's annual all-star game. During the early 1960's she played many top American nightclubs, including, in New York, the Copacabana (1960), the Basin Street East (1962), and the Royal Box of the Americana (1963).

Proud of her training in religious music, Miss Reese early incorporated a distinctive feature into her nightclub act, the performance of a Negro spiritual during each set; and in January 1962 she brought the Meditation Singers to the Copacabana with her. The following month she began touring with them in a two-act show entitled "Portrait of Della Reese," which was recorded by RCA Victor and filmed for a TV special by National Telefilm Associates. During the first act Miss Reese introduced gospel singing in words and song with the help of the Meditations and then showed the evolution of blues singing, with the support of her sister, Marie Waters, a blues singer. In the second half of the program she illustrated the gospel and blues beat in popular music by singing standards and selections from her albums.

After hearing one of her early albums on the RCA label, *Della: The Lady is a Tramp*, a reviewer for *Time* (February 8, 1960) wrote that Della Reese "projects a vivid image—that of a tender roughneck who wears her heart square on her agitated chest, where it belongs." Although her romantic ballads are well received by audiences, it is her exciting delivery of jump tunes, blues, and gospels that always brings down the house. Distinctive to her style is an unusually full-bodied voice of seemingly glass-shattering proportions and an eccentric manner of pronouncing lyrics through clenched teeth so that vowels become distorted and extra syllables are added. "Melancholy Baby" comes out "Melancholy Ba-aye-by" and "Put On a Happy Face" becomes "Put-uh On-uh a Happy-uh Face-uh." After hearing her in a Toronto nightclub, Blaik Kirby of the Toronto *Globe and Mail* (November 21, 1968) wrote, "Miss Reese's singing style is definitely mannered, but somehow in a way that seems natural rather than objectionably artificial."

Endowed with an engaging personality, mercurial humor, and earthiness, Della Reese has been in demand for appearances on radio and television. She has performed sixty-eight times on the Robert Q. Lewis CBS radio show and has made more than 300 guest appearances on TV, including the *Ed Sullivan Show*, the *Perry Como Show*, the *Mike Douglas Show*, the *Merv Griffin Show*, the *Joey Bishop Show*, the *Pat Boone Show*, and *Hollywood Palace*. In London she appeared on the BBC *Palladium Show* and with Johnny Carson on Granada TV's *Granada Special*; in Rome she cohosted a television special with Caterina Valente. She has substituted for Johnny Carson on the *Tonight Show*.

Della Reese was therefore eminently qualified to become the first woman to host a TV variety show. *Della* was presented five days a week during the 1969-70 season on TV stations in such major northern cities as New York, Washington, Boston, Detroit, Cleveland, and San Francisco, and in nine southern cities. The hour-long shows, 250 segments in all, were taped and then syndicated to the participating stations by RKO General. The format was light, with an emphasis on entertainment rather than talk. "We want people to snap their fingers and tap their feet, to relax and enjoy themselves. We're not going to settle the world's problems," she told Jo Ann Harris of the Washington *Post* (June 8, 1969), a few months before the show had its première in late August. Besides singing on each show, Miss Reese would introduce two or three guests like Johnny Mathis, Wilson Pickett, Jackie Curtis, John Hartford, or Eartha Kitt.

When her TV show was not renewed for the 1970-71 season, Miss Reese resumed her nightclub appearances. Among the top clubs where she has appeared in recent years are the Flamingo and Sands hotels in Las Vegas, Harrah's Club in Reno

and at Lake Tahoe, Cocoanut Grove in Hollywood, the Fairmont Hotel and Basin Street West in San Francisco, the Fontainebleau Hotel in Miami Beach, the Caribe Hilton in San Juan, and El Morocco in Montreal. She has also performed at the Palace and Apollo theatres in New York, the Michigan Theatre and the Masonic Temple in Detroit, the Chicago and Regal theatres in Chicago, and the Shrine Auditorium in Los Angeles. Besides the United States and Canada, the singer has toured South America, Europe, Japan, and Australia.

Della Reese's popularity as a recording artist has grown apace with her career in nightclubs and television. From 1965 to 1969 she recorded for the ABC label and, since September of 1969, for Avco Embassy Records. In recent years her singles of "Bill Bailey" and "It Was a Very Good Year" have gone over the million mark in sales, and she has recorded a number of other popular single discs, including "Sunny," "Games People Play," and "Why Not Now?" Among her best-selling albums have been *Amen!* and *Story of the Blues* on Jubilee; *Classic Della, Moody, Della by Starlight,* and *Della with Brass* on RCA; *I Like It Like Dat* and *Della Reese Live* on ABC; and *Della on Strings of Blue* and *Black is Beautiful* on Avco Embassy.

Black-haired, brown-eyed Della Reese is five feet eight inches tall with a well-proportioned figure that has been described as "Junoesque." Until the age of nineteen she weighed about 230 pounds, but since that time she has kept her weight between 135 and 165 pounds through almost constant dieting. Around 1951 Miss Reese married Vermont Taliaferro, and she was later married to Leroy Basil Gray, an accountant. Both marriages ended in divorce. According to an August 30, 1961 account in *Variety*, she was at that time married to Mercer Ellington, the son of Duke Ellington. In her 1963 interview with Jack Leahy of the New York *Sunday News* she said that in 1961 she had been briefly married but that the marriage had been annulled when her husband's previous divorce, obtained in Mexico, had been declared illegal. Miss Reese has one daughter, Deloreese, whom, according to the Leahy article, she adopted in 1961. With her daughter, who is nicknamed Dumpsey, she lives in a cliffside house in the Hollywood Hills. In her spare time Miss Reese enjoys sketching, writing prose and poetry, playing chess, collecting clocks, and, of course, listening to music. Her favorite vocalists are Ray Charles, Frank Sinatra, Carmen McRae, Aretha Franklin, and Lena Horne. In 1968 she made her TV acting debut as a discotheque owner in a segment of the ABC program *The Mod Squad*.

References

Ebony 17:107+ Jl '62 pors
N Y Daily News p59 N 12 '69 por
N Y Sunday News Mag p4 D 29 '57 por; p4 S 8 '63 por
N Y World-Telegram and Sun p21 D 18 '59
Toronto Globe and Mail p27 N 23 '68 por
Washington (D.C.) Post D p12 D 4 '70
Who's Who in America, 1970-71
Who's Who of American Women, 1972-73

RIAD, MAHMOUD (rē'äd mä-mōōd')

Jan. 8, 1917- Foreign Minister of the United
Arab Republic
Address: Ministry of Foreign Affairs, Cairo,
United Arab Republic

For almost a quarter of a century the man who has
been Egypt's spokesman on international affairs
has been Mahmoud Riad, the Foreign Minister of
the United Arab Republic. A confidant of the late
Egyptian President Gamal Abdel Nasser, Riad has
continued to serve as Foreign Minister in the present
government headed by Anwar Sadat. After serving in the 1948 Palestine war, Riad was chairman
of the Egyptian delegation to the Israel-Egypt
Mixed Armistice Commission which, under United
Nations guidance, worked out armistice negotiations
following that conflict. At the present time, he is
his country's chief representative during negotiations to bring a permanent peace following the
renewed Arab-Israeli conflict of June 1967.

Mahmoud Riad was born in Egypt on January 8,
1917. He was educated at the Egyptian Military
Academy and at the General Staff College, where
he received his doctorate in engineering. While at
the academy, Riad struck up a friendship with
Gamel Abdel Nasser, who was a year younger than
he. The friendship was cemented when the two
young men later served as instructors at the academy and found that they more or less shared the
same political philosophy.

In 1948, when the Arab states invaded Israel
after that nation proclaimed its independence, Riad
served as an officer in the Egyptian army, where he
impressed his associates as a "nonmilitant military
man." With the defeat of the Arab forces, Riad
entered the world of diplomacy when he represented Egypt at the armistice talks initiated by the
United Nations in late 1948 and early 1949. The
delegations at the armistice talks were half civilian
and half military.

While still in the army, Riad acted as deputy
to Brigadier Seif-ed-Din of the Egyptian delegation. While serving in that post, Riad was one of
those who carried out the original so-called
"Rhodes" formula, which, evolving from forty days
of deliberations, enabled Arab and Israeli delegates
to conduct armistice negotiations without talking
directly to each other.

The painstaking negotiations were held in a hotel
on the Greek island of Rhodes under the guidance
of the United Nations' Dr. Ralph J. Bunche, who
continued the work of Count Folke Bernadotte,
the original mediator who had been assassinated
in Jerusalem. During those forty days, Bunche
shuttled back and forth between the Israeli and
Arab delegations until an armistice was formally
signed on February 24, 1949 by Egypt and Israel.
Although an armistice was proclaimed, no general
peace treaty emerged from the negotiations, and
the Arab nations continued their policies of political
warfare, economic boycott, local incitement, and
blockade of the Suez Canal.

After the armistice Riad, who remained in the
army, was named his government's representative

MAHMOUD RIAD

to the Egyptian-Israeli Mixed Armistice Commission, which was instituted by the United Nations
to help preserve peace along the lines of demarcation. Meanwhile, Riad kept up his close association
with Nasser, who had become convinced that the
future of Egypt and the well-being of her people
lay in the overthrow of the feudal monarchy of
King Farouk. Known for its royal extravagance, the
Farouk regime was rife with corruption and had
long delayed needed reforms.

Led by Nasser, on July 22, 1952, a group of
young officers called the Free Officers Committee
staged a swift and bloodless coup that deposed
King Farouk. Both Riad, who was by then a colonel,
and Anwar Sadat, the present president of the
United Arab Republic, were members of the committee. After the new government was set up, Riad
was named director of Arab affairs in the Foreign
Ministry, and he served in that post until 1955,
when he was named Egyptian ambassador to Syria.
There he played a major role in bringing that nation and Egypt into a political union known as the
United Arab Republic. Although Syria broke away
from the union in 1961, Egypt kept that name.

In 1958 Riad returned to Egypt to serve as
Nasser's counselor on foreign affairs. He remained
in that post until early in 1962, when he was
named Cairo's permanent representative to the
United Nations. As Nasser's chief spokesman at the
United Nations, Riad became embroiled in Egypt's
feud with Israel, using his position for verbal attacks on the Jewish state. He accused Israel of
developing an atomic bomb and materials for bac-
teriological warfare, and he said that he saw no
prospect for conciliation between the two countries.
Riad pointed out that Egypt was committed to returning Israel to the Arab refugees, who were, he
contended, the rightful owners of the land. According to him, the Jewish state was an artificial creation, held together only by foreign aid and charity.

Succeeding Mahmoud Fawzi, a career diplomat,
Riad was called back to Egypt in March 1964 by
Nasser, who named him Foreign Minister. Accord-
ing to the New York *Times* (September 30, 1967),
Fawzi "was better known . . . in the international

diplomatic community, but Riad . . . wielded considerable influence. His close ties with President Nasser's inner circle and his military background were considered crucial factors." As Foreign Minister, Riad drew even closer to Nasser, accompanying him to all major meetings of Arab and African leaders. He also embarked on diplomatic missions throughout the world, including trips to the Soviet Union. Keeping up his personal contacts with the United Nations, he returned to its New York-based headquarters each year to deliver his country's policy speech when the General Assembly convened.

Establishing closer ties with other Arab countries also took up much of Riad's time. In November 1966 he announced that Egypt and Syria had agreed to exchange ambassadors and enter into a defense agreement. The two countries, at odds since 1961 when Syria pulled out of the United Arab Republic, also agreed to take steps "toward political coordination."

The most pressing problem confronting Riad continued to be the steadily deteriorating relations with Israel. The situation came to a head in May 1967, when the United Nations peace-keeping force withdrew at Nasser's insistence. On the withdrawal of the United Nations troops, the Egyptian army quickly reoccupied the Gaza Strip and closed the Gulf of Aqaba to Israeli shipping. On June 5, 1967 full-scale war broke out between Israel and the Arab nations, but within six days the Israelis defeated the Arab nations, captured the Gaza Strip, occupied the Sinai Peninsula to the Suez Canal, and took Old Jerusalem and other Jordanian and Syrian territory. On June 10, 1967 the fighting was halted by cease-fire agreements arranged by the United Nations. According to unconfirmed reports from the Middle East, Riad was a moving force in the negotiations and helped persuade Nasser to accept a cease-fire.

Ever since the cease-fire Riad has labored to achieve what he might consider to be a just peace agreement between the Arab states and Israel. Hopes for peace were once again shattered in 1968, when sporadic fighting broke out between Israel and Egypt, and artillery duels across the Suez Canal became a daily occurrence. When Palestinian guerrillas and terrorists raided Israeli-held territory, Israeli troops retaliated by staging ground forays into Arab lands and by penetrating deeply into the United Arab Republic by air. The crisis took on worldwide implications when the Soviet Union increased its military and economic aid to the United Arab Republic, sent more than 10,000 military personnel to that country, and set up anti-aircraft missile bases there.

In August 1970 the United Arab Republic and Israel agreed to a ninety-day standstill cease-fire. Peace negotiations, under United Nations auspices, began August 25, and on September 28 the Arab world was stunned by the death of Nasser, one of the most commanding and charismatic figures in Arab history. The quest for peace in the Middle East continued, however, with the reins of government passing smoothly to Anwar Sadat, who retained his old friend and comrade-in-arms, Riad, as head of the Ministry of Foreign Affairs.

The largely fruitless negotiations dragged on. As the Arab spokesman, Riad announced that his group would not negotiate directly with the Israelis; instead he insisted that the talks be held under the auspices of the United Nations or of the Big Four: the United States, Great Britain, France, and the Soviet Union. Israeli delegates preferred direct talks with their Arab counterparts, although they did not altogether rule out indirect talks.

Both sides were intransigent concerning conditions for negotiations. The United Arab Republic took the stance that meaningful talks could not get underway until the withdrawal of Israel from Arab territories taken in the June 1967 war, and the return of Palestinian refugees to their lands. Israel, in turn, adopted the posture that any sort of withdrawal was out of the question, unless it received absolute guarantees of her security and the protection of her people. That could only come about, Israeli Premier Golda Meir asserted, when the United Arab Republic proved that it genuinely desired to conclude a "true peace" in the Middle East.

Through the years the indirect negotiations inched on, broken off from time to time by mutual charges on the part of the antagonists of breaches of the cease-fire agreement. Meanwhile, there was an unofficial truce of the Suez Canal, since the cease-fire, which had been renewed up until March 7, 1971, technically expired. A United Nations General Assembly resolution of November 22, 1967 proved to be the first breakthrough in what had been up to then a stalemate. The United Arab Republic offered to abide by the resolution that provided in particular for the withdrawal of Israel's armed forces from "territories occupied" during the six-day war, for an end to the Arabs' state of belligerency against Israel, and for Arab recognition of Israel's sovereignty and borders.

Israel rejected the resolution, maintaining there could be no discussion on borders, the return of Palestinian refugees, or other details before the Arabs showed a willingness to negotiate a peace treaty. Mrs. Meir defined the main points of Israel's position in a statement to the Knesset on December 29, 1970, calling for "our right to defensible agreed and recognized boundaries, united Jerusalem—the capital of Israel—and our maintaining the cease-fire lines until a contractual and binding peace is reached." Israel opposed letting Dr. Gunnar V. Jarring, the United Nations intermediary in the Arab-Israeli conflict, interpret the "withdrawal" clause or determine at what stage in the overall peace settlement Israel would have to pull back its troops from the occupied territories.

Riad charged the United States with frustrating a Middle East settlement through its support for Israel. Instead of honoring its previous commitments to support an armistice, he said, the United States supplied new jet fighters for Israel and failed to insist on Israeli withdrawal from Arab territories as spelled out in the United Nations resolution. According to Riad, because the United States refused to bring effective pressure on Israel, it was to blame for "the complete and very serious deadlock" in the search for peace.

As the negotiations slowly progressed, the antagonists' positions moved perceptibly closer, with both sides making concessions. Although both the United Arab Republic and Israel modified their positions as the negotiations went into their fifth year, Riad did not rule out the possibility of all-out hostilities breaking out again. "We are at war today," Riad said. "We shall be at war for as long as our territory is occupied. Egypt could resume fighting again if it was forced to. We can choose our moment and we naturally reserve the right to liberate our territories."

Mahmoud Riad and his wife, Sawsan, live with their three adolescent sons in what the Foreign Minister has described as a "not too modern" apartment in the exclusive suburb of Zamalek, on an island in the Nile at Cairo. Riad has thinning, dark hair, heavy eyebrows, and a bushy moustache. Of medium height and stockily built, he dresses immaculately in dark suits and discreet neckties, and sometimes wears dark-rimmed and heavy plastic eyeglasses. No matter what the pressures brought to bear on him, he remains a softspoken and deliberate speaker, who never raises his voice. Whenever he gets the chance, he relaxes by going fishing in the Red Sea.

References

N Y Times p2 S 30 '67 por; p2 S 26 '69 por
International Who's Who, 1970-71
Who's Who in the World, 1971-72

RICHARDSON, ELLIOT L(EE)

July 20, 1920- United States Secretary of Health, Education and Welfare
Address: b. Department of Health, Education and Welfare, 330 Independence Ave., S.W., Washington, D.C. 20201; h. 1100 Crest Lane, McLean, Va. 22101

The public career of Elliot L. Richardson has proven his adage that "a Harvard Law Review man can do any job well," for, since leaving Harvard, the Massachusetts lawyer has distinguished himself as an Assistant Secretary of the Department of Health, Education and Welfare (HEW) and as United States Attorney for Massachusetts, both under President Dwight D. Eisenhower; as Attorney General and Lieutenant Governor of Massachusetts; and, most recently, as Under Secretary of State and Secretary of Health, Education and Welfare in the Nixon Cabinet. Aided by his keen intellect and impressive administrative ability, Richardson mastered the complexities of American foreign policy and initiated important administrative reforms during his year and a half as number two man in the State Department, and those talents have stood him in good stead in his most challenging post to date, as HEW Secretary. A mammoth and complex bureaucracy that administers the nation's social welfare programs through such agencies as the Public Health Service and the Social Security Administration, HEW is under constant fire from critics who oppose its programs

ELLIOT L. RICHARDSON

or who accuse it of ineffectiveness and bureaucratic bungling. Much of Richardson's attention since taking office in June 1970 has been directed toward promoting the Nixon administration's controversial Family Assistance Plan, a reform of the department's archaic welfare program.

Descended from early New England settlers, Elliot Lee Richardson was born in Boston, Massachusetts on July 20, 1920 to the late Edward P. Richardson, an eminent physician and professor at Harvard Medical School, and Clara (Shattuck) Richardson. He is related to many of Boston's most prominent families, who made their fortunes and reputations in law, banking, medicine, education, or politics. Although both his grandfathers and several uncles were doctors, and his two brothers followed in their footsteps, Elliot early decided on a career in politics. Like the rest of the family, however, he attended Harvard College.

Richardson claims to have spent most of his time at Harvard drawing cartoons for the Lampoon, but he managed to receive his B.A. degree cum laude in 1941. After spending a short time at Harvard Law School, he found his studies interrupted by World War II. As a first lieutenant in the Fourth Infantry Division of the United States Army, Richardson took part in the landing at Normandy and amassed an impressive record for daring and heroism, receiving a Bronze Star and two Purple Hearts. (His comrades nicknamed him "Lucky" and "Fearless Fosdick.") When he returned to Harvard in 1945, Richardson went on to become editor and president of the Harvard Law Review. In 1947 he was awarded the LL.B. degree cum laude and then clerked for Judge Learned Hand of the United States Court of Appeals in 1947-48 and for Supreme Court Justice Felix Frankfurter in 1948-49. (Frankfurter was so impressed that he proposed Richardson for the presidency of Harvard in 1953, when he was only thirty-three years old.) Late in 1949 Richardson became an associate in the reputable old Boston law firm of Ropes, Gray, Best, Collidge and Rugg, but he found that the private practice of law "didn't match the satisfaction of doing a good job for the public." After a stint as an aide to Massachusetts Senator Leverett Saltonstall in 1953-54 he returned to the law firm until 1957, when President Eisenhower appointed him Assistant Secretary for Legislation in the Department of Health, Education and Welfare. During that tour of duty he wrote the National Defense Education Act and developed legislation on social security, public health, and juvenile delinquency. From April to July 1958 he served as the department's acting head.

Returning to Boston in 1959 after President Eisenhower appointed him United States Attorney for Massachusetts, Richardson quickly earned a reputation as a relentless prosecutor. One of his best-known cases was the tax evasion conviction of Bernard Goldfine, the textile manufacturer whose gifts to White House aide Sherman Adams considerably embarrassed the Eisenhower administration. Richardson returned to his law practice in 1961 as a partner in Ropes and Gray. A year later he lost a Republican primary contest for state attorney general to Edward Brooke, now a United States Senator, but in 1964 he was elected Lieutenant Governor of Massachusetts. Not content with ceremonial duties, Richardson took an active role as Governor John Volpe's lieutenant, coordinating the state's health, education, and welfare programs, and heading the task force that initiated the state's Mental Health Act. Elected Attorney General in 1966, Richardson pushed through consumer protection laws and crime prevention legislation and prosecuted consumer fraud and unfair trade practice cases.

In 1969 Elliot Richardson was chosen Under Secretary of State at the recommendation of William P. Rogers, Nixon's newly appointed Secretary of State. The two men had developed a close rapport and mutual confidence while serving together in the Eisenhower administration, and Rogers declared that the Massachusetts lawyer would act as his "alter ego" in the State Department. Although he had little formal experience in foreign policymaking, Richardson was launched into an active and vocal role soon after being sworn into office on January 24, 1969. In February, while representing the United States at a Paris meeting of the Organization for Economic Cooperation and Development—a forum of nineteen European nations, Canada, the United States, and Japan—Richardson pledged the Nixon administration to a policy of increased free trade. In September 1969 the administration entrusted Richardson with an important exposition of its foreign policy when, speaking before the International Studies Association in New York City, he announced that "a cohesive and dynamic new policy" was "being crafted," which would take a more flexible and less entangling attitude to the country's overseas commitments in an effort to avoid a new Vietnam. Richardson took an active part in the policymaking and preliminary negotiations that attended the United States-Soviet Strategic Arms Limitation Talks (SALT) that opened in Helsinki in November 1969, and he represented the United States at a NATO meeting that month to consider a Warsaw Pact proposal for an all-European security conference in 1970.

As Under Secretary of State, Richardson attended meetings of the National Security Council and served as chairman of the council's under secretaries committee. By the time that he left the State Department in June 1970 many observers acknowledged him to be the department's most influential voice at the White House, with an especially close working relationship with Nixon's key foreign policy adviser Henry A. Kissinger. Richardson's attempts to introduce personnel and administrative reforms into the labyrinthine depths of "Foggy Bottom" endeared him to the department's dissident, "young Turks." Following their suggestions, he decided to revitalize the largely moribund Foreign Service Board and became its head in June 1969. In that post he set out to make more effective use of foreign service personnel and to bring more unity to the various branches of the foreign service, including the United States Information Agency, the Agency for International Development, and the Peace Corps.

Although rumors of a change at HEW had been circulating for some time, practically everyone—including Richardson—was surprised when President Nixon chose him to replace Robert H. Finch, who became a White House adviser. Declaring that he was "returning to an old love," Richardson was sworn in by the President on June 24, 1970. His record as a progressive Republican made him a popular choice at HEW, and Nixon asserted that his credentials as a strong innovative administrator made him "the best qualified man in the country" to put the department's tangled affairs in order.

When Richardson took over at HEW he found it in a state of confusion, with outrageous instances of administrative disorder, duplication of services, inefficient budgeting of funds, and a sadly demoralized staff. A civil rights aide had been ousted, apparently for his liberal views, Education Commissioner James E. Allen Jr. had been fired after openly opposing the Vietnam war, and mass resignations were being received from officials who felt that the administration was shifting to the right on domestic problems. Many top-echelon positions needed to be filled, especially in the Office of Education. Since Richardson had served as Assistant Secretary a few years after the department was established in 1953, HEW had doubled in size, and as a result had become unwieldy and snarled in bureaucratic red tape. With an annual budget of some $65 billion, HEW employs over 100,000 persons who administer 260 federal programs, and it finances more than 40,000 institutions and agencies.

To put HEW's administrative house in order, Richardson set out to promote simplifications in the processing of grants, consolidation of existing programs, and, in keeping with President Nixon's concept of the "New Federalism," decentralization of authority to give greater administrative responsibility to state and local governments. He made the administration's Family Assistance Plan (FAP) the centerpiece of HEW legislation, calling it a progressive attempt to "end the depressing cycle of dependency" that has characterized previous welfare programs. FAP would establish a federally financed minimum annual income at the rate of $1,600 for a family of four, require recipients to register for job training, and provide various work incentives. The bill had passed the House in the spring of 1970, but in the Senate it met a hostile reception, both from conservatives who thought it would increase the welfare rolls and from liberals who felt that it differed little from previous plans. Richardson's meticulous and deliberate presentation of the bill before the Senate Finance Committee won respect from the Senators and from HEW aides, but the bill was bogged down by filibusters and never came to a vote in the Ninety-First Congress. It was scheduled for early action in the Congress that convened in January 1971.

Committed to Nixon's middle-of-the-road stand on school desegregation, Richardson has had to face both the traditional animosity of the South toward HEW and the criticisms of civil rights activists. In August 1970 he announced that the department had abandoned its policy of cutting off federal funds to school districts that refused to desegregate. Instead, the department would turn over cases to the Justice Department for legal action, which, he contended, would be more effective. At a news conference in January 1971 Richardson asserted that more schools had been desegregated in 1970 than in any year since 1954, although some reporters questioned the validity of the statistics used by the HEW Secretary. He also announced that for the first time the South exceeded the North in its desegregation rate. In answer to protests that the government was doing little to prevent the discriminatory firing of black teachers and principals when schools are consolidated and integrated, Richardson said that his department had issued warnings to offending schools. Like the rest of the administration, Richardson opposed the Democratic-sponsored Emergency Health Personnel Act, which was signed into law on December 31, 1970. The HEW head had asked Congress to defer action on the bill, because he contended that the program, designed to bring doctors into urban ghettoes and poor rural areas, would not further the health reform package to be introduced by the administration in 1971.

Richardson has been active in Boston civic affairs and is a former president of Boston's World Affairs Council, secretary and trustee of the Massachusetts General Hospital, and chairman of the Greater Boston United Fund Campaign. He is a trustee of Radcliffe College and a member of the board of overseers of Harvard College. Richardson has published articles in the *Harvard Law Review*, *Atlantic Monthly*, and the *Boston University Law Review*. He is a member of the Council on Foreign Relations, a fellow of the American Academy of Arts and Sciences, and a fellow of the American Bar Foundation.

In public Elliot Lee Richardson often appears to be the epitome of the "Boston Brahmin"— aristocratic, coolly reserved, and possessed of an assurance verging on arrogance. His intimates, however, know him to be a warm, witty man who loves parties, adventurous travel, and outdoor sports. Richardson is six feet tall and keeps trim with tennis, skiing, and canoeing. He also enjoys fishing and birdwatching. On August 2, 1952 he married Anne Francis Hazard, a graduate of Radcliffe College, and they have three children, Henry, Nancy, and Michael. The HEW Secretary is an inveterate doodler and an accomplished watercolorist. His church is the Unitarian.

References

> Fortune 84:88+ O '71 pors
> N Y Post p22 Je 13 '70 por
> N Y Times p44 Je 8 '70 por
> Washington (D.C.) Post F p1+ Ja 3 '71 por
> Who's Who in America, 1970-71
> Who's Who in American Politics, 1969-70

RIKLIS, MESHULAM

Dec. 2, 1923- Corporation executive
Address: b. c/o Rapid-American Corp., 711 5th Ave., New York 10022; h. 5 E. 80th St., New York 10021

Meshulam Riklis, the chairman of the board of the Rapid-American Corporation, the Glen Alden Corporation and, until 1969, of the McCrory Corporation, is a spectacular performer in the world of corporate finance. An Israeli immigrant, he began his career in the early 1950's as a teacher of Hebrew, working part time as a research analyst in a Minneapolis brokerage house. Within less than ten years he had gained control of a multi-million dollar conglomerate, including one of the largest retail chains in the United States, applying what he has called "the effective nonuse of cash," or, the technique of using credit to acquire undervalued companies whose assets could be used for further acquisitions. One acquaintance, quoted by Oscar Schisgall in *The Magic of Mergers; The Saga of Meshulam Riklis* (Little, 1968), has said of Riklis: "He is like a chess player whose sole objective is to win the game. He plans the moves ahead carefully. But he also plans alternate moves. If one fails he is ready with another. What drives a man like him is the *excitement* of the game."

An eighth-generation descendant of Baal Shem Tov, the founder of the Hasidic movement, Meshulam Riklis is the only son of Pinhas and Betty (Guberer) Riklis. He was born on December 2, 1923 in Istanbul, Turkey, where his father, then the export manager of the Jaffa citrus exchange, had gone on business. Soon after his birth, the family returned to Palestine, where Meshulam and his sister Aviva (now Mrs. Joseph M'Aman) grew up in a moderately well-to-do section of Tel Aviv, in a cultural and intellectual atmosphere. Riklis' business acumen was already evident when, as a boy, he made kites and sold them to his friends, later expanding his enterprises to include the sell-

MESHULAM RIKLIS

ing of marbles and the raising of silkworms for profit.

Riklis was educated at the Herzlia Gymnasium, which his father had also attended, and which has nurtured a number of Israel's leaders. A bright student, concerned more with practical matters than with abstract discussion, he showed a special aptitude for mathematics and tutored his school-mates in that subject. After graduating, he entered a kibbutz, but finding that life in an agricultural cooperative did not appeal to him, he left after a year. In 1942, after serving for a time as codirector of youth activities and military training at the Herzlia Gymnasium, he joined the British Eighth Army. Rejected for officer training because at eighteen he was considered too young, he served for four years as chauffeur and assistant to Jewish chaplains in the combat zones of North Africa and Italy. After his discharge in 1946, Riklis, now a married man, took a job as a clerk with an export firm but found that his homeland did not afford him the opportunities he desired to make a big splash in the world of business and finance.

After some deliberation, Riklis decided in 1947 to move to the United States, with accumulated savings of about $3,000. He studied for a year at the University of New Mexico and then, to obtain more specialized training in finance, transferred to Ohio State University at Columbus, where he became a member of Pi Mu Epsilon, the honor society in mathematics. To make ends meet, he and his wife took jobs as teachers of Hebrew. In one of his courses at the university Riklis learned that a number of business firms had cash assets and receivables exceeding the total value of their stock, and he concluded that a businessman could build a corporate empire through the judicious acquisition of such undervalued companies.

After obtaining his B.A. degree from Ohio State in 1950, Riklis began to work for a master's degree there, but lack of finances forced him to interrupt his graduate work before he was able to complete his thesis. Moving to Minneapolis in 1951, he and his wife took jobs as teachers of Hebrew at the Talmud Torah School. Since his

teaching schedule enabled him to hold two jobs, Riklis also worked part time as a junior security analyst in the research department of the Minneapolis stockbrokers Piper, Jaffray, and Hopwood. According to Palmer Jaffray, one of his former employers, he "worked harder and asked more questions than any man in the office." After several months as an analyst he obtained a stockbroker's license. His teaching job at the Talmud Torah School—which served some of the wealthiest Jewish families in Minneapolis—helped him to obtain a number of customers, and his recommendations generally paid off, largely as a result of a rise in stock market prices in 1952. Within a year, Riklis' income had increased from $50 to $400 a week. Meanwhile he was looking around for an opportunity to enter the world of corporate finance.

In 1953 Riklis organized an investment syndicate of about a dozen partners and after thorough investigation persuaded its members to acquire a controlling interest in the undervalued Marion Power Shovel Company, which he felt was an ideal base for acquiring other companies. The syndicate bought 10,000 shares of the company's stock but, to Riklis' dismay, sold them a few months later at a 30 percent profit. On Riklis' recommendation the Minneapolis syndicate next invested $300,000—representing 30 percent of the stock and a seat on the board of directors—in Balcrank, Inc., a Cincinnati manufacturer of diversified appliances. More concerned with immediate gain than with long-range goals, the partners again sold out, this time for a profit of 100 percent.

Setting his sights on a more ambitious project, Riklis made plans for the syndicate to acquire control of the highly respected Gruen Watch Company of Cincinnati. Controlling interest in the company, whose assets included a factory in Switzerland valued at $5,000,000, could be obtained for about $1,500,000. It was his plan to sell the factory in Switzerland and invest the proceeds in expanding and diversifying the company's activities. Riklis arranged for the syndicate to gain control of Gruen by pledging $750,000 and borrowing an equal amount, and he invited Edward Weitzen, a former vice-president of the Bulova Watch Company, to become the company's new president. After Weitzen took office in January 1955, however, he overruled Riklis' plans for diversification and sale of the Swiss factory. His position was upheld by a sixteen-to-four vote of the company's directors, who apparently felt that Riklis had no interest in Gruen except as a tool for acquiring other companies. After his defeat, Riklis resigned from the board of directors.

In the fall of 1955 Riklis persuaded a group of investors to put up $400,000 to acquire a controlling interest in the Rapid Electrotype Company of Cincinnati, the second-ranking manufacturer of electrotype plates in the United States, which had liquid assets of about $1,600,000. Riklis personally negotiated with the company's aging chief executive, Peter Schotanus, who agreed to sell his 10 percent of the company's stock after Riklis offered him $28 a share—$10 above the market price. To obtain an equity in the syndicate's holdings, rather than merely acting as paid adviser, Riklis invested his own assets, amounting to $25,000, in the new venture. Elected board chairman and chief executive officer of Rapid Electrotype—his first corporate executive position —in November 1955, he moved the company's headquarters to New York City and settled with his family at Kings Point, Long Island.

Intending to expand further in the office equipment business, Riklis acquired some 40 percent of the Smith-Corona Typewriter Company's stock for Rapid Electrotype. When, however, his efforts to gain control of Smith-Corona were frustrated by that company's management, he quickly divested himself of its stock. He next directed his attention to the American Colortype Company, a manufacturer of greeting cards and metal signs. Although the company had immediate assets of over $10,000,000, a controlling interest could be obtained for an investment of $4,500,000. Using the proceeds from the sale of the Smith-Corona stock as a partial payment, Riklis gained control of American Colortype in 1956, becoming its board chairman and chief executive officer. His goal to obtain a solid base on which to build his projected corporate empire was realized in January 1958, when Rapid Electrotype and American Colortype were merged under his direction into the Rapid-American Corporation.

As president and board chairman of Rapid-American, Riklis steadily expanded its operations. IIis first step was to acquire a controlling interest in Butler Brothers—also known as the BTL Corporation—a West Coast merchandising firm. While retaining control of BTL, Riklis sold its assets in 1959 and used the proceeds to buy United Stores, which controlled the McCrory-McLellan chain of variety stores. In 1960 BTL Corporation, United Stores, and McCrory-McLellan were merged into a single operating company, the McCrory Corporation, under the control of Rapid-American, which owned some 30 percent of its stock. The new corporation, which comprised some 600 stores and had assets totaling about $70,500,000, elected Riklis as its chairman.

Acquisitions for McCrory over the next two years included the Oklahoma Tire and Supply Company (OTASCO), a chain of some 400 stores in the South and Southwest; National Shirt Shops, a chain of men's furnishings; and the lucrative women's specialty store chain, Lerner Shops. With the acquisition of over 50 percent of the stock of the H. L. Green chain of variety stores, the McCrory-McLellan stores became McCrory-McLellan-Green. Riklis received a boost in prestige when in May 1962 the Ford Foundation made a $5,000,000 investment in the Rapid-American Corporation.

With the recession of 1962, Riklis took advantage of the decline in stock prices and bought more McCrory stock for Rapid-American, increasing its holdings in the McCrory Corporation to 51 percent. Soon, however, Riklis' corporate empire was faced with a struggle for its survival. An article in *Barron's* in the fall of 1962, entitled "Meshulam Riklis Is Trying to Build a Retail Empire in a Hurry," charged that McCrory stock was vastly overpriced. The McCrory Corporation's earnings fell far short of what company officials had predicted, and as a result, stock prices sharply declined. To acquire control of McCrory, Rapid-American had borrowed heavily from banks, which were now pressing for repayment. For a time, Rapid-American appeared to be nearing the brink of bankruptcy. Resisting demands that he resign, Riklis managed to obtain a respite of eight months from the bankers—long enough to enable him to diagnose the ills of his enterprises and take remedial steps. He dismissed McCrory's professional managerial staff, liquidated much of its inventory, eliminated stores that were not showing a profit while concentrating on those that showed promise, and sold most of Rapid-American's operating properties. By mid-1963 Riklis' enterprises had withstood the test of survival.

To enhance the strength and prestige of Rapid-American and McCrory, Riklis negotiated for the acquisition of a controlling interest in the Glen Alden Corporation, a highly respected conglomerate, headed by his long-time friend Albert A. List. Its enterprises at the time included coal, textile, leather tanning, and building materials industries, as well as the RKO-Stanley Warner movie theatre chain. In October 1964 the McCrory Corporation acquired a 33 percent interest in Glen Alden, increasing its holdings to 49.3 percent a few months later. Riklis succeeded List as chairman of the board of Glen Alden in October 1965.

Having decided to turn the Glen Alden Corporation into a consumer packaged goods company, Riklis engineered its acquisition of control of such dry-goods concerns as International Playtex and the BVD Company, while arranging for it to divest itself gradually of its coal, leather tanning, and motion picture theatre interests. In September 1968 Glen Alden acquired what has been described as its "crown jewel," an 88 percent interest in the $300,000,000 Schenley Industries, one of the leading distillers of liquor in the United States. In concluding the Schenley transaction, which took about three years to complete, Riklis relied largely on promissory notes, in keeping with his principle of "buying companies with their own money."

For the McCrory Corporation, Riklis obtained control of S. Klein Department Stores and of the women's specialty shops Best & Company, in 1966. The latter firm was liquidated in 1970, when its New York real estate was sold to Aristotle Onassis. Other firms acquired by Riklis in recent years include Leeds Travelwear and the men's clothing manufacturers Joseph H. Cohen and Sons and Cross Country Clothes, which are under the direct control of Rapid-American. In July 1971 Riklis offered to put up $10,000,000 to back a dissident group of former associates of Bernard Cornfeld, the ousted founder of Investors Overseas Services Ltd. (I.O.S.), in trying to wrest control of that company from its present management. He revealed that in 1970 a subsidiary of Rapid-American had acquired 450,000 shares of I.O.S. stock, intending to gain control of the company.

In June 1969 Riklis relinquished the chairmanship of the McCrory Corporation to Samuel Neaman of S. Klein, while retaining a vice-chairmanship. He continues to serve as chairman of Rapid-American and Glen Alden and is, with an annual salary of $375,000, one of the highest-paid executives in the United States. With a 10.9 percent stock interest, he is virtually able to control the entire $1.7 billion Rapid-American complex. Although Riklis has been subjected to lawsuits and a barrage of criticism, he has taken pains to remain within the limits of legality and to avoid conflict with government authorities. In his view, a merger should never be a mere concentration of power but should aim toward greater efficiency of operation, improved service to the public, increased earnings for stockholders, and more benefits for employees.

In 1966 Riklis obtained his M.B.A. degree from Ohio State University after completing his thesis, describing the steps he took to build his corporate empire. His wide-ranging philanthropic activities include contributions to civil rights movements and refugee relief. He has endowed a chair at Brandeis University, contributed a building to the Jewish Theological Seminary, and made funds available for the reconstruction of his old school, Herzlia Gymnasium. On his initiative a program was instituted making available twenty $4,000 scholarships each year to children of McCrory Corporation employees. Among the honors that Riklis has received over the years is the 1965 Man of Achievement award of the Anti-Defamation League of B'nai B'rith; the 1965 Distinguished Achievement award of New York University; and the 1967 Eternal Light medal of the Jewish Theological Seminary.

Meshulam Riklis has been a citizen of the United States since 1955. He and his wife, the former Judith Stern, whom he married on December 17, 1944, make their home in a six-story town house on New York's fashionable East Side. They have two daughters, Simona and Marcia, and a son, Ira. A short man of slight build, with graying hair, Riklis—who is known as Rik to his associates—still speaks with a trace of an Israeli accent and enlivens his conversation with anecdotes and quotations from the Talmud. In spite of a nagging ulcer, he appears low-keyed and relaxed. Riklis collects modern art. His other recreational activities include tennis, golf, boating, skiing, bridge, listening to music, and reading books on mathematics and history. The key to his success is said to be his talent for cultivating personal relationships. According to Schisgall, Riklis "prefers the diplomatic way. He never uses a club. He relies on logic, on persuasiveness, on a friendly approach."

References

Forbes 107:24+ Mr 15 '71
N Y Times III p1+ F 7 '65 por
Time 91:98+ Ap 5 '68 por
Schisgall, Oscar. The Magic of Mergers;
  The Saga of Meshulam Riklis (1968)
Who's Who in America, 1970-71

RILES, WILSON (CAMANZA)

June 27, 1917- Educator; California State Superintendent of Public Instruction
Address: b. California State Department of Education, 721 Capitol Mall, Sacramento, Calif. 95814; h. 4246 Warren Ave., Sacramento, Calif. 95822

The first black man ever to hold statewide elective office in California is Wilson Riles, who heads the state's educational system, a jurisdiction comprising more than 4,500,000 children in 1,100 school districts, an annual budget of $2.5 billion, and an administrative staff of 2,300. Riles, previously director of California's educational programs for the disadvantaged, was elected State Superintendent of Public Instruction and Director of State Education in November 1970, when he scored a stunning upset over conservative firebrand Max Rafferty, the incumbent. Although Riles is a Democrat and Rafferty a Republican, the election was nonpartisan, in accordance with California law, which aims at keeping politics out of education. Although liberal by Rafferty's standards, Riles is really a moderate, a cool, quiet administrator, primarily interested in the welfare of school children, who prefers to avoid or defuse such politically inflammatory issues as the forced busing of children for integration's sake. He has made it a matter of policy not to issue "a mandate . . . for the integration of schools" because "when you're saying that a black child has to sit next to a white child to learn, I don't believe that." Riles's post automatically makes him a regent of the University of California, a trustee of California's state college system and secretary and executive officer of the State Board of Education.

Wilson Camanza Riles is the son of Wilson Roy Riles and Susie Ana (Jefferson) Riles. He was born on June 27, 1917 near Alexandria in backwoods Louisiana, where his father was a crew chief in a turpentine camp. Orphaned at eleven, he was adopted by a childless couple who had been friends of his parents. After graduating from McDonogh High School in New Orleans, Louisiana, he moved to Flagstaff, Arizona, where relatives of his worked in sawmills. In Flagstaff he "discovered" Arizona State College (now Northern Arizona University), where he paid his way by working in a National Youth Administration program. "I would never have made it had not that school been there," he told Wallace Turner of the New York Times (November 6, 1970). "I don't know what I would have made of my life without that. So I get out of sorts with people who want to limit opportunity for the young."

Sensitive to racial prejudice, Riles made a practice at Arizona State of arriving at classes early, so that anyone who sat next to him would do so by his or her own choice. His extracurricular activities were in the college's honorary dramatic fraternity and writers club. The person who most influenced him in his choice of his lifework was Mildred Kiefer, one of his professors. After taking his B.A. degree, in 1940, Riles began his professional career as an elementary school teacher. From 1943 to 1946 he served in the United States Army Air Corps, in the ranks of private and corporal, and after his discharge he returned to Arizona State to earn his M.A. degree in school administration.

After taking the advanced degree, in 1947, Riles worked in Arizona public elementary schools as a teacher and administrator for seven years. At the same time he did volunteer work with the American Friends Service Committee. Riles, from childhood an active member of the African Methodist Episcopal Church, later said that he had been "really influenced" by the Quakers with whom he worked. "There's God in every man. If you appeal to the best in people, they respond with the best."

Almost always, when Riles left a position it was at the urging of his wife. "I would tell him," she has recalled, "'I can't stay in this little town any longer' or 'It's time for you to move along.'" In 1954 he moved to Los Angeles to become executive secretary of the Pacific Coast region of the Fellowship of Reconciliation, an old, established religious peace organization.

In 1958 Wilson Riles left the Fellowship of Reconciliation to become chief of the California State Department of Education's Bureau of Intergroup Relations, an equal-opportunities watchdog. "This was prior to the Fair Employment Act," he later recounted. "So what I did was work with boards and point out that whenever you don't hire the most qualified person, you're hurting the students. There were no loud speeches. We just worked and worked."

In 1965 the California legislature created a federally subsidized $100,000,000 compensatory education program for disadvantaged children, and Riles was placed in charge of the program. Four years later Max Rafferty, then in his second term as State Superintendent of Education, promoted Riles to Deputy Superintendent in charge of special education. "What he really succeeded in doing," Riles told Louie Robinson in an interview for an article in *Ebony* (May 1971), "was to take me away from the program and put me in a window-dressing position."

Rafferty was a man on fire with the opinion that permissiveness and progressivism were undermining learning and contributing to social disorder. Known nationally as the most vociferous champion of old-fashioned hickory-stick schooling among American educators, he spent his energy as State Superintendent chiefly, or at least most noticeably, in denouncing the liberal humanistic approach to education and preaching a return to small community school systems, financed as minimally as possible by state or federal government and oriented around drilling in the three R's and patriotic indoctrination. He also denounced teacher strikes, sex education in the schools, drug abuse by students, campus demonstrations, and administrative softness in handling those problems.

Riles too is against unstructured, standardless schooling, but he viewed Rafferty's rhetoric as simplistic and divisive, a counterproductive answer

WILSON RILES

to California's mounting educational problems. He felt, for example, that it was senseless to talk about community control without first talking about adequate resources. "Suppose you drew another ring around Watts and said, O.K., you people, this is yours, you operate the schools," he once observed. "That sounds democratic, except for one thing: that area has a very low tax rate, and to impose on people a job, a duty, a responsibility without any money is one of the greatest copouts we can perpetrate."

He came to the conclusion that "public education in California can't stand four more years of Max Rafferty" and that he could not "in conscience" shirk challenging Rafferty at the polls if no one else was willing and able to do it. After sounding out leading liberal Democrats and Republicans to assure himself that there was reasonable hope of forging a successful anti-Rafferty coalition, Riles consulted his wife and children about his decision to run for State Superintendent. "My family didn't want me to get hurt," he later revealed. "But I told them, 'Listen, I was born in rural Louisiana. I know every problem you can imagine. Talk about working your way through college—I worked my way through elementary school. The worst things that can happen to me have already happened.'"

In announcing his candidacy, in February 1970, Riles accused Rafferty of using his nonpartisan post as an instrument of political ambition (Rafferty had staged an energetic, noisy, unsuccessful campaign for the State Senate in 1968); of not following up his talk about "quality education" with significant attempts to implement that ideal; and obstructing his (Riles's) special education programs. He added that he too deplored the widening abuse of drugs and student and faculty dissidence but that he would not make "political" issues of them.

In a field of nine candidates, Rafferty and Riles finished first and second, respectively, in the June 1970 primary, with 48.6 and 25.2 percent of the votes cast. In the campaign preceding the November runoff election, Rafferty had the support of conservative Republican Governor Ronald Reagan, while Riles won the endorsement not only of liberals but of some important figures generally considered to be outside the progressive camp, most notably S. I. Hayakawa, the president of San Francisco State College. Such endorsements as Hayakawa's deflated an apparent abortive attempt by Rafferty to link Riles with the extreme left. Riles concentrated his attacks on the financial problems of the California school system. In the five years beginning in 1966, California moved from sixth place down to twenty-fourth among the states in expenditures per pupil in elementary and secondary schools. That decline in educational budget has been chiefly attributed to Governor Reagan, so that Riles knew that it would remain even if he were in Rafferty's place. But he argued that Rafferty aided and abetted the problem, while he, Riles, would fight it. He related the financial problem to what he alleged was a regression in reading scores of California children, but Rafferty contended that under his administration California's national ranking in student achievement had risen.

At the polls on November 3, 1970, the voters of California elected Riles over Rafferty, 3,156,144 votes to 2,681,831. The following day the victorious candidate told Wallace Turner of the New York Times (November 6, 1970): "The main problem now is to work out a way to get funds for the schools. Bond issues and school finance measures have failed all over the state. We need to depend on the state general fund, not local property tax revenues." In a press conference on December 6, 1970 he elaborated: "The ideal would be to have the schools financed one-third by the local tax payers, one-third by the state, and one-third by the federal government. But until we can get that kind of contribution from the federal government, the state's share should be at least fifty percent. I can see no justification for the present system whereby the kind of education a child gets depends on where in the state he lives. I don't think that's equity." He also went on record in favor of state support for parochial and other private schools, in the form of transportation, textbook, and lunch subsidies viewed as "child benefits." And he said he would encourage every school district in the state to designate several of its schools as "experimental," to offer parents more options regarding the kind and location of their children's schooling. But the State Department of Education would have to play a more unifying role, because individual school districts were spending millions of dollars blindly on experimental programs that had already proved failures elsewhere. "In education we have the most fragmented research efforts of any institution I know about."

Riles took office at the beginning of January 1971. In his first meeting with his staff he said that he planned to achieve an integrated department without using strict racial quotas. "If there are 15 percent minorities in the state and you go out and look at your staff and you don't have 15 percent minorities, then you know you're not doing it." Regarding school integration, he later expressed

the view that, while "integration is a good concept," its promotion "purely as a way to help minority students" is not good. "It is never sold on the right basis: to be able to function in a multiracial society is just as important for the white child as it is for the black child."

Later in January, Riles announced that he would press for early childhood education, instruction about drugs, and more relevant curricula. He said that he planned to reorganize the State Department of Education in such a way as to facilitate accountability of local school districts to the State Curriculum Commission and to enable the department to serve as a center and clearinghouse of research into school programs and their results. At a news conference in March he expressed his opposition to the "open classroom," the informal, unstructured school advocated by such educators and education critics as Harvey Scribner, Charles Silberman, and the Reformists. "There are these middle-class people who will teach their youngsters anyhow, and they want them to go to school and have a nice, unpressed experience. But there are disadvantaged youngsters too. Let's not kid them. Let's teach them what they have to have in society in order to make it." Schools should establish goals for each grade "in performance terms."

Wilson Riles and Mary Louise Phillips were married on November 13, 1941. They have four children: Michael Leigh, Narvia (Mrs. Ronald Bostick), Wilson C. Jr., and Philip Gregory. Riles is six feet four inches tall, weighs about 200 pounds, and has deep brown skin, brown eyes, black hair flecked with gray, and a clipped mustache. His presence is quietly imposing and his manner confident, self-possessed, and alert. In repose his face is earnest and brooding, but it easily breaks into a warm smile, and in his relations with others he is outgoing, congenial, and democratic. Riles is a member of Phi Delta Kappa, the education honor society, and his favorite recreation is golf, although he seldom has time for it nowadays. After dinner at home he often returns to his office to work into the late evening at the job for which he is paid $35,000 a year. In 1965 George Pepperdine College bestowed an honorary doctor of laws degree on him.

References

Ebony 26:54+ My '71 pors
Life 70:30+ F 26 '71 pors
N Y Post p22 N 14 '70 por
N Y Times p28 N 6 '70 por

ROBINSON, FRANK

Aug. 31, 1935- Baseball player
Address: b. Baltimore Orioles, Baltimore Memorial Stadium, Baltimore, Md. 21218

BULLETIN: On December 2, 1971 Frank Robinson was traded by the Baltimore Orioles to the Los Angeles Dodgers.

The time is ripe for the first black manager in major-league baseball, and the man with the most obvious qualifications for that distinction is Frank Robinson, the slugging superstar of the American League's Orioles. The Baltimore right fielder, now a mellow, sage seventeen-year veteran of the base paths, was reputed to be a "problem" player, given to inscrutable moods, when he was with the Cincinnati Reds of the National League in the late 1950's and early 1960's. But even then he was a perennial All-Star and a leader to his teammates, especially the younger ones, and statistics attested to his power at the plate. In what Steve Jacobson of *Newsday* (October 8, 1970) called "one of the worst misjudgments of talent in baseball," Robinson was traded to the Orioles in 1965. He went on to lead Baltimore to the world championship and to become the first winner of the Most Valuable Player award in both leagues. Robinson's slugging was still at the level of his career totals going into the 1971 season: a .303 batting average (seventh among active players), 1,455 runs batted in, and 475 home runs (fifth among active players and tied, with Stan Musial, for twelfth all-time). In addition to playing in the regular season, Robinson has been managing the high-calibre Santurce Cangrejeros of the Puerto Rican League winters since 1968, and a major-league all-star team managed by him defeated the New York Yankees in an exhibition game in the spring of 1971.

The youngest of ten children of Ruth Shaw, Frank Robinson was born on August 31, 1935 in a hospital in Beaufort, Texas. His father was Frank Robinson, the third and last husband of Ruth Shaw, who had previously been married to Burton Shaw and John Grisby. Father and mother separated when Frank was an infant, and when he was four Ruth Shaw moved, with her children, to California, finally settling in Oakland, where she still lives.

In his autobiography, *My Life Is Baseball* (Doubleday, 1968), written with Al Silverman, Robinson described the West Oakland neighborhood where he grew up as "a rough, mixed neighborhood, mostly Negroes but also Mexicans and a lot of Orientals." He went on: "It wasn't a bad, Harlem-type ghetto and there was never any trouble over race. . . . I never ran into any problem over being a Negro until my first year in the minor leagues." Growing up, he was, by his own description, "a tall, gangling, skinny kid," and a "loner." Off the athletic field, the center of his life, he spent his leisure sequestered in the darkness of motion picture theatres, when he had the price of admission. Because his mother seldom had money for anything beyond bare necessities, he usually earned his own spending money by delivering newspapers.

Robinson was good at sandlot and schoolboy sports in general, but baseball was always his forte. "Football and basketball," he has said, "for me were things to do while waiting for the baseball season." His first and most influential baseball mentor was George Powles, a ubiquitous Oakland coach dedicated to helping young people, especially the disadvantaged. Robinson played under Powles with the Bill Erwin Post 237 team of the American Legion Junior League and with the Mc-

FRANK ROBINSON

Clymonds High School team, as third baseman and, occasionally, pitcher. In high school he played varsity football as a defensive back briefly, until his injuries caused him to quit. Playing as a forward with the high school basketball team—on which Bill Russell, who later went on to pro fame, was a teammate—he made All-City in his senior year. His scholastic record was much less brilliant. "I never felt schoolwork was that important," he has explained. "I knew what I was going to be—a professional baseball player—and that was it."

Signed by Cincinnati scout Bobby Mattick when he graduated from high school, in 1953, Robinson was assigned to the Reds' Class C Pioneer League team in Ogden, Utah, where he was shocked and hurt to discover that he couldn't go to the movies because the town's only motion picture theatre was for whites only. On the diamond he began at third base but was soon switched to the outfield, at his request. His fielding at that time was only fair, but his speed was good and his arm superior, and at the plate he batted .348, led the team in home runs (seventeen), and hit twenty doubles and six triples. He batted in eighty-three runs and scored seventy himself.

With Columbia, South Carolina of the Class A South Atlantic League, Robinson batted .336 and hit twenty-five home runs in 1954 and tallied .390 and ten homers in 1955. His two years in the South were not entirely pleasant, because of segregation and because of the racial slurs occasionally hurled by fans in such cities as Macon and Augusta, Georgia. When he was called up to Cincinnati in 1956 he was, in his own words, "in a shell," and one of the team's coaches described him as "a lost soul," with "no companionship, no guidance." But he batted .290, hit thirty-eight home runs, and was named National League Rookie of the Year. He maintained a batting average just under .300 for five years, and during that period his other averages included thirty-three home runs and ninety runs batted in per season. In 1960 his slugging average or extra-base-hit percentage, was .595, the highest in the league.

Robinson's daring batting stance, with body close to the plate and head over it, makes him vulnerable to "bean" balls. When with the Reds he led the National League six years in times hit by pitched balls (total, 118). The worst beaning he suffered occurred in June 1958, when a fast ball thrown by Camilo Pascual hit him in the head. Opposing infielders often injured him too, sometimes possibly as retaliation for the threat he posed to them with his reckless, flashing spikes, especially when sliding into second to break up a double play. He is still a demon of the base paths, although he seems to evoke less animosity with his running and base-stealing now. "Everybody knows he's a good hitter," Eddie Kasko, an infielder with the Reds, once observed, "but I never saw a baserunner with greater instincts. Faster yes, better no."

Bill DeWitt replaced Gabe Paul as general manager of the Reds after the 1960 season. Trying to tighten the club's budget, DeWitt asked Robinson to accept a cut in his high salary, and in the argument that followed accused him of not working hard enough on the field. Robinson, a conscientious person with a deceptively insouciant style and an antipathy for "false hustle," noted in his autobiography that he has "never forgotten" the remark by DeWitt "that ruined our relationship forever."

In his reckless bachelor days, Robinson occasionally allowed himself to fall into situations of which he is now ashamed. The worst was a fracas in a Cincinnati restaurant in February 1961. In that incident he pulled out a pistol to frighten off a man threatening him with a knife. Arrested for carrying a concealed weapon, he was dismissed with a reprimand and a $250 fine, but not before spending the night in jail—because, according to Bard Lindeman in the *Saturday Evening Post* (August 27, 1966), Bill DeWitt did not respond to a telephone call for help. In Lindeman's paraphrase, DeWitt said that "the middle of the night was no time to have to deal with a bail bondsman and a desk sergeant." The incident hardened the animosity between the general manager and the outfielder.

"A man learns from his stupidities," Robinson commented after the gun incident, and he deliberately redeemed himself by his performance on the diamond the following season. With a .323 batting average, 124 runs batted in, thirty-seven homers, and twenty-two stolen bases (out of twenty-five attempted), he paced the Reds to their first pennant in two decades and was voted the Most Valuable Player in the National League. "I've never seen such a dramatic change in one player," Jim Brosnan, then a teammate, later observed. "Frank became the club's leader that year."

The best year of Robinson's career was 1962, when he had a .342 batting average, 136 runs batted in, 134 runs scored, thirty-nine home runs, and eighteen stolen bases. His worst was 1963, when, plagued by injuries, he had a .259 average, twenty-one home runs, and ninety-one runs batted in. In 1964 he batted .306, hit thirty-eight doubles, six triples, and twenty-nine home runs, and batted

in ninety-six runs. His career fielding average to that point was .986. In 1965, his last season with the Reds, his batting average was .296, he hit thirty-three homers, and he batted in 113 runs. During his decade in the National League his annual averages had been .303 at the plate, 101 runs batted in, thirty-two home runs, and thirty-two doubles.

Ostensibly because the Cincinnati club needed pitching strength, the Reds traded Robinson to the Baltimore Orioles in December 1965 in exchange for pitchers Milt Pappas and Jack Baldschun and outfielder Dick Simpson. Dick Sisler, then the Reds' manager, later commented: "The front office wasn't aware of how many ways he [Robinson] helped the club. Johnny Edwards was the player representative . . . but when the team played baseball, Robinson was the leader. He played when he was hurt . . . never asked out. The only rest he got was when I sat him down."

Robinson, who had been paid a record salary in Cincinnati, contracted for an even higher one, $67,500, when he arrived in Baltimore, and he immediately proved that he was worth it. In the 1966 season he paced the Orioles to the American League pennant and took the league's triple batting crown, with a .316 average, forty-nine home runs, and 122 runs batted in. Two feats by Robinson stood out during the season: he hit the first home run ball to go clear out of Baltimore's Memorial Stadium, and in a game against the New York Yankees in Yankee Stadium he preserved an Oriole victory with a spectacular leaping catch that landed him over the grandstand wall, sprawling amid the fans in the bleachers.

Hitting two home runs, Robinson led the Orioles to victory over the Los Angeles Dodgers in four straight games in the 1966 World Series. The honors heaped on him in addition to the Baseball Writers Association of America's Most Valuable Player award and the Babe Ruth award for best series player included the Hickok Professional Athlete of the Year award, the Associated Press' Male Athlete of the Year citation, the Sid Mercer Memorial award, the Clark Griffith award, the Rogers Hornsby Award, and Sport magazine's Man of the Year citation. The Orioles raised his salary to $100,000.

Robinson's worst accident on the base paths was a collision at second base on June 27, 1967 in which he suffered a brain concussion that resulted in double vision. When he returned to the lineup on July 29 his vision had not yet completely cleared, but by the end of August his eyesight was almost back to normal. Despite the handicap, he batted second in the American League, with .311, and he hit thirty home runs and batted in ninety-four runs. His twenty-seventh home run was the four-hundredth of his career—a mark reached by only three other active players in the American League. But the Orioles, meanwhile, had slumped, and the slump carried over into 1968. In the latter year Robinson, waylaid by the mumps and hampered by an arm injury, fell to a .268 batting average and only fifty-two runs batted in.

Resurging in 1969, Robinson batted .308, hit thirty-two home runs, and batted in 100 runs, and the Orioles won the American League pennant—but lost the World Series to the New York Mets. In 1970 Robinson averaged .306 at the plate, hit twenty-five home runs, and batted in seventy-eight runs. Along with fellow hitters Don Buford, Brooks Robinson, Paul Blair, and Boog Powell and pitchers Dave McNally, and Jim Palmer, he boosted the Orioles to another pennant, and in the World Series the Orioles defeated the Cincinnati Reds, 4-1. In June 1971 Robinson became the eleventh player in major league history to hit 500 home runs. That season he helped the Orioles to win their third American League pennant in a row, but the team lost the World Series to the Pittsburgh Pirates.

The Santurce Cangrejeros, managed by Robinson since 1968, are virtually a major league team, rated above Triple-A. In Robinson's first season in Puerto Rico, in the winter of 1968-69, the team won the league pennant, and the exhibition all-star team coached by him beat the New York Yankees at Fort Lauderdale, Florida on March 13, 1971, 7-4. Big leaguers who have played under him as well as with him agree that he manages with the same do-or-die effectiveness with which he plays. "He'd be a heck of a manager," Dave Johnson, an Oriole teammate and a member of Robinson's all-star team, observed after the game with the Yankees. "He understands people. He has real good temperament. He wants to win, and people feel that and react to it."

Frank Robinson and Barbara Ann Cole were married on October 28, 1961. They have two children, an adopted son, Frank Kevin, and a daughter, Nichelle. The Robinsons have two homes, one in Baltimore, where they live during the baseball season, and the other in the La Dera Heights section of Los Angeles. Robinson is six feet one inch tall and weighs about 193 pounds. His legs are thin but his arms and shoulders are muscular. He has been described as "confident, in a relaxed way," as a "gentle ribber" with a "wry sense of humor," and as "not outgoing," although he does not hesitate to approach younger players who need encouragement or friendly moral support. His favorite recreations are going to the movies, listening to music, and playing with his children. On the diamond he bats and throws righthanded. His 1971 salary is $130,000, the highest of the Orioles and one of the highest in the history of baseball. To those who have criticized him for what they consider his lack of racial militancy, Robinson has responded: "I am happy to see progress in civil rights, but I don't believe in mixing sports with civil rights. . . . That is my way. Everybody goes his own way."

References

Look 34:83+ My 5 '70 pors
Sport 47:48+ Mr '69 pors
Sports Illus 18:33+ Je 17 '63 pors; 33: 26+ O 5 '70 pors
Robinson, Frank. My Life Is Baseball (1968)

ROGERS, FRED M(cFEELY)

Mar. 20, 1928- Television producer and host; clergyman
Address: b. Mister Rogers' Neighborhood, WQED, Pittsburgh, Pa. 15213; h. 1300 Beechwood Blvd., Pittsburgh, Pa. 15217

An estimated four million young children daily enjoy a half hour of quiet rapport with soft-spoken Fred Rogers, the creator and host of the Peabody Award-winning *Mister Rogers' Neighborhood*, a low-keyed Public Broadcasting Service show that outdraws its raucous, high-budgeted commercial competitors in juvenile programming, including the animated cartoon offerings. Rogers, trained in music, theology, and psychology, entered television out of concern for the medium's impact on preschool emotional development. After a decade of experience in both commercial and noncommercial television, he began developing his present show in the early 1960's, for the Canadian Broadcasting Corporation. In the United States the Eastern Educational Network started carrying the program in 1965-66, and the following year National Educational Television picked it up. The series, which is produced at station WQED in Pittsburgh, is now aired in color by the more than 200 stations in the Public Broadcasting Service network, and within the areas served by those stations it is watched consistently in one-third of the households, according to a Harris survey. In terms of families with children under six watching public television, it has an audience pull of 58 percent.

Sensitive to the feelings and fears of children aged three and up, Rogers attempts to provide a friendly, emotionally healthy haven for growth in the midst of television's commercial din. He is less concerned with teaching numbers, letters, shapes, or colors than with reinforcing the young listener's sense of his intrinsic worth and dignity as a unique individual and with helping him face common childhood crises with courage rather than terror or bewilderment. Serenely and with artful effortlessness, *Mister Rogers' Neighborhood* explores the developing child's interior drama through songs, puppetry, and conversation—with a mixture of fantasy and reality, which are clearly differentiated. Rogers, executive producer of the show, writes the scripts and the songs, gives voice to most of the puppets, and talks to his young audience with unmistakable respect and empathy. "Before we got so mobile in this country," he has said, "there was always a grandparent or an uncle who could give a child undivided attention. I think that I'm this adult male who stops in."

Fred McFeely Rogers was born in Latrobe, Pennsylvania on March 20, 1928 to James Hillis Rogers and Nancy (McFeely) Rogers. His father was a prosperous manufacturer of silica brick, which is used in steel furnaces. With his sister, Nancy (Mrs. Daniel Gordon Crozier), Rogers grew up in Latrobe. At Latrobe High School he was president of the student council and editor of the yearbook, and while in high school he wrote

FRED M. ROGERS

features for the local newspaper, the Latrobe *Bulletin*.

After graduating from high school, in 1946, Rogers studied briefly as a Romance language major at Dartmouth College before matriculating as a music composition major at Rollins College in Winter Park, Florida. His original intention was to begin studies for the Presbyterian ministry immediately upon graduation from Rollins, but what he saw on television made him change his mind. Appalled by the children's shows offered on the home screen, he decided to enter the television field with the ultimate aim of helping to upgrade them.

In 1951 Rogers took his bachelor's degree in music *magna cum laude* and found employment with the National Broadcasting Company, where he knew Niles Trammel, then president of the network. At the NBC television studios in New York City he was at first an assistant producer of the *Voice of Firestone* and the *NBC Television Opera* and later the network floor director of *Your Lucky Strike Hit Parade* and the *Kate Smith Hour,* among other shows. In 1953 he went to nascent noncommercial television station WQED in Pittsburgh and a year later he launched on the station a daily hour-long program, *Children's Corner,* which he produced, wrote, and performed. The show, which ran on WQED for seven years, won the 1955 Sylvania Award for the best locally produced children's program in the country, and NBC aired thirty segments of it in 1955 and 1956.

While working at WQED, Rogers attended Pittsburgh Theological Seminary, where he won the Jennie Rigg Barbour Award and the Homiletic Prize. He received the bachelor of divinity degree *magna cum laude* in 1962, and shortly afterward the Pittsburgh presbytery of the United Presbyterian Church ordained him, charging him specifically with the mission of working with families, and especially children, through the mass media.

From WQED, Rogers went to the Canadian Broadcasting Corporation in Toronto, Canada. The progenitor of his present *Mister Rogers' Neighborhood* show was *Misterogers,* a fifteen-minute daily program aired over the CBC in 1963-64. The show, lengthened to half an hour, was broadcast in Pittsburgh in 1964-65, and the following year the Eastern Educational Network bought 100 of the completed programs. When production funds ran out in 1967, stations carrying the show announced its imminent cancellation. Audience response was so strong that new funding was sought, and the Sears, Roebuck Foundation came forward with a grant of $150,000. National Educational Television matched the sum, and a new series of *Misterogers' Neighborhood,* as the show was then called, went into production for national distribution. Sears, Roebuck Foundation grants, renewed periodically, remain the chief support of *Mister Rogers' Neighborhood,* and the Corporation for Public Broadcasting now contributes to both production and distribution costs.

A typical program in the *Mister Rogers' Neighborhood* series opens with Fred Rogers arriving "home" and singing "Won't You Be My Neighbor?" while changing from business to leisure attire. He chats realistically about things of interest to children, usually including some childhood fear or crisis, such as the arrival of a new baby, the death of a family pet, moving to a new house, or the notion that one might be sucked down the drain with the bath water. In some instances he reassures his audience dramatically, as when he demonstrates that haircuts don't hurt by submitting to one on camera or when he takes the terror out of medical injections by receiving one in view of his audience. Then he goes to the Neighborhood of Make Believe to deal with the same theme or problem, often whimsically, on the fantasy level. The Neighborhood of Make Believe is inhabited by friendly puppets, including King Friday XIII, and visited by human guests. The latter include, regularly, Betty Aberlin, the program's ingenue, and, occasionally, famous leaders in the arts or other fields. Among the visitors to give command performances at Make Believe Castle have been pianist Van Cliburn, opera baritone John Reardon, and blind saxophonist Eric Kloss (who dispelled childhood misconceptions about sightlessness, such as its being a punishment for naughtiness). Others received in royal audience by King Friday have included Garry and Barry Nelson, the twin basketball stars, who helped make the point that the uniqueness of individual personality transcends physical similarities.

In a booklet designed to help adults understand some of the ways *Mister Rogers' Neighborhood* "encourages children to grow," Rogers and his associates point out that Mister Rogers constantly assures the child watching him: "There's only one person in the whole world like you, and I like you just the way you are." But he also reminds the child what he has in common with other children, helps him recognize jealousy, rage, sadness, and trust as "facets of loving and being loved," and demonstrates to him that "feelings are mentionable as well as manageable." The show "encourages sustained watching and listening and feeling" as "skills essential to learning" and stimulates "creative play," which is as essential to a child's "personality and cognitive development," as creative work is to fulfillment for adults. It instills the hope-building concepts that "each age of life has value" and that "each person within himself or in affiliation with others can achieve constructive change for mankind's good."

Rogers plans his shows in collaboration with psychologists at the Arsenal Family and Children's Center, a division of the Western Psychiatric Institute at the University of Pittsburgh, where he has done graduate work in child care and development and where he is a consultant in creative media for children. Margaret B. McFarland, the director of the center, after spending many hours observing the interaction between Rogers and the children at the center, said: "I'm deeply impressed with the support he is able to give them in working with the task of growing up or in coping with the problems that confront them. Their responses to this program are different than to the usual television entertainment for children. Children tend to talk to Mister Rogers during the program; their faces are mobile, reflecting varied feelings; they are prone to get up and respond actively to suggestions. Children seem to respond to Mister Rogers' leaving the television screen as though they have been separated from a meaningful adult." Johnny Costa, the musical director of *Mister Rogers' Neighborhood,* has explained Rogers' success with children this way: "Grownups say to kids, 'Get out of my way. I've got important things to do.' Here's a man who cares, and these kids know it. He says, 'You're you, and you're worth something.'"

His friends attest that off camera Rogers speaks and acts in exactly the same easy, gentle manner that he does on television. But beneath his cheery, peaceful demeanor is a seriousness and intensity, especially when he is talking about the "grave responsibility" of anyone who programs for children or about those commercial children's shows that bombard their impressionable audiences with violence and unwittingly teach them to get their way by manipulating others or to value some huckstered toy or other product over their own inner resources. Even some well-intentioned quasi-educational programs sometimes go too far, he believes, in treating young children like "trained seals" rather than as "thinking, understanding human beings."

"Primarily, I believe, we must approach it [children's programming] with a sincere respect for the child and his very existence," Rogers explained in an interview for an article in *Presbyterian Life* (February 15, 1969), adding that there should be required training in an institute for children's programming. "We'd never think of putting anybody on the air to do the news who didn't know how to pronounce Vietnam. But we put on the most important programming, as far as I'm concerned, with people who don't know what their own audience is really dealing with."

That Rogers knows what his audience is dealing with is the consensus of thoughtful critics, including Eliot A. Daley, who wrote in *Look* (December 2, 1969): "His face-to-face personal encounter with the individual child elicits an uncanny rapport. . . . Rogers takes great pains to provide a secure framework for a fantasy laboratory within which children can exercise the capacity for imaginative thought that will later power them to insight and accomplishment in adult affairs. What sets *Mister Rogers' Neighborhood* apart from other television experiences children enjoy (or suffer) is that it enables their fantasy to become a time of growth rather than diversion."

Rogers has recorded six albums for children: *King Friday XIII Celebrates* (made in the early 1960's and now out of print), *Won't You Be My Neighbor?* (1967), *Let's Be Together Today* (1968), *Josephine, the Short-necked Giraffe* (1969), *You Are Special* (1969), and *A Place of Our Own* (1970). All were released by Small World Enterprises Inc. Nineteen of the songs he wrote for his recordings and television programs were published, primarily for the benefit of parents and other adults involved in the development of children, in *Mister Rogers' Songbook* (Random House, 1971). The songs include "Everybody's Fancy," "Wishes Don't Make Things Come True," and "Sometimes People Are Good" ("But the very same people who are good sometimes/Are the very same people who are bad sometimes").

In addition to the Peabody Award for best children's television program (1969), *Mister Rogers' Neighborhood* has received, among other honors, three Emmy nominations (two in 1968 and one in 1969) and a *Saturday Review* television award (1970). The *Saturday Review* citation praised Rogers for his "uncompromising respect for the integrated growth and unhurried development of the growing child" and the program for "sensitizing and opening them [preschool children] to the essential mutuality of the civilized human condition on its affective, emotional, and cognitive levels."

Fred Rogers is six feet tall, weighs 155 pounds, and has blue eyes and neatly trimmed and combed black hair. He always, at least on television, wears a tie, with jacket or sweater. Unhurried but brisk in his daily pace, he confesses to "a compulsion about being on time." One of his favorite desserts is apple pie with ice cream. He does not smoke or drink hard liquor, but he takes an occasional glass of wine because his wife likes to serve it on festive occasions. His preference is for sacramental wine, because "it tastes like soda pop." Beyond his own television program, Rogers devotes considerable time and energy to the general movement for the protection of children against harmful television fare. At the 1970 White House Conference on Children he was chairman of the panel on mass media, which recommended that the government establish an organization able to oppose effectively television stations and sponsors who exploit the gullibility of children, and he has addressed and consulted with Action for Children's Television, a national group that wants the FCC to ban commercials and other huckstering from children's television and to require all stations to broadcast a minimum number of hours for all age groups.

Fred Rogers and Joanne Byrd were married on July 9, 1952. They have two sons, James, born in 1959, and John, born in 1961. Mrs. Rogers, a pianist, sometimes helps her husband with his compositions. The Rogers live most of the year in a home they own in the Squirrel Hill section of Pittsburgh, from which Fred drives to station WQED and the Arsenal Family and Children's Center. The family also owns a house on Nantucket Island, where it spends its summer vacations. During the vacations, Rogers blocks out his programs for the coming television season, working, preferably, through midnight into the small hours of the morning. For recreation, he swims and boats with his sons or walks in the surf with them, collecting stones polished by the sea. Indoors, he and his wife enjoy playing his new songs on two old pianos. Calling his work with children on television "a direct offering of care," he has said: "This is the kind of work that I always wanted to be involved in. This is no stepping stone for me. People say, 'What's next?' and I say, 'This is next.' "

References

Look 33:102+ D 2 '69 pors
N Y Times II p21+ N 16 '69 por
Nat Observer p1+ Ag 4 '69 por
Newsweek 73:97+ My 12 '69 por
Parade p14 My 9 '71 pors
Washington (D.C.) Post D p1 Jl 7 '69 pors

RUCKELSHAUS, WILLIAM D(OYLE) (ruk'əls-hous)

July 24, 1932- United States government official; lawyer
Address: b. Environmental Protection Agency, Washington, D.C. 20460; h. 11124 Luxmanor Rd., Rockville, Md. 20852

At a time when all men and all nations face the common threat of a dangerously deteriorating life-support system on earth, the man who holds the most comprehensive authority over environmental pollution control in the United States is William D. Ruckelshaus, director of the Environmental Protection Agency. Ruckelshaus became familiar with many of the problems of pollution control during the early 1960's as a member of the Indiana Attorney General's staff, drafting the Indiana Air Pollution Control Act of 1963 and prosecuting corporations and municipalities under its provisions. After one outstanding term in the Indiana legislature, in which he was elected majority leader, the Republican lawyer made an unsuccessful attempt to unseat United States Senate Democrat Birch E. Bayh, in 1968. Ruckelshaus joined the Nixon administration early in 1969 as an assistant attorney general and was chosen in November 1970 to launch the newly-created Environmental Protection Agency, which was established to centralize regulatory powers formerly dispersed among many governmental agencies.

During the year that the Environmental Protection Agency has been in operation Ruckelshaus has revealed himself to be a vigorous enforcer of water and air quality standards, and he has infused his agency with an enthusiastic spirit that observers liken to that of the Peace Corps in its early days. He acknowledges, however, that he can accomplish his job only if society drastically changes its attitude toward the environment. "We must all learn that we are the victims of a point of view . . . which has long been obsolete," the EPA director observed in a recent speech. "This viewpoint holds that man can conquer nature. We have clung to this vision with such tenacity that we now inherit the spoils of a three-hundred-year war against nature."

Heir to a family tradition of politics and law, William Doyle Ruckelshaus was born on July 24, 1932 in Indianapolis, Indiana to John K. and Marion (Doyle) Ruckelshaus. His family has been prominent in Republican politics in Indiana since the early 1900's when his grandfather, a county prosecutor, was Republican county chairman. His father, who was active in shaping the platforms of every Republican convention between 1920 and 1960, considered running for the United States Senate in the 1940's but decided that a Roman Catholic could not win.

At Portsmouth Priory School in Rhode Island, Ruckelshaus was an all-state football and basketball player until a football injury to his right knee ended his participation in school-boy athletics. After two years at Princeton Ruckelshaus was inducted into the United States Army because, he has recalled, his father was chairman of the local draft board and was concerned over his lack of application to his studies. Two years in the Signal Corps as a drill instructor apparently had the desired effect, for Ruckelshaus returned to Princeton University and obtained the B.A. degree *cum laude* in 1957.

Having decided on a law career, Ruckelshaus earned an LL.B. degree from Harvard in 1960. He was admitted to the Indiana bar the same year and joined his family's Indianapolis law firm of Ruckelshaus, Bobbitt, and O'Connor, where he remained until 1968. In 1960 he was also appointed a state deputy attorney general, and in 1963 he became chief counsel of the Attorney General's office. His environmental control activities there were conducted in conjunction with the state board of health.

After forming a Republican Action Committee and leading a reorganization of the Marion County party, Ruckelshaus made a stunning debut as a political candidate in 1966, when he was elected to the Indiana House of Representatives by a wide margin. During his initial year in the legislature he became the first freshman Representative ever elected majority leader, and Indiana political reporters voted him the year's most outstanding Republican legislator and first year legislator. His political aspirations received a setback in 1968, however, when he lost by 62,639 votes to incumbent Birch Bayh in a bid for the United States Senate.

Ruckelshaus was one of a number of defeated Republican candidates to be brought into the Justice Department by Attorney General John N. Mitchell after the 1968 election. As head of the civil division, he handled negotiations with angry student demonstrators who gathered in Washington to protest the Cambodian invasion in the spring of 1970. In contrast to the administration's hard-nosed response to the November 1969 antiwar protests, Ruckelshaus' attitude was conciliatory, and he persuaded Mitchell to let the demonstrators hold a rally behind the White House. Following his success at avoiding a violent confrontation in the Capital, Ruckelshaus was called upon to mediate with demonstrators in New Haven, Connecticut during the Black Panther trial and to tour college campuses for the Justice Department in order to improve communications with students.

During the early days of Nixon's Presidency, it was generally conceded that the administration was failing to display a strong commitment to environmental quality control. However, as the ecology movement mushroomed in the United States and the White House felt mounting pressure on the issue from political opponents—especially Senator Edmund Muskie, front-runner for the 1972 Democratic Presidential nomination—the administration's stance grew more responsive. In July 1970 President Nixon sent to Congress reorganization plans for the establishment of an Environmental Protection Agency that would absorb portions of the departments of the Interior, Agriculture, and Health, Education and Welfare, as well as several other agencies. The new agency was to have an annual budget of $1.4 billion and a staff of 5,800 employees. By centralizing environmental control in one body operating independently of any Cabinet department, the Nixon administration hoped not only to create efficiency but to eliminate conflict of interest over the pollution issue, for in the past departments had often acted both as industry promoters and as industry regulators. For example, the Department of Agriculture, which tends to champion the cause of farmers, was the agency charged with policing their use of pesticides.

Ruckelshaus was named director of the Environmental Protection Agency on November 6, 1970, and his appointment was approved by the Senate on December 2, 1970, the same day that the new agency officially opened. Ruckelshaus lost little time in showing that he meant to enforce the regulatory powers assigned to him. On December 10 he shocked a convention of big city mayors in Atlanta, Georgia when he announced in a speech that Atlanta, Detroit, and Cleveland would be given 180 days to stop polluting interstate waterways or face federal court action. Ruckelshaus claimed that those three cities had fallen behind previously negotiated schedules to bring their sewage treatment plants up to certified federal standards. The mayors subsequently retaliated by pointing out that they had not received promised federal funding. While acknowledging that hundreds of millions of dollars authorized by Congress to expand municipal sewage treatment facilities had so

WILLIAM D. RUCKELSHAUS

far failed to reach cities across the nation, Ruckelshaus insisted that municipalities must be held responsible for adhering to established water standards whether or not they receive federal assistance. Furthermore, he predicted confidently that money allotted under new legislation on water pollution control would be distributed.

Cities have not been the only water quality violators singled out by Ruckelshaus. As of the summer of 1971 he had filed suits with the Justice Department against several industrial polluters, including United States Plywood Champion Papers, Jones and Laughlin Steel, ITT-Rayonier, and ARMCO Steel. The EPA director was given wider regulatory control than that afforded by recourse to individual court actions when a new permit system was enacted on July 1, 1971, under the authority of a seventy year old law regulating obstructions to navigable waterways. Some 40,000 United States companies dumping wastes into rivers and bays are now required to detail the content of the effluent before securing a permit that is issued by state pollution control agencies and approved by the EPA. If an industry's wastes do not meet water quality standards it will be required to adhere to a strict cleanup schedule or lose its permit.

In December 1970 Ruckelshaus had his first major confrontation with an air polluter, the Union Carbide ferroalloy plant of Marietta, Ohio, which had become a symbol of corporate resistance to pollution control. The federal government first became concerned about the Union Carbide plant in 1967, when a Public Health Service study showed that the factory's soot and sulphur dioxide emissions were causing a sharp increase in respiratory diseases among inhabitants of surrounding Ohio and West Virginia towns. Union Carbide refused to cooperate with the federal government in submitting to inspections, and in April 1970 the Ohio plant was ordered to adhere to a cleanup schedule set by a federal pollution abatement conference. The company was instructed to reduce sulphur dioxide emission by 40 percent by October 1970 and by 70 percent by April 1972 and to reduce fly ash emission by 25 percent by September 1971. Union Carbide did not meet the October 1970 deadline and in December informed Ruckelshaus that it would not be able to meet the other deadlines. The EPA director ordered the firm to meet the 40 percent reduction immediately by burning low-sulphur coal and to meet the rest of the timetable as stipulated. Union Carbide announced that it could comply with the immediate reduction, but that it would have to meet the rest of the schedule by closing parts of the Marietta plant and laying off 625 employees. Ruckelshaus has expressed disbelief that the company could not find a satisfactory alternative to the layoffs, and he has refused to back down in the face of what Ralph Nader has termed "environmental blackmail."

Although the Union Carbide case might at first glance seem an unmitigated case of corporate villainy, the company does have serious problems that it shares with other industries trying to comply with air pollution standards. Low-sulphur fuels are more expensive and are often in short supply, and a commercially feasible method of extracting sulphur oxides from fuel in a plant has yet to be discovered. Soot, on the other hand, can be removed with comparative ease, but many cost-conscious companies are reluctant to install scrubbers to remove ash unless they can install sulphur oxide removal equipment at the same time. Ruckelshaus, however, has urged industry to use the technological equipment available without waiting for the ultimate technology. To encourage industries to cut down on their emissions of sulphur oxides, the Nixon administration submitted legislation to Congress in 1971 for a graduated sulphur oxide tax.

Another technology that has yet to be perfected is the production of a non-polluting automobile engine, but Detroit has been ordered to reduce carbon monoxide emission 90 percent by 1975 under provisions of Senator Muskie's 1970 Clean Air Act. In May 1971 the automobile industry informed Ruckelshaus that it could not meet the 1975 deadline. Without Congressional approval the EPA director is empowered to extend the deadline for one year, but as of late 1971 he had made no decision on the matter.

Even if the automobile industry does perfect a clean engine by 1975, it will not be on the market in time to alleviate the problems of the states, which were instructed by Ruckelshaus in May 1971 to meet strict nationwide clean-air standards by July 1, 1975. Authorized by the Clean Air Act of 1970, the standards set the maximum amount of sulfur oxides, soot, photochemical oxidants (the irritating chemicals in smog), carbon monoxide, and nitrogen oxides (released by most fuels when burned) per cubic meter of air. In many major American cities adherence to the regulations would entail restrictions on automobile use, the implementation of low-pollution public transportation systems, and higher electricity costs that would be passed on to the consumer.

Although the major thrust of the EPA is directed toward air and water pollution control, Ruckelshaus has taken action on other environmental issues. In March 1971 he requested the Interior Department to delay granting a permit for construction of the controversial trans-Alaska pipeline, pending a thorough study of an alternative route through Canada that may be less hazardous to the environment. While conservationists applauded that move, they were not so happy when, a few days later, Ruckelshaus refused to enact a total ban on DDT and the herbicide 2,4,5T. Reporting that he found the chemicals were not an imminent hazard to humans, the EPA director announced that they would be subjected to further studies, along with the pesticides dieldrin, aldrin, and mirex.

On May 12, 1962 William D. Ruckelshaus married Jill Elizabeth Strickland, and they have five children—Catherine, Mary, Jennifer, William, and Robin. Ruckelshaus' first wife, a classmate at Harvard Law School, died early in 1961. A husky man, six feet four inches tall and weighing 195 pounds, Ruckelshaus relishes sports and considers himself the best bass fisherman in North America. In public the EPA director is often bookish and even solemn, but his friends, who call him "Ruck," describe him as a witty storyteller. Ruckelshaus was voted Man of the Year by the Indianapolis Junior Chamber of Commerce in 1967. He is a member of the American Political Science Association, the Indianapolis Council on Foreign Relations, and the Columbia Club of Indianapolis. His religion is the Roman Catholic.

References

> Look 35:20+ My 4 '71 pors
> N Y Times N 12 '70 por
> Who's Who in America, 1970-1971

SADAT, ANWAR (EL-)

Dec. 25, 1918- President of the United Arab Republic
Address: The Presidency, Cairo, United Arab Republic

On September 28, 1970 Egyptians were thrust into a frenzy of grief by the death of Gamal Abdel Nasser, Egypt's leader for almost two decades and the most powerful figure in the Arab world in generations. Yet with an impressive show of political stability, the reins of government passed smoothly to Anwar Sadat, who was sworn into office on October 17, 1970 for a six-year term as president of the United Arab Republic (Egypt's official name since 1958). Sadat, a close personal friend and loyal supporter of Nasser, was one of the original group of Egyptian army officers who began plotting with Nasser in the late 1930's for the overthrow of the feudal monarchy that finally took place in 1952. (Most of the other dozen plotters are dead or have lapsed into obscurity.) Sadat's role in Nasser's Egypt was primarily that of a publicist for the regime, and he served as editor of the semiofficial newspaper *Al Gomhuriya* for a time and as Nasser's representative on visits to many nations. He also held posts in the government and was vice-president when Nasser died.

When Sadat was elected to the presidency many observers prophesied that he would exert little real power, but within a year he had aborted a coup, purged the government of his rivals, and emerged as a strong and popular leader.

Anwar el-Sadat was born on December 25, 1918 in Talah Monufiya, a village in the Nile Delta, to a military hospital clerk and his Sudanese wife. The Sadats were poor but devout Moslems, and they saw to it that Anwar attended a local religious primary school, where he studied the Koran. He received his secondary education at a school in Cairo.

As a youth Sadat longed to become an army officer and to oust the British, who continued to hold considerable power in Egypt even after their protectorate was formally abolished in 1936. When the Abbassia Military Academy was opened to members of the lower and middle classes in 1936, Sadat was admitted, and it was there that he met Gamal Abdel Nasser, who was just eleven months his senior. The two soon became close friends. In the winter of 1938, after graduating from the military academy, Sadat, Nasser, and ten other officers stationed at the garrison town of Mankabad in upper Egypt formed what Sadat has described as a "secret revolutionary society dedicated to the task of liberation." Their group became the nucleus of the Free Officers Committee that seized power from the Farouk regime some fourteen years later.

To weaken the hold of the British over neutral Egypt in World War II, Sadat collaborated clandestinely with the Germans, but his efforts met with little success. His assignment of smuggling a cashiered Egyptian general into German hands was bungled when first a getaway car broke down and then an airplane crashed on takeoff. The general was captured and imprisoned by Egyptian authorities. Then Sadat began working with two inept Nazi spies in Cairo who, it became apparent, were more interested in drinking and women than in spying. One of their escapades led to their arrest along with Sadat, and in October 1942, following a court-martial, the Egyptian army officer was dismissed from the service and imprisoned.

Sadat remained in a detention camp for two years while his fellow conspirators paid his family $200 a month, which he described as "a balm to my soul," in his book on the Egyptian revolution entitled Revolt on the Nile (Day, 1957). He continued, "All those who have fought for an ideal know that it is not the fear of death or torture that causes a man to weaken but the thought of what may happen to his wife and children who are weak and defenseless." In November 1944 he escaped from the camp and went into hiding in Egypt, continually changing disguises and residences and working at a variety of odd jobs, including selling used tires and driving a cab.

As he related in Revolt on the Nile, Sadat was an impetuous and romantic revolutionary in those early days. "I was always eager to step up the pace, but Gamal [Nasser], a man of deliberation, acted as a restraining influence. . . . My idea was to blow up the British Embassy and everybody in

ANWAR SADAT

it. . . . Gamal listened attentively and then . . . said, 'No.' " Sadat was again imprisoned in 1946 after a series of terrorist attacks against pro-British officials. Although he stoutly maintained his innocence, he served almost three years in prison on charges of involvement in the assassination of Finance Minister Amin Osman Pasha, whom he called "a die-hard Anglophile." While in prison, Sadat missed out on the fighting between Israel and the Arab nations after Israel proclaimed independence in 1948. Sadat described that period of imprisonment as "the most terrible years of my life." Released from prison in 1949, Sadat worked as a newspaper reporter until some of his influential friends were able to get his army commission restored in 1950. He was then stationed as a captain at Rafah in the Sinai Desert, where his main revolutionary duty was to maintain liaison between Nasser's Free Officers Committee and civilian terrorist groups.

The conspirators' plans to overthrow Farouk came to fruition on the night of July 22, 1952, when the Free Officers Committee led by Nasser staged a swift and bloodless coup d'etat. Sadat, who had been summoned back from Rafah to Cairo by Nasser on July 21, almost missed the event. Finding no further message from Nasser upon his return to Cairo on July 22, Sadat decided to take his children to the movies. When he returned home, Sadat discovered that he had missed Nasser and that the revolution had started without him. By the time he arrived at Cairo military headquarters, it had already surrendered, but Nasser gave him the job of announcing the news of the coup on the morning of July 23. On Egyptian radio Sadat reported to the world that the Free Officers Committee had seized power and demanded the abdication of King Farouk. He then was given the task of flying to Alexandria to oversee the departure of Farouk on July 26. "From the bridge of the destroyer, I watched Farouk pass into the twilight of history," Sadat recalled in his book. "The sailors round me were jubilant. Suddenly I felt faint. For three days I had not slept. I had lived on my nerves. Now I was feeling the effect of those long hours of tension. I had to be helped down the gangway."

At first the new government was nominally headed by General Mohammed Naguib, but by 1956 Nasser, the real power behind the revolt, had seized control as Premier and president of the Egyptian republic. Although Sadat served as a member of the military junta's Revolutionary Command Council and in a number of other posts, Nasser did not give his friend a truly leading role in the new government. According to Edward R. F. Sheehan (New York *Times Magazine,* November 29, 1970), "Nasser never entrusted [Sadat] with important jobs because he did not consider him efficient." At first Sadat was appointed director of army public relations, and then he became editor of *Al Gomhuriya,* the semigovernment newspaper, for which he wrote scathing anti-Western editorials during the Suez crisis. From 1954 to 1956, Sadat was a minister of state, and in 1957 he was appointed secretary general of the National Union, the forerunner of the present Arab Socialist Union, Egypt's only political organization. In 1961 he exchanged that job for the presidency of the National Assembly, where he remained until 1968. During the mid-1950's he served as secretary general of the Islamic Congress, a short-lived body established by Nasser to promote Moslem unity, and in 1958 he was chairman of the Afro-Asian Solidarity Conference. During the 1960's Sadat represented his government on a number of ceremonial visits to the Soviet Union, Czechoslovakia, Mongolia, North Korea, and the United States, and he served as one of Nasser's trouble-shooters in Yemen, where the United Arab Republic supported the republicans in a civil war.

Nasser was wary of letting anyone get too much power in his government, but he seems to have trusted Sadat more than anyone else. Therefore, while others fell from favor, Sadat maintained his prominence. From 1962 to 1964 he was a member of the Presidential Council, and from 1964 to 1967 he was one of four vice-presidents, until Nasser abolished the post in the aftermath of the June 1967 war with Israel.

Following a lengthy illness President Nasser reestablished the vice-presidency in December 1969 and named Sadat to the post, reportedly because he was the only man he trusted not to take advantage of the position. When Nasser suffered a fatal heart attack on September 29, 1970 Sadat became president, under the terms of the nation's constitution, for up to sixty days, in which time the National Assembly was to choose a successor. On October 7, 1970 the legislative body unanimously nominated Sadat, apparently because he was uncontroversial and had agreed to share the nation's leadership with his rivals. Speaking before the National Assembly after his nomination, Sadat pledged to work toward Nasser's goals: the recovery of Arab lands occupied by Israel; the unification of the Arab nations; the definition of "the enemies of our nation"; the maintenance of a non-aligned posture between the major world powers; the support of national liberation movements in other countries; and the defense of Egypt's social-

ist goals. In a national presidential referendum on October 15, 1970 Sadat received a 90.4 percent "yes" vote from the 7,000,000 Egyptians casting their ballots, and he was sworn into office for a six-year term two days later.

Sadat took office in the midst of an uneasy truce with Israel. In March of 1968 Nasser had launched a "war of attrition" against Israel, vowing to continue until his country regained its territory occupied by Israel in 1967. During the summer of 1970, however, Nasser had agreed to a ninety-day ceasefire, beginning in August, and to negotiations with Israel through United Nations mediator Gunnar V. Jarring. A bitter foe of Israel, Sadat had reportedly been strongly opposed to the ceasefire, and some observers doubted at the time he took over the government that he would continue Nasser's policy of cautious receptivity to negotiations. Yet, once in office, Sadat agreed to a ninety-day extension of the truce, beginning in November, and in late December, Israel agreed to rejoin the peace talks that it had boycotted since August in protest against the Egyptian buildup of missiles in the Suez Canal zone.

In an interview with James Reston for the New York *Times* (December 28, 1970), Sadat stated that his nation's primary demand for peace in the Middle East was that Israel give up "every inch" of territory she had captured from the U.A.R. in June 1967. If she did, said Sadat, the U.A.R. would recognize the rights of Israel as an independent state and was prepared to negotiate Israel's "rights of passage" through the Gulf of Aqaba and the Strait of Tiran. However, he stipulated that Israel's "rights of passage" through the Suez Canal would depend on settlement of the "[Palestinian] refugee problem." Sadat agreed to one more extension of the ceasefire, until March 8, 1971, but since then he has refused further extensions until progress has been made in peace negotiations with Israel. Despite the absence of a formal truce, hostilities between the two nations had not broken out as of late November 1971.

In January 1971 Sadat dedicated the Aswan Dam, Nasser's largest domestic project, which had been under construction for ten years. Another of Nasser's dreams, for Arab unity, moved closer to realization under Sadat's aegis when a loose confederation of Arab states, called the Federation of Arab Republics, was agreed upon in September 1971 by Egypt, Libya, and Syria. (Egypt and Syria merged to form the United Arab Republic in 1958, but Syria withdrew from the union three years later.)

Anwar Sadat and his wife, Gehan, who is half English, live in an elegant mansion in the Giza section of Cairo, near the Nile River. They have three daughters and a son named Gamal. By a previous marriage Sadat has three daughters, all married, and several grandchildren. Charming and genial in manner, the Egyptian president speaks with a deep voice and is fluent in English, German, and Persian. Although lacking the charisma of his predecessor, Sadat is imposing in appearance—tall, lean, impeccably dressed, with very dark hair, eyes, and skin, and a dark callous in the center of his forehead from years of praying with head to the ground. He is an avid reader whose tastes range from classical Islamic literature to the novels of Lloyd Douglas and Zane Grey, and he has expressed the desire to retire to his village eventually, where he can write and "lead his own life." Besides *Revolt on the Nile,* whose style one British critic described as "jaunty journalese," Sadat has written an unpublished political novel entitled "The Prince of the Island."

References

N Y Post p24 O 3 '70 por
N Y Times p16 Sep 30 '70; p47 O 21 '70 por
N Y Times Mag p30+ N 29 '70 por; p6+ Jl 18 '71 pors
Time 97:23+ My 17 '71 pors
International Who's Who, 1970-71
Sadat, Anwar. Revolt on the Nile (1957)

SAKHAROV, ANDREI D(MITRIYEVICH)

May 21, 1921- Soviet physicist; social philosopher
Address: b. P. N. Lebedev Physics Institute, Leninsky Prospekt 53, Moscow, U.S.S.R.

Albert Einstein once wrote, with reference to the dilemma faced by the scientist whose discoveries are used for destructive purposes: "The line of demarcation does not lie between scientists and non-scientists but between responsible, honest people and the others." Einstein's standards of responsibility and honesty for the scientist are epitomized in the life of physicist Andrei D. Sakharov, the man perhaps most responsible for the development of the Soviet hydrogen bomb. Since the late 1950's this "Oppenheimer, Teller, and Hans Bethe all rolled into one," as Harrison E. Salisbury has called him, has grown, in Salisbury's words, into "a philosopher and social architect on a world scale." Salisbury made the description in introducing *Progress, Coexistence, and Intellectual Freedom* (1968), the American translation of Sakharov's major statement of his world-view. In the daring essay Sakharov lucidly analyzed the human condition today, in and out of the Soviet Union, and painstakingly elaborated his vision of a future in which East and West will meet in a common ground of democratic socialism, free in large measure of the tensions and repressions that now afflict men and nations. In 1970 Sakharov and other Soviet physicists founded the Committee for Human Rights, an organization dedicated to promoting in their country the principles expressed in the Universal Declaration of Human Rights.

Official biographies of Andrei Dmitriyevich Sakharov offer no information about his family background or early life other than the facts that he was born on May 21, 1921 and graduated with honors in physics from Moscow State University in 1942. Apparently because of the remarkable ability he demonstrated as a student, he was ex-

empted from military service and permitted to pursue his studies throughout the World War II years. In 1945 he became an associate at the P. N. Lebedev Physics Institute of the U.S.S.R. Academy of Sciences in Moscow. There he worked with Igor Tamm, the specialist in quantum mechanics who later, in 1958, won the Nobel Prize for Physics. Under Tamm's guidance, Sakharov obtained his doctorate in physical and mathematical sciences in 1947—a formidable achievement, because in the Soviet Union the doctorate is usually awarded to older, more experienced scientists. In the same year Sakharov published his first scientific paper, "Generatsiya zhestkoy komponenti kosmicheskikh luchey" (Generation of the Hard Component of Cosmic Radiation).

Before 1948 neither Sakharov nor Tamm was involved in the frenetic weapons research program that Joseph Stalin had instituted during the war. Sakharov's work in theoretical physics was leading, however, according to Harrison E. Salisbury, into the "critical field of thermonuclear reactions, of fusion physics, of the H-bomb, and of what lay beyond." In 1948 Sakharov published the articles "Vzaimodeystvie elektrona i pozitrona pri rozhdenii par" (Electron-Positron Interaction During Pair Production) and "Temperatura vozbuzhdeniya v plazme gazovogo razryada" (Excitation Temperature in Gaseous Discharge Plasma). In the latter he outlined the principle for the magnetic thermal isolation of high-temperature plasma (ionized gas) and thus significantly altered the course of Soviet research on controlled thermonuclear reactions and, with it, the focus of his own work. From 1948 to 1956 he was engaged almost exclusively in research connected with nuclear weapons, and a virtual press blackout was imposed on his activities. Only later was it disclosed that he had been a—if not the—major contributor to the development of the Soviet hydrogen bomb. It has been established that in 1950 Sakharov and Tamm formulated the theoretical basis for controlled thermonuclear fusion, the means whereby hydrogen bomb power could be employed for the generation of electricity and other peaceful ends. The extent of Sakharov's achievement was such that in 1953, without having to go through the intermediate stage of corresponding membership, he became the youngest scientist ever to be elected a full member of the prestigious Soviet Academy of Sciences. In 1959 he began to work with Mikhail A. Leontovich on the theoretical aspects of controlled fusion.

Sakharov's first public statements after years of enforced silence presaged the role he was later to play as a critic of his society. In the fall of 1958 he and a colleague, Yakov B. Zeldovich, published an article in *Pravda* advocating educational reforms that contradicted the official pronouncements of Premier Nikita S. Khrushchev. Pointing out that mathematicians and physicists were most creative during the earlier stages of their careers, Sakharov and Zeldovich criticized Khrushchev's plan to incorporate job training into most high school curricula. Such a course, they argued, was detrimental to students gifted in science, who needed accelerated programs to prepare them for early entry into the universities. The debate continued for several years, and ultimately substantial revisions were made in secondary school education along lines proposed in the Sakharov-Zeldovich article. The changes included increased emphasis on scientific method and the principles of the new mathematics.

In the early 1960's Sakharov took part in a public controversy between the classical, Mendelian geneticists and the followers of Trofim D. Lysenko, an agronomist who had virtually controlled the Soviet life sciences during Stalin's regime. Although Lysenko's claim that environment could alter the heredity of plants had been largely discredited after Stalin's death, his views had considerable appeal for Khrushchev, who was seeking solutions to Russia's agricultural problems. Threatened with a resurgence of Lysenkoism, a number of Soviet scientists protested, in the popular press and in scientific journals, that Lysenko's practices had done irreparable damage to Soviet genetics and biology. In 1963 Sakharov supported the classical geneticists and, despite warnings from Khrushchev, he and his colleagues were instrumental in breaking Lysenko's hold over Soviet science. More importantly, he also helped the scientific community gain a considerable degree of immunity from political control.

For Sakharov, as for many of his colleagues, Lysenkoism portended a far greater menace, a return to Stalinism, signs of which were apparent even before Khrushchev's fall from power in 1964. Not only had the promise of liberalization that Khrushchev had made in his famous denunciation of Stalin in 1956 not been kept, but the atmosphere in the arts and sciences was becoming increasingly repressive. By 1966 the trials of the writers Andrei D. Sinyavsky and Yuli M. Daniel on charges of having slandered the Soviet Union in books published abroad had convinced many Soviet intellectuals that however great a risk dissent involved, the risk of silence was even greater. As the historian and literary critic Sidney Monas pointed out, the "divisive impact" of the trials polarized the Soviet public. In a wave of protest that followed the conviction of the two writers, Sakharov and other intellectuals wrote to Leonid I. Brezhnev, the new Communist party leader, warning him that the Soviet people would not accept a recurrence of Stalinism. Later that year Sakharov was one of the most outspoken critics of the government after it issued a decree making public demonstrations illegal.

In analyzing Sakharov's career, Harrison E. Salisbury discerns a parallel between the evolution of his social consciousness in the mid-1960's and the expanding focus of his scientific research. Whether Sakharov refused to continue with weapons research in 1965 is not certain, but from that time on the titles of his articles suggest a shift in interest from nuclear physics to theoretical studies concerning the structure of the universe. In 1965 he published an article dealing with the initial stage of an expanding universe and the appearance of nonuniformity in the distribution of matter. The following year he published a study of the "quark structure" and mass of ultra-active particles. ("Quarks" are, in the hypotheses of some physicists, the basic components, or building blocks, of protons.) In a highly original paper published by the Joint Institute for Nuclear Research at Dubna in 1969, Sakharov postulated a universal sea of "antiquarks" as a possible explanation for the symmetry physicists had observed in the balance of matter and antimatter.

Sakharov's controversial 10,000-word "manifesto" was circulated widely in the Soviet Union in manuscript form without official sanction before its publication in the New York *Times* on July 22, 1968 under the title "Progress, Coexistence, and Intellectual Freedom." Its basic theses were that "the division of mankind threatens it with destruction" and that "intellectual freedom is essential to human society." Sakharov saw among the chief dangers facing mankind the perpetuation of "intellectually simplified, narrow-minded mass myths" that make nations a prey to hysteria and the dogmatism of "cruel and treacherous demagogues." Among such myths he cited racism, nationalism, and the "proletarian infallibility" of the Stalinist and Maoist cults. Demonstrating with unmistakable precision and authority the futility of a nuclear arms race, Sakharov advocated a rapprochement of rival political systems based on an enlightened public opinion. While attributing much of the existing world tension to United States military involvement in Vietnam, Sakharov was also critical of the Soviet Union's "irresponsible encouragement" of the Arab nations in their conflict with Israel. Among the current dangers facing mankind that Sakharov discussed were hunger, overpopulation, and pollution of the environment.

While examining the prospects for a rapprochement between the two great powers, Sakharov exposed what he considered the utter betrayal of Communist ideals during the Stalinist regime. He went on to condemn "neo-Stalinist" tendencies under the present Soviet government, notably, the continued imprisonment of dissidents, the repression of national minorities, and the rigid censorship imposed on writers, who, he asserted, should be free to express "not only true but also dubious ideas." Departing sharply from Communist orthodoxy, Sakharov challenged the Marxist prediction of an inevitable breakdown of capitalism from internal contradictions. "Both capitalism and socialism are capable of long-term development, borrowing positive elements from each other and actually coming closer to each other in a number of essential aspects," he wrote. Greater emphasis on the moral responsibility of government will, in Sakharov's views, ultimately achieve needed reforms in both countries, leading to a "convergence" of the two systems in democratic socialism.

Sakharov concluded his essay with a "four-stage plan for cooperation." In the first stage a democratic evolution of socialism in the Soviet Union would occur through ideological debate and possibly the development of a multi-party system; in the second, vital social reforms would occur in the United States and other capitalist countries. These would include the elimination of racism and militarism and a transition to greater collective ownership of the means of production. In the third stage, the two great powers would cooperate in devoting a portion of their national incomes to the promotion of economic progress in the underdeveloped countries. Foreseeing a progressive convergence of ideals and growth of intellectual freedom and economic prosperity during the fourth stage, Sakharov anticipated that by the year 2000 a workable world government could become a reality.

Published by W. W. Norton & Company in 1968 under the title *Progress, Coexistence and Intellectual Freedom,* with introduction and notes by Harrison E. Salisbury, Sakharov's essay was hailed by Western observers as a document of major importance, particularly in view of Sakharov's stature as a leading Soviet scientist. Although some critics found the work unduly schematic and utopian, Sakharov's enlightened humanism was generally praised. In a report to members of the Book-of-the-Month Club, Clifton Fadiman commented: "The least one can say is that an intellectual conscience exists and flourishes in Soviet Russia, and that in Andrei Sakharov it would seem to have found its spokesman."

Prospects for the liberalization of Soviet life seemed particularly bleak after the invasion of Czechoslovakia by the Soviet Union and its Warsaw Pact allies in August 1968. Nevertheless, in the long run the invasion had the effect of intensifying dissent, since the Czech experiment in democratic socialism had pinpointed the very reforms Sakharov and other intellectuals sought to achieve in their own country. Writers and artists, traditionally the most outspoken, were the first to protest. They were joined in September 1968 by scientists and technicians at the Obninsk nuclear research center, who publicly denounced restrictions on freedom of thought. Although the dissenters constituted a minority of the scientific community, the government was sufficiently alarmed to issue strong admonitions to the scientists.

Sakharov responded to the warnings by continuing his campaign for intellectual freedom while carrying on his independent research in physics. On March 19, 1970, he and physicist Valery F. Turchin and historian Roy A. Medvedev issued a manifesto commenting on the threat thought control poses to scientific and technological progress. A few months later, Sakharov appealed to Brezhnev for the release of the biologist Zhores A. Medvedev, a leading critic of Lysenko, who had been forcibly detained in a mental hospital after advocating a freer exchange of scientific information. Sakharov's letter to Brezhnev, in which he reminded the party chief of the "potential threat to the freedom of science" posed by the arrest, is believed to have been largely responsible for Medvedev's release on June 27, 1970. With less success, Sakharov also spoke out in behalf of former Major General Pyotr Grigorenko, a critic of the invasion of Czechoslovakia, who had been sent to a mental institution in 1969; and the mathematician Revolt I. Pimenov, who was exiled to Siberia in October 1970 for allegedly slandering the Soviet state.

On November 4, 1970 Sakharov and two colleagues in the field of physics—Andrei N. Tverdokhlebov and Valery N. Chalidze—created the Committee for Human Rights, an autonomous, nongovernmental organization, that seeks to apply the humanitarian principles of the Universal Declaration of Human Rights within the Soviet Union. The stated principles guiding the committee stress cooperation with the government in "creating and implementing guarantees of human rights." The committee's first recruit was reportedly the Nobel Prize-winning author Aleksandr I. Solzhenitsyn. Although Sakharov's name was not specifically mentioned, he was apparently the intended target of government and Communist party spokesmen who in late 1970 censured the staff of the P. N. Lebedev Institute for what they regarded as ideological shortcomings.

On December 29, 1970, in an open letter addressed jointly to Soviet President Nikolai Podgorny and United States President Richard Nixon, Sakharov appealed for justice both in the case of two Jews sentenced to death in an alleged air hijack plot in Leningrad and that of the American black militant educator Angela Davis, facing murder and kidnapping charges in connection with a California courtroom shootout. "I call on freedom-loving people in the United States, the U.S.S.R., and all the world to act against injustice, terror, and oppression, wherever they take place," he concluded.

Despite some abortive efforts to have him expelled from the U.S.S.R. Academy of Sciences for his ideological unorthodoxy, Andrei D. Sakharov apparently continues to be held in high esteem in the Soviet Union, especially among his colleagues. Although his work has been mainly confined to the P. N. Lebedev Institute in Moscow, he has on occasion traveled to scientific conferences elsewhere. In 1958 he attended the second international atomic conference in Geneva, and in the summer of 1968 he was at a conference on general relativity in Tiflis, where he reportedly met with American scientists. Sakharov has been decorated with the Order of Lenin, and he holds a Stalin prize. Colleagues have mentioned his name as a possible candidate for a Nobel Peace Prize. In 1969 the American Academy of Arts and Sciences elected him to membership. Personal data on Sakharov is scant and photographs of him, if such exist, are for some reason not readily available, at least in the West.

References

Guardian p1 D 30 '70
N Y Times p16 Jl 22 '68
Sat R 54:24 Ja 16 '71
Brumberg, Abraham. In Quest of Justice (1970)
International Who's Who, 1971-72
Prominent Personalities in the USSR (1968)
Sakharov, Andrei D. Progress, Coexistence, and Intellectual Freedom (1968)
Who's Who in the USSR, 1970-71
Who's Who in the World, 1971-72
World Who's Who in Science (1968)

SARGENT, FRANCIS W(ILLIAMS)

July 29, 1915- Governor of Massachusetts
Address: b. State House, Boston, Massachusetts
02133

After John A. Volpe joined President Richard Nixon's Cabinet as Secretary of Transportation, in January 1969, his unexpired term as governor of Massachusetts was filled by Francis W. Sargent, who had been lieutenant governor under Volpe. An independent Republican who enjoys exceptional nonpartisan popularity in the nation's most sophisticated Democratic stronghold, Sargent was elected governor in his own right in November 1970, when he defeated Boston mayor Kevin H. White, the Democratic gubernatorial candidate, by 1,044,022 votes to 790,111. Sargent came to elective office from a distinguished two-decade career as administrator of state departments concerned with natural resources and public works. As governor, he has captured national attention by signing two precedent-shattering state laws: the Massachusetts "no-fault" auto insurance law and a statute challenging the legality of the Vietnam war. Governor Sargent's current term expires in January 1975.

The scion of an old Yankee family, Francis W. Sargent was born in Hamilton, Massachusetts on July 29, 1915 to Francis Williams Sargent and Margery (Lee) Sargent. He was educated at the elite Noble and Greenough School in Dedham, Massachusetts and at the Massachusetts Institute of Technology. After taking a special degree in architecture at M.I.T., in 1939, he joined the architectural firm of Sargent and Sweeney. During World War II he served as an infantry ski trooper in Europe, earning the Bronze Star and the Purple Heart, among other decorations, and reaching the rank of captain.

After the war, having decided that he "wanted to live a quiet life" close to nature, Sargent opened, on Cape Cod, the Goose Hummock Shop, a sporting goods store with a charter boat service for fishermen. "The last thing I wanted," he has said, "was to go back into architecture or into politics." But a crusade he waged against certain commercial fishermen who were using surf nets for mass catches brought him to the attention of Massachusetts Governor Robert F. Bradford, who asked him to become State Director of Marine Fisheries in 1947. Sargent agreed to fill the post for one winter—and remained in it for ten years. In 1951 he was named United States commissioner on the International Commission for the Northwest Atlantic Fisheries, and he served in that position for eleven years concurrently with his state duties.

From the Division of Marine Fisheries, Sargent moved to the Massachusetts Department of Natural Resources, in 1956. During three years as Commissioner of Natural Resources he also served as chairman of the Massachusetts Water Resources Commission and the Atlantic States Marine Fisheries Commission. At the request of President Dwight D. Eisenhower he directed a special United States Outdoor Recreation Resources Commission in Washington, D.C. for four years, beginning in 1959. When the federal commission's assignment was done, President Kennedy asked Sargent to remain in Washington as head of the National Park Service, but he turned down the offer. "I missed New England," he later explained, "and I missed the climate here at the statehouse. Later on, for the same reasons, I turned down an offer from then Governor Pat Brown of California to become director of parks and recreation in that state."

In 1962 Sargent ran unsuccessfully for the Massachusetts State Senate, and the following year he returned to appointive state office as director of the Division of Fisheries and Game. From 1964 to 1966 he was chairman of the Merrimac Valley Flood Control Commission, and while in that position he also served as Commissioner of Public Works in Massachusetts, in 1965 and 1966, and as adviser to the California Department of Parks and Recreation, beginning in 1964. Over the years he had become an influential, nonpartisan friend of many Massachusetts state legislators, and as commissioner of Public Works he used that influence to gain passage of a state law eliminating the power of ten Greater Boston communities to veto Interstate Highway System plans, a local power that hobbled highway development and threatened the loss of millions of dollars in federal subsidies.

With his eye, distantly, on the governorship, Sargent ran for lieutenant governor of Massachusetts, beside fellow Republican John A. Volpe, the incumbent governor, in 1966, and he won election easily. A little over two years later, when Volpe moved into the Nixon Cabinet, Sargent was sworn in as governor, on January 22, 1969. Whereas Volpe had alienated the predominantly Democratic (3-1) state legislature by his absences from the state in behalf of Nixon's candidacy during the Presidential campaign, Sargent, already respected and trusted by the legislators, was received with open arms, and he and Maurice A. Donahue, the Democratic president of the State Senate, pledged mutual cooperation. The pledge was honored during Sargent's first two years in office—the two years of Volpe's unexpired term—and the cooperation continued after Sargent won election as governor in his own right.

The first major problem facing Sargent in office was a budgetary crisis precipitated by exorbitant welfare costs. By executive order, he changed the eligibility rules for Medicaid to save the state $17,500,000, and at his request the legislature passed a measure authorizing a new tax on corporations and other "special interests" that would increase revenues by some $100,000,000. At about the time that he signed the tax bill into law he vetoed a $92,500,000 appropriation for pay raises for state employees, returning it to the legislature with the request that $25,000,000 be whittled from it. Also in 1969, Sargent, with the help of Senator Donahue, pushed through the legislature a government reorganization plan, effective two years later, in accordance with which the sprawling state bureaucracy has been arranged into ten Cabinet-level departments.

Sargent was the only United States governor to participate in the antiwar demonstrations on Vietnam Moratorium Day, October 15, 1969, when he delivered an address castigating the war to a crowd on historic Lexington green. The constitutional legality of the massive, prolonged American military expedition in Indochina, conducted by Presidential fiat without an explicit declaration of war by Congress, was uniquely challenged in the Massachusetts legislature's Shea bill, named for its chief sponsor, Representative H. James Shea. The bill, authorizing Massachusetts citizens to refuse combat duty in undeclared foreign wars and requiring the state Attorney General to defend in the courts those who so refuse, was signed into law by Sargent on April 2, 1970. As the Governor pointed out when signing it, the statute was designed for court testing, for presenting "our highest tribunal with the grave question of whether and under what circumstances an individual may be required to serve in an armed conflict that lacks a formal Congressional declaration of war." Later in 1970 the legislature approved the holding of a public referendum on the war.

In her syndicated newspaper column published in the New York *Post* and other newspapers on April 6, 1970, Mary McGrory described the Massachusetts climate of opinion that made possible the enactment and signing of the Shea bill: "Nixon lost Massachusetts to Hubert Humphrey in 1968 and nothing he has done since has much endeared him to its large university and progressive elements. Sargent vetoed a proposed visit by Vice-President Agnew, the scourge of the Northeastern liberal community, war resisters, and 'so-called intellectuals' [and the proscription against Agnew extended through the 1970 elections]. . . . 'This is Kennedy country,' the Governor says. Its potential majority apparently has been conditioned by Kennedy antiwar views. 'This isn't like any other state,' says Sargent with some pride."

The law challenging the legality of the war was the first such statute enacted in any state in the United States, and it has inspired efforts at similar legislation in Rhode Island, California, New York, Illinois, and Ohio. Another pioneering Massachusetts measure was the "no fault" auto insurance law, signed by Sargent in August 1970. The key feature of that law, which applies only to compulsory bodily injury insurance, requires that claims of less than $2,000 be paid by the injured party's insurance company, without litigation, regardless of who was at fault in the accident. As Sargent and the legislative backers of the plan predicted, it began saving the insurance companies money as soon as it went into operation, in January 1971. In the first quarter of 1971 there was a reduction of 36 percent in bodily injury claims, and the average claim was for $131, as compared to $205 the year before. But the companies were niggardly in passing along the savings to consumers in the form of reduced premiums, and on April 23, 1971 Sargent warned: "If the industry continues to block the benefits of no-

FRANCIS W. SARGENT

fault for the consumer, I will file legislation with heavy penalties to block that blocking."

In 1970 the Massachusetts legislature also passed important witness immunity, mental health, unit pricing, public housing, and environmental protection laws. Particularly impressive was the legislation in the two latter areas. The ecology statutes included a $250,000,000 municipal water pollution control bond issue, and the core of the housing program enacted was authorization of a new lending ceiling for the quasi-public Massachusetts Housing Finance Agency, enabling it to loan money for 20,000 to 25,000 housing units, about one-fourth of which will be low income.

On the debit side, Sargent was disappointed at the legislature's failure to approve an environmental quality control council, a private right of action (in environmental protection) bill, civil service and county government reform, highway safety improvement, an increase in the number of justices on the State Supreme Court, the phasing out of the special justice system in the District Courts, and a referendum on cutting the size of the State House of Representatives. Also disappointing was its passing of a self-serving Senate redistricting plan and a bill giving police powers to Registry men; its craven shirking of the unpopular task of reining a Vietnam veterans' bonus program whose cost is running out of control, into tens of millions of dollars; and its failure to pass a measure that would have funneled gas tax money into mass transportation, a $300,000,000 transit authority bond issue, alcoholism treatment and rehabilitation programs, and legislation concerned with the pressing public problem of drug abuse.

In the spring of 1971 the legislative recommendations Sargent was planning or working on included tax relief for home owners, to attract new industry to Massachusetts; extension of no-fault auto insurance to cover property damage; and an amendment to the state constitution that would make it possible for eighteen-year-olds to vote in state elections. In his relations with Washington, the Governor was petitioning for federal subsidies for mass transit.

In an article on Sargent in the Washington *Post* (September 25, 1970), David S. Broder observed: "He has raised the art of bill signing to heights unknown in America since the halcyon days of the Great Society. . . . Sargent's feat is in some respect greater, because he has been grabbing the bills and the glory from an opposition controlled body." As instances, Broder cited the signings of the Shea bill and "his greatest triumph of head-line-stealing," the no-fault auto insurance bill. "His decision [to sign the no-fault bill] was announced on live television and the climactic moment, when Sargent scrawled his signature on the bill and dramatically announced, 'Now the crisis is on us,' was even picked up by the national television news shows—an incredible public relations coup for the governor."

Governor Sargent is a member of the Boston Museum of Science Corporation, the advisory board of Cape Cod Community College, the visiting committee of Harvard University, and the board of fellows of Boston University, a director of the Massachusetts Society for the Prevention of Cruelty to Animals, a trustee of the Boston Zoological Society and the New England Aquarium, and an overseer of Old Sturbridge Village. Among the honors he has received are honorary degrees from Staley College, Southeastern Massachusetts University, and Framingham State College. His church is the Unitarian.

Francis W. Sargent and Jessie Fay were married on June 11, 1938. They have three children: Fay (Mrs. James McLane), Jessie, and F. Williams Sargent Jr. As one Boston political columnist has observed, Sargent has "all the natural requisites to be the complete politician." He is tall, lean, and handsome and has a winning smile, a good sense of humor, a faultless memory for names and faces, and a charming manner that comes over well on television. As a public speaker, he used to fill about four speaking engagements a week before he assumed the duties of governor. Those duties have also reduced the time that he spends at such outdoor activities as hunting, skiing, fishing, mountain climbing, and sailing. Sargent has said that his basic aim in the governorship is "to make this government work not for the politicians but for the people."

References

N Y Times p44 D 15 '68
Washington (D.C.) Post H p1+ D 19 '68
Who's Who in America, 1970-71

SARTRE, JEAN-PAUL (CHARLES AYMARD)

June 21, 1905- French writer
Address: b. Les Temps Modernes, 30 rue de l'Université, Paris 7, France

NOTE: This biography supersedes the article that appeared in *Current Biography* in 1947.

The term existentialism, coined by Gabriel Marcel in the mid-1940's, may be applied generally to any philosophy of human existence that is oriented descriptively around the philosopher's own fluid, anguished consciousness, as opposed to "essentialist" world-views, based on preconceived categories. More specifically, it applies to the movement of thought that began in the nineteenth century with the Danish Christian rebel Soren Kierkegaard's rage against Hegelian idealism, a monolithic philosophical system that tried to give truth an "eternal" set and thus dehumanized it, "mocking" the "poor existing individual" whose "situation" is not a completed, stable fact but "a process of becoming." "What such a man needs instead," Kierkegaard wrote, "is precisely an explanation of how the eternal truth is to be understood in determinations of time by one who, as existing, is himself in time." Kierkegaard's theme, transmuted by the German philosophers Edmund Husserl and Martin Heidegger, has been secularized in the philosophy, psychology, fiction, theatre, and criticism of Jean-Paul Sartre. With his message that "man makes himself" despite his "contingency" in an "absurd" world, the French thinker has been a prodigious intellectual force in an age of changing, ambiguous values, a seminal influence in such diverse areas as the anti-novel, New Wave cinema, and Third World revolutionary ideology. Sartre's chief publisher in France is Gallimard. In the United States his books have been published by French and English Publications Inc., Knopf, Braziller, Random House, and the Modern Library, among others.

An only child, Jean-Paul Sartre was born in Paris, France on June 21, 1905 to Jean-Baptiste Sartre, a French naval officer, and Anne Marie Schweitzer, a first cousin of the famous African jungle physician Albert Schweitzer. Shortly afterward his father died, leaving him permanently "without a superego," as Sartre confesses in *Les Mots* (1964; *The Words*, 1964), his unreservedly candid, irony-filled childhood memoir.

Until 1916, when she remarried, Anne Marie Sartre and her son lived with her parents, Charles and Louise Schweitzer, mostly in Paris, where the grandfather, a bilingual Alsatian language teacher, founded the Modern Language Institute. Sartre recalls the grandparental home as a "hothouse" of bourgeois hypocrisy where role-playing was taken seriously and where he became the worst "imposter" of the lot. An ugly little "toad" of a boy, without friends his age, he assiduously played at being the prodigy his doting, authoritarian grandfather assumed him to be. The grandfather's image of him was self-fulfilling, because by pretending to read Sartre taught himself actually to do so, at the age of three or four, and by plagiarizing he learned to write stories, five or six years later. He retreated from life "into words," which he regarded as "the quintessence of things," more real than the objects they denote. The Schweitzers' shallow, bifurcated religious faith (Lutheran on the grandfather's side, Roman Catholic on the grandmother's) left him cynical about all religion, but, like his grandfather, he retained the theological concept of the Holy Spirit, in the sense of a divine muse immanent among men chiefly for the purpose of inspiring a literary "elect." Having what he calls "an imagination of epic cast," he viewed himself as one of the elect.

At the end of *Les Mots* Sartre refers vaguely to the development of what has been called his "aesthetic of opposition," saying that he "shall speak later on" about how he "discovered my ugliness—which for a long time was my negative principle." "I came to think systematically against myself, to the extent of measuring the obvious truth of an idea by the displeasure it caused me."

Much of Sartre's elementary education was received from tutors hired by his over-protective grandfather. In school, as he recalls, his genius was not immediately apparent because of faulty spelling habits, slowness in answering, and difficulty in getting "used to democracy." But at Lycée Henri IV in Paris he "became, without effort, a rather good student." In 1924 he graduated from the lycée and entered the École Normale Supérieure at the University of Paris. At the university he and Simone de Beauvoir began their lifelong companionship, with a pact pledging mutual loyalty in times of need but permitting "contingent loves." Another student with whom Sartre formed a friendship was Raymond Aron, the eminent political pundit. That friendship was later ruptured by political differences, as was Sartre's association with Albert Camus.

After taking his agrégé in philosophy, in 1929, Sartre served in the meteorological section of the French army (1929-31) and taught at a lycée in Le Havre (1931-33). At the suggestion of Raymond Aron, he went to Germany in 1933, as a teaching fellow at the French Institute in Berlin, for the purpose of studying Edmund Husserl's phenomenology, a methodology for examining the structure, or laws, of consciousness without preconceptions or reflective notions. Husserl bracketed all questions about the reality of subject and object in order to treat the immediate phenomena of consciousness, no matter what their content, with equal seriousness. When that is done, he asserted, consciousness is aware of itself purely as "intentionality," a self-transcending outward thrust, and the object of that thrust is a "given," whether it be a "real" chair out in the room or a centaur that exists only in the imagination's field of "nothingness."

Following his year in Germany, Sartre taught philosophy successively at the Lycée de Laon and at the Lycée Pasteur, in the Paris suburb of Neuilly. While teaching, he elaborated the psychological implications of phenomenology, as he saw them, in *La Transcendance de l'égo* (1936; *The Transcendence of the Ego*, 1957), *L'Imagination* (1936; *Imagination*, 1962), *Esquisse d'une théorie des émotions* (1939; *The Emotions*, 1948), and *L'Imaginaire* (1940; *The Psychology of Imagination*, 1961). In those works he stressed the creative power of consciousness, the active "making" of the imagination as opposed to the inert impression-collecting of the memory.

Well into adulthood Sartre struggled to free himself from the Platonic subjectivism ingrained

JEAN-PAUL SARTRE

in him in boyhood, from that "lucid blindness," as he called it, in which the names of things were more real than the things themselves. The emancipation was apparently consummated in a mescalin-triggered experience he described in his autobiographical novel *La Nausée* (1938; *Nausea*, 1949), the book that first brought him fame in France. Roquentin, the novel's anti-hero, suddenly begins to see familiar objects in a new light, as "frightening" manifestations or instances of the "gelatinous" universal "dough out of which things are made." "The veil is torn away. . . . Words had vanished and with them the meaning of things . . . the feeble points of reference that men have traced on their surface." He is left despondent, suffocating "at the bottom of this immense weariness," aware that existence, the living of life at any given moment, is inevitably "viscous." But he finally sees that he can give a "hardness" at least to his past life—his life as lived up to the present existential moment—by transmuting it into art, into a story. "People . . . would read this novel and think about my life as something precious and almost legendary. . . . And I might succeed, with the past—and only with the past— in accepting myself." Outside of *La Nausée*, Sartre's fictional output in the 1930's was confined to short stories, collected in *Le Mur* (1939; *The Wall*, 1948).

After military service at the beginning of World War II (1939-40) and incarceration as a prisoner of war in Germany (1940-41), Sartre returned to Paris. He served in the Resistance, contributed to underground publications, and taught at the Lycée Condorcet until 1944, when he began devoting all of his time to writing. Soon he became the center of a literary circle whose locus was the Café Flore in the Saint Germain des Prés section of Paris.

In the meantime, Sartre had been reading the works of the German philosopher Martin Heidegger, who brought together Husserl's concept of intentionality and Kierkegaard's insight that there is a rift at the center of man's being. He is never at one with himself and is always becoming something other than he is. Heidegger pictured man as the *Dasein,* the anguishingly free project—ultimately a project toward death—wherein being finds its "there" or its "here and now," the locus of meaning in an otherwise amorphously absurd world.

After absorbing Heidegger's thought, Sartre wrote his massive tome on phenomenological ontology, *L'Être et le néant* (1943; *Being and Nothingness,* 1956). That otherwise lugubrious work contains a succinct summation of the author's world-view at that time: "Man can will nothing unless he has first understood that he must count on no one but himself: that he is alone, abandoned on earth in the midst of his infinite responsibilities, without help, with no other aim than the one he sets himself, with no other destiny than the one he forges for himself."

In *L'Être et le néant* and subsequent works Sartre refined his theory that "existence precedes essence," by which he meant that the human being is not a set character whose actions are determined by its nature but, rather, a project always in progress. The configuration of one's past actions indicates a fundamental, pattern-setting choice, but the configuration can be changed unpredictably by present or future free choices. Sartre defined essence as "a constant ensemble of properties" and existence as "a certain effective presence in the world." At any given moment that presence is a lie, inasmuch as the conscious person (termed the *pour soi* by Sartre) can never be a thing, an object (termed *en soi*) to himself, is always at odds with himself, always transcending himself. The authentic person frankly recognizes the constant ambivalence within himself. The man of truly bad faith (*mauvaise foi*) believes the lie, allows himself to be petrified into an object by the image others have of him, by the role society imposes on him, or simply by self-deception.

During the war Sartre inspired Parisian audiences with his play *Les Mouches* (1943; *The Flies*), a subtly anti-Nazi adaptation of the Orestes legend. It was also under the Occupation that *Huis clos* (1944; *No Exit*) was first produced. In that play three characters condemned to hell are surprised to find that there is no explicit punishment until they realize that the lights never go out and that their eyes never close, so that they are never free of the transfixing "look of the other" that denies the infinite possibilities for change in human beings. "There is no need for grills. Hell is other people."

For the postwar theatre Sartre wrote *La Putain respectueuse* (1946; *The Respectful Prostitute*); an indictment of racial oppression in the American South; *Morts sans sépulture* (1946; *The Victors*), about an ordeal of conscience among French Resistance fighters; and *Les Mains sales* (1948; *Dirty Hands*), an anti-Stalinist play that dramatizes, perhaps better than any other work, his view that a choice of action in the present can give meaning to, or illuminate the meaning of, one's past actions. For the cinema Sartre wrote *Les Jeux sont faits* (1947), a fantasy about a couple who return from the dead determined to be lovers in life but who are thwarted by *mauvaise foi.*

During the postwar period, when existentialism became an international fad, Sartre delivered a popularized, hastily written explanation of his philosophy in a Saint Germain des Prés nightclub, and the talk was published as *L'Existentialisme est un humanisme* (1946; *Existentialism,* 1947). Also in the postwar era, he began publishing, in 1947, the series of volumes, called *Situations,* containing his critical essays, and he wrote *Les Chemins de la liberté* (1945-49; *The Roads to Freedom,* 1947-51), a Dos Passos-like trilogy of novels about a group of young intellectuals and Bohemians in Paris before and during World War II. In the 1950's he wrote the plays *Le Diable et le bon Dieu* (1951; *The Devil and the Good Lord*), in which a group of peasants who accept the benevolence of a land-owning feudal tyrant discover that complacency is futile as long as others are oppressed; *Kean* (1954), about an actor who, even in life, needs spectators to assure him of the reality of the role he is playing; and *Les Séquestrés d'Altona* (1959; *The Condemned of Altona*). The latter, ostensibly about a former Nazi who is tormented by the possible significance history will put on his acts but who nevertheless owns up to them, in reality expressed Sartre's view on French military suppression of the independence movement in Algeria, then a colony of France.

Sartre applied existential psychoanalysis to racial bigotry in *Réflexions sur la question Juive* (1947; *Anti-Semite and Jew,* 1948) and to literary biography in *Baudelaire* (1947; translation, 1949) and *Saint Genêt* (1952; translation, 1963). He analyzed the anti-Semite as a person afraid of his own liberty, whose bigotry permits him to persuade himself "that his place in the world has been marked out in advance"; he saw Baudelaire as someone who decided to live his adult life as if he were a disobedient child under his mother's gaze; and he explained Jean Genêt as an orphan, judged delinquent by society, who decided to play, with a vengeance, the role assigned him.

Beginning with his clear call for a *littérature engagé* in *Qu'est-ce que la littérature?* (1947; *What is Literature?,* 1949), Sartre has, over the years, become progressively more committed to social and political action and progressively more Marxist (but not doctrinaire Communist) in his sympathy for the "rising peoples" of the Third World. In keeping with his basic tenet that "one is free to act but one must act to be free," he believes in taking sides on important public issues despite ambiguities in the issues themselves. In the pages of his monthly review *Les Temps Modernes* (founded 1945) he exposed Soviet forced labor camps in the early 1950's and denounced the Soviet suppression of the Hungarian revolt in 1956. His *Critique de la raison dialectique* (1960) suggested a turn in the direction of Marxist economics, the view that scarcity of goods is the prime motivating factor in society and politics, and in an interview four years after the publication of the book he said: "Compared to a child who dies of hunger, *La Nausée* has not much weight. . . . The exploitation of man and undernourishment relegate to a secondary position metaphysical evil, which is a luxury. Hunger, and nothing else, is an evil. . . . Do you think that I could read Alain Robbe-Grillet in an underdeveloped country? I consider him a good writer, but he addresses himself to the comfortable bourgeois. . . . [But] in New Guinea I could read Kafka."

In 1960 Sartre demanded—in vain—to be arrested like others who had signed a declaration of solidarity with young men refusing to fight in Algeria, and in 1961 right-wing terrorists bombed his Paris apartment. In 1967 he headed the international War Crimes Tribunal set up by Bertrand Russell to judge American military conduct in Indochina. The student rebellions of 1968 radicalized him even further, and in 1970 he assumed nominal editorship of two radical left-wing publications, *La Cause du Peuple* and *Tout*, when the young men who had been editing them were jailed. In June 1970 he and Simone de Beauvoir were arrested briefly for distributing *La Cause du Peuple* on Left Bank streets. A series of articles published in *La Cause du Peuple* and *Tout* in 1970 led to Sartre's arrest and indictment in June 1971 on charges of libeling the police. He told reporters that he considered the four counts of defamation against the police to be "another turn in repression and a trial of strength." His case was expected to come to trial late in 1971.

Jean-Paul Sartre is a short, walleyed man whose friends testify to his kindness, patience, attentiveness, vitality, naturalness, and good humor. But according to Alfred Kazin in the *Reporter* (July 1, 1965) he has frequent "black moods" and an "air of always moving along an abyss." In keeping with his philosophy that life is a game board on which one creates both the game and its rules, Sartre himself has referred to his fundamental lack of seriousness, his "incredible levity." Detached from possessions and modest in his life style, Sartre has always lived in small, spare quarters. His present home is a Montparnasse apartment not far from the residences of his mother and Simone de Beauvoir. In 1965 Sartre legally adopted his editorial assistant, Miss Arlette Kaim, then twenty-eight years old.

When Sartre writes, he does so with furious intensity. No longer viewing literature as he once did, as a sacred vocation for the redemption of one's fellow men, he continues to write because "it's a habit." "Culture doesn't save . . . it doesn't justify. But it's a product of man: he projects himself into it, he recognizes himself in it; that critical mirror alone offers him his image." In mid-1971 Sartre released the first two volumes of his long-awaited study of Gustave Flaubert entitled *L'Idiot de la Famille*. Sartre was awarded the Nobel Prize for literature in 1964, but he rejected it because he did not wish to be "transformed into an institution." He has also rejected the Legion of Honor.

References

Life 57:87+ N 6 '64 pors
N Y Post p26 O 25 '64 por
Beauvoir, Simone de. The Force of Circumstance (1965)
Contemporary Authors vol 9-10 (1964)
Richter, Liselotte. Jean-Paul Sartre (1970)
Sartre, Jean-Paul. The Words (1964)
Who's Who in France, 1965-66

SAUL, RALPH S(OUTHEY)

May 21, 1922- Former stock exchange executive; banker
Address: b. First Boston Corp., 225 Franklin St., Boston, Mass. 02110

Ralph S. Saul's tenure as president of the American Stock Exchange, which began in November 1966, coincided closely with a period of crisis in the securities industry—a "speculative orgy," to use his term, followed by the deepest market slump in thirty years. As a former official of the Securities and Exchange Commission, Saul was unusually well-qualified to direct Amex, which is second only to the New York Stock Exchange among the nation's securities markets, in cooperating with the federal regulatory agency to serve the interests of the public as well as industry. In guiding Amex through Wall Street pitfalls, Saul emerged as one of the most forward-looking of the country's financial leaders, a resourceful initiator of long-range proposals to modernize the wasteful, outmoded structure within which the exchanges now operate. Thus it was "with reluctance" that the governing board of Amex accepted Saul's resignation on March 16, 1971, when he announced that he planned to join the First Boston Corporation, a leading investment banking and securities firm, as vice-chairman. Saul was succeeded at Amex by the exchange's executive vice-president, Paul Kolton.

Ralph Southey Saul was born in the Flatbush section of Brooklyn, New York on May 21, 1922, the son of Walter Emerson Saul, a machinist at the Brooklyn Navy Yard, and Helen Douglas (Coutts) Saul. When Ralph was five years old, the family, which included a younger daughter, moved to Roslyn, Long Island. His childhood was described in a New York *Post* (September 22, 1966) profile as "neither affluent, nor deprived, just happy." He attended the public schools of Roslyn, and on graduating from high school in 1940 he won a scholarship to the University of Chicago. To pay part of his college expenses, he worked as a waiter, clerk, and hospital aide. He intended to specialize in American history and economics, but in 1943, while still an undergraduate, he enlisted in the Navy for World War II service. Obtaining a commission, he was assigned as a radar and gunnery officer to the USS *Lamson*, a destroyer plying the South Pacific.

When he was discharged from the service with the rank of lieutenant in 1946, Saul returned to the University of Chicago to complete his under-

RALPH S. SAUL

graduate work. He was undecided about his plans for a career, and though he had been interested in teaching American history, he now wavered between government work and the law. In his senior year he took and passed an examination for the United States Foreign Service. After he had graduated with a B.A. degree in 1947 he was appointed to the American Embassy staff in Prague. Serving there during the time that the Communists were tightening their control of the Czechoslovakian government, Ralph Saul found his job "depressing."

At the end of about a year in the Foreign Service, in September 1948 Saul entered the Yale University Law School. He was granted the LL.B. degree in June 1951 and was admitted to the District of Columbia bar in 1951 and to the New York bar in 1952. For about a year, in 1951-52, he worked as a law associate in the firm of Lyeth & Voorhees in New York City. Then he went up to Albany as a confidential law assistant to the Governor of New York, Thomas E. Dewey. When Dewey left office two years later, in 1954, Saul returned to New York City to become a staff attorney with the Radio Corporation of America (RCA), working on diverse legal matters, some of them involving securities and stocks and bonds. Saul found that work stimulating and in August 1958 joined the federal regulatory agency for the stock markets, the Securities and Exchange Commission in Washington, as an associate director of the trading and exchange division. Although he had intended to stay "just a few years," his interest in regulation became more intense as he began to shape policy affecting broad social issues.

In 1961 Saul was put in charge of the SEC's special study of the securities market investigating reports that stock swindles and financial mismanagement were rampant on Wall Street. He played a key role in uncovering the fraudulent practices of Gerard A. and Gerard F. Re, father-son investment specialists who were indicted and eventually convicted on charges of stock market rigging. (Specialists are floor brokers responsible for maintaining stable markets in assigned stocks.)

The 1962 SEC report drafted under Saul's supervision dealt with "manifold and prolonged abuses by specialists and floor traders" that clearly pointed to "a general deficiency of standards and a fundamental failure of controls." The investigation forced the resignation of Edward T. McCormick, then president of the American Stock Exchange, and resulted in extensive reforms in security dealings on the American board.

Business and government leaders commended Saul's expert handling of the difficult and somewhat sensitive securities reorganization. When the study was completed in 1963 he was named director of the trading and markets division of the Securities and Exchange Commission. Two years later, although feeling a "real wrench" in leaving Washington, Saul resigned his government post, in July 1965, to become vice-president for corporate development at Investors Diversified Services in Minneapolis, a managing company for five mutual funds with assets of more than $5 billion. Leslie Gould, the financial editor of the New York *World Journal Tribune* (September 13, 1966) later wrote that after seeking "greener pastures than civil service" and moving to Investors Diversified Services, Saul launched "a front-end load contractual mutual fund purchase plan." Gould went on to say, "One of the SEC study's sharpest criticisms of the mutual funds was front-end loads on contractual plans."

A regard for public service partly motivated Saul's acceptance in November 1966 of an appointment to the presidency of the American Stock Exchange, the nation's second-largest trading arena. He regards the exchange, which was founded in 1849, as a quasi-public institution. Amex had been headed since 1962 by Edwin D. Etherington, who had become president at the height of the scandals and had been required to introduce the reforms recommended by Saul's special study group. The members of the committee who had given Saul's name to Amex' board of governors from a field of some thirty-five candidates felt that he would be a forceful administrator and an effective representative in the exchange's association with Washington authorities.

Some Wall Street brokers were startled by Saul's nomination, and a few commentators in the press thought it ironic that the one-time investigator and critic of the exchange should be made its president. Opponents of the selection of Saul suggested that the decision to appoint someone so closely identified with the SEC was a "sellout" to government pressure. Unembarrassed by his succession of roles, Saul said that in view of the housecleaning at Amex, "the events of the past are not really relevant to 1966." He considered his SEC experience an asset because he believes that Amex has a public regulatory responsibility under the law.

On taking office Saul affirmed his belief that the "American Exchange will continue to be an innovator and to remain responsive to the public and to the needs of the industry." In one of his first undertakings he launched a construction program for the renovation of the trading floor to provide more space and easy access to counters and to install automatic equipment and computers to facilitate commercial transactions. He was eager to upgrade the American board and to dispel the impression on Wall Street that it was a second-class institution. Saul believed that his major task was to guide Amex's compliance with the law, since the "public, the Congress and the SEC expect it." Although he refused to consider himself the "top cop," he steered the American Exchange into a closer relationship with the SEC and encouraged more extensive self-regulation.

At the same time Saul stood firmly against innovations that he considered harmful to Amex members. He criticized 1967 SEC proposals that grew out of regulatory concern mainly about the selling of mutual fund shares, but that would have far-reaching effect on the structure of commission rates, outlawing, for instance, the practice of give-ups (fee-splitting). "Does it make sense to perform surgery on the entire securities business to meet a problem which perhaps can be met through a more limited approach?" he asked in a speech before the Investment Brokers of Washington in March 1967. ". . . If there are abuses in the use of give-ups, these should be pinpointed and defined in discussions between the SEC and the industry."

The year 1967 saw frenzied activity in the stock market, completely reversing the downward trend of the previous year. More than one billion shares were traded over 690,000,000 shares in 1966. The unprecedented trading of the first few months of 1967 yielded a daily turnover of 4,500,000 shares. When the daily volume soared to more than 6,000,000 shares in mid-July, Saul issued a warning about the "serious level of speculative activity on the American Exchange" and cautioned brokers to moderate their customers' enthusiasm. The continuing speculation increased trading by more than 25 percent over 1966, drove up the price of the average Amex stock by 68 percent, and pushed price-earnings ratios from 11.7 to 18.2. Although he looked forward to unlimited growth opportunities and record sales, Saul was concerned with the heavy concentration of activity in low-priced issues with rapidly rising price-earnings ratios. Speculation had always been a major problem for Amex, since its listings included newer, smaller, and less stable companies. Shares of stock selling on the American Exchange were generally less expensive and had a greater potential for volatility because there were relatively few shares outstanding and available for trade.

To help curb speculation Saul suspended margin buying on some of the more active stocks and expanded the market surveillance program to catch sharp stock-price fluctuations. Almost 400 Amex employees engaged in surveillance of trading, and approximately $5,600,000 was appropriated for surveillance efforts so that "fair and orderly auction markets" could be maintained. Despite those attempts to improve the self-regulatory activity of the American Exchange, there were isolated reports of stock fraud, manipulation, and price-rigging involving respected brokerage houses and some underworld figures. "Surveillance is no substitute for a member's responsibility to supervise its own organization," Saul pointed out. ". . . It cannot insure against loss or risk of investment in an equity market."

When the stock market continued to act erratically, the Amex board revised its requirements for listing new issues. Saul believed that the fullest disclosure of details on the floating of new issues was the best defense against stock manipulation. He wanted to raise the qualifications for listings and reduce the volatility of their shares. Companies were required to have at least 300,000 publicly held shares, amounting to at least $2,000,000, to have earned at least $300,000 in the prior fiscal year and have a minimum of $3,000,000 of net tangible assets. Amex also sought to impose reverse splits in corporations with shares selling for less than $5, in order to reduce the number of outstanding shares but double the dollar value of the shares. In 1967 Amex' board of governors approved 120 new listings to achieve a thirty-year high.

As a result of the steady expansion in volume during the spring and summer of 1968, both the American and New York Stock Exchanges closed their doors on Wednesday, instituting a four-day trading week to allow brokerage houses to catch up with the backlog of orders. The comprehensive automation program at Amex helped to reduce manual clerical operations, especially in the processing of odd-lots and some round-lot limit orders. Amex raised listing fees to defray the cost of its streamlined market procedures, including a computerized clearance system, high-speed tickers, and sophisticated stock watch and surveillance programs. During 1969 some 1.2 billion shares traded hands, with an average daily volume of almost 5,000,000 shares. Amex listed 1,000 issues representing 2.6 billion shares valued at $67 million. The average price of shares traded was $24, up from $6.76 in 1962. Only 11 percent of volume was in shares selling for less than $5 compared with 42 percent in 1962.

With so great an expansion in the market, change became inevitable. "The most rational approach to the problems of growth is a cooperative one," Saul maintained in support of a proposal made by an Amex-financed study group calling for an interindustry body—composed of brokers, bankers, and institutional investors—to reorganize the structure of the securities business. In a letter to Amex members in November 1970 he wrote that "organizations conceived in other times and under other circumstances may no longer be adequate in many respects to meet the needs of an industry that has expanded and diversified into something different from what it was thirty years ago." The following month he disclosed in a speech before the Bond Club in New York that the American Stock Exchange had proposed to the New York Stock Exchange the consolidation of certain technological services and facilities of the two major exchanges, a proposal that may lead to joint long-term planning of some of the operations of the securities industry.

Ralph S. Saul belongs to the American Bar Association, the Bond Club of New York, and the Sierra Club in San Francisco, a conservationist society. He is the director of the executive committee for the Downtown-Lower Manhattan Association, a member of the finance committee of the State Traffic Safety Council, and a member of the advisory councils of the New York Institute of Finance, Center for the Study of Financial Institutions at the University of Pennsylvania Law School, and New York University Men in Finance. During 1968 and 1969 he served as chairman of the USO campaign in New York City, and he is honorary chairman of the Wall Street committee for the Wiltwyck School for Boys. He was awarded an honorary LL.B. degree by Alfred University in 1968.

Conveying a sense of confidence in appearance and manner, Saul is six feet two inches tall and weighs 200 pounds. The impression he gives of strength and solidity is tempered by his soft smile and gentle manner. He married his high school sweetheart, Betty Jane Bertschinger, on June 16, 1956, and they have a son, Robert Southey, and a daughter, Jane Adams. Saul reads extensively, plays tennis for fast exercise, and also enjoys swimming.

References

Bsns W p150+ O 29 '66
N Y Post p39 S 2 '66 por; p75 N 7 '66 por
N Y Times p1+ Ag 16 '66 por; p51 Ag 17 '66 por
N Y World Journal Tribune III p1 N 6 '66
International Who's Who, 1970-71
Who's Who in America, 1970-71
World Who's Who in Finance and Industry (1970-71)

SCAMMON, RICHARD M(ONTGOMERY)

July 17, 1915- Elections analyst; statistician; political scientist
Address: b. Elections Research Center, 1619 Massachusetts Ave., N.W., Washington, D.C. 20036; h. 5508 Greystone St., Chevy Chase, Md. 20015

Not excepting the years he spent as director of the United States Census Bureau, from 1961 to 1965, Richard M. Scammon has dedicated most of his career to studying elections, both at home and abroad. Currently he continues his election watching as director of the nonprofit Elections Research Center and as political analyst for the National Broadcasting Company and *Newsweek*. Since his goal is not the promotion of a particular issue or candidate but the assessment of the political pulse of the nation, he remains nonpartisan and commands respect for his objectivity. At a time when the New Left and the New Right challenge traditional social and political values, Scammon sees the American center, consisting of the middle- and lower-middle-class citizenry, as having the determining voice in national elections.

Richard Montgomery Scammon was born on July 17, 1915 in Minneapolis, Minnesota to Dr. Richard Everingham Scammon, a physician and professor of anatomy at the University of Minnesota Medical School, and Julia (Simms) Scammon. More attracted to politics than to medicine, even in his teens Scammon became a sharp observer of electoral contests and underwent his first election ordeal at thirteen, when Herbert Hoover defeated Al Smith, his favorite in the 1928 Presidential race. After his graduation from high school in Minneapolis at sixteen, he entered the University of Minnesota, where he majored in political science and government and obtained the B.A. degree in 1935.

Scammon then spent the following academic year at the London School of Economics, studying under Harold Laski, who described him as "the ablest American student" he had ever had, and under Herman Finer. When Scammon returned to the United States he attended law school briefly because he found it not to his liking. He then enrolled in the graduate school of the University of Michigan where in 1938 he took the M.A. degree in political science for his dissertation on "The Special Pattern of Political Behavior in the Administrative County of London, 1922-37."

Weary of formal schooling, Scammon rejected the idea of studying for a Ph.D. degree in favor of practical experience in his field. His first job was that of assistant to the director of the popular weekly public affairs program heard on radio as the "University of Chicago-N.B.C. Round Table of the Air." He worked with the show for two and one half years until he entered the United States Army during World War II. From 1941 to 1946 he served in England, France, and Germany, spending the final year as a political officer with the military government in occupied Germany. Discharged with the rank of captain in 1946, he stayed on in Berlin in a civilian job as chief of the elections and political parties branch of the Civil Administrative Division of the United States Military Government in Germany. As such, he held considerable responsibility for developing licensing policies for political parties and setting up the machinery for West German elections. In 1948 Scammon returned to Washington to head the State Department's division of research for Western Europe.

When the foundation-supported Elections Research Center was founded in 1955, Scammon was appointed its first director. He has continued in that post until the present, except for his one four-year leave of absence as director of the United States Census Bureau. (Even during that period he went on working at the Center in his spare time.) An important elections evaluation agency, the Elections Research Center was established as a nonprofit division of the Governmental Affairs Institute for collecting, organizing, and interpreting election results in local and national contests. All those data are brought together and published in *America Votes; A Handbook of Contemporary American Election Statistics*, which has appeared every two years under the imprint of the

University of Pittsburgh Press since 1956. The book not only provides statistics by state, of the vote since 1945 for president, governor, senator, and congressman, and statistics, by county and ward, of the vote in the most recent election for president, governor, and senator, but also contains basic political information such as the special situations obtaining in each state. So invaluable has the book proved to historians and political analysts who were previously obliged to use scattered and often incomplete sources of information that it is sometimes referred to as the "Bible of United States election statistics."

Through the years Scammon has established a reputation as a first-rate statistician, political soothsayer and psephologist or elections expert, with considerable influence on Washington newsmen and political bosses who rely on his conclusions. He can reel off voting patterns with minute figure breakdowns for districts, counties, and even precincts, throughout the United States. "Mention your home town to him," William Whitworth wrote in an admiring *New Yorker* (September 20, 1969) profile, "and the chances are that Scammon remembers which way it went in the last Presidential election, recalls watching your neighbors vote and knows which parts of town are inhabited by the gentry." Scammon travels a great deal to observe elections at firsthand so that he can weigh the effects that the social, political, and economic characteristics of a community have on voter trends. He chats with the people, looks out for signs of wealth and poverty, evaluates the racial and ethnic mix, and attends sports and cultural activities to get clues to the life style of a given area. That experience with people, politics, and government has given him a record of consistently accurate evaluations that Scammon continues to perfect. Because he deals with both political parties he has to be careful about his impartiality. Richard Scammon has jokingly compared his own role to that of a garbage collector and he has said that data, like garbage, can not be "partisan."

In February 1961 President John F. Kennedy appointed Scammon to head the Bureau of the Census, the principal fact-finding and statistical agency of the United States Government. Sanguine as usual, as the national "nose-counter" Scammon maintained that America could feed a population of 400,000,000 and remained unconcerned about a population explosion. While conceding that more Americans would eventually exacerbate problems in housing, transportation, education, and welfare, he was unwilling to sound the tocsin of doom or "underrate man's ingenuity in conquering his environment," as he pointed out in an article he wrote in collaboration with Frances Spatz Leighton for *American Weekly* (November 5, 1961). According to Scammon, "The land is still there; we've just opted not to live on it." He fears that talk about a population explosion may become a substitute for the critical evaluation of American institutions. His suggestions for coping with the future call for astute, constructive planning and an education that will enable old and young to

RICHARD M. SCAMMON

adjust to a new concept of living. "Our problem will not be over-population," Scammon insists, "but under-thinking."

In addition to his official duties at the Census Bureau, Richard Scammon served as an adviser to Presidents Kennedy and Johnson and to the Democratic party, proving himself invaluable for interpreting trends, for analyzing voting patterns for gains and losses in local Democratic contests, and for gauging the public mood. He chaired a Presidential Commission in 1963-64 on registration and voter participation that found election laws "unreasonable, unfair, and outmoded." Voting requirements often discriminated against the poor, the aged, the illiterate, and the rural resident. To secure broader voting rights the Commission proposed several recommendations, including a ban on literacy tests, poll taxes, and harsh residency requirements, extending the vote to eighteen-year-olds, and creating more comfortable polling establishments. Scammon discovered that voter turn-out paralleled education and income and varied with social class, age, sex, and geography. More men voted than women, more middle-aged than young or old, more whites than Negroes, and more suburban residents than city dwellers. Writing in the New York *Times Magazine* (November 17, 1963), Scammon suggested that more meaningful issues, candidates with more charisma, and the end of the one-party system in the South would "stimulate response from the 'uncaring citizens.'"

Resigning from the Census Bureau in February 1965, Scammon returned to the Elections Research Center because he was concerned that "he was losing his grip on the data." Those data are the facts and figures of election returns, which Scammon believes are the clearest, most precise, and definitive indices of how groups vote in America. After evaluating the demographic materials, Scammon constructed a composite portrait of the typical voter as a white, suburban, middle-aged, middle-income American. Although that estimate did not apply to all regions of the country, it was substantiated by figures gathered from the nation as a whole. Further breakdowns of the statistics showed that the more affluent and better educated American voted Republican, while city dwellers voted Democratic more often than rural residents. Scammon's conclusions flatly contradicted popular misconceptions that the black, the young, and the poor determined the outcome of elections, since the Negro vote approximated only 10 percent of the total and young people were far outnumbered by the thirty-five to sixty-four age group. Less than half of the eligible voters in their twenties bothered to register for voting. "It is the middle-aged voter who wields the decisive electoral power . . . and even with the enfranchisement of eighteen-year-olds, the average age will still be over forty-five, Scammon observed in *Business Week* (September 5, 1970). Identifying the rising suburban vote as an indication of the increased importance of the middle class, he estimated that new economic gains by the laboring class would swell the ranks of the lower middle-class with persons with the same concerns for housing, education, and personal safety shared by other members of suburbia. Scammon interpreted that to mean that groups which once divided on bread and butter issues were realigning on social issues such as race, crime, campus unrest, war, and street riots.

One of the few professional analysts to concentrate on the American political center rather than on the Right or the Left, Scammon expounded his theories on the electorate in the book *The Real Majority: An Extraordinary Examination of the American Electorate* (Coward-McCann, 1970). His collaborator was Ben J. Wattenberg, a journalist and former White House aide of President Lyndon B. Johnson. "The real majority," according to the authors, " is where it has always been—right smack in the center." They hold the view that the middle-class, middle-aged, middle-thinking citizens comprise the great bulk of the American electorate; any changes, if and when they occur, will be evolutionary and centrist in outlook. Any American politician who veers to the extreme Right or Left will therefore court defeat. Social issues have superseded the pocketbook as the voters' main concern. *The Real Majority* soon became the "chic" book along the Washington cocktail circuit.

Scammon is a political consultant to *Newsweek* and to the National Broadcasting Company's news elections unit, which provides the facts and figures for key precincts on which election night computer projections are based. He served as a consultant to the Louis Harris Polls, and though he once opposed the use of polls during election campaigns, he now believes that they "are the best thing for democracy since the direct primary, since they permit the voice of the majority to be heard against that of the clamorous minority." Called a "one-man think tank" by William Whitworth, Scammon lectures widely and writes for popular magazines in a vernacular that appeals to laymen. In 1965 he collaborated with Ben J. Wattenberg on *This U.S.A.* (Doubleday), an upbeat look at the American nation based on the 1960 census data. Some reviewers thought the authors too optimistic about problems of population growth.

In 1958 Scammon led an official American delegation to observe elections in the U.S.S.R. He served as chairman of the United States Select Commission on Western Hemisphere Immigration (1966-68), as president of the National Council on Public Polls (1969) and as senior research consultant to the National Advisory Commission on Civil Disorders. He belongs to the American Academy of Political and Social Sciences, the Academy of Political Science, and both the American and Canadian Political Science associations.

A veritable giant of a man, Scammon stands six feet five inches tall and weighs 280 pounds. Bald, bespectacled, and paunchy, he speaks at a breakneck pace, laughs heartily, and exudes a restless energy even when he is sitting still, chomping a cigar. Although his eyes are piercing, they radiate good humor. On February 20, 1952 Richard M. Scammon married the former Mary Stark Allen, and they have a daughter, Anne. He views himself as "an independent liberal Democrat" or "a man of the center," and sides more with Dr. Pangloss than with Tiresias when scanning the future.

References

New Yorker 45:50+ S 20 '69 por
Who's Who in America, 1970-71

SCHEEL, WALTER (shāl)

July 8, 1919- Vice Chancellor and Foreign Minister of the Federal Republic of Germany
Address: b. Auswärtiges Amt, Bonn, Federal Republic of Germany; h. Schleichstrasse 6, Bonn, Federal Republic of Germany

A "man of the middle," West Germany's Vice-Chancellor and Foreign Minister, Walter Scheel, is largely responsible for the Federal Republic's recent diplomacy of rapprochement with the Soviet bloc, which he views as "the German contribution towards a pan-European policy of equitable settlement, closer cooperation, and the securing of peace." An authority on technical aid to underdeveloped countries, Scheel gained much of his experience in foreign affairs while serving from 1961 to 1966 as Minister for Economic Cooperation. Since 1968 he has been national chairman of the small Free Democratic party, which holds a balance-of-power position in West German politics. Scheel was appointed to his present Cabinet post by incoming Chancellor Willy Brandt in October 1969, after leading his party into a coalition with the Social Democrats. As a result, the Christian Democrats were excluded from the government for the first time in the history of the German Federal Republic.

A native of the industrial Rhineland, Walter Scheel was born on July 8, 1919 in Solingen—a town noted for the manufacture of high-quality cutlery—into a Protestant family of craftsmen. His father was a wheelwright and carriage builder. As a boy, he witnessed the political struggles in his native city, where the Communists enjoyed considerable strength in the 1920's. He obtained his secondary education at the Reform-Realgymnasium in Solingen, and after graduating in 1938 he began his apprenticeship with a local mercantile bank.

In 1939 Scheel was drafted into military service and assigned to the Luftwaffe. As a pilot with a night interceptor squadron operating over France and Russia he downed four Allied planes and earned two Iron Crosses. He was discharged in 1945 with the rank of first lieutenant. After the war he managed a small razor blade factory owned by his wife's family and was for a time on the staff of the Solingen Steel Works. In the early 1950's he was a shareholder and manager of Intermarket and Interfinanz—firms engaged in market analysis and the buying and selling of business enterprises. He also headed several business associations and in 1953 became an independent consultant to business and industry.

Scheel's interest in politics in the early postwar years was motivated by his concern for rebuilding the nation's economy. "I was fascinated by the tasks involved in creating a liberal economic system," he has said, as quoted by Hans Gresmann in *Interplay* (August 1970). In 1946 he joined the Free Democratic party (FDP), whose adherents claimed to be successors of the constitutional liberals of the 1848 revolution and of the liberal industrialists and academicians of Imperial and Weimar Germany. Scheel soon rose to the chairmanship of a local FDP organization and then to membership in the FDP executive committee of North Rhine-Westphalia. In 1948 he was elected to the city council of Solingen, and two years later he won election to the Landtag (state legislature) of North Rhine-Westphalia, at Düsseldorf, where he devoted much of his effort to economic reconstruction and regional planning.

Elected to the Bundestag—the lower house of the federal legislature—in 1953, Scheel became a member of the executive of the federal FDP organization, allying himself with its younger and more progressive faction. As the party's expert on economic and financial matters he was named chairman of its economic affairs committee. From 1955 to 1969 Scheel also was a representative of the Federal Republic in the European Parliament, and in 1956-57 he was a member of West Germany's parliamentary delegation to the European Coal and Steel Community. In 1958 he was elected vice-chairman of the Liberal section in the European Parliament and chairman of its committee for cooperation with developing countries. In the latter position he traveled to Asia, Africa, and Latin America, acquiring a solid background in the field of international development aid. About that time Scheel also served on the presidium of the German Africa Association.

When, as a result of the general election of September 1961, West Germany's ruling Christian Democratic Union (CDU)—together with its Bavarian affiliate, the Christian Social Union (CSU)—no longer commanded a majority in the Bundestag, federal Chancellor Konrad Adenauer was compelled to take the FDP into a coalition government. Although during the 1950's Scheel

WALTER SCHEEL

had sometimes vigorously opposed Adenauer's policies in the Bundestag, the Chancellor admired his expertise in international economic relations and appointed him to the newly created post of Minister for Economic Cooperation in the coalition Cabinet, installed on November 14, 1961. In addition to administering West Germany's $750,000,-000-a-year foreign aid program, Scheel, as Minister for Economic Cooperation, also took on the responsibility of acting as deputy to Foreign Minister Gerhard Schröder.

Scheel embarked on his task with enthusiasm, traveling abroad and promoting the concept of development aid among West Germany's population. In his program he emphasized sound economic principles rather than political considerations and stressed the need for encouraging self-help among nations. He pointed out that because of the growing importance of the developing countries, the industrialized nations of the West would benefit from an enlightened development aid policy which, by raising living standards, would create new markets for Western products.

Calling for increased involvement of private business in governmental foreign aid programs, Scheel advocated an "aid by trade" policy that would require a willingness on the part of West German firms to transfer manufacturing facilities to developing countries and import products from those countries, and he urged businessmen not to shy away from dealing with state-controlled enterprises. In July 1962 Scheel embarked on an extended tour of Latin America to coordinate West Germany's aid with that of the United States and with the programs of such regional organizations as the Alliance for Progress.

Although the development aid program under Scheel's direction seemed more or less successful, some observers doubted its effectiveness in Africa. In 1962 Scheel had insisted that development aid should not become a weapon in the cold war, but West German officials later admitted that projects were sometimes undertaken to meet the growing competition of Communist East Germany. After charges were made in *Der Spiegel* that German financial aid to African nations was often misappropriated or squandered on worthless projects, Scheel announced in January 1965 that all West German aid to Africa would be thoroughly reexamined.

Another aspect of West German development aid was the establishment of a volunteer program —the Deutsche Entwicklungsdienst (German Development Service)—modeled on the Peace Corps of the United States. The program was launched in 1964 with some 800 trainees. By 1965 some 6,000 persons from underdeveloped countries were annually invited to come to West Germany for agricultural or industrial training. Additional thousands were aided by scholarships and special training programs sponsored by West German business firms abroad with the help of government subsidies.

The CDU-FDP coalition government of Ludwig Erhard—who had succeeded Adenauer as Chancellor in October 1963—collapsed on October 27, 1966 when the FDP withdrew its four Cabinet members, in opposition to the Chancellor's insistence on increasing taxes to meet a budgetary deficit. After unsuccessful efforts by the leaders of the FDP and the Social Democratic party (SPD) to arrive at a coalition agreement, a "grand coalition" government of the CDU and the SPD was installed on December 1, 1966 under the chancellorship of Kurt Kiesinger, leaving the FDP, with forty-nine of the 496 Bundestag seats, as the sole party of opposition.

Meanwhile, Scheel's stature within the FDP was growing, and Thomas Dehler, the party's elder statesman, recommended Scheel as future party chairman shortly before his death in July 1967. In September 1967, after FDP chairman Erich Mende announced his intention to resign, the FDP's federal executive nominated Scheel to the party chairmanship. Scheel was elected chairman at the party congress at Freiburg in January 1968 with 216 out of 251 votes.

As the leader of the opposition, Scheel—who had also been elected vice-president of the Bundestag in September 1967—guided the party's policies closer to those of the SPD. When a federal assembly met in West Berlin on March 5, 1969 to choose a successor to the retiring president of the Federal Republic, Heinrich Lübke, the eighty-three FDP delegates voted almost unanimously for the Social Democratic candidate, Gustav Heinemann, thus ensuring his victory. Scheel, who engineered his party's vote, thereby forged an unprecedented unity within FDP ranks and paved the way for an SPD-FDP coalition.

During the campaign that preceded the general election of September 28, 1969, the FDP called for a "partnership for progress" with the SPD and demanded reform measures. The FDP received only 5.8 percent of the vote—only slightly more than the 5 percent it needed for continued representation—and thirty seats in the Bundestag. The SPD, with 224 seats, had won enough of a victory so that an SPD-FDP coalition would have a twelve-vote majority among the 496 voting members of the Bundestag.

After the thirty-four-member FDP executive had given its approval with only two dissenting votes. Scheel began full-scale discussions with SPD leader Willy Brandt, rejecting a last-minute bid by Chancellor Kiesinger for a CDU-FDP coalition. A cornerstone of their program was an Eastern policy aimed at "acceptance of the realities" in Central Europe. On October 3, 1969, after minor differences over domestic policy had been ironed out, the party leaders announced agreement on a basis for a coalition government.

Brandt became Chancellor on October 21, 1969, and on the following day the coalition Cabinet of eleven Social Democrats and three Free Democrats was installed. Taking office as Vice-Chancellor and Foreign Minister, Scheel resigned as Bundestag vice-president but retained the FDP chairmanship and took charge of the 8,000-member Foreign Office staff. During his early months in office, he took part in negotiations concerning West German acceptance of the nuclear nonproliferation treaty, reassured Israel of his government's continued friendship, toured Asian countries, and initiated preliminary talks for agreements with the Soviet Union and Poland. On a trip to Spain in April 1970 he made an unprecedented demand for a meeting with leaders of the outlawed opposition to the government of Generalissimo Francisco Franco. As temporary president of the European Economic Community (EEC) council of ministers in the summer of 1970, he engaged in talks concerning Great Britain's bid for membership in the Common Market.

Some observers questioned Scheel's effectiveness as Foreign Minister, noting that he was often overshadowed by Brandt, who liked to take the initiative in conducting foreign policy. In the spring of 1970 Scheel was criticized for not having acted decisively enough in the case of West German Ambassador Karl von Spreti, who was kidnapped and killed by leftist guerrillas in Guatemala. Scheel's position was further weakened by severe setbacks suffered by the FDP in state elections held in June 1970 in North Rhine-Westphalia, Saarland, and Lower Saxony. Nevertheless, he was reelected party chairman later that month with 298 out of 384 votes.

On July 26, 1970 Scheel went to Moscow at the head of a twenty-five-member delegation to engage in discussions for a nonaggression treaty. Fearing that undue concessions might be made to the Soviet Union, the Christian Democrats turned down Scheel's invitation to send a delegate to the talks. On August 7 Scheel and Soviet Foreign Minister Andrei Gromyko concluded a treaty that committed the two powers to resolve any conflicts by peaceful means; to respect the territorial integrity of all European states; to renounce territorial claims against any other country; and to regard all boundaries, including Poland's western border at the Oder-Neisse line and the border between East and West Germany, as inviolate. Not included in the treaty, but attached in separate notes, were statements affirming West Germany's view that the German people had the right to seek reunification of the country "through free self-determination" and asserting the continued rights and responsibilities of the Western Allies in Berlin and in Germany as a whole. The treaty was hailed at home and abroad as a landmark in East-West relations and enhanced Scheel's stature as a diplomat.

A second major step in West Germany's new Eastern policy was taken in November 1970, when Scheel came to Warsaw to conclude a treaty with Poland. Initiated by Scheel and Polish Foreign Minister Stefan Jedrychowski on November 18, the treaty normalized relations between the two countries and accorded mutual recognition—although it did not give legal finality—to the Oder-Neisse frontier. West Germany thus relinquished its claim to some 40,000 miles of territory that had been German before World War II. Although the treaty did not refer to the problem—raised by Scheel—of the status of some 1,000,000 Germans living east of the Oder-Neisse line, an understanding was reached that the problem would be dealt with on an informal basis. The treaty was formally signed on December 7, 1970.

Meanwhile the SPD-FDP coalition government was placed in jeopardy when, in early October, Mende and two other FDP Bundestag members defected from the Free Democratic ranks and joined the CDU. Although the defection reduced the coalition's majority to six votes, Scheel and Brandt expressed confidence that their government would survive, declaring that West Germany's domestic economic conditions, as well as its foreign relations, had improved considerably. The outlook for the coalition brightened in November 1970, when the FDP scored substantial gains in state elections in Hesse and Bavaria.

In 1968 Scheel became president of the World Liberal Union (or Liberal International). His book, *Konturen einer neuen Welt*, published in Düsseldorf in 1965, deals with aid to underdeveloped countries. Scheel also edited the volume *Perspektiven deutscher Politik* (1969). Among his many decorations is the Döring medal, conferred on him in 1969, and the Federal Republic's Great Cross of the Order of Merit (Grosses Bundesverdienstkreuz) with star.

Walter Scheel was first married in 1942 to the former Eva Kronenberg, who died in 1966, and he has a son from that marriage. He was married a second time, in 1969, to Dr. Mildred Wirtz of Munich, a roentgenologist, who had been widowed and has a six-year-old daughter. In 1970 the Scheels became the parents of a daughter, Andrea Gwendolyn who—according to *Time* (August 17, 1970)—was named after Andrei Gromyko. The easygoing, affable West German Foreign Minister has gray-blue eyes and receding gray hair and is noted for his appeal to women, his quick wit, his flair for telling jokes, his gourmet tastes, his expensive cigars, and his preference for informal dress. Scheel enjoys Bach organ works and modern art. His home in the fashionable Venusberg section of Bonn is decorated with wooden masks that he acquired on his trips to Africa. He also has a house in a secluded valley in the Austrian Alps. Hans Gresmann described him in the *Inter-*

play article as an "elegant conversationalist with a bent for facile irony" and "the very opposite of an ascetic, a man wholly without angularities and rough edges."

References

N Y Times p5 O 24 '69 por
Time 94:26 O 31 '69 por; 96:17 Ag 17 '70 por
International Who's Who, 1970-71
Wer ist Wer? (1969-70)
Who's Who in Germany (1964)

SCHILLER, KARL (AUGUST FRITZ)

Apr. 24, 1911- Minister of Economics and Finance of the Federal Republic of Germany; economist; university professor
Address: b. Bundesministerium für Wirtschaft, Bonn-Duisdorf, Federal Republic of Germany; h. August-Bolten-Weg 6, Hamburg-Blankenese, Federal Republic of Germany

The "supreme overlord of the West German economy," Dr. Karl Schiller, Minister of Economics and Finance of the Federal Republic of Germany, is both a university scholar and a public official. A member of West Germany's Social Democratic party since 1946, and a professor of economics at the University of Hamburg since 1947, Schiller helped to direct the post-World War II reconstruction of the city of Hamburg and the recovery of West Berlin from the crisis brought about by the construction of the Berlin wall in 1961. As Minister of Economics in the "grand coalition" government of Kurt Kiesinger, Schiller effected West Germany's recovery from the recession of 1966-67 by "orchestrating" harmony among the country's divergent economic interests. Continuing as Economics Minister in the Cabinet of Willy Brandt, which came to power in 1969, Schiller added the portfolio of Finance to his responsibilities in May 1971. His influence on the international monetary scene has made him one of Europe's most powerful men. Highly respected among his countrymen, Schiller was given a top rating for political ability in a public opinion poll conducted by the London *Times* among West Germans in the fall of 1969.

Karl August Fritz Schiller was born on April 24, 1911 in Breslau, Silesia (now the Polish city of Wroclaw) to Carl Schiller, an electrical engineer, and Marie (Dreizehner) Schiller. He grew up in Kiel, the capital of Schleswig-Holstein, where his family had moved soon after his birth and attended the Hebbel-Schule, a Realgymnasium, or nonclassical secondary school, there. After passing his Abitur, at the head of his class, in 1931, he studied economics and sociology at the universities of Kiel, Frankfurt, Berlin, and Heidelberg. He obtained a diploma in political economics in 1934 and then served for a year as an assistant lecturer at the University of Heidelberg while studying for his doctorate under Professor Carl Brinkmann. His dissertation, "Arbeitsbeschaffung und Finanzord-

KARL SCHILLER

nung," which dealt with public works programs and government finances, drew some negative criticism from governmental authorities, who noted that he relied almost completely on sources from the pre-Nazi era in researching it.

On obtaining his doctorate (Dr. rer. pol.) at Heidelberg in 1935, Schiller returned to Kiel, where he headed a research group at the university's Institut für Weltwirtschaft (Institute for World Economy) until 1941. From 1939 to 1941 he also taught at the University of Kiel as a Privatdozent, having qualified as a university lecturer with a thesis on market regulation in international agriculture. Although as a government employee he was automatically enrolled in the National Socialist party, he has said that he steered clear of its activities and once told an interviewer that his enlistment in the German army in 1941 was motivated by his desire to escape the party's demands. Schiller served with the intelligence section of the Wehrmacht and saw action on the Russian front with the 290th Infantry Division, rising to the rank of Oberleutnant (first lieutenant).

Although Schiller was offered an assistant professorship at the University of Rostock in 1944, while still in the army, he never taught in that city, which became part of the Soviet occupation zone at the end of the war. Instead he returned to the University of Kiel after his discharge in 1945, where he remained as a guest professor until 1946. Appointed in 1947 to a professorial chair in the faculty of economics and social science at the University of Hamburg, he became, in addition, director of the university's Institut für Aussenhandel und Überseewirtschaft (Institute for Foreign Trade and International Commerce) and of its socioeconomic seminar. A specialist in economic theory, political economics, and international trade, and a leading exponent of the principles of the British economist John Maynard Keynes, he also became an authority on problems of economic growth in underdeveloped nations, after making several study trips abroad. In 1956 Schiller was elected to a two-year term as rector of the University of Hamburg, becoming the youngest man ever to serve in that post.

In 1946 Schiller joined the newly reconstituted Social Democratic party (SPD), and in the years that followed helped to change its orientation from a doctrinaire Marxism to a broadly-based liberalism. The principle of "competition as far as possible; planning as far as necessary," which he advanced in a speech delivered at a party congress in Bochum in 1953, became a basic part of the SPD's liberal Godesberg program that was adopted in 1959.

As head of an advisory commission to formulate a program for the rebuilding of the war-torn city of Hamburg, Schiller issued a comprehensive report entitled "Denkschrift zur künftigen Entwicklung Hamburgs" ("Memorandum on the Future Development of Hamburg") in 1947. Known as the Schiller Report, it became a blueprint for Schiller's own activities as senator (or commissioner) for economics and commerce of the free Hanseatic city of Hamburg from 1948 to 1953, when he presided over the reconstruction of the city as a major world seaport and the revival of its shipbuilding industry and merchant marine. Schiller also served from 1949 to 1953 in the Bundesrat, or upper house of the West German federal parliament, where, among other matters, he promoted legislation against obstacles to free competition. From 1949 to 1957 he was, in addition, a member of Hamburg's Bürgerschaft (House of Burgesses), acting, beginning with 1954, as spokesman on economic affairs for its SPD faction.

In the wake of the crisis engendered by the building of the Berlin wall by East German Communist authorities in August 1961, Willy Brandt, then the mayor of West Berlin, called on Schiller to help alleviate the economic hardships resulting from the city's isolation. As West Berlin's senator of economic affairs from 1961 to 1965, Schiller took steps to obtain effective federal legislation to provide aid for the city and promoted tax incentives that helped stem the exodus of workers. In 1962 and 1963 he visited the United States and consulted with President John F. Kennedy and other government officials, as well as business leaders, in an effort to draw more American investments to West Berlin. Under Schiller's supervision, West Berlin's economy not only surmounted its crisis but actually experienced a considerable upsurge.

Elected deputy chairman of the SPD's economic policy committee in 1962, Schiller succeeded Heinrich Deist as chairman of that committee two years later at the Karlsruhe party congress, which also elected him to the SPD executive board. In 1965 Schiller won a seat in the Bundestag, the lower house of the federal parliament, as a representative of Berlin, becoming at the same time deputy chairman of the SPD parliamentary faction and its spokesman on economic policy. In 1966 he was elected to the ruling presidium of the SPD. Schiller also served the federal government from 1963 to 1966 as a member of the scientific advisory council of the Ministry of Economic Cooperation.

A sharp recession and financial crisis in the fall of 1966 led to the collapse of the Cabinet of Chancellor Ludwig Erhard and the inauguration, on December 1, of West Germany's first "grand coalition" government, headed by Christian Democratic Chancellor Kurt Kiesinger and Social Democratic Vice-Chancellor Willy Brandt. At Brandt's urging, Schiller was appointed Minister of Economics in the new Cabinet, and he immediately began to deal with the economic crisis by means of a policy of "controlled expansion." Through "concerted action" of labor, industry, and government, Schiller tried to harmonize investments, wage demands, and other economic factors, with the aim of stimulating a general upturn in business. The principles of Schiller's new economic policy were embodied in a "law for the promotion of stability and growth of the economy," adopted in June 1967, that was inspired in part by the United States Employment Act of 1946.

To increase the country's productive capacity, Schiller instituted special "pump-priming" public works programs, to be funded by short-term borrowing. At the same time, to balance the budget, taxes were raised, while reductions were made in military expenditures, farm subsidies, and some welfare benefits. When, in his view, the economy needed a boost, Schiller urged trade union leaders to make greater wage demands. In the fall of 1967 he personally mediated a labor dispute in the metals industry of North Baden-Württemberg, and he took a hand in reviving the impoverished coal industry of the Ruhr area by formulating a plan to place the coal mines under a single holding company that would be aided by government funds.

By mid-1967, the downward trend of the West German economy had begun to reverse itself, and in April 1968 Schiller could report to the Bundestag that the country had withstood the recession. By the summer of 1968 Schiller's policies had established virtually full employment and restored economic growth without jeopardizing price stability. An international monetary crisis in November 1968 brought increasing pressure from abroad for upward valuation of the West German mark. In response, Schiller, while resisting demands for revaluation, made some concessions to the Federal Republic's Western European trading partners by reducing import taxes and tax rebates on exports.

By March 1969 Schiller had become convinced that upward valuation of the mark was necessary to combat inflation, a position that was reportedly urged on him by Karl Blessing, president of the Bundesbank. In May Schiller recommended revaluation as the only practical means of stemming the "import of inflation" from abroad. The rejection of his proposals by Kiesinger and Finance Minister Franz-Josef Strauss almost broke up the government coalition. Continuing inflation made currency revaluation a major campaign issue in the weeks that preceded the national election of September 28, 1969. Schiller's persuasive advocacy of revaluation contributed considerably to the SPD's success in obtaining a plurality of Bundestag seats in the election.

A new coalition government of Social Democrats and Free Democrats, under the Chancellorship of Willy Brandt, took office on October 21, 1969, with Schiller continuing to serve as Minister of Economics. Three days later, in its first major action, the Brandt government formally increased the value of the mark from $.25 to $.273. Defending the new valuation, Schiller called it "the golden mean—courageous but not foolhardy." To help West German farmers to recover the losses they would sustain from revaluation, Schiller arranged for them to obtain aid from the European Economic Community's farm fund.

A minor crisis erupted in the Brandt Cabinet in February 1970, when the Chancellor rejected a series of anti-inflationary tax measures proposed by Schiller, fearing that their adoption could have an adverse effect on SPD candidates in forthcoming local elections. The crisis was resolved with Brandt's refusal to accept Schiller's resignation and with the adoption of compromise anti-inflation measures. To stabilize the economy further, Schiller introduced legislation imposing surcharges on personal and corporate taxes and suspending tax writeoffs on investments in July, and announced wage and price guidelines in October 1970. When on May 13, 1971 Finance Minister Alex Möller resigned, charging that excessive budget demands by other members of the government had made it impossible to balance the budget, Brandt placed Schiller at the head of a newly created "super-ministry," combining the portfolios of Economics and Finance.

At the time Schiller assumed his dual Cabinet post, Europe was again shaken by a currency crisis, and inflation in Germany was mounting beyond all predictions. Although the crisis was largely the result of a massive influx of unwanted United States dollars into European markets, many observers blamed Schiller for having touched it off by his statement, early in May 1971, that since the United States was not going to devalue the dollar, the Common Market nations should allow their currencies to float against the dollar. According to *Time* (May 17, 1971), "The money crisis began when some remarks by Schiller led money speculators to believe that Germany would soon raise the official value of the mark. . . . Speculators immediately started selling dollars for marks, hoping to make a quick profit."

At a meeting of Common Market representatives at Brussels on May 8, 1971 Schiller's proposals for floating Common Market currencies against the dollar, in fixed relationship with each other, as a step toward establishing a common European currency, was opposed by French Finance Minister Valéry Giscard d'Estaing. He feared that West Germany would dominate any new currency union. A compromise was finally reached, under which the margin of fluctuation of the currencies was allowed to expand. On the following day the West German government began to float the mark within the permitted range, at the same time introducing new monetary controls to stop the influx of speculators' dollars. In June 1971 Schiller announced plans for a major tax reform, aimed at bringing "justice and simplicity" to the tax system by shifting the burden from low-income groups to the more affluent. Declaring that the floating of the mark had "proved itself very well," Schiller said, as quoted in the *Wall Street Journal* (August 26, 1971), that the current monetary crisis presented a "unique chance" to reform the international monetary system. The possibilities of international monetary reform were discussed at a four-day meeting of the International Monetary Fund and World Bank, presided over by Schiller, that opened in Washington, D.C. on September 27, 1971.

A supporter of Chancellor Brandt's *Ostpolitik*, Schiller has visited the Soviet Union and other Communist countries to stimulate trade. In July 1970 he was named president of the European Economic Community's Council of Ministers, with major responsibility for dealing with the question of British membership in the Common Market. He has maintained friendly relations with United States officials, but he takes a dim view of what he considers American protectionist policies, notably the 10 percent surcharge on nonquota imports announced by President Richard Nixon in August 1971.

Among Schiller's published works are the books *Aufgaben und Versuche; Zur Neuen Ordnung von Wirtschaft und Gesellschaft* (1953), a collection of essays and speeches on new concepts of economy and society; *Der Ökonom und die Gesellschaft; Das freiheitliche und das soziale Element in der Wirtschaftspolitik* (1964), an examination of the role of the economist in society; and *Aufgeklärte Marktwirtschaft; Kollektive Vernunft in Politik und Wirtschaft* (1969), a study of rationality in politics and economics. He is also a prolific contributor to magazines, symposia, and reference works. In addition to his academic and political activities, he has served on the boards of directors of the Dortmunder Bergbau Aktien-Gesellschaft, a mining company, and the Hamburger Hafen- und Lagerhaus Aktien-Gesellschaft, a harbor warehouse company.

Dr. Karl Schiller has been married three times. He was divorced in 1970 from his second wife, the former Annemarie Vogt, to whom he had been married since 1951. On May 21, 1971 he married Dr. Etta Eckel, a lawyer with the North Rhine-Westphalia finance ministry. Schiller, who is a grandfather, has two married daughters, Barbara and Bettina, from his first marriage; another daughter, Christa, and a son, Michael-Tonio, are from the second marriage. A slender man, five feet seven inches tall, Schiller has a youthful, boyish face that belies his age, and he wears custom-tailored suits and horn-rimmed glasses. Respected for his scholarship, wit, and rhetorical skill, he laces his writings and speeches with catchy slogans, bon mots, and quotations from literature. He speaks English fluently, but his French is less than perfect. Often working fifteen hours a day, he has a reputation as a perfectionist, but he welcomes differences of opinion among his staff. His self-assurance has led some observers to detect a hint of arrogance in his manner. Schiller collects rare

stones as a hobby, and for relaxation he reads, listens to music—classical and jazz—and goes to the theatre. In 1968 the popular West German magazine *Der Stern* named him "man of the year." The German Federal Republic conferred its Great Cross of the Order of Merit (Grosses Bundesverdienstkreuz) with star on Schiller in 1969.

References

N Y Times p68 N 21 '68 por; p43 My 8 '71 por
Washington (D.C.) Post L p1+ S 26 '71 por
International Who's Who, 1971-72
International Year Book and Statesmen's Who's Who, 1971
Kürschners Deutscher Gelehrten-Kalender, 1970
Persönlichkeiten der Gegenwart. Heft 9. Karl Schiller: Ein Porträt (1969)
Wer ist Wer? (1969-70)
Who's Who in Germany (1964)

SCHRANZ, KARL

Nov. 18, 1938- Austrian ski racer
Address: b. Skifabrik Franz Kneissl, Kufstein/Tirol, Münchnerstrasse, Austria; h. A-6580, St. Anton, Arlberg, Austria

Among Alpine racers, who usually peak in their early twenties, Karl Schranz of Austria is, at thirty-two, the reigning "grand old man" of the slopes. Since 1957 Schranz has won more than 100 official ski races, far more than any other member of the Fédération Internationale de Ski, the world amateur skiing association. He garnered his first FIS world championships, in downhill and combined slalom events, in 1962, and captured the giant slalom title in 1970. In both 1969 and 1970 he won the World Cup, the highest FIS award, based on the total number of points accrued by a skier in his best downhill, slalom, and great slalom finishes during a season. After seriously considering retirement in 1970, Schranz returned to competition, apparently with his eye on the 1972 Winter Olympics. (He has yet to win an Olympic gold medal.) Because there is no direct remuneration in amateur skiing, the Austrian champion earns his living by serving as a public relations agent and technical adviser with Skifabrik Franz Kneissl, manufacturers of ski equipment.

Karl Schranz was born on November 18, 1938 in the ski resort village of St. Anton, high in the Austrian Alps, to Anton Schranz, an official with the Austrian Federal Railway, and Anna Roith Schranz. He has four siblings, Arnold, Gertraud, Helmut, and Anton. Schranz began skiing in childhood. When he, as an adolescent, was developing his speed and prowess on the slopes, the Austrian national ski team was perfecting the advanced techniques that put it into world leadership. That leadership was personified in Tony Sailer, who won an unprecedented three gold medals in the 1956 Winter Olympics.

Schranz's first important adult victories were in the Arlberg-Kandahar competition, held in his hometown, in which he won the downhill championship in 1957, 1958, and 1959. In the latter year he also took the downhill at the Lauberhorn-Alpine meet at Wengen, Switzerland, and in January 1960 he won the slalom in the Hahnenkamm competition at Kitzbühl, Austria.

The annual amateur ski racing tour consists of some twenty-eight meets, held between December or early January and March. The Winter Olympics and the FIS world championships are special, quadrennial meets. In his first Olympic effort, at Squaw Valley, California in 1960, Schranz finished far out of contention, but in the 1962 FIS world championships at Chamonix, France he won the downhill and combined slalom races. At the beginning of the 1963 racing season Schranz won the downhill at Wengen by four seconds, a run-away triumph. In reporting the event for the western edition of the New York *Times* (January 15, 1963), Robert Daley wrote: "His secret, they are saying in the Alps today, is in holding most of his weight on the rear of his ski. . . . It is difficult to hold Schranz's tight crouch for three and a half minutes at such speed. He is virtually leaning backward."

Handicapped by an arm injury, Schranz finished no better than second in any phase of the 1964 Winter Olympics, held at Innsbruck, Austria. In 1965 he won the combined title at Wengen and the downhill at St. Anton, and the following year he took both the downhill and combined titles at Wengen, the combined at Kitzbühl, and the special slalom in the Émile Allais Cup championships at Megève, France. In the Tyrolean championships at Hochgurgl, Austria in December 1967 he won the slalom, posting times of 48.2 and 53.2 seconds for a total of 101.4 seconds.

In the Olympic slalom at Grenoble, France in 1968 Schranz clocked 1 minute 39.23 seconds, half a second faster than Jean-Claude Killy of France. The judges declared Killy the winner, however, because, according to them, Schranz had missed two gates on the densely foggy course. Early in 1969 Schranz won the downhills at St. Anton, Hahnenkamm, and Wengen. The Wengen victory—which paced the Austrian team to a sweep of the meet—set a record for the 4,260-meter course: 3 minutes 1.60 seconds. Schranz clinched the World Cup in March 1969 by winning the du Maurier Cup international giant slalom at Beaupré, Canada.

His first victory in the 1970 Alpine skiing season was in the giant slalom at Adelboden, Switzerland on January 5. He zigzagged the 1,600-meter course in 1 minute 41.85 seconds in the first heat and 1:40.91 in the second, for a total time of 3:22.76. At Megève, France on January 23 he won the downhill, completing the 3,369-yard course (which has a drop of 926 yards) in 2 minutes 12.80 seconds. He trailed Patrick Russel of France and Gustavo Thöni of Italy in World Cup points until February 10, when he won the giant slalom in the world Alpine ski championships at Val Gardena, Italy. The Val Gardena track is 1,563 meters long,

KARL SCHRANZ

with sixty-eight gates. Schranz covered it in heats of 2:15.15 and 2:04.4, for a total of 4:19.19.

Dan Jenkins reported from Val Gardena for *Sports Illustrated* (February 23, 1970): "The Austrians had got off to their most dreadful start ever in the men's slalom. . . . In the opening event no Austrian finished the race. Schranz and Harald Rofner fell, Heini Messner missed a gate and Herbert Huber . . . never even started. But good Old Schranz, who is sort of the Sam Snead of ski racing, brought them back all right, as he has so often done. Schranz was simply magnificent in about the most tiring and rugged giant slalom race the world championship has ever staged."

Schranz's second straight World Cup title was assured when the closest contender, Russel, was knocked out of the running by Schranz's teammate Werner Bleiner in the giant slalom at Voss, Norway on March 13. William Johnson reported on the occasion in *Sports Illustrated* (March 23, 1970): "The young hotshots—Russel, Jean Noel Augert, Alain Penz of France and Thöni of Italy, the combined bronze winner—simply could not bring down the King. At thirty-one, Schranz reigned again. And though he was once renowned for his sour manner, Karl was all sunshine now."

Johnson quoted Schranz as saying that the season just completed was his last. "I have decided to stop amateur racing . . . now that I am on top." There was a rumor that he might become coach of the Austrian team. He was already a respected mentor to his younger teammates, such as Karl Cordin, inspiring in them emulation of what has been called his "fierce and fearless approach." There was also speculation that he might follow Billy Kidd of the United States into the newly formed professional circuit, the World Professional Skiing Championships.

But Schranz changed his mind, and in the autumn of 1970 he began practising in preparation for the 1971 season. Close observers believe that a prime factor in his decision to return to competition is his desire to win an Olympic gold medal, the one conspicuous lacuna in his trophy collection. Accordingly, such observers predict that he will remain an active amateur until the next Winter Olympic games, which are scheduled to take place in Sapporo, Japan in 1972.

Many ski writers have observed that Schranz, contrary to the general rule in skiing, seems to improve with age. Maturity has made him, in the opinion of at least one expert observer, the "wisest" of skiers. A writer in *Austrian Information* (March 1970) said of him: "The 'old' Schranz has one great advantage over his younger competitors: there is a fatalistic strain in him. He knows that one cannot force a victory. Experience has taught him that taking too great a risk can end in disaster. He made those mistakes himself when he was younger."

Schranz's major duty as an agent of the Kneissl Company is to flaunt the manufacturer's name or symbol (a star) on his gear. He also gives the company technical advice and tests new equipment for it. His remuneration for those tasks has been estimated at $50,000, in addition to bonuses of $4,000 for each victory. In the past, such income was considered incompatible with amateur status, but, the Fédération Internationale de Ski, facing the fact that skiers must have some form of livelihood while spending ten months a year competing or training for competition, has relaxed its pecuniary rule. The International Olympic Committee is expected to do likewise, if only for reasons of uniformity. But if reports are true, it is likely to do so only after the retirement of Avery Brundage, the octogenarian who heads the committee. According to Marc Hodler, president of the FIS, Brundage's dedication to the definition of amateurism as an "avocation without gain of any kind" is "a personal battle and his last battle."

Karl Schranz is about five feet nine and a half inches tall, weighs between 160 and 165 pounds, and has brown eyes and light brown hair. His physical strength is obvious, particularly in his legs, which have been described as "thick, heavy." A bachelor, Schranz leads a quiet life, relishing, in his sedentary moments, good books and music. He skis for recreation when he is not doing it in, or in preparation for, competition. He also enjoys swimming, playing soccer and tennis, and running. His church is the Roman Catholic. Dan Jenkins described his visit with Schranz in his *Sports Illustrated* article. "Two rooms of his family hotel in St. Anton overflowed with trophies. He had been a marvel and he knew why: 'I win because I like it better than anyone else,' he said. 'I love training. . . . I don't drink, smoke, or eat spaghetti. I've never felt bad a day in my life. When I win I go to bed at nine o'clock and everyone else celebrates. All I ever wanted to be was a ski racer and I am very happy.' "

References

Austrian Information 23:4 Mr '70 pors
N Y Times p1+ F 19 '68
Newsday p57 Mr 20 '69
Newsweek 73:58 F 3 '69 por
Sports Illus 32:26+ F 23 '70; 32:58+
    Mr 23 '70 por
Time 95:48 Mr 23 '70

SCOTT, DAVID R(ANDOLPH)

June 6, 1932- Astronaut
Address: b. NASA Manned Spacecraft Center, Houston, Tex. 77058

The first three flights to land men on the moon, staged by the National Aeronautics and Space Administration between July 1969 and February 1971, were chiefly feats of engineering in which the astronauts served primarily as test pilots. More specifically scientific was the twelve-day lunar expedition of Apollo 15, led by Colonel David R. Scott of the United States Air Force in July and August 1971. The selenological trove brought back to earth by Scott and his two Air Force crewmates is contributing significantly to cosmogony, and the two final flights in the Apollo program, scheduled for March and December 1972, are expected to abet that science further. After the completion of Apollo, NASA reportedly intends to apply its resources to earth-oriented projects, such as the orbiting Skylab manned space station and the space shuttle, until technology makes possible a permanent base on the moon, probably about 1980.

One of two sons of an Air Force brigadier general, David Randolph Scott was born at Randolph Air Force Base in San Antonio, Texas on June 6, 1932. His father, Tom W. Scott, who now lives in retirement with Mrs. Scott in La Jolla, California, told a reporter for the New York *Times* (August 15, 1971) how David and his brother were raised: "They were taught respect for their elders. . . . They still address me as 'Yes, sir' and 'No, sir.' "

In childhood Scott suffered various allergic ailments, including severe attacks of asthma, but he outgrew them, and as a high school student he was an outstanding swimmer with a strong physique. After attending military academies and other schools in Texas, California, and the Philippines, he graduated from Western High School in Washington, D.C., where the entry under his name in the 1949 yearbook read: "Has a dislike for pokey people. Ambition to fly in the Air Corps. Shows unusual mechanical ability."

Scott's appointment to the United States Military Academy was delayed by the requirement that he have his teeth straightened, and while undergoing orthodontia he attended the University of Michigan for a year. At West Point the intensely competitive but popular Scott pursued both studies and extracurricular activities with his characteristic diligence and vigor. In his senior year he was captain of the water polo team, and scholastically he ranked fifth in a class of 633.

In 1954 Scott received a B.S. degree at West Point and was commissioned an officer in the United States Air Force. After training at Webb and Laughlin Air Force bases in Texas and Luke Air Force Base in Arizona, he flew for four years (1956-60) with the Thirty-second Tactical Fighter Squadron at Soesterberg Air Force Base in the Netherlands. As a jet fighter pilot he demonstrated his cool presence of mind in two dangerous situations: after losing an engine over the North Sea he brought his plane to a landing on the Dutch coast, and on another occasion he made an emergency landing on a golf course when his plane suffered an engine flare-out.

In the early 1960's Scott earned an M.S. degree in aeronautics and astronautics at the Massachusetts Institute of Technology, with a dissertation on interplanetary navigation. In 1963, when he was an advanced student at the Aerospace Research Pilot School at Edwards Air Force Base in California, Scott was named an astronaut. His first flight for NASA was an earth-orbital mission with Neil Armstrong in Gemini 8 in March 1966. On the first day of that flight, which was to have lasted three days, Scott and Armstrong achieved the first docking in space, a link-up with an unmanned Agena rocket. No sooner had they done so when a short circuit in a thruster mechanism sent their craft into a harrowing spin, and they were forced to splash down prematurely in the Pacific, after only twelve hours aloft. Scott's second space assignment was to pilot the command module of Apollo 9 in earth orbit for ten days in March 1969. On that occasion Scott's companions, James A. McDivitt and Russell L. Schweikart, tested the spaceworthiness of the then new LM, the lunar landing module.

In preparation for the flight of Apollo 15, Scott, Lieutenant Colonel James B. Irwin, and Major Alfred M. Worden trained themselves in science, especially geology, through field trips, reading, and instruction from experts. "I really got hooked on geology," Scott has said. "I had always liked history, and when I was a fighter pilot in Europe, flying over North Africa and Greece, I became fascinated with the archeological ruins. Archeology became a sideline of mine. When I got to geology, I could see the similarities with history and archeology and soon felt myself on familiar ground. ... Gradually we made the transition from engineers and test pilots to men who could think geology."

The 107,000-pound Apollo 15 blasted off from Cape Kennedy, Florida at 9:34 A.M. EDT on July 26, 1971. After orbiting the earth for three hours it headed for the moon, 250,000 miles away, at an initial speed of 24,218 miles per hour. Three days later, as they approached their destination, Scott, Irwin, and Worden donned black eye shades and conducted the first of their scientific experiments: making detailed observations on the flashbulb-like blips of light reported by previous moon explorers. The strange phenomena are believed to be the effect, on the retina or directly on the brain, of high-energy cosmic rays.

On July 29, 1971 Apollo 15 entered lunar orbit, and the following day, while Worden remained in the orbiting command ship *Endeavour*, Scott, accompanied by Irwin, piloted the lunar module *Falcon* down to a landing north of Salyut Crater in the Hadley-Apennine region of the moon. Scott and Irwin remained on the moon three days, exploring more than seventeen miles of the stark, undulating terrain in the Jeep-like runabout *Rover 1*, taking photographs and motion pictures, setting up scientific apparatus, and collecting 175 pounds of moon dust and rock.

DAVID R. SCOTT

The most important sample collected was a small fragment that Scott immediately recognized as anorthosite, the crystalline "Genesis rock" that probably formed the moon's original crust some 4.6 billion years ago. (On earth, where early geological history has been erased by the erosion of water and wind, the oldest rocks are only about 3.4 billion years old.) Another important item was an eight-and-one-half-foot-long core sample extracted from the lunar soil with great difficulty by means of a hollow drill. The core, containing fifty-seven separate layers of soil, is expected to reveal changes in the sun's radiation as it hit the moon over the course of the last 2.4 billion years.

A color television camera mounted on *Rover 1* and controlled from Mission Control in Houston televised to earth many of the astronauts' activities on the moon, up to and including the lift-off in *Falcon* on the afternoon of August 2. As the lunar module left the moon's surface, television and radio audiences heard the Air Force song "Off We Go Into the Wild Blue Yonder" blaring tinnily from a small tape player the astronauts had smuggled aboard Apollo 15. After *Falcon* docked with the *Endeavour*, Scott and Irwin transferred to the latter and the lunar module was released and sent crashing back to the moon. Apollo 15 remained in lunar orbit for two more days, as the astronauts aimed the command ship for the course it would take back to earth and released a small lunar satellite that is expected to relay scientific information to earth for a year.

At 5:23 P.M. on August 4, Apollo 15 began its return trip to earth. In the course of the journey Major Worden spacewalked, retrieving motion pictures of the lunar surface from the experimental bay of the service module. On the afternoon of August 7 the *Endeavour* separated from the service module, reentered the earth's atmosphere, and splashed down in the Pacific, 333 miles north of Hawaii. A waiting team of sailors from the U.S.S. *Okinawa* plucked the astronauts from the sea and took them by helicopter to the aircraft carrier, whence they were flown via Hawaii to the United States mainland. They were debriefed—

until August 24—but not quarantined, because the previous quarantining of moon explorers for possible contamination by lunar "germs" proved to be unnecessary. A week after their return, Dr. Charles A. Berry, their physician, revealed that their condition did not "fit the pattern" established by previous space voyagers. He said that both Scott and Irwin had irregular heart beats while on the moon's surface; that Irwin suffered from dizziness for six days after splashdown; and that all three astronauts registered below normal in a circulatory system test, designed to indicate the heart's capacity to support bodily work.

Blond, blue-eyed David R. Scott is six feet tall and weighs 175 pounds. The trim, muscular astronaut is an abstemious physical-fitness zealot who rises at six every morning to jog two miles and who regularly swims, surfs, skis, and plays handball. His chief non-athletic hobby is photography. He is reported to be a man of "computer-like practicality" and old-fashioned patriotism, and friends say that he is not as quiet as he may seem to the superficial observer. Scott and Ann Lurton Ott, the daughter of an Air Force brigadier general, were married in 1959. They have two children, a girl, Tracy, born in 1961, and a boy, Douglas, born in 1963. Like many other NASA families, the Scotts live in the elite Houston suburb of Nassau Bay, in a comfortable brick house built to their specifications.

References

N Y Post p51 Mr 5 '69 por; p20 Jl 31 '71 por
N Y Times p20 Mr 17 '66 por; p17 Jl 27 '71 por; p44 Ag 15 '71 por
Newsday p6 Mr 3 '69
Washington (D.C.) Post B p1 O 20 '63 por; C p4 Jl 25 '71 por
Who's Who in America, 1970-71

SCOTT, GEORGE C(AMPBELL)

Oct. 18, 1927- Actor
Address: b. c/o Twentieth Century-Fox Film Corp., 444 W. 56th St., New York 10019

Granite-faced George C. Scott, an intense, bravura performer who rose to fame as a chilling "heavy" *par excellence* in the late 1950's and early 1960's, is now recognized unanimously as one of the finest all-around actors in American theatre, television, and cinema. On the stage his roles have ranged from Shakespearean interpretations to the varying comic heroes of Neil Simon's three-play *Plaza Suite* (1968), and on television he is best known for his 1963-64 dramatic series *East Side, West Side*. In Hollywood he has been nominated for three Academy Awards, for his roles in *Anatomy of a Murder* (1959), *The Hustler* (1961), and *Patton* (1970), but since 1962 he has asked that his name be kept out of the Oscar competition, the politics of which he regards as professionally "demeaning." Disregarding his request, the Academy of Motion Picture Arts and Sciences awarded an Oscar to

Scott for his portrayal of General George S. Patton Jr. in April 1971, but the actor refused to accept it.

The grandson of a coal miner and the son of a mine surveyor, George C. Scott was born in the mountain hamlet of Wise, Virginia, in rural Appalachia, on October 18, 1927. When mining slumped in 1929, the Scotts moved to Michigan, where the father, George D. Scott, found work at the Buick assembly plant in Pontiac and, later, at the Ex-Cel-O Corporation, manufacturers of precision machine tools, in Detroit. With his older sister, George C. Scott grew up in the motor city.

As a child Scott was not only athletic but sensitive, thanks to his mother, Helena Scott, whom he remembers as his "creative" parent. "My mother was an elocutionist and a poet," he told Christina Kirk in an interview for the New York *Sunday News* (March 8, 1970). "She would read her own things to groups and once in a while over the radio." When Scott was eight his mother died, and four years later his father remarried. The elder Scott, who worked his way up from salesman to vice-president of the Ex-Cel-O Corporation, was at last report living in retirement in California.

From the age of ten or so Scott's favorite activity was writing fiction—none of it ever published—but his classmates at Redford High School in Detroit apparently remember him primarily as a baseball player. Enlisting in the United States Marines as soon as he graduated from high school, in 1945, he spent four years in the corps, burying bodies at Arlington National Cemetery and, in his free time, as he has recalled, "picking up a solid drinking habit that stayed with me from then on."

On his discharge from the Marines, Scott entered the School of Journalism of the University of Missouri, in Columbia, Missouri. Although he still liked to write short stories, he realized after a couple of years in college that journalism was not for him, because he was too "shy" in interviewing, too "uninquisitive," and too reluctant "to impose . . . on other people long enough to find out about them." When the university dramatic club was casting for *The Winslow Boy*, he tried out, half-heartedly but successfully, for the role of Sir Robert Morton, the barrister. "The minute I got on stage, I knew . . . that this was what I had to do," he later recounted, and he was quoted in *Life* (March 8, 1968) as explaining that he found in acting an instant therapy for boredom with himself: "I became an actor to escape my own personality. . . . Through acting you come full circle in your personality and, oh, what a grand time you can have along the way being wonderful people through your characters."

In addition to roles in seven University of Missouri productions, Scott played Chester Norton in a production of *Personal Appearance* at the Stephens College Playhouse, on a nearby girls' campus. In 1953 he dropped out of college to seek his fortune in the professional theatre. For five years he did stock work—more than 125 roles—where he could find it, in Toledo, Ohio, Washington, D.C., and Ontario, Canada. Between roles he supported himself by manual labor, mostly construction work for his brother-in-law, a Washington, D.C. contractor. Beset with marital problems at home and feeling oppressed by "the expectation of failures" in the theatre, he drank ever more heavily, and his bouts with the bottle often ended in barroom brawls, according to Christina Kirk. He spent at least one night in jail, and his nose was broken four times. (A fifth fracture occurred later, when he was mugged in New York City.)

Early in his lean years Scott vainly stormed both Hollywood and Broadway. Returning to New York in 1956, he settled in Greenwich Village and, while working nights as an IBM check-sorting machine operator at a Wall Street bank, spent his days making the rounds of casting offices. He was at the point of feeling about to die "from living on my own sour juices" when fortune, in the person of a mutual friend, introduced him to Joseph Papp, founder and producer of the New York Shakespeare Festival. Scott auditioned for Stuart Vaughn, who was preparing to direct Papp's production of *Richard III*, and got the title role. When he performed it in November 1957, critics were stunned by his interpretation, which Rex Reed later described as "the meanest Richard III ever seen by human eyes." Scott has recalled: "Richard III brought me a good agent, Jane Deacy. She found me TV work, and I haven't been off stage since."

Later in the 1957-58 Shakespeare series Scott won a Clarence Derwent Award for his portrayal of the cynical philosopher Jacques in *As You Like It*, an interpretation described by critic Walter Kerr as "caustic, ruthlessly intellectual yet innately good-humored . . . easily the most stimulating and the funniest Jacques I have ever seen." During the same theatrical season Scott garnered four major awards, including Theatre World and Obie citations, for his silkily evil performance as Lord Wainwright, the dandified, conscienceless poisoner in José Quintero's revival of *Children of Darkness* at the Circle in the Square in Greenwich Village. Immediately after the run of *Children of Darkness*, he went to Hollywood to make his first film appearance, as Grubb, a loathsome zealot in the psychological western *The Hanging Tree* (Warner Brothers, 1959).

To critical applause, Scott made his Broadway debut in November 1958 in the short-lived melodrama *Comes a Day*, in which he played Tydings Glen, a financially successful but psychopathic sadist to whom a greed-blinded mother betroths her daughter. After seeing Scott in *Comes a Day*, film producer-director Otto Preminger signed him to play the coldly relentless prosecuting attorney in the courtroom melodrama *Anatomy of a Murder* (Columbia, 1959), a role that brought him an Academy Award nomination but no Oscar. After witnessing the ferocious competition for votes among Oscar nominees, he decided never again to have anything to do with that "beauty contest in a slaughterhouse." When he was nominated for an Oscar two years later for his portrayal of a vulpine gambling gangster in *The Hustler* (Twentieth Century-Fox), he asked the Academy of Motion Picture Arts and Sciences to withdraw his name, but the request was ignored.

Back on Broadway, Scott starred in *The Andersonville Trial* (1959-60), as the prosecuting judge advocate in the post-Civil War trial of the com-

GEORGE C. SCOTT

mandant of a notorious Confederate prison camp, and in *The Wall* (1960-61), as an heroic Jewish resistance leader in the Warsaw ghetto during World War II. Hoping to establish a prototype for regional theatres that would decentralize and revitalize the American theatre, Scott and Theodore Mann founded the Theatre of Michigan in 1961. Their plan was to produce plays in Detroit and take them to Broadway only after they had proven successful regionally. This they did with *General Seeger*, about dishonesty in contemporary military public relations, and *Great Day in the Morning*, about an Irish Catholic household in St. Louis. But *General Seeger*, with Scott in the title role, ran only two days on Broadway early in March 1962 and *Great Day in the Morning* closed after thirteen performances the following month. Rather than let the Theatre of Michigan go into bankruptcy, Scott paid off the company's debts with his own savings, $70,000.

On television in the late 1950's and early 1960's Scott had major roles in dramas on *Kraft Television Theatre*, *Dow Hour of Great Mysteries*, *NBC Sunday Showcase*, *Esso Theatre*, *Kraft Mystery Theatre*, *Omnibus*, *Playhouse 90*, *Play of the Week*, *Armstrong Theatre*, *The Virginian*, *Dupont Show of the Month*, *Hallmark Hall of Fame*, and *Ben Casey*. For his performance as Karl Anderson in the *Ben Casey* offering *I Remember a Lemon Tree* he was nominated for an Emmy Award by the National Academy of Television Arts and Sciences in 1962. In return for a substantial investment by CBS-United Artists Television in the Theatre of Michigan Company he committed himself to a television series, and the dramatic program worked out with his consultation, but not entirely to his satisfaction, was *East Side, West Side*, in which he played an angry social worker in the slums of New York. The series, aired in hour-long weekly segments over the CBS network in 1963-64, was boldly realistic by television standards, and it won a National Critics Award. (There were also several Emmy nominations for Scott and the show, but CBS boycotted the Emmy Awards that year.) However, Scott was constantly engaged in script arguments with the CBS

Program Practices Department, and by the time the series came to an end he had concluded that "it is probably impossible to do a serious show on a weekly basis." In general, Scott has often said, television is inimical to good acting, and he found this to be especially true in series work.

After directing Scott as a British gentleman-detective in the thriller *The List of Adrian Messenger* (Universal, 1963), and as Abraham in *The Bible* (Twentieth Century-Fox, 1966), film director John Huston called him "one of the finest actors I have ever worked with." (During the filming of *The Bible*, Scott became a close friend of another member of the movie's cast, Ava Gardner.) In the mid-1960's Scott's Hollywood credits also included *Dr. Strangelove* (Columbia, 1964), an outrageous satire on the possibility of a nuclear Armageddon in which Scott played bomb-loving General Buck Turgidson; *Not With My Wife, You Don't,* (Warner Brothers, 1966), a more frothy military comedy, the least satisfactory of all of his film vehicles; and *The Flim-Flam Man* (Twentieth Century Fox, 1967), a superior comedy starring Scott as a sly old traveling con man.

With the New York Shakespeare Festival in the summer of 1962 Scott gave one of his favorite interpretations, Shylock in *The Merchant of Venice,* which he played straight, as Shakespeare created the character, and not, as one critic has pointed out, in the usual contemporary "sympathetic" manner. A writer for *Look* (November 6, 1962) called his portrayal "a revelation": "There was a strength and pride to Scott's usurer, and a depth of feeling that made him, and not Antonio, the tragic hero of the trial scene." Also Off Broadway, in the 1962-63 season, Scott played Ephraim Cabot in a revival of O'Neill's *Desire Under the Elms.* When the Actors Studio Theatre presented Chekhov's *The Three Sisters* as part of the World Theatre Season in London in May 1965, Scott gave what one observer described as a "distinguished" performance in the role of Vershinin, but the production as a whole was given a standing boo by the audience and British critics mercilessly panned it. With the Repertory Theatre of Lincoln Center in late 1967 Scott portrayed Benjamin Hubbard in a revival of *The Little Foxes.* On Broadway later in the same season, and into 1968-69, Scott and Maureen Stapleton starred in Neil Simon's *Plaza Suite,* a trio of one-act comedies united by their setting, a suite in Manhattan's Plaza Hotel. Emory Lewis of *Cue* (February 24, 1968) was in accord with most critics when he hailed the two actors for their "display of astonishing versatility."

In the waning 1960's Scott returned to Hollywood to make *Petulia* (Warner Brothers-Seven Arts, 1968), a glossy satire on bankrupt love in affluent San Francisco, in which he played an emotionally bereft physician, just divorced, who has an affair with a kooky married woman (Julie Christie). The high point of his cinematic career was his meticulously researched, epic portrayal of General George S. Patton Jr., the flamboyant, gutsy World War II tank commander who became a legend in his own time, in *Patton* (Twentieth Century-Fox, 1970). Judith Crist, reviewing the film in *New York* (February 9, 1970), reflected the critical consensus: "The beauty of this multi-million-dollar production . . . is that it neither romanticizes nor glorifies. All the glory emanates from Scott, who dominates the large screen as no single actor has, in my memory, making us party to the very depths of the soldier's soul. It is a stunning accomplishment from an actor who has never been less than excellent but proves perpetually that he can be better than ever."

For his portrayal of Patton, Scott was named best actor of the year in the New York Film Critics poll in December 1970. Two months later, in balloting by the more than 800 members of the actors' branch of the Academy of Motion Picture Arts and Sciences, Scott was nominated for the Academy Award as best actor. From Spain, where he was then filming "The Last Run," Scott sent the Academy a telegram in which he said: "Once again, I respectfully request that you withdraw my name from the list of nominees. . . ."

During 1971 Universal Studios released *They Might Be Giants,* a comedy in which Scott portrays a paranoid amateur detective psychoanalyzed by a woman psychiatrist (Joanne Woodward). On television in recent years he played the good farmer in Arthur Miller's drama about the Salem witch trials *The Crucible* (CBS, May 4, 1967) and the novelist with a split personality in David Shaw's comic fantasy *Mirror, Mirror, Off the Wall* (NBC, November 21, 1969), and he directed a TV version of *The Andersonville Trial* (Public Broadcasting Service, May 7, 1970). His previous television credits included Trock in *Winterset* and the police lieutenant stalking the alcoholic priest in *The Power and the Glory.*

A dedicated professional who hates show business and is interested in a good performance, a satisfied audience, and the judgment of posterity, Scott has no desire to be a superstar whose acting is indistinguishable from his own personality. Nor does he believe in becoming the character he plays, as some "Method" actors try to do, in keeping with the slogan, "Be, do not act." "I get a mental vision of the character and try to project it," he has explained, and one observer has said of him: "Scott . . . can sense a character in a gross script the way a sculptor can detect a man in a block of marble."

George C. Scott and Coleen Dewhurst, an actress with whom he has often worked, were first married in 1960. Divorced in the mid-1960's, they remarried in 1967. They have two sons, Alexander and Campbell, and Scott has three other children by previous marriages, to Carolyn Hughes, an amateur actress, and Patricia Reed, a professional singer and actress. The Scotts live in a ten-room, 250-year-old house on a thirty-three-acre farm in South Salem, Westchester County, New York, where they grow vegetables and keep several dogs and ponies as pets. "Watching him with animals," Rex Reed wrote in the New York *Times* (March 29, 1970), "you can see that he is a gentle man. A sour green apple with a soft core, hounded by the furies all his life." Scott's recreations are watching baseball and playing softball, golf, tennis (only because his wife does), chess, and cards, and he has been a movie buff since childhood. If former reports still hold true, he is a chain smoker. In politics he is an independent who leans, moderately, in the same direction as his wife, a progressive, activist, antiwar Democrat.

Scott is a strapping six-footer with a deep, raspy voice, thin lips, graying brown hair, and a strong, battered, pale face. His smile has been described as "one-sided" and his eyes as resembling those of "a cautious spaniel." According to Frances Herridge of the New York *Post* (March 31, 1958), he "has the self-contained, assured manner of a person who could never fawn or ask for favors," and others have testified that he is an idealist whose temper explodes at dishonesty, injustice, and hypocrisy. Scott has been found "charming" by most who have met him, including Ira Mothner, who wrote in *Look* (November 6, 1962): "Scott is not only a supercharged actor, he is a supercharged man. He has a robust sense of humor and a gift for mimicry, and he will take over the entire living room to act out a joke." But Dan Knapp of the Washington *Post* (March 21, 1970) got the impression that, "beneath all the easy laughter, something large, dark, and ferocious is eating away at him." Regarding alcohol, Scott told Christina Kirk in the New York *Sunday News* interview: "I still drink, but it no longer bothers my life as much."

References

N Y Post p35 Ap 29 '67 por
N Y Sunday News II p18 Mr 8 '70 pors
N Y Times II p15+ Mr 29 '70 por
Biographical Encyclopaedia & Who's Who of
 the American Theatre (1966)
Who's Who in America, 1970-71

SEGAL, ERICH (WOLF)

June 16, 1937- Author; university professor
Address: b. Dept. of Classics, Yale University, New Haven, Conn. 06520; h. Ezra Stiles College, Yale University, New Haven, Conn. 06520

In 1970 and 1971 when the market for old-fashioned sentimentality in fiction and motion pictures seemed dead beyond recall, Erich Segal scored sensationally both in the bookstores and at the box office with *Love Story*, a simple, lachrymose romance about a Radcliffe girl from a poor family who marries a rich Harvard athlete, works to support him through law school when he is disinherited, and dies of leukemia just when he is through with his studies and beginning his law career. Some literati panned the novella as maudlin and bathetic, especially after the popular success of the film, but the general public saw *Love Story* as a tender tale, in tune with the real, or emerging, attitudes of contemporary youth. One in five Americans read the slim book, and countless others waited patiently in lines outside of theatres for their turn to have their hearts rent. The versatility of *Love Story*'s author is evident in the range of other products that have come from Segal's hand, including the Beatles' surrealistic cartoon feature film *Yellow Submarine* (United Artists, 1968) and scholarly books on

ERICH SEGAL

classical literature. His most important work, in his own view, is his teaching of classics and comparative literature at Yale University, where he has been on the faculty since 1964.

Erich Wolf Segal was born in Brooklyn, New York on June 16, 1937 to Cynthia (Shapiro) Segal and the late Samuel M. Segal, an orthodox rabbi. Of his father he has said: "It was he who instilled in me the love of learning and who made me take Latin as well as Hebrew." Avocationally, Rabbi Segal was a sculptor, artist, and musician of more than average talent, and musical competence was one of the traits he passed on to Erich, who plays the piano well. Erich Segal has two younger brothers, Thomas, a Boston business man, and David, an off-Broadway lighting designer.

In Brooklyn, Segal attended the Crown Heights Yeshiva and Midwood High School, where he registered straight A's. Too frail for most varsity sports, he took up running for therapeutic reasons, after injuring a leg in a canoe accident when he was sixteen, and he made the high school track team. (He has run ten miles daily ever since.) Continuing to attend Midwood even after the Segals moved to West 79th Street and Broadway in Manhattan—where the father was rabbi of the Mount Neboh Congregation—Segal followed a breathtaking daily schedule, commuting to and from Brooklyn and then going to classes at the Jewish Theological Seminary in Manhattan. Summers, he attended the Institut Monnivert outside Lausanne, Switzerland.

In 1954 Segal graduated from high school and entered Harvard College, where he ran track and, with composer Joe Raposo, wrote the annual *Hasty Pudding* show for 1958. When he took his B.A. degree, in 1958, he was both class poet and Latin salutatorian. In 1959, when he earned his M.A. degree from Harvard University, he met Ali MacGraw—the star of the film version of *Love Story*—during a theatrical production at nearby Wellesley College, and the two remained friends thereafter.

While working for his Ph.D. degree, Segal was a resident teaching fellow in classics at Harvard's

Dunster House. Lance Morrow, an undergraduate resident of the house at the time, reminisced about Segal in *New York* (April 27, 1970): "He had a gemlike ego, an almost amphetamine enthusiasm. . . . He seemed an implausible academic, [one] who ran marathon races as a hobby, sang with the Dunster Dunces, wrote music, lyrics, and would, it seemed at the time, wind up like Noel Airman, tinkling the 'South Wind Waltz' after dinner to successive generations in the junior common room."

During his graduate years Segal earned money by working part-time helping to doctor plays in their Boston tryouts, and he himself wrote a revue, *Voulez-Vous?*, that was staged in Boston. It ran only five days, partly because audiences were deterred by heavy snows. Relatively more successful was *Sing, Muse!*, a musical spoof on the Trojan War written by Segal, with music by Joe Raposo, that ran for thirty-nine performances off-Broadway in New York in the 1961-62 season. Judith Crist panned it unreservedly, but other critics found some good in the musical. "Mr. Segal can turn out sparkling lines, full of conceits and interior rhymes . . . ," Howard Taubman observed in the New York *Times* (December 7, 1961). "But a rhymester bemused by his own bravura technique can become tedious. When Mr. Segal learns to relax a little, he will be easier to take and his stuff will be funnier." Richard Rodgers was so impressed with *Sing, Muse!* that he invited Segal to collaborate on a musical with him. Eventually they did write a musical together, but it was never finished, or at least never produced.

Harvard granted Segal his Ph.D. degree in 1964, upon acceptance of his dissertation, "Roman Holiday Humor: The Plays of Plautus as Festival Comedy," in 1964. After receiving the degree Segal went to Yale University as a visiting lecturer. He became an assistant professor at Yale in 1965 and advanced to his present position of associate professor three years later.

Strictly as characters, aside from the story line, the star-crossed hero and heroine of *Love Story* were based on a young man and woman Segal had known, in separate connections. The plot was inspired by a student conversation that he overheard, about two people he had not known, in 1968. Moved, he decided to write a fictional version of the tale he heard. "I sat down and started writing immediately," he recalled in an interview with Phil Casey of the Washington *Post* (February 11, 1971). "The story poured out of me. I changed everything except the girl's death and the fact that she supports her husband through graduate school."

He first wrote *Love Story* as a film script, which he finished in a few weeks. The scenario was rejected by every motion-picture studio in the United States, and one producer sent back the advice: "You've got to get with it, Segal. This is soap opera stuff." On the advice of his agent, Mrs. Lois Wallace, Segal rewrote the script as a novel. But in the meantime actress Ali MacGraw read the original scenario and persuaded executives at Paramount Pictures to film it, with her in the role of the tragic heroine, Jenny. Production began in November 1969, with Ryan O'Neal starring opposite Miss MacGraw and Arthur Hiller directing.

After the shooting of the film began, Harper & Row bought *Love Story* in its novel form, and the 131-page volume was published on February 4, 1970. The reviews were generally less than enthusiastic but most were no harsher in tone than the observation of William McPherson of the Washington *Post* (January 31, 1970) that "fairy stories are still nice to read," and a few critics were charmed by the simplicity and gentleness of the book. The outstanding anathema was hurled by S. K. Oberbeck in *Newsweek* (March 9, 1970): "The banality of *Love Story* makes *Peyton Place* look like *Swann's Way* as it skips from cliché to cliché with an abandon that would chill the blood of a *True Romance* editor."

Love Story zoomed to the top of the best-seller lists, where it remained for months. It headed the New York *Times Book Review* list until the middle of February 1971, and it was still number two on that list in March 1971. By the end of April there had been twenty-one hardcover printings of the book, totaling 500,000 copies. The first paperback run by the New American Library had been 4,325,000 copies, the largest single printing in the history of movable type. There have been twenty-three foreign translations of the book, some supervised by Segal, who reportedly speaks some eight or nine languages and has a reading knowledge of several others. Early in 1971 it was leading the best-seller lists not only in the United States but in England, France, Italy, Brazil, Japan, and Germany.

When the film *Love Story* was released in December 1970, John J. O'Connor of the *Wall Street Journal* (December 22, 1970) called it "Sam Richardson, Charles Dickens, and old Irene Dunne movies put into the modern idiom." The assessment of other critics ranged from "outstanding modern romantic drama" (*Variety*, December 16, 1970) to "a love idyll [that] . . . heralds the return of the weepies . . . [that] one had hoped might have been laughed off the screen forever" (Pauline Kael, *New Yorker*, December 26, 1970). At the box office the film was an unqualified, phenomenal success, and the reviewer for *Cue* (December 26, 1970) "even saw David Merrick dabbing his eyes." The movie was nominated for seven Oscars.

In a poll of 500 critics, librarians, and people in publishing *Love Story* was recommended for candidacy for a 1971 National Book Award, but the five judges on the NBA's fiction panel threatened to quit if it was not removed from the list of nominations and the National Book Committee yielded to their demand. When the rejection of *Love Story* was revealed, William Styron, one of the fiction jurors, explained to a reporter that "it . . . simply doesn't qualify as literature." Segal's reaction was: "I honestly don't think I should be placed on the same page with Saul Bellow and John Updike . . . [but] it was a moral breach to take me off.' At that very time, Segal himself was an NBA judge in another category, arts and letters.

Segal's screen credits include, besides *Love Story* and *Yellow Submarine, The Games* (Twentieth Century-Fox, 1970), an Olympic marathon epic, and Stanley Kramer's *R.P.M.* (Columbia, 1970), a film about campus revolution with the message that the adults responsible for Hiroshima and Vietnam should not be surprised at violent revolt against their world by the young. The reviews of both films were generally bad, the common complaint being oversimplification and contrivance. In October 1971 United Artists released *Jennifer on My Mind*, a black, mock-sentimental comedy about a death from heroin overdose that was scripted by Segal and directed by Noel Black. Mr. Black will also direct the filming of "Railroad Bill," Segal's western scenario about a Negro outlaw.

Among his peers Segal is much more highly respected for his scholarly writings than for his Hollywood, stage, and fictional work. In addition to papers published in professional journals, he has written the book *Roman Laughter: The Comedy of Plautus* (Harvard University Press, 1968). He has also edited *Euripides* (Prentice-Hall, 1968), a collection of critical essays, and translated three of Plautus' comedies, *The Braggart Soldier, The Brothers Menaechmus,* and *The Haunted House.* The three translations were published in one volume by Harper and Row in 1969. Scholars reviewing his books have called his translations "excellent," his interpretations "refreshing," "sensitive," and "peruasive," and his writing style "terse," "witty," and suitable for lay as well as academic readers.

Erich Segal is a short (five and a half feet), wiry, swarthy man with a handsome face, long black, frizzy hair and sideburns, remarkably white teeth, dark, prominent eyes, and lithe, animated fingers. According to some who know him, he is "ultra-sensitive," a characteristic hidden beneath his glib, rapid-fire speech and frenetic, hyperkinetic manner. Robert McG. Thomas Jr., writing in the New York *Times* (December 20, 1970), described him as a "constant, booming" conversationalist. "His gestures are varied, expansive, and frequent. They engage all comers in a friendly, open-handed welcome; they caress every point; and they try to express the all but overwhelming joy he feels at just being alive."

A bachelor "with intermittent qualms," he has been keeping steady company lately with a young woman from Paris, but he rules marriage out at this time, according to an article in the New York *Sunday News* (March 7, 1971), because his life is "too turbulent." He relishes the turbulence, the publicity, and the busy schedule he now follows, jetting to book-and-author luncheons, motion picture conferences, television panel shows, and lecture and speaking engagements around the country. No matter how busy he is, he always takes time out for his daily run, and every April he participates in the Boston Marathon, in which his best finish to date was fiftieth (in a field of 1,500). He also rides a bicycle as often as he can, al-

though he owns a Mercury Cougar. Another of his favorite recreations is playing Richard Rodgers' songs on the piano in his living room. He does not smoke, and he seldom drinks anything alcoholic other than a little wine.

Typical of Segal's attire are the rumpled suede or corduroy suits, suede shoes, leather pants, and golf shirts that, along with books, clutter his bachelor apartment in Yale's Ezra Stiles College. The other pop celebrity on the Yale campus, Charles Reich, author of *The Greening of America,* also lives in Ezra Stiles College. As a professor Segal is respected by his colleagues and popular with students, who have described his lectures as "living theatre" and "star performances." His undergraduate course, Classical Civilization, fills the 600-seat Sterling Law Auditorium three times a week. In addition, he conducts a seminar in comparative literature for graduate students. Segal was a Guggenheim fellow (1968), and he is a member of the National Advisory Committee of the Peace Corps.

References

Life 68:R Ap 24 '70 pors
Macleans Mag 84:40+ Jl '71 pors
N Y World Journal Tribune mag p14 Ja 13 '62 por
White Plains (N.Y.) Reporter Dispatch p6 Mr 2 '71
Directory of American Scholars (1969)

SHELEPIN, ALEKSANDR (NIKOLAEVICH) (shel-yep'ēn)

Aug. 18, 1918- Soviet official
Address: Central Council of Trade Unions, 42 Leninsky Prospect, Moscow, U.S.S.R.

Like Joseph Stalin before him, Nikita Khrushchev ruled the Soviet Union both politically, as first secretary of the Communist party's Politburo, and governmentally, as chairman of the Council of Ministers, the Soviet cabinet. When Khrushchev was deposed in 1964, Leonid Brezhnev succeeded him as party chief, while Aleksei Kosygin assumed the premiership. Now that there are rumors of a new power struggle within the Soviet hierarchy, or at least in the Politburo, many Western Kremlin watchers see Aleksandr Shelepin as the Politburo member most likely to succeed Brezhnev. Shelepin, a hard-liner in both foreign and domestic affairs, aided in the rise of Khrushchev and played perhaps the key role in his deposition. Since then his ostensible power has declined, but Soviet experts point out that he is a shrewd, resilient political maneuverer, that he is young by Kremlin standards, and that he enjoys a strong following in the Komsomol (Young Communist League) and the KGB (the secret police), both of which he has headed, and in the Central Council of Trade Unions, which he now chairs.

The son of a middle-class railroad office worker, Aleksandr Nikolaevich Shelepin was born on August 18, 1918 in Voronezh, Russia, the Soviet

ALEKSANDR SHELEPIN

Union. He was educated at the Moscow Institute of History, Philosophy, and Literature. After serving as a squadron commander in the war against Finland (1939-40), he joined the Komsomol and rose steadily up its ranks, filling positions having mostly to do with the improvement of Soviet standings in world athletic competitions and with relations with international youth and student organizations.

In October 1952 Shelepin was elected to the Communist party's 195-member Central Committee, and the following month he was elected first secretary of the 18,000,000-member Komsomol. In the struggle for power following the death of Stalin, in 1953, he threw his influence as leader of the Komsomol behind Nikita Khrushchev. He mobilized Soviet youth for service in agricultural projects that were initiated by Nikita Khrushchev, and then, when Khrushchev and his associates accelerated the areal development of Kazakhstan and Siberia, he recruited hundreds of thousands of young people to migrate to those bleak, virgin areas as miners and industrial and construction workers. He also performed the more difficult task of indoctrinating the Komsomol membership to accept Khrushchev's shattering revelation of Stalin's crimes and his denunciation of Stalin's "cult of personality" without losing their faith in the Communist system itself.

In his book *The 100 Most Important People in the World Today* (1970), Donald Robinson described Shelepin's leadership of the Komsomol: "He was charged with 'molding the rising generation in the party's image' and he went at it with an iron hand. He resurrected the old anti-religious movement among youth, and smashed down hard on 'heretical' trends that surfaced in the Komsomol. 'Nihilism' and 'hooliganism' he angrily tagged them. . . . On various occasions he charged the Komsomol members with being slackers, poorly versed in Communism . . . while indulging such 'alien' tastes as 'vulgar dancing, abstractionist painting and sculpture.' He fiercely attacked the great Boris Pasternak when he won the Nobel Prize for Literature."

Robert M. Slusser in his chapter on Shelepin in *Soviet Leaders* (1967), edited by George W. Simmonds, observed: "Shelepin's world outlook, rooted in the experiences of his formative years during the great purge, took shape and found expression in his work as the first secretary of the Komsomol. Intense devotion to the ideology of Communism; loyalty to party leadership combined with an ability to maneuver adroitly in intraparty conflicts and pick the winning side; and a messianic sense of Russian patriotism combined with an unrelenting hostility to the non-Communist world viewed through the prism of a rigid party ideology—these characterize Shelepin's views."

In the midst of his tenure as first secretary of the Komsomol, Shelepin was elected a deputy in the Council of Nationalities of the Supreme Soviet, the U.S.S.R.'s parliament, in March 1954. Four years later he resigned his Komsomol office to accept Khrushchev's appointment of him to the chairmanship of the Committee on State Security, the Soviet secret police agency, better known as the KGB. Under his administration the state security force was, by his own account, purged of the last vestiges of the police terrorism for which it had been notorious under Lavrenti P. Beria in the Stalin years. In his final report as secret police chief, Shelepin was able to boast: "The state security organs have fully liquidated distortions in their work and violations of Socialist legality. . . . The state security organs have been reorganized, greatly reduced in number, deprived of their improper functions, and freed of careerist elements."

Shelepin left the KGB when he was moved up to the ten-member Secretariat of the Communist party's Central Committee in 1961. In the Secretariat he was the party's watchdog on law enforcement and judicial processes, and his power in that sphere was greatly enhanced in November 1962, when he was put in charge of a new Party-State Control Committee, which was invested with broad investigative powers. At the same time, he was named deputy chairman of the Council of Ministers.

According to Robert M. Slusser, "It can be assumed that Shelepin was a prime agent in the ouster of Khrushchev in October 1964, although the secrecy that surrounded that event, together with Shelepin's customary reticence and circumspection, makes proof difficult." Slusser pointed out that events following Khrushchev's deposition indirectly confirm the assumption. At the plenary session of the Communist party's Central Committee in November 1964, the committee hurriedly elected Shelepin to the Politburo, without the usual formality of making him first a candidate. And in subsequent statements Shelepin made veiled criticisms of Khrushchev's "loquacity and unsystematic working methods," and he differed sharply from Khrushchev on two key issues, relations with China and the United States. In February 1965 Shelepin told a conference of the Mongolian Workers party: "No matter how great our differences have been, they cannot and must not serve as the basis for a split in the socialist camp and the entire Communist movement." And he sharply attacked the whole course of United States foreign policy, from Hiroshima to Vietnam, in a meeting at Pyongyang the following August. During 1965 Shelepin traveled extensively, leading Soviet missions to Egypt, North Vietnam, North Korea, and Switzerland.

It has been speculated in some Western circles that the Party-State Control Committee under Shelepin may have been too assiduous in its investigations of party activities. Whatever the reason, Shelepin was stripped of his two government posts, deputy premier and chairman of the control committee, in December 1965. He kept his party posts, however, so that along with Brezhnev and Suslov he was the only member of both the Central Committee's Secretariat and its Politburo. He also remained prominent in foreign affairs. In January 1966, for example, he visited North Vietnam as head of a Soviet aid mission and, promising more aid to the Hanoi regime, he vowed to help Vietnam fight off "American aggression." The speech was generally regarded as the toughest ever made against the United States by a Soviet leader since the days of Stalin.

Apparently Shelepin's line in foreign affairs was too hard for the prevailing mood of the Soviet hierarchy. In 1967, after he urged the Arabs to become more hawkish toward Israel, he was removed from the Communist party Secretariat (but not the Politburo) and assigned to head the Central Council of Trade Unions. Henry Kamm, who was then chief of the New York *Times* Moscow bureau, later reported in the *Times* (August 10, 1060): "All experts were agreed that for a member of the ruling Politburo this was a serious demotion. . . . Yet as I left Moscow, the same experts were convinced, without further knowledge, that Shelepin was now the major threat to Brezhnev's power."

Personal information about Aleksandr Shelepin is hard to come by. He is of medium height and weight, and Donald Robinson in his book has written of him: "A sturdy, dark-haired chap with handsome, straight features—but very thin lips—he is a neat dresser who could easily pass for a London financier or a Wall Street lawyer. If he possesses any sense of humor, he keeps it well concealed." Shelepin has been decorated with two Order of Lenin medals and an Order of the Red Star medal.

References

N Y Post p45 D 10 '65 por
N Y Times p13 Ag 10 '60 por; p4 N 17 '64 por; p20 Jl 12 '67 por
Newsweek 77:68 Ja 4 '71
International Who's Who, 1970-71
Prominent Personalities in the USSR (1968)
Robinson, Donald. The 100 Most Important People in the World Today (1970)
Simmonds, George W., ed. Soviet Leaders (1967)
Who's Who in America, 1970-71
Who's Who in the USSR, 1965-66
Who's Who in the World, 1971-72

SHIKLER, AARON (A.)

Mar. 18, 1922- Painter
Address: b. c/o Davis Galleries, 231 E. 60th St., New York 10022; 44 W. 77th St., New York 10024

During the period of decline of representational art that followed World War II, the New York City artist Aaron Shikler has held in his work to a realism that he believes to be "an ongoing, vital, ever sustained" part of the American tradition. In the painstaking manner of the old masters, with grace and technical facility, he paints landscapes, portraits, still-lifes, and genre pieces, at times somewhat impressionistic in the handling of light. The paintings for which Shikler is likely to become best known and remembered are the official White House portraits of the late President John F. Kennedy and his widow, Mrs. Jacqueline Kennedy Onassis.

Aaron A. Shikler was born into a middle-class Jewish family in Brooklyn, New York on March 18, 1922, the only son of Frank Shikler, a tailoring contractor, and Annie (Blei) Shikler. He has four older sisters, Eve Altman, Jean Rieder, Mollye Geller, and Julia Gerstenhaber. He grew up in Brooklyn and obtained his early instruction in art at the High School of Music and Art in Manhattan. An enthusiastic student, he found his training "an exciting experience all around," as he told Sally Hammond in an interview for the New York *Post* (March 2, 1971). "It was a marvelous school to go to, and I couldn't thank Mayor La Guardia enough for having set up the school." He graduated in June 1940.

With the help of scholarships Shikler continued his education at the Tyler School of Fine Arts of Temple University and at the Barnes Foundation Collection in Merion Station, near Philadelphia, where he took courses from 1941 to 1943. During World War II he left school to serve in the Army as a private in the infantry from 1943 to 1946. He then resumed study at Temple University's art school, which awarded him the B.S. degree in fine arts and the B.S. degree in education in 1947 and the Master of Fine Arts degree in 1948. For further graduate work he enrolled in 1949 in the Hans Hofmann School of Fine Arts in New York City. His three years of study under Hofmann, a leading exponent of abstract expressionism, however, appears not to have had a noticeable influence on the development of his own style.

Once asked why he had chosen a career in painting, Shikler replied, "I am enamored and always have been by the smell of oil paint." Critical recognition and commercial reward came slowly to him, however. To earn a living he took a job for a time painting pictures of ballet dancers for a wholesale firm. "I was so embarrassed at putting my name to this chintzy work that I signed them Phil I. Steen," he disclosed in the New York *Post* interview. The opening of a gallery in Manhattan by his friend and onetime fellow art student Leroy Davis helped immensely to advance Shikler's career. He held the first

AARON SHIKLER

of his one-man exhibitions at the Davis Galleries in 1953. In addition to periodic one-man shows, he presented his work in group shows at the Davis and also in several joint shows with David Levine, the caricaturist and painter, who, like Shikler, studied with Hofmann, but may be said to work in a nineteenth-century tradition.

At the Davis Galleries in January 1955 Shikler, Levine, and another friend, Seymour Remenick, displayed self-portraits and portraits of each other in a show characterized by "thoughtful and searching realism," according to a review in the New York Times (January 29, 1955). The small oil portraits of antique dealers amid their cluttered surroundings that made up Shikler's February 1957 show won the praise of critics both as character studies and as gracefully executed complex compositions. In the spring of 1958 he joined several other young painters in an exhibition of landscapes at the Davis called "Hudson River Revisited." His solo show in the fall of that year was devoted to small still-life arrangements. Along with portraits and interiors, his later shows included conversation pieces, or groups of figures, such as his canvas of the early 1960's in which eight female members of the family are preparing a young woman for her wedding. His figures in pastel became as deftly painted as his pictures in oil, and by 1964 he was exhibiting watercolors also of exceptional craftsmanship.

In their comments on Shikler's work many art critics have been particularly appreciative of his control of light. One reviewer remarked on the "quite magical lighting" of some of his early portraits. Bennett Schiff appraised his still-life canvases in the New York Post (December 7, 1958), noting the purity of texture and distinctive character of each flower, bottle, or other object. "What is not to be overlooked here—it might easily be because it is done with such subtlety—is the use he makes of lighting," Schiff wrote. "His objects, all of which he obviously has great affection for, are balanced in an atmosphere of quiet light, set off by and yet a part of the beautifully painted backgrounds." Discus-

sing his landscapes in the New York Times (April 1, 1958), Dore Ashton observed that Shikler "has a special affinity for the oblique lights, the sudden shifting lights that occur when great clouds descend toward the horizon." She went on to say, "His paintings, in fact, are touched with the romance of the sky found in the Dutch painter Ruysdael."

Among the more recent painters that Shikler's work has been said to call to mind on occasion are Edouard Manet, Walter Sickert, and Andrew Wyeth. Reviewing his joint show with Levine at the Brooklyn Museum in the spring of 1971, David L. Shirey, who much preferred the still lifes to the portraits, asserted in the New York Times (April 28, 1971), "Mr. Shikler carries around the phantoms of Vuillard, Bonnard, Sargent and Degas and employs their styles with extraordinary virtuosity to limn contemporary faces. But not their feeling." Some other critics, however, have found Shikler close in spirit as well as in technique to painters like Sargent and Degas and have commented on the emotional depth with which he at times invests his human subjects.

Shikler's pictures are often especially appealing when they combine portraiture with still life, such as Meditation. In his small-size portrait of the Duchess of Windsor, who sat for him in her Manhattan apartment, the setting includes an antique desk of the William and Mary period, a pet pug dog, and a framed photograph of the Duke of Windsor, along with many additional details of the room. Among the other celebrities whose portraits Shikler has painted are the actress Joanne Woodward and Senator Abraham A. Ribicoff. Esquire magazine commissioned him to do portraits of John F. Kennedy, Charles de Gaulle, and Winston Churchill for its covers, and Sports Illustrated commissioned pictures of two sports figures. Once just for fun, some years ago, he copied John Singer Sargent's picture "Mrs. Edward L. Davis with her Son, Livingston Davis," but gave Mrs. Davis the features of Mrs. Jacqueline Onassis and her son those of Shikler's agent.

Besides painting pictures of his own children, in natural poses, Shikler has done portraits of Lauren Bacall's children and Paul Newman's children, among others. In an article for McCall's (March 1971) he discussed the painter-subject relationship, the effort of the painter "to penetrate the mystery of another human being," who is likely to be on guard or fearful of being misunderstood. When his subject is an adult, Shikler explained, the artist is a "protagonist"; but when he is painting a child, he becomes somewhat like a "spy." "He catches the child, seizes him at a moment, unawares," Shikler wrote. ". . . It is not that the child is less mysterious than the adult; he is less self-conscious, more likely to be taken by surprise."

The children of Peter Lawford and his former wife, Patricia (Kennedy) Lawford, are among those whose portraits Shikler has painted. He has speculated that Mrs. Onassis had seen his pictures of her nieces and nephew or had come to know his work from visits to the Davis Galleries, of which she is a client. In late 1967 she commissioned him to paint pastel portraits of her two children. Caroline Kennedy, then ten years old, and John Kennedy, seven years old, were each at an age that their mother thought particularly becoming. The following year during afternoons at Mrs. Onassis' apartment in New York, Shikler made many studies of the children, some of heads and others of full figures usually in informal poses. At Mrs. Onassis' suggestion he also painted a pastel conversation piece in which she is shown reading to her children.

Obviously pleased with his work, Mrs. Onassis then asked Shikler to paint her official White House portrait, commissioned by the White House Historical Association. As he related in the *McCall's* article, he did not want to do a portrait that would be like most of those of the First Ladies decorating the walls of the White House: "a dreary, uninspired lineup of patrician or Middle-American faces, of carefully composed, pompously gowned nonpersons." Yet he realized that his painting would have to be in keeping with White House tradition. "I needed to paint a picture of the First Lady of the Land at the same time that I painted a picture of Jacqueline Bouvier Kennedy Onassis."

Beginning in the winter of 1968 he made dozens of sketches of Mrs. Onassis in a long, black skirt and white blouse. Some of them, which he has called "un-White House," were made to increase his understanding of his subject. When he and Mrs. Onassis decided on a sketch suitable for developing into an official portrait, the completed picture, enlarged and in oil, proved disappointing. He then began the series of sketches that led to the finished White House portrait, in which Mrs. Onassis, wearing a floor-length, long sleeved gown, probably of Givenchy design, is standing in front of the fireplace in her apartment. In the background are pink-tinged peonies and a French eighteenth-century bust of a child. The light of the late afternoon sun softens the terra cotta and peach colors that pervade the canvas. Shikler has said that his intention was not simply to capture Mrs. Onassis' beauty, but to reveal a haunted expression in her eyes and an inner tension and strength.

Sometime before Shikler finished the painting in February 1970, Mrs. Onassis had proposed that he also undertake the official portrait of the late President John F. Kennedy. Since Shikler had seen Kennedy on only one occasion from a distance, he had to work from photographs of his subject. Studying about twenty-five of them, he found that one of Kennedy's most characteristic gestures was to stand with his arms folded across his chest. That posture was the one Shikler chose for his portrait of a young, slim President whose head is bowed in deep thought. With few exceptions, White House portraits of former Presidents are frontal, but in the Kennedy picture, the eyes are downcast instead of looking directly at the painter. Shikler had in mind the mood of Kennedy at the time of the Cuban missile crisis. "I wanted to show him as a President who was a thinker," he told Sarah Booth Conroy of the Washington *Post* (February 5, 1971). ". . . I wanted to show a courage that made him humble."

The White House Historical Association paid Shikler $15,000 for each of the portraits, which were then kept in a vault under tight security measures until the official unveiling scheduled for the spring. In late January 1971, however, the Washington *Post* columnist Maxine Cheshire asserted that a close duplicate of the official portrait of Mrs. Onassis would appear on the cover of the March issue of *McCall's* magazine as part of a first-person story by Shikler about the painting of the portraits. In submitting his article, which had the approval of Mrs. Onassis, he had taken the precaution of having the release date set three months in advance. When, however, Maxine Cheshire printed the version of the *McCall's* portrait in her column on February 2, 1971, thus appearing to scoop both the magazine and the historical association, the *McCall's* story was quickly released and the date of the unveiling of the portraits at the White House was moved up to February 5, 1971. The artist himself sees considerable difference between the small pastel on the *McCall's* cover and the official oil portrait, which is 56 and ¾ inches by 41 inches in size. Probably in part because of the commotion over the magazine story, the portrait of Mrs. John Fitzgerald Kennedy attracted more public comment than that of the President. In reply to some criticism that the portraits were too "modern" or "impressionistic" for the White House, Shikler maintained, as quoted in the Washington *Post* (February 5, 1971), "Both portraits are straight American representational, tempered by a vast study of European tradition."

Besides the Davis Galleries and the Brooklyn Museum, Shikler has had exhibitions at the Art Institute of Chicago (1962), the National Academy of Design (1959, 1961, 1963, and 1965), the Gallery of Modern Art (1965), the Butler Institute of American Art (1959 and 1961), and the New Britain (Connecticut) Museum of Art (1964). His work is represented in the collections of the Metropolitan Museum of Art, the Hofstra University's art museum, the National Academy of Design, and other institutions. Among his awards are the Tiffany Foundation Award (1957), the Ranger Award (1959), the Proctor Prize of the National Academy of Design (1959 and 1961), and the Thomas B. Clarke Prize (1962). He contributed two chapters to *Pastel Painting* (1968) by E. L. Sears. He is a member of the National Academy of Design and the Century Association.

On October 4, 1947 Aaron Shikler married Barbara Lurie, whom he had met in art school. Their children are Cathy, fifteen years old, and Clifford, ten years old. A trim, slight man, Shikler stands five feet five inches tall, weighs 140 pounds, and has brown eyes, gray-brown hair, and a freckled forehead. He shares his neo-Gothic studio on Manhattan's West Side with David Levine, with whom he also teaches a class in painting. His hobby is watching professional football.

References

McCall's 98:76+ Mr '71
N Y Post Mr 2 '71 por
N Y Times Ap 28 '71
Newsweek 77:84 My 3 '71 por
Washington (D.C.) Post C p1+ F 5 '71
Who's Who in American Art (1970)
Who's Who in America, 1970-71

SHUMWAY, NORMAN E(DWARD)

Feb. 9, 1923- Surgeon; university professor
Address: b. Stanford University School of Medicine, Palo Alto, Calif. 94304; h. 1291 Pitman St., Palo Alto, Calif. 94301

The 1970's will be the decade of transplantation, just as the 1960's was the decade of open-heart surgery, according to Dr. Norman E. Shumway, who is also convinced that future cardiac therapy is more likely to depend on transplantation than on the use of an artificial heart. Many of the basic techniques that have made transplantation possible were developed from Shumway's pioneering laboratory research on dogs at the Stanford University School of Medicine, where he has been head of the division of cardiovascular surgery since 1964. A highly skilled surgeon, he has himself performed many human cardiac transplant operations since early 1968 and has advanced other forms of cardiovascular surgery.

Norman Edward Shumway was born to Norman Edward and Laura (Vander Vliet) Shumway on February 9, 1923 in Kalamazoo, Michigan, where his father operated a creamery. With the intention of becoming an engineer he entered the University of Michigan, but after two years joined the United States Army as a private for World War II service. As a result of an aptitude test given in the Army, he was selected for the premedical program at Baylor University, where he completed his undergraduate work. He obtained his M.D. degree from Vanderbilt University in 1949. The following year he interned in the hospitals of the University of Minnesota, where he became a medical fellow in surgery in 1950. During the Korean war he served, from 1951 to 1953, in the Medical Corps of the United States Air Force, in which he advanced to the rank of captain. Resuming his study at the University of Minnesota, he earned his Ph.D. degree in surgery in 1956. His dissertation was "Experimental Surgery of the Heart and Great Vessels under Hypothermia." He remained at the university for two more years as a special trainee in the National Heart Institute, where he had been a research fellow from 1954 to 1956.

At Minnesota, Dr. Shumway studied under the general direction of Dr. Owen H. Wangensteen, head of the department of surgery, who had instituted a graduate research program in the science of surgery. Among the surgeons trained by Wangensteen was Dr. C. Walter Lillehei, a specialist in open-heart operating procedures, who himself became a teacher of Shumway and also

of the South African surgeon Dr. Christiaan N. Barnard, one of Shumway's classmates. Another teacher at Minnesota who had an enduring influence on Shumway's work was Dr. F. John Lewis, credited with having performed the first true open-heart operation, in 1952.

In 1958 Shumway joined the faculty of the Stanford University School of Medicine as an instructor in surgery, becoming also a member of the surgical staff at the university's hospitals. He advanced quickly, to assistant professor in 1959, to associate professor in 1961, and to full professor in 1965. Since 1964 he has also been head of the division of cardiovascular surgery. Some of the students that he trained at Stanford now direct cardiovascular surgery programs in other medical schools.

An early contribution of Dr. Shumway to the techniques of cardiovascular surgery was a new procedure, reported in April 1959, for correcting a birth defect involving transposition of the heart's great vessels through "bypass" surgery. Much of his success in open-heart surgery, the field in which he first came to wide professional attention, was due to his persistent experimentation in the surgical laboratory. "The best arena for the training of good surgeons," he once observed, "is the dog laboratory."

Working with Dr. Richard Lower, then a resident in surgery at Stanford, Shumway performed an operation in December 1959 in which the heart of one dog was transferred to another. The dog receiving the heart, a mongrel two and a half years old, lived for eight days after the transplant. The operation demonstrated that it was technically possible to maintain blood circulation in the recipient by a substitute heart and that the heart itself could withstand total separation from the donor body. In previous heart transplant operations, animals had died quickly because of blood clots. To avoid that eventuality Shumway and Lower tried a new technique, leaving in the patient parts of the heart, including part of the atrial system, areas where veins return blood to the heart. The heart tissue and arteries were then sutured.

Over the next six to eight years Shumway and his colleagues refined their technique through experimentation on some 300 dogs, performing about 200 heart transplants and achieving a survival rate of 60 to 70 percent. One dog with a transplanted heart lived for about a year before being killed for purposes of testing. In November 1967, as reported in the *Journal of the American Medical Association*, Dr. Shumway disclosed that he and other surgeons at Stanford felt that they had achieved enough expertise in their work on dogs to undertake a human heart transplant—whenever the suitable recipient and donor appeared at the same time. He explained that the ideal recipient would be a patient for whose fatal heart ailment there was no corrective surgery or treatment, and the ideal donor would be a person dying of causes unconnected with heart disease. Ideally, both would be relatively young. The heart would have to be removed within a half hour of death or oxygen starvation would damage it beyond use, although when operating on dogs the Stanford team had been able to prolong the viability of the heart for several hours by immersing it in cold salt water.

By late 1967 surgeons had achieved considerable success in transplantation of certain organs other than the heart: four children were being kept alive by transplanted livers and more than 600 men and women with incurable renal disease had survived kidney transplant operations. Then, on December 3, 1967, in Capetown, South Africa, Dr. Christiaan N. Barnard implanted the heart of a twenty-five-year-old girl, an accident victim, in a Lithuanian-born businessman, Louis Washkansky. Using the technique that Shumway had developed, Barnard proved that it was medically possible for a dying patient to get a second chance at life with a heart not his own. Washkansky died of pneumonia eighteen days later.

On January 6, 1968 the world's fourth human heart transplant and the first adult transplant in the United States was performed by Dr. Shumway at the Stanford Medical Center. His patient was Mike Kasperak, a fifty-four-year-old steel worker near death from heart damage caused by a virus infection. The heart donor was a forty-three-year-old housewife, Virginia Mae White, who had died of a cerebral hemorrhage. After the surgery Dr. Shumway and his colleagues watched closely for signs of the hazards of implantation, many of which had become better understood from the extensive work on kidney implantation and from Washkansky's death.

Transplantation hazards primarily concern immunological rejection. The body's natural internal defense system attacks the new heart as foreign matter, just as it would attack a germ. When immunosuppressive drugs are administered to reduce the body's strength in rejecting the transplanted organ, defense against infection is also weakened. In postoperative care of transplant patients physicians have to walk a fine line between giving too little medication and having the new organ rejected, and giving too much medication and having the patient succumb to infection.

Although the immunity problem was considered a crucial one for Kasperak, his chances for recovery also involved damage to lungs, liver, and kidney from long-standing heart disease. Dr. Shumway and his team of specialists fought for fifteen days to save his life. When Kasperak died on January 21, 1968, Shumway pointed out in a news conference, "He survived a fantastic galaxy of complications. Any one of these complications would have been lethal had it not been for the cardiac transplant." He also noted that during the time that Kasperak's circulation was being maintained by the transplanted heart he had survived kidney failure, liver failure, and three major operations. That fact offered "some hope" despite the patient's death. The deterioration of Kasperak's condition before surgery, however, led Dr. Shumway to remark in the *Journal of the American Medical Association* that although "the severely ill and the comatose are the patients with whom we must

DR. NORMAN E. SHUMWAY

work . . . there may very well be a level of organ function below which we should not perform such an operation."

Many shades of opinion on the subject of organ transplantation were soon being expressed both in professional circles and in the popular press. In March 1968 three cardiologists, not directly involved with heart transplantation, called for a moratorium on heart transplants until the six that had been performed were fully evaluated. They contended that nothing had been learned from transplants. Dr. Shumway, testifying before a subcommittee of the Senate Government Operations Committee, rejected the proposed moratorium, although he endorsed the idea of a Presidential commission to study the ethical and sociological issues associated with transplantation. He suggested that some day heart transplants would become standard medical technique, and that by that time improved storage methods would make it unnecessary for surgeons to postpone operating until the coincidental death of a donor.

Before long the high mortality rate among early transplant patients discouraged surgical teams in most medical centers, as initial overoptimism turned to pessimism. The team led by Shumway at Stanford, however, continued to perform cardiac transplantations regularly when medically indicated. By the end of 1970 twenty-six patients had received new hearts at Stanford, nine of whom were then living, one for more than two years. The Shumway survival rate compared favorably with worldwide figures: just fourteen patients survived the 140 or more operations elsewhere. During 1970 the Stanford team had performed only eight heart transplants, but Shumway predicted a general renewal of interest in that operation in 1971, along with an increase in the survival rate to one year for over 50 percent of the heart transplant patients at Stanford. He maintained that surgeons have extended their knowledge with each transplant operation, improving methods of handling cardiac rejection and various surgical techniques involved in the procedure.

According to Dr. Shumway, moreover, cardiac transplantation is not so difficult an operation as certain types of open-heart surgery, and it has therefore been undertaken in some hospitals by unqualified teams with inadequate experience in treating rejection. He has argued that a transplant operation is not primarily a surgical exercise; if it were, almost all patients would survive. A transplant team needs specialists in many disciplines to handle unfamiliar diseases that appear and other nonsurgical problems. Doubtful that a manmade device can approach the human heart in efficiency of performance, Shumway foresees increasing resort to transplantation in cardiac therapy. He believes that new attitudes will develop with respect to both the donor and recipient. In an article for *Stanford M.D.* (Spring-Summer 1968), based on his Congressional testimony, he wrote, "The hopelessness and profound grief associated with catastrophic brain injury may be alleviated to some extent by the fact that another human can be helped by transplantation of a crucial organ system. . . . We are at the threshold of a wondrous new era in medicine, and doctors will need help to realize fully its potential."

Aside from his work on heart transplantation, some of Dr. Shumway's major accomplishments have been in the field of open-heart surgery, particularly the transplantation of valves. At a meeting in February 1968 of the Pacific Coast Surgical Association, a team of Stanford surgeons, including Shumway, reported that they had successfully replaced defective aortic heart valves with transplants in thirty-five out of forty patients. The cause of death of five patients was not malfunctioning of the transplanted valves. Shumway also developed techniques for total surgical correction of "blue baby" heart defects, greatly reducing the risk of death that earlier procedures had entailed.

Dr. Shumway is a diplomate of the American Board of Surgery and the American Board of Thoracic Surgery and a member of the American Surgery Association, the Society of University Surgeons, the American Association for Thoracic Surgeons, the Society of Thoracic Surgeons, and the Halstead Society. He is the author or coauthor of professional articles on cardiac surgery and related subjects. One of his colleagues has described him as "the least flashy, most dedicated of doctors for whom the patient is first." Others have commented on his appetite for long hours of work, his vast curiosity, and his receptiveness to new ideas and the views of his associates.

When he was a student in Minneapolis, Norman E. Shumway met Mary Lou Stuurmans, a nurse whom he married on June 21, 1951. They have four children, Sara Jane, Norman Michael, Lisa Anne, and Amy Martha. A pleasant-looking man, Dr. Shumway is slender and tall, just under six feet in height, and has smooth features and gray hair. Although he is known to be tough-minded, his demeanor is quiet and gentle, without a trace of stuffiness. His hobby is Egyptology, and for outdoor recreation he takes an occasional skiing trip with his children.

References

Look 34:43+ D 29 '70 por
N Y Post p35 Ja 11 '68 por
N Y Sunday News p133 Ja 2 '71 por
N Y Times p24 Ja 8 '68 por
Stanford M.D. 7:3+ Spring-Summer '68 por
International Who's Who, 1970-71
Who's Who in America (1970-71)
World Who's Who in Science (1968)

SINGH, (SARDAR) SWARAN (sing)

Aug. 19, 1907- Indian Minister for External Affairs
Address: b. Ministry of External Affairs, South Block, Central Secretariat, Government of India, New Delhi, India; h. 7 Hastings Rd., New Delhi, India

A record of nineteen uninterrupted years of service in the Indian legislature and Cabinet ranks Sardar Swaran Singh, Minister for External Affairs, among the most durable and dependable figures in the national government. At one time or another he has held nine of the eighteen portfolios, including those of Minister of Steel, Mines, and Fuel and Minister of Defense. Because of his vast parliamentary and administrative experience in both domestic and foreign affairs, he has been called "a man of crisis" and "the utility infielder of the Indian Cabinet." Well known for his integrity, his objectivity, and his apparent lack of personal ambition, he has never been privately identified with any particular political clique. "I am a public servant," he once said, "and I cannot afford the luxury of factional loyalties and ideological affinities."

Sardar Swaran Singh was born in the village of Shankar, Jullunder District, in East Punjab, India on August 19, 1907. ("Sardar," literally "commander," is roughly the Sikh equivalent of "esquire," and "Singh," literally "lion," is a name carried by virtually all Sikhs, although not all persons named Singh are Sikhs.) His father, Sardar Pratap Singh, of Sikh peasant origin, served as a noncommissioned officer with the rank of jemadar in the Indian Army. Swaran Singh attended the Government College of Punjab University in Lahore, where in 1930 he took his B.S. degree with honors and his M.Sc. degree in physics. After teaching physics briefly at Khalsa College in Lyallpur, he studied at the Law College of Punjab University. In 1932 he returned to Jullunder with his LL.B. degree to set up a law practice.

Assiduously pursuing his career in criminal law, Singh did not become directly involved in India's nationalist movement, playing no perceptible role, for instance, in Mahatma Gandhi's civil disobedience campaigns of the 1930's or the 1942 Quit India drive. Unlike many Indian statesmen, he has no record of imprisonment for resistance to the British rule. The distinguished reputation and large clientele that he acquired over the years as a lawyer, however, made him a likely choice of the Sikh political organization, the Akali Dal (literally, the Army of the Servants of God), in recruiting candidates to run in the 1946 elections to the Punjab legislative assembly. Singh campaigned successfully under the banner of the Akali legislative wing, the Panthic party, which then joined the Congress party in the assembly, as it had often done before, to form a government.

For about six months after his election Singh, who was made secretary of the Panthic party, served as a parliamentary secretary in the Cabinet of Malik Khizar Hayat Khan Tiwana, Premier of Punjab. He then advanced to the leadership of his party and took over the portfolio of Minister of Development, Food, and Civil Supplies in the Punjab government. From 1947 to 1949 he served as Minister of Home, General Administration, Revenue, Irrigation, and Electricity and in 1952 was Minister of Capital Projects and Electricity.

Meanwhile, in 1947, Singh had undertaken the first in a long series of assignments involving negotiations between India and Pakistan when he was appointed to the Radcliffe Commission formed by the British government to draw the boundary between India and what would become Pakistan and to divide the assets of the Punjab between the two new, independent countries. In March 1947 he was also named a member of the Security Council, which advised the central government on problems relating to law and order as the partition drew near.

It was in Punjab, and especially among the Sikh community, that the knife of partition was most keenly felt. One of the effects of partition was to intensify the conflict between two factions of the Akali Dal—particularly over its relationship with the Congress party, which insisted on a reorganization of East Punjab along secular lines and rejected Akali demands for the establishment of a separate Sikh state. In 1948 the Akalis split, and most members of the Panthic party—including Singh—remained in the Congress party. For Singh, the decision meant a commitment to national, secular politics within the Congress party fold instead of the possible development of a local political base.

Because he had never sided with either Akali faction, Singh emerged as one of the potentially strongest of the former Panthic party leaders. That potential reportedly caused the Congress party's Chief Minister of Punjab, Pratap Singh Kairon (also a former Akali), to maneuver Singh into the national Parliament and Cabinet. Singh became a member of the upper house, Rajya Sabha (Council of States), in 1952 and in May 1952 was appointed Minister of Works, Housing, and Supply in the Cabinet of Prime Minister Jawaharlal Nehru. With that move to New Delhi, Singh began a long ministerial career divided almost equally between administration and diplomacy.

"He is a very modest, very clear-headed, and very hard-working colleague," Nehru once observed in reflecting on the qualities that prompted him to call on Singh for many chores in addition

SWARAN SINGH

to those formally assigned. Although still a relative newcomer to national political and government circles, Singh was chosen to lead the Indian delegation to the 1954 and 1955 sessions of the United Nations Economic and Social Council, held in Geneva. After the 1957 general elections, which won him a seat in the lower house, Lok Sabha (House of the People), as representative of a Punjab constituency, he was appointed to head the newly created Ministry of Steel, Mines, and Fuel.

Over the next several years Singh contributed greatly to the development of India's industry. The country's First Five Year Plan envisaged a rapid expansion of heavy industry centered on the construction, with foreign assistance, of four (later three) steel plants to be publicly owned and operated by the newly created Hindustan Steel Limited. As Minister of Steel, Singh was responsible for the implementation of the overall project and for the necessary but difficult negotiations with the three assisting countries (the United Kingdom, West Germany, and the Soviet Union). That all three plants were operating before Singh left the ministry in 1962 was a tribute to his administrative skill and quiet determination. His proficiency in diplomacy was also an asset when, as Minister of Steel, he led a delegation to Moscow in May 1959 to negotiate credit for development and another economic delegation to Tokyo in May 1961.

In the Cabinet formed by Nehru soon after the 1962 general elections, Singh was put in charge of the Ministry of Railroads. He set about reorganizing India's rundown railway system and temporarily retained his position as Minister of Railways even after he had been appointed Minister of Food and Agriculture in September 1963 to cope with an acute food crisis. Briefly, in June and July 1964, he held the portfolio of Minister of Industry and Supply. Before becoming Minister of External Affairs, then, Singh had dealt with some of the major economic problems of India. Moreover, all of his posts both in state and national government were recognized—because of licensing and other responsibilities—as offices with high potential for patronage and personal gain. Yet Singh's reputation for integrity remained undiminished. Despite his pre-occupation with domestic matters during his first twelve years in the Cabinet, he worked with growing authority for the betterment of India's relations with other nations.

Prime Minister Nehru himself held the portfolio of external affairs, but he shared some responsibility in foreign relations with Defense Minister V. K. Krishna Menon and looked increasingly to Swaran Singh to play a supporting role. In October 1959 and January 1960 Singh attended the conference to demarcate the Punjab border between India and Pakistan and to resolve outstanding issues regarding exchange of assets and personal property. He has been given major credit for the success of the conference in reaching a settlement. Further talks in which Singh participated produced agreement over the division of the five rivers of Punjab between India and Pakistan and resulted in the Canal Waters Treaty of September 1960.

During 1960, also, Singh was a member of the Indian team for the New Delhi talks between Nehru and Chinese Premier Chou En-lai over the Sino-Indian border conflict. Following the Chinese invasion of India in 1962, Singh took part in a series of talks, beginning in December 1962, with Pakistani officials over the disputed state of Kashmir. Shortly before the start of the talks, however, Pakistan recognized the Communist border claims at the expense of Indian claims. Little was accomplished during the next few months and discussions broke off in May 1963.

On the death of Nehru in May 1964, Lal Bahadur Shastri was chosen for the Prime Ministership. He initially followed his predecessor's example by retaining the foreign affairs portfolio for himself. Soon after taking office in June, however, Shastri suffered a mild heart attack. The following month, recognizing his inability to carry out duties beyond those of Prime Minister, he turned the responsibility for foreign affairs over to Singh, to whom he had earlier given the portfolio for industry and supply. On July 19, 1964 Swaran Singh became India's first full-time Minister of External Affairs.

With a typical lack of fanfare, Singh began his diplomatic duties with a trip to India's neighbors, Afghanistan, Nepal, Burma, and Ceylon. His approach won immediate approval from Indians who believed that a retrenchment in India's international activities was long overdue and who saw India's immediate neighbors as being among those with whom India's relations most needed repair. In working to improve relations with Pakistan, Singh tried in general, and at times in vain, to have a ceasefire maintained along the troubled India-Pakistan border until the Kashmir and other disputes could be resolved.

On October 25, 1965, when Pakistan's Foreign Minister Zulfikar Ali Bhutto raised political questions at the U.N. Security Council meeting called to discuss the collapse of the India-Pakistan ceasefire, Singh led the Indian delegation in the first walkout of the Security Council since the Soviet Union had left the debate over Iran in 1946. He continued to boycott the discussion until it returned to the issue of troop withdrawals for which the session had been intended. Singh was Shastri's closest adviser at the Tashkent meeting on the Kashmir problem, which began on January 4, 1966, under the auspices of the Soviet Union. When Shastri died on January 11, Singh inherited the primary responsibility for India's acceptance and implementation of the Tashkent agreement for promoting friendly relations.

Singh continued as External Affairs Minister until November 1966, when Prime Minister Indira Gandhi transferred him to the Ministry of Defense. The transfer took place in the context of a sudden Cabinet reshuffle believed to be brought about in part by political considerations involving the government's preparation for the 1967 elections. The move was thus apparently in no way related to Singh's management of India's foreign affairs. In a similar sudden Cabinet shuffle in late June 1970, Mrs. Gandhi returned Singh to the Ministry of External Affairs to replace Dinesh Singh (Swaran Singh is not related to him), with whose conduct of foreign policy she had been reportedly dissatisfied.

The return of Swaran Singh to the foreign ministery, was widely interpreted as an attempt by Mrs. Gandhi to repair some of the deterioration in India's relations with the United States that had occurred under his predecessor. To some observers the sudden stopover in New Delhi of a Soviet Deputy Foreign Minister in mid-July 1970 constituted evidence of Soviet concern that the removal of Singh's predecessor might mean a cooling of India's relations with the Soviet Union. Singh's policies, however, have never been identified with either the East or West but adhere to his country's traditional course of nonalignment. On August 9, 1971, nevertheless, India signed a twenty-year friendship treaty with the Soviet Union. Indian officials stated that the purpose of the treaty was to discourage a possible attack from Pakistan on India.

Imposing in appearance, though modest in manner, Swaran Singh stands over six feet tall, wears a turban in Sikh tradition, and has a gray beard and sweeping mustache. According to *Newsweek* (August 3, 1964), "He is not a religious man but he is said to wear about his person all the 'five K's,' prescribed by Sikh religious tenets: *kanga* (a small comb), *kara* (an iron wrist bangle), *kirpan* (a small sword), *kesh* (hair), and *kachara* (underwear)." He is married to the former Sardarni Charanjit Kaur and has four daughters. His family life in New Delhi is somewhat austere, free from notoriety and ostentation.

References

Forum Service p20+ Ag 22 '64 por
N Y Times p1+ Jl 18 '64 por; O 7 '67 por
Newsweek 64:30+ Ag 31 '64
India Who's Who, 1968-69
International Who's Who, 1970-71
International Yearbook and Statesmen's Who's Who, 1970
Nalanda Yearbook and Who's Who in India and Pakistan, 1958
Who's Who, 1970-71

STAGGERS, HARLEY O(RRIN)

Aug. 3, 1907- United States Representative from West Virginia
Address: b. Room 2366, Rayburn House Office Bldg., Washington, D.C. 20515; h. New Creek Dr., Keyser, W.Va. 26726

West Virginia's Second District—a constituency of some 400,000 people in the mountainous eastern part of the state—has been represented in Congress since 1949 by Harley O. Staggers. As assistant Democratic Whip, Staggers is influential in lining up his party's voting in the House of Representatives, and he wields further influence as chairman of the House Interstate and Foreign Commerce Committee, which is concerned with such matters as broadcasting, securities and exchange, power and fuel transmission, railroads, civil aeronautics, weather bureaus, and national health. Representative Staggers, who once characterized himself as a "Johnson man," leans to the liberal side in his voting, at least on domestic matters.

Harley Orrin Staggers was born in Keyser, Mineral County, West Virginia on August 3, 1907 to Jacob Kinsey Staggers and Frances Winona (Cumberledge) Staggers. He was educated in Mineral County public schools and at Emory and Henry College, a Methodist-controlled four-year liberal arts school in Emory, Virginia. Throughout high school and college he worked after classes and during vacations at various farm, railroad, and factory jobs.

After taking his B.A. degree, in 1931, Staggers taught mathematics and science and coached athletics at Norton High School in Norton, Virginia until 1933, when he became football coach at Potomac State College in his hometown. In 1935-36 he did graduate work at Duke University, and after his return to Virginia he served as sheriff of Mineral County, an elective position, for four years. For one year, beginning in 1941, he was right-of-way agent for the West Virginia State Road Commission, and he served briefly as West Virginia director for the Office of War Information, in 1942. In World War II he served in both the Atlantic and Pacific theatres of operations as a Navy Air Corps navigator with, finally, the rank of lieutenant commander. During the immediate postwar years he farmed in Keyser and served as Mineral County director of rent control.

Elected by the voters of West Virginia's Second District in November 1948, Staggers took his seat in the House of Representatives when the Eighty-first Congress convened two months later, and he has kept it ever since, through eleven consecutive biennial elections. At first assigned to the Committee on Veterans' Affairs and the Committee on the Post Office and Civil Service, he moved to the Interstate and Foreign Commerce Committee in 1951.

Staggers became assistant Democratic Whip in January 1955, at the beginning of the Eighty-fourth Congress. During that Congress he unsuccessfully introduced a bill proposing that a Secre-

HARLEY O. STAGGERS

tary of Peace be added to the President's Cabinet, to be concerned with "promotion of international understanding, interchange of ideas, and education in the problems of peace." Because of the serious problem of unemployment in his constituency, he also proposed the creation of a domestic "Marshall Plan." For the same reason he opposed the Eisenhower administration's bid for moderate reductions in import tariffs and he strove, successfully, to have Green Bank, West Virginia chosen as the site for the National Radio Astronomy Observatory.

When the Natural Gas Act was passed in 1958, Staggers successfully sponsored an amendment favorable to the coal industry. In the early 1960's he headed Commerce subcommittee hearings that resulted in a bill calculated to strengthen the Securities and Exchange Commission, particularly in its power to protect stock market investors against fraud. At the same time he began writing a "truth in packaging" bill, designed to protect the consumer against deception in supermarket and drugstore products. After three years of effort the bill was enacted into law in diluted form in 1966, as the Fair Packaging and Labeling Act. The act empowered the Secretary of Health, Education, and Welfare and the Federal Trade Commission to establish standard weights and measures for packaged commodities and to require that specified information appear on labels.

When Oren Harris resigned his House seat early in 1966 to become a federal judge in Arkansas, Staggers succeeded him in the chairmanship of the Committee on Interstate and Foreign Commerce. Whereas Harris had been considered, in the words of one reporter, "friendly" toward the broadcasting industry, Staggers initiated a tough attitude of vigilance against, as he said, "any trend toward monopolistic control over what this nation's television viewers see and hear and think." In committee hearings in the late 1960's he repeatedly took members of the Federal Communications Commission to task for forgetting the FCC's "role as a guardian of the public interest" and as a creature of the Congress. He was especially angered at what he considered the FCC's tendency to make, without consulting Congress, major licensing decisions in favor of established broadcasters and against such insurgents as pay television entrepreneurs. In other areas in the late 1960's Staggers' committee counseled the House to pass legislation to force striking airline employees back to work and to require auto manufacturers to equip their vehicles with adequate tires.

The *Congressional Quarterly* tabulated Staggers' votes in the House vis-à-vis the conservative coalition as 13 percent in accord and 75 percent opposed in 1965 and 1966. In the first session of the Ninetieth Congress, in 1967, his tallies in the same categories were 30 and 54 percent. His votes in accordance with Johnson administration policy in the Ninetieth Congress were 79 percent in domestic affairs and 78 percent in foreign. In 1969, after President Nixon took office, his tallies were 100 percent in accord with the administration in foreign policy but only 48 percent in domestic.

Among specific matters on which Staggers registered a pro vote were extension of the Arms Control and Disarmament Agency, but with a reduced appropriation (1968), the Vocational Rehabilitation Act (1968), financial sanctions against college students involved in serious campus disturbances (1968), abolition of the Electoral College (1968), and increases in railroad and federal retirement benefits (1970). Staggers and Representative Paul G. Rogers of Florida were the prime movers in the House of the Emergency Health Personnel Act of 1970, which enabled the federal government to put on the payroll of the Public Health Service physicians, nurses, and other health professionals working in city slums, rural areas, and other doctor-poor localities.

Harley Orrin Staggers and Mary Veronica Casey of Keyser were married on October 4, 1943. They have two sons, Harley Orrin Jr. and Daniel Casey, and four daughters, Margaret Ann, Mary Katherine, Frances Susan, and Elizabeth Ellen. According to TV columnist Lawrence Laurent of the Washington *Post* (March 15, 1967), "nothing in Staggers' appearance inspires awe. He is silver-haired and usually soft-spoken." But Laurent added that on the rare occasions when his ire is raised he takes on "the appearance of an angry cherub." An active Methodist, Staggers taught Sunday school for many years in Keyser. The Representative is a member of the West Virginia Farm Bureau, the Keyser-Mineral County Chamber of Commerce, the American Legion, the Veterans of Foreign Wars, the Disabled American Veterans, the Amvets, the Loyal Order of Moose, the Knights of Pythias, the Elks, and the Lions Club. His honors include honorary degrees from Emory and Henry College and Elkins College.

References

U S News 60:10 Ja 10 '66 por

Biographical Directory of the American Congress, 1774-1961 (1962)
Congressional Directory (1970)
Who's Who in America, 1970-71
Who's Who in American Politics, 1969-70

STELLA, FRANK (PHILIP)

May 12, 1936- Painter
Address: b. c/o Lawrence Rubin Gallery, 49 W. 57th St., New York 10019

Exclusively interested in nonreferential abstract art throughout his career, Frank Stella, a leader in the development of Minimal Art, is a major figure in the contemporary art world at an age when most painters are still seeking their first one-man shows. At thirty-three Stella received what amounts to "old master" accreditation when he was honored with a retrospective exhibition at the Museum of Modern Art in New York in the spring of 1970.

Because they involve the salient traits of three-dimensional work, Stella's "shaped" paintings indicate that he is moving into three dimensions—the direction, in the opinion of some leading critics, in which all of the best painting must sooner or later move. In recent years he has worked with huge, shaped, and decorative canvases that, like murals, demand their own architectural contexts for proper display. From the spareness and austerity of his earlier "stripe" paintings, with their black, aluminum, and copper, he has evolved into a freer lyricism, in which he has abandoned himself to a joyous and decorative use of color. For a man sometimes given to ambivalence and ambiguity, Stella has been remarkably forthright in defining the artist's mission. "The idea in being a painter is to declare an identity," Stella has said in conversation. "Not just my identity, an identity for me, but an identity big enough for everyone to share in. Isn't that what it's all about?" Stella defines a painting as a special kind of object—"one that's intended to be a painting."

Frank Philip Stella was born on May 12, 1936 in Malden, Massachusetts, a Boston suburb, to Dr. Frank Stella, a gynecologist and Constance Aïda (Santonelli) Stella. The painter vaguely remembers having attended "sentimental" art classes at his grammar school in Malden. In junior high school he became interested in pastels, but was put off by the technical aspects of conventional realistic drawing. "I wasn't very good at making things come out representationally," he recalls, "and I didn't want to put the kind of effort that it seemed to take into it."

In 1950 Stella entered Phillips Academy at Andover. There he studied painting with the abstractionist artist Patrick Morgan and soon became intensely interested in Mondrian. "I got the point of Mondrian right away," he says. "I liked it, and I liked organizing things in blocks, abstractly.... I wanted to paint just squares or something comparable." Most of the works he painted at Andover were, in fact, geometrical (usually rectangular) compositions in rather small formats.

After graduating from Andover in 1954, Stella entered Princeton University. Although he majored in history, he continued to study painting—first with William Seitz and later with Stephen Greene. Through the influence of those men, both of whom were involved in the avant-garde, Stella began visiting galleries and museums in New York City.

What attracted him to Abstract Expressionism was "the size of the paintings and the wholeness of the gesture." Stella had always enjoyed house-painting, and the fact that abstract expressionists used larger brushes appealed to him. Most of the paintings Stella produced at Princeton, including his covers for the college literary magazine, *Nassau Lit*, were abstract expressionist, and for his research project in his junior year he wrote an essay comparing Hiberno-Saxon manuscript illuminations with the works of Jackson Pollock.

In his final year at Princeton, Stella began to reject the abstract expressionist concept of the artist "as a terrifically sensitive, ever-changing, ever-ambitious person" and started searching for a simpler, more straightforward style. In January 1958 he saw the first exhibition of Jasper Johns's flag and target paintings. Impressed by Johns's use of simple motifs and rhythm and repetition, Stella began painting in a "transitional" style, which consisted of compositions containing single or multiple box forms placed in various contexts of bands or stripes. Those transitional paintings were shown at a group exhibit at the Allen Memorial Art Museum of Oberlin College in May 1959 and later that year at the Malden Public Library.

After obtaining his B.A. degree from Princeton in June 1958, Stella moved to New York City, where he settled into a storefront studio on the Lower East Side. He supported himself by working as a housepainter three or four days a week, and continued, for a while, to paint in his transitional style, using out-of-style commercial colors that he purchased for a dollar a gallon. In late 1958 he began working on an innovative series of "black" paintings, which impressed critics by their monumental simplicity and austere aesthetic. Stella has explained: "Everybody was tired, the field was open. All you had to do was do it."

The "black" paintings, which eliminate the complicating box forms of Stella's transitional style, consist entirely of simple stripe patterns—rectangular, notched, and diamond-shaped. Symmetrically arranged with equal emphasis over the entire field of the canvas, they extend right out to the framing edge. The stripes, two and one-half inches wide, were painted freehand with a housepainter's brush and the narrow spaces between them were left as unprimed canvas. For reasons of economy, Stella built his stretchers of ready-made one-by-three's; the deep stretcher thus created served to set the painting off from the wall, emphasizing its "objecthood" and the two-dimensionality of its surface. Since that was one of the effects Stella was seeking, he has retained that device.

The "black" paintings brought Stella immediate recognition by the New York art world. *Club Onyx* appeared at a group show at the Tibor de Nagy Gallery in April 1959, and *Clinton Plaza* was exhibited at a group show at the Leo Castelli Gallery in October. (The latter was the first painting that Stella sold outside his immediate circle of friends.) A third "black" painting, *Jill*, was selected by Adolph Gottlieb for exhibition at the Metropolitan Young Artists Show at New York's National Gallery of Arts Club in December. Most impor-

FRANK STELLA

tant, when Dorothy Miller selected four "black" paintings for the Museum of Modern Art's "Sixteen Americans" exhibition (December 16, 1959-February 14, 1960), Stella, at twenty-three, became the youngest artist included in that prestigious show.

In the statement he prepared for the exhibition catalogue the critic and sculptor Carl André wrote: "Art excludes the unnecessary. Frank Stella has found it necessary to paint stripes. . . . [He] is not interested in expression or sensitivity. He is interested in the necessities of painting." Then director of the Museum of Modern Art's collections, Alfred H. Barr Jr. found himself "baffled" by Stella's paintings but "deeply impressed by their conviction," while William S. Rubin wrote in *Art International* (January 1960) that he was "almost mesmerized by their eerie, magical presence." *Marriage of Reason and Squalor*, one of the "black" paintings, was bought by the Museum of Modern Art, the first work by Stella to be acquired by a museum.

After completing the "black" paintings, Stella started on a series of works executed in metallic aluminum paint. Black had suggested chiaroscuro shading to him, therefore implying a three-dimensionality that he then wanted to avoid. The aluminum surface seemed a sound choice, since it repelled the eye and made visual penetration difficult. Like the "black" series, the "aluminum" paintings consisted of simple stripe patterns, but some of those patterns were inflected in ways that did not conform to the rectangular edge of the canvas. Not wanting leftover corners, and not knowing what else to do with them, Stella simply cut them out, creating thereby the first contemporary "shaped canvases." The "aluminum" paintings were exhibited at Stella's first one-man show at the Leo Castelli Gallery in the autumn of 1960.

In his "copper" series, executed immediately after his "aluminum" paintings, Stella diverged even more widely from the rectangle, creating L-, U-, and other radically shaped canvases by cutting the framing edge to fit his surface patterns. Five of the six paintings in the series were damaged by exposure in 1960; Stella repainted them the following year.

From the radical shaping of the "copper" series, Stella returned to the simplest shape possible in his "Benjamin Moore series," named after a brand of alkyd paint, which he used straight as it came from the can. The series consists of six square monochromatic stripe paintings, one each in red, orange, yellow, blue, green, and purple. The "Benjamin Moore" series was exhibited at Stella's first one-man European show, at the Galerie Lawrence in Paris in November 1961. In the summer of 1962 Stella forsook the monochromy of his "Benjamin Moore" series to begin work on a series of grisaille and multicolored concentric squares and metered mazes in which, for the first time, he explored the possibilities of polychromy. All rectangles, those paintings consisted of striped sequences of different light values and different hues.

Having briefly given up the investigation of shape to explore color, Stella returned to shape with a vengeance in his "purple" series of 1963. Called "portraits" and named after such friends as Leo Castelli and Ileana Sonnabend, the purple paintings are all polygons—among them a trapezoid, pentagon, hexagon, triangle—in which Stella not only shaped the outside edge of the canvas but also cut a parallel shape out of the inside. The painting itself, therefore, serves as a framing edge for the internal space.

Before painting the "purple" series, Stella had spent the summer of 1963 as artist-in-residence at Dartmouth College in Hanover, New Hampshire. There he began experimenting with joining wedge-shaped or chevron-shaped areas of stripes to create complex trapezoidal and starlike forms and with using more than one metallic color in a single painting. Those "Dartmouth" series experiments were further developed in the "Notched V" series of 1964-65. The Notched V's, formed by cutting the bottoms out of the basic chevron form of the Dartmouth paintings, began with a single unit and reached their most complex form in the *Empress of India*, in which four V's in four different metallic colors are juxtaposed in a single painting.

Although the Notched V paintings, combining polychromy with marked shaping, stand at the center of Stella's concerns during 1964 and 1965, he also worked on two other series. The "Moroccan" series, executed in fluorescent colors on square formats, ranges from an initial two-color painting to *Sidi Ifni*, the final work in the series, in which Stella uses ten different Day Glo colors in a single painting. The "Running V" series, also executed during that period, consists of monochromatic works, painted in metallic colors, in which tracks of multiple stripes (as many as twenty-seven) trace an inflected path across a large (up to twenty-three feet wide), unbroken field.

In 1965 Stella embarked on a radical departure in his development with the "irregular polygon" series, the salient characteristic of which is the interpenetration of contrasting geometrical shapes that are unbroken by stripes. The paintings also marked the first time that Stella conceived of an

entire series in advance. He chose eleven different shapes and built stretchers for each shape in quadruplicate, thus allowing himself four possibilities to explore color combinations for each image. "It doesn't matter whether the first painting of each shape is good or bad," Stella said, "it gives me a start. If I see in it something that I like—or something that I don't like—it's still something to react against and it sets the way I'll go with the next few pictures."

It was a breakthrough series, in which Stella found himself more open, flexible, and free. But he paid for his liberation with some failures that some critics regarded as overcomplicated. Selections from the "irregular polygon" series were shown at Stella's first one-man museum exhibition at the Pasadena Art Museum in California in October 1966, and the same show was later mounted at the Seattle Art Museum Pavilion.

With his launching of the "protractor" series in the fall of 1967, Stella began work upon the most daring and monumental of his artistic conceptions to date. The first of his paintings to employ circular forms, the "protractor" series was planned as a group of ninety-three paintings, consisting of thirty-one differently shaped canvas formats, arrived at through an ingenious use of protractors, each one to be realized in three different designs. Stella refers to those designs as "interlaces," "rainbows," and "fans." Except for a brief digression into the tangential "Saskatchewan" series, in which circular forms are used within rectangular frames, Stella has continued to work on the "protractor" series to the present, and about three-quarters of it had been realized by the time of his retrospective exhibition at the Museum of Modern Art, from March 26 to May 31, 1970.

The retrospective exhibition contained sixty works, consisting of forty-one paintings and nineteen drawings that reviewed Stella's entire artistic development from the "transitional" paintings onward. A modified version of the exhibition later circulated under the auspices of the museum's international council to the Hayward Gallery, London; Stedelijk Museum, Amsterdam; Pasadena Museum of Art, California; and Art Gallery of Toronto, Ontario. Published by the museum in conjunction with the exhibition, William S. Rubin's monograph on Stella contained 176 pages, eighty-three illustrations, and a bibliography with 192 entries.

Not all reviewers felt that Stella's work warranted so much critical and curatorial concern. In a lengthy review in the *New Yorker* (May 9, 1970) Harold Rosenberg categorized Stella's painting as "chessboard aesthetics" and "an adjunct of aesthetic theology." In the New York *Times* (April 5, 1970) Hilton Kramer noted, "On one level, . . . [a] Stella exhibition is more like a seminar on aesthetics than an exhibition of paintings," but, impressed by the lush, fluorescent color of his latest works, he added "On another level, however, the spectator is offered a very rich and complicated optical experience." And Douglas Davis wrote in *Newsweek* (April 3, 1970): "The retrospective reveals . . . a carefully structured career that has become seduced by the sensuousness of its own medium—to the point where it no longer represents the cutting polemic edge of vanguard art. Frank Stella is a painter now. He is no longer a logician."

In addition to the one-man shows already mentioned, Stella has had one-man exhibitions at the Leo Castelli Gallery in New York in 1962, 1964, 1966, 1967, and 1969; at the Ferus Gallery in Los Angeles in 1963; at the Galerie Lawrence in Paris in 1964; at the David Mirvish Gallery in Toronto in 1966 and 1968; at Kasmin, Ltd., in London in 1966 and 1968; at Galerie Bischofberger in Zurich in 1967; at the Washington (D.C.) Gallery of Modern Art in 1968; at the Irving Blum Gallery in Los Angeles in 1968 and 1969; at Bennington College in 1968; at the Rose Art Museum of Brandeis University in 1969; at the Mayaguez campus of the University of Puerto Rico in 1969; and at the Lawrence Rubin Gallery in New York in 1970. His work has appeared in many important group exhibitions that helped shape the consciousness of the avant-garde during the 1960's, among them "Toward a New Abstraction" at the Jewish Museum in New York in 1963; "Post-Painterly Abstraction" at the Los Angeles County Museum of Art in 1964; "The Shaped Canvas" at the Solomon R. Guggenheim Museum in New York in 1964; and "Three Americans," with Kenneth Noland and Jules Olitski at the Fogg Art Museum of Harvard University in 1965. It has been included in the Venice Biennale in 1964, the São Paulo Bienal in 1965, and other international group shows. When Brandeis University distributed its creative arts awards in 1968, Stella received the painting citation. His paintings are owned by major museums and important private collectors throughout the world.

Among the schools where Stella has taught or lectured are Yale University (1965), the University of Saskatchewan (1967), and Brandeis University (1969). He did not accept an offer to become artist-in-residence at the University of California in 1967 because he refused to sign the state's loyalty oath.

Frank Stella married Barbara Rose, the art critic, in 1961. By that marriage, which ended in divorce, the couple had two children, Rachel and Michael. Small and slender, Stella was described by a reporter for Newsweek (April 3, 1970) as "coming on as casually as he talks—hair rumpled, baggy sweat shirt streaked with acrylic stains, his trousers matching, his bridgework missing." An ardent tennis player, in 1966 Stella performed in Robert Rauschenberg's Open Score, a "happening" consisting of a tennis game in which the rackets were wired for the transmission of sound. In 1967 he designed the sets and costumes for Merce Cunningham's dance composition Scramble, and in 1968 he designed some stained glass windows, inspired by his "Saskatchewan" series, for a projected building by Philip Johnson.

"I always get into arguments with people who want to retain the 'old values' in painting," Stella has said. "If you pin them down, they always end up asserting that there is something there besides the paint on canvas. My painting is based on the fact that only what can be seen is there. . . . If the painting were lean enough, accurate enough, or right enough, you would just be able to look at it. . . . What you see is what you see."

References

Kunstwerk 18:125 Ap '65 por
Life 64:44+ Ja 19 '68 pors
Time 90:64 N 24 '67
Rubin, William S. Frank Stella (1970)
Who's Who in American Art (1970)

STILL, CLYFFORD

Nov. 30, 1904- Artist
Address: b. c/o Marlborough-Gerson Gallery, 41 E. 57th St., New York 10022

Although considered one of the most influential of the abstract expressionist painters, until 1969 Clyfford Still had not shown his work in New York City for more than seventeen years. He then allowed several important paintings to be included in group shows at the Museum of Modern Art and the Metropolitan Museum of Art and gave his new dealer, Marlborough-Gerson, permission to mount a major retrospective. Previously Still had had only two museum retrospectives, at the Albright Gallery in Buffalo in 1959 and at the Institute of Contemporary Art in Philadelphia in 1964. As for one-man exhibitions, he had had only four in New York City and three in San Francisco—far fewer than any artist of comparable stature and achievement. Still has always shunned group shows and has made it extremely difficult for anyone, whether museum representative or private collector, to purchase his works.

Still pursues those policies not to be willfully "eccentric," "cantankerous," or "iconoclastic"—words that often crop up in the literature about him—but because of his apocalyptic vision of art and his messianic view of the role of the artist. "A painting in the wrong hands," he has said, "is a highly dangerous force." For many years Still taught so that he would not have to sell his paintings, creating in the process a body of theory and practice that offered younger painters the first viable alternative to cubism in abstract art. Rejecting the art scene, which he excoriates as "a fraudulent arena of poltroon politicians and charlatan hucksters who pretend they love art for the vile sake of exploitation," and rejecting New York City, which he looks upon as the Sodom of the art world, Still moved in 1961 to a small farm in Maryland, where he lives and works in isolation.

Clyfford Still was born on November 30, 1904 in the farm country of Grandin, North Dakota, and he divided his childhood years between his father's homestead in Bow Island, southern Alberta, Canada, and a family home in Spokane, Washington, where his father worked as an accountant. As a child, Still painted at every opportunity, stealing time between farm chores to do so. Since his family considered artists "sissies," he

CLYFFORD STILL

began signing his paintings "Clyfford" to save them embarrassment, a practice he continues to this day.

Still first visited New York City in 1924, mainly for the purpose of touring its art museums and galleries. After waiting in the rain for several hours for the Metropolitan Museum of Art to open, he was disappointed when he got inside, because the long awaited masterpieces seemed alien to him. While in New York City he also enrolled briefly (some reports say for fifteen minutes, some for forty-five) at the Art Students League; in either case, he left convinced that they had nothing to teach him. At that time, he once explained, art schools were "putrefying with Bauhaus teaching."

In 1933 Still obtained a B.A. degree from the University of Washington in Spokane, where he had been awarded a scholarship in art. That same year he became a teaching fellow at Washington State University, from which he received an M.A. degree in 1935. Unlike many artists, Still refused throughout the Depression to work for the WPA, on the ground that he never considered his art a "social utility." Instead he spent the summers of 1934 and 1935 as a fellow at the Trask Foundation in Saratoga Springs, New York, and from 1935 to 1940 he was an instructor at Washington State University. From 1940 to 1941 he was an assistant professor there. During that period he painted realistic landscapes of the American West and a series of distorted figure studies in which the men were all bony and angular and the women bloated and pregnant. His first one-man show, at the San Francisco Museum of Art in 1943, consisted of twenty-two paintings in that style.

Between the fall of 1941 and the summer of 1943 Still was too busy drawing blueprints in the aircraft and shipbuilding industries of Oakland and San Francisco to do much painting. In the fall of 1943 he accepted a position as professor at the Richmond Professional Institute, a division of the College of William and Mary in Richmond, Virginia. There he resumed painting in earnest, adopting an increasingly nonfigurative style. Although there are references to the figure in most of Still's works before 1946, the emphasis shifted

to the expressive possibilities of abstract elements in themselves. His canvases of that period consisted of upward-thrusting areas with shredded, jagged contours, darkly colored in tenebrous browns and blacks, with the paint applied in slabs almost as thick as bas-relief.

When fourteen of those paintings were exhibited at Still's first one-man show in New York City at Peggy Guggenheim's Art of This Century Gallery in 1946, they were generally seen to have mythic and surrealist connotations, somewhat related to Adolph Gottlieb's "pictographs" and Mark Rothko's "dream landscapes" of the same period. In an introduction to the catalog of the exhibition, Rothko said that Still had created a new "generic myth," transforming every shape into an "organic entity, inviting a multiplicity of associations." Still himself said that these paintings were "of the Earth, the Damned, and the Recreated"; they were even given mythic titles: *Nemesis of Esther III, Buried Sun, Theopathic Entities.* However, Still has since repudiated those titles, along with any surrealistic or mythic connotations attributed to the paintings. (In a biography prepared for the catalog of his Philadelphia exhibition, Mrs. Still wrote: "All titles associated with work were applied by gallery for their personal interests.")

In 1946 Still returned to the West to teach at the California School of Fine Arts in San Francisco. Except for a brief interval in 1947-48, when he returned to New York City to organize and plan the program for a group of painters which became known as "Subjects of the Artist," he remained there until 1950. During that period, and particularly after 1948, when he initiated and directed an advanced painting class, Still's influence became a significant force in contemporary American art. Together with Mark Rothko he stimulated what was known as the "San Francisco Renaissance."

Still's ascendancy over so many younger painters, according to British critic Kenneth Sawyer, occurred because "he offered them the first alternative to cubism the new generation could take seriously." What he advocated, in both his teaching and painting, was a rigorous rejection of everything cubism implied: its relational design contained within the picture frame, its implied horizon line and recessive space, its small scale, and perhaps most important, its "well-madeness" or "prettiness," a symbol, to him, of Western European decadence.

His wholly nonfigurative paintings, which emerged in 1947, are the antithesis of all that. As critic Irving Sandler has described them in his *The Triumph of American Painting* (Praeger, 1970): "They are generally composed of vertical paint-incrusted areas of flat color whose contours are jagged. The areas are not separable forms against a background but function as zones of a holistic field. The accent is on openness. No horizontals knit the verticals that might break the continuous plane. The areas that spread to the canvas edges are cut off, appearing to expand beyond the picture limits."

Furthermore, Still's paintings cannot even remotely be considered "pretty" or "in good taste."

Sandler goes on to say: "Indeed, his pictures suggest that he deliberately renounced painterly graces, sensuousness, and sophistication: the forms are ragged, looking as if they were arbitrarily drawn; the colors are dry and repeated in unrefreshing sequences; and the surfaces, consisting of paint troweled on with palette knives, are scabrous. In sum, these canvases, while elating, are nevertheless rude and dour."

During the late 1940's and early 1950's Still exhibited more actively than at any other period. He had one-man shows in San Francisco at the California Palace of the Legion of Honor in 1947 and at Metart, a gallery formed at his suggestion by his students at the California School of Fine Arts, on his retirement from that school in 1950. He also had one-man shows at the Betty Parsons Gallery in New York City in 1947, 1950, and 1951.

In 1950 Still moved to New York City, where he continued to live, with occasional trips to San Francisco, until 1961. During his New York sojourn he taught briefly at Hunter and Brooklyn colleges. During 1948 and 1949 he had painted several canvases entirely in black; during the 1950's he keyed up his palette, achieving greater sensuousness than he had managed before. He also began painting in enormous dimensions and opened up his pictures by lightening the textures and simplifying the field. At the same time he reduced the expanses of bare canvas, sized but without ground, in his paintings.

Appearing for the first time in a group exhibition, in 1952 Still allowed his work to be included in the Museum of Modern Art's prestigious "Fifteen Americans" show, in which the work of his close friend Jackson Pollock was also introduced to the museum-going public. In his statement for the catalog of the exhibition, at which seven of his paintings dating from 1947 to 1952 were shown, Still said: "We all bear the burden of . . . tradition on our backs but I cannot hold it a privilege to be a pallbearer of my spirit in its name." Flouting tradition, he made the museum wait for two years before allowing it to purchase one of his works it had exhibited.

Not until 1959 did Still again exhibit his work, when the Albright Gallery in Buffalo offered him a retrospective show under unusual circumstances: he was permitted to select, install, and catalog his own work, while all competing modern canvases were banished from sight. Earlier, Still had turned down the offer of a one-man show at the Venice Biennale for fear that it would be misinterpreted as catering to "the praise of Vanity Fair."

The exhibition at the Albright Gallery consisted of seventy-two works, covering twenty-three years of Still's artistic evolution. Writing in November 1959, *Art News* critic Hubert Crehan found an "imposing grandeur" in the paintings. "The meaning of his work," he said, "is a defiant gesture toward an authoritarian past and a portent that the lost causes of freedom in the old world may be redeemed in the new." In the New York *Times* (November 15, 1959) the critic Dore Ashton was not as favorably impressed. While acknowledging Still's "singular imagery" and recognizing that his

technically "bad" painting was deliberate and in keeping with his anti-elegant attitude, she felt that "there always seems to be one too many ruffles in his compositions" and concluded that his paintings were "products of an excessive sentimentalism of awesome proportions." Having found such a congenial setting at the Albright Gallery, in 1964 Still donated thirty-one paintings, then valued at more than $1,000,000, to that museum, now known as the Albright-Knox Gallery. Made on condition that all the works be kept together, the gift represents one of the most generous gestures ever made by a contemporary artist.

Still had another retrospective exhibition in 1963, when thirty-two of his major oils constituted the inaugural show of the University of Pennsylvania's Institute of Contemporary Art. The show was organized by the art institute's then acting director, Ti-Grace Sharpless, who is now the Ti-Grace Atkinson of radical feminism fame. In *Time* (November 29, 1963) a reviewer commented on the amount of activity that occurs in a Still painting near the edges of the canvas, "where colorful jigsaw puzzle pieces are chopped off as if they had turned the corner into a new dimension," and found in the show proof that Still "ranks among the few skilled practitioners of abstract expressionism."

After a hiatus of seventeen years, Still again showed his work publicly in New York City in 1969. Six of his major paintings were included in the Museum of Modern Art's "Abstract Expressionism" exhibition, five were displayed in the Metropolitan Museum of Art's centennial show, "New York Painting and Sculpture: 1940-70," and a major retrospective was mounted by his new dealer, Marlborough-Gerson. Still, who once said, "I'd rather have my paintings burned or destroyed than let them go to certain dealers or collectors," has not explained why he is again exhibiting in the "Sodom" of the art world, or why he has affiliated with a gallery that is considered the General Motors of the art market.

The gallery exhibition consisted of forty-five oils and gouaches dating from 1943 to 1966. In the works of the 1960's, seen in New York for the first time, the painting is thinner, freer, and more atmospheric, the color brighter and more lyrical, leading several reviewers to compare them with Monet's late lily pads. Irving Sandler announced in the New York *Times* (December 21, 1969) that "Still re-emerges at this time as a giant of contemporary art," while David L. Shirey observed in *Newsweek* (December 22, 1969): "The powerful, mostly large-scale paintings . . . transcend the label of Abstract Expressionism and become epochal, timeless statements of man in raw, basic confrontation with himself."

Six feet tall, Clyfford Still stands as straight as a martinet and has silver hair and black eyes. He lives with his wife and his daughter Sandra, who devote themselves to photographing and cataloging his works. Before she became adept at photography, Mrs. Still used to make sketches of all her husband's paintings, for the purpose of identification. Still's studio, which is in a Victorian house in Maryland, contains more than 750 works, some dating as far back as 1920, with a probable market value of several million dollars. Their intrinsic value to Still cannot be calculated. "Let no man undervalue the implications of this work," he once wrote, "or its power for life—or for death—if it is misused."

References

Newsweek 74:105 D 22 '69 por
Time 70:105 N 25 '57; 82:76 N 29 '63 por
Miller, Dorothy, ed. 15 Americans (1952)
Sandler, Irving. The Triumph of American Painting (1970)
Sharpless, Ti-Grace. Clyfford Still (1963)

STOCKHAUSEN, KARLHEINZ (shtôk'hou-zen)

Aug. 22, 1928- Composer; conductor
Address: b. Studio für Elektronische Musik, Westdeutscher Rundfunk, Wallrafplatz 5, Cologne, Federal Republic of Germany; h. Marienburgerstrasse 17a, 5 Cologne-Marienburg, Federal Republic of Germany

Ever since Karlheinz Stockhausen created the first purely synthetic music in 1952, his innovations in the composition of musical and extra-musical sounds have become more and more radical. Early in his career he used the new medium of electronic music to evolve concepts of form that dispensed with the traditional ideas of development, repetition, and variation. Those concepts led in turn to the creation of a new system of musical notation, a new vocabulary, and also, the idea of a new spherical concert hall in which music would converge on an audience from loudspeakers placed in every direction. Over the years Stockhausen has shifted from a style that allows for virtually complete control over the structure, sound elements, and interpretation of his works to one that relies a great deal on the whims of chance and improvisation. The wide range of his inventiveness has met with an equally wide-ranging critical response. To some, especially the young, including the Beatles, he is a genius and a prophet, to others a sensationalist and a cabaret clown. Notwithstanding all the controversy, Stockhausen's disciples and detractors alike agree, as the critic Peter Heyworth remarked in a profile for the *Observer* (April 25, 1971), that "no composer has made so deep an impact on the evolution of music in the past fifteen years."

Karlheinz Stockhausen was born on August 22, 1928 in the village of Mödrach near Cologne, Germany to Simon and Gertrud (Stupp) Stockhausen, who came from peasant stock. His mother, was confined to a mental hospital, and in 1941 she was eliminated by the Nazis as a "useless member of society." His father, who was a schoolmaster, was killed in 1944 after serving five years in the army. The orphaned Stockhausen was sent to a state school at Xanten where, for a time, he had a chance to continue the musical studies he had begun at home. His education was interrupted towards the end of the war when he was drafted to serve as a medical orderly and stretcher-bearer at the front. Not until 1946 was he able to resume his studies, and the following year he graduated from the secondary school in Bergisch-Gladbach.

In 1947 Stockhausen entered the Hochschule für Musik in Cologne in order to prepare for a career in teaching. At the Hochschule, Stockhausen studied music, helping to support himself by playing in a jazz combo and by accompanying a traveling magician with improvisations at the piano. Until 1950 he studied piano with Hermann Schroeder and eventually became a student of the noted Swiss composer Frank Martin. In 1951 he moved to Paris to study composition with Darius Milhaud and Oliver Messiaen. The latter composer, who taught at the Paris Conservatory, also instructed Pierre Boulez, with whom Karlheinz Stockhausen formed a close and lasting friendship. For a while Stockhausen was intrigued by some of the experiments in *musique concrète* ("concrete music" produced by recording everyday sounds, or their distortions, on tape), but he soon decided it had limited value as an art form. By contrast, the new medium of electronic music seemed to provide infinite possibilities, some of which Stockhausen already had tentatively begun to explore in 1952. He discussed the problems of electronic music in a correspondence he had conducted with Dr. Herbert Eimert at the West German Radio Station in Cologne, and in 1953, when Eimert concluded the preliminary arrangements for an electronic studio at the station, he appointed Stockhausen as its permanent staff member.

Before Stockhausen's appointment, Cologne Radio had already become a major force in German musical life through its efforts to promote new music. By 1945 it offered nightly broadcasts of contemporary music arranged with the collaboration of such composers as Hindemith, Schoenberg, and Stravinsky. Several years later its ample resources were used to commission works by young, avant-garde composers, performances of which were given by orchestras and choirs trained by the station's music department. When Cologne Radio undertook to sponsor the International Vacation Courses for New Music in Darmstadt, composers representing every modern trend had unparalleled opportunities to be heard. Stockhausen himself attended those courses in 1951—the year in which his *Kreuzspiel* (Crossing Game) for oboe, bass clarinet, piano, and three percussion players had its première. It was his first work to have a significant impact on contemporary German music.

Two works composed in the early 1950's—*Kontra-punkte* (Counterpoint) and *Electronic Studies 1 and 2*—illustrate the diversity of his experimentation during the early part of his career. The first, a serial piece written for ten instruments, was conducted by Hermann Scherchen at the 1953 Festival of New Music in Cologne. An immensely difficult work, in which pairs of instruments and extreme note values are played off against each other, it met with a mixed reception. Some years later Stockhausen himself found the piece inadequate, because it seemed far too traditional compared to his electronic music.

Stockhausen's electronic music, even such early compositions as the 1953 *Studies,* represents a radical departure from the most modern works written for conventional instruments. And although Stockhausen has since written far more complex electronic works, his rationale for switching to the new medium has remained fairly consistent: namely, that it allows a composer to transcend the limits of "preformed instrumental sounds," to create not only the structure of a work but the acoustical elements it employs. As such, he thinks it offers a unique opportunity to compose a totally "integrated" work.

On the subject of Stockhausen's intentions, and those of the new music in general, no one has been more prolific a commentator than Stockhausen himself, who has written a spate of articles, analyses, and program notes and has lectured and taught. Many critics deplore his volubility, but they nonetheless agree that the unprecedented gap between public taste and contemporary music inevitably puts avant-garde composers on the defensive. Since Stockhausen is the most radical member of the group, his tendency to "explain" himself, especially recently, is thus more pronounced and more understandable. In the 1950's his lectures and articles also dealt with the innovations of other composers, primarily those of Anton Webern, from whom he derived his "pointillistic" method of composition (one that emphasizes the properties of notes rather than their arrangement). Together with Herbert Eimert, in 1955 Stockhausen provided a forum for other composers of the Webern school by establishing a journal on serial music entitled *Die Reihe (The Row).* Other articles he wrote during that period concerned the applicability of modern acoustical theories to electronic music. They were based upon ideas he developed while studying phonetics and communications science at the University of Bonn from 1952 to 1954 and were related to his own compositions.

He put his new insights to work in an early piece called *Gesang der Jünglinge* (Song of the Youths) 1956, which is still considered one of his best. Here the fluting soprano voice of a young boy blends with complex electronic sounds to provide a musical setting for a text from the The Old Testament's Book of Daniel (the song of praise sung by Shadrach, Meschach, and Abednego in the fiery furnace). At the first performance of *Gesang der Jünglinge* in Cologne, the music, which is on tape, was carried throughout the hall by five loudspeakers.

Innovations of a different kind characterized two compositions that Karlheinz Stockhausen wrote in 1956 for conventional musical instruments: *Klavierstück XI* (Piano Piece XI) and *Nr. 5 Zeitmasze* employed the technique of "variable" or "multivalent" form to allow performers to improvise on the basic elements of composition. In *Klavierstück XI,* which consists of nineteen fragments, the pianist is free to arrange the fragments at will and to select from a range of designated tempos, touch, and dynamics those he wishes to use. The piece concludes when any one fragment has been played three times. With so much left to the whim of the

KARLHEINZ STOCKHAUSEN

performer, the composition naturally varies from one performance to another. The same is true of *Zeitmasze,* which allows the performer to alter tempos and to improvise in passages similar to cadenzas. In the actual cadenzas, however, the material is predetermined by the composer. Tempo is the most unpredictable element in the work, for Stockhausen wanted to demonstrate, as he said, that time is experienced most acutely when "all sense of time is lost." Like the first piece, *Zeitmasze* belongs to the genre of variable form or "aleatoric" music initiated by the American composer John Cage.

Another problem that engaged the attention of Stockhausen at that time was what he has called "spatial" or "directional" music—the stereophonic rendition of works in concert performance. He first attempted to achieve that effect in 1957, when he composed *Gruppen* (Groups), a "spatial" work for three orchestras, which had its premiere in Cologne on March 24, 1959. Three orchestras, each with its own conductor, were set up in different parts of the hall, the music converging on the audience in the center. In introducing the music, Stockhausen remarked that the orchestras play "partially independently in different tempi; from time to time they meet in common rhythm; they call to each other and answer each other; for a whole period of time one hears only music from the left, or from the front, or from the right. The sound wanders from one orchestra to another." One of the best taped performances of *Gruppen* was given at Expo '70 in Osaka, Japan, where the spherical auditorium Stockhausen intended for his works had been specially constructed at the German pavilion.

Although Stockhausen had become one of Germany's most talked-about composers by the late 1950's, his music still had not attracted much of a following abroad. In 1958, when he toured the United States and Canada for the first time, critics reported the bewilderment and shock that audiences experienced on hearing his "strange" sounds. Six years later, when Stockhausen returned to the United States, the reaction to his work was far more positive. The main works featured were

Zyklus for a Percussionist and *Refrain*, both compositions of variable form music that date from 1959, and *Kontakte* (Contacts), also composed in 1959, a work combining both electronic and traditional instruments. Critics were struck by the novel use of rhythmic progression in *Zyklus* and by the intriguing sonorities of *Refrain*, which, however strange, was unquestionably satisfying. The most compelling work was *Kontakte*, whose effect on one New York *Times* critic (January 7, 1964) was that of an "aural landscape of considerable fascination."

The year of Stockhausen's second American visit also witnessed the United States première of his musical play, *Originale*, which was introduced at the New York Avant-Garde Festival in Judson Hall on September 8, 1964. Fully living up to the promise of its title, the play evoked the same laughter, catcalls, and frenzied applause that had greeted it at its German première in Cologne in 1961. The cast consisted of acrobats, jugglers, musicians, poets (including Allen Ginsberg) and a variety of fauna (including birds, dogs, hens, and a chimpanzee). It also featured street musicians playing early Stockhausen and a beautiful lady cellist, astride a balcony railing, playing Bach. The objective of the "absurd, improvised drama," according to a critic in the New York *Herald Tribune* (September 9, 1964) was to add another dimension to Stockhausen's ideas about spatial music by having the entire troupe "personify musical patterns" in an attempt to "establish a human bridge with the audience." Although critics felt that *Originale* failed to elicit the kind of audience participation that provides real communication, they recommended it as a "dazzling display of inventiveness."

Despite his obvious gift for spectacle and showmanship, Stockhausen is often disturbed by the fact that audiences respond primarily to the "paraphernalia" of his compositions and only secondarily to the music, which is his main consideration. As he emphasized in his liner notes for the Nonesuch recording of *Momente* (1963; revised in 1965), his purpose is to explore the "purely musical range of problems of tone-color composition." In *Momente* he tried to achieve that goal through the instrumentation: a soprano, four choirs, eight brass instruments, two Hammond organs, and percussion (some of it produced by the chorus). In one version he built audience reaction into the piece by having the chorus shout: "Bravo, bis, awful, marvelous, phony." When *Momente* was performed on March 1, 1964 in Buffalo, New York, the audience seconded those sentiments, and some critics were once again impressed by Stockhausen's musical imagination and by what one reviewer called his ability to "embrace, reorder, and transform" experience.

In *Mixtur* (1964) Stockhausen carried his experiments with tone-color composition one step further by transforming electronically the sounds of the "live" orchestra. That same year he wrote two works in which microphones are employed as extensions of musical instruments, namely, *Mikrophonie I* and *Mikrophonie II*. Much of the sound in those compositions emanated from the various types of friction produced by "exciting" an ancient, five-foot tam-tam. Stockhausen has remarked that they illustrate a point that is central to new music, particularly electronic: the need to devise the *materials* of composition, not just their arrangement.

By the mid-1960's avant-garde composers had transformed audience receptivity to such a degree that they had acquired a considerable following. Riding the cresting wave of popularity, Stockhausen served as visiting professor at the University of California for the academic year of 1966-67 and gave many concerts in the United States. For the young and the "hip" in particular he is one of the most charismatic figures in new music today, a prophet of the Age of Aquarius. Stockhausen's appeal to that audience has increased since the composition of *Hymnen* in 1967, a collage of anthems that yearns for a "oneness" transcending barriers of race, religion, and nationality. In an interview with Peter Heyworth for the New York *Times* (February 21, 1971), Stockhausen revealed the religious and mystical bent that has governed such of his recent compositions as *Hymnen, Stimmung* (Tuning), and *Mantra*. Speaking of the need to develop "a technique of getting in touch with the intuitive," he elaborated on the role of the composer as a spiritual guide who, through his music, "brings us to essentials." After the New York première of *Hymnen* at Philharmonic Hall on February 25, 1971 some critics doubted that Stockhausen had achieved those objectives, but even the sceptical Harold C. Schonberg observed that "the music meant a good deal to the young audience, which listened intently and clearly entered into its spirit." He concluded that the audience's reaction might well be the best indication of Stockhausen's stature as a composer.

Karlheinz Stockhausen spends much of his time when not on tour with his family, which consists of his second wife, Mary Bauermeister, an accomplished painter and sculptress, and their two children. The family receives few visitors other than those concerned with music, for the voluble Stockhausen, who is equally articulate in French, English, and German, sees little value in talk for the sake of talk itself. He equates life with work. His personality is reflected in the simple and austere beauty of his home that he designed himself in the hilly countryside east of Cologne.

It would be difficult to improve on Peter Heyworth's description of Stockhausen in his *Observer* profile: "He is a tall, well set-up man who looks younger than his forty-two years. Only surprisingly delicate hands, silky brown hair that falls on to his shoulders and huge, solemn eyes (he does not laugh easily, and least of all at himself) suggest someone out of the ordinary." Although he subscribes to no single theology, Stockhausen remains as fundamentally religious as he was when he attended the state school as a child, where prayer constituted his only retreat into privacy. His scarring early experience with the Nazis has left him wary of all political ideologies. Mystical though he is in outlook, he has the technological expertise to apply effectively his most far-out ideas.

References

Christian Sci Mon p4+ Jl 22 '68 por
London Observer p9 Ap 25 '71 por
N Y Times II p13+ F 21 '71 por
Sat R 50:63+ S 30 '67 por

Ewen, David, ed. The World of Twentieth
Century Music (1969); Composers Since
1900 (1969); Composers of Tomorrow's
Music (1971)
International Who's Who, 1971-72
Who's Who in America, 1970-71
Who's Who in Music, 1970-71
Who's Who in the World, 1971-72
Wörner, Karl H. Karlheinz Stockhausen;
Werk & Wollen 1950-1962 (1963)

MICHAEL TILSON THOMAS

THOMAS, MICHAEL TILSON

Dec. 21, 1944- Conductor; pianist
Address: b. Boston Symphony, Symphony Hall,
251 Huntington Ave., Boston, Mass. 02115;
h. 303 Commonwealth Ave., Boston, Mass.
02115

Michael Tilson Thomas' rise to musical fame has
been dramatic, and the rapidity with which he
has achieved prominence is only one aspect of
the drama. He literally burst upon the scene when
he pinch-hitted for the ailing William Steinberg,
conductor of the Boston Symphony Orchestra, on
October 22, 1969 in New York. Just before that
occasion he had been appointed assistant conductor of that orchestra, at the age of twenty-five,
and at the close of the 1969-70 season was named
its associate conductor. In February 1971 he was
appointed director of the Buffalo Philharmonic
Orchestra, to assume leadership at the beginning
of the 1971-72 season. Charming, young, and
gifted, he brings to mind the early career of
Leonard Bernstein in terms of personality and
especially the circumstances of his New York
debut. Indeed, some music critics have called
Thomas the "Lenny of the Seventies."

Michael Tilson Thomas was born on December
21, 1944 in Hollywood, California, the only child
of Theodore and Roberta Thomas. With the exception of his mother, a teacher in the Los Angeles city school system, his family has a theatrical background. Theodore Thomas went to
Hollywood years ago to write material for Paul
Muni, Michael's uncle, and is now a director and
writer for films and television in Los Angeles.
Thomas' paternal grandparents, Boris and Bessie
Thomashefsky, were founders and stars of the
Yiddish theatre in New York. Music and science,
however, rather than the theatre, were the main
interests of Thomas from childhood. He could
play the piano by ear at the age of five, read
music by eight, and began formal piano studies
at ten, but in school he became absorbed in crys-
tallography and chemistry. Although he continued
music lessons throughout his teens—piano with
John Crown and Muriel Kerr and harpsichord
with Alice Ehlers—it was not until he entered the

University of Southern California in 1962 that he
became firmly committed to music.

Enrolling in the university with advanced standing, since he had attended classes there during
his last two years at North Hollywood High
School, Thomas embarked on a topsy-turvy course
of study. He was taking graduate courses as a
sophomore, had to fulfill freshman requirements
as a senior, and earned extra credits in architecture and Asiatic studies, among other subjects, as
well as music. He maintains that he almost
majored in Asiatic studies.

In distinction to being a product of the music
conservatory, where the student is likely to fall
under one person's influence, Thomas considers
himself a university product, educated to understand varied approaches to music. Citing the comment of Aldous Huxley, "Los Angeles is the place
where geniuses go to die," in an interview with
Howard Klein in the New York *Times* (March 29,
1970), Thomas noted that he was able to learn
from the top musicians. Besides studying piano
with John Crown, he studied conducting with
Ingolf Dahl, who as Thomas' mentor also taught
him structural analysis, music history, and ear
training. He was pianist for Gregor Piatigorsky's
master cello classes, accompanied violinist Jascha
Heifetz, assisted Pierre Boulez in orchestra rehearsals, and was also acquainted with Igor Stravinsky and Robert Craft.

Thomas graduated from the University of
Southern California in 1968 with a master's degree in music. On graduation day he received an
award for being its outstanding alumnus. Long
before graduation Thomas had launched his conducting career. For four years beginning in 1963
he was conductor of the Young Musicians Foundation Debut Orchestra, a resident company of
the Los Angeles Music Center. Serving as piano
soloist as well as conductor, he performed the
music of Igor Stravinsky, Pierre Boulez, Karlheinz
Stockhausen, Lukas Foss, and Ingolf Dahl for the
Monday evening concert series. Some of those performances were premières.

In 1966 Thomas went to Bayreuth, Germany to study in Friedelind Wagner's classes. Thomas did not care for Richard Wagner's music but wanted to acquire a rationale for his dislike of the composer. An orchestra coach for the Bayreuth Festival became ill just five days after Thomas had arrived, and he was given the assignment of assisting Boulez on the production of *Parsifal*, with the result that he learned to love Wagner's operas. He also assisted Boulez in the Ojai, California festival in 1967 and became chief conductor of the festival in the summers of 1968 and 1969.

During 1968 and 1969 Thomas divided his time between the East Coast and West Coast. He conducted the Youth Concerts of the Los Angeles Philharmonic and was guest conductor with the Boston Philharmonia, a cooperative group, in which he was first heard by the Boston Symphony Orchestra's William Steinberg. In 1968 he also prepared the orchestra for the Heifetz-Piatigorsky concerts in Los Angeles. When he appeared at the Berkshire Music Center in Tanglewood, Massachusetts as a conducting fellow in 1968, he won the Koussevitzky Prize. During that summer season he conducted Stanley Silverman's *Elephant Steps*, an "occult opera." Returning to Tanglewood the following summer, again as a conducting fellow, he assisted Erich Leinsdorf in the preparation for Alban Berg's opera *Wozzeck*.

Not neglecting the piano, Thomas also appeared in chamber music recitals. A concert with cellist Lawrence Lesser at Town Hall, New York was praised by Theodore Strongin in the New York *Times* (April 24, 1969) as ideal chamber music, with both musicians' exhibiting virtuoso abilities. Singling out Debussy's Sonata for Cello and Piano as a high point, Strongin wrote, "It was played with brilliant attention to detail and a sense in depth of color, line and proportion. It was a magical performance."

Thomas was appointed assistant conductor of the Boston Symphony in the fall of 1969, but that apprenticeship was perhaps the shortest in musical history: about ten days. Around Columbus Day, Thomas made his debut in Boston in an afternoon performance. The music critic Louis Snyder, of the *Christian Science Monitor* (October 17, 1969), found that Thomas led Charles Ives's *Three Places in New England* "stunningly to the heart and to the ear" and reported "thunderous applause" at the concert's end. Then on October 22, 1969 the Boston Symphony played in Philharmonic Hall in New York City. During the intermission Steinberg went to the hospital suffering from fatigue, and Thomas completed the program: Robert Starer's Concerto for Violin, Cello and Orchestra and Richard Strauss's *Till Eulenspiegel*. Reviewing the concert in the New York *Times* (October 23, 1969), Harold C. Schonberg observed, "A tall, thin young man, he came on stage with an air of immense confidence and authority, and showed that his confidence was not misplaced."

More important to Thomas' career, however, was the fact that Steinberg had to reduce his conducting schedule for the rest of the season. Although the circumstances surrounding Thomas'

unexpected debut in New York were exciting and newsworthy, his opportunity to gain experience on a routine basis was more significant. During the rest of the 1969-70 season he led thirty-seven concerts with the Boston orchestra.

In an interview with the New York *Times* music critic Allen Hughes, published three days after his New York debut, Thomas expressed a desire to conduct all kinds of compositions, from symphonies to Monteverdi vocal music. He likes to plan programs that ignore traditional concepts of chronological or stylistic order, caring more about contrast or unexpected similarity between compositions. "My credo is to resist the dogmatism of the *avant* and *arrière garde*. My idea of a performance is one that presents new ideas about the music," he told Howard Klein of the New York *Times* (March 29, 1970). On occasion he finds it effective to break the orchestra into small units. Thomas feels free to pick and choose from all centuries and styles because of his broad musical education. His unorthodox programming ideas come naturally, he has explained: "There have been a lot of polar influences in my musical development —but I don't feel . . . that I am really a disciple of any idea or person." Thomas' education involved the head-on collision of conflicting ideas, which he finds stimulating.

The complexity of his orientation has led critics to discuss Thomas' programming as well as his abilities as a conductor. After hearing a program that included a twelfth-century organum by Pérotin, the première of Karlheinz Stockhausen's *Punkte* (*Points*), and a Schumann symphony, Louis Snyder remarked in the *Christian Science Monitor* (January 11, 1971), "Over the past few weeks . . . Thomas and the Boston Symphony have turned Symphony Hall into a kind of musical version of a Revere Beach fun house—full of unexpected surprises and harmless jolts. . . . No sooner does the tonal floor seem comfortably firm under foot than one is plunged onto a tilting, spinning, rippling plane of sound, unfamiliar maybe, but curiosity-provoking."

Another program contrasted Lou Harrison's Canticle No. 3 for only seven performers with Carl Nielsen's big Fifth Symphony, both of which heavily exploit percussion and brass. The two extremes were bridged by a Haydn symphony. Harold C. Schonberg called Thomas' program at Philharmonic Hall in New York on March 17, 1971 "an example of unusual and even defiant juxtapositions" (New York *Times*, March 19, 1971). Played side by side were Bach and Schönberg, then Stravinsky and Tchaikovsky. To top it off, the Tchaikovsky was a selection from *Swan Lake*, usually reserved for pop concerts and ballet performances. Believing that some of Tchaikovsky's best music is in his ballet scores, Thomas intends to do parts of *The Sleeping Beauty* and *The Nutcracker* in the future.

The critical reception to Thomas' conducting has been warm. Schonberg discerns a few unpolished areas, particularly in rhythm and stick technique, but finds that Thomas is charismatic, has "talent to burn," and approaches music in a subjective manner, managing to make even Webern sound charming and almost romantic. Winthrop Sargeant described Thomas in the *New Yorker* (April 11, 1970) as an "extraordinary phenomenon" and went on to say, "Not that 26-year-old conductors haven't shown remarkable technical accomplishments in the past. . . . But Mr. Thomas is different. He is, apparently, a fully mature maestro. . . . His beat is clear, and since I last watched him it has become more reserved and modest." Thomas himself has pointed out that since leading the Boston group his style has changed: he uses fewer motions.

At the close of the 1969-70 season Thomas was appointed associate conductor, the first to hold that position since Richard Burgin, who retired in 1965. In May 1970 he made his London debut with the London Symphony Orchestra. Once again, he was a last-minute substitute, this time for the ailing Gennadi Rozhdestvensky of the Soviet Union. London audiences and critics applauded him enthusiastically. During the summer of 1970 he conducted at Tanglewood, the Ravinia Festival in Chicago, and the Mostly Mozart Festival in New York, at which Mozart's Requiem was performed. He gave that work an "astonishingly mature reading," according to Raymond Ericson of the New York *Times* (August 30, 1970), who also observed that "Mr. Thomas made the performance very much his own without lapsing into exaggeration."

A heavy schedule for the 1970-71 season required Thomas to conduct the Boston Symphony Orchestra in more than forty concerts at home and on a European tour and to appear as guest conductor with the Buffalo, Rochester, and Japan Philharmonic orchestras. On February 22, 1971 it was announced that Thomas had been chosen director of the Buffalo Philharmonic, an appointment effective at the beginning of the 1971-72 season. He told a reporter of the Washington *Post* (March 17, 1971) that in Buffalo he expected to delve into the music of the late twelfth century up to Bach, reserving the contemporary repertory for Boston, with which he will continue as associate conductor. His contract with the Buffalo orchestra runs until 1973, at which time the Boston orchestra will be without a leader, since Steinberg intends to resign from that post in 1972. Thomas' name is among those favored in speculation in musical circles as to Steinberg's successor.

Thomas has already established a strong rapport with the Boston Symphony Orchestra through both live performances and recordings. It was Thomas who led the orchestra in its first recording under the Deutsche Grammophon label, conducting Ives's *Three Places in New England* and Carl Ruggles' *Suntreader*. Issued in October 1970, it was nominated for a Grammy Award as the best classical album of that year. A disc of Debussy, with Thomas serving as pianist with members of the orchestra, was released a month later. Commenting on both records in the New York *Times* (December 6, 1970), Howard Klein said, "By identifying with Debussy, Ives, and Ruggles, one gets the impression that this is one conductor who is not out for the dubious glory of leading the same orchestras . . . in the same classic-romantic repertory. . . . With the death of Szell, the twilight of the great classic-romantic conductors grows darker. With the emergence of Thomas the future brightens." Under Thomas' direction the orchestra has also recorded the Schumann violin concerto, Tchaikovsky's Symphony No. 1, and Piston's Symphony No. 2.

Boyishly enthusiastic, high-strung, and friendly, Michael Tilson Thomas can talk at length about many subjects. He has dark-brown hair, blue-green eyes under prominent eyebrows, and an engaging smile. He stands six feet one inch tall and weighs 160 pounds. With his time completely occupied by music—in addition to conducting rehearsals and performances he studies scores all morning and composes a little for his own enjoyment—he sees fewer movies than he would like to. But he maintains his interest in geology and chemistry.

References

Hi Fi/Mus Am 20:6 Jl '70 pors; 20:MA7 S '70 por
N Y Times p23 O 25 '69; II p17+ Mr 29 '70 por
N Y Times Mag p36+ O 24 '71 pors
Newsweek 75:86 Ap 13 '70 por; 77:67 Mr 1 '71 por
Sr Schol 97:22+ O 26 '70 pors
Time 96:57 S 14 '70 por
Washington (D.C.) Post E p1+ Mr 17 '71 por

TIJERINA, REIES LOPEZ (tē-he-rē'nä)

Sept. 21, 1926- Spanish-American social activist; former clergyman
Address: c/o Alianza Federal de los Pueblos Libres, 1010 3d St. N.W., Albuquerque, N.M. 87101

Among the ethnic minorities struggling to attain justice in the United States, the Spanish-speaking people of the American Southwest—descendants of Spanish settlers and indigenous American Indians—have as their militant champion the fiery and colorful Texas-born sharecropper's son and former preacher Reies Lopez Tijerina. In 1963 he founded the Alianza Federal de Mercedes (Federal Alliance of Land Grants)—now the Alianza Federal de los Pueblos Libres (Federal Alliance of Free City States)—to advance claims of impoverished Spanish-Americans of New Mexico to land granted to their ancestors by Spanish viceroys in Mexico and the Mexican government but taken from them in the aftermath of the Mexican War. To dramatize those claims and draw attention to the plight of Spanish-Americans, Tijerina has in recent years been engaged in a determined and sometimes violent guerrilla-type struggle against state and federal authorities, and he has gone to prison as a result of his activities. In 1967 he gained international attention when members of his

REIES LOPEZ TIJERINA

Alianza staged an armed raid on the town of Tierra Amarilla in northern New Mexico and briefly occupied the Rio Arriba county courthouse.

Reies Lopez Tijerina was born on September 21, 1926 in a one-room adobe hut on the outskirts of Falls City, Texas, some 120 miles from the Mexican border, one of ten children of Antonio and Herlinda Tijerina, of whom three died in infancy. He has four surviving brothers, Anselmo, Ramón, Margarito, and Cristóbal, and two sisters, María and Josefa. His father, who claimed that he was heir to a Spanish land grant near Laredo, Texas, made his living for a time as a sharecropper, but clashes with landowners who frequently demanded the entire crop at harvest time forced the Tijerina family to become migrant farm workers. Tijerina remembers his mother, who died when he was a small boy, as a robust and strong-willed woman and a devout Roman Catholic, whose constant prayers and Bible recitations fed his mystical religious visions. His paternal grandfather, Santiago Tijerina, told his grandchildren of the depredations once visited on Spanish-American farmers by Texas rangers and vigilante mobs.

By the time he was seven, Reies Tijerina was working in the fields with the other members of his family. Because the Tijerinas were often on the move, his formal education was fragmentary. Despite hardships, he had a relatively contented childhood. "We were happy in poverty," he told Peter Nabokov, as quoted in *Tijerina and the Courthouse Raid* (Univ. of New Mexico Press, 1969). "Earthly possessions didn't bother me, but I was always attracted . . . by that fascinating power that is justice." In 1939 the Tijerina family moved to Michigan to work in the beet fields and remained there for about five years. During that period Reies Tijerina acquired the nickname *abogado sin libros* (lawyer without books), because he would take up an argument and hold his ground against all comers. To his father's dismay, he began to talk back to the ranch owners who hired the family.

The religious faith implanted in Tijerina by his mother was enhanced by a copy of the New Testament given to him by a Baptist minister when he was in his mid-teens, and he was especially inspired by its message that the meek would someday inherit the earth. By the time he was about eighteen he had decided to make his career in the ministry and, transcending the Roman Catholic faith in which he was reared, he entered a Bible college in Ysleta, Texas that was operated by the Latin American council of the Assemblies of God church, the largest of the Fundamentalist sects known as Pentecostal. A former school official remembers him as a "very sincere student" who developed some "rather far-out ideas." Suspended from the Bible college about 1946, reportedly because he had dated a girl in violation of school regulations, Tijerina married and became a circuit preacher in the Assemblies of God Church.

During his first year in the ministry, Tijerina traveled throughout the Southwest and lived for a time in solitude in a cave near El Monte, California, where he experienced "great illuminations." He became convinced that all religions were essentially the same and that there were only "the two strong powers of good and evil." In 1947 he walked all the way from Illinois to Texas to be at the bedside of his dying grandfather. Later that year he became pastor of the Assembly of God Church in Victoria, Texas, but his unorthodox ideas brought him into conflict with the church authorities. In 1950 his ministerial credentials were revoked after he had told his congregation to stop paying tithes, since the church was supposed to help the poor rather than take from them. He then became a nondenominational minister and, after giving away his worldly possessions, traveled and preached throughout the United States, depending on charity for his sustenance. A collection of his sermons and Biblical interpretations of this period was later privately published under the title *Hallará Fe en la Tierra?* (Will There Be Faith on Earth?).

The abject poverty that he encountered in his travels gradually channeled Tijerina's efforts in a more practical direction. In the early 1950's he conceived of a "community of justice and harmony" and, putting his idea into practice, he persuaded seventeen Spanish-American families to pool their resources and buy 160 acres of desert land in Pinal County, Arizona. Known as Valle de la Paz (Valley of Peace), Tijerina's utopian community was at first successful, but it was soon confronted with the hostility of the surrounding community. Its residents were subjected to harrassment and violence and its buildings were burned to the ground.

In the spring of 1957 Tijerina, who was then still living on the site of the Valle de la Paz settlement, was twice charged with grand theft after some allegedly stolen property was found in his possession. The charges were later dismissed because of insufficient evidence. In July, however, Tijerina was arrested on charges of having helped his brother Margarito break out of an Arizona jail where he had been held for extradition to Indiana as a parole violator. The following month, while the hearings on the case were in progress,

Tijerina jumped bail and became a fugitive, reportedly because his life had been threatened and he feared for his safety. While hiding out in California in the fall of 1957, Tijerina—according to his own account—had a "messianic vision," which he interpreted as a divine call to go to New Mexico and take up the fight for the restoration of old Spanish land grants—a problem in which he had become interested a few years earlier.

The land grant question involves millions of acres of land in what is now the American Southwest that had been given to Spanish settlers by kings of Spain in the sixteenth century and to their descendants by the Mexican government in the nineteenth century. Tijerina and his supporters claim that although the Treaty of Guadalupe Hidalgo, under which most of the American Southwest had been ceded to the United States by Mexico in 1848, guaranteed private and communal landholdings, in subsequent years many of the descendants of the Spanish settlers were illegally deprived of their land. In northern New Mexico, where Tijerina concentrated his campaign, Spanish American farmers had for some decades been engaged in a struggle to regain the 594,500-acre Tierra Amarilla land grant, one of 1,715 land grants given to settlers in the American Southwest during the period of Mexican rule.

During the late 1950's, while still a fugitive, Tijerina spent some time in Mexico, where he researched the land grant question in libraries and unsuccessfully tried to interest Mexican government officials in the problem. After coming to New Mexico with a small band of followers, Tijerina conducted a clandestine campaign among persons involved in land grant disputes, inspiring them with hope for the eventual restoration of their lands. In 1960 he settled in Albuquerque, where he worked for a time as janitor at a Presbyterian church while continuing his secret organizing activities and his studies of the land grant problem. By late 1962, after the statute of limitations on the Arizona charges against him had expired, Tijerina was able to conduct his activities more openly.

The Alianza Federal de Mercedes was founded at Alameda near Albuquerque on February 2, 1963 by Tijerina and thirty-seven of his supporters. At its September convention, attended by representatives of some fifty land grants, a constitution was drawn up, declaring the aim of the Alianza to be the restoration to Spanish land grant heirs of all properties and rights covered by the treaty of Guadalupe Hidalgo. In October the Alianza was registered for incorporation by the state of New Mexico. An organizational headquarters was established in a block of real estate in Albuquerque, purchased with money acquired from the sale of the Valle de la Paz properties.

Combining evangelistic fervor with Spanish-American folk rhetoric, Tijerina stumped the rural communities of New Mexico. "He does not make a speech; he enacts the history of the village," Stan Steiner wrote in *La Raza* (Harper & Row, 1970) describing Tijerina's style. "He performs all the roles in the historical pageant he recites. He is the lawyer, judge, victim, preacher, sufferer, farmer, oracle, avenger, and holy prophet." In 1963 and 1964 Tijerina made trips to Washington, but received little more than lukewarm expressions of sympathy for the Alianza's demands from Congressmen and government officials. During the summer of 1964 he led a motorcade into Mexico but was expelled for engaging in political activities in violation of his visitor's permit. Also in 1964, Tijerina began a daily ten-minute local radio program called "The Voice of Justice."

In 1965 the Alianza created a legal action fund and assigned lawyers the task of establishing claims against the federal and state governments. Tijerina went to Spain in the spring of 1966 to search the archives of Seville and Madrid for documents relating to the land grant question. At its September 1966 convention the Alianza—which now claimed a membership of some 20,000 in five states—included among the topics to be discussed discrimination against Spanish-speaking pupils in public schools and the high rate of Spanish-American casualties in the Vietnam conflict.

Led by Tijerina, a group of Alianza members took over the Echo Amphitheater, a campground in the Kit Carson National Forest, on October 15, 1966, proclaiming the reestablishment of the Pueblo de San Joaquín del Rio de Chama, a nineteenth-century land grant, and electing a mayor and governing council. On October 22 they "arrested" two forest rangers in the area and placed them on trial for trespassing. Soon thereafter, the Alianzans were dispersed by state and federal officers, and federal charges were later drawn up against Tijerina and several associates. In the spring of 1967 there was widespread arson and vandalism—allegedly fomented by followers of the Alianza—against Anglo-American-owned ranches and federal lands in northern New Mexico. A cordial meeting between Tijerina and New Mexico Governor David F. Cargo on April 21 got nowhere, and as the violence continued to mount, District Attorney Alfonso Sanchez took the offensive against the Alianza. Fearing imminent arrest, Tijerina resigned as president and disbanded the organization, only to reconstitute it a few days later as the Alianza Federal de los Pueblos Libres. On June 3, 1967 the Alianza met at Coyote, in southern Rio Arriba county, to confront Forest Service officials with demands for federally held land grant territory. Responding to rumors that another violent takeover attempt was imminent, Sanchez ordered the meeting to be broken up, and ten Alianza members—including two of Tijerina's brothers—were arrested on charges of unlawful assembly.

The polarization of forces in northern New Mexico climaxed on the afternoon of June 5, 1967, when some twenty armed Alianza members raided the town of Tierra Amarilla, occupied the Rio Arriba county courthouse and jail for about two hours, and wounded the jailer and a state patrolman in an exchange of gunfire with police. The raiders fled, taking with them a newspaper reporter and a deputy sheriff as hostages. The aim of the raid was, according to Tijerina, to make a citizens' arrest of District Attorney Sanchez, who was mistakenly believed to have been at the Tierra Amarilla courthouse at the time. The raid touched off what has been called the largest manhunt in New Mexico's history. Some 350 National Guardsmen—commanded by General John Pershing Jolly—were called into action and were joined by about 200 state policemen and by local sheriffs, armed ranchers, and Jicarillo Apache police. Tanks, helicopters, and patrol cars were used in the search. Most of the alleged raiders were soon rounded up. Tijerina was arrested on June 10 and charged with kidnapping and other offenses before being released on bond six weeks later. The Tierra Amarilla incident had made Tijerina a hero of the New Left, and in September 1967 he attended the much publicized National Conference for New Politics in Chicago, where a resolution endorsing the goals of the Alianza was unanimously adopted.

After a five-day federal trial at Las Cruces, New Mexico, Tijerina was found guilty on November 11, 1967 of having assaulted two Forest Service rangers at the Echo Amphitheater in 1966, but he remained free on bail pending appeal. In May and June 1968 Tijerina played a key role in the massive Poor People's Campaign in Washington, D.C., where he clashed with some of its black leaders, charging them with squandering campaign funds, neglecting the needs of non-Negro minorities, and ignoring the land-reform proposals of the late Rev. Martin Luther King Jr. During the summer of 1968 Tijerina entered the race for governor of New Mexico as the candidate of his newly-created People's Constitutional party. He was disqualified by the state supreme court, however, because of his federal felony conviction.

After a month-long trial at Albuquerque, on December 14, 1968, Tijerina won acquittal on three charges, including kidnapping, in connection with the Tierra Amarilla raid. In his defense, which he conducted himself after dismissing his court-appointed attorney, he emphasized his right to try to make a citizen's arrest of Sanchez for infringing on the rights of Alianza members. Although the acquittal was considered a major victory for Tijerina, he continued to face charges on some lesser counts in connection with the raid.

In a new upsurge of militancy, in June 1969 Tijerina unsuccessfully tried to make citizen's arrests of United States Supreme Court appointee Warren E. Burger for "decisions detrimental to the civil rights of minority groups"; Los Alamos Laboratory director Norris Bradbury for his role in the development of weapons of mass destruction; and Governor Cargo "for conspiring to deprive us of our lands and rights." Later that month, he had another confrontation with Forest Service officers near Coyote and was arrested on charges of aiding in the destruction of government property and of threatening and assaulting a federal official. He was convicted on those charges by a United States district court in Albuquerque on October 10, 1969, and three days later, after the United States Supreme Court refused to review his conviction in the Echo Amphitheater raid, he began to serve a two-year prison term at the federal prison at La Tuna, Texas. Brought to trial on two remaining charges of assault and false imprisonment stemming from the Tierra Amarilla raid, Tijerina was convicted by a district court jury on November 26, 1969 and was sentenced on January 5, 1970 to concurrent state prison terms of one to five and two to ten years. The United States Parole Board voted on May 25, 1971 to release Tijerina—who had in the meantime been transferred to Springfield, Missouri—from federal prison, so that he could begin to serve his state sentences.

Tijerina not only wants to establish a separate but equal community of Spanish-Americans on land-grant territory within the state of New Mexico, but he also hopes that such communities may someday come into being in other Southwestern states. Although the aims of the Spanish-Americans are distinct from those of the Mexican-Americans, or chicanos, Tijerina has established close ties with such chicano leaders as Cesar Chavez and Rodolfo (Corky) Gonzáles. He has also received support from federal antipoverty agencies and the Presbyterian Church, and from such scholars as Professor Clark Knowlton of the University of Texas, one of the Alianza's foremost champions. On the other hand, United States Senator Joseph M. Montoya of New Mexico once called Tijerina an "exploiter, discredited charlatan, impostor, and racist," who "takes the savings of people . . . to fatten his purse." In response to widespread charges that he is a Communist or Castroite, Tijerina has said, as quoted by Stan Steiner: "Communism is just another European political system to me, just as corrupt as any other political system. We don't need it."

Reies Lopez Tijerina was first married about 1946 to Mary Escobar, a fellow Bible student. They separated about 1963 and were later divorced. By his first marriage, Tijerina has three sons: Reies Jr. (also known as David), Danny, and Noah; and three daughters: Rosemary (or Rosa), Rachel, and Iradeala. His second wife, the former Patsy Romero, is a descendant of a New Mexico land-grant family. With their two children, Iris Isabel and Carlos, they maintain an apartment in the Alianza building in Albuquerque. The entire family is intimately involved in Alianza affairs. A stocky, sharp-featured, hazel-eyed, and intense man, Tijerina is described by Richard Gardner in Gritò! (Bobbs-Merrill, 1970) as "a man of contradictions, with myriad flaws and failings and a number of hidden conflicts." Some years ago Tijerina rejoined the Roman Catholic Church because, as he explained to Gardner, "my people expect it."

References

N Y Times Mag p20+ Jl 16 '67 por
Gardner, Richard. Gritò! Reies Tijerina and the New Mexico Land Grant War of 1967 (1970)
Jenkinson, Michael. Tijerina (1968)
Nabokov, Peter. Tijerina and the Courthouse Raid (1969)
Steiner, Stan. La Raza; The Mexican-Americans (1970)

TRAMPLER, WALTER

Aug. 25, 1915- Violist
Address: h. 33 Riverside Drive, New York
10023

To the habitual concertgoer in New York City, the distinguished viola virtuoso Walter Trampler seems virtually ubiquitous, appearing, as he does, in concert after concert ranging from Renaissance to avant-garde music, either as soloist or as a member of an ensemble. As he takes his seat the music lover knows that, whatever else the imponderables of the evening's performance may be, he can count on the predictable qualities of Trampler's playing: a complete mastery of technique, thorough musicianship, a high order of intelligence, irreproachable intonation, and silken tone—if not the biggest kind of viola sound. German-born, Trampler immigrated to the United States in 1939 and has been a naturalized citizen since 1944. Over the years he has become widely known to record collectors, who especially treasure his much acclaimed performances of the six Mozart string quintets with the Budapest String Quartet. Since 1962 Trampler has been a professor of viola and chamber music at the Juilliard School of Music in New York City.

A product of the rich Central European musical culture, Walter Trampler was born in Munich, Germany on August 25, 1915, the son of Johann Trampler, a violinist with the orchestra of the Munich State Opera, and Willy (Jaeger) Trampler, an amateur pianist. Johann Trampler, who envisioned his son as *the* future great European violinist, first tucked a violin under Walter's chin when the boy was five. Although he was still too tiny to hold a quarter-size violin with comfort, Walter began to study the instrument at the age of six, with his father as his teacher, and continued under his tutelage until 1930. He studied academic subjects at the Volks Schule in Munich from 1920 to 1924 and at the Real Gymnasium, also in Munich, from 1924 to 1930. As a violin student at the State Academy in Munich, he was also required to study viola for a year, in addition to taking courses in music theory, history, and related disciplines.

Although he originally turned to the viola only in order to learn the clef and to qualify himself for playing in quartets, Trampler soon transcended introductory knowledge. First-rate violists are always in shorter supply than first-rate violinists, and soon Trampler found himself in great demand. His first quartet experience was with three young beer-drinking companions of his, and from that he graduated to playing piano quartets with a trio. He graduated from the State Academy of Music in 1934.

Although his father still entertained grandiose visions of a career as virtuoso violinist for his son, Walter Trampler accepted an invitation to join the Strub Quartet as violist and another to join the All-German Radio Symphony Orchestra in Berlin as first violist. He found the prestige of playing in a famous quartet irresistible and saw in

WALTER TRAMPLER

his post with the All-German Radio Symphony Orchestra the prospect of "instant fame."

In an interview with Carlie Hope Simon that was published in New York radio station WNCN's program guide (August 1970), Trampler recalled that he "lived not so happily in Berlin." "I was too young," Trampler explained, "and felt lonely and left out, though I had many friends there later." He soon became too busy to indulge in self-pity, however, playing on the radio and touring with the Strub Quartet, performing with the great pianist Edwin Fischer in his chamber orchestra, mastering the string quintet repertory, and appearing at summer music festivals on the Continent. He stayed with both the Strub Quartet and the All-German Radio Symphony Orchestra until 1939.

Appalled by political developments in Nazi Germany, Trampler came to the United States in 1939 after a short stopover in France. That same year he was appointed associate professor at the Rollins College Conservatory of Music in Winter Park, Florida, but he felt that his future lay with a major symphony orchestra rather than with a university. Nevertheless he remained at Rollins until the end of the academic year of 1941-42, meanwhile performing in the summers of 1940 and 1941 at the Berkshire Music Center at Tanglewood, Massachusetts, to which he had been steered by Serge Koussevitzsky. After hearing him there, its manager offered him a post with the Boston Symphony Orchestra, and in October 1942 Trampler joined the renowned organization, both as member and as soloist.

"In the summer of '43," Trampler told Carlie Hope Simon, "I got very patriotic. I was very much a German who'd come here and wanted to do something for America. So I went to work in a factory that made cones for the propeller shafts of PT boats. Dull work!" In the spring of 1944 Trampler was drafted into the Medical Corps of the United States Army, and he soon entertained troops in the hospital wards overseas by playing popular songs on a cheap violin borrowed from Rembert Wurlitzer. He was accompanied by a Texan G.I., who played on a portable reed organ.

Later Trampler served in the Military Government Division.

Discharged in 1946, Trampler decided not to return to the Boston Symphony. He had had, he felt, enough regimentation in the United States Army to last him for some time. Instead he turned to acting lessons, hoping that his strong Teutonic accent would prove useful for German roles in American motion pictures. "I don't know if I was any good, but I loved it," he recalled during his WNCN interview. "They pushed me and encouraged me, but after six months, I got cold feet." He was also discouraged by the fact that Hollywood stopped grinding out anti-Nazi films.

With three musician friends, in 1947 Trampler organized the New Music Quartet, not only to perform contemporary works in public but also to hold private readings of new compositions. The competition was formidable, consisting of such groups as the Budapest String Quartet, the Quartetto Italiano, and the Juilliard Quartet, but Trampler was confident that the New Music Quartet would meet a special need. He now believes that when it was disbanded in 1956, it was well on its way to leading all the others. He still regrets the loss of its *gemütlichkeit*. "The thing I'll always remember about the quartet," he told Carlie Hope Simon, "is that we had such hilarious times together. In the early years, when our rehearsals often lasted up to eight hours a day, we spent many of those hours just telling stories and laughing."

Since the dissolution of the New Music Quartet, Trampler has followed a free-lance career as soloist and chamber music instrumentalist. Starting in 1955, he was a guest artist with the Budapest String Quartet and the Juilliard String Quartet; in 1958, 1959, and 1960 he was a featured artist at the Casals Festival in San Juan, Puerto Rico; and from 1953 to 1956 he was both a member of the faculty and soloist at the Aspen Music Festival in Colorado. Since 1956 he has made annual tours of Europe, and in 1963 he toured the Far East. With the Budapest String Quartet he made many highly esteemed recordings for the Columbia label, including Brahms's Quintet Number 1 in F, Opus 88 and Number 2 in G, Opus 111; Beethoven's Quintet in C, Opus 29; Dvorak's Quintet Number 3 in E flat, Opus 97; and Mozart's six string quintets. Trampler can also be heard on recordings for Mainstream, Music Guild, Composers Recordings, Inc., and RCA Victor.

Trampler has played quartets with the Beaux Arts Trio, quintets with the Juilliard String Quartet, duets with such flutists as Claude Monteux, and joint violin-viola recitals. Most recently he has been a stalwart of the Chamber Music Society of Lincoln Center, which, when it performs at Alice Tully Hall, commands sell-out audiences that overflow onto the stage. Wherever he appears, he can always be singled out from the other performers by what Allen Hughes of the New York *Times* once called his "wavy hair of near-Lisztian length and a markedly dramatic performance style." To Hughes the violist seems "a welcome reincarnation of a nineteenth-century virtuoso."

By combing the literature for seldom performed works that feature the viola and the viola d'amore, on which he is equally accomplished, Trampler has become something of a musicologist. His repertory is vast, ranging from seventeenth-century music to contemporary compositions that he has commissioned or that were written especially for him. Once his need to ferret out new scores even led to some international intrigue. On November 16, 1963, at a Musica Aeterna concert at the Grace Rainey Rogers auditorium of the Metropolitan Museum of Art he introduced a viola concerto by Jan Vanhal, a Czech contemporary of Franz Joseph Haydn, the score of which had been discovered two years earlier in Sofia, Bulgaria by Reba Paeff Mirsky. When Mrs. Mirsky showed the concerto to Trampler in New York, he was thwarted in his desire to perform it by the fact that the orchestral parts were missing. With the aid of Professor T. K. Nikolov of the Sofia Medical School the missing orchestral parts were found and shipped to the Rockefeller Institute in New York City on the assumption that they would get out of Bulgaria more easily if they looked like scientific material.

After encountering an almost monotonous success with contemporary music, Trampler came a cropper at Alice Tully Hall on November 21, 1970, when he and his violist wife, Karen Phillips, premièred Larry Austin's "Walter," a mixed-media biographical profile commissioned for him by the Chamber Music Society. It featured the violist dancing with his wife, smoking cigarettes, changing his clothes, and indulging in other musical and nonmusical activities at one side of the stage, while films flickered from a screen and bizarre noises squawked from a tape recorder. In the last section, "Go to the Young People," the Tramplers strolled out into the audience, playing their instruments as they went.

"'Walter' bombed at Tully Hall on Saturday night," Allen Hughes announced in the New York *Times* on November 23, 1970. "'Walter' bombed because it lacked the fantasy, the imagination, the wit, the illuminating vision that make a successful mixed-media work open up new worlds of revelation and perception and joy. . . . This was the kind of product that gives mixed-media a bad name." But Carman Moore of the more untrammeled *Village Voice* (December 10, 1970) rallied to the defense of "Walter" because he felt that it satirized the ritualistic element of concerts and audiences who fantasize romantically about concert stars at the same time that they are frightened by new art. "As for the outraged listeners," Moore wrote, "it was like when Dad discovered daughter Molly the Sunday school teacher smoking pot as she pored over, of a Saturday night, her well-thumbed New Translation Bible. Trampler, if not Austin, is moving right-mindedly toward erasing music's performance gap."

Very much involved with students and their causes, Trampler has been teaching viola and chamber music at the Juilliard School of Music in New York City since 1962. "The artist has to participate a little in the lives of the students," he told Carlie Hope Simon, "go to the university campuses, spend some time, talk with the students, and listen to them in turn. You can't expect students just to join *you* for two hours. I don't think the artist today has the right to exclusivity in society." He prides himself on the fact that when he joined the faculty of Juilliard in 1962, there were two viola students, while, by 1970, there were eighteen.

It was at Juilliard that Trampler met his present wife, Karen Phillips, a viola student whom he married in December 1968. By an earlier marriage, to Margaret Stark on May 15, 1959, he has two children, Janet and Anthony. The Tramplers live in a hospitable apartment on Riverside Drive that is crowded with Victorian antiques, music stands, and instrumental scores. They also have a clapboard house in Connecticut, where they like to spend their weekends. Students from Juilliard often pitch in with the housecleaning, but Trampler himself "loves to play carpenter," according to his wife. The Tramplers like to give simple but elegant dinners for about six people—occasions that are usually enlivened by the violist's skill as a raconteur.

Music critics have often commented on the strikingly attractive presence that Trampler brings to the concert stage—not surprising in a man who once entertained ambitions to be an actor. One of the most graphic descriptions is that of Carlie Hope Simon: "On stage Walter Trampler is nothing short of magnificent. His figure, graceful as a fencing-master's, is strung with thin tension. Under the lights, his long hair is molten silver, spilling sparks over his ruffled shirt front to the silver buckles on his shoes. A character right out of the nineteenth century, at its most dashing."

References

N Y Post p15 N 28 '70 por
N Y Times II p19 N 15 '70 por
Who's Who in America, 1970-71
Who's Who in the World, 1970-71

TRENKLER, FREDDIE

1920(?)- Comedy ice skater
Address: b. c/o Solters & Sabinson, Inc., 62 W. 45th St., New York 10036; 6121 Santa Monica Blvd., Los Angeles, Calif. 90038

The greatest clown on ice, Freddie Trenkler has delighted audiences with his pantomime and virtuoso skating for over three decades. Born in Vienna, Trenkler began his career as a comic with European ice carnivals and skated with Sonja Henie's ice revues throughout the 1940's. Since 1955 he has been the comedy star of the Ice Capades. A pixieish little clown in a colorfully patched tramp costume, Trenkler experiences Chaplinesque adventures on ice, managing always to outsmart and outskate the bullies who plague him.

Alfred Trenkler was born in Vienna, Austria to Max Trenkler, a department store comptroller, and

FREDDIE TRENKLER

his wife Magdalena. Freddie has two brothers and two sisters, none of whom took up skating. His recent publicity releases place his birthdate around 1920, although earlier press notices seem to suggest an earlier date. He declines to reveal the exact date of his birth and told a United Press International reporter in 1969, "This isn't just a case of vanity with me. I'm thinking of the children in the audience. If they found out my real age, they might be disappointed. They would think, 'Here is a man who could be my grandfather.'"

Trenkler began skating at the age of eleven on one of Vienna's public rinks, and he later took figure skating lessons from Karl Schaeffer, a former Austrian Olympic figure skater. Although Trenkler's father encouraged him to be a figure skater, and the boy won the Viennese international junior figure skating championship, his heart was never really in figure skating. What he enjoyed much more were the free-skating events, in which he could execute spins and jumps as he pleased and experiment with bits of clowning.

Around 1936 Trenkler had the opportunity to fill in for the clown at an ice show in Vienna, and his act was such a success that he began touring with amateur ice carnivals throughout Austria, Czechoslovakia, Romania, Hungary, and Germany. Late in 1937 he came to the United States and appeared professionally at Madison Square Garden at an ice show in December of that year. Trenkler returned to Europe, but in 1940 he was back in the United States at the invitation of Sonja Henie, who asked him to join her ice revue. Trenkler was soon the star comedian in both Miss Henie's annual *Hollywood Ice Revues,* in which she appeared, and in her productions staged at the now defunct Center Theatre in New York. The latter included *Stars on Ice, Hats Off to Ice, Icetime,* and *Howdy, Mr. Ice.* Trenkler also was featured in Miss Henie's film *The Countess of Monte Cristo* (Universal, 1948). After the *Hollywood Ice Revue* disbanded in 1955 Trenkler was invited to join the *Ice Capades.* He accepted and has toured with it ever since.

The character of Trenkler's comedy act has changed very little over the years. As he told Kaspars Dzeguze of the Toronto *Globe and Mail* (November 2, 1970) he has generally "followed [Charlie] Chaplin's characters in feeling" when planning his skits. "There's the little guy," he explained to Dzeguze, "not quite fit for society, so authority or some bully comes by to push him around, even though he's done nothing." But Freddie Trenkler's little tramp always outwits the policeman, sergeant, fire chief, or jealous boyfriend who is trying to persecute him. For example, in one act the clown's persecutor is a tall policeman. His escapades with Trenkler have already left him sprawling on the ice, when the clown comes skating toward him at breakneck speed only to stop a fraction of an inch from the policeman's nose, spraying his face with ice. In his flirtations with girls Trenkler's clown is also Chaplinesque, the impudent but shy little guy whose flirting amuses the girl and awakens her interest. Years ago he invented a routine reminiscent of an act now famous from the TV show *Laugh-In* in which he plays an old man sidling up to a girl on a park bench. For most of his skits Trenkler wears the same tramp costume that he has had since early in his career. When the need arises he patches it, and it now contains none of the original fabric.

Trenkler has said that he invents his skits not on the ice, but locked away by himself in a room. What he tries to engineer is a series of surprises for the audience that will make it laugh. Many years ago the clown outlined his technique for Helen Ormsbee of the New York *Herald Tribune* (July 23, 1944): "Suppose . . . the audience sees a banana peel on the ground, but the clown doesn't see it. . . . Sure enough, he slips. The audience was waiting for that. But watch him; he manages not to fall. That is a surprise and people laugh because the clown was smarter than they thought. Now he starts to walk away, pleased with himself. Here is the very moment he trips over something else, and down he goes. This surprise gets a bigger laugh. . . . After one or two surprises like those . . . perhaps there will be another and another. The clown must think always ahead of the people who are watching, and he must make things come out differently from what they expect. Like when I skate very fast right down to the front of the stage. People think I can't stop and I will be tumbling on them."

Trenkler's clowning is vastly abetted by his skating virtuosity. Quick stops are among his favorite tricks, and it has been estimated that he can stop on a dime at thirty miles per hour. With the Ice Capades he is billed as the "Bouncing Ball on the Ice," because of the peculiar bouncing style of skating he sometimes uses—and because of the many preplanned falls he bounces up from during his routines. A few years ago Trenkler estimated that he expends as much energy in his act as would be required to sprint two miles with three-pound skates on each foot. Trenkler concludes his routine with a spectacular finish. In one he grabs on to a wire and swings over the ice like Tarzan with his rope, finally catapulting through a small opening six feet off the ice at the end of the rink. In another variation, he is skating leisurely off the ice until he jumps on a concealed trampoline and disappears through the second story window of a paper house.

Occasionally, Trenkler likes to leap from the rink into the lap of a startled member of the audience. He usually chooses a motherly, middle-aged matron, because the audience responds best to her discomfiture. Once, however, he received a surprise when the woman whose lap he had chosen began hugging him and refused to let him go. Trenkler's only serious injury occurred in 1958 when he fell onto a wooden barrier to avoid endangering the audience. At that time he had an ending to his act in which he would break away from a speed skating sequence by grabbing a wire that would send him swinging over the audience. One night, however, the wire was unsteady and the clown let go of it, being careful to aim himself where there were no people. The accident occurred on the night that the program was being televised on the *Ed Sullivan Show* and Trenkler's mishap was viewed by millions. As a result of his fall, he had to keep off the ice for several weeks while he recovered from broken ribs and other injuries.

Although he has been clowning on ice professionally for over thirty years, Freddie Trenkler claims he has given no thought to retirement. He has said, however that he would like to establish skating schools around the country, where he could teach his art of ice pantomime. Trenkler spends all but six weeks of the year on the road, and he divides his vacation between Europe and the house he maintains in Milton, Massachusetts. On June 15, 1961 he married Gilberte ("Gigi") Naboudet, a French skater with the Ice Capades who has since retired from professional ice skating. She and their daughters, Margaret and Pamela, accompany Trenkler on his peregrinations as much as possible. By a previous marriage, to Josephine Barnum, a former American figure skating champion and Ice Capades skater, Trenkler has a son, Alfred Williams, who attends Milton Academy in Milton, Massachusetts. His first wife, Margery Luce of Forest Hills, New York, was not a professional skater. A quiet, mild-faced man with a lilting Viennese accent, Trenkler is five feet three inches tall, weighs about 130 pounds, and has blue eyes and blond hair. To keep in shape Trenkler takes long, brisk walks, and he plays golf and tennis occasionally. A good skier, he gave up that sport when he discovered that it was making him develop a different set of leg muscles. Trenkler became an American citizen in 1948.

References

N Y Herald Tribune IV p1 Jl 23 '44; p14 S 8 '51
N Y World-Telegram and Sun p5 S 8 '58
San Antonio Express D p16 O 31 '69
Toronto Globe & Mail p14 N 2 '70 por
Washington (D.C.) Post B p5 Ja 10 '69

TREVINO, LEE (BUCK)

Dec. 1, 1939- Golfer
Address: b. P.O. Box 26854, El Paso, Tex.
79926; h. 16020 Homestead St., El Paso, Tex.
79927

LEE TREVINO

Fun has returned to the professional golf circuit, where tense quiet usually reigns, in the person of Lee Trevino, a voluble, happy-go-lucky clubhouse hustler who rose the hard way, from dirt-poor Mexican-American origins, to become the hottest prize-winner in the Professional Golfers Association. The irrepressible Trevino, whose self-taught flat swing makes polished pros shudder, was regarded by many as a flash in the pan when he won the United States Open Tournament in 1968. Confounding the naysayers, he has, over the past four years, finished well in more tournaments (at least tenth place in seventy-six) and won more money ($597,461, not counting unofficial earnings) than any other pro, and in 1971 he became the first player to win the United States, Canadian, and British opens all in the same year. Trevino, with his loud, flamboyant manner, big grin, and constant flow of wisecracks, is a natural gallery pleaser, second in popularity only to Arnold Palmer.

Lee Buck Trevino was born into a fatherless home on the outskirts of Dallas, Texas on December 1, 1939. There are some discrepancies among biographical sources, but apparently he and his two sisters were raised by their mother, Juanita Trevino, who sometimes worked as a domestic, and their maternal grandfather, Joe Trevino, a gravedigger who had immigrated from Mexico. The house in which the family lived was a four-room frame building, without electricity or plumbing, that stood in a hayfield next to the fairway of the Glen Lakes Country Club. When Trevino was six he began emulating the golfers on the other side of the fence, using an old club he had found and cut to size and playing on a two-hole course he dug in his own yard. In teaching himself, he developed a style that George Nobbe, writing in the New York Sunday *News* (June 23, 1968), described as "a horrendously flat baseball swing."

After completing seventh grade, Trevino quit school and went to work as assistant to the greenkeeper at the Glen Lakes Country Club. On the side he caddied, and at the end of the day he would shoot a few holes. When he played his first full eighteen holes, at the age of fifteen, he shot a 77.

Lying about his age, Trevino joined the United States Marines when he was seventeen. During the second of two two-year hitches, he played with the Third Marine Division golf team in tournaments in Japan, Formosa, and the Phillipines, and in the course of doing so he began taking his game seriously for the first time. After his discharge from the Marines, in 1961, he worked as pro at Hardy's Pitch-N-Putt, a par-3 course in Dallas. To supplement his salary at Hardy's he "hustled" strangers by offering to play them for money with a gimmick that ostensibly put him at

a disadvantage, such as an improvised club with an adhesive-wrapped Dr. Pepper soft-drink bottle for a head. "I can hit a ball 100 yards with a Dr. Pepper Bottle," Trevino told Myron Cope of *Sports Illustrated* (June 17, 1968). "In fact, I never lost a bet using that bottle." But in the same interview he admitted that his penchant for gambling was not so lucrative off the links. "If there's a little poker game nearby and if I got $500 I'll blow it. Or if I got $5 I'll blow that. I got to bust that poker game or it got to bust me. Unfortunately, I don't bust many poker games." Elsewhere he consoled himself: "That's what money is for, though, right? To have fun."

As his game improved Trevino thought more and more about joining the pro tour. The Class A card that automatically admits a player to the tour is obtained by four years work as a club pro and matriculation at the business school run by the Professional Golfing Association in Dallas. Trevino attended the school and, after four years at Hardy's he asked his employer to sign a form verifying his length of service there. The employer refused, probably, ironically, because he valued Trevino highly and did not want to lose him. Furious, Trevino quit the job and began looking for someone to pay his expenses at the scattered tournaments that do not require a Class A card.

His first patron was Bill Gray, a government employee in Dallas who had not much more money than Trevino but sponsored him in the 1965 Texas State Open, the Mexico City Open, and the Panama Open (in which Trevino placed first, second, and fifth, respectively). The second was Martin Lettunich, a millionaire El Paso cotton farmer who got him a job as assistant pro at the Horizon Hills Country Club outside of El Paso. At Horizon Hills, a sandy, windswept course, Trevino had plenty of time to practice his line-drive shots, with the ball kept low to stay out of the wind, and develop excellent control. When he finally obtained his Class A card in 1966 the club paid his way to the United States Open at the Olympic Country Club in San Francisco, where he tied for fifty-fourth and won only $600.

Discouraged and in bad financial straits, Trevino was reluctant even to send in the $20 registration fee for the 1967 United States Open trials. But his wife sent the money, and Trevino qualified with the lowest round in the nation, 69 and 67 for a total of 136. In the Open itself, at the Baltusrol Country Club in Springfield, New Jersey, he surprised everyone by finishing fifth and winning $6,000. In the thirteen PGA tournaments he played that year he was out of the money only twice, and he finished the season with over $28,000 in winnings. The Metropolitan Golf Writers Association named him Rookie of the Year.

In 1968 Trevino had already won $54,000 when he arrived in June at the United States Open at the Oak Hill Country Club in Rochester, New York. In winning that tournament he became the first player in history to shoot four sub-par rounds in the Open (69, 68, 69, 69). He also tied Jack Nicklaus' Open scoring record, set the year before, with his 5-under-par 275. To win, Trevino endured tremendous pressure in a three-day duel with Bert Yancey and remained calm and consistent on the last day while Yancey faded and Nicklaus made a furious but futile comeback. Trevino is only the third man ever to make the United States Open his first major tournament victory. The Open was worth a small fortune to him in endorsements and business deals, and later in the year, in winning his second major tournament, the Hawaiian Open, he garnered an additional $25,000 first prize. He finished 1968 with $125,675 in official PGA prize money and more than $6,000 in unofficial earnings. After the tour he represented the United States, unsuccessfully, in the World Cup Tournament in Italy.

In February 1969 Trevino had his third big win, the $20,000 first prize in the Tucson Open. In April he did poorly in the Masters Tournament in Augusta, Georgia because the hilly course there is not well suited to his line drives. After the tournament he said—to the dismay of the local golfing establishment—that he never wanted to play there again, but eventually he learned, by practice, how to maneuver the Augusta course and he has returned there to participate in tournaments.

Also in April 1969, Trevino was second in the Tournament of Champions at Rancho La Costa, California, losing to Gary Player in the final holes. In September he was second again, throwing away a six-stroke lead—and $40,000—in the last three holes to give Billy Casper the Alcan Golfer of the Year Tournament. The following month he and Orville Moody won the World Cup for the United States in Singapore, where Trevino took individual honors with a 9-under-par 275.

Trevino began the 1970 tour auspiciously, again winning the Tucson Open and walking off with $40,000 as winner of the National Airlines Open in Miami. He suffered reverses in the summer, losing the Colonial National and British opens, dropping out of the Philadelphia Open, and being disqualified from the Westchester Open for oversleeping, but his overall number of high finishes made him the top money winner for the year, with over $157,000, as well as the leader in performance points based on tournament finishes, with 1,533.1 points in thirty-three events.

After thirteen months without a victory, Trevino had the best winning streak of his career between April and July 1971, taking the Tallahassee, the Danny Thomas Memphis, and the Canadian, the United States, and the British opens. Trevino's earnings of $197,210 were the highest on the circuit when, early in August, after celebrating Lee Trevino Day with the citizenry of El Paso, Texas, and Juarez, Mexico, he went to Elephant Butte, New Mexico on a fishing trip. While on the trip, on August 9, 1971, he was stricken with appendicitis and rushed to St. Anne's Hospital in Truth or Consequences, New Mexico, where he underwent an emergency appendectomy in the early morning hours of August 10. He returned to competition in September but the effects of the illness, surgery, and hospitalization lingered, drastically reducing his efficiency on the links. After missing the cut in four tournaments he bounced back to win the Sahara Invitational in Las Vegas at the end of October. His purse from that event, $27,000, and later events brought his earnings for the year to $231,202.

Among the products Trevino has endorsed for payment are Faultless golf balls, Blue Bell underwear, Stylist shoes, and Dr. Pepper, the soft drink that used to receive free publicity from him. In partnership with Jess Whittenton, the former pro football player, he has set up his own business agency, Lee Trevino Enterprises Inc., which is packaging a television series called *Golf Celebrity* and planning a luxury apartment complex in El Paso to be called Casa Trevino.

Trevino talks incessantly, in a running stream of jokes and repartee with the gallery. "The only time I stop yakking," he has said, "is when I'm asleep. I even had to quit smoking on the golf course because I nearly choked to death while I was talking." While some close observers sometimes find his wisecracking irritating, they generally agree that he is at base a good sport and a gentleman. Essentially a humble man, he aims much of his wisecracking at himself. Generous, he usually follows a tournament victory by writing a check for several thousand dollars to a local orphanage or charity.

Lee Trevino is swarthy, stands five feet seven and a half inches tall, and weighs 185 pounds. On his right forearm he has a tattoo reading "ANN," a reference to an old girlfriend who sent him a "Dear John" letter when he was in the Marines. His first marriage ended in divorce after the birth of one son, Richard, and he married his present wife, Claudia Ann Fenley, on August 24, 1964. By Claudia—who controls the family finances—he has two children, Lesley Ann and Tony Lee. He has explained his money-making motivation as a desire "to slice a hunk of life for me and my kids." With children other than his own he is also generous, financing impromptu hot dog-and-soda pop parties for crowds of them at tournaments. Children as well as adults belong to the immense following known as "Lee's Fleas."

References

Newsweek 78:57+ Jl 19 '71 pors
Sport 47:61+ F '69 pors
Sports Illus 28:49+ Je 17 '68 pors
Time 98:47+ Jl 19 '71 pors

TRUSSELL, RAY E(LBERT)

Feb. 7, 1914- Physician; hospital administrator
Address: b. Beth Israel Hospital, 10 Nathan D.
Perlman Pl., New York 10003

Anyone who doubts the shameful inadequacy of
the medical care received by Americans need only
consider the low international ranking of the
United States in male life expectancy (twenty-
second) and infant survival (eighteenth). If, as
its critics claim, the American medical profession
is generally complacent about its failure to meet,
adequately and comprehensively, the health needs
of all citizens, there are some outstanding exceptions. One of them is Dr. Ray E. Trussell, the
director of the Beth Israel Medical Center in Manhattan. As New York City Commissioner of Hospitals, from 1961 to 1965, Trussell significantly
upgraded the quality of care in municipal hospitals through sweeping reforms that were bitterly
fought by some elements in the medical establishment, and the codes he imposed on proprietary
hospitals and nursing homes set standards that
could well serve the nation as a whole. Previously,
while actively directing the Columbia University
School of Public Health and Administrative Medicine, Trussell led team studies of prepaid medical
care in New York City, found it deplorable (except in some large voluntary—private but nonprofit
—institutions, usually affiliated with research centers or medical schools), and warned that if com-
mercialized medicine and private health insurance
agencies did not put their own house in order,
a desperate public would eventually force the
government to do so.

Ray Elbert Trussell was born in Toledo, Iowa
on February 7, 1914 to Ray E. and Verna (Cannon) Trussell. Orphaned early in childhood, he
was raised by his grandmother, first in Iowa and
later in California. Trussell began his college
studies at Chaffey Junior College in Ontario, California, in 1931-32, then transferred to the University of Iowa, where he took his B.A. degree, with
a Phi Beta Kappa key, in 1935. He worked his
way through the College of Medicine at Iowa as
a laboratory instructor and research assistant and
received the M.D. degree in 1941.

After his internship at the University of Iowa
Hospital, in 1941-42, Trussell taught preventive
medicine at the university's College of Medicine
for a year, in 1942-43. From 1943 to 1946 he was
an epidemiologist with the United States Army in
the Pacific theatre of war, and during his Army
service he won the Bronze star and reached the
rank of major. After his military discharge he
earned a master's degree in public health at Johns
Hopkins University, in 1947.

DR. RAY E. TRUSSELL

In 1947 Trussell moved to Albany, New York
to teach at Albany Medical College and to work
as an epidemiologist with the New York State
Department of Health. From 1950 to 1955 he was
director of the Hunterdon (New Jersey) Medical
Center, a rural community service, and at the
same time he was clinical professor of preventive
medicine at the New York University-Bellevue
Medical Center in New York City. In 1955 he
joined the faculty of Columbia University in Manhattan as associate dean of the College of Physicians and Surgeons and director of the School of
Public Health and Administrative Medicine.

As director of the Columbia School of Public
Health and Administrative Medicine, Trussell
supervised long and thorough studies of private,
nonprofit health insurance plans, such as Blue
Cross and Blue Shield. The major surveys were
sponsored by the State of New York and by the
Teamsters Union's Joint Council 16 in New York
City, both of which were concerned with rising
costs and deteriorating care. Begun in the late
1950's and in 1960, the surveys were completed
in the early 1960's, when thick, fully documented
reports were submitted to the sponsoring agencies.

The Teamster project concentrated on a sample
group of 406 union members and their families
and the treatment they received in 101 hospitals
in the New York City metropolitan area. Trussell
and his associates—notably his wife, Dr. Mildred
A. Morehead, also a physician—reported that one-
fifth of the patients received bad care; another
fifth received only fair care; twenty out of sixty
hysterectomies performed were unnecessary; and
only five out of thirteen Caesarian deliveries were
necessary and competently executed. The worst
offenders by far were the small proprietary (profit-
making) hospitals, most of them unaccredited. In
those institutions fully one-half of the patients received poor care; many admissions were unnecessary and many hospitalizations were protracted
unnecessarily, apparently for monetary reasons;
and 71 percent of the physicians were not certified specialists. The report recommended that

health insurance services boycott the unaccredited institutions. It also suggested that the laity paying for health insurance be represented on the governing or advisory boards of the services.

In the report for New York State, Trussell and codirector Frank Van Dyke said, in sum, that medical care in New York City was the worst in the state and that organized medicine was "doing little" about it. "Only when the medical profession is willing to use financial sanctions against its less well prepared members, as one method to protect the public, can assurance be given of the sincerity of the profession as the professed guardian of public health."

Some members of the New York County Medical Society charged, in a series of articles in the society's house organ, *New York Medicine*, that Trussell's findings were politically motivated "distortions." Contrary to his assertions, they claimed that 95 percent of medically insured patients in New York City received care of the highest quality. Trussell responded at a meeting of the society: "The immediate challenge to physicians and hospitals is to solve the problems facing their paying patients—and there are many problems that will not go away regardless of sanctimonious editorials. . . . An irresponsible series of articles should not be allowed to lull the largest county medical society in the world into a false sense of security. We at Columbia do not publish lightly or with carelessly gathered data. . . . We find this medical society being asked by the Comita Minora to support Blue Cross payments to small unaccredited hospitals by opposing proposed legislation to the contrary. Since these hospitals . . . have the weakest medical staffs and the poorest facilities, are we to assume, nevertheless, that the society thinks they are satisfactory for 'just plain folks'? . . . . And the issue of discrimination against Negro physicians has not even been mentioned—a social issue that can no longer be buried."

At the request of Mayor Robert F. Wagner, Trussell took leave of absence from Columbia University on March 1, 1961 to assume control of the New York City municipal hospital system, the largest and most complex city system in the world, with twenty-one facilities, fourteen of them large general-care institutions, and an annual budget even then passing the $250,000,000 mark.

As Commissioner of Hospitals, Trussell liberalized the dissemination of birth control information and devices; initiated a pilot project for a round-the-clock suicide prevention telephone service; upgraded psychiatric services for children; and improved ambulance service. At the same time he put his influence behind the national movement toward a federal health insurance plan, especially for old people. "The long range goal is complete coverage . . . ," he said in 1962. Pointing out that he and his colleagues had found three times as much illness as the ill themselves recognized, he added: "There is a vast unmet medical need in the population and particularly among old people."

But the major problem to which Trussell addressed himself was the critical and worsening shortage of professional personnel in the municipal hospitals of New York City. He solved the physician shortage by raising the salary scale and by developing a system in which medical schools and strong voluntary hospitals assumed the responsibility for professional services in most of the general-care municipal hospitals. The affiliation of which he was most proud was that effected between the Columbia School of Physicians and Surgeons and Harlem Hospital. "The results were immediate improvements in patient care," Dr. Howard A. Rusk later recounted in the New York *Times* (October 9, 1966). "Adequately paid, full-time chiefs of service were appointed, attending staffs were increased, and more fully qualified interns and residents appointed."

"There were, of course, howls of protest from the superseded doctors on city hospital medical boards, and in the case of Elmhurst Hospital in Queens, a mass resignation of the board and a law suit," Joseph R. Hixson wrote in the New York *Herald Tribune* (August 1, 1965). "But the Commissioner won in every case. He also won his battle to regulate operations in the city's private hospitals so that, for instance, only qualified physicians can cut into a patient's abdomen. And he instituted strict construction standards for nursing homes, often the sites of disastrous fires." An editorial writer in the New York *Times* (June 7, 1965) noted that Trussell's codes for proprietary hospitals and nursing homes "not only have raised their standards but have provided yardsticks that should be useful in the legislation Congress now is writing for medicare." The editorialist concluded that "the whole concept of community hospital planning has advanced under his leadership."

Because the university refused to extend his leave of absence further, Trussell returned to his posts at Columbia in June 1965. A little over three years later, in December 1968, he left Columbia University to assume his present position as director of the Beth Israel Medical Center. Beth Israel's central facility is a 536-bed, acute-care hospital overlooking Stuyvesant Square in Manhattan. The center also includes the nearby 375-bed Bernstein Institute, for addictive diseases, and a clinic in Harlem. In addition to its own facilities, Beth Israel administers two city institutions in poor neighborhoods: the Gouverneur Health Services Center, with a substantial Chinese-American clientele, and the Judson Treatment Center, with a largely Puerto Rican clientele. When Trussell took over the Beth Israel complex, it was running at an annual deficit of $700,000 at its main center, $500,000 in its work with narcotics addicts, and $600,000 at Gouverneur and Judson. Thirty percent of Beth Israel's patients and 20 percent of its outpatients were dependent on Medicaid, the New York State program subsidizing health care for the poor. When the State cut back the program in 1969, Trussell warned of the disastrous effect the cutback would have on care for the poor in such facilities as Gouverneur and Judson. "It is unthinkable," he told the press, "that we should have to refuse to serve these people."

Beth Israel has the most ambitious methadone program in the United States. Trussell was a pioneer advocate of methadone, a synthetic drug that enables physicians for the first time to treat large numbers of drug addicts as outpatients (the only feasible way to treat them, the shortage of hospital space being what it is). Drunk in daily doses, the synthetic removes the craving for heroin and takes the "kick" out of it, thus enabling the addict to lead a normal life as a contributing member of society. Although methadone is addictive, withdrawal from it is far less an ordeal than withdrawal from heroin. "Give me a million dollars," Trussell has said, "and I will get a thousand addicts off the street."

Trussell is the author of *Hunterdon Medical Center: The Story of One Approach to Rural Medical Care* (1956) and, with Jack Elinson, *Chronic Illness in a Rural Area: The Hunterdon Story* (1959). Both books were published for the Commonwealth Fund by Harvard University Press. In addition, he has written monographs and medical journal articles on such subjects as public health administration and trichomoniasis. He is a fellow of the American Public Health Association and the New York Academy of Medicine and a member of the New York chapter of the American Medical Association, the New York County Medical Society, the Association of Teachers of Preventive Medicine, and the Sigma Xi and Alpha Omega Alpha fraternities.

Dr. Ray E. Trussell and Dr. Mildred A. Morehead were married in 1961. By a previous marriage Trussell has three grown children: Ray, Peg, and Susan. In addition to their Greenwich Village apartment, Trussell and his wife have a house that overlooks the bay at Northport, Long Island. It was originally a summer home, but they have had it winterized and spend weekends there year round, commuting by automobile. Trussell's favorite recreation is swimming, but even on the beach he usually has his nose in paper work. Barbara Yuncker in the New York *Post* (June 10, 1962) described him as "hard-driving," with a "complex personality." "He constantly encompasses a staggering load of detail and is an enormously exacting (though often generous) boss."

References

N Y Post mag p2 Je 10 '62 por; p39 Ag 22 '65

Who's Who in America, 1970-71

TUNNEY, JOHN V(ARICK) (tun'ē)

June 26, 1934- United States Senator from California; lawyer
Address: b. New Senate Office Bldg., Washington, D.C. 20510; h. 500 Rotunda, Mission Inn, Riverside, Calif. 92501

California's junior Senator, John V. Tunney, is the leader of the younger generation of Democratic politicians in his state and an increasingly dependable vote getter. In November 1970 he defeated the incumbent Senator George Murphy by 619,000 votes, the largest plurality given a Democratic

JOHN V. TUNNEY

candidate in California in the twentieth century. His victory is of national significance because top G.O.P. dignitaries stumped the state for his opponent. Tunney, the son of Gene Tunney, former world's heavyweight boxing champion, is a lawyer who had earlier served three terms as the Representative of California's Thirty-eighth Congressional District, south of Los Angeles. A dovish liberal, Tunney favored the withdrawal of all American troops from Vietnam by the end of 1971 and the conversion of defense industries to peacetime production to deal with unemployment and to help solve the problems of environmental pollution.

John Varick Tunney was born in New York City on June 26, 1934, the second of four children of Gene (James Joseph) and Mary Josephine (Lauder) Tunney. His brothers are Gene Lauder and Jonathan R. Tunney, and his sister is Mrs. Joan T. Wilkinson. Their father had become the heavyweight boxing champion of the world when he won the title from Jack Dempsey in 1926. The following year he won a rematch against Dempsey in what is known as the "long count" fight: Tunney was knocked down in the seventh round, but on a technicality was given a long count and got up to win. It was an incident to which Gene Tunney referred on two occasions when his son's elections were so close that a winner was not declared until the next morning.

The children of Gene Tunney, however, never knew their father as a boxer. After marrying a wealthy society girl, Tunney went into business and became a millionaire and director in some two dozen well-known corporations. The family lived in Stamford, Connecticut until John was six years old. They then moved to a small farm in Amenia, New York, but about seven years later returned to Stamford. John attended private schools, graduating from Westminster High School in Simsbury, Connecticut in 1952. Afterward he enrolled in Yale University, where he majored in anthropology. According to *Time* (November 16, 1970), "Clouded by his father's shadow, he was an indifferent student." Nevertheless, he obtained the B.A. degree in 1956.

Shortly before his graduation from college, Tunney had changed his mind about an intended career in business and decided to enter the University of Virginia Law School. There he met Edward M. ("Ted") Kennedy, who became his roommate in his second year. When the younger Kennedy took time out from his law studies to help manage Senator John F. Kennedy's reelection campaign, Tunney, who had switched his political affiliation from Republican to Democrat, went along for his first close contact with electioneering. On an earlier excursion from the Charlottesville campus he had studied in 1957 at the Academy of International Law at The Hague. In 1959 he won the Appellate Court Competition at the University of Virginia, earned the LL.B. degree, and was admitted to the bar in Virginia and New York.

Tunney joined the Wall Street law firm of Cahill, Gordon, Reindel & Ohl as an attorney. Within a year, in April 1960, he was called into the Air Force and assigned to legal work in the Advocate General's Office at March Air Force Base near Riverside, California. During his three years in the Air Force he advanced in rank from first lieutenant to captain. On a thirty-day leave in 1961 he toured Latin America with Edward Kennedy. He also found a change from military duty in teaching business law in 1961-62 at the Riverside branch of the University of California. In 1963, on his release from the service, he decided to settle down in Riverside. He took the California bar examination and opened a private law practice.

Later in the year Tunney was urged by state Democrats to run for a seat in the House of Representatives from the Thirty-eighth California Congressional District. That burgeoning inland area south of Los Angeles includes wealthy Palm Springs and the Imperial Valley farming region in its two counties of Riverside and Imperial. At that time roughly 60,000 of its population of about half a million were impoverished Mexican-Americans, many of them migrant workers. The conservative Thirty-eighth District had reportedly elected a Democrat only once.

As soon as John Tunney decided to run for Congress his kin turned out to help him campaign in a style reminiscent of the Kennedys. His older brother, Gene, though without professional political experience, left his job as a La Jolla stockbroker to become campaign manager; and his younger brother, Jonathan, worked as field coordinator in the outlying areas of Riverside and Imperial counties. His wife and sister-in-law handled coffee klatsches and helped mobilize some 2,000 volunteers. In addition, Gene Tunney made two trips to California on his son's behalf, bringing along his friend Jack Dempsey. The two prizefighters drew large crowds at dinners and barbecues showing films of their two title fights and boosting the young politician. As reported in *Time* (November 16, 1970), President John F. Kennedy told Edward Kennedy to advise Tunney to drop the name "Varick," by which he had always been called. Tunney hesitated until a poll showed that 66 percent of his potential constituents associated the name with Russia and Com-

munism. Ironically, "Varick" was the surname of a Revolutionary War ancestor of Tunney.

In the 1964 elections national attention focused on the Presidential race between Democratic President Lyndon B. Johnson and Republican Barry Goldwater. The greatest controversy within California, however, was generated by the presence on the ballot of Proposition 14, which called for a state constitutional amendment nullifying California's antidiscrimination Rumford Act. Although Tunney's own polls showed that Proposition 14 would pass, he took the risk of opposing the conservative measure. Tunney's polls also showed that he had progressed from being a three-to-one underdog in April to a narrow winner just before the election. On November 3, 1964 Tunney defeated incumbent Representative Patrick Martin by fewer than 10,000 votes. While Johnson swept the state, the Democratic Senator Pierre Salinger lost his seat to George Murphy, and Tunney, as the only Democratic candidate to unseat an incumbent, won the biggest victory for his party in the state.

When he sought reelection to the House for two additional terms, Tunney piled up a larger margin each time. Unopposed for renomination in the party primary of June 1966, he outpolled in Riverside County the combined total of Governor Edmund G. Brown and Los Angeles' Mayor Sam Yorty, who were running for the gubernatorial nomination. Republican strategists marked Tunney as a prime target in the November election, but their party's candidate, Robert R. Barry, won only 46 percent of the vote as compared with Tunney's 54 percent.

At the time of his 1968 campaign one of the major issues in the state involved the strike by grape pickers in Imperial County and the national grape boycott organized in support of the strikers. Tunney favored union bargaining rights for farm workers, but declined to take a position on the boycott, saying it was not the business of a Congressman. A writer for *Newsweek* (October 14, 1968) observed that the evident contrast between the urbane Tunney and his agrarian constituents led him to play down his "star quality" and stress bread-and-butter issues. Because of the national mood that it was "time for a change," his posters did not identify him as a Democrat. He concentrated, instead, on such accomplishments as having obtained a grant to eradicate pink bollworm in the cottonfields, a reprieve on a local naval arsenal, and a government labor camp in the Coachella Valley. On November 9, 1968 he defeated Robert O. Hunter with more than 60 percent of the vote, in the same election in which Republican Richard Nixon carried the state against Democrat Hubert H. Humphrey to win the Presidency.

During his six years as a Representative, Tunney served on the House Committee on Interior and Insular Affairs, with appointment to its subcommittees on Indian affairs, public lands, and irrigation and reclamation. In the Eighty-ninth Congress, from 1965 to 1967, he was also a member of the Post Office and Civil Service Committee, but in 1967 he was transferred to the more influential House Committee on Foreign Affairs. He served on that committee's subcommittees on foreign economic policy, the Far East and the Pacific, and State Department organization and foreign operations.

Most often Tunney voted with the Democratic liberals. According to a *Congressional Quarterly* voting study, he supported President Johnson 72 percent of the time and opposed him 6 percent of the time on a selection of 230 Johnson-issue roll call votes during the Ninetieth Congress, in 1967 and 1968. Most of his domestic legislative efforts were directed toward serving his constituents and expanding welfare provisions. For example, he sponsored a bill to allow elderly widows to keep their social security benefits if they remarry. He also sponsored a bill to provide federal grants to any community that wanted to start its children in school before kindergarten.

On foreign policy questions alone, Representative Tunney backed the President 93 percent of the time during 1967-68. While Johnson was still in office he supported United States involvement in Vietnam. By 1969, however, he had become critical of the United States position on the Vietnam war, and he was among the minority who voted against the resolution endorsing President Nixon's efforts to achieve "peace with justice" in Vietnam. In debate he argued that the administration had "missed opportunities" to speed United States withdrawal, especially in its refusal to pressure the Saigon government into broadening its political base. Early in 1969 Tunney, who had made a field trip to South Vietnam the preceding spring to investigate conditions in the countryside, disputed optimistic reports from that country about the success of pacification efforts in the villages. During 1970 he tried in the House to restrict United States military aid to Cambodia to small arms and ammunition and communications equipment.

Not long after his 1968 victory at the polls Tunney had come to be regarded by California Democratic leaders as a likely contender for the Senate seat held by Republican Senator George Murphy. Although Tunney did not announce his candidacy until January 1970, he began in 1969 to elicit goodwill from all factions of the badly split state Democratic party and to build up recognition throughout California by engaging in such newsworthy ventures as descending in diving gear some 175 feet in Santa Barbara Bay to investigate a disastrous oil leak. It soon seemed to some political observers, however, that his failure to support the grape boycott would cost him votes among liberals. Although he had joined a march in May 1969 supporting the strike, his general neutrality is thought to have encouraged the more liberal Democratic Representative George E. Brown Jr. of Los Angeles to declare his candidacy for the Senate nomination in the June 1970 primary. And Brown had been opposed to the Vietnam war from the beginning.

With his eye on battles against both the liberal Brown in June and the conservative Murphy in

November, Tunney tried to create an image of himself as a moderate who would have the best chance of winning the race for the Senate, to amplify his somewhat recently acquired opposition to the Vietnam war, and to convince voters of his determination to save the environment from pollution. Once again his brothers gave up their jobs to help with his campaign, which was described in the *Christian Science Monitor* (May 26, 1970) as "slick, professional and apparently well financed." The election was close, but Tunney won.

The ensuing Tunney-Murphy contest, vituperative on both sides, proved to be one in which issues ran "second to candidate personalities and their slickness in grabbing news space," according to *Newsday* (October 19, 1970). Tunney did, however, attack the Republican effectively on economic issues, citing the growing unemployment rate in California. His own advocacy of law and order neutralized that issue and disarmed his opponent. In an all-out effort to elect Republicans, President Nixon and other party notables went to California to make speeches for Murphy. But their intervention did not help their candidate, whose bid for reelection may very well have been weakened by conflict-of-interest charges in connection with his position as consultant to Technicolor Inc. Benefiting by the ticket splitting practices of Californians, Tunney won by 54 percent of the vote, while Republican Ronald Reagan retained the governorship by 53 percent.

In the weeks following his election to the Senate, Tunney became more outspoken, particularly on the subjects of the Vietnam war, unemployment in the aerospace industry, and legal aid services in California. Urging a quick withdrawal of American troops from Southeast Asia, he continued to oppose supplying anything beyond small arms to the Cambodian government, asserting that greater commitment would be against the national interest of the United States. In deciding whether to approve the development of the supersonic transport plane (SST), Tunney conducted hearings in California in the aerospace industry, where the SST was viewed as an aid to the crippled industry. When he later studied testimony gathered in Senate hearings, he concluded that the SST would not really solve unemployment and would cause serious environmental problems. Therefore, he urged the federal government to help the aerospace industry to convert to water-pollution control systems or other systems to meet domestic needs. He also came out in support of the California Rural Legal Assistance program (CRLA) after Governor Reagan vetoed its continuation late in 1970. It was given a six-month extension pending further study.

To enable Tunney to claim seniority over other freshmen Senators, Murphy resigned his Senate seat on January 2, 1971 so that Tunney could be sworn in before the convening of the Ninety-second Congress. At thirty-six he became the youngest Senator in Washington. He was appointed to the Judiciary Committee, the Public Works Committee, and the Committee on the District of Columbia. In association with the senior California Senator, Democrat Alan Cranston, he introduced a bill early in the first session of the Ninety-second Congress to establish a federal ecological preserve in the Santa Barbara Channel to protect the coast against effects of badly planned oil drilling. Tunney has asserted that he would endorse some form of revenue sharing as long as it included controls on how the money is used locally. On questions of Congressional reorganization, he has urged reform of the seniority system in determining committee chairmen. And he has advocated reducing the number in the Senate required to cut off a filibuster from two-thirds to three-fifths, but has maintained that some limited form of the filibuster is valuable in protecting Senate minorities.

As a member of Congress, Tunney has attended various international conferences, including several meetings of the Anglo-America Inter-Parliamentary Conference; the Ditchley Foundation Conference in England in 1966 and 1968; and the American Assembly Conference, cosponsored by Columbia University, in Shimoda, Japan in 1969. He is a member of the board of councilors of the Center for Urban Affairs of the University of Southern California and in 1967-68 was a member of the University of Chicago's Center for Policy Study on Urban Environment. He serves on the board of trustees of the California Indian Legal Services and was legal adviser in 1962 to the Riverside area Aiding Leukemic Stricken American Children. In 1967 he was named a Chubb Fellow of Yale University.

While studying at The Hague in the summer of 1957, John V. Tunney met an attractive blond native of Holland, Mieke Sprengers of Nijmegen, whom he married on February 5, 1959 after further visits to the Netherlands. They have three children—Edward Eugene (whose first name was taken from his godfather, Edward Kennedy), Mark Andrew, and Arianne Sprengers Tunney. Husky and athletic in build, Tunney is six feet three inches tall and weighs about 190 pounds. He has blue eyes, light-brown hair, and a gleaming smile. In the early years of his political career he was often compared in the press to the Kennedy brothers, with his Eastern speech pattern, heavy shock of hair, vigorous manner, gregariousness, glamourous social life, and celebrated family. His church is the Roman Catholic. He is fond of many sports—golf, tennis, skiing, swimming, sailing, scuba diving, and mountain climbing.

References

Christian Sci Mon p4 O 13 '70 por
N Y Herald Tribune p12 N 22 '64 por
N Y Post p47 Ja 27 '65 por
Time p21 N 16 '70 por
Washington (D.C.) Post B p2+ Ja 5 '65 por
Congressional Directory (1971)
Who's Who in America, 1970-71
Who's Who in American Politics, 1969-70
Who's Who in California (1968)

TVARDOVSKY, ALEXANDR T(RIFONOVICH)
(tvyär-dôf'ski)

June 21, 1910- Soviet writer; editor
Address: b. c/o Union of Soviet Writers, 52 Vorovskaya St., Moscow, U.S.S.R.

BULLETIN: Alexandr T. Tvardovsky died on December 17, 1971.

A steady campaign against liberal tendencies in the arts in the U.S.S.R. culminated in the resignation in February 1970 of the poet Alexandr Tvardovsky as editor of the foremost Soviet literary magazine, *Novy Mir* (New World). His departure marked the end of an era, bringing "incalculable loss to Russia and the world," as the noted translator and critic Max Hayward remarked. Despite a tense political atmosphere during his editorship in the post-Stalin era he had made *Novy Mir* a forum for some of the best and most controversial writers. Using his influence with the Communist party (he was a candidate member of the Central Committee until 1966) and his prestige as a poet, he skillfully pursued an editorial policy of publishing works of quality that might otherwise have been relegated to the underground press. His persistent efforts to publish the banned works of Alexandr Solzhenitsyn, however, proved all too threatening to the Soviet literary establishment. When the Writers' Union replaced four members of his editorial staff with conservatives, Tvardovsky resigned.

While Tvardovsky is perhaps better known in the West as an editor, he is also a distinguished and popular poet. Partly because of his background and the vernacular in which he writes, he is sometimes labeled a "peasant" poet, though his work has little of the distinctly personal lyricism characteristic of peasant poetry. Like the nineteenth-century poet and editor Nikolai Nekrasov, Tvardovsky uses narrative poetry to discuss the important issues of his time, following a tradition that makes his work as editor and poet inseparable.

Alexandr Trifonovich Tvardovsky himself has provided the best account of his development as a writer in a brief autobiographical sketch published in 1959. Born on June 21, 1910 in Zagorye, a town in the Smolensk region, Russia, he grew up on what he jokingly terms the family "estate," twenty-seven acres of brush-covered, swampy land that his father, Trifon Gordeyevich, a blacksmith, had labored hard to acquire. Far more resourceful culturally than financially, his father had equipped the home with a supply of books and on long winter evenings would often read aloud from the Russian classics or sing folk ballads. In that atmosphere Tvardovsky began to write early, mostly short narrative verse in which he tried to capture the lilting rhythms of Pushkin's poems. Confident of his ability, he was somewhat disillusioned when a schoolteacher reared on the Symbolists convinced him that all good contemporary poetry should be obscure. Thereafter, Tvardovsky recalls, he tried to write as "incoherently" as possible, but not succeeding too well, turned to prose. For a time he wrote brief news items for some of the Smolensk newspapers, and in one of them, *Smolenskaya Derevnia* (Smolensk Countryside), his first published poem, "New Hut," appeared when he was fourteen.

For many writers of his generation, Tvardovsky has observed, early acclaim fostered "dangerous illusions." In 1928, almost totally uneducated, relying solely on his youth and talent, he set off for Smolensk, determined to support himself as a writer. He spent most of his two years there "haunting editorial offices," barely subsisting on an income derived from hack writing jobs and the few poems he published. Similarly unsuccessful in Moscow, where he stayed briefly after some poems were accepted by the journal *Oktiabr* (October), he returned to Smolensk to resume his education. With the help of a Communist party official, he entered the pedagogical institute there without taking entrance examinations, and on his own made up the secondary school courses he had missed. In 1936 he transferred to the Moscow Institute of History, Philosophy and Literature, from which he graduated in 1939. While a student there, he also became a member of the Communist party.

Before leaving Smolensk, Tvardovsky had completed *Land of Muravia*, published in the magazine *Krasnaya Nov* in 1936. His long narrative poem concerns a rebellious peasant who resists collectivization and searches for a legendary land that has neither communes nor kolkhozes (collective farms). The late poet Samuel Marshak found it a mark of Tvardovsky's integrity that despite his enthusiasm for collectivization, he could honestly present both sides of the conflict. With great wit and sympathy, Tvardovsky depicts his recalcitrant hero's attempts to flee the new order as simply one of many understandable responses to social change. Some of Tvardovsky's shorter early poems were published in the collections *The Road* (1934), *Village Chronicle* (1939), and *Zagorye* (1941).

Tvardovsky was drafted in 1939, and after serving in the Belorussian campaign of 1939, became a front-line correspondent in the battle against Finland and in World War II. His firsthand knowledge of war provided the material for a book about a Russian soldier, *Vasily Tyorkin*, written and serialized during the war as a cycle of poems and awarded a Stalin Prize in 1946. Tvardovsky's most popular work, it is both a convincing portrait of a common soldier and a parable of a nation's courage. Allowing himself far more narrative and philosophical scope in that work, Tvardovsky comments on the bewildering chaos of war as he accompanies his hero through each stage of battle. Although he exposes Tyorkin to every possible adversity, his compassion for him never lapses into sentimentality. For Tvardovsky's characteristic approach is humor, and in his rendering Tyorkin emerges as a comically bemused but resourceful soldier—a lovable folk hero—whose reactions to the war parallel those of the nation as a whole.

ALEXANDR T. TVARDOVSKY

Shortly after completing *Vasily Tyorkin*, Tvardovsky published two other powerful works on the subject of war: *A House By the Roadside* (1946) and *Native and Foreign Land* (1947). The first focuses on the fate of a soldier's wife who, after spending most of the war in a German prison camp with her children, struggles to find her way "home." Although her husband too has survived, the poem ends on a note of uncertainty, for the place at which the couple expects to be reunited has long since been destroyed. *Native and Foreign Land*, a series of war sketches in prose, details the panic and suffering endured by the population during the initial Soviet defeats. Ironically, it was this work—a celebration of quiet dignity and strength—that branded Tvardovsky as a "defeatist." By the time of its publication a singularly repressive period had set in, the "Zhdanov era," in which the very theme of war had become anathema and writers were obliged to produce ideologically "constructive" works. Under those conditions, Tvardovsky chose one of the few honorable defenses available to Soviet writers—silence.

The years from 1947 to 1953 were a sterile period in Soviet literature, and when Tvardovsky succeeded Konstantin Simonov as editor of *Novy Mir* in 1950, he found it virtually impossible to publish works of quality. However, in the abortive thaw that followed Joseph Stalin's death in March 1953, he registered his protest, both as editor and poet, against the years of silence and regimentation. In June of that year six chapters of his long poem *Horizons Beyond Horizons* appeared in various journals, and in the following months *Novy Mir* featured several outspoken articles, the most unequivocal being V. Pomerantsev's "On Sincerity in Literature." Shortly thereafter writers realized that their demand for "sincerity" had been premature; on August 11, 1954, as part of a series of reprisals, the Writers' Union dismissed Tvardovsky as editor for having promulgated "idealistic" and "nihilistic" views.

In the four years before Tvardovsky was reinstated, he continued to work on *Horizons Beyond*

Horizons, a complex work consisting of sixteen chapters that are, in effect, self-contained episodes. The setting is that of a journey: one that Tvardovsky literally made to the Far East in 1950 to observe the Korean war; metaphorically, it is a journey back in time to retrace his life in the Stalin era. In her essay on Tvardovsky in *Soviet Leaders* (1957) Vera Dunham commented on the poem as confessional literature: "The work is, in fact, a personal diary with topical digressions— the story of an intellectual of the mid-generation, and of his conscience."

Critics have often singled out for attention three chapters of *Horizons Beyond Horizons:* In one, "Conversation about Literature," the poet narrates a "discussion" he has with several passengers on the train who criticize him for writing cowardly, superficial works that have no bearing on life. When he, in turn, blames this on the whole system of literary controls, a voice from an upper berth breaks in to ridicule the poet's rationalization. The stranger is an editor, but of a special sort—"a phantom, no other than the embodiment of the author's own fear," Vera Dunham notes. Thus the conversation amounts to a brief allegory on the evils of censorship. More personally revealing is the chapter entitled "A Childhood Friend," describing the poet's encounter in Siberia with an old friend who is bound westward after seventeen years in a concentration camp. After a brief, awkward conversation the two men head in opposite directions, just as their lives had in the past. Left with the shameful recognition that he had chosen the easier alternative, Tvardovsky writes: "In many ways, I know,/His had greater integrity and strength." The culmination of these painful disclosures comes in the chapter called "That's the Way it Was," in which Tvardovsky insists that only by its refusal to bury the past can his generation atone for its complicity with Stalinism.

Awarded a Lenin Prize in 1961, Tvardovsky's poem helped to reinforce the concessions writers had won from Nikita S. Khrushchev during the early phase of his campaign of de-Stalinization. In the winter of 1962, however, when Khrushchev felt the campaign threatened to backfire, he reversed his policy on the arts and sharply curtailed the limits of intellectual freedom. Tvardovsky used his influence to ease the attacks on writers and, for a time, even persuaded Khrushchev that liberalism need not become a prelude to sedition.

What most impressed Khrushchev at this time was a reading of Tvardovsky's hilarious anti-Stalinist satire, *Vasily Tyorkin in the Other World.* Although begun in 1954, it could not be published until it received Khrushchev's approval in 1963. Its hero is the same Vasily Tyorkin whom Tvardovsky had described in the war years, except that in the later poem Tyorkin dies in battle and descends into purgatory, only to find it equipped with all the bureaucratic machinery he had known in life: questionnaires in quadruplicate, censors, sectors, divisions, departments. With brilliant wit, Tvardovsky depicts the incredulous Tyorkin wan-

dering through a netherland in which the rules of nonexistence are strictly prescribed. Here, too, censors rebuke writers for failing to heed the "latest directives," while the editor of the official purgatory organ, the *Cemetery Gazette,* ponders the "proper angle." Even more daring than the thrusts at censorship, however, is Tvardovsky's image of a capitalist and communist otherworld coexisting under one roof, with only a transparent wall between. Toward the end of the poem Tyorkin turns out to be considerably less dead than he had appeared, and after a struggle he makes his way back to life in this world. In his closing remarks Tvardovsky reminds his readers that his farce was motivated by a serious purpose: "One thought alone possessed me: If I could cope with this one,/ I could cope with any."

Tvardovsky managed to cope far better with the conservative opposition of Khrushchev's era than that of the years following. When he had resumed the editorship of *Novy Mir* in 1958, he had sought to fill in much of the historical record that had been obliterated by the purges and enforced silence of the Stalinist regime by publishing the memoirs of writers, diplomats, and generals. To critics who feared that such accounts would damage the nation's image, he replied, "Everything that is talented and truthful in art is beneficial to us."

Growing repressiveness in the intellectual climate manifested itself in 1966 in the sentencing of the writers Andrei Sinyavsky and Yuli Daniel for publishing presumably anti-Soviet works abroad. During that year Tvardovsky was not reelected to the Central Committee at the 23d Party Congress, and the stage version of *Vasily Tyorkin in the Other World* was temporarily removed from the repertory. Nonetheless, he continued to defend writers who withstood political attack. In March 1966 he wrote a moving obituary on the poet Anna Akhmatova, who had long been a victim of Stalinist repression. Tvardovsky's tribute to Akhmatova clearly alluded to the senseless persecution of writers also under the current regime.

In 1967 the official policy on the arts appeared thoroughly ambiguous; despite repeated attacks on *Novy Mir* for publishing works critical of Soviet society, Tvardovsky was awarded another Order of Lenin, and his complete works were published in five volumes. However, with the rigid constraints on intellectual freedom that followed the Soviet-led suppression of liberalization in Czechoslovakia in 1968, Tvardovsky found himself in serious jeopardy. He refused to endorse the invasion of that country and renewed his protest against the treatment of Alexandr Solzhenitsyn, whose major works had been banned in the Soviet Union since 1966. Largely because of his defense of Solzhenitsyn, Tvardovsky was subjected to a barrage of attacks, that ultimately forced him to resign from *Novy Mir* in 1970. Since then the only recognition accorded him has been a minor award, the Order of the Red Banner, which Tvardovsky received on his sixtieth birthday in June 1970 for his "services in the development of Soviet poetry."

The issue at stake in the debate over Solzhenitsyn was precisely what Tvardovsky had fought for throughout the post-Stalin period: the right to publish works that depict "reality as it is, in all its complexity, in its real contradictions and movements." That became apparent to Western readers when the March 13, 1970 issue of the *Guardian* published a translation of a long letter Tvardovsky had written two years earlier to Konstantin A. Fedin, secretary of the Writers' Union. Urging him to lift the ban on Solzhenitsyn's novel *The Cancer Ward*, Tvardovsky wrote: "Solzhenitsyn concerns us now, and not simply by himself, but because through circumstances he stands at the crossroads of two opposed tendencies in the social consciousness of our literature, one which strives to go back, the other which strives to progress in accordance with the irreversibility of the historical process." Publication of his works, he added, would be "to the indisputable benefit of Soviet literature in its present crisis." Although Alexandr Tvardovsky himself has since become a victim of that crisis, like Solzhenitsyn, he remains one of the writers whom Soviet intellectuals most respect.

References

N Y Times Mag p10 D 19 '65 por
Newsweek 75:58+ Mr 2 '70 por
Time 95:41 Mr 2 '70 por

Alexandrovna, Vera. A History of Soviet Literature 1917-1962 (1963)
International Who's Who, 1970-71
Prominent Personalities in the USSR, 1968
Simmonds, G. W., ed. Soviet Leaders, 1967
Who's Who in America, 1970-71
Who's Who in the Soviet Union, 1965-66

VASARELY, VICTOR (vas-ə-rel'ē)

Apr. 9, 1908- French artist
Address: Socio-Cultural Center for the Plastic Arts, Château de Gordes, Gordes, Vaucluse, France

Retinal, or optical, kineticism is static art that moves "magically," by the calculated effect of precisely arranged geometric color-forms on the retina of the observer. Because of its relation to optical illusion, retinal kineticism was generally viewed as a para-artistic genre, suitable mostly for parlor games or psychology text illustrations, until the mid-1960's. Then, its way paved by the hard-edged Pop art reaction against egocentric slap-dash abstract expressionism, Op art finally gained recognition as the art form perhaps most in accord with developments in science and technology and the aesthetic needs of a polychrome city of the future that those developments make inevitable. At about that time the American painter George Rickey observed: "The primary source for the artistic use of optical phenomena is not the teaching of [Josef] Albers on color but the painting and influence of Vasarely." Victor Vasarely, a Budapest-born French citizen who describes himself as a "craftsman" of "plastic abstractions," be-

VICTOR VASARELY

gan his visual research in childhood and started producing Op art professionally in the early 1930's, when he was a commercial graphic designer. For the past two decades his work, with its ingenious permutations of space, light, and movement, has reflected an ever more refined mastery of techniques complementary to the wave mechanics of contemporary physics, and the results are, in the words of Grace Glueck (New York *Times*, January 30, 1966), "the most dazzling retinal spectaculars in contemporary art."

Vasarely is an articulate theoretician as well as a disciplined craftsman, and in his theory as in his craft he is an antiromantic, anti-Renaissance revolutionary, out to subvert the very art establishment that has made him a millionaire. An aesthetic socialist, he believes in and works on the principle that the personalized, unique work of art, ownable only by the affluent and explainable only by an anointed elite, must give way to impersonal "multipliables," coded creations as reproducible as phonograph records are in music and needing no appreciation beyond the act of perception itself. Most of Vasarely's experimentation and creation is now carried out, in collaboration with ten assistants, at the Socio-Cultural Center for the Plastic Arts, housed in the sixteenth-century Château de Gordes in the village of Gordes, near Avignon in southern France.

Victor Vasarely was born on April 9, 1908 in Pecs, Hungary to a gentleman-farmer of the same name and Anna (Csiszar) Vasarely. The high social background of the family became an empty advantage when, during Vasarely's childhood, the warring Communist and fascist factions in Hungary displaced the traditional aristocracy, leaving such families as the Vasarelys relatively impoverished. Even as a child Vasarely was fascinated by "movement in a plane." He liked to draw trains and animals in motion; to create a "crude little cinema" by drawing double images with his finger on steam-clouded storm windows; and to experiment with the three-dimensional effects of tracing-paper transparencies and with the *Moiré* phenomenon—the micro-universe of changing linear networks—visible in gauze bandaging. In school he was fascinated by the isobar maps in geography class and the isoclinical, isochronous, and isochromatic lines in physics. While growing up, he filled whole notebooks with linear designs (which he calls "births"), and his eye constantly drew him to "escape" and "dream" in the cross-hatching of old engravings, the metamorphoses that occur in the interstices of twisted grill works, and the like.

In 1925 Vasarely graduated from the Lycée Isabelle in Budapest and entered the University of Budapest to study medicine, but two years later political conditions forced the curtailment of classes at the university and he dropped out, never to return. While studying at the Poldini-Volkmann Academy of Painting in Budapest in 1927 he supported himself by working as a bookkeeper in a ball-bearing factory. In addition to his tasks at the ledger he designed some advertising posters for his employer, and in 1929 he quit his job to study under Sándor Bortnyik, who had just opened a Bauhaus-type school in Budapest. (The Bauhaus was the revolutionary German school of design, founded by architect Walter Gropius, in which all teaching was based on the principle that form should follow function in architecture, industrial design, and city planning. In all fields and at every stage of training, Bauhaus students were taught the pure arts only in conjunction with applied craftsmanship, with special emphasis on the mechanics of mass production.) "The famous axonometric perspective, so dear to Kupka, was our daily bread in Master Bortnyik's studio in Budapest," Vasarely later wrote in his artistic journal, which he calls his "rough notes." "Before this, representing a cube in transparency was conceivable only by means of six lozenges, a law well known to Italian perspective. We would set up the four perpendiculars at the four points of the basic square, but inclining them to the right or to the left: at equal distance from the first, a second square could be constituted. The working drawing thus obtained gave us a cube, but its components were indeed two perfect squares and only two lozenges. The same procedure could likewise be followed with other figures of plane geometry."

Feeling "stifled" in Hungary, Vasarely moved to Paris in 1930, and on July 25 of the following year he and Claire Spinner, also an artist, were married there. In collaboration with his wife he designed geometric prints for a fabric manufacturer in 1931 and 1932, and thereafter he did graphic creations for printing companies in and around Paris. (His affluence dates from 1935, when he began doing pharmaceutical ads.) Optical kineticism, implicit in his drawings of 1931-32, became more explicit in the axonometric-perspective drawings of checkerboards, harlequins, zebras, tigers, prisoners, Martians, and the like that he executed between 1933 and 1938. "The ambiguity of these drawings," he later observed, "did not result from the *trompe-l'oeil*, due to a given perspective, but from an as yet mysterious space that appeared in the plane." One of his more extraordinary works of the early 1930's,

utilizing antecedents of his later color-forms, was *Fille-Fleur*, which he has called "an instinctive work that reassures me I have followed one fundamental path throughout my career."

Not yet seeing his true course, Vasarely took what he calls a "wrong" turn in 1938, into Futurism, the portrayal of the movement of figures through simultaneity, or sequences of positions. (The best known Futurist device was a multi-legged figure, suggesting the action of walking.) For thirteen years Vasarely did no more Op work, but the long detour was not entirely a waste of time. During it he came for the first time to a real appreciation of painting, which as a commercial graphic artist he had previously deprecated. And, as he has said, he discovered "in certain Futuristic canvases and in Paul Klee's pen-and-ink drawings . . . analogies with my networks, as later in the work of Pevsner, in a composition by Albers. . . . Was this pure coincidence?"

Vasarely's independence as an experimenter was strengthened when, toward the end of World War II, he found a quasi-patron in Denise René. He helped her found the Galerie Denise René in Paris and began exhibiting there regularly, as he still does. (In New York he exhibits at the Sidney Janis Gallery.) Immediately after the war he turned out for the gallery dozens of commercially successful Symbolist and abstract expressionist paintings. "I could have gone on," he later said, "but what I had learned from the Bauhaus made me rebel."

Two experiences rescued Vasarely from the "wrong track." Through the "oceanic feeling" he experienced while vacationing on the island of Belle-Isle, off the coast of Brittany, in the summer of 1947 he recognized "the inner geometry of nature" and the fact that "pure form-color could represent the world." The experience was reflected in his paintings by ever greater emphasis on a purified ellipsoid form, which became for him "the synthesis of a whole world, engendering in me a unitary philosophy. . . . I can no longer admit an inner world and another, an outer world, apart. . . . The languages of the spirit are but the supervibrations of the great physical nature."

The second experience took place in the summer of 1948, on the first of his annual vacations at Gordes. At the time he wrote in his notebook: "Southern towns and villages devoured by an implacable sun have revealed to me a contradictory perspective. Never can the eye identify to what a given shadow or strip of wall belongs: solids and voids merge into one another, forms and backgrounds alternate. . . . Identifiable things are transmuted into abstractions, and, passing over the threshold of the Gestalt, begin their independent life." About the time that he underwent the Belle-Isle and Gordes experiences, and afterward, Vasarely was reading Teilhard de Chardin's *The Phenomenon of Man* and numerous works on relativity, wave mechanics, cybernetics, and astrophysics. Later he wrote: "A sentence (was it by Bohr, Dirac, De Broglie, Wiener, Dauvillier, or Heisenberg?) struck me vividly: "In the last analysis, matter-energy could be considered as deformation of space. . . . Pure physics suddenly revealed itself before my dazed eyes as the new poetic source. . . . The traditional landscape disappears, certainty-uncertainty alternate. . . . Could the universe be one grandiose equation?"

What Vasarely calls his crystal period, with its vestiges of figurative or representational elements, gave way gradually, just before and after 1950, to his Denfert period—an allusion to the Denfert-Rochereau station of the Paris subway, where, years before, he used to wait for the train to take him home to Aceuil. While waiting, he would meditate on the crackle designs in the station's tile wall. "Was it really 'chance' that had perfectly framed them?" he later wrote in his journal. "I had the impression of curious landscapes when the crackles were horizontal, of bizarre cities or phantoms when they were vertical. . . . The tiny crackle due to a break on the level of the molecular structure became identified with great geosynclinals and went even beyond, in my imagination. The incubation of the plastic theme was a lengthy one, and it was only in about 1948 that I made my first Denfert drawings from memory."

In 1951 he had the small linear drawings enlarged to wall scale and exhibited them under the title "photographisms." Transposed on transparencies, the networks were projected and used as settings for a ballet. Seeing his direct work appear in gigantic form without losing its character, he realized that "the intervention of the machine made it possible to go beyond the human scale." In *Sonata-T* (1953) and similar "deep kinetic" works, he translated his drawings into large plexiglass constructions, transparent screens, placed at varying angles so as to create different combinations of linear patterns. Later, in his "refractions," he added deforming glass and mirror effects to achieve a constant shift of images.

In 1955 the Galerie Denise René held an exhibition that brought together for the first time the works of artists in various kinetic fields (Agam, Soto, Calder, Duchamp, Tinguely, Bury, and Jacobsen). It was in the "Yellow Manifesto" that he wrote for that exhibition that Vasarely invented the term *plastique cinétique*, elaborating thus: "The screen is flat, but, by permitting movement, it is also space. . . . We are at the dawn of a great epoch. The era of plastic projections on screens, flat or in depth, in daylight or darkness, is beginning. . . . At a time when mankind has extended its knowledge to cover both macro- and micro-cosmos, how can an artist get excited about the same things that made up the day-to-day world of the painter of the past, restricted as it was to what came within his immediate sense range—his home, the people he knew, his garden. . . . Henceforth art will adequately express the cosmic age of atoms and stars." The term "Op art" did not come into use until ten years later, when the first exhibition in the United States devoted exclusively to that branch of kinetic art was held at the Museum of Modern Art in New York City.

Over the years Vasarely was developing, in accordance with the relativity principle of wave mechanics, his "planetary folklore," an alphabet of some thirty geometric forms and about the same number of colors capable of practically infinite arrangements for varying, calculable effects. Actually, he does not consider form and color separately, but as a form-color whole, or "plastic unity." "Every form is a substratum of color, every color is the attribute of a form." Marcel Joray, in his introduction to the magnificently illustrated volume *Vasarely* (Editions du Griffon Neuchâtel, 1965; distributed in the United States by Wittenborn and Company), commented: "A vocabulary of elementary color-forms fitting into a square enables him to give to modern architecture its plasticity. Not by means of a superadded polychromy, but through a true integration. Perhaps, thanks to the idea of planetary folklore, all those dreary, ugly city blocks will some day make way for more human and truly radiant dwelling centers."

Vasarely's plastic ABC's, completed in the mid-1950's, did not begin to reach full utilization until the 1960's, when the artist started to integrate color into his work with unprecedented, brilliant variety. In such paintings as *Cham* (1965) dazzling retinal vibrations are effected by the use of small color forms that expand and contract against contrasting color grounds. Some of his works of the late 1960's, such as *Tri-Dim* (1969), might suggest a departure from Op art if he were not during the same period also doing such paintings as those in the *Ond* and *Vega* series, with their undulating hills and bulges, now convex, now concave. In *Axo-77*, among other 1969 works, he created a third and fourth dimension, expressing both volume and movement through the backward and forward shifts of two cubes.

Major examples of Vasarely's work since 1964 may be seen in *Vasarely II* (Editions du Griffon Neuchâtel, 1970; distributed in the United States by Wittenborn). Like the antecedent volume, the book was designed out by the artist himself, meticulously, so as to stand as a self-sufficient work of art. (One printing form had to pass through the press twenty-six times to meet his requirements.) In his preface to the book, Marcel Joray wrote: "He has undertaken vast studies to enable him to use that modern tool . . . the computer. Already his manually wrought works are being executed . . . [by] programming, the form-colors being ciphered. . . .The Gordes foundation . . . is a decisive step in the direction of . . . the collaboration of builders and artists [from which] the plastic beauty of the cities of tomorrow will soon burst forth." In his introductory note to the volume, Vasarely wrote: "This volume is my tribute to the multitude, my sly salute to youth, my admiration before the facts of progress . . . my conviction that to make men see is to make them joyous and civilized." Elsewhere he has said that the function of his shimmering, shifting, retina-discombobulating work is not, like that of sensibility-oriented traditional art, to transmit emotions to the heart, but rather to reach the "refined mind" through the retina, "to stimulate us and provide us with wild joys. . . . The immaterial spirit has had its day. Man is henceforth defined as the highly diversified summit of a material universe, in which every event, and therefore himself as well, proceeds from the wave-particle duality. An ambiguous world, enigmatic even, expressed in quanta by some, in plastic equivalents by others."

Just as the medieval synthesis expressed itself in the Gothic cathedrals, Vasarely believes, the new synthesis must express itself in the collaborative building of the polychrome city. Accordingly, the works of which he is most proud are the architectonic integrations, usually murals or gates, that he has done for building complexes at the University of Caracas, the Essen (Germany) Pedagogical College, the University of Montpelier, the Hilton Hotel in Brussels, the Jerusalem Museum, the University of Bonn, the University of Paris, and the Olympic Speed Ring in Grenoble, France, among other projects. Vasarely creates the prototypes or master plans for his multipliable drawings, paintings, and plexiglass constructions and leaves their execution to his assistants. Besides living and working in Gordes he apparently still has a house in the Paris suburb Annet-sur-Marne.

Victor and Claire Vasarely have two sons, André, a physician, and Jean-Pierre, a painter who shares his father's interest in kinetics. According to a writer in *Construire* (June 4, 1969), he is a tall, slender man with a stiff carriage, an animated manner, and the vestige of a Hungarian accent. His favorite recreations are chess and billiards. When Grace Glueck interviewed him for the New York *Times* she found him to be "softspoken, courteous, and handsomely tailored in a pearl gray suit. . . . His appearance didn't hint at the visual revolutionary that he is." Miss Glueck observed that Vasarely wished not to hoard his plastic alphabet, but rather to share it with others, in true scientific spirit. "The 'star' artist and the 'solitary genius' have had their day, he notes. He believes that groups of investigators, collaborating with scientific and technical discipline, will create the art of the future. . . . Plastic works . . . are nourishment to which all are entitled, as they're entitled to knowledge and vitamins." As John Canaday observed in the New York *Times Magazine* (February 21, 1965), the motto of the Op art movement might well be, "From impersonality, universality."

References

Time 83:75 My 1 '64; 95:56+ Je 22 '70
Barnett, Cyril. Op Art (1970)
Ferrier, Jean-Louis. Entretiens avec Victor Vasarely (1969)
Vasarely, Victor. Vasarely (1965); Vasarely II (1970)

WALTERS, BARBARA

Sept. 25, 1931- Broadcaster
Address: b. National Broadcasting Company, 30 Rockefeller Plaza, New York 10020; h. 171 W. 57th St., New York 10019

One of the most adept interviewers in a medium overstocked with talk shows is Barbara Walters, the cohost and commentator of NBC-TV's *Today*.

Knowledgeable, direct, and unpretentious, Miss Walters almost always succeeds in relaxing her guests—who vary from the most over-interviewed celebrities to unknowns quaking with stagefright—and in getting them to answer the questions of greatest interest to *Today* viewers. The program has been on television since 1952, offering a low-pressure format of news, weather, feature stories, and interviews to early risers. (It is aired weekdays from 7 to 9:00 a.m. Eastern Standard Time.) After several years of TV production and scriptwriting, Miss Walters joined *Today* in 1961 as a writer and occasional on-the-air feature reporter. Since assuming her present position in 1964, she has appeared daily with host Hugh Downs and, in recent years, cohost Joe Garagiola, Miss Walters is also a commentator on the NBC radio program *Monitor*.

Barbara Walters became accustomed to meeting celebrities at an early age, since her father is Lou Walters, founder and proprietor of New York's Latin Quarter and other nightclubs. She was born to Walters and his wife, the former Dena Selett, on September 25, 1931 in Boston, Massachusetts. Miss Walters has an older sister Jacqueline who, herself mentally retarded, helps to teach retarded children. Barbara grew up in Boston, New York, and Miami Beach, and attended Miami Beach High School and two private institutions in New York City—the Fieldston School and Birch Wathen School. In 1954 she graduated from Sarah Lawrence College in Bronxville, New York with a B.A. degree in English.

For a time during college Miss Walters thought she would like to be an actress, but after graduation she began working toward a master's degree in education and planned to teach. In the meantime, she took a speedwriting course and briefly held a job as an advertising agency secretary. All thoughts of teaching apparently vanished, however, when she landed a job as assistant to the publicity director of WRCA-WRCA-TV, NBC's New York outlet. Chosen to participate in the station's training program for TV producers, Miss Walters soon moved out of the publicity department into a position as a producer and writer at WRCA-TV. Later she moved to WPIX-TV as women's-program producer.

Practised in researching, writing, filming, and editing, Miss Walters was hired as a news and public affairs producer and writer for the CBS Television network. Officials assigned her to the network morning show—*Today*'s competition—where she wrote material for Dick Van Dyke, Will Rogers Jr., Jack Parr, and Anita Colby. That job, apparently, proved to be a dead end, because she left CBS to embark on what she has called her "dark ages years," in which she worked for a theatrical public relations firm. Eventually she was hired as a writer by Dave Garroway, then host of *Today*. Primarily she remained behind the scenes preparing scripts slanted towards women for others to present, but occasionally she would be given a chance to do a feature story on the air. One such assignment took her to India and Pakistan with Mrs. John F. Kennedy.

While Barbara Walters toiled in the background, a number of women came and went on the show in the position known as the *"Today* girl." From the beginning it had been the policy of the program to look for names that would be recognized by the sponsors, and over the years the ranks of *"Today* girls" included Lee Ann Meriwether, Helen O'Connell, Florence Henderson, Betsy Palmer, Pat Fontaine, and Maureen O'Sullivan. Although many of those women were accomplished in other fields, none of them could present credentials as newswomen, and all they were called upon to do was to smile prettily, indulge in small talk, and read commercials. Everyone agreed that a different kind of woman was needed, but no one seemed to have any clear idea of what kind. No one, that is, except Barbara Walters. She has recalled to interviewers that she would say to herself, "Hey fellas, look at me, I'm right here, how about me?" but that she never found the courage to say it aloud. Then one day the veteran actress Maureen O'Sullivan, *Today's* latest "girl," became tired of presiding over the teacups and abruptly resigned. Hugh Downs and the producer, Al Morgan, told Miss Walters that she could take her place on a trial basis, with the understanding that her writing job would be waiting if things did not work out.

Contrary to the network's apprehensions that the public would not cotton to an "educated woman," it soon became apparent that *Today's* earnest and intelligent female reporter—no one ever called her the *"Today* girl"—was a popular success. Several months after Barbara Walters had begun appearing regularly on the program Hugh Downs told Hyman Goldberg of the New York *Herald Tribune* (August 22, 1965), "She's the best thing that's happened to the show since I've been on it." If the public appreciated her obvious professionalism before the camera, the show continued to benefit from her behind the scenes work, and to this day she continues to produce and write most of her material. Acutely aware of the issues and personalities that interest the public, she expends great effort and displays formidable tenacity to obtain her interviews. Reportedly she worked for two years to get Dean Rusk on the show and ended up by scoring a coup when Rusk gave her his first interview after leaving the post of Secretary of State.

Miss Walters' feature stories for *Today* have included an investigation of anti-Semitic housing practices in Grosse Pointe, Michigan, a film essay on loneliness in New York City, coverage of a Presidential breakfast, and a moving report on the life of Robert Smithdas, a deaf and blind poet. For the sake of firsthand reporting, she has visited a nunnery and a girls' reform school and worked as a Playboy bunny. She was the first to secure television interviews with Truman Capote, the notoriously shy Fred Astaire, and with the painter Andrew Wyeth. She has interviewed Presidents Johnson and Nixon, their consorts, and Mamie Eisenhower. Mrs. Rose Kennedy, matriarch of the Kennedy family, has answered her questions on the air as have Edward, Ethel, and the late Rob-

BARBARA WALTERS

ert F. Kennedy. She once filmed a two-part interview with the late Martin Luther King Jr.'s widow Coretta and her children. Other famous guests of hers have included Golda Meir, Prince Philip, Princess Grace of Monaco, the late Judy Garland, and Ingrid Bergman.

Although her questions have occasionally been described as uncomfortably probing, Miss Walters seldom seems to alienate her subjects, and she is acknowledged to have an uncanny ability to get people to open up and talk about themselves. She told Ben Gross of the New York *Sunday News* (January 19, 1969) that for her a good interview was "one that brings out some thing concerning a guest that he hasn't revealed about himself before." "For example," she explained, "while talking with Truman Capote a year or so ago, he made this remark: 'It's my essentially tragic nature that makes me do the frivolous things I do.'" Miss Walters has revealed some of the secrets of her success with people in *How to Talk With Practically Anybody About Practically Anything* (Doubleday, 1970), in which she intersperses her advice on how to achieve social ease with anecdotes about her famous friends and guests. As of December 1970, the book was in its seventh printing and nearing the best-seller ranks.

Since coming into her own on the *Today* show Miss Walters has received many assignments from the NBC network. On NBC Radio she is a commentator on *Monitor* and formerly held the same position on *Emphasis*. She has participated in network television specials such as *The Pill*, produced by the staff of *Today* in 1967, and *From Here to the 70's*, for which she headed up the segment entitled "The Sexual Revolution." In July 1969 she was sent to Caernarvon, Wales to cover the investiture of Prince Charles as the Prince of Wales.

Barbara Walters and Lee Guber, a theatrical producer and owner of summer theaters, were married on December 8, 1963. They have an adopted daughter, Jacqueline Dena. Although she claims never to get enough sleep, Miss Walters successfully manages to maintain a family life despite her grueling schedule. To appear before the cameras at seven each morning, she must rise at 4:30 a.m., and she is seldom home from work before 5:00 p.m. An attractive green-eyed brunette, five feet five inches tall and weighing 115 pounds, the TV interviewer wears conservative but stylish designer dresses, most of which she buys retail at Bonwit Teller. Her speech betrays a slight lisp and an accent that she calls "Boston with a New York overlay." Miss Walters has worked extensively for retarded children, and she is a former honorary chairman of the National Association for Help to Retarded Children. She has twice been named to the *Harper's Bazaar* list of "100 Women of Achievement" and Houston, Texas has named her Woman of the Year. Although Miss Walters readily acknowledges that television does not offer equal opportunities to women and that she has had to fight for her more serious assignments, she remains a moderate on the issue of women's liberation. "I am for many of the things that women's lib is for—like day care centers and employment opportunities," she told Judy Klemesrud of the New York *Times* (August 27, 1970). "But I don't want a total revolution in the state of women. I like the feminine role. I like being a mother, and having my home revolve primarily around my husband's life."

References

Cue 39:1 D 26 '70 por
N Y Herald Tribune mag p8 Ag 22 '65 pors
N Y Post p31 Ag 1 '65 por
N Y Sunday News II p29+ Ja 19 '69 por
N Y Times II p15 Jl 2 '67
Newsday p93 N 1 '65 pors
Newsweek 73:73 My 19 '69 por

Walters, Barbara. How to Talk With Practically Anybody About Practically Anything (1970)

WATSON, ARTHUR K(ITTREDGE)

Apr. 23, 1919- United States Ambassador to France
Address: b. United States Embassy, 2 Avenue Gabriel, Paris 8, France; h. 260 West St., New Canaan, Conn. 06840

In March 1970 President Richard Nixon named as Ambassador to France Arthur K. Watson, then board chairman of the World Trade Corporation, the global arm of the International Business Machines Corporation, the computer giant built by his father. As head of World Trade for nearly two decades, Watson became known in European—and especially French—business and governmental circles as an enlightened, cosmopolitan capitalist, who had translated the ethic of American free enterprise into a commitment to barrier-free trade worldwide. When his ambassadorial nomination was announced, Governor Nelson Rockefeller of New York predicted that Watson's "outstanding ability to communicate the American spirit to

others" would "do much to strengthen the historic ties between the peoples of France and the United States."

Arthur Kittredge Watson was born on April 23, 1919 in Summit, New Jersey to Thomas J. Watson Sr. and Jeanette (Kittredge) Watson. The father was a traveling salesman who rose to the top of the National Cash Register Company and then, in 1914, became general manager of the Computer-Tabulating-Recording Company, manufacturers of meat slicers, grocery store scales, and business machines. Under his direction the company developed into IBM, of which he became president in 1923. He coined the motto "Think" for IBM and the slogan "World peace through world trade" for the International Chamber of Commerce.

Watson has an older brother, Thomas J. Jr., now the board chairman of IBM, and two sisters. In raising his sons, Thomas J. Watson Sr., an old-fashioned authoritarian with a formidable personality, imposed standards of achievement and decorum similar to those with which he ran IBM, where employees were required to conform to a strict set of rules ranging from white shirts to teetotalism. The development of Arthur K. Watson's internationalist attitudes dates from his childhood, when he began accompanying his father on trips abroad.

Watson was educated at the Hotchkiss School and at Yale University, where he took his bachelor's degree in international affairs in 1942. During World War II he reached the rank of major with the United States Army ordnance corps in the Philippines. At the end of the war he wanted to stay in the Philippines, as manager of IBM's Manila office, but his father thought he needed more preparation for a managerial position. Returning to Yale, Watson studied Russian, French, German, and Spanish. He joined IBM as a salesman in 1947 and quickly climbed the corporate ladder. When the IBM World Trade Corporation was formed in 1949 to handle IBM's manufacturing and marketing abroad, he was elected a director and vice-president. Five years later he became president of the wholly owned subsidiary, and in 1963 he was elected board chairman. Beginning in January 1966 he held the position of vice-chairman of the IBM board of directors in addition to his World Trade post.

Under Watson's leadership the World Trade Corporation's sales rose during the 1960's from $372,000,000, or 21 percent of IBM's total revenues, to $2.5 billion, or 35 percent of the total. Seventy-five percent of the subsidiary's revenues came from its European, African, and Middle Eastern operations. In France it had two manufacturing plants, employed more than 14,000 people, accounted for 69 percent of the installed computer business, and was one of the country's four top exporters. Sixty-eight percent of the installed computers in Germany came from World Trade, as did 77 percent of those in Italy and 40 percent of those in the United Kingdom. In 1968 in the United Kingdom the company reportedly earned $80,000,000 before taxes on revenues of $300,000-

000. The following year its after-tax return on capital worldwide was 26 percent and its profits made up 40 percent of the IBM total.

But to Watson the financial success of the World Trade Corporation was no more important than the principle that "commerce can transmit ideas from people to people rather than from government to government." During his regime, as now, one of the key elements in the company's policy of cultivating goodwill in host countries was a preference for natives in hiring. Of its 74,000 employees in Europe, only 236 were United States citizens, and the majority of managerial positions in Paris were filled by Europeans. Another element was an emphasis on language skills. An American seeking a company post in another country was required to learn the language of the country, and foreign administrators and those engineers and technicians needing greater fluency in English were sent to the United States for a year or more.

Political ties in the Watson family have been mixed. Thomas Watson Sr. was a supporter of Franklin Roosevelt and Dwight D. Eisenhower and a family friend of the Kennedys. Thomas Jr. was a strong supporter and friend of John and Robert Kennedy and he has filled some of the executive positions at IBM with former Kennedy aides. Arthur is a Republican and has reportedly been a substantial contributor to the party.

As president of the World Trade Corporation, Watson was present at the United States exhibition at the Moscow Trade Fair when Richard Nixon, then Vice-President, officiated at the opening of the exhibition in July 1959. (On that occasion, speaking Russian, Watson persuaded Soviet Premier Nikita S. Khrushchev to watch a demonstration of an IBM computer.) He first came close to a public political role when, in 1967, he and David Rockefeller formed the Emergency Committee for American Trade, a lobby dedicated to combatting a growing protectionist sentiment in Congress. Testifying before the House Ways and Means Committee in 1968, Watson asserted that "import quotas and orderly marketing ceilings are inconsistent with a free enterprise economic system."

Watson was in Miami during the 1968 Republican National Convention, at which Richard Nixon was nominated for the Presidency, and he accompanied Governor Nelson A. Rockefeller of New York on a fact-finding tour of Latin America for President Nixon in 1969. On March 2, 1970 the President named him to succeed Sargent Shriver as Ambassador to France. The following month Watson resigned his IBM and WTC posts, and in May 1970 he presented his credentials to French President Georges Pompidou.

The Ambassador has served as a director of the Continental Corporation, the Continental Insurance Company, the Federal Reserve Bank of New York, and Pan American Airways. He is a trustee of the Carnegie Endowment for International Peace, the Hotchkiss School, the Metropolitan Museum of Art, the Presbyterian Hospital of New York, the Sloan Foundation, and the Ethel Walker School and a fellow in the Corporation of Yale University. For his contributions to international

ARTHUR K. WATSON

cooperation he has been awarded the French Legion of Honor and the Vatican's Equestrian Order of St. Sylvester.

Arthur K. Watson and Ann C. Hemingway were married on July 10, 1948. They have six children: Ann Carroll, Jane White, Caroline Trowbridge, Arthur Kittredge, Stuart Hemingway, and David John. The boys live in Paris with their parents. The girls, who are older, are continuing their education in the United States. For the girls' sake the Watsons are keeping open "Orchard Farm," their seventy-three-acre estate in New Canaan, Connecticut. The family also owns a summer house on Penobscot Bay in Camden, Maine, and Watson has a sloop docked there.

The Watsons took with them to Paris their collection of Royal Copenhagen figurines and some favorites among the paintings they own: a Monet, a Corot, a Gauguin, a Childe Hassam, and an Andrew Wyeth. In mid-1971 they were preparing to move from the old ambassadorial residence to a much larger building recently purchased by the United States government on the Faubourg St. Honoré, not far from the United States Embassy offices.

Watson, who is known to his peers as "Dick" for some inscrutable reason, is tall (six feet two) and slim and has brown eyes and a full head of white hair. He is soft-spoken, and his quiet manner has impressed some observers as "reserved" or "patrician" and others as "aloof" and even "cold." But friends report that he can be "super-affable," that he likes to tell funny stories, sometimes bordering on the "risqué," and that he often plays the guitar, and sings at parties. He is known for his tact, his ability to keep discussions directly on the point, and for his good taste in clothes—from conservative business suits to brocade jackets and Bermuda shorts for less formal occasions. According to his wife, he is a better cook than she. In French and Spanish he is fluent, or "quite passable" as one auditor reported, and he speaks some German. Watson has said that his "best friend" is his brother, with whom he shares a love of sailing.

References

N Y Post p37 Ap 26 '71 por
N Y Times p6 Mr 4 '70 por; p16 My 9 '70
Washington (D.C.) Post A p6 Mr 4 '70
International Who's Who, 1970-71
Rodgers, William. Think; A Biography of
    the Watsons and IBM (1969)

WELCH, RAQUEL

Sept. 5, 1940- Actress
Address: b. c/o Twentieth Century-Fox Studios,
10201 W. Pico Blvd., Los Angeles, Calif. 90064

By projecting the image of a willful Amazon, who is at the same time sensual, tough, and unfettered, Raquel Welch has become the current sex goddess. Guided by the artful promotion of her husband, Patrick Curtis, Miss Welch first gained fame as an international cover girl during the mid-1960's and has since starred or been featured in over a dozen films, including *Fantastic Voyage, Bedazzled, Fathom, 100 Rifles,* and *The Magic Christian.* Although even her loyal fans admit her acting powers have not been tested by her appearances in a string of undistinguished films, Raquel Welch's vehicles gross huge profits, and she has been ranked among the top ten female attractions at the box office since 1968. Her most ambitious role to date was that of the transsexual Myra bent on conquering Hollywood and mankind in *Myra Breckinridge.* The highly publicized screen version of Gore Vidal's best seller was universally condemned by critics when Twentieth Century-Fox released it in 1970.

Raquel Welch was born Raquel Tejada in Chicago, Illinois on September 5, 1940 to Armand Tejada, a Bolivian immigrant of Castilian Spanish extraction, and his American wife, Josephine (Hall) Tejada. Miss Welch's parents later divorced, after having another daughter and one son. About 1942 the family moved to La Jolla, a small community near San Diego, California. There her father, a structural stress engineer, worked in a General Dynamics plant, and the family lived in a small stucco house just two blocks from Wind and Sea Beach, a well-known surfing center. Raquel attended La Jolla public schools, studied ballet with a local instructor named Irene Clark, and won her first beauty contest at fifteen. She later became Miss La Jolla, Miss San Diego, and Maid of California.

At La Jolla High School Raquel was a cheerleader, belonged to the dramatic club, and was vice-president of the senior class. Although she had apparently decided on an acting career long before graduating in 1958 her ambitions were thwarted during her first few years after school. There followed more beauty contests, a job as weather girl for a television station in San Diego, and a year of acting classes at San Diego State College. On May 8, 1959, she married her high school sweetheart, James Westley Welch, and the couple soon had two children, a son Damon and a daughter Tahnee.

By 1963 the Welches had parted company and Raquel turned up in Dallas, Texas, where she modeled at Neiman-Marcus and worked as a cocktail hostess. (The couple obtained a divorce in 1964.) She apparently wanted to embark on a stage career in New York City and was working her way East with that in mind, but she soon returned to California, picked up her children in La Jolla, and settled in Hollywood. Making the rounds of studios, she obtained bit parts in two films, *A House Is Not a Home* (Embassy, 1964) and Elvis Presley's *Roustabout* (Paramount, 1964), but she accomplished very little until she met Patrick Curtis, a former child actor who was working in the Hollywood public relations firm of Rogers and Cowan.

Within three weeks of their first encounter, Curtis left Rogers and Cowan and founded Curtwel Productions with Miss Welch. That autumn she appeared in *Life* magazine (October 2, 1964) as a promising young actress. Curtis then obtained a modest assignment for her in a teenage beach movie called *A Swingin' Summer,* but her role was prominent enough to prompt a *Variety* reviewer to remark: "It's hard to look away when she's in view."

Twentieth Century-Fox signed a contract with Miss Welch and gave her a featured role in *Fantastic Voyage,* a science-fiction film about a team of scientists who are reduced to microscopic proportions in order to enter the bloodstream of an ailing man and cure him. When the film was released in 1966 Bosley Crowther of the New York *Times* (September 8) called Raquel Welch "a newcomer who is the most pneumatic-looking thing in a skin-diving suit that has yet appeared on the screen."

By the time *Fantastic Voyage* was released Miss Welch was in England on loan to Hammer Film Productions, where she starred in *One Million Years B.C.* (Twentieth Century-Fox, 1967), an inept Grade B drama about love in the stone age. "It was the kind of movie you do just to go to Europe and hope everyone will forget," Miss Welch told an interviewer for a *Time* cover story (November 28, 1969). As a cave girl named Loana Shell, she uttered only three words in the entire film, but her fur bikini won her hordes of admirers.

Pat Curtis had no intention of letting Raquel Welch languish among the dinosaurs. Executing what the *Time* cover story called "a slick transatlantic crossruff," Curtis billed the unknown actress to the European press as America's answer to Ursula Andress, and she soon became the darling of European magazine photographers and *paparazzi.* By shipping the hoopla back to the United States, the astute Curtis made his charge an instant celebrity there. On August 26, 1966 *Life* magazine ran a story on Raquel Welch calling her "the most photographed woman of 1966." According to *Life's* count, she had appeared so far on a total of ninety-two European and sixteen American magazine covers. But perhaps the greatest publicity triumph of Curtwel Productions in Europe was the marriage of its partners, which took place in Paris on St. Valentine's Day 1967. When the bride appeared in her loosely crocheted white minidress a hundred photographers tried to storm the city hall where the ceremony took place.

Meanwhile, Miss Welch was starring in a series of low-budget films by European producers. The first was *Shoot Loud, Louder . . . I Don't Understand* (Embassy, 1966), a surreal Italian comedy in which she played a prostitute loyal to Marcello Mastroianni. After that came *Fathom* (Twentieth Century-Fox, 1967), in which Miss Welch was a kind of female James Bond; *The Biggest Bundle of Them All* (MGM, 1968), in which she played a member of an inept gang that kidnaps Vittorio De Sica; and *The Oldest Profession* (Goldstone, 1968), an omnibus film about prostitution through the ages. The only film in which Miss Welch appeared during that period that was hospitably received by the critics was *Bedazzled* (Twentieth Century-Fox, 1967), an irreverent British comedy based on the Faust legend that was written by *Beyond the Fringe* creators Peter Cook and Dudley Moore. As Lilian Lust, Miss Welch stole the show from the other six Deadly Sins.

Curtwel Productions returned to the United States in time for the Academy Award presentations of 1967, where Miss Welch wore a low-cut, skin-tight culotte outfit that caused a sensation. After accompanying Bob Hope on his Christmas tour of South Vietnam in 1967, she was called "the pin-up girl of this war" by gossip columnist Earl Wilson (New York *Post*, December 30, 1967).

Settled once again in Hollywood after her European sojourn Raquel Welch starred in a bloody western entitled *Bandolero!* (Fox, 1968) with James Stewart and in *Lady in Cement* (Fox, 1968), another sequel in Frank Sinatra's Tony Rome detective series. Then she went to Spain to appear in *100 Rifles* (Twentieth Century-Fox, 1969), about an Indian uprising in Mexico in 1912. A reviewer for *Time* magazine (November 28, 1969) called *100 Rifles* "execrable," but when Miss Welch made love on screen with black actor Jim Brown it marked the first such interracial scene in a major film, and audiences flocked to see it. Next she made *Flareup* (MGM, 1969), a tepid thriller in which she starred as a go-go dancer pursued by a demented killer. In *The Magic Christian* (Commonwealth United, 1970), based on Terry Southern's novel, Miss Welch played a cameo role as a whip-wielding slave driver commanding a galley full of bare-breasted female oarsmen.

Early in 1968 Twentieth Century-Fox bought the film rights to *Myra Breckinridge*, Gore Vidal's controversial best seller about homosexuality, transsexualism, and Hollywood. The central figure of the book is Myron/Myra, a man who becomes a woman through surgery, and for the film Fox decided they had to cast the male and female roles separately. They settled on Miss Welch to play Myra reportedly on the basis of the reasoning of the film's producer Robert Fryer: "If a man were going to become a woman, he would want to become the most beautiful woman in the world. He would become Raquel Welch." With the

RAQUEL WELCH

acerbic celebrity interviewer Rex Reed cast as Myron, and Mae West and John Huston assigned to supporting roles, production on *Myra Breckinridge* began in September 1969.

By the time it was released in June 1970 *Myra Breckinridge* resembled, according to Stanley Kauffmann of the *New Republic* (July 19, 1970), "an abandoned battlefield after a lot of studio forces tussled and nobody won." Gore Vidal had quit as screenwriter, the script had been rewritten several times, Mae West had insisted on writing her own scenes, and the proceedings had been enlivened by a number of feuds, most notably Miss Welch's with the director Michael Sarne and with Mae West.

"Rather astonishingly," wrote Howard Thompson in the New York *Times* (June 25, 1970), "the picture starts strongly, dazzlingly and hilariously in a flow of rich color imagery and filthy language from what must surely be the gamest cast of the season. But rot soon sets in." Most other reviewers found the film putrid from the beginning. Although the critics agreed that Miss Welch had made a game try, no one felt that she had achieved new acting distinction as Myra, and Raquel watchers were distressed to see her clothed in mannish 1940's-type suits and involved in scenes of fairly explicit sodomy and autoeroticism.

During the late summer of 1970 Raquel Welch began working on "A Private Disgrace" on location in Cyprus. Described as "a modern drama with Greek tragedy overtones," the film is coproduced by Curtwel Productions. Miss Welch starred in *Raquel*, her first television special, on April 26, 1970. After it was telecast on CBS, Ben Gross wrote in the New York *Daily News* (April 27), "It was evident that this Hollywood sex goddess is no Barbra Streisand as a singer or a Lauren Bacall as an actress. . . . However, . . . she displayed an eagerness to please and an amiable TV personality." The show was produced by Curtwel Productions, which has several other specials in production for other stars.

Separated from her husband in March 1971, Raquel Welch filed for a divorce in September.

Before their split, Curtis and Miss Welch and her two children, whom he adopted, lived in a spacious Beverly Hills house that she has described as "English colonial style with a pool." Miss Welch is dark-haired, tawny-skinned, and about five feet five inches tall. Her much publicized measurements are 37-22½-35¾. According to several sources she underwent plastic surgery on her nose before going into films. Although she is determined to obtain better roles and prove herself as an actress, Miss Welch is candid in assessing her career thus far: "I consider all of the roles that I have done as camp," she told Kay Gardella of the New York *Daily News* (April 12, 1970). "They have not been things of my choice. They've been things that the studios have put me in. So I guess the best way to survive them is to play them to the hilt. If writers are going to put such cliché characters in their scripts, you might as well give it all you've got."

References

Esquire 73:123+ My '70 pors
N Y Times II p15 S 11 '66 por
Sat Eve Post 240:32+ N 18 '67 pors
Show 1:63+ Je '70 pors
Time 94:85+ N 28 '69 pors
Who's Who in America, 1970-71
Who's Who of American Women, 1970-71

WILDER, THORNTON (NIVEN)

Apr. 17, 1897- Writer
Address: h. 50 Deepwood Dr., Hamden, Conn. 06517

NOTE: This biography supersedes the article that appeared in *Current Biography* in 1943.

Paying no heed to the changing literary fads of social propaganda, pessimism, and obscenity, Thornton Wilder has searched beyond the topical American scene in his plays and novels for that which is universal and eternal in ancient myths, historic events, the confining life of a New England village, and inquiry into the realm of the unknowable. One Pulitzer Prize in fiction and two in drama testify to the relevance in the 1920's, 1930's and 1940's of his preoccupation with moral and spiritual fundamentals.

More recently Wilder's work has been the subject of an increasing number of book-length studies by both American and European scholars. Often performed now as modern classics, *Our Town* and *The Skin of Our Teeth* are credited with helping to revitalize a tradition-gagged American theatre. Wilder's bold innovations in drama and fiction are of superb craftsmanship. "He is—in the best sense of the term—a stylist," Richard H. Goldstone has pointed out, "a man who writes with urbanity, discrimination, and clarity."

The second son in a family of four children (two boys and two girls), Thornton Niven Wilder was born on April 17, 1897 in Madison, Wiscon-

sin to Amos Parker and Isabella Thornton (Niven) Wilder. Both of his parents were New Englanders with strong religious convictions. He has described Amos Wilder, a Congregationalist, as "a very strict Calvinistic father." His mother was the daughter of a Presbyterian minister. Thornton's brother, Amos Niven Wilder, became a Congregational minister and taught for many years at the Harvard School of Divinity.

Until the age of nine Thornton Wilder was reared in Madison, where his father edited the *Wisconsin State Journal*. In 1906 Amos Wilder obtained an appointment as American consul general in Hong Kong and moved his family to China. After several months there, during which Thornton attended a German day school, Mrs. Wilder took the children back to the United States and enrolled them in schools in Berkeley, California. Five years later they rejoined Amos Wilder, who had been transferred to the consulate in Shanghai. Thornton was sent as a boarding pupil to the English China Inland Mission School at Chefoo for a year. On returning to California in 1912, he went to the Thacher School in Ojai, but a year later entered the Berkeley High School, from which he graduated in 1915. While in high school he became fascinated with the theatre, eagerly attending performances of plays, mostly of the nineteenth century, that were presented at Ye Liberty Theatre in Oakland.

Wilder's first published writing, prose pieces, appeared in the literary magazine of Oberlin College, where he studied from 1915 to 1917. Transferring to Yale University, he contributed short plays, as well as essays, to the *Yale Literary Magazine*, which in his senior year published serially his first full-length play, *The Trumpet Shall Sound*. Military service in World War I, as a corporal in the Coast Guard artillery, delayed his graduation by a year.

When Wilder left Yale with the B.A. degree in 1920, he went to Rome to study archeology at the American Academy. His field trips greatly affected his perspective on human events, making them seem objectively insignificant and somewhat absurd. In a *Paris Review* interview with Richard H. Goldstone (*Writers at Work*, 1959), he discussed a central theme of his writings that developed from his study in Rome: "an unresting preoccupation with the surprise of the gulf between each tiny occasion of the daily life and the vast stretches of time and place in which every individual plays his role."

From his year in Italy, Wilder also derived the atmosphere for his first novel, *The Cabala* (Boni, 1926), which he began writing in Rome. The title refers to an influential and aristocratic circle of men and women living in Rome who want to preserve the past in society, religion, and politics. Wilder completed *The Cabala* while employed as a member of the faculty of the Lawrenceville School in Lawrenceville, New Jersey, where he taught French from 1921 to 1928. During a two-year leave of absence for writing and study he worked for his M.A. degree in French literature, awarded by Princeton University in 1926.

Neither *The Cabala* nor *The Trumpet Shall Sound,* which was produced by the American Laboratory Theatre in New York in 1927, gave promise of Wilder's developing into a writer of wide popular appeal. With the publication of *The Bridge of San Luis Rey* (Boni) in 1927, however, he became an international celebrity almost overnight. The novel climbed on the best-selling list, won the Pulitzer Prize for fiction in 1928, and was filmed for the first of three times in 1929. Episodic like *The Cabala,* but more unified in structure and theme, *The Bridge of San Luis Rey* tells the stories of five people killed in the collapse of a bridge in Peru in the eighteenth century and at the same time poses a number of theological and philosophical questions about the nature of love and the meaning of their deaths. The bringing together by accident or fate of a group of unrelated characters at some crucial moment in their lives became a widely imitated fictional device.

Remote also in time and place, the events of *The Woman of Andros* (Boni, 1930), which Wilder wrote largely during a year of travel in Europe, take place on the Greek island of Brynos not long before the dawn of Christianity. Although the plot follows in part Terence's *Andria,* Wilder turned that comedy into a tale of human suffering. Describing the novel as "one of the most classic things . . . in our language," Bernard Grebanier observed in *Thornton Wilder* (1964), "Bathed in transparent light, like the light peculiar to Greece itself, it is caressed by the air of Platonism." But in the Depression year of its appearance, some social-minded reviewers denounced its graceful style and philosophic concern as escapism, an evasion of a realistic treatment of today's critical problems.

In *Heaven's My Destination* (Harper, 1935) Wilder as a novelist moved into contemporary America with the story of George Brush, an ingenuous, sincere, and righteous man who makes himself ridiculous and at times unlikeable by trying to live strictly according to his religious principles. Because of confusion as to whether Wilder intended a sober, satirical, or humorous novel, *Heaven's My Destination* is considered his most misunderstood work. In his interview with Goldstone, Wilder explained that the novel is "a very autobiographical book," in which he tried to come to terms with the narrow and didactic religious influences of his youth. "The comic spirit is given to us," he said "in order that we may analyze, weigh, and clarify things in us which nettle us, or which we are outgrowing, or trying to reshape."

Wilder had made his first cross-country lecture tour of the United States in 1928-29. From 1930 to 1936 he held the post of lecturer in comparative literature at the University of Chicago. Free to devote half the year to writing, he spent several summers at the MacDowell Colony near Peterborough, New Hampshire. He was therefore very much involved in the American scene when he wrote *Heaven's My Destination.* As a playwright, he had earlier made the transition from what has been called "the realm beyond actual-

THORNTON WILDER

ity," in the three-minute plays of *The Angel That Troubled the Waters* (Coward, 1928), to a more recognizable actuality, in the six plays of *The Long Christmas Dinner and Other Plays in One Act* (Yale Univ. Press, 1931).

In presenting his own times in his one-act plays, such as "Pullman Car Hiawatha" and "The Happy Journey to Trenton and Camden," Wilder "tried to capture not verisimilitude but reality," as he wrote in the preface to a collection of his later, full-length plays, *Three Plays* (Harper, 1957). He freed his stage of scenery and traditional props, condensed years or hours into minutes, and used a Stage Manager where necessary to set the scene and comment to the audience somewhat in the manner of a Greek Chorus. His innovative techniques reflect his appreciation of "the theatre's power to raise the exhibited individual action into the realm of idea and type and universal."

The experimental devices of Wilder's short plays anticipated those of his first major play, *Our Town.* Conventionally staged in tryouts in Princeton and Boston, it had a generally unenthusiastic reception. The decision of Wilder and the producer Jed Harris to present the play on Broadway without scenery and with a minimum of props perhaps saved *Our Town* from oblivion as a celebration of the joys and sorrows of life in a specific place at a specific time. It began a long run at the Henry Miller Theatre on February 4, 1938, startled but delighted critics, and won the Pulitzer Prize for drama.

Grover's Corners, the town of *Our Town,* is modeled after Peterborough, Wilder's summer retreat. But, as he explained in his preface to *Three Plays,* "*Our Town* is not offered as a picture of life in a New Hampshire village. . . . It is an attempt to find a value above all price for the smallest events in our daily life. I have made the claim as preposterous as possible, for I have set the village against the largest dimensions of time and place."

Also in his preface Wilder suggested that "one way to shake off the nonsense of the nineteenth-century staging is to make fun of it." To parody the old-fashioned theatre he wrote *The Merchant of Yonkers, A Farce in Four Acts,* based loosely on Johann Nestroy's 1842 Viennese play, *Einen Jux will er sich Machen.* His slapstick comedy opened on Broadway, in a production directed by Max Reinhardt, in December 1938, but closed after only twenty-eight performances.

Wilder's second long-run, Pulitzer Prize-winning play, *The Skin of Our Teeth,* sets routine family life against vast dimensions of time in a way strikingly different from *Our Town.* In its multiple symbolism and fusion of past and present it owes much to James Joyce's *Finnegans Wake.* The members of the Antrobus family and their maid, Sabina, live both in prehistoric times and in a New Jersey suburb of the twentieth century. They confront the ice age, the flood, and finally war, in man's continuing struggle for survival. Its première in New York in the midst of wartime crisis, at the Plymouth Theatre on November 18, 1942, gave the play immediate relevance.

Because of its farcical humor in characterization and dialogue, its satiric wit, and unorthodox staging, *The Skin of Our Teeth,* has been described as "daffy" and "cock-eyed," as well as "brilliant." A comedy of deeply serious intent, it was written, Wilder has said, "under strong emotion," on the eve of the American entry into World War II. When the play opened on Broadway he was serving overseas in the United States Army Air Intelligence. He was commissioned a captain in 1942 and was promoted to lieutenant colonel before being discharged in 1945.

His service in Italy and his meditating about the war as resistance to absolute power very likely inspired Wilder's *The Ides of March* (Harper, 1948), a many-sided portrait of Julius Caesar. An appealing and tragic figure, the Caesar of the novel bears little resemblance to the dictators Hitler and Mussolini. Wilder's experiment in historical fiction consists of a series of extracts from letters, diaries, writings of Roman authors, and various other "documents," almost all of them invented, but remarkable for the authenticity of their Latin style. His next novel, *The Eighth Day* (Harper, 1967), is contrastingly traditional in form. The absorbing narrative begins with a murder and a miscarriage of justice in a Midwestern town at the turn of the century. And in unraveling that mystery, Wilder ponders the greater mystery of human destiny and of the design of creation. *The Eighth Day* won the National Book Award in 1968.

During the span of nearly twenty years between his two novels Wilder's stature as a playwright had grown internationally. For presentation at the Edinburgh Festival in Scotland in 1954, he contributed *The Matchmaker,* a "slightly modified version" of *The Merchant of Yonkers,* focusing attention even in its change of title on Dolly Levi, a heroine of his own, not Nestroy's, creation. The revised play was then produced with commercial and critical success in London and New York. A musical adaptation, *Hello, Dolly!,* scored at the box office on Broadway in 1964.

In 1955 Wilder returned to the Edinburgh Festival for the première of another of his plays, *The Alcestiad,* an allegory based on the Alcestis myth of Greek antiquity. The festival production, which used the title *A Life in the Sun* over the author's protests, had a disappointing reception. But translated into German, the play fared well in performances in Switzerland, Germany, and Austria. Wilder, who has a profound love and knowledge of music, wrote the libretto for an opera by Louise Talma based on the German version of *The Alcestiad.* It had its world première in Frankfurt in March 1962. An opera derived from Wilder's short play, "The Long Christmas Dinner," with libretto by the playwright and music by Paul Hindemith, had been produced in Mannheim in December 1961.

For some years Wilder had been working on an artistic summing up on the theme of "our lives and errors" in a projected double cycle of seven one-act plays each, to be called "The Seven Ages of Man" and "The Seven Deadly Sins." Two plays from the first cycle, "Infancy" and "Childhood," and one play from the second, "Someone from Assisi," were produced under the title *Plays for Bleecker Street* in early 1962 at the Off-Broadway Circle in the Square Theatre, on the arena stage for which Wilder had specifically written the plays.

Among Wilder's other contributions to the theatre, which he regards as "the greatest of all art forms," are his English translations of several plays in foreign languages, including Jean-Paul Sartre's *The Victors* (from *Morte sans sepulture*). He has occasionally performed in his own plays, particularly in the roles of Stage Manager of *Our Town* and Mr. Antrobus of *The Skin of Our Teeth* in summer stock theatres. For motion pictures he wrote the script of Alfred Hitchcock's *Shadow of a Doubt* (1943). His contributions to the preparation of the many screen, radio, and television scripts based on his work appear to be inconsiderable, but he did serve as a consultant in the filming of *Our Town* (1940).

As Charles Eliot Norton Professor of Poetry at Harvard University Wilder gave a series of lectures in 1950-51 entitled "The American Characteristic in Classic American Literature." He has lectured at many other universities, both in the United States and abroad. One of his subjects has been Gertrude Stein, who exerted a strong influence on his work. In the role of cultural ambassador he visited three South American countries on an educational mission for the State Department in 1941 and headed the American delegation to the UNESCO Conference of Arts in Venice in 1952.

Thornton Wilder is the first recipient of the National Book Committee's National Medal for Literature, presented at a White House ceremony in 1965. Wilder's countless other honors include a dozen degrees from American and foreign universities, the Peruvian Medal of the Order of Merit, and the German Goethe-Plakette and Peace Medal of Pour le Mérite. Wilder is a Democrat and a Congregationalist.

During the early 1960's Wilder retired to the obscure Arizona town of Patagonia to concentrate for a few years on writing and on research into scholarly problems regarding the dating of the plays of Lope de Vega. Decades ago, with royalties from *The Bridge of San Luis Rey*, he built a house in Connecticut, not far from the Yale library, where he spends much of his time. He is a bachelor and shares his home with his sister, the novelist Isabel Wilder. Meeting him in New Haven in 1966, Paul Horgan admired his "warm, witty, self-teasing" humor. "He was ruddy, full-fleshed, his fringe of hair and his clipped mustache were whiter than gray," Horgan observed in *Book-of-the-Month Club News* (March 1967). During the interview for the *Paris Review* Goldstone found that Wilder's eyeglasses acted as a mask: "Unobscured, the eyes—cold light blue—reveal an intense severity and an almost forbidding intelligence." Others have been more impressed by the boundless vitality and acute awareness of Wilder, who wrote so poignantly in *Our Town* about the difficulty of fully realizing life while it is being lived.

References

    N Y Times Bk R p1+ Je 20 '65 por; p1+ Ap 9 '67 por
    N Y Times Mag p28+ Ap 15 '62 por
    Sat R 50:25+ Ap 1 '67 por
    Gould, Jean. Modern American Playwrights (1966)
    Grebanier, Bernard. Thornton Wilder (1964)
    Papajewski, Helmut. Thornton Wilder (1968)
    Stresau, Hermann. Thornton Wilder (1971)
    Twentieth Century Authors (1942; First Supplement, 1955)
    Two Hundred Contemporary Authors (1969)
    Who's Who in America, 1970-71
    Writers at Work: The Paris Review Interviews 1st series (1959)

WILHELM, (JAMES) HOYT

July 26, 1923- Baseball player
Address: h. 6075 Chriskin Dr., Columbus, Ga. 31904

In baseball, where a pitcher's career expectancy is to reach thirty-five or so, knuckleball magician Hoyt Wilhelm continues to confound the sports' actuarial tables as he approaches fifty. The journeyman relief hurler owes his astounding durability at least in part to his strange delivery, which not only baffles batters but is—and always has been —easy on his arm. Unlike the traditional knuckleball hurler, Wilhelm did not develop the erratic "flutter" pitch as he grew older, to compensate for a strained, tired arm, but used it from the beginning of his career. That career goes back, professionally, thirty years, twenty of them in the major leagues, where he has been shunted from team to team and league to league as one manager

HOYT WILHELM

after another has falsely assumed that his playing days could not possibly extend to another season. As of the end of the 1970 season Wilhelm held the major-league pitching records for most game appearances (1,042), most games as a relief pitcher (990), most games finished (635), most victories in relief (124), lowest lifetime earned-run average (2.50), and most consecutive errorless games played by a pitcher (246, between 1963 and 1968). His mound totals were 124 wins of his own and 347 saved for others. Wilhelm, who has been the only pitcher to lead both the National (1952) and American (1959) leagues in the ERA category tallied the best ERA of his career in 1967, when he was forty-four years old. In ranking the pitchers he faced during his career as a slugger, Ted Williams places Wilhelm among the five toughest to hit.

The knuckler, at least the one Wilhelm throws, is misnamed. Wilhelm, a right-hander who uses two or three fingers in gripping the top of the ball, presses not his knuckles but the flat of his fingernails against the seam. In his delivery there is no twist of the elbow or shoulder, the twist of the wrist is relatively gentle, and speed is not necessary for the effectiveness of the pitch. It leaves his hand like a butterfly floating on the wind and travels toward the plate "dead," without the spin of other pitches. (But Wilhelm sometimes deliberately makes it turn *once*.) It moves straight through the air until it reaches the batter, when it falls, rises, or darts to the left or right unpredictably. Even Wilhelm himself does not know what it is going to do. It is sufficient for him to know only that it will go over the plate, and the difficulty of mastering even that degree of control over the knuckler is one of the reasons it is not used by more than a handful of pitchers. Wilhelm attributes his mastery basically to a "knack." "You can take a kid who can throw hard and teach him a curve or slider," he has observed. "But a knuckleball pitcher is born, not made." Occasionally he uses curves or sliders to keep batters guessing, and, more rarely, he used to use a fast ball. His primary problem throughout his career has been that he cannot use the full force of his magic against batters unless he has behind the plate that rare catcher who will not be just as baffled as the batter.

One of eleven children in a dirt-poor family of tenant farmers, James Hoyt Wilhelm was born in Huntersville, North Carolina on July 26, 1923. His father early saw his potential as a baseball pitcher and encouraged him to cultivate it. "Hoyt never had trouble getting out of chores if there was a game to be played," one of his brothers, Gary Cooper Wilhelm, who also showed promise as a pitcher, has recalled. The father was eventually rewarded with a 150-acre farm of his own, after Wilhelm became successful in baseball. Wilhelm's mother died in 1954.

Wilhelm first heard of the knuckleball as a child listening to radio broadcasts of games pitched by Dutch Leonard, then the foremost exemplar of the genre in professional baseball, and his only instruction in Leonard's pitch was a detailed description of it that he came across in a newspaper. He taught himself the strange delivery chiefly for fun, to surprise other children playing catch with him, but soon he realized that it was a unique asset, and, luckily, Ben Brown, his coach at Cornelius (North Carolina) High School, agreed with him. Wilhelm has said of Brown, "He did a lot to instill confidence in me."

When he graduated from Cornelius High School in 1942 Wilhelm was signed by Mooresville of the Class D North Carolina State League, and as a starting pitcher with that club he won ten games and lost three in the 1942 season. After the season he was drafted into the United States Army for service in World War II, in which he won a Purple Heart for wounds received in the Battle of the Bulge. After the war he returned to the minors and labored there for six more years, winning ninety-seven games and losing sixty-one for, successively, Mooresville, Knoxville, Jacksonville, and Minneapolis. His extraordinarily long minor-league apprenticeship was attributable to a combination of two factors: his temperamental unaggressiveness, or tendency to be content with his lot, and the blind spot that scouters of major league talent have for pure knuckleball pitchers.

Throughout his minor league career Wilhelm was a starting pitcher. He became a relief hurler —one sent to the mound as a replacement in crises— when he moved up to the majors as a member of the New York Giants in 1952 because the Giants needed a stronger bullpen and, besides, in the experience of Giant manager Leo Durocher knuckleballers were synonymous with relievers. In his first time at bat with the Giants, Wilhelm hit the only home run of his major league career, and in his first season he appeared in seventy-one games, more than any other National League pitcher. He saved eleven games for other pitchers and was himself credited with fifteen wins and debited with three losses. The first rookie ever to lead the league in both winning percentage (.833) and earned-run average (.243), he was runner-up to Joe Black for Rookie of the Year.

With a 12-4 record—tied for best in the National League that year—Wilhelm helped the Giants win the pennant in 1954, and in the ensuing World Series he pitched scoreless innings in each of two games. During four years with the Giants, he saved forty-one games, won thirty-eight, and lost sixteen. Most Giant catchers, like catchers generally, found it impossible to handle his pitches, and one, Ray Katt, set an all-time record for passed balls in one inning. But Wilhelm found an ideal receiver in Wes Westrum, who caught his erratic pitches as if by magic.

In 1956 Westrum left the Giants and Wilhelm had his worst season with the New York club, losing nine games while winning only four. The Giants, needing starting pitchers anyway, traded Wilhelm to the St. Louis Cardinals, and with the Cardinals in 1957 he pitched fifty-five innings and was credited with one win and four losses. As the season was drawing to an end he was waived out of the National League, to the Cleveland Indians of the American League, for whom he tallied 1-0 before the season came to an end. In 1958, when his record was 3-10, he began the season with the Indians and ended it with the Baltimore Orioles, who bought him on waivers.

When Wilhelm left the Indians his morale was in shreds, but he regained his confidence under Baltimore manager Paul Richards, who recognized that he was neither an ordinary relief hurler nor a typical knuckleballer. (Relief pitchers, however good, are generally viewed as men who cannot maintain their strength for long stretches, and knuckleballers have usually been fastballers past their prime who adopted the unusual pitch to make up for loss of speed.) With Cleveland, Wilhelm had done some starting—his first in the majors —and Richards started him on a regular basis. In what remained of the 1958 season Wilhelm won only one game out of four for Baltimore, but the one victory was extraordinary—a no-hitter against the New York Yankees on September 20, 1958.

With Baltimore, Wilhelm had a congenial battery mate in Gus Triandos, and Paul Richards enhanced Triandos' quick reflexes with an outsized mitt (forty-one inches in circumference, later outlawed in major league baseball). At the beginning of the 1959 season he had a victory streak of nine straight games, and his 1959 totals were fifteen wins, eleven losses, and an ERA of 2.19, the lowest in the American League. In the two following seasons his mound records were 11-8 and 9-7. But Gus Triandos left the Orioles in 1962, and no one else on the club could catch Wilhelm. In trying to handle his knuckleball, various Baltimore catchers tied the league record for passed balls in a game six times and in an inning twice. While his ERA was 1.94, his best up to that time, the catching problem showed up in his winloss record, 7-10. The Orioles reluctantly traded him to the Chicago White Sox.

In six years with the White Sox, Wilhelm won forty-one out of seventy-four decisions and saved ninety-eight games, and his overall earned-run average was 1.86. But his catcher, J. C. Martin, set a league record for passed balls, with thirty-two. In the American League expansion draft of 1968, Wilhelm was picked by the new Kansas City Royals, who promptly traded him to the California Angels, with whom he pitched 5-7 in 1969. On September 8, 1969 the Atlanta Braves, desperate for pitchers to help them win the National League's western division title, bought him on waivers. In the last three weeks of the season he won both of the games that were his, saved four, and helped Cecil Upshaw save another. The Braves won the title and the team's management credited the difference between winning and losing the flag to Wilhelm's solid end-of-season performance.

In 1970 Wilhelm pitched for the Braves until September 21, 1970, when the Chicago Cubs bought him. His combined tallies in Atlanta and Chicago in 1970 were fifty-three appearances, six wins (out of eleven decisions), and thirteen saves. On November 30, 1970 the Cubs traded him back to Atlanta, for first baseman Hal Breedan. The following year he had pitched in only three games and had no record when the Braves announced his unconditional release, on June 21, 1971. "I think I can pitch if I just get a chance," he told reporters. Wilhelm got that chance in July, when he signed a contract with the Spokane Indians, a Dodgers-affiliated team in the Pacific Coast League. After a month, in which he proved himself in eight games, he moved back up to the major leagues with the Los Angeles Dodgers.

Wilhelm is six feet tall and weighs 190 pounds. "He has a slender knobby look—not the thick bulk and ponderous waist that Cy Young had when he finally quit at forty-four," Bill Furlong observed in *Sport* (November 1968). "Wilhelm takes care of himself." To keep himself in trim he hunts quail, fishes, and runs around the outfield a few times before a game. His favorite sedentary recreation is listening to country and western music.

Hoyt and Peggy (Reeves) Wilhelm were married on September 19, 1951. They have three children, Patti, Pam, and Jim. The Wilhelms live in Columbus, Georgia, Mrs. Wilhelm's home town. The self-effacing, publicity-shy knuckleballer speaks with a slight, soft drawl, and his manner has been called "shoulder-shrugging, easy-going." Eddie Stanky who was his manager with the White Sox, once said of him: "He has the ideal temperament. . . . Nothing bothers him." As he was nearing his thousandth game in the majors, Wilhelm observed: "The next 1,000 are going to be a lot easier."

References

Christian Sci Mon p12 My 6 '67
N Y Sunday News p28 Je 28 '59 pors
N Y Times p32 Mr 14 '69 por
Newsweek 73:127 Ap 21 '69 pors
Sat Eve Post 232:25+ Ag 1 '59 pors
Sport 46:64 N '68 por
Sports Illus 31:128 S 22 '69 por
This Week p15 Ag 16 '59 por
Libby, Bill. Star Pitchers of the Major Leagues (1971)
Who's Who in Baseball, 1971

WODEHOUSE, P(ELHAM) G(RENVILLE)
(wŏŏd'hous)

Oct. 15, 1881- Writer
Address: c/o Simon and Schuster, 630 5th Ave., New York 10020

Ever since the Edwardian era, P. G. Wodehouse, the master of inspired inanity, has been entertaining a guffawing world readership with a uninterrupted flow of light genre novels that he has described as "musical comedies without the music." The fictive world that Wodehouse evokes is a loony Arcadia peopled with gentle caricatures of the British gentry of a bygone day—imbeciles in spats, surrounded by freakish or obnoxious relatives, practising ritualized chivalry no matter how intricate their misadventures. The most famous of Wodehouse's seedy, befuddled aristocrats, the antihero of many of his novels, is Bertie Wooster, a "stage dude" (Wodehouse's epithet) who is rescued at every turn by his omniscient, imperturbable valet, Jeeves. The Wodehouse canon, which grows by a book or two a year, now totals more than ninety works of light fiction. Sean O'Casey dismissed Wodehouse as "English literature's performing flea," and Wilfrid Sheed, aiming to praise with accuracy rather than dismiss completely, has called him a "genre hack" of "the high colloquial." Hilaire Belloc, however, termed him "the best writer of English now alive," while Evelyn Waugh once observed that his "universality" was unique in the twentieth century for a writer of "ephemeral" comedy. "Three full generations have delighted in Mr. Wodehouse," Waugh said a decade ago. "He satisfies the most sophisticated taste and the simplest." In Great Britain, Wodehouse has been published by Barrie and Jenkins since 1917, and in the United States he was published by Doubleday until 1951, when Simon and Schuster became his publisher.

"The name of Wodehouse," *Burke's Peerage* notes, "first occurs in Norfolk in 1402, when John Wodehouse was made constable of Castle Rising." Pelham Grenville Wodehouse is a member of the Norfolk branch of the Wodehouse family, headed by the Earl of Kimberly, as is manifest in the unusual pronunciation of his name, peculiar to Norfolk. The third of four sons, Wodehouse was born in Guildford, Surrey, England on October 15, 1881 to Henry Ernest Wodehouse, a British judge in Hong Kong, and Eleanor (Deane) Wodehouse, the daughter of an English clergyman. Mrs. Wodehouse gave all of her sons formidable names. P.G. was named after his godfather, Colonel Pelham Grenville Von Donop. His brothers were named Philip Peveril John, Ernest Armine, and Richard Lancelot Deane.

Until the age of four, Wodehouse lived with his parents in Hong Kong. From four until eight he lived with a family in Croydon, England to which the Wodehouses entrusted all of their sons. He received his elementary education in boarding schools on the island of Guernsey and in Dover, England and his secondary education at Dulwich College, a prep school not far from London. He

P. G. WODEHOUSE

spent his holidays with relatives, including his aunt Mary, a novelist who was the prototype for Bertie Wooster's harridan Aunt Agatha.

An outstanding student, especially in Latin and Greek composition, Wodehouse became one of the four Senior Scholars in his class at Dulwich. His extracurricular activities were Rugby, cricket, and editing the school magazine, the *Alleynian*. When he graduated, in 1900, his father, who had been forced by bad health to retire from the bench prematurely, was unable to send him to Oxford University. Instead he obtained for him a job as executive trainee with the Hong Kong & Shanghai Bank in London. While at the bank, Wodehouse wrote humorous verse, fiction, and articles for various publications. In 1901 he joined the staff of the London *Globe,* and three years later he took over that newspaper's humorous column, "By the Way."

In addition to his newspaper column, Wodehouse wrote encore lyrics for productions at the Aldwych Theatre in the West End and a spate of juvenile novels about prep school life, including *The Head of Kay's* (1905) and *The Pothunters* (1909). In one of the boys' books, *Mike* (1909), he introduced Psmith, the compulsive mouther of stilted rhetoric who became the hero of *Psmith in the City* (1910), *Psmith, Journalist* (1915), and *Leave it to Psmith* (1923). In his first adult novel, *Love Among the Chickens* (1908), he created Ukridge, the absent-minded scrounger with futile dreams of money who later appeared as the central character in short stories collected in *Ukridge* (1924).

Regarding the United States as "the land of romance," Wodehouse visited New York City—"an amazingly attractive city . . . then"—in 1904 and settled there, in Greenwich Village, in 1909. His income, which had been minimal in England, was swelled on this side of the Atlantic by the money the *Saturday Evening Post* paid him for short stories and serialization rights to a score of his novels, beginning with *Something New* (1914). The latter was the first of his books about the mad ménage of Blandings Castle, including Lord Ems-

worth, who is infatuated with his prize-winning pig, the Empress of Blandings; the butler Beach; and Lord Emsworth's foppish son, the Honourable Freddie Threepwood, among others. Wodehouse later revisited the Shropshire castle in a long series of books, including *Fish Preferred* (1929), in which there are two intricate comic romances, one of them involving Ronnie Fish, an amateur handicapper; *Uncle Fred in the Springtime* (1939), in which the Empress is the object of a kidnapping plot; *Pigs Have Wings* (1952), in which she almost loses the prize for fattest pig at the Shropshire Agricultural Fair; and *No Nudes is Good Nudes* (1970), in which an American millionaire and Lord Emsworth argue over whether the nude in a painting is the Empress of Blandings or one of the millionaire's ex-wives.

The Wooster and Jeeves characters were developed in short stories, collected in *My Man Jeeves* (1919), *Jeeves* (1923), and *Carry On, Jeeves* (1927.) Other collections of short stories by Wodehouse have included *The Heart of a Goof* (1926), titled *Divots* in the United States, *Meet Mr. Mulliner* (1928), *Mr. Mulliner Speaking* (1930), *The Man Upstairs* (1930), *Louder and Funnier* (1932), and *A Few Quick Ones* (1959). Wodehouse is a fast writer, once he has a plot in mind. As his career progressed he realized that his difficulty in thinking up plots was slowing his production, and he began to treat plots as precious commodities to be husbanded rather than spent quickly. Consequently, he wrote more and more novels and fewer and fewer short stories.

The first novel that Wodehouse constructed around Wooster and Jeeves was *Thank You, Jeeves* (1934). That was immediately followed by *Brinkley Manor* (1934), which had been serialized in the *Saturday Evening Post* as *Right Ho, Jeeves*. More recent novels in the series include *The Return of Jeeves* (1954), *Right You Are, Jeeves* (1960), *Jeeves in the Offing* (1960), and *Stiff Upper Lip, Jeeves* (1963). Among the characters in the latter are Roderick Spode, "who has the kind of eye that can open an oyster at sixty paces," Madeline Basset, "a soppy girl, riddled from head to foot with whimsy," and Stephanie Byng, "as loony a young shrimp as ever wore an upswept hairdo."

In the second and third decades of the century Wodehouse wrote drama criticism for *Vanity Fair* and lyrics for Broadway and the West End. Most of his work as a lyricist was in collaboration with Jerome Kern and playwright Guy Bolton on the shows *Oh, Boy* (1916-17), *Oh, Lady! Lady!* (1917-18), *Leave It to Jane* (1917-18), *Sally* (1920-21) and *Sitting Pretty* (1923-24). Out of that collaboration came such songs as "Till the Clouds Roll By," "The Siren's Song," and "Bill" (written for *Oh, Lady! Lady!* but dropped from that musical and later used by Kern in *Show Boat*), and *Oh, Lady! Lady!* became the basis for Wodehouse's novel *The Small Bachelor* (1926), set in Greenwich Village.

Wodehouse's work for the theatre also included adaptations of *The Play's the Thing* (1926-27), based on the Hungarian of Ferenc Molnár, and other foreign comedies. In two brief stints in Hollywood in the 1930's he assisted Guy Bolton on the script for the musical *Rosalie* (MGM, 1937) and worked on the screen adaptation of his own novel *A Damsel in Distress* (RKO, 1937). He did not work on the adaptations of his *Piccadilly* (MGM, 1937) or *Step Lively, Jeeves* (Fox, 1937).

As Alex Campbell has noted (in the *New Republic* for May 16, 1970), Wodehouse later wrote several novels and short stories in which "he characteristically turned [Hollywood] into a surrealist wonderland, peopled by powerful producers who had on their staffs not just yes men but also assistant nodders, and where alarm bells rang and lights flashed when a writer tried to make a bolt for it—'Alert the guard! One of our authors has escaped from his cubicle!' " Among Wodehouse's Hollywood stories is *Laughing Gas* (1936) in which an English gentleman goes to Hollywood to rescue his cousin from a vamp, and *The Old Reliable* (1951), in which an aging star, writers, and others vie for possession of a diary presumed to be scandalous.

In the period between the two world wars, Wodehouse was an international commuter, with a town house in London and a villa in Le Touquet on the French Riviera. Taken into custody as an enemy alien by the invading Germans at Le Touquet in 1940, he was interned in a camp at Tost in Upper Silesia. While at the camp he wrote *Money in the Bank* (1942), about a bumbling nobleman who forgets where he put the diamonds into which he has converted his fortune.

In June 1941 Wodehouse was moved from Tost to the Adlon Hotel in Berlin, where he was kept under house arrest. There a representative of the Columbia Broadcasting System approached him with the suggestion that he give a series of talks, via shortwave, to the American radio public, and Wodehouse, a political innocent, foolishly agreed. In June and July 1941 he gave five talks in which he made light of his experiences and the war. In Britain, which was then under Nazi siege, Wodehouse's reputation plummeted, and there was a strong movement in some circles to try him for treason throughout the war. The movement might have succeeded had not such ranking intellectuals as Malcolm Muggeridge, George Orwell, and Evelyn Waugh come to his defense. Orwell's argument in behalf of Wodehouse was published in *Windmill* magazine in July 1945.

After the war, Wodehouse lived in Paris until 1947, when he returned to the United States. *Full Moon*, a Blandings Castle novel that he had begun during his internment, was published in 1947. His other postwar publications included *Spring Fever* (1948), *Uncle Dynamite* (1948), *The Mating Season* (1949), and *Nothing Serious*. Later he published *Angel Cake* (1952), titled *Barmy in Wonderland* in England, about a hotel clerk who invests his inheritance on Broadway; *Cocktail Time* (1958), an Uncle Fred story; and *French Leave* (1958), about two British girls looking for rich husbands on the Riviera. Simon and Schuster has initiated a program of reissuing

out-of-print Wodehouse classics; Barrie and Jenkins is publishing autographed editions of the Wodehouse canon; and both companies have published omnibus volumes of his work. The BBC ran a television comedy series based on the Wooster-Jeeves stories in 1965.

Reviewing *The Girl in Blue* (1971), James Finn wrote in the *New Republic* (April 24, 1971): "*The Girl in Blue* has all the Wodehouse virtues . . . the sure use of cliché . . . the easy entrance into another display of love frustrated and love fulfilled, of fortunes supposedly gained and fortunes apparently lost, . . . of Americans and Englishmen bumping into each other's eccentricities. . . . His zany characters live in a world . . . in which family relations, family retainers, and money get entangled but never succeed in keeping young lovers apart."

In 1952 Mr. and Mrs. Wodehouse bought the ten-acre estate in Remsenburg, Long Island, where they still live. Wodehouse became an American citizen in 1956, and in the same year he published *America, I Like You*, an account of his long love affair with the United States. With the passing of the years the wartime animosity toward Wodehouse in his native land dissipated, and he was gratified when, in a gesture of reconciliation, Oxford University bestowed an honorary doctor of letters degree on him in 1959 and when, two years later, a group of prominent British literati headed by Evelyn Waugh marked the eve of his eightieth birthday with a ceremony of "homage and reparation."

P. G. Wodehouse (known as "Plum" to family and friends) and Ethel Rowley, who is also a native of England, were married on September 30, 1914. Mrs. Wodehouse has a daughter by a previous marriage. Wodehouse is a tall, freckled man, robust for his age, temperamentally shy but with a cheerful disposition, an optimistic outlook, and a sense of humor in conversation. Every morning he does calisthenics, then works at his electric typewriter until noon. In the early afternoon he usually takes a walk with his old friend, Guy Bolton, who lives nearby, before doing a couple more hours of work. He enjoys watching soap operas on television, and golf, swimming, and motoring have been listed as other recreations of his. He and his wife have a houseful of dogs and cats and are the patrons of the P. G. Wodehouse Shelter, a Bide-a-Wee home for cats and dogs in Eastport, New York.

References

New Yorker 47:43 My 15 '71 por
French, Robert Butler Digby. P. G. Wodehouse (1966)
Twentieth Century Authors (1942; First Supplement, 1955)
Voorhees, Richard. P. G. Wodehouse (1966)
Who's Who, 1970-71
Who's Who in America, 1970-71
Who's Who in the World, 1971-2
Wodehouse, P. G. Performing Flea (1953); Over Seventy (1957); Author! Author! (1962)

WOLFE, TOM

Mar. 2, 1931- Journalist; artist
Address: b. New York Magazine, 207 E. 32d
St., New York 10016

While Truman Capote is generally recognized as
the chief exponent of the new literary genre known
as the "nonfiction novel," Tom Wolfe is credited
by many critics with creating the nonfiction short
story. Wolfe describes himself more modestly, as
"a proponent of what has been called the 'New
Journalism.'" "I believe," he has said, "that it is
possible to achieve a nonfiction form that combines the emotional impact usually found only in
novels and short stories, the analytical insights of
the best essays and scholarly writing, and the deep
factual foundation of 'hard reporting.'" Wolfe burst
spectacularly upon the American literary horizon
in the mid-1960's with his *outré* articles on pop
culture for *New York* (then a supplement to the
Sunday edition of the New York *Herald Tribune*),
the magazine for which he still writes. Many of
his short pieces were collected in *The Kandy-
Kolored Tangarine-Flake Streamline Baby* (1965)
and *The Pump House Gang* (1968), and two long
articles by him were brought together in the controversial *Radical Chic and Mau-Mauing the Flak
Catchers* (1970). His other book, *The Electric
Kool-Aid Acid Test* (1968), is a report on Ken
Kesey's psychedelic-oriented Merry Pranksters.
Wolfe sometimes illustrates his work with pen-
and-ink drawings.

Some have described the wild rush of Wolfe's
prose, with its unorthodox use of italics, exclama-
tion marks, and repetitions of letters to suggest
prolongation of vowels, as "aural," but Wolfe himself has categorized its patterns as "logical," simulating stream of consciousness in himself or as he
imagines it in his subjects. A writer for *Newsweek*
(February 1, 1965) has observed: "Wolfe's prose
is as outrageous as his clothes. For the who-what-
where-when-why of traditional journalism he has
substituted what he calls 'the wowie!' Wolfe's
wowie is a seemingly anarchic barrage of metaphor
explanations. . . , neologisms, hip phrases, nonsense words, ellipses, onomatopoeia, learned references to Greek myths and the Pre-Raphaelites,
and architectural, medical, and comic-strip allusions." Karl Shapiro has said of Wolfe: "Tom
Wolfe is more than brilliant. . . . He is more than
urbane, suave, trenchant. . . . Tom Wolfe is a god-
dam joy. . . . Also, not to insult him, he writes like
a master."

Liz Smith, writing in *Status* (January-February
1966), described Tom Wolfe as having "a kind of
stubborn Southern Remembrance of Things Just
Past" and "the Virginia-born resentment of the
entire Eastern Seaboard clique's old leftover F.D.R.
liberalism and snobbism." Thomas Kennerly Wolfe
Jr. was born in Richmond, Virginia on March 2,
1931 to Thomas K. Wolfe Sr. and Helen Perkins
(Hughes) Wolfe. Before his retirement his father
was professor of agronomy at Virginia Polytechnic
Institute, editor of the *Southern Planter*, and director of distribution for the Southern States Coopera-

tive. Wolfe has a sister, Mrs. Murphy Evans of
Raleigh, North Carolina.

The book that most impressed Wolfe in early
childhood was Dixie Willson's *Honey Bear*, a story
in verse, with Art Nouveau drawings, about a baby
kidnapped by a friendly bear. "The poetry still
haunts me," Wolfe told Charles Monaghan of the
Washington *Post* (September 1, 1968), adding that
allusions to it appear often in his writing. "That
book set two things that I pursue in my writing.
First is rhyming poems used as narrative. . . . The
second thing *Honey Bear* suggests is what might
be done by blending drawings with print."

Later in childhood Wolfe became fascinated by
the Arthurian legend and composed his own additions to the stories of King Arthur. After reading
Emil Ludwig's biography of Napoleon, he tried
writing his own life of the historic French leader,
cribbing freely from Ludwig. At fourteen he discovered James T. Farrell's *Studs Lonigan* and James
M. Cain's novels. Shortly afterward he read John
Steinbeck's *In Dubious Battle* and began reading
the fiction of Thomas Wolfe (no relation), and at
sixteen he had "the great experience of discovering Faulkner." In counterpoint to his literary
interests, he played baseball, usually on the mound.

Wolfe obtained his secondary education at St.
Christopher's School in Richmond, where he was
coeditor of the school newspaper. In 1947 he
graduated from St. Christopher's and entered
Washington and Lee University in Lexington, Virginia, where he majored in English. At Washington and Lee he was sports editor of the campus
newspaper, one of the founders of the literary quarterly *Shenandoah*, and a pitcher on the baseball
team. He took his B.A. degree *cum laude* in 1951.

According to Terry Coleman, who interviewed
him for the *Guardian* (March 3, 1966), Wolfe tried
out as a pitcher for the old New York Giants when
he was twenty-one. Failing the try-out, he rejected
his professional baseball aspirations and matriculated at Yale University instead. Although his field
of specialization in graduate work was American
studies, the chief influences on him were the Russian postrevolutionary writers, such as the Brothers
Serapian group. "They were nonpolitical and said,
'We're for our talent,'" Wolfe explained to Charles
Monaghan in the Washington *Post* interview. "They
were in the Gogol tradition. . . . The Serapians experimented with all kinds of things, including
stream of consciousness."

Wolfe left Yale toward the end of 1956 and
received his Ph.D. degree a few months later.
"After five years in graduate school," he has recalled, "I very much wanted a break from the
academic life and went into the only field where
I thought I could make a living—newspaper work.
To tell the truth, I immediately found it glamorous. Nobody else did at that late date (December
1956), but I looked at it like the original 1922
Chicago cub reporter."

After a six-month apprenticeship as general assignment reporter for the Springfield (Massachusetts) *Union*, Wolfe joined the staff of the Washington *Post* in June 1959. He did local and Latin
American reporting for the *Post* and won 1960

Washington Newspaper Guild awards for foreign reporting (coverage of Cuba) and humor (stories and drawings of the 1960 Senate civil rights filibuster). Although the editors of the *Post* viewed him as their developing star feature writer, Wolfe was not entirely satisfied with the kind of writing he was required to do. "I didn't subscribe to the theory that every documented sparrow that falls within our circulation area you have to write about," he later told an interviewer for *Newsweek* (February 1, 1965).

In April 1962 Wolfe left the *Post* to become an artist-reporter for the New York *Herald Tribune.* During the four-month newspaper strike in 1963 he went to California to do an article for *Esquire* magazine on customized cars—automobiles with lowered chassis, souped-up engines, and added fins and chrome—and their young aficionados. In California, as Terry Coleman of the *Guardian* noted, he found a youthful new society, with a new life style and enough affluence to realize it. "Practically every style recorded in art history is the result of the same thing," Wolfe told Coleman. "A lot of attention to form plus the money to make monuments to it."

After months in California, Wolfe returned to New York with plenty of notes but no story. Byron Dobell, the managing editor of *Esquire*, anxious because a two-page illustration for the story was already locked into the printing presses, badgered him for the article, to no avail. "Finally I told Byron Dobell . . . that I couldn't pull the thing together," Wolfe later recounted. "O.K., he tells me, just type out my notes and send them over." Wolfe did, and Dobell ran the rough memorandum just as it was.

Liberated from traditional journalistic form by the *Esquire* piece, Wolfe poured out forty more torrentially impressionistic articles within two years. Most were written for the New York *Herald Tribune's* Sunday magazine *New York*, many for *Esquire*, and some for other magazines, such as *Harper's Bazaar.* His subjects included stock car racing, gangster society in Las Vegas, Cassius Clay, disc jockey Murray the K ("The Fifth Beatle"), Cary Grant, Huntington Hartford, and the pop, teen and "camp" worlds. One of the most successful of the articles was "Girl of the Year," about socialite-underground film star Baby Jane Holzer, written for *New York*. Commenting on it later, Wolfe wrote: "Baby Jane Holzer . . . is the most incredible socialite in history . . . a living embodiment of almost pure "pop" sensation . . . the hyper-vision of a whole new style of life in America. . . . But she is not the super-hyper-vision. The super-hyper-vision is Las Vegas . . . the Versailles of America . . . created after the war, with war money, by gangsters . . . the first uneducated, prole-petty-burgher Americans to have enough money to build a monument to their style of life."

In 1965 Wolfe supplanted Edward Albee as the chief subject of controversy at literary cocktail parties in the United States. "As the most spectacular journalist in years," Liz Smith reported in her *Status* article, "Wolfe caused severe jealousy and outrage pangs throughout the U.S. literary establishment when he sprang right out

of Pop Culture's forehead to become a star practically overnight. Seldom has anyone seen such visceral envies, such backbiting bitchiness, such voodoo malevolence directed at any writer-especially after he took on the *New Yorker* magazine." In his attack on the *New Yorker*, in two articles in *New York* (April 11, and 18, 1965), Wolfe dismissed the sacrosanct magazine as "mummified." Dwight Macdonald, a *New Yorker* staff writer and the patriarch of the New York literati, retaliated by anathematizing Wolfe as a "para-journalist."

Miss Smith went on: "He [Wolfe] was, by degrees, tasteless, brilliant, inaccurate, witty, perverse, undisciplined, electric, perceptively scary, exhibitionistic, and absolutely of the moment. His subject matter often trembled like Jell-O about to collapse . . . but there was no one else around who could touch him. The other 'soft' journalists just stood tongue-tied atop Roget's Thesaurus and watched him, the *noirest* of the *bête noires*, absquatulate with most of the fame and fortune." She added: "It wasn't only the literary establishment that took umbrage at Wolfe's elliptical verbosity, his maddening super-baroque style, or the agglutinated argot of his private visions. . . . His readers, and even the very heroes and heroines of his tales for our time seemed to resent him every bit as much as his literary peers. Of course, untold numbers of people were applauding."

Twenty-three of the articles were brought together, along with eighteen satiric drawings by Wolfe, in *The Kandy-Kolored Tangerine-Flake Streamline Baby* published by Farrar, Straus and Giroux in June 1965. The collection entered the bestseller list within two weeks of its publication and remained there for months. Reviewing the book when it was published in England by Jonathan Cape in 1966, John Gross wrote in the *Observer* (March 6, 1966): "Mr. Wolfe's writing *is* gimmicky (those italics are infectious), personalized rather than personal, artificially pepped-up. . . . [But] how else does one write about the man who paints monsters on Weirdo shirts with an airbrush, or the publisher of *Confidential*, or

Bob B. Soxx and the Blue Jeans. . . . Gibbonian irony would be lost on 'the first tycoon of teen'. . . . In some ways he is a literary equivalent of the Pop painters. Like them he borrows freely from commercial art and the comic strips. . . . Unlike the snobs who condemn pop culture en bloc, Mr. Wolfe is at least using his eyes and his ears. His whole pose, in fact, is that of an indulgent aesthete who even parodies himself by praising *Confidential* as a classic of the *esthétique du schlock*."

He continued to write for *New York* after it survived, as an independent weekly, the death of the *Herald Tribune* in 1966 and the demise of the *World Journal Tribune* in 1967. A second collection of his short pieces, including articles on Hugh Hefner, the publisher of *Playboy*, and Carol Doda, a San Francisco go-go dancer, was published under the title *The Pump House Gang* by Farrar, Straus, and Giroux in 1968. Reviewing it in the *National Observer*, (August 26, 1968), Bruce Cook wrote: "There is his notorious style, with its hyped vocabulary, run-on sentences, and wild punctuation. . . . But style aside, Tom Wolfe has a distinctive way of looking at things, of trapping significant experience in remote corners."

Simultaneously with that collection, Farrar, Straus, and Giroux published *The Electric Kool-Aid Acid Test*, an account of his travels with the Merry Pranksters, the group of freaked-out, LSD-dropping hippies headed by Ken Kesey. Through his contact with the Kesey group, Wolfe became aware of the current wave of experimentation with consciousness. "Everything that Kesey tried went far beyond the whole question of drugs," he told Lawrence Dietz in an interview for *New York* (August 19, 1968), "to this whole matter of self-realization and what you're going to do with yourself on the frontier beyond catastrophe. . . . I thought I'd never finish [the book]. . . . I was reading books on brain physiology, on religions, on sociology, books on psychology, cognitive psychology, all sorts of things. I was gradually coming to the realization that this was in a way a curious, very bizarre, advance guard of this whole push towards self-realization. . . . People are trying to avoid facing up to . . . [the fact] that people are free all of a sudden. . . . They really aren't needed in the work force in the old way. . . . I think there's going to be a tremendous boom in self-realization. . . . It'll take many different guises. . . . The thing to buy at this point in history would be a good self-realization company. . . . Arthur Murray's dance studio and Fred Astaire studios: they're a very crude type of self-realization business. . . . Dale Carnegie courses do the same thing. In the future, though, they'll come right out and deal with the psyche."

In April 1969 twenty-one members of the Black Panther party, the black revolutionary group, were indicted in New York on bomb plot charges. Murray Kempton, the journalist, among others, doubted that the Panthers were guilty as charged and set about to raise money for their defense and to publicize their plight, because, as he explained, "if they cannot be saved from being tried as strangers, they have no chance to be tried fairly at all." The culmination of Kempton's efforts was a party the following winter at the Park Avenue apartment of Leonard Bernstein, the conductor, and his wife, to which a hundred members of the social elite were invited, along with representatives of the Black Panther party. Tom Wolfe attended the party and wrote an issue-length article about it for *New York* (June 8, 1970). The article was again published later in 1970 as the first segment of *Radical Chic and Mau-Mauing the Flak Catchers* (Farrar, Straus, and Giroux). The second segment of the book was a report on the rebellious younger generation in San Francisco's Chinatown. Reviewing the book in the *New York Review of Books* (December 17, 1970), Jason Epstein wrote: "According to Wolfe, the people who attended Mrs. Bernstein's party were not moved by an innocent love of justice but by a snobbish infatuation with the unruly poor. It was, he says, 'nostalgie de la boue'—what used to be called slumming—and not a quixotic interest in fair play that brought these rich, fashionable, and clever people together to hear Donald Cox, a Panther field marshall. . . . Wolfe's sin is a lack of compassion and his intellectual weakness a tendency to panic when he finds himself beyond his depth, frailties that commonly accompany moments of great personal or public stress." Reviewing the book for the Washington *Post*'s *Book World* (December 6, 1970), Richard Freedman saw it differently: ". . . his attitude is that the Panthers are demeaned by such occasions."

Freedman continued: "The companion piece eking out this slim volume lacks the formal perfection of 'Radical Chic,' but is almost as much fun. 'Mau-Mauing the Flak Catchers' shows in gruesome detail how the government's poverty programs have neutralized the ghetto gangs of San Francisco by the simple expedient of cutting their leaders in on the swag."

Tom Wolfe is six feet tall, weighs 175 pounds, and has blue eyes, light brown hair, and a face that has been described as "boyish." Wolfe reportedly approves of Kurt Vonnegut Jr.'s description of him: "The artist sees himself as an Edwardian fop with a ploughboy's 3-by-8 wrists, and loves him." Vonnegut has also called him "a genius who will do anything to attract attention." Wolfe used to attract attention with his clothes, such as white suits, before the men's fashion revolution developed. Despite his image, he is reported to be soft of voice, gentlemanly in manner, and "vulnerable." Wolfe has said that his favorite recreation is window shopping and that he has no religious, political, or club affiliations. Among the authors he reads and rereads are Max Weber and Friedrich Nietzsche. He is a bachelor.

References

Guardian p7 Mr 3 '66
Newsweek 65:44+ F 1 '65 pors
New York 1:42+ Ag 19 '68 por; 3:4 Je 8 '70 por
Status 2:42+ Ja-F '66
Contemporary Authors vol 15-16 (1966)
Who's Who in America, 1970-71

YAHYA KHAN, A(GHA) M(UHAMMAD) (yä-hē'ə kän)

Feb. 4, 1917- President of the Islamic Republic of Pakistan; army officer
Address: President's House, Rawalpindi, Pakistan

BULLETIN: General A. M. Yahya Khan resigned as President on December 19, 1971 and the following day was succeeded in office by Zulfikar Ali Bhutto.

A professional soldier, General A. M. Yahya Khan became Pakistan's third President on March 25, 1969, when he took over the reins of government as chief martial law administrator and supreme commander of the armed forces. Six days later he proclaimed himself president, retroactive to the date he assumed power. He succeeded Field Marshal Mohammad Ayub Khan, Pakistan's President for more than a decade, who relinquished office after some five months of a steadily mounting crescendo of civil conflict. Yahya Khan, a close associate and loyal lieutenant of Ayub Khan, had no political experience when he took office, but as commander in chief of the army since 1966 he held the power needed to restore some degree of stability to a country lacerated by strife.
A native of British India's Northwest Frontier Province—now a part of West Pakistan—Agha Muhammad Yahya Khan (the title Khan is an inherited mark of distinction in the Moslem world) was born on February 4, 1917 in the town of Chakwal, in the Jhelum district, not far from the city of Peshawar. His father, Khan Bahadur Agha Saadat Ali Khan, was a superintendent of police. Like his predecessor, Yahya Khan is of Pathan, or Indo-Iranian, stock. He belongs to an aristocratic family, the Qizilbash, whose name stands for "red heads" or "red turbans." The Qizilbash are descended from the military elite of Nadir Shah, a shepherd boy who, after becoming ruler of Persia, defeated the Mogul empire of India and conquered the city of Delhi in 1739.
Yahya Khan attended the Government College at Lahore and obtained his B.A. degree from Punjab University in 1936. He then entered the Indian Military Academy at Dehra Dun, where he had the distinction of being selected as the King's Cadet. Commissioned a lieutenant in 1938, he was assigned to the Second Battalion of the Worcester Regiment and took part in operations in the Northwest Frontier region. After about a year he was transferred to the Third Battalion of the Baluch Regiment. During World War II, Yahya Khan served with his regiment in the British Eighth Army for more than five years and saw action in several theatres of war, including Egypt, the Sudan, Iraq, Libya, Cyprus, and Italy. He and a fellow officer were captured in Italy by the Germans but escaped. Yahya Khan was successful in making his way to France; the other officer, Major P. P. Kumaramangalam—who later became commander in chief of the Indian army—was recaptured.

GEN. A. M. YAHYA KHAN

After the war, Yahya Khan attended Staff College at Quetta, and after graduating in 1946 he served in various instructional and staff positions there. When Pakistan was separated from India and became a sovereign nation within the British Commonwealth in August 1947, Yahya Khan was the only Pakistani instructor at Quetta, and he was given the responsibility for establishing the first Pakistani Staff College. Promoted to lieutenant colonel in October 1947, he served as commander of various battalions, and in 1950 he became a general staff officer at a divisional headquarters. In 1951 he was promoted to brigadier and placed in command of an infantry brigade, and later he served as a brigadier general in the corps headquarters staff.
In 1957, at forty, Yahya Khan became the youngest major general in the Pakistani army. Serving as chief of the army general staff from 1957 to 1962, he helped bring about the reorganization and modernization of the army and its adoption of new weapons systems and tactical concepts. According to British sources, Yahya Khan was closely associated with the military coup of October 1958 that ousted Pakistan's first President, Iskander Mirza, and brought Ayub Khan into power and in the period that followed he was said to have played a key role in the administration of martial law. Concurrently with his military duties, Yahya Khan served in 1959 as chairman of the Federal Capital Commission, established to select a suitable site for a new national capital and to formulate plans for its design. When the Capital Development Authority was created in 1960 to oversee construction of the new capital, to be known as Islamabad, Yahya Khan was appointed its first chairman.
From December 1962 to August 1964 Yahya Khan served in East Pakistan as general officer, commanding. As commander of an infantry division in the 1965 war with India over the disputed territories of Jammu and Kashmir he distinguished himself in the Chhamb-Jaurian valley campaign and was awarded the Hilal-i-Jurat, Pakistan's second highest military honor. In March 1966 **Yahya**

Khan became deputy commander in chief of the army, with the rank of lieutenant general. He attained the highest position in the Pakistani army in September 1966, when he succeeded Mohammad Musa as commander in chief, with the rank of general. Ayub Khan reportedly promoted him to that post over the heads of seven generals with greater seniority. In 1968 Yahya Khan visited Moscow, where he may have negotiated a deal for the purchase of Soviet weapons by Pakistan.

Meanwhile, popular dissatisfaction with Ayub Khan's regime was mounting. Part of the discontent has been attributed to the government's failure to win the 1965 war against India. Furthermore, Ayub Khan's system of "basic democracy," which placed the country's political power in the hands of an indirectly chosen "electoral college" of men loyal to the president, gave the average Pakistani little voice in a government marked by corruption and bureaucratic inefficiency. The average Pakistani was also demoralized by the state of the economy. Despite the impressive gains achieved by the third five-year plan, instituted in 1965, peasants and factory workers were convinced that the cream of economic development was being skimmed off by a tiny clique of businessmen and army officers who monopolized government, industry, agriculture, and commerce. Twenty-two multimillionaire families controlled the economic life of the country.

The most immediate threat to the stability of Ayub Khan's regime lay in the differences between East and West Pakistan. Although united into a single country by a common religion, the two regions are separated by an enormous geographical, cultural, and economic gap. The Bengalis of East Pakistan, numbering some 73,000,000 of Pakistan's 128,000,000 people, occupy only 55,126 of the country's 310,403 square miles and are separated from their Urdu-speaking compatriots in the West by some 1,000 miles of Indian territory. Far less prosperous than the West Pakistanis, the East Pakistanis have generally been relegated to a second-class status, while the top posts in government, the military, and the economic establishment are occupied by West Pakistanis. Furthermore, the greater part of public and private investment funds for economic development had been allocated to West Pakistan, despite East Pakistan's greater need. Dissatisfaction in East Pakistan centered around Sheik Mujibur Rahman, a popular political figure, who had spent nearly a decade in prison for his separatist views, and who demanded a kind of semi-autonomous status—known as *purbodesh*—for East Pakistan. Another leading opponent of Ayub Khan's regime, former Foreign Minister Zulfikar Ali Bhutto, advocated a federal structure for Pakistan and had a large following among university students.

Violent student demonstrations broke out in several cities of West Pakistan in November 1968, and the unrest soon spread to the eastern part of the country. In a speech on February 21, 1969 Ayub Khan, acknowledging most of the major grievances against his regime, pledged to institute parliamentary government under a system of direct adult suffrage and promised that he would not seek reelection as president in the general elections scheduled for March 1970. But his efforts to soothe growing popular dissatisfaction proved futile. In the weeks that followed, the situation deteriorated, especially in East Pakistan, where governmental control had virtually broken down. On March 25, 1969 Ayub Khan resigned, declaring that he "could no longer preside over the destruction" of Pakistan, and turned power over to the army, which, he said, was the only "remaining legal and effective organ" in the country.

Immediately following Ayub Khan's resignation, General Yahya Khan declared martial law throughout the country and proclaimed himself chief martial law administrator and supreme commander of the armed forces. To help him, he named the deputy commander of the army and the heads of the navy and air force as deputy chief martial law administrators and designated two military men as administrators of martial law in East and West Pakistan. In his proclamation he abrogated Pakistan's 1962 constitution and dissolved the National Assembly and the provincial assemblies. Under the martial law regulations he sharply curtailed civil liberties, banned all strikes and political demonstrations on the threat of severe penalties, and set up military courts. In his nationwide address on March 26, 1969, he said: "My sole aim in imposing martial law is to protect life, liberty, and property of the people and put the administration back on the rails." On March 31, 1969 Yahya Khan declared himself president of Pakistan, retroactive to March 26.

Soon after coming to power, Yahya Khan took steps to restore political stability and return the country to civilian constitutional rule. By July 1969 limited political activity had been restored, and in August a civilian Council of Ministers was appointed. Addressing the nation on November 28, 1969, Yahya Khan announced that general elections would be held on October 5, 1970 to choose delegates to a constitutional convention. After drafting a constitution that was approved by the president, the convention would then become Pakistan's National Assembly. If the convention were unable to draft an acceptable constitution within 120 days, it would be dissolved and new elections would be held. Yahya Khan also declared that the country would be reorganized along federal lines and that the four provinces—Sind, West Punjab, Northwest Frontier, and Baluchistan—into which West Pakistan had been divided up to 1955, would be restored.

In preparing for national elections, full political activity resumed on January 1, 1970, although the country continued under martial law. In an address on March 28, 1970 Yahya Khan announced that the elections would be held on the principle of "one man, one vote"—a boon to East Pakistan with well over half the population. To reduce regional conflicts at the national level, elections for regional legislatures would be held within seventeen days of the national elections.

In June 1970 a fourth five-year plan was launched, allocating 53 percent of the total public investment to East Pakistan, and including a family planning program to control population growth. Other economic measures instituted by Yahya Khan include steps to raise minimum wage rates, to curb business monopolies, and to increase tax revenue. Attacking corruption, he brought charges against hundreds of former government officials for allegedly corrupt practices.

Despite Yahya Khan's reforms for East Pakistan, however, unrest continued to build there, and in the December 1970 national elections Sheik Mujibur Rahman's Awami League scored a stunning victory with a platform calling for Bengali autonomy. When the Pakistani president refused to convene the newly elected legislature, in which the Awami League held a majority, Sheik Mujib called for massive protest strikes in Bengal, seized effective control of the government there, and declared it the independent state of Bengal. Yahya Khan responded by sending West Pakistan troops into Bengal in March, and they soon quelled the rebellion, although rebel guerrillas continued to operate. Among reports of massacres and widespread atrocities by government troops, millions of East Pakistanis poured over the border into India, rekindling animosities between Pakistan and that country. By late 1971 President Yahya Khan was girding his country for war with India, while trying to find a suitable settlement to the civil war in East Pakistan.

A. M. Yahya Khan was married on April 4, 1944, to the Begum Fakhira Yahya. They have a son, Agha Saadat Ali Khan, and a daughter, Yasmeen Yahya. A short and stocky man with graying hair, Yahya Khan is an extrovert who enjoys social functions and lively discussions and is adept at dealing with others. At the time Yahya Khan took office, Patrick Keatley of the *Guardian* (March 26, 1969) noted that he was "perhaps more flexible in manner and more attuned to the political world than Ayub Khan" and that he had "a reputation as a tough administrator" with a "capacity for physical endurance . . . matched by a quick intellect." An avid sportsman and outdoorsman, Yahya Khan enjoys golf and shooting, but he also indulges in the more sedentary joys of reading. An amateur boxer in his youth, he became a patron of the Pakistan Amateur Boxing Association in 1966. Yahya Khan speaks English and Persian in addition to his native Urdu. His religion is that of the Shiite Moslems, the heterodox sect of Islam with a large following in Iran and southern Iraq but with only a minority among the Moslems of Pakistan. His civil awards are the Hilal-i-Pakistan and the Sitara-i-Pakistan.

References

Guardian p1 Mr 26 '69 por
N Y Times p6 Mr 26 '69 por
Nat Observer p5 Mr 31 '69 por
Newsweek 77:35+ Mr 22 '71 por
Time 93:32 Ap 4 '69 por
Washington (D.C.) Post A p16 Ap 1 '69
International Who's Who, 1969-70
Who's Who, 1970-71
Who's Who in America, 1970-71

ZABALETA, NICANOR (thä-bä-lä′tä)

Jan. 7, 1907- Harpist
Address: b. P.O.B. 886, San Juan, Puerto Rico 00902; h. 1400 Ashford Ave., San Juan, Puerto Rico 00907

The king of the harpists, Nicanor Zabaleta is a virtuoso performer on one of the most difficult of all musical instruments. Famed for decades among musical connoisseurs throughout the world, Zabaleta is relatively unknown to the general public because his chosen instrument is not usually the focus of sustained attention by audiences and critics. Nonetheless, Zabaleta has attained an unequaled reputation as a concert harpist in an era in which solo harp performances are neither familiar nor fashionable. Moreover, during a career spanning five decades, he has done much to restore the harp to prominence. This has been accomplished not only by his skill as a performer and by his thousands of concert appearances but also by his dedication to the task of increasing the literature of the harp. Not only has Zabaleta unearthed long-forgotten music for the harp by composers of the past, but he has also induced contemporary composers to write new harp works that he has added to his repertory.

Born on January 7, 1907 in the city of San Sebastián, the capital of Guipúzcoa province in the Basque region of northern Spain, Nicanor Zabaleta is the son of Pedro Zabaleta, a painter and musician, and of the former Isabel Zala. He has one brother, Diogenes. Zabaleta grew up in comfortable middle-class surroundings and developed a passion for music early in life. When he was seven he began to study the harp, and the following year he entered the Madrid Conservatory, from which he graduated in 1920 with highest honors. He made his concert debut in San Sebastián in 1918.

Zabaleta obtained his secondary education at the Colegio del Sagrado Corazón and at the Colegio de Lecaroz, both in San Sebastián, devoting himself to preparation for a career in business. He continued his harp studies with enthusiasm, but during those student years he looked upon his interest in music as an avocation. By the time he completed his secondary education in 1923, Zabaleta had given up the idea of becoming a businessman and decided to make music his profession. He began his musical career as an orchestral musician in San Sebastián and Madrid, while continuing his harp studies under such renowned Spanish harpists of the period as Vicenta Tormo de Calvo, Luisa Menárguez, and Pilar Michelena.

In 1925 Zabaleta moved from Madrid to Paris, where he completed his harp studies under Marcel Tournier and studied fugue and composition with Marcel Samuel-Rousseau and Eugène Cools. He became a concert harpist and recitalist about 1929 and soon was well known in most of the major cities and cultural centers of Europe and in Latin America. When a fungus infection of his fingers forced him to interrupt his concert career, he taught for four years at the Caracas (Vene-

NICANOR ZABALETA

zuela) conservatory. As he told an interviewer for *Time* (December 14, 1953), since he did "not have the teacher's mentality," he returned to the concert stage after his recovery.

Zabaleta made his American debut on July 5, 1934, when he appeared at Lewisohn Stadium in a concert conducted by his countryman José Iturbi. Commenting on his performance as soloist in Debussy's *Danse Sacrée et Danse Profane* and Ravel's *Introduction et Allegro* for harp, flute, clarinet, and string quartet the reviewer for the New York *Times* (July 6, 1934) wrote that Zabaleta "had an enthusiastic reception" and that his "musicianship commended him to a large audience."

One of Zabaleta's distinctive characteristics as an artist is his intense and driving sense of obligation to his craft. He feels a personal responsibility to enrich and enlarge the literature of the harp, a once-flourishing musical literature that he found sadly diminished because of neglect by composers and musicologists since the early nineteenth century.

Since there was little music available for solo harp when he began his career as a concert harpist, and since he had "no ability for composing," as he explained to the reporter for *Time* (December 14, 1953), Zabaleta was faced with the alternatives of depending on harp arrangements of works originally written for other instruments or of building a new harp repertory on his own by searching out lost harp works of the past and by persuading contemporary composers to write new works for the harp. Convinced that many harp works of high quality, dating from periods when the harp had been a popular instrument, were buried and forgotten in the libraries and manuscript collections of Europe, Zabaleta embarked on a one-man crusade to revive the harp and its literature.

Zabaleta's dedication and fervor, and the long, tedious hours he spent in research, were rewarded by many important musical discoveries. In addition to anonymous Spanish and Portuguese harp works of the sixteenth, seventeenth, and eighteenth centuries, he has rediscovered many forgotten works by known composers, some of whom were not generally thought to have composed works specifically for the harp. Among the lost works restored to the harp repertory as a result of Zabaleta's research were sonatas, concertos, songs, and other items of harp music by such composers as Beethoven, Handel, Johann Sebastian Bach, Carl Philipp Emanuel Bach, Johann Baptist Krumpholtz, Georg Philipp Telemann, François-Adrien Boieldieu, Carl Czerny, Friedrich Wilhelm Rust, Georg Christoph Wagenseil, Johann Ladislaus Dussek, Ludwig Spohr, Alonso de Mudarra, and Antonio de Cabezón. Many of those works are included in Zabaleta's collection *Original Harp Repertoire,* published by Schott in Mainz, West Germany in 1955.

The other phase of Zabaleta's campaign to rejuvenate the literature of the harp has met with equal success. Major harp works by contemporary composers written for his use include Peggy Glanville-Hicks's *Sonata for Harp* (1951); Germaine Tailleferre's *Sonata* (1953); Darius Milhaud's *Concerto for Harp and Orchestra* (1954); Joaquín Rodrigo's *Concerto for Harp and Orchestra* (1954); Heitor Villa-Lobos' *Harp Concerto* (1955); Alan Hovhaness' *Sonata* (1955); Ernst Křenek's *Harp Sonata* (1955); and Salvadore Bacarisse's *Prelude, Aria and Passepied* (1965). Other modern composers who have written for Zabaleta, or whose works he has introduced include Virgil Thomson, Walter Piston, Marcel Tournier, Alberto Ginastera, Jacobo Ficher, and Teodoro Valcárcel. Although the bulk of Zabaleta's repertory consists of works written for him and works that he has discovered, he occasionally includes harp arrangements of works composed for other instruments—such as the piano, harpsichord, violin, or vihuela—in his concerts.

Since his New York debut in 1934, Zabaleta has continued to pursue an active concert career. Over the years, he has given more than 2,500 recitals in the United States, Europe, Latin America, the Middle East, and Japan. Since the 1950's he has appeared at Town Hall in New York City almost annually. His Town Hall concerts are among the most eagerly awaited events of the New York musical season, particularly since a program comprised entirely of works performed on and written for the harp is now such a rarity.

In addition, Zabaleta has performed as a soloist with more than 150 of the world's leading symphony orchestras, among them the Israel Philharmonic, the Warsaw Philharmonic, the Madrid National Symphony, the London Royal Philharmonic, the Salzburg Mozarteum, and the Philadelphia Orchestra. He has taken part in the Casals Festival in Puerto Rico and in other international music festivals, including those at Berlin, Bucharest, Edinburgh, Granada, Prague, Santander, Venice, Lucerne, and Osaka.

Among Zabaleta's many recordings are the albums *Music for the Harp* (Counterpoint), *Five Centuries of the Harp* (Everest), and *Spanish Harp Music of the 16th and 17th Centuries* (Archive). For the Deutsche Grammophon Gesellschaft label, Zabaleta has recorded concertos by Mozart and Carl Reinecke, with the Berlin Philharmonic; concertos by Ginastera, Tailleferre, and Saint-Saens with the Orchestre National de Paris; and various works by Handel, Debussy, Hindemith, Ravel, Milhaud, and others. Zabaleta's recordings are often accompanied by liner notes written by himself.

In his concert performances, Zabaleta uses a harp built to his own specifications—with eight pedals instead of the conventional seven, the additional one serving to stop the vibrations of the lower wire strings. His virtuosity is all the more impressive because of the many technical limitations that reduce the musical possibilities of the harp as a solo instrument, such as its limited coloristic and expressive range and its lack of volume and emphasis.

Those problems notwithstanding, critics have been virtually unanimous in their acclaim of Zabaleta as a musical craftsman. A critic for *Musical America* (March 1957) wrote in a review of one of Zabaleta's Town Hall recitals: "He revealed the full character of the harp as a solo recital instrument. Its strength lies in the wonder of color that can be coaxed from its glistening strings, from the intricate counterpoint it is capable of tackling, and from the purity of its sound." Similarly, Harold C. Schonberg, reviewing another Town Hall concert in the New York *Times* (February 6, 1960), praised the "delicacy, subtlety, and immense control" of Zabaleta's performance and suggested that he "might be termed the Segovia of the harp, for he brings to his music the same type of dedication, style, and high art that the guitarist brings to his."

In the same vein, Eric Salzman described Zabaleta in the New York *Times* (February 4, 1961) as "an elegant master of his instrument" who is "very much part of the classical tradition in music," while Ronald Eyer wrote in the New York *Herald Tribune* on the same date that Zabaleta is "a musician of the most serious purpose and deep penetration. He has also the heart of a poet, as a good harpist . . . should have." A *London Times* critic, commenting on Zabaleta's performances in London in November 1964, wrote that "Nicanor Zabaleta is one of that select company of artists who, in the course of history, have lifted the instrument of their choice to new honour among men." More recently, Irving Kolodin wrote in the *Saturday Review* (February 20, 1971), following a concert at Alice Tully Hall in New York's Lincoln Center: "Harpists of the Zabaleta stripe (which is, of course, the royal purple) do not traffic in the demonstrative, the overt, or the ostentatious. They are the patricians of their profession, for whom a pure harmonic, a sparkling glissando, or a glistening arabesque calls for plaudits on behalf of their deftness in the low end of the dynamic scale as a bruising *fortissimo* arouses the beast in piano fanciers."

Nicanor Zabaleta makes his home in San Juan, Puerto Rico with his wife, the former Graciela Torres Alcaide, a graduate of Wellesley College, whom he married on February 22, 1952. They have two children, Pedro and Estela. A vigorous man of medium build, Zabaleta is five feet seven inches tall, weighs 160 pounds, and has graying hair and green eyes. He collects coins as a hobby. His religion is the Roman Catholic. In 1959 Zabaleta was awarded the Grand Prix National du Disque Français and the Harriet Cohen International Music Prize. He continues to go on international concert tours, and during summers he has taught a master harp class at the Accadèmia Musicale Chigiana in Siena, Italy.

References

Grove's Dictionary of Music and Musicians (1955)
Slonimsky, Nicholas. Baker's Biographical Dictionary of Musicians (1958)
Thompson, O., ed. International Cyclopedia of Music and Musicians, 1964
World of Music (1963)

ZIEGLER, RONALD L(EWIS)

May 12, 1939- White House press secretary
Address: b. The White House Office, 1600 Pennsylvania Ave., N.W., Washington, D.C., 20500; h. 2008 Fort Drive, Alexandria, Va. 22307

As press secretary to President Richard Nixon since the beginning of his administration and as his press assistant during the Presidential campaign, Ronald L. Ziegler has often been criticized by newsmen for being evasive, misleading, and incommunicative. But although they may chafe at his unwillingness to interpret news on his own or to fill in certain kinds of background details, they realize that he is doing exactly the job that Nixon chose him to do: serving as a transmission channel for whatever the President wants to be known about any given subject at any given time. The carping of the journalists is therefore accompanied by a certain grudging respect. John Carroll of the Baltimore *Sun*, for example, once commented: "He's a P.R. man. He doesn't care about the public's right to know and all that. He's the kind of press secretary I'd probably have if I were President."

The son of Louis Daniel Ziegler, a metal company production manager, and of Ruby (Parsons) Ziegler, a former public health nurse, Ronald Lewis Ziegler was born on May 12, 1939, in Covington, Kentucky. His ancestry is German and Scotch-Irish. He attended Dixie Heights High School in Covington, where he was the star fullback on the football team and attained all-state football honors. In 1957, on a football scholarship, Ziegler entered Xavier University in Cincinnati.

During the summer of 1958 Ziegler visited his parents, who had moved to Los Angeles a few months earlier for business reasons. Liking California so much that he decided to remain there, he transferred to the University of Southern California that September. At the university Ronald Ziegler majored in marketing (or, according to another source, in politics and government) and graduated with a B.S. degree in 1961.

RONALD L. ZIEGLER

A big man on campus, Ziegler was an officer of Sigma Chi fraternity, busied himself in the Young Republicans, and handled public relations for a wide variety of campus events, ranging from the Miss USC contest and the televised crowning of the Sweetheart of Sigma Chi to the university's Model United Nations and Richard M. Nixon's visit to USC during the 1960 Presidential campaign. He supported himself by working part time and summers as a tour guide at Disneyland and, during his senior year, by managing the high-rise apartment house in which he lived.

After his graduation Ziegler worked briefly as a salesman for the Proctor & Gamble Distributing Company. Already acquainted with many people at the headquarters of the California state Republican organization because of his work as a volunteer, in October 1961 Ziegler was appointed press officer of the Republican State Committee. Working mainly from his office in the State Capitol Building at Sacramento, and also traveling extensively throughout California, Ziegler got to know members of the state legislature and party officials. His duties included the writing of press releases and related materials, taking full charge of press arrangements for state conventions and other functions, and editing the monthly California Republican News. Ziegler held that post until May 1962, when he became an assistant to Herbert G. Klein, now President Nixon's director of communications, and at that time chief press aide in Nixon's California gubernatorial campaign.

During the campaign Ziegler became something of a protégé of H. R. ("Bob") Haldeman, campaign manager for Nixon and now one of his closest advisers. Haldeman was also vice-president in charge of the Los Angeles office of the J. Walter Thompson Company, America's largest advertising agency, and after Nixon's defeat in November he asked Ziegler to come and work for him there. Ziegler began with J. Walter Thompson in December 1962, became a junior account executive less than a year later, and in 1964

became a full account executive, the youngest in the Los Angeles branch of the agency. Managing such choice accounts as Walt Disney Productions, 7-Up, Blue Chip Stamps, Sea World, Continental Airways, and radio-TV station KNBC in Los Angeles, Ziegler was responsible for annual billings totaling more than $2,000,000. During his stint with the advertising agency, he gained experience as an administrator and became familiar with the problems and intricacies of television news coverage.

At the same time Ziegler sustained his lively interest in politics. In 1964 he attended the Republican Convention in San Francisco and worked part time in George Murphy's victorious senatorial campaign and in 1966 spent his vacation handling press relations in Robert H. Finch's successful campaign for the lieutenant-governorship of California.

When, in 1968, Haldeman became "chief of staff" of the Nixon For President Team, he brought Ziegler with him, and in June of that year Ziegler, taking leave from J. Walter Thompson, became chief assistant to Herbert G. Klein, who was again serving as Nixon's chief press aide. This time Ziegler had a small staff of his own. Acting, according to a reporter for the New York Times (August 3, 1969), as "in effect, head scoutmaster for the press," Ziegler conducted press briefings, arranged news conferences, prepared and distributed press releases, set up transportation schedules for reporters, and even took care of their baggage. According to journalist Jules Witcover in The Resurrection of Richard Nixon (Putnam, 1970), Ziegler's ability was demonstrated not only by his efficiency, but by his effective dissemination of "noninformation" when campaign requirements made it necessary for him to hold off reporters and buy time for his candidate.

"Ziegler was ideal for the role," Witcover wrote. "Himself a pretty good football player . . . he was well trained to execute the plays given to him and not to be overly concerned with the philosophy behind them. Bright and properly wide-eyed as required in any political dispenser of the truth . . . Ron for all his boyish charm was sharp and capable. He had one major advantage that made him particularly valuable and particularly effective in his job; he was a card-carrying 'flack'—a PR man. . . . He was never torn, as some of his colleagues who had been reporters often were, between protection of his candidate and the public's right to know. . . . Young Ron, though sociable and likable if excrutiatingly evasive, always knew which team he was on, and wanted it that way."

In recognition of what Joseph Albright of Newsday (November 16, 1968) called his vital qualities of "youth, the ability to sell a product, and the skill to make things run on time," Ziegler was elevated to the White House staff soon after Nixon's victory in the November 1968 election. On November 15 Ziegler was named a special assistant to the President, in keeping with Nixon's intention not to have a press secretary. Soon afterward, however, Nixon decided to name

Ziegler press secretary after all, fearing that a lesser title like special assistant might tarnish Ziegler's image and dilute his authority as an official spokesman. When he was officially appointed press secretary on January 20, 1969, Ziegler became, at twenty-nine, the youngest man ever to hold the $30,000-a-year post.

As press secretary, Ziegler meets with White House correspondents at 11 A.M. and 4 P.M. each day—the regularly scheduled press briefings—to make announcements concerning President Nixon's schedule, activities, policy decisions, and executive actions, and to answer questions on current events and issues. He is also available at all times to communicate any news that might break from the President, and he advises the President and other members of the executive staff on matters pertaining to the news media.

Not surprisingly, Ziegler is one of the best-informed men in the Nixon administration. His twelve-hour day begins at 6:30 A.M., when he is picked up at his home by an official limousine. During the drive to his office in the White House, he scans four major newspapers, a forty-page mimeographed summary of international and domestic news developments, and summaries of intelligence reports on problem areas and issues. All the while, he jots down notes on topics that he expects to be the focus of questions from reporters. On his arrival at the White House he confers with Haldeman, John Ehrlichman, Henry Kissinger, George P. Shultz, and other key Presidential aides and staff heads. He also sits in on meetings between the President and his advisors and subordinates, meets on his own with cabinet officers and other government officials, and supervises the activities of his own staff. Ziegler talks with the President several times a day and also has access to him at any time that the news situation may require Nixon's immediate attention, a privilege that Ziegler uses with discretion.

Before the beginning of each daily briefing, Ziegler prepares his announcement list and his answers to anticipated questions in writing. He is usually, but not always, punctual, often reads his answers from his prepared text and refuses to extemporize or clarify, although he may leaven his refusal with a good-humored joke. When he expects an issue to come up that requires specialized background, he brings along Kissinger or some other expert to discuss it with reporters. Ziegler is not averse to admitting ignorance when questioned on a subject for which he is not prepared and presides over press briefings in a firm, assured, and sometimes jovial manner.

Many newsmen questioned Ziegler's appointment as press secretary because he lacked journalistic experience and had only a limited knowledge of national and world affairs. They saw in him an advertising man whose job it would be to sell the President and his policies rather than to relay useful information to the news media. Especially during the early months of his incumbency Ziegler was criticized for displaying what some journalists considered an unwarranted self-confidence, for occasionally misinforming or mis-

leading reporters, and for evasive, confusing statements couched in what John Pierson of the *Wall Street Journal* (December 29, 1969) called "Madison Avenue fuzziness."

On one occasion, for instance, when questioned at the conclusion of a thirty hour halt on B-52 bombing raids over South Vietnam, Ziegler volunteered a circuitous statement which, when deciphered, said that the bombing had not been resumed, when in fact it had. The White House had to call in a senior official to clarify the matter. On another occasion Ziegler denied to reporters that President Nixon had influenced the Army's decision to drop its case against Green Berets accused of murdering a South Vietnamese agent, only to backtrack and reverse himself later.

Since then, Ziegler has tried to remedy many of those deficiencies and has learned to capitalize on his most important asset—his personality. Most members of the White House press corps genuinely like him and realize that much of what they criticize in Ziegler's official behavior is not his fault. As Candace D. Hopkins pointed out in "Press Relations with President Nixon," an unpublished study for American University, "Ziegler is held on a tight leash by his President. He is only allowed a small radius of latitude. This is after all one of the major characteristics of the Nixon Administration."

Unlike some of his predecessors, Ziegler plays no part in shaping Presidential policy, nor does he try to demonstrate his knowledge or his rapport with members of the press by substantial "backgrounding" in off the record chats and meetings. A communications channel from President Nixon to the news media, he reveals only what the President wants to have revealed. Ziegler is too skilled and disciplined to allow reporters to trick him into giving away anything that President Nixon does not want him to give away. Small wonder that, according to some newsmen, Ziegler has had to master the difficult art of ambiguity.

On July 30, 1960 Ronald L. Ziegler married Nancy Lee Plessinger, whom he met in the first grade in Covington, Kentucky, and later dated when she became a cheerleader in his high school. With their small daughters, Cynthia Lee (Cindy) and Laurie Michelle, they live in a white brick colonial house in the Belle Haven section of suburban Alexandria, Virginia. Once described by James Naughton in the New York *Times Magazine* (May 30, 1971) as a "fresh-faced, dark-haired, clean-cut athletic young man," Ziegler weighs about 190 pounds and stands six feet tall. He dresses conservatively. Although his gruelling schedule allows him little recreation, he occasionally plays touch football with reporters and White House staffers. Ziegler is a Presbyterian.

References

N Y Times Mag p9+ My 30 '71 pors
Washington (D.C.) Post E p5 Mr 17 '71 por; mag p4+ Jl 4 '71 pors
Who's Who in America, 1970-71
Who's Who in American Politics, 1969-70

ZUMWALT, E(LMO) R(USSELL), JR.

Nov. 29, 1920- United States Chief of Naval Operations
Address: b. Navy Department, The Pentagon, Washington, D.C. 20350; h. Admiral's House, Naval Observatory, Washington, D.C. 20390

Rapidly declining enlistment rates are forcing the traditionally hidebound military services of the United States to accommodate themselves to the dawning of the age of Aquarius. The pioneering concessions to the liberated spirit of contemporary youth have been made by the Navy, under the enlightened leadership of Admiral E. R. Zumwalt Jr., the youngest Chief of Naval Operations in history. Formerly Commander of United States Naval Forces in Vietnam, Zumwalt was chosen CNO over thirty-three senior admirals by Secretary of Defense Melvin Laird and nominated by President Richard Milhous Nixon in April 1970. He assumed the post three months later, succeeding Admiral Thomas Moorer, who became Chief of the Joint Chiefs of Staff. As CNO, Zumwalt has boosted Navy morale and personnel recruitment and retention by eliminating the senseless, abrasive, and demeaning regulations that enlisted men refer to as "chicken————" and by generally allowing sailors as free a life style as is compatible with necessary discipline. His relaxation of rules regarding such matters as grooming, dress, and shore leave is essentially a humanization and modernization of outdated tradition, based on a policy designed to "treat our Naval personnel with dignity, discipline, compassion, maturity, and intelligence, but most of all with twentieth-century common sense."

On November 29, 1920, three generations after his ancestors emigrated from Switzerland to the United States, Elmo Russell Zumwalt Jr., known to his friends as Bud, was born in Tulare, California. Zumwalt's father is a physician at the Naval Weapons Center at China Lake, California. His mother, also a physician, died in 1938. He has a brother, James, and two sisters, Irene and Saralee. According to Lloyd Shearer in *Parade* (March 14, 1971), Zumwalt "inherited sensitivity, compassion, a strong affinity to duty, and the rare ability to empathize" from his parents, and Zumwalt Sr. told Shearer: "Bud got a lot of love, time, and communications from us as a boy, and that's why he developed into a very secure man without a vestige of hostility in his personality." The father also observed that Zumwalt is "not afraid of change" and that "his strong suit is human relations." He quoted one of the Admiral's aides: "Once you work for Zumwalt, you become his slave for life."

At Tulare High School, Zumwalt was an A student, a tackle on the football team, and the valedictorian of his class. After graduating from Tulare High, in 1938, he studied at the Rutherford Preparatory School at Long Beach, California for a year while waiting for a service academy appointment. His original intention was to become an Army physician, but an old Irish whaling

sailor, a friend of his father's, visited the Zumwalt home, and the exciting sea adventures that he recounted changed Zumwalt's mind. He asked Senator Hiram Johnson, his sponsor, to change his service academy appointment from West Point to the United States Naval Academy, and Johnson complied.

At Annapolis, Zumwalt was a company commander, a regimental three striper, president of the Trident Society, vice-president of the Quarterback Society, a debater, and two-time winner of the academy's public speaking contest. His attitude toward meaningless regulations was reflected in the fact that in his class of 615 cadets he ranked twenty-fourth scholastically but 275th in conduct. Classmates remember him as "a ladies' man," "a great orator," "a fellow who got on well with everybody."

In June 1942 Zumwalt was commissioned an ensign and assigned to the destroyer USS *Phelps*, on which he served for a year. "He may be a good officer," one of his superiors on the *Phelps* was quoted as saying in *Time* (December 21, 1970). "But it was difficult to tell because he was seasick the first three months." From the *Phelps*, Zumwalt went to the combat information center of the destroyer USS *Robinson*, where he remained through the end of the war. He was awarded the Bronze Star for his performance in the Battle of Leyte Gulf and rose to the rank of lieutenant.

As hostilities were coming to an end, in August 1945, the task force of which the *Robinson* was a part captured several Japanese ships. Zumwalt, commanding an American crew of twenty, took over one of the ships, the gunboat *Ataka*, and sailed it up the Yangtze and Whampoo Rivers as the spearhead of the Allied occupation of Shanghai.

After the war, when he was considering returning to civilian life, Zumwalt applied for a Rhodes scholarship and reached the final selection stage before being turned down. In the immediate postwar years he was executive officer aboard the destroyers USS *Saufley* and USS *Zellars* and a professor of naval science in the NROTC program at the University of North Carolina. In the early 1950's, when his rank was lieutenant commander, he commanded the USS *Tills* and, in the Korean war, was navigator of the USS *Wisconsin*. In the latter assignment he received a Letter of Commendation with Ribbon and Combat V. After attending classes for a year at the Naval War College in Newport, Rhode Island, he headed the Shore and Overseas Section of the Bureau of Naval Personnel at the Department of the Navy in Washington, D.C., from 1953 to 1955. Vice Admiral James F. Calvert, who graduated from Annapolis with Zumwalt, has said: "If anybody tells you he spotted Bud as a potential CNO in the 1950's, he's kidding you."

During the last half of the 1950's, in the rank of commander, Zumwalt served successively as commanding officer of the destroyer USS *Arnold J. Isbell*, as lieutenant detailer at the Bureau of Naval Personnel, as executive assistant and senior aide in the office of the Assistant Secretary of the Navy for Personnel and Reserve Forces, and as commanding officer of the guided missile frigate USS *Dewey*. From the *Dewey* he went, in the rank of captain, to the National War College in Washington, D.C., for ten months of study, in 1961 and 1962.

While attending the War College, Zumwalt delivered a lecture, "The Problems of Succession in the Kremlin," the brilliance of which was the talk of the college. Assistant Secretary of Defense for International Affairs Paul Nitze heard about it and had him assigned to his staff as a desk officer, and when Nitze became Secretary of the Navy, in 1963, he took Zumwalt along as his executive assistant. Nitze has recalled: "I threw everything at him . . . NATO affairs . . . the details of the blockade in the Cuban crisis. . . . He was a tower of strength. He had energy and intelligence." For his work with Nitze, Zumwalt was awarded the Legion of Merit.

In July 1965 Zumwalt was selected for the rank of rear admiral and made commander of Cruiser-Destroyer Flotilla Seven, and in the latter assignment he won the Gold Star in lieu of a second Legion of Merit. Beginning in August 1966, he set up the Division of Systems Analysis within the Office of the Chief of Naval Operations, and during the two years he spent developing the division he served as the personal representative of the CNO within the Department of Defense and before Congress. For his display of "acumen, integrity, tact, and diplomacy" he was awarded the Distinguished Service Medal.

Zumwalt went to Vietnam as Commander of United States Naval Forces and Chief of the Naval Advisory Group in the United States Military Command there in September 1968, and the next month he was elevated to the rank of vice admiral. For his service in Vietnam he received a Gold Star in lieu of a second Distinguished Service Medal. While in Vietnam, Zumwalt reflecting on changes in the nature of war and in the attitudes of young personnel, "picked up a whole new set of ideas" about the way the contemporary Navy should be run. He tested those ideas as best he could in his war theatre command, and after becoming Chief of Naval Operations, in July 1970, he began applying them to the entire Navy.

In his directives, known as "Z-Grams," Zumwalt has ordered that "a wide variety of hair styles, if maintained in a neat manner, is acceptable," including "full and partial beards," and that a sailor is not required to stay sequestered on base or on board ship while his beard is growing; that beer may be dispensed in enlisted men's barracks and that stronger alcoholic beverages may be kept in quarters with individual rooms; that civilian clothes may be worn at shore installations and neat work clothes may be worn to and from assignments to avoid endless changes in uniform; that a day of liberty in port not terminate in the evening but extend to the morning after; that watches be expanded to leave more weekends free; that ships berthed together pool their watches so that more men are free; that low-cost charter flights be planned for families wishing to visit men deployed far from home; that make-work

ADM. E. R. ZUMWALT JR.

and "panic painting" (for making an impression on visiting senior officers) be eliminated; that barracks and personnel inspections, if held at all, not be allowed to interfere with weekend liberty; and that services at commissaries and exchanges be increased and that waiting time in any line be kept to a maximum of fifteen minutes.

In addition, Zumwalt has abolished the prerequisite of a major command at sea for the rank of admiral; widened freedom of choice in assignments; made a computer in the Pentagon available for matching exchanges of duty stations; set up a grievance system in which groups fully representing all personnel consult regularly with Zumwalt; appointed a personnel ombudsman; and toured virtually all installations himself, hearing the men out.

The Admiral is determined to raise the Navy pay scale, "even at the expense of ships." "If we must err," he has said, "it should be in favor of people rather than hardware." This attitude is especially commendable when one considers that cuts in the defense budget mean that the Navy will probably suffer an estimated 30 percent reduction in ships, from 900 to 600. To offset the reduction, Zumwalt is putting much of the money available into gas turbine gunboats as well as hydrofoils and air-cushion craft that are two to three times faster than conventional ships. Zumwalt's concern for maintaining Naval strength is in keeping with the Navy's preoccupation with the threat that the Soviet Union, in its view, poses on the seas. While understanding young people's apathetic response to talk of a Communist "menace," he predicts that events will force a change in that attitude within a few years.

A few Navy mossbacks refer to Zumwalt as a "Popularity Jack," suggesting that his permissiveness is primarily at the service of his own ego. But that jaundiced view of the Admiral's patent popularity is gainsaid by the practical effect of his progressive policies. In large measure because of those policies, the drop in Navy enlistment and reenlistment rates has been halted, if the statistics of his first four months in top command indicate a continuing trend. According to those statistics, the enlistment rate was 35 percent and the re-enlistment rate was 15 percent, compared to rates of 21 and 8.5 percent for the comparable period in the year previous. Recruiting ads have become hip, or "cool," in tone and message, stressing that the Navy was "where the mod look began." There is special emphasis on the recruiting of blacks, in keeping with a desire to bring the Negro representation in the Navy up to the 12 percent level it is at in the national population, and conditions are being reformed to make the Navy a more congenial home for minorities. Zumwalt has issued tough directives to end all vestiges of discrimination everywhere, from off-base housing to the kinds of food, books, and grooming and cosmetic aids available.

E. R. Zumwalt and Mouza Coutelais-du-Roche, a Franco-Russian, were married in Shanghai, where they met, on October 25, 1945. They have four children: Elmo R. 3d, James G., Ann F., and Mouza C. Zumwalt is six feet one inch tall, weighs 185 pounds, and has brown eyes and black hair. He keeps in athletic trim by running two miles a day and by playing tennis or swimming regularly. In his reading he prefers current political and sociological works to military books. The Admiral is a member of the United States Naval Academy Alumni Association, the Naval Institute, and the Alfalfa Club of Washington. He describes himself as a Protestant in religion but acknowledges no political affiliation.

References

N Y Times p21 Jl 2 '70 por
Parade p4+ Mr 14 '71 pors
Time 96:16+ D 21 '70 pors
Who's Who in America, 1970-71

PHOTO CREDITS

NECROLOGY

ACHESON, DEAN (GOODERHAM) Apr. 11, 1893-Oct. 12, 1971 United States Secretary of State (1949-53); lawyer; Under Secretary of Treasury (1933); Assistant Secretary (1941-45) and Under Secretary of State (1945-47); one of chief architects of post-World War II policy of containment of Soviet Union through United States military strength and political alliances; helped formulate Truman Doctrine, Marshall Plan, North Atlantic Treaty Organization, and policies leading to United Nations "police action" in Korea and the creation and arming of Federal Republic of Germany; adviser to Presidents Kennedy, Johnson, and Nixon; received 1970 Pulitzer Prize for book *Present at the Creation; My Years in the State Department*. See *Current Biography* (February) 1949.

Obituary

N Y Times p1+ O 13 '71

ADAMS, ROGER Jan. 2, 1889-July 6, 1971 Chemist; chairman of the department of chemistry and chemical engineering at the University of Illinois (1926-54); awarded the National Medal of Science in 1965 as "the one recognized leader" in organic chemistry for many years. See *Current Biography* (June) 1947.

Obituary

N Y Times p28 Jl 8 '71

ALLEN, JAMES E(DWARD), JR. Apr. 25, 1911-Oct. 16, 1971 United States Commissioner of Education with rank of Assistant Secretary in the Department of Health, Education, and Welfare (1969-70); resigned in controversy with Nixon administration over school desegregation and Vietnam war policies; as New York State Commissioner of Education (1955-69), promoted liberal, urban-oriented reforms; mediated New York City teachers' strike (1968). See *Current Biography* (June) 1969.

Obituary

N Y Times p1+ O 19 '71

ALLMAN, DAVID B(ACHARACH) July 18, 1891-Mar. 30, 1971 Former president of the American Medical Association (1957-58); prominent Atlantic City surgeon; named New Jersey's outstanding citizen in 1956. See *Current Biography* (February) 1958.

Obituary

N Y Times p49 Mr 31 '71

ARBENZ GUZMAN, JACOBO Sept. 14, 1913-Jan. 27, 1971 Former President of Guatemala (1951-54); part of an army junta that overthrew longtime Ubico dictatorship in 1944 and established a constitutional elective government; known as the "Red Colonel" in the United States because of his leftist leanings and strong nationalism; ousted by a United States-backed right-wing military coup in 1954. See *Current Biography* (September) 1953.

Obituary

N Y Times p39 Ja 28 '71

ARMAND, LOUIS Jan. 17, 1905-Aug. 30, 1971 French civil servant; engineer; president of Euratom, Western Europe's atomic energy community (1958-59); as general manager (1949-55) and board chairman (1955-57) of Société Nationale des Chemins de Fer, directed reconstruction and modernization of French railways; elected to Académie Française (1963). See *Current Biography* (September) 1957.

Obituary

N Y Times p36 Ag 31 '71

ARMSTRONG, (DANIEL) LOUIS July 4, 1900-July 6, 1971 Jazz trumpeter; singer; band leader; nicknamed Satchmo; grew up where jazz was born, in the black New Orleans red-light district Storyville; was a prime force in developing the gutsy Storyville sound into a national art form; known and loved by millions around the world for his instrumental virtuosity, raspy voice, wide smile, and ebullient personality; composed "I Wish I Could Shimmy Like My Sister Kate," among other songs, but was most successful commercially with recordings of pop songs, notably "Mack the Knife" and "Hello, Dolly!" See *Current Biography* (April) 1966.

Obituary

N Y Times p1+ Jl 7 '71

ASTOR, JOHN JACOB, 1st BARON OF HEVER May 20, 1886-July 19, 1971 Former publisher of the *Times* of London; bought the *Times* in 1922 and remained its chief proprietor until 1959, when his son Gavin succeeded him; relinquished family control of the newspaper to Lord Thomson, Canadian publisher, in 1966; Conservative Member of Parliament (1922-45); active in British philanthropic and press organizations. See *Current Biography* (May) 1954.

Obituary

N Y Times p36 Jl 20 '71

BALABAN, BARNEY June 8, 1887-Mar. 7, 1971
Motion picture executive; president (1936-64) and
chairman (1964-66) of Paramount Pictures Corporation; helped to found the Midwestern movie
theatre chain of Balaban & Katz, of which he became president in 1942; a leader in the financial
aspects of the film industry. See *Current Biography*
(October) 1946.

Obituary

N Y Times p36 Mr 8 '71

BEALL, J(AMES) GLENN June 4, 1894-Jan. 14,
1971 Former United States legislator from Maryland; moderate Republican who served in the
House of Representatives (1942-52) and the Senate (1952-64). See *Current Biography* (April)
1955.

Obituary

N Y Times p39 Ja 15 '71

BELL, DANIEL W(AFENA) July 23, 1891-Oct.
3, 1971 United States government official; banker; Under Secretary of the Treasury (1940-45);
member of Price Decontrol Board (1946-47); appointed by President Harry S. Truman as chief of
Financial Survey Mission to the Philippines, with
rank of Ambassador; president (1945-59) and
board chairman (1954-62) of American Security
and Trust Company. See *Current Biography*
(October) 1946.

Obituary

N Y Times p44 O 5 '71

BERLE, ADOLF A(UGUSTUS), JR. Jan. 29, 1895-
Feb. 17, 1971 Lawyer; statesman; economist; one
of the original brain trusters of Roosevelt's New
Deal; Assistant Secretary of State for Latin American Affairs (1938-44); cofounder and chairman
(1952-55) of the Liberal party; professor of corporation law at Columbia University (1927-64)
and author of books on economics; partner in the
New York law firm Berle & Berle (1919-70). See
Current Biography (June) 1961.

Obituary

N Y Times p1+ F 19 '71

BERRYMAN, JAMES THOMAS June 8, 1902-
Aug. 11, 1971 Cartoonist; on staff of Washington
Evening Star (1924-64); won Pulitzer Prize (1950)
for satirical cartoon "All Set for a Super-Secret
Session in Washington." See *Current Biography*
(July) 1950.

Obituary

N Y Times p32 Ag 13 '71

BLACK, HUGO L(A FAYETTE) Feb. 27, 1886-
Sept. 25, 1971 Associate Justice of United States
Supreme Court (1937-71); one of the most distinguished jurists in the court's history; briefly
a member of Ku Klux Klan in early 1920's, but
later repudiated membership; as United States

Democratic Senator from Alabama (1927-37),
supported New Deal programs of President Franklin D. Roosevelt; member of Supreme Court's liberal, activist wing; staunch defender of Constitution and Bill of Rights; wrote, or took part in,
landmark decisions favoring freedom of expression,
racial desegregation, rights of defendants in criminal cases, and equal apportionment of voting
power; retired shortly before his death. See *Current Biography* (May) 1964.

Obituary

N Y Times p76 S 26 '71

BLANCHFIELD, FLORENCE A. Apr. 1, 1884-
May 12, 1971 United States Army Nurse Corps
Colonel; nurse; superintendent of the Army Nurse
Corps during World War II; largely instrumental
in securing full military rank for nurses in the
Army, was first woman ever to receive a regular
commission (1947). See *Current Biography* (Sep-
tember) 1943.

Obituary

N Y Times p48 My 13 '71

BLATTENBERGER, RAYMOND Jan. 19, 1892-
Apr. 26, 1971 Printer; former government official;
was associated with Edward Stern & Company
of Philadelphia as employee and executive officer
(1917-53); as United States Public Printer directed
the Government Printing Office in Washington,
D.C. (1953-61), the world's largest printing
operation. See *Current Biography* (March) 1958.

Obituary

N Y Times p50 Ap 28 '71

BLAUSTEIN, JACOB Sept. 30, 1892-Nov. 15,
1970 Corporation executive; organization official;
founder (1910) and president (1933-37) of American Oil Company; president of American Jewish
Committee (1949-54); unofficial adviser to five
United States Presidents; delegate to San Francisco Conference on United Nations Organization
(1945) and to U.N. General Assembly (1955).
See *Current Biography* (April) 1949.

Obituary

N Y Times p40 N 16 '70

BOURKE-WHITE, MARGARET June 14, 1906-
Aug. 27, 1971 Photographer; one of world's foremost photo-journalists; member of original staff
of *Life* magazine (1936); noted for stark realism
of her pictures of Depression and World War II;
photographed world's leading statesmen; collaborated with Erskine Caldwell on book *You Have
Seen Their Faces* (1937), documenting poverty
in rural South; conducted long and heroic struggle
against Parkinson's disease. See *Current Biography*
(January-February) 1940.

Obituary

N Y Times p1+ Ag 28 '71

BOYD ORR, JOHN BOYD ORR, 1st BARON Sept. 23, 1880-June 25, 1971 British nutritionist; established the Rowett Research Institute in Scotland and other institutes that served as international centers for nutritional study; first director of the United Nations' Food and Agriculture Organization (1945-49); credited with having averted famine in Europe after World War II; recipient of the Nobel Peace Prize in 1949. See *Current Biography* (June) 1946.

Obituary

N Y Times p1+ Je 26 '71

BRADDOCK, E(LIZABETH) M(ARGARET BAMBER) Sept. 24, 1899-Nov. 13, 1970 Labour member of the British Parliament from Liverpool (1945-70); known as "Battling Bessie"; outspoken champion of social reform, noted for her colorful oratory. See *Current Biography* (July) 1957.

Obituary

N Y Times p32 N 14 '70

BUDD, EDWARD G(OWEN), JR. Mar. 23, 1902-May 20, 1971 Industrialist; executive vice-president (1943-46), president (1946-65), and board chairman (1965-67) of Budd Company, manufacturers of railroad cars, automobile body components, and other products. See *Current Biography* (July) 1949.

Obituary

N Y Times p34 My 22 '71

BURNS, H(ENRY) S(TUART) M(ACKENZIE) Apr. 28, 1900-Oct. 21, 1971 President and chief executive officer of Shell Oil Company (1946-60); presided over its growth as one of largest producers of crude oil in United States, served as board chairman of American Petroleum Institute. See *Current Biography* (May) 1954.

Obituary

N Y Times p42 O 22 '71

BYINGTON, SPRING Oct. 17, 1893-Sept. 7, 1971 Actress; appeared in Broadway productions, and in seventy-five motion pictures, usually in supporting roles, portraying dithering, effervescent matrons; attained considerable popularity in starring role of Lily Ruskin, "America's favorite mother-in-law," in CBS television comedy series *December Bride*, which began in 1954 and ran five seasons. See *Current Biography* (September) 1956.

Obituary

N Y Times p46 S 9 '71

CAMPBELL, E. SIMMS Jan. 2, 1906-Jan. 27, 1971 Illustrator; as a cartoonist for *Esquire* since 1933 created voluptuous odalisques and Eski, the magazine's white-mustachioed, bulging-eyed connoisseur of feminine pulchritude; contributed cartoons and illustrations to *Playboy, Life*, the *New Yorker*, and other magazines; first Negro artist hired by national publications. See *Current Biography* (January) 1941.

Obituary

N Y Times p40 Ja 29 '71

CERF, BENNETT (ALFRED) May 25, 1898-Aug. 27, 1971 Publisher; editor; columnist; lecturer; jokesmith and raconteur; president of Modern Library since 1925; founder (1927), president (1927-65), and chairman (1965-70) of Random House; won landmark court battle (1933) lifting censorship ban on Joyce's *Ulysses;* published works of Kafka, Proust, O'Neill, Faulkner, and other literary giants; compiled over twenty anthologies of humor; regular panelist on popular CBS television show *What's My Line?* since 1952. See *Current Biography* (September) 1958.

Obituary

N Y Times p1+ Ag 29 '71

CHANEL, GABRIELLE (BONHEUR) Aug. 19, 1883(?)-Jan. 10, 1971 French fashion designer; one of the most influential couturiers of the twentieth century; revolutionized women's fashions after World War I with the straight, simple, uncorseted lines of the "Chanel look"; after a fifteen-year hiatus reopened her Maison Chanel in Paris in 1954; introduced women to short hair, costume jewelry, and the famous Chanel suit, a collarless braid-trimmed cardigan jacket and slim, graceful skirt; created the world-famous Chanel No. 5 perfume; subject of Broadway musical *Coco* (1969). See *Current Biography* (September) 1954.

Obituary

N Y Times p1+ Ja 11 '71

CHIPERFIELD, ROBERT B(RUCE) Nov. 20, 1899-Apr. 9, 1971 Former United States Representative from Illinois (1938-1960); chairman of the House Foreign Affairs Committee (1953-54) and ranking Republican on the committee during the Eisenhower administration. See *Current Biography* (September) 1956.

Obituary

Washington (D.C.) Post C p4 Ap 10 '71

CHISHOLM, (GEORGE) BROCK May 18, 1896-Feb. 2, 1971 Canadian psychiatrist; head of World Health Organization (1946-53); lectured widely, stirring controversy by condemning "the Santa Claus myth" and other "pathological sore spots" of Western culture. See *Current Biography* (July) 1948.

Obituary

N Y Times p34 F 5 '71

CLARK, J(OSEPH) J(AMES) Nov. 12, 1893-July 13, 1971 Retired Admiral, United States Navy; commanded aircraft carriers in the Pacific during World War II and the Seventh Fleet during the Korean War; an expert on carrier warfare who outspokenly championed the role of air power in the Navy. See *Current Biography* (January) 1954.

Obituary

N Y Times p38 Jl 14 '71

CORTNEY, PHILIP Jan. 16, 1895-June 11, 1971 Industrialist; former president of Coty, Inc. and Coty International Corporation; chairman of United States Council of International Chamber of Commerce (1957-59); founded La Maison de France (1947) to stimulate economic cooperation with France; author of *The Economic Munich* (1945). See *Current Biography* (January) 1958.

Obituary

N Y Times p48 Je 16 '71

DAVIS, BENJAMIN O(LIVER), SR. July 1, 1877-Nov. 26, 1970 United States Army officer; first American Negro to attain rank of brigadier general (1940); as special adviser to European Theatre commander during World War II and assistant to inspector general (1945-47), worked to ease racial tensions and end discrimination in armed forces; retired (1948) after fifty years of service. See *Current Biography* (December) 1942.

Obituary

N Y Times p30 N 28 '70

DE KRUIF, PAUL (HENRY) Mar. 2, 1890-Feb. 28, 1971 Author; bacteriologist; medical history popularizer; coauthor, with Sidney Howard, of the play *Yellow Jack* (1934) and author of more than a dozen books, including the best sellers *The Microbe Hunters* (1926) and *The Hunger Fighters* (1928); former contributing editor of *Reader's Digest*. See *Current Biography* (July) 1963.

Obituary

N Y Times p38 Mr 2 '71

DEWEY, THOMAS E(DMUND) Mar. 24, 1902-Mar. 16, 1971 Government and political leader; was elected district attorney of New York County (1937) on his record of investigating and prosecuting racketeers and other figures of organized crime; Republican Governor of New York for three terms (1943-55); unsuccessful Republican candidate for President (1944 and 1948), member of a New York City law firm (since 1955). See *Current Biography* (September) 1944.

Obituary

N Y Times p1+ Mr 17 '71

DODD, THOMAS J(OSEPH) May 15, 1907-May 24, 1971 United States Democratic Senator from Connecticut (1959-71); zealously anti-Communist member and vice-chairman of Senate Internal Security subcommittee; special assistant in Justice Department (1938-54); executive trial counsel at Nuremberg war crimes trials (1945-46); member of House of Representatives (1953-57); censured by Senate for irregularities in his financial affairs (1967); defeated in bid for third Senate term (1970). See *Current Biography* (September) 1959.

Obituary

N Y Times p43 My 25 '71

DONNELLY, WALTER J(OSEPH) Jan. 9, 1896-Nov. 12, 1970 United States diplomat; a leading authority on Latin American affairs; held various diplomatic posts in Latin America (1929-50); Ambassador and High Commissioner for Austria (1950-52); High Commissioner for West Germany (1952). See *Current Biography* (September) 1952.

Obituary

N Y Times p40 N 13 '70

DUVALIER, FRANÇOIS Apr. 14, 1907-Apr. 21, 1971 President of Republic of Haiti since 1957; a ruthless dictator who suppressed all opposition through torture, terrorism, and murder; kept his black countrymen in abject poverty and ignorance; proclaimed himself President for Life in 1964; designated his son, Jean-Claude, as his successor in 1971; a physician and former public health officer, relished his nickname of "Papa Doc." See *Current Biography* (September) 1958.

Obituary

N Y Times p1+ Ap 23 '71

ELIOT, GEORGE FIELDING June 22, 1894-Apr. 21, 1971 Author; lecturer; radio commentator; during World War II was military correspondent and analyst for the New York *Herald Tribune* and the Columbia Broadcasting System; wrote columns on military affairs for General Features Syndicate (1950-67); author of books on military subjects, including *If Russia Strikes* (1949). See *Current Biography* (January-February) 1940.

Obituary

N Y Times p44 Ap 22 '71

ETTINGER, RICHARD P(RENTICE) Sept. 26, 1893-Feb. 24, 1971 Publisher; co-founder (1913), president (1913-49), and board chairman (1949-71) of Prentice Hall Inc. See *Current Biography* (December) 1951.

Obituary

N Y Times p40 F 25 '71

EVANS, HERBERT M(cLEAN) Sept. 23, 1882-Mar. 6, 1971- Physician; endocrinologist; discoverer of Vitamin E; taught at Johns Hopkins University (1908-15) and University of California at Berkeley (from 1915); headed Institute of Experimental Biology at Berkeley (1930-52). See *Current Biography* (July) 1959.

Obituary

N Y Times p26 Mr 8 '71

FERNANDEL May 8, 1903-Feb. 26, 1971 Motion picture comedian; known for equine, mobile face with radiant, toothy smile and indignant, wide-eyed pout; since 1930, one of France's leading box-office attractions; during a four-decade career played some four film roles a year, ranging from warmhearted bumpkins flailing against odds to the pugnacious anti-Communist Italian village priest in the Don Camillo series. See *Current Biography* (October) 1955.

Obituary

N Y Times p60 F 28 '71

FRAZER, JOSEPH W(ASHINGTON) Mar. 4, 1892-Aug. 7, 1971 Industrialist; with Henry J. Kaiser founded in 1945 the Kaiser-Frazer Corporation, which became the nation's fourth largest producer of automobiles before halting production in 1953; president of Willys-Overland Motors, Inc., manufacturers of low-priced passenger cars and jeeps (1939-43). See *Current Biography* (March) 1946.

Obituary

N Y Times p59 Ag 8 '71

GARCIA, CARLOS P. Nov. 4, 1896-June 14, 1971 President of Philippines (1957-61); led anti-Japanese guerrilla forces during World War II; member of Senate (1941-53); Vice-President (1953-57); Minister of Foreign Affairs (1954-57); adhered to pro-American foreign policy; promoted agrarian reform and industrialization. See *Current Biography* (June) 1957.

Obituary

N Y Times p46 Je 15 '71

GIPSON, LAWRENCE HENRY Dec. 7, 1880-Sept. 26, 1971 Historian; head of history and government department (1924-46) and research professor (1946-52) at Lehigh University; author of fifteen-volume *The British Empire Before the American Revolution* (1936-70); received Bancroft Prize (1950) and Pulitzer Prize (1962), among other awards. See *Current Biography* (October) 1954.

Obituary

N Y Times p38 S 27 '71

GIVENS, WILLARD E(ARL) Dec. 10, 1886-May 20, 1971 Educator; executive secretary of National Education Association (1935-52); superintendent of public instruction for Hawaii (1923-25); superintendent of public schools in San Diego (1927-28) and Oakland (1928-35), California; helped found World Confederation of Organizations of the Teaching Profession (1946); adviser and delegate to UNESCO. See *Current Biography* (September) 1948.

Obituary

Washington (D.C.) Post B p4 My 22 '71

GLUECK, NELSON June 4, 1900-Feb. 12, 1971 One of the foremost Biblical archeologists of the century; since 1947 president of Hebrew Union College in Cincinnati, now called the Hebrew Union College-Jewish Institute of Religion; discovered King Solomon's mines and many other ancient sites in Palestine, using the Bible as his guide. See *Current Biography* (July) 1969.

Obituary

N Y Times p75 F 15 '71

GOLDBERG, RUBE July 4, 1883-Dec. 7, 1970 Cartoonist; satirized American folkways and modern technology with his comic drawings of zany, complicated inventions designed to achieve simple ends; creator of such comic strip characters as "Boob McNutt" and "Lala Palooza"; editorial cartoonist (1938-63) for New York *Sun, Journal-American,* and King Features Syndicate; won Pulitzer Prize (1948) for cartoon warning of dangers of nuclear weapons. See *Current Biography* (September) 1948.

Obituary

N Y Times p1+ D 8 '70

GRACE, ALONZO G(ASKELL) Aug. 14, 1896-Oct. 19, 1971 Educator; Connecticut State Commissioner of Education (1938-48); director of Educational and Cultural Relations Division of American Military Government in Germany (1948-49); held administrative posts at University of Chicago and New York University; retired (1970) as dean of University of Illinois College of Education. See *Current Biography* (January) 1950.

Obituary

N Y Times p36 O 23 '71

GUGGENHEIM, HARRY F(RANK) Aug. 23, 1890-Jan. 22, 1971 Publisher; industrialist; philanthropist; scion of philanthropic family that became rich through mining operations; in 1939 with his wife Alicia Patterson founded *Newsday,* the Long Island newspaper that is now the nation's largest suburban daily; headed the Solomon R. Guggenheim Foundation and the Daniel Guggenheim Fund for Aeronautics. See *Current Biography* (October) 1956.

Obituary

N Y Times p1+ Ja 23 '71

GUTHRIE, SIR (WILLIAM) TYRONE July 2, 1900-May 15, 1971 Theatrical director and producer; noted for imaginative stagings; director of Stratford (Ontario) Shakespeare Festival (1953-55); founded Tyrone Guthrie repertory theatre in Minneapolis (1963); author of *Top of the Ladder* (1950) and other plays; knighted in 1961. See *Current Biography* (July) 1954.

Obituary

N Y Times p1+ My 16 '71

HARRIDGE, WILL(IAM) Oct. 16, 1885-Apr. 9, 1971 Former president of the American League of Professional Baseball Clubs (1931-58); served as American League administrator for twenty years before assuming presidency. See *Current Biography* (September) 1949.

Obituary

N Y Times p59 Ap 11 '71

HARRINGTON, RUSSELL C(HASE) Nov. 9, 1890-Aug. 7, 1971 United States government official; commissioner of the Internal Revenue Service during Eisenhower administration (1955-58); instituted reforms in revenue collection procedures; introduced employee training programs; awarded Alexander Hamilton gold medal for meritorious service (1958). See *Current Biography* (April) 1956.

Obituary

Washington (D.C.) Post C p4 Ag 9 '71

HART, THOMAS C(HARLES) June 12, 1877-July 4, 1971 Retired Admiral, United States Navy; was on active duty for half a century, through World War II, in which he commanded Asiatic Fleet and, later, sat on Navy's General Board; filling a vacancy, served as appointed Republican United States Senator from Connecticut (1945-47). See *Current Biography* (January) 1942.

Obituary

N Y Times p2 Jl 5 '71

HAYWARD, LELAND Sept. 13, 1902-Mar. 18, 1971 Producer; former theatrical agent for Judy Garland, Clark Gable, and other stars and literary agent for Ernest Hemingway, Edna Ferber, and other writers; began producing with *A Bell for Adano* (1944); producer or coproducer of *South Pacific, The Sound of Music,* and other Broadway successes, as well as motion pictures and TV shows; cofounder of Southwest Airways (1946). See *Current Biography* (February) 1949.

Obituary

N Y Times p1+ Mr 19 '71

HEFLIN, VAN Dec. 13, 1910-July 23, 1971 Actor; won Oscar for supporting role of alcoholic scholar in film *Johnny Eager* (1942); among his other Hollywood credits were the homesteader in *Shane* (1953) and the mad bomber on the plane in *Airport* (1970); on Broadway, played the sardonic reporter in *Philadelphia Story* (1939), the tragic longshoreman in *A View from the Bridge* (1955), and Louis Nizer in *A Case of Libel* (1964), among other roles. See *Current Biography* (July) 1943.

Obituary

N Y Times p28 Jl 24 '71

HICKENLOOPER, BOURKE B(LAKEMORE) July 21, 1896-Sept. 4, 1971 United States Republican Senator from Iowa (1945-69); Governor of Iowa (1943-45); influential member of Senate Foreign Relations Committee; chairman of Joint Congressional Committee on Atomic Energy; cosponsored Atomic Energy Act of 1954; author of amendment to 1962 foreign aid bill, denying aid to countries expropriating United States-owned property; moderately conservative in his voting record. See *Current Biography* (May) 1947.

Obituary

N Y Times p41 S 5 '71

HILL, HARRY W(ILBUR) Apr. 7, 1890-July 19, 1971 Retired Vice-Admiral, United States Navy; during World War II commanded amphibious forces that captured Okinawa and other islands in the Pacific; commandant of the National War College (1946-49); superintendent of the United States Naval Academy (1950-52). See *Current Biography* (July) 1950.

Obituary

N Y Times p38 Jl 21 '71

HOLLAND, SPESSARD L(INDSEY) July 10, 1892-Nov. 6, 1971 Governor of Florida (1941-45); United States Senator (1946-70); generally voted with conservative Southern Democratic bloc in Senate, but played major role in effecting passage of 24th Amendment to Constitution (1946), abolishing poll tax. See *Current Biography* (February) 1950.

Obituary

N Y Times p85 N 7 '71

HORSFALL, FRANK L(APPIN), JR. Dec. 14, 1906-Feb. 19, 1971 Physician; virologist; research director; staff member of Rockefeller Institute for Medical Research (1934-60); president and director of Sloan-Kettering Institute for Cancer Research (since 1960). See *Current Biography* (January) 1961.

Obituary

N Y Times p30 F 20 '71

HOUSSAY, BERNARDO ALBERTO Apr. 10, 1887-Sept. 21, 1971 Argentine physiologist; shared 1947 Nobel Prize in Medicine and Physiology for discovery of role of pituitary hormones in sugar metabolism; faculty member of University of Buenos Aires from 1907; headed physiology department of its faculty of medicine (1919-43, 1945-46, 1955-57); research professor (1957-68); opponent of dictatorship of General Juan Perón. See *Current Biography* (January) 1948.

Obituary

N Y Times p50 S 22 '71

HULL, HELEN R(OSE) 1888-July 15, 1971 Author; educator; published some sixty short stories and twenty novels, including *Heat Lightning* (1932) and *Through the House Door* (1940); usually wrote about marriage and family life; taught fiction writing at Columbia University (1915-56). See *Current Biography* (May) 1940.

Obituary

N Y Times p26 Jl 17 '71

HURLEY, ROY T. June 3, 1896-Oct. 31, 1971 Industrialist; president (1949-61) and board chairman (1952-61) of Curtiss-Wright Corporation; a leading spokesman for expansion of aircraft industry for military purposes; served in managerial posts with Bendix Aviation Corporation and Ford Motor Company in 1930's and 1940's; deputy chief of ordnance of United States Army during World War II. See *Current Biography* (June) 1956.

Obituary

N Y Times p3 N 0 '71

ISELIN, COLUMBUS O'D(ONNELL) Sept. 25, 1904-Jan. 5, 1971 Oceanographer; director of the Woods Hole Oceanographic Institution (1940-50, 1956-57); oversaw tenfold expansion of Woods Hole during World War II; received Medal of Merit in 1948. See *Current Biography* (November) 1948.

Obituary

N Y Times p40 Ja 6 '71

JACKSON, WILLIAM H(ARDING) Mar. 25, 1901-Sept. 28, 1971 United States government official; lawyer; investment banker; deputy director of Central Intelligence Agency (1950-51); adviser and special assistant to President Dwight D. Eisenhower for foreign policy and national security affairs. See *Current Biography* (March) 1951.

Obituary

N Y Times p36 S 29 '71

JOHNSON, ALVIN (SAUNDERS) Dec. 18, 1874-June 7, 1971 Educator; economist; helped found (1919) the New School for Social Research; taught at Columbia, Yale, and other universities;

president of New School (1928-45); editor of *New Republic* (1917-23); author of scholarly works, novels, and autobiography *Pioneer's Progress* (1960). See *Current Biography* (August) 1942.

Obituary

N Y Times p1+ Je 9 '71

KATZ-SUCHY, JULIUSZ Jan. 28, 1912-Oct. 28, 1971 Former Polish diplomat; university professor; Ambassador to United Nations (1947-51); Ambassador to India (1957-62); appointed (1964) to chair of international relations and diplomatic history at University of Warsaw, but ousted (1968) because of liberal views; defected to Denmark (1970); assistant professor of political science at University of Aarhus (1970-71). See *Current Biography* (June) 1951.

Obituary

N Y Times p44 O 29 '71

KELLY, MERVIN J(OE) Feb. 14, 1894-Mar. 18, 1971 Physicist; former president and board chairman of Bell Laboratories; headed military research at Bell labs during World War II and after; adviser to NASA after his retirement from Bell in 1959. See *Current Biography* (October) 1956.

Obituary

N Y Times p32 Mr 20 '71

KENT, ROCKWELL June 21, 1882-Mar. 13, 1971 Artist; created oil paintings, watercolors, lithographs, woodcuts in vigorous, romantic-realistic style reflecting affinity with ruggedness in nature; author of several books, including autobiography, *It's Me O Lord* (1955); illustrated his own and other books, including Chaucer and Shakespeare; exponent of left-wing causes; winner of Lenin Peace Prize (1967). See *Current Biography* (November) 1942.

Obituary

N Y Times p1+ Mr 14 '71

KHRUSHCHEV, NIKITA S(ERGEYEVICH) Apr. 17, 1894-Sept. 11, 1971 First Secretary of Soviet Communist party (1953-64) and Chairman of Council of Ministers (Premier) of Soviet Union (1958-64); ebullient leader of Communist bloc during crucial years of cold war era; instituted de-Stalinization policy after denouncing excesses of Stalin regime (1956); suppressed Hungarian revolt (1956); adopted peaceful coexistence policy toward West, but engaged in several confrontations with United States, culminating in Cuban missile crisis (1962); came into conflict with Chinese Communist leaders over strategy toward West and other issues in late 1950's; lived in retirement after enforced resignation from government and party posts in October 1964. See *Current Biography* (July) 1954.

Obituary

N Y Times p1+ S 12 '71

KNATCHBULL-HUGESSEN, SIR HUGHE (MONTGOMERY) Mar. 26, 1886-Mar. 22, 1971 British diplomat; Ambassador to neutral Turkey during World War II; victim of a famous spy case; had his secret papers describing the Normandy invasion stolen by a servant who sold them to the Germans. See *Current Biography* (March) 1943.

Obituary

N Y Times p40 Mr 23 '71

KNATHS, (OTTO) KARL Oct. 21, 1891-Mar. 9, 1971 Abstract painter, variously described as a cubist with poetic qualities of expressionism or a cubist with representational elements vaguely suggestive of Cape Cod landscapes; achieved recognition at a time of declining popularity of cubism in the United States. See *Current Biography* (July) 1953.

Obituary

N Y Times p40 Mr 12 '71

KOLLMAR, RICHARD Dec. 31, 1910-Jan. 7, 1971 Radio and stage actor; producer; with his wife Dorothy Kilgallen broadcast *Breakfast with Dorothy and Dick* on WOR New York (1945-63); portrayed title role in long-running radio detective program *Boston Blackie*. See *Current Biography* (February) 1952.

Obituary

N Y Times p30 Ja 9 '71

KROLL, JACK June 10, 1885-May 26, 1971 Trade union leader; vice-president of Amalgamated Clothing Workers of America (1928-66); close associate of union's president, Sidney Hillman; directed CIO Political Action Committee and co-directed AFL-CIO Committee on Political Education. See *Current Biography* (September) 1946.

Obituary

N Y Times p36 My 28 '71

LARKIN, OLIVER W(ATERMAN) Aug. 17, 1896-Dec. 17, 1970 Educator; author; won 1949 Pulitzer Prize in history for *Art and Life in America;* taught art at Smith College (1925-64); retired as professor emeritus of Smith in 1964. *See Current Biography* (July) 1950.

Obituary

N Y Times p30 D 19 '70

LEMASS, SEÁN F(RANCIS) July 15, 1899-May 11, 1971 Irish statesman; fought with the I.R.A. (1916-22); helped found Fianna Fáil, the governing party of the Irish Republic; as Cabinet member in several governments under Prime Minister

Eamon de Valera (1932-59), was charged with developing industries; Prime Minister (1959-66). See *Current Biography* (March) 1960.

Obituary

N Y Times p46 My 12 '71

LEWIS, OSCAR Dec. 25, 1914-Dec. 16, 1970 Anthropologist; author; developed theory that a "culture of poverty" exists that transcends national differences; wrote vivid, best-selling books on the Mexican and Puerto Rican poor, including *The Children of Sánchez, Pedro Martínez,* and *La Vida,* which won the 1967 National Book Award. See *Current Biography* (April) 1968.

Obituary

N Y Times p42 D 18 '70

LLOYD, HAROLD (CLAYTON) Apr. 20, 1893-Mar. 8, 1971 Motion picture comedian; began film career in 1914; in 1917 invented the stereotype of the wide-eyed, bespectacled, cliff-hanging innocent that eventually made him the highest-paid male star of the silent and early talkie screen; altogether, made some 500 motion pictures, including one-reelers; compiled scenes from them in *Harold Lloyd's World of Comedy* (1962). See *Current Biography* (September) 1949.

Obituary

N Y Times p1+ Mr 9 '71

LUKAS, PAUL May 26, 1895-Aug. 15, 1971 Actor; appeared on Broadway stage and in scores of Hollywood films, usually portraying urbane Continental types; best known for his performance as Kurt Mueller in the Broadway production of Lillian Hellman's anti-Nazi play, *Watch on the Rhine* (1941), and in its motion picture version, which earned him an Academy Award as best actor in 1943. See *Current Biography* (February) 1942.

Obituary

N Y Times p38 Ag 17 '71

LUSK, GEORGIA L(EE) May 12, 1893-Jan. 5, 1971 Educator; Democratic Representative in the United States Congress from New Mexico (1947-48); served eight years as New Mexico State Superintendent of Public Instruction. See *Current Biography* (October) 1947.

Obituary

N Y Times p40 Ja 6 '71

McGREGOR, G(ORDON) R(OY) Sept. 26, 1901-Mar. 8, 1971 Canadian air lines executive; president of Air Canada (formerly Trans-Canada Air Lines) for twenty years (1948-68); president of International Air Transport Association (1953-54). See *Current Biography* (March) 1954.

Obituary

N Y Times p41 Mr 9 '71

MALVERN, GODFREY (MARTIN) HUGGINS, 1st VISCOUNT July 6, 1883-May 8, 1971 Former Prime Minister of Rhodesia; physician; Prime Minister of Southern Rhodesia (1933-53) and the Central African Federation of Nyasaland, Northern Rhodesia, and Southern Rhodesia (1953-56); a moderate, was opposed to present Rhodesian government policies. See *Current Biography* (November) 1956.

Obituary

N Y Times p62 My 9 '71

MANNA, CHARLIE Oct. 6, 1925-Nov. 9, 1971 Comedian; noted for discreet topical humor; became an overnight hit with monologue about an eccentric astronaut (1961); appeared in nightclubs and theatrical productions, on most major television variety shows, and on such recordings as *Manna Overboard!* and *Manna Alive!* See *Current Biography* (January) 1965.

Obituary

N Y Times p50 N 11 '71

MARTIN, THOMAS E(LLSWORTH) Jan. 18, 1893-June 27, 1971 Former Republican Senator from Iowa; lawyer; served in the United States House of Representatives (1939-54); defeated veteran Senator Guy M. Gillette in 1954; supported Eisenhower's flexible farm price support program. See *Current Biography* (March) 1956.

Obituary

N Y Times p40 Je 29 '71

MATTSON, HENRY (ELIS) Aug. 7, 1887-Sept. 8, 1971 Artist; noted for lyrical seascapes and landscapes; received Harris Silver Medal (1931), Clark Prize (1943), and other awards; represented at Metropolitan Museum of Art, Whitney Museum of American Art, and Corcoran Gallery of Art. See *Current Biography* (January) 1956.

Obituary

N Y Times p30 S 11 '71

MAXON, LOU R(USSELL) July 28, 1900-May 15, 1971 Business executive; philanthropist; founder (1927) and head of Maxon Inc., one of the top advertising agencies in the United States, and among the first to use sports as a means of reaching mass audiences; public relations director of Office of Price Administration (1943). See *Current Biography* (August) 1943.

Obituary

N Y Times p50 My 19 '71

MORÓN, ALONZO G(RASEANO) Apr. 12, 1909-Oct. 31, 1971 Educator; sociologist; first Negro president of Hampton Institute in Virginia; Commissioner of Public Welfare (1933-36), assistant to governor (1959), and Commissioner of Educa-

tion (1960) of Virgin Islands; later deputy regional director of Department of Housing and Urban Development at San Juan, Puerto Rico. See *Current Biography* (October) 1949.

Obituary

N Y Times p44 N 1 '71

MOWERY, EDWARD J(OSEPH) Mar. 8, 1906-Dec. 19, 1970 Journalist; won 1953 Pulitzer Prize for local reporting for his seven-year investigation that led to the vindication of a Brooklyn man wrongly convicted of murder; reporter for the New York *World-Telegram and Sun* (1942-54); wrote syndicated column during the 1960's. See *Current Biography* (November) 1953.

Obituary

N Y Times p38 D 21 '70

NASH, OGDEN Aug. 19, 1902-May 19, 1971 Poet; poked gentle fun at human foibles with his witty, unconventional rhymes, often disregarding rules of grammar, spelling, and prosody to obtain desired comic effect; contributed verse to *New Yorker* and other magazines; author of some twenty books, including *I'm a Stranger Here Myself* (1938), *You Can't Get There From Here* (1957), and *Bedriddance* (1970); wrote lyrics for Broadway musical hit *One Touch of Venus* (1943). See *Current Biography* (April) 1941.

Obituary

N Y Times p1+ My 20 '71

NEVINS, ALLAN May 20, 1890-Mar. 5, 1971 Historian; professor of American history at Columbia University (1931-58) and a founder of its oral history program; senior research associate of the Huntington (California) Library (1958-69); authority on the Civil War and American economic history; author or editor of over sixty books; winner of Pulitzer Prizes for 1932 biography of Grover Cleveland and 1936 study of Hamilton Fish. See *Current Biography* (October) 1968.

Obituary

N Y Times p1+ Mr 6 '71

NIEBUHR, REINHOLD June 21, 1892-June 1, 1971 Protestant theologian; architect of "Christian realist" philosophy, stressing fallibility of man and combining pragmatism with Biblical precepts in solution of human problems while rejecting both utopianism and cynicism; influential spokesman for non-Communist left; taught at Union Theological Seminary (1928-71); author of many books, including two-volume *Nature and Destiny of Man* (1943); recipient of Presidential Medal of Freedom (1964). See *Current Biography* (November) 1951.

Obituary

N Y Times p1+ Je 2 '71

NOGUÈS, AUGUSTE (PAUL) 1876-Apr. 20, 1971 French general; Vichy administrator of Morocco during World War II; after the war was sentenced *in absentia* to twenty years hard labor for blocking French resistance efforts in Morocco. See *Current Biography* (February) 1943.

Obituary

N Y Times p44 Ap 22 '71

NYE, GERALD P(RENTICE) Dec. 19, 1892-July 17, 1971 United States Senator from North Dakota (1925-45); nominally Republican but essentially Populist-Isolationist, for the farmer and small businessman and against the military-industrial complex; used his important Senate committee posts to expose malfeasance in public office, beginning with the Teapot Dome scandal, and to advocate nonintervention in World War II; was later employed in government posts concerned with problems of the elderly. See *Current Biography* (November) 1941.

Obituary

N Y Times p28 Jl 19 '71

PADILLA, EZEQUIEL Dec. 31, 1890-Sept. 6, 1971 Mexican Foreign Minister during World War II; organized hemisphere defense against Axis while keeping Mexico out of war; one of signers of U.N. charter at San Francisco (1945); urged anti-Communist, pro-United States policy after war; as secretary of public education (1928-30), helped create Mexico's modern school system. See *Current Biography* (July) 1942.

Obituary

N Y Times p48 S 8 '71

PENNEY, J(AMES) C(ASH) Sept. 16, 1875-Feb. 12, 1971 Chain store executive; in 1902 founded J. C. Penney Company, a chain of department stores now numbering 1,660 and comprising the nation's fifth largest merchandizing enterprise; president of his business from 1913 to 1917 and honorary chairman or director since then; pioneered with profit-sharing and preached business precepts based on the Golden Rule. See *Current Biography* (December) 1947.

Obituary

N Y Times p1+ F 13 '71

PEREIRA, I(RENE) RICE Aug. 5, 1907-Jan. 11, 1971 Artist; abstract painter who experimented with geometric forms, light, and color; held sixty-work retrospective at Whitney Museum (New York) in 1953. See *Current Biography* (November) 1953.

Obituary

N Y Times p42 Ja 13 '71

POOR, HENRY VARNUM Sept. 30, 1888-Dec. 8, 1970 Artist; noted for his paintings, murals, and ceramics; executed murals and frescoes for public buildings; taught painting at Columbia University and other institutions; founder (1946) and first president of Skowhegan (Maine) School of Painting and Sculpture. See *Current Biography* (April) 1942.

Obituary

N Y Times p38 D 9 '70

PORTAL OF HUNGERFORD, CHARLES FREDERICK ALGERNON PORTAL, 1st VISCOUNT 1893-Apr. 23, 1971 Royal Air Force Marshal; Chief of the British Air Staff during World War II; administered atomic energy research facilities at Harwell (1945-51). See *Current Biography* (March) 1941.

Obituary

N Y Times p33 Ap 24 '71

POWER, THOMAS S(ARSFIELD) June 18, 1905-Dec. 7, 1970 United States Air Force officer; commander of Strategic Air Command (SAC), the world's most powerful missile-deploying force (1957-64); led first large-scale bombing raid on Tokyo (1945); helped plan atomic bomb attacks on Hiroshima and Nagasaki (1945); deputy commander of SAC (1948-54); chief of Air Research and Development Command (1954-57); attained rank of full general in 1957. See *Current Biography* (April) 1958.

Obituary

N Y Times p50 D 8 '70

PROUTY, WINSTON L(EWIS) Sept. 1, 1906-Sept. 10, 1971 United States Republican Senator from Vermont (1959-71); member of United States House of Representatives (1951-59); sponsored Older Americans Act (1970) to improve income of aged poor. See *Current Biography* (July) 1960.

Obituary

N Y Times p30 S 11 '71

RAKOSI, MATYAS Mar. 14, 1892-Feb. 5, 1971 Former Hungarian Communist party leader (1945-56); left Hungary for the Soviet Union in 1940 and became Soviet citizen; returned to Hungary in 1944 as a general in the Soviet army and largely engineered the Communist takeover there; exiled to the Soviet Union in 1956. See *Current Biography* (March) 1949.

Obituary

N Y Times p32 F 6 '71

RAMAN, SIR (CHANDRASEKHARA) VENKATA
Nov. 7, 1888-Nov. 21, 1970 Indian physicist; won
Nobel Prize in Physics (1930) for discovery of
the Raman Effect, a tendency of light, when dif-
fused, to change wave length and color; conducted
pioneering research in musical acoustics and crys-
tallography; professor at University of Calcutta
(1917-33); director of Bangalore Institute (1933-
47); became director of Raman Research Institute
in 1947. See *Current Biography* (November)
1948.

Obituary

N Y Times p83 N 22 '70

**READING, STELLA (CHARNAUD ISAACS),
MARCHIONESS OF** Jan. 6, 1894-May 22, 1971
British social worker and organization official;
founder (1938) and chairman of Women's Volun-
tary Services for civil defense; helped sponsor
Women's Home Industries Ltd. (1947); became
first female member of House of Lords in 1958.
See *Current Biography* (April) 1948.

Obituary

N Y Times p60 My 23 '71

**REITH, JOHN CHARLES WALSHAM, 1ST
BARON** 1889-June 16, 1971 British broadcasting
executive and government official; as director general of British Broadcasting Corporation (1927-
38), shaped its image of dedicated public service
and defense of national institutions; championed
freedom from government interference and resisted influx of commercial broadcasting; served
in several Cabinet posts. See *Current Biography*
(November) 1940.

Obituary

N Y Times p44 Je 17 '71

RIVERS, L(UCIUS) MENDEL Sept. 28, 1905-
Dec. 28, 1970 United States Representative from
South Carolina since 1940; key figure among conservative Southern Democrats; chaired House
Armed Services Committee since 1965; powerful
champion of American military might who urged
escalation of Vietnam war and development of
new weapons systems. See *Current Biography*
(October) 1960.

Obituary

N Y Times p1+ D 29 '70

ROBERTSON, A. WILLIS May 27, 1887-Nov. 1,
1971 United States Democratic Senator from Virginia (1946-66); member of United States House
of Representatives (1933-46); influential chairman of Senate Banking and Currency Committee;
favored conservative, anti-inflationary economic
policies; sponsored wildlife conservation legislation; became consultant to International Bank for
Reconstruction and Development (1966) after defeat in Senate primary race. See *Current Biography* (December) 1949.

Obituary

N Y Times p38 N 2 '71

ROPER, ELMO (BURNS, JR.) July 31, 1900-
Apr. 30, 1971 Public opinion analyst; one of the
first developers of modern public opinion polls;
acquired fame in 1936 when he predicted Presidential vote within 1 percent accuracy by utilizing
the sampling techniques of marketing research.
See *Current Biography* (January) 1945.

Obituary

N Y Times p36 My 1 '71

ROYALL, KENNETH C(LAIBORNE) July 24,
1894-May 25, 1971 United States government official; lawyer; Secretary of War (1947); first Secretary of the Army (1947-49) after President Harry
S. Truman restructured government, uniting armed
forces under Defense Department; senior partner
of law firm of Royall, Koegel & Rogers (1949-
67). See *Current Biography* (January) 1947.

Obituary

N Y Times p42 My 27 '71

RUSSELL, RICHARD B(REVARD, JR.) Nov. 2,
1897-Jan. 21, 1971 United States Senator from
Georgia since 1933; one of the most highly respected and influential members of the Senate and
its senior member; leader of the Senate's Southern
Bloc; unsuccessfully sought Democratic Presidential nomination in 1952; chairman of Armed Services Committee (1951-69); President Pro Tem-
pore of the Senate since 1969. See *Current Biography* (November) 1949.

Obituary

N Y Times p1+ Ja 22 '71

SCHUSTER, M(AX) LINCOLN Mar. 2, 1897-
Dec. 20, 1970 Publisher; editor; founder with
Richard L. Simon in 1924 of Simon & Schuster
and partner until 1966; achieved great financial
success with self-help and culture-for-the-masses
books (like Dale Carnegie's *How to Win Friends
and Influence People* and Will Durant's *The Story
of Philosophy*); established Pocket Books, popular
paperback line, with Simon and others; edited
A Treasury of the World's Great Letters (1940).
See *Current Biography* (July) 1941.

Obituary

N Y Times p38 D 21 '70

SEPHERIADĒS, GEŌRGIOS S(TYLIANOU) Feb.
29, 1900-Sept. 20, 1971 Greek writer; former diplomat; received 1963 Nobel Prize in Literature,
under pen name George Seferis; works in English
translation include *The King of Asine and Other
Poems* (1948), *Poems* (1960), and *Collected
Poems, 1924-1955* (1967); translated works of
T. S. Eliot and Ezra Pound into Greek; served as
Ambassador to Great Britain (1957-62) and in
other diplomatic posts; issued public declaration
(1969) against Greek military regime. See *Current Biography* (May) 1964.

Obituary

N Y Times p40 S 21 '71

SERLIN, OSCAR Jan. 30, 1901-Feb. 27, 1971 Former producer and director; was associated with Paramount Pictures as a talent scout and eventually an associate producer (1932-37); produced the Howard Lindsay-Russel Crouse play *Life with Father,* which opened on Broadway in 1939 and ran for 3,213 performances. See *Current Biography* (March) 1943.

Obituary

N Y Times p60 F 28 '71

SHVERNIK, NIKOLAI (MIKHAILOVICH) May 19, 1888-Dec. 25, 1970 Former Soviet government official; a close associate of Stalin; head of Soviet trade unions (1930-48); president of the Supreme Soviet (Parliament) of the Soviet Union (1946-54); one of the few Old Bolsheviks to survive Communist party purges. See *Current Biography* (October) 1951.

Obituary

N Y Times p32 D 25 '70

SIROKY, VILIAM May 31, 1902-Oct. 6, 1971 Premier of Czechoslovakia (1953-63); Vice-Premier (1945-53); Minister of Foreign Affairs (1950-53); helped to found Czechoslovak Communist party (1921); member of its Central Committee from 1930 until his retirement from public life in 1966; closely adhered to orthodox Communist policies of Soviet Union. See *Current Biography* (April) 1957.

Obituary

N Y Times p50 O 7 '71

SKOURAS, SPYROS P(ANAGIOTES) Mar. 28, 1893-Aug. 16, 1971 Motion picture magnate; came to United States as poor Greek immigrant; gradually acquired theatre chain, which he built into motion picture empire; president of Twentieth Century-Fox Film Corporation (1942-62); resigned after controversy over losses incurred by film *Cleopatra* but remained with company as board chairman; after retirement (1969), became chairman of Prudential-Grace Shipping Lines; noted for philanthropy. See *Current Biography* (June) 1943.

Obituary

N Y Times p38 Ag 17 '71

SLIM, WILLIAM JOSEPH SLIM, VISCOUNT Aug. 6, 1891-Dec. 14, 1970 Retired British Army officer; led the Allied campaign that liberated Burma from the Japanese in World War II; chief of the Imperial General Staff (1948-52); constable and governor of Windsor Castle (1964-70). See *Current Biography* (June) 1945.

Obituary

N Y Times p48 D 15 '70

SMITH, (OLIVER) HARRISON Aug. 4, 1888-Jan. 8, 1971 Publisher; editor; founded Jonathan Cape and Harrison Smith, Inc., early publishers of William Faulkner, in 1929; president and associate editor of the *Saturday Review* (1938-66); edited *From Main Street to Stockholm* (1952), a volume of Sinclair Lewis' letters; since the 1940's a staunch advocate of women's rights in articles and lectures. See *Current Biography* (December) 1954.

Obituary

N Y Times p30 Ja 9 '71

SOONG, T.V. 1894-Apr. 25, 1971 Leading financier of the Chinese Nationalist regime for twenty years before it fled the mainland in 1949; introduced reforms in banking, finance, and currency as Minister of Finance; founded Bank of China (1936); held government posts as Foreign Minister and Premier. See *Current Biography* (March) 1941.

Obituary

N Y Times p46 Ap 27 '71

STANLEY, W(ENDELL) M(EREDITH) Aug. 16, 1904-June 15, 1971 Biochemist; shared 1946 Nobel Prize in chemistry for pioneering work on nature of viruses; developed influenza vaccine during World War II; professor of biochemistry and virology and director of virus laboratory at University of California (1948-69). See *Current Biography* (April) 1947.

Obituary

N Y Times p48 Je 16 '71

STRANG, RUTH (MAY) Apr. 3, 1895-Jan. 3, 1971 Educator; author; taught education at Teachers College, Columbia University, from 1924 to her retirement as professor emeritus in 1960; wrote extensively on student personnel and guidance administration and child psychology. See *Current Biography* (December) 1960.

Obituary

N Y Times p39 Ja 5 '71

STRAVINSKY, IGOR (FEDOROVICH) June 17, 1882-Apr. 6, 1971 Russian-born composer; most significant musical innovator of the twentieth century; ushered in the era of modern music with *Le Sacre du Printemps,* which caused a riot when it was premièred in Paris on May 29, 1913; in early ballets *The Firebird* and *Petrouchka* introduced bold new rhythms, polytonality, and extensive use of orchestral timbres; subsequently adopted more classical, astringent style in such pieces as *L'Histoire du Soldat* (1918), *Les Noces* (1923), and *The Rake's Progress* (1951); composed his last works, including *Agon* (1957) and *Abraham and Isaac* (1964), in the serial idiom. See *Current Biography* (April) 1953.

Obituary

N Y Times p1+ Ap 7 '71

SWITZER, MARY E(LIZABETH) Feb. 16, 1900-Oct. 16, 1971 United States government official; director of Office of Vocational Rehabilitation (1950-67); administrator of Social and Rehabilitation Service of Department of Health, Education, and Welfare (1967-70); received Albert Lasker Award (1960) for work in behalf of physically handicapped. See *Current Biography* (January) 1962.

Obituary

N Y Times p77 O 17 '71

TAMM, IGOR (EVGENYEVICH) July 8, 1895-Apr. 12, 1971 Soviet physicist; corecipient of the Nobel Prize in Physics (1958); recognized mainly for his work during the 1930's and 1940's in uniting Einstein's theory of relativity with quantum mechanics; pioneered in the development of peaceful uses for atomic energy. See *Current Biography* (December) 1963.

Obituary

N Y Times p46 Ap 14 '71

THOMAS, J(OHN) PARNELL Jan. 16, 1895-Nov. 19, 1970 United States Republican Representative from New Jersey (1937-50); chairman of House Committee on Un-American Activities (1947-50); zealous anti-Communist crusader; gained national attention during committee investigation of alleged Communist influence in Hollywood (1947) and hearings leading to perjury conviction of Alger Hiss (1948); convicted on charges of padding his Congressional payroll and imprisoned (1950). See *Current Biography* (September) 1947.

Obituary

N Y Times p44 N 20 '70

TISELIUS, ARNE (WILHELM KAURIN) Aug. 10, 1902-Oct. 29, 1971 Swedish biochemist; received 1948 Nobel Prize in Chemistry for his contributions to the biochemical study of serum proteins and his perfection of methods of electrophoresis and adsorption analysis; professor of biochemistry at University of Uppsala, Sweden from 1938 until retirement; president of Nobel Foundation (1960-64), then chairman of Nobel Committee for Chemistry. See *Current Biography* (April) 1949.

Obituary

N Y Times p34 O 30 '71

TONG, HOLLINGTON K(ONG) Nov. 9, 1887-Jan. 9, 1971 Nationalist Chinese diplomat; journalist; Ambassador to the United States (1956-58); after American journalism education served as correspondent, editor, or publisher of many English- and Chinese-language newspapers in China and, later, Taiwan; wrote first official biography of Chiang Kai-shek in English (1937); Ambassador to Japan (1952-56). See *Current Biography* (December) 1956.

Obituary

N Y Times p34 Ja 11 '71

TSALDARIS, CONSTANTIN 1884-Nov. 15, 1970 Premier of Greece (1946-47); Deputy Premier and Foreign Minister (1947-50); leader of right-wing Populist party; architect of Greece's post-World War II pro-Western, anti-Communist foreign policy. See *Current Biography* (November) 1946.

Obituary

N Y Times p40 N 16 '70

TUBMAN, WILLIAM V(ACANARAT) S(HAD-RACH) Nov. 29, 1895-July 23, 1971 President of Liberia since 1944; immensely popular chief executive of the republic founded by freed American slaves in the nineteenth century; extended full citizenship rights to the nation's aboriginal inhabitants; stewarded Liberia's economic growth by encouraging foreign investment. See *Current Biography* (January) 1955.

Obituary

N Y Times p1+ Jl 24 '71

ULLMAN, JAMES R(AMSEY) Nov. 24, 1907-June 20, 1971 Author; mountain climber; world traveler; wrote nearly a score of books of adventure, many of them about or based on his own experiences, such as the novels *The White Tower* (1945), about an Alpine ascent, and *River of the Sun* (1951), about exploration in the Amazon jungle; among his works of nonfiction were two histories of mountain climbing, *High Conquest* (1941) and *The Age of Mountaineering* (1954); also wrote several and produced many plays, including Sidney Kingsley's Pulitzer Prize-winning *Men in White* (1933-34). See *Current Biography* (October) 1945.

Obituary

N Y Times p32 Je 21 '71

VAN SLYKE, DONALD D(EXTER) Mar. 29, 1883-May 4, 1971 Biochemist; conducted research at Rockefeller Institute for Medical Research (1907-48) and Brookhaven National Laboratory (1948-70), where he organized the departments of biology and medicine; recognized for his discoveries in chemistry, physiology, and medicine with many awards, including the National Medal of Science (1965). See *Current Biography* (January) 1943.

Obituary

N Y Times p46 My 6 '71

VILAR, JEAN (LOUIS CÔME) Mar. 25, 1912-May 28, 1971 French theatrical director and actor; brought moderately-priced high-quality theatre to masses as director (1951-63) of state-subsidized Théâtre National Populaire and starred in many of its productions; founded Avignon Festival (1947); staged opera productions and acted in motion pictures. See *Current Biography* (April) 1962.

Obituary

N Y Times p26 My 29 '71

WHITE, MARGARET BOURKE See Bourke-White, M.

YOUNG, WHITNEY M(OORE), JR. July 31, 1921-Mar. 11, 1971 Civil rights leader; social worker; executive director of the National Urban League (since 1961) and promoter of its programs to improve opportunities for blacks in housing, employment, and welfare. See *Current Biography* (April) 1965.

Obituary

N Y Times p1+ Mr 12 '71

BIOGRAPHICAL REFERENCES

American Architects Directory, 1970

American Bar, 1965

American Catholic Who's Who, 1970-71

American Medical Directory, 1965

American Men of Science 11th ed (1955-70)

Annuario Pontificio, 1965

Asia Who's Who (1960)

Author's & Writer's Who's Who (1960)

Baseball Register, 1967

Biographical Directory of the American Congress, 1774-1961 (1962)

Biographical Encyclopaedia & Who's Who of the American Theatre (1966)

Biographical Encyclopedia of Pakistan, 1955-56

Biographic Directory of the USSR (1958)

Burke's Peerage, Baronetage, and Knightage, 1963

Canadian Parliamentary Guide, 1967

Canadian Who's Who, 1967-69

Catholic Who's Who, 1952

Celebrity Register (1963)

Chemical Who's Who, 1956

Chi è? (1961)

China Yearbook, 1963-64

Chujoy, A., and Manchester, P. W., eds. Dance Encyclopedia (1967)

Clerical Directory of the Protestant Episcopal Church in the U.S.A., 1965

Concise Biographical Dictionary of Singers (1969)

Congressional Directory (1971)

Congressional Quarterly Almanac, 1971

Contemporary Authors (1962-70)

Contemporary Poets of the English Language (1970)

Debrett's Peerage, 1964

Department of State Biographic Register, 1970

Dictionary of Latin American and Caribbean Biography (1971)

Dictionnaire de biographie française (1964)

Directory of American Judges (1955)

Directory of American Scholars (1969)

Directory of British Scientists, 1966-67

Directory of Medical Specialists (1965)

Ewen, D., ed. Composers of Today (1936); Living Musicians (1940); First Supplement, (1957); Men and Women Who Make Music (1949); American Composers Today (1949); European Composers Today (1954); The New Book of Modern Composers (1961); Popular American Composers (1962); Composers Since 1900 (1969)

Feather, Leonard. Encyclopedia of Jazz (1960); Encyclopedia of Jazz in the Sixties (1966)

Foremost Women in Communications (1970)

Grove's Dictionary of Music and Musicians (1955)

Hindustan Year Book and Who's Who, 1963

Hochn, M. A., ed. Catholic Authors (1957)

Hvem er Hvem, 1964

International Motion Picture Almanac, 1971

International Television Almanac, 1971

International Who's Who, 1971-72

International Who's Who in Poetry (1958)

International Year Book and Statesmen's Who's Who, 1971

Japan Biographical Encyclopedia & Who's Who, 1964-65

Jews in the World of Science (1956)

Junior Book of Authors (1956)

Kelly's Handbook to the Titled, Landed and Official Classes, 1964

Kleine Slavische Biographic (1958)

Kraks Blå Bog, 1964

Kürschners Biographies Theater-Handbuch (1956)

Kürschners Deutscher Gelehrten-Kalender, 1966

Leaders in Education (1971)

McGraw-Hill Modern Men of Science (1966-68)

Martindale-Hubbell Law Directory, 1970

Middle East and North Africa, 1968-69

More Junior Authors (1963)

Nalanda Year-Book and Who's Who in India and Pakistan, 1958

National Cyclopaedia of American Biography current vols A-K (1926-67)

New Century Cyclopedia of Names (1954)

Nordness, Lee, ed. Art USA Now (1963)

Nouveau Dictionnaire National des Contemporains (1961-63)

Official Catholic Directory, 1968

Panorama Biografico degli Italiani d'Oggi (1966)

Poor's Register of Directors and Executives, 1964

Prominent Personalities in the USSR (1968)

Quién es Quién en la Argentina, 1958-59

Quién es Quién en Venezuela, Panama, Ecuador, Colombia, 1956

Robinson, Donald. 100 Most Important People in the World Today (1970)

Slonimsky, Nicholas. Baker's Biographical Dictionary of Musicians (1958)

Thomas, S. Men of Space (1960-68)

Thompson, O., ed. International Cyclopedia of Music and Musicians, 1964

Turkin, H., and Thompson, S.C. Official Encyclopedia of Baseball (1959)

Twentieth Century Authors (1942; First Supplement, 1955)

Two Hundred Contemporary Authors (1969)

Vem är Det, 1971

Warfel, H. R. American Novelist of Today (1951)

Webster's Biographical Dictionary (1963)

Wer ist Wer? (1969-70)

Who is Who in Music (1951)

Who's Who, 1971-72

Who's Who in Advertising (1963)

Who's Who in America, 1970-71

Who's Who in American Art (1970)

Who's Who in American Education, 1967-68

Who's Who in American Politics, 1969-70

Who's Who in Art (1970)

Who's Who in Australia, 1965

Who's Who in Austria, 1959-60

Who's Who in Baseball 1971

Who's Who in Belgium (1962)

Who's Who in California, 1965

Who's Who in Canada, 1969-70

Who's Who in Chicago and Illinois (1950)

Who's Who in Colored America, 1950

Who's Who in Engineering, 1964

Who's Who in Finance and Industry (1972-73)

Who's Who in Foreign Correspondence, 1956-57

Who's Who in France, 1965-66

Who's Who in France (Paris), 1953-54

Who's Who in Germany (1964)

Who's Who in Insurance, 1971

Who's Who in Israel, 1969-70

Who's Who in Italy, 1957-58

Who's Who in Latin America Pts 1-7 (1946-51)

Who's Who in Library Service (1966)

Who's Who in Malaysia, 1967

Who's Who in Music, 1969

Who's Who in New York, 1960

Who's Who in New Zealand (1965)

Who's Who in Philosophy (1952)

Who's Who in Publishing (1965)

Who's Who in Railroading in North America (1959)

Who's Who in Space, 1966-67

Who's Who in Spain, 1965

Who's Who in Switzerland: 1968-69

Who's Who in the Arab World, 1967-68

Who's Who in the East, 1972-73

Who's Who in the Midwest, 1970-71

Who's Who in the Netherlands, 1962-63

Who's Who in the South and Southwest, 1971-72

Who's Who in the Theatre (1967)

Who's Who in the United Nations (1951)

Who's Who in the USSR, 1965-66

Who's Who in the West, 1970-71

Who's Who in the World, 1971-72

Who's Who in World Aviation and Astronautics (1958)

Who's Who in World Jewry (1965)

Who's Who of American Women, 1972-73

Who's Who of British Engineers, 1970-71

Who's Who of British Scientists, 1969-70

Who's Who of Southern Africa, 1968

Who's Who of Rhodesia, Mauritius, Central and East Africa, 1965

Wie is Dat? (1956)

Women Lawyers in the United States (1957)

Wood, C. TV Personalities vols 1-3 (1955-57)

World Biography (1954)

World Diplomatic Directory, 1951

World Who's Who in Commerce and Industry, 1968-69

World Who's Who in Science (1968)

PERIODICALS AND NEWSPAPERS CONSULTED

ALA Bul—American Library Association Bulletin
After Dark—After Dark
Am Artist—American Artist
Am Assn Univ Women J—Journal of the American
  Association of University Women
Am Bar Assn J—American Bar Association Journal
Am Hist R—American Historical Review
Am Pol Sci R—American Political Science Review
Am Scholar—American Scholar
Am Sociol R—American Sociological Review
Am W—American Weekly (discontinued)
America—America
Américas—Américas (incorporating Bul Pan Am
  Union)
Ann Am Acad—Annals of the American Academy
  of Political and Social Science
Arch Forum—Architectural Forum, The Magazine
  of Building
Arch Rec—Architectural Record
Archaeology—Archaeology: A Magazine Dealing
  with the Antiquity of the World
Art N—Art News
Arts—Arts
Arts & Arch—Arts & Architecture
Atlan—Atlantic Monthly
Aviation W—Aviation Week and Space Technology

Barrons—Barron's
Bet Hom & Gard—Better Homes and Gardens
Book-of-the Month Club N—Book-of-the-Month
  Club News
Book W—Book Week
Bsns W—Business Week
Bul Atomic Sci—Bulletin of the Atomic Scientists

Can Hist R—Canadian Historical Review
Cath World—Catholic World
Chem & Eng N—Chemical and Engineering News
Christian Sci Mon—Christian Science Monitor
Colliers—Collier's (discontinued)
Commonweal—Commonweal
Cong Digest—Congressional Digest
Cong Q—Congressional Quarterly Weekly Report
Coronet—Coronet
Cosmop—Cosmopolitan
Cue—Cue
Cur Hist—Current History

Dance Mag—Dance Magazine

Ebony—Ebony
Ed—Education
Ed & Pub—Editor & Publisher
Ed Res Reports—Editorial Research Reports
Encounter—Encounter
Esquire—Esquire
Etude—Etude (discontinued)

Facts on File—Facts on File
For Affairs—Foreign Affairs
For Policy Bul—Foreign Policy Bulletin
Forbes—Forbes
Fortune—Fortune

Guardian—Guardian (formery Manchester Guardian)

Harper—Harper's Magazine
Hi Fi—High Fidelity; The Magazine for Music
  Listeners
Hi-Fi/Stereo R—Hi-Fi/Stereo Review
Holiday—Holiday
House & Gard—House & Garden

Illus Lond N—Illustrated London News

J Am Med Assn—Journal of the American Medical
  Association

Ladies Home J—Ladies' Home Journal
Lib J—Library Journal
Life—Life
London Observer—London Observer
Look—Look (discontinued)

McCalls—McCall's
Macleans Mag—Maclean's Magazine
Mag Wall St—Magazine of Wall Street and Business
  Analyst
Mlle—Mademoiselle
Mus Am—Musical America
Mus Courier—Musical Courier (discontinued)
Mus Mod Art—Museum of Modern Art Bulletin

NEA J—Journal of the National Education Associa-
  tion
N Y Herald Tribune—New York Herald Tribune
  (discontinued)
N Y Herald Tribune Bk R—New York Herald Trib-
  une Book Review (discontinued)
N Y Post—New York Post
N Y Rev of Books—New York Review of Books
N Y Sunday News—New York Sunday News
N Y Times—New York Times
N Y Times Bk R—New York Times Book Review
N Y Times Mag—New York Times Magazine
N Y World-Telegram—New York World-Telegram
  and Sun (discontinued)
N Y World Journal Tribune—New York World
  Journal Tribune (discontinued)
Nat Geog Mag—National Geographic Magazine

Nat Observer—National Observer
Nation—The Nation
Nations Bsns—Nation's Business
Nature—Nature
New Engl Q—New England Quarterly
New Repub—New Republic
New Statesm—New Statesman
New York—New York Magazine
New Yorker—New Yorker
Newsday—Newsday
Newsweek—Newsweek

Opera N—Opera News

Playboy—Playboy
Pol Sci Q—Political Science Quarterly
Pop Sci—Popular Science Monthly
Ptr Ink—Printers' Ink (discontinued)
Pub W—Publishers' Weekly

Read Digest—Reader's Digest
Reporter—The Reporter (discontinued)

Sat Eve Post—Saturday Evening Post
Sat Night—Saturday Night
Sat R—Saturday Review
Sch & Soc—School and Society
Sci Am—Scientific American
Sci Mo—Scientific Monthly (combined with Science)
Sci N L—Science News Letter
Science—Science (incorporating Sci Mo)

Show—Show (discontinued)
Show Bsns Illus—Show Business Illustrated (discontinued)
Spec—Spectator
Sport—Sport
Sports Illus—Sports Illustrated
Sr Schol—Senior Scholastic

Theatre Arts—Theatre Arts (discontinued)
This Week—This Week Magazine
Time—Time
Times Lit Sup—London Times Literary Supplement
Toronto Globe and Mail—Toronto Globe and Mail
Travel—Travel

U N Rev—United Nations Review
U S Dept State Bul—United States Department of State Bulletin
U S News—U.S. News & World Report

Variety—Variety
Village Voice—Village Voice
Vision—Visión
Vital Speeches—Vital Speeches of the Day
Vogue—Vogue

Wall St J—Wall Street Journal
Washington (D.C.) Post—Washington Post
Wilson Lib Bul—Wilson Library Bulletin

Yale R—Yale Review

CLASSIFICATION BY PROFESSION—1971

ADVERTISING
Ford, Eileen
Ziegler, Ronald L.

AGRICULTURE
Borlaug, Norman E.
Morton, C. B. Rogers
Polyansky, Dmitry S.

ARCHITECTURE
Otto, Frei
Owings, Nathaniel A.
Vasarely, Victor

ART
Diebenkorn, Richard
Gould, Chester
Guston, Philip
Hirschfeld, Albert
Max, Peter
Millett, Kate
Morris, Robert
Shikler, Aaron
Stella, Frank
Still, Clyfford
Vasarely, Victor

ASTRONAUTICS
Scott, David R.

AVIATION
Prescott, Robert W.
Scott, David R.

BUSINESS
Borch, Fred J.
Brock, William Emerson, 3d
Brown, George H.
Buckley, James L.
Chalk, O. Roy
Cromer, 3d Earl of
Ford, Eileen
Graham, Katharine
Iacocca, Lee A.
Karinska, Barbara
Kelly, John B., Jr.
McGannon, Donald H.
Max, Peter
Morton, C. B. Rogers
Murphy, Franklin D.

Perot, H. Ross
Prescott, Robert W.
Riklis, Meshulam
Saul, Ralph S.
Watson, Arthur K.

DANCE
Béjart, Maurice
Berkeley, Busby
Dowell, Anthony
Erdman, Jean
Feld, Eliot
Hawn, Goldie
Karinska, Barbara
Keeler, Ruby
McKayle, Donald
Mazzo, Kay
Moore, Mary Tyler

DIPLOMACY
Aichi, Kiichi
Cromer, 3d Earl of
Lopez Bravo, Gregorio
Maurer, Ion Gheorghe
Singh, Swaran
Watson, Arthur K.

ECOLOGY
Ruckelshaus, William D.

EDUCATION
Berio, Luciano
Bok, Derek C.
Brown, George H.
Diebenkorn, Richard
Drinan, Robert F.
Duffey, Joseph D.
Erikson, Erik H.
Fleisher, Leon
Ginsberg, Mitchell I.
Greer, Germaine
Horgan, Paul
Kemeny, John G.
Lowenstein, Allard K.
McGill, William J.
Millett, Kate
Monod, Jacques
Morris, Robert
Murphy, Franklin D.
Riles, Wilson
Schiller, Karl
Segal, Erich
Shumway, Norman E.
Trampler, Walter

ENGINEERING
Gibson, Kenneth A.
Iacocca, Lee A.

FASHION
Fairchild, John B.
Ford, Eileen
Karinska, Barbara

FINANCE
Cromer, 3d Earl of
Perot, H. Ross
Riklis, Meshulam
Saul, Ralph S.
Schiller, Karl

GOVERNMENT, Foreign
Aichi, Kiichi
Allende, Salvador
Barber, Anthony
Boumedienne, Houari
Carrington, 6th Baron
Colombo, Emilio
Cromer, 3d Earl of
Gierek, Edward
Healey, Denis
Hoveyda, Amir Abbas
Husak, Gustav
Lopez Bravo, Gregorio
McMahon, William
Maurer, Ion Gheorghe
Médici, Emílio Garrastazú
Ne Win
Paisley, Ian
Pastrana Borrero, Misael
Polyansky, Dmitry S.
Riad, Mahmoud
Sadat, Anwar
Scheel, Walter
Schiller, Karl
Shelepin, Aleksandr
Singh, Swaran
Yahya Khan, A. M.

GOVERNMENT, U.S.
Abzug, Bella
Badillo, Herman
Bazelon, David L.
Bentley, Helen Delich
Blatchford, Joseph H.
Brock, William Emerson, 3d
Brown, George H.
Buckley, James L.
Carter, Jimmy

Chiles, Lawton
Drinan, Robert F.
Fletcher, Arthur A.
Foster, John S., Jr.
Gibson, Kenneth A.
Ginsberg, Mitchell I.
Hanks, Nancy
Holton, Linwood
Klein, Herbert G.
Lowenstein, Allard K.
McCloskey, Paul N., Jr.
Moorer, Thomas H.
Morton, C. B. Rogers
Moss, Frank E.
Richardson, Elliot L.
Riles, Wilson
Ruckelshaus, William D.
Sargent, Francis W.
Scammon, Richard M.
Staggers, Harley O.
Trussell, Ray E.
Tunney, John V.
Watson, Arthur K.
Ziegler, Ronald L.

INDUSTRY
Bentley, Helen Delich
Borch, Fred J.
Gierek, Edward
Gonzalez, Efren W.
Iacocca, Lee A.
Perot, H. Ross
Riklis, Meshulam
Watson, Arthur K.

INTERNATIONAL RELA-
TIONS
Blatchford, Joseph H.
Cromer, 3d Earl of
Singh, Swaran
Watson, Arthur K.

JOURNALISM
Bentley, Helen Delich
Gould, Chester
Graham, Katharine
Hirschfeld, Albert
Klein, Herbert G.
Tvardovsky, Alexandr T.
Wolfe, Tom

LABOR
Fitzsimmons, Frank E.
Fletcher, Arthur A.
Hernandez, Aileen C.

LAW
Abzug, Bella
Badillo, Herman
Barber, Anthony
Bok, Derek C.
Drinan, Robert F.
Holton, Linwood
Klein, Herbert G.
Kunstler, William M.
Lowenstein, Allard K.
McCloskey, Paul N., Jr.
Moss, Frank E.
Pastrana Borrero, Misael
Richardson, Elliot L.
Ruckelshaus, William D.
Saul, Ralph S.
Tunney, John V.

LIBRARY SERVICE
Doms, Keith
Gonzalez, Efren W.

LITERATURE
Auden, W. H.
Burroughs, William S.
Horgan, Paul
Perelman, S. J.
Sartre, Jean-Paul
Segal, Erich
Quayle, Anthony
Tvardovsky, Alexandr T.
Wilder, Thornton
Wodehouse, P. G.

MEDICINE
Allende, Salvador
Erikson, Erik H.
Monod, Jacques
Murphy, Franklin D.
Shumway, Norman E.
Trussell, Ray E.

MILITARY
Boumedienne, Houari
Foster, John S., Jr.
Médici, Emílio Garrastazú
Moorer, Thomas H.
Ne Win
Scott, David R.
Yahya Khan, A. M.
Zumwalt, E. R., Jr.

MOTION PICTURES
Berkeley, Busby
Brel, Jacques
Bresson, Robert

Dassin, Jules
Eastwood, Clint
Forman, Milos
Gould, Elliott
Hawn, Goldie
Henderson, Florence
Jackson, Glenda
Keach, Stacy
Keeler, Ruby
McNair, Barbara
Moore, Mary Tyler
Perelman, S. J.
Prince, Harold
Quayle, Anthony
Redford, Robert
Scott, George C.
Segal, Erich
Welch, Raquel
Wodehouse, P. G.

MUSIC
Arroyo, Martina
Baker, Janet
Berio, Luciano
Brel, Jacques
Fleisher, Leon
Getz, Stan
Ginastera, Alberto
Hampton, Lionel
Henderson, Florence
Kirkpatrick, Ralph
Ludwig, Christa
McNair, Barbara
Mingus, Charles
Penderecki, Krzysztof
Prince, Harold
Reese, Della
Rogers, Fred M.
Stockhausen, Karlheinz
Thomas, Michael Tilson
Trampler, Walter
Zabaleta, Nicanor

NONFICTION
Auden, W. H.
Bouton, Jim
Erikson, Erik H.
Greer, Germaine
Horgan, Paul
Kemeny, John G.
Kunstler, William M.
Millett, Kate
Nearing, Scott
Perelman, S. J.
Sakharov, Andrei D.
Segal, Erich
Sartre, Jean-Paul
Wodehouse, P. G.
Wolfe, Tom

ORGANIZATIONS
Doms, Keith
Fitzsimmons, Frank E.
Gonzalez, Efren W.
Hanks, Nancy
Hernandez, Aileen C.
Kelly, John B., Jr.
Kunstler, William M.
Lowenstein, Allard K.
Millett, Kate
Muhammad, Elijah
Tijerina, Reies Lopez

PHILOSOPHY
Millett, Kate
Sartre, Jean-Paul

PHOTOGRAPHY
Evans, Walker

POLITICS, Foreign
Aichi, Kiichi
Allende, Salvador
Arafat, Yasir
Barber, Anthony
Boumedienne, Houari
Câmara, Helder Pessoa
Carrington, 6th Baron
Colombo, Emilio
Gierek, Edward
Healey, Denis
Hoveyda, Amir Abbas
Husak, Gustav
Lopez Bravo, Gregorio
McMahon, William
Maurer, Ion Gheorghe
Médici, Emílio Garrastazú
Ne Win
Paisley, Ian
Pastrana Borrero, Misael
Polyansky, Dmitry S.
Riad, Mahmoud
Sadat, Anwar
Scheel, Walter
Schiller, Karl
Shelepin, Aleksandr
Singh, Swaran
Yahya Khan, A. M.

POLITICS, U.S.
Abzug, Bella
Badillo, Herman
Blatchford, Joseph H.

Brock, William Emerson, 3d
Buckley, James L.
Carter, Jimmy
Chiles, Lawton
Drinan, Robert F.
Duffey, Joseph D.
Fletcher, Arthur A.
Gibson, Kenneth A.
Holton, Linwood
Klein, Herbert G.
Lowenstein, Allard K.
McCloskey, Paul N., Jr.
Morton, C. B. Rogers
Moss, Frank E.
Richardson, Elliot L.
Ruckelshaus, William D.
Sargent, Francis W.
Scammon, Richard M.
Staggers, Harley O.
Tijerina, Reies Lopez
Tunney, John V.
Ziegler, Ronald L.

PSYCHOLOGY
Bazelon, David L.
Brothers, Joyce
Sartre, Jean-Paul

PUBLISHING
Chalk, O. Roy
Fairchild, John B.
Graham, Katharine
Murphy, Franklin D.

RADIO
Brothers, Joyce
McGannon, Donald H.
Walters, Barbara

RELIGION
Câmara, Helder Pessoa
Drinan, Robert F.
Duffey, Joseph D.
Lord, John Wesley
McIntire, Carl
Medeiros, Humberto S.
Muhammad, Elijah
Paisley, Ian
Rogers, Fred M.
Tijerina, Reies Lopez

SCIENCE
Borlaug, Norman E.
Erikson, Erik H.
Foster, John S., Jr.

Gonzalez, Efren W.
Kemeny, John G.
Monod, Jacques
Odishaw, Hugh
Sakharov, Andrei D.
Scott, David R.

SOCIAL SCIENCE
Brown, George H.
Duffey, Joseph D.
Erikson, Erik H.
Horgan, Paul
McGill, William J.
Nearing, Scott
Sakharov, Andrei D.
Scammon, Richard M.
Schiller, Karl

SOCIAL SERVICE
Blatchford, Joseph H.
Câmara, Helder Pessoa
Ginsberg, Mitchell I.
Hernandez, Aileen C.
Kunstler, William M.
Perot, H. Ross
Tijerina, Reies Lopez

SPORTS
Barry, Rick
Bench, Johnny
Bouton, Jim
Clarke, Ron
Conigliaro, Tony
Frazier, Joe
Goolagong, Evonne
Kelly, John B., Jr.
Plunkett, Jim
Robinson, Frank
Schranz, Karl
Segal, Erich
Trenkler, Freddie
Trevino, Lee
Wilhelm, Hoyt

TECHNOLOGY
Foster, John S., Jr.
Kemeny, John G.
Odishaw, Hugh

TELEVISION
Bench, Johnny
Bouton, Jim
Brothers, Joyce

Eastwood, Clint
Greer, Germaine
Hawn, Goldie
Henderson, Florence
Jackson, Glenda
McGannon, Donald H.
McNair, Barbara
Moore, Mary Tyler
Quayle, Anthony
Redford, Robert
Reese, Della
Rogers, Fred M.
Scott, George C.
Walters, Barbara

THEATRE
Béjart, Maurice
Berkeley, Busby
Brel, Jacques
Dassin, Jules
Erdman, Jean
Gould, Elliott
Henderson, Florence
Hirschfeld, Albert
Keach, Stacy
Keeler, Ruby
Ludwig, Christa
Jackson, Glenda
McNair, Barbara

Moore, Mary Tyler
Perelman, S. J.
Prince, Harold
Quayle, Anthony
Redford, Robert
Sartre, Jean-Paul
Scott, George C.
Segal, Erich
Wilder, Thornton
Wodehouse, P. G.
Vasarely, Victor

OTHER CLASSIFICATIONS
Gebel-Williams, Gunther

CUMULATED INDEX—1971

For the index to the 1940-1950 biographies, see CURRENT BIOGRAPHY 1950 Yearbook. For the index to 1951-1960 biographies, see CURRENT BIOGRAPHY 1960 Yearbook. For the index to 1961-1970 biographies, see CURRENT BIOGRAPHY 1970 Yearbook. The dates after names indicate monthly issues and/or yearbooks in which biographies and obituaries are contained.

Gould, Eliott Feb 71
Grace, Alonzo G(askell) obit Dec 71
Graham, Katharine (Meyer) Jan 71
Greer, Germaine Nov 71
Guggenheim, Harry F(rank) obit Mar 71
Guston, Philip Feb 71
Guthrie, Sir (William) Tyrone obit Jul 71
Hampton, Lionel (Leo) Oct 71
Hanks, Nancy Sep 71
Harridge, Will(iam) obit Jun 71
Harrington, Russell C(hase) obit Oct 71
Hart, Thomas C(harles) obit Sep 71
Hawn, Goldie Dec 71
Hayward, Leland obit Apr 71
Healey, Denis (Winston) Dec 71
Heflin, Van obit Sep 71
Henderson, Florence Apr 71
Hernandez, Aileen C(larke) Jul 71
Hickenlooper, Bourke B(lakemore) obit Oct 71
Hill, Harry W(ilbur) obit Sep 71
Hirschfeld, Albert Jan 71
Holland, Spessard L(indsey) obit Dec 71
Holton, (Abner) Linwood, (Jr.) Feb 71
Horgan, Paul Feb 71
Horsfall, Frank L(appin), Jr. obit Apr 71
Houssay, Bernardo Alberto obit Nov 71
Hoveyda, Amir Abbas Oct 71
Hull, Helen R(ose) obit Sep 71
Hurley, Roy T. obit Dec 71
Husak, Gustav Oct 71
Iacocca, Lee A(nthony) Oct 71
Iselin, Columbus O'D(onnell) obit Feb 71
Jackson, Glenda Dec 71
Jackson, William H(arding) obit Nov 71
Johnson, Alvin (Saunders) obit Jul 71
Karinska, Barbara Jan 71
Katz-Suchy, Juliusz obit Dec 71
Keach, Stacy Nov 71
Keeler, Ruby Dec 71
Kelly, John B(renden), Jr. Jun 71
Kelly, Marvin J(oe) obit May 71
Kemeny, John G(eorge) Feb 71
Kent, Rockwell obit Apr 71
Khrushchev, Nikita S(ergeyevich) obit Oct 71

Kirkpatrick, Ralph Sep 71
Klein, Herbert G(eorge) Feb 71
Knatchbull-Hugessen, Sir Hughe (Montgomery) obit May 71
Knaths, (Otto) Karl obit Apr 71
Kollmar, Richard obit Feb 71
Kroll, Jack obit Jul 71
Kunstler, William M(oses) Apr 71
Larkin, Oliver W(aterman) obit Feb 71
Lemass, Seán F(rancis) obit Jun 71
Lewis, Oscar obit Feb 71
Lloyd, Harold (Clayton) obit Apr 71
López Bravo, Gregorio Jul 71
Lord, John Wesley May 71
Lowenstein, Allard K(enneth) Sep 71
Ludwig, Christa Mar 71
Lukas, Paul obit Oct 71
Lusk, Georgia L(ee) obit Feb 71
McCloskey, Paul N(orton), Jr. Nov 71
McGannon, Donald H(enry) Feb 71
McGill, William J(ames) Jun 71
McGregor, G(ordon) R(oy) obit Apr 71
McIntire, Carl Oct 71
McKayle, Donald (Cohen) Jun 71
McMahon, William Sep 71
McNair, Barbara Nov 71
Malvern, Godfrey (Martin) Huggins, 1st Viscount obit Jun 71
Manna, Charlie obit Dec 71
Martin, Thomas E(llsworth) obit Sep 71
Mattson, Henry (Elis) obit Nov 71
Maurer, Ion Gheorghe Sep 71
Max, Peter May 71
Maxon, Lou R(ussell) obit Jul 71
Mazzo, Kay Jul 71
Medeiros, Humberto S(ousa) Nov 71
Médici, Emílio Garrastazú Oct 71
Millett, Kate Jan 71
Mingus, Charles Feb 71
Monod, Jacques Jul 71
Moore, Mary Tyler Feb 71
Moorer, Thomas H(inman) Apr 71
Morón, Alonzo G(raseano) obit Dec 71
Morris, Robert Apr 71
Morton, Rogers C(lark) B(allard) Nov 71
Moss, Frank E(dward) Dec 71

Mowery, Edward J(oseph) obit Feb 71
Muhammad, Elijah Jan 71
Murphy, Franklin D(avid) Mar 71
Nash, Ogden obit Jul 71
Nearing, Scott Oct 71
Nevins, Allan obit Apr 71
Ne Win Apr 71
Niebuhr, Reinhold obit Jul 71
Noguès, Auguste (Paul) obit Jun 71
Nye, Gerald P(rentice) obit Sep 71
Odishaw, Hugh Feb 71
Orr, John Boyd See Boyd Orr, John Boyd Orr, 1st Baron obit Sep 71
Otto, Frei (Paul) Oct 71
Owings, Nathaniel A(lexander) May 71
Padilla, Ezequiel obit Oct 71
Paisley, Ian (Richard Kyle) Jan 71
Pastrana Borrero, Misael Jul 71
Penderecki, Krzysztof Jun 71
Penney, J(ames) C(ash) obit Mar 71
Pereira, I(rene) Rice obit Feb 71
Perelman, S(idney) J(oseph) Mar 71
Perot, H(enry) Ross Jul 71
Plunkett, Jim Sep 71
Polyansky, Dmitry S(tepanovich) Mar 71
Poor, Henry Varnum obit Jan 71
Portal of Hungerford, Charles Frederick Algernon Portal, 1st Viscount obit Jun 71
Power, Thomas S(arsfield) obit Jan 71
Prescott, Robert W(illiam) Jul 71
Prince, Harold Apr 71
Prouty, Winston L(ewis) obit Oct 71
Quayle, Anthony Dec 71
Rakosi, Matyas obit Mar 71
Raman, Sir (Chandrasekhara) Venkata obit Jan 71
Reading, Stella (Charnaud Isaacs), Marchioness of obit Jul 71
Redford, Robert Apr 71
Reese, Della Sep 71
Reith, John Charles Walsham, 1st Baron obit Jul 71
Riad, Mahmoud Nov 71
Richardson, Elliot L(ee) Mar 71
Riklis, Meshulam Dec 71
Riles, Wilson (Camanza) Dec 71
Rivers, L(ucius) Mendel obit Feb 71

Robertson, A. Willis obit Dec 71

Robinson, Frank Jun 71

Rogers Fred M(cFeely) Jul 71

Roper, Elmo (Burns, Jr.) obit Jun 71

Royall, Kenneth C(laiborne) obit Sep 71

Ruckelshaus, William D(oyle) Jul 71

Russell, Richard B(revard, Jr.) obit Mar 71

Sadat, Anwar (el-) Mar 71

Sakharov, Andrei D(mitriyevich) Jul 71

Sargent Francis W(illiams) Jun 71

Sartre, Jean-Paul May 71

Saul, Ralph S(outhy) Feb 71

Scammon, Richard M(ontgomery) Mar 71

Scheel, Walter Feb 71

Schiller, Karl (August Fritz) Dec 71

Schranz, Karl Jan 71

Schuster, M(ax) Lincoln obit Feb 71

Scott, David R(andolph) Oct 71

Scott, George C(ampbell) Apr 71

Seferis, George See Sepheriades, G. S. obit Nov 71

Segal, Erich (Wolf) Apr 71

Sepheriades, Georgios S(tylianou) obit Nov 71

Sorlin, Oscar obit Apr 71

Shelepin, Aleksandr (Nikolaevich) Feb 71

Shikler, Aaron (A.) Dec 71

Shumway, Norman E(dward) Apr 71

Shvernik, Nikolai (Mikhailovich) obit Feb 71

Singh, (Sardar) Swaran Mar 71

Siroky, Viliam obit Nov 71

Skouras, Spyros P(anagiotes) obit Nov 71

Slim, William Joseph Slim, Viscount obit Feb 71

Smith, (Oliber) Harrison obit Feb 71

Soong, T. V. obit Jun 71

Staggers, Harley O(rrin) Mar 71

Stanley, W(endell) M(eredith) obit Sep 71

Stella, Frank (Philip) Apr 71

Still, Clyfford Sep 71

Stockhausen, Karlheinz Dec 71

Strang, Ruth (May) obit Feb 71

Stravinsky, Igor (Fëdorovich) obit May 71

Switzer, Mary E(lizabeth) obit Dec 71

Tamm, Igor (Evgenyevich) obit Jun 71

Thomas, J(ohn) Parnell obit Jan 71

Thomas, Michael Tilson May 71

Tijerina, Reies Lopez Jul 71

Tiselius, Arne (Wilhelm Kaurin) obit Dec 71

Tong, Hollington K(ong) obit Feb 71

Trampler, Walter Nov 71

Trenkler, Freddie Jun 71

Trevino, Lee (Buck) Nov 71

Trussell, Ray E(lbert) Jan 71

Tsaldaris, Constantin obit Jan 71

Tubman, William V(acanarat) S(hadrach) obit Sep 71

Tunney, John V(arick) Jun 71

Tvardovsky, Alexandr T(rifonovich) May 71

Ullman, James R(amsey) obit Sep 71

Van Slyke, Donald D(exter) obit Jul 71

Vasarely, Victor Feb 71

Vilar, Jean (Louis Côme) obit Sep 71

Walters, Barbara Feb 71

Watson, Arthur K(ittredge) Sep 71

Welch, Raquel May 71

White, Margaret Bourke See Bourke-White, M. obit Oct 71

Wilder, Thornton (Niven) Nov 71

Wilhelm, (James) Hoyt Jul 71

Wodehouse, P(elham) C(renville) Nov 71

Wolfe, Tom Jan 71

Yahya Khan A(gha) M(uhammad) Jan 71

Young, Whitney M(oore), Jr. obit Apr 71

Zabaleta, Nicanor Jun 71

Ziegler, Ronald L(ewis) Nov 71

Zumwalt, E(lmo) R(ussell), Jr. Jun 71